WIT

WITHDRAWN

THE FAR EAST

THE FAR EAST

A History of the Impact of the West
on Eastern Asia

by

PAUL HIBBERT CLYDE

*Professor of History
in Duke University*

New York

PRENTICE-HALL, INC.

1948

PRENTICE-HALL HISTORY SERIES

PRINTED IN THE UNITED STATES OF AMERICA

To Mary Kestler Clyde

*We are by nature observers,
and thereby learners.*
——*Emerson*

PREFACE

THE Japanese attack at Pearl Harbor, December 7, 1941, was one expression of powerful and complex revolutionary forces which have been stirring in the Orient for more than half a century. Japanese militarism was only one manifestation, though admittedly an important one, of a restless Asia seeking new orders for old. Considered historically, Asia's contemporary revolution is a child of westernization and modernization. Its character has been shaped by the impact of European and American thought and action upon the traditional cultures of the East. The societies which will emerge from the present chaos of change have not yet taken shape. They are being fashioned by patterns of thought and action which arise out of Asia's own long and rich past, and also by patterns which are new and in large measure still foreign, namely the confused and often mutually hostile philosophies of the West. To those who seek an historical introduction to this eastern Asia, to a revolution that we in part have created and with which we are now inextricably involved, the following pages are addressed.

The story is modern. It concerns principally growing contacts between the Western world and the Far East in the nineteenth and twentieth centuries. In consequence, this book contains no extended account of the early history of the Chinese, the Japanese, or of other East Asiatic peoples. Rather, the stress so far as Asia's history is concerned is on the modern institutional life of the Far East, where such knowledge is essential to an understanding of modern contacts. The approach to the subject is derived from more than twenty years of classroom discussion with American university students seeking their first intellectual contacts with Asia. To them, the natural approach to the field of things Asiatic lies through our own contacts with the modern Far East.

Even this limited approach is too vast to be treated in detail in a single volume. I have therefore limited or subordinated many phases of the subject and have emphasized those events or movements most closely concerned with the central story of Western contacts and resulting modernization. Phases of the subject which have been subordinated may be followed adequately in the references listed. Since

v

history does not take place in a vacuum, I have introduced a considerable measure of interpretation. Moreover, in a book designed primarily for Americans, I have felt justified in devoting larger space to the activities of Americans and to critical appraisal of American policies than is given to the treatment of other countries. In the final chapters, which deal with events that are immediately contemporaneous, interpretation must be regarded of course as tentative and subject to revision.

The limitations set by the theme of these pages still leave a subject so large and a liability of error so great that I have called upon the time and generosity of many of my colleagues in the field of far eastern studies. Their response has been most cordial and helpful. Without in any sense minimizing my debt to others, I mention especially those who have worked through most of the semi-final draft of the manuscript: Meribeth Cameron, of Milwaukee-Downer College; Homer H. Dubs, of University College, Oxford; Lennox A. Mills, of the University of Minnesota; and John Gilbert Reid, of the Department of State. Criticism and constructive suggestions on single chapters or groups of chapters were given by: Thomas A. Bailey, of Stanford University; Knight Biggerstaff, of Cornell University; Claude A. Buss, of Stanford University; George B. Cressey, of Syracuse University; Allan B. Cole, of Claremont College; Rupert Emerson, of Harvard University; John K. Fairbank, of Harvard University; Bruno Lasker, of the Southeast Asia Institute; Kenneth S. Latourette, of Yale University; Owen Lattimore, of The Johns Hopkins University; the late Harley F. MacNair, of the University of Chicago; Earl H. Pritchard, of Wayne University; Lawrence K. Rosinger, of the Foreign Policy Association; G. Nye Steiger, of Simmons College; Laurence E. Salisbury, editor of the *Far Eastern Survey;* Maxwell S. Stewart, of the Public Affairs Committee; Amry Vandenbosch, of the University of Kentucky; and Richard L. Watson, Jr., of Duke University. These scholars are not responsible, of course, for errors in fact or judgment I may have made. Their assistance, however, is gratefully acknowledged. If in any case I have failed either here or by letter to express this debt, I trust that my failure will be understood as an oversight. Special editorial assistance was given by George Kao, of the Chinese News Service; suggestions on Chinese politics were given by P. M. A. Linebarger. Among those who cannot be mentioned here individually are the many authors whose works I have quoted or from which I have drawn parts of the story and the interpretation. Members of the staff of the Duke University libraries who have given freely of their time in aiding my research include: Miss Evelyn Harrison, Mrs. Spears Hicks, Miss Gertrude Merritt, Miss Helen Oyler, and Miss Allene Ramage. I am also indebted to Mrs. Marjorie F. Scarlett, who typed the entire manuscript, and to Mrs. Betty Miller Unterberger and Mr. John Chalmers Vinson, who assisted in making the index.

PAUL H. CLYDE

Duke University

ACKNOWLEDGMENTS

In addition to the credits given throughout the text, grateful acknowledgment is made to the following publishers and individuals, who have given permission for material to be used from the items listed:

American Council, Institute of Pacific Relations, Inc., New York
  E. Herbert Norman, *Japan's Emergence as a Modern State* (1940)
D. Appleton-Century Company, Inc., New York and London
  G. B. Sansom, *Japan: A Short Cultural History* (New York, 1931)
  Reginald F. Johnston, *Twilight in the Forbidden City* (London, 1934)
William Blackwood & Sons Ltd., Edinburgh and London
  Alexander Michie, *The Englishman in China* (2 vols., New York, 1900)
The Cambridge University Press, London
  The Cambridge Modern History
The Contemporary Review, London
  Hugh Byas, "The Communist Movement in Japan," CXLI (1932)
Doubleday & Company, Inc., New York
  Tyler Dennett, *Roosevelt and the Russo-Japanese War* (1925)
Far Eastern Survey, American Council, Institute of Pacific Relations, New York
  Andrew J. Grajdanzev, "Korea Divided," XIV (1945)
Foreign Affairs, New York
  Henry L. Stimson, "The Nuremberg Trial: Landmark in Law," XXV (1947)
Harcourt, Brace and Company, Inc., New York
  A. Whitney Griswold, *The Far Eastern Policy of the United States* (1938)
Harper & Brothers, New York
  Henry L. Stimson, *The Far Eastern Crisis* (1936)
Harvard University Press, Cambridge, Mass.
  Merle Fainsod and others, *Japan's Prospect* (1946)
Institute of Pacific Relations, New York
  Irving S. Friedman, *British Relations with China: 1931-1939* (1940)
The Johns Hopkins Press, Baltimore, Maryland
  E. B. Price, *The Russo-Japanese Treaties of 1907-1916 Concerning Manchuria and Mongolia* (1933)
  W. W. Willoughby, *Japan's Case Examined* (1940)
Kelly & Walsh, Ltd., Shanghai
  H. A. Giles, *Gems of Chinese Literature* (Verse) (2nd rev. ed., 1923)
  H. B. Morse, *The Gilds of China* (2nd ed., 1932)

Longmans, Green & Co., Inc., New York
  M. [E. R.] Huc, *A Journey Through the Chinese Empire* (2 vols., 1859)
  H. B. Morse, *The International Relations of the Chinese Empire* (London, 1910-1918)
L. B. Lippincott Company, Philadelphia
  J. O. P. Bland and E. Backhouse, *China Under the Empress Dowager* (1912)
Louisiana State University Press, Baton Rouge
  M. Frederick Nelson, *Korea and the Old Orders in Eastern Asia* (1945)
The Macmillan Company, New York
  The Cambridge Modern History
  Engelbert Kaempfer, *The History of Japan* (1906)
McGraw-Hill Book Company, Inc., New York
  P. M. A. Linebarger, *Government in Republican China* (1938)
Minnesota Law Review, University of Minnesota
  Nathan April, "An Inquiry into the Juridical Basis for the Nuernberg War Crimes Trial," XXX (1946)
Publishers' Weekly, New York, and Frank E. Taylor
  Frank E. Taylor, "Censorship of Writers and Publishers in China," CL (1946)
G. P. Putnam's Sons, New York
  Bayard Taylor, *India, China, and Japan* (1855)
  F. W. Williams, *The Life and Letters of Samuel Wells Williams* (1899)
Princeton University Press, Princeton, New Jersey
  Harold M. Vinacke, *Modern Constitutional Development in China* (1920)
Charles Scribner's Sons, New York
  Sir Henry Yule, ed., *The Book of Ser Marco Polo* (3rd rev. ed., 1926)
Smithsonian Institution, Washington, D. C.
  John F. Embree, *The Japanese* (1943)
Stanford University Press
  M. E. Cameron, *The Reform Movement in China* (1931)
  Yamato Ichihashi, *The Washington Conference and After* (1928)
  Thomas E. LaFargue, *China and the World War* (1937)
The University of Chicago Press
  Tatsuji Takeuchi, *War and Diplomacy in the Japanese Empire* (1936)
The University of Illinois Press, Urbana
  Earl H. Pritchard, *Anglo-Chinese Relations during the Seventeenth and Eighteenth Centuries* (1929)

CONTENTS

LIST OF MAPS

LIST OF CHARTS

THE ROMANIZATION OF CHINESE AND JAPANESE

CHINESE personal and place names, many of which appear in the following pages, are of course written by the Chinese in Chinese characters. These characters are intelligible only to students of the Chinese language. Thus Chinese personal or place names are reproduced in the phonetic languages of the West by writing the sound, a process known as transliteration, or romanization. Within China itself, Chinese characters are pronounced in various ways. The Mandarin or Peking dialect is, however, generally regarded as standard. This would seem to solve the matter, but unfortunately the sounds of the Mandarin dialect do not always have exact equivalents in English. Thus the Mandarin sounds must be indicated by some conventionalized system of English letters and accents in which the English letters do not necessarily have the normal English sound but instead represent certain Mandarin sounds.

The problem is one with which Western sinologists have long experimented. As yet the results are somewhat less than adequate. The most commonly used system is the Wade and Giles spelling, which is in general followed in this book. However, in recent decades, as news from the Far East has commanded more space in the Western press, there has come into common use a postal or journalistic spelling, which I have often used in these pages to avoid confusing the student unfamiliar with the Wade-Giles spelling. For example, we spell the name of the old capital of the Manchu Empire in journalistic style as Peking; the Wade-Giles spelling would be Pei-ching. A closer approach to the pronunciation would be Bei-jing. The explanation lies in the fact that the commonly used transcriptions for Chinese words are defective, chiefly in three respects: 1) they fail to use the letters *b, d, g,* and they use *j,* not with its hard sound, but for a sound closer to the English *r;* 2) they use English vowels to represent the Chinese semi-vowels in such syllables as *tzu* and *shih;* 3) the un-English apostrophe in the Wade and Giles romanization is frequently forgotten and dropped, with the result that different Chinese pronunciations are represented by the same English letters. Since speakers of English inevitably tend to pronounce words as they are spelled, such words as "Peking" are pronounced in a way that would be unintelligible to a Chinese.

The following is a simplified guide to pronunciation in the Peking dialect according to the Wade system.

Vowels: (as in Italian)

a as in "father"

e as in "Edward"

i like the *e* in "me"

o like "aw" (but often like the *u* in "cut")

u as in "lunar"

ê like the *u* in "under"

ih like the *e* in "her" (no real equivalent in English)

ü like French *u* or German *ü*

ŭ is practically unpronounced

Consonants: The apostrophe following a consonant indicates aspiration; the lack of the apostrophe indicates the lack of aspiration, which sounds to our ears very much like voicing. Therefore:

(*Unaspirated*)	(*Aspirated*)
ch sounds like the *j* in "jam"	*ch'* as in "chin"
k like the *g* in "gun"	*k'* as in "kin"
p like the *b* in "bat"	*p'* as in "pun"
t like the *d* in "doll"	*t'* as in "tap"
ts and *tz* sound like *dz*	*ts'* and *tz'* like the *ts* of "Patsy"
j between French *j* and English *r*	

Most of the other consonants are similar to those in English.

Note: Other systems of romanization are used in other Western languages. In newspapers and popular books the diacritical marks ' ^ " ˇ are commonly omitted; as a result many irregularities occur which are due chiefly to the dropping of the apostrophe; also *k* or *k'* are often substituted for *ch* or *ch'* before *i*.

A more recent system of romanization which, though not commonly used, has many features which recommend it, is the Homer H. Dubs revision of C. S. Gardner's romanization. It is an attempt to modify the Wade and Giles spelling to avoid the difficulties noted above. It also represents the distinction between *ts* and *ch,* and *hs* and *s* before the vowels *i* and *ü.* This distinction is retained in most of China. Actually, only a specially devised alphabet can be entirely phonetic, but the Dubs' spelling attempts to assist Occidentals in pronouncing Chinese words while at the same time being suitable for the work of the sinologist.

Some examples of the three systems mentioned are given on the following page.

Chinese characters	Postal or journalistic spelling	Wade-Giles spelling	Dubs spelling
浙江	Chekiang	Che-chiang	Je-jiang
廣東	Kwangtung	Kuang-tung	Guang-dung
保定	Paoting	Pao-ting	Bao-ding
北京	Peking	Pei-ching	Bei-jing
北平	Peiping	Pei-p'ing	Bei-ping
天津	Tientsin	T'ien-chin	Tien-dzin
成都	Chengtu	Ch'eng-tu	Cheng-du
湖北	Hupeh	Hu-pe	Hu-be
牯嶺	Kuling	Ku-ling	Gu-ling
桂林	Kweilin	Kuei-lin	Guei-lin
大理	Tali	Ta-li	Da-li
定縣	Tinghsien	Ting-hsien	Ding-hsien
潼關	Tungkwan	T'ung-kuan	Tung-guan
鄭縣	Chenghsien	Cheng-hsien	Jeng-hsien
蘭州	Lanchow	Lan-chou	Lan-jou
貴陽	Kweiyang	Kuei-yang	Guei-yang
張伯苓	Chang Po-ling	Chang Po-ling	Jang Bo-ling
新京	Hsinking	Hsin-ching	Sin-jing
汲縣	Chihsien	Chi-hsien	Ji-hsien
支塘	Chihtang	Chih-t'ang	Jzh-tang
四川	Szechuan	Ssu-ch'uan	Sz-chuan
熱河	Jehol	Je-ho	Re-ho
青島	Tsingtao	Ch'ing-tao	Tsing-dao
濟南	Tsinan	Chi-nan	Dzi-nan
清苑	Tsingyüan	Ch'ing-yüan	Tsing-yüan
西康	Sikang	Hsi-k'ang	Si-kang
西安	Sian	Hsi-an	Si-an
孫逸仙	Sun Yat Sen	Sun I-hsien	Sun Yi-sien
廣州	Canton	Kuang-chou	Guang-jou
上海	Shanghai	Shang-hai	Shang-hai
武昌	Wuchang	Wu-ch'ang	Wu-chang
重慶	Chungking	Ch'ung-ch'ing	Chung-ching
延安	Yenan	Yen-an	Yen-an
開封	Kaifeng	K'ai-feng	Kai-feng
昆明	Kunming	K'un-ming	Kun-ming

In both Chinese and Japanese personal names, the surname comes first, followed by the given name. However, in the following pages it has seemed best to use the form with which American readers are most familiar. Thus, for example, Li Hung-chang, Fêng Yü-hsiang, Chiang K'ai-shek, but T. V. Soong. The same procedure has been followed with Japanese names. However, fewer Japanese given names are known to the American public, and in general the rule of given name followed by surname has been adopted. For the romanization of Japanese words, the Hepburn system is used. Here pronunciation is relatively simple; each syllable ends in a vowel, with the exception of the few syllables ending with the consonant n. There are as many syllables in a word as there are vowels. No syllable is accented, though there are long vowels which really constitute two syllables, as in Ōsaka. Consonants in Japanese are sounded much as they are in English. Vowels are sounded as follows: a as in father; i as "ee" in feet; u as "oo" in food; e as in met; o as in home.

BIBLIOGRAPHICAL INTRODUCTION

The subject of the westernization and modernization of the Far East is a field so vast that even a survey would have been impossible were it not for the special studies by many scholars covering particular subjects or periods. I have drawn freely on the research and writing of hundreds of authors whose works are cited in footnotes or listed in the bibliographical suggestions listed for each chapter. If in any case I have misstated a fact or interpretation, I should appreciate having it called to my attention by the author or by others. The works cited and listed, though extensive, are not exhaustive. They are designed to give the beginner some indication of the variety of the materials and some direction to the better secondary sources, primarily in the English language. The footnote citations serve not only to indicate some of the more important sources from which material has been drawn, but also to lend weight to points of interpretation.

For the beginning American student who seeks to go beyond general reading in secondary sources listed, the following suggestions are made:

Bibliographies.

S. F. Bemis and G. G. Griffin, *Guide to the Diplomatic History of the United States, 1775-1921* (Washington, 1935), a very complete guide. E. H. Blair and J. A. Robertson, *The Philippine Islands, 1493-1898* (55 vols., Cleveland, 1903-1909), Vol. LIII, 1908. Hugh Borton, S. Elisseff, and E. O. Reischauer, *A Selected List of Books and Articles on Japan in English, French, and German* (Washington, 1940). The Library of Congress, Division of Bibliography, *The Japanese Empire: Industries and Transportation* (Washington, 1943). Henri Cordier, *Bibliotheca Sinica* (5 vols., 2nd ed., Paris, 1904-24). Henri Cordier, *Bibliotheca Indosinica* (4 vols., Paris, 1912-13). Henri Cordier, *Bibliotheca Japonica* (Paris, 1913). Institute of Pacific Relations, *Korea for the Koreans. . . .* (New York, 1943), contains twelve pages of annotated bibliography. R. J. Kerner, *Northeastern Asia: A Selected Bibliography* (2 vols., Berkeley, 1939), contains titles in Chinese and Japanese as well as Western languages. Oskar Nachod, *Bibliography of the Japanese Empire, 1906-1926* (2 vols., London, 1928). Fr. von Wenckstern, *A Bibliography of the Japanese Empire* (Vol. I, Leiden, 1895; Vol. II, Tokyo, 1907).

Collections of Treaties, etc.

Carnegie Endowment for International Peace, *Treaties and Agreements with and Concerning China, 1919-1929* (Washington, 1929). China, the

Maritime Customs, *Treaties, Conventions, etc., between China and Foreign States* (2 vols., 2nd ed., Shanghai, 1917). Henry Chung, *Korean Treaties* (New York, 1919). Hertslet's *China Treaties* (2 vols., 3rd ed., London, 1908). League of Nations, *Treaty Series* (London, 1920 ff.). J. V. A. MacMurray, ed., *Treaties and Agreements with and Concerning China, 1894-1919* (2 vols., New York, 1921). W. M. Malloy, ed., *Treaties, Conventions, International Acts, Protocols and Agreements between the United States and Other Powers* (3 vols., Washington, 1909-1923). W. F. Mayers, *Treaties between the Empire of China and Foreign Powers* (3rd ed., Shanghai, 1901). David Hunter Miller, ed., *Treaties and Other International Acts of the United States of America* (7 vols. to date, Washington, 1931-1942), a scholarly and meticulous work of editing. W. W. Rockhill, *Treaties and Conventions with or Concerning China and Korea, 1894-1904* (Washington, 1904).

Executive, legislative, and diplomatic documents.
France. Documents Diplomatiques Français, 1871-1914 (Paris, 1929-1937).
Germany. Die grosse Politik der Europäischen Kabinette, 1871-1914 (Berlin, 1921-1927).
Great Britain. The British *Parliamentary Papers* (London, 1801 ff.), contain excellent material for both the nineteenth and twentieth centuries. A second valuable series for reference is *British and Foreign State Papers* (London, 1841 ff.). See, too, *Parliamentary Debates* (London, 1812 ff.); *British Documents on the Origins of the World War, 1898-1914,* ed. by G. P. Gooch and H. W. V. Temperley (11 vols., London, 1927-1938).
League of Nations. Official Journal (Geneva).
Russia. Krasnyi Arkhiv, Vols. 1-85 (Moscow, 1922-1937).
United States. Papers Relating to the Foreign Relations of the United States (Washington, 1861, and subsequent years); annual volumes contain selections from American diplomatic correspondences with liberal sections devoted to the Far East. The Department of State, *Press Releases* (Washington) are of value on current developments in American policy. Much material covering the Far East is to be found in various United States Congressional documents such as the Executive Documents, Miscellaneous Documents, and the *Reports* of Committees of the Senate and the House of Representatives. Illuminating material from the debates in Congress is in *The Annals of Congress* (1789-1824), *Register of Debates* (1825-1837), *The Congressional Globe* (1833-1873), and *The Congressional Record* (1873 to date).

Many of the more definitive studies on aspects of modern far eastern history are scattered throughout an extensive periodical literature, in the journals of learned and professional societies, and in popular and semi-popular periodicals.

The following, though not a complete list of such journals, includes the more useful ones printed in the English language:

Amerasia (New York)
American Historical Review
American Journal of International Law (Washington, D. C.)
American Political Science Review
Annals of the American Academy of Political and Social Science (Philadelphia)
Asia and the Americas (New York)
Bulletin of the School of Oriental Studies (London)
Chinese Social and Political Science Review (Peking)
Contemporary Japan (Tokyo)
Far Eastern Quarterly (New York)
Far Eastern Review (Shanghai)
Far Eastern Survey (New York)
Harvard Journal of Asiatic Studies (Cambridge, Mass.)
International Review of Missions (Oxford)
Journal of the American Oriental Society (Baltimore)
Journal of the Burma Research Society (Rangoon)
Journal of the Malayan Branch of the Royal Asiatic Society
Journal of Modern History
Journal of the North China Branch of the Royal Asiatic Society
Journal of the Royal Asiatic Society
Journal of the Royal Central Asian Society
Journal of the Thailand Research Society
Kyoto University Economic Review (Kyoto)
Memoirs of the Research Department of the Toyo Bunko (Tokyo)
Nankai Social and Economic Quarterly
Oriental Economist (Tokyo)
Pacific Affairs (New York)
Pacific Historical Review
Philippine Social Science Review (Manila)
Political Science Quarterly
T'ien-hsia Monthly (Shanghai)
The Times Literary Supplement (London)
Transactions and Proceedings of the Japan Society (London)
Transactions of the Asiatic Society of Japan (Tokyo)
Transactions of the Korean Branch of the Royal Asiatic Society
United States Naval Institute Proceedings

CHAPTER 1

THE PEOPLES AND THE LANDS IN WHICH THEY LIVE

THE geography of eastern Asia is as much a part of American international politics today as was the geography of Cuba half a century ago or the geography of the Mississippi Valley in the year 1800.

This is the more striking since, for most Americans during the greater part of this country's history, geography as a field of realistic interest has tended to reach only from the Atlantic seaboard to the Pacific coast, and from the 49th parallel to the Gulf of Mexico and the Rio Grande. When in 1898 President McKinley acknowledged that he was somewhat uncertain just where the Philippine Islands might be, his confession was one to which most of his fellow countrymen could also subscribe. The political geography of Asia, when it was thought of at all, was considered a subject which might well be left to academicians with a fancy for strange and outlandish regions of the world. In our nineteenth century a $64 question on the geography of Asia would have been meaningless, because anyone answering the $16 question would have been marked as a near geographical genius. To be sure, there were Americans—traders, business men, sea-captains, missionaries, and historians—who were not strangers to Asia's lands and peoples. But, apart from these special groups, very few Americans were possessed of any systematic politico-geographical knowledge of China, Japan, India, or lesser countries of the East.

Today, when most American school boys are more familiar with Buna, Biak, and Bataan than with Buffalo, Butte, and Baltimore, this capacity of the nineteenth-century American mind to ignore half the world's physical surface and more than half its peoples seems hardly credible. Yet, as typical of the times, a popular school history, published in 1863 in New York, advised its readers that "China, a vast country of eastern Asia, may be almost said to have no history of any interest to the general reader, it has so few revolutions or political changes to record." [1] Certainly a country with so little history could have no geography of any consequence.

---

[1] Marcius Willson, *Outlines of History* (New York, 1863), 286-287.

There are of course many historical factors which explain the willingness of Americans to neglect all save the geography of their own country. Here it is sufficient to suggest that as the American built his new society in the United States, he found satisfaction in certain negative rather than positive realities of geography because these realities (the Atlantic Ocean, for example) enabled him to achieve that *separation* from Europe so ardently desired. Geography, indeed, was the means by which the Old World of Europe might be held at a distance; not a means by which cultural, political, or economic influence would be furthered. Later, when this American had acquired a coastline on the Pacific, he saw, to be sure, visions of a great commerce with Asia; he even pictured the Pacific as an American lake; yet he was more than ever dominated by a philosophy of political isolation, and it was thus very satisfying for him to note that the Pacific Ocean was wide and the "teeming millions" of Asia were far away. If, as many of our forefathers saw it, there was little reason to be concerned about the political geography of Europe (since it was largely a matter of the sinister rivalries of kings), there was even less to recommend the geography of Asia, inhabited as that continent was by Oriental despots and a heathen, uncivilized society.

"The march of events," however, often has scant respect for man's deep-rooted and hallowed habits and traditions. The military and naval campaigns of World War II have given to thousands of Americans an undreamed of familiarity with those same distant lands which their fathers and grandfathers had called strange and outlandish. The old and convenient American-made stereotypes of Asia and the Asiatic are no longer convincing. The Chinese, or the "Chinaman," as most Americans called him in the late nineteenth century, was a coolie, a species of unskilled cheap laborer. He was poverty-stricken, dirty, illiterate, and heathen, though sometimes endowed, it was said, with a fine simple honesty. It was also observed that there was a seemingly limitless number of Chinese with insatiable ambitions to enter the laundry business. Some Americans knew the Chinese villain of American fiction, personalized by the dark ways of Dr. Fu Manchu, and there was the popular conception of the Chinese as a philosopher, oblivious to the passage of time. Even more than the Chinese, the Japanese were mentally stereotyped "as a quaint little people devoted to cherry blossoms and Mount Fuji." It is quite true that the people were little, that they liked both cherry blossoms and Mount Fuji, but as a contemporary student has said, they were not thereby quaint by any means.[2] Now,

[2] John F. Embree, *The Japanese* (Washington: The Smithsonian Institution, 1943), 36. Both Chinese and Japanese of course had their own mental stereotypes of Americans.

as a result of the broadened geographical horizons that have come to us out of World War II, there are fewer Americans who can be satisfied with this kind of capsule human geography. Yet it is hardly surprising that as a people we are not so geographically minded even now as our new and dominant position among the nations would seem to demand.

The human, the political, the economic, and the social geography of eastern Asia can no longer be dismissed as remote, inconsequential, or quaint. It is the United States that has recently bestowed independence on a young Asiatic nation, The Republic of the Philippines. It is the United States that is in military occupation of the once powerful Japanese Empire where it has undertaken to chart the course of 75 million people toward the philosophy and the institutions of democracy. On the continent of Asia from Manchuria to Canton, millions of Chinese have clung to the hope that a special representative of the President of the United States—a former Chief-of-Staff of the United States Army —would bring internal peace to a China long ravaged by foreign aggression and by civil war. Truly, our present geographical interests exceed the most fantastic dreams of our forefathers.

The United States has emerged from World War II with powers, material and spiritual, which make it the potential leader of that free geographical world for which we supposedly fought. That world has yet to be created, for freedom, in the ultimate sense, is the achievement of peace, not of war. Whether we achieve victory in peace as we did in war will be determined in some considerable degree by the use to which as a people we put our new politico-geographical power. There is and there will be the temptation for the United States, like other newly rich empires, to enter the world of Asia to dominate it and fatten on its resources. This we shall have to recognize as the old doctrine of geographical isolationism in a new form, the theory of self-protection beyond the physical borders of the nation. Old labels may

---

In pre-war years the Japanese came to accept the idea that Americans were soft and weak; many Chinese had the impression that all Americans were wealthy. Many Americans tended to underrate Japan not only because she was "quaint" but also because she was an "imitator." "Most anthropologists realize that every culture is made up of a vast dough of borrowed culture with a small pinch of original invention. Americans, for instance, speak a 'borrowed' language, and use a 'borrowed' script, their legal system is largely borrowed, and their religion is also no original invention. Furthermore, even in the field of industrial development, most of the basic inventions involved are by no means original to America—e.g., the wheel, the steam engine, wireless communications. Similarly, most Japanese culture is borrowed—her script, her Buddhist religion, her industrial development. But, as with other peoples, on the basis of existing and borrowed cultural materials, the Japanese have been able to develop new combinations to suit their own cultural tradition. Japan is not to be underestimated in ability to borrow, adapt, and invent so far as her material resources and international contacts permit." *Ibid.*, 36-37.

change, and old forms of imperialism to which the American people have never taken kindly may become a new isolation of expansion. Will the new geographical reach of the American people exceed its grasp of those progressive principles that world leadership will demand?

Our story therefore must logically begin with some systematic introduction to those lands in which the peoples of the Far East are living.

THE CONTINENT OF ASIA

The Far East, as we shall see, though an immense area in itself, is but a part of the world's largest continent, Eurasia. It was in this continent, probably somewhere in the hinterland of the Arabian Sea, that the race-home of man was located, somewhere in the area which is the traditional site of the Garden of Eden.[3] Asia, alone, is pre-eminent among all the continents in both size and altitude. Covering one third of the land-surface of the world, Asia comprises some 17 million square miles. It is larger than the combined area of North and South America, which is something more than 14 million square miles, and more than four times the size of Europe, which in reality is but a peninsula on the western rim of Asia. If considered in terms of linear distance, Asia extends for some 6,000 miles from east to west and for more than 5,000 miles from its most northerly to its most southerly point. In matters of altitude also, Asia has no rival. Mount Everest, towering 29,141 feet, surpasses Mount McKinley in Alaska (20,300 feet), and Mount Aconcagua in the Andes (22,834 feet). There are 18 peaks in Asia exceeding 23,000 feet. However, the most compelling characteristic of Asia's physical formation is neither its unique size nor its towering altitudes, but rather "the gigantic development of plateau" extending for some 9,000 miles in a great arc from the eastern Mediterranean to the Bering Strait, widening in some areas to nearly 2,000 miles in the heart of the Tibetan tableland. As geographers measure this plateau, it covers nearly two fifths of Asia's land mass, but it supports only a limited and mostly pastoral population.

THE POPULATION

Of the estimated two billion inhabitants of the world, more than half —some estimates suggest two thirds, or 1,300,000,000—live in Asia. Most of this multitude lives (exists might be a better word) in the southern and eastern fringes of the continent: in India, China, Japan, Korea, and the East Indies. Important, too, is the fact that the overwhelming proportion of this vast population are tillers of the soil. Just prior to

[3] Lionel W. Lyde, *The Continent of Asia* (London, 1933), 18.

World War II, Japan was the only Asiatic country with a highly developed industry, and even in Japan some 50 percent of the population still lived by the soil.

Base map according to J. Paul Goode, plotted according to Alber's Area Projection.

THE CLIMATES OF ASIA

The climates of Asia are sufficiently varied to satisfy the most extreme tastes, yet there are certain broad features which may be said to affect the continent as a whole. Of these the best known, and, to European navigators the most useful, was the monsoon (from the Arabic "season"), seasonal winds blowing south and westerly from the heart of the continent in the winter or dry season, and north and easterly from the Indian Ocean in the summer or wet season. It was on the spring or summer monsoon that the European navigators sailed to Canton from the sixteenth to the mid-nineteenth century, and it was on the winter monsoon that they turned their course homeward. But of greater importance to the population of Asia was the fact that the wet monsoon brought the seasonal rains which in southern Asia made it possible for so many to live on the land. Farther inland, where the moisture did not reach, were the arid and semi-arid regions of the Mongolian plateau where the land maintained only a sparce population.[4]

GEOGRAPHICAL CONTROLS ON POPULATION AND CULTURE

Relief and climate in Asia are reflected not only in the distribution of Asia's population but also in its racial and cultural traits. Here a word of contrast and comparison with Europe is suggestive. In Europe, communication both by land and by sea was relatively easy; there was great variety of relief so concentrated in area as to promote the intermingling of peoples; yet there were also natural geographic units favorable to the creation of nation-states. In Asia, immense size, virtually impassable barriers of mountain and desert, and extreme variations of climate precluded, in the main, communication over the continent as a whole.[5]

Furthermore, it should be observed that geography not only separated the great civilizations of Asia one from another, it also maintained their remoteness until very recent times from other centers of civilization such as western Europe. Again, it may be emphasized that much of our story will be concerned with the manner in which man has combatted this Asiatic isolation and this remoteness. Quite early in the story it will appear that it was Western man from Europe and later from America who seized the initiative. In the modern sense, it is Western man and his civilization that have invaded Asia. It was he who set the objectives, determined the rules by which they should be obtained, and imposed on the vanquished Oriental the penalties of defeat. In terms of our current vocabulary, Western man was the aggressor at a time when aggression paid great dividends.

THE FAR EAST

The eastern half of Asia, with which these pages will be primarily concerned, may be labelled conveniently *The Far East*. More specifi-

---

[4] George B. Cressey, *Asia's Lands and Peoples* (New York, 1944), ch. ii; Daniel R. Bergsmark, *Economic Geography of Asia* (New York, 1935), Pt. I, chs. i-v; Lyde, *The Continent of Asia*, Pt. I, chs. i-xiii.

[5] Lyde, *The Continent of Asia*, ch. xiii, "Some 'Controls.'"

From Paul Monroe, "China: A Nation in Evolution." The Macmillan Company,
New York, 1928.

cally, it comprises those lands of the Asiatic continent and adjacent islands which lie east of longitude 90° east of Greenwich. These include, on the mainland: eastern Siberia, Korea or Chosen, the Republic of China and certain borderland territories—Manchuria, Mongolia, Sinkiang or Chinese Turkestan, and Tibet; and to the south, Burma, Siam (Thailand), Indo-China, and British Malaya; and the insular areas: the Japanese Empire, the Republic of the Philippines, and the East Indies.

To Americans of the eighteenth and nineteenth centuries as well as to Europeans, the term Far East was more descriptively suggestive than it is to us today, since, in those days, mariners sailing to China skirted Africa and sailed eastward. Thus in a very real sense China and the lands immediately surrounding it were the Far East, the ultimate destination of these early mariners.[6] In the course of time, the term has come to be used with a variety of connotations that are not always self-explanatory. It is sometimes used as a synonym for the equally indefinite "eastern Asia"; sometimes it is used to denote political areas such as China, Japan, etc.; and sometimes to depict those areas where Chinese culture and its derivatives have been predominant.

---

[6] For Americans today the term Far East is less appropriate, since, as the geographer George B. Cressey has pointed out, for us in the United States the region is now neither east nor far.

CHINA

Historically and culturally the civilization of the Far East is the civilization of China, and so, it is to the geographical features of this China that we must first give attention. Since 1911, China has been called a republic, and before that time it was called an empire, a term which is sometimes misleading, since China, the Middle Kingdom, was the senior and superior member of a Confucian family of nations rather than a politico-geographical area, though to be sure she did have definite borders and frontier posts. It is notable, too, that only in modern times has the Western world become reasonably familiar with this geographic China. The vague conceptions of the Far East entertained by Europe in the Middle Ages persisted beyond the thirteenth century, even in the face of new knowledge carried back to Europe by such travellers as Corvino, Croce, Odoric, and Marco Polo. When Polo told and wrote of a new Far East, he was called an impostor, for his fellow Europeans were still inclined to believe the "accretions of legend and romance" handed down from the days of Rome, according to which there was the land of "Seres" at the end of the overland route eastward, and there was "Thin" (China) at the end of the sea route. It was not until the sixteenth century that it was "recognized that the land of the 'Seres' (Cathay) and 'China' were the same."[7]

CHINA: GEOGRAPHICAL LIMITS

Thus it has always been easier and more significant, historically speaking, to delimit China in a cultural sense than to do so in terms of geographical boundaries. This, let it be emphasized again, is because in the long view China has been a society and a civilization rather than a sovereign nation-state in the Western political sense of that term. Nevertheless, during modern times, during the Manchu regime (1644-1912), China—the Middle Kingdom—was contained within politico-geographical boundaries whose location, at least in certain instances, was reasonably stable and well understood. This China consisted of 18 provinces known as China Proper.[8] Its area was approximately 1,500,000 square miles, comparable to the area of India. It was here in China Proper that most of the Chinese lived. Beyond China Proper

---

[7] John K. Wright, *The Geographical Lore of the Time of the Crusades* (New York, 1925), 271. See also: Sir Percy Sykes, *A History of Exploration* (New York, 1934), 8; M. Cary and E. H. Warmington, *The Ancient Explorers* (London, 1929), 160.

[8] The 18 provinces were: Anhui, Chekiang, Fukien, Honan, Chihli (now Hopei), Hunan, Hupeh, Kansu, Kiangsi, Kiangsu, Kwangtung, Kwangsi, Kweichow, Shansi, Shantung, Shensi, Szechwan, and Yünnan.

were certain outlying dependencies: Manchuria (the Chinese called it the Three Eastern Provinces), Mongolia, Sinkiang (meaning New Dominion, sometimes called Chinese Turkestan), and Tibet. Greater China, which included China Proper and the dependencies, has an area estimated as in excess of four million square miles.

PHYSICAL CHARACTERISTICS OF CHINA PROPER

The physical setting provided by China Proper has encouraged through the centuries the growth of a distinctive and a stable society. Here the Chinese were shut off from other major civilizations by great natural barriers: the sea on the east and south; mountains of great altitude in the west; desert and steppe in the north. Where, as in the north, the natural barrier seemed inadequate, the early Chinese built a Great Wall to insure their isolation.[9] Within these great natural and artificial barriers is a territory distinguished by much physical variety and by two large river systems that flow eastward: the Huang Ho or Yellow River in the north, and the Yangtze River in the center.

THE YELLOW RIVER BASIN

The Huang Ho or Yellow River, so called because of the color of the loess which it carries, loess which the Chinese call by a name meaning yellow earth, drains a basin of some 600,000 square miles with a population of perhaps 100,000,000. From its source in the mountains of Tibet, the river wanders for 2,500 miles to the sea. The loess soil of the region is unusually fertile, and so it is not surprising that the first centers of China's earliest civilizations were on the loess plains of the Yellow River Valley or that these areas are among the most densely populated in China today. But if the Yellow River has brought life, its floods have brought destruction and death, whence comes its traditional name, "China's Sorrow." The earliest Chinese records recount the ravages of these great inundations and also the migrations of the entire river bed in its lower reaches. It would appear that the river has emptied into the sea at times as far north as Tientsin and at others as far south as the channel of the Yangtze near Shanghai. When, in times of unusually high water, floods do occur, they are particularly destructive. In the great floods of 1887-89 it is estimated that 2,000,000 lost their lives either by drowning, or by starvation from the resulting famine.[10]

---

[9] Probably begun in the third century B.C., the Great Wall, designed to protect the northern states of Ch'in, Chao, and Yen from raids by the barbarians of what is today Mongolia, stretches for more than 1,500 miles from the eastern edge of Turkestan to the Gulf of Chihli near the town of Shanhaikwan.

[10] Walter H. Mallory, *China: Land of Famine* (New York, 1926), 49-52.

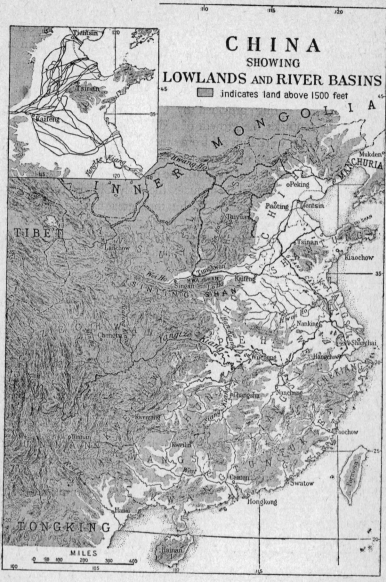

The essentially mountainous character of western and southern China is illustrated. Scale 1:20,000,000. The inset shows changes in the lower course of the Huang Ho and the seaward extension of the shoreline. *Courtesy of the "Geographical Review," published by the American Geographical Society of New York.*

THE YANGTZE BASIN

Cutting eastward across the central part of China Proper is the greatest of China's rivers, the Yangtze. Like the Huang Ho, it also rises in the mountains of Tibet. Its course stretches for 3,200 miles. With its tributaries it drains approximately 756,000 square miles, in which live about 180,000,000 people. Even in an air age, the Yangtze is still the main highway for trade, commerce, and for life in general throughout central and interior China. It is not by chance that China's greatest city and seaport, Shanghai, is situated near the mouth of this river.

Lesser but still important rivers of China Proper include the Hsi Kiang and the Huai. The Hsi Kiang basin includes most of the four southern provinces of Kwangtung, Kwangsi, Kweichow, and Yünnan. The area is some 390,000 square miles, with a population of 60,000,000. Between the Huang Ho and the Yangtze is the Huai River, which rises in Honan and flows through Anhui into Kiangsu.

Several great river systems are in the border lands of Greater China. The Amur through much of its course forms the boundary between North Manchuria and Soviet Siberia. The large central Manchurian plain is drained by the Sungari, a tributary of the Amur. The Tumen and Yalu Rivers separate Korea from Manchuria and the Maritime Province. Far to the south, the Salween and the Mekong, which rise in the Tibetan plateau, flow parallel southward for 900 miles through Chinese territory, then through the peninsula of southeastern Asia, the former emptying into the Gulf of Martaban, the latter reaching the sea through Indo-China and Cambodia.

THE DIVERSITY OF THE CHINESE TERRAIN

Physical diversity is one of the most pronounced features of the Chinese scene. Land forms present a great variety of types. In northeast China, there is the great plain of the Yellow River and large mountain formations in Shantung. In central China there are the Yangtze lowlands, the central mountain system, and to the west the great basin of Szechwan, which foreigners call the Red Basin. In South China are the mountains of the southern Yangtze basin, the Hsi Kiang lowlands, the plateau and mountains of Kweichow and Yünnan.[11]

---

[11] The principal mountain systems of China originate in the far west in the Pamir plateau and lie generally from west to east in three major chains or lesser systems: 1) the T'ien Shan, running northeasterly into northeastern Siberia; 2) the K'un Lun, south of the T'ien Shan and separated from the latter by the Takla-Makan and Gobi deserts, terminates in the Khinghan Mountains of Manchuria and their extensions across Siberia to the Sea of Okhotsk; and 3) the Trans-Himalaya, which break on the Sino-Tibetan

THE CHINESE CLIMATE

Climate in China is as varied as the landscape, but in the overall picture the monsoon has a unifying influence. Summer with its winds from the south is the wet season; winter with its winds from the interior of the continent is dry. Since the overwhelming population of China

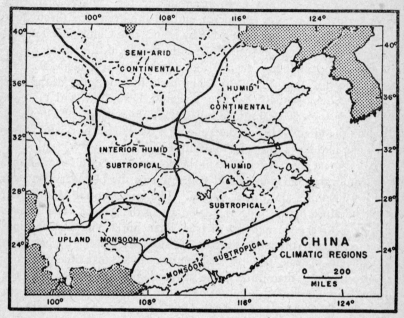

United States, Department of State. Division of Map Intelligence and Cartography.

lives on farms, it is vitally dependent upon the weather, and the coming of rain too soon or too late, too little or too much, means certain hardship and often death to thousands and sometimes millions.[12]

MINERAL RESOURCES OF CHINA

History bears witness to the fact that China's natural resources endowed her amply for the maintenance of a highly developed pre-industrial society. The years since 1937 have also demonstrated China's remarkable capacity to resist a powerfully armed invader despite lack of industrialization and the lack of equipment for her own troops. Her

border to form two systems, the one crossing China northeastwardly to Hopei, the other southeastwardly and then paralleling the coast from Kwangsi to Chekiang. G. B. Cressey, *Asia's Lands and Peoples*, 50-60.

[12] Cressey, *Asia's Lands and Peoples*, 60-65.

resistance has been part of the march from semi-colonialism to member-ship among the so-called Great Powers in the United Nations. Cul-turally there can be no doubt that the Chinese merit the distinction of being a great people; but the question whether China is a Great Power in the sense in which political realists use the phrase remains for the future to answer. China's future political power is likely to bear a close relation to her industrial strength, and this in turn will be de-pendent in some major degree on her mineral resources and techno-logical skills. China possesses plentiful reserves of coal, antimony, and tungsten; lesser reserves of iron and tin; and very limited reserves of sulphur, copper, and petroleum. Based on these, her own resources, in so far as they are known, and in the light of her immense population, her industrialization in the near future is likely to be within fairly modest limits. Nevertheless, in this respect her prospects are more favored than those of other peoples on the Pacific slope of Asia.[13]

We should be reminded, too, that though the exquisite products of China's handicraft shops and factories have commanded the admiration of the artistic world for many centuries, China remains the least in-dustrialized of all the larger powers. Until the outbreak of World War II, factory industry on a large scale (principally cotton mills) was con-fined to a few great cities such as Shanghai, and to an unusual degree was owned by foreign capital. The necessary retreat of "Free" China into the interior stimulated the beginnings of war industries in areas of western China previously untouched. With the coming of peace, the National Government announced extensive plans for further industrial-ization. The part which these plans will play in China's future are as yet unpredictable. During the past 50 years China's industrialization has been retarded by many factors: unstable political conditions, lack of capital, lack of modern transportation, the physical isolation of large

[13] Coal. China ranks fourth among the powers in surveyed and estimated reserves, following the United States, the Soviet Union, and Canada.

Oil. Thus far the prospects of oil reserves have not been encouraging.

Hydroelectric power. This source had not been developed in China prior to World War II. The greatest potential area is in South China.

Iron. Total known reserves are about 1,302,600,000 tons, very limited for a country of China's size and population. China's iron consumption in pre-war years including imports was about 600,000 tons annually. This is a per capita consumption of three pounds compared with 1,000 pounds in the U. S.

Tungsten. This ferroalloy derived from wolfram is plentiful. China at times has supplied the greater part of the world market. Tungsten is mined principally in Kiangsi.

Manganese. Found in Kwangsi in quantities sufficient for domestic needs.

The shortage of iron and the distances between metallurgical coke and iron ore will be among the limiting factors in China's development of heavy industry. See Cressey, *Asia's Lands and Peoples*, 75-83.

areas, limited natural resources, and the weight of tradition which emphasized agriculture and the importance of the family as the unit of society. As a result, in 1937 more than 70 percent of the industrial capital in China was foreign investment, and total industrial capital was infinitesimal as compared with that of Europe or the United States. Apart from certain special areas such as South Manchuria and the region of Shanghai, industrialization in China is still largely in the blueprint stage. Pre-war industry as it existed was centered largely in such areas as: Dairen, Mukden (iron, coal, soya-bean products), Tientsin (coal, salt, cement), Tsingtao, Tsinan (coal and cotton textiles), Shanghai, Nanking (cotton and silk textiles, cigarettes, flour-milling), Hankow (iron), Hongkong, Canton (silk, shipbuilding).[14]

FORESTS

One of China's deficiencies in terms of natural wealth is her lack of great forest resources. Although the picture of China as a deforested land has often been exaggerated, the fact remains that for a land of her size and population, timber resources are inadequate. Some of the best forests are in eastern Manchuria.[15]

THE CHINESE PEOPLE

But the most striking feature of the Chinese landscape is its human inhabitants. The good earth of China has supported more of mankind than any comparable area of the world. Throughout their history almost all Chinese have been farmers, and the great majority of them remain so to this day. The rich maturity of China's pre-industrial civilization was supported by the toil of millions of peasants who have been "farmers for forty centuries." Everywhere in China there is the pressure of man on the available arable land. The population of Greater China is of course unknown but has been estimated as in the neighborhood of 475,000,000. This population is by no means evenly distributed; on the contrary, it is mostly in China Proper, with the heaviest concentrations along the coast and in the central Yangtze Valley and Szechwan. Population is centered where land is most productive, and despite the ravages of war, flood, drought, and pestilence, population appears to be increasing four or five million per year. Already there are about 1,500 persons per square mile of agricultural land. In the view of most students of the subject, China is overpopulated. Millions of her people never have an opportunity to live. Cressey hazards

---

[14] See Cressey's discussion, *Asia's Lands and Peoples*, 163-165.
[15] Mallory, *China: Land of Famine*, 28, 37.

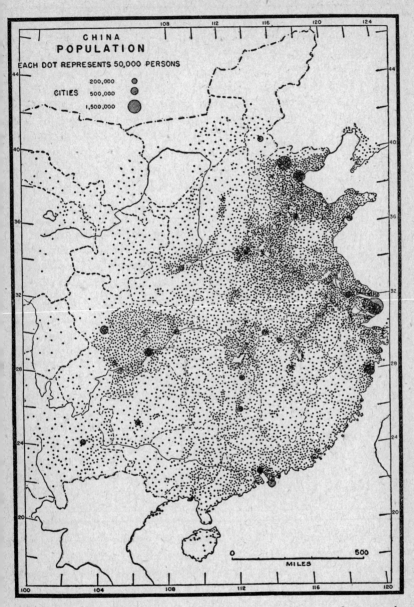

United States, Department of State. Division of Map Intelligence and Cartography.

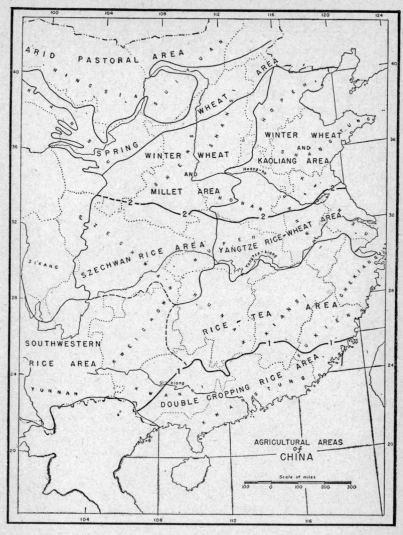

United States, Department of State. Division of Map Intelligence and Cartography.

the guess that 100,000,000 may have died of famine in the past century.[16] Human life and human labor remain among the cheapest of commodities in China. This continuing and increasing pressure of im-

---

[16] The heaviest concentrations of Chinese population are in the following widely scattered provinces: Szechwan, 52,703,000; Shantung, 38,000,000; Kiangsu, 36,469,000; Kwangtung, 32,452,000; Honan, 34,289,000.

mense population upon limited resources is a major controlling factor in China's future.

The Chinese of course are not all alike. Lin Yutang has reminded us that the southerner differs as much from the northerner in temperament, physique, and habits, as do the people of the Mediterranean from those of Scandinavia. Very generally, however, the Chinese, by reason of their physical environment, have developed great powers of stamina and resistance. Those who did not, did not survive.[17] The capacity of the Chinese as a farmer has often been told. His great food crops in the north are such grains as wheat, millet, and kaoliang; in the regions of the Yangtze and the south the grain food is rice, developed in many varieties. Tea is grown in the temperate regions of the lower Yangtze and the south. Pork has long been prominent in the diet of the northerner; fish and poultry in that of the southerner. The staple crops have been and still are raised largely by vast expenditure of human labor. The use of animals is the exception rather than the rule, and machine power in agriculture has hardly as yet made its appearance. The problem of agriculture is further aggravated by the effects of deforestation, by lack of scientific seed culture and selection, by failure to eradicate pests, and by the lack of adequate irrigation control. Of course, the fundamental importance of agriculture is not unrecognized in China. For nearly a decade prior to the Sino-Japanese undeclared war of 1937, many Chinese reformers considered the direct improvement of rural China as the nation's main route to salvation. During the war and particularly after 1941 the theorists turned to industrialization as the solution, on the theory that the lowly status of the farmer, his burdens of debt, can only be lifted by the nation's capacity to develop modern industry.[18]

MANCHURIA

From many points of view, the area known as Manchuria is one of the most important regions of China. Prior to the Japanese invasion of 1931, it consisted of what the Chinese called the Three Eastern Provinces, Fengtien (Liaoning), Kirin, and Heilungkiang, with a total area of about 400,000 square miles, which is somewhat larger than the com-

[17] In addition to the Chinese, the sons of Han, there are many other races within China. In Manchuria there are more than a million Manchus. In the far southwest there are from 15 to 20 million peoples of various stocks: Thai, Shan, Lolos, and others. Mongol, Tungan, and Turkish stocks each account for some two million.

[18] Kuo-heng Shih, *China Enters the Machine Age* (Cambridge, 1944), xvi. For the position of the farmer in China see in particular Hsiao-tung Fei, *Peasant Life in China* (New York, 1946).

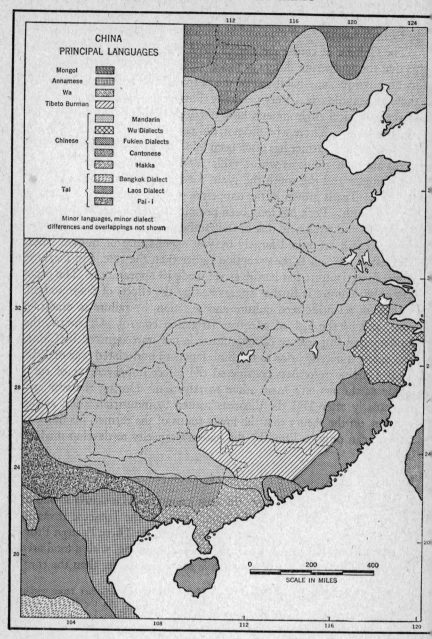

CHINA
PRINCIPAL LANGUAGES

Mongol
Annamese
Wa
Tibeto Burman

Chinese
Mandarin
Wu Dialects
Fukien Dialects
Cantonese
Hakka

Tai
Bangkok Dialect
Laos Dialect
Pai - i

Minor languages, minor dialect
differences and overlappings not shown

SCALE IN MILES

United States, Department of State.   Division of Map Intelligence and Cartography.

bined areas of Texas and New Mexico.   Both by reason of its natural
resources in minerals, timber, and rich agricultural plain, and also because of its geographical position with respect to other lands—Siberia,
Korea, and Japan—Manchuria has enjoyed a unique position in recent
Chinese history.   In the first decade of the twentieth century, it became

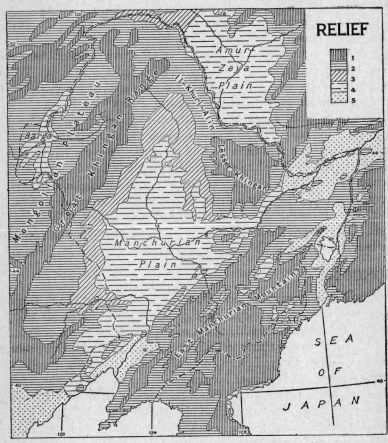

MANCHURIA.   The numbers refer to: 1, mountains; 2, uplands and higher foothills;
3, lower foothills; 4, plains; and 5, lowlands.   *Courtesy of the "Geographical Review,"
published by the American Geographical Society of New York.*

the battleground of imperialistic rivalry between Japan and Russia.
Manchuria is the only part of China served adequately by railroads.   Of
an approximate 15,000 miles of railroad in all China in 1940, half of this
mileage was in Manchuria.   The opening of the country by railroad
construction, and the removal of the old Manchu restrictions on im-

migration have brought millions of Chinese immigrants from Shantung and Hopei in the past fifty years. From a figure of 14 million in 1910, Manchuria's population rose to 25 million in 1926, and to some 40 million in 1940. In this way Manchuria has been a safety valve for population pressures in North China. Manchuria is made up of a huge central agricultural plain (138,000 square miles) comprising the basins of the Liao River in the south and the Sungari in the center and the north. This plain is almost surrounded by mountains.

Here in Manchuria in the twentieth century have occurred the most spectacular agricultural and industrial developments in all Asia. With a continental climate of long cold winters and short hot summers, with new and rich soil, and with pioneer peasant settlers from North China, where similar crops are grown, Manchurian agriculture has been able to produce for export. The crop for which the area is known in the export trade is the soya bean and its products. In some recent years Manchuria has produced more than half the world supply. The spectacular industrial developments in coal and iron mining and smelting are in South Manchuria, which Japan claimed as a sphere of influence after 1905. Here the city of Dairen ranked second among China's seaports. The eastern mountain regions are famous because they contain the best and largest of China's timber reserves.

MONGOLIA

Lying between central Soviet Siberia on the north, and China Proper to the south, are great grass plains, the Gobi Desert, and the bordering foothills and mountains of Mongolia, a territory which in the last years of the Manchu dynasty prior to 1912 covered an area of something more than one million square miles. Mongolia has usually been considered as being in two parts. Inner Mongolia was the southern region lying just north of the Great Wall. When the Chinese Republic was established in 1912, this area was divided into four provinces: Chahar, Jehol, Ningsia, and Suiyuan.[19] The remaining vast area to the north, commonly known as Outer Mongolia, was a dependency of both the Manchu empire and the later Republic. Under the Republic, China continued to claim suzerainty over it, but in reality it has been virtually independent since 1921, and in still more recent years has been organized as two republics under the protection of the Soviet Union: the Mongolian People's Republic, with its capital at Ulan Bator (Urga), and the

---

[19] Their respective areas in square miles are: 107,500; 74,300; 106,100; and 112,500. Suiyuan is approximately the size of the state of Arizona.

Tuvinian People's Republic, with its capital at Kizil Khoto.[20] Prior to World War II the population of all Mongolia was roughly estimated at about three million, and of these some 65 percent were Chinese peasant farmers, colonists who had pushed into the marginal-land provinces of southern Inner Mongolia where it is possible for agriculture to encroach on the grasslands of the nomads. For most of Mongolia, however, life is a matter of grass. The Mongols have traditionally been nomads raising flocks of sheep, horses, cattle, and camels, moving about the semi-arid Gobi where grass could be found. The degree to which the Chinese farmer has been able to penetrate Mongolia from the south has been determined by rainfall, and, indeed, many of the political currents which have swept back and forth across Mongolia in recent decades are indications of the conflict between the settled agriculture of the Chinese invader and the nomadic animal husbandry of the Mongols. The customary political organization of the Mongols has been the banner or clan, and the power of Lama Buddhism has been dominant.

SINKIANG

Northwest of China Proper and southwest of Mongolia is Sinkiang or Chinese Turkestan, some 706,000 square miles in area, with its capital at Tihwa (Urumchi). Larger than the combined areas of the Canadian provinces of Alberta and British Columbia, Sinkiang has a population of only about 4,500,000. Most of these are Turki in race and Mohammedan in religion. Although the Chinese population has numbered only about 10 percent of the total, Sinkiang during most of its modern history has been under greater or less Chinese control. The ancient silk routes from Europe to the Far East passed through this territory along the southern edge of the Tarim Basin. Here are the ancient caravan towns of Lop Nor, Yarkand, and Kashgar. Yarkand was the northern terminus of the Karakorum Pass from India. Today the more important road from China to the west follows the old route from Sian in Shensi through Lanchow to the Jade Gate at the end of the Great Wall, but at this point turns northwest toward the T'ien Shan, Heavenly Mountains. Dividing here, one route passes south of the T'ien Shan to Kashgar, the other north to Tihwa, the capital. From Tihwa westward, roads connect with the Turko-Siberian railway not far distant in Soviet Russian territory.

---

[20] This is the area marked on most maps as Tannu Tuva. It comprises a basin of the valley of the Yenisei. The people are a Finno-Turki strain. By 1946 Tannu Tuva had been formally incorporated in the U. S. S. R., and the Mongolian People's Republic had become an independent state under Soviet patronage.

In 1878, Sinkiang, previously a dependency, was formally incorporated as the nineteenth province of China. However, in the modern period since the rise of Mohammedanism in this area, China's political control has been precarious. At the beginning of World War II, Soviet influence was supreme. At the end of the war, Chinese influence was reviving.

United States, Department of State. Division of Map Intelligence and Cartography.

Sinkiang is a land of rugged mountains, arid plains, and scattered oases where only irrigation makes possible the existence of small cities. The population of Kashgar is some 35,000. Beyond these oases there is little agriculture. Sinkiang has been only a minor element in world politics in modern times. Recently, however, it has assumed greater importance, for it is the western gateway between Greater China and the

Soviet Union, just as many centuries ago it was the roadway over which passed Marco Polo and other early travellers from Europe. It was across these barren lands that Europe and China first exchanged ideas in the days of Greece and Rome. Now, in our own day, new and revolutionary ideas are again passing over the same route.

TIBET

Tibet, the Roof of the World, is a land of high mountains and high plateau separating China from India. Under the Manchus before 1912, its relationship to China was that of an "outer territory" or "dependency," a relationship which the reader will find more understandable in the light of the Confucian political theory of states discussed in Chapter 13. Since 1928, Tibet has been divided into two parts: Outer Tibet and Inner Tibet. The former maintains a semi-independent status, and is ruled by its Lama (Buddhist) religious hierarchy from the picturesque capital at Lhasa. The area of Outer Tibet is some 350,000 square miles, and the population about 1,500,000. Inner Tibet comprises the two Chinese provinces of Ch'inghai and Sikang (respectively 271,000 and 143,000 square miles) with a combined population of approximately two million. Racially, the native Tibetans are not Chinese but are related in physical type to various peoples of the steppe and desert country to the north.

Tibet has been the great physical barrier between the oldest cultures of middle and eastern Asia: the Indian and the Chinese. The entire area may be considered as a vast mountain, since 75 percent of the land has an elevation of 10,000 feet. Here are some of the highest mountain systems of the world: the Himalayas, the Karakorum, and the K'un Lun. The Tsang Po Valley just north of the Himalayas in southern Tibet has the least elevation and is the most populous region of Outer Tibet. Lhasa is located in this region. These physical characteristics have had much to do with the practical autonomy and semi-independence which the country has maintained. In modern times, Chinese influence has been the most persistent though not always the most effective. It has been rivalled at times by British influence from India.

The economic life of Tibet centers about the migratory herdsmen who raise yak, and about a small peasantry engaged in agriculture (barley, peas, and wheat), and wool-spinning and weaving as a household industry. Government in Outer Tibet is headed by the Dalai Lama, who is nominally supreme in both civil and religious affairs.

TRANSPORTATION

In the modern age of nations, the development of wealth and power has been inseparable from the factor of communications. This has applied in peace as well as in war. It is not possible here to treat in any detail the subject of communications in relation to Greater China's economic status and her political position among the powers, but it should be noted that the lack of modern railway and highway transportation has been and remains one of the serious handicaps on the road of Chinese modernization. As late as 1940, the total railway mileage in China was less than 15,000, and, as noted, half of this was concentrated in Manchuria and North China. For purposes of contrast only, it may be noted that railway mileage in the United States is about 240,000. Be this as it may, the fact remains that China's history both ancient and modern is unintelligible without recognition of the limited means of communication that have been available. This lack of effective communication has fostered the growth of sectionalism. With the exception of the very poor, often impassable, imperial roads joining the provincial capitals, the rivers were the only highways. As late as 1944, nine of the provinces were without railroads. The motor highways which now exist are a modern innovation. The first such road was built in Hunan in 1912. National planning of a system of highways was undertaken in 1932, and by 1937 there were 68,000 miles in operation, one fourth of which were surfaced. The most famous road in China, however, is the Yünnan-Burma highway, known to the West as the Burma Road. This approach to China's backdoor winds its tortuous way over mountain and valley for 596 miles from Kunming to Wanting on the Yünnan-Burma border. The section from Kunming to Hsiakwan was originally built in 1935 by the provincial government of Yünnan. The war-famous Hsiakwan-Wanting section was begun in the winter of 1937; through traffic on the entire road was opened late in 1938. In a very literal sense this was accomplished not by power machinery of an industrial age but by the manual labor of 160,000 men, women, and children working with spades, picks, and baskets. Before the close of World War II, American engineering skill had built the Ledo Road linking Burma and the Burma Road with Assam and India.

THE SEAPORTS OF CHINA

In concluding this brief survey of China's geographical position, it is worth-while to note that during the past four and one-half centuries, and particularly during the past one hundred years, European civilization, commercial and cultural, has been approaching China by way of the sea from the east. China's foreign commerce in the nineteenth and twentieth centuries has been conducted almost exclusively through a few great seaports: Dairen and Tientsin in the north, Shanghai at the mouth of the Yangtze, Canton and British Hongkong in the south. Nearly all foreign commercial and industrial capital (and much Chinese capital also) was invested in or near these ports and in lesser ports such as Swatow, Amoy, Foochow, Ningpo, Tsingtao, Newchwang, and Antung. It was in these cities on the seaboard, or in inland cities on the Yangtze, such as Hankow, that foreign trade, concessions, and influence developed. China's education and her growth in westernization, whether material or cultural, was felt therefore most deeply on the seaboard.

The recent war has altered this picture in some degree, and the future may alter it even more. Maritime or seaboard China is still dominant. However, interior and western China have acquired a new importance. During the war it was in western China that the National Government was able to survive. It was in northwest China that the rival power of the Chinese Communists was able to acquire its greatest strength. It is also in the interior and the west that China's ancient culture is meeting the young and vigorous cultural drive of Soviet Russia. The Pacific Ocean is no longer the only door to China.

SOVIET SIBERIA

Half of all Siberia lies within our definition of the Far East. In addition, much of southwestern Siberia borders Greater China along the long frontier of Sinkiang. Stated in another way, this is to say that all of Greater China's northern frontier and half of her western frontier touch the territories of the Union of Soviet Socialist Republics. The largest state of the Russian Union is the Russian Soviet Federated Socialist Republic, which includes three fourths of all Russian territory and had a pre-war population of 109,000,000, most of whom resided in European Russia. This enormous state reaches from Leningrad in Europe across Siberia to the Pacific Ocean, a distance of some 5,000 miles. Within that portion of this vast territory which lies directly north and northeast of China are a great variety of geographical regions and a number of special autonomous political divisions such as the Yakutsk Autonomous Soviet Socialist Republic centering about the valley of the Lena River; the Buryat Mongol Autonomous Soviet Socialist Republic in the area directly east of Lake Baikal; and the Jewish autonomous province known as Birobidjan, west of Khabarovsk in the great northern bend of the Amur River. Far again to the west against the frontier of Sinkiang are the huge Kazakh Soviet Republic and the smaller republics of Kirgiz and of Tadzhik.

In the modern age since the opening of the sea route to China, the Russo-Chinese frontier—the longest political boundary in the world— has played a relatively minor role in world politics. In part this may be explained by the inhospitable character of much of the country and the consequent sparseness of population. Yet it should be recalled that these have not always been forgotten lands. In the thirteenth century the Mongols came out of this heart of Asia and, turning both to the east and west, moved to the conquest of China and of much of Europe. Now, in the twentieth century, geographic prophets have attributed new and greater meaning to the Russo-Chinese frontier. Eastern Europe and most of Siberia is what Sir Halford Mackinder called the "Heartland," of which he said: "Who rules East Europe commands the Heartland; who commands the Heartland commands the World-Island [Eurasia]; who rules the World-Island commands the World." [21] The idea was the inspiration of Karl Haushofer and German so-called "science" of geopolitics.[22] One does not need, however, the assistance of geopolitics to recognize the new significance, political and cultural, which now attaches to the long Russo-Chinese frontier as a result of the Soviet-Russian renaissance now felt in every region of Siberia.

The area of Siberia is some five million square miles. Much of this territory lies along the Arctic Circle, where the ground is permanently frozen. Nevertheless, Siberia farther south is extremely rich in timber, in minerals, and in young agricultural land. Western Siberia is preeminently an agricultural region. South central Siberia, which lies west of Lake Baikal, is a mountainous region. Here in the Kuznets and Minusink Basins are some of Russia's great coal fields. Farther to the east, the coastal areas of Siberia on the Pacific are known as the Maritime Territory, and north of this the Khabarovsk Territory. Off these shores are the valuable Pacific fisheries. Like other regions of southern Siberia, these extreme eastern areas have witnessed a very rapid development, agricultural, industrial, and urban, since 1930. The expansion of agriculture, the birth of heavy industry, a rapid influx of immigrants from European Russia, and a feverish building of cities have been characteristic of this amazing frontier growth.

There are two great transportation systems in Siberia, the one very

---

[21] Halford Mackinder, *Democratic Ideals and Reality: A Study in the Politics of Reconstruction* (New York, 1942), ix.

[22] Hans W. Weigert, *Generals and Geographers* (New York, 1942), ch. vi.

old, the other quite new. The former is the system of magnificent rivers flowing to the north into the Arctic Ocean: the Ob, the Yenisei, and the Lena. The latter is the system of railroads running east and west across southern Siberia. The Trans-Siberian Railroad, which since the beginning of the century has linked European Russia with Vladivostok and with the cities and ports of Manchuria and North China, is now a double-track system. Other major systems originating in European Russia and in southwestern Siberia now penetrate deeply toward the southeast across the Kazakh Republic to within a limited distance of the Sinkiang frontier. A third major line, the construction of which has been covered with considerable secrecy, may be regarded as an expansion of the Trans-Siberian system. This is the Baikal-Amur Railway. Originating at Taishet or possibly at Nizhneudinsk on the Trans-Siberian west of Lake Baikal, the line survey runs far north of the Lake, then turning eastward reaches the Amur near its mouth at Komsomolsk, and continues to the sea opposite Karafuto. Late in 1946 it appeared that construction had not been completed.

These railroads, the Trans-Siberian and the Baikal-Amur, together with the great Amur River, provide ample outlets from eastern Siberia to the Pacific in the warm season of the year. But all Russian ports on the Pacific are ice-bound during the winters, and as a consequence Russian far eastern policy for the past century has sought and at times has achieved control of ice-free ports in South Manchuria. Indeed, Manchuria and Korea have peculiar geographical significance not only for China and Japan but also for the future of eastern Siberia.

The geographical significance of Siberia, however, does not lie solely in its extraordinary industrial development nor in its 5,000 mile boundary against Greater China. The advent of an air age has altered the relation of Siberia to North America across the Arctic Circle and by way of Alaska. The Arctic is no longer an impassable barrier between North America and Eurasia. Moreover, during World War II a new air road from America to Asia was developed by way of the Alaska-Siberia route. This route was from Fairbanks, Alaska, to Seimchan or Yakutsk, then south across Mongolia to China—a completely new approach to Asia.[23]

Finally, it may be observed that today the great bulk of the population in Asiatic Russia is Russian, and this predominance of the Russian immigrant stock is yearly becoming more pronounced. Among the Asi-

---

[23] Owen Lattimore, "New Road to Asia," *Nat. Geog. Magazine,* LXXXVI (1944), 641-676.

atic stocks are the Tadziks, the Turkmen, and the remnants of many ancient tribes of paleo-Asiatic or Mongolian derivation.[24]

JAPAN

Contrasting with the continental position and the great areas of China and Siberia is the maritime and small empire of Japan. Before World War II, this empire was made up of two major political divisions: 1) Japan Proper, consisting of four major islands and hundreds of small ones close by, with an area of 147,707 square miles, which is less than the area of California; 2) the outlying colonies which, when added to Japan Proper, gave a total area of 260,759 square miles, which is somewhat less than the area of Texas or the Republic of Chile.[25] Japan's insular position and her formation as a great chain of islands reaching from the Kuriles in the far north to the Pescadores and Formosa in the south have affected the nation's history and influenced its culture. Early in Japan's history, her proximity to China enabled her to draw heavily upon China's wealth in Confucian and Buddhist learning. Likewise, Japan's insular position enabled her at a later time to maintain a long period of political isolation.

JAPAN PROPER

There are four major islands in Japan Proper. Beginning in the north, the first of these is Hokkaidō (Yezo), 34,276 square miles. This island, slightly larger than the state of Maine, is the most recently settled of the major islands. Honshū (Hondo), 87,000 square miles, is the main island on which the great cities such as Tokyo and Ōsaka are located. It is slightly larger than the state of Utah. The third major island is Shikoku (island of four provinces), 7,000 square miles, where two rice crops are grown annually. The fourth, in the south, is the island of Kyūshū (island of nine provinces), 14,000 square miles, about twice the size of the state of New Jersey.

OUTLYING INSULAR TERRITORIES AND COLONIES

Beyond these main islands of Japan Proper were many others which were added to the empire in the course of its expansion.

1. Karafuto. This is the southern half (from the 50° parallel south) of the island of Sakhalin off the mouth of the Amur. This territory,

[24] See Aleš Hrdlička, *The Peoples of the Soviet Union* (Washington, 1942), 22-29.
[25] Manchuria, which under the name of Manchukuo was controlled by Japan from 1932 to 1945, was regarded officially as an independent state and was not incorporated in the Japanese Empire.

with an area of 13,934 square miles, was acquired from Russia in 1905; presumably it will be restored to the Soviet. The island is valuable for its fisheries and its oil deposits.

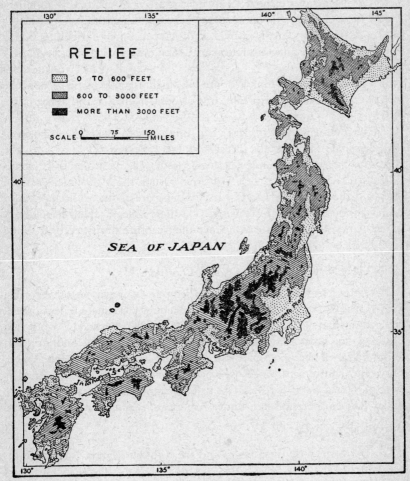

RELIEF

▦ 0 TO 600 FEET

▨ 600 TO 3000 FEET

▩ MORE THAN 3000 FEET

SCALE |___0___75___150__| MILES

SEA OF JAPAN

RELIEF OF JAPAN PROPER. *From Daniel R. Bergsmark, "Economic Geography of Asia."*

2. The Kurile Islands or Chishima (thousand islands). This is a long chain of volcanic peaks, 32 in number, extending some 700 miles northeastward from Hokkaidō toward the southern tip of the Kamchatka Peninsula. The area of the Kuriles (from the Russian *kurit*, to smoke) is 6,146 square miles.

3. The Ryukyu (Liu Ch'iu) Islands. This chain of 55 islands lying

21970

southwest of Japan Proper is divided into two groups named from their principal islands: Okinawa and Sakishima. Acquired by Japan in 1879, these islands have an area of 864 square miles.

4. The Island of Formosa (Taiwan), south of Ryukyu and opposite the Chinese coast of Fukien, is somewhat larger than the state of Maryland. Acquired by Japan in 1895, it developed a rich agriculture, particularly in sugar. Its restoration to China was pledged at the Cairo Conference, 1943.

5. The Pescadores (Hokoto) are 64 small islands (area 50 square miles) off the southwestern coast of Formosa. Japan acquired them in 1895.

6. The Bonin Islands (Ogasawara Jima), 615 miles south of Tokyo, include some 97 tiny islands (area, 30 square miles).

7. The South Sea Islands (Nanyo), under Japanese mandate from 1919 until World War II, consist of three groups, the Mariana, the Caroline, and the Marshall Islands. In all, there are about 623 islands and nearly a thousand lesser reefs (area, 840 square miles). They have been under American administration since their capture during World War II.

CONTINENTAL TERRITORIES OF JAPAN

The largest colony of the Japanese Empire as it was before World War II was Chosen, or Korea, with an area of 85,000 square miles, somewhat more than half the area of California. In 1905, Japan also acquired by lease the Kwantung Territory in South Manchuria, and during World War I she took over the German leased territory at Kiaochow, in Shantung province, which she controlled until 1922. At the close of World War II, Korea was divided into two zones, the northern under Russian, the southern under American, administration.

PHYSIOGRAPHY

Japan Proper, with the Kuriles and the Ryukyu Islands, is essentially a mountain chain lying off the coastline of Asia. Geologically the land is of recent origin, containing some 500 volcanoes, of which 60 have been recorded as active. Between the mountain zones of Japan proper are the lowlands, representing about one fourth of the area, which support the bulk of Japan's wet rice agriculture. Climate varies from the humid subtropical to the humid continental type. Climatic conditions are affected both by the nearness of the islands to the mainland and their location in the path of the monsoons. Winters are less severe than in adjacent areas of the continent. In late summer the islands suffer from typhoons blowing north from the tropics.

NATURAL RESOURCES

Half of Japan is covered with forests which provide fuel, building material, fiber for industry (paper, rayon), and food (fruit, nuts, etc.). Although rivalled by industry in the immediate pre-war years, agriculture remained dominant in the Japanese economy. In 1920, slightly more than 50 percent of the gainfully occupied population was engaged in agriculture; in 1936, slightly less than 50 percent. A striking feature is that not more than 20 percent of Japan Proper is regarded as arable land. The mean size of the Japanese farms is a little more than two and one-half acres, but 70 percent of the farms are below this figure. Cultivation is highly intensive and the use of machinery is the exception rather than the rule. The dominant crop, rice, uses about 40 percent of the crop land. Barley, wheat, and oats are second as food crops, followed in the southern sections by fruit and tea. Extensive areas have been devoted to the mulberry tree in the production of silk worms. In recent years live stock, though increasing, remained limited both because of physical limitations in land and certain cultural habits. Prior to World War II, 27 percent of Japan's farmers were tenants, whereas 43 percent owned part of their farms and rented additional land.

Fishing is one of the great sources of food for Japan; the industry employs more than 650,000 full-time fishermen. Where part-time workers are included, the industry in normal times has contributed income to 20 percent of the population. Fish in the Japanese diet has occupied the place of meat in the Western diet.

Japan's mineral wealth does not place her among the most favored nations, yet her mineral resources are not without importance. Her estimated coal reserves are significant but fall far short of those in China, Siberia, Australia, or Indo-China, her nearest neighbors. Oil in relation to demand is scarce. Whereas the Japanese per capita reserve prior to 1937 was some seven million barrels, that in the United States was 140 million. Throughout the Far East, Japan's petroleum resources on the eve of World War II were far inferior to those in the East Indies (British and Dutch), and probably to those of Siberia. In water power Japan is relatively wealthy, though her potential resources in this respect do not compare with those of the United States. In iron ore reserves she ranked fifth among countries of the western Pacific, and her heavy industry has been in part dependent on foreign sources. Prior to World

War II she was self-sufficient in sulphur, limestone, and nearly so in manganese, chromium, and copper.

POPULATION

Population and the so-called "population problem" in Japan Proper have been among the most controversial questions in recent far eastern history. This problem of population is of relatively recent appearance. From 1721 until 1852 Japan's population remained practically stationary —about 27,000,000. But between 1872 and 1940 there was an increase from 34,000,000 to 73,000,000. Since it was estimated that this popula-

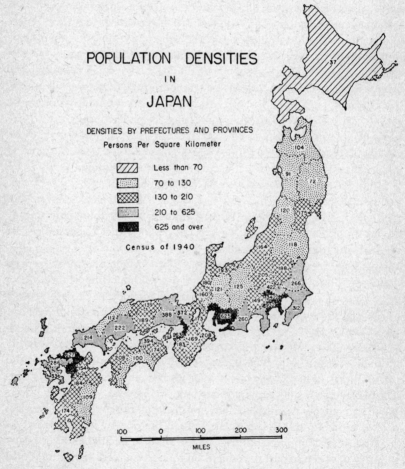

POPULATION DENSITIES
IN
JAPAN

DENSITIES BY PREFECTURES AND PROVINCES
Persons Per Square Kilometer

Less than 70
70 to 130
130 to 210
210 to 625
625 and over

Census of 1940

United States, Department of State. Division of Map Intelligence and Cartography.

tion would continue to increase until about 1970, Japan's problem was to find "productive occupation for the increasing numbers" in a land where there were already 3,000 persons per square mile of arable land. Emigration had little effect on the problem, the main efforts for relief between 1920 and 1940 being in industrialization and military expansion.

FOREIGN TRADE AND THE PORTS

In the years between World War I and World War II, Japan could be described as a country "nearly self-sufficient in food, deficient in primary materials, and rapidly achieving an advanced, though still incomplete, stage of industrialization." [26] In this picture foreign trade played an increasingly important part after 1920. Principal exports included raw silk, cotton tissues, and metal products, while imports were primary materials, mechanized equipment, and raw cotton.

Some of the chief cities and ports of Japanese industry and commerce include: Tokyo (the capital, formerly Yedo), with a population of over 6,000,000; Ōsaka (the Pittsburgh of Japan), 3,200,000; Nagoya (in central Japan, famous in the history of Japanese porcelain and pottery), 1,200,-000; Kyoto (the former Heian, the second permanent capital, noted for its silks, and embroideries), 1,150,000; Yokohama (the seaport of the capital, on Tokyo Bay), 800,000; Kobe (the center of the shipping industry), 1,000,000.

KOREA

The long and troubled story of Korea's political history is unintelligible without due consideration to the country's geographical position. Not only in the late nineteenth and early twentieth centuries but also on many previous occasions, Korea has been a political hot spot of the Far East. Ethnographically the Koreans are a distinct people. They have their own language and literature, their own dress and mores, but their geographical position and, at times, their seeming political ineptitude have combined to give them a rather unhappy modern history. Their long Confucian subserviency to China gave way at the turn of this century to colonial subserviency to Japan. Moreover, Korean nationalism, driven into hiding by the Japanese conqueror, was further weakened by its own internal dissensions. The resulting uncertainties for future Korean nationhood were reflected in the Cairo Declaration, which called for an independent Korea not immediately, but "in due course."

[26] Guy-Harold Smith and Dorothy Good, *Japan: A Geographical View* (New York, 1943), 73.

Korea is a mountainous land. Plains and valleys comprise only about one fifth of the total area of 86,000 square miles, which is just half the size of Japan Proper. The predominant mountains, the Taihaku range, follow the eastern shoreline and drop abruptly into the Japan Sea. As a consequence, there are few good harbors on the northeastern coast. Most of Korea's rivers rise in these eastern mountains and flow westward into the Yellow Sea or into the Yalu and Tumen river systems on the border of Manchuria. Climate is subject to greater extremes than those which prevail generally in Japan. The area of cultivated land in recent years, some 11 million acres, is relatively larger in respect to total area and population than is that of Japan Proper. But as against this, it is to be noted that 80 percent of Korea's population of over 23,-000,000 derives its meager living from agriculture. As in both Japan and China, human labor, not machinery, is the motive power in agriculture. The major crops parallel those of Japan but the yield is far less. In some recent years 40 percent of Korea's rice crop has been shipped to Japan, while cheaper millet was imported by Korea from Manchuria. As in so many other parts of the world, so in Korea, farm tenancy and debt present a repelling picture of economic and social maladjustment. Somewhere between three and four out of every five Korean farmers were tenants on the eve of World War II.[27]

More than 70 percent of Korea is covered with forest, but commercial timber is confined largely to the northern areas bordering Manchuria. Gold, iron, and coal are the principal minerals. Industrialization has made rapid progress since 1930. Seoul, or Keijo, the centrally located capital, is the largest city, with a population of over 700,000.

While Korea was a colony of Japan after 1910, it acquired a considerable Japanese population. By 1940, this population numbered 630,000, engaged for the most part in industry, railroading, merchandising, and government service. Conversely, Korean "cheap" labor migrated to Japan; statistics indicate that in the immediate pre-war years Koreans in Japan exceeded the number of Japanese in Korea.

Since 1875, Korea has been controlled in succession by China, by Russia, and by Japan. At the close of World War II, it was Russia and the United States that contended for the right to shape Korea's future. In Korea, geography is the father of international politics.

SOUTHEASTERN ASIA

The remaining section of the Far East to be mentioned is commonly referred to as Southeastern Asia. It consists of two geographical areas.

[27] H. K. Lee, *Land Utilization and Rural Economy in Korea* (Shanghai, 1936).

The first is a large peninsula of the continent comprising three political divisions: Burma, Siam (Thailand), and Indo-China. The dominant historical culture of this semi-continental area is Buddhist.[28] The second area includes the peninsula of Malaya, and the archipelagoes of Netherlands India and the Philippines. So it is basically an insular and maritime region where the predominant culture, with the exception of the Philippines, is Mohammedan. It would be difficult to exaggerate the historical, the economic, or the strategic role which this area has played in modern times. The Straits of Malacca have been the maritime gateway to the Far East since the beginning of the sixteenth century. The East Indies were the great source of the spice trade. In more recent times, Malaya has been a main producer of the world's rubber, tin, oil, and many tropical products. Both economically and strategically, Southeastern Asia has been and remains one of the key areas of the world. Since World War II, its political significance has increased rather than diminished as a result of the nationalistic movements through which its peoples are seeking to break the bonds of colonialism. For many centuries the peoples of Southeastern Asia have not been their own political masters. Here the colonial empires of Britain, France, Holland, and the United States have met, and here also a great variety of colonial techniques have been applied. Nevertheless, in any attempt to determine the culture values of this vast and populous region, it must be remembered that India, both Buddhist, Hindu, and later Moslem, was the source of the culture of Southeastern Asia, except for Annam, which received its philosophical heritage from China.

BURMA

Burma, for many years a part of the British Empire in India, in 1937 became a semi-selfgoverning colony of the empire. Only a little smaller than Texas, Burma has an area of 262,000 square miles and a population of 16,000,000, of whom there are some 11 million Burmese, more than one million Karens, one million Shans, one million Indians, and some 200,000 Chinese. Burma's population is predominantly agricultural, and there is no problem of overpopulation, there being only some 60 persons per square mile. Rice is grown in southern Burma; millet, cotton, and beans, further north. The concentrations of population are in the valley of the Irrawaddy and the Sittang. Oil is present in commercial quantities. Rangoon, a city of half a million, near the mouth of the

---

[28] Considering the area from the broadest historical point of view, it should be noted that Indonesia received Hindu acculturation first, then Buddhist, and finally Moslem. Cambodia was affected by both Hindu and Buddhist culture.

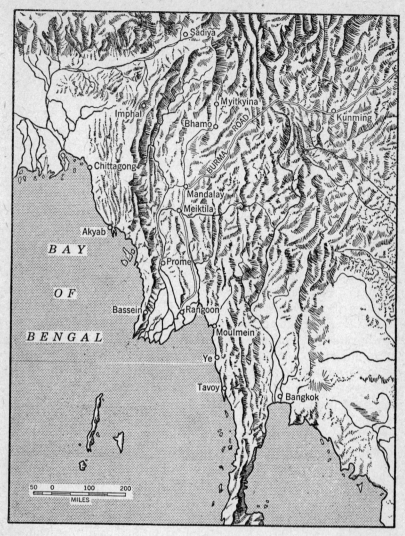

RELIEF OF BURMA.

Irrawaddy, was until recently the only gateway to Burma, since the country is sealed off on the west, north, and east by high mountains. Even with the completion of the Burma Road into Yünnan, and the now unused Stilwell (Ledo) Road to India, the principal commercial avenues to Burma are likely to remain the maritime routes in the south. Much of eastern Burma is a plateau where the predominant population is composed of Shans, and where because of the elevation (3,000 to 4,000 feet) the climate is temperate.

SIAM (THAILAND)

Wedged between Burma on the northwest and Indo-China on the northeast is Siam, which, until invaded by Japan during World War II, was the only country of Southeastern Asia which had been permitted to retain its independence. Siam is slightly smaller than the Republic of France, and has a population of about 16,000,000. Here, too, as in Burma, there is a rice economy and no serious population pressure. For many years Siam has been an important exporter of rice, tin, and rubber. The best agricultural land is in central Siam; the north is mountainous; the northeast contains forests, grassy plains, and some rice lands; the south is a part of the Malay Peninsula, where tin is mined and rubber is grown. The predominant people are the Thai.

INDO-CHINA

East of Siam is the French colonial empire of Indo-China, with an area of 286,000 square miles and a population of 24,500,000. There are five political divisions or provinces. In the south is Cochin-China, occupying the Mekong Delta. The principal city and the capital is Saigon. The central Mekong Valley is occupied by Cambodia. Along the eastern coast against the South China Sea is the province of Annam with its coastal plain backed by mountains. To the west of Annam in the interior and in the mountains of the upper Mekong is the state of Laos; in the far north, bordering China, is Tonkin, through which flows the Red River. Here the important cities are Hanoi and Haipong.

Throughout Indo-China more than 70 percent of the people are Annamese, a stock showing strong Chinese cultural influence. The Cambodians, the principal lesser stock, have a culture derived from India. Since more than half of Indo-China is mountainous, population tends to be unevenly distributed with heavy concentrations in the delta lands, particularly in Tonkin. Most of the country, too, lies in the tropics. Its principal products are rice, rubber, tea, and coffee. The area is fairly well endowed with minerals basic to heavy industry.

MALAYA

British Malaya is a long peninsula stretching southward from Burma and Siam almost to the equator. At its southern tip is located an island on which is the city of Singapore, founded by Sir Stamford Raffles in 1819. Tin and rubber have made Malaya and Singapore famous. The area is 51,000 square miles (approximately the size of North Carolina), and the population is about 5,500,000. Politically the area consists of British crown colonies, federated native states under close British control, and unfederated states which are British protectorates. Prior to World War II cultivated land was devoted approximately 65 percent to rubber, 14 percent to rice. Malaya's share of world production of rubber was from 40 to 50 percent, and of tin, 30 percent.

THE EAST INDIES

The East Indies form the largest and richest archipelago in the world with an area of approximately one million square miles located entirely within the tropics. The extent of the islands from east to west is greater than the breadth of continental United States. Most of the archipelago has long been the major holding of the Dutch colonial empire, known as the Netherlands Indies or Netherland India. Smaller areas in Borneo and New Guinea are British possessions, and half of the small island of Timor is a remnant of the Portuguese colonial empire.

The principal islands of Netherland India are: Sumatra, Java, the Celebes, and parts of Borneo and New Guinea. The total area is 753,-000 square miles with a population in excess of 70 millions, of which more than half live in the two islands of Java and Madura. Rice is the principal grain crop. Java's huge agricultural population, about 950 persons per square mile, is explained by the unusual fertility of her tropical soil. Plantation agriculture financed by Dutch and foreign capital and employing scientific methods has developed the following products for the export trade: rubber, copra, coffee, tea, cinchona, kapok, sugar, tobacco, and palm oil. Prior to World War II the Netherlands Indies produced 90 percent of the world's quinine supply, 85 percent of the pepper, and a third of the world's rubber. The more important petroleum resources are in Sumatra and Borneo. The prevailing racial stock is Malay.

THE PHILIPPINES

The Philippine Islands are of particular interest to American students because it is in the Philippines that the United States has experimented with the problems of training a subject people for self-government and independence. From 1898 until 1946, the Philippines were an American colonial possession—an unincorporated territory of the United States.

The Philippine archipelago consists of more than 7,000 islands, great and small, lying within the tropics off the southeast coast of Asia. The

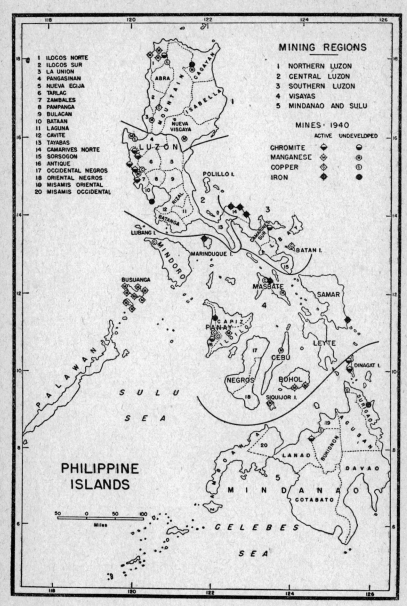

MINING REGIONS

1 NORTHERN LUZON
2 CENTRAL LUZON
3 SOUTHERN LUZON
4 VISAYAS
5 MINDANAO AND SULU

MINES : 1940

	ACTIVE	UNDEVELOPED
CHROMITE		
MANGANESE		
COPPER		
IRON		

1 ILOCOS NORTE
2 ILOCOS SUR
3 LA UNION
4 PANGASINAN
5 NUEVA ECIJA
6 TARLAC
7 ZAMBALES
8 PAMPANGA
9 BULACAN
10 BATAAN
11 LAGUNA
12 CAVITE
13 TAYABAS
14 CAMARIVES NORTE
15 SORSOGON
16 ANTIQUE
17 OCCIDENTAL NEGROS
18 ORIENTAL NEGROS
19 MISAMIS ORIENTAL
20 MISAMIS OCCIDENTAL

PHILIPPINE
ISLANDS

50   0   50   100
Miles

United States, Department of State. Division of Map Intelligence and Cartography.

area of 115,600 square miles is a little larger than that of the state of Arizona. The principal islands are: Luzon in the north, Mindanao in the south, Mindoro, Negros, Panay, Samar, Leyte, and Bohol in the center. Since 1946, the population has probably been in excess of 17,-000,000.[29]

During the twentieth century, the economic life of the islands has rested to an increasing degree on the development of a sugar industry. Tobacco, hemp, copra, timber, and fish are other important agricultural resources. By 1946, only some 25 percent of the potential agricultural land had been brought under cultivation. Since 1930 there has been notable development of a mining industry producing gold, chrome, copper, iron, and manganese. Chrome deposits, estimated as among the world's largest, are in the Philippines. Lead, molybdenum, asbestos, zinc, platinum, and sulphur are present in commercial quantities. Low grade bituminous coal is also plentiful. No good coking coal has been discovered, but there is a considerable field for the development of hydroelectric power.

During the half century of American control, the Philippine agricultural economy gravitated toward a few products, such as sugar, for which there was a ready and open American market. The result was to encourage an agricultural economy dependent on free access to the American market. However, both climate and the resources of the land make possible a self-sufficient economy in foodstuffs. For many reasons, industrialization is not likely to be rapid. It has been indicated that though there is much mineral wealth, coal is lacking.

The Filipino people can be classified into 43 ethnographic groups employing 87 languages and dialects, yet with the exception of probably less than 100,000 negroid peoples, they all belong to the great Malay group. Ethnologically, therefore, it is not diversity but homogeneity that distinguishes the Filipino. The diversity is cultural and religious rather than racial.[30]

GEOGRAPHICAL FACTORS NOT STATIC

In concluding this brief geographical introduction to our story of modern contacts between the West and the Far East, it is well to remind ourselves that the force of geographic factors does not remain static. Their influence is not fixed and absolute but changing and relative. In the sixteenth and seventeenth centuries, the Far East was viewed by

---

[29] In 1918, the figure was 10,314,310; in 1939, it was 16,000,303.

[30] Major religious and cultural groups include: Roman Catholics, 12,603,000; Aglipayans, 1,573,000; Mohammedans, 678,000; Pagans, 626,000.

Europeans as a remote region; it could be reached only by a long and arduous ocean voyage of many months; its products were rare and expensive luxuries; and its peoples and their cultures belonged to another world. By the later nineteenth century distance had shrunk and knowledge had increased. The Far East was still distant from Europe, and also now from America, but it was no longer remote. Months of travel by sailing ship were now measured as weeks by steamship; silk and tea might still be luxuries, but they were no longer rare. If the Far East remained another world, it was now regarded as a world to be conquered by European and Western civilization. And now in our own day, that conquest, certainly in terms of geography, has been achieved. The United States and China are now separated only by days and hours. Tin and rubber from the mines and plantations of Asia, and a host of other products have entered into the daily consumption of Western industry. Moreover, the language, if not the substance, of Western economic, social, and political thought seeks to remake the whole cultural pattern of Asia. Some would even suggest that the battles of Western political philosophy—the struggles of capitalism, democracy, constitutionalism, fascism, socialism, and communism—are being fought and determined as much in the Far East as in Europe or in America. Asia is no longer merely a geographical area providing a source of raw materials and a market for manufactures. Industrialization is already at work in the Far East. Present-day Japanese life rests on industry; Siberia has already become an industrial frontier; and China has blueprinted its plans for an industrial future. Indeed, a new civilization is now being fashioned in the Far East. In Japan alone the United States is attempting to remake the political character of an entire people. The geography of the Far East has become the geography of American international politics.

CHAPTER 2

CHINA: A BRIEF HISTORICAL RETROSPECT

THE civilization of China is one of the oldest and one of the richest known to man. Yet in the United States until very recent years surprisingly little attention has been paid to it. This is the more curious because for more than a century the American people has thought of itself as the friend of China, and because, during this same period, the government of the United States has held rather firmly to well defined and friendly principles in its relations with China. Indeed, the United States has often been considered the defender of China's political integrity. Nevertheless, the richness of China's thought and culture has occupied an extraordinarily small corner in the scheme of American education or in the recesses of American thought. Europe, in contrast with America, has often been more conscious of the intellectual gifts which China could offer, but even in the case of Europe, this enthusiasm for things Chinese has been sporadic. The result is that though there is a long history of intercourse between China and the Western world, in the main, the two civilizations have had little mutual understanding. In general, this state of affairs has prevailed until very recent times. Thus, before entering on the story of the growth of contacts between China and the West, it will be worthwhile to review briefly some of the high lights of China's history and her philosophy; for without some knowledge of these there can be no understanding of our contacts with China in the nineteenth and the twentieth centuries.[1]

PREHISTORIC CHINA

The traditional accounts of early Chinese history begin before the time of Hsia, a dynasty supposed to have held sway in northern China from 1994 to 1523 B.C., and to have included such mythical or legendary figures as Huang Ti, Yao, Shun, and Yü, the last being the alleged founder of the Hsia. But all this is mostly a matter of myth.[2]

---

[1] This chapter should be regarded as merely suggestive of the larger outlines of Chinese history and culture which deserve much broader reading in the references cited.

[2] The basic study is H. G. Creel, *The Birth of China* (New York, 1937). See also K. S. Latourette, *The Chinese: Their History and Culture* (3rd ed., New York, 1946).

BEGINNINGS OF HISTORIC CHINA

What may now be called the beginnings of China's history as opposed to legend lie in the five centuries of the Shang or Yin dynasty, *ca.* 1523 to 1027 B.C., the capital of which was at Anyang in the north-central valley of the Yellow River. Even at this early date, the men of Shang had developed a remarkable system of writing which employed most of the important principles involved in modern Chinese written characters. Government, particularly in the cities, appears to have been rather highly developed. Time was calculated by a calendar frequently adjusted to keep it in tune with the seasons. This was important. In an agricultural country and among a credulous people, a king might easily lose favor if the seasons went astray.[3] Shang was also a period of warfare which finally resulted in the defeat and destruction of the dynasty.

THE CHOU (JOU) DYNASTY, 1027-256 B.C.

The long and justly famous Chou dynasty is usually divided into a number of periods which cannot be treated here in detail. Though the origin of the people of Chou is uncertain, they appear to have come from the regions of the modern Shensi and Kansu. The early Chou state covered most of the lower Huang Ho Valley. The capital shifted from time to time. At one period it was in Shensi near modern Sian. After some two and one-half centuries, the Chou kings no longer were able to control the country; consequently, their dominions were broken into a number of semi-independent states. During the period of Middle Chou, 771-474 B.C., the scope of the Chinese realm expanded into the Yangtze Valley, while the Late Chou, 473-256 B.C., was again a period of interstate warfare from which was to emerge the power of Ch'in. Yet, despite its feudal warfare, Chou was a classical age. It was the period of Confucius, perhaps also of that vague figure, Lao-tzŭ, and of other great philosophers who have left their stamp on every succeeding generation in China's long history. In addition, it was a period when the Chinese appear to have absorbed ideas from beyond their own borders.[4]

---

[3] Cf. this responsibility of the sovereign with the theory of the Mandate of Heaven discussed later, p. 55.

[4] The most useful general history of China is Latourette, *The Chinese.* An extremely brief survey, convenient as an introduction, is L. Carrington Goodrich, *A Short History of the Chinese People* (New York, 1943).

CHINA BECOMES AN EMPIRE

From 221 to 207 B.C., China passed under the control of Ch'in (Tsin), one of the extreme western states of the late Chou period. By advancing eastward, this people came to control the richest agricultural areas, overcame the rival states, and made their king the "First Emperor" Shih Huang Ti. This emperor linked together the sectional walls already constructed on the northern frontier into the Great Wall, thus emphasizing what was Chinese and what barbarian.[5] Within its short lifetime, the Ch'in Empire grew to include the entire area between the Great Wall and the Yangtze and eventually most of the territory south of that river as far as Tonkin in Indo-China. In this manner, Ch'in, from which the name China probably comes, created the idea of an all-embracing state inside the Great Wall, an idea which was to have great significance in later Chinese history.

Ch'in was thus witness to the beginnings of one of the greatest revolutions in China's history, a revolution comparable only with that now taking place in twentieth-century China. This early revolution sought to destroy the ancient feudal system, laying the foundations for a relatively centralized bureaucratic state. The extent of this ruthless social upheaval is suggested by the fact that the kings of the earlier feudal China were aristocrats claiming divine ancestry and, together with the nobility, were the sole possessors of political power, whereas Liu Pang, founder of the Han dynasty, 202 B.C., was born a poor peasant. The contributions of the Ch'in revolution, however, were not entirely constructive. Shih Huang Ti is remembered also for his "burning of the books" by which he vainly hoped to narrow and discipline the course of Chinese intellectual development.[6]

THE EARLIER OR WESTERN HAN, 202 B.C.-A.D. 9
THE HSIN, A.D. 9-23
THE LATER HAN, A.D. 25-220

It is hardly surprising that the Chinese have liked to call themselves the Sons of Han, for Han is one of the rich and moving periods in China's long history.

The forces which had struck at the political and social system of the old feudal China also prepared the way for an era of discovery, expan-

---

[5] The Chinese recognized the frictions between themselves and "barbarians" long before the Ch'in.

[6] C. P. Fitzgerald, *China: A Short Cultural History* (London, 1935), 133-155.

sion, and conquest which made China a world power dominating the eastern half of Asia. These conquests belong mainly to the period of the Earlier Han and for the most part to the reign of Emperor Wu, 141-87 B.C. The energy of Han leaders extended the empire to the east to include South Manchuria, the southern fringe of Outer Mongolia, and the vast central Asian basin of Sinkiang or modern Chinese Turkestan.

The brief interregnum of the Hsin dynasty, A.D. 9-23, notable principally for the rule of Wang Mang and his efforts to imitate ancient Confucian models, was followed by the resumption of Han rule and the conquest of new lands.[7]

Han culture enriched China's life in almost numberless ways: in literature and the arts, in government, science, and industry. Here was begun the painstaking search and research to rediscover the proscribed classics. Here was laid the foundation for the Confucian conquest of the Chinese mind. In some ways, however, it was a new Confucianism, not concerned with finding a principle of moral authority. An authoritative and stable state already existed in Han, and so Confucianism, tinged by the atmosphere in which it was reborn, acquired an authoritative and religious tone, becoming in time the state cult.[8]

The creative qualities of Han reveal themselves in many ways. A solar calendar was developed with great mathematical accuracy. A seismograph detected earthquakes so slight that people did not notice them. Glazed pottery was being made at the close of the Han period. Elaborately embroidered silks were woven for both the domestic and the foreign trade. Han ladies improved on nature with face powder and various shades of rouge. Literature became richer in expression. Manuscripts were collected in an Imperial library. Paper appears to have been made from rags, and the first standard histories were written.

POLITICAL DIVISION: THE "DARK AGES," A.D. 220-590

The four centuries which followed the collapse of the later Han empire may be likened in some degree to Europe's "Dark Ages." The fall of Han, prefaced by that inveterate evil, the inordinate power of irresponsible elements near the throne, was accompanied, like the fall of Rome, by barbarian invasions, though in the case of China the cultural

[7] Cf. H. H. Dubs, "Wang Mang and his Economic Reforms," *T'oung Pao*, 35 (1939-1940), 219-265.

[8] Fitzgerald, *China*, 213-222; Richard Wilhelm, *A Short History of Chinese Civilization* (New York, 1929), 171-175; John K. Shryock, *The Origin and Development of the State Cult of Confucius* (New York, 1932).

and intellectual collapse was less devastating. In the end, the Chinese absorbed their conquerors and preserved the native language and literature. Whereas formerly the center of Chinese civilization had remained in the north, it now spread southward, a result of barbarian pressure, to include the Yangtze Valley, which to this time might have been described as colonial territory. In general it was a period in which old elements of civilization were severely damaged but not ruined. The empire was gone and was replaced by barbarian kingdoms, yet these displayed a "marked tendency to preserve Chinese civilization as a desirable thing." [9]

In this age of invasion, political confusion, and rival kingdoms, Buddhism became an integral part of Chinese thought and all but conquered the Chinese mind. Reaching China first in the first century A.D., Buddhism was able to capitalize on the political downfall of the Confucian Han. If Buddhism did not conquer China, it at least became the most important influence of foreign origin introduced in historic times. It modified Chinese life profoundly, but in the end was itself transformed by China.

The age of confusion helped along a movement at least as old as Han times—the transformation of the early philosophy of Taoism into a religion. Confucian neglect of the mystical world opened the way to both Buddhism and Taoism. Previously the latter had possessed no doctrine of an after-life. It now became the keeper of the spirit world with promises of immortality, of making old men young, and of creating gold by chemical processes.

As for the miscellany of the age, tea was mentioned for the first time in Chinese literature; the sedan chair as a mode of conveyance had come into being, as had also dice as a means of losing one's wealth.

THE SUI DYNASTY, 590-618

After these long centuries of political disunion, China was again united under the short-lived Sui dynasty. Conquests were renewed in central Asia; Formosa was invaded; and missions sailed south to the East Indies, presumably in the hope of developing commerce. At home, better communications were created by the building of a great canal through the heart of north-central China. This was the work of several million forced laborers. Though its military power was great, and its contributions to China's economy considerable, Sui could not long survive the popular resentment created by its extravagance and its intolerance.

---

[9] Wilhelm, *Chinese Civilization*, 206; Goodrich, *History of the Chinese People*, ch. iii.

THE T'ANG DYNASTY, 618-906

The new sovereigns of T'ang China were destined to lead the country through what is usually called the most brilliant period of its history. For purposes of administration the country was divided into provinces. Education was officially encouraged. Civil service examinations were stressed as in the previous Sui dynasty. Though the state cult of Confucius was later favored, religious tolerance in general prevailed. Laws were codified, and commerce was encouraged by further extension of the canal system. In the middle of the eighth century the T'ang Empire covered not only the greater part of what is now China Proper but also south and central Manchuria, and the vast area of Turkestan far to the west. It was T'ang China which challenged the growing political power of the Buddhist and other alien religions, subjecting them to the State or suppressing them. Architecture and sculpture reached new peaks of excellence. Ch'ang-an, the capital of T'ang China, with a population of nearly two million in 742, was one of the world's finest cities architecturally. This city formed the model for Japan's first permanent capital, Nara. T'ang, too, was the great age of Chinese poets: Po Chu-i, Li Po, Tu Fu, Wang Wei, and Wei Ying-wu. Two great encyclopedias were compiled. The short story, formerly dealing only with the world of spirits, entered the more human and mundane field of life and love. Block printing was invented. A list of the brilliant cultural inventions and attainments of T'ang China could be further lengthened. Yet for all the cultural greatness which filled the land, later T'ang emperors had not learned how to avoid the corruption of a wealthy court.

THE SUNG EMPIRE, 960-1279

With the fall of the T'ang Empire, China again fell into political confusion. The Khitans, a Mongol people, occupied Mongolia and Manchuria, while in other parts of the empire there were successful secessionist movements. Between 907 and 960 a succession of the so-called "Five dynasties" maintained a precarious hold on what was left of the T'ang Empire. These dynasties were: the Later Liang, the Later T'ang, the Later Tsin, the Later Han, and the Later Chou. In general it was a period of rule by "licentious tyrants," of such sensual refinements as the binding of women's feet (an imposition which seems first to have been imposed upon dancing girls), and of a general breakdown in the entire economic and political structure of society. Out of this chaos, however, rose the Sung dynasty, which, with the exception of the years 1127-1135, ruled China from 960 to 1279. The Sung Empire at its height (about 1100) covered virtually all China south of the Wall. On the north, however, it was bordered by the two powerful states of Hsi-hsia and Liao, the latter including southwestern Manchuria, part of northeastern China, and Inner Mongolia. It was the failure of the Sung to check the power of the border states that eventually forced the dynasty to retreat south of the Yangtze River. Nevertheless, Sung China was a period of general advancement in the livelihood of the people. Even the common folk now began to sit on chairs instead of the floor. Unhappily, there was little improvement in the lot of the common people after Sung times. Ceramics reached their highest degree of excellence. Because of the movement of population southward there was much expansion of the overseas trade along the coasts of southeast Asia and on to India. The Sung government attempted to regulate this commerce and reaped rich profits from it. Another innovation of Sung times was the use of explosive powder for warfare. Although known in China for many centuries, it had been used previously only in the making of firecrackers, and in religious and festive ceremonies. Sung was also a period of renaissance in the arts and in education. Unlike T'ang, where the poets excelled, under Sung the writers of prose took the lead. There was also advance in the science of algebra, probably introduced through the Arab trade. In religion and philosophy, the influence of Buddhism continued to decline, giving place to a new school of thought called Neo-Confucianism, which took what it wanted from both Taoism and Buddhism, discarding the rest. All in all, the civilization of Sung China probably outstripped any of its contemporary rivals so that Shao Yung might well have said: "I am happy because I am a human and not an animal; a male, and not a female; a Chinese, and not a barbarian; and because I live in Loyang, the most wonderful city in all the world." [10]

THE YÜAN DYNASTY OF THE MONGOLS, 1260-1368

Sung China, however, was under almost constant threat from rude peoples on the north and west: the Khitan, the Tangut, and the Jurchen. The Khitan state, which called itself the Liao dynasty, stretching across southwestern Manchuria and into China, was able to exact tribute from the Sung court. A second power, which eventually overcame the Khitans, was the Jurchen, which occupied the Amur country. Much later, in 1644, they were to conquer China. A third threat to China came from a Tibetan people, the Tangut, who ruled a state in Kansu

[10] Quoted by Goodrich, *History of the Chinese People*, 159.

called Hsia, with its capital at Ning-hsia. However, in the thirteenth century it was before Mongol power that Sung China was to fall. By the end of that century, the greater Mongol Empire extended from the eastern seaboard of China and as far north as the Amur in a continuous broad belt across the heart of Asia to the borders of Arabia and far into European Russia. The Mongols, in their advance upon China, controlled Mongolia by 1204, overran Korea in 1231, and made Khanbaliq (Peking) their eastern winter capital in 1260. Under Kublai Khan's generals, Yünnan was conquered in 1254, Annam was reduced to vassalage in 1258, and two unsuccessful expeditions were dispatched against Japan. China, indeed, had become merely a part of the world empire. It was the period when, as will be seen in later chapters, the world was shrinking: ideas as well as goods travelled the caravan routes from Peking to the Danube.

THE MING, 1368-1644, AND THE CH'ING (TSING), 1644-1912

With the fall of the Mongol power after a century of rule, China passed under the control of its last native Chinese dynasty, the Ming, which in mid-seventeenth century was overcome by another alien conqueror, the Manchus, who ruled until the establishment of the Republic in 1912. These last dynasties will be treated in greater detail in subsequent pages. Here it remains to set forth in limited detail some Chinese ideas on philosophy, religion, and government as these have developed out of China's long past. The emphasis will be only on those ideas and practices which bear most directly on the misunderstandings which were to arise as China and Europe were drawn into more intimate contact during the nineteenth century.

PHILOSOPHY AND RELIGION

It would indeed be a sad and futile pursuit to attempt an understanding of modern China through a mere recital of the rise and fall of dynasties or the comings and goings of kings, however important at times these things may be. A little reading in Chaucer, Shakespeare, Milton, Burke, or Dickens is likely to be more enlightening than memorizing the names and dates of the English kings. So in China, with rare exceptions, those who fashioned the mind of society were not always the emperors but rather the writers, the teachers, religious leaders, and philosophers.

Most of the fundamentals of historic Chinese religion and philosophy are exceedingly old. As a matter of convenience, the history of Chinese thought has been divided by one of China's brilliant contemporary philosophers, Hu Shih, into three main periods: the Sinitic age, extending from the beginnings to the ascendancy of Buddhism in the fourth century A.D.; the Buddhist age, 300 to 1100; and finally, the age of the Chinese Renaissance, having its origins in the rise of secular Neo-Confucianism in the eleventh century.

SINITICISM: THE NATIVE RELIGION OF CHINA

The native religion of the Chinese people, which Hu Shih has called Siniticism, probably dates from pre-historic times and includes all such later phases of its development as Taoism, Confucianism as a state religion, and Moism. It was a product of the combined cultures of the Shang and the Chou periods. Among other things, it contributed to the Chinese mind a profound belief in ancestor worship, in divination, in the concept of *Shang-ti* (the Lord on High) or *Hao-t'ien* (August Heaven), and in the idea of retribution for good and evil. These ideas, which had satisfied the Chinese of the early Chou period, failed, however, to meet the needs of men when, in the later years of the dynasty, political disorder and human distress were widespread. Popular discontent was given eloquent expression in the famous *Book of Poetry,* the most widely read of all books in the sixth century B.C. The poets of ancient China were thus paving the way for the appearance in the next century (570 to 420 B.C.) of the founders of Chinese philosophy: Lao-tzǔ,[11] Confucius, and Mo Ti. These men must therefore be studied in their relation to the decaying Sinitic religion and to the critical, skeptical atmosphere of their age. All three were revolutionary in their thinking. Applying the language of modern politics to ancient religion, Lao-tzǔ represented the extreme Left; Confucius, the Center, though leaning toward the Left; Mo Ti, the Right. Lao-tzǔ was a thorough heretic in religion and a revolutionary in philosophy. Confucius was a humanist and an agnostic. Mo Ti, devoutly religious, sought to preserve Siniticism by purifying it and infusing it with new life.

TAOIST PHILOSOPHY AND RELIGION

Of the personal identity of Lao-tzǔ, little, if anything, is known. Indeed, his very existence is doubted by some scholars. But the teachings ascribed to him have affected China profoundly. His philosophy resented the notion that God is a personal being, and sought to replace it by the idea of *Tao* (the Way or Road or Process). To Lao-tzǔ the *Tao*

---

[11] Contemporary scholarship, in particular the researches of Professor Homer H. Dubs, is inclined to date Lao-tzǔ, not as an older contemporary of Confucius, but at a much later period—that is, in the third or fourth century B.C.

was a natural process, something "being so of itself"; thus there was no need to construct any divine plan or purpose; "the *Tao* always does nothing; and yet it achieves everything." This was a quietistic philosophy which, if applied, would affect every phase of society. In politics the best government was the least government. Literature, knowledge, civilization were undesirable, for "when the world knows beauty to be beauty, there is ugliness; when it knows goodness to be good, there is evil."

Posterity has dealt with Lao-tzŭ much as it has dealt with other great teachers. Although he probably did not consider himself a religious leader, he was credited by later generations with founding a religion. Early chroniclers affirmed that he was born of a virgin. The wisdom ascribed to him and preserved by his followers was published, probably with much padding, in the second century B.C. in a work called the *Tao-Te-Ching*. Many of the virtues which Lao-tzŭ extolled, such as patience, humility, calmness, and deliberation, appealed to thoughtful men, but his quietistic doctrines, reminiscent of some forms of Hindu philosophy, were beyond the understanding of the masses. Hence, out of Lao-tzŭ's "natural way," succeeding generations of priests built the religion of Taoism, a thing miraculous and supernatural. In time Taoism became "the most elaborate and complicated system of magic, myths, spells, charms, incantations, demonology, and all similar forms of superstitious practice that any society has developed." [12] Taoism's control of the world of spirits gave it a foremost place in the scheme of ancestor worship. Man's every act was affected by spirits, either friendly or hostile. Herein lay the power of the Taoist priest to determine the appropriate time for building a house, for celebrating a wedding, or for burying a corpse. Here, too, the practical, matter-of-fact Chinese mind found relief in a world of the unreal: the world of nature, of romance, and of spirits—a world of mysteries. The secret healing power of herbs, the reviving virtues of aphrodisiacs, the wonders of astrology and alchemy—all these and many more were the stock in trade of the Taoist priest. Taoism was superstition, but it was also poetry.

CONFUCIANISM: THE TRADITIONAL PHILOSOPHY

The history of China without Confucius would be like the history of America without Washington and Jefferson. China, of course, has not always been dominated by the lives of those who professed to be Confucians. Yet Confucianism has affected China more profoundly and

[12] Paul Monroe, *China: A Nation in Evolution* (New York, 1928), 102.

continuously than any other philosophy. It gave to China a remarkable humanistic philosophy, a recognition that the true bases of society are social and mundane as well as divine.

Confucius was not merely an academic theorist. He was also a practical statesman, who, however, spent most of his life moving about the country engaged in teaching. Most of his students were young men of the upper classes for whom politics was the only honorable profession. Confucius presented to them a code of high moral ideas of such force that it became the dominant philosophy of official China and, until 1911, remained as authoritative as the Bible was, until a century ago, in Western thought. In fact, Confucianism was so much a part of the Chinese character that it was in a sense taken for granted. "The Chinese," to quote the American sinologue, Homer H. Dubs, "said little about it, just as Burke rarely quotes the Bible. Yet this [Confucian] tradition was in the background of every educated person's mind, since every candidate for official position concentrated on it for years, memorized longer accounts of the Confucian classics than our ancestors memorized from the Bible, and, what is more important, became expert in applying it."

The Bible of Confucianism, the Confucian classics, consists of the Four Books and the Five Canons. The Four Books include: (1) the *Analects,* or dialogues of Confucius with his disciples; (2) the *Book of Mencius,* containing the sayings of this sage; (3) the *Great Learning,* an outline of Confucian ethics; and (4) the *Doctrine of the Mean,* a similar treatise. The Five Canons contain: (1) the *Book of Changes,* an elaborate book of divination with a philosophical interpretation of the sixty-four hexagrams; (2) the *Book of History,* a fragmentary history covering the period 2400-619 B.C.; (3) the *Book of Poetry,* a collection of more than three hundred poems of the Chou period; (4) the *Book of Rites,* dealing with ceremonial procedure: and (5) the *Spring and Autumn Annals,* a history of the state of Lu.[13] To these basic works must be added the voluminous commentaries, comprising thousands of volumes, produced through the tireless industry of Confucian scholars both ancient and modern.

The classics and the commentaries provided a minutely detailed plan for human conduct. It was not sufficient to describe how Confucius spoke or acted. Details were provided as to his posture when in bed and the length of his night shirt. All life, in a word, was measured by the Confucian code. Thus it was possible for a wise man to be master

---

[13] See E. D. Thomas, *Chinese Political Thought* (New York, 1927), 28 ff.

of himself at all times and in all circumstances. No detail was considered too small to merit regulation.

Since Confucius was a humanist, his philosophy, broadly considered, was a code of conduct by which man might govern himself in his relations with his fellow men. These relations included five which were considered of prime importance: the relation of prince and minister, of parent and child, of husband and wife, of elder and younger brother, and of friend and friend. Five constant virtues were stressed: benevolence, righteousness, propriety, wisdom, and fidelity. The application of these virtues to human relations would, in the Confucian view of things, achieve the true end of life. Life would be simple; the family, happy; and social relations, harmonious. Confucianism expressed the practical, matter-of-fact, mundane tendencies in the Chinese character. Thus Confucianism was not a supernatural religion. To the Confucianist, the idea that men "live in order to die, as taught by Christianity, is incomprehensible." When his disciples asked concerning the gods, Confucius replied that he knew little about them. He appears to have been mildly skeptical of the supernatural, on the theory that if man could not understand life, it was unreasonable to suppose that he could understand death. Yet Confucianism included and inculcated the state religion and the sacrifices to the gods, although in Hsün-tzu it denied the existence of all gods. Confucius attended these and taught them. But the common accompaniments of supernatural religion were left to the state and the people, whereas Confucianism attended to mundane matters. There was a state priestcraft but no Confucian priestcraft. The concept of a future life was vague; it was not non-existent. Matters such as apostolic succession, miracles, sacraments, and the future life were left for other cults to manage as they would. Without the promise of rewards or punishment from the unknown spiritual world, Confucianism directed man in his duty both to his family and to society as a whole.

BUDDHISM

Buddhism was introduced to China about the beginning of the Christian Era.[14] Gautama, the traditional founder, is said to have been born in northern India on the border of Nepal about 563 B.C. Despite his noble birth he became dissatisfied with the transient character of worldly things, renounced the world, and began his wanderings in search of truth. His problem was the perplexing one of achieving re-

[14] The term "Buddha" is not a proper name but a title meaning "The Enlightened One."

lease from the burden of constant trouble that besets human life and of achieving the spiritual training necessary to that end. Whether Gautama regarded himself as the founder of a religion or merely as a teacher of ethics need not be argued here. The fact of importance is that from his central theme, the moral life with its virtues of love, wisdom, and the suppression of desire, his followers did erect a religion whose influence has been of the greatest significance. Centuries after Gautama's death his followers divided, and it was the northern as distinct from the southern Buddhist movement that spread its influence to Nepal, Tibet, Mongolia, Cochin China, China, Korea, and Japan. The most influential sect in this northern school of Buddhism developed the idea of the Western Paradise (Heaven), a concept which was lacking in Gautama's original teaching. Buddhism thus concerns itself deeply with man's spiritual life as contrasted with Confucianism, which is interested primarily in the earthly life. One would look in vain in Confucian writings for any mention of, or emphasis upon, this life as a probation for winning heavenly rewards.

China in many ways might have appeared an unpromising field for Buddhism. The emphasis on introspection and the inner life did not seem to harmonize with the practical philosophy of the Confucian mind. Buddhism in its exhortations to the celibate life could, it would seem, have little appeal in a land of ancestor worship.[15] Yet Buddhism was widely accepted in China and for some eight centuries was dominant in Chinese thought. This is explained by the fact that during the years of its introduction, leading intellectuals of China were already deeply immersed in the closely related speculations of Lao-tzŭ, while among the common people popular Taoism was widely practiced. Buddhism appealed therefore both to the learned and to the illiterate. Its elaborate ritual made a natural appeal to the masses. As a religion it was more dignified and comprehensive than Taoism, while as a philosophy it possessed the spiritual warmth so lacking in the Confucian ethical code of conduct. Here lay the explanation of a China "dazzled, baffled and conquered" by an alien faith. Indeed both Buddhism and Taoism became popular because Confucianism seemed to have failed, in that it did not prevent the downfall of the deeply Confucian Han dynasty. Hence Chinese leaders experimented for a period of centuries with various other religions.

Buddhism, however, brought more to China than the spiritual satisfactions of religion. Indian science and art came too. Chinese astron-

[15] Buddhism adjusted itself to ancestor veneration. Who could tell better than the Buddhist priest what became of the spirits of deceased ancestors?

omy was enriched; the written language became less rigid through the adoption of foreign terms; Chinese sculpture and painting took on new and deeper forms; block printing was used in the making of Buddhist and other books. These were permanent contributions to China's culture. In time, Buddhism as a religion tended to give place to the rising influence of Neo-Confucianism; yet much of the nobility of Buddhist thought and spirit remained.

THE CHINESE AND THEIR GOVERNMENT

In China every Confucian, appalling as it may seem, was a potential political scientist, if not a real one. From the earliest times philosophy concerned itself primarily with ethics and politics. Confucius, it will be recalled, was a statesman as well as a teacher. Politics was regarded as the most desirable profession for a young man of "good" family. The ruling class in China was the educated class, and education, in turn, meant mastery not only of the Confucian classics but also of the voluminous commentaries on them which later scholars had produced. Political problems were discussed in terms of the classics. An apt quotation from the classics could clinch a political argument. There was, in fact, a sort of Confucian monopoly on scholarship, maintained through the simple expedient of passing only Confucians in the civil service examinations. These examinations were the most important means of entrance to government service, and thus to posts of honor.

Since Chinese government has been affected more by Confucianism than by any other philosophy, it is worth while to inquire into the nature of its more important political precepts. These precepts came to be so deeply rooted as to be taken for granted by the ruling bureaucracy which so largely controlled the country.

Among the first precepts is that of unity, both social and political. To Western students familiar only with the chaotic and amorphous China of the early twentieth century, it may be surprising to find that Confucius taught: "As Heaven has not two suns, so the people should not have two kings." This was a doctrine frequently invoked when the state was threatened with political division.

Closely allied with this concept of political unity was the doctrine of Heaven's Mandate, which appears to have been taught by Confucius, but more particularly by his disciple Mencius. This doctrine teaches that the supreme earthly ruler, the emperor, is elevated to his position through the favor of Heaven. The emperor is therefore the Son of Heaven, and by Heaven's Mandate maintains his rule. But Heaven does not lose control of its mandate. When an incapable or wicked ruler ascends the throne, Heaven withdraws the mandate and bestows it on some righteous noble. It then becomes the duty of this noble to rebel, to overthrow the emperor, and to ascend the throne himself. In expounding this doctrine, Confucius was really idealizing the method by which dynasties in China had been said to have been overthrown.

A number of important implications follow very naturally from this convenient doctrine of the Mandate of Heaven. It is a justification for rebellion—a very significant point to the practical Chinese mind. It is also a justification for conquest, once the conquest has been achieved successfully. It may sanction submission on the part of a conquered people to the conqueror, since the latter undoubtedly holds the Mandate of Heaven.[16] However, the conqueror may also be resisted, for Mencius, one of the greatest of Confucian adherents, taught that Heaven sees as the people see and hears as the people hear. Therefore a conqueror who did not improve the lot of the people might be resisted. In modern times China has twice applied these political principles. She accepted the rule of the Mongols (1280-1368) and of the Manchus (1644-1912) so long as these foreigners conferred substantial benefits upon her. She overthrew their rule once they had lost the Mandate of Heaven.

The virtue of political loyalty was also affected by the doctrine of Heaven's Mandate. Although loyalty in the Confucian code was honored frequently to an extreme degree, it was not an absolute virtue. When the ruler had lost the Mandate of Heaven, it was the duty of the subject to be disloyal. The Western concept of the divine right of kings, demanding absolute loyalty to the throne, did not exist in the Confucian scheme of things. On the contrary, Confucianism called upon the people to pass judgment on their sovereign. Hsün-tzu, one of the great Confucian teachers of the third century B.C., said: "The people are the water and the prince is the boat; the water can support the boat, but it can also sink it."

Again, the doctrine of Heaven's Mandate justified only a very limited use of force by a conqueror, for a conquest is not achieved by fighting but only by securing the favor of Heaven. Hence force is only to subdue recalcitrants against the Will of Heaven. As a result, Chinese, generally speaking, have been pacifists. Mencius taught that there were no righteous wars although some wars might be better than others. Lao-tzŭ and Mo Ti likewise condemned war. Virtue was more likely

---

[16] This explains why the Japanese fostered Confucianism in Manchuria after 1931, and in North China after 1937. Some devout Chinese Confucians who accepted the Japanese conquest did so undoubtedly because of this doctrine.

to impress Heaven than brute force. Consequently, Confucianism justified military expeditions only when they could be interpreted as designed to restore order and preserve peace in a neighboring state.[17] The record of Chinese history, to be sure, may appear as a contradiction of all this theorizing about peace, for actually the Chinese have warred as generously as other peoples; but their wars of conquest were conducted mostly by rulers who were not Confucians.[18] The Confucian theory alone does not of course explain why the Chinese have in general avoided wars of conquest. Economic considerations have also played an important part. But it does appear that, had there been no Confucian pacifism, China would have warred upon its neighbors to a much greater extent than it has. In general, the Chinese have preferred to let their neighbors alone, provided the neighbors did not meddle in Chinese affairs.[19]

THE MACHINERY OF GOVERNMENT

The first Western traders and diplomats to reach China in the sixteenth and seventeenth centuries were both surprised and annoyed by the discovery, which they soon made, that the Chinese had their own peculiar ideas in the matter of business and government, and that these ideas frequently ran counter to the rules commonly accepted among Europeans. Since each side was convinced that its own ways were the right ways, it was difficult to find a common ground. Much of this difficulty can now be traced to that wide gulf which separated the Western from the Chinese way of running a government. What then constituted the every-day working ideas and machinery of Chinese politics?

In seeking an answer to this question, the Western student might do well to forget the kind of government he may see in the capital of the United States. The machinery of China's metropolitan government was remarkably simple. The emperor's government was furthermore a thing apart from the people, not a thing of the people. An ancient Chinese poet expressed the idea when he wrote:

> Work, work,—from the rising sun
> Till sunset comes and the day is done

---

[17] Japan's declarations that her conquests in China were for the purpose of restoring peace in Asia are derived directly from this doctrine.

[18] However, the whole question of Chinese pacificism is a touchy one and cannot be disposed of easily. Most of China's dynasties were set up by brute force.

[19] On this conception of Chinese unity and political theory, cf. H. H. Dubs, "The Concept of Unity in China," *Annual Report of the American Hist. Association*, III (1942), 3-19.

I plough the sod
And harrow the clod,
And meat and drink both come to me
So what care I for the powers that be? [20]

A Chinese boy was not likely to think of his country or his government as something of which *he* might one day be president.

There was also another vital difference. Whereas in Europe and in the New World of European ideas the individual was the unit of society, in China the family was the unit. This being so, it followed logically that the basic human relationships were those within a family and those between families. As the father was the head of the family household, so the emperor was the father of the family-state. Here the ideal which controlled man was not statute law but the virtue of filial piety. Man's body was a sacred inheritance from his parents. In the broader political sense this was interpreted to mean that careless living, disloyalty to a worthy prince, dishonesty in official duty, faithlessness toward friends, or lack of courage were sins against filial duty. So long as men conformed to the virtue of filial piety, there would be harmony in society, and consequently there would be little need for a government to pass laws. The form of government and the laws of government were of only secondary importance. It was not the structure of government, but the officials, who make government just or unjust. Laws, so it was said, did not create a good society; it was rather the officials who made and interpreted and enforced the laws. This will suggest why it was that the Chinese, particularly the Confucians, rarely excited themselves over such ideologies and structural forms as autocracy or democracy, anarchism or socialism, capitalism or communism. They held that people could not agree as to what these terms meant anyway. The important thing in government as in society at large was not structure and law, but men.[21] In a word, the Chinese rested their government on a social rather than on a political and legal basis.

THE FORMAL POLITICAL STRUCTURE OF GOVERNMENT

If in modern times the Chinese have given more thought to the political superstructure of their basically social government, it is because Europeans and Americans have forced them to do so. What, then,

---

[20] H. A. Giles, *Gems of Chinese Literature* (Verse) (2nd rev. ed., Shanghai, 1923), 12.

[21] The Confucian statement is: "Let there be the men and the government will flourish; but without the men, their government decays and ceases."

was the political framework of China's government under the Manchus (1644-1912) when this revolution in political thinking was imposed upon her?

The Manchu administration may be considered conveniently under four headings:

1. The emperor, the court, and the Manchu nobility.
2. The central or metropolitan administration.
3. Provincial administration.
4. Local government in the township and village.[22]

At the head of the state was the emperor, possessed of theocratic, patriarchal, and autocratic powers—"the Son of Heaven." He was held accountable for any famine, flood, or pestilence that befell the people, because such things were believed to be a consequence of his sins. As the father of the nation, he was clothed in theory with autocratic, absolute powers; yet these powers were not to be exercised in an arbitrary manner, but in conformity with customary practices established through the ages. The succession passed in the male line to whichever son an emperor might choose; the offspring of concubines were not excluded. When there was no direct heir, the succession passed to a lateral branch of the family of a younger generation. The new emperor was thus adopted as the son of his predecessor and performed the ancestral rites to the spirits of the departed sovereigns.

The authority of the Manchu emperor was not confined within definitive politico-geographic boundaries as was the case with European sovereigns. The territory over which he exercised direct rule included eighteen provinces, known as China Proper, and four great dependencies: Mongolia, Manchuria (which enjoyed a privileged status because it was the homeland of the dynasty), Tibet (after 1700), and Sinkiang (after 1789). Beyond these dependencies lay the vassal or tributary states, varying in number from time to time and recognizing, according to Confucian political ideas, the overlordship of the Middle Kingdom. Payment of tribute was one tangible evidence of vassalage (it was repaid by imperial gifts), and its bearers had come, in the course of Chinese history, from such distant lands as Arabia, Malabar, Ceylon, and eastern India, as well as from the adjacent kingdoms of Indo-China, Ryukyu, Sulu, and Korea.

As legislator and administrator, this autocratic Manchu emperor was bound by powerful controls: custom—the unwritten constitution of the

[22] For a detailed discussion see H. B. Morse, *The Trade and Administration of China* (3rd rev. ed., London, 1921), ch. ii.

Empire, and precedent as defined in the edicts of his predecessors. He was influenced and not infrequently controlled by the opinions of his ministers and by those of his personal attendants within the palace. Under the guidance of these latter, he selected his empress from a group of daughters of Manchu nobles. Secondary consorts might be chosen from the same group. Finally he might favor himself with an unlimited number of concubines from the families of Manchu nobles and freemen.

The nobility consisted of the imperial clansmen who traced their descent directly to the founder of the dynasty; the hereditary nobility who were direct descendants of the eight princes who co-operated in the conquest of China; and finally, a number of Chinese families such as the household of the Duke of Yen, a descendant of Confucius.

Usually the function of the metropolitan administration at Peking was negative rather than positive: to check rather than to direct the actions of the provincial officials. In the middle of the nineteenth century, however, increasing contacts with Western states forced the central government, though reluctantly, to assume a more positive responsibility.

The administrative divisions of the central government included:

1. The Inner Cabinet or Grand Secretariat. (Though of great importance under the Mings, this body had under the Manchus become less significant. Membership, which was limited to six, conferred the most coveted honor to which Chinese officialdom might aspire.)

2. The Grand Council. (This group was the emperor's chief advisory body, whose membership usually did not exceed five.)

3. The Tsungli Yamen (1861-1901). (First organized as a ministry of foreign affairs, this body tended to function as a sort of cabinet, taking over in large part the work of the Grand Council.)

Under the direction of these policy forming bodies, administration was conducted by the following boards:

1. The Board of Civil Office, controlling appointment to all official posts: the patronage.
2. The Board of Revenue, controlling such finances as were paid to the imperial treasury.
3. The Board of Ceremonies.
4. The Board of War, controlling the provincial (Chinese) military, not the Manchu military.
5. The Board of Punishments, a department of criminal justice dealing primarily with wayward officials.

6. The Board of Works, controlling official buildings throughout the empire.

To these boards at a later time were added:

7. The Board of Foreign Affairs (Wai-wu Pu), replacing the Tsungli Yamen in 1901.
8. The Board of Commerce, in 1903.
9. The Board of Education, also in 1903. Prior to this date the educational system had been controlled by the College of Literature (Han-lin Yüan).

There was also the Court of Censors, which, through its unlimited power to criticize, was a constant check, in theory at least, upon the activities of the throne and of the highest officials.

PROVINCIAL ADMINISTRATION

Under this rather impressive but rather passive metropolitan administration, the provinces of China enjoyed a large measure of autonomy. So long as the actions of provincial leaders did not run completely counter to Peking's general instructions and so long as the appropriate revenues were forwarded promptly to the capital, a province was free to administer local affairs largely as it saw fit. This did not mean, however, that Peking had no control in the province. All provincial officials from the highest to the lowest were appointed, promoted, transferred, and dismissed by the central government. Appointment was made usually for a three-year term, and high officials were not assigned to office in the province of their birth. It followed that the personnel was constantly changing and that every official ruled among strangers. Officials sent to a given capital were likely to be chosen from various factions or cliques in order that each might act as a check on his fellows. Against Western notions of centralized control, this Chinese system must appear inadequate, but the fact that it worked remarkably well is due to the deeply rooted social philosophy of Confucianism on which the society rested. Some features of the system, such as the lack of reciprocal responsibility among the provinces, were mildly amusing. If cases of brigandage occurred in the province of Kiangsi, the provincial authorities would probably drive the outlaws across the border into Fukien. It was then the duty of that province to deal with the matter.

The principal official of the provincial administration was a viceroy or governor. With him might be associated a Tartar general in command of the local Manchu garrison. There were also a treasurer who transmitted the revenues to Peking, a judge who passed on appeals from prefectural and district courts, a salt commissioner who controlled both the manufacture and sale of this article, a grain commissioner in some provinces, and a literary chancellor who supervised the civil service examinations.

LOCAL GOVERNMENT

For purposes of administration, the province was divided into a number of units, the most important of which was the county. A number of counties (from two to six) formed a prefecture, while two or more prefectures were grouped in a circuit under a supervising official known as the *taotai*. The county (*hsien*) was composed of a walled city and the adjacent country with its towns and villages. In the case of larger cities, only half or a third of the city was included. The magistrate, supposedly a master of all the arts and problems of government, was the chief official. His functions were as many and varied as the problems of mankind. He collected all local revenues with the exception of special taxes such as the salt tax and *likin,* the latter being an internal transmit levy. He was judge in first instance in cases both civil and criminal. He was registrar of land; he was famine and pestilence commissioner, and custodian of official buildings. In general, it was his business to preserve law and order and to have a care for both the physical and the moral welfare of his people. Within a county, the towns and villages were governed by their own officials, who were nominated by the village elders and confirmed in office by the magistrate. Within the village lay the real government of China, where the spirit of the family or the unity of the family expressed itself in a larger loyalty to the land which had supported the family or the clan. The government of the village was communal and largely invisible, for there were no mayor and councillors; it was a moral government of the elders based on "custom and usage, the unwritten law." This was the only government that most Chinese knew. As for Peking and the metropolitan administration, the villagers considered that "heaven was high and the emperor far away."

THE TRADITIONAL EDUCATION

Although schools did exist in the China of the Manchus and although some schools were subsidized, formal public education was not regarded as the function or duty of government. The wealthy employed private tutors for their children and in some cases established a free school as an act of benevolence, but the average Chinese boy enjoyed no formal schooling. At the close of the nineteenth century, not more than three percent of the people were literate. However, as Arthur W. Hummel has suggested, the word "literate" is apt to be misleading when applied to a people so compact socially and so deeply rooted in their culture as are the Chinese. A Chinese, for instance, may not be able to read, and yet he may possess extraordinary traditional skills which make him almost a cultured man.

The small literate group, however, provided the scholars, and scholarship in turn was of high importance since only through learning could men rise to official position and honor. The basis of education was the Confucian classics and their commentaries, a knowledge of which required a much more extensive scholarship than, for example, a thorough knowledge of English literature. The commentaries, of which there were thousands of volumes, had also to be mastered. In addition, the extensive Chinese histories had to be known. Therefore there was much emphasis on memory. To be able by memory and in appropriate style to apply a classical phrase to the solution of a philosophical problem of politics was the goal of the scholar. Science, mathematics, and the development of independent and critical thought were regarded as of little consequence in fitting a man for the responsibilities of government.

Scholarship achieved its rewards when the candidate had passed one or all of the civil service examinations prescribed and conducted by the metropolitan government. This was the only proper avenue to public office and official distinction. There were four series of examinations, the first being held in the county and prefectural cities twice every three years. In the county only some two percent of the candidates were permitted to pass. These were admitted a few weeks later to the prefectural examinations, where somewhat more than fifty percent were likely to be successful. These men were now eligible for minor posts and could qualify to enter the provincial examinations held every three years in the provincial capitals. In great examinations halls, as many as 14,000 candidates ate the food they brought along, wrote their essays, and slept in their "cells" for three separate sessions of three days each. During these sessions the candidates were permitted no recesses. Once a session had commenced and walls between the rows of cells had been bricked up, the gates of the hall were locked, and none, not even the chief examiner, might enter or leave. Those who became mentally unbalanced under the strain of this supreme literary effort might be hoisted over the wall to their friends on the outside; those who became ill or died were left inside until the session was finished. Successful candidates in the provincial tests were eligible for the metropolitan examinations in Peking. In these about six percent passed, and they, in turn, might enter the palace examinations held in the presence of the emperor.

The significance of the Chinese examination system can hardly be overestimated. It was the great carrier of tradition. It helped, under the Ming and Manchu dynasties, to freeze the old and rich Chinese culture into a fixed pattern. It encouraged reliance upon the wisdom of the past; it discouraged freedom and independence of thought and thus prepared the way for a cultural decline which was hastened by the concurrent impact of an expanding Europe on China. It was the principal agent by which Confucianism monopolized scholarship, and by which scholarship, in turn, monopolized politics. But it went even further. The examinations became a principal road to wealth as well as to official position. This wealth was usually invested in land. The landed gentry, the silk-gowned, frequently controlled public opinion. The official did well to defer to this class, for he was a member of it either in his person or in his interests, or in both.[23]

---

[23] Too frequently there was a wide gulf between theory and practice in the administration of the examination system.

In addition to entry into the civil service through the examinations, many officials were admitted through the recommendation of their relatives who had attained high position. While this practice was looked down upon, a considerable fraction of the lesser officials entered office through this *yin* system.

CHAPTER 3

JAPAN: A BRIEF HISTORICAL RETROSPECT

THE Chinese and the Japanese peoples are, in many essentials, the product of a single civilization, the civilization of China. From early historical times, Japan has drawn heavily upon the arts, letters, and philosophy of China. There is much then that is common in the social and cultural life of these two great Oriental states. Yet their differences are as arresting as their similarities. In contrast with the Chinese, the Japanese mind has lacked an absorbing interest in ethical controversy. The Chinese have been characterized by a profound *social* pride in their race and its culture; the Japanese have been distinguished by a tendency toward extreme political and national vanity. The Chinese, historically speaking, cared little for China as a political unit, but they have clung tenaciously to the great cultural heritage of their past. The Japanese, in contrast, have twice attempted to discard their own heritage for an alien culture, and yet in the abstract they are virile nationalists. There are, to be sure, many qualifications which must be applied to these general statements, nevertheless they suggest the problem of understanding two peoples so alike yet so dissimilar.

The history of Japan, when measured in terms of China's past, is a comparatively brief story. When Confucius in the sixth and fifth centuries B.C. was teaching an ethical philosophy of human relationships to an already highly cultured society, Japan was a battleground of rude and warring tribes whose exploits are recorded dimly in myth and legend.

The origins of the Japanese are not known with certainty, but it does seem clear that "the race is a compound of elements drawn in prehistoric times from different parts of the Asiatic mainland, and perhaps from Indonesian islands such as Borneo, Java, the Celebes, and the Philippines." [1] In this compound of racial stocks the Mongolian strain is strong, if not predominant.

In the first century of the Christian Era, at a time when Han culture

---

[1] G. B. Sansom, *Japan: A Short Cultural History* (New York, 1931), 3. The writer is indebted to this excellent work for much in the following summary of Japan's early history.

was already penetrating the Japanese islands by way of Korea, the clans of Kyushu moved eastward along the Inland Sea and set up a central state in the province of Yamato. Through succeeding centuries the little state of Yamato attempted to extend its authority, and, by the close of the sixth century, it exercised some control over western, central, and eastern Japan as far as Sendai. Since the authority of Yamato was still subject to challenge by rival chieftains, it was thought well to fortify its dynastic claims by evidence of its allegedly divine origins. This evidence was provided in two official compilations: the *Kojiki* or *Records of Ancient Matters,* and the *Nihongi* or *Chronicles of Japan,* completed respectively in 712 and 720.[2]

According to the picturesque story contained in these ancient works, the islands of Japan were the first-born offspring of the god Izanagi and his goddess Izanami. They also created Amaterasu-omi Kami (Heaven Shining Great Deity) or the Sun Goddess. Other details of creation were produced in like manner. Finally the Sun Goddess sent her grandson to rule the earth. He made his first appearance in the island of Kyushu, bearing the sacred mirror, sword, and jewel as pledges of his divine mission to rule Japan forever. From Kyushu the divine grandson, now the Emperor Jimmu, moved eastward, conquering as he went, and created the new state of Yamato on February 11, 660 B.C., according to the official record.

Such is the myth by which the sovereigns of Yamato attributed divine sanction to their early conquests and to their later efforts to win from rival chieftains acceptance of their rule. In addition to their excursions into the supernatural, the early chroniclers allowed themselves a good deal of imaginative freedom in the treatment of historical fact, as for instance when they place the eastward march of Jimmu in the seventh century B.C. It is probable, as already noted, that it took place about the beginning of the Christian Era. Many other legendary details in the story of Jimmu require the same correcting perspective of scholarship. The chronicles, indeed, are more interesting for what they have revealed indirectly to historical scholarship. For example, the first symbols of Japanese sovereignty—the mirror, sword, and jewel—appear to have originated neither in Japan nor in the heaven of the Sun Goddess, but in China, for such objects were unknown in Yamato until this state was influenced by the metal culture of China. So in general it may be said that the compilers of the chronicles picture events of the legendary

---

[2] For English translations of these see: B. H. Chamberlain, translator, *Kojiki or Records of Ancient Matters* (2nd ed., Kobe, 1932); W. G. Aston, *Nihongi: Chronicles of Japan* (2 vols., London, 1896).

age with the cultural trappings of the seventh and eighth centuries A.D. Yet these early myths are of great historical importance. By inventing and preserving myth for both political and religious ends, the early chroniclers of Japan created the foundations of an extreme nationalistic philosophy which was revived by official Japan in the late nineteenth and in the early twentieth centuries with disastrous consequences.

THE INTRODUCTION OF CHINESE CULTURE

Chinese influence, coming by way of Korea, was felt in Japan as early as the first century A.D. This infiltration was promoted by a succession of wars among the early Korean kingdoms which enabled the Japanese to maintain a foothold in southern Korea for many years. It is not surprising then that sometime before the beginning of the fifth century the Chinese language and script were known in Japan. In 405 A.D. the arrival of a Sino-Korean scholar, Wani by name, as tutor to the heir apparent of Yamato, signified that the Chinese written language had been officially adopted by the Japanese court. Such events as this paved the way for the general Chinese cultural impact which followed. Before this movement is summarized, however, a word should be said on Japan's indigenous culture.

JAPAN'S NATIVE CULTURE

Politically the early Japanese were organized in patriarchal clans called *uji*. Attached to the clans were guilds, known as *be* or *tomo,* the households of which were held together by common occupations rather than by ancestry, as in the case of the clan. The guild was subordinate to the clan and in time usually merged with it. The regions of Japan occupied by the Yamato people included a number of such clans, the Imperial Clan simply being the most powerful. This clan ruled directly only in its own lands. Its authority over other clans was exercised indirectly through their chieftains.

Shinto, the Way of the Gods, was the indigenous cult of the Japanese, although it was not known by this or any name, for that matter, until the sixth century A.D. The material culture of this early Japan was crude indeed, but its religious and social life was of a comparatively high order. Shinto was a pantheism, a nature worship, based on "appreciation rather than fear." It follows that

. . . much that is kindly and gracious in the life of the Japanese to-day can be traced to those sentiments which caused their remote ancestors to ascribe divinity not only to the powerful and awe-inspiring, such as the sun and the moon and the tempest, or to the useful, such as the well and the cooking pot, but also to the lovely and pleasant, such as the rocks and streams, the trees and flowers.[3]

In this "religion of love and gratitude rather than of fear," the Sun Goddess occupied a position of paramount importance, for she was both the central divinity in this early worship and also the ancestress of the Imperial House. Purity was the essence of religion. Uncleanliness, even the material uncleanliness of the person, was to be avoided. Preparation for religious observance consisted in washing the body and in putting on clean garments. Herein, deeply rooted in time and tradition, lies the origin of a modern characteristic of the race: its desire to be scrupulously clean. In general then it may be said that early Shinto was a simple nature worship. It is to be distinguished in this form from the later institutionalized Shinto (see p. 431) fostered by the official class for political purposes. Shinto is sometimes described loosely as ancestor worship. However, it should be noted that

ancestor worship as practiced in Japan, is a cult imported from China. The objects of worship of the early Japanese were nature deities, and not their own deified ancestors. It is true that the noble families claimed descent from the gods whom they worshipped, but making your god into an ancestor and making your ancestor into a god are not the same thing.[4]

Within the three centuries, 350 to 645, Japan's indigenous culture, based on the clan system, was revolutionized by China's civilization, coming primarily by way of Korea. The suggestion has already been made that these revolutionary, cultural changes were hastened by an influx of Sino-Korean immigrants from the Japanese sphere of influence in southern Korea. By the sixth century, these foreign influences were playing upon a Japan in which the power of the central government tended to increase while the power of the Imperial Family declined. Actual authority was shifting from one to another of a small group of increasingly powerful clans that sought to control the throne. It was in the midst of such conflicts that Buddhism from China began to play a dominant role in Japan. While one clan championed the indigenous Shinto, another—the Soga family—championed Buddhism and Chinese learning in general. The final victory of Soga over their rivals thus promoted a cultural revolution. From the sixth century

[3] Sansom, *Japan*, 45.
[4] Sansom, *Japan*, 53.

onward Japan was vitally affected by Chinese thought, and at times she was dominated by it.

THE FATHER OF JAPANESE CIVILIZATION

Japan at the close of the sixth century was distinguished by a confused, not to say chaotic, society. The old clan system had crumbled under the power of a few vigorous families, who as yet failed to comprehend the significance of the new Chinese cultural heritage. The first leader to challenge the creators of this political vacuum was Shotoku Taishi, who, as regent in 604, issued a code of moral injunctions superior to any previous political philosophy known in Japan. It enunciated a new concept of the state. This code accepted the theory that ultimate power resides with the emperor, and the principle that while obedience is demanded of inferiors to superiors, the latter are also entrusted with duties to inferiors. Shotoku Taishi sought in Chinese political theory for a unifying force that could break the heritage of clan and caste barriers, and he thereby laid the foundations for a new political and economic life. Some of his principles were implemented in the *Taikwa* or Great Reform of 645-650. These measures contemplated a new system of taxation, of local government, and of land tenure. In theory they all involved a greater centralization of power; but in practice, powerful families who could not be deprived expediently of their lands were confirmed in their titles on the questionable assumption that they now held their lands from the throne. In addition they were given official posts or court rank. The central government also undertook to appoint governors for the provinces; but here too the practice was to confirm the existing authority of the most powerful local chief. Theoretically, all this amounted to a political reorganization, but in reality the emphasis in the Great Reform was on the economic rather than on the political. The forces which controlled the court were not concerned primarily with the extension to remote regions of their direct political control. Their immediate concern was to find a more effective means of collecting wealth from the provinces.[5]

By the later code of *Taiho* (Great Treasure) of 701-704, the administrative machinery of a reformed central government was devised. Unhappily, this code tended to preserve the interests of the court aristocracy of birth at the expense of other groups in the populace. This is a significant example of how the Japanese of this period adopted frequently merely the form of the Chinese system to the neglect of the vital

[5] The basic study is K. Asahawa, *The Early Institutional Life of Japan* (Tokyo, 1903).

principle that in China the official aristocracy was not one of birth but
of learning.

Yet the reforms were not without value. Under the inspiration of
Chinese learning a beginning had been made toward political unification. Buddhism, as the new state religion, assisted to this end, for it
gave to the Japanese a new faith and culture never provided by the
simple beliefs and rituals of Shinto.

THE CIVILIZATION OF NARA, 710-784

The city of Nara presented in the eighth century the most strikingly
tangible evidence of Chinese influence upon Japan. Men's thoughts
were here translated into the design and material structure of Japan's
first great city and her first permanent capital.[6] Previously the custom
had prevailed of changing the seat of government with each new reign
in order to avoid the contamination which accompanied death. The
central government at Nara functioned as a bureaucracy patterned on
the forms of the T'ang dynasty and buttressed by the ever increasing
influence of Buddhism as the state religion. Buddhism indeed was one
of the chief instruments of government which sought to strengthen
its control through appointing the "right" men as chief abbots of the
powerful monasteries. The architecture of Buddhist temples with their
brilliant decorations and sculpture dotted the landscape. An increasing
population brought new lands under cultivation, promoted the building
of roads, established new provinces, and subjugated regions as far distant as southern Kyūshū. Numerous embassies, sent to the T'ang
court in China, enriched the intellectual life from that inexhaustible
source of learning. Within the limited group that composed the Imperial Court at Nara, literature and the fine arts flourished. The *Kojiki*
and the *Nihongi* (written in Japanese and in Chinese respectively) were
completed in the early years of Nara. The poetry of Nara preserved
in the great anthology, the *Manyoshiu* (Collection of One Thousand
Leaves), has never since been surpassed in Japanese literature.

Politically, however, Nara witnessed a decline in the sovereign's
power through the growing influence of the great Fujiwara clan over
its powerful rivals. The fact that laws were frequently not enforced
at all was not a surprising circumstance, since the militia was an ill-fed
rabble of farmer conscripts. Economically the government lived far
beyond its means. The building of Nara itself, with its lavish expenditures on temples and bronze images, and the purchasing of favor
with the Buddhist priesthood by means of generous gifts from the pub-

[6] The Chinese capital at Sian was the model for the city of Nara.

lic domain reduced the farmers to the level of slaves, while provincial officials amassed fortunes and Buddhist orders waxed wealthy through their control of land.[7]

JAPAN IN THE HEIAN PERIOD, 784-1185

The four centuries that followed the Nara period are in many respects the most fascinating in Japanese history. While the men and women of Nara were absorbed by the new interest in things Chinese, their successors in the age of Heian had a deeper understanding of what had been acquired from China and a more critical attitude as to the place and form it should assume in its new home. The enthusiasm for Chinese thought and institutions remained strong until the closing years of Heian, but it tended to express itself through criticism which sought to adapt the new ideas to the peculiar background and needs of Japan. Even the Buddhism of Japan became somewhat nationalistic.

At the beginning of the period the Buddhist church, by reason of its tremendous power, was in a position to intimidate government. The capital was accordingly moved to Heiankyo (City of Peace), known today as Kyoto, where it was to remain until the Restoration of 1868. By this move the administration escaped the domination of the great Nara temples. This was the work of the Emperor Kammu, in many respects the most brilliant and capable of all Japan's sovereigns. Having curbed the political power of Buddhism, Kammu resolved further that its religious power must be fused with the native Shinto to create a national religion supporting the throne. This task was entrusted to two learned priest-patriots, Kobo-Daishi and Dengyo-Daishi, the founders respectively of the Shingon and Tendai sects of Japanese Buddhism. Kobo-Daishi reconciled Buddhism with Shinto through a convenient doctrine which stated that the Buddhas had in part revealed themselves in Japan as Shinto deities. Thus a foreign Buddhism became a patriotic Japanese Buddhism and a safe bulwark of the central government.

The new capital, Kyoto, the largest and most spacious city Japan had yet known, modelled after the T'ang capital of Ch'ang-an, became one of the world's most beautiful cities. Surrounded by and built into natural scenic beauty, it personified with its great palaces and temples the early maturity of Japanese artistic expression. This was the setting in which the Imperial Court, the court nobility (*Kuge*), the men of letters, and, to an even greater degree, the women of letters, produced the

---

[7] An exhaustive treatment of early Japan is R. K. Reischauer, *Early Japanese History* (2 vols., Princeton, 1937).

classical works of Japanese literature. The second great anthology, the *Kokinshiu* (Poems, Ancient and Modern), was completed in 922. The age also created Japan's ablest women of letters: Lady Murasaki no Shikibu, author of the *Genji Monogatari*[8] (*ca.* 1004), and Lady Sei Shonagon, author of the *Makura-no-soshi* (Pillow Sketches). Kyoto was a cultured and refined city but its life was effeminate. It is natural then that its great literature should have been that of belles-lettres: the novel and poetry, and diaries and essays in the sophisticated manner. Such dull pursuits as theology and law were left to the scholars who still wrote in Chinese with little literary style.

The literary triumphs of Heian stand in bold relief against the political decline of the Imperial Family and of the civil aristocracy, the *Kuge,* or court nobles. Sovereigns less competent than the great Kammu became puppets in the hands of the powerful Fujiwara family, which after driving out its rivals monopolized most of the high offices of state. Child emperors, the off-spring of Fujiwara consorts, were placed on the throne, while heads of the Fujiwara house administered the state as regents (*sessho*) or as civil dictators (*kampaku*). Ambitious and capable men who were not members of the Fujiwara clan were thus forced to seek their fortunes in distant provinces. There, by various means, they acquired great manors and built the foundations of a frontier military society in striking contrast with the civilian effeminacy of the Kyoto aristocracy. These new landed barons had no interest in the stability of the central government. On the contrary, their ambition was to strengthen their own local independence. During the last century and a half of the Heian era, the feudal barons (*buke*) with their well-trained soldiers (*bushi*) were completely beyond the control of Kyoto. The once powerful Fujiwara were forced indeed to seek the aid of some of the new military upstarts to maintain order in the Imperial capital itself. In the conflicts which ensued between the frontier warrior clans of Taira and Minamoto, the old civil government of Kyoto collapsed. For a few years the Taira held control, only to meet defeat at the hands of their Minamoto rivals in the naval battle of Dan no ura, 1185.

KAMAKURA AND THE GROWTH OF FEUDALISM, 1185-1338

Yoritomo, the victorious Minamoto chieftain, had thus become by the fortunes of war the military master of Japan. What sort of government would he erect in a state where power in terms of land and fight-

---

[8] The term "monogatari" means "narrative." It is applied chiefly to fiction and sometimes to histories. Murasaki, like Fielding, created the prose epic of real life.

ing men had passed from the throne and its civilian nobility to a new group of landed magnates in the provinces supported by their hardy military followers? Yoritomo's answer was a unique system, known as the shogunate, which may be said in general to have survived until the Imperial Restoration of 1868. It is not possible to describe this system accurately within brief compass, but some of its major features may at least be suggested. These include the shogunate, the feudal magnates, and the throne.

Yoritomo established his government at Kamakura, 300 miles eastward from the Imperial capital at Kyoto. A dual purpose was served by this selection, since Kamakura was a natural center from which to control his own vassals, and it was far removed from the pleasures and the effeminate life of the civilian court. The atmosphere of Kyoto was not designed to nurture the rugged and frugal qualities which Yoritomo demanded of his warriors (*bushi*), the knights of Japanese feudalism, later known as *samurai*. In 1192, the Emperor conferred on Yoritomo the title, Sei tai shogun (barbarian-subduing generalissimo), thereby investing him with supreme command of all military forces. The title itself was not new. It had been conferred previously on military commanders commissioned to lead a particular military expedition against the barbarians in the northern frontier, but with Yoritomo the title became hereditary. This gave to the title immeasurably greater significance. Yoritomo's appointment as shogun marked the inception of a feudal and military administration which came to be known as the Bakufu.[9] During periods of able administration, the power of the Bakufu was for practical purposes supreme. The shogun was, in a sense, the head of a military dictatorship deriving his actual power from the strength of the Minamoto clan and its vassals.[10] Within this sphere, the administration of Kamakura was direct and exclusive.

However, it must be recalled that Yoritomo, while acting in the capacity of a military dictator, recognized the sovereignty of the throne and considered himself as exercising authority delegated by the throne. To state the matter another way, the appearance of the shogunate did not put an end to the throne, although it did for centuries strip the

---

[9] *Bakufu* means literally "tent government." The term was used originally to designate the headquarters of an army in the field. Later it designated the administrative headquarters of a military dictator.

[10] During the time of the Minamoto shoguns and the Hojo regents, the lands of the Minamoto and their vassals were scattered thickly throughout eastern Japan, and more thinly in other areas. Sometimes the lands of a vassal lay within the domain of some independent lord. The authority of the shogun was thus likely to vary from complete military control in some areas to a rather shadowy suzerainty in others.

throne of all save *de jure* authority. Successive emperors continued to reign in Kyoto, where the throne retained at times "a certain social prestige and a certain negative authority." This fact was not unimportant. In so far as Japan possessed a concept or a symbol of national unity, that concept found expression, vaguely, to be sure, in the throne. The significance of this real although weak theory of Imperial authority is suggested by the fact that Yoritomo probably did not conceive of himself as the ruler of all Japan nor did he probably think of Japan in terms of national unity. The twelfth century had, as already indicated, created a feudal society dominated by great landed barons who, within their own domains, were virtually independent. The barons did not recognize the military power of the throne, for the throne no longer possessed such power. The barons would, however, recognize the military power of the shogun, in so far as it was expedient to recognize his power. They were the more likely to do this since the shogun's legal authority, derived from the throne, carried with it such national prestige as the throne possessed.

THE HOJO REGENCY, 1205-1333

With the passing of Yoritomo, the shogunate in turn was soon controlled by an able line of regents who ruled for the shoguns, just as in previous centuries Fujiwara regents had acted for the emperors. The Japan of the thirteenth century thus presented the amazing spectacle of a country headed by a sovereign who was emperor in name only, whose vestigial functions were assumed by an abdicated emperor, and whose real power was delegated to a hereditary military dictator (the shogun), but wielded in reality by a hereditary regent acting for the dictator. Impossible as such a system may seem, the fact that it worked well for a century was due largely to the capacity of the Hojo regents. The country enjoyed a government which was more stable, honest, and efficient than it had previously known. It was, moreover, a period of spiritual advance. Great teachers such as Honen (1133-1212), Shinran (1173-1262), and Nichiren (1222-1282), forsaking classical Chinese for Japanese, stimulated the people and made of Buddhism a popular religion affecting the moral and intellectual life of the entire people.

In the midst of this moral and political advance, the shogunate was called upon to repel the Mongol invasions of Kublai Khan, who by 1263 had become emperor of China. In 1274 and again in 1281, the Mongol armies were driven back by the Japanese defenders, and their fleets destroyed by providential typhoons. The Hojo regents, their vassals, and their feudal allies had proved themselves equal to the military task of defense, but as has so often been the case they were unequal to the task of domestic reconstruction which followed. The finances of the shogunate were exhausted. Increased taxes led to local rebellions. Vassals who had fought in defense of the nation, and priests whose prayers had brought the typhoons demanded rewards, but there were no new lands for the Hojo to bestow. In these circumstances power momentarily returned to the throne when the Emperor Go-Daigo, aided by rebellious generals, destroyed Kamakura and with it the Hojo regency in 1333.

An Imperial restoration, however, was not to be. Ashikaga Takauji, a general who had assisted in the fall of Kamakura, not only turned upon his emperor and allies but also championed a rival emperor, who in 1336 appointed Takauji as shogun. A new shogunate was thus established which was to persist until 1573.

THE ASHIKAGA SHOGUNATE, 1336-1573

In the political sense, the Ashikaga period had little to recommend it. For a time (1336-1392), rival dynasties claimed the Imperial throne, while most of the country was little more than a battleground of feudal strife. This confused picture of fourteenth-century strife was in reality essentially a struggle among contending factions to control feudal privileges in the form of lands or vassals. The fifteenth century, with its almost continuous feudal warfare, its epidemics, and famines, served only to add unhappy detail to a scene dominated by political and economic chaos. After 1477 the Ashikaga shoguns themselves were reduced to political impotence and the Imperial court was penniless and destitute.

THE CULTURE OF KAMAKURA AND OF THE ASHIKAGA

The cultural life of Japan naturally reflected the revolutionary changes which marked the ascendancy of the Kamakura military caste. In religion, Buddhism underwent what might be termed a reformation. It became the popular religion of the people, became distinctly Japanese in character, and thus became national. The formal Buddhism of the Fujiwara period gave place to new protestant sects, and to the appearance in Japan of Zen Buddhism. The religious conflicts of this reformation period suggest striking parallels to the religious struggles of Europe. The battle of creeds, the appearance of saints, the sacrifice of martyrs, the intolerance of religious bigots—all these are represented in the religious history of Japan during the Kamakura shogunate. Yet it seems justifiable to say that in general Japan happily did not experience the vicious religious intolerance of Europe. If anything, her peoples revealed a tendency to religious indifference rather than a tendency to the fanaticism of the zealot.

The most striking religious development of the Kamakura period was the growth of Zen Buddhism. Zen doctrines had been known as early as the Nara period, but Zen as a separate sect appeared with the shogunate. Zen cast aside the formulae of institutionalized religion and faith in the saving power of a redeemer. Salvation could be achieved only through the individual's effort to discover the meaning of the universe. The broad and intense appeal made by Zen Buddhism to the fighting men of the Bakufu may be explained in a number of ways. Zen was self-reliant, did not depend on scriptures, was unencumbered by any intricate philosophy. Its stern injunction to self-examination, its freedom from the emotional, its stress upon individualism —each and all of these made an appeal to the rugged warriors of the Bakufu. Zen as the religion of the soldier was to become in succeeding centuries a vital influence in the intellectual, the social, and the political life of the entire nation.

Apart from its religious philosophies, Kamakura contributed little of cultural value. Its poetry, collected in the *Shin Kokinshu* anthology, though possessing merit was distinctly inferior to that of Heian. The prose of the period was confined largely to a number of military novels, the *Hogen Monogatari* and the *Heike Monogatari,* distinguished chiefly for their ornamental style. Sculpture and painting, however, were revived. Kamakura produced vigorous men whose vigor was reflected in the art of the period. An active, virile realism replaced the conventional, tired spirit of the later Heian art.

Culturally, the Ashikaga period promoted a mingling of the provincial military-feudal society with the older metropolitan, civilian society of Kyoto. The Ashikaga shoguns, unlike their predecessors, set up their residence in Muromachi, a quarter of Kyoto. This meant that the military caste gravitated to Kyoto, where it could not but be influenced by the old civilian culture of Heian. Military men who rose to power in these unpredictable years coveted the cultural trappings which their newly found wealth could buy in the capital. Merchants, and to some degree, artisans, profited by the extravagance of the provincial military upstarts, but the peasant-farmer found no relief from the extortions of government officials and landlords. Family loyalties to a large degree superseded clan loyalties.

In this maze of economic, political, and social maladjustment, growth of the arts, however, was unprecedented. This seeming contradiction

may be explained in a number of ways. The feudal gentry who flocked
to the capital sought to hide their boorish background by displaying
an interest in things cultural. The rough soldier became a leader of
fashion. Thus the monks and the artists who possessed the heritage
of an earlier age were sustained and became the cultural leaders of the
Ashikaga. It was a period, as noted, when Zen Buddhism flourished.
In a military age, it is significant that it increased its power by peaceful
means. A revival was also noticeable in the indigenous cult of Shinto.
Although Shinto had been relegated to a secondary position by the influence of Buddhism, it was far from being completely lost. Shinto
was, it would seem, inseparable from the Japanese consciousness both
in its relationship to the throne and in the simple concepts of nature
worship on which it was based.[11]

The extravagance and the dissipation of the age were reflected in the
architecture patronized by the Ashikaga shoguns. Vast sums were expended on the Kinkakuji (Golden Pavilion) and the Ginkakuji (Silver
Pavilion). Wealthy barons rivalled each other in the construction of
costly palaces and in indulgence in aesthetic amusements, while in contrast, squalor infested the countryside, and an impoverished emperor
sought a livelihood by selling examples of his own calligraphy. The
wealthy, too, could afford to pass their time in the practice of a new
diversion, the *cha-no-yu* (tea ceremony), by which sophisticated virtues
such as urbanity and courtesy were developed. Those members of
genteel society who so desired enriched the aesthetic nature through
the art of *ikebana* (flower arrangement). These and other refinements
of an artificial, corrupt, and profligate society produced, nevertheless,
some of Japan's greatest artists—names such as Sesshu, Chodensu, Ma-
sanobu, and Motonobu. Their exquisite designs found expression not
only on the utensils used in the tea ceremony, on flower vases and mural
scrolls, but also on the elaborate masks and robes worn by actors in the
newly developed *No* or lyrical drama.[12]

THE ERA OF DICTATORS, 1568-1615

The restoration of stable government in Japan following the political
anarchy of the Ashikaga shogunate was the work of three men of ex-

---

[11] Sir George Sansom observes that Shinto, when least influential, retained a greater
vitality than is admitted by those critics who attribute its revival in the nineteenth century
to conscious and deliberate political motives. Cf. Sansom, *Japan*, 369.

[12] *No* means "ability." The *No* drama, developed during the Ashikaga period, possessed remote origins. In its early forms it was little more than a kind of "rhythmic
posturing" to the accompaniment of drums and other instruments. The dramatic elements of lyrical drama were later introductions.

ceptional ability: Oda Nobunaga, Toyotomi Hideyoshi, and Tokugawa Iyeyasu.[13] Nobunaga (1534-1582), the son of an obscure feudal chieftain, after building and consolidating a military following, occupied Kyoto, and, by 1568, with the overthrow of the last of the Ashikaga, was installed as shogun *de facto*. With the aid of his principal general, Hideyoshi, and his effective ally Iyeyasu, Nobunaga carried his conquests against his remaining feudal rivals and, in particular, against the militant monkish orders of the Buddhist church whose power stood as a barrier to the establishment of any centralized authority. So successful was Nobunaga in his conquest of the church and of feudal rivals that at the time of his death (1582) he controlled more than half of the provinces of Japan.

This work of unification was carried on by Hideyoshi (1536-1598), who, in 1584, was created *kwampaku* (regent or civil dictator) by the emperor. It is signficant that men of Hideyoshi's power still coveted titles bestowed by a neglected and penniless court. By 1587, Hideyoshi, by breaking the resistance of the Satsuma clan, completed his conquest of Kyūshū. Three years later, he could regard himself as the military master of all Japan. His military ambition, however, was not satisfied. In 1592 and again in 1597 he dispatched armies, numbering as many as 200,000 men, to Korea with the avowed purpose of conquering China. Only the death of the Japanese Napoleon in 1598 brought these unhappy and aggressive exploits to a close.

Out of the civil war which followed the passing of Japan's greatest military genius, power passed into the victorious hands of Iyeyasu (Battle of Sekigahara, 1600). By 1615, opposition had been completely suppressed and the foundations laid for the last and greatest of the shogunates—the Tokugawa.

THE SYSTEM OF THE TOKUGAWAS, 1603-1868

Hideyoshi had conquered the barons; it remained for Iyeyasu and his successors to build and consolidate a political, social, and economic structure that would preserve the conquest. The son of Hideyoshi was set aside (and later slain), and in 1603 Iyeyasu accepted from the throne the coveted title of shogun. Japan now entered upon a period of government more stable than any she had previously enjoyed. Iyeyasu broke with the past by building a new capital in eastern Japan, Yedo

---

[13] Proper names in Japanese, as in Chinese, give the family name first, followed by the given name. In later chapters of this volume where reference is made to personalities whose names have appeared repeatedly in Western literature and in the daily and periodical press, the more familiar Western practice is followed.

(later known as Tokyo). Like Yoritomo, he sought freedom from the enervating influences and traditions of the Imperial Court which, as formerly, remained at Kyoto. But Yedo was not to be merely a second Kamakura. Iyeyasu conceived the new capital to be not only the military camp of the former Bakufu but also the political, commercial, and cultural center of the state. From Yedo Castle, today the permanent residence of the emperors, Iyeyasu and successive Tokugawa shoguns ruled Japan. The shogun, himself, and his bureaucracy ruled directly a fourth of the country, including most of the important cities. Officers of this government were drawn exclusively from the hereditary vassals of the Tokugawa clan—the *daimyo* (lords, literally "great name") and the *samurai* (knights). The remainder of the country was divided among other *daimyo*. Of these, some 50 percent were known as *fudai* (inside lords), since they too were either branch families or vassals of the Tokugawa. The remainder, the *tozama* (outside lords), were regarded as potential foes of the shogunate. Outstanding among such clans were Satsuma, Choshu, Tosa, and Hizen, all of which were later to win fame as "the western clans" and as the leaders of the Restoration of 1868. Inasmuch as these clans possessed great wealth and constituted the greatest potential threat to the shogunate, they were subjected to numerous restrictions and disabilities. They were excluded from all offices in the Yedo government. The *daimyo* were required to spend every second year at the shogun's capital (the law of *sankin kotai*) and to leave their wives and children as permanent hostages of their loyalty to the shogunate. The *tozama* were excluded from the emperor's court at Kyoto and were not permitted to form alliances among themselves. Also, in the early years of the Tokugawa regime, feudal holdings were redistributed so as to place *fudai* lords at strategic points where they might crush attempted *tozama* risings against the shogunate. The building of feudal castles was strictly limited, if not proscribed. The movement of travellers from one province to another was carefully checked. Where surplus wealth might encourage a *tozama* lord to revolt, the shogun did not hesitate to "honor" such lord with a command to expend it on public works. As late as 1753 the *daimyo* of Satsuma was ordered to repair at great cost the levees of the Kiso River, 750 miles from his fief. By these and other means, the shogunate was able to maintain predominance over the *tozama* lords while at the same time leaving them complete autonomy in the government of their fiefs. Even in the matter of revenue, the *daimyo* within each fief retained full administrative power, levying and collecting taxes according to the laws of the fief. The system was thus pre-eminently feudal. The revenues of the shogunate were not national; they were derived from the vast Tokugawa estates. The armies were likewise feudal. The Tokugawa forces were composed of the direct feudal retainers of the clan, though in time of emergency the barons might be called upon to furnish contingents of fighting men. The very existence of these semi-independent feudal armies was, obviously, an ever-present threat to the shogun's authority. This was particularly true in western Japan, the home of the *tozama* lords.

THE SOCIAL STRUCTURE OF TOKUGAWA JAPAN

The Tokugawas had created a system of centralized feudalism. While their rule was as yet less than 40 years old (1640), they had adopted and enforced a national policy of exclusion and seclusion, which, though isolating Japan from the world about her, conferred upon her more than two centuries of unbroken peace. Military power, astute statecraft, and freedom from foreign influence all contributed to the unprecedented stability of the early Tokugawa government. The foundation of that stability was, however, social as well as political. Tokugawa administrators sensed the importance of maintaining the economic and social *status quo*. Their efforts were therefore directed toward the creation of a crystallized social order. During the constant civil strife of the Ashikaga period, men of ambition might rise from lowly origin to positions of privilege. No such shifting was to be permitted under the new dictatorship. The social order under the Tokugawas was rigid and conventional.

At the peak of the social edifice was the emperor, who with his civilian court nobility, the *kuge,* resided at Kyoto. In matters of theoretical honor, the emperor and his court were unrivalled; but since they were without property, they were dependent on income granted by the shogun and were subject to the commands and the supervision of Yedo; thus their honor was little more than a hollow pretense.

Second in the social scale stood the feudal nobility of various grades, headed by the shogun himself. The *daimyo* might lack that essence of unadulterated honor on which the civilian court was fed; but what he lacked in honor, he possessed in the abundant material wealth which flowed from his feudal fief. Ranking below the *diamyo* were the *hatamoto,* who were lesser vassals of the Tokugawa, and the *gokenin,* who filled minor administrative posts in the shogunate. Below these again were the *samurai,* the knights or hereditary fighting men. They were vassals either of the shogun or of other barons, and to them was reserved the privilege of wearing the two swords, the badge of knighthood. Their incomes, paid by their lord, were small, as befitted men trained to live a frugal and austere life and to find happiness in the honor of their calling. During the Tokugawa period there were some two million of these *samurai,* representing about 400,000 households. Since after 1615 there were no longer any wars to fight, the *samurai* became a social parasite living upon the toil of the peasantry.

Contrasted sharply with the above gradations of aristocratic and privileged society were the commoners. Even here social distinctions were no less severe. The farmer, in matters of honor at least, was the aristocrat of the plebs. He provided the rice on which his social superiors fed more generously than did he himself. His was the honor not only to produce the food but also to pay a good portion of the taxes. In return, he was conceded a "living," sometimes only a bare existence, and a generous share of social honor among his fellow commoners. Some of the more fortunate farmers might on occasion be elevated to the *samurai* class. In the case of the Satsuma clan, some of the *samurai* were also farmers. Generally speaking, however, the farmer could count on few rewards in a life of incessant toil. Privileged society paid lip service to the value of agriculture, but in practice it showed little concern for the agriculturist.

Next in the social scale of plebian society was the artisan, whose honored position was logical in a state dominated by the military man. The artisan fashioned the sword, and the sword was the soul of the *samurai.* Artistic craftsmanship was its own reward.

Below the artisan was the merchant, who enjoyed the contempt of society as a whole. He produced nothing, so it was thought, yet he waxed rich by disposing of what others had produced. During the Tokugawa period, the merchant's power greatly increased until through his growing control of the national wealth he could exploit the privileged classes just as these classes exploited the peasant.

Finally, at the bottom of the social scale were the *eta,* scarcely to be counted as members of human society. The *eta* were bound to hereditary occupations involving some form of pollution, or social ostracism: those who handled the bodies of the dead, executioners, beggars, and professional entertainers.

THE SOCIAL PATTERN—*BUSHIDO*

The intellectual pattern of this military-feudal society was the ethical philosophy of *Bushido,* the Way of the Warrior. It was derived in part from Confucian doctrine. Since the Tokugawa shoguns recognized that their continued power depended on maintaining the political, economic, and social *status quo,* and since the foundations of their society were deeply rooted in the past, they adopted this past, at least such portions of it as were convenient, as the model both for the present and the future. They sought indeed to make their particular order an unchanging order. They realized, however, that if they were to freeze society, they must subject the commoners as well as the privileged feudal classes to a conventional code of social behavior more formal than anything Japan had previously known. Such a code was provided by *Bushido.*

The term *Bushido* is of comparatively recent origin. The cult, or the set of ideas of which it is the label, is, on the contrary, of ancient origin. These ideas were analogous in some degree to European concepts of chivalry. Principles in the code of *Bushido* varied from time to time. They did not become highly conventionalized until well into the Tokugawa period and then became so, as already indicated, to serve a specific political objective of the ruling military caste. Historically, the philosophy found its origins in early conceptions of the soldier's duty. In periods of strife there was need for standards of loyalty among fighting men. Thus, "rectitude, courage, benevolence, politeness, sincerity, honor, disdain of money, and self-control" constituted a set of ideals pointing the way for the *samurai.* Since virtue is only as strong as those who profess its practice, it may be assumed that the *samurai* rarely achieved the philosophical ideal. In the early days of feudalism, this warrior code was largely a mere sentiment between lord and vassal based on direct personal service and contact in battle; but in the Tokugawa period, it assumed the form of a tangible and systematized creed for controlling in times of peace the turbulent qualities of the *samurai.* Furthermore, the period of peace imposed by Tokugawa supremacy made it more than ever necessary to control the commoners and, in particular, the rising middle classes. *Bushido* therefore achieved a new significance as an ethical guide applied by the rulers to privileged and unprivileged society alike.

CHAPTER 4

EARLY WESTERN CRUSADERS

T HE history of Western contacts with the Far East is a long and fascinating story. It reaches back into the pre-Christian Era. These pages, however, are concerned only with years that are distinctly modern and contemporary—the nineteenth and twentieth centuries. But modern events find their origins in the remote past. A study of the French Revolution involves some delving into the much earlier society of feudalism. And so, in seeking to understand the conflicts between the West and the Far East during the past century and a half, it will be of advantage to review, even superficially, events and problems of earlier centuries. What, then, was this pre-nineteenth century heritage in the relations of Europe and the Far East?

THE EARLIEST REFERENCES TO CHINA

The time at which Europe gained its first knowledge of China is not known with certainty. Perhaps it was as early as the sixth or even the seventh century B.C. In 128 B.C. the Chinese emperor Wu Ti dispatched the embassy of Chang Ch'ien into west central Asia. The results of this mission were notable. Force and diplomacy extended Chinese influence west of the Pamir divide; regular communication with western Asia was established; and, finally, an indirect trade between China and Europe developed.[1]

Thus there grew at the beginning of the Christian Era a remarkable overland traffic in silk from China to the Roman World. The direct overland route stretched from Antioch through Samarkand, Kashgar, Lop-nor, and across Central Asia to the Sera metropolis of Ch'ang-an in western China. Alternate water routes extended from the Red Sea and the Persian Gulf to western India, whence they joined the land route by way of Khotan, or continued eastward by the sea route as far as the modern Hanoi in Indo-China. This traffic was due primarily to the

---

[1] For a detailed account of early relations between Europe and China consult G. F. Hudson, *Europe and China* (London, 1931), which covers the period to 1800.

See also, Harry E. Burton, *The Discovery of the Ancient World* (Cambridge, 1932), 90-104.

Roman demand for silk, not to any Chinese demand for the products of Rome.

The European demand for Chinese silk continued during the first six centuries of the Christian Era. In the sixth century, however, "the smuggled moth" was producing silk in Europe, where the silk industry had been established at Constantinople. The Roman World, and ultimately Europe as a whole, were freed from dependence on China's silk. The early romance of the China trade was for the time being ended.

The sixth century likewise witnessed the rise in Central Asia of the Turks and their advance westward until they had effected diplomatic contacts with the Roman World at Constantinople. This did not lead to direct Roman contacts with China, but it created in Byzantine Greek literature, from Turkish sources, the most revealing picture of China to appear in European literature prior to the accounts of Marco Polo. This was the work of Simocatta, an Egyptian Greek, writing about 630. But, though Europe had lost its interest in China, the annals of the T'ang dynasty contain much on the population and wealth of Byzantium.

THE NESTORIAN MISSIONS

When Christianity, in one or other of its various forms, first reached China is not known. Tradition would have it that Saint Thomas preached there. More substantial evidence attaches to the work of the Nestorian missionaries. The Persian Church, augmented by Nestorian disciples, who were expelled from the Roman Empire, had by the close of the fifth century become Nestorian in doctrine. Its missionaries were active in Mesopotamia, India, and Central Asia, and from there finally reached China. The record of this Nestorian effort has been preserved on a monument erected at Sian in 781, though not discovered until the seventeenth century.[2] From this and other sources it now appears that the Nestorians reached T'ang China about 635, where they were honorably received by the emperor. Churches were built in several cities and though at times the faith was persecuted it appears in general to have been tolerated for two centuries, until, in 845, the missionaries were commanded by the emperor to renounce their priestly calling and "to cease to pervert the institutions of the country."[3]

[2] Sian is the generally used modern spelling for Hsian (Wade-Giles romanization). In the spelling Hsianfu, the *fu* ending is a Manchu dynasty form which has not been used in Nationalist China. Again, the T'ang dynasty name was Ch'ang-an, not Hsian. The beginning student of far eastern history and geography must be prepared to face some of the confusion which arises from changes in place names and from varying forms of romanization.

[3] L. C. Goodrich, *A Short History of the Chinese People* (New York, 1943), 128-129.

THE ARAB TRADE

In Chinese history the period of the Five Dynasties (907-960) and of the Sung dynasty (960-1279), though marked by political weakness, was nevertheless distinguished for cultural brilliance. The Chinese were moving southward and thereby were increasing the relative importance of the Yangtze Valley and the southern coast. A very considerable foreign trade was conducted at Ch'üan-chou (Zayton) in Fukien, and at Canton in Kwangtung. This trade was both encouraged and rigidly controlled by the Sung emperors, who derived a substantial revenue from it. Most of the foreign merchants in this trade were Moslem Arabs, who in general seem to have been well treated, were permitted to settle in the country, to take Chinese wives, to adjust disputes among themselves according to their own laws, and, in some cases, to hold high office in the state. There was, too, among these southern foreigners a colony of Jews. It was this Arab trade which was to carry eventually to Europe a knowledge of Chinese tea. Meanwhile, Islam straddled the trade routes between Europe and the Far East while Europe's energies were consumed in the monstrous political failure of the Crusades. Following close upon these disasters came the Mongol invasions of Europe. The time had come when in Europe both church and state would seek an escape from this new challenge from Central Asia.[4]

THE RENEWAL OF EUROPEAN INTEREST IN CHINA

Christian Europe was beset in the thirteenth century by unprecedented dangers. On the south and southeast lay the fanatical power of Islam. Directly to the east was the rising threat of the Mongol Empire, whose armies in 1222 invaded Europe and defeated the Russians on the Dnieper. Simultaneously other Mongol armies were advancing eastward upon North China. Before the close of the thirteenth century, the empire built by Chingiz Khan and his successors sprawled across the map of Eurasia from the western borders of Russia to the Pacific. Trade routes from Europe to China, closed for more than four centuries, were again opened. Europe was soon to expand upon the meager knowledge of China which it had gained in the days of the silk trade. The motives inspiring this new European interest in China and the empire of the Tatars were various. Christian Europe was not averse to the possibility of an alliance with the Mongols and the Chinese against the Moslems. The Crusades, quite apart from their spiritual results, had created a new demand for the wares of the East. Finally, the

---

[4] Goodrich, *A Short History*, 147-149.

Roman Catholic Church recognized in some measure the new opportunity to carry Christianity to the pagan world. Faith, fear, and the desire for material gain combined to inspire the embassies which Europe was soon to dispatch into Central Asia and the Far East.

The first ambassador of the Catholic Church was a Franciscan, John de Plano Carpini. He delivered a papal letter to the Great Khan at his Mongolian capital in 1246. The Khan's reply was not encouraging. Instead of agreeing to accept Christianity, he counselled the Pope to proceed to the East and there pay homage to the Mongol power. The next Christian missions to the East were sent by Louis IX of France. The first of these, headed by Andrew of Longomeau and designed to secure a treaty of alliance against the Moslems, was rebuffed in 1249. The second of Louis' embassies, sent in 1252, was in charge of a Flemish Franciscan, William of Rubruck. He, like Carpini, was received at the camp of the Great Khan in Mongolia. Neither of them reached China, though both recorded the information they obtained concerning that country.

THE POLOS IN CHINA

Kublai Khan, as ruler of the eastern Mongol dominions, set up his capital at Cambaluc (Khanbaliq, the modern Peking or Pei-p'ing) in 1264. There the Khan received two Venetian merchants, Nicolo and Maffeo Polo, whose travels in Asia had been prompted by neither political nor religious, but rather by commercial, motives. Now, however, they were commissioned by the Khan with letters to the Papacy asking that a hundred scholarly missionaries be sent to the Mongol capital. The Papacy responded by dispatching two Dominicans who turned back to Europe before the journey was well begun. The Polo brothers, less timorous than their ecclesiastical brethren, returned in 1275 to Kublai's capital, taking with them Nicolo's son Marco. All three entered the service of the Khan and continued to serve him for seventeen years, enjoying both honor and advancement. *The Book of Marco Polo,* written at the close of the century after the return of these intrepid travellers to Europe, gave to the West its first comprehensive picture of China. Marco records the existence in China of Europeans carried there captive by the Mongols. His, too, was the first European account to record the name Zipangu (Japan).

It was just as the Polos were returning for the second time to Europe that the first zealous Roman missionary, John of Monte Corvino, in 1289, was carrying a papal letter to the Khan. Arriving at Cambaluc about 1293, he was permitted to preach, to erect a church, and to be assisted by missionaries sent subsequently to join him. In 1307 the Pope created him Archbishop of Cambaluc, and when, in 1328, Corvino died, there had been created a Christian community of several thousand enjoying the favor of the Mongol dynasty. This favor was a feature of the Mongol policy of cultivating foreign religions as a counterpoise to the Confucian philosophy of their conquered subjects, the Chinese. With the collapse of the Mongol rule in 1368, the Christian community established by Corvino appears to have vanished. Under the subsequent Ming rulers foreign creeds and isms which had been patronized by the Mongols were suppressed.

The fall of the Mongol power interrupted the revival in the silk trade between China and Europe. It also tended to center the attention of Europe upon the spice trade. During the period when the Mongols controlled Persia, prior to its conversion to Islam, Italian traders were permitted direct access to India. They were able easily to lower the fantastic prices charged by the Egyptian middlemen in the spice trade. Thus when the Mongol power fell and European traders could no longer trade directly with India, but on the contrary were subject to the exactions and wars of a hostile Islam, a demand was thereby created for a new route to the land of spices. This demand was created just at a time when the European conception of India and the Far East was overcoming the incredulity which had greeted the accounts of Marco Polo.[5]

THE ALL-SEA ROUTE TO CHINA

From as early as 1291 Europe had played with the idea of a sea route to the East. Not until two centuries later was this dream brought to fulfillment when, in 1488, Portuguese navigators reached and passed the Cape of Good Hope. Ten years later (1498-1499), Vasco da Gama reached Calicut in India from Lisbon, and returned with a valuable cargo of pepper. Successors of da Gama reached Malacca in 1511. From these advanced trading posts, which now for the first time could be reached by an unbroken sea voyage, the Portuguese advanced to Java, Siam, Indo-China, and the southern coasts of China Proper. Meanwhile, they had, by their naval warfare against the Arabs, become the commercial masters of the Arabian Sea. The Portuguese could contemplate with satisfaction their control of the sea route from Lisbon to Malacca.

The China which Portuguese traders were soon to visit was ruled by

[5] For convenient readings on European knowledge of China during the early and medieval periods, see Henry Yule, *Cathay and the Way Thither* (2 vols., London, 1866).

the last of the great Chinese dynasties, the Ming (1368-1644). The first century of Ming rule had been a period of commercial and maritime vigor dominated by a forceful naval diplomacy. Chinese fleets penetrated the South China Sea and the Indian Ocean, returning with tribute-bearing embassies. After 1421, when the Ming capital was moved from Nanking to Peking, maritime interests were subject to increasing neglect. Yet some remnants of the trade remained, for when Portugal's emissary, Albuquerque, reached Malacca, he found a Chinese trading squadron of five junks.[6]

THE FIRST PORTUGUESE REACH CHINA

The first Portuguese reached China from Malacca in 1514. This was a commercial and unofficial enterprise, and though the mariners were not permitted to land, they disposed of their goods at a considerable profit. This auspicious beginning led in 1517 to an official Portuguese mission headed by Thomas Pires, who was conducted to Canton in a pepper-laden Portuguese squadron commanded by Fernam d'Andrade. The embassy was well received at Canton and permission was requested for it to proceed to Peking. In this it was supported by the Canton merchants whose commercial interests had been furthered temporarily by the arrival of the Portuguese in Malacca. Accordingly, in 1519 Pires was ordered to proceed to Peking. But no sooner had he reached the capital than he was hustled back to Canton and imprisoned. In 1522 the Chinese attacked and destroyed the Portuguese trading post at Canton, though another which survived for some years was soon established nearby at Lappa. Later, Portuguese traders were driven from Ningpo and Amoy. These misfortunes are not difficult to explain. Reports had already reached the Ming court that the Portuguese, far from being bent solely on peaceful commerce, were intent on conquest. Meanwhile, too, Simon d'Andrade, a brother of Fernam, who had reached Canton with a Portuguese license to trade, had outraged Chinese officialdom by his insolence and by piratical forays along the coast. Consequently, the Portuguese could blame only themselves for their diplomatic and commercial failure.

. . . Truculent and lawless, regarding all Eastern peoples as legitimate prey, they [although professing Christianity] were little if any better than the contemporary Japanese pirates who pillaged the Chinese coasts. The Ming [emperors of China] can scarcely be censured for treating them as freebooters.[7]

---

[6] Goodrich, *A Short History,* ch. vii.

[7] K. S. Latourette, *The Chinese: Their History and Culture* (2nd rev. ed., 2 vols. in one, New York, 1934), I, 313.

THE PORTUGUESE POST AT MACAO

The informal trade and the intermittent conflicts waged by the Chinese and the Portuguese along the coasts as far north as Ningpo gave place in 1557 to a somewhat more formal intercourse. In this year the Portuguese established themselves at Macao, a small peninsula joined by a narrow neck of land to Hsiang Shan (Island of Hsiang), which lies in the delta to the south of Canton. Portuguese occupation of this desolate spot appears to have been arranged quite informally, though in part it may have been a reward for assistance in the suppression of Chinese piracy. At all events the foreigners were permitted to remain, assisted to this end no doubt by a little well-placed bribery, and later by the payment of an annual rent. Across the narrow isthmus, the Chinese constructed a wall with one gate in order that the movements of the Westerners might be the better controlled. Here the Portuguese traders were under the jurisdiction of the Chinese authorities. They themselves, however, were usually allowed to handle cases involving only their own subjects. Beyond this, Chinese control, territorial, judicial, and fiscal, was absolute.[8] It remained so until 1849, at which time the Portuguese began to persist in a claim to exclusive jurisdiction. Macao, nevertheless, was not recognized as Portuguese territory until the Protocol of Lisbon was signed in 1887. Macao, from the time when the Portuguese first settled there until the cession of Hongkong to Great Britain in 1842, remained the summer residence of Westerners engaged in the Canton trade. During the later nineteenth century its importance declined steadily.

CHINA'S POLICY AND THE PORTUGUESE TRADE

The question naturally arises why China, after her expulsion of the Pires mission and her subsequent experience with the Portuguese lawlessness, tolerated these foreign merchants at all. In part it may be explained by the tendency of the Chinese Imperial Court to assert an authority which it was either unwilling or unable to enforce. Certainly the emperor could not bestow his Imperial favor on surly Western barbarians who had respect neither for the dignity of the empire nor for its control over neighboring tributary states. Yet if there was profit to be derived from a limited commerce with the barbarian, he might be permitted to trade informally at a few ports. This was practical and therefore good Chinese doctrine. Actually the Chinese merchants at Canton desired the trade; there were provincial officials who for a con-

---

[8] H. B. Morse, *The Chronicles of the East India Company Trading to China* (5 vols., Oxford, 1926-29), I, 8-9.

sideration would permit the trade; and at Peking, metropolitan officials, likewise for a consideration, might pretend ignorance that there was any trade with the barbarian at all. The consequence was that the trade prospered while the question of diplomatic recognition was ignored.[9]

THE DEVELOPMENT OF CATHOLIC MISSIONS

The rediscovery of China by Portuguese traders renewed and intensified the missionary interest of the Roman Catholic Church. Francis Xavier, who, in 1549, introduced Catholicism to Japan, was the first zealot in the new campaign to convert the Chinese. Xavier, however, died off the coast of Kwangtung (1552), thwarted in his ambition to carry Catholic Christianity to China. Several missionaries who subsequently sought to enter the country were denied admittance. From these failures came the resolve to train in the Chinese language a selected group of Jesuits who might appeal to Chinese officialdom not on religious grounds but rather through other scholarly attainments. So it was that Matteo Ricci, an Italian, a student of mathematics and astronomy, who had joined the Society of Jesus in 1571, came to Macao in 1582. At first garbed in the robes of a Buddhist monk, he contented himself with winning the interest and respect of Chinese officials through his scientific knowledge. His Buddhist robes were later discarded for the dress of a Chinese Confucian scholar, not without effect, for in 1601 he received permission to reside and preach in Peking, where he continued to live until his death in 1610.[10]

The religious propaganda of Ricci, his associates, and successors, based on their appeal to the scientific and scholarly interests of Chinese officialdom, met with notable success. Among the converts were many princes of the blood, mandarins, and other courtiers. As aids in their mis-

---

[9] The system of foreign trade which prevailed under the Mings is the key to the politico-commercial difficulties which were to plague China's relations with the Western powers during the later eighteenth and nineteenth centuries. Under the Mings, foreign trade was considered primarily as an instrument for controlling the vassal states, not as a source of government revenue. Local officials, however, found in this trade a door to great wealth. The system worked very well in early Ming times, but with the arrival of the European barbarians (the Portuguese and those who followed them), who did not consider themselves as tributaries, it was subjected to new and powerful pressures. To high Chinese officials at Macao, the Portuguese, who frequently acted in defiance of all law and custom, were "like a tumour on the back." Teh-ch'ang Chang, "Maritime Trade at Canton during the Ming Dynasty," *Chinese Soc. and Pol. Science Rev.* XVII, No. 2 (July, 1933), 279-282. Note also J. K. Fairbank, "Tributary Trade and China's Relations with the West," *Far Eastern Quarterly,* I (1942), 129-49; and J. K. Fairbank and S. Y. Teng, "On the Ch'ing Tributary System," *Harvard Journal of Asiatic Studies,* VI (1941), 135-246.

[10] K. S. Latourette, *A History of Christian Missions in China* (New York, 1932), 91-98.

· sionary work, the Jesuits employed every intellectual, scientific, and mechanical device which the Europe of their day could suggest: clocks, horological instruments, gauges, glass prisms, mathematical and astronomical instruments, and geographical, architectural, literary, and religious books. Ricci prepared for the Chinese a map of the world, on which he tactfully placed China in the middle; his followers corrected the Chinese calendar; others were appointed by the emperor to the post of state astronomer. A century after Ricci's arrival at Canton, the K'ang-hsi emperor granted freedom of worship to the Roman churches throughout the empire.

PERSECUTION AND ITS CAUSES

These official favors did not exempt the missionaries from persecution. In 1616 and again in 1664 some of the Jesuits were expelled from Peking and forced to return to Canton or Macao. In fact it is surprising that in the seventeenth century there was not more persecution. Neo-Confucianism under the Ming emperors was inclined to be fixed and intolerant; Buddhism and Taoism were permitted but were regulated closely. The Imperial Court under the late Mings and under the first Manchu rulers did not look with favor on an exclusive, authoritarian, and dogmatic religion such as Catholicism. Actually, seventeenth-century China, whatever its limitations may have been, was more tolerant than Catholic Europe. At the very moment when the Papacy was seeking tolerance for its monks in China, Alva, as agent of the Counter Reformation, was seeking to crush by the sword heresy in the Netherlands. A Church which denied tolerance to Europe, insisted upon it from the Chinese. And when finally Christianity was proscribed by Peking (1724), responsibility rested upon the missionaries rather than upon Chinese officialdom.

THE RITES CONTROVERSY

For some fifty years after the arrival of Ricci, the Jesuits were the only Christian missionaries in China, but in the following century they were joined by representatives of the Dominicans (1631), the Franciscans (1633), the Augustinians (1680), and the Paris Foreign Missions (1683). With the arrival of these competing orders, many of the policies toward doctrine and procedure which had been adopted by the Jesuits were attacked by the late comers. These disputes may be classified under three heads, all of importance to the theological mind of the times. They involved the major question whether Christianity as practiced by the Church should compromise with Chinese culture in order to appear less antagonistic to China's political and social institutions. Under the first group of controversies was the question whether Chinese classical terms, such as *T'ien* (Heaven), known to all Chinese scholars, should be used by the missionary and given a Christian connotation. In the second group fell such questions as to whether Chinese converts should be forbidden to engage in ceremonies honoring Confucius and the ancestors. Finally, there were numerous miscellaneous problems. Would the Church permit masses to "be said for the souls of the non-Christian ancestors of [Chinese] Christians?" [11]

Ricci and his immediate followers had recognized that if Christianity was to make progress in China, it must accommodate itself to some of the beliefs and practices of Confucianism and ancestor worship. Thus he maintained that the ceremonies to Confucius and to ancestors were civil and not religious acts. Therefore a convert to Catholicism could participate in them without violating his religion. Some of the Jesuits themselves doubted the moral basis of this liberal policy, but by the Franciscans and by the Dominicans such practices were stoutly opposed. Furthermore, the Jesuits permitted use of the Chinese character *T'ien* (Heaven) in referring to the Christian God. The rival orders asserted that *T'ien-chu* (Lord of Heaven) was the correct character. These disputes raged on among the missionaries for the better part of a century, and finally were carried for settlement both to the emperor in Peking and to the Pope in Rome. In 1700, the Manchu K'ang-hsi emperor decided in favor of the Jesuits, while in Rome the Papacy supported their critics. The resulting situation was ludicrous. No missionary could go to China as a representative of the Roman Church unless he accepted the Papacy as the final authority on the true significance of China's religious ideographs; such missionaries as accepted this authority, the Manchu emperor would not receive. The net result of this extraordinary episode was that in 1724 all missionaries, save a few who were retained for scientific work, were expelled.[12] Despite this development, the Church fared better than it deserved. Many of its converts retained

---

[11] Latourette, *A History of Christian Missions in China,* 132-135. Stated in other words, the question was how far should a Christian participate in the society in which he lives? To the Church of the time the question appeared to be one of life or death; the issues were debated bitterly by the rival orders; nationalistic rivalries to which priests were not immune were injected; and ultimately all ecclesiastical and learned Europe participated in the debate until, so far as the Church was concerned, it was silenced by Rome. *Ibid.,* 134-135.

[12] A full and excellent discussion of the origin and development of anti-missionary feeling and anti-foreignism in China during the seventeenth and eighteenth centuries is given in Earl H. Pritchard, *Anglo-Chinese Relations during the Seventeenth and Eighteenth Centuries* (Urbana, 1929), ch. vi.

their faith, and courageous missionaries more interested in the work of salvation than in theological disputation entered China secretly at the risk of their lives to minister to the faithful and to win new converts.[13] Moreover, it should be noted that although in its spiritual mission the church had enjoyed only the most qualified success, the intellectual influence of the Jesuits on late Ming China was very considerable.

THE SPANIARDS REACH THE PHILIPPINES

Less than a decade after the first Portuguese navigators reached Canton, Spanish explorers were crossing the Pacific after rounding Cape Horn. In March, 1521, Ferdinand Magellan, a Portuguese by birth but sailing under the flag of Spain, discovered the Mariana or Ladrone (Robber) Islands, and later in the same month reached Samar in the Philippines. At Cebu, Magellan found a native population engaged in trade with China. Junks from Siam visited in Philippine waters, while in the markets of Cebu brass gongs and a variety of articles gave evidence of an extensive trade with the Chinese.

The Spaniards, however, were not seeking the Philippines or China, but the Spice Islands which lay to the south. As it happened, these islands, by the line of demarcation of 1494, lay, as did also the Philippines, in the Portuguese half of the world. It was not, then, until some years later that Spain undertook conquest and exploration of the Philippines. Manila was founded in 1571, by which time the Chinese trade with the islands was considerable. In this trade the Spaniards were soon involved, for they had failed to find in the Philippines the coveted wealth of the Spice Islands, and they could not trade directly with China, which was recognized as lying within the Portuguese sphere. Herein lies the explanation of the rapid increase in the Chinese commerce with Manila and in the Chinese population of that city—an increase so rapid that Spanish colonizers resorted on a number of occasions to massacre. Some of Spain's adventurers at Manila contemplated the conquest of China, naïvely suggesting that less than one hundred soldiers could handle the matter.

THE DUTCH IN THE FAR EAST

Fresh from their successful struggle for national independence, the Dutch reached the Far East at the beginning of the seventeenth century.

[13] Commenting on the Bull "Ex quo singulari" of Pope Benedict XIV, July 11, 1742, which condemned Chinese ceremonies and chose the expression *T'ien-chu* for God, *The Catholic Encyclopedia* (London, 1908), III, 671-672, observes: "Rome having spoken, no more can be said here on the question, but it may be noted that the Bull "Ex quo singulari" was a terrible blow to the missions in China. . . ."

Organization of the United Dutch East India Company signalized the emerging commercial supremacy of the Netherlands and its determination, with England, to destroy the colonial and mercantile monopoly of Spain and Portugal. The Dutch attempted to open trade at Canton in 1604, and again in 1607, but on both occasions permission was denied, probably at the instigation of the Portuguese at Macao. In retaliation, the Dutch attacked Macao unsuccessfully in 1622. Subsequent attacks on the Portuguese were conducted from a new Dutch base on the Pescadores Islands near Taiwan (Formosa). Here too the Dutch carried on trade with Chinese from the mainland, until under pressure from Chinese authorities they were forced to retire to Formosa (1624), where on the west coast of the island they constructed a factory (trading post) and a fort known as Zelandia Castel. Here the Dutch were advantageously situated for the development of their trade between the East Indies and Japan, and for the formalizing of their relations with China. In 1662, however, they were driven from Formosa by Cheng Ch'eng-kung, known popularly as Koxinga, a partisan of the last Ming aspirants who had not yet been suppressed by China's new Manchu rulers. Two decades later the Dutch, who meanwhile had assisted the Manchus in the overthrow of Koxinga's mushroom state (Formosa, Amoy, and part of Fukien), were permitted, along with the English, to trade at Amoy, but such were the exactions of the Manchu military that the trade was soon virtually abandoned.

During the seventeenth and the eighteenth centuries the Dutch sent four embassies to Peking (1656, 1667, 1685-86, and 1795) seeking formal contacts with the Manchu Court and commercial concessions. The ambassadors were required to perform the humiliating *kotow* (nine prostrations), in return for which they received only meager commercial privileges. After 1729 the Dutch traded regularly at Canton.

The Dutch were the first representatives of the Protestant faith in China. Though they sent no missionaries to the Far East, their traders, who had tasted the bitterness of religious persecution in Europe, did not fail to warn the Chinese against the political and social dangers inherent in the Roman Catholic system, in which the spiritual allegiance of Chinese converts was transferred from Peking to Rome.

THE ENGLISH REACH CHINA

Although the English had preceded the Dutch in their efforts to open trade with China, their first ship and the envoys were lost at sea in 1596. The first English vessel to reach Canton was dispatched in 1635 by the English East India Company. This was followed by a squadron of English vessels, commanded by Captain John Weddell, sent by the

Courteen Association. Weddell arrived at Macao in 1637, proceeded to Canton, met at first with opposition from the Chinese, but was finally permitted to engage in trade. The English sent ships regularly to Canton after 1699, which is the date probably marking the beginning of their permanent factory there.

Other European nations played an inconspicuous role in this early China trade. The first French ship to reach Canton arrived in 1698; the first Danish ship in 1731; the first Swedish ship in 1732; and the first Russian ship in 1753. The first American ship, *The Empress of China,* sailed for China in 1784.

FIRST RUSSIAN CONTACTS WITH CHINA

While western Europeans in the sixteenth and seventeenth centuries were making their first contacts with China by the all-sea route, Russians, too, were moving to the East by way of Siberia. These first adventurers were composed of a motley aggregation of explorers, fur traders, and fugitives from the law. Some of them reached the Pacific slope, while across Siberia appeared permanent settlements at Tobolsk, Tomsk, Yakutsk, Nertchinsk, and other points. In far eastern Siberia there was a natural tendency for the Russians to move south into the valley of the Amur River. Here they came into conflict with tribal peoples who, theoretically at least, recognized the overlordship of China. For some years there was intermittent conflict between the Russians and the Chinese at Albazin, a Muscovite outpost on the upper Amur. Not until 1689 was a boundary settlement effected by the Russo-Chinese Treaty of Nertchinsk, China's first treaty with a Western power. As a result of this settlement, in which the Chinese negotiators were assisted by Jesuit advisers, Peking retained and extended its sovereignty over the Amur Valley. A number of Russian embassies were sent subsequently to Peking during the eighteenth century. A settlement of the Russo-Chinese northwestern boundary was reached in 1727, and permanent trading posts were established on the frontier. Permission was also given for establishment of a Russian church in Peking, and China sent to St. Petersburg her only embassy to a foreign court.

THE WEST DISCOVERS JAPAN

When Marco Polo was writing of his adventures in China, he recounted that

Chipangu is an Island toward the east [from China] in the high seas, . . . and a very great Island it is. The people are white, civilized, and well-favoured. They are Idolaters, and are dependent on nobody. And I can tell you the quantity of gold they have is endless. . . . You must know that he [the king of this island] hath a great Palace which is entirely roofed with fine gold, just as our churches are roofed with lead, insomuch that it would scarcely be possible to estimate its value.[14]

Marco Polo himself did not visit Japan. What he wrote was based upon hearsay. It was, indeed, more than two centuries after the travels of the Polos before Europeans set foot on the shores of Japan. The account generally accepted relates that in 1542 Portuguese sailors voyaging from Macao to Siam were blown from their course to the shores of Tanegashima, a small island off the southern coast of Kyūshū, where they instructed the natives in the use of firearms. These visitors were followed closely by Fernando Mendez Pinto, to whom the discovery of Japan is usually credited. He, too, appears to have impressed the Japanese with the admirable qualities of the gun. More Portuguese ships soon appeared, for the feudal lords of southern Japan took readily to the idea of trade with the foreigners.

These commercial contacts with southern Japan soon aroused the interest of the Portuguese monks. Francis Xavier, a Jesuit who had been preaching in Goa, Travancore, and Malacca, was inspired to visit the Japanese mission field. In this he was influenced by Anjiro (Yajiro), a Japanese who had been carried to Goa on a Portuguese ship. In company with a brother missionary, Father Fernandez, Xavier landed at Kagoshima in August, 1549. For more than two years he pursued in this new field the most successful mission of his life. The Japanese, far from repelling the foreigner, welcomed both his commerce and his religion.

The [Portuguese] Merchants in exchange for their European and Indian commodities, as raw silk, fine stuffs, druggs, wines, medicines, and a great variety of other both natural and artificial curiosities, became possess'd of immense treasures, and the golden marrow of the country. The fathers of the Society [of Jesus] on their side gain'd the hearts of the people, always greedy of novelties, by the meek and comfortable doctrine of the Gospel. . . .[15]

THE GROWTH OF CATHOLIC MISSIONS

Xavier, during his stay in Japan, moved from Kagoshima in Satsuma to Hirado and later to Kyoto, vainly seeking an audience with the em-

---

[14] Sir Henry Yule, ed., *The Book of Ser Marco Polo* (3rd rev. ed., New York, 1926), II, 253-254.

[15] Engelbert Kaempfer, *The History of Japan* (New York, 1906), II, 154.

peror. In November, 1551, he left Japan, and died the following year off the coast of southern China. Other Jesuits, however, followed him to Japan, where their work soon testified to their vigorous spirit and to the tolerance of the Japanese. The missionaries were heard respectfully by all classes of the people, including Buddhist priests. This may be accounted for partly by certain similarities between the rites and ceremonials of Buddhism and Catholicism. Since, too, Catholicism was introduced directly from India, many Japanese assumed that it was a reformed Buddhism. Some of the Japanese feudal lords in their official edicts referred to Catholicism as "the New Buddhism from the Western Nations." It may of course be questioned whether many of the Japanese converts possessed any profound understanding of the new Western religion, for it has been noted that "Japanese is a difficult language and Christianity is hard to explain."

Other causes, too, contributed to the early success of Christianity in Japan. The feudal barons desired the profits of the foreign trade, and those in southern Japan, where most of the trade was conducted, were eager to increase their own power at the expense of the shogun's government. These barons observed the deference paid by the Portuguese traders to the missionaries. They concluded that where the missionary was, there too would be the trader. In Kyūshū, the barons, on occasion, ordered the mass conversion of their retainers to Christianity and even instigated persecution of the Buddhists; but if no foreign ship arrived, the populace was as often commanded to revert to the native faith.

Although the Japanese were attracted by the learning and dignity of the Jesuits, they were at a loss to understand their intolerance.

[The] . . . Jesuits did not study the feelings of others, and their zeal easily took the form of an aggressive bigotry, though it must be granted that they displayed a splendid courage which undoubtedly gained them the respect of the military class. Xavier . . . made the bad mistake of insisting that all the dead who had not been Christians during their lifetime would burn forever. To a people who had never believed seriously in the flames of hell, and who paid to the memory of their ancestors a most reverent devotion, this was a revolting doctrine.[16]

Thus, while gaining many converts through one influence or another, the missionaries aroused bitter opposition to themselves and their creed. Their main strongholds were in Kyūshū but they enjoyed some success, too, in Kyoto, where a group of Jesuits was received by the shogun and

[16] G. B. Sansom, *Japan: A Short Cultural History* (New York, 1931), 408.

also by Nobunaga (1568), who befriended them in his desire to curb the political power of Buddhism.

THE SPANIARDS IN JAPAN

Until 1592 the Portuguese were the only Europeans to reach Japan. When Philip II of Spain ascended the throne of Portugal in 1581, he confirmed his Portuguese subjects in the exclusive right to the Japan trade. Four years later the Papacy conferred upon the Jesuits the sole right to enter Japan as missionaries. It was just at this time (1591), that Hideyoshi, planning the conquest of China, sent an embassy to Manila demanding that the Spaniards there recognize them as their suzerain. The Spanish governor sent two missions to Japan, carrying among their number four Franciscan friars, who, in the guise of ambassadors, entered Japan in violation of the papal order. Other priests who soon followed were permitted to remain on the understanding that they should not preach Christianity. Having accepted this prohibition, the priests proceeded immediately to violate it by conducting services in Nagasaki, Kyoto, and Osaka. Hideyoshi had at first been disposed favorably toward the foreign priests, but he had become suspicious of political implications in the Jesuit policy and conduct. In confirmation of his fears, he now observed the Spanish priests openly defying his authority, and promoting, as in China, sectarian feuds with their Jesuit colleagues. Finally, the idle boasting of a Spanish pilot to the effect that the missionary was preparing the way for political conquest led Hideyoshi to act. In February, 1597, six Franciscans, three Japanese Jesuits, and seventeen Japanese laymen were crucified at Nagasaki. In explanation of this vigorous act, it should be noted that ten years earlier, Hideyoshi, after subduing the *daimyo* of Satsuma, where most of the Christians lived, had issued an edict ordering the foreign missionaries to leave Japan within twenty days. This edict was directed against the priests, not against their religion, for the Japanese desired to continue the Portuguese trade. The edict was in consequence modified to permit priests to accompany the Portuguese ships but not to remain in Japan. But for a number of reasons the law was not enforced effectively. Priests defied the law; some of them were protected by friendly barons in Kyūshū; Hideyoshi's attention was diverted both by war at home and abroad. Thus, when the first crucifixions occurred in 1597, the Spanish priests could not plead ignorance of the law. Hideyoshi, it will be observed, did not interfere with the Jesuits. Probably he feared stoppage of the valuable Portuguese trade.

THE FOREIGN POLICY OF IYEYASU

With the passing of Hideyoshi (1598), political control in Japan passed into the hands of Tokugawa Iyeyasu, the able founder of the last great shogunate. Iyeyasu's views on foreign policy and trade were probably more enlightened than any which prevailed even in Europe at the time. During his rule the Portuguese, the Spaniards, the Dutch, and the English were all welcomed in Japanese ports. The exclusion edict against foreign priests was not revoked; neither was it enforced. Spanish monks from Manila again entered Japan, and in 1608 the Papacy rescinded the restriction which had granted the field solely to the Jesuits.

In 1600 the first Dutch ship reached Japan. It was one of a fleet of five vessels which had sailed by way of the Straits of Magellan, and, blown from its course, sought shelter in the Japanese harbor of Bungo. The pilot of the vessel was an English sailor, Will Adams, who, because of his natural wit and ability, was promptly employed by Iyeyasu as adviser in matters of commerce and navigation. Other Dutch ships arrived in 1609, and a Dutch factory was built at Hirado, an island near Nagasaki. News of these successes brought the first English ship to Hirado in 1613. Iyeyasu, influenced by Adams, offered the English a charter for free trade and urged them to construct a factory at his capital, Yedo, the modern Tokyo. The short-sighted English Captain Saris preferred to remain with his factory and trade at Hirado. There the business was handled incompetently and abandoned in 1623 at a time when the Dutch trade was prospering.

Iyeyasu was likewise interested in developing closer commercial relations with Spain. He communicated with the Spanish authorities in the Philippines, offered to open the ports of eastern Japan to Spanish ships, and allowed it to be understood that the edicts against the missionaries would not be enforced. But it soon appeared that Spain was more likely to send missionaries than traders to Japan. Iyeyasu grew suspicious of Spanish motives. The Dutch and English asserted that priests were not essential to trade. Accordingly, in 1612 Iyeyasu proscribed the Christian faith. All the Franciscan churches and many of the Jesuit establishments were destroyed. Some Japanese converts were executed in Yedo (1613), and in the following year suppression of the faith was ordered throughout the empire. However, most of the foreign missionaries were not harmed at this time, and many of the local barons refused to act against the native Christians in their domains.

Hidetada, who succeeded Iyeyasu in 1616, executed some Spanish priests, yet the laws were still not fully enforced. The government sought rather to have the priests leave the country voluntarily, whereas native Christians were induced by peaceful means to abandon the faith. Actually this policy failed, for the priests were defiant, and most of the converts clung to their new-found religion.

THE POLICY OF EXCLUSION AND SECLUSION

The Catholic priesthood and their converts were, it seemed to the shogun, creating a rival authority in Japan which the shogunate was no longer willing to tolerate. Accordingly, in 1624 the Spaniards were ordered to leave the country. Direct relations between Japan and the Philippines were severed. Then in 1636 Iyemitsu, son and successor of Hidetada, proscribed Japanese trade on the high seas. No Japanese vessel might proceed abroad; no Japanese subject could lawfully leave his country; those doing so and attempting to return would suffer death. For this revolutionary policy, Catholic Christianity was in part responsible. Many Japanese converts had gone abroad to receive instruction at Macao or Manila, whence they returned to propagate the faith in their native land. This practice was now stopped, while at the same time foreigners who were permitted to remain in Japan were sharply controlled. The Dutch were still permitted to trade at Hirado, but at Nagasaki the Portuguese were forced to conduct their commerce virtually as prisoners on a small artificial island, known as Deshima.

These virile measures did not end the trouble. The Shimabara revolt of 1637, a movement occasioned by feudal oppression and Christian persecutions, involved a large number of Japanese converts and was believed to have been incited by the missionaries. The government acted promptly. Spanish and Portuguese subjects were forbidden to visit Japan. Furthermore it was decreed that if any Portuguese ship came to Japan, the vessel and cargo would be burned and the crew put to death. A Portuguese embassy of 73 persons, seeking to prove Portuguese innocence of the Shimabara revolt, met exactly this fate. All were sentenced

. . . to be beheaded, excepting twelve men of the lowest rank, who were sent back to Macao, to bring their countrymen the news of this unhappy success, along with a most proud and threatening message from the Emperor, containing in substance, that should the King of Portugal himself, nay the very God of the Christians, presume to enter his dominions, he would serve them in the very same manner.[17]

---

[17] Kaempfer, *The History of Japan*, II, 166-167.

A second embassy sent to Japan after Portugal had regained her independence from Spain failed also.

JAPAN IN SECLUSION

In this manner Japan entered upon a long period of exclusion and seclusion. The Dutch, to be sure, were permitted to carry on a limited trade confined to the island of Deshima in Nagasaki harbor, and the Chinese could send a few junks annually to the same port. Except for these contacts Japan was excluded from the outside world, and was to remain so for more than two centuries. It was indeed an extraordinary shift from the original policies of Iyeyasu. What would have happened had Japan not adopted the policy of exclusion lies in the field of speculation. It is suggestive, however, to recall that during the period of exclusion (1638-1854) the Western powers built and consolidated their colonial empires. Had Japan been in more intimate touch with world affairs perhaps she too would have played a leading role in those struggles.

CHAPTER 5

THE CANTON TRADE

THE sixteenth and seventeenth centuries, as we have seen in the previous chapter, gave promise of a rich and permanent intercourse, both material and cultural, between Europe and the Far East. In China there was an intelligent and on the whole a tolerant audience ready to listen while Jesuits lectured on Europe's science. In Japan, the commercial and economic ideas of Tokugawa Iyeyasu far surpassed in liberality the economic policies of contemporary leaders in Europe. Yet by 1638 Japan had closed her doors to all foreign intercourse save for the annual Dutch ship and a few Chinese junks at Nagasaki. China likewise adopted a policy of cultural if not commercial exclusion. Repelled by the exclusive philosophy of the Catholic Church and by the quarrelsome character of its rival religious orders, the Chinese government expelled the missionaries in 1724. Thus the trade between Europe and Japan was ended, while such trade as remained with China enjoyed only a precarious, unstable existence. This China trade, dominated in the sixteenth century by the Portuguese, passed during the seventeenth century into the hands of the Dutch, who by the beginning of the eighteenth century were in turn surrendering it to their English rivals.[1]

The eighteenth century was in fact notable for two distinct though perhaps related movements in the relations of the West (Europe) and the Far East. The first was the rise and the decline in Europe of a pronounced Chinese influence: artistic, cultural and intellectual.[2] The second was the development of what was known as the Canton trade. It was this trade, maintained in the curious circumstances which pre-

[1] For a brief summary account of European expansion in the period covered by this and the preceding chapter, see Charles E. Smith, *A History of Western Civilization* (2 vols., Baton Rouge, 1936-37), II, 153-169.

[2] The early modern Chinese and Japanese influence upon Europe manifested itself in many ways: 1) After 1655, illustrated books on China were published in Latin, Dutch and French; 2) The Trianon de Porcelaine of Louis XIV at Versailles was Chinese in design; 3) Similar influence marked English architectural landscape designs in the eighteenth century; 4) Europe's China-collecting mania in the same century developed substitute native industries. Joseph Downs, "The China Style in Europe," in *The China Trade and Its Influences* (New York, 1941), 8-12.

vailed at Canton from 1750 to 1839, which precipitated the nineteenth-century conflict between the West and the Far East.

CHINA'S INFLUENCE UPON EUROPE:
EARLY EIGHTEENTH CENTURY

At the beginning of the eighteenth century polite society in Europe spoke of Chinese art with ease and familiarity. The brilliant masquerades of the French court were dominated by the art of China. The work of many of Europe's rococo artists was enriched if not inspired by the elaborate arts of southern China. To Europeans, the word porcelain connoted China; in England it actually was called "china," and it still is. Lacquer ware, a rarity in the time of Louis XIV, was almost a commonplace in eighteenth-century France. Europe was influenced, too, not only by Chinese styles in ornamentation, but also by Chinese technical skills in the coloring of silks.

Side by side with these Chinese influences upon the Paris *salon* were others playing upon the intellectual life of so-called "enlightened" Europe. European philosophers such as Leibniz, LaMettrie, and Quesnay found in Confucian philosophy support for the rational basis of their systems of "pure thought." The physiocrats derived in part their notions on the economic nature of the state from their conception of conditions in ancient China. Lastly, it may be noted that in the late eighteenth century, Europe's "Back to Nature" crusades, and the development of a sentimental nature-worship found some of their inspiration in the form and symbolism of the Chinese garden. This particular enthusiasm was the final and the most extreme form of China's cultural influence upon Western society.

As the eighteenth century drew to a close, China ceased to be a source of vital inspiration to either the art or the philosophy of Europe. This was due in part to the altered views and changed status of the Jesuits. To a great degree the intellectual bridge between China and Europe had been built by the Jesuits. They had found in China something akin to the ideal state, and they had so reported it to Europe. But the expulsion of the missionaries by China, and the later dissolution of the Jesuits in Europe destroyed the main carrier of Chinese thought and influence.[3]

CULTURAL ENTHUSIASM BECOMES SKEPTICISM

With the passing of the Jesuit contact, Chinese cultural influence not only ceased to reach Europe—such influence as persisted there was

---

[3] See Adolf Reichwein, *China and Europe* (New York, 1925), for a full discussion of intellectual and artistic contacts in the eighteenth century.

subjected to attack. The authenticity of the early Chinese annals was questioned. In England (1790) Chinese philosophy was dismissed by one writer as virtually worthless. Save for a few remnants here and there, the China of art, letters, and philosophy had by 1800 all but disappeared from the European mind. Yet quite another China was already making its appeal to Europe. This was a material China rather than an aesthetic one; an economic China rather than an intellectual one. Unlike the China which had appealed to the intellectuals of the European enlightenment, this was a China that appealed to the moneyed barons of the English East India Company. It was a China of statistics and markets, and, so the barons hoped, of larger and larger profits.

Thus it was that as the later eighteenth century advanced, Europe's cultural interest in China was replaced by a growing commercial interest —an interest which tended more and more to be monopolized by the British, which is to say, by the powerful English East India Company. This did not mean of course that other nationals were excluded from the trade of the China coast, but their share in it was circumscribed by political events. For instance, the Portuguese who had dominated the early trade (1517–ca. 1600), maintained themselves continuously at Macao during the seventeenth, eighteenth and nineteenth centuries, enjoying the profits of a small but lucrative, if not always an honorable trade. The Dutch, who dominated the eastern trade in the seventeenth century, failed to maintain this lead against the British in China. France, defeated by Britain in the colonial struggle, was unable to bid seriously for the China trade. So it was that as the eighteenth century advanced, the China trade became more and more the property of the English East India Company. Britain's victories in the colonial wars, her established position in India, and her primacy in the industrial revolution all served to stimulate her trade with the Far East. In fact, from 1750 until 1834 it may be said that China's relations with Europe were essentially her relations with the English East India Company. For most of this period China's foreign trade was confined to the single South China port of Canton. Thus, this commerce came to be known as the Canton trade. The peculiar circumstances surrounding this trade, the attitudes of the Chinese toward the foreign barbarians, and of the foreign barbarians in turn toward the "heathen" Chinese—all these had created by 1839 a crisis in the relations between Great Britain and China. It was this crisis and the wars which followed it that were to determine the relations of China and the West for the succeeding century (1840-1940). An analysis therefore of the Canton trade in the years before 1839 cannot be dismissed as a mere academic pursuit.

THE CANTON TRADE: EARLY DEVELOPMENT

The trade at Canton in the seventeenth century had been granted by China as a monopoly to the Portuguese, and as late as 1681 the Portuguese by reason of this grant and because of their establishment at Macao were still successful in excluding all other nationals from this commerce. However, when in 1685 the emperor of China declared all ports open to foreign commerce, the English East India Company was granted the right to establish a factory—that is, to trade—at Canton.[4] Since subsequent efforts to trade at ports other than Canton did not prove successful, the Company centered its efforts at Canton, to which ships were dispatched regularly after 1715. The increase in the size and value of the trade encouraged the Company to maintain a regular staff at Canton and Macao. The French also set up a factory at Canton. Thus the tendency for the foreign trade to gravitate to Canton was well under way when the Chinese government, in 1757, speeded the movement by decreeing that all the foreign trade should be confined to this city. From this time on the English East India Company's trade prospered.[5] By the close of the century the Canton trade had become in large measure a British trade, monopolized by the English East India Company.[6]

THE CATHCART MISSION, 1787

The primacy enjoyed by British trade was not, however, a reflection of British satisfaction with the commercial system which prevailed at Canton. On the contrary, the British, like all other foreign traders in China, regarded these conditions as exceedingly irksome. Accordingly, in 1787 Lieutenant Colonel Charles Cathcart was appointed by the British government as special envoy to the emperor of China. Cathcart was to go to Peking and there negotiate for a commercial depot where British merchants might store their goods pending sale, and where Chinese merchants might do business with them. The later exercise of extraterritoriality by foreigners in China was suggested by the provision

[4] On the trade of various countries at Canton, see the tables compiled by Earl H. Pritchard, "The Struggle for Control of the China Trade," *Pacific Historical Review*, III (1934), 280-295.
[5] H. B. Morse, *The Chronicles of the East India Company Trading to China 1635-1834* (Oxford, 1926), I, 294; II, 137. Hereafter cited as *Chronicles*.
[6] See the analysis of the eighteenth-century trade with China by Earl H. Pritchard, "The Struggle for Control of the China Trade," *Pacific Historical Review*, III (1934), 280-295.

that in this depot Chinese would remain under Chinese jurisdiction, the English under English jurisdiction.

Because of the death of the ambassador, this embassy did not reach Peking. It was, nonetheless, symptomatic of British dissatisfaction with what they regarded as China's unreasonable exactions in the Canton trade.

THE MACARTNEY EMBASSY, 1793

A second effort to deal with commercial conditions at Canton through diplomatic pressure at Peking was made by the British government in 1792-93. The head of the new embassy, Lord George Macartney, had already distinguished himself in India, where he was known as an administrator of great capacity.

Lord Macartney was received in audience by the emperor without performing the humiliating *kotow*.[7] During the sojourn of the mission in China, he was accorded "with every mark of respect, of honour, and of courtesy," and this despite the fact that the ambassador was cut off completely from all communication with the outside world. In matters of ceremony Macartney had little to complain of save that the members of his embassy were virtually "prisoners in silken bonds." But in the business which had brought Lord Macartney to China not the slightest progress was made. The ambassador had hoped to put Anglo-Chinese relations on a treaty basis, to open such ports as Ningpo, Chusan, Tientsin, and others to trade, to obtain a clear statement of all tariffs, duties, and other levies, and to secure the right for an English minister to reside at Peking. All were refused, and the ambassador was virtually reprimanded for his impertinence in making requests that ran counter to China's custom. Thus the Macartney embassy, while it could and did inform the British public on the general state of Chinese society, was unable to show any positive advantages gained for British trade.

THE AMHERST MISSION, 1816

While England remained involved in the wars of the French Revolution and the Napoleonic Era, her merchants at Canton continued to bow to regulations which in the view of the Foreign Office were "scarcely compatible" with "civilized society." In 1816, however, Lord Amherst was appointed special ambassador to the Chinese emperor. Specifi-

---

[7] The best account of the Macartney embassy is Earl H. Pritchard, *The Crucial Years of Early Anglo-Chinese Relations 1750-1800* (Pullman, Wash., 1936), chs. vii-ix. Note also the same author's exhaustive study of the *kotow* in "The Kotow in the Macartney Embassy to China in 1793," *Far Eastern Quarterly*, II (1943), 163-203.

cally, Lord Amherst was to seek a firmer basis for the British trade by having it placed under the direct protection of the emperor, where presumably it might escape the exactions imposed upon it by local authorities.

When Amherst arrived at Tientsin, the Chinese promptly insisted that he perform the *kotow* when received in audience by the emperor. Although his instructions were not emphatic on this point, Lord Amherst decided against performance of the *kotow* in any circumstance.[8] It was his Lordship's view that the nine humiliating prostrations before the emperor would serve the purposes of British trade in the nineteenth century no better than they had served the Dutch in the seventeenth and eighteenth centuries.[9] So it came about that the Chinese court, disgruntled by Amherst's refusal to *kotow,* hustled him by night to the imperial summer palace, the Yüan Ming Yüan ("the round flowery garden"). Without affording him opportunity to rest, to change his attire, or to secure his credentials, the officials attempted to push and haul the ambassador into an immediate audience. When Amherst resisted this treatment, his embassy was ordered to leave.

Like Macartney before him, Amherst had failed to secure a single concession from the Chinese. But worse than this, his embassy, and thus his government, had been grossly and wilfully insulted. However, the utter failure of the mission served to clarify the alternatives facing British policy at Canton. To English commercial interests and to the government it was becoming increasingly clear that English trade at Canton might follow one of three policies: 1) complete submission to a commercial system prescribed and controlled wholly by the Chinese; 2) complete abandonment of the trade (an unlikely course, since the trade was profitable even under the worst conditions); and 3) the application of force to compel the Chinese to do business on terms dictated by the West.

---

[8] The English view on the significance of the *kotow* was expressed in a letter by Sir T. Metcalfe and the Select Committee of the English East India Company to Lord Amherst: "If the ceremony of the Kotow was merely a form of obeisance on entering into the presence of a Sovereign no objection could exist to its performance, . . . but when it is peremptorily insisted upon as an acknowledgment that the Emperor of China is the Sovereign of the Universe and demanded as a Duty from other Potentates being his vassals, it is scarcely possible to suggest any circumstances that could induce a compliance and its humiliation requires most deliberate consideration." Quoted in H. B. Morse, *Chronicles,* III, 263.

[9] The Dutch embassies to Peking previously noted all conformed to Chinese demands by presenting tribute and performing the *kotow* in some form. By so doing the Dutch appear to have gained nothing. No additional commercial liberties or concessions were granted them. Their humility appears, however, to have confirmed the Chinese in their belief that all nations were inferior to China.

THE ANGLO-CHINESE CONFLICT IN 1800

By way of summary it may here be said that by the beginning of the nineteenth century there had already developed at Canton a clash between the fundamentally different cultures of England and China. The origins and the development of this conflict, and the unhappy shadows which it cast toward the future have been summarized ably in the following basic points:

1. England's first interest in China was promoted by the desire of private traders, as organized in the East India Company, to make profits, and to find a market for woollens and a purchasing place for silk.
2. The monopolistic East India Company continued to be the sole connecting link between England and China until 1833 despite the governmental attempts to establish relations in 1793 and 1816.
3. The tea trade served as the great binding link between the two peoples.
4. A very extensive anti-foreign attitude did not exist in China before the first quarter of the 18th century. It was generated by hatred of the missionaries, and was then increased by quarrels with, and arrogant treatment of, the steadily increasing number of foreign traders who came to China.
5. Between 1723 and 1757 the most prominent feature in the relations between the English and the Chinese was the growth of restrictions. Between 1757 and 1795 the most important factor was the growth in the volume, and the increasingly arrogant way in which the Chinese applied the restrictions.
6. The fundamental cause of the trouble between the English and the Chinese was a cultural one. Conflict was inevitable if the two civilizations were once brought together in an extensive way. It was the function of trade to bring them together, and as contacts, driven on by the basic factors of economic relationship, increased, the conflict of culture grew.[10]

Thus, many years in advance of any actual military conflict, conditions had been created which made war inevitable. On the part of the Chinese mandarins there was often the deeply imbedded, and not wholly unjustified, fear that the Western barbarian culture would breach the walls of Chinese exclusiveness. This attitude resulted in a China that "was haughty and aloof." It is important then to survey in some detail those "arrogant regulations" at Canton which the British traders and the British government regarded as "scarcely compatible" with "civilized society."

---

[10] Earl H. Pritchard, *Anglo-Chinese Relations during the Seventeenth and Eighteenth Centuries* (Urbana, 1929), 189-190.

THE "IRREGULARITIES" OF THE CHINESE TARIFF

The foreign merchants, whether English, American, Dutch, or French, engaged in the Canton trade were concerned primarily, as merchants have always been, with profits. Profits in turn depended in some considerable degree on the extent to which and the manner in which the Chinese taxed the trade; and as will be seen presently, both the extent to which and the manner in which the Chinese taxed the trade were regarded by the foreigners as unreasonable.

In China the practice of taxing the foreign and the domestic trade appears to antedate the Christian Era. At the close of the seventeenth century, the K'ang-hsi emperor, one of the most famous of the Manchus, instituted what might be termed a regular tariff. So it came about that when the Ch'ien-lung emperor (1736-1796) was reigning in the middle eighteenth century, at a time when the English East India Company was fast assuming leadership in the Canton trade, China had developed and was applying a tariff policy, remarkable in that it was designed to encourage the import and discourage the export trade. Such a policy was not likely to win British or other foreign approval.

One notable feature of the Chinese tariffs appealed to the foreigners—the system was authorized by Peking. A system in which fiscal policy originated in the central government was quite understandable to western Europeans. But these same tariffs, though fixed by Peking, were interpreted and applied by local or provincial authorities, who functioned only nominally under the Peking government. Here was a matter of the utmost importance. For the most part it would appear that the rates sanctioned by Peking were reasonable. But when these rates were interpreted and applied by the local customs authorities, the tariff became far from reasonable—at least, such was the constant complaint of the foreign traders at Canton.

This complaint was not without some foundation. Certainly the chief Chinese customs officials and their staffs had every reason to seek rapid and ready fortunes. Each chief together with his staff enjoyed only a short term in office. He had paid heavily for the office; he continued to pay for the favor of the higher authorities; he was required to see that fixed contributions reached the Imperial government; and he would indeed be short-sighted not to make provision for his own later days of retirement. All these ends he accomplished by a constant though irregular pressure on the foreign trade. The unpredictable exactions meant fortunes to the customs bureaucracy but they were an abomination to the foreign traders.

British traders frequently voiced their protests in Parliament. They complained that from the moment a foreign vessel reached Canton her business was delayed by underlings of the custom house on all manner of frivolous pretexts for the purpose of extorting unauthorized charges. The duty on imports was levied "in an arbitrary manner by low, unprincipled men, who openly demand bribes." The merchants thus claimed that the actual duties paid were of uncertain amount, and that local "exactions" far exceeded the rate prescribed by the Imperial tariff. In general, the merchants held that, though the Imperial rates appeared to be moderate, they were so little regarded in practice that it was scarcely possible to name any fixed charge, save on a few articles.[11] In fact, the policy of the local officials at Canton was to keep the foreigner in ignorance of the actual tariff schedule. As a result, some of the duties collected appear to have been ten times the amount authorized by Peking. Such seem to have been the "exactions" in the case of cotton imports. Yet even these unauthorized charges left an ample margin of profit to the foreign trader, and, it may be added, the traders made no real effort to discover what proportion of the charges they paid were in fact authorized by Peking. In summary, it may be said then that the foreigners disliked a tariff system which was arbitrary and unpredictable; but so long as profits were great they were not likely to do much about it.

THE CANTON MONOPOLY—THE CO-HONG

In the early nineteenth century, British traders, so it was said, found China "difficult to enter as Heaven and as difficult to get out of as Chancery."[12] This was merely a way of saying that the Canton trade was a monopoly, and that the Chinese, at least a favored few of them, were the monopolists. There was of course nothing shocking to the English East India Company in the fact of monopoly. The Company was itself a monopoly. But when Chinese traders exacted monopoly profits at the expense of Western traders, monopoly as a principle lost much of its virtue.

The monopoly system which prevailed at Canton from 1757 to 1842 bore resemblance in some respects to commercial institutions and practices of Europe in the Middle Ages, namely, to the staple and the gild merchant or hanse. In Europe the gild merchant was a society whose primary purpose was to secure and hold a monopolistic privilege of

---

[11] See Stanley F. Wright, *China's Struggle for Tariff Autonomy 1843-1938* (Shanghai, 1938), 1-5.

[12] C. Northcote Parkinson, *Trade in the Eastern Seas, 1793-1813* (Cambridge, 1937), 58, quoting Charles Reade.

carrying on trade. In China, the Co-hong, which corresponded to the
gild merchant, was an instrumentality of Imperial politics as well as of
trade.[13]

The origins and character of the Co-hong are not without interest.
At the beginning of the eighteenth century, although the foreign trade
had gravitated to Canton where it was restricted in many ways, it was
not subject to any *consistent* regulation. Private bargaining had a good
deal to do with what each ship was required to pay in the matter of fees.
But in 1702 Peking appointed a single Canton merchant, who might be
called the emperor's merchant, charged with handling the entire business of the foreign traders. This system satisfied no one save the emper-
or's merchant. Therefore he soon found it expedient to admit other
Canton firms, on payment of a fee, to a share in the foreign trade.

Against the power of these Chinese firms and of the Hoppo (the commissioner of customs at Canton), the foreign traders found no redress
from what they considered to be their legitimate grievances. They
were denied liberty to trade with whom they would. They were not
free to engage Chinese servants in the factories. They were restricted
in buying provisions for the factories and the ships. Sometimes they
were denied the privilege of re-exporting unsold goods duty free.

In 1720 the Canton merchants who shared in the foreign trade formed
themselves, presumably with the approval of local officials, into one
body, the Co-hong, in order the better to control the price that might be
demanded from the foreigners for cargoes of silk and tea. Exactions
and monopolistic controls on the trade thus continued to increase. A
practice had arisen by 1736 whereby every foreign vessel was to be
"secured"; that is, it was to be assigned to a security merchant who was
to be responsible not only for the sale of the inbound cargo and provision
of an outbound cargo, but also for every operation connected with the arrival and departure of the ship. Imperial decrees of 1755 required that
in future only Hong merchants could act as security merchants, and in
1760 the Co-hong was again established. Eleven years later, in 1771, it
was dissolved by the Kwangtung yiceroy, only to be re-created in 1782 as
"The Twelve," later "The Thirteen Security Merchants," or Co-hong,
again charged by Peking with sole control of the foreign trade. This
newly created Co-hong was more closely controlled by the government,
being directly subject to the Hoppo, and was made the instrument for
exacting a great revenue from the foreign trade, for the benefit primarily
of the Hoppo, and indirectly, through him, of the Canton officials and

[13] H. B. Morse, *The Gilds of China* (2nd ed., Shanghai, 1932), 11-38.

the Court of Peking.[14] The Co-hong was to insure that foreigners observed the rules of the government and was to act as the sole medium of communication between the government and the foreign traders. These functions were thus superimposed on its monopolistic control of the trade itself. Thus this merchant gild, the Co-hong,

. . . operated in close touch with the agents of government, receiving their full support on the one hand, and on the other serving as the channel through which was transmitted the stream of wealth in which the officials [of government] expected to share largely. . . .[15]

THE END OF THE ENGLISH EAST INDIA COMPANY'S MONOPOLY, 1833

In 1833 occurred an event of great significance. The English East India Company's monopolistic charter giving it exclusive control of English trade at Canton expired and Parliament did not renew it. So far as England was concerned, the trade was now open to any British merchant who had a mind to engage in it. This change foreshadowed grave complications in the commercial relations of Chinese and foreigners. Prior to 1833 the English traders at Canton had been under the control of a mere commercial agent, the chief factor of the Company there; but after 1833, with the abolition of the Company's monopoly, his Britannic Majesty was to be represented in the Canton trade by a "com-

---

[14] Pritchard, *Anglo-Chinese Relations*, 141-142. The Hong merchants were among the world's greatest business men and traders of this period. Most popular with the American traders at Canton was the Hong merchant, Houqua (Wu Ping-ch'ien). He is described by Thomas W. Ward of Salem as "very rich," "just in his dealings," "a man of honour and veracity," who "loves flattery and can be coaxed." Joseph Downs, "The American Trade with the Far East," in *The China Trade and Its Influences* (New York, 1941), 15.

It is also worthy of note that when an American ship, *The Columbia*, reached Canton, members of her company were struck by the Chinese method of doing business. "*The Chinese Merchant* is very particular in his business, and very nice in his calculations, and no part of his affairs appear to be unnoticed by him. In making a bargain they are very shrewd; when closed they are *faithful* as to quantity, but for quality you must be constantly on your guard or else it is certain the Goods will not turn out as expected, and the only satisfaction you will get from them is that you ought to have looked sharper, and at the same time will try to console you by this remark, that on another Voyage you will be better acquainted with the mode of doing business at Canton. Upon the whole, the Candour that is about the Chinese merchant makes some amends for the general complaint against them, that they *will* cheat you, if they can—therefore, your business is to see that *they shall not.*" John Boit, "Log of the Columbia, 1790-1792," *Massachusetts Historical Society Proceedings,* LIII, 265-266.

[15] Morse, *The Gilds of China*, 78. See also, John Barrow, *Travels in China* (Philadelphia, 1805), 414. Barrow was private secretary to the Earl of Macartney during the latter's mission to China.

missioned officer not only as a protector of his subjects and an overseer of their commercial activities, *but as a political and diplomatic representative*" of the British Crown.[16]   The Crown was not likely to bow without protest to those real or supposed indignities and to the "exactions" under which, at China's will, the *Fan-kwei* (foreign devils) had previously traded at Canton.   Between 1833 and 1839 three major problems, none of which was essentially new, matured and finally precipitated the first Anglo-Chinese war (1839-42), usually called the Opium War.

LORD NAPIER AND THE QUESTION OF DIPLOMATIC EQUALITY

On December 10, 1833, Lord Napier, a Scottish peer of distinction, received a royal commission as First Superintendent of [British] Trade at Canton.[17]   On his arrival at Macao (July, 1834), he proceeded to carry out his instructions, which, although they appeared proper enough from the Western point of view, were, if pressed, bound to result in conflict.   Napier was required to announce his arrival "by letter to the Viceroy."   He interpreted this to mean that he could not communicate through the Hong merchants.   At the same time he was instructed not to arouse Chinese prejudice or to endanger the trade; he was not to call for armed assistance save in "extreme cases"; yet he was advised by Lord Palmerston that "the establishment of direct communications with the Imperial court at Peking would be desirable."   Neither Palmerston nor Napier appear to have realized that all these diplomatic eggs could not be carried in one basket with safety.

Accordingly, at Canton, Napier announced his arrival by a letter to the Viceroy, which, of course, the latter refused to receive.   This refusal was natural enough, for Napier had violated three important rules by which the Chinese controlled the foreigners.   He had proceeded from Macao to the Canton factories, which were located on the bank of the river outside the walled city, without asking and receiving China's official permission; he had attempted direct communication with the Viceroy, instead of using the medium of the Hong merchants;

---

[16] The italics are mine.   See W. C. Costin, *Great Britain and China 1833-1860* (Oxford, 1937).

[17] He was assisted by Sir John Francis Davis and Sir George Best Robinson as Second and Third Superintendents, respectively, both of whom succeeded to the post of First Superintendent in the years following Napier's death.   The fact that these officials were Superintendents of Trade precluded any possibility of their being treated as diplomatic equals by the Chinese officials.   A merchant as such did not enjoy a station of honor in the official social scale of either Chinese or Japanese society.

finally, he had termed his communication a *letter* instead of a *petition,* the form required by China of inferior tributary or vassal states. The issue was thus clearly drawn. The Viceroy regarded Napier as a barbarian whose business was merely that of a commercial agent. Napier, on the other hand, was asserting for himself and his government a status of diplomatic equality between high representatives of The Middle Kingdom and of Great Britain.

Napier died at Macao (October, 1834), and was succeeded by Sir John Francis Davis, who, because the Chinese had stopped the trade and because of the resulting protests of the English traders, adopted a quiescent policy, awaiting further instructions. Meanwhile there was division in British opinion both in the Far East and at home.

Charles Elliot, Robinson's successor at Canton (1836), began his China career with the conviction that China could be "reformed" by a policy of caution and conciliation. Accordingly, he accepted the indignity of announcing his arrival in a *petition* transmitted by the Hong merchants. Thus Elliot was permitted to go to Canton, where he arrived on April 12, 1837. New instructions, however, forbade him to address further *petitions* or to employ the Hong as a medium of communication. Thus the conflict on the principle of diplomatic equality continued. China, however, was not as yet prepared to accept this concept of equality among states.[18]

THE LEGAL PROBLEM OF JURISDICTION

The abolition of the English East India Company's monopoly at Canton precipitated in aggravated form another problem of long standing. This was the question of legal control over foreigners engaged in the trade. The problem was by no means academic, since some of the foreign traders and the crews of the foreign ships could scarcely be classed as the cream, so to speak, of Western society. Both traders and seamen were, by and large, a rough and ready lot, and at times they might well

---

[18] Had Napier or Elliot known more of China's remote history they might have confounded the Mandarins by citing a case from the Han dynasty in which China had received the ruler of a foreign state as an equal. In 52 B.C. Shan-yu Hu-han-hsieh, a claimant to the Hun throne, seeking the aid of China, was granted permission to visit the court. In debating the procedure to be followed, most of the Chinese court officials urged that he be treated as a guest, i.e., as an equal of the emperor, since it would be better to attach the barbarians by kindness and generosity than to alienate them by harshness. This procedure was accordingly followed. It is at least interesting to speculate on what might have been the results to Anglo-Chinese relations in 1834 had Napier astonished the Canton Viceroy by quoting this Confucian precedent from the ancient and venerable records of the Former Han dynasty. See Homer H. Dubs, translator, *History of the Former Han Dynasty,* II, 189-191.

be described as an intractable crowd. Remembering then the suspicions and prejudices of the Chinese populace toward the foreigners, and the jealousy of the Mandarins, it is not surprising that truculent foreign sailors on shore after the long and irksome sea voyage should become involved in altercations sometimes resulting in serious injuries and even death. Before 1833 the East India Company had controlled its licensed traders by the threat of withdrawing their license, but after 1833 Napier exercised no such authority.

More serious in Western eyes were those cases in which the Chinese demanded the surrender to Chinese justice of a foreigner accused of homicide in which a Chinese was the victim. There was a long history of cases in which the Chinese and the foreigners had clashed on this point. In 1780, the Chinese strangled a French seaman who had killed a Portuguese, despite evidence establishing a case of self-defense. In 1784, an English subject accidentally killed a Chinese. The Chinese demanded his surrender, held the captain of his ship a hostage, and threatened stoppage of the trade. The accused was accordingly handed over and was strangled. This case led to the abortive British mission to Peking (1788), seeking exclusive British jurisdiction over British subjects in all cases. In 1807, drunken British sailors killed another Chinese. When the British refused to surrender any of the alleged culprits, the ship's security (Hong) merchant was permitted to pay a heavy bribe, whereat the Mandarins altered the charge to that of accidental killing, the culprit thus escaping on payment of a small fine. In 1820, to cite another case, a Chinese was accidentally shot by a foreigner. Simultaneously another foreigner committed suicide. The Chinese officials decided to accept the second act as balancing the former: a rather neat method of keeping the scales of justice in balance.

THE CASE OF TERRANOVA

One of the most notorious cases illustrative of the jurisdictional conflict was the Terranova affair. Terranova was an Italian seaman serving on the American ship *Emily* of Baltimore. In 1821, he was accused by the Chinese of having caused the death of a Chinese woman. Although convinced of his innocence and thoroughly aware that the Chinese would not give him a fair trial according to Western standards, the American merchant consul at Canton and the officers of the ship surrendered Terranova after the Chinese had stopped all American trade. Terranova was strangled and the credit of the American merchants was saved.

In this conflict of jurisdictional interests all the faults or misunder-

standings were by no means on one side. It would appear that the
Chinese authorities had no well fixed desire to shield their own nationals
from punishment; but they insisted that justice should take its course
according to well established Chinese ideas and methods. These the
foreigners regarded as barbarous. At least until 1844 American traders
generally adopted the view that they must abide by Chinese law. The
settled British policy after 1784 was never to surrender one of their
nationals to Chinese justice. The foreigners came more and more to
the view that whatever merits Chinese law might possess in theory, its
practice was entirely unsuitable to Westerners.

The contrary Chinese view is equally understandable. Prior to the
coming of the Westerners, China's foreign relations were confined
substantially to bordering vassal states which acknowledged their inferiority. If Chinese law had been accepted by these vassals, there
seemed to be no good reason why special legal concessions should be
made to the Western barbarians.

Again it should be noted that the foreigners, who considered themselves extremely practical, argued that no matter what China's legal
theories might be, her courts were utterly corrupt. In cases involving
foreigners, money, it was said, was more effective than evidence. A
Chinese judge was disposed to give more credence to the testimony of
a "civilized" Chinese than to that of an "uncivilized" barbarian. Furthermore, torture was applied inevitably to any victim who refused to
confess. This method of extracting a confession, by no means unknown in the Western world at the time, appeared more sinister when
applied by "yellow" men against "white."

Finally, it should be observed that the Chinese legal theory of responsibility was thoroughly obnoxious to the English and other foreigners at Canton.

The Yellow River bursts its banks; the governor of Honan begs the
emperor to deprive him of his titles, since he is responsible. A son commits
an offence; the father is held responsible. A bankrupt absconds; his family
are held responsible in body and estate. A shopman strikes a blow and goes
into hiding; his employer is held responsible for his appearance. A province
is overrun by rebels; its governor is held responsible. . . . The result is
that nothing which occurs goes unpunished; if the guilty person cannot be
found, convicted and punished, then the responsible person must accept the
consequences—father, family, employer, village, magistrate, or viceroy.[19]

---

[19] H. B. Morse, *The International Relations of the Chinese Empire* (London, 1910), I,
56.

THE OPIUM TRADE

Opium more than any other single article of commerce fashioned China's relations with the "Western barbarians" in the first half of the nineteenth century. "The engrossing taste of all ranks and degrees in China for *opium*," wrote John Francis Davis in 1836, "a drug whose importation has of late years exceeded the aggregate value of every English import combined, deserves some particular notice, especially in connection with the revenues of British India, of which it forms an important item." [20] The opium trade with China, like many attractive but forbidden practices, was illegal, immoral, but financially fattening. How had this traffic come to dominate British and to a lesser degree the imports of other powers at Canton? Many factors contributed to this unhappy condition. China presented a vast market of those willing to consume the drug. The Peking government though frequently sincere in its opposition to the traffic was impotent against smugglers and its own corrupt officials. In Bengal, the East India Company and later the Crown itself were deeply involved in the opium monopoly and the revenue which sprang from it. Finally, among all nationalities there were traders eager to make an "honest" dollar in an illegal traffic. [21]

The precise time at which opium was first used by the Chinese is not generally known. The opium-producing poppy occurs in Chinese literature of the T'ang period (618-906), at which time opium seems to have been used for medicinal purposes. In India opium was eaten, but it remained for the Chinese to popularize its use for smoking. This practice was derived evidently from the smoking of tobacco introduced to China by Spaniards from the Philippines early in the seventeenth century. The Dutch, who controlled Formosa for a time after 1624, mixed opium with tobacco as a preventive, so it was thought, against malaria. From Formosa the habit spread to Fukien, where the Chinese refined the practice by eliminating the tobacco. In 1729, the vermilion pencil of the Yung-cheng emperor first prohibited the importation and sale of opium for smoking but imposed no penalties on the buyer or smoker. Despite this prohibition the importation of foreign opium increased rapidly, the trade being conducted in large part by the Portuguese at Macao. The demoralizing effects of the drug were so apparent by 1799 that the emperor renewed the edict against importation

---

[20] John Francis Davis, *The Chinese* (London, 1836), II, 453. The author was chief superintendent of British trade at Canton.
[21] D. E. Owen, *British Opium Policy in China and India* (New Haven, 1934), 17.

and banned cultivation of the poppy in China. The foreign smuggling trade was thus directly affected, and through it, as will be seen, the entire legitimate trade.

The circumstances and manner in which the traffic was conducted varied. As indicated, it was at first centered at Macao and then at Whampoa. About 1822 the rapacity of the Portuguese and pressure from the Chinese drove it to other channels. Thenceforth it was conducted largely at Lintin Island in the broad estuary of the Canton River. Lintin was in fact the center of a great smuggling trade in legitimate articles of commerce as well as in opium. Here the opium was stored in armed receiving ships for delivery to Chinese smugglers on orders from Canton.

All the foreign nationalities represented at Canton engaged in the opium traffic. The best opium came from Bengal and Behar in British India, where its manufacture was a monopoly of the English East India Company. The traffic was prohibited at an early date to the "Company ships" and thus, so far as the British flag was concerned, was handled by private or "country ships" licensed by the Company. American, French, and other ships carried Persian and Turkish rather than Indian opium.[22] Imports to China of the Indian drug rose from 4,580 chests valued at $4,159,250 in the year 1818-19, to 9,535 chests valued at $10,-425,076 in 1827-28. In 1832, the total opium imports were estimated at 23,670 chests valued at more than $15,000,000.[23]

The fact that the opium trade continued to prosper long after it had been prohibited by Peking was due to a number of considerations. In the first place, there was no great demand in China for the products of the West. The foreign traders paid for their cargoes of silk and tea in specie or Spanish silver. The trade was thus heavily balanced in China's favor. Gradually a market was found in China for ginseng, furs, sandalwood, and cotton goods, but these failed to balance the trade until opium entered the market in large quantities.[24] So effectively did opium alter the balance that by 1830 it was unfavorable to China. Likewise, if opium was a balance to the trade as a whole, it was also

---

[22] The China trade in opium was not a monopoly of European powers. "In the period prior to 1820 Americans had developed a profitable monopoly in traffic in Turkish opium; had carried to China quantities of Persian and Turkish drug sufficient to threaten the East India Company's interest in the trade; and had made a far from insignificant use of opium in their commerce to China." Charles C. Stelle, "American Trade in Opium to China, Prior to 1820," *Pacific Historical Review*, IX (1940), 425-444.

[23] Davis, *The Chinese*, II, 454; Morse, *Chronicles*, IV, 383.

[24] Raw cotton from India, however, did balance the British trade perhaps as early as 1791. See Pritchard, *The Crucial Years*, 144.

profitable to special interests. It served the revenues of British India. It filled the pockets of unscrupulous traders, both foreign and Chinese, and of Chinese officials who for a consideration closed their eyes to an illicit traffic. Occasionally some overzealous official might try to enforce the law; but not until 1836 was there "any real attempt to stop, or even to check, the trade."

The emperor might prohibit the trade, and might renew the prohibition by repeated edicts; the [Canton] viceroy might issue his proclamation in strict accordance with the Imperial orders, and both viceroy and Hoppo might enjoin on the Hong merchants to obey the law; but viceroy, Hoppo, governor, admiral, magistrate, and down to the smallest person with the slightest connexion with a government office, all connived at the continuous breach of the law provided only that they found therein their personal profit.[25]

Had China enforced the ban against opium in 1800, the problem of suppression might have been comparatively simple. But when, as we shall see, nearly forty years later the law was applied, the traffic had grown to such proportions, and was so involved with the legitimate trade and with political questions that any arbitrary attempt by China at prohibition could not but lead to most serious consequences.

SOCIAL RESTRAINTS ON THE FOREIGNER AT CANTON

It must now be apparent that the commercial intercourse of Chinese and foreigners at Canton was saturated with political, economic, and legal difficulties of the greatest delicacy. To these were added lesser irritants, of little consequence in themselves, yet, when added to larger grievances, of vital importance in shaping foreign attitudes.

If the foreigner was aggrieved when China dictated the terms on which he might conduct his trade, he was exasperated when his personal life was treated in like manner. At Canton, the foreign factories were situated on the river bank just outside the walled city. To this city the foreigner was denied access. His movements at Canton were confined to the narrow limits of the factory grounds.[26] He was denied

---

[25] Morse, *The International Relations of the Chinese Empire,* I, 56.

[26] "The factories comprise a pile of buildings, about a quarter of a mile square, through which they [the foreigners] may range, without molestation. In front of these is an open space, not more than a hundred yards long, and fifty wide, where they may take the air; but this esplanade is generally so choked up with barbers and fortune-tellers, venders of dogs and cats, quack medicines, and trinkets, with a host of strangers, come to gaze at the foreigners, that it is difficult to move." W. H. Medhurst, *China* (London, 1842), 285-286.

the use of sedan chairs—the most honorable conveyance for travel.   He could not row on the river and only on rare occasions was he permitted to visit the flower gardens on the opposite bank.   The markets of the walled city, with their variety of wares, were as far removed from his view as though they had been on the opposite side of the globe.   He could hire Chinese servants only by connivance, not by right.   Neither wives nor other foreign women could accompany the traders to Canton.   These were required to remain at Macao, to which all the traders were also forced to return at the close of the trading season.[27]   Official China, which made these rules, looked upon the foreigner as a lower order of being and treated him accordingly.   Since there were virtually no contacts between the foreign traders and the officials there was little hope of such barriers being lowered.   And yet, in contrast with these imposed social restraints, there were frequently the most friendly and intimate relations among the traders, their Chinese agents, and the Hong merchants.   At times the foreigner did become restive, yet he was also timid.   Despite all its impositions the Canton trade was profitable. On the whole, the foreign trader was inclined to bear exasperating regulations rather than risk stoppage of the trade.   If he desired or sought the diplomatic support of his government, he was also fearful of what the consequences of government interference might be.

THE CALM BEFORE THE STORM

The Canton trade was, in brief, much more than a mere rivalry of merchants.   It was a clash between essentially different commercial, legal, and political systems.   To the foreigner, as Arthur Smith observed, it was "one long illustration of the Chinese talent for misunderstanding."   Yet to the complaints of the foreigner the Chinese had a ready and plausible answer.

Why do you come here?   We take in exchange your articles of produce and manufacture, which we really have no occasion for, and give you in return our precious tea, which nature has denied to your country; and yet you are not satisfied.   Why do you so often visit a country whose customs you dislike?   We do not invite you to come among us; but when you do come and behave well, we treat you accordingly.   Respect then our hospitality, but don't pretend to regulate or reform it.[28]

---

[27] See Charles T. Downing, *The Fan-Qui or Foreigner in China* (2nd ed., London, 1840), III, 199-200.

[28] John Barrow, *Travels in China*, 413.

CHAPTER 6

THE FIRST COMMERCIAL TREATIES

B Y 1834, when the East India Company lost its monopoly in the China trade, the stage appeared to be set at Canton for armed conflict between Great Britain and China. Would war prove to be the only answer? When and on what pretext would it occur? Neither Peking nor London understood fully the basic conflict, submerged as it was under surface irritations; and, since in 1834 neither government was prepared to adopt a positive policy on any of the issues involved, war was delayed. However, in 1835, when Palmerston returned to the British Foreign Office and Captain Charles Elliot was sent to Canton as Chief Superintendent, Britain determined to seek *direct communication* with Chinese officials upon terms of *diplomatic equality*. The appearance off the China coast in July, 1838, of a small British squadron was designed to put teeth in the new policy, but the Chinese gave no indication of receding from their position of superiority.

Coincident with these developments, China displayed a new interest in the problem of the illicit opium traffic. At Peking two groups sought the favor of the Tao-kuang emperor (1821-1850). The one favored legalization of the opium trade as a means of controlling it. The other, opposed to all compromise, would have nothing but complete enforcement of the existing ban. In January, 1839, word reached Canton that the emperor had sanctioned full enforcement of the law and that an Imperial commissioner, Lin Tse-hsü, would soon reach the city to "scrub and wash away the filth" of opium. It appeared that the emperor, who since his accession in 1820 had enjoyed some success in reforming a licentious court and a corrupt government, now proposed to rid his country of the incubus of opium.

COMMISSIONER LIN AT CANTON

Commissioner Lin reached Canton in March, 1839. Within eight days he had ordered the foreign merchants to surrender all opium in their possession, and to give bond on penalty of death that they would import no more. To insure the enforcement of these demands, Chinese troops and war junks surrounded the foreigners in their factories on the river bank while all foreign trade was temporarily stopped.

This situation was without precedent. The foreign merchants were confronted by a remarkable phenomenon—a Chinese official bent on enforcement of the law regardless of consequences. Accordingly Captain Elliot, acting on behalf of the foreign community, surrendered more than 20,000 chests of British-controlled opium. To the astonishment of all, this comfortable fortune, later valued at $6,000,000, was mixed with salt, lime, and water and sluiced into the river.

There still remained the question of the bond which Lin had demanded. Some foreign merchants of various nationalities gave a voluntary pledge to abstain from the traffic. Lin, however, ignored this, insisting on a bond which Elliot described as a "monstrous instrument" committing the merchants on penalty of death to the impossible: control of the future commercial policies of their respective governments. Accordingly, the British merchants, under Elliot's orders, retired to Macao, leaving the Canton factories in the hands of some twenty-five Americans (May 24, 1839). In July a Chinese was killed at Kowloon, a result of rioting between Chinese and British and American sailors. Fines and imprisonment were imposed on the sailors by Captain Elliot, but Lin demanded surrender of the accused on a charge of murder. When this was refused, food supplies were cut off from Macao, and the British, now ordered to leave, took refuge in August on the barren and mountainous island of Hongkong opposite the Kowloon Peninsula. In November, the Chinese, attempting to seize the accused seamen, sent a fleet of war junks against the British naval force at Hongkong. When this effort failed, Peking banned all British trade. The answer to this act was war.[1]

WAS THIS AN "OPIUM WAR"?

A good deal of historical controversy has been centered on the causes of and the responsibility for the war which followed. On either side of middle-of-the-road interpretations have been two extreme views. The first of these traditionally accepted interpretations was that England fought a war to force opium on the Chinese, a view which for under-

---

[1] This account of initial hostilities is at variance with the record left by Commissioner Lin. According to the Chinese version, the Lin Wei-hi homicide case was not the cause of the naval engagement of Chuenpi (Nov. 3, 1839). Lin's version relates that a British merchant ship, having signed the bond, was on its way to Whampoa to trade, when Elliot appeared on the scene to stop it. Thus the immediate clash arose out of Chinese protection of legitimate trade and an English effort to obstruct it. See T. F. Tsiang, "New Light on Chinese Diplomacy 1836-49," *Journal of Modern History*, III (1931), 584.

standable reasons was popular in the United States, especially with those Americans who wished to bolster their anti-British bias with the notion that China was the innocent victim of British perfidy. The second traditionally accepted interpretation, stemming in the main from nineteenth-century British official opinion, was that war was the only means through which Chinese pretensions of exclusiveness and superiority could be broken down and replaced by principles of diplomatic equality, and that therefore opium was purely incidental. Neither of these extreme views can now be accepted in the light of evidence made available by historical scholarship. The war of 1839-1842 was the result of a number of forces, not of controversy over one particular question. The basic fact which is now clear is that fundamental differences in both the theory and the practice of government as between England and China made conflict inevitable since neither side was sufficiently conditioned toward compromise and concession. On the single point of official contacts, the positions taken by the two governments were irreconcilable. The issue would be decided eventually by war.

However, the outbreak of this conflict at the particular time when it occurred cannot be detached from the problems created by the opium traffic. Opium was the *immediate* cause of the war. It happened that two forces converged in the years between 1833 and 1839. There was the British demand for a changed system of intercourse brought to a head by the abolition of the East India Company's monopoly, and at the same time there was an unprecedented expansion of the opium trade. This growth in an illegal traffic, connived at by both Chinese and foreigners, had produced serious economic consequences within China. In particular it meant that China's commodity exports were insufficient; silver was being exported to pay for opium to the detriment of the country's currency and finance. Herein lay the basic cause for China's effort to prohibit rigidly the opium traffic.[2]

THE COURSE OF HOSTILITIES

Great Britain's demands upon China now included: 1) payment for the seized British opium, 2) treatment of British officials "in a manner consistent with the usages of civilized Nations, and the respect due to the Dignity of the British Crown," 3) cession of an island off the China coast to insure the future security of British trade and to protect British merchants against "the arbitrary caprice either of the Government at

---

[2] The best summary of the causes of the war will be found in P. C. Kuo, *A Critical Study of the First Anglo-Chinese War* (Shanghai, 1935), 194-199. See also D. E. Owen, *British Opium Policy in China and India* (New Haven, 1934), 167-175.

Peking, or its local authorities at the Sea-Ports"—a demand which
might be waived if an otherwise satisfactory treaty were forthcoming.
These British demands were delivered to Chinese officials at the Pei-ho
in August, 1840, but without result. A British squadron then blockaded Canton and demanded payment for the opium; when this was not
forthcoming the city was bombarded (January, 1841). The local Chinese officials now promptly offered concessions. A draft treaty was
concluded but later disavowed by both governments. Hostilities were
renewed as spring approached. Canton lay at the mercy of the British
fleet and was "ransomed" for $6,000,000. These disastrous events
brought dire punishment on the head of the unfortunate Commissioner
Lin. Although he alone among Chinese officialdom had enforced the
emperor's law, his reward was removal from office and banishment to
Ili.

Meanwhile Sir Henry Pottinger had arrived off the coast as Britain's
chief representative. A British fleet moved northward, meeting no
effective resistance. Early in August, 1842, Nanking, the southern capital, was at the mercy of British guns. The war was ended. The military defeat of China was decisive. A small British force, never more
than 7,000 effectives, had broken what remained of Manchu military
prestige. It was the beginning of a century of military defeats for
China. Helpless and humbled, she sought peace on the deck of a
British battleship, the *Cornwallis,* as it lay in the river off Nanking.[3]
Legally the days of China's exclusiveness and superiority were at an
end. During the ensuing century the "barbarians" would dictate the
terms on which China might trade and enjoy peace.

THE TREATY OF NANKING AND TREATY
OF THE BOGUE

The formal settlement of the first Anglo-Chinese war was embodied
in two treaties: the Treaty of Nanking, August 29, 1842, and the supplementary Treaty of Hoomun Chai, signed at the Bogue, October 8,
1843.[4] The two treaties contain the basic principles which were to

[3] During preparation of the treaty, the Chinese diplomats, Ch'i-ying and I-li-pu, visited
Pottinger on the *Cornwallis* "to pave the way to free and unrestrained intercourse," an
ideal which the high officers of both nations sought to promote by delivering "many fine
speeches" and by the consumption of "much cherry brandy." Lieut. John Ouchterlony,
The Chinese War (London, 1844), 443-444. This work is a contemporary British view
of the military and naval operations. The Chinese names are sometimes transliterated
variously: Ch'i-ying (Kiying, or Keying), I-li-pu (Elepoo). Of the Chinese negotiators,
Ch'i-ying alone was at this time an Imperial commissioner.

[4] For texts of all important nineteenth-century treaties with China, see China, the
Maritime Customs, *Treaties, Conventions, etc., between China and Foreign States* (2 vols.,
2nd ed., Shanghai, 1917).

govern China's international status for a century. Later treaties between China and foreign states modified or amplified details, but the
basic structure of principles contained in the first treaties remained
with little change.

Five ports, Canton, Amoy, Foochow, Ningpo, and Shanghai, were
opened to the residence and trade of British merchants. At these ports,
Britain was to appoint consular officers.

The island of Hongkong was ceded to Great Britain "in perpetuity."

The Co-Hong was abolished, and British merchants were "to carry
on their mercantile transactions with whatever persons they please."

China was to pay a total indemnity of $21,000,000: $6,000,000 for the
surrendered opium; $3,000,000 to cover debts owed by Hong merchants
to British subjects; $12,000,000 for expenses occasioned by the war.

Correspondence between the chief British representative and high
Chinese officials was to be under the term "a communication," not "a
petition."

China agreed to a uniform and moderate tariff on exports and imports, which came to be known as the five percent ad valorem treaty
tariff. The duties fixed at this time were not to be increased save by
mutual agreement. Thus for the ensuing 88 years, that is until 1930,
China was unable to fix her tariffs of her own free will. In 1842, however, it should be noted that China did not realize the importance of
this act; nor was there anything in the nature of a plot on the part of
British negotiators to violate China's sovereign rights beyond meeting
and correcting the circumstances in which the trade had been conducted. The British purpose was not to control China's fiscal policies
but to provide a *modus operandi* for the foreign trade. Since this trade
was still relatively small, and since isolation was still China's prevailing
philosophy, the principle of tariff autonomy had at the time little of the
significance which in later years it acquired.[5] Another motive behind
the tariff clause of the treaty was the aggressive free trade philosophy
that existed in Britain. In general the free traders felt that they had
a divine mission to impose their creed on the world.

The first treaty settlement likewise included provision for extraterritorial jurisdiction in criminal cases (Treaty of the Bogue, Art. IX)
—a second major infringement on China's exercise of sovereignty. It
will be recalled that for many years the foreign traders and their governments had condemned Chinese notions both of the theory and the
practice of justice. At Macao the Portuguese had sought to retain exclusive jurisdiction over their nationals, and in 1833 the British, by

[5] S. F. Wright, *China's Struggle for Tariff Autonomy* (Shanghai, 1938), 45-48.

order-in-council, provided their own court at Canton with criminal and admiralty jurisdiction. In this matter, as in the tariff, it was only in later years that China awoke to the full implications of harboring in her seaports a foreign population over which her courts had no power.

Although China regarded opium as the primary cause of the war, the first treaty settlement, aside from stipulating the payment of $6,000,000 for the opium seized, mentioned the traffic not at all. In the British view, China was free to legalize and control imports or to prohibit them, but enforcement of the latter course would be China's responsibility. The Chinese would not agree to legalization, and thus, on this important question the treaty was silent.

Finally, Britain secured the principle of most-favored-nation treatment. Art. VIII (Treaty of the Bogue) stated "that should the Emperor hereafter, from any cause whatever, be pleased to grant additional privileges or immunities to any of the subjects or Citizens of such Foreign Countries, the same privileges and immunities will be extended to and enjoyed by British Subjects."

OTHER POWERS SECURE TREATIES

The new status enjoyed by Great Britain and her traders in China prompted other powers to seek treaty relations. Between 1844 and 1847 three treaties were concluded by China: with the United States (July 3, 1844); with France (October 24, 1844); and with Norway and Sweden (March 20, 1847). Of these, by far the most important was the American. Its significance may best be seen by reviewing briefly the growth of American interests in China in the decades following the Revolutionary War.

EARLY AMERICAN INTERESTS IN CHINA

The conceptions which one people hold of another change with time and circumstance, and to this statement American views on China are no exception. Even before the days of independence some American intellectuals had expressed themselves on China. Benjamin Franklin (1771) hoped America would increase in likeness to her. Thomas Jefferson (1785) held that China's policy of non-intercourse was ideally adapted to American use. John Quincy Adams (1822) praised the Chinese for recognizing the virtues of the decimal system. But to most Americans, certainly prior to 1830, China was merely a vast and remote empire—as much a curiosity as though it belonged to another planet.

John Ledyard, an American who accompanied Captain Cook to the Pacific (1776-1781), was among the first to tell his countrymen how furs

from the northwest coast of America sold in Canton at enormous profit.
The result was a voyage by the *Empress of China,* the first American
ship to sail direct for Canton (1784).[6] The trade, thus begun, soon
prospered. The Americans, like the European traders, sought Chinese
silk and tea, and they encountered the same difficulties as the Europeans
in finding an outbound cargo. Furs, ginseng, sandalwood, opium, and
silver constituted main items in the China-bound cargoes, and various
routes were followed by the ships in the early American trade.

Between 1784 and 1811 Americans were the most serious rivals of the
British in the tea trade at Canton. Their ships were neither so large
nor so numerous as those of the English East India Company, yet in
the season 1805-06 they carried from Canton 11 million pounds of tea
in 37 ships, as against British exports of 22 million pounds in 49 ships.[7]

The position of the Americans at Canton contrasted in some respects
with that of the British. The Americans traded with greater individual
freedom, but they possessed neither the financial backing nor the prestige of the English company, nor did they enjoy any naval protection
from their home government. The first official representative of the
United States in China was Major Samuel Shaw, who, after a number
of voyages to the Far East, was named consul, without salary, at Canton
by the Continental Congress acting on the recommendation of John
Jay. It would seem that the early American trader felt little need for
official support so long as he was permitted to trade on equal terms with
his British rivals. But as the tension grew between the British and the
Chinese after 1834, the indifference of American merchants to official
backing disappeared. In May, 1839, after Lin had forced the surrender

---

[6] The *Empress of China,* 360 tons, carried as cargo "furs, foodstuffs, and genseng—a
wild root worth its weight in gold in the Orient as the 'dose of immortality.'" Robert
Morris financed the voyage. Joseph Downs, "The American Trade with the Far East,"
in *The China Trade and Its Influences* (New York, 1941), 13.

[7] The American ships were frequently exceedingly small—35 to 50 tons—compared
with European East Indiamen of 1,500 tons. They made up in speed what they lacked
in size. From 1846 to 1849 the *Sea Witch* of Howland and Aspinwall, was the world's
fastest ship. Her second voyage from Canton to New York was made in 74 days (1849).
See Joseph Downs, "The American Trade with the Far East," in *The China Trade and
Its Influences* (New York, 1941), 14. The initiative that was to be characteristic of the
early American traders in the Far East was expressed by Obadiah Brown, shipmaster of
Providence, in 1736: "If I should never Venter nothing, I should never have nothing."
Ibid., 16.

For a "List of Ships Arriving at the Port of Canton and Other Pacific Ports, 1799-1803,"
see the compilation by Howard Corning in The Essex Institute, *Historical Collections,* Vol.
LXXVIII, Oct., 1942. Extracts from the memorandum book of Sullivan Dorr, an Amer-
ican merchant at Canton in these years, are given in *ibid.,* April, 1942. See also K. S.
Latourette, *History of Early Relations Between the United States and China (1784-1844)*
(New Haven, 1917).

of foreign-owned opium, a group of Americans at Canton memorialized Congress to send a commercial agent to negotiate a treaty, and a naval force to protect persons and property.[8]   Although expressing no sympathy with the opium traffic, they found no excuse for the "robbery" committed on the British.   They foresaw that England would use armed force, and they believed "that this is necessary."   They recommended that the United States take *joint* action with England, France, and Holland to secure: 1) resident ministers at Peking; 2) a fixed tariff on exports and imports; 3) the liberty of trading at ports other than Canton; and 4) Chinese assent to the principle that, until their laws are made known and recognized, punishment for offenses committed by foreigners against Chinese or others shall not be greater than is applicable to a like offense by the laws of the United States or England.   The American traders believed that the appearance in Chinese waters of a fleet including American, British, and French ships would effect the necessary revision in the system of trade "without bloodshed."   Britain they believed would use armed force, and they regarded this as necessary or "there will be no dealing with the Chinese."

When the opium crisis broke at Canton, the Americans turned over their opium to Captain Elliot for surrender to the Chinese; but when the English withdrew to Macao, and later to Hongkong, the Americans remained at Canton (much to the disgust of Elliot), conducting the while a lucrative business in carrying to Canton cargoes of British goods when British ships were no longer permitted to enter the river.   These events during 1839-40 focussed for the first time American public attention, both official and non-official, on the Canton trade.

In the broad sense, Americans appeared ill-prepared to formulate a political policy toward China.   A fair proportion of Americans who thought about China at all harbored all manner of distorted, if not fantastic, notions concerning her.   The most prevalent opinion was that the Anglo-Chinese war was "another item in the sad catalogue of [British] outrages on humanity." [9]   When in 1841 John Quincy Adams suggested in an address that the principle of equality among states was the real cause of the war in China, the idea was so shocking to the editor of the *North American Review* that he refused to print Adams' manuscript.   After the first American Protestant missionaries, Elijah C. Bridgman and David Abeel, were sent to Canton in 1829, the missionary

---

[8] For a selected group of representative documents on American policy see Paul H. Clyde, *United States Policy Toward China: Diplomatic and Public Documents, 1839-1939* (Durham, N. C., 1940).

[9] *Niles Register*, LXI (October 30, 1841), 130.

press dwelt heavily on the vices of the "heathen Chinese." The Chinese were frequently pictured as masters of deceit, of cruelty, of gambling and rioting, of indolence and superstition. Worst of all was their preference for rice rather than for salvation. To many religious Americans there was a shocking satisfaction in the thought that China's "depravity" offered an unlimited field for American missions.[10] Nor were these opinions merely the fulminations of fanatics. After seventeen years in China, S. Wells Williams, one of the ablest of missionaries, succumbed at times to the prevalent conclusion:

It is much easier [he wrote] loving the souls of the heathen in the abstract than in the concrete encompassed as they are in such dirty bodies, speaking forth their foul language and vile natures exhibiting every evidence of depravity.[11]

Many an American was at a loss to know what to believe about China. He could read that the Chinese had "some very esteemable qualities" but were "false, dishonest and distrustful"; that they were "base" yet "more civil than" Americans; that their government was a system of unwarranted oppression in a society remarkable for its thrift and industry.

THE FIRST ENUNCIATION OF AMERICAN POLICY

Out of the background of these confused and inadequate ideas on China there was to emerge an official policy which, surprising as it may seem, expressed so exactly the real interests of Americans that it survived for a century. President Tyler, on December 30, 1842, four months after the Treaty of Nanking had been signed, asked Congress to authorize appointment of a resident commissioner in China to protect the commercial and diplomatic affairs of the United States. This post was conferred upon Caleb Cushing of Massachusetts, brilliant lawyer, member of the Committee on Foreign Affairs, and intimate friend of the President. To Daniel Webster, Secretary of State, fell the task of preparing Cushing's instructions. The American envoy was to secure entry of American ships and cargoes into the open ports on terms as favorable as those enjoyed by the English. He was to employ the utmost tact; to impress the Chinese with the peaceful character of his mission; to visit Peking if possible; but in no case was he to perform

---

[10] *Missionary Herald* (Boston), XXXVIII (August, 1842), 336.
[11] F. W. Williams, *The Life and Letters of Samuel Wells Williams* (New York, 1899), 174.

the *kotow*. The instructions were concluded with these significant words—the essence of American policy:

Finally, you will signify, in decided terms and a positive manner, that the Government of the United States would find it impossible to remain on terms of friendship and regard with the Emperor, if greater privileges or commercial facilities should be allowed to the subjects of any other Government than should be granted to the citizens of the United States.

THE MISSION OF CALEB CUSHING

Cushing reached Macao on February 24, 1844, welcomed neither by the Chinese, nor by the British, nor by the American communities. The treaties of Nanking and the Bogue were already in operation; Commodore Lawrence Kearny of the United States Navy had (on October 8, 1842) already requested of China and had been granted most-favored-nation treatment for Americans.[12] Thus the question arose as to what Cushing could do which had not already been done.[13]

In the face of Chinese procrastination, Cushing intimated that he would proceed to Peking. This threat brought an Imperial commissioner to Macao, and soon thereafter the first American treaty was signed (Treaty of Wang-hea [Wang Hiya], July 3, 1844).[14] Although this treaty followed in general the principles contained in the British treaties, it was superior in point of clarity and in extending the principle of extraterritoriality to include civil as well as criminal cases (see Arts.

[12] For discussions of the extension of most-favored-nation treatment in the first China treaties see T. F. Tsiang, "The Extension of Equal Privileges to Other Nations than the British after the Treaty of Nanking," *Chinese Soc. and Pol. Science Rev.*, XV (1931-32), 422-444. Varying conclusions are reached by Thomas Kearny, "The Tsiang Documents," *ibid.*, XVI (1932-33), 73-104.

[13] The Manchu emperor's formal approval of the equal extension of trading privileges had been given November 15, 1843, before the arrival of Cushing in China. Kenneth Ch'en, "The Cushing Mission: Was It Necessary?" *Chinese Soc. and Pol. Science Rev.*, XXIII (1940), 3-14.

[14] For a scholarly editing of this treaty see Hunter Miller, ed., *Treaties and Other International Acts of the United States of America* (Washington, Department of State), IV. The prompt conclusion of the American treaty, once negotiations were begun, was due to Chinese "abhorrence of Cushing's intention to go to Peking." Ping Chia Kuo, "Caleb Cushing and the Treaty of Wanghia, 1844," *Journal of Modern History*, V (1933), 51.

Ten years after the American treaty had been signed, there was still told in Macao a story "to the effect that, when Cushing went out in state to meet Keying, he was attended by the Portuguese band belonging to the governor, and that the drum-major of the band made such an impression upon the Chinese authorities by his portly size, and the glitter of his full-dress uniform, that they imagined him to be the American mandarin, and wasted several profound salutations upon him before the mistake was discovered." Bayard Taylor, *India, China, and Japan* (New York, 1855), 480.

XXI, XXIV, XXV).[15] Thus the American treaty rather than the
British became the basic document in China's foreign relations until the
treaties of Tientsin were signed in 1858. Whereas the commercial
policy set forth by Webster was in the main approved by American
opinion, criticism of the Cushing mission was not lacking, although
for the most part it was political in character—directed at the gold braid
and plumes worn by the "pompous" Cushing rather than at the purposes of the mission. Journals such as *Hunt's Merchants' Magazine,*
which a few months previously had bitterly denounced England's
motives in China, reversed themselves, found excuses for England's
behavior, and supported her policy of treaty relations. And in Congress
there was spirited support for Cushing since no one knew "just how
much of our tobacco might be chewed [in China] in place of opium." [16]

The Franco-Chinese treaty (October, 1844) followed the model of
the British and American treaties. The French diplomats, however,
appeared also in the role of "protectors" of Catholic missions. Their
request that permission be granted to build Roman Catholic missions
in the five treaty ports, and for toleration to Chinese and foreign
Christians, was granted by the emperor, though not as a part of the
treaty. These concessions were extended later to Protestants.

THE RECEPTION OF THE FIRST TREATIES

The first treaty settlement viewed in retrospect reveals graphically its
deep significance, but it must not be assumed that all this was clear to
the contemporaries of Lin, Ch'i-ying, Pottinger, and Cushing. The fact
that a handful of British troops and a small fleet had forced the Manchu
court to terms did not signify necessarily that all was now well. The
treaties themselves were an experiment. Would they in practice satisfy
either the foreign traders and their governments or the reluctant Manchu court? Behind this question was a broad and vital problem. Did
China's signature of the first treaties mean that she had broken positively and willingly with the past? Would her doors now be opened
widely to Western influence, or, by evasion of the treaties, would she
await the day when these doors might be closed again to a presumptu-
ous, barbarian world? Between 1842 and 1856 many of these questions
were answered, but as always, new questions arose as old ones were
solved.

[15] For discussions of the development of extraterritoriality in China see: W. W. Willoughby, *Foreign Rights and Interests in China* (2 vols., rev. ed., Baltimore, 1927); C. S.
Lobingier, compiler and ed., *Extraterritorial Cases* (Manila, 1920).

[16] *Congressional Globe,* 27th Cong., 3rd sess., 325.

CHINA'S REACTION TO THE TREATIES

In 1843 some of the English congratulated themselves in the belief that China had experienced a complete conversion. This impression was encouraged by the cordiality of Ch'i-ying's relations with Pottinger.[17] Yet despite all this cordiality, Pottinger reported that China remained an empire, and that the Chinese remained a people "who have no notion, however small, of international law and rights." Since Pottinger meant *Western* law there was a measure of truth in his remark.

Indeed the Manchu failure of 1842 was due in considerable measure to ignorance of the West. Even some of China's most distinguished dignitaries thought "it was because England had only a queen" that many of her subjects dared to be so unruly in China.[18] Chinese scholars found the barbarian character "unfathomable" since it would do anything for profits. But there were reasons other than ignorance and misunderstanding for China's capitulation. The Manchu military structure had been designed to control the Chinese people—not to resist invasion from the sea. In Peking, the court, ever sensitive to public opinion, feared rebellion in the provinces—always an indication that the dynasty was loosing the Mandate of Heaven.[19]

THE LABORATORY OF THE NEW TREATIES

The laboratory in which the new treaties were to be tried consisted of the five treaty ports: Canton, Amoy, Foochow, Ningpo, and Shanghai. In all these ports save Canton, the foreigner was a stranger, and to the vast population in the interior he was all but unknown. Much was thus likely to depend on the first contacts between Chinese and foreigners at the new ports. This was doubly true because the main Chinese objection to the treaties was the opening of additional ports.

AMOY, FOOCHOW, AND NINGPO

Only two of the first treaty ports were destined to develop as great centers of the foreign trade: Shanghai and Canton. For a few years, commerce, particularly in black tea and in contract coolie labor to Cuba,

---

[17] W. C. Costin, *Great Britain and China 1833-1860* (Oxford, 1937), 111.

[18] T. F. Tsiang, "New Light on Chinese Diplomacy 1836-49," *Journal of Modern History,* III (1931), 586.

[19] J. F. Fairbank, "Chinese Diplomacy and the Treaty of Nanking, 1842," *Journal of Modern History,* XII (1940), 1-30. "The Manchu court did not understand England's motives and feared the unknown. It also feared that the British advance might precipitate rebellion in the coastal provinces. . . . Only an opportunist of Ch'i-ying's gifts could have succeeded in the two-faced role demanded by the intransigence of the court and the firmness of the invader." 29-30.

flourished at Amoy. Trade at Foochow was negligible. Until the middle of 1844 not a foreign ship had entered its harbor. As a port Foochow suffered because its harbor was poor, its population, under official encouragement, was anti-foreign, and its location was too close to Amoy. In the same way Ningpo was too close to Shanghai. Ningpo's later fame was due to missionary rather than commercial enterprise.

THE UNIQUE POSITION OF SHANGHAI

Shanghai was opened to foreign trade on November 17, 1843. Situated on the Whangpoo River about twelve miles from where it joins the Yangtze at Woosung, and having a native population of some 270,000, it was already an important center of China's inland and coasting trade. Robert Fortune, the Scottish botanist, who travelled widely in China in the decade of the forties, wrote of Shanghai's pre-eminence in the foreign trade.[20] Here traders were no longer hampered by such monopolistic agencies as the Co-hong. There were business and opportunity for all. In 1844 forty-four foreign ships of a total tonnage of more than 8,000 entered Shanghai. Eight years later the number of ships was 182, with a total tonnage of 78,000. Shanghai exports were valued in 1846 at $7,000,000; in 1853, at $23,000,000. By 1852 Shanghai accounted for more than half of China's export trade. Many factors contributed to this rapid growth. The city bordered the great silk-producing areas; its situation at the mouth of the Yangtze was ideal for both the import and the export trade; its inhabitants were free from the unhappy memories and the violent anti-foreignism so pronounced at Canton.

ORIGINS OF THE SHANGHAI INTERNATIONAL SETTLEMENT

The treaty status under which foreign merchants lived at the new ports was a peculiar, not to say unique, system. At Canton and at many of the ports opened subsequently, the treaty powers obtained from China, that is from the emperor, grants of land known as "concessions," where the traders could erect commercial structures and residences. The concession was leased by China to the foreign power concerned; the power subdivided the land into lots, granting these on long-term leases to its subjects and in some cases to other foreigners. Sometimes, as later at Tientsin, there were at one time in one open port as many as eight separate foreign concessions. The foreign community of each concession provided, under authority of its home government,

[20] See Robert Fortune, *Three Years Wanderings* (London, 1847), ch. vii.

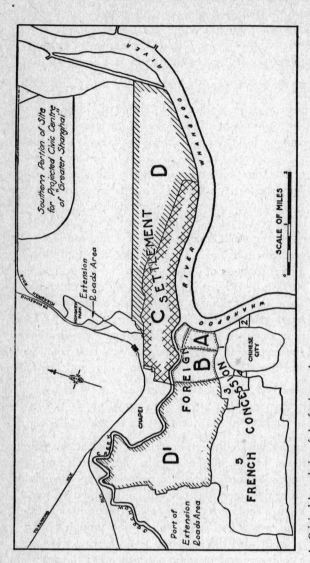

A. Original boundaries of the foreign settlement.
B. Extension of the settlement boundaries, 1848.
C. The "American Settlement," 1863; incorporated with the foreign settlement the same year.
D. Further extension of the settlement, 1899.
D¹. Extension of 1899.

1. Original French concession, 1849.
2. Extended, 1861.   4. Extended, 1900.
3. Extended, 1900.   5. Extended, 1914.

The projected civic center of Shanghai is a project of the municipal government of the Chinese City.

SHANGHAI, THE INTERNATIONAL SETTLEMENT AND THE FRENCH CONCESSION.

its own municipal government for the concession. Over this municipal government the consul of the given power presided. Thus at a given treaty port there came to exist, in contiguous concession areas, a number of separate municipal governments, each exercising independent authority.

At Shanghai the system was somewhat different. Since the local Chinese authorities there objected to the concession system, the first British consul accepted a plan whereby the Chinese authorities set apart an area of land on the river bank in which British subjects might acquire lots from Chinese owners. A British purchaser, having reached an agreement with a Chinese owner, reported it to the British consul, who in turn reported it to the Chinese local authority, the *taotai*. This latter functionary then issued to the British subject, through his consul, a title in the form of a perpetual lease, under which the foreign buyer paid a small annual rent to the Chinese government, the theory being that all land belonged to the emperor and could not be alienated by outright sale.[21]

The Shanghai "settlement," as this area and its peculiar system came to be known, was at first restricted to British control. Foreigners of non-British nationality secured land therein through the consent of the British consul. This proved particularly objectionable to Americans, and so in time the right of all foreigners to lease land within the settlement and to register such land at their own consulates was recognized. In this manner a system developed whereby each consul exercised jurisdiction over his own nationals in the common settlement area, and at the same time participated with his fellow consuls in supervision of settlement affairs.[22]

When the Shanghai settlement was first established, it was supposed that the area would be inhabited exclusively by foreigners, and for some eight years this was so. In 1853 there were only 500 Chinese residents, most of whom were servants or shopkeepers supplying the needs of the 200-odd foreign residents. In this same year, however, Chinese authority in areas adjacent to the settlement having broken down completely as a result of rebellions and civil war, the foreign area was soon

---

[21] *Report of the Hon. Mr. Justice Feetham to the Shanghai Municipal Council* (4 vols., Shanghai, 1931-32), I, 27. The *taotai,* an official of the central government, was the officer of an administrative division called a "circuit." At Shanghai he was also superintendent of customs.

[22] For a brief period, separate American and French settlements existed at Shanghai, but in 1863 the American was merged with the British, forming the basis of what was to be known as the International Settlement. The French area continued to remain separate and came to be known as the "French concession," though the term is not strictly accurate.

swarming with homeless and often destitute Chinese refugees. By 1854 the Chinese population of the settlement exceeded 20,000. In this manner the whole character of the settlement was changed, and it became imperative that this unorganized community consisting of groups of foreigners belonging to different nations, each group living under its own national laws and subject to the jurisdiction of its own consul, should provide itself with effective municipal authority for internal administration and for protection against the rebellions and civil wars on its borders. To accomplish this it was necessary for the foreign settlement community to acquire some degree of unity under a municipal constitution having the approval of the consular authorities. Such a constitution was adopted by the foreign merchants (known as the "renters" of settlement land) in 1854. Under this instrument adequate governing powers over the Shanghai Settlement were placed in the hands of an elected and exclusively foreign municipal council. Here then was a situation unforeseen and in no sense anticipated at the time the first treaty settlement was made (1842-44).

FOREIGN RELATIONS AT CANTON

While the new foreign trade at Shanghai grew rapidly under conditions that were generally amicable, its corresponding growth at Canton was marked by friction, mob violence, and open armed conflict. To understand this contrast, one should recall that at Canton the foreign traders and some Chinese had long been in contact and in many cases had made fortunes; but at Canton, too, had arisen the grievances, real and imaginary, and the hatreds finally producing war. At Canton the foreigner had been subjected to "insults" by the populace and by high-handed Chinese officials. At Canton these same officials had bowed outwardly at least before the power of British guns. Now that the war had been won, the British proposed to assert after their own fashion their newly won privileges of equality. But the Chinese populace and many of the officials were by no means prepared to concede all this. The issue was soon drawn. No sooner had the city been officially opened in its new status as a treaty port (1843) than the intensity of its anti-foreignism became apparent. The mere presence of Caleb Cushing in South China and his threat to proceed to Peking called forth a popular manifesto from Canton: "Ye men of America may truly dread local extermination." [23] Foreigners were not permitted access to the walled city, and Governor Davis of Hongkong regarded this "degrad-

---

[23] Cushing to the Sec. of State, July 24, 1844 (Sen. Ex. doc. 67, 28th Cong., 2nd sess.), 21.

ing" exclusion as a factor "provoking the insolence of the people." The treaties, to be sure, did not provide explicitly for entrance into the city, but the British claimed that denial of the privilege violated the spirit of the treaties and indicated the resolve of both officials and populace to preserve the old exclusive superiority. Because of this intensity of feeling, it was agreed in 1846 to postpone the "opening" of the city. The temper of the populace, however, did not improve. Foreigners, including Englishmen and an American, were stoned in a nearby village in 1847; a British fleet attacked the Bogue Forts and blockaded the river; the viceroy thereupon agreed to open the city in April, 1849, but this settlement was not approved by the emperor. Peking in fact was torn between the demands of the foreigners and those of its own people. Until 1848, Ch'i-ying at Canton attempted at least to keep the local people within the strict limits of the treaties, but his successors, Hsü Kwang-chin and Yeh Ming-ch'en, as will be seen, encouraged anti-foreignism and thus contributed to a second war, which was now in the making.[24]

GROWING TENSION AFTER 1848

After 1848 tension between Chinese and foreigners at Canton increased. Commissioner Hsü, Ch'i-ying's successor, was eminently anti-foreign. For some time he refused even to receive John W. Davis, the newly arrived American commissioner, and he made it clear to Sir Samuel George Bonham (Davis' successor at Hongkong) that it was impossible to open the city. This stand prompted the remark by a French observer that: "Sooner or later she [England] will have to take up the task she left unfinished at Nanking. . . ." Meanwhile the people of Canton were jubilant over Hsü's "peaceful" victory. Efforts by Bonham to establish relations with high officials in Peking either by a visit to the Pei-ho or through the Nanking viceroy also proved futile. China was adhering to a strict interpretation of the treaties. Diplomacy was to be conducted through the Canton viceroy and through him alone. Though legally correct, this doctrine was not of a character to appeal to Palmerston, who had already reached the conclusion that

the Time is fast approaching when we shall be obliged to strike another Blow in China. . . . These half-civilized Governments such as those of China, Portugal, Spanish America, all require a Dressing every eight or

---

[24] T. F. Tsiang, "New Light on Chinese Diplomacy 1836-49," *Journal of Modern History,* III (1931), 590-91. It is difficult to weigh responsibility for conditions at Canton. Governor Davis wrote: "I am not the first who has been compelled to remark that it is more difficult to deal with our own countrymen at Canton, than with the Chinese government."

Ten years to keep them in order. Their minds are too shallow to receive an Impression that will last longer than some such period and warning is of little use. They care little for words and they must not only see the Stick but actually feel it on their Shoulders before they yield to that only argument which to them brings conviction the argumentum Baculinum.[25]

In 1852 the easy-going Bonham, always a "cautious administrator," was succeeded at Hongkong by Sir John Bowring, "a man of precipitation, of definite ideas, and of a reforming zeal." [26] Yet the coming crisis was delayed. Granville's instructions were explicit. China should be asked to observe her engagements, but the British envoy was "to avoid all irritating discussions." Britain in 1852 was not as yet ready for war.

---

[25] Quoted by Costin, *Great Britain and China, 1833-1860*, 149-150.

[26] The author, among other things, of the hymn, "In the Cross of Christ I Glory."

CHAPTER 7

THE *ARROW* WAR AND THE SETTLEMENT

THE crisis confronting the Manchu Empire in the decade 1850 to 1860 was perhaps no less acute than that faced by Commissioner Lin at Canton in 1840. Great Britain had won the first war but there was some reason to believe that she had lost the peace. By 1850 most of the foreigners in the five ports regarded the first treaty settlements as inadequate if not a complete failure. The major question was whether this settlement could be revised by diplomacy or would require resort to arms. This problem was resolved ultimately by conditions of political disintegration within China: conditions which, in a sense, deprived the Manchu government of both the will and the power either to enforce the treaties and their broad implications upon its subjects, or to repudiate them completely. The days of the great K'ang-hsi emperor (1662-1722) and the Ch'ien-lung emperor (1736-1796) were long since past. With all her vast population, China lacked a great leader.

Should an Emperor arise among them [wrote M. Huc] possessed of a great intellect, a will of iron, a reformer determined to come at once to a rupture with the ancient traditions, and initiate his people into the progressive civilization of the West, we believe that the work of regeneration would proceed with rapid strides. . . .

[But] the Young Mantchou prince who in 1850 ascended the Imperial throne, will probably not be the great and powerful reformer of whom we have spoken. He commenced his reign by degrading and putting to death the statesmen who, during that of his predecessor, had seen themselves compelled, under the English cannon, to make some concessions to the Europeans. The high dignitaries who form his council have been chosen among the most obstinate partisans of the old *regime,* and the ancient traditions; and in place of the tolerant sentiments manifested by those who opened the five ports, have come all the old traditional antipathies. Every device has been tried to elude the obligation of treaties; under the influence of the new policy, the relations between the Consuls and the Mandarins have become embittered, and the concessions of the late Emperor almost illusory.

It is evident to the least clear-sighted, that the object of the Manchou government is to disgust Europeans, and break off all intercourse with them; it would gladly have nothing to do with them at any price. China has, however, now been brought too near to Europe for it to be permitted any longer to lead this isolated life in the midst of the world. . . .[1]

These were indeed prophetic words. In the mid-nineteenth century China possessed neither the power to repel the "barbarian" nor the leadership to create a new China adjusted to a new world. Future conflict was inherent in these facts. This conflict was to develop out of three major sources: 1) the decline of Manchu power, hastened by the T'ai-p'ing and other rebellions; 2) the refusal of the official hierarchy to adjust itself to the new order of foreign intercourse with its broad social and economic implications; and 3) the growing co-operation of the treaty powers in their quest for wider and more stable commercial relations with The Middle Kingdom.

THE T'AI-P'ING REBELLION

Rebellion is an old institution in China, sanctioned by Confucian philosophy, and essential in the theory of the Mandate of Heaven. When a dynasty, for whatever reason, lost its ability to rule, it was obvious that Heaven had withdrawn the mandate. The duty of the subject to rebel was then clear. This ancient theory was to enjoy wide application in nineteenth-century China. In the two decades which preceded the first British war, revolts had occurred with alarming frequency in Kwangsi, Shansi, Kweichow, Kiangsi, Hainan, Hupeh, and Formosa. All were indicative of growing political discontent. They aggravated, too, the Manchu problem of dealing with the troublesome foreigners. While pirates swarmed and looted along the coasts, floods in the Yellow River Valley drove thousands to brigandage. Secret political societies bent on rebellion (a not unusual feature in Chinese society) flourished as rarely before.

Fundamentally the causes of unrest in the middle nineteenth century lay in the fact that in China "economic change had outrun the growth of social theory." Population had increased out of proportion to the land under cultivation. As a result of this, of the growth of internal and foreign trade, and of the inequalities of an antiquated tax system, the peasant was degraded to virtual serfdom. Thus a permanent, floating "population of paupers" provided the raw material for rebellion.[2]

[1] M. [E. R.] Huc, *A Journey Through the Chinese Empire* (2 vols., New York, 1859), I, 412-13.
[2] G. E. Taylor, "The Taiping Rebellion: Its Economic Background and Social Theory," *Chinese Soc. and Pol. Science Rev.*, XVI (1933), 545-549.

In these circumstances there appeared one, Hung Hsiu-ch'üan, a native of the Canton district, the youngest and brightest son of a farm family. Young Hung passed the local examinations, but failed repeatedly in the provincial tests. To this background of disappointment and failure were added illness, visions, and some contacts with the Reverend Issachar Roberts, an American Baptist missionary at Canton. With the mental and spiritual equipment thus provided, Hung resolved that he was commissioned to restore the worship of the true god. His original organization, the *Pai Shang-ti Hui* (Association of God Worshippers), soon recruited an enormous following from disaffected elements in Kwangsi. At first the movement appeared as religious, iconoclastic, and, superficially at least, seemed to bear some resemblance to Protestantism. As the movement grew, its devastating armies moved north to the Yangtze and captured Nanking, where its capital was established in 1853. Meanwhile Hung had bestowed upon himself the title, *T'ien-wang* (Heavenly King), professed to rule over the *T'ai-p'ing T'ien-kuo* (The Heavenly Kingdom of Great Peace), and had set for his purpose the overthrow of the Manchu dynasty. In this new theocracy God was the Heavenly Father; Christ, the Divine Elder Brother; the *T'ai-p'ing Wang* (Hung, himself), the Divine Younger Brother. The Bible of the movement was the New Testament revised sufficiently to justify the claims of the Divine Younger Brother. Such was the notable achievement of this "soured and disappointed member of the learned proletariat."

THE REBELLION AND THE FOREIGN POWERS

During the winter of 1853-54, Hung and his rebels advanced to the north and reached the outskirts of Tientsin. They were unable to reach Peking. Yet for another decade they dominated the Yangtze Valley in defiance of Manchu authority. A rebellion so wide-spread, promoting a government which threatened to rival if it did not overthrow the Manchus, could not but command the attention of the foreign powers. If the T'ai-p'ing were Christians, would they not be more amenable than the Manchus to foreign treaty relations, to the commercial, social, and political concepts of the Westerners? This importance of defining their relation to the rebels was brought home to the powers in 1853, when the Chinese walled city of Shanghai, on the very border of the foreign settlements, was captured by a rebel band known as the "Small Swords." Civil war had thus reached the edge of the settlements, while retreating Imperial authorities deserted the Shanghai customs house. This raised the question whether Shanghai had become a free port, since the Chinese government was no longer capable of collecting the duties. British and American consular authorities notified their nationals that the consuls themselves would collect the duties during the absence of Imperial authorities. The British consul required his merchants to deposit promissory notes, which in fact were never paid, while the Americans were at the disadvantage of having to pay in specie. Merchants who had no consular representative enjoyed favorable discrimination and paid nothing. British policy stipulated too that the Shanghai settlement was to remain neutral in the civil strife which surrounded it; but in reality foreign merchants constantly gave aid to the rebels in the sale of supplies. Many ships entered and cleared the port without the payment of duties. It was in these circumstances of confusion, discrimination, and uncertainty that the rate-payers of the settlement established the Municipal Council.[3]

THE FOREIGN INSPECTORATE OF CUSTOMS AT SHANGHAI

From this crisis at Shanghai, a crisis which had destroyed temporarily the power of the Peking government, and threatened likewise the whole treaty structure built by the foreigners, there emerged a remarkable institution—the Foreign Inspectorate of Customs. By agreement between the *taotai* and the consuls of the three treaty powers, England, the United States, and France (June 29, 1854), provision was made for appointment of a board of foreign inspectors, for the creation of an adequate customs machinery, and for regulations which should define the relation of the Inspectorate to the *taotai*, the consuls, and the commercial public. At first the appointing power was given to the consuls, and it was the purpose of the British consul (Alcock) that the British should control the new Inspectorate, but within a year the British Foreign Office had ruled that the foreign inspectors were officials of China and not the nominees and delegates of foreign countries. Thus was formed the nucleus of a new Chinese customs administration, officered by foreign inspectors, which, in 1858, was extended to all the treaty ports, where it became a model of efficient and honest government.[4]

---

[3] For a detailed description of Shanghai in these years see Earl Cranston, "Shanghai in the Taiping Period," *Pacific Historical Review*, V (1936), 147-160.

[4] For detailed studies of the customs problem at Shanghai in this period see: J. K. Fairbank, "The Provisional System at Shanghai," *Chinese Soc. and Pol. Science Rev.*, XVIII (1934-35), 455-494, and XIX (1935-36), 65-124; "The Creation of the Foreign Inspectorate of Customs at Shanghai," *ibid.*, XIX (1935-36), 469-514, and XX (1936-37), 42-

THE COOLIE TRADE

Although the creation of the Municipal Council and the Foreign Inspectorate of Customs tended after 1858 to stabilize conditions at Shanghai, other movements, disruptive and demoralizing, continued to harass the relations of foreigner and Chinese. It was in these years that the coolie trade was matured into a species of refined frightfulness unsurpassed in the most colorful and profitable years of the slave trade. The gradual emancipation of black slaves turned the attention of planters, particularly those in Cuba and Peru, to alternate sources of cheap, steady, and effective labor. As early as 1839 there had been some emigration of British East Indians to British Guiana; but flagrant iniquities associated with this trade soon brought its stoppage by the British government. Nevertheless, the value of coolie labor had been established and new sources of supply were sought and found in China. Just when the first coolies were shipped from China is uncertain; but it is clear that by 1847 the trade was growing rapidly. Nominally the coolies migrated as voluntary contract laborers committed to work for a term of years under specified conditions contained in their contract. In reality most of the migration could hardly be described as voluntary, for thousands of unsuspecting coolies were kidnapped both by foreigners and by their Chinese agents. Once the victim was confined on the coolie ship, his contract was likely to be of no value. Most of the ships were floating hells in which the wretched prisoners festered and often died before reaching American shores.

In a sense the coolie trade was more inhumane than the slave trade. The slave, having no prospect of freedom, entertained little hope of a better life; the coolies, on the contrary, were beguiled with the promise of gainful labor and eventual return to their native land with the profits of their toil. Many failed even to reach their destination. Ships sailing from Hongkong were under stricter supervision than those from ports on the China coast, yet of the 23,928 coolies shipped from Hongkong between 1847 and 1857, bound for Cuba, more than 3,000 died on the voyage. When food and water supplies failed, those in the worst stages of disease were sometimes thrown overboard while still alive. Naturally as these reports reached the China ports, violence in the recruiting of coolies increased. In Cuba and Peru the coolies with their contracts were sold at auction. Some found decent owners but the majority worked in conditions of extreme cruelty.

100; "The Definition of the Foreign Inspector's Status (1854-55): A Chapter in the Early History of the Inspectorate of Customs at Shanghai," *Nankai Social and Economic Quarterly*, IX (1936), 125-163.

Expatriation and emigration were alike prohibited by Chinese law, but the Manchu government was powerless and seemingly unwilling to attack this evil infesting the treaty ports and Macao. The British recognized at an early date that the coolie trade was defensible neither on humanitarian nor on economic grounds. Bonham noted that it was on a par with slave trade, and that the continuance of its abuses might easily threaten immense Anglo-Indian-Chinese commercial interests. But the English Passenger Act (1855), which curbed some of the worst abuses under the British flag, served largely to concentrate the coolie business at Portuguese-controlled Macao. The court at Peking was also emboldened to prohibit coolie emigration by Imperial edict. Concurrently, representatives of the United States in China sought legislation to prohibit American participation. In 1856 Dr. Peter Parker, Commissioner of the United States in China, warned Americans that they would forfeit protection of their government if they became involved in the trade. In 1860 a report to ·Congress revealed that foreigners were chartering American vessels and that the trade was thus being thrown to an alarming degree into American hands. Congress acted with some promptness, passing in 1862, despite its preoccupation with civil war, an act which barred American citizens and ships from the traffic. Unfortunately, most of the powers remained indifferent to the evils of the trade and it continued for some years. In 1874, after the United States and Great Britain had jointly condemned Portugal for harboring the evil at Macao, the business was finally prohibited there. In retrospect the coolie trade remains one of the blackest pages in the record of the nineteenth century. In the middle of that century it served to aggravate the already difficult relations between China and the foreign commercial powers.

THE CONVOYING SYSTEM

Another unhealthy feature of Sino-foreign relations was a peculiar system of convoy employed in the Chinese coasting trade. At many periods in Chinese history both Chinese and Japanese pirates had preyed upon the native coasting trade. In the nineteenth century, the weakness of the Manchu dynasty plus general economic distress opened a wide field for Chinese pirates to loot the cargoes of their own countrymen. Foreign ship-owners (at first mainly Portuguese) soon discovered in this situation a new road to profits. With well-armed ships they offered (for a generous monetary consideration) their services as convoys. At first their charges were reasonable and Chinese junk owners willingly accepted this protection. In time the greed of the convoy agents increased; their charges became extortion; and their services were literally forced upon the helpless coasting traders. Those who declined the service of convoy frequently met death at the hands of these violent plunderers. The immediate results were two-fold: 1) much of China's coasting trade passed under foreign flags, since the pirates were more apt to respect these; 2) most of the foreign nations represented on the China coast became involved in the vicious system of convoying. Bowring reported to Lord Clarendon that British vessels had by 1854 "almost superseded Portuguese lorchas" in the traffic.[5] So desperate indeed was the plight of the Chinese traders that in 1857 they appealed to their pirate fellow-countrymen for protection. Some of the Portuguese convoy ships were defeated by the Chinese pirates, but the evils of the convoy system lingered on for many years. Convoying did little to reconcile the Chinese to the presence of foreigners in their ports or on their coasts.

THE OBLIGATIONS OF EXTRATERRITORIALITY

The coolie trade and the system of convoying were the work of the lawless and unscrupulous among the foreign community. Most of the Western governments frowned from the first upon such practices, yet these same governments were at times notably negligent in their obligations toward China. The application of extraterritoriality was a case in point. In acquiring extraterritorial jurisdiction over their nationals in China, the treaty powers had won a legal right of the greatest consequence. The practice of extraterritoriality, however, carried with it grave responsibilities, which for many years most of the powers treated with shameful disregard. At first only the British recognized and sought to meet their extraterritorial obligations.

Since under the extraterritorial grants China had surrendered the power of her own courts over foreigners, it became the duty of the treaty powers to provide competent consular courts in the treaty ports, and jails where criminals might be incarcerated. Prior to 1857, Great Britain alone took adequate steps to meet this need. A British criminal court, provided for in 1833, functioned at Canton after 1839. By act of Parliament (1843) British legal jurisdiction was authorized on foreign soil, as a result of which machinery was provided for the administration of extraterritoriality in China, including provision for jails. In contrast, habitual American criminals in the China ports

[5] At Ningpo, for example, Chinese coasting and fishing vessels by 1857 were paying annually $200,000 "protection" money to Portuguese lorchas that were "masters of this part of the coast." G. W. Cooke, *China . . . in 1857-58* (London, 1858), 129-134.

could be confined only on a national ship, or, as frequently happened, by courtesy, in a British jail.   In 1858 American criminals were released from the British jail in Shanghai because the American consul had no funds for jail expenses.   Two years later the United States provided its first appropriation for consular jails in China.[6]

THE GROWTH OF THE OPIUM TRADE

Since 1842 the opium trade had continued to grow and to prosper. Although opium had provided the occasion for the first Sino-British war, the subsequent treaties had evaded the problem of control.   Thus, while by the laws of China the importation of opium was still prohibited, foreigners and Chinese conspired to flood the market with this contraband and destructive drug.[7]   It has been estimated that between 1840 and 1858 the annual imports increased almost three hundred percent. The effects upon the Chinese were devastating; but so long as the Chinese government would not or could not enforce its laws, there was little hope that the foreigners would forego a trade so profitable.

DEMANDS FOR TREATY REVISION

By 1854, despite the growth of profitable trade at Shanghai and Canton, it was evident that the relations of China and the treaty powers were far from healthy.   The abuses of extraterritoriality, the traffic in coolies, convoying, the opium trade, and the gun-boat policy at Canton, all served to reinforce the official Chinese view that the foreign barbarians were an uncouth and troublesome lot with whom China should have as few dealings as possible.   On his part, the foreigner, both merchant and consul, was convinced that China had no respect for treaties, and no understanding of the benefits of free commerce and free access to markets.   The foreigners now regarded the treaties of 1842-44 as inadequate not only because China had frequently evaded them but also because under these treaties foreign trade was confined to the five ports; the foreign trader was still a stranger to China's vast interior; the foreign diplomat was still a stranger to Peking.   Both the American and the French treaties of 1844 provided for revision after twelve years, and the British claimed this same privilege on the basis of most-favored-nation treatment.   Under this claim the British held that the Treaty of Nanking would be subject to revision in 1854.

---

[6] For an extended treatment see G. W. Keeton, *The Development of Extraterritoriality in China* (2 vols., London, 1928).

[7] *The Times* correspondent reported, 1857: "At present the [opium] trade is as open and as unrestrained in all the cities of China as the sale of hot-cross buns on Good Friday is in the streets of London."   Cooke, *China . . . in 1857-58,* 179.

BRITAIN SEEKS NEW PRIVILEGES

The scope of Britain's policy of treaty revision was contained in instructions from Clarendon to Bowring (Feb. 13, 1854). The British government insisted on China's recognition of the *right* of immediate revision, but the actual revision might be delayed at Bowring's discretion in view of China's domestic strife due to the T'ai-p'ing Rebellion. Meanwhile, Bowring was to seek co-operation with the Americans and the French, whose treaties would also soon be subject to revision. In his negotiations with China he was to seek "access generally to the whole interior of the Chinese Empire as well as to the cities on the coast: or failing this, . . . free navigation of the Yangtze Kiang and access to the cities on its banks up to Nanking. . . ." He was to effect legalization of the opium trade, in order that it might be limited and controlled; and to seek abolition of internal transit duties on goods imported or purchased for export. He was also to secure suppression of piracy and regulation of the coolie trade. Finally, the British government desired "the permanent and honourable residence at the Court of Peking of a Representative of the British Crown" or provision for direct and unobstructed correspondence with that government. These official British objectives also represented approximately those general principles which were beginning to appear in French and American policy.

The desire of the British to be represented diplomatically at Peking indicated, among other things, that they were no longer willing to tolerate the Chinese system whereby the Canton viceroy was entrusted by Peking with the actual conduct of foreign affairs. With this official alone the foreigners were expected to deal, and their experience had not recommended the system. In 1848 John W. Davis, the American commissioner, after great difficulty, secured an interview with the viceroy for the purpose of presenting his credentials. He was treated "with extreme rudeness" by both viceroy and governor. In fact, after 1852 "the practice of ignoring the foreign representatives became a part of the settled policy of the Chinese government." [8]

A French diplomat remained at Macao fifteen months vainly awaiting a personal interview with a qualified Chinese official. Of the various successors of Davis in the period to 1855, none succeeded in securing an interview. The high commissioner was always "too busy," and in any event would have to await the dawn of "an auspicious day." Two American commissioners, Humphrey Marshall and Robert McLane,

---

[8] H. B. Morse, *The International Relations of the Chinese Empire* (3 vols., London, 1910-1918), I, 411.

went to Nanking hoping to make direct contact with responsible officials, only to be referred back to Canton. Thus in 1854 when Clarendon instructed Bowring on British policy, the foreign traders and most of their consular and diplomatic associates were of a mind not only to extend their commercial rights but also to convert China, forcibly if necessary, to Western concepts of international law, diplomacy, and commercial intercourse in general.

LIMITED CO-OPERATION AMONG THE TREATY POWERS

England's plan for treaty revision did not imply an immediate resort to war. There was to be no precipitate action. Actually the British government hoped for a co-operative policy with France and the United States. Already Britain had made friendly gestures toward the Americans in China. She had made it clear that she sought no exclusive privileges for herself, and she had conceded the claim of the United States for equal rights in the Shanghai settlement.

Among American merchants in the treaty ports there was very general support for Britain's policy of treaty revision. This was natural because the interests of British and American traders were in many respects identical. Some support for British policy was contained, too, in the dispatches of various American commissioners.[9]

In fact, some significant features of later American policy in China were enunciated by American commissioners in these years when the first treaties were on trial. Humphrey Marshall (1853-54), though described by Bonham as "a very coarse headstrong man" who had "never been out of Kentucky," wrote with profound understanding that

the highest interests of the United States are involved in sustaining China— maintaining order here, and gradually engrafting on this worn-out stock the healthy principles which give life and health to governments, rather than to see China become the theatre of a widespread anarchy, *and ultimately the prey of European ambition.*[10]

Marshall, while suspicious of both Britain and Russia, favored a co-operative diplomatic intervention by the powers to end China's internal turmoil. Robert McLane, who succeeded Marshall (1854), took an active part in organizing the Foreign Inspectorate of Customs at Shang-

---

[9] Full-ranking ministers were not appointed by the United States to China until after the Treaties of Tientsin, 1858.

[10] Marshall correspondence. U. S., H. Ex. doc. 123:33-1 (734), 210-13. Italics are mine.

hai. He was the first American to apply fully the co-operative policy. In 1854 he accompanied Bowring to the Pei-ho in a vain effort to effect treaty revision at this gateway to Peking. This was after McLane had been repeatedly rebuffed at Canton by what he described as the "discourtesy and repulsiveness" of Commissioner Yeh. Dr. Peter Parker (1855-57), successor to McLane and a former medical missionary in China, was a vigorous advocate of what he considered American interests in Asia. He hoped to secure the revision of the American treaty of 1844, but on learning that his privilege was to be denied him, he advocated occupation of Formosa as a means of forcing China to observe her treaty obligations.[11]

In view then of the harmony between British and American expressions of policy, England's proposals through Lord Napier to Secretary Cass (March, 1857) for a three-power alliance (the United States, France, and Great Britain) to effect revision of the treaties, were not surprising. These proposals were of course declined, yet the dangers threatening American interests in China did prompt the appointment of William B. Reed as envoy extraordinary and minister plenipotentiary to the court of Peking.

PRETEXTS FOR WAR

By the early autumn of 1856, with the crisis of the Crimean War already past, Great Britain had determined on a diplomatic and naval move toward Peking to hasten revision of the treaties, to expand commercial intercourse, and to destroy the exclusiveness of Yeh's policy at Canton.

A SO-CALLED JUDICIAL MURDER

In this forward policy, Britain might count on the support of France, for in February, 1856, a French Catholic missionary, Auguste Chapdelaine, had been put to death by Chinese authorities at Sinlin in Kwangsi. Chapdelaine and some of his converts had been arrested on a charge that they were rebels—a natural enough charge, for Kwangsi had witnessed the beginnings of the T'ai-p'ing Rebellion with its frosting of Christian flavor. The arrest, torture, and execution of the foreign priest and his followers are thus understandable according to official Chinese ideas of the time. The Chinese magistrate could likewise

---

[11] Parker correspondence. U. S., Sen. Ex. doc. 22:35-2 (983), 1081-83, 1208-10. Of Commissioner Yeh, Parker wrote that he "stands alone and pre-eminent in his insane and insufferable conduct towards foreigners. . . . The same demeanor on the part of an official of his rank of any other nation would be deemed an outrage justifying summary redress. . . ." *Ibid.*, 760.

rest his case on the fact that under the treaties no foreigners were allowed beyond the treaty ports. Furthermore, the testimony of Catholic missionaries themselves reveals that they indoctrinated their Chinese converts with the idea of looking to "France as their support and liberator" against persecution.[12]   China's fault of course lay in the fact that the execution of the priest violated the extraterritorial rights of France.

News of this so-called "judicial murder" reached Canton in July, 1856. It was not unwelcome to Napoleon III.   France was now in a position not only to assist Great Britain in forcing, if need be, a revision of the treaties, but also to aid the Catholic Church by political means in the spiritual conquest of China.   By October, 1856, France and England were able to agree upon a common policy of force.

THE AFFAIR OF THE LORCHA *ARROW*

The incident which was to precipitate hostilities between Great Britain and China found its origin in a system by which Chinese coasting vessels acquired temporary register under foreign flags.   During 1853-54 southern Chinese rebels held positions so strong in the regions of Canton and Kowloon that communications between Whampoa (the Canton anchorage) and Hongkong were frequently broken so far as the passage of Chinese vessels was concerned.   Even Commissioner Yeh asked help from the despised foreigners.   In 1855 English and American authorities in order to maintain trade between Hongkong and Canton believed it was necessary to grant "English and United States flags with a passport to Chinese lighters for a single trip to and from Canton and Whampoa to be immediately returned and filed at the consulates by which they were issued." [13]   Out of this situation arose various ordinances of the colonial government of Hongkong permitting residents of the colony, including Chinese, under prescribed conditions, to use the British flag on their vessels for this limited purpose.   In time this right by ordinance was abused.   Some vessels used the protection of the British flag to engage in the smuggling trade; others carried the flags of various foreign powers with no authority whatsoever for doing so; sometimes merchant consuls without authority from their governments issued foreign registry to native craft.   As a result it was soon difficult for Chinese authorities to distinguish between the legitimate and the illegitimate use of foreign flags by native craft.

The lorcha *Arrow,* owned by a Chinese who had resided in Hong-

---

[12] *Missions Etrangères* (Paris), Vol. DL.   Quoted by W. C. Costin, *Great Britain and China* (Oxford, 1937), 202.
[13] Parker correspondence.

kong for ten years, and commanded by a British subject, was boarded by Chinese police (Oct. 8, 1856) while it was lying at anchor in the river at Canton. Twelve of her Chinese crew of fourteen were arrested on charges of piracy and removed to a Chinese war-junk. Harry Parkes, British consul at Canton, promptly demanded release of the captives on the ground that the *Arrow* was a British ship carrying colonial registry from Hongkong, that she had been boarded without communication first having been made to the British consul, and that the British flag had been hauled down by the Chinese police. Sir John Bowring supported Parkes by demanding an apology and guarantees for the future. The prisoners were eventually handed over by Yeh (Oct. 22), but Consul Parkes refused to accept this release since the captives were accompanied neither by a Chinese officer of rank nor by an apology.[14] British naval forces therefore attacked the forts guarding the approach to Canton. On October 29, the walls of the city were breached, but though the British could attack the city, they had insufficient forces to occupy it. In the heat of these proceedings the American flag too was fired upon by Chinese forts—a fire which was returned by American ships of war. Trade was now at an end, yet Commissioner Yeh refused all concessions.

In England, Bowring's actions were approved despite vigorous criticism from the Opposition; and now that France was prepared for full co-operation in treaty revision, the British government appointed Lord Elgin to head Her Majesty's special embassy.[15] Elgin's mission was not merely to solve local grievances at Canton or elsewhere. He was to extend the opportunities for foreign trade and to establish diplomatic representation at Peking. In other words he was to revise the treaties thoroughly.

---

[14] The argument was advanced that the *Arrow* was not entitled legally to British protection since her Hongkong registry had expired a few days before her crew was seized. This fact was unknown to Parkes, the British consul, and to the Chinese who authorized the seizure. The point was regarded as irrelevant by the law officers of the Crown, since in their minds the real question was one of international law between England and China as defined by the supplementary Treaty of the Bogue, 1843. Since the *Arrow* possessed a sailing letter as specified by that treaty, she was, according to English legal interpretation, a British vessel. On the question whether the British flag was flying, and whether it was pulled down by the Chinese, the evidence is contradictory, but appears to support the British charge. For a full discussion see Costin, *Great Britain and China*, 206-230.

[15] The attack in the House of Commons on Bowring's policy rested on: 1) distrust of Bowring's honesty, 2) the question of the legality of his actions, and 3) the question of the political wisdom of his demands upon Yeh. These considerations had no effect upon Palmerston, who termed Yeh "one of the most savage barbarians that ever disgraced a nation." This was hardly a considered judgment.

ARMED CONFLICT INEVITABLE

War was now certain. The "murder" of the French priest and the affair of the *Arrow* were the convenient pretexts for armed action, the real causes of which were far more fundamental than these incidents. China's exclusion policy was regarded by Britain as a menace both to her actual and to her potential commercial interests, while the conduct of Chinese officials—that of Yeh in particular—was looked upon as an insult to the Crown. With the British policy deriving from these sentiments Napoleon III was happy to be associated. A victorious war in China would appeal to French business, and, by avenging the death of a priest and providing religious guarantees for the future, would not be unwelcome to French Catholics or to the Papacy. In extenuation of these official views it may be noted that the powers and their nationals had suffered grave indignities in China. The treaties had been consistently broken by China, though she was not the sole offender in this respect. In addition, her officials had given little evidence of adjusting themselves to a world of Western trade and law. Yet this was not surprising. Nations rarely recognize voluntarily the need for change or appreciate their own attitude as an obstacle to change. It was natural and it was easier for China to see the foreigners as barbarians to be repelled, not as envoys of a "superior" or more powerful civilization.

THE WAR

After much delay due to diversion of British contingents to suppress the Indian Mutiny, British and French forces bombarded and captured Canton in December, 1857. British marines seized the venerable but proud and obstinate High Commissioner Yeh as this portly gentleman sought to escape over the back wall of his yamen. Fifteen months later he died, a prisoner of war, in India. Until 1860, Canton was ruled by Chinese officials acting at the command of a British and French commission.[16]

Britain and France, on February 11, 1858, were joined by the representatives of the United States and Russia, William B. Reed and Count Putiatin, respectively, in simultaneous notes to Peking making clear the united demand of the powers for treaty revision and religious toleration, and suggesting negotiations at Shanghai. To the Chinese demand that negotiations be conducted at Canton, the representatives of the powers replied by sailing north to the mouth of the Pei-ho, at the very

[16] See "Conversations with Yeh" by *The Times* correspondent, in Cooke, *China . . . in 1857-58*, 396-432.

gateway to Peking. Alarmed by this manoeuvre, the Chinese court appointed the viceroy of Chihli to negotiate, but his powers were regarded by Lord Elgin and Baron Gros (France) as inadequate. It was their view that only an advance to Tientsin would bring the Chinese to terms. To this end they demanded the surrender of the Taku forts guarding the mouth of the river, and when this was refused, the forts were stormed and taken (May 20). Peking thereupon promptly appointed officials whose powers were regarded as adequate. Negotiations leading to new treaties were now conducted with all four powers, concurrently but separately. Before the end of June, 1858, the four treaties of Tientsin had been signed: the Russian on the 13th, the American the 18th, the British the 26th, and the French the following day.[17]

THE TREATIES OF TIENTSIN, 1858

The treaties of Tientsin must be viewed as a revision of and an enlargement of principles and practices set forth in the first treaties of 1842-44. Since England and France had employed force, it was their treaties which embodied the new and valuable concessions, which, however, by reason of the most-favored-nation clause would be enjoyed likewise by Russia and the United States.[18] In this sense the four treaties constituted a single settlement having a profound influence upon China's relations with the West.

The new and significant privileges won by the treaty powers in the Tientsin Treaties included:

1. The right to maintain a resident minister at Peking, or the right of the minister, at the discretion of the British government, to visit the capital. The British minister should "not be called upon to perform any ceremony derogatory to him as representing the sovereign of an independent nation on a footing of equality with that of China."

2. The right of travel in all parts of the interior under passports issued by the foreign consuls and counter-signed by the local Chinese authorities.

3. The right of foreign ships to trade on the Yangtze River, and the opening of additional treaty ports.[19]

---

[17] See Miller, *Treaties*, VII, 793-930, for text and notes on the American treaty.

[18] It has been stated with some justification that "it became ingloriously, yet very profitably, the role of the United States pacifically to follow England to China in the wake of war, and to profit greatly by the victories of British arms." Tyler Dennett, *Americans in Eastern Asia* (New York, 1922), 159.

[19] To the five ports opened by the treaty of 1842 were added: Chefoo in Shantung, Chinkiang in Kiangsu, Hankow in Hupeh, Kuikiang in Kiangsi, Kiungchow in Hainan, Newchwang in Manchuria, Swatow in Kwangtung, Wenchow in Chekiang, and Nanking in Kiangsu.

4. The right of missionaries to protection by the Chinese authorities, since "the Christian religion, as professed by Protestants or Roman Catholics, inculcates the practice of virtue, and teaches man to do as he would be done by." [20]

SIGNIFICANCE OF THE TIENTSIN TREATIES

The Tientsin Treaties were of such moment as to justify a further statement on the policy embodied in them. It is to be noted that they represented a common policy on the part of the four powers, for although England and France alone had used force, the United States and Russia insisted on most-favored-nation treatment.

The most striking concession was the right of residence of foreign ministers at Peking, or at least the right of these ministers to visit the capital. The delay and evasion which China had practiced constantly in dealing with the foreign governments would now be more difficult.

The grant of toleration to Christians, to missionaries, and to their Chinese converts has been a subject of much controversy. To toleration in principle there could be no objection; but in 1858 toleration was won as a result of war, and was granted in the clause of a treaty exacted as a result of war. The missionaries, particularly the Catholics, were already well aware that many elements in Christian doctrine had proved disruptive of China's cultural heritage; yet, since the object of the missionaries was to make this heritage subservient to Christianity, it was natural that they should welcome the new treaty status for themselves and for their religion. Neither is it surprising that after 1858 many Chinese felt quite justified in regarding Christianity as a political as well as a religious weapon of the West.

The right of foreigners to travel in the interior was another concession on which opinions have differed widely. The traders of 1858 had complained bitterly of the restrictions which confined them to the treaty ports. They were businessmen intent on profits, and these same profits, they felt, would depend in turn on freedom of access to the entire country. Against this point of view the Chinese could argue that the people were not yet ready to receive foreigners beyond the port towns, and that because the foreigner enjoyed extraterritoriality and would when in the interior be far removed from his nearest consul, China could exercise over him only an ineffective control.

Since, too, the powers were now bent on expanding their commerce

---

[20] All quotations are from the British treaty. In addition, the extraterritorial rights of foreigners were further defined in criminal cases. Indemnities demanded by the British totalled four million taels; by the French, two million taels.

with China, the opening of additional treaty ports (nine in China and one in Formosa) could not long be delayed. Nevertheless, the opening of the additional ports did occasion trouble, and in the case of Nanking the port was not opened until 1899. On the other hand, the admission of foreign vessels to the trade of the Yangtze could not be easily defended. It was the great artery to the richest areas of China. The fact that the foreigners could demand and be granted access to China's coasting and inland trade is the most eloquent testimony to the decay of the Manchu dynasty.

LEGALIZATION OF THE OPIUM TRADE

Following the Tientsin settlement, negotiations were adjourned to Shanghai, where a revised schedule of rates in the conventional tariff was adopted, providing for a general five percent duty on exports and imports. But more significant than this revision was the legalization of the opium trade at a duty of 30 taels per 100 catties.[21] This new legal status of opium was a triumph for British policy, which, since 1842, had been consistent, and probably sound, despite the fact that it appeared to support a nefarious traffic. The British argument ran as follows. Since the Nanking settlement, the importation of opium, a contraband trade, had increased rapidly. Although most of the opium was produced in India, other sources of supply were available, and therefore prohibition by the British authorities was not likely to prove effective in stopping the trade, though it would materially reduce Indian revenue. It was the business of China to enforce her laws against an illicit traffic. England would not give protection to subjects violating China's laws, but neither would she undertake to enforce the laws for China. Since China had failed to enforce the law against opium, the trade should be legalized at a fixed duty and supervised strictly.[22]

The attitude of the United States at this time to the opium question is also of interest. Minister Reed had been instructed that his government would not seek legalization of the opium traffic, and thus the treaty which Reed signed at Tientsin made no mention of opium. But

---

[21] One catty equals one and one-third lbs.

[22] J. F. Fairbank, "The Legalization of the Opium Trade before the Treaties of 1858," *Chinese Social and Political Science Review*, XVII (1933), 215, points out that while the Imperial government in Peking took no steps to levy an official impost on opium trade before 1858, nevertheless "the unofficial or private taxation of the traffic by local [Chinese] authorities, . . . appears to have been put gradually on a more regular basis." Thus the taxing of opium was applied by the Chinese authorities at some of the ports before the legalization clause was written into the treaties of 1858. Legalization served two purposes: it provided China with needed revenue, and it stabilized an important item of the foreign trade by placing it on a treaty basis.

later, in discussions with Lord Elgin, Reed came to the view that "any course is better than that which is now pursued." He therefore supported the principle of legalization and his action in this respect was accepted by his government.

THE RENEWAL OF HOSTILITIES

The treaties of Tientsin were approved by the Chinese government in 1858 before the British and French forces left Tientsin. They were not to become effective, however, until ratified copies had been exchanged *at Peking*. This was done without difficulty in the case of the Russian treaty. The new Russian minister, General Ignatiev, proceeded to Peking by the old overland route and was promptly received. The British, the French, and the American envoys, accompanied by ships of war, arrived at the mouth of the Pei-ho in June, 1859. Here it was discovered that the Chinese had strengthened the forts at Taku and had blocked the river's mouth. The envoys were informed, but only when it was too late, that they would be received at P'ei-t'ang ten miles farther north on the coast, but that China would repel any attempt to enter the river at Taku. The British and French therefore attempted to storm the forts and break the barrier—an attempt in which they failed utterly, and accordingly were forced to return to Shanghai.[23]

Hostilities had thus been precipitated and a second chapter in the *Arrow* War was now inevitable. Again it should be noted that the question of responsibility is difficult to assess. The British envoy, Frederick Bruce, had been instructed that it would be desirable for him to "reach Tientsin in a British ship of war," but that since definite rules of procedure could not be laid down in London the envoy was to use discretion when "to give way" and when "to stand firm." Thus Bruce, faced with dilatory Chinese correspondence and evasion followed by the blocking of the river at Taku, had come to the conclusion that this was the time "to stand firm." When he insisted on the approach through Taku and Tientsin he was not violating his instructions but he was demanding something not granted by the British treaty. Actually neither British nor French policy in this instance could be justified in law. Both the policy and Bruce's decision were political. They rested on the conviction, for which there was considerable ground, that the Peking

---

[23] During the engagement, the commander of the American naval forces, whose country was neutral, had none the less come to the assistance of his British cousins, explaining his action with the statement that "blood is thicker than water." This was doubtless scientifically true, but it had little bearing on the commander's official instructions.

government had no intention to honor the extensive new concessions which it had been forced to grant at Tientsin the previous year.

MR. WARD CROOKS THE KNEE

Meanwhile John E. Ward, the American envoy, restricted neither to any route or place for the exchange of his country's treaty, proceeded to P'ei-t'ang. At Tungchow the Chinese provided carts which carried him and his mission to Peking.[24] This was unfortunate for the dignity of the United States. Ward, a native of Georgia, was a Southern gentleman of some distinction, but being sadly ignorant of the finer points of Oriental procedure, he permitted the Chinese to take full advantage of his inexperience. He should have demanded sedan chairs, the mode of conveyance used by high Chinese officials. The cart in which he did ride was the kind of vehicle used to carry Korean and other tribute-bearers to the Chinese capital. Over this cart floated banners describing Ward as a tribute-bearer from the United States. This of course was further evidence that the Manchu Court did not accept the Tientsin treaties in letter or spirit.[25]

Arrived in Peking, Ward was requested to perform the *kotow,* which of course he refused to do, and with what must have been a splendid dignity informed the Chinese officials that "although he was willing to 'bend the body and slightly crook the right knee,' he was accustomed to kneel only to God and woman." [26] Thoroughly disgusted, Ward returned to P'ei-t'ang where copies of the ratified American treaty were exchanged.

BURNING THE SUMMER PALACE

Meanwhile British and French reinforcements reached the Pei-ho. On August 21, 1860, the Allies stormed the Taku forts and advanced on

---

[24] The Ward correspondence is in U. S. Sen. Ex. doc. 36-1:(30), 569 ff. Further details are in the diary of S. Wells Williams, *Journal of the Royal Asiatic Society,* North China Branch, XLII (1911), 102 ff. For discussion of these events see also Great Britain, *Parliamentary Debates* (C) CLVI, 919-952; CLVII, 781 ff.

[25] The attitude of the Manchu Court to Ward and thus to the United States is revealed in an Imperial rescript to the Privy Councillors. "The American chieftain [Ward] can on no account be allowed to ride in a sedan chair in the capital. But after landing at Pei-t'ang, he can well be allowed to sit in a sedan chair for the land journey to a point beyond Tientsin, at which he should change to a boat. As soon as he reaches Tungchow, let him sit in a carriage or a mule chair, but not in a sedan chair. . . . explain this clearly to the chieftain beforehand, in order to avoid possible last minute wrangling." T. F. Tsiang, "China after the Victory of Taku, June 25, 1859," *The American Historical Review,* XXXV (1929), 79-84.

[26] Tyler Dennett, *Americans in Eastern Asia* (New York, 1922), 342.

Tientsin and Peking. The Chinese retired in confusion, and when the foreigners entered the capital, the degenerate Manchu emperor had already fled with his court to Jehol, ostensibly on a hunting trip. During the Allied march on Peking, thirty-nine foreigners (twenty-six English, and thirteen French, including the private secretary of Lord Elgin who had replaced Bruce as Britain's plenipotentiary) were captured by the Chinese. At the time, the victims were presumably protected by a flag of truce, but the Chinese appear to have believed that by holding these hostages, they would bring the Allies to adopt a more moderate policy. Twenty of the prisoners were already dead when the remaining survivors were released. As a result, Lord Elgin ordered the burning of the emperor's Summer Palace (Yüan Ming Yüan) situated outside the city, an architectural monument which the French troops had already occupied and looted.[27] In Elgin's view China would have no peace with Britain until by the destruction of the Summer Palace a price had been paid for her "foul deed."

THE PEKING CONVENTION, 1860

With the Chinese capital now at their mercy, the Allied envoys proceeded to the exchange of the ratified treaties of 1858, and to exact new concessions embodied in the Conventions of Peking, 1860. The Emperor of China expressed "his deep regret" that a "misunderstanding" had occurred at Taku the previous year; agreed that the British minister might "reside permanently" at Peking; consented to additional indemnities,[28] and to the opening of Tientsin as a treaty port; legalized the coolie trade under regulation; and consented to the cession of Kow-

---

[27] The Summer Palace extended over an area more than six miles in length, situated at the foot of the first range of hills some five miles to the northwest of Peking. The grounds, which might be described as a great private park, included: residences, temples, pagodas, gardens, and artificial hills, some of them 300 feet in height, surrounding a lake. "There were forty palaces in all, the imperial yellow everywhere predominating, even to the tiles of the turned-up roofs, ..." Quoted from Rennie's *British Arms in China* by Lieut. Colonel W. Hill James, "Recollections of the Chinese War," *Macmillan's Magazine*, LXXI (1895), 247.

[28] The Chinese understanding of the nature of war indemnities at this time is not without interest and humor. A memorial of an Imperial commissioner (July 14, 1859) sets forth that ". . . it is an old established practice with the foreign barbarians that after a war between two countries, the country seeking peace, must pay an indemnity to the country consenting to it. . . . If the barbarians after their defeat [at Taku] ask us for peace, they will be afraid of our demanding an indemnity from them. On the other hand, if we should ask them for peace, they would undoubtedly demand compensation from us, ... We must forestall any such eventuality. Therefore at the interview of the 9th your slave ordered my aides to request the American chieftain [Ward] to transmit to the English barbarians our demand for an indemnity. This was only to stop them from demanding any from us." T. F. Tsiang, "China after the Victory of Taku," 82.

loon on the mainland opposite Hongkong. The French convention secured the restoration to the Roman Catholic Church of all property confiscated since 1724, a provision which was to work great hardship on Chinese who had acquired the property. The fact does not appear to have troubled the French government or the Church. Both found a convenient justification for taking the property in an Imperial edict of 1846, which had promised restoration of religious establishments to Roman Catholics. The Chinese text of the French convention (which was not authoritative) also contained a troublesome provision allowing French missionaries to rent and purchase land and to erect buildings in all provinces.[29]

The most curious phase of events in China during 1860 remains to be told. It was in this year that rebel bands associated with the T'ai-p'ing were threatening to advance upon the wealthy and populous city of Shanghai with its growing foreign settlement. In this extremity the Chinese authorities appealed to the English and French for protection, and these latter agreed to defend the Chinese city and the foreign settlement against any attack. On August 21, 1860, the British troops, assisted by some French, repelled the rebels from the walls of Shanghai. It was on this very day that British and French troops in the north were storming the Taku forts and beginning their march on Peking.

CONCLUSION

The second treaty settlement with China was now complete, for in reality the treaties of 1858 and 1860 were one settlement. These treaties were also a logical sequel to the earlier treaties of 1842-44. Within a period of twenty years the Western powers had forced a diplomatic and commercial revolution upon China. The days when the Canton viceroy might "insult" a British superintendent of trade were passed. Henceforth the ministers of Western powers would reside in Peking as representatives of states that claimed equality with The Middle Kingdom. The Western barbarian had arrived; he had reached the Forbidden City, the Dragon Throne, and the Son of Heaven himself.

. [29] For a full discussion of the social and political complications arising from this alleged right of Catholic missionaries see Paul H. Clyde, *United States Policy Toward China* (Durham, 1940), 107-112.

Chapter 8

THE RUSSO-CHINESE FRONTIER TO 1860

THE longest, and perhaps the least generally known, land frontier in the history of modern political geography is a tortuous line which lies between China and Asiatic Russia. From the northern tip of Korea, a few miles from Vladivostok and the Korean port of Yuki, it runs northward along the Ussuri River to the junction with the Amur; then up the course of that river and on westward through a vast expanse of desert and mountain that divides in uncertain fashion Mongolia from Siberia. Far to the west it veers southward into the heart of Central Asia between Sinkiang (Chinese Turkestan) and Kirghiz (Russian Turkestan). Until very modern times this boundary was little more than a species of geographical mystery winding its often unchartered way through a remote continent. But during the past century the Russo-Chinese frontier has given to history some of its most significant chapters. Russian commerce, imperialism, and communism have all crossed this frontier to play their part in the Western world's impact on China and Japan.

RUSSIAN EXPLORATION AND COLONIZATION IN SIBERIA

Russian expansion eastward across the Ural Mountains into Siberia began in the sixteenth century in the time of John the Dread (1533-1582). Cossack adventurers, seeking to escape the law, fled to Siberia, conquered the native chieftains, and, with these territorial prizes taken in the name of Russia, purchased pardons from the tsars. Russian peasants sought relief from oppressive government by migrating to the Siberian frontier. By 1638 a motley crew of these hardy pioneers had pushed eastward as far as the Lena River, where Yakutsk was founded. Behind them, settlements had already appeared at Tobolsk (1587) and at Omsk on the Irtish. In general, this pioneering advance was promoted rather than retarded by the character of the country and its native inhabitants. Native tribes offered relatively little resistance, and although the rivers flowed to the north, the portages between their upper tributaries were neither long nor impassable.

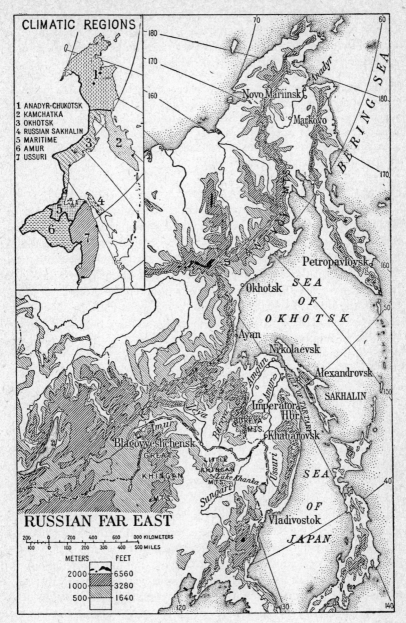

CLIMATIC REGIONS

1 ANADYR-CHUKOTSK
2 KAMCHATKA
3 OKHOTSK
4 RUSSIAN SAKHALIN
5 MARITIME
6 AMUR
7 USSURI

BERING SEA

Novo Mariinsk

Markovo

Petropavlovsk

SEA
OF
OKHOTSK

Okhotsk

Ayan

Nikolaevsk

Alexandrovsk

SAKHALIN

Imperators
Hbr
Khabarovsk

BUREYA
MTS.

Blagoveshchensk

GREAT

KHINGAN

LITTLE
KHINGAN
MTS.

Lake Khanka

MTS.

Sungari

Ussuri

SEA

OF

JAPAN

Vladivostok

RUSSIAN FAR EAST

200   0   200   400   600   800 KILOMETERS
100   100   200   300   400   500 MILES

METERS   FEET
2000   6560
1000   3280
500   1640

*Courtesy of the "Geographical Review," published by the American Geographical
Society of New York.*

The principal though not the sole incentive for this Russian push into Siberia was the desire to impose upon the natives the fur tribute, or *iasak*. In theory at least, Siberia became a colonial enterprise controlled for this purpose by the Muscovite state.

The local administration, military in character, sought alliance with the native upper classes as a guarantee of security and regular delivery of the fur tribute. For utilitarian reasons the Muscovite government adopted a benevolent attitude toward the natives, and tried to prevent their enslavement and compulsory baptism, but it had considerable difficulty in carrying out its policies through its local agents.[1]

FIRST CONTACTS WITH CHINA

The establishment by 1650 of Russian towns and religious outposts in Trans-Baikalia (the region between Lake Baikal and Manchuria) led inevitably to contacts with China—contacts both in arms and in diplomacy. The Cossacks appear to have entered the basin of the Amur and to have reached the river itself near the present site of Blagovestchensk in 1643. Five years later other Cossacks discovered the Shilka, a tributary of the upper Amur, directly east of Lake Baikal. In 1649 a vigorous Cossack, Khabarov by name, sailed down the Amur from Shilka, slaughtering natives, plundering their villages, seizing crops, and exacting tribute from those who surrendered to his arms. On the upper Amur, Albazin was founded as a frontier fort, while on the lower Amur, at its junction with the Ussuri, the Cossacks defeated the first Manchu-Chinese force sent against them.

RUSSO-CHINESE DIPLOMACY

This forcible occupation of the Amur Valley had been preceded and was to be followed by a long series of Russian diplomatic, semi-diplomatic, and religious missions to Peking. The earlier of these missions had all failed to obtain an audience with the Chinese emperor since they presented no tribute. One envoy did however carry back a letter from the Chinese court, but it is recorded that this letter "was of no use to anybody because nobody in Moscow could read it."[2] The Chinese court welcomed neither the envoys nor the depredations of their countrymen in the Amur Valley. So it was that toward the close of the seventeenth century while diplomacy got nowhere at Peking the

[1] George V. Lantzeff, "Beginnings of the Siberian Colonial Administration," *Pacific Historical Review*, IX (1940), 47-52.

[2] Gaston Cahen, *Some Early Russo-Chinese Relations*, translated and edited by W. Sheldon Ridge (Shanghai, 1914), 1.

For Russo-Chinese relations, 1602-1676, see the monumental work by John F. Braddeley, *Russia, Mongolia, China. . . .* (2 vols., London, 1919).

two powers pursued fruitlessly on the undefined boundary in the Amur Basin an irregular and dangerous border warfare. Actually neither China nor Russia desired war. Peace was the objective of both powers, but the ends for which peace was sought were not identical. Russia sought commerce: the exchange of furs for Chinese products. China sought, not commerce, but the stabilization of her traditional suzerainty over the principal peoples (Turguts, Kalmuks, and Eleuths) forming border or tributary states between herself and Russia. The problem of reaching an understanding was complicated further by Russo-Chinese ignorance of the extent and power of their respective empires, and when the Treaty of Nertchinsk was finally concluded (1689), Latin was chosen as the language of official intercourse, a fact which gave to Jesuit missionaries at Peking strategic posts as indispensable interpreters.

THE TREATY OF NERTCHINSK (1689)

The immediate origins of this famous treaty, the first concluded by China with a Western power, are found in two letters in Latin from the K'ang-hsi emperor of China which reached the tsar in 1685. These letters gave evidence of a conciliatory policy to which Russia responded by the appointment of Theodore Alexievitch Golovin as "High Ambassador Plenipotentiary" to meet the representatives of China and with them to fix the frontier and determine commercial relations. It was not, however, until nearly four years later that the envoys of the two powers met in the summer of 1689 at Nertchinsk, east of Lake Baikal and about 180 miles from the present city of Chita. The Russian negotiators had about 1,000 troops to reinforce their diplomatic arguments; the Chinese had about 10,000, plus a fleet of river boats and artillery. This disparity in military strength was not without effect on the subsequent negotiations. The treaty which resulted was for China a diplomatic triumph.

The treaty provided: 1) that the boundary should be at the Argun River, the Gorbitsa (a left bank tributary of the Shilka), and along the watershed between the basins of the Lena and the Amur to the sea;[3] 2) Albazin was to be destroyed and its garrisons withdrawn; 3) deserters were to be subjected to extradition; 4) commercial relations were to be maintained by the merchants of both countries provided with official letters.

By this agreement the Manchu dynasty achieved a settlement of its

---

[3] Actually the frontier was fixed specifically only at one point. "There was no clear delimitation of any part of the region to the northeast of Nertchinsk, for the simple reason that it was quite unknown. . . . The country to the southwest of Nertchinsk, Trans-Baikalia and all the remainder of Siberia were left without delimitation of frontiers." Cahen, *Russo-Chinese Relations,* 16.

northern frontier that was to prevail with little change for more than a century. For the time being the Russians were excluded from the Amur Valley, but they had won an important concession in the right of their merchants to enter China for trade.

THE TREATY OF KIAKHTA (1727)

For many years following the Nertchinsk settlement the Amur Valley played only an insignificant role in the affairs of Russia and China. Russian ambitions were centered for the time in Europe. China was engaged in the conquest of border states such as Mongolia, Turkestan, Tibet, and Indo-China. Meanwhile the center of such Russo-Chinese trade as there was shifted to Kiakhta, from which a subsequent treaty settlement (1727) takes its name.[4]

The Treaty of Kiakhta defined the frontier westward from the Gorbitsa; future deserters were to be extradited and punished; a Russian commercial caravan of 200 men was to be admitted every three years to Peking; several frontier posts were designated where commodities might be exchanged; ambassadors and diplomatic mail were to be received with dispatch; Russia might maintain in Peking a church, a priest, three curates, and five language students. These modifications were important in themselves but in addition they signified a change in Russian policy: the decline of Russian state commerce and the triumph of the private traders.

In the broadest historical sense these early years of limited Russo-Chinese intercourse were full of deep significance for later generations. From them China had learned virtually nothing of Russia, whereas Russia used every returning embassy and caravan as the carriers of ideas as well as commodities.

In spite of hindrances and obstacles placed in the way by the Chinese, not one of the twelve caravans, of the Russian commercial agents [in the period 1689-1730], or of the four diplomatic missions failed to bring back precise information on the economic and military condition of China. . . . Such information was not wasted: the nineteenth century, if not the eighteenth, knew how to use it.[5]

---

[4] See William Coxe, *Account of the . . . Commerce between Russia and China* (London, 1780), 211-215.

Russo-Chinese commerce in these early years was one of barter. Russian exports included: furs (sea-otter, beaver, fox, sable, ermine, gray squirrel), and cloth of various types. Russian imports from China included: raw silk (smuggled into Kiakhta), raw and manufactured cotton, teas ("much superior in flavor and quality to those which are sent to Europe from Canton"), and porcelain "of all sorts."

[5] Cahen, *Russo-Chinese Relations*, 127.

THE NEW IMPORTANCE OF THE AMUR

There were few developments of importance in Russo-Chinese relations from 1727 until well into the nineteenth century. Yet these intervening years did forecast the renewal of rivalry on the Amur. By 1795, when the Ch'ien-lung emperor abdicated, the Ch'ing (Manchu) empire, having reached the height of its power, was already suffering from internal decline. The Pai-lien Rebellion, suppressed in 1804, was the first major evidence that the dynasty was losing the Mandate of Heaven. Later rebellions were to cripple its power permanently, coinciding as they did with the impact on China of the Western maritime powers (Opium War, 1840; *Arrow* War, 1857). It is notable, then, that in these same years (1847-1860) China was called upon to meet new problems on her northern frontier. Russia had determined on a territorial advance, which could be made only at the expense of China.

THE CH'ING POLICY IN MANCHURIA

Although China had won a diplomatic victory at Nertchinsk (1689), she failed in the years following to consolidate her hold on the Amur country. While the Manchus themselves tended to migrate southward to China, Chinese migration to Manchuria was prohibited. Therefore the Amur Valley persisted as an uncolonized, undeveloped, and unprotected frontier.

The first tangible signs of renewed Russian interest in this area appeared in 1828, when the tsar ordered surveys of the region. However, it was not until 1847 that Russia undertook seriously the task of advancing the frontier beyond the unsurveyed line of the Treaty of Nertchinsk. It was in this year that the tsar appointed Count Nicholas Muraviev governor-general of eastern Siberia, with instructions to pursue special investigations of the Amur question. This renewed Russian interest in the Far East had been prompted by a number of developments. The British as a result of the Opium War had opened a new maritime door to the China trade, eclipsing the Russian caravans at Kiakhta. The activities of the British navy in the Pacific spurred the Russians with the desire to establish ports on their own Pacific coastline. Both eastern and western Siberia had grown in importance to Russia, particularly after 1825. The growth of settlements in Kamchatka, the expanding activities of the Russian-American Company in Alaska, and the development of the whaling industry in the Bering Sea—all these prophesied the growing importance of Russia's Pacific and China frontier. It is hardly surprising therefore that between 1847 and 1854 Russia reached a number of decisions which were to launch her on the new policy of the "Easterners" under the leadership of Muraviev.[6]

THE POLICY OF MURAVIEV

The new governor-general applied his policy with promptness and decision. His first agents sailed down the Amur in 1848. This river, it will be recalled, was wholly within the territory of the Manchu empire according to the terms of the Treaty of Nertchinsk. The following year Russian officers explored the coasts of the Sea of Okhotsk as far south as the mouth of the Amur. This was a preliminary survey in Russia's general plan to prevent occupation of the area by potential enemies: Great Britain and France. Nikolaievsk was founded at the mouth of the Amur (August, 1850). These were the first major violations of the Nertchinsk Treaty. They were to be followed by a vigorous pursuit of the new policy. Russian posts were founded at De Castries, Mariinsk, and Imperatorski Bay in 1852. Sakhalin Island was annexed in 1853.[7]

Up to this point China paid little attention to the Russian advance and seems to have ignored the deep significance of the new aggressive policy. Chinese border authorities were negligent and most of the Manchurian troops had been withdrawn by 1853 to meet in China Proper the threatening northward march of the T'ai-p'ing rebels. Even had this not been the case China's position in 1853 did not appear on the surface at least to be threatened seriously on the northern frontier. Officially the policy of the Russian government was still one of respect for the terms of the Nertchinsk Treaty. Nevertheless, by 1854 Muraviev had received the tsar's mandate to settle directly with Peking all questions concerning the eastern boundary. He was thus freed from all interference by the "Westerners" in the Russian ministry of foreign affairs. He was free to pursue his own grandiose scheme of making Russia a power on the Pacific, and, if need be, "the protector of China."[8]

The Crimean War had already broken out in Europe. In the Pacific the two great commercial pioneers, the Hudson's Bay Company and the Russian-American Company, had agreed to remain neutral, but this did not deter Great Britain and France from attacking Russia's Pacific base

[6] T. C. Lin, "The Amur Frontier Question between China and Russia, 1850-1860," *Pacific Historical Review*, III (1934), 1-27.

[7] Russian interest in Sakhalin was evident as early as 1806-07, following still earlier attempts to open trade with Japan. W. G. Aston, "Russian Descents in Saghalien and Itorup in the Years 1806 and 1807," *Trans. of the Asiatic Society of Japan*, I (1882), 78-86.

[8] Anatole G. Mazour, "Dimitry Zavalishin: Dreamer of a Russian-American Empire," *Pacific Historical Review*, V (1936), 26-37.

at Petropavlovsk. The real value of the Amur as a road for the transport of Russian supplies to the Pacific could no longer be denied even by the "Westerners." As a result, in April, 1854, Muraviev, on the pretext of military necessity, the defense of Kamchatka, sent his first major expedition down the entire length of the Amur. No attempt was made by the Chinese frontier forces to question or stop the Russians. More troops and munitions of war descended the river the following year, and the tsar informed Muraviev that the left bank of the Amur was now indispensable to Russia.

Now that Russia had occupied the river with her transports, contacts with the border Chinese authorities were inevitable. The first direct Russo-Chinese negotiations at Mariinsk in 1855 proved abortive. In 1856 Muraviev ordered his third major expedition down the river. The Chinese authorities protested, but the Russians replied with the stationing of garrisons at strategic points on the left bank of the river.

THE MISSION OF COUNT PUTIATIN

Meanwhile Russia was preparing a double diplomatic assault on Peking. While Muraviev was yet on the Amur, Count Putiatin was sent to Peking to secure for Russia whatever commercial concessions should fall to England and France as a result of the *Arrow* War. He was also to seek a settlement of the Amur question. Putiatin was refused entry at Kiakhta but reached the mouth of the Pei-ho in August, 1857, by way of the Amur and the ocean route. To his overtures, the Chinese replied tersely that Russia should observe her treaty obligations. Blocked in his mission, Putiatin joined the British, French, and American envoys at Canton, and proceeded north again with them to Tientsin, where in June, 1858, the four commercial treaties were signed. His influence on the Amur question was negligible. Not so that of Muraviev.

During the progress of the *Arrow* War, Muraviev had not been idle in the north. Early in May, 1858, he succeeded in bringing the Chinese into conference at Aigun, where he demanded virtually the boundary which today divides Manchuria from Siberia. China's protests received but scant consideration. On May 28, 1858, the Aigun Treaty was signed. In it Russia acquired all the territory on the left or northern bank of the Amur, while the land lying between the Ussuri River and the sea (the present Maritime Province) was to be held in joint control by both powers.[9] The Aigun agreement was thus signed two weeks be-

[9] The Chinese text of the treaty refers, in the case of territory to be held in common, only to the right bank of the Amur from the Ussuri to the sea, and not to the entire Maritime Province as is implied in the Russian text. T. C. Lin, "The Amur Frontier Question . . . ," 21.

fore Putiatin signed the Russian Treaty of Tientsin, and without his knowledge.

CHINA REJECTS THE AIGUN SETTLEMENT

Although China was in no position to dispute successfully Muraviev's advance, she refused to accept the Aigun Treaty in its entirety. China was prepared to cede those territories north of the Amur not already occupied by Chinese subjects, but she was not prepared to dispose of the Ussuri country. The local Kirin provincial authorities were accordingly commanded to prevent Russian encroachments. But this gesture was of no effect. When these officials failed, Peking might, and in fact did, order punishment of these helpless underlings. She might declare null and void the joint-control clause of the Aigun Treaty. Actually, China's impotence and Russian strength remained unchanged. The vigor of Muraviev's invasion may be judged when it is recalled that by 1859 there were more than fifty Russian settlements on the left bank of the Amur. Russia had taken the Amur by force, and by force she proposed to hold it.

THE ANNEXATION OF THE MARITIME PROVINCE

Having thus pushed her boundary to the river, and having commenced penetration of the Trans-Ussuri region, Russia now directed her final attack through diplomacy in Peking. Early in the summer of 1859 General Ignatiev had reached the Chinese capital to exchange the ratified copies of the Russian Treaty of Tientsin. In addition it was his purpose to cultivate Russian interests in other ways. In his first diplomatic overtures he sought additional commercial privileges and the outright cession to Russia of the Trans-Ussuri lands. These requests were promptly refused, and the envoy was informed that China did not regard the Aigun settlement as binding. Here matters might have rested until such time as Muraviev was again prepared to use force. But, happily for Russia, other powers came unwittingly to her aid. By October, 1860, the British and French Allies, having broken Chinese resistance between Peking and Taku, had occupied the capital. The Manchu Dynasty appeared to be on the verge of total collapse. The T'ai-p'ing rebels were laying waste the central coast; the capital lay at the mercy of British and French arms; the Summer Palace had already been looted and burned, while a cowardly emperor and his renegade court had fled to the mountains of Jehol. Baffled and perplexed by the misfortunes that pursued the dynasty, Prince Kung, brother of the emperor, remained in Peking to seek a settlement with the victorious "barbarians."

Here was Russia's opportunity. Ignatiev played on the fears of the frightened Prince. He would intervene, so he said, with the Allies, and thus save Peking itself from the destruction that had already consumed the Summer Palace. For these services to China he would ask only an insignificant return: the rectification of a frontier, the cession of the Trans-Ussuri country. Prince Kung was not deceived, but assuredly he was defeated. On November 14, 1860, he signed with Ignatiev the convention which among other things ceded the Manchurian coastline to Russia.[10]

In large part Muraviev's dream had now been realized. By the close of 1860, Russian policy in China had enjoyed a success unparalleled by that of any other state. Like the United States, she had not participated as a belligerent in the *Arrow* War, yet she was to reap all the advantages, commercial and diplomatic, won by England and France in the Treaties of Tientsin. In the north, through a policy of force, but without declaration of war, she had opened the Mongolian frontier to her traders and had advanced her boundary along the course of the Amur and far south along the Pacific coast to the northern tip of Korea. By conquest and colonization, yet without war in the legal sense, she had deprived the Manchu empire of 350,000 square miles of territory. Manchuria was cut off from the sea on the east, whereas Russia possessed a new and broad road to the ocean. Before Ignatiev signed the convention which transferred the Maritime Province, Russia proceeded to consolidate her new lands. At the southern extremity of the new coastal territory Muratiev selected the harbor and site of Russia's future fortress on the Pacific. The founding of Vladivostok, "dominion of the East," was a fitting culmination to the work, aggressive, unscrupulous, but successful, of one of Russia's greatest empire-builders.[11]

---

[10] The treaty also provided for a settlement of the far western frontier and for a resumption of the right of Russian merchants to proceed from Kiakhta to Peking. Other trading posts would be established to the west. A convention governing the overland trade was concluded March 4, 1862.

This relation between Prince Kung and Ignatiev in 1860 was the first of a series of similar "deals" in which China, hard pressed by some of the great powers, was to appeal to Russia for protection. The second instance occurred immediately following the Sino-Japanese War, 1895, when China appealed to Russia and other powers against Japan; the third occurred in 1923, when Sun Yat-sen made his agreement with Soviet envoy Joffee. In each case Russia exacted a high price for her support. In each case China was, or believed herself to be, in extreme danger. T. F. Tsiang, "China, England and Russia in 1860," *The Cambridge Historical Journal*, III, No. 1 (1929), 115-121.

[11] G. F. Wright, *Asiatic Russia* (2 vols., New York, 1902), I, 214.

CHAPTER 9

JAPAN: THE COLLAPSE OF THE POLICY OF EXCLUSION, 1800-1865

JAPAN experienced during the nineteenth century a revolution, the consequences of which it would be difficult to exaggerate. There are two major effects of this revolution which are of importance to this narrative. As a result of the first (the subject of this chapter), the 250-year-old policy of exclusion and seclusion was ended and replaced by a broad policy of intercourse with the West. As a result of the second (treated in Chapter 10), dual government, the shogunate, and the system of feudalism were replaced by a centralized administration, carried on in the name of the Mikado, and clothed in 1889 with a constitution deriving its form, if not its spirit, from Western political models.

The collapse, in the middle of the nineteenth century, of Japan's policy of exclusion was a result not only of external pressures exerted by foreign states, but also of revolutionary social pressures within Japan itself. To put the matter another way, when in 1854 the Japanese signed a treaty with the United States, they were not reacting solely to American naval power. On the contrary, they were reacting also, and perhaps primarily, to the fundamental needs of their own society. For nearly 250 years the Tokugawa shoguns had sought to maintain a planned and fixed social economy. Unfortunately for the Tokugawas, their society did change even if their plans did not. Thus, by mid-nineteenth century, Japan was living under a regime which was no longer adequate to meet new conditions. A new national policy, both internal and external, was imminent. The ways in which Japan had outgrown her social-political-economic structure may be understood best by reviewing some aspects of her government and society during the Tokugawa period (1603-1868).

POLITICAL OBJECTIVES OF THE TOKUGAWA SHOGUNS

After the Tokugawa Bakufu had enforced (1638) the policy of exclusion and seclusion, it set about to freeze society in the then existing pattern of feudal-military-dictatorship. This was the system which had bestowed power on the Tokugawas, and therefore the one which that family judged most likely to preserve power in its hands. To this end the Bakufu set up various measures for the control of the *daimyo*. In addition it sought to crystallize the institutions and the social classes of feudal society. All economic and social class distinctions were to be observed rigidly. The privileged few, the military, would retain the privilege of being supported by the commoners, the peasants. The peasants in turn, the great bulk of society, would continue to enjoy the privilege of supporting their legal and social betters, the military. Society, so ran the theory, would thus preserve a perfect contentment and a perfect peace, since every man would be in his proper station and would be expected to stay there. Indeed for more than two centuries the Tokugawas did preserve this legal framework of society. To this degree they were successful. They failed, however, to note that no government is likely to survive which seeks merely to maintain society unchanged.

THE PHILOSOPHY OF CONTENTMENT

It should be noted that even from the earliest Tokugawa times there were flagrant evils within the structure of the feudal society. For example, the peasants, particularly those under the Tokugawas and their vassals, were "slaves" in both body and mind to the ruling military classes. The latter sought "to paralyze the mind of the lower class permanently." They set up laws which stripped the farmers, merchants, and artisans of their natural resources, and taught them, as a matter of ethics, to be contented with their miserable lot.[1] The shogunate sought to impress these ideas on the people not so much by "rules of law" as by "rules of ethics" made public through the medium of admonitory placards advising families to live harmoniously, servants to be faithful, masters just, while everybody was to be frugal, industrious, virtuous, and above all was to keep in his proper station in life.

THE NATIONAL POLICY

This philosophy of a static, crystallized, and contented society appeared natural and attainable to the early Tokugawa shoguns. For a number of reasons the Bakufu felt sure of itself. In the first place Iyeyasu greatly strengthened his position when he cut loose from Kyoto and the Imperial Court to rule Japan from Yedo, the center of his military power, and destined to become the greatest city of the empire. It was here the Tokugawas built their great castle; here they issued the

---

[1] Yosaburō Takekoshi, *The Economic Aspects of the History of Civilization of Japan* (3 vols., New York, 1930), I, 526.

regulations which deprived the Imperial Court of every administrative function, leaving to it only its "ancient dignity" and its empty ceremonials. From Yedo the Tokugawas issued the decrees by which they held in subjection their vassals and the great *tozama* barons. From Yedo, in a word, they ruled Japan by what was "in essence martial law."

In the second place, the policy of exclusion and seclusion adopted in 1638 appeared as an effective safeguard against change. By it, an alien religion—Christianity—had been suppressed; foreign aggression had been forestalled; and a curb placed on domestic agrarian revolts with which many native Christian converts had been associated. Thus by closing Japan's doors, the Tokugawa shoguns hoped to preserve their peculiar Japanese society. They did not foresee that they would have to do this at a time when their society would be shifting from an agricultural to a mercantile economy.[2]

PEACE PROBLEMS OF A MILITARY STATE

When the Tokugawa shoguns set themselves this task of perpetuating a military-feudal society in times of unbroken peace, they assumed a burden of no mean proportions. They were indeed proposing to maintain a large and unproductive military caste (the *samurai*) at the expense of the underprivileged civilian. Obviously this problem was all the more difficult once the nation had cut itself off from all foreign sources of supply.

This difficulty and others confronting the old feudal order did not become apparent immediately—not indeed until the seventeenth century was well advanced, by which time revolutionary forces were already undermining the whole structure. To begin with, in conditions of unbroken peace, there were of course greater opportunity and greater need for the development of a mercantile class. Furthermore, it was not long until this class was in a position to exploit the military class, the nobility.[3]

---

[2] For a survey of Japanese commerce prior to and during the Tokugawa era see Yetaro Kinosita, *The Past and Present of Japanese Commerce* (New York, 1902). The decline of the agricultural economy is treated by Matsuyo Takizawa, *The Penetration of Money Economy in Japan* (New York, 1927).

[3] The student may well wonder how a group, the mercantile class, that had relatively limited legal rights and no military power could reach a point where it was able to exploit the military classes. Two considerations appear to be of basic importance.

The first of these was the development of Yedo as a large city which had to be supplied in part by imported food and which demanded a large supply of manufactured luxuries. This forced the spread of a money economy and made the merchants absolutely necessary. The development of Yedo as a large city and as a great consuming center was brought about by the rule that the families of the *daimyos* must reside there. Had the *daimyos* remained in their rural hamlets, their consumptive habits, as well as those of their retainers, would have developed less rapidly, and the spread of a money economy

Nobility in turn sought by heavier taxation to shift its increasing burden
of debt to the peasant. Under these new peacetime pressures the old
agricultural economy began gradually to give way to a new mercantile
economy in which economic power passed into the hands of the rice
brokers of the rising cities. These men had no predilections in favor of
a military feudal state once that system ceased to serve their interests.
In fact they were already creating not only a new society of business but
also one of culture.

THE CULTURE OF GENROKU

Early in the Tokugawa period, these economic and social changes
which were already well under way were reflected in the cultural life
of Genroku, the era-name applied to the years 1688-1703. By this time
the merchant-commoners had attained a position of real economic importance. The *samurai* retained their dignity, but the commoners—the
merchants, traders, rice-brokers, and bankers—"had most of the money
and most of the fun." [4] Genroku, indeed, mirrored the new and rising
money-power of the townsmen. Government edicts, which continued
to oppress the peasants, used the softer tones of "advice" when addressed
to the merchants. The Bakufu continued to preach frugal simplicity,
all the while spending its money lavishly and setting the pace in extravagance which in reality only the wealthy commoners could afford.
These latter centered their pleasures in the new culture of *ukiyo* (floating world)—a world of new bourgeoisie who spent their fortunes in
theaters and restaurants, in public bath-houses and luxurious brothels.
It was this life which produced a new popular and plebeian literature, the
ukiyo-sōshi, and a new popular pictorial art, *ukiyoe,* depicting the lives
and pleasures of the newly rich commoners. All this was new and vital,
even if rather wicked, and it contrasted strangely with the formal, empty
ritualism that had overtaken the culture of the civilian and the military
aristocracy—the *No* drama, the poetry contests, the flower arrangement
(*ikebana*), and the tea ceremony (*cha-no-yu*). The most despised of
all commoners in the feudal order of things, the merchant, was acquiring his own peculiar culture, and the ability to pay for it.

---

and the rise of a class to cater to these expensive consumptive habits would have been
much slower.

In the second place, the upper, that is, the military classes, became dependent on the
merchants because of these increased consumptive habits. Having acquired a taste for ease
and luxury and being inclined to compete with each other in their manner of living, the
nobility was willing to mortgage its future to the merchants in order to maintain its expensive consumptive habits. The military classes did not liquidate the merchants because
without them the necessary food and luxuries would not have been forthcoming.

[4] G. B. Sansom, *Japan: A Short Cultural History* (London, 1932), 463.

THE INTELLECTUAL ATTACK ON FEUDALISM

It was not alone in the lives of the rich commoners that feudalism had ceased to be useful. Many intellectuals of eighteenth-century Japan lived in a world of changing ideas, some of them quite foreign to the planned feudal society of the Tokugawa Bakufu. For instance, Bushido in the hands of peace-time philosophers was no longer a customary code for warriors but rather a system of practical ethics "striving to meet the needs of a peaceful society." The orthodox Confucian teaching, promoted by the early Tokugawas in a futile effort to prevent free inquiry, declined under the influence of Yamazaki Anzai (1618-1682) and his followers. In its place there appeared the beginnings of an anti-Chinese school of thought which turned to Japan's own ancient literature, revived the almost-forgotten indigenous cult of Shinto, of which the neglected emperor was the visible deity, and thus set afoot the idea that the shogun was at best a mere delegate of the throne, and at worst, in the eyes of his enemies, the *tozama* lords, a usurper.

THE ECONOMIC ATTACK ON FEUDALISM

This intellectual turmoil of Tokugawa times may be traced back to the failure of the Bakufu to meet the economic problem of food supply. This problem in turn could not be solved so long as the Tokugawas refused, as they did, to alter the social institutions and barriers of their feudal society. For a number of reasons, the country after 1725 was no longer able to support a general rise in the standard of living. The peasant, whose lot was dreadful even in the best of times, was rendered desperate by a shrinking income and by a rising standard of living enjoyed by all classes save his own. The Bakufu itself was by no means blind to the fact that something was wrong. Its "brain-trust" of Confucian scholars gave the closest attention to economic problems, but most of these men failed to see "that the wealth of Japan was adequate neither in amount nor in distribution to the needs of her society." Landlordism and tenant penury, famine and pestilence, infanticide and abortion, the kidnapping and buying of city children to avoid the expense of raising them for labor on the farms—these were the commonplace symptoms of Japan's malady.[5]

In the cities, despite gaiety and extravagance, signs of trouble were evident. The wealth of the merchants was a product of the exploitation

---

[5] The lot of the peasants under the *tozama* lords was on the whole much less severe. See Hugh Borton, "Peasant Uprisings in Japan of the Tokugawa Period," *Transactions of the Asiatic Soc. of Japan,* 2nd series, XV, No. 16 (1938), 1-258.

and the impoverishment of other classes. By the eighteenth century this impoverishment had reached deep into the purses of the military classes. The income of *daimyo* and *samurai* was measured in rice. But most of the military men lived a good part of the year in cities where they needed money which could only be secured by selling rice on terms fixed by the rice-brokers, bankers, and merchants. In fact the time had come when the commoner could buy not only the noble's rice, but his title as well. The old class distinctions were becoming blurred —farmers deserted their farms for the city; wealthy merchants became landlords; bankers were adopted by purchase into *samurai* families, while *samurai* surrendered their honor and position to seek wealth as commoners.[6] Against all these changes and calamities in its planned society, the edicts of the Bakufu had been in vain. As a consequence, when Japan entered upon the nineteenth century neither her government nor her social-economic system was adequate to the nation's needs. A revolution had long been in the making, and the shogunate had long since lost its ability either to control or to lead.[7]

THE WORLD BEYOND JAPAN

It will be well perhaps to recall that while Japan was living within the exclusive walls of the Tokugawa dictatorship, Western states were developing a new society, new theories of government, new conceptions of national wealth, and new colonial empires. Between 1638 and 1854, the period of Japanese seclusion, Europe witnessed the Glorious Revolution in England, the perfecting of the absolute monarchy in France, the victory of England over France in the great colonial wars in America and India, the revolt of the thirteen English colonies, the French Revolution, the wars of Napoleon, and the beginnings of the Industrial Revolution with its emphasis on economic doctrines of *laissez faire*. By the first half of the nineteenth century, popular middle-class nationalism had triumphed over the crumbling edifice erected by Metternich. Both Europe and the United States (the latter had become a power on the Pacific with the acquisition of the Oregon Territory in 1846) were prepared for a new era of commercial and industrial expansion. Western commerce was already invading every area of the globe. It certainly

---

[6] By 1850 a regular though illegal charge had been fixed for the entry of a commoner into a *samurai* family. Sansom, *Japan*, 513-14.

[7] The shogunate's principal claim to primacy in the early nineteenth century was that it set the pace in an age of debauchery. Shogun "Iyenari [1818] kept sixteen concubines and twenty-four mistresses, who gave him fifty-nine children and made the shogun's palace a brothel." Takekoshi, *The Economic Aspects*, III, 169.

could not by-pass Japan for long. Already in 1840-42, England had fought successfully her first commercial war in China.

Japan's knowledge of this changing and threatening Western world was imperfect, and colored by lack of perspective. Yet the shogunate was by no means in complete ignorance of external affairs. Some considerable body of information had entered Japan through the medium of the Dutch at Nagasaki.

EARLY NINETEENTH CENTURY ATTEMPTS TO OPEN JAPAN

Late in the eighteenth and early in the nineteenth centuries a number of Western powers made half hearted efforts to open Japan to trade. All of these attempts failed, for prior to 1850 no Western power was of a mind to force the issue with Japan. Yet by 1850 the United States was becoming as interested in Japan, as it had previously, since 1842, been interested in China. Shipwrecked American seamen from the North Pacific whaling fleet cast upon Japanese shores were often treated as criminals. Some died from exposure; others were required to trample and spit on the Cross; all were exhibited in cages to the public gaze. Furthermore America's expanding trans-Pacific trade from San Francisco to China passed through Japanese waters. Japanese ports were needed as coaling stations for the new trans-Pacific steamships. American business was already anticipating the opening of a lucrative trade with Japan.[8]

---

[8] Such knowledge as the West had of Japan during the first half of the nineteenth century, it had learned from two principal sources: 1) the writings of men associated with the early Dutch factory at Deshima, such as Engelbert Kaempfer's, *History of Japan,* first published in 1727; the lectures of Carl Peter Thunberg at Upsala (1784); and the published notes of Isaac Titsingh, director of the Dutch factory, 1779-1784; 2) the writings of a few nineteenth-century contemporaries who resided in Japan such as: Philip Franz von Siebold, physician to the Dutch factory, 1823-29; Captain Wassili Golownin, Russian officer held prisoner by the Japanese, 1811-13; and the Dutch agents G. F. Meijlan, Hendrik Doeff, J. F. van Overmeer Fischer, and J. H. Levyssohn. Many early nineteenth-century general works on Japan were based on the writings of these men.

Knowledge of Japan was increased too by the number of foreign ships touching Japan's forbidden shores between 1790 and 1850. During 1797-1809 the Dutch, involved in the Napoleonic Wars, chartered (eight American, one Danish, one Bremen) neutral vessels for the annual voyage from Batavia to Nagasaki. Private attempts to trade with Japan were made by Americans in 1800, 1803, 1807, 1837; by Englishmen in 1803, 1818, 1823. A Russian diplomatic mission failed at Nagasaki, 1804. A request by William II of Holland that Japan open her doors was declined, 1844. The American Commodore James Biddle was informed in 1846 that the exclusion policy would not be abandoned. Shunzo Sakamaki, "Western Concepts of Japan and the Japanese, 1800-1854," *Pacific Historical Review,* VI (1937), 1-14.

PERRY'S EXPEDITION—A "ROMANTIC NOTION"

Influenced by these various motives, by petitions to Congress, and by what appeared to be an influential public interest, President Fillmore in 1852 selected Commodore Matthew C. Perry, a distinguished naval officer and a brother of the hero of Lake Erie fame, to command a naval expedition designed to open Japan to trade.

Public reaction to the mission was divided. While optimists hoped for its success, the pessimists referred to it as a "romantic notion" and "a matter of ridicule abroad and at home." [9] This was not surprising since both in the United States and Europe inadequate knowledge had produced strange and varied opinions of Japan and the Japanese. Estimates of Japan's area ranged from 9,000 to 266,000 square miles; of population density, from 184 to 4,000 per square mile; and of total population, from 15,000,000 to 50,000,000. Yedo alone was said to have a population of at least 10,000,000. The Japanese of the "lower orders" were said to have a yellow complexion, "like the color of cheese." [10]

With a fleet of four ships, Perry entered Yedo (later Tokyo) Bay and anchored off Uraga, July 8, 1853. His arrival did not take the Japanese by surprise, for they had been warned of his coming by the Dutch, yet the appearance of the American squadron precipitated one of the great crises of Japanese history. While unaware of the real nature of this crisis, Perry proceeded to the task before him with firmness, dignity, and tact. He impressed the officials of the shogun's government with the power of his fleet—it contained the first steamers seen in Japanese waters—and with his own good will. He refused to retire to Nagasaki or to deal through the Dutch there. He demanded treatment suitable to the representative of a great power. In this behavior he was justified when, in opposition to Japanese law, President Fillmore's letter was received by two high officials of the shogun's court. Then Perry sailed away, but not without informing the Japanese that he would return the next year with a more powerful fleet to receive their answer. [11]

THE SHOGUN'S DILEMMA

Perry's visit confronted the shogun with the most serious decision ever faced by the Tokugawas. An Iyeyasu would have decided the matter

---

[9] Ignazo Nitobe, *The Intercourse Between the United States and Japan* (Baltimore, 1891), 43-44.

[10] Shunzo Sakamaki, "Western Concepts of Japan and the Japanese, 1800-1854," 1-14.

[11] Payson J. Treat, *Diplomatic Relations Between the United States and Japan* (2 vols., Stanford University, 1932), I, 11.

on his own responsibility. Now, however, the shogunate had come on sorry days, and, faced with an issue of unparalleled importance, it took the unprecedented step of seeking the advice not only of the *daimyo* but also of the emperor. The preponderant opinion favored repelling the foreigner, but some few recognized the futility of armed opposition.

Indeed, Perry was already hastening his return, spurred by rumors that French and Russian squadrons planned to visit Japan. This time with an augmented fleet of seven vessels he entered Yedo Bay, February 13, 1854. Fortunately, the far-sighted minority at the shogun's court had prevailed, and so at Yokohama the negotiation of a treaty proceeded amid social activities of the utmost gaiety. Gifts presented to the Japanese by the United States included a miniature railway, telegraph, books, and a variety of liquors. All these delighted the Japanese no end.[12]

NATURE AND IMPORTANCE OF PERRY TREATY

The treaty signed by Perry and the representatives of the shogun, March 31, 1854, viewed superficially, was in many respects a disappointment. In reality it was little more than a convention covering shipwreck and supply. It provided: for peace; for the opening of two ports for supplies (Shimoda immediately and Hakodate a year later); for good treatment for shipwrecked American sailors; for a limited trade under Japanese regulations; for supplies for American ships; and for the most-favored-nation principle. Plainly, Perry had not secured a full commercial treaty. Yet the treaty he did secure was a remarkable achievement viewed in the light of more than two centuries of Japanese exclusion. His success was due to many factors: his own "firmness, sagacity, tact, dignity, patience and determination"; the strength of his great naval squadron, the like of which the Japanese had never before seen;[13] and his declaration that more ships would be sent if the just de-

---

[12] See Francis L. Hawks, compiler, *Narrative of the Expedition of an American Squadron to the China Seas and Japan, Performed in the Years 1852, and 1854, under the Command of Commodore M. C. Perry, United States Navy* (published by order of Congress, A. O. P. Nicholson, Washington, 1856), 375. See also S. Wells Williams, "A Journal of the Perry Expedition to Japan (1853-1854)," *Transactions of the Asiatic Soc. of Japan*, XXXVII (1910).

Young officers in Perry's fleet saw Japan as a country of beautiful landscapes, of annoying and ridiculous spies, of Japanese officials who were "old fogies," and of "pretty women" of little virtue, because they indulged in mixed bathing "without rag enough to cover a thumb nail." *With Perry in Japan: The Diary of Edward Yorke McCauley,* edited by Allan B. Cole (Princeton, 1942).

[13] The effect of the fleet on the Japanese was not lessened by the fact that Perry's instruction forbade resort to force save in self-defense or to avenge an insult.

A number of incidents, trivial in themselves, served none the less to elevate the Americans in the eyes of the Japanese. When for instance the Japanese noticed some Chinese

mands of the United States were not met. Reinforcing these attributes of Perry, the diplomat, were others over which he had no control, but without which he might well have failed: the recent frequent appearance of Russian vessels in Japanese waters; Japanese knowledge of China's defeat in 1842; and, above all, those internal developments, described in the first pages of this chapter, which had made Japan ripe for revolution.[14]

Perry's success was one of the most significant events in American history, though it was not so recognized in the United States at the time. Little attention was paid to it in the press, and it was almost ignored by President Pierce in his annual message to Congress, perhaps because it had been the work of a Whig government. Actually Japan's exclusion policy had been ended. The decision which effected this momentous change was made by the shogun's government, but the United States had provided the occasion which forced the decision.[15]

TREATIES WITH OTHER POWERS

Representatives of other powers soon followed Perry to Japan and secured treaties similar though not identical with that of the United States. A British admiral, Sir James Stirling, negotiated a treaty at Nagasaki (October, 1854). The Russian Admiral, Count Putiatin, secured his treaty at Shimoda (February, 1855). Finally the Dutch were released from their commercial confinement at Nagasaki and given a new treaty (January, 1856). The most-favored-nation clause made the provisions of each treaty the common property of the four powers, and expanded somewhat the rights Americans had won in the Perry treaty. These total and enlarged rights held by the four powers in 1856 included: 1) permission to secure supplies at Shimoda, Hakodate, and Nagasaki; 2) permission to trade through Japanese officials and under their regulations at these ports; 3) right of male residence at Nagasaki;

---

deck-hands among Perry's crews, they asked in tones of "contempt and disgust": "Is it possible that you have Chinese among your men?" The Japanese were assured with promptness but with some lack of candor that: "These men are *the servants of our sailors.*" This reply seems to have reinstated the Americans in the good opinion of the Japanese. Bayard Taylor, *India, China, and Japan* (New York, 1855), 434.

[14] Until recently Perry enjoyed more fame in Japan than in the United States. A monument was erected by the Japanese on the shore of Yedo Bay to his memory and his achievement.

[15] Perry and the officers of his expedition were unaware of the real nature of the crisis in domestic Japanese affairs. The success of this first visit was thus attributed solely, though erroneously, to Perry's plans and his ability. A member of Perry's staff thus wrote: "I have reason to know that the final success of the Expedition was owing to no fortunate combination of circumstances, but wholly to the prudent and sagacious plan pre-arranged by its Commander." Taylor, *India, China, and Japan,* 440.

4) permission to appoint consuls at Shimoda and Hakodate; and 5) a limited extraterritorial jurisdiction.[16]

FIRST TREATIES APPROVED BY MIKADO

Three of these treaties (the American, the British, and the Russian) were approved by the emperor in February, 1855. The importance of this was not realized at the time by the foreign powers. The treaties had been negotiated with the shogun's government and they were signed under the title of "tycoon" (great lord). By the foreigners it was assumed that the shogun was the proper authority to control diplomatic affairs. This of course was so; but what the foreigner did not know was the extent to which the authority of the shogun had already been weakened by internal dissension. This explains why the shogunate, when Perry arrived, was unwilling to accept full responsibility for signing a treaty. It had therefore referred the matter for approval to the emperor. Since the shogun's influence with the Imperial Court was still strong, the Imperial approval was given. With this approval the shogun could for a time silence the powerful opposition to the new policy.

The Imperial approval insured general acceptance of the treaties, but the fact that the shogunate almost failed to secure the Throne's favor revealed how the might of the Bakufu had declined. It had not been the habit of the Tokugawas or their predecessors to consider the will of the Throne. They did so now because their old supremacy was little better than a political fiction, because they recognized the power of their feudal enemies, the *tozama* lords, and because there was bitter dissension within the Tokugawa clan itself. Indeed even among those elements who favored signing the treaties, the feeling was strong that no further concessions should be made to the foreigner—no general trade would be permitted and foreign contacts would be held to the bare treaty minimum.[17]

TOWNSEND HARRIS IN JAPAN

Shortly after the Perry treaty was concluded, the American government sent its first consul general to reside at Shimoda. He was Townsend Harris of New York, a merchant familiar with the Far East, and a man of excellent mind and character. Harris travelled by way of

---

[16] For the texts of these various treaties, see G. H. Gubbins, *The Progress of Japan 1853-1871* (Oxford, 1911), 227-265.

[17] See Gubbins, *The Progress of Japan,* ch. iii.

Siam, where he nogotiated a treaty granting extraterritoriality and a conventional tariff. He reached Shimoda on August 21, 1856.

The village of Shimoda, some 60 miles from Yedo, on the southern extremity of the Izu Peninsula southwest of Yedo Bay, was possessed of an exceptionally poor harbor which had been all but ruined by a tidal wave the previous year. The town, shut off from the hinterland by ranges of hills, was remote from the high roads and markets, and, in a word, was peculiarly ill-adapted to the needs of Harris. The Japanese had hoped to isolate the consul, if one came, and the selection of Shimoda was admirable for this purpose. Here Harris was in virtual quarantine not only from the United States but also from Japan. Fourteen months elapsed before he was visited by an American naval vessel, and eighteen months before he received additional instructions from the Department of State. On one occasion he wrote in his journal that for ten months he had not received a letter from the United States; that his supply of Western food was exhausted; and that he had lost so much weight it appeared that a vice-consul had been cut out of him.

The principal objective of the Harris mission was to secure a full commercial treaty. The prospects of success were small. From the moment Harris landed, the Japanese used every device of obstruction and deceit to discourage and defeat him. They asserted that he had no right to land since Japan had not approved his coming. With reluctance they assigned him an old temple as a residence. It was infested with mosquitoes, cockroaches, and large rats. The market sold him roosters that were too tough to eat. Police constantly guarded the temple on the pretext of protecting him. Wherever Harris or his Chinese servants went they were spied upon with the utmost suspicion. Japanese officials lied to him in the most flagrant manner. All this and much more Harris bore with patience until after some months he was able to write in his journal: "The Japanese officials are daily becoming more and more friendly and more open in their communications with me. I hope this will grow and lead to good results by and by." [18] This turn for the better in the relations between Harris and the shogun's officials must be attributed in large part to the patience, firmness, and unfailing honesty of this lonely bachelor American diplomat. He had set for himself a high goal. He proposed to serve the interests of his own

---

[18] Many aspects of Japanese social life, manners, and customs are depicted in the brilliant novel by Gisaburô Jûichiya, *Tôjin O-Kichi* ["O-Kichi, 'The Foreigner'"] (Tokyo, 1927), wherein this lady is depicted as the concubine of Harris, and the cause of many natural calamities which followed the coming of foreigners to Japan.

country by leading Japan to a policy of full commercial intercourse, yet in so doing he was resolved not to take advantage of Japanese ignorance and lack of experience in international affairs. Harris, indeed, had become Japan's first instructor in world politics.

RESULTS OF THE HARRIS MISSION

In June, 1857, Harris witnessed the first official fruits of his labors when the Japanese signed a convention which among other things granted formally to the United States all that was contained in the British, Russian, and Dutch treaties. This was merely a preliminary. The great work still remained. Harris had asked for an audience with the shogun in Yedo at which he would present a letter from the President. After much delay the request was granted. Harris himself described the astonishment of the officials as he stood in the presence of the shogun and looked "the awful 'Tycoon' in the face," spoke "plainly to him," heard his reply—and all this without any trepidation, or any "quivering of the muscles of the side." [19] Without the support of gunboats or marines Harris had won a diplomatic victory of the greatest magnitude.

It now remained for Harris to approach his main task—negotiating a full commercial treaty. He sought to convince the shogunate that the limited intercourse established by the first treaties was no longer adequate or practical. By January, 1858, the shogunate had agreed to the principal terms of a treaty. As the details of the treaty were perfected, Harris continued to act as instructor to the Japanese in diplomacy and international law. He continued to be that rare type of patriot who believed that the honor of his own country depended on its consideration for the rights of others.[20]

When the treaty was completed, Harris waited impatiently month after month for the Japanese to sign. In July an American warship reached Shimoda bringing news of the Tientsin Treaties recently forced upon China. Harris saw in these reports both a danger and an opportunity. If the Europeans now turned their guns on Japan, his own policy would be in jeopardy. Could this potential threat from English and French warships be used to frighten the shogunate into signature of

---

[19] *Living Age*, LX (Feb 26, 1859), 570. For extended accounts of Harris in Japan see: M. E. Cosenza, ed., *The Complete Journal of Townsend Harris* (New York, 1930); and Carl Crow, *He Opened the Door of Japan* (New York, 1939). Only once did the Japanese mention a prostration similar to the *kotow,* and when Harris replied that its mere mention was repugnant, the matter was dropped.

[20] Contemporary testimony to the diplomatic skill and statesmanship of Harris was later given by his colleagues and, in a sense, his diplomatic rival, the first British minister at Yedo. Sir Rutherford Alcock, *The Capital of the Tycoon* (2 vols., London, 1863), I, ch. x.

the new treaty with America? Harris believed it could and, in this, he was right. Despite bitter division of opinion in the shogunate, the treaty was signed July 29, 1858. It was a great personal victory for Harris, and a great diplomatic victory for his country. The treaty provided for diplomatic representation at the capitals of both powers, for the opening of new treaty ports where consuls might be stationed, for extraterritoriality, civil and criminal, for prohibition of the opium trade, for the freedom of foreigners to practice their religion, for a conventional tariff, and for the principle of most-favored-nation treatment.

The Harris treaty became the fundamental document in Japan's foreign relations until 1894. European powers accepted it as a model for their new treaties concluded in the months immediately following: the Dutch, August 18; the Russian, August 19; the British, August 26; and the French, October 7.[21]

DOMESTIC POLITICS AND FOREIGN AFFAIRS

The shogunate had signed the Harris treaty. Could it enforce acceptance of the new policy by its enemies at home? These latter included not only the *tozama* lords but also powerful leaders within the Tokugawa family itself. During 1857 powerful opposition against the pro-foreign policy of the shogunate had again reasserted it. When therefore the shogunate sought the emperor's consent to signature of the Harris treaty, the request was denied. This explains why Harris was kept waiting. Furthermore, his treaty represented a new policy adopted by the *Bakufu without the consent of the Mikado*. The enemies of the Tokugawas were quick to see that by opposing this liberal foreign policy of the shogunate they could appear as loyal supporters of the "divine" emperor against a "usurping" shogun. It was clear too that the balance of power in Japan had so shifted as to enable the Imperial Court to issue orders to the Bakufu. Therefore the shogun was told by the Court that the new treaties could be accepted only until such time as the foreign barbarians could be expelled and the old policy of exclusion resumed. In this way the Imperial Court at Kyoto became the center of an anti-foreign, anti-Bakufu party, deriving its support from the *tozama* lords (the so-called "western clans," Satsuma, Choshu, Hizen, and Tosa), from disgruntled allies of the Tokugawa clan, and from branch families of the Tokugawa house itself, such as the Mito group. Japan was on the brink of civil war in which the new treaty rights and the very lives of the foreigners would be subject to attack.

[21] For the Harris treaty and conventions see Hunter Miller, ed., *Treaties, etc.* . . . (Washington, 1931-   ), VII, 598-648, 947-1170.

THE TREATIES IN JEOPARDY

July, 1859, was a critical month both for the shogunate and for the new treaty powers. So great was the danger of murderous attacks upon foreigners, that the shogunate, refusing to open Kanagawa, which lay on the *Tokaido* highway between Yedo and Kyoto, encouraged the foreigners to settle at Yokohama, farther down the bay and destined soon to become one of Japan's great seaports. The immediate danger was two-fold. So-called ultra-patriots, *samurai* and *ronin,* who had detached themselves from their clans, were anxious to embarrass the shogunate by attacking foreigners. Many of the foreigners in turn had come directly from residence in China, where too frequently they had acquired the habit regarding the Oriental as an inferior to be treated with little respect. This being so, it is surprising that in the years 1859 to 1865, when foreigners were denounced by every fanatical supporter of the Throne, only twelve Westerners were killed. Two cases having important repercussions on foreign relations may be mentioned. When in January, 1861, the interpreter at the American legation, Heusken by name, was murdered, the foreign representatives with the exception of Harris retired from Yedo to Yokohama in protest against the shogun's failure to give the legations adequate protection. Harris took the broader view that the administration was doing everything in its power. He therefore remained in Yedo, where for a time he was the only foreign diplomatic representative.

THE MURDER OF RICHARDSON

The second case had more serious consequences. In September, 1862, C. L. Richardson, a Britisher visiting from Hongkong, was killed on the highway near Yokohama while riding with three compatriots, two men and a woman. The assassins were *samurai* in the feudal procession of the father of the Lord of Satsuma, a leader of the anti-shogun and anti-foreign party supporting the Throne. This influential personage had just served upon the shogun a summons ordering him to appear in Kyoto to explain his conduct before the Throne. There are various accounts as to what happened. There is no proof that Richardson intended to be offensive. Nevertheless, he and his companions failed to dismount while the feudal procession passed by. For this he sacrificed his life, and his companions were wounded. Although foreigners in Yokohama demanded immediate military action, saner counsel prevailed. Early in the following year (1863), the British government made the following demands: 1) payment of an indemnity of

100,000 pounds; 2) an indemnity of 25,000 pounds to be paid by the Satsuma clan, and 3) trial and execution of the assassins in the presence of a British naval officer.

These demands came at a most unhappy moment in the shogun's career. He had already been summoned to Kyoto to explain his conduct, which could mean only that those opposed to his government and his policy were now in control of the Throne. This proved to be true, for the emperor ordered that all ports be closed to foreign commerce. Meanwhile, the negotiations on the British demands continued at Yokohama, where the British and the French now offered to use their naval forces on behalf of the shogun against the anti-foreign lords. This offer the shogun declined. On June 24 the British indemnity was paid and the powers notified of the emperor's exclusion decree. Their reply declared that the treaties must be enforced, which, of course, the shogun fully realized. For the moment his policy would be one of delay, while he entertained the hope that some change could be effected in the attitude of his domestic enemies.

CHOSHU ATTACKS THE FOREIGNERS

According to the Imperial decree, the expulsion of the foreigners and the discarding of the treaties were to be carried out by the shogun's government. But when June 25 passed without action on the part of the shogunate, the Lord of Choshu, a *tozama daimyo* whose lands controlled the western entrance to the inland sea, fired on an American ship lying off Shimonoseki. Later, French and Dutch vessels were also fired upon. Consequently, one American and several French war vessels hastened to attack the Choshu forts. It was evident that the shogun was unable to control the western barons. The British had already determined to take action against Satsuma to enforce compliance with the demands arising out of the Richardson affair. Accordingly, a British squadron appeared at Kagoshima in August, 1863. Here negotiations broke down, and the resulting bombardment, assisted by a typhoon and fire, resulted in the destruction of more than half the town. Without securing acceptance of their demands, the British sailed away. Three months later envoys from Satsuma called upon the British *chargé,* agreeing to pay the indemnity and to continue the search for the guilty. They also requested assistance in securing in England a naval vessel for their clan. The significance of the incident is obvious. Anti-foreignism in Satsuma was in part a cloak hiding a determination to destroy the shogunate.

And now events took an unusual turn at Kyoto, where the anti-foreign and anti-shogunate forces were in control. Dissension appeared in these councils, where Choshu leaders were accused of attempting to seize the person of the emperor. Choshu troops were therefore ordered to leave the capital, and when they attempted a *coup d'état,* the shogun was ordered by the emperor to deal with the rebellious clan. At this juncture, Sir Rutherford Alcock, the British minister, returned to Japan determined to unite the foreign powers in a joint expedition against Choshu. The purpose of this was to give support to the shogunate in the hour of its need and to demonstrate to the hot-headed clans that it was no longer safe to tamper with the treaty rights of foreigners. Alcock's plan was supported by his diplomatic colleagues, and so, contrary to his instructions from London, he set about to organize a joint naval expedition, consisting of British, Dutch, and French ships, and one small American vessel, which sailed from Yokohama in August, 1864. No negotiations preceded the engagement off the Choshu coast. The fleet went straight to the task of silencing the batteries. On Choshu this lesson was as effective as the previous affair at Kagoshima. Clan leaders agreed to open the straits, not to repair the forts or to build new ones, and to pay an indemnity covering the cost of the expedition. This clan, too, now turned to the West for armaments and advice that would create an effective military machine. Since the shogun could not permit the foreign powers to negotiate with a single clan, a convention was soon concluded whereby the indemnities were assumed by the shogunate. Payment of large sums, however, proved most embarrassing to the government, and since the powers were more interested in new treaty ports and new concessions, the opportunity was favorable for a second naval demonstration.

Under the leadership of the new British minister, Sir Harry Parkes, it was planned to assemble the naval forces of the powers at Osaka, close to Kyoto, where pressure could be most effectively brought to bear upon the anti-foreign forces surrounding the Throne. This time no American vessel participated, for none was available. The demands stated that two thirds of the Shimonoseki indemnity would be remitted if Hiogo and Osaka were opened immediately, if the emperor gave his approval to the treaties, and if the tariff were reduced to a general five percent. The reply was delivered on the final day permitted by the Allies' demands. The emperor, and this was most important of all, had agreed to ratify the treaties; the tariff would be reduced; and the full indemnity would be paid, for Japan was not prepared to open Hiogo and Osaka until 1868. Thus the most serious problem, the opposition of the imperialists to the treaties, was disposed of. The western *daimyo* were no longer aligned against the foreigners, but their determination to over-throw the shogunate and restore the emperor still remained.

The first phase of Japan's nineteenth-century revolution was now complete. The two-centuries-old policy of exclusion and seclusion had been abandoned not only by the weakened shogunate but also by the Throne, which derived its power from the vital western clans. Japan had now accepted full treaty relations with the major Western powers. These treaties as in the case of those with China imposed certain serious limitations upon Japan's sovereignty—extraterritoriality and the conventional tariff.

JAPAN, 1868-1889: THE RESTORATION OF AN EMPEROR AND THE ESTABLISHMENT OF CONSTITUTIONAL GOVERNMENT

B Y 1865 the contending clan factions that controlled political power in Japan had accepted as a basic plank in the national policy the principle of diplomatic and commercial intercourse with the West. This, as already stated, was the first phase of the nineteenth-century revolution. But by whom should this new policy be controlled and carried on? The general economic distress, the weakness of the shogunate, its lack of national confidence, and more specifically its bankrupt prestige in the eyes of the western (*tozama*) clans—all these and other factors foreshadowed the need for sweeping changes in the whole structure of Japanese government, if indeed the nation was to acquire a position of strength in its relations with the foreign commercial powers. Neither dual government, the shogunate, nor a military feudalism was designed to serve Japan adequately in her new relation with the outside world. The need was for a strong national government capable of controlling the clans, and of creating a unified political structure which might deal with the foreigners on terms of equality.

LEADERSHIP OF THE WESTERN CLANS

The most vigorous and effective spokesmen of all elements disgruntled with the existing social and economic order, whether *daimyo*, *kuge, samurai, ronin,* merchants, or peasants, were certain able *samurai* of the western clans, who by capacity and experience had already become the real controllers of clan policy, the *daimyo* being reduced to the role of mere puppets.[1]

It was men of this stamp who planned and executed in its initial stages the political revolution which, between 1867 and 1889, destroyed

---

[1] Takamori Saigo and Toshimichi Okubo, *samurai* of Lord Shimazu of Satsuma; and Koin Kido, *samurai* of Lord Mori of Choshu, may be cited as examples. They were supported by distinguished members of the court nobility (*kuge*) such as Saneyoshi Sanjo and Tomoyoshi Iwakura.

the shogunate, stripped the Tokugawas of their lands and power, restored the emperor as the supreme ruler, abolished the feudal order, and bestowed upon the nation a centralized and constitutional but not a democratic government. This revolution, effected in scarcely more than twenty years, was destined to place Japan before the turn of the twentieth century in that exclusive company known as "the Great Powers." It was a political, an economic, and in some degree a social revolution of transcending importance not only to Japan but also to China, to Europe, and to the United States.[2]

THE END OF THE SHOGUNATE

The first step in these revolutionary changes occurred in 1867, when the *Daimyo* of Tosa demanded the resignation of the Tokugawa shogun and the restoration of all power to the emperor. Since this demand was supported by the *Daimyos* of Satsuma, Choshu, and Hizen, and by the strongest branch families of the Tokugawa clan itself—the *Daimyos* of Owari and Echizen—the shogun was forced to comply, consoled by the thought that he would doubtless be chosen as chief adviser to the emperor under the new regime. This, however, was not the purpose of the revolutionists. These men were impelled by a number of motives: 1) their newly found loyalty to the Throne, 2) their hatred of the Tokugawa family, and 3) their own personal clan ambitions for power. When, therefore, the Tokugawas and their allies realized that the western clans were bent on their total destruction, they resorted to arms. In the brief civil war which followed, they were defeated. This was the end of Tokugawa power, and likewise the end of the shogunate and the ancient system of dual government.[3] These stirring events opened the way for the restoration to full sovereign power, in theory at least, of a boy emperor, Mutsuhito, fourteen years of age, destined to go down in history as one of Japan's greatest rulers. He bore with dignity the reign-name of *Meiji* (enlightened government) from 1867 to 1912.

THE IMPERIAL OATH, 1868

The question is frequently asked: "Why did not the young, revolutionary *samurai,* who engineered this Restoration, particularly those representing the powerful clans of Satsuma and Choshu, erect a new shogunate under their own control?" There was a time indeed when the

---

[2] Here we are concerned with the political revolution. Its economic and social features will be discussed in Chapter 27.

[3] It will be apparent later that the principle of dual government survived under new forms. See Chapter 33.

Restoration was interpreted largely as a product of clan ambition and intrigue.   Local and personal ambitions were indeed present, but they formed only a part of the larger revolutionary picture involving economic and social maladjustments that could not be met merely by substituting one shogunate for another.   It must be remembered that if the younger *samurai* provided the personal leadership of the Restoration, the big merchants of Osaka and Kyoto financed it.   Such a movement cannot be interpreted solely within the narrow view of feudal clan rivalries.   Moreover, the emperor was the logical person to wear the official mantle of authority under the new regime.   Though often neglected by the shoguns and sometimes relegated to a position of abject poverty, the emperor, or rather "the magic power of the Throne," was "such as to evoke the most passionate feelings of loyalty which were never completely dissipated." [4]   This loyalty was soon developed by the Restoration leaders into a cult of emperor-worship deriving its immediate background from historical studies that stressed the "divinity" of the Imperial Family and the "illegitimate" character of Tokugawa rule.[5]   Fundamentally the new emperor-worship rested on what has been called a revival of "pure Shinto"—a Shintoism, which, purged of Buddhist influence, was to stress as never before the emperor as the central and supreme deity of the nation.[6]

Since many of the *daimyo* and the *samurai* feared that power in the new regime would be monopolized by a few younger revolutionary leaders, these latter caused the young emperor, Mutsuhito, to issue in June, 1868, an Imperial Oath setting forth the principles on which the new Imperial rule was to rest.   This charter, a sort of Japanese Declaration of the Rights of Man, recognized, sometimes in ambiguous terms, the principles of public discussion and debate by both the high and the low, called for the abandonment of "absurd" practices of former times, and for the pursuit of knowledge wherever it might be found in order that the nation might be strengthened.[7]   Although the framers of this charter had in mind the *samurai,* and not the people as a whole, it was to this same charter that the liberals of later nineteenth-century Japan appealed in their struggle for representative government.   Even in 1868 the Imperial Oath was indicative of something far more significant than mere political expediency.   It was an expression "of the anti-feudal

---

[4] E. Herbert Norman, *Japan's Emergence as a Modern State* (New York, 1940), 27.
[5] See Chapter 3.
[6] D. C. Holtom, *Modern Japan and Shinto Nationalism* (Chicago, 1943), chs. i and ii.
[7] For text of the Imperial Oath see W. W. McLaren, "Japanese Government Documents," *Trans. of the Asiatic Society of Japan,* XLII, Pt. 1 (Tokyo, 1914), 8.

aspirations of the masses of people," whether disillusioned *samurai*, ambitious capitalists, or half-starved peasants. In a word, social forces, anti-feudal in philosophy, were demanding a new political structure—a national structure for the state.[8] In 1868, however, these new forces were extremely vague, and the framework of the new political order had not taken definite shape even in the best Japanese minds. For some fifteen years after the Restoration, one temporary administration followed another. All these passing executive councils were headed nominally by Imperial princes, by *kuge* or by *daimyo*, but the real power remained in the hands of younger *samurai* advisers. Actually there could be little progress toward a political house-cleaning until the debris of feudalism as a legal institution had been removed.

THE ABOLITION OF FEUDALISM

It has already been pointed out that for many years economic and social adjustments had been taking place extra-legally in Japanese society, adjustments which revealed the incapacity of the feudal structure to meet new needs. The Restoration of 1868 in bestowing political power on the young *samurai* leaders of the western clans gave them also the opportunity to destroy political feudalism and thus to clear the ground for a truly national government.

The initiative in this development came again from the western clans of Satsuma, Choshu, Hizen, and Tosa, whose *daimyo* in 1869 returned their feudal domains to the emperor. These lords had been advised by their *samurai* leaders, who now controlled the emperor, that they were surrendering power only to receive greater power. Indeed the western barons took up their residence in Tokyo, the former Yedo, to which the emperor had moved, and placed their troops at the disposal of the sovereign's government. Thus strengthened in their position, the young *samurai* leaders were able through the emperor "to invite" the remaining *daimyo* to surrender their lands, and to follow this "invitation" with an Imperial rescript (1871) abolishing fiefs and clans. Feudalism as a political structure was thus destroyed.

This sweeping change in the political edifice affected materially every class of society. Most of the *daimyo* viewed the change with apprehension but they knew better than to oppose the great western clans. Then, too, they were consoled with annual pensions of one tenth of the nominal revenue from their former fiefs. Indeed, their financial position was greatly improved because: 1) the nominal income was higher than the actual income; 2) they were no longer burdened with the support

---

[8] Norman, *Japan's Emergence*, 91 ff.

of their *samurai;* and 3) their debts in most instances were assumed by the new central government or were cancelled. Some of the barons won political distinction in the new government, and most of them retained their social prestige in the new national nobility which was soon to be created.

Far different were the effects upon the *samurai.* This class numbered about 450,000 families in 1871. The *samurai's* income from his feudal lord, measured in rice, was already small. By the decree of 1871 this income was cut in half; but he was permitted to lay aside the badge of his class, the two swords, and to enter the field of business or finance. All this, however, was highly bewildering to men whose sole profession had been that of bearing arms, who regarded the state (fief) as owing them a living, and whose mental horizon was restricted to the military philosophy of *Bushido.* They now faced a society which deprived them of half their income, deprived them of their monopoly in bearing arms (the new conscript national army was made up largely of commoners), and, worst of all, a society which directed them toward the despised walks of business. Some of the lesser *samurai* adjusted themselves with relative ease to the new order. Some indeed were to emerge as the leaders of modern Japanese business. But the majority could not make the adjustment. These malcontents, and their intellectual descendants, as we shall see, were destined to play a significant role in Japan's later bid for world power.[9]

Capitalistic groups, bankers, rice brokers, and wealthy merchants, welcomed the Restoration and the abolition of feudalism. Among these groups were families such as Mitsui and Sumitomo who had financed the Revolution of 1868-71. For these services they were not to go unpaid. Many of the debts owed to these capitalists were assumed by the new government.

Most significant of all, the effects stemming from the abolition of feudalism were those directly touching the farmers. In 1871 probably 80 percent of Japan's population was composed of farmers, a majority of whom were independent cultivators. Yet within a few years "tenant land occupied 30 percent of the area cultivated," a tendency which was accelerated in later years. In a word, the surreptitious acquisition of land by the new capitalistic landlord class, which had been going on before the Restoration, was now legalized; the peasant was freed from feudal obligations and became nominally a free-holder paying, not a

---

[9] See Chapter 28.

tax in kind on the value of his crop, but a money tax on the value of his land. When in feudal days taxes were collected, the principle followed was "to see that the peasants had just enough to live on and no more." Thus under the "paternal" care of the feudal lord, the peasant "neither died nor lived." "In the new society [after 1871] they [the peasants] were free to choose their own fate; to live or die, to remain on the land or sell out and go to the city." [10] Thus the way was opened for the dispossession of the peasantry and the creation of "modern Japanese agriculture with its unique tenant-landlord relations." [11]

THE ERA OF ENLIGHTENED GOVERNMENT

The Restoration and the abolition of feudalism, together with the earlier adoption of the new policy of commercial intercourse with the great Western maritime powers, were an essential prelude to the creation of a new Japan.

Prior to the Restoration, foreign travel had been forbidden. Japan's knowledge of the Western world was confined to what she had learned from the Dutch at Nagasaki, from the foreigners who had come in the wake of Perry, and from the limited company of Japanese who had gone abroad with or without government approval. It was a new and strange world that they saw. The scope of the impressions carried back to Japan by the first travellers in these years is illustrated by the report on the shogun's mission to the United States in 1860. Its observations covered every human activity from the constitutional position and behavior of the President to the plumbing and etiquette of the bath room.

When the President of this country is to be elected, four of five of the leading men of the government choose a candidate who is nominated by the party convention. . . . Anyone of good character except a negro may be elected president. . . . The President and members of the government sometimes go for a walk wearing ordinary clothes without any bodyguard, and no one recognizes them or speaks to them. When the President or other high officials go to a private house they remove their hats. It seems that the people think a great deal of their country but not half so much of their President.[12]

---

[10] Norman, *Japan's Emergence,* 142-143. For population estimates and vocational distribution see Royichi Ishii, *Population Pressure and Economic Life in Japan* (London, 1937), and A. E. Hindmarsh, *The Basis of Japanese Foreign Policy* (Cambridge, 1936).

[11] For a full discussion of the economic and social consequences of this movement see Norman, *Japan's Emergence,* ch. v, and Chapter 27 of this volume.

[12] M. K. Yanagawa, [Diary of] *The First Japanese Mission to America* (1860), translated by Junichi Fukuyama and Roderick H. Jackson (Kobe, 1937), 24, 50.

THE NEW EDUCATION

Significant among the reforms of early Meiji were those in education. Here Japan's enthusiasm for the new world of the West appeared to recognize no barriers. Following the mandate of the Imperial Oath (1868), that knowledge should be sought wherever it might be found, a department of education was set up (1871) under a law which proclaimed that "all people, high or low, and of both sexes, should receive education, so that there should not be found one family in the whole empire, nor one member of a family, ignorant and illiterate." This was a radical departure from previous policy and practice. Education in feudal Japan had been restricted to men of privileged society. Now elementary education was to be compulsory. It was based on a modification of the American primary and secondary systems. Boys and girls, six years of age, were required to attend a four-, later increased to a six-year course. They were given instruction in elementary subjects plus special character training closely associated with reverence for and loyalty to the emperor. Secondary education prepared students for an immediate vocation or for entrance into a university. Normal schools turned out an ever-increasing supply of elementary teachers, and in a few years the personnel needs of Japan's expanding trade and industry were met by commercial schools. Elementary training for girls was similar to that for the boys; secondary education, however, stressed woman's role as wife and mother; and it was not until 1902 that the government made provision for higher education for women. Yet in this limited program for women, Japan was in advance of many Western states. In the organization of her universities for men Japan tended to follow the French model, and throughout the entire educational system the German insistence on vocational training was notable.

From whatever angle it be considered, this was a revolution in education, quite as striking as the political and economic revolutions of 1867-1871. The Japanese clamored for the new education with an unbounded but at times undiscriminating enthusiasm. Many mistakes were made, laws were frequently altered, and hurriedly trained teachers taught what they themselves did not understand. It was above all an educational system founded and shaped by the new Restoration government, a system which imparted to Japan's rising generations the strength and likewise the weakness of her revolutionary leaders. Two positive accomplishments are traceable to the new education: it created a literate people, and a nation technically abreast of the modern mechanical world of science. But as a purely intellectual force, the new education in the late nineteenth century did not create, in fact it was never intended to create, a democratic philosophy for free men. There was no Thomas Jefferson in Japan's historical heritage. Consequently, while Japan imported precipitately a thousand forms and techniques of American education between 1870 and 1890, its spirit and its ideals did not thrive in the new environment.[13] From the standpoint of the leaders of post-Restoration Japan education could be useful only as it helped in the transition from a mediaeval to a modern autocratic state, only as it prevented "the predatory powers of America and Europe" from gaining "a stronghold in the economic life of the islands." Therefore education was limited to specific purposes: "national unification, unquestioning loyalty, the acquirement of modern scientific and economic technique and the perfection of national defense."[14]

THE MATERIAL TRANSFORMATION

The technical, material transformation of Japan was rapid and dramatic. Every Western mechanical device of the time in trade, business, commerce, and transportation soon found its place in the Japanese scene. Foreign architecture and city planning appeared first in the seaports of Yokohama and Kobe. Japanese in foreign trade put on foreign dress, and, even in later days of the twentieth century, those who were not too discriminating might be seen taking their summer evening stroll through the bazaars of Yokohama clad in a hard straw hat, white cotton gloves, a cane, native geta (wooden clogs), and for the finishing touch, a suit of American model BVD's. A postal system and telegraph were in use by 1868. In 1872 the first railroad, 18 miles long, began business. In 1897, 3,000 miles of railroad, mostly government owned, were in operation. In all these activities and many others the initiative of the government was evident either through organization or subsidy. Shipping lines such as Nippon Yusen Kaisha (Japan Mail) (1885), and Osaka Shosen Kaisha were organized. Tonnage increased from 59,000 in 1885 to 1,115,000 in 1907. The textile industries were promoted by every modern means designed to improve and standardize the product and to assure its acceptance by the public. To meet the needs of currency reform and national credit, national banks, after the American model, made their appearance after 1872. The Central Bank of Japan was formed in 1882 as the financial bulwark of the government. This

[13] For a full discussion of Japan's unique politico-religious philosophy, see Holtom, *Modern Japan and Shinto Nationalism*.
[14] Hugh L. Keenleyside and A. F. Thomas, *History of Japanese Education* ([Tokyo], 1937), 73; see in particular ch. iii.

was followed among others by the Yokohama Specie Bank (1887) to finance foreign trade and to control exchange.

Japanese cities soon showed a rapid growth. Tokyo's population increased during the years 1882 to 1904 from 900,000 to 1,870,000; Osaka's, 1883 to 1904, from 309,000 to 1,020,000; Yokohama's, 1883 to 1904, from 59,000 to 330,000; Nagoya's, 1887 to 1905, from 140,000 to 290,000.

National finances showed an equally striking growth, as indicated by the following table:

Fiscal Year	Receipts	Expenditures
1869-70	¥20,900,000	¥20,700,000
1880-81	63,300,000	63,140,000
1890-91	106,400,000	82,125,000
1900-01	295,800,000	292,750,000
1907-08	619,795,000	619,796,000

And so statistics could be compiled in the fields of finance, communications, banking, industry, and trade, to reveal (during the closing decades of the nineteenth century)[15] the dramatic transformation of agricultural Japan into a semi-commercial-industrial state.

APPEARANCE OF REPRESENTATIVE INSTITUTIONS

The overwhelming enthusiasm of the Japanese for the newly discovered Western world was affected naturally enough by Western political philosophy and especially by the dominant liberalism of the nineteenth century. What philosophy and structure of government would Japan erect on the foundations of her Meiji Restoration? Her new educational program indicated already that the new government would be nationalistic and centralized in a peculiarly Japanese sense. Would it also be democratic, based on a popular constitution, a bill of rights, a broad franchise, political parties, and economic individualism, as understood by powerful industrial and middle class groups in the Western democracies?

The answer to these questions must be found in the sphere of domestic Japanese politics following the return (1873) of the Iwakura mission from Europe and America. Impressed by the strength of the West, the members of this mission soon emerged as leaders of a so-called peace party in opposition to a war party composed of more belligerent *samurai,* who, for reasons to be explained later, desired a foreign war in

---

[15] For a series of essays on Japan's material development, 1870 to 1905, see Shigenobu Okuma, ed., *Fifty Years of New Japan* (2 vols., New York, 1909).

Korea and Formosa.[16] The war party soon withdrew from the government and thus formed a nucleus of potential political opposition. To strengthen its position, the government created a Ministry of Home Affairs, which had immediate control over prefectural and city governments. The opposition then attempted to assassinate Iwakura and demanded a national elective assembly. This the government refused, and a series of rebellions followed. As a concession, the government did call an Assembly of Local Governors (1875) which proved to be a rubber stamp for approval of government policies.

While the government continued to live under the protection of press censorship, it succeeded in defeating a desperate rising by opposition leaders from Satsuma (1877). The Satsuma Rebellion led by Saigo was a protest against the general policy of the government—against the conscription law (1873), against the importance of capitalistic interests in the new government, and against the refusal of the government to employ the ex-*samurai* in foreign war—a composite policy which threatened the very existence of *samurai* traditions. When, however, despite suppression of the rebellion, further assassinations of government leaders followed, prefectural assemblies were established (*fuken-kai*). This was a step, though a faltering one, toward representative government, because the franchise in the assemblies was limited; prefectural governors initiated and could veto all bills, leaving to the assemblies nothing but the privilege of discussing budgets and finding new ways to raise new taxes. Nevertheless these assemblies encouraged the opposition to agitate for a national assembly. In response to the incessant demands of Itagaki, the government, while opposing anything in the form of a national parliament, did permit (1880) the calling of municipal assemblies.

A CONSTITUTION PROMISED; POLITICAL PARTIES

The immediate origins of the Imperial edict granting a national parliament are to be found in the flagrant financial corruption of Satsuma and Choshu, ex-*samurai* who controlled the government. When these practices were exposed publicly in 1881 by Okuma, there was mob violence in Tokyo. Government property was destroyed, and the police were defied. A frightened government sought refuge behind the Imperial apron strings, while an Imperial rescript announced that a national parliament would be created in 1890. For this turn of events the Satsuma and Choshu leaders had only themselves to blame. They had

---

[16] Leaders of the war party included: Taneomi Soejima, Takamori Saigo, Taisuke Itagaki, Shimpei Eto, and Shojiro Goto.

excluded from office or had relegated to minor posts their colleagues from the less powerful clans: Shigenobu Okuma of Hizen, and Taisuke Itagaki and Shojiro Goto of Tosa. It was this disgruntled but able opposition which now used the pretext of graft in high places to force the issue of a national parliament, and its natural concomitant, political parties.[17]

A so-called Liberal Party (*Jiyuto*) was organized by Itagaki in 1881, and a so-called Progressive Party (*Kaishinto*) by Okuma in 1882. These parties issued elaborate platforms. The *Jiyuto* advocated a one-house legislature, universal suffrage, a "strong" foreign policy, and many features of the French system of government. Some members of the party leaned toward republican ideas. The *Kaishinto* favored a bicameral legislature, limited manhood suffrage, administrative reform, and a national but non-imperialistic foreign policy. A third party, the Imperialist (*Rikken Teiseito*), also appeared in 1882. It favored absolute monarchy. Organized by Genichiro Fukuchi, it accepted literally the idea of restoring full power to the emperor. Thus in theory these parties represented widely divergent views on the future constitution: the *Jiyuto* stood theoretically for popular sovereignty after the manner of Rousseau; the *Kaishinto* wanted a more restricted constitutional regime on the British model; the *Teiseito,* if there was to be a constitution at all, wanted essentially the Prussian system.[18]

It cannot be said that these platforms were completely meaningless, theoretical as they were. Historically they represent the first unsteady gropings of the Japanese toward modern and liberal government. Yet it must also be remembered that these first platforms had no solid foundation in the traditions of Japanese thought. In reality therefore the parties did *not* represent political principles as set forth in the platforms. Instead they were personal followings of particular political leaders. In this sense they were patterned after the Oriental idea that government is a matter of men rather than of law.

CONSTITUTIONAL PREPARATIONS

Meanwhile, as the political parties clamored for a popular and liberal constitution, the government set about the task of drafting a document

---

[17] It is not to be assumed that Itagaki and Goto were concerned primarily with the purification of Japanese politics. They, like many members of the government, began as poor *samurai* and died immensely wealthy.

[18] See Harold S. Quigley, *Japanese Government and Politics* (New York, 1932), ch. xii.

which would preserve the power of oligarchy. It created a commission on constitutional investigation headed by Hirobumi Ito. In 1884, a new nobility was created to draw together and unify the conservative and aristocratic elements that were to dominate the new government.[19] It was also decided to fashion the executive department prior to the adoption of the constitution. This would enable the executive to become a functioning organism familiar with its duties before it would be required to adjust itself to a parliament. Accordingly a cabinet (*naikaku*) was set up in 1885 modelled on the German cabinet of that day. Then in 1888 a new privy council was named with Ito, head of the constitutional commission, as president. This pre-constitutional executive included the men who were to control the Japanese state for many years: Hirobumi Ito, Tsuyoshiaki Inouye, Aritomo Yamagata, and Arinori Mori of Choshu; Masayoshi Matsukata, Iwao Oyama, Tsugumichi Saigo, and Akuyoshi Yamada of Satsuma; Kanjo Tani of Tosa; and Baye Enomoto of Hizen. In this group were all those who were later to become the original Genro (Elder Statesmen). As further preparation for the constitutional regime, a merit system was introduced into the civil service, and new codes were prepared in both public and private law.

Japanese law of the earlier Restoration period had been derived from early Japanese law, which in turn had been borrowed from China in the seventh and later centuries and codified extensively in the Tokugawa feudal society. As the Western powers entered into treaty relations with Japan, they objected to submitting their nationals to Japanese law and consequently demanded and secured extraterritorial jurisdiction, as they had also done in the case of China. The Restoration government in its desire to preserve the national independence was quick to recognize that the abolition of extraterritoriality would depend on the speed and effectiveness with which Japan adopted principles of jurisprudence acceptable to Europeans and Americans. Accordingly, a penal code and a code of criminal procedure, begun in 1873 and completed in 1880, were adopted in 1882. They were strongly influenced by French law. Revisions of the code of criminal procedure appeared in 1890, and of the penal code in 1908. The larger task of constructing a civil code, begun in 1870, was completed and the code put into effect in 1899, in which year extraterritoriality was terminated. The basis of the civil law was also French, though it drew contributions also from the German and other law. A

---

[19] Quigley, *Japanese Government and Politics,* 31-32; McLaren, "Japanese Government Documents," 88-90.

code of civil procedure was operative as early as 1891, and the commercial code, German in origin, was adopted, as was the civil, in 1899.[20]

THE DRAFTING OF THE CONSTITUTION

From the foregoing it will be noted that some of the more important instruments of a new government had been created and were in operation before the constitution itself was created. While this procedure lent stability to political affairs in a period of transition, it also enabled the ruling faction, headed by Ito, to maintain its monopoly of power.

The foundations of a constitutional regime had been laid as early as 1868, when the Charter Oath was proclaimed. Two years later, in 1870, Ito visited the United States, where he studied the American constitutional system, delving deeply into the pages of the *Federalist*. More important in shaping Ito's ideas, however, was the advice of General Grant given in 1879, that Japan in designing a constitution should give full regard to her own peculiar traditions. Then in 1882, a year after the emperor had promised a constitution, Ito studied in Germany, where the successes of Bismarck had brought new prestige to the political philosophy and institutions of Prussia. Back in Japan and commissioned in 1884 to draft a constitution, Ito called on the services of three able assistants, all of whom had travelled abroad: Tsuyoshiaki Inouye, Myoji Ito, and Kentaro Kaneko. With Ito these men constituted a bureau attached to the Imperial Household, thus precluding political pressure from the liberals. When the draft of the constitution was completed, it was ratified by the privy council created by Ito for this specific purpose and to be maintained under the constitution as the highest advisory body to the sovereign. Finally, when the work was complete, Emperor Mutsuhito on February 11, 1889, the anniversary of the traditional founding of the state of Yamato in 660 B.C., bestowed the constitution as a royal gift upon his people. Every precaution had been already taken to insure an obedient and peaceful acceptance by the people at large. Tokyo under a special Peace Preservation Ordinance was subject to a sort of quasi-martial law. Most of the radical newspapers had already been suppressed, while the press in general was under strict instructions to refrain for the time being from all critical comment. As a consequence the public reception was peaceful.[21]

[20] Quigley, *Japanese Government*, 36-37; Masaakira Tomii, "The Development of Japanese Legal Institutions," in S. Okuma, ed., *Fifty Years of New Japan* (2 vols., New York, 1909), I, 231-250; K. Takayanagi, *The Reception and Influence of Occidental Legal Ideas in Japan* (Tokyo, 1929).
[21] W. W. McLaren, *A Political History of Japan* (New York, 1916), 186; Quigley, *Japanese Government*, 39-43; G. E. Uyehara, *The Political Development of Japan* (Lon-

THE BASIC CHARACTER OF THE CONSTITUTION

The Constitution, drafted by a small group of Meiji leaders, bestowed as a gift by the emperor, and accepted obediently by the people, denied any opportunity for criticism.   It has been most aptly described by a Japanese student of politics as "a document embodying Japanese political principles under the cloak of representative institutions." [22]   To the aristocrats of the Privy Council viewing Ito's work in the light of Japan's traditional political ideas, the Constitution may well have appeared as a singularly progressive affair, but as Uyehara again remarks, the aristocrats had not only "defeated the extreme doctrines of Liberalism, but also [had] lost sight of the true principle of representative institutions." They had, in fact, created a framework of government which all but denied any "available avenue for democratic development," and which was admirably designed to perpetuate "the oligarchical absolutism in which it began its career." [23]   What then were the essential principles in the new constitutional political order?

THE ESSENTIALS OF JAPANESE GOVERNMENT:
1. THE LAW

The fundamental law of the Empire consisted of: the Constitution, the Imperial House Law, Imperial ordinances, statutes, and international treaties.[24]

The nature of the Constitution is best revealed by the position of the emperor.   Since the Constitution was a gift of the Throne, only the emperor could initiate amendments.   These required the consent of the House of Peers (*Kizoku-in*) and the House of Representatives (*Shugi-in*).   Interpretation of the Constitution rested with the courts, and, in a case of dispute, with the Privy Council.[25]

The Imperial House Law occupied a unique position.   It could not be affected by legislation, was beyond the control of the Diet, could

---

don, 1910), 109-123.   The official interpretation of the constitution is by Hirobumi Ito, *Commentaries on the Constitution of the Empire of Japan,* translated by Myoji Ito (2nd ed., Tokyo, 1906).

[22] Uyehara, *Political Development,* 119.

[23] Quigley, *Japanese Government,* 42.

[24] For an excellent and concise summary of the organization of Japan's government on which I have drawn heavily, see R. K. Reischauer, *Japan: Government-Politics* (New York, 1939), ch. iv.

[25] The complete text of the Constitution, the Imperial House Law, and other documents is given in: Quigley, *Japanese Government;* McLaren, "Japanese Government Documents"; Tatsuji Takeuchi, *War and Diplomacy in the Japanese Empire* (New York, 1935).

be amended only by the emperor with advice of the Imperial Family Council and the Privy Council. The Imperial House Law, not the Constitution, determined the succession.

Great powers were exercised by the emperor through Imperial ordinances of three kinds: 1) prerogative—Imperial House Law; 2) administrative—executive acts in the interest of the general welfare; 3) emergency—to meet emergencies when the Diet was not in session. These last required, at time of issue, approval by the Privy Council (*Sumitsuin*), and ultimately by the Diet, unless repealed before a new session. It is thus clear that in a very large field the ordinance powers of the emperor were beyond legislative control.

Statutes were enacted by majority vote of both houses of the Diet, whose powers over legislation were the same, save that money bills were to be presented first in the lower house. The emperor's veto power over all laws was made absolute. In practice, most legislation was initiated by the government.

Treaties were to be ratified by the emperor with the consent of the Privy Council. Treaties were to be regarded as superior to ordinary law, were not subject to change by ordinance, but could not be in conflict with the Constitution or the Imperial House Law.

2. THE ARISTOCRATS

Japanese government was dominated after 1889 by an aristocracy composed of: the Imperial Family, the Genro (Elder Statesmen), and the House of Peers. In this group were the former *kuge* (the civilian court nobility), the *daimyo* (the former great feudal lords), and *buke* (feudal barons), those *samurai* who engineered the Restoration in 1868, wealthy merchants and capitalists who financed the Restoration, and finally, a select few from the professional classes elevated to the new nobility.

The Position of the Emperor

The emperor's powers as defined by the Constitution were extremely broad. He possessed the rights of sovereignty, exercised them within the Constitution, convoked and prorogued the Diet, dissolved the House of Representatives, issued ordinances, determined the organization of the government, and acted on appointments and dismissal of all officials, save in those cases where other provision was made by the Constitution. He exercised the administrative and command powers over the army and navy, declared war, made peace and concluded treaties, proclaimed martial law, conferred all high official ranks and honors, appointed and removed judges.   All these constitutional powers and prerogatives of the emperor were to be exercised *only* on the advice of his advisers, whether ministers of state, ministers of the Imperial Household, or chiefs of the general staffs of the army and navy.   The emperor, in a word, reigned but did not rule.   The problem of Japanese government in any period after 1889 was to discover what individuals and groups ruled through the sovereign.

The Imperial Family Council

This body advised the emperor on the conduct of Imperial Family affairs within the provisions of the Imperial House Law.   The Council included the Princes of the Blood who had attained majority.   The Imperial Family during the constitutional period remained one of the wealthiest in Japan.

The Genro (Elder Statesmen)

From shortly after the promulgation of the Constitution until 1931, the most powerful group in Japanese government and politics was the Genro.   This group was extra-constitutional.   It was composed of trusted and tried statesmen who had assumed leadership in the making of new Japan, approximately in the years 1880-1900.   These men exercised the real power in government under the Constitution.   No important decisions were made without their consent.   In fact they made the decisions.   It was not until about 1922 that their supreme control in all important affairs of state, domestic and foreign, began to be questioned.   The Genro illustrate clearly the fact that while constitutional government in Japan often appeared to be Western in structure and performance, actually it was not so.   The Genro as personalities, not as constitutionalists, were the real makers of the new Japan in the later years of Meiji.   They included: Hirobumi Ito (Choshu), maker of the Constitution, Aritomo Yamagata (Choshu), the builder of Japan's modern army, Kaoru Inouye (Choshu), influential in the drafting of the Constitution and reforms in taxation, Iwao Oyama (Satsuma), a great soldier, and Masayoshi Matsukata (Satsuma), of great prominence in taxation and finance.   These were the original members.   Later, General Taro Katsura (Choshu), and Kimmochi Saionji (Kuge) were added.   All have now passed from the scene and with them have gone not only the institution itself, but also the ablest men of modern Japan.[26]

[26] Ito was assassinated, 1909; Katsura died, 1913; Inouye, 1915; Oyama, 1916; Yamagata, 1922; Matsukata, 1924; Saionji, 1940.   It is significant that no Genro was ever assassinated in Japan or by a Japanese.   But as indicative of the weakening prestige of the group, attempts were made on the life of the aged Saionji.

The House of Peers

This body, the upper house of the legislature, included: 1) all Princes of the Blood who had reached majority; 2) princes and marquises twenty-nine years of age; 3) representatives of counts, viscounts, and barons, elected by their orders for terms of seven years; 4) Imperial appointees selected for life because of distinguished service to the state or in recognition of scholarship; 5) representatives of the Imperial Academy elected by their colleagues for seven-year terms; and 6) elected representatives of the highest tax-payers from each prefecture. This was a body distinguished for its conservatism of blood, wealth, and title. Its power was guaranteed by the Constitution. When the position of the Imperial Family, the Genro, and the House of Peers is noted, it must be clear that the framers of Japan's Constitution did not intend to erect a democratic structure in the Western sense of that term.

3. THE BUREAUCRACY

The bureaucrats were the civil office holders. Their position was based on ability and on appointment. Their loyalties were toward the aristocrats rather than to the common people. Of first importance among the bureaucratic elements was the Imperial Household Ministry. The Lord Keeper of the Privy Seal and the Minister of the Imperial Household headed this group. Both, because of their close personal relationship with the emperor, had great influence as advisers of the Throne. It was through them that audience with the sovereign was secured. These ministers were appointed by the emperor on the advice of the Prime Minister.

The Privy Council

The second group in the bureaucracy was the Privy Council. Created, as already noted, in 1888, it was designed to review and accept the Constitution and to be the highest constitutional advisory body to the emperor. Its membership numbered twenty-six, appointed for life by the emperor on the advice of the Prime Minister and with the approval of the President of the Council. Ministers of state were *ex-officio* councillors. The advice of the Council has been sought in all the following cases: a change in the order of succession, institution of a regency, amendment of the Imperial House Law, amendments to the Constitution, cases calling for fundamental interpretation of the Constitution, emergency Imperial ordinances, and treaties. The Council proved to be extremely unpopular with the House of Representatives but its prestige with the aristocracy remained high. It proved itself an effective curb against democratic or representative tendencies.

The Civil Service

The great body of civil servants—the rank and file of bureaucracy—numbering nearly half a million members, was selected by competitive examination. Usually the most rigid application of these examinations was in the Foreign Office (*Gaimusho*), whereas in the Home Ministry they have been less effective in competition with the spoils system.

4. THE MILITARISTS

In no modern state, save perhaps Prussia, has the professional soldier played so influential a role in politics as in Japan.[27] His influence has been exercised through a number of military boards and officials. The Board of Field Marshals and Fleet Admirals (*Gensuifu*) was most significant in war time since only Imperial princes were raised to these supreme ranks in times of peace. Much more important was the Supreme War Council (*Gunji-Sangi-in*) consisting of the field marshals, fleet admirals, chief of the general staff, chief of the navy staff, minister of war, minister of the navy, as well as additional high-ranking officers appointed by the emperor. It was this Council that controlled the policy of the fighting services. The emperor acted on its advice. Actual administration of the army was by the minister of war, the chief of staff, and the inspector-general of military education; navy administration was by the chief of the naval staff and the minister of the navy. All save the inspector-general had direct access to the Throne, being thus on a footing of equality with the prime minister and above the other members of the ministry. Both service ministers were required to be high-ranking officers on the active list. They were selected by the premier but only with the approval of the respective chiefs of staff. The services thus had the power to destroy any cabinet by forcing the resignation of the service ministers and refusing to nominate new ones.

---

[27] The army and the navy liked to think of themselves as unique guardians of the Throne and of the so-called "national spirit." In practice, however, they have been the most flagrant violators of the commands of the Throne. An Imperial rescript addressed to the army (1882) set forth that: "Service men should not involve themselves or interest themselves in politics." Under the Constitution they cannot vote. Nevertheless no group in Japanese society has been more jealous of its political fortunes than the military. See the concise discussion of this subject in K. W. Colegrove, *Militarism in Japan* (Boston: World Peace Foundation [World Affairs Books No. 16] 1936); see also E. E. N. Causton, *Militarism and Foreign Policy in Japan* (London, 1936), and O. Tanin and E. Yohan, *Militarism and Fascism in Japan* (New York, 1934).

Special Powers of Emperor

Supreme Commander Army and Navy.
Rules Affairs of Imperial Household under Imperial House Law.
Confers Honors on advice of Minister of Imperial Household.
Promulgates Imperial ordinances which are executed by Cabinet.
Controls foreign affairs which are conducted by the Cabinet.
Convokes and prorogues Diet.
Appoints some members of House of Peers.
Dissolves House of Representatives.

Privy Council

Appointed by Emperor;
the highest constitutional advisory
body to the Throne. Cabinet
ministers are ex-officio members.
Advises Emperor on both
domestic and foreign affairs.
Appointments for life on
nomination of Prime Minister.

The Imperial Diet

All statutes require a majority vote of
both houses, but are subject to the
Emperor's veto; most bills are
presented by the Government, not by
a member of the Diet; power to
approve or reject Imperial ordinances;
has no control over Imperial House
Law; power to approve but not to
initiate amendments to the Constitution.

House of Peers

Membership: Princes of the Blood, Princes and
Marquises; representatives of Counts, Viscounts,
Barons; Imperial appointees for life selected
because of special service to the State; representatives of Imperial Academy; representatives
of the highest tax payers. Legislative powers
equal to those of House of Representatives.

House of Representatives

Members elected for 4 years (manhood suffrage after
1925). Convoked annually by Emperor. Has power,
usually not exercised, to initiate legislation. Financial
bills introduced first in House of Representatives. Has no control
over "fixed" expenditures in budget. Membership
representative of varying political parties. "Party"
cabinets more or less responsive to House of Representatives prevailed
1918-1932.

The people elect.
Manhood suffrage
after 1925.

PRINCIPAL FEATURES OF THE GOVERNMENT

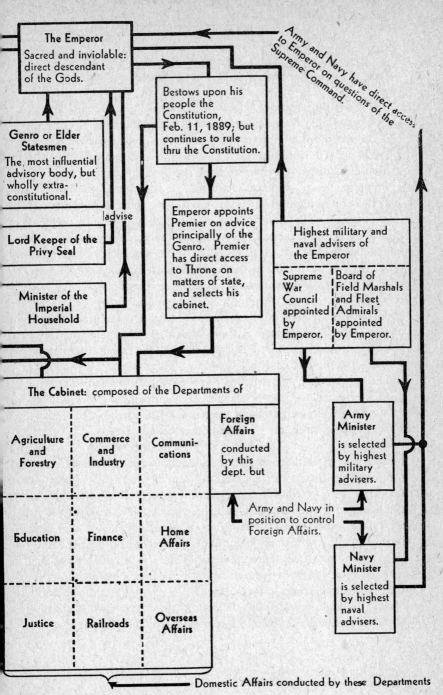

The Emperor
Sacred and inviolable: direct descendant of the Gods.

Army and Navy have direct access to Emperor on questions of the Supreme Command.

Bestows upon his people the Constitution, Feb. 11, 1889; but continues to rule thru the Constitution.

Genro or Elder Statesmen
The, most influential advisory body, but wholly extra-constitutional.

advise

Lord Keeper of the Privy Seal

Minister of the Imperial Household

Emperor appoints Premier on advice principally of the Genro. Premier has direct access to Throne on matters of state, and selects his cabinet.

Highest military and naval advisers of the Emperor

Supreme War Council appointed by Emperor.

Board of Field Marshals and Fleet Admirals appointed by Emperor.

The Cabinet: composed of the Departments of

Agriculture and Forestry	Commerce and Industry	Communi- cations	Foreign Affairs conducted by this dept. but
Education	Finance	Home Affairs	
Justice	Railroads	Overseas Affairs	

Army Minister
is selected by highest military advisers.

Army and Navy in position to control Foreign Affairs.

Navy Minister
is selected by highest naval advisers.

Domestic Affairs conducted by these Departments

5. THE POLITICIANS AND THE HOUSE OF REPRESENTATIVES

The Constitution provided for a bicameral legislature or diet which the Japanese call *gikai*. The purpose of the framers was to prevent the legislators from indulging in hasty legislation and to give decisive legislative power (in the House of Peers) to the aristocracy.[28] The House of Representatives, according to the *Commentaries,* was to regard itself as "representatives of the people of the whole country," though prior to 1925 there were high property qualifications both for candidates and for the franchise. The Constitution required annual sessions of the Diet which were supplemented frequently by extraordinary sessions caused by frequent dissolutions. Originally the House of Representatives consisted of 300 members, but this number was increased to 381 in 1900, and to 466 in 1925, when manhood suffrage was adopted. All statutes required approval by the House of Representatives as well as by the House of Peers. The same applied to amendments to the Constitution and to Imperial ordinances if these latter were to remain in effect after the Diet came into session. However, the Diet, and consequently the House of Representatives, has held but limited control over the nation's finances. All items of so-called "fixed expenditures" were beyond its power: salaries, expenses of the Imperial Household, fixed budgets of administrative branches of the government, etc., such as the army and navy. Furthermore, the Constitution provided, in Article LXXI, that: "When the Imperial Diet has not voted on the budget, or when the budget has not been brought into actual existence, the government shall carry out the budget of the preceding year." Thus the framers of the Constitution were careful not to place control of the national purse in the hands of the representatives of the people. This is not to say that the people were denied all influence in government. As will be seen in subsequent pages, their demands for a broadened franchise could not be ignored, and their representatives in the lower house were able to increase their power by practicing techniques of obstruction. Nevertheless, the aristocratic framework of the Constitution and the tradition of rule by the upper (feudal) classes remained after 1890 as substantial obstacles to the development of representative and responsible government.

---

[28] Quigley, *Japanese Government,* 160; Ito, *Commentaries,* 71; H. Furuya, *Système representatif au Japon* (Brussels, 1899), 69.

6. THE MINISTRY AND THE CABINET

Under the Constitution no formal provision was made for a cabinet. The Constitution merely noted that: "The respective Ministers of State shall give their advice to the emperor, and be responsible for it." All laws, ordinances, rescripts, etc., required the countersignature of a minister of state. But, as noted, a cabinet was created in 1885 and it continued to function as the ministry under the Constitution. The prime minister was selected by the emperor on the advice of the Genro. Not until 1918 was he in any sense responsible to the majority party in the House of Representatives. This is another way of saying that the cabinet's first responsibility was to the emperor, and only secondly to the Diet.

Such, in brief, are some of the main features of Japan's national government as established by the Constitution of 1889. How this government functioned during the rapid changes of the twentieth century will be discussed in subsequent chapters.[29] For the moment it is sufficient to note that the essential features of the constitutional structure as it emerged in 1889-1890 left the control of government in the hands of a small, privileged oligarchy.

JAPANESE LITERATURE, 1868-1889

These stirring political and constitutional changes, culminating in 1889, were accompanied by new and revolutionary trends in Japan's intellectual and literary world. During the early years of Meiji (1868-85) three Western philosophies vied for supremacy among Japan's intellectuals: 1) Anglo-Saxon utilitarianism; 2) the Christian concepts of mankind's freedom and brotherhood; and 3) German nationalism. All these were advocated vigorously in those turbulent years when the Japanese seemed willing to replace *everything* that was native with *anything* that was foreign. Confusion in act was linked with confusion in thought. How would the Japanese mind adjust itself to a wholly new set of social and political manners? Class distinctions had been abolished; Buddhist priests were raising families and letting their hair grow; men walked the streets in foreign clothes with long swords jutting from their hips; many Shinto shrines and Buddhist temples were torn down simply because they were old in an age that would tolerate only the new; priceless treasures of painting and sculpture were

---

[29] See Chapters 24 and 27.

sold to foreign collectors for little more than a song for the same reason; there was talk of romanization of the Japanese *kanji* (characters), of adopting free marriage, and of Christianizing the nation. And if this were not confusion enough, there was more at the most exclusive club in Tokyo, where Yamagata, the builder of Japan's army, and Ito, the architect of the Constitution, learned the waltz and the two-step.

One of the greatest literary figures of the period was Yukichi Fukuzawa. Of *samurai* family, he forsook the *samurai* tradition, devoted himself to the study of economics and political philosophy, and founded the school which grew into Keio University. Here many leaders of late Meiji Japan were educated in the utilitarian philosophy of the new politics, morals, and manners. A prolific writer, Fukuzawa ranged over the field of human knowledge from politics and morals to household economy. As the unrelenting advocate of Western ideas, he had no peer.[30]

Translations of many Western literary and political classics soon appeared on the Japanese market. *Earnest Maltravers, Hamlet, Aesop's Fables, The Lady of the Lake, Arabian Nights, Julius Caesar,* and many others followed in quick succession. Most of the translators, significantly, were not literary men but students of politics, economics, and government.

---

[30] Tadao Kunitomo, *Japanese Literature since 1868* (Tokyo, 1938), 1-11. See also *The Autobiography of Fukuzawa Yukichi* (Tokyo, 1934). The range of some of Fukuzawa's better known works is suggested by the following titles: *Gakumon-no-Susume* (Need of Learning), *Seiyo Jijo* (Western Life), *Sekai Kunizukuski* (Countries of the World), *Kyuri Zukai* (Illustrated Plain Talks on Science).

CHAPTER 11

CHINA, 1860-1894: THE LULL BEFORE THE STORM

WHEN Kuo Sung-tao, who had been appointed the first Chinese Minister to England (1867), returned to Peking, he said, to the consternation of his colleagues in the capital: "Confucius and Mencius have deceived us."[1] By this he meant not that he was converted to Western ideas, but that he recognized there were ways other than the Chinese of governing civilized countries. For a distinguished Chinese official to recognize that there were Western governments that were both "civilized and rational" was almost an unprecedented departure. Yet this was the central idea which during the latter half of the nineteenth century made its first impress on the Chinese mind. It was a lesson in intellectual readjustment that many Chinese were loath to learn, and which they learned but imperfectly. Indeed, from 1860 until the close of the century the Western powers vacillated between hope and despair of China's capacity to adjust herself to a "modern" world. It must therefore be the purpose of this chapter to relate in some detail the course of China's relations with the West following her humiliating defeat in the years 1858-1860. If these relations were at times unhappy in the extreme, if they formed but a prelude to greater tragedies to come, it will be helpful to recall that most of the statesmen, the politicians, the diplomats, and the merchants—Chinese and Europeans—who shaped these events were concerned in the main with immediate objectives—the opening of treaty ports, the regularizing of diplomatic intercourse, or the preservation of an ancient and hallowed Chinese political system. Neither Chinese nor foreigners sensed adequately, nor could they be expected to have done so, that China was already on the threshold of the most revolutionary era in her long and rich history.

---

[1] Quoted by E. R. Hughes, *The Invasion of China by the Western World* (London, 1937), 107.

A DISCREDITED DYNASTY

In 1861, as the first ministers of the treaty powers took up their residence in Peking, it seemed that the days of the Manchu dynasty might well be numbered. It was no longer a conquering power. It had superimposed its control on China's native and ancient culture, but as in the case of previous conquerors, the Manchu culture had been submerged and lost in that of China. In the early years of the dynasty when wisdom and vigor prevailed, the rule of the Manchus was accepted, even welcomed, since it appeared to hold the Mandate of Heaven. Now in the nineteenth century the favor of Heaven was in question. From within, China was plagued with natural calamities— flood, famine, and pestilence—and their inevitable concomitants, and with political revolts culminating in the T'ai-p'ing Rebellion; from without, she faced the increasing pressure of the Western powers whose superior force had exacted an enlarging array of treaty rights, not wholly unwelcome to Chinese merchants but wholly repugnant to the men who ruled China—the *literati*. To these men, the foreign impact meant humiliating treaties that degraded the Son of Heaven to the level of a Western sovereign; the defiling of the capital where foreign diplomats lived in the very shadow of the Forbidden City; and worse than these, the spread of subversive doctrines carried by traders, by diplomats, or by missionaries, all of whom were protected by treaties, while they taught alien social and religious ideas designed to supplant China's indigenous culture through which the *literati* maintained their power.

PEKING IN 1860 TO 1861

Peking in 1860 was a "deserted" city—deserted by its emperor and his court. The Imperial entourage had fled to the mountains of Jehol when the British and French advanced on the capital. Now that the panic was passed, the Court must return to set up an administration capable of enforcing the new treaties of 1858 and 1860. To this nervous capital came also, in the spring of 1861, Frederick Bruce and M. de Bourboulon, the British and French Ministers, respectively. Anson Burlingame, the new American Minister, arrived a few months later. These ministers were permitted to set up permanent residence in Peking, but when a representative of Prussia appeared, the Chinese, although granting him the commercial privileges won by the treaty powers, refused him residence at the capital. This was significant because it revealed the power still exercised by the extreme anti-foreign party at court. Even while members of this court were in virtual exile at Jehol in 1860, they still clamored for the impossible—the execution of all foreign prisoners. It was evident then that many members of the nobility had not learned the lesson which the *Arrow* War was supposed to teach.

THE ROLE OF PRINCE KUNG

When the Court fled from Peking, Prince Kung, brother of the emperor, had remained in the capital to treat with the foreigners. He was an able statesman, conscious in some degree of his country's inability to resist the foreign powers, yet handicapped by the stifling atmosphere of his training and background. To him fell the task of re-establishing friendly relations with the powers, of securing the emperor's approval of the conventions of 1860, and of reconciling the ignorant, anti-foreign court party with China's obligations under the new treaties.

The prospects for success were not bright. The Hsien-feng emperor, a mental and physical degenerate, had died at Jehol in August, 1861. Two court factions seeking control promptly appeared. The one was headed by reactionary Manchu princes; the other by an equally reactionary and anti-foreign concubine who in 1856 had borne the sovereign his first and only son. Anti-foreignism, characteristic of the Court during the entire Hsien-feng period, left ample room, as noted, for factionalism, and so it came about that under the influence of her enemies, the emperor had at his death named an administration from which she and Prince Kung were excluded. These circumstances drove the former concubine, now the junior Empress Dowager Tz'u-hsi, and Prince Kung to join forces. The princes were ruthlessly crushed. Since Prince Kung had saved the throne for her son, Tz'u-hsi repressed her violent anti-foreign views, perhaps in gratitude, perhaps because it was expedient. Thus by the end of 1861 there was some reason to hope that China's foreign relations were entering on happier times.

THE END OF THE T'AI-P'ING REBELLION

While this palace revolution was running its course at Peking, the Manchu government was still threatened in Central China by the T'ai-p'ing rebels. This rebellion, now in its second decade, had not only weakened the authority of the dynasty but also had complicated China's relations with the foreigners. Although the foreign powers, after a period of uncertainty, had determined to remain neutral in China's civil war, and had later given their support to the Manchus, many foreigners had reaped handsome commercial profits through trading with the rebels. But there could be no security for foreign interests in general so long as the lower Yangtze was ravaged by rebel and Imperial armies.

The eventual destruction which overtook the T'ai-p'ing must be credited neither to Chinese nor to foreign military action, but to the fact that the rebellion itself had failed. The rebels had outlived whatever usefulness they may originally have possessed. An Englishman visiting the rebel capital at Nanking in 1861 wrote: "I have no hope of any good ever coming of the rebel movement. No decent Chinaman will have anything to do with it. They do nothing but burn, murder and destroy." [2]

If China was slow in meeting the threat of the T'ai-p'ing, she was not wholly without resolve. It was indeed the T'ai-p'ing revolt which brought into prominence two of China's all too few great nineteenth-century leaders, Tsêng Kuo-fan of Hunan and Li Hung-chang of An-hui. These men, unlike so many of their colleagues, had fought the rebellion from its beginnings; but it was not until after 1860 that they achieved, with foreign assistance, any major success.

Among the foreigners who entered the Chinese service to fight the T'ai-p'ing were: Frederick Townsend Ward, an American soldier of fortune, of Salem, Massachusetts, organizer of a Chinese force known as the "Ever Victorious Army"; and Major Charles George Gordon of the British army, who took command of the "Ever Victorious Army" in 1863 after Ward's death. The military campaigns of Tsêng, Li, and their foreign colleagues, together with the aid of the British and the French governments, resulted in the slow but effective destruction of the rebel military power on the lower Yangtze. The city of Soochow, one of the strongest rebel bastions, fell in December, 1863. Two years later the T'ai-p'ing "Heavenly King," debauched and degenerate, committed suicide; his capital Nanking fell before the armies of Tsêng Kuo-fan. [3]

So ended the T'ai-p'ing Rebellion. During its course through the middle decades of the century, twelve of the richest provinces were devastated; some 20 million people were exterminated; poverty was everywhere; and the dynasty was almost destroyed. In a word, the movement was first an agrarian revolt, secondly a religious and moral

[2] Alexander Michie, quoted by E. T. Williams, *A Short History of China* (New York, 1928), 281.

[3] For an able sketch of Tsêng, see T. K. Chuan, "Tsêng Kuo-fan," *T'ien Hsia Monthly*, II, No. 2 (Feb., 1936), 121-137; see also A. E. Hake, *The Story of Chinese Gordon* (2 vols., 7th ed., London, 1884-85).

movement, and thirdly a rebellion against a dynasty which appeared to have lost the Mandate of Heaven. In some respects the rebellion had played a decisive part in the relations of China and the West. It helped, among other things, to encourage European intervention in China. For instance, the conclusion of the treaties of 1858 and 1860 stamped the T'ai-p'ings as rebels. They could be regarded no longer as potential allies of the Western powers, nor as potential successors to the Manchus. Furthermore, the indemnities for the *Arrow* War depended on the fate of the Peking dynasty.[4] These were not inconsequential factors in the decision of the foreign powers to intervene in support of the moribund Manchu rule.

THE CO-OPERATIVE POLICY, 1861-67

In a number of ways the years following the Peking settlement of 1860 gave promise of peaceful and constructive adjustment in China's relation with the powers. This was due very largely to the personalities of the four principal ministers who had established their legations in Peking: Anson Burlingame of the United States; Sir Frederick Bruce of Great Britain; M. Berthemy of France; and General L. de Balluseck of Russia, known popularly as the "Four B's." In this group Burlingame soon achieved a leadership which was the more remarkable since his country was involved in civil war, and since he, himself, was a novice in the diplomatic techniques of commercial imperialism.

Since Burlingame was under instructions to "consult and cooperate" with his diplomatic colleagues, he described for Secretary Seward in 1862 the principles through which the United States might apply a "co-operative" policy. These principles, approved by Seward, included:

1. No acquisition of Chinese territory by the United States.

2. No interference "in the political struggles of the Chinese further than to maintain our treaty rights."

3. Active assistance, in co-operation with other powers, to Chinese authorities in maintaining treaty rights against pirates, bandits, and rebels to the end that should the other powers "menace the integrity of the Chinese territory then the very fact that we had acted with them for law and order would give us greater weight against such a policy."

To Burlingame the danger of foreign aggression in China was very real.

---

[4] G. E. Taylor, "The Taiping Rebellion," *Chinese Soc. and Pol. Science Rev.*, XVI (1933), 612-614.

Here are over three hundred millions of people who are without arms—industrious, patient and wealthy and who, it is thought would be but too happy to submit to any power that would protect them.

To meet this danger Burlingame reiterated the principle already expressed by Humphrey Marshall.

If the treaty powers could agree among themselves to guarantee the neutrality of China and together secure order in the treaty Ports and give their moral support, at least, to that party in the Empire which would most favor a stable government—the interests of humanity would be subserved. The Treaty powers are practically doing this now, but how long they may remain in agreement it is impossible to imagine.

From 1862 until he retired as American Minister in 1867, Burlingame and his three colleagues applied the co-operative policy with remarkable success. In essence the policy achieved two things. First: China, confronted by united diplomatic action from the powers, was held to a stricter observance of the treaties, and this lessened the danger of resort to the gunboat policy. Second: as a result of this increased diplomatic stability, there was less temptation to individual powers to take advantage of China's weakness.

The co-operative policy, so long as it was applied, served to protect China's integrity at the hands of foreign aggressors. However, China's ills in the decade of 1860 could not be laid solely at the door of British, French, and Russian commercial exploitation. China also suffered grievously from enemies within. In this connection Burlingame's testimony is of great historic interest.[5]

The trouble here now is, that we are dealing with a regency which, in a few years, must hand over its doings to the Emperor and those he may call around him. The regency dare not depart in the smallest particular from the old traditions, and yet these will not do for these times. They [the Peking authorities] are distrustful of us, and are afraid of their censors and distant local authorities. Besides, there is a large anti-foreign party here. There are members of the foreign board who, if left to themselves, would at once place China in perfect international relations with us; but sitting with them are spies, who paralyze them in their action with us, to fall, as they frequently do, far short of their promises. In their weakness they . . . in-

---

[5] Cf. the attempt of the Washington Conference (1921-22) to provide by co-operative action an opportunity for China to cope with internal problems. (Chapter 25).

vite menace, and . . . cause us, almost to despair of holding, with dignity, any relations at all with them.[6]

So long as the "Four B's" interpreted the policies of the powers at Peking, China, in spite of her political weakness—her aptitude for evasion—enjoyed from the powers a liberal measure of understanding. But as Burlingame had said, it was impossible to predict when the powers would disagree, when the co-operative policy would be abandoned, when patience on either side would be exhausted and aggression be resumed.

PIN CH'UN'S MISSION TO EUROPE

China did appear to be frozen in "the old traditions." Yet there were tangible signs of what the West would call "progress." Even before 1860, there was a small but growing interest in things European. Two books treating foreign countries appeared in 1844 and 1848, respectively. Ministers of the Chinese Foreign Office frequently appealed to Burlingame, Bruce, Robert Hart, the Inspector-General of the Chinese Maritime Customs, and W. A. P. Martin of the T'ung Wen Kuan (the government foreign language school) for information and advice on foreign affairs. But, when it was first suggested that China might be the better informed by stationing diplomatic representatives abroad, all sorts of objections were raised.

As a temporary substitute for regular diplomatic intercourse, China did send to Europe in 1866 a mission of investigation composed of Pin Ch'un, a former district magistrate, and three students of the T'ung Wen Kuan. Since all were of low official rank, no questions of official etiquette would arise. The mission visited widely throughout Europe in France, England, Holland, Denmark, Russia, Germany, and Belgium. It appears to have paid little attention to questions of politics, but was greatly impressed by the spotless hotels, the brightly lighted streets where it "rained all day, yet there is no mud," and by Queen Victoria "unable to act without the sanction of a parliament." [7]

THE BURLINGAME MISSION

More significant was China's invitation in 1867 to Burlingame, then retiring as American Minister, to serve as China's first official envoy to

---

[6] Quotations are from Burlingame's official correspondence with Secretary Seward, United States Department of State, *China Despatches,* printed in Paul H. Clyde, ed., *United States Policy toward China* (Durham, 1940), 59-64.

[7] Knight Biggerstaff, "The First Chinese Mission of Investigation Sent to Europe," *Pacific Historical Review,* VI (1937), 307-320.

the treaty powers. The Foreign Office took this unprecedented action in the hope that misunderstandings might be removed, that there might be closer contact with foreign governments, and, most important, that in the approaching revision of the treaties the powers might be persuaded to show forbearance on the theory that China was already "progressing" as rapidly as could be, and that demands for further concessions would be inexpedient. Burlingame had so won the confidence of Peking that he was considered the ideal envoy to achieve these ends. Associated with him on a basis of equality in the mission were Chih Kang, a Manchu, and Sun Chia-ku, a Chinese.

The mission was received in America with an enthusiasm not unlike that which small boys accord a circus. Burlingame, an idealist and above all an orator, gave free reign to his own eloquence. He pictured China, the oldest nation, seeking westernization and progress through America, the youngest of nations. He pictured a China that stood with arms extended to receive "the shining banners of Western civilization"—strange sounding words to the conservative ears of Prince Kung and his associates in Peking.

In Washington the envoys were received by President Johnson. Burlingame and Secretary Seward then concluded (July 28) eight supplementary articles to the American Treaty of Tientsin. These articles provided: that China might appoint consuls at United States ports; that Americans in China and Chinese in the United States should enjoy complete freedom of religion; and that rights of residence and travel were to be open to the nationals of both countries. Moreover, the United States disavowed "any intention or right to intervene in the domestic administration of China in regard to the construction of railroads, telegraphs or other material internal improvements," China being conceded the right to determine the time for such improvements; and, finally, China and the United States recognized "the inherent and inalienable right of man to change his home and allegiance. . . ." [8]

On September 19 the mission reached London, where it received Lord Clarendon's assurance that the British government would show forbearance in seeking further commercial concessions and would deal

[8] For the Burlingame mission, see Knight Biggerstaff, "The Official Chinese Attitude toward the Burlingame Mission," *American Historical Review*, XLI (1936), 682-702; and Knight Biggerstaff, "A Translation of Anson Burlingame's Instructions from the Chinese Foreign Office," *Far Eastern Quarterly*, I (1942), 277-279. These studies have modified and supplemented earlier interpretations in F. Wells Williams, *Anson Burlingame and the First Chinese Mission to Foreign Powers* (New York, 1912), and Johannes von Gumpach, *The Burlingame Mission* (Shanghai, 1872).

only with the central government in seeking redress for wrongs to British subjects.[9]

From London the mission visited Paris, Belgium, Prussia, Denmark, Sweden, Holland, and Russia. While in Russia, on February 23, 1870, Burlingame died of pneumonia. Meanwhile, although the foreign press in the treaty ports had heaped abuse on the mission, declaring that it did not represent the real purposes of Peking, the Chinese government did ratify the Seward-Burlingame articles, thus demonstrating its faith in an envoy who, though exceeding the stricter limits of his instructions, had presented China's case with ability and enthusiasm.[10]

A summary appraisal of the Burlingame mission leads to a number of conclusions. It represented a radical departure from Chinese practice, even if it be assumed that Peking was seeking only to obstruct "progress" in the approaching treaty revision. Moreover, the Seward-Burlingame articles, taking the form of a treaty, were soon to prove embarrassing to both governments. In contrast, the policy of Great Britain as expressed by Lord Clarendon was substantial and sound. While expressing sympathy for China in a most difficult period of her development, it placed responsibility for treaty enforcement squarely on the shoulders of the Peking government.

THE PROBLEM OF TREATY REVISION

The British Treaty of Tientsin was subject to revision in 1868, but, as already noted, Lord Clarendon had assured Burlingame that the British government would exercise forbearance. This was significant. Chinese officialdom was convinced that the treaties offered too much; the British, and most of the foreign merchants in the ports, that they conceded too little. There was always the danger, too, that attacks upon foreigners by lawless and anti-foreign elements of the Chinese populace would lead to a resumption of the gunboat policy. Americans like all foreigners were subject to these attacks. In 1866, for example, the American vice-consul at Newchwang in South Manchuria was entrusted with arms and ammunition so that the American community

---

[9] Great Britain, *Parliamentary Papers, 1868-69,* Vol. LXIV, China, No. 1.

[10] It may be questioned whether Burlingame ever saw his official instructions, concerning the sources for which there is some dispute. He certainly did not follow them. In writing Seward he claimed a rank to which he was not entitled, and implied that his position was superior to that of Chih Kang and Sun Chia-ku, which it was not. Finally, the negotiation of the supplementary articles was a most liberal interpretation of the instruction to initiate only routine negotiations. See Biggerstaff, "The Official Chinese Attitude," 688-9.

at this port might protect itself from armed ruffians. S. Wells Williams, secretary of the American legation at Peking, noted that

. . . if we expect that the Chinese authorities at such times will always wish or dare to protect us, it is likely that we shall be disappointed. They readily assent that the treaties require them to afford us all the protection in their power, but as individuals, they may have their own opinion about the expediency or possibility of doing much for us against their countrymen; or, as at Niuchwang [Newchwang], sometimes may have no reliable or adequate force to help them.
. . . The first treaties . . . [are] so far beyond the ideas of the people at large, that their rulers become discouraged in trying to carry them out.[11]

Skillful diplomacy was needed if the legitimate rights of the powers were to be observed, the uncompromising demands of the merchants curbed, and Chinese officialdom convinced that its best interests would be served by educating its people to a fuller observance of the treaties. A few liberal officials at Peking did have some understanding of all this, and had sought the opinions of provincial governors and viceroys as early as 1867. Many of these latter counselled a rigid resistance to the foreigner. A few officials, such as Li Hung-chang, advocated a more progressive policy. Discarding the view that foreigners were a plague on Chinese soil, he observed with brutal frankness that "the outrageous craft and malignity of the Chinese exceeds even that of the foreigners." It was good sense for China to adopt those modern instruments of industry and politics which had given strength to the West.

The foreign merchants in the treaty ports and Hongkong also had their ideas on what should be done. They were already appealing to their home governments on the subject of treaty revision to redress their real or imagined grievances. However, Sir Rutherford Alcock, British Minister at Peking, believed that China could better be induced to adopt a liberal and progressive policy if coercion were not applied. He recognized that a moderate policy would never satisfy the merchants, and he added that they had no claim to consideration since they refused to appreciate the difficulties of reform and progress in a land as old as China, and since they themselves were guilty of "fraudulent practices and want of good faith." Accordingly, Lord Clarendon decided to delay pressing for treaty revision until 1872-73, when the young T'ung-chih emperor would attain his majority. In this decision the other treaty powers concurred.

---

[11] United States, Department of State, *China Despatches,* Vol. 23, No. 33, printed in Clyde, *United States Policy toward China,* 73-75.

There was thus for the time being a disposition on the part of the powers to view the China problem with sympathy and forbearance. But this intelligent self-interest made no appeal to the traders who wanted the profits of expanding trade and wanted them promptly.[12]

THE DEVELOPMENT OF CHRISTIAN MISSIONS

The question of treaty revision and in fact the larger problem of China's social relations with the West were connected intimately with the so-called missionary problem. The reader is already familiar with some aspects of Roman Catholic missions in China during the sixteenth, seventeenth, and eighteenth centuries. In the nineteenth century, coincident with the opening of China and Japan, Protestant Christendom became active in the field of foreign missions. In 1805 the London Missionary Society sent Robert Morrison to China. He travelled on an American ship, because the English East India Company, fearful of offending the Chinese, refused him passage on a Company ship.[13] The American Bible Society also entered the field. During the first year of its work in China (1822) the Society distributed 500 copies of the New Testament. Eighty years later it was giving away more than half a million copies, including an elegantly bound edition to the far-from-pious Empress Dowager on her sixtieth birthday.[14]

After 1830 American Protestantism was represented in China by an expanding group of churches and missionary societies.[15]

THE TREATY STATUS OF MISSIONARIES

Christianity and those who preached it had acquired an international legal status in China as a result of the toleration clauses of the Tientsin Treaties of 1858; the Russian and the French treaties permitted the missionaries *to travel* with passports in the interior. The Chinese text of the Franco-Chinese Convention of 1860 conceded the right of missionaries *to reside* in the interior, to acquire land, build churches, schools, etc., and to propagate Catholic doctrine without hindrance. The French text, which was the authoritative text, contained no such concession, and was kept secret from the other legations at Peking for

---

[12] See Alexander Michie, *The Englishman in China* (2 vols., New York, 1900), II, 321.

[13] See K. S. Latourette, *A History of Christian Missions in China* (New York, 1932), 212.

[14] D. Mac Gillivray, ed., *A Century of Protestant Missions in China* (1807-1907) (Shanghai, 1907), 574.

[15] See Latourette, *A History of Christian Missions in China*, 365-409; Mac Gillivray, *A Century of Protestant Missions in China*, 332, 366, 429, 527, 530; Julia C. Emery, *A Century of Endeavor 1821-1921* (New York, 1921), 61.

ten years. Whatever the explanation of this discrepancy in the texts of the Franco-Chinese Convention, its effects were explained clearly by Frederick F. Low, American Minister at Peking in 1870:

The missionaries of this [Roman Catholic] Religious Faith have, in addition to the right of residence as Bishops and Priests, assumed to occupy a semi-official position which places them on an equality with the native officers where they reside. They also claimed the right to protect the native Christians from persecution, which practically constituted the missionaries the arbiters of their disputes and the judges of their wrongful acts, and removed this class from the control of their native rulers. The absolute right of the Roman Catholic Clergy to exercise, in the name and by the authority of the French Government, a protectorate over native Christians was claimed . . . and insisted upon by some of the earlier representatives of France in China.[16]

Chinese officialdom feared and resented these pretensions of the missionaries. Not only did the official see immediate political implications involving his own power, he was also suspicious of Christianity because it was an alien and exclusive faith frequently in conflict with fundamental concepts of Chinese social and religious life. It will not be difficult to understand then how easily the ignorant and superstitious masses might be aroused to attacks upon missionaries and their property. All classes of the Chinese found ample evidence to support their distrust of the foreign missionary. His fundamentalist and intolerant dogmas could scarcely be reconciled with Chinese philosophy, essentially tolerant, practical, and mundane. Christian love and Christian intolerance were difficult for many Chinese to reconcile. Christian theory did not seem to be practiced with much vigor by the foreign merchants in the ports. From these critical conclusions grew others less critical, born of ignorance and fanaticism. It was common belief that Christian hospitals and orphanages purchased from indigent mothers hapless infants, whose eyes were extracted to compound direful drugs which when taken converted the victim to Christianity.

THE TIENTSIN MASSACRE

From a background of such suspicion, hatred, and fear, came the so-called Tientsin Massacre of 1870. A Chinese mob destroyed a Roman Catholic orphanage and adjoining church, and killed the French consul,

---

[16] Low to Secretary of State, Hamilton Fish, Peking, Dec. 5, 1870. Printed in Clyde, *United States Policy toward China*, 108-112.

two priests, ten nuns, three Russians, and some thirty Chinese servants. Alarm soon spread to many of the treaty ports, and French, British, and American warships appeared off Tientsin. The demands of France led to the death penalty or banishment of some of the perpetrators. China paid an indemnity of 250,000 taels and sent a mission of apology to France. Peking proposed a number of rules to govern and safeguard the work of missionaries, but only the American Minister was willing even to discuss them.

Thus less than ten years after Burlingame had reached China, and two years after negotiation of the Burlingame-Seward Treaty, the policy of patience and forbearance was headed for rough weather. The responsibility for the Tientsin Massacre cannot be laid to one country or one group of individuals. It must be shared by Chinese officials and agitators, by the missionaries, their church, and their governments. The Chinese government in failing to protect the foreigners had violated the treaties, but as Minister Low said:

. . . One of the great underlying causes of the unrest of the Chinese, which exhibits itself in hostility towards foreigners is to be found in the unwise action and illegal assumptions of the Roman Catholic Missionaries; which assumptions have, to a great extent, the countenance and support of the French Government.[17]

An earlier crisis than that at Tientsin had been averted only because France's able Minister, M. Berthemy, had "informed the missionaries that their assumptions were not warranted either by treaty right or good policy."

Many Protestant missionaries held views similar to the Catholics. Minister Low gave the essence of a complex problem when he wrote:

An ill-defined suspicion pervades the native [Chinese] mind that some political design lies beneath the honest exterior of the missionaries, and they are constantly watching with a suspicious eye for the hidden mystery which they can neither see nor understand.

If the Officials could be undeceived in regard to the real purposes of the missionaries, and if the missions in China could be conducted by really honest and sagacious men I doubt if anything more than a passive resistance would be met with, which would soon be overcome by friendly intercourse and mutual forbearance.[18]

---

[17] Clyde, *United States Policy toward China*, 108.

[18] Paul H. Clyde, "Frederick F. Low and the Tientsin Massacre," *Pacific Historical Review* II (1933), 100-108.

During the remainder of the nineteenth and on into the twentieth century China's relations with the West continued to be complicated by the political and other implications of the Christian missionary movement. A balanced picture of the missionary at work must of course give full weight to the sincerity and humanity with which many of the missionaries labored. Many of them lived in almost complete isolation, and sacrificed themselves willingly in the cause of Christianity. The educational and the medical work of the missions brought forth the highest praise. Nevertheless, George F. Seward, while American Minister at Peking (1876-1880), found that the majority of the grievances with which the legation was called upon to deal concerned missionaries. He regretted a situation which made the diplomatic agent of the American government the right arm of the propagandists of the Christian faith.[19] The established and learned classes of Chinese officialdom did not soon forget that the church of Notre Dame des Victoires at Tientsin was built on the former site of an Imperial temple, the cathedral at Canton on what had been the viceroy's yamen, and the P'ei-t'ang (Pehtang) cathedral at Peking on ground from which its towers looked down upon the Imperial Palaces.[20]

---

[19] United States, *Foreign Relations, 1876*, 47-48. Circular letter, Seward to United States consuls in China, Mar. 3, 1876.

[20] When in 1885 the Empress Dowager Tz'u-hsi moved into the palaces on the Central Lake she objected to the proximity of the cathedral from which her movements could be spied upon by the "foreign devils." L. C. Arlington and William Lewisohn, *In Search of Old Peking* (Peking, 1935), 135-136.

Chapter 12

CHINA, 1860-1894: THE LULL BEFORE THE STORM (CONTINUED)

CHINA, by 1860, had been forced to make important concessions to the treaty powers. Equality in diplomatic correspondence had been wrung from her in 1842; residence of the foreign envoys at Peking in 1858-60. It was understandable, too, that despite these developments, China should cling to whatever remnants of her tradition of superiority that still remained.

THE AUDIENCE QUESTION

Principal among these was the matter of audience for the foreign envoys in the presence of the emperor. When a minister from a treaty power reached China, he would, if Western practice were followed, be received in audience by the emperor to present his credentials. However, such an audience would imply that the Son of Heaven was a mere equal of Western sovereigns, an admission conservative Peking was not prepared to make. As late as 1867 the Court had been most careful in its instructions to the Burlingame mission to guard against committing the emperor on this point. Consequently all requests for audience made by the envoys in Peking had been denied. From 1861 to 1873 the Chinese Foreign Office was able to evade and delay a decision on the ground that the emperor was a minor. But this excuse could not be used indefinitely. The powers were in general agreement that eventually the audience must be insisted upon.[1] It seemed that 1873, the year of the emperor's coming of age, would be the appropriate time.

The audience was granted finally on June 29, 1873. During the previous four months the ministers of the Foreign Office and the foreign envoys had engaged in an unprofitable wrangle, the former demanding

---

[1] The Chinese attitude toward the audience question may be stated in this way. Apparently the Court was not unwilling to grant Imperial audiences during the 1860's. It merely demanded that foreign envoys conform to certain ceremonial usages to which the foreign envoys objected. Hence came the desire of the Chinese to postpone grappling with the question. Note W. W. Rockhill, *Diplomatic Audiences at the Court of China* (London, 1905).

that the foreigners kneel before the throne. Three bows were finally accepted as a substitute. Then came the appointed day when the T'ung-chih emperor entered the *Tzu Kuang Ko* (Throne Hall of Purple Effulgence) located in an Imperial park adjacent to but not in the Imperial Palace. The Japanese ambassador, Soyeshima, outranking his European colleagues, was received first and alone. Then the representatives of the Western powers were led in together by Prince Kung: General Vlangaly of Russia, Frederick F. Low of the United States, Thomas F. Wade of Great Britain, M. de Geofroy of France, and M. Ferguson of the Netherlands. All bowed three times as they advanced to the center of the hall and placed their letters of credence on the Dragon Table. After the reading of a congratulatory address in French the emperor acknowledged receipt of the letters by a slight inclination of the head and a few words in Manchu addressed to Prince Kung. The envoys now stepped backwards bowing repeatedly until they had reached the entrance to the Hall. The entire ceremony had taken less than half an hour.

So ended the first audience granted the foreign powers since the establishment of treaty relations. It was an event of primary importance to the powers, for as Minister Low had said, friendly relations could not be cultivated unless the "arrogance and conceit" of high Chinese officials was curbed by a ceremonial recognition that China was no more than equal with the foreign barbarians. On the surface therefore the powers could pride themselves on a diplomatic, ceremonial victory. Their triumph, however, was not so complete as they supposed. The Manchu-Chinese Court had succeeded in snubbing the foreigners at the very moment their equality was seemingly recognized. The *Tzu Kuang Ko* was a pavilion used for receiving tribute missions from the rulers of lesser kingdoms such as Korea, Burma, and the Ryukyu Islands. Furthermore, the envoys were not permitted to enter the grounds by the main gate but through a side entrance, just as lesser officials were required to enter at the side gate of a yamen. Finally, the Chinese account of the audience notes particularly that the foreign ministers were admitted "after an interval of some duration"; that is, after they had been kept waiting, a favorite method of making a caller feel his inferiority.[2]

In reality, therefore, the audience had accomplished very little, for the Peking authorities were convinced that they had succeeded in maintaining their superior position. Moreover, a year and a half later

---

[2] For further details see L. C. Arlington and William Lewisohn, *In Search of Old Peking* (Peking, 1935), 101-103, 330-332.

(January 12, 1875) the T'ung-chih emperor died of smallpox. Under the influence of the Empress Dowager Tz'u-hsi, and against all precedent, the Court named as successor, Tsai-tien, a child of the same generation as the deceased monarch. The new sovereign, the Kuang-hsü emperor (1875-1908), was a son of Tz'u-hsi's sister and of Prince Chun, her most ardent supporter in the Imperial Family. For the next fourteen years Tz'u-hsi, as regent, was again the ruler of China in fact, and in name. This development did not bode well for China's relations with the treaty powers.

THE MARGARY AFFAIR

As Minister Low had predicted, the Imperial audience did not prove a panacea for all the ills to which the foreigners were heir in China. In fact, the audience had no sooner been granted than events occurred which threw China's foreign relations into diplomatic turmoil.

Foreign traders in the Far East had long speculated on the possibilities of reaching China's western provinces of Kweichow, Yünnan, and Szechuan by way of the Burma border. One expedition from British India had proceeded to Bhamo on the upper Irrawaddy in 1868; a second expedition, under the command of Colonel Horace A. Browne, was organized in 1874 to enter Yünnan. The British legation in Peking was asked to provide passports and an interpreter from the consular service. For this post Minister Wade selected Augustus Raymond Margary, who, travelling overland with six Chinese, reached Bhamo on January 17, 1875.

In February the Browne expedition left Bhamo. It was preceded by Margary and his Chinese, whose purpose was to discover whether the route might be travelled in safety. The answer to this question was given when Margary and five of his Chinese associates were killed by what seems to have been the premeditated act of armed Chinese. Responsibility for this outrage is not easily placed. The Burmese sovereign was opposed to the opening of trade routes, as were also the local Chinese authorities in Yünnan. The border tribes were irresponsible and frequently beyond Chinese control; yet the local Chinese authorities could scarcely be absolved of negligence if not connivance. What is really significant is that the murder of Margary was seized upon by British Minister Wade as an appropriate incident to be used in forcing a settlement with Peking of all outstanding Anglo-Chinese questions.

Wade formulated his demands promptly: 1) China to send a mission of investigation accompanied by British officers; 2) permission for a second expedition from India; 3) 150,000 taels to be placed at the British Minister's disposal; 4) the emperor to grant a fitting and satisfactory audience to Her Majesty's Minister; 5) British goods to be freed from all *likin* taxation; and 6) all British claims to be satisfied at once. On second thought Wade reduced his demands to the first three. In London the government approved one and two but reserved judgment on point three.

The Chinese government accepted the demands in principle but objected to the blunt manner of Wade's diplomacy. It was not until August, 1876, that he met with Li Hung-chang at Chefoo, where on September 13 an agreement known as the Chefoo Convention was signed. It was ratified by China four days later, but by Great Britain not until July, 1885, which delay suggests that governments sometimes have difficulty in making up their minds.[3]

THE CHEFOO CONVENTION

The Chefoo Convention was an impressive document embodying three sections. The first, which dealt with the Yünnan-Margary case, provided for the issuance of proclamations in the provinces, for the drawing up of regulations for the Burma-Yünnan frontier trade, for a second mission from India, for the stationing for five years of British officers at some city in Yünnan, for an indemnity of 200,000 taels for the families of those murdered, for expenses incident to the whole case, and for the claims of British merchants. Finally, China was to send a mission of apology to London.

Section two of the Convention dealt with "Official Intercourse." China was to invite the foreign powers to consider with her a code of procedure and official etiquette designed to insure proper treatment of the foreign ministers at Peking and of the consuls at the treaty ports. China was also to invite the powers to consider with her means of insuring more effective administration of justice at the treaty ports.

Section three, dealing with trade, provided for the opening of additional treaty ports (Ichang, Wuhu, Wenchow, and Pakhoi), for stationing a consul at Chungking, and for the opening of several ports of call on the Yangtze. Other clauses provided for defining more clearly the foreign settlement areas in the ports.

In general it may be said that the Chefoo Convention was a sub-

---

[3] For text of the Chefoo Convention see China, The Maritime Customs, *Treaties* (2 vols., 2nd ed., Shanghai, 1917), I, 491-505. Note S. T. Wang, *The Margary Affair and the Chefoo Convention* (New York, 1939).

stantial supplement to Britain's treaties of 1842, 1858, and 1860, in that
it secured practically all the concessions the British Minister had been
demanding over a period of nearly two years, the major exception being
the failure to have Viceroy Tsen and others brought to trial. However,
the Convention was not well received by representatives of the other
treaty powers. There were objections from the Russians, the Germans, and the French, a point of importance since by the nature of its
content most of the Convention required the ratification of these powers
also. In general, too, British merchants were opposed to it, on the
ground that it would be better to hold China to a strict observance of
the 1858 settlement than to require new concessions of her.

SEWARD AND TREATY QUESTIONS

Perhaps the most penetrating analysis of the complexities of China's
relations with the powers at this time was given by the American Minister in Peking, George F. Seward, a nephew of William H. Seward.
The period of Seward's ministry at Peking, 1876-1880, was one in which
there were few, if any, conclusive achievements in the foreign relations
of the Chinese Empire. But it was a period in which every problem
arising out of China's new treaty relations was debated vigorously by
the diplomats in Peking; a period in which every method of extortion
was used on the one side, and every method of obstructionism and
evasion on the other. What Seward had to say is of importance not because of his concrete accomplishments (he could claim few, if any), but
because of the light he throws upon the clash of interests in China.[4]

The attitude of the American Minister toward the Chinese was both
realistic and liberal. He was convinced that the Chinese would grant
nothing, indeed that they would not even negotiate, except under coercion, and that they had no intention of carrying out existing treaty stipulations wherever an avenue of escape could be found. Yet he believed
that the foreigner must be willing to compromise with the Chinese view
and to recognize Chinese sovereignty as far as was practicable. He opposed the most extreme demands of Minister Wade, and he recognized
and accepted the justice of China's claim that railroads should not be
built on her soil without her consent. Like Burlingame, Seward favored the co-operative policy, but when the British Minister used the
Margary incident as an excuse for demanding of the Chinese a settle-

[4] The ablest treatment of Seward's diplomacy in China is an unpublished manuscript
study, Harry R. Lynn, *George F. Seward and China Treaty Questions 1876-1880*, University of Kentucky, 1932.

ment of commercial and other extraneous matters, Seward declined to co-operate.

On questions of the administration of justice and the operations of extraterritoriality in China, Seward was equally expressive. The Chinese held that by no treaty had they given foreigners permission to disregard or violate their laws. They insisted that the true meaning of extraterritoriality was not that foreigners were at liberty to break Chinese laws, but merely that in case of infraction they should be punished by their own officials. Seward firmly opposed this position. He pointed out that while it was obviously clear that Americans in China should not be permitted to outrage Chinese public sentiment,

things . . . which are not offences in the United States cannot be dealt with as such in the consular courts. It is our own system of law which these courts are empowered to administer and not Chinese law.[5]

LIKIN AND THE TAXATION OF FOREIGN GOODS

Since the foreign merchants and their governments were interested in China primarily because of the rewards of commerce, the subject of taxation of foreign merchandise was constantly before the diplomats. The principle of the conventional tariff embodied in the treaties of 1843 and later years had by no means solved all the problems incident to this question. Among the more important and difficult of these problems of commerce was *likin* taxation. *Likin* was a species of internal customs duty, levied at various stations upon goods in transit within the Empire. Rates were determined locally, and varied widely among the different provinces. Seward regarded *likin* as in contravention of the treaties, and hence illegal on the ground that this form of taxation had only been applied generally after the treaties of 1858, which expressly forbade additional taxation on foreign goods. The whole business was complicated by the fact that other internal customs duties, similar to *likin,* did antedate all the treaties with China. These duties, if they were in force in China in 1844, had been regarded as legal under the treaties. The American treaty of 1858 set up a procedure for commuting these legal internal levies by a single payment amounting to one half of the tariff duty, and specified that no further taxes were to be levied. *Likin* obviously was an additional tax, and therefore under the treaties illegal. Levied first in 1853 during the T'ai-p'ing Rebellion as a temporary means of securing funds to meet extraordinary conditions,

---

[5] United States, Department of State, *China Despatches,* Vol. 50. Seward to Evarts, Washington, April 15, 1879.

its application spread widely after 1857, and by 1874-76 it had become general throughout China and Manchuria.[6]

In 1876, when the Chefoo Convention was concluded, there was virtual agreement among the foreign envoys that *likin* was illegal, but it was also recognized that the tax was of great importance to the local or provincial governments which might well refuse to surrender it even if so demanded by Peking.

IMMIGRATION: PRINCIPLE AND PRACTICE

While these problems, brought into discussion by the Chefoo Convention, were still being debated, China's relations with the United States were disturbed by the results of the emigration of Chinese laborers to California. During the nineteenth century Chinese emigration had been of two kinds: free emigration of coolie laborers, for the most part to California and Australia; contract-labor emigration to Cuba and Peru, known as the coolie trade. After 1862 the coolie trade was prohibited to American ships, and was brought under rigid regulation in British vessels sailing from Hongkong. Nevertheless, until 1874 this nefarious trade continued to flourish from the Portuguese settlement at Macao. No better example can be found of man's inhumanity to man than this business in human flesh. S. Wells Williams wrote in 1866 from Peking that "the most flagitious acts have been committed by the [Chinese] natives upon each other, under the stimulus of rewards offered by foreigners to bring them coolies." Burlingame reported that in the season 1865-66 there were sent to Cuba alone, mostly from Macao, 13,500 coolies at a cost of nearly $3,000,000.[7] Until this vicious traffic was brought to an end in 1874 there were small grounds for Western moralizing on the short-comings of China in international affairs.

In contrast with the pitiable condition of the Chinese coolie laborer in Cuba and Peru, the free laborer who came to California enjoyed a personal and an economic freedom he had not known in China. So relatively prosperous, indeed, was the lot of these immigrants that by 1880 there were 75,000 Chinese in California—nine percent of the population. They had been attracted by news of the rich opportunities offered in the gold fields, by the demands for labor in the building of the first transcontinental railroad, and by the retail trade in San Francisco and other towns. At first the Chinese were welcome as laborers.

[6] Shao-Kwan Chen, *The System of Taxation in China in the Tsing Dynasty, 1644-1911* (New York, 1914), 103 ff.
[7] United States, Department of State, *China Despatches*, Vol. 23, No. 27, and Vol. 24, No. 130, printed in Paul H. Clyde, ed., *United States Policy toward China* (Durham, 1940), 76-79.

They provided cheap convenient labor, able to live on "the smell of a greasy rag." In the beginning, too, their qualities of industry and docility were thought of as virtues. This attitude prevailed until the great depression of the seventies, at which time the cry was raised that the "Chinaman" was robbing the white man's dinner pail and destroying his standard of living. The "Chinaman's" virtues now became vices. The New York *Nation* noted derisively in 1883 that on the Pacific Coast the Chinese were perpetuating "those disgusting habits of thrift, industry, and self-denial. . . ."[8] It became clear, to those who wished so to think, that the Chinese had many other vices. They lived to themselves, frequently in hovels. They were impervious to the beneficent influence of Americanization. They gambled. They smoked smuggled opium, and, since they had no wives with them, they consorted with prostitutes. There was some truth in all these charges, but no evidence has yet been unearthed to indicate that in these respects the Chinese were any worse, or better, than virile immigrant "Americans" of Irish and other foreign descent who at this time made up the vociferous element on the Pacific Coast.

Violence against the Chinese in word and deed reached a shameful intensity in 1877. San Francisco harbored the backwash of the depression of 1873: the scum of the labor market, rowdies, and political adventurers. In this group were many Irish, naturalized and unnaturalized, who readily accepted the leadership of one Denis Kearney, an Irish-born, recently naturalized agitator, famous for his hypnotic power over the mob. It was Kearney who shouted as he held a noosed rope in his hand, "The Chinese must go!" "Christian" followers of Kearney held that the Chinese didn't have souls, and even if they did, they weren't worth saving. So the Chinese were attacked, their store windows broken, their freshly laundered clothing trampled in the gutter, their queues snipped with scissors, their bodies kicked and stoned. Finally, there were boycotts of Oriental labor, and cold-blooded murdering of some of the Chinese.[9]

THE CHINESE BECOME A POLITICAL QUESTION

What was basically an economic and sociological problem now became political. Western politicians and members of Congress were

---

[8] Quoted by Thomas A. Bailey, *A Diplomatic History of the American People* (2nd ed., New York, 1942), 428.

[9] See: M. R. Coolidge, *Chinese Immigration* (New York, 1909), chs. i-vii; R. W. Paul, "The Origins of the Chinese Issue in California," *Miss. Valley Hist. Rev.*, XXV (1938); and the study by H. F. MacNair, *The Chinese Abroad* (Shanghai, 1924).

determined to get rid of the Chinese. The attitude of the eastern states was one largely of indifference. To the rather sanctimonious East, a western editor wrote:

Let a colony of these Asiatic brethren, with souls to save, camp down beside Boston Common, with their filthy habits, their criminal practices, and their nasty vices, and how long would it be before Beacon Hill would sniff the polluted atmosphere, and all the overgodly of New England would send up their prayers for relief.[10]

This political battle against the Chinese had a long background. As early as 1855 a governor of California was denouncing the Chinese to satisfy his constituents; anti-Chinese memorials were in circulation; and anti-Chinese bills were being offered in the legislature. Charges were made that the Chinese in California, like those in Cuba and Peru, were under servile contracts. The Civil War quieted the agitation for a time, and the transcontinental railroad construction which followed absorbed all available Chinese labor. The Central Pacific was finished in 1869, at which time the roads were employing nearly 10,000 men, of whom some 9,000 were Chinese who were noted to be "peaceable, industrious and economical, apt to learn and quite as efficient as white laborers." However, in defiance of all forecasts, the completion of the railways did not usher in prosperity. On the contrary, land values failed to rise; thousands of white and Chinese laborers were thrown out of employment; the California State Democratic platform of 1869 was rabidly anti-Negro, anti-railway, and anti-Chinese. The Republicans too found it expedient politically to be nominally anti-Chinese. In 1876 the California Senate sent to Congress, in the guise of an impartial investigation of the Chinese, a viciously partisan document designed to inflame race prejudice and win the election. Against this testimony were the words of a former American minister at Peking, J. Ross Browne, usually regarded as severe in his judgments of the Chinese:

[The Chinese] do not seek to interfere in our political struggles; they are peaceful and law-abiding; they are always willing to bear their equal burden of taxes; and all they ask is to be treated with common humanity. It is a noticeable fact that the only strenuous opposition to them is from an alien population [the Irish], who upon the principle of discrimination urged against the Chinese would themselves be excluded. But the fault is not so

---

[10] *San Francisco Argonaut,* II, 5 (Jan. 19, 1878), quoted by Bailey, *A Diplomatic History,* 430.

much with the laboring classes who pour into our country from Europe, as with the political charlatans who mislead them.[11]

All this made it abundantly clear that Seward and Burlingame had misjudged the future when in 1868 they had written into their Sino-American treaty "the inherent and inalienable right of man to change his home and allegiance." It now appeared either that this principle itself was not valid, or that many Americans were not so closely wedded to it as had been supposed. At any rate, the American government was faced with the embarrassing task of informing China that her people were not wanted here.

Prompt action by the federal government could not be delayed, for in 1879 Congress passed a law prohibiting any ship from bringing to the United States more than fifteen Chinese on any one trip. President Hayes vetoed the bill on March 1, 1879, on the ground that it was virtual exclusion and therefore in violation of the Burlingame Treaty. In the West, Hayes was burned in effigy, while the East greeted his act as "wise and manly." Thereupon the President sent to China a commission composed of James B. Angell, William H. Trescot, and John F. Swift. One who is unfamiliar with the background traced in the preceding paragraphs, and who reads only the instructions of Secretary Evarts to the commission, June 8, 1880, might well suppose that in that year it was the United States rather than China that had suffered injury. The commissioners were to concern themselves with: 1) "making our [commercial] privileges more clear, more secure and more extensive"; 2) impressing upon the Chinese that if they could collect *likin* and other "discriminatory" taxes, they could also prevent their collection; 3) entertaining any ideas the Chinese might have for reconciling the systems of jurisprudence, American and Chinese, in applying extraterritoriality in China; and 4) explaining to the Chinese why "this Government finds great public interests to require in our relations to China and the movement of its population to our Pacific coast, what may appear to be a modification of our universal hospitality to foreign immigration." [12] On November 17, 1880, the commission signed two treaties with China, the one commercial, the other giving the United States the right to "regulate, limit or suspend" but not to "absolutely prohibit" the immigration of Chinese laborers. When in response to this new treaty status Congress suspended Chinese immigration for twenty years, President Arthur vetoed the measure, April 4, 1882, as "unreasonable," that

---

[11] United States, Department of State, *China Despatches*, Vol. 25, No. 1.

[12] United States, Department of State, *China Instructions*, Vol. 3, No. 1.

is, not within the meaning of a "suspension." Again East and West were divided, but compromise was found in a second bill, in 1882, suspending Chinese immigration for ten years, a measure which the President accepted. The law of 1882 was amended and strengthened in 1884, and two years before it was due to expire it was made more rigid, in 1892, on the eve of a presidential election. Chinese exclusion had become a national policy.

Even this diplomatic settlement and the legislative program against the Chinese did not for a time put an end to anti-Chinese riots in the United States. Twenty-eight Chinese were murdered in Wyoming in 1885; the federal government was powerless to intervene in what was purely a state matter. The best that Congress could do was to vote an indemnity.[13]

THE IMPLICATIONS OF CHINESE EXCLUSION

The facts of the Chinese immigration question in the late nineteenth century lead to conclusions which are not pleasant. On a number of points the evidence is perfectly clear. Most of the Chinese in the United States were here legally; as a group they were industrious and peaceable; their vices may have been different but it would be a wise man who could affirm that they were worse than those of other immigrants, or for that matter of native-born Americans. Indeed, the Chinese had been encouraged to come to the United States not only by economic opportunity but also by the diplomacy of two Americans, Seward and Burlingame. Burlingame was undoubtedly influenced by idealism, Seward by the more mundane considerations of cheap labor. Their combined motives resulted in the writing of a treaty in 1868 which embodied the ideal and the principle of free immigration. Within twelve years this ideal had become unworkable. Thereupon the problem was permitted to fall into the hands of demagogues, agitators, political hoodlums, and others who thought of themselves as "100 percent American." By them the Chinese question was never considered upon its merits. Their policy of total exclusion was as barren in statesmanship as was the naïve "free immigration" of Burlingame and Seward.

END OF THE CHINESE EDUCATIONAL COMMISSION

Among the unforeseen results of the new policy of Chinese exclusion was one of great importance. In 1872, as a consequence of the efforts of Tsêng Kuo-fan and Li Hung-chang, the Chinese government had sent to the United States the first of several groups of students who were to study modern American ways as a preparation for government serv-

[13] Coolidge, *Chinese Immigration,* chs. ix-xvii.

ice in their native land. Most of these Chinese boys were located in homes of the small towns of the Connecticut Valley. Their training would fit them, it was hoped, for leadership in the development of a modern China. In 1881, when their high-school work was completed and they were about to enter upon their technical training, the students were recalled to China, and the sending of future contingents was cancelled. A promising experiment in American-Chinese relations was thus terminated abruptly. Although this decision of Li Hung-chang and the Tsungli Yamen resulted from a number of considerations (among which were the too thorough Americanization of the students, the cost of the experiment, etc.), it was also due to what the Chinese regarded as American repudiation of the reciprocal clauses of the Burlingame Treaty and the adoption of a discriminatory policy toward Chinese immigration.[14] Some Chinese were not slow in reflecting on the fact that though the Chinese were invited to the American heaven, they were not wanted in the Americans' country.

POLITICAL DESTINIES CONTROLLED BY THE STARS

In a sense it may be said that the years 1880 to 1898 form a period of reaction and stagnation in China's relations with the West. The hopes expressed by Burlingame in 1868 had not been fulfilled. The progressive tendencies shown by Tsêng Kuo-fan and Li Hung-chang were giving place to parochial conservatism with which China had been frequently over-blessed. An attitude of inaction, of evasion, and of philosophical helplessness possessed the Peking administration. This meant that toward the close of the century, when various powers were about to increase their pressure upon some of China's border states (Indo-China, Korea, etc.), China was unprepared mentally and physically to meet the onslaught. China was not solely responsible for this, but regardless of responsibility, she was to pay dearly for her failure to modernize her processes of thought and action.

China's great lack in this period was that of positive, dynamic statesmanship. Even the powerful Li Hung-chang in 1883 could do no more than bewail his country's fate.

. . . China [he said] had no friends. Russia was menacing her on the north. Germany had invaded her territory at Swatow. Japan had taken the Loo-Choo [Ryukyu] Islands. England held Hongkong, and was forcing upon her a traffic in opium that meant the misery and ruin of her peo-

[14] Thomas E. LaFargue, "Chinese Educational Commission to the United States," *Far Eastern Quarterly*, I (1941), 59-70. See also Yung Wing, *My Life in China and America* (New York, 1909). See further Thomas E. LaFargue, *China's First Hundred* (Pullman, Wash., 1942).

ole. France was sending an expedition to dismember her empire. The United States had passed an act excluding Chinese from her soil, Chinese, alone, of all the races in the world.[15]

The answer to this dismal picture, as the foreigners saw it, was given to Li by John Russell Young who had become American Minister at Peking in 1882. In his conversations with the powerful viceroy, Young points out that China had largely herself to blame. "She must first show the world [said Young] that she has a Government. There is now no government in Peking." It was Young's view that Peking was simply "trifling" in foreign affairs. The most ordinary questions that could be settled in an hour were allowed to drag on for months with no results. The Tsungli Yamen showed not the remotest desire to encourage diplomatic relations. The inevitable results were irritation and friction.

Minister Young found little encouragement in the fact that the ups and downs of Peking politics were controlled as much by the movement of comets as by the practical needs of the times.[16]

TRADE, FINANCE, AND INVESTMENT

It is pertinent to recall at this point that most of the problems that have been touched upon in this and the preceding chapter, whether diplomatic, political, religious, or social, had come about because Westerners had established themselves in China under a system of treaties designed to promote international trade among national states—a system in which governments acted as the protectors of their merchant nationals. In the middle of the nineteenth century, the impact of the foreign trader, confined as he was to the treaty ports, appears to have brought about no general dislocation in China's economy, though some competent students consider that the foreign impact was an important contributing cause to the T'ai-p'ing Rebellion. However, in the early Canton trade, and as late as the 1870's, tea and silk amounted to more than 90 percent of China's exports. Not until the last quarter of the century did China's foreign trade show marked signs of growth and diversification. Trade routes had been shortened by the opening of the Suez Canal; freight was carried in steel steamships; and London

---

[15] United States, Department of State, *China Despatches,* Vol. 65, No. 230, Aug. 8, 883, report of a conversation between Li Hung-chang and John Russell Young, American Minister at Peking.

[16] United States, Department of State, *China Despatches,* Vol. 64, No. 136, Peking, February 21, 1883.

merchants communicated with their agents in Shanghai by cable. A the end of the century approached, the variety of China's exports in creased; silk and tea accounted for only 50 percent of exports; and, wha was perhaps of greater importance, China became an importer of cot ton goods, kerosene, glass, flour, soaps, and a wide variety of consume goods. The significance of this lay in the fact that China was under going a commercial revolution which her politicians, "controlled by the comets," failed to understand.

With this commercial revolution, too, came the first signs of a stil more fundamental economic and financial revolution. It was abou 1870 that the foreigner became interested in capital investment in China The first foreign railroad was built from Shanghai to Woosung in 1876 but prejudice was so strong that in 1877 it was purchased by the Chinese torn up, and shipped away to Formosa to rust. However, in 1881, L Hung-chang's influence brought about the opening of the Tongshan railroad. The Shanghai-Tientsin telegraph was opened in 1882. Some Chinese, indeed, were overcoming their prejudice against mining devel opment, as evidenced by the opening of the Kaiping mines in 1878 The period also witnessed appearance of the first Chinese steam navi gation company and the opening of iron works in the Yangtze Valley These enterprises, whether Chinese or foreign, required financing and foreign machinery, and these came from abroad. Here then were the first beginnings of foreign investment in China (other than that con nected immediately with foreign trade at the ports), and of foreign bor rowing by the Chinese government. The first of these government loans was made in 1865 from an English bank.[17]

Unfortunately, only a few Chinese statesmen such as Li Hung-chang and Chang Chih-tung sensed the inevitable advance of Western com merce, finance, and investment; recognized some of the revolutionary changes these things were about to force upon China; and felt the de mand for political reform to meet the times. It would indeed have been strange had China been prepared for the revolution which was slowly forcing itself upon her entire structure. Her economy was a social, agricultural, and family economy; that of the West was political, com mercial, and national. The West, recognizing the efficacy of economic power, had created national states which emphasized "the relation of the state to the economic activity of the people." China, on the contrary, had detached economics from politics. "Traditional China," as Profes sor Remer has said, "was a civilization, not a state."[18]

[17] A. G. Coons, The Foreign Public Debt of China (Philadelphia, 1930), 1-2.
[18] C. F. Remer, Foreign Investments in China (New York, 1933), 37-38.

CHINA AND HER DEPENDENT STATES: RYUKYU, ILI, ANNAM, SIKKIM, AND KOREA; THE SINO-JAPANESE WAR

IT HAS already been suggested in these pages that the increasing nineteenth-century contacts between Westerners and the Chinese involved forces more complex than the balance sheet of a trader, the catechism of a missionary, or the etiquette of a diplomat. In their various callings, trader, missionary, and diplomat carried to China a Western civilization which was well on its way to Europeanize the world. It was a vigorous and an aggressive civilization which assumed that man's material and, in some degree, even his spiritual, salvation rested on the national state and the colonial empire, on the Industrial Revolution and the development of commerce, on the conversion of the heathen to Christianity, and on the acceptance by "remote and backward peoples" such as the Chinese of Western ideas of international law. But all these concepts were foreign to the traditional thought of nineteenth-century China. She could accept them only through changes which in the light of her own civilization would be in the broadest sense revolutionary, and, as was indicated at the close of the preceding chapter, China was not yet prepared to undertake a revolution.[1] It is true that the Seward-Burlingame Treaty (1868) had conceded to China "the right to decide the time and manner and circumstances" of westernization; but treaties fail frequently to control "the march of events." So it was that between 1870 and 1895 China's position in the Far East was challenged by the powers not only at Peking but also on the borders of the Empire in the "vassal"

---

[1] The traditional Chinese view of history had something to do with the slowness of Chinese modern adjustment. According to the traditional view, "dynasty succeeded dynasty, each following the same cycle of rise in virtue and decay in vice—the same play presented over and over again, but each time with a new cast. It was this view of Chinese history which T. T. Meadows had in mind in mid-nineteenth century when he coined his famous description of the Chinese as the most rebellious but the least revolutionary of peoples. A change of dynasty meant new personnel, not new institutions." Meribeth Cameron, "The Periodization of Chinese History," *Pacific Historical Review,* XV (1946), 173.

or "tributary" or, to use a better term, the dependent states. During this period the Middle Kingdom lost whatever control, *de facto* or *de jure,* it had exercised previously in the Ryukyu Islands, in Indo-China, in Burma, in Korea, and in other areas.[2] Thereby a fundamental principle of Chinese government—the relation between the superior and the inferior state—was destroyed. States which had recognized the overlordship of Peking were to become either independent, or the colonies of foreign powers. To understand how this came about and the consequences to China resulting from it, one must review briefly certain Chinese concepts of government.

CONFUCIAN INTERNATIONAL THEORIES

The Confucian system of China in its bearing on international relations rested on the principles of familism and the inequality of nations. The world was regarded as a unit, natural rather than legal in organization. China Proper, the Middle Kingdom, was the controlling center area where men were civilized and thus understood and lived by the Confucian rules of propriety. All who lived outside this area were "barbarians," a term denoting anything from savagery to a state of civilization different from and therefore inferior to China's. As border states became civilized, that is, Confucianized, the Confucian system was extended to them. The relation between China and these border, Confucianized states, was that of the elder and younger brother. It was a relation not always definite or uniform, but it was apt to include the following: 1) China, the superior, taught and admonished the lesser state; 2) the lesser state might be under close supervision or the contacts might be largely ceremonial; 3) the lesser sovereign received investiture from the Chinese emperor; 4) the lesser state could be required to furnish men and supplies when China engaged in missions of "correction"; 5) tribute-bearing missions from the lesser state were sent to China, thereby recognizing the primacy of China in the Confucian family of nations.[3]

In theory, and generally in practice, China did not seek through these means to control directly the internal affairs of the border states. In fact the border states were largely autonomous so long as their rulers kept the peace, lived with their peoples on the Confucian model, and

---

[2] In some cases (e.g., Burma, Sikkim, Annam) China had not exercised any control for a very long time, so that despite theoretical dependence upon China, these states were really independent *de facto.* This was one reason why France and Britain paid little attention to Chinese claims of overlordship.

[3] I have here drawn heavily upon M. Frederick Nelson, *Korea and the Old Orders in Eastern Asia* (Baton Rouge, 1945). Tribute-bearing missions usually received in return gifts of greater value than those they had brought.

performed the ceremonial and other duties of their inferior status. In practice, however, many of the men who have controlled China have been politicians rather than pure Confucian theorists. It was possible for such men to use the theory of the superior and the inferior state to serve the ends of what today would be called power politics, and thus to make the border states mere colonies of the Middle Kingdom.

IN SUMMARY

The basic difference between the Chinese and the Western concept of international affairs was that the Chinese system did not rest primarily on any concept of the "state" or "sovereignty" as understood in the West.

With their concept of the natural world order, with government the centrifugal force of moral precepts, expanding from a central core through example and voluntary emulation, the Chinese developed no concept of the 'state' or of 'sovereignty.' China was the center of an entire world system, a powerful core around which were grouped many weaker satellites, none able to compare with it in power, wealth, culture, and virtue. With all influence flowing outward, with no competing cultures or authority against which the barriers of definite boundaries need be raised, China had no need for the legal concept of the state or of sovereignty. Its control was through ideas which could be confined within no physical boundaries. The marking off of a certain territory within which its word was the highest law and beyond which its precepts were unrecognized, was not contemplated in Chinese theory. Not only was the field of Chinese influence unlimited by physical boundaries, but its field of action embraced the entire social life of man, not certain fields which were deemed public.[4]

These controls were applied "through propaganda, appeal to reason, and example, not through the enactment of law, enforced by the authority of the state." None of this was understood by the Western powers when in the nineteenth century they sought to open relations with China's border states. To the West it appeared that China was the "suzerain" over various "vassal" or "tributary" states. This was of course so; but these terms did not connote identical forms of control in the Western and in the Chinese system of things.

While China remained the center and the superior in a Confucian community of nations, and while China had no vital contacts with other civilizations, all was well; but when in the nineteenth century Western states sought relations not only with China but also with the border

---

[4] Nelson, *Korea*, 102-103.

states, such as Korea, they precipitated a conflict between the Confucian theory and Western concepts of international law and the legal equality of states. In Korea, for instance, they found a people "which to them was neither sovereign enough to conduct independent relations nor subject enough to throw responsibility for its actions on China."

THE CASE OF THE RYUKYU ISLANDS

The island kingdom of Ryukyu, the chain of small islands reaching from Kyūshū in southern Japan southward to Formosa, had sent tribute to China since late in the fourteenth century, a fact which placed it in the Confucian community of states over which China presided. However, feudal Japan also exercised certain political claims over Ryukyu. The royal family of Ryukyu was said to be related to the Minamoto clan; this may explain why it was that the Ryukyuans sent tribute to Japan in the fifteenth century. Early in the seventeenth century the Japanese *Daimyo* of Satsuma attacked the islands, brought the northern group under his immediate control, leaving the southern group semi-independent, a species of tributary status. Thus in the middle of the nineteenth century the unfortunate little state found itself tributary to both China and to Japan. In 1871 some Ryukyu islanders, wrecked on the shores of Formosa, were murdered by the aborigines. When China in response to Japanese overtures disclaimed responsibility for acts of the Formosans, Japan sent a military expedition to Formosa (1874). In addition, the Japanese continued to occupy a portion of the island, pending a settlement of the dispute with China. This was finally secured through British mediation; China agreed to identify the families of the murdered men and to pay for the roads Japan had built in Formosa. The significant implication of this settlement was that Japan was able to establish a legal claim to be protector of the Ryukyu islanders. For a time China refused to accept this view, and Ryukyu continued tribute missions to Peking. Attempts at mediation by General U. S. Grant in 1879 also failed, but in that year the Ryukyuan king was removed to Tokyo, where he was granted a title of nobility, and the islands were incorporated into Japan as a prefecture under the name of Okinawa. In 1881 China accepted a situation which she was powerless to alter.[5] The Ryukyu incident is important because in this case Japan had succeeded in breaking the Confucian concept of international relations, and in substituting for it the Western code of state responsibility.

---

[5] Payson J. Treat, *Diplomatic Relations between the United States and Japan 1853-1895* (2 vols., Stanford University, 1932), I, 473-475, 568-569; II, 71-78, 98-104, 126-127, 141-144.

THE CASE OF KOREA

The case of Korea was to be of far greater international consequence than that of Ryukyu. The earliest European contacts with Korea had occurred in 1593 when the Spanish Jesuit, Gregorio de Cespedes, administered spiritual consolation to Japanese Christian soldiers during Hideyoshi's abortive invasion.[6] A number of Dutch sailors were shipwrecked on Korean shores in the seventeenth century, and later escaped to Japan.[7] Some attempts were made to open trade toward the end of the eighteenth and the beginning of the nineteenth century.[8] During these developments Catholic Christianity reached Korea by way of the Jesuit mission in Peking, and later French priests entered the country surreptitiously. The conflict between Christianity and Confucianism, and the increase in the number of converts (there were 9,000 in 1839) led in that year to persecution and to the death of many converts, including three priests. When in 1846 France sought explanations, she was informed that Korea was subordinate to China, to whom all questions of foreign relations must be referred.[9] By this statement Korea was attempting to avoid relations with the West rather than to describe accurately her own status, for actually she had negotiated directly with foreign states such as Japan, though with no other states that were outside the Confucian system.

After 1860 a number of powers attempted to trade with Korea: the British and the Russians in 1861, the French the following year. To a second Russian mission in 1866 the Koreans declared that they were a dependent state of China. This Korean policy, in so far as it was followed from 1863 until 1898, may be ascribed to the regent, father of an infant king, who was vigorously anti-Western and anti-Christian, and who carried the title Tai wun kun.[10]

FRANCE IN KOREA, 1866

In 1866 a great wave of anti-Christian persecution virtually wiped out the Christian community of some 18,000 converts, while only three of

[6] Ralph M. Cory, "Some Notes on Father Gregorio de Cespedes, Korea's First European Visitor," *Transactions*, Korean Branch, Royal Asiatic Society, XXVII (1937), 1-55.

[7] Hendrick Hamel, "An Account of the Shipwreck of a Dutch Vessel . . . , together with the Description of the Kingdom of Corea," *Transactions*, Korean Branch, Royal Asiatic Society, IX (1918), 91-148.

[8] J. H. Longford, *The Story of Korea* (London, 1911), 226; and W. E. Griffis, *Corea: The Hermit Nation* (7th ed., London, 1905), 359.

[9] Charles Dallet, *Histoire de l'église de Corea* (2 vols., Paris, 1874), II, 339-341.

[10] G. H. Jones, "The Taiwon Kun," *Korean Repository*, V (1898).

a score of French priests escaped with their lives. A French force from China prepared to attack Korea, and the Peking government was informed that since China disclaimed any authority over Korea, France herself would seek satisfaction. The military-naval expedition which followed suffered a decisive defeat and for a time France abandoned any further action. The fact that China did not assume any responsibility for the acts of Korea confirmed France in the belief that China had voluntarily surrendered any claim to suzerainty over this former vassal or tributary state.[11]

THE UNITED STATES AND KOREA

The United States, too, showed an official interest in Korea in 1866, when Secretary of State William H. Seward, thinking that Korea was about to be partitioned, proposed a joint Franco-American expedition. The French had brought back from Korea word that an American merchant ship, the *General Sherman,* had been wrecked on the Korean coast and that the natives had burned her and killed the crew. To Burlingame's inquiries at Peking, China replied that her connections with Korea were only "ceremonial." Seward's joint expedition was not undertaken, but American naval vessels did some charting on the Korean coast, and it was decided to seek a treaty with Korea for the protection of Americans shipwrecked on her coasts.[12] When the American naval expedition reached Korea in May, 1871, it was fired upon. In retaliation, it destroyed a number of Korean forts, but got no treaty.[13] Indeed, the Koreans made it clear to China that they hoped to continue the old Confucian relationship, and they hoped China would make this clear to the barbarians. This, China made little effort to do. Thus American diplomats in Peking, like their French colleagues, continued to hold the view that China had recently renounced control over Korea's foreign affairs in order to avoid responsibility for Korea's involvements with Western powers.

JAPAN AND THE OPENING OF KOREA

Japan sent a mission to Korea in 1868 to announce the restoration of the emperor and to seek the re-opening of relations. However, this mission and subsequent ones in 1869 and 1871 were treated with scant respect by the Tai wun kun's government since Japan was regarded as a

---

[11] United States, *Foreign Relations, 1866,* 536; *1867,* Pt. I, 420 ff.

[12] United States, *Foreign Relations, 1870,* 33.

[13] C. O. Paullin, *Diplomatic Negotiations of American Naval Officers, 1778-1883* (Baltimore, 1912), 282-328.

traitor to Confucian society because of her adoption of Western ways. However, in 1875 a Japanese gunboat engaged in marine surveys on the Korean coast was fired upon. Here, then, was an incident which could serve to bring Korea into treaty relations with Japan, and at the same time detach Korea from its Confucian dependency on China.

MORI'S MISSION TO CHINA, 1876

Recognizing however that her success in Korea might well depend on the attitude of China, Japan first dispatched to Peking a mission under Yurei Mori to seek a more definite Chinese avowal of Korea's independence. China however continued to maintain that the relationship was that of "dependence yet no control." Nevertheless, Li Hungchang agreed to aid Japan in securing a friendly reception at Seoul.[14]

The mission which Japan sent to Korea soon secured a treaty (February 26, 1876) which opened three Korean ports to trade and provided for diplomatic intercourse.[15] In English translation, Article I reads: "Chosen, being an independent State (*tzu chu*), enjoys the same sovereign rights as does Japan." Some Chinese historians have, however, translated this article more favorably to China. For instance: "Chaohsien [Chosen or Korea] being an autonomous (*tzu chu*) state, shall enjoy the rights of equality with Japan."[16] Nevertheless, despite arguments over the precise meaning of Article I, certain points are quite clear. The Japanese at this time intended by their treaty to make Korea "independent" as the West understood that term, whereas China on the other hand had no intention to alter the ancient relation in any way. As for the Korean government, the best that can be said is that it signed a "Western treaty" with Japan, making at the same time a mental reservation to continue the old Confucian relation with China.

CHINA LOSES THE DEPENDENCIES OF ILI, ANNAM, BURMA, SIKKIM

Korea's status, hanging as it did at this time between an ancient Confucian ideology and a modern Western one, was soon to be clarified by events in China's other dependencies. In 1881 the inroads of Russia in

---

[14] T. F. Tsiang, "Sino-Japanese Diplomatic Relations, 1870-1894," *Chinese Soc. and Pol. Science Rev.*, XVII (1933), is the best Chinese interpretation based on extensive Chinese sources. See also T. C. Lin, "Li Hung-chang: His Korea Policies, 1870-1885," *Chinese Soc. and Pol. Science Rev.*, XIX (1935-36).

[15] Text in *British and Foreign State Papers*, LXVII, 530-533.

[16] Shuhsi Hsu, *China and Her Political Entity* (New York, 1926), 109. *Tzu chu* is usually translated "self-governing" or "autonomous," rather than "sovereign" or "independent."

the northwest resulted in the loss by China of the western part of Ili, which was ceded to Russia.[17]   In 1885 the long story of French penetration into Indo-China dating back to the days of Louis XVI was completed.   In that year Annam, which had been a dependent state of China since Han times, fell completely under the control of France.[18] At virtually the same time, Burma ceased to be a dependency of China. It had been a vassal state of China since its conquest by Kublai Khan in 1284.   Lower Burma had passed to British control in 1862.   Now in 1886 the British extended their jurisdiction over all Burma.   China recognized British sovereignty in Burma, and Britain agreed that Burma might continue to send decennial tribute missions to Peking.[19]   Only one mission, that of 1895, was ever sent.   Finally in 1890 China recognized a British protectorate over Sikkim.[20]   All of these treaties concerning Ili, Annam, Burma, and Sikkim revealed that the old Chinese relationship to these states (dependence yet no control) was giving place to a new Western and legalistic relationship in which these states were recognized by China as the colonies or protectorates of Western powers. It was therefore apparent that Japan's attempt to establish the independence of Korea in 1876 was not an isolated occurrence but rather a part of a larger movement by which the dependencies of China were being detached from dependence on Peking.[21]

THE NEW CHINESE POLICY TOWARD KOREA

China was not slow in recognizing the danger of losing her ancient Confucian control over Korea. Following the loss of Ryukyu, Li Hung-chang noted that: "We can no longer refrain from devising ways and means for the security of Korea." [22]   Accordingly, China adopted a three-fold course of action: she urged Korea to strengthen her military forces; she increased her diplomatic contacts with Korea in the hope of exercising greater influence at Seoul; and she urged Korea to conclude treaties with those powers which, unlike Japan and Russia, would be

[17] British and Foreign State Papers, LXXII, 1144.

[18] British and Foreign State Papers, LXXVI, 246 ff. See also H. I. Priestley, France Overseas (New York, 1938), 216-222.

[19] China, The Maritime Customs, Treaties (2nd ed., 2 vols., Shanghai, 1917), I, 506-508.

[20] Ibid., 513-515.

[21] For a more detailed summary of this movement see M. J. Bau, The Foreign Relations of China (New York, 1922), II, "The Loss of Dependencies (1860-1895)." See also H. B. Morse, The International Relations of the Chinese Empire (3 vols., London, 1910-18), II. Morse provides the most detailed accounts.

[22] T. C. Lin, "Li Hung-chang," 219.

unlikely to have territorial ambitions. Of these powers the United States was the first to show a renewed interest in treaty relations with Korea. Commodore Robert W. Shufeldt was sent by the Navy Department to seek, with Japanese aid, a commercial treaty. The mission failed, but Shufeldt was encouraged by Li Hung-chang to seek a treaty through China's good offices. In 1882 the first American-Korean treaty was concluded. It provided among other things for the exchange of diplomatic and consular officers, for trade with Korea on the most-favored-nation principle, and included the provision:

If other Powers deal unjustly or oppressively with either Government, the other will exert their good offices, on being informed of the case, to bring about an amicable arrangement, thus showing their friendly feelings.[23]

Li had asked, and Shufeldt had refused, to include a clause acknowledging the dependence of Korea upon China. This matter was disposed of by a letter from the Korean king to the President acknowledging the subservient status.[24] However, the United States took the position, stated by Frederick T. Frelinghuysen, the Secretary of State,

that we have not regarded the aid lent to us by Chinese officials in bringing about this treaty as in any way an assertion of China's administrative rights over Corea . . . but that we regarded Corea as de facto independent, and that our acceptance of the friendly aid found in China was in no sense a recognition of China's suzerain power.[25]

EUROPEAN TREATIES WITH KOREA

The principal European powers were quick to follow the example of the United States in securing treaties through China's good offices: Great Britain, November 26, 1883; Germany, November 26, 1883; Italy, June 26, 1884; Russia, June 25/July 7, 1884; and France, June 4, 1886.[26] In each case Korea, while negotiating as a sovereign power in terms of the treaty, set forth in accompanying letters her dependent position upon China.

---

[23] Text of the treaty in United States, *Statutes at Large*, XXIII, 720-725.

[24] United States, *Foreign Relations, 1888*, Pt. II, 255-256.

[25] United States, Department of State, *China Instructions*, Vol. 3, No. 30.

[26] For the texts of these various treaties see *British and Foreign State Papers*, LXXIV, 86-93, 633-640; LXXV, 308-316, 510-518; and LXXVII, 500-507. For a full discussion of the final and the preliminary British treaties see E. V. G. Kiernan, *British Diplomacy in China, 1880-1885* (Cambridge, England, 1939), chs. vi-vii.

KOREAN POLITICS AND CHINESE RELATIONS, 1882

Prior to the conclusion of these treaties, the international status of Korea had been affected by other developments. The first of these was China's intervention in a palace revolution at Seoul; the other, the conclusion of certain Sino-Korean trade regulations.

There were two major factions at the Korean court: the one, led by the family of the queen, favored relations with foreign powers; the other, led by the Tai wun kun, was, as already noted, intensely antiforeign. The rivalry of these two factions, together with bad economic conditions, led to a conspiracy (1882) to do away with the queen. The plot failed, but in the course of the fighting Korean mobs attacked the Japanese legation and drove its occupants to the coast, where they were rescued by a British ship. Both Japan and China now stepped into the picture by sending troops to restore order. China, claiming to act in her traditional Confucian capacity, seized the Tai wun kun and sent him to Tientsin for punishment. Japan on her part exacted from Korea an agreement providing for an apology, an indemnity, the right to station a legation guard at Seoul, and the right of travel in the interior.[27] To the Western powers all this was thoroughly confusing. Here was China intervening in the internal affairs of Korea, for which she professed to have no responsibility, using troops to restore order, issuing proclamations in the name of the king, and carrying off a member of the Royal House to answer for his deeds. On the other hand, here was Japan ignoring the Chinese and dealing directly with Korea.

The second development of 1882 was the conclusion by China and Korea of new regulations on trade. This agreement, while asserting that there was no change in Korea's status "as a boundary state of China," gave to the Chinese discriminatory advantages over other foreigners in matters of residence, travel, trade, and import duties. These advantages were granted exclusively to China because Korea was a tributary kingdom. Again the question before the Western powers was how this sort of thing could be reconciled with their own Korean treaties negotiated on the assumption that Korea was now independent.

It was evident after 1882 that Chinese control over and intervention in Korea was becoming more pronounced. High Chinese military officers even proposed the annexation of Korea and war with Japan.[28] Li, however, adopting measures short of this, sent P. G. von Mollendorff to

---

[27] United States, Department of State, *China Despatches,* Vol. 61, No. 27, Young to Frelinghuysen, incl. 8, Oct. 2, 1882.

[28] T. F. Tsiang, "Sino-Japanese Diplomatic Relations, 1870-1894," 76-77.

Korea as Inspector-General of Korean Customs. He also sent a number of Chinese "commercial agents" who would "actually assist the King to decide political issues" under the guise of their title. Indeed, Korea had ceased to be merely a Confucian appendage of China, for Li Hung-chang was now asserting, "I am King of Corea whenever I think the interests of China require me to assert that prerogative." [29]

THE TIENTSIN CONVENTION, 1885

Japan too had become active in Korea. She gave her support to the progressive or reform party. By 1884 the Japanese minister at Seoul openly criticized the policies of China, adding that Japan would welcome complete Korean independence.[30] In December, 1884, the Korean Progressives seized the king and called upon the Japanese for military protection. Yüan Shih-k'ai, commanding Chinese troops, promptly drove the Japanese to the coast and restored the king to his conservative counsellors. For this affair, the Japanese exacted from Korea a mild treaty including an indemnity; but they also sent a mission headed by Hirobumi Ito to Tientsin to discuss the Korean question with Li Hung-chang. The Treaty of Tientsin (April 18, 1885) which resulted was a partial though not a complete victory for Japan. The two powers agreed to withdraw their troops from Korea, and, in the case of future disturbances, neither would send troops *without notifying the other*.[31] Thus, Japan gained a position of equality with China in the matter of military intervention.

KOREA BECOMES A CHINESE "PROTECTORATE,"
1885-1894

Between 1885 and 1894 Li Hung-chang so strengthened his control over Korea that the country became a Chinese protectorate rather than a dependent state in the old Confucian sense. Li accomplished this end by various means. To the control which he already exercised through foreigners in the employ of the Korean government and through Chinese commercial agents, he added the appointment of Yüan Shih-k'ai as Chinese Resident in Korea, a post superior to that of a mere diplomatic representative. By the control which he exercised through these agents, Li attempted to destroy any idea in the minds of the powers that Korea was fully sovereign. There are numerous examples of the length to

[29] United States, Department of State, *China Despatches*, Vol. 65, No. 230, Young to Frelinghuysen, Aug. 8, 1883.
[30] Alfred Stead, ed., *Japan by the Japanese* (London, 1904), 189-191.
[31] *British and Foreign State Papers*, LXXVI, 297-298.

which Li was prepared to go to maintain his "kingship" in Korea. When in 1886 members of the Korean government were seeking Russian aid to re-establish "independence," Li threatened to depose the king if that were necessary to stop the movement. At the same time Li's influence was able to remove from the Korean scene Lieutenant George C. Foulk, American naval *attaché* and *chargé* at Seoul, when he attempted to carry out his instructions to regard Korea as an independent state.[32] Other Americans also interested themselves in the efforts of the Korean king to free himself of Chinese control. Among these were O. N. Denny, the king's American adviser, whose opposition to Chinese influence in Korea was expressed in the United States Senate by Senator Mitchell of Oregon.[33] The net result of this futile effort to bring the United States to the aid of Korean independence was the dismissal of Denny. Finally, Li sought economic as well as political influence at Seoul. In 1885 China obtained a monopoly in the Korean telegraph, and attempted to get control over future loans sought by the Korean government. So successful indeed was Li's policy that in 1892 even Japan approached Korea through China when seeking satisfaction for losses occasioned by certain Korean embargoes on the exportation of beans to Japan.[34]

IMMEDIATE BACKGROUND OF THE SINO-JAPANESE WAR

The issue between China and Japan concerning the international status of Korea was clear by the early months of 1894. Summarized briefly it was this: 1) the impact of the West had already deprived China of her principal dependent states, Burma, Annam, Ili, and Sikkim— Korea alone remained; 2) Korea too appeared to be headed toward what the West called "sovereign independence" (this was indicated by the Japanese treaty of 1876, the American treaty of 1882, and the European treaties of 1883 and after); 3) Li Hung-chang, however, was determined to preserve China's influence in this strategic peninsula against the designs of either Japan or Russia, and to do so by Western as well as Confucian techniques if that were necessary; and, finally, 4) since no one of the Western powers, despite their treaties, was prepared to assert the fact as well as the principle, of Korean independence, the way was left open for Japan to do so. And when the time at last came for Japan to

---

[32] Harold J. Noble, "The United States and Sino-Korean Relations, 1885-1887," *Pacific Historical Review*, II (1933), 292-304. See also Payson J. Treat, "China and Korea, 1885-1894," *Political Science Quarterly*, XLIX (1934), 506-543.

[33] *Congressional Record*, XIX (1888), 8135-8140.

[34] United States, Department of State, *Korea Despatches*, Vol. 10, Nos. 396 and 399.

implement her policy of upholding Korean independence, she enjoyed a special advantage. It was relatively easy for her to give the impression that her motives were benevolent—to rescue Korea from China and Russia, and to bestow upon the Hermit Kingdom the independence, the sovereignty, and the progressive outlook which Japan herself enjoyed. It is perhaps needless to add that Japan's motives relative to Korea were no more benevolent than those of any other power.

KOREA: A EUROPEAN PROBLEM

However, even in 1894 Korea was not a question concerning Japan and China alone. It had already become "a sort of focal point for great European rivalries, as well as for Asiatic antagonisms." [35] When in 1885 it was rumored that Russia was to seize Port Lazarev, the British occupied Port Hamilton, an island off southern Korea, but Russia pursued a cautious policy mildly supporting Japan and the United States against Chinese pretensions.[36] England's policy in these years was dominated by the idea of preventing "the Russians from encroaching on Korea and from securing an ice-free port." It was against this background of European rivalries that the Japanese policy of 1894 was launched.

By 1894, Japan's political position in Korea was woefully weak, but her economic position was showing steady growth. Ninety percent of Korea's foreign trade was with Japan. Li had made strenuous efforts to counter Japan's economic advance. He was slowly acquiring an army and navy, and was creating at Port Arthur a respectable naval base. He was also planning a railway from Shanhaikwan to the Manchurian border near Vladivostok. News of this latter project created considerable excitement in Russia, where in 1891 the decision was made to build the Trans-Siberian Railway. This was looked upon in Europe as a decision of the utmost importance, and it was viewed with misgivings by both China and Japan. The Japanese believed that if Russia completed her system of communications, her advance into eastern Asia could not be stopped; yet they also believed that Korea must be independent or controlled by Japan if the Empire was to be secure.[37] The

---

[35] William L. Langer, *The Diplomacy of Imperialism, 1890-1902* (2 vols., New York, 1935), I, 168. Note ch. vi for a discussion of European aspects of the crisis.

[36] The Russian view of the conflict over Korea, like the British, was thoroughly realistic. The Russian Foreign Office held that: "The conflict between China and Japan is the natural result of a diplomatic struggle between these governments for political and economic influence in Korea." "First Steps of Russian Imperialism in Far East (1888-1903)," from Krasny Archiv., *Chinese Soc. and Pol. Science Rev.*, XVIII (1934), 246.

[37] Langer, *The Diplomacy of Imperialism*, I, 172.

Japanese also had domestic worries on their minds. The constitutional government inaugurated in 1890 was not going well. Cabinets that considered themselves responsible only to the emperor were faced with a succession of recalcitrant diets which refused to accept naval estimates presented by the government until appealed to directly by the emperor.[38] With young and inexperienced parliamentarians in this mood, some of the bureaucrats and militarists in the government were ready to welcome a foreign war that would unite the political home front in bonds of patriotism.

IMMEDIATE PRELIMINARIES TO WAR

From 1871 until 1894 the peace party in Japan, headed in the later years by Hirobumi Ito, maintained its ascendancy over the militarists, and consequently there was no war over Korea. But after 1890 the "obstructive" tactics of the Diet gave the war party its opportunity. Only a pretext was needed, and this was soon forthcoming. The *Tong Hak* ("Eastern Learning Society"), originally a Korean religious sect, had acquired a political complexion, had drawn into its membership the politically oppressed, and had assumed a program which was anti-foreign, anti-Christian, and anti-Japanese. When as a result rebellion finally occurred in the southern provinces, Korean government troops sent to quell the disturbance were themselves defeated. Acting on the advice of Yüan, Li Hung-chang promptly decided to send Chinese troops (June 6, 1894), and, in accord with the Tientsin Convention, notified Japan that he was doing so. Untactfully, China's notice referred to "our tributary state." Japan replied the same day that she too would send troops owing to the "grave nature" of affairs in the peninsula, and added that she had "never recognized Korea as a tributary state of China." By the time the Chinese and the Japanese troops arrived, the Koreans had already suppressed the revolt. Two hostile foreign armies faced each other before Seoul. A miracle perhaps could have prevented a clash, but miracles were not happening at Seoul. Japan proposed joint Sino-Japanese action to effect financial, administrative, and military reforms in Korea. China replied that she would not interfere in the internal administration of Korea and added that Japan had no right to do so. Japan then turned to the Korean government, demanding a declaration indicating whether or not Korea was tributary to China. When Korea's reply proved unsatisfactory to the Japanese, their troops seized the king, and a reorganized Korean government ordered Japan

---

[38] Tatsuji Takeuchi, *War and Diplomacy in the Japanese Empire* (Garden City, 1935), 109-110.

to expel the Chinese troops. The Sino-Japanese War had begun. The declarations were issued on August 1, 1894.[39]

THE WAR

The diplomatic front was by no means favorable to Japan when she embarked on a policy of war. Britain, having supported China, indicated that she would not agree to Japanese annexation of Korean territory. Russia too gave her diplomatic support to China, seemingly on the theory that it was better to have Korea controlled by a weak China than by a young and vigorous Japan. As a result, Japan gave assurances to the powers that she had no designs on Korean territory, was interested only in Korean reform, and, in the interests of European commerce, would refrain from attacking Shanghai. These assurances were accepted, probably because it was believed generally in the West that Japan would be defeated. But these early forecasts were shattered by the September victories of Japanese arms at Pingyang and the Yalu. It soon became evident that Chinese forces were no match for the small but relatively efficient Japanese military machine.[40]

Indeed a diplomatic revolution was already under way. British opinion, reacting to the Japanese victories, contemplated a complete reorientation of British far eastern policy. On October 6, the British invited France, Germany, Russia, and the United States to intervene jointly to seek a settlement that would include: Korean independence, a European guarantee to Korea, and indemnity for Japan. The proposal was dropped when Germany and the United States refused to join. Li Hung-chang himself also sought the support of Europe and America to end the disastrous war before China was completely humbled. During the winter months of January and February, 1895, the Japanese had taken Wei-hai-wei; their armies were crossing southern Manchuria; and in early March they had occupied Newchwang and Yingkow, from which they might soon advance on a frightened and humiliated government in Peking. Here the Empress Dowager, instead of building a navy, had employed government funds to rebuild the Summer Palace, now embellished with an atrocious triumph, the Marble Boat, which was made mostly of wood. But the Marble Boat was small comfort to Chinese Admiral Ting Ju-Chiang, who committed suicide at Wei-hai-wei when forced to surrender to the Japanese, who had not spent their

---

[39] See W. M. Junkin, "The Tong Hak," *Korean Repository,* II (1895), 56-60; and "Russian Documents Relating to the Sino-Japanese War, 1894-95," *Chinese Soc. and Pol. Science Rev.,* XVII (1933-34), 480-515.

[40] Langer, *The Diplomacy of Imperialism,* I, 173-175.

money on marble boats. When at this juncture the United States offered its good offices to both belligerents, Japan replied significantly that
her objectives would not be reached "until China finds herself in a position to approach Japan directly on the subject of peace."

Indeed Li did send a succession of peace missions to Japan. Finally,
when all these failed, when hope of European aid or of a victory for
Chinese arms had vanished, Li Hung-chang himself accepted the
humiliating task of asking for peace. As he left for Japan he still hoped
for a diplomatic victory through European intervention, though he was
warned by Denby that what China needed was "a sincere, friendly *rapprochement* with Japan."

THE TREATY OF SHIMONOSEKI, APRIL 17, 1895

Japan's military and naval victory marked the beginning of a new era
in the Far East, the effects of which were to be felt almost as much in
Europe as in Asia. The immediate question was: "What would be
Japan's demands?" The tables were now turned. At Tientsin in 1885
Ito had been forced to accept what China was willing to give. At Shimonoseki in 1895 it appeared that China would be forced to give whatever
Ito demanded. The specific nature of Japan's demands was not known
until they were presented to the Chinese on April 1. They included:
1) China to recognize the full and complete independence of Korea;
2) China to cede to Japan Formosa, the Pescadores, and the Liaotung
Peninsula in South Manchuria; 3) China to pay an indemnity of 300,-
000,000 taels; 4) China to conclude with Japan a new treaty of commerce, granting Japan among other things most-favored-nation treatment, and opening seven new treaty ports. Since neither Europe nor
the United States was prepared to come actively at this time to China's
aid, Li was forced to accept Japan's terms with some modifications.
The Treaty of Shimonoseki (sometimes known as Bakan) was signed
April 17, 1895.[41]

EFFECTS OF THE WAR AND THE PEACE IN JAPAN

The efficacy of war as a stabilizer of Japanese politics was immediately
evident. By the declaration of war Ito and Japan's Elder Statesmen
achieved notable results. The nation was unified; peace prevailed between the government and the Diet; huge war budgets (one of 150,000,-

---

[41] For full text and separate articles, see John V. A. MacMurray, compiler and ed.,
Treaties and Agreements with and concerning China, 1894-1919 (2 vols., New York,
1921), I, 18-25. Hereafter cited as MacMurray, *Treaties*. The indemnity was fixed at
200,000,000 taels, and four ports were to be opened.

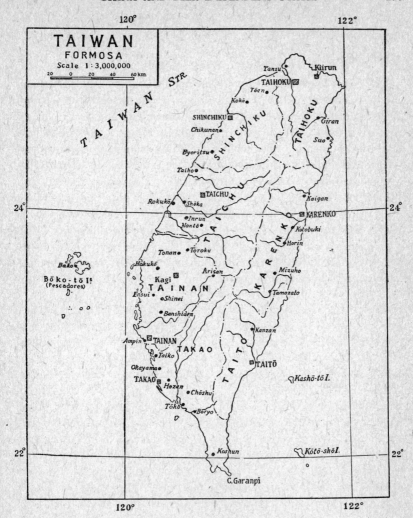

000 yen) were passed without a dissenting vote; in February a resolution was adopted unanimously to appropriate any amount of funds needed for the prosecution of the war.[42]   Japan had indeed taken the first step in what was to be a vigorous policy of expansion on the Asiatic continent.   With Port Arthur and the Liaotung Peninsula in her possession she could look forward to a controlling influence at Peking.   In a word she had made it clear that both territorially and diplomatically

---

[42] Takeuchi, *War and Diplomacy in the Japanese Empire*, 112-16.

she proposed to be a part of whatever imperialistic pressures were exerted upon China.

CHINA'S NEW POSITION

For China the results of the war were not less momentous. The proud Middle Kingdom had been defeated by a people looked upon not only as inferior but also, by reason of their westernization, as traitors to the Confucian family of nations. In naval, in military, and in political affairs, the Manchu government was revealed as inefficient and corrupt. To a few thoughtful Chinese it already appeared that the dynasty had lost the Mandate of Heaven. Now with Japan's victory the old Confucian theory of international relations, which China had maintained for centuries, was destroyed and replaced by Western concepts of treaties and international law. There was no longer in theory or in fact a far eastern Confucian family of nations. China was no longer the Middle Kingdom for there were no longer any border, dependent states that recognized her superior status.

CHAPTER 14

THE AFTERMATH OF THE SINO-JAPANESE WAR, 1895-1899

THE Treaty of Shimonoseki placed Japan in the company of the so-called Great Powers; but it did much more than this. It precipitated a new and a dramatic era in the relations of China and the West. Until 1895, the major interest of the Western states in China was commerce. The traders had purchased China's silk and tea, and in return they had sold to China silver, opium, ginseng, sandalwood, furs, and, in the later years of the century, an expanding assortment of manufactured textiles, flour, and kerosene. There had been little penetration by the trader *into* China. Business was conducted in the treaty ports on the coast. Here to be sure the foreign merchants and their governments had surrounded themselves with certain protective agencies—the conventional tariff, extraterritoriality, concessions, and settlements—but apart from these guarantees to commerce, neither governments nor merchants had been concerned primarily with China as a great frontier for capital investment or with the political controls which might be imposed upon China to that end. Between 1895 and 1899 much of this was changed, for in these years China did become a market for the investment, principally, of railroad capital. This development, considered so vital by the industrialized states of the West, took the form of an international scramble by the powers for exclusive economic concessions and spheres of political interest. For a time it appeared that a complete political partitioning of China was imminent. The roots of this movement antedate of course the Sino-Japanese War, but it was Japan's victory in that war and her threat to dominate North China by the annexation of Port Arthur and Liaotung which precipitated the movement and endowed it from this time on with the full flavor of power politics.

THE TRIPLE INTERVENTION

The ink was dry, but no more than dry, on the seals of the Treaty of Shimonoseki, when six days after its conclusion, that is, on April 23,

1895, the representatives of Russia, Germany, and France in Tokyo presented to Count Hayashi, deputy foreign minister, notes which said that

. . . the possession of the Peninsula of Liaotung, claimed by Japan, would be a constant menace to the capital of China, would at the same time render illusory the independence of Korea, and would henceforth be a perpetual obstacle to the peace of the Far East.

The three powers, protesting that in this manner they were giving new proof of their friendship, "advised" Japan to renounce possession of Liaotung. For a week the diplomatic scales hung in uneasy equilibrium. On May 1, Japan offered to give up all of Liaotung save the southern tip with Port Arthur. This offer the three powers refused, and on May 5, Japan accepted their "advice" without qualification. She asked, however, that the Treaty of Shimonoseki be ratified in its original form prior to the retrocession, and that she be given additional indemnity. This the powers granted. Ratification took place at Chefoo, May 8, where significantly a Russian squadron, wearing the gray paint of war and with its decks cleared for action, lay at anchor. The Liaotung Peninsula was returned to China by a convention signed November 8, 1895, in which China agreed to pay an additional indemnity of 30,000,000 Kuping taels.[1]

The Triple Intervention ended the temporary truce in Japan's domestic politics. During the Shimonoseki negotiations Prime Minister Ito and Foreign Minister Mutsu knew that an unfriendly European intervention was in the making. Accordingly, Mutsu, in an effort to forestall action by the powers, had insisted that Japan make no territorial demands on the mainland, but he was overruled by pressure of the military and naval staffs. The generals were determined to have a strategic foothold on the continent. Therefore, when the Japanese public, elated with the news of military and naval triumphs, learned that its government had bowed to a European intervention, indignation was widespread, and was not quieted until on May 10 the emperor sanctioned an Imperial rescript stating that the retrocession in no way compromised the dignity or honor of the nation.[2] Actually the government was well aware that Japan had won the war, but had lost the peace. For the brief duration of the war she had bid for and had held

---

[1] Text, MacMurray, *Treaties,* I, 50-53.
[2] Tatsuji Takeuchi, *War and Diplomacy in the Japanese Empire* (Garden City, 1935), 116-119.

diplomatic leadership in the Far East. It will be remembered that none of the Great Powers was willing to intervene to "save" China during the war. Then, with military victory achieved, Japan made certain her diplomatic defeat by permitting the militarists to have their way in demanding a territorial concession from which Japan could dominate Peking.

EUROPEAN BACKGROUND OF THE INTERVENTION

The reasons which led to this dramatic three-power intervention are now reasonably clear to the historian, as are also the reasons why Britain did not participate. Up to the war, English policy had been decidedly pro-Chinese. However, it also favored independence for Korea while opposing any thought of Japanese annexations on the continent. Japan's demands were therefore disturbing to the British, for they upset whatever balance of power there was in the Far East; yet at the same time the British admired Japan's aggressive efficiency, and they were not insensible to the fact that the commercial clauses of the peace settlement would be very profitable to British business in China.

Russia's problem created by the Japanese peace terms could not be rationalized so easily. In general, Russian policy in the long view was aiming at acquisition of an ice-free port on the Pacific. For Russia, the Sino-Japanese War had come too soon: the Trans-Siberian was not completed and Russian plans were as yet immature. As a result of Japan's victory, Russia was forced to decide whether to seek a temporary understanding with Japan, or by diplomatic pressure and the threat of war to force the Japanese out of Manchuria at once. Under the guidance of Count Witte and with the assurance of German and French support, Russia adopted the latter policy. The Russians saw numerous advantages in this course. It would exclude Japan from any share in the partition of China (a partition which the Japanese were already considering),[3] and it would make Russia appear as the savior of China, which thus would dispose Peking favorably to subsequent Russian territorial demands.

Germany's participation in the intervention is explained largely by the fear that a partition of China was possible and that it would be well to be active in the events leading to that end. The Germans already had their eyes on several bases in the Far East, and the views of the German Foreign Office were influenced by von Brandt, who for a quarter of a century had been the leading German diplomat in the Orient.[4]

---

[3] *Die Grosse Politik*, IX, No. 2231.

[4] See Max von Brandt, *Drei Jahre Ostasiatischer Politik, 1894-1897* (Stuttgart, 1897).

Furthermore, anything which encouraged the Russians to become involved in eastern Asia would presumably react to German advantage in Europe.

The participation of France is explained by "considerations of general policy." France feared that the Japanese would resist, and that they would be joined by the British, which thus would precipitate a general conflict. Therefore, France favored letting the Japanese have their gains while the powers would seek their own territorial compensation elsewhere in China. When, however, Russia decided to act, France joined in the interest of the Dual Alliance.[5]

FINANCING THE WAR AND THE PEACE

While Japan paid for her diplomatic defeat with humiliating loss of her territorial gains in Manchuria, China paid for her unpreparedness with cold cash. Her efforts to float domestic loans during the war had failed. Chinese bankers had little interest in Li Hung-chang's Korean or Manchurian policies. Consequently, the Peking government financed the war with two loans totalling some £4,635,000 from the British Hongkong and Shanghai Bank.[6] After the war, China was confronted with the Japanese indemnity totalling 230,000,000 Kuping taels (about $172,000,000 gold). The Russians were particularly anxious that this bill should be paid, and thus effect the Japanese evacuation of Liaotung; but they were equally concerned that the indemnity be met in such fashion as to leave China in a kind of politico-financial dependence upon Russia, which thus would prevent the extension of British financial influence at Peking. In this desire, the Germans and the French shared. The result was a Franco-Russian loan to China, July 6, 1895, of 400,000,000 francs. The political motive behind the loan was indicated by China's pledge not to grant to any foreign power any right of supervision or administration over any of its revenues, unless the same rights were extended to the Russian government.[7] Witte, Russia's minister of finance, had won the first round in the financial battle for dominance at Peking. The Germans who had not been admitted to the Franco-Russian loan now joined the British bankers in a loan of £16,000,000, March 23, 1896.[8] Two years later, March 1, 1898, the

---

[5] See Emile Bourgeois and Georges Pages, Les Origines . . . de la Grande Guerre (Paris, 1921), 251-253, quoted by Langer, The Diplomacy of Imperialism, I, 185; also Auguste Gérard, Ma Mission en Chine, 1894-1897 (Paris, 1918).

[6] Arthur G. Coons, The Foreign Public Debt of China (Philadelphia, 1930), 5; text of contracts in MacMurray, Treaties, I, 11-18.

[7] Coons, The Foreign Public Debt of China, 6-8; texts in MacMurray, Treaties, I, 35-42.

[8] Text in MacMurray, Treaties, I, 55-80.

Anglo-German banking group extended another loan in the sum of £16,000,000.[9] The era of international European rivalry to finance and to control China had begun.

THE RUSSO-CHINESE AGREEMENTS OF 1896

The indemnity loans, virtually forced upon China by Russia and France in 1895, were not of course to be considered as adequate compensation for "the diplomatic aid" these powers had given Peking. The shape of future Russian policy was made clear during 1896. Since 1891 the Russians had been engaged in construction of the Trans-Siberian Railway. It was obvious that such a huge undertaking involving a line some 5,000 miles in length was not designed primarily to connect European Russia with Vladivostok or any other port which, like it, was ice-bound four or five months each year. What Russia wanted was a port in southern Korea or Manchuria; but in the months immediately following the peace this was out of the question unless she was prepared to fight Japan. However, by February, 1896, Russian fortunes in Korea took an unexpected turn for the better. The Koreans had not taken kindly to Japan's energetic suggestions on reform, and, when the Japanese Minister was implicated in the murder of the Korean queen, the king fled to the Russian legation in Seoul, from which for some time he ruled the country.[10] Even this development did not result in immediate Russian seizures in Korea.

In Europe, Witte was developing Russia's far eastern plans with deliberation. In December, 1895, he chartered the Russo-Chinese Bank, ostensibly a private corporation but officially approved and inspired. Baron Rosen called it a "slightly disguised branch of the Russian treasury." The capital came from French banks. The new concern was to be the financial arm of the new Trans-Siberian Railway. Its powers were notable in that it could collect taxes, finance the business of local government, coin money, and secure commercial and industrial concessions such as railroads.[11] Its founders likewise assumed, unofficially of course, that the granting of special concessions to Russia would be promoted by a judicious bestowal of "financial gifts" upon suitable Chinese officials in Peking.

---

[9] Text in MacMurray, *Treaties*, I, 107-112.

[10] Payson J. Treat, *Diplomatic Relations between the United States and Japan 1895-1905* (Stanford University, 1938), 4; William F. Sands, *Undiplomatic Memories* (New York, 1930), 66-69.

[11] C. Walter Young, *The International Relations of Manchuria* (Chicago, 1929), 11. In 1910 the bank was merged with the Banque du Nord to form the Russo-Asiatic Bank (Banque Russo Asiatique).

Another phase of the Russian far eastern plan concerned the route of the Trans-Siberian Railway from Lake Baikal to Vladivostok. To run the line wholly in Russian territory north of Manchuria and the Amur would entail 350 miles of additional construction through difficult terrain. If, however, it were run directly across Central Manchuria it would be the first step to Russian control of all Manchurian commerce and to the present and future railroad systems of North China. For a time, however, the Russians made little headway at Peking. The Chinese Minister at St. Petersburg was without authority; Li Hung-chang was under a temporary shadow; some of the Peking officials were leaning toward the British and the Germans, so that when in March and April, 1896, Count Cassini, the Russian Minister at Peking, began to push the Trans-Siberian project, he met with no encouragement from the Chinese. The latter were well aware that the Russian railway demands could not be pushed aside, but they hoped to strike a better bargain by sending Li Hung-chang to the coronation of the new tsar. Actually this arrangement was exactly what Witte wanted. Li was met at Port Said by Witte's agent, Prince Esper Ukhtomskii, whose colorful writings on the cultural and philosophical unity of the Russians and the Asiatics were well known. It was the role of the Prince to prepare Li for Witte's more practical proposals on Russo-Chinese industrial unity in Manchuria. The argument as presented to Li was that Russia had plenty of territory and therefore no designs on that of China; that culturally the tie between the two nations was great; that by building the railroad across Manchuria, Russia would be in position to aid China against attack; and finally that China herself was not in a position to finance or build the road. There seems little doubt that Li was bribed handsomely by Russian agents, but his decision was probably made basically on other grounds. He had given up hope of aid from England after the "desertion" of 1895; he hated Japan intensely. Therefore an alliance with, and concessions to, Russia seemed the natural answer. If Russia were refused she would probably force her demands in time anyway.[12]

As a result, Russia got her railway concession in Manchuria, and Li in return secured a defensive military alliance. In point of time the alliance came first. This secret alliance, known as the Li-Lobanov Treaty, was signed on June 3, 1896. It was to remain in force for fifteen years.

---

[12] See: E. J. Dillon, *The Eclipse of Russia* (London, 1918); J. O. P. Bland, *Li Hung-Chang* (New York, 1917); A. Yarmolinsky, ed., *The Memoirs of Count Witte* (New York, 1921), of great value but incomplete and unreliable in Witte's estimates of his own role; Valentine Chirol, *The Far Eastern Question* (London, 1896).

Among other things it provided: 1) for mutual assistance against any Japanese aggression, 2) for the use of Chinese ports by Russia in the event of war, and 3) for China's consent to the construction of the Trans-Siberian across Manchuria, construction and operation of the road to be accorded to the Russo-Chinese Bank. Although rumors of this agreement soon became public, it was not until many years later that the exact nature of the alliance was revealed.[13]

THE CHINESE EASTERN RAILWAY AGREEMENTS, 1896

What the public did learn was that on September 8, 1896, the Russo-Chinese Bank and the Chinese government had agreed to the construction and operation by the Chinese Eastern Railway Company of a line of railway from Manchouli on the western border of Manchuria to Pogranichnaya (Suifenho) on the southeast border near Vladivostok. The statutes of the new Chinese Eastern Railway Company were to conform to Russian law; the president was to be named by China; but the Russian general manager would exercise the greater power. The political nature of the line was indicated by the fact that over the "lands actually necessary for the construction, operation, and protection of the line" the Company was to have "the absolute and exclusive right of administration." China was to grant reduced tariff rates to goods entering or leaving by the line; there was to be no interference with the movement of Russian troops or munitions; and the Company was to have "the complete and exclusive right to operate the line."[14]

These terms were confirmed when in December, 1896, the Russian government sanctioned the statutes of the Chinese Eastern Railway Company. These statutes in addition obligated the Company to construct telegraph lines, and to carry free the Russian mails. Although the Chinese government was to adopt measures for the protection of the line, the statutes provided that "the preservation of law and order on the lands assigned to the railway and its appurtenances shall be confided to police agents appointed by the Company." After eighty years the railroad was to become Chinese property without payment. After thirty-six years from its completion China could purchase it by paying to the Company the full outlay with interest.[15] Construction of the Chinese Eastern Railway was completed in 1904. From this great trunk line nearly 1,000 miles in length, Russia hoped to build a political and

[13] See: MacMurray, *Treatises,* I, 78-82; Young, *The International Relations of Manchuria,* 253-257.
[14] MacMurray, *Treaties,* I, 74-77.
[15] MacMurray, *Treaties,* I, 84-88.

commercial empire, an empire providing easy access to the Pacific, and insuring Russian economic dominance in North China. This was the Russian policy that Witte called "peaceful penetration."

THE YAMAGATA-LOBANOV AGREEMENT, JUNE 3, 1896

Li Hung-chang was not the only distinguished Oriental guest at the Russian coronation in 1896. Japan was represented by Aritomo Yamagata, the most powerful of the Choshu clansmen, father of the modern Japanese army, and, in his day, the leading exponent of the military tradition. The Japanese wanted a compromise settlement of Russo-Japanese rivalry in Korea, a compromise that would maintain the balance until the army and navy expansion program could be effected. Accordingly, Yamagata proposed to the Russians that the two powers divide Korea at the 38th parallel into a northern Russian sphere and a southern Japanese sphere, an arrangement which would have given the Japanese control of Seoul, the capital. But the Russians turned down the offer. For the present they regarded it as good policy to play along with England and the United States, respecting the integrity of Korea, and, in the long run, they hoped to get control of the entire peninsula, especially the more highly developed and richer south with its strategic naval harbors of Fusan, Gensan, and Masampo. As a result, two general and unsatisfactory compromise agreements were reached. At Seoul the Russian and Japanese representatives advised the Korean king to return as soon as possible to his palace from his refuge in the Russian legation. The Japanese were to withdraw most of their troops. This understanding reached at Seoul (May 26) was supplemented by the Yamagata-Lobanov Agreement made at Moscow (June 9). Both powers would support the Korean king's efforts to restore and maintain order; both would guarantee foreign loans so that adequate police could be maintained and foreign intervention avoided. Korea was thus recognized as a Russo-Japanese joint problem. A secret article provided that in case it became necessary to send troops to Korea, the two powers would consult with a view to fixing a neutral zone between their spheres of action. This meant that Korea had become a kind of joint protectorate.[16]

GERMANY AND THE FAR EAST

The German intervention against Japan in 1895 had been prompted not only by the desire to involve Russia in the Far East and thus weaken

---

[16] William L. Langer, *The Diplomacy of Imperialism 1890-1902* (New York, 1935), I, 405-407; Isabella Bishop, *Korea and her Neighbors* (2 vols., London, 1898), II, 307-310.

the Franco-Russian alliance in Europe but also by the German ambition to secure a naval and commercial base in China. All during the last quarter of the nineteenth century, Germany had possessed very able scientific as well as diplomatic representation in the Far East. To diplomatic and political knowledge concerning Asia from such men as von Brandt was added scientific, geographic, and social-economic data from such authorities as Ferdinand von Richthofen, perhaps the outstanding European authority of the time on China. It was he who dramatized for Europe the dire consequences that must follow when Asiatic labor should be turned loose upon the world. It was he also who first pointed out the strategic and economic advantages of Kiaochow on the South Shantung coast; but for a time Germany appeared to be more interested in various islands on the Korean coast, in Weihai-wei, Chusan, Woosung, Amoy, Samsah Bay, and Mirs Bay.[17]

The German decision to take Kiaochow was made in the summer of 1897. This decision rested on the enthusiasm of the Kaiser, on the reports of Admiral von Tirpitz, who was in command of the German far eastern fleet in 1896, and on the reports of German harbor-construction engineers.[18] To avoid any collision with Russia, whose fleet had already wintered at Kiaochow, thus setting up a sort of priority in the place, the Kaiser appealed to the Tsar and was seemingly given a green light. In September, Germany notified China of her need for this harbor. Apparently the plan was for the German fleet, uninvited, to winter at Kiaochow—a friendly but unmistakable gesture calculated to bring the Chinese to terms. But the way was made easier when on November 1, 1897, two German Catholic missionaries were killed by Chinese robbers in southern Shantung. On November 14, Admiral von Diederich landed German troops at Kiaochow Bay. For a time the Chinese government refused to come to terms. The mandarins were encouraged by the Russians to resist, but by January, 1898, the Russian opposition had subsided, and on March 6, Germany secured her agreement with China. This convention was prefaced with the remark that "the Imperial Chinese Government consider it advisable to give a special proof of their grateful appreciation of the friendship shown to them by Germany." [19] How deep this "friendship" was, and how significant its results, may be judged from the terms of the con-

---

[17] German commercial and colonial activity in the Pacific area dates back to the activities of Hamburg merchants in Samoa (1857); by 1885 Germany had possession of a large section of New Guinea, and of the Bismarck and the Marshall Islands.

[18] Alfred von Tirpitz, *My Memoirs* (2 vols., New York, 1919), ch. viii.

[19] MacMurray, *Treaties*, I, 112-113.

vention. It provided among other things: 1) for a so-called "neutral" zone 50 kilometers wide surrounding Kiaochow Bay, in which zone China would permit the free movement of German troops, and in which China would take no measures without the consent of Germany; 2) for the lease to Germany for 99 years of both sides of the entrance to Kiaochow Bay, including the port of Tsingtao as a naval base; 3) for the exercise by Germany during the term of the lease of sovereign powers over the leased area; 4) that should Germany return the territory to China prior to the expiration of the lease, China would "cede to Germany a more suitable place"; 5) that Germany should not "sublet" the territory to another power; 6) that Germany might construct two railways in Shantung: a) from Kiaochow to Tsinan, and b) from Kiaochow to Ichow and Tsinan, construction and operation to be handled by a Sino-German company in which the nationals of both powers might invest; 7) that German nationals might mine coal within 30 *li* (10 miles) of the railways; and, finally, 8)

the Chinese Government binds itself in all cases where foreign assistance, in persons, capital or material, may be needed for any purpose whatever within the Province of Shantung, to offer the said work or supplying of materials in the first instance to German manufacturers and merchants engaged in undertakings of the kind in question.[20]

RUSSIA LEASES PORT ARTHUR

Germany's descent upon Kiaochow necessitated changes in Russia's plans. She had considered Kiaochow herself in the winter of 1895-1896, and her Foreign Minister, Muraviev, was violently opposed to the German occupation. Although the Germans had taken the one good naval harbor in North China, there were still plenty of harbors in Korea. Back in Moscow in 1896 Li Hung-chang had even advised the Russians to take a Korean port. But when in late 1897 Russia turned to Korea, attempted to make a Russian the financial adviser of the king, and attempted to oust a Britisher, M'Leavy Brown, from control of the Korean customs, she was met with the appearance of a strong Anglo-Japanese squadron in the harbor of Chemulpo. Accordingly, late in November, 1897, the Russian government began to consider occupation of the harbor of Talienwan on the Liaotung Peninsula in South Manchuria a few miles northeast of Port Arthur. In Peking

---

[20] For full text of the convention see MacMurray, *Treaties,* I, 112-116; see also W. L. Godshall, *The International Aspects of the Shantung Question* (Philadelphia, 1923).

the Chinese government, though petitioned by some of the most powerful viceroys, such as Chang Chih-tung, to seek an alliance with Japan and England, had already determined on a policy of surrender. And so, on March 27, 1898, less than three weeks after Germany had leased Kiaochow, China leased to Russia for twenty-five years the southern tip of the Liaotung Peninsula containing Port Arthur and Talienwan (Bay). This was the spot from which Russia, France, and Germany had ousted Japan three years earlier. North of the leased area was to be a neutral zone stretching to the base of the peninsula. Finally, the convention granted to the Chinese Eastern Railway Company the right to connect Talienwan by rail with the main line in Central Manchuria. Thus, to use the terms of the agreement, Russia's naval forces had secured "an entirely secure base on the littoral of northern China," and the two sovereigns had fulfilled their desire "of still further-strengthening the friendly relations existing between the two Empires." [21]

FRANCE LEASES KUANG-CHOU WAN

During the winter of 1897-98 when Germany and Russia were maturing their plans at Kiaochow and Port Arthur, France did not appear disposed to play an active role in China. French political leaders were paying lip service to the principle of China's integrity. Yet it was obvious that France was not unaffected by the German and Russian moves. Since 1885 France has possessed a great empire of colonies and "protectorates" in Indo-China. In that year China had renounced sovereignty over Annam, had agreed to respect Franco-Annamite agreements, and had promised to open two cities in Yünnan to French commerce.[22] In 1895, French influence, now more strongly entrenched in northern Indo-China (Annam and Tongking), was looking to industrial concessions across the frontier in China's southern provinces.

[21] For a discussion of the negotiations preceding the Russian seizure, see Langer, The Diplomacy of Imperialism, II, 445-461; text of the lease agreement is in MacMurray, Treaties, I, 119-122.
The crisis in Russo-Japanese relations occasioned by the Russian lease of Port Arthur was cushioned by the inconclusive Nishi-Rosen Agreement, April 25, 1898, by which both powers agreed to limit materially their political freedom in Korea whereas Japan retained a considerable measure of economic freedom there. Both powers of course recognized the "independence" of Korea. The agreement revealed a cleavage in Japanese counsels between the younger statesmen (Kato and Hayashi) who favored resistance to Russia and alliance with England, and the older generation, represented by Ito, which sought at least temporary agreements with Russia. Text in Korea: Treaties and Agreements (Washington: Carnegie Endowment for International Peace, 1921), 24-25; and British and Foreign State Papers, XCII, 1068-69.
[22] Herbert Ingram Priestley, France Overseas (New York, 1938), 216-230.

Within a month of the famous Triple Intervention of that year, France reaped her first reward. On June 20, 1895, it was agreed that

. . . for the exploitation of its mines in the provinces of Yunnan, Kwangsi, and Kwangtung, [China] may call upon, in the first instance, French manufacturers and engineers. . . .

The principle that the railways of Annam might be extended into China was also agreed upon.[23] Following close on the heels of this agreement, France in June, 1896, secured from China a concession to construct a railroad in Kwangsi from the border of Tongking to Lung-chow. In the same year a French expedition explored the interior of the island of Hainan, and in January China promised France never to alienate it to any other power. It is not surprising then that France was ready with new demands on China once Germany and Russia had taken action at Kiaochow and Port Arthur. The gains of France were extensive. On April 10, 1898, China agreed not to alienate any of her territories on the border of Tongking (northern Annam.)[24] On the same day China agreed: 1) to grant France a concession for a railroad from Tongking to Yünnan-fu; 2) to lease to France for 99 years the bay of Kuang-chou as a naval station and coaling depot; and 3) to appoint Frenchmen as advisers to the newly proposed Chinese postal service.[25] These measures were designed not only to give France a strategic foothold and industrial concessions in South China, but also to draw Chinese commerce away from British influence at Hongkong and Canton, and to center it under French control in the Gulf of Tongking.

GREAT BRITAIN: KOWLOON, THE YANGTZE VALLEY, WEI-HAI-WEI

The British government during 1897-98 had failed to place any effective restraints on the development of German, Russian, or French policy in China. British policy had been basically commercial rather than political, but it could hardly remain unaffected by the new position now occupied in China by the other great European powers. In other words, if leaseholds, preferential concessions, and special spheres were to be the order of the day, it behooved England, so ran the argument, to have her share. From February through July, 1898, the British

[23] Text in MacMurray, *Treaties,* I, 28-30. In 1914 the French railroad preference in Yünnan and Kwangsi was made absolute.
[24] Text of exchange of notes, MacMurray, *Treaties,* I, 123-124.
[25] See texts of these various agreements, MacMurray, *Treaties,* I, 124-125, 128-130.

secured from China a series of agreements of the utmost importance. China agreed: 1) never to alienate any territory in the Yangtze Valley (February 11); 2) that the Inspector-General of the Chinese Maritime Customs should be a British subject so long as British trade predominated (February 13); 3) to lease Wei-hai-wei to Britain as a naval harbor "for so long a period as Port Arthur shall remain in the occupation of Russia" (July 1); 4) to extend the British territory of Kowloon by a lease for 99 years of the entire peninsula lying between Deep Bay and Mirs Bay (June 9). With this British advance should be noted also the Anglo-German loan to China (March 1, 1898) in the amount of £16,000,000, and various preliminary agreements between the Hongkong and Shanghai Banking Corporation and Chinese authorities concerning the financing of the Shanghai-Nanking Railway (May 13) and the Peking-Newchwang Railway (June 7).[26] By November, 1898, the British had secured nine railroad concessions totalling 2,800 miles; the Russians, three concessions, 1,500 miles; the Belgians, one concession, 650 miles; the French, three concessions, 300 miles.[27] This scramble intensified the desire of the powers to define more specifically the limits of the spheres which each claimed. Diplomatic pressure was continually exerted on Peking to this end.

These developments culminating in the spring and summer of 1898 made it quite clear that the integrity of China was worth very little. Germany, Russia, and France had all expressed great respect for this principle, but their leaseholds, and their railroad and non-alienation agreements made it perfectly clear that these protestations were not to be taken too seriously. It was clear that an era of special and exclusive privilege was dawning in China. Britain disliked the tendency, for she had more to gain in an open market where all traded on terms of equality. But no power, not even the United States, would align itself with the British. Consequently, Downing Street, having protested, decided to join the robbers.[28] In London, opponents of this policy of

---

[26] For the texts of these various agreements see MacMurray, *Treaties*, I, 104-402 *passim*.
[27] Details on railroad concessions in: P. H. Kent, *Railway Enterprise in China* (London, 1907); Philip Joseph, *Foreign Diplomacy in China, 1894-1900* (London, 1928), chs. xii-xiv; and R. S. McCordock, *British Far-Eastern Policy, 1894-1900* (New York, 1931), ch. iv.
[28] Of British policy at this time it should be said that the only way to stop Russia in Manchuria was to fight her, and Britain had no intention of doing this. For one thing, it would have been a doubtful war fought at the end of sea lines of communication 12,000 miles long. Geography would have favored Russia. Britain preferred the maintenance of China's integrity, but she had no intention of going to war to uphold it. There was little chance that she could stop Russia, since no other great power was prepared to join in the crusade.

imitation spoke in sarcastic terms of "Port Arthur Balfour" and "a triumph of diplomatic incompetency." The Opposition called Wei-hai-wei, "Woe! Woe! Woe!" The fact was that the four great powers of Europe had begun the serious business of tampering with Chinese sovereignty. To be sure, each of the leasehold agreements carefully reserved to China her full sovereignty in the leased areas. But as Langer has said: "This was mere camouflage and the statesmen knew it." [29] The most serious phase of the business was that in 1898 there were no unity of purpose within China herself, no constructive program of reform and resistance, and no able leadership.

THE ONE HUNDRED DAYS OF REFORM

One futile effort the Chinese did make to extricate themselves. In 1898 China was not without her political reformers. Among these was K'ang Yu-wei, known as the "Modern Sage," a Cantonese who had read widely, if not deeply, in Western political thought, and who was impressed with the need of a political house-cleaning. After many years of writing and preaching moderate reform, K'ang came to Peking in 1898 as under-secretary to the Board of Works just at the moment when the powers were appropriating their leaseholds and attempting to define their spheres. Appalled by the spectacle of China's weakness, K'ang appealed to the Son of Heaven to assume the role of emperor-reformer after the fashion of Peter the Great.

> If Your Majesty will . . . prefer to remain in the old grooves of the Conservatives, then your territories will be swallowed up, your limbs will be bound, your viscera will be cut out, and Your Majesty will scarcely manage to retain your throne or to rule over more than a fragment of your ancient Empire.[30]

The sovereign to whom this appeal was addressed was the Kuang-hsü emperor, a young man not yet thirty, who owed his position as sovereign to the imperial manoeuverings of his aunt, the Empress Dowager Tz'u-hsi. Even after the Kuang-hsü emperor became of age, the august lady had continued to control him. It is not surprising then that he saw in K'ang's memorial both a means of asserting his own authority and also of rescuing his country from destruction.

On June 11, 1898, appeared the first Imperial decrees ushering in the

---

[29] Langer, *The Diplomacy of Imperialism*, II, 479-480.
[30] Wen Ching [Lim Boon-keng], *The Chinese Crisis from Within* (London, 1901), 53-54.

famous "Hundred Days of Reform." China was to have able diplomatic representation abroad, and officials were ordered to recommend men "who are not enveloped in the narrow circle of bigoted conservatism." China was to have a new order in which all the nation would unite in a march to progress. High conservative officials were advised to seek education in Europe. Decrees followed each other in rapid succession. The old education was to be replaced by "practical" subjects; modern schools and colleges were to be established in every province; a transportation and mining bureau would be set up in Peking; the army would be reorganized; useless government posts would be abolished; foreign works on politics and science would be translated. From June to September, some forty decrees attempted to remake an old people into a new. It is small wonder that they failed. The reformers lacked experience, and the young emperor was in no sense a second Peter the Great. Undoubtedly he was well intentioned, but he was emotionally unstable and intellectually diffuse. He possessed no adequate appreciation of the practical difficulties of constructive reform or of the conservative forces, personified by the Empress Dowager, that would oppose him.[31]

Recognizing that their plans of reform would certainly fail unless this conservative opposition were removed, the reformers conspired to seize the Empress Dowager and Jung Lu, her most trusted adviser and commander of the northern army, and, though the evidence is conflicting, perhaps to do away with both of them. The plot, however, was discovered; K'ang and some of the reformers fled; and on September 21, the Empress Dowager again seized control of the government. The attempted reform had failed because of the impetuous ineptitude of the reformers, the worthy but misdirected zeal of the emperor, the determined opposition of most of the conservatives, and finally the fact that "the lethargic mass of the people was not stirred" by any popular understanding of, or desire for, reform. Many of the reformers suffered summary execution. But the leaders, K'ang Yu-wei and Liang Chichao, escaped to British Hongkong, where in safety they could read the decrees condemning them to death by "slicing." For ten years the Kuang-hsü emperor lived on, a prisoner of the Regent Empress Dowager. That he was permitted even this existence was due among other things to: the intervention of the powers, the Regent's fear of provoking the southern liberals, and the desire to hide the fact that China was again ruled by a woman.

---

[31] For a full discussion of the reforms of 1898 see Meribeth E. Cameron, *The Reform Movement in China* (Stanford University, 1931), ch. ii.

In the closing months of 1898 it was the fashion among the foreigners in Peking to dismiss Kuang-hsü's reforms as a case of misguided zeal, in the light of which it is easier to understand the determination of the Chinese conservatives to have their way. Nevertheless the Empress Dowager never ceased to protest her own enthusiasm for reform. Judged by practical results this zeal was not very great. The principal results were the recruiting of additional men for the army by questionable methods, and an audience which the Empress Dowager held for the wives of foreign diplomats in Peking. The ladies noted the "courteous amiability" of the Empress Dowager, and that was all. As yet there was no evidence that Tz'u-hsi herself was to become a more zealous reformer than Kuang-hsü.[32]

CHINA'S RESISTANCE STIFFENS

The return of the Empress Dowager to power could not be interpreted as a victory for progressive or patriotic forces in Chinese life, but it was coincident with a stiffening of the government's opposition to further foreign demands. In March, 1899, when Italy demanded the lease of San Men Bay, and the setting aside of the greater part of Chekiang province as a sphere of influence, she received a polite but firm refusal. In fact, no further major concessions were secured by the powers during 1899 or the early months of 1900. Energies were consumed in evaluating and defining concessions already held. There were many disputes as to boundaries of sphere, some of which were ironed out by diplomatic exchanges. For instance, the Anglo-Russian rivalry over railroad concessions in Manchuria and North China was alleviated somewhat by an exchange of notes, April 28, 1899, in which the British agreed not to seek railway concessions north of the Great Wall, while Russia pledged herself not to seek similar concessions in the basin of the Yangtze.[33]

Nevertheless, as the last days of the year 1899 and of the nineteenth century approached, the far eastern situation was filled with dire forebodings. In addition to the naval leaseholds secured by Germany, Russia, France, and Great Britain, hardly a square foot of Chinese territory remained which was not already claimed or about to be claimed as a sphere of influence. The Russians claimed Manchuria and were extending their influence into Mongolia. From Shantung the Germans

---

[32] See: Cameron, *The Reform Movement in China,* 47-55; Princess Der Ling, *Old Buddha* (London, 1929), ch. xxvi, and *Two Years in the Forbidden City* (New York, 1911).

[33] Text in MacMurray, *Treaties,* I, 204.

were looking westward into the northwest provinces. Great Britain was firmly entrenched in the great Yangtze Valley. France was encroaching on concessionary rights in Yünnan, Kwangsi, and the greater part of Kwangtung. Japan, though not as yet a serious contender, had secured, on April 26, 1898, China's assurance not to alienate any portion of the province of Fukien opposite Japanese Formosa.[34] In the view of many a Chinese editor the time was not far distant when Europe would "slice China as a ripe melon."[35]

[34] Text, MacMurray, *Treaties,* I, 126.
[35] Edward T. Williams, *China: Yesterday and Today* (5th ed., rev., New York, 1935), 489.

CHAPTER 15

THE UNITED STATES AND THE PHILIPPINES, 1898-1913

IT HAS been said that in the months and the years which preceded May 1, 1898, no idea was perhaps so remote from the mind of the American people as the conquest and acquisition of the Philippine Islands. Yet within the year which followed this date, the United States had taken unto itself a great colony, 7,000 miles from San Francisco across the Pacific; had projected itself into the main currents of world politics; and had discarded, so it seemed, some of its most deeply rooted traditions. It was as though the habits and dress of an old century had given place to the more modish styles of the new.

THE TRADITION OF WESTWARD EXPANSION

To Americans there was, to be sure, nothing new in the simple acquisition of contiguous territory. That was an old American custom. The nineteenth century was filled with the territorial advance of Americans through Louisiana and Florida, through Texas to the Rio Grande and California, and across Kansas plains to Oregon. The movement was completed by mid-century. The natural limits of westward continental expansion had been reached. Was it not now the business of Americans to remain at home to develop what they already possessed? Nevertheless, a new extra-continental, overseas expansion had already been foreshadowed and was soon to begin. The interruption was only temporary. In Seward's purchase of Alaska, 1867,[1] there was the suggestion of the earlier ideas of Commodore Perry in Japan and Peter Parker in China that the United States needed coaling and naval stations on far eastern islands: Formosa, the Ryukyus, and the Bonins.[2] As early as 1854 President Pierce and Secretary of State Marcy tried but

---

[1] On the Alaska purchase see: V. J. Farrar, *The Annexation of Russian America to the United States* (Washington, 1937); F. A. Golder, "The Purchase of Alaska," *American Historical Review*, XXV (1920), 411-425; T. A. Bailey, "Why the United States Purchased Alaska," *Pacific Historical Review*, III (1934), 39-49; and the popular account in F. R. Dulles, *America in the Pacific* (Boston, 1932), ch. vi.

[2] Tyler Dennett, *Americans in Eastern Asia* (New York, 1922), 272, 284-291.

failed to annex the Hawaiian Islands by treaty. The Midway Islands were easier marks. A thousand miles northwest of Hawaii, they were occupied by an American naval force in August, 1867. In 1878 the American Navy acquired the use of a harbor in the far distant Samoan Islands of the South Pacific, and a decade later, the State Department resisted German encroachment there with vigor.[3] This official American interest in Samoa and the harbor of Pago Pago, 5,600 miles from Panama, was significant because it was an

. . . assertion by the United States, not merely of a willingness, but even of a right, to take part in determining the fate of a remote and semi-barbarous people, whose possessions lay far outside the traditional sphere of American political interests.[4]

And, if Americans had not been seriously interested previously in annexing Hawaii, the Senate in 1887 secured an equivalent, the exclusive right for the United States to use Pearl Harbor as a naval station,[5] and by 1893, Americans were debating with a good deal of heat the proposals of the Harrison administration to bring the Islands under the American flag. Against the pro-expansionist arguments of Captain Alfred T. Mahan, that the islands controlled the commerce of the North Pacific and were strategically essential, were those of the anti-expansionists and anti-annexationists: men such as Carl Schurz, E. L. Godkin, editor of *The Nation,* and James Gordon Bennett, Jr., publisher of the Democratic *New York Herald.* This triumphant opposition to expansion expressed views running the gamut from the constitutional and ideological objections of Schurz to the polemics of Godkin, who asserted that if Hawaii were admitted to the Union,

men would come into our Senate worse than those from Nevada, Wyoming and Idaho and which will be sent from Utah, Arizona, New Mexico and Oklahoma after they are admitted into the Union.[6]

BLOCKING THE NEW MANIFEST DESTINY

It is thus proper to note that in the decades which preceded immediately the Spanish-American War the American mind as it contemplated the Pacific had not kept pace with "the march of events."

---

[3] George H. Ryden, *The Policy of the United States in Relation to Samoa* (New Haven, 1933), chs. vii-x.

[4] John Bassett Moore, *Cambridge Modern History,* VII, 663.

[5] Charles P. Howland, ed., *Survey of American Foreign Relations 1930* (New Haven, 1930), ch. vi gives a general survey of islands of the Pacific.

[6] E. L. Godkin, "Hawaii," *The Nation,* 56 (1893), 96.

The official arm of the United States had already carried the Stars and Stripes far out into the Pacific, to Alaska and the Aleutians, to Midway and to Samoa, and finally to Pearl Harbor. Yet the vast majority of politically minded Americans had no interest in these places, no understanding of why their government was projecting itself into foreign fields, and certainly no thought of setting up a colony in Asia itself. Disciples of the New Manifest Destiny, of imperialism, there were, but they were few compared with those Americans who followed the more timid and conscientious philosophy of Grover Cleveland, called by the expansionists "the Buffalo lilliputian!"[7] Even American "big business," usually considered the spearhead of imperialism, was, in the main, content to stay at home. In 1893 no less a person than the vice-president of the Great Northern Railroad was saying publicly that

he [the Chinaman] is as poor as a rat, and has nothing with which to pay for our high-priced products except silk handkerchiefs and bamboo pipes. . . . The Great Northern is coming here to do business with the Pacific slope, not with Asia.[8]

THE NEW FAR EASTERN POLICY IN THE MAKING

Nevertheless, on the eve of the Spanish-American War a new far eastern policy for the United States was taking shape in the minds of a handful of Americans. Policy up to this time had been shaped by commercial rather than political aims.[9] The new policy, although by no means nation-wide as yet in its appeal, gained ground rapidly after 1890 under the leadership of a group of dynamic spokesmen.

The patron saint of the new and large policy of expansion, John Louis O'Sullivan, close associate of Polk, Pierce, and Buchanan, and coiner of the phrase "Manifest Destiny," died in 1895, but his philosophy was kept alive by John Fiske, the historian, Josiah Strong, a Congregational clergyman, Professor John W. Burgess of Columbia University, under whom Theodore Roosevelt sat as a student, and Captain Alfred Thayer Mahan, whose lectures at the Naval War College were later published

[7] For further readings on the beginnings of American imperialism in the Pacific, see: J. W. Pratt, *Expansionists of 1898* (Baltimore, 1936), ch. i, "The New Manifest Destiny"; H. W. Bradley, "The American Frontier in Hawaii," *Proceedings,* Pacific Coast Branch, American Historical Association, 1930; Allan Nevins, *Grover Cleveland* (New York, 1934), ch. xxx; C. C. Tansill, *The Foreign Policy of Thomas F. Bayard, 1885-1897* (New York, 1940), ch. xii; A. T. Volwiler, "Harrison, Blaine, and American Foreign Policy, 1889-1893," *American Philosophical Society Proceedings,* LXXIX (1938), 637-648.
[8] *The New York Times,* Jan. 8, 1893.
[9] A. Whitney Griswold, *The Far Eastern Policy of the United States* (New York, 1938), 8.

under the title, *The Influence of Sea Power upon History*.[10] The composite doctrine which emerged from the writings and speeches of these men and others was that the United States had come of age; that it could no longer be held within the old continental borders; that the commerce of the world was beckoning to American enterprise; that benighted areas and backward peoples were calling to the beneficent forces in American civilization; in a word, that we could no longer ignore the responsibilities of the "white man's burden" to civilize, to Christianize, and (it was added by a few) to commercialize less fortunate peoples.

THE BACKGROUND FOR WAR

To a notable though limited degree, therefore, the stage was already set for new adventures in American foreign policy when, on April 19, 1898, the Congress of the United States passed the joint resolution which precipitated the Spanish-American War. Actually, the roots of this war were connected only remotely, if at all, with the white man's burden and the larger policy it entailed. There were few Americans indeed in the spring of 1898 who entertained any notion that the war with Spain would place the United States among the great colonial powers, much less that the principal new colonies would lie on the fringe of Asia some 7,000 miles from San Francisco. There was in fact no official suggestion that, if war came, it was to lead to colonies at all. On the contrary, the war resolution voiced traditional principles associated with the Monroe Doctrine: Cuba was and ought to be free "of right"; the withdrawal of Spain was demanded; the President was instructed to secure these ends by use of the armed forces; and there was express denial of any intent on the part of the United States to annex Cuba.

THE POPULAR VIEW OF THE WAR

Most Americans viewed the outbreak of war as the inevitable result of what they called Spain's long record of corrupt, oppressive, and cruel rule in the island of Cuba. Then came the destruction of the *Maine* in Havana harbor on February 15, 1898, with a loss of more than 250 officers and men. While some sections of the American press called for restraint, the yellow journals yelled for war and a "Free Cuba." The demands for war came from mass meetings, from university students, and from members of the clergy. Responsibility for the *Maine* disaster remains unfixed to this day, but the average Ameri-

[10] J. W. Pratt, *Expansionists of 1898* (Baltimore, 1936), chs. i, vi, and vii.

can of 1898 agreed with the Assistant Secretary of the Navy, Theodore Roosevelt: "The *Maine* was sunk by an act of dirty treachery on the part of the Spaniards. . . ." [11]   In all of this there was not the slightest hint of any public American interest in the Philippines. [12]

ROOSEVELT LOOKS TO THE PHILIPPINES

While Congress, no less than the public, clamored for a war to free Cuba, the Assistant Secretary of the Navy, Theodore Roosevelt, worked behind the scenes with equal effect for a war to annex the Philippines, islands whose very existence, as well as their Spanish ownership, was unknown to the American public.   It was Roosevelt who selected Commodore George Dewey, a man who would "be equal to the emergency," to command the American Asiatic squadron in October, 1897.   It was Roosevelt, too, who on a Saturday afternoon (February 25, 1898), when Secretary Long was away from the office, cabled Dewey to hold himself in readiness, and, in the event of war, to destroy Spanish power in the Philippines. [13]

THE MAN FOR AN EMERGENCY

When Commodore Dewey received the appointment as commander of the Asiatic squadron, the United States, as in 1941, was not prepared for war in the Far East.   "The latest official report relative to the Philippines on file in the office of naval intelligence bore the date of 1876."   Unlike the great European powers, the United States had no colony or naval leasehold in Asia.   The nearest American naval station was at Pearl Harbor in the Hawaiian Islands.   The fleet which Dewey assembled in the British harbor of Hongkong consisted of seven vessels with a total displacement of 20,378 tons, and a total complement of 1,524 officers and men.   When war was declared and Hongkong could no longer be used as a base for supplies and repairs, Dewey moved his

---

[11] Roosevelt to Diblee, Feb. 16, 1898, Roosevelt Papers, Library of Congress, quoted by T. A. Bailey, *A Diplomatic History of the American People* (2nd ed., New York, 1942), 502.

[12] For the background of the Spanish-American War see the following: E. J. Benton, *International Law and Diplomacy of the Spanish-American War* (Baltimore, 1908); F. C. Chadwick, *The Relations of the United States and Spain: Diplomacy* (New York, 1909), 411-587; A. L. P. Dennis, *Adventures in American Diplomacy, 1896-1906* (New York, 1928), ch. iii; Orestes Ferrara, *The Last Spanish War*, trans. from the Spanish by William E. Shea (New York, 1937); Walter Millis, *The Martial Spirit* (Boston, 1931), not always reliable; J. W. Pratt, *Expansionists of 1898* (Baltimore, 1936); M. M. Wilkerson, *Public Opinion and the Spanish-American War* (Baton Rouge, 1932); J. E. Wisan, *The Cuban Crisis as Reflected in the New York Press, 1895-1898* (New York, 1934).

[13] Dewey tells in his *Autobiography* how on Roosevelt's advice he used senatorial influence, combatting similar influence used by other officer candidates, to secure the Asiatic naval command.   *Autobiography of George Dewey* (New York, 1916), 167-170.

fleet 30 miles up the China coast into the Chinese waters of Mirs Bay, "an isolated locality" where "independent of international complications" supplies could be received secretly and temporary repairs effected. "We appreciated that so loosely organized a national entity as the Chinese Empire could not enforce the neutrality laws," [14] wrote Dewey. Roosevelt was right. Here indeed was a man who could "be equal to the emergency."

THE BATTLE OF MANILA BAY

Dewey's fleet sailed for the Philippines on April 27. On the morning of May 1, while it was yet dark, his ships, disregarding the danger of mines, passed the guns of Corregidor, and sent the Spanish fleet to the bottom as it clung to its base at Cavite. Dewey promptly established a blockade of the bay and city of Manila, while he informed Washington that the city could be taken, but that 5,000 men would be needed to hold it. In Washington, the decision to send troops to the support of Dewey involved many questions. No political policy as to the future of the Philippines had yet emerged, and even the future of the immediate military policy, now forced upon the consideration of the government by Dewey's victory, was in a formative and tentative stage. For what specific purposes were the troops to be sent? Were they to engage in the conquest of the entire archipelago? How many troops would be sent? Illogically, the last question was answered first. The fact was that Dewey's dramatic victory had taken the country by surprise. Neither the government nor the people were prepared for the vital decisions which the victory demanded. What is more, Theodore Roosevelt, who was more responsible than anyone else for Dewey's presence in Manila Bay, was now a colonel commanding a regiment of Rough Riders. Thus McKinley's cabinet, groping for an immediate and future policy, dispatched troops to Manila, where by the end of July some 8,000 had arrived. This was to make possible the eventual capture of Manila, but it did not clarify the political atmosphere in the islands. Filipino nationalists with American encouragement and assistance had taken the field against Spain, and with Dewey's approval harassed the outskirts of Manila while the American commodore awaited the arrival of an American army.

NATIONALISM IN THE PHILIPPINES

Who were these Filipino patriots, who, like the Americans, were fighting against Spain?

Prior to the Spanish conquest of the islands in the sixteenth century,

---

[14] *Autobiography of George Dewey,* 175-190 *passim.*

there was no strong national or political structure in the Philippines. With the completion of the Spanish conquest, which by the close of the sixteenth century reached all parts of the archipelago save Palawan and the Moro country, the islands passed under a unified control. Slavery was abolished in law, if not in fact, and the natives were converted speedily to Christianity. Economic progress, however, under the Spanish regime was slow. Agricultural methods remained antiquated until well into the nineteenth century, while excessive restrictions on trade hampered commercial development. Under remnants of feudal theory, Spain at first controlled all the land, conducting its administration through the *encomienda* system. With the failure and subsequent abolition of this system, the control of local affairs passed largely into the hands of the regular clergy, known as the friars. This was natural enough at the time. The clergy, as missionaries, were close to the natives; they had mastered the native tongues, and had frequently protected their converts from the injustice of the *encomenderos*. In addition, the union of church and state in the Philippines "was apparently even more intimate" than the corresponding union in Spain. Thus, while in law the governor general might appear all powerful, he acted, and usually wished to act, in close collaboration with the hierarchy of the religious orders. The system contributed much by bringing Christianity to the Filipino, but it also meant that he lived "through more than two centuries of political stagnation." [15] The nineteenth century in contrast saw the beginnings of a political awakening, drawing its inspiration from liberal movements in Europe and the democratic struggle within Spain itself.[16] In part, too, the movement was a revolt against the increasingly oppressive rule of the friars. In their jealousy of anything which suggested a political awakening, the friars watched over the meetings of municipal councils, gave decisions on questions of public works, supervised the police, the prisons, and charities, and censored the theater. They owned 400,000 acres of the most fertile farm lands, which they rented to some 60,000 tenants at rates which the latter regarded as onerous. Out of these circumstances and many others was created the anomalous situation in which the friars were resented and even hated by a populace which held the doctrines and sacraments of the Church in the deepest reverence.[17]

---

[15] Maximo M. Kalaw, *The Development of Philippine Politics, 1872-1920* (Manila, 1926), 1-19.

[16] Austin Craig and Conrado Benitez, *Philippine Progress Prior to 1898* (Manila, 1916), 128-129. Revolts occurred in the years 1807, 1811, 1814, 1820, 1828, 1837, 1844, 1854, 1863, 1869, and 1872.

[17] W. C. Forbes, *The Philippine Islands* (2 vols., Boston, 1928), I, 50-54.

LEADERS OF THE PHILIPPINE REVOLT

The last quarter of the nineteenth century produced a number of Filipino students, writers, and political agitators who became aggressive in their demands for reform. Marcelo H. Del Pilar attacked the friars as the principal enemy of both the church and the state. Jose Rizal wrote political novels revealing the social, political, and economic backwardness of his people. These books, though condemned by the friars, found their way secretly into thousands of homes.[18] Rizal, a man of education, culture, and letters, who had studied abroad, founded in 1892 the Liga Filipina, through which he hoped to raise the economic, social, and educational life of his people. Whether he contemplated political revolution is a matter of dispute. Far more radical in method and purpose were Andres Bonifacio and Emilio Aguinaldo, who were associated with a new secret society, the Katipunan. This organization, definitely plebeian and revolutionary, contemplated destruction of the power of Spain, of the friars, and of the great landlords. Discovery of its plans resulted in a premature revolt in 1896. Rizal, unjustly accused of inspiring the rising, was executed, and thereby was to become the Philippine national hero. During 1897 the revolt was suppressed. Several of the rebel leaders who were paid to leave the islands claimed that Spain had promised reforms. These were not forthcoming, whether promised or not. The result was that on the eve of the Spanish-American War sporadic revolts were again occurring even though most of the leaders were in exile.[19]

THE RETURN OF AGUINALDO

Aguinaldo, one of the exiles, was at Singapore when Dewey entered Manila Bay. The Commodore, advised of this fact by an American consul, first encouraged and then actively aided Aguinaldo's return to Manila on an American dispatch boat, where he was assisted further with supplies and rifles from the Cavite arsenal in recruiting a new revolutionary army. On May 24, 1898, five days after his arrival, Aguinaldo proclaimed his revolutionary government and announced his purpose to liberate the islands from Spain. On June 23, the revolutionary government named Aguinaldo president, and adopted a constitution

---

[18] Two of Rizal's books, *Noli Me Tangere* and *El Filibusterismo,* have appeared in English translation by Charles Derbyshire as *The Social Cancer* (Manila, 1912), and *The Reign of Greed* (Manila, 1912).

[19] Kalaw, *The Development of Philippine Politics,* chs. iii-v; George A. Malcolm, *The Government of the Philippine Islands* (Manila, 1916), chs. iii-iv.

proclaiming independence. On August 6, this government petitioned foreign powers for recognition of its belligerent status and for independence in the Philippines.[20] A week later, after the newly arrived American troops had occupied lines which Aguinaldo's insurgents had thrown about the city, Manila capitulated to the American forces. This occurred only a few hours after a protocol of peace had been signed at Washington by the United States and Spain, August 12, 1898 (August 13, 5:30 A.M. Manila time).

THE EMBARRASSMENTS OF VICTORY

From May 1, 1898, the date of Dewey's naval victory, until February 6, 1899, when the Senate ratified the Treaty of Paris by a margin of only two votes, the government and the people of the United States were embarrassed by an unforeseen naval victory which had given them a tropical archipelago and some six or seven million little brown wards. At first the experience was intoxicating. When the news came of Dewey's triumph,

the country went wild with excitement. 'Dewey Days' were celebrated in the principal cities. Streets were renamed for Dewey. Young women wore 'Dewey' sailor hats, sipped 'Dewey' cocktails, chewed 'Dewey Chewies'—a new brand of gum—and wrote letters on 'Dewey blue' stationery. Men smoked cigars made of Sampson [Havana] filler and Dewey [Manila] wrappers, while those who were so inclined resorted to the corner saloon and called for Dewey brand whiskey. Meanwhile the President notified Congress that: 'At this unsurpassed achievement the great heart of our nation throbs, not with boasting or with greed of conquest, but with deep gratitude that this triumph has come in a just cause. . . .'[21]

When this tumult and shouting had subsided somewhat the country was faced with the serious problem of what to do with these Oriental fruits of victory.

THE EMERGENCE OF A POLICY

Any uncertainty in the original intent of Roosevelt and other supporters of a policy of expansion was swept away by Dewey's victory. The expansionists now wanted annexation of all the Philippines. While Roosevelt led his Rough Riders to Cuba in late May, Senator

[20] Malcolm, *The Government of the Philippine Islands*, 117-128.
[21] H. R. Lynn, *The Genesis of America's Philippine Policy* (Lexington, 1935), in manuscript, 8.

Henry Cabot Lodge urged the larger policy on a hesitant McKinley and his Secretary of State, Judge William R. Day, but with little immediate success. Then, early in July, the Congress, by joint resolution, annexed the Hawaiian Islands, and by the time Manila fell, public opinion and pressure groups, always effective instruments on government, were swinging definitely toward the larger policy. There were petitions to Congress and to the State Department picturing the Philippines as the key to far eastern commerce. Publications of the Protestant churches favored annexation almost unanimously, for church editors saw God's hand and new mission fields in Dewey's victory.[22]

Powerful forces in international politics also played on the uncertain views of McKinley and his cabinet. Great Britain and Germany were dominated by their bitter colonial rivalry. Each was determined that the Philippines should not fall into the hands of the other if by chance the unpredictable United States turned them loose. Great Britain, whose attitude when the war began was in doubt, later urged retention of the islands by Washington. England did not wish to be placed in a position where she would have to oppose German claims directly. Unquestionably, the Germans were interested. They had hoped to prevent the war. They were alarmed by signs of Anglo-American friendship and the prospects of American commercial rivalry in Asia. During the war German public opinion, favorable to Spain, again aroused American suspicions, still sensitive over the Samoan affair. Then too, there was the story, widely believed, that at Manila the German admiral, von Diederich, had interfered with Dewey's blockade, and had withdrawn only when threatened by Captain Chichester of the British squadron. This was a far cry from what actually happened, but the incident served none the less to arouse American resentment, and so to support the advocates of American annexation.[23] Japan's attitude at the time was not very significant. She was not as yet a great power. Her influence, such as it was, was added to England's, urging American annexation. If the United States did not take the islands, Japan, while not refusing them herself, would accept an international protectorate in which she should share.[24]

---

[22] Griswold, *The Far Eastern Policy of the United States,* ch. i.

[23] T. A. Bailey, "Dewey and the Germans at Manila Bay," *American Historical Review,* XLV (1939), 59-81; L. B. Shippee, "Germany and the Spanish-American War," *American Historical Review,* XXX (1925), 754-777.

[24] P. J. Treat, *Diplomatic Relations between the United States and Japan 1895-1905* (Stanford University, 1938), ch. iv; J. K. Eyre, Jr., "Japan and American Annexation of the Philippines," *Pacific Historical Review,* XI (1942), 55-71.

THE PROTOCOL OF PEACE

The Protocol of Peace,[25] drawn up by McKinley's cabinet and signed with Spain, August 12, was diplomatically vague concerning the future status of the islands, though it foreshadowed occupation of at least part of them. It stated (Article 3) that:

The United States will occupy and hold the city, bay, and harbor of Manila pending the conclusion of a treaty of peace which shall determine the control, disposition, and government of the Philippines.

The implications of the Protocol were soon reflected in the appointment by McKinley of a peace commission dominated by expansionists. Whitelaw Reid, and Senators Cushman K. Davis of Minnesota and William P. Frye of Maine were definite for annexation. Judge William R. Day, who gave up the State Department to be on the commission, was uncertain. Senator George Gray of Delaware opposed annexation to the last. While the commissioners sailed toward Paris, John Hay was crossing from the London embassy to become Secretary of State, and to be one of the decisive influences on McKinley's final decision (October 26): "The cession must be of the whole archipelago or none."

THE TREATY OF PARIS[26]

The Treaty of Paris was not signed until December 10, 1898, for Spain's opposition to relinquishment of the Philippines was persistent and bitter. The Spanish commissioners had not been slow to point out that in their view the United States could not claim the Philippines by right of conquest since Manila had been captured several hours aftei the signing of the Protocol of Peace. Thus the Treaty, which set up American sovereignty in the Philippines, Puerto Rico, and Guam, and provided for Spain's withdrawal from Cuba, also stipulated that the United States pay Spain $20,000,000

One more hurdle remained: ratification of the Treaty by the Senate. This was secured February 6, 1899, by the dangerously narrow margin of two votes. It was preceded by some of the most dramatic debates in the Senate, in the press, and on the public platform. The arguments centered primarily on the Philippines. In Congress the opposition to expansion and imperialism was led by Senator Hoar (Representativ-

[25] Text printed in Forbes, *The Philippine Islands,* II, 425-426.
[26] Text of the Treaty is printed in Charles B. Elliott, *The Philippines: to the end o: the Commission government* (Indianapolis, 1917), 479-483.

from Massachusetts). His eloquence opposing imperialism[27] failed to curb the popular enthusiasm for empire either within or outside Congress. Even then the result was in doubt until news of the outbreak of the Filipino insurrection against American control (February 4) raised the issue of national honor and strengthened the hands of the annexationists. Certainly one of the most momentous decisions of American history had been made. The United States had acquired a dependency—a dependency which was already in armed revolt against its new master. Truly, this country was entering the arena of world politics the hard way. She had fought a war to free Cuba; she had won a distant archipelago whose people did not welcome her. For the Filipino patriot, it was a case of a new master for an old.

THE BEGINNINGS OF AMERICAN GOVERNMENT IN THE PHILIPPINES

The McKinley administration took prompt action in assuming its new responsibilities in the Philippines. An American military government of occupation was instituted immediately after the fall of Manila.[28] Local civil authorities were soon functioning under American military supervision in Manila and Cavite. Meanwhile, in January, 1899, before ratification of the Treaty of Paris, McKinley appointed a commission of investigation headed by Dr. J. G. Schurman of Cornell University. The preliminary and final reports of this commission submitted to the President in November, 1899, and January, 1900, respectively (in published form the report filled four large volumes), were a comprehensive and, on the whole, accurate picture of the Philippine problem.[29] While in the islands, the commission attempted to make clear "the liberal, friendly, and beneficent attitude of the United States" coupled with the fiat that its "supremacy . . . must and will be enforced." Back in Washington, it recommended a territorial form of government since "the Filipinos are wholly unprepared for independence, and if independence were given to them they could not maintain it." Acting on the report, McKinley now took steps, through appointment of the second, or Taft, Commission, to provide a government in which there should be a gradual swing to civilian in place of military government. In addi-

---

[27] *Congressional Record*, 31: 6661 (July 5, 1898).

[28] See Charles B. Elliott, *The Philippines: to the end of the military régime* (Indianapolis, 1916).

[29] See United States Philippine Commission Annual Reports, Washington: *Report for 1900* (Schurman Commission) in 4 vols.; *1901*, 2 vols.; *1902*, 2 vols.; *1903*, 3 vols.; *1904*, 3 vols.; *1905*, 4 vols.; *1906*, 3 vols.; *1907*, 3 vols.; *1908*, 2 vols., and appendix; *1909-16*, 1 vol. annually.

tion to William Howard Taft, as its president, the second commission, a truly distinguished body, included: General Luke E. Wright of Tennessee, a gracious Southern gentleman, learned in the law; Henry C. Ide from New England, who had been chief justice in Samoa; Dean C. Worcester, who had served with the first commission, and Bernard Moses of the University of California, a mature student of history and economics.

MANILA IN THE SUMMER OF 1900

The Manila which awaited the arrival of the Taft Commission in June, 1900, was not the tropical paradise that many Americans imagined. In some sections houses were crowded together with no space for streets or even alleys. The wretched dwellers crept "through human excrement under one another's houses to reach their own." Six or eight persons lived in rooms not large enough for one. Throughout the islands, save for the antiquated and polluted Spanish water system, "there was not a reservoir, not a pipe line, and not an artesian well." Plague was in every alley of Manila; the morgue was filled with victims of cholera; smallpox was killing forty thousand annually; tuberculosis, fifty thousand; every second child died before it was a year old. Indeed, "the Philippines had the unenviable distinction of having the highest infant mortality rate in the world." [30]

The reception of the Commission, unlike the climate at Manila, was distinctly chilly. A month before its arrival, General Arthur MacArthur, who had been at Manila since 1898, had been made military governor. He was absorbed in the task of putting down the insurrection. As a professional soldier, he saw the complex question of the Philippines as a simple matter of crushing the insurgents with rifle and bayonet and then enforcing law and order by military discipline. He resented the arrival of a civilian commission which was soon to take over all legislative authority, including control of appropriations. [31]

BASES OF AMERICAN POLICY AND ADMINISTRATION

In these unfavorable and discouraging circumstances the Commission began its work. Many minds had contributed to the Instructions which the Commission was required to apply. Judge Ide was responsible for keeping appropriations out of the hands of the army, and thus for curbing the militarists. In the main, the Instructions were the work of the

---

[30] Victor Heiser, *An American Doctor's Odyssey* (New York, 1936), 38-39.

[31] Henry F. Pringle, *The Life and Times of William Howard Taft* (2 vols., New York, 1939), I, 169.

Secretary of War, Elihu Root, and Taft, President of the Commission. On questions of fundamental, immediate concern, the policy was definite, even arbitrary. In the Philippines the United States was supreme. No promise of independence was to be given.[32] With the exception of trial by jury and the right to bear arms, the Filipino was to enjoy all the guarantees of the American Bill of Rights. From this point the policy was subject to broad interpretation. The Filipino was to be given the greatest possible influence and participation in government for which his education and increasing experience would fit him. Americans today may take pride in the words of the Instructions which reminded the Commission that the system of government which it was to build in the islands was

. . . designed not for our satisfaction, or for the expression of our theoretical views, but for the happiness, peace and prosperity of the people of the Philippine Islands, and the measures adopted should be made to conform to their customs, their habits, and even to their prejudices, to the fullest extent consistent with the accomplishment of the indispensable requisites of just and effective government.[33]

Where, however, local customs interfered with "the rule of law and the maintenance of individual freedom," custom must give way.

THE BEGINNINGS OF CIVIL GOVERNMENT

The second Philippine commission carried out its instructions with vigor and, on the whole, with tact. The period of transition from a military to a full civil administration remained complicated by the fact that the military governor retained the executive power until July 4, 1901, when Taft became the first civil governor. Taft's appointment was a victory not only for himself but also for the American principle that civil government should be established as rapidly as possible. From his arrival in Manila, Taft had held that the army was a necessary evil but not an agent to encourage the establishment of a well-ordered civil government. Actually, long before July, 1901, the major task of the army, suppression of the insurrection, had been completed in all save

[32] For many years, after Dewey had assisted Aguinaldo's return to Manila, there was bitter debate on the question: Did the United States promise independence to the Philippines at this time? The answer would seem to be "that the United States by properly accredited agents made no promises of independence, but that the actions of certain Americans led the Revolutionists to draw inferences, exaggerated by their hopes." Malcolm, *The Government of the Philippine Islands,* 121-122. See also Dean C. Worcester, *The Philippines Past and Present* (new ed., New York, 1930), ch. ii.

[33] Text printed in Worcester, *The Philippines,* 792-798.

remote districts. Aguinaldo had been captured by General Funston's forces on March 23, and on April 19 he took the oath of allegiance to the United States. The way had thus been paved for the rapid extension of local civil government.

FILIPINOS INCLUDED IN COMMISSION GOVERNMENT

Firm in its conviction that for decades the Filipinos would be incapable of self-government, and that independence was not to be thought of, the Taft Commission was equally determined to avoid the charge that a handful of Americans were running the islands without consulting their little brown brothers. Accordingly, to the American membership of the Commission were added three Filipinos of wealth who were not adovcates of independence: Benito Legarda, Jose R. de Luzuriaga, and T. H. Pardo de Tavera. Legarda and de Tavera were among the organizers of the native Federal Party, which favored peace, allegiance to the United States, and eventual admission to the Union as a state. The inclusion of Filipinos on the Commission was by no means welcome to all Americans, but Taft, as governor, was less concerned with exploitation of the material resources of the islands than with understanding the character and potentialities of the Filipinos. He was quick to note that they were proud, sensitive, and resentful of any suggestion that their race was inferior. While there was a tendency for some Americans to regard the Filipinos as "niggers," [34] there was no color line in the Philippine policy of the Commission. It maintained a paternal, if not always a democratic, attitude toward the Filipino; an attitude which Taft liked to express in the phrase "our little brown brothers." This made no appeal either to MacArthur's staff or to the rank and file of the American army of occupation. Soldiers of this young army of imperialism sang with gusto a refrain which ended:

> He may be a brother of William H. Taft,
> But he ain't no friend of mine! [35]

THE PERIOD OF THE TAFT POLICY

The administration of the United States in the Philippines from 1901 to 1913 may best be described as the period of the Taft policy. Taft as Civil Governor, then as Secretary of War, and finally as President gave direction and continuity to these years. The Taft slogan, "The Philip-

---

[34] Pringle, *The Life and Times of William Howard Taft*, I, 174.
[35] Mrs. William Howard Taft, *Recollections of Full Years* (New York, 1917), 125.

pines for the Filipinos," was applied as a political doctrine with the
utmost caution. By 1907, however, Filipino political aspirations were
given some recognition with the election of the first Philippine Assembly which, as the lower house, was to share the legislative power
with the Commission. Since the governor-general (previously the civil
governor) did not possess the power of veto, the principal check on legislation rested in the power of Congress to nullify. Taft described the political development of the whole period when he said that it was a process of making a paternal government less paternal.[36]

THE MATERIAL AND CULTURAL ADVANCE

The years of the Taft policy brought some material and cultural ad-
vances to the Philippines. The revival and growth of trade and industry were revealed in the revenues of the insular government. Courts
were established applying a new code of civil procedure over which
presided judges summoned from the United States. Taft had described
justice as he first found it in the native courts by saying that it "stinks
to Heaven." While Dr. Victor G. Heiser was commissioner of public
health, the death rate from all causes was reduced from 27.46 per 1,000
in 1905, to 18.32 per 1,000 in 1913. After long negotiations with the
Vatican, the vexed problem of the friar lands was only partially settled
in December, 1903, when the Philippine government purchased most of
them for the generous price of $7,239,000. Substantial beginnings were
made in the field of public education, replacing the inadequate system
of monastic control which had prevailed in Spanish days. English was
made the basic language of primary instruction.[37]

THE AMERICAN PEOPLE AND THE PHILIPPINES

The relationship of the American people to American policy in the
Philippines, 1898-1913, has not yet received definitive treatment by the
historian. Nevertheless, some features of the story are reasonably clear.
To summarize, its origins are to be found in the ambitions of the small
but articulate Roosevelt-Lodge group to direct the United States toward
colonial empire and sea-power.[38] McKinley's government, the Congress, and the American people, all engaged in fighting a war to free

[36] Roosevelt as President described the program as one "of changing a government of
Americans assisted by Filipinos into a government of Filipinos assisted by Americans.
. . ." Forbes, *The Philippine Islands*, I, 139.
[37] For extensive discussions of Philippine progress in these years see: Forbes, *The
Philippine Islands;* Worcester, *The Philippines Past and Present;* and David P. Barrows,
History of the Philippines (rev. ed., Yonkers-on-Hudson, 1925).
[38] Griswold, *Far Eastern Policy*, 34.

Cuba, had no interest in and little knowledge of these ambitions until Dewey's victory revealed new vistas in Manifest Destiny. Even then the popular enthusiasm barely carried the treaty of annexation through a divided Senate, and in later years McKinley felt it necessary to place responsibility for annexation on Divine Providence.[39] Perhaps he might better have attributed it to his desire to follow the popular clamor. Thus the Philippines were taken, not in pursuit of a well established national policy, but because "the march of events rules and overrules human action." Nevertheless the issue of empire was not yet settled. Though anti-imperialism was the slogan of the Democrats in the presidential campaign of 1900, the sweeping victory of the Republicans was not a mandate on imperialism, for the campaign was a confusion of many issues.[40]

UNANSWERED QUESTIONS

At the outbreak of the Spanish-American War no idea was more remote from the mind of the American people than the conquest of the Philippine Islands. What is more, after the decision to retain the islands was made, American public opinion developed very little interest in a philosophy of empire and very little understanding of its new responsibilities in colonial administration. The task of planning and administering the government which we gave to the Philippines was the essence of paternalism. Its success, however, was not due to any magic in the ideology of paternalism, but rather to the character of Taft himself. It was his capacity and his personality that made paternalism work. His policy bridged a wide and deep chasm between the proud, sensitive, resentful, politically immature Filipino and an American pub-

---

[39] The President explained to a group of Methodists: "The truth is I didn't want the Philippines and when they came to us as a gift from the gods, I did not know what to do about them. . . . I walked the floor of the White House night after night until midnight; and I am not ashamed to tell you, gentlemen, that I went down on my knees and prayed Almighty God for light and guidance more than one night."

"And one night late it came to me this way—I don't know how it was, but it came: (1) that we could not give them back to Spain—that would be cowardly and dishonorable; (2) that we could not turn them over to France or Germany—our commercial rivals in the Orient—that would be bad business and discreditable; (3) that we could not leave them to themselves—they were unfit for self-government—and they would soon have anarchy and misrule over there worse than Spain's was; and (4) that there was nothing left for us to do but to take them all, and to educate the Filipinos, and uplift and civilize and Christianize them, and by God's grace do the very best we could by them, as our fellow-men for whom Christ also died. . . ." *The Christian Advocate,* Jan. 22, 1903.

[40] T. A. Bailey, "Was the Election of 1900 a Mandate on Imperialism?" *Mississippi Valley Historical Review,* XXIV (1937), 43-52.

lic which lacked interest and almost forgot that it owned an Asiatic dependency.   Back in 1897-98, as McKinley pondered over the problem of an American empire, his mind had travelled between political extremes. Before the war he had seen annexation as "criminal aggression"; after the fall of Manila he came to view annexation as "benevolent assimilation."   It was Taft, not McKinley and not the American people, who found and applied in the Philippines a middle course between these extremes.

CHAPTER 16

THE OPEN DOOR AND THE INTEGRITY
OF CHINA, 1899-1905

WE HAVE seen (Chapter 14) how the Sino-Japanese War, 1894-95, precipitated a train of events, resulting, in 1896-98, in a movement threatening the partition of China. This movement, against which the spineless Manchu government seemed helpless, had, by 1899, reduced strategic areas in China to a semi-colonial status. For example, Tsingtao, under lease, had become a German city protected by a German squadron; the Chinese derived such consolation as they might from the fact that sovereignty in the abstract was reserved to Peking. Beyond Tsingtao throughout populous Shantung province, the birthplace of Confucius and thus China's Holy Land, German capital had acquired a practical monopoly in railroad and mining development. The stage was thus set in China for an era of special monopolistic privilege for German capital in Shantung, for Russian capital in Manchuria, for British capital in the Yangtze Valley, and for French capital in the areas bordering Indo-China.

This state of affairs, whereby large areas of China had fallen into a sort of industrial-investment servitude to the great powers of Europe, would not have come about but for the inability of Peking to protect its territory and to enjoy the respect that power invites. In reality Peking was not only weak, it was growing weaker. There was no intelligent leadership in China's capital, and popular discontent among the masses suggested that the dynasty had lost the Mandate of Heaven, and that the foreigner with his leaseholds, his railways, and his Christianity was not looked upon by the Chinese people as an adequate substitute for Heaven's favor.[1] After 1898 the political and military impotence of Peking and the lack of a national consciousness in the Chinese people served as constant invitations to the great powers in their quest and rivalry for markets which could be controlled politically. Thus, once the first steps had been taken in 1897-98 to cut the Chinese melon, once the leaseholds

---

[1] For background manifestations of political weakness, anti-dynastic, and anti-foreign reactions see Paul H. Clyde, *United States Policy toward China* (Durham, 1940), ch. xxix.

and spheres had been acquired, the powers were under the temptation to cut deeper—to make "spheres" into protectorates, and protectorates into annexations. This threat to China's sovereign existence was, it should be remembered, an important by-product not only of China's weakness but also of that intense European imperialistic rivalry which was to result finally in the World War of 1914.

During the years 1899 to 1905, which are to be reviewed in this chapter, China, politically helpless, played a confused, passive role in her vain efforts to resist the pressure of the powers. A sort of political football, she was kicked about by the contending powers, restrained only by their own mutual jealousies. The period is dominated by a series of striking historical events, all intimately related to one central problem: "Was China to be a sovereign, independent state?" In noting the answer which the powers gave to this question in the years 1899-1905 we shall discuss: 1) the enunciation of an open door policy for commerce; 2) the threat to China's territorial integrity arising from the Boxer troubles; 3) the new far eastern balance of power created by the Anglo-Japanese Alliance, 1902; and 4) implications of the Russo-Japanese War.

1. THE OPEN DOOR POLICY

The major interest of the powers in China during the nineteenth century, as we are aware, was in the main commercial. After the first treaty settlement of 1842-44, these commercial interests were pursued by the various powers within the limitations imposed by the most-favored-nation clause contained in all the treaties.[2] Commercial privileges or concessions extended by China to one power were thus automatically enjoyed by all. As a result, the principle of equal commercial opportunity was maintained with a fair measure of support from all the powers, and in particular from the United States and Great Britain.[3] When in the winter of 1897-98 Germany and Russia launched the scramble for naval leaseholds and spheres of influence, the British at first opposed the idea. They were confident that a free and open market for British commerce and capital was the best guarantee of their continued economic supremacy in China. Realizing, however, that it could not hope for success by playing a lone hand, the British government appealed

---

[2] For texts of the most-favored-nation clause in the various nineteenth-century treaties, see China, The Maritime Customs, *Treaties, Conventions, etc. between China and Foreign States* (2 vols., 2nd ed., Shanghai, 1917).

[3] In this respect American policy had been consistent since 1843, when Webster wrote the first instructions to Cushing. Clyde, *United States Policy toward China*, ch. iii. The background of the British attitude is given in Lord Charles Beresford, *The Breakup of China* (New York, 1899).

to the United States in March, 1898, and again in January, 1899, for some form of joint action to maintain the open door.[4] Neither President McKinley nor Secretary of State John Sherman was disposed to act on the British suggestion. Neither possessed any deep understanding of previous American policy in China, and anyway American eyes were turned toward Cuba, not Kiaochow or Port Arthur. Accordingly, Britain, as we have seen, went into the business of leaseholds (Kowloon extension and Wei-hai-wei) and spheres of influence (Yangtze Valley) on a magnificent scale.

THE REVIVAL OF AMERICAN POLICY

One may well ask why any administration could be so unresponsive to the call of historic American policy. The principle of most-favored-nation treatment was as old as American independence itself and had been applied in European as well as in far eastern treaties. The State Department had been advised repeatedly by Ambassador John Hay in London and Minister Charles Denby in Peking that the leaseholds and the spheres threatened not only equal opportunity in commerce but the territorial and political integrity of China as well.[5]

Only on the basis of a number of factors can we explain our costly mistake of 1898 in failing to defend the principle of equal opportunity. Principal among these were: 1) Sherman's incompetence in diplomacy and his fear of being "used" by the British; 2) the preoccupation of government and people with Cuba and the war; and finally, 3) the fact that the material American commercial stake in China was small—hardly two percent of the total United States foreign trade.

Slowly, and with hesitant steps, the American government moved to reassert its interests and its historic policy in China. In the winter of 1898-99 Lord Charles Beresford, returning to England from China, aroused his American friends with a picture of China preserved by an Anglo-American open door policy. The idea fitted well into the new and larger concepts acquired by American business men after Dewey's victory of May, 1898, at Manila Bay.[6] The reasonableness of the picture depended on preserving China as a free market. The American government began to react to the pressure of these ideas in the early fall and winter of 1898. The Anglophile John Hay was now secretary of state. McKinley told the Paris Peace Commission (September 16) and the

---

[4] The relevant correspondence is treated in A. L. P. Dennis, *Adventures in American Diplomacy 1896-1906* (New York, 1928), ch. viii, with documents.

[5] Dennis, *Adventures in American Diplomacy,* 198, 202, 205.

[6] See Julius W. Pratt, *Expansionists of 1898* (Baltimore, 1936), 278.

Congress (December 5) that the sale of American products in China could not be prejudiced by exclusive treatment. But the President was still uncertain of his course, for the second British overture for joint action on the open door was rebuffed in January, 1899, despite the fact that more than 1,000 American missionaries in China were at one with American business in wanting now a "strong" policy from Washington.

In the late summer of 1899 an American policy finally emerged. It was a direct product of British initiative. The principal details may be told briefly. During the early summer, A. E. Hippisley, an Englishman, and an official of the Chinese Customs Service, renewed in Washington his old friendship with W. W. Rockhill, who had seen much diplomatic service in Asia, and was now Hay's chief adviser on far eastern affairs. Hippisley's views on the open door were given to Rockhill in a memorandum dated August 17. Rockhill, having revised and expanded the document, presented it for the approval of McKinley and Hay, August 28. On September 6, Secretary Hay, drawing heavily on Rockhill's draft, sent his now famous open door notes to Great Britain, Germany, and Russia.[7]

NATURE OF THE HAY OPEN DOOR NOTES

What, then, was the character of the policy set forth in Hay's notes to the powers? Specifically, the notes asked for equal *commercial* opportunity within the spheres of influence. The spheres, it would seem, to use Rockhill's words, were accepted "as existing facts" about which the United States could do nothing. Therefore the notes carefully avoided any mention of those foundation stones on which the spheres rested—preference and monopoly in mining and railroad concessions and capital investment. Each power addressed was also asked to adhere to certain stipulations[8] whereby equal commercial opportunity might be maintained, and to co-operate with the United States in securing the adherence of other powers.

The replies addressed to Hay by the powers were carefully qualified; some were evasive; and one, Russia's, virtually rejected the whole idea of equal opportunity. Most of the powers professed great enthusiasm for

---

[7] Similar though not identical notes went to Japan (Nov. 13), to Italy (Nov. 17), and to France (Nov. 21). The most exhaustive treatment of the enunciation of the open door policy is A. Whitney Griswold, *The Far Eastern Policy of the United States* (New York, 1938), ch. ii; texts of the Hippisley memorandum, Rockhill memorandum, and drafts of the final notes are in Griswold, 475-500.

[8] Each power within its sphere was asked: 1) not to interfere with the treaty ports; 2) not to impede equitable administration of the Chinese Customs tariff; and 3) not to charge discriminatory railroad rates or harbor dues.

the "principle" of the open door, but even Great Britain's acceptance was made dependent "on similar assent" by the other powers. To meet this disheartening result, Hay resorted to the game of international bluff. He announced, March 20, 1900, that he regarded the replies as "final and definitive." [9] The phrase fooled nobody except perhaps the American people, which was left with the impression that its government had won a brilliant diplomatic victory over predatory powers in China. Actually, the United States had not done so. It had reaffirmed its adherence to a basic principle, equal commercial opportunity. It had attempted also to secure the adherence of other powers. It had failed to get unqualified acceptance of the principle, and it had failed to attack the basic problem—the spheres of influence. The phrase "sphere of influence" was merely a convenient label meaning special privilege in mining, railroad construction, and investment. So long as the spheres remained in a politically enfeebled China there could be small hope for equal commercial opportunity. This was no secret to Hay or Rockhill, but they also knew that the American people were neither willing nor prepared to seek destruction of the spheres by force. In reality the two United States policies of isolation on the one hand and the open door in China on the other were incompatible, since the latter could only be made effective if diplomacy were supported by action. American policy and diplomacy toward China at the turn of the twentieth century reads, as will be seen, like a preview of policy and diplomacy there from 1931 to 1941.

2. THE BOXER MOVEMENT AND CHINA'S INTEGRITY

It is not belittling the Hay policy of 1899 to say that it was inadequate to protect either immediate American commercial interests or the historic American principle of equal opportunity. One need only recall that "in the Far East the powers were dealing with the fate of an empire of upward of three hundred million souls and no less than five major states were disputing the spoils." [10] This was not the sort of thing to be arrested by polite diplomatic notes. The spheres were still there. These spheres were designed to give preferential treatment in railroad, mining, and investment concessions. The question was: How could even Hay's modest request for equal commercial treatment be honored against such a background? [11]

---

[9] United States, *Foreign Relations, 1899,* 142.

[10] William L. Langer, *The Diplomacy of Imperialism* (New York, 1935), II, 677.

[11] It is Langer's conclusion that to this point "the efforts of Hay, then, had no practical bearing on the situation as it was at the turn of the century." II, 688. Tyler Dennett,

The first test of the effectiveness of the Hay policy came in 1900 with the outbreak of the Boxer troubles.[12] Anti-foreign movements were not new. For a decade the diplomatic correspondence had been heavily weighted with accounts of attacks on foreign persons and property.[13] After China's defeat in 1895, and particularly after the German politico-economic invasion of Shantung in 1897-98, anti-foreignism increased rapidly among the ignorant masses in Chihli, Shantung, Shansi, and South Manchuria.

The first attacks by the Boxers and their accomplices were directed against Chinese converts to Christianity and the missionaries who sought to protect their spiritual wards. Protests from the Ministers at Peking had anything but the desired effect, for the Empress Dowager, who sympathized with the anti-foreign movement, urged viceroys and governors to give encouragement to those who resisted "the foreign aggressor." [14] Thus the movement spread while the foreign powers continued to regard the Boxers as rebels rather than as allies of the Peking government. The powers were unbelievably slow to realize the gravity of the situation. Not only did the Boxers surround and lay siege to the foreign legations in Peking, they also cut the railroad to Tientsin, and defeated and forced back British Admiral Seymour and his force of some 2,000 men who attempted to break through to the rescue of be-leaguered foreigners in the Peking legations. By mid-June, 1900, the Peking government, now controlled by anti-foreign factions, was giving open support to the Boxers, who entered Peking, June 13, cutting tele-graphic communications with the outside. Peking was isolated. On June 17, foreign naval forces bombarded and took the Taku forts below Tientsin. By June 19, when German Minister von Ketteler was killed in Peking, Imperial Chinese troops had joined the Boxers, and attacks on the besieged legations had begun. The famous relief expedition, finally organized by the powers, did not reach Peking until August 14, by which time many gallant defenders of the legations had fallen, while the movement itself, spreading to Manchuria and to areas southwest of Peking, had claimed many additional victims.[15]

John Hay (New York, 1933), 295, gives the following comment on the whole negotiation: "It would have taken more than a lawyer to define what new rights had been recognized, or acquired, or even what had actually been said."

[12] For the character of the Boxer movement see G. N. Steiger, *China and the Occident* (New Haven, 1927).

[13] Clyde, *United States Policy toward China,* 199.

[14] United States, *Foreign Relations, 1900,* 85-86.

[15] The best narrative accounts are Paul H. Clements, *The Boxer Rebellion* (New York, 1915), Pt. II; and Steiger, *China and the Occident,* chs. vii and viii.

RUSSIA OCCUPIES MANCHURIA

Meanwhile, in Manchuria, the Boxers attacked the Chinese Eastern Railway, forced the Russians out of Mukden, and Tsitsihar, and laid siege to the Russian section of Harbin. This development was not entirely unwelcome to some members of the Russian government. General Kuropatkin, the Minister of War, had greeted news of the Boxer outbreak with the exclamation: "This will give us an excuse for seizing Manchuria." [16] Count Witte wanted only "peaceful penetration," but the Boxer attacks were an invitation to Kuropatkin's soldiers. By October, 1900, Russia was in complete military control of Manchuria. This was the same Russia that less than a year earlier had turned down Hay's open door proposals. It now appeared that Russia intended to convert her Manchurian sphere into a Russian province. The threat was not only to equal commercial opportunity but also to China's territorial integrity.

UNITED STATES POLICY DURING 1900

During the first half of 1900, Edwin H. Conger, American Minister at Peking, while constantly warning his government of the chaos in North China, co-operated with his diplomatic colleagues in joint representations and protests to the Chinese government. This was in line with the Hay notes of 1899 which had invited the powers to resume the so-called co-operative policy reminiscent of Burlingame. Yet between March and June, 1900, the Department of State reversed itself, repudiated the idea of co-operation, and told Conger that his country would act "singly and without the co-operation of other powers." Seemingly there was little appreciation in Washington of what was happening in China. On the eve of the attacks on the Peking legations, Rockhill was telling Hay that the Boxer movement was not likely to "cause any serious complications." Following this, the Department, its course still unpredictable, effected another partial about-face, informing Conger that he now might act "concurrently" with other powers "if necessity arises." [17]

Nevertheless, the pressure of events in China was forcing Hay toward another and more fundamental enunciation of American policy. The Secretary knew that some of the powers, Russia and Germany in particular, were willing to use the Boxer troubles to enlarge their spheres of

---

[16] Langer, *The Diplomacy of Imperialism*, II, 695.

[17] Dennis, *Adventures in American Diplomacy*, 216-220; Griswold, *Far Eastern Policy of the United States*, 79-80.

influence and, if possible, to gain further political control in them. Diplomatic wrangles over organization of the international relief expedition were already revealing how tense was the rivalry. While, therefore, on June 10, Hay instructed Conger that

we have no policy in China except to protect with energy American interests, and especially American citizens and the legation,

he informed the powers by circular note, July 3, that the United States aimed

. . . to seek a solution which may bring about permanent safety and peace to China, preserve Chinese territorial and administrative entity, protect all rights guaranteed to friendly Powers by treaty and international law, and safeguard for the world the principle of equal and impartial trade with all parts of the Chinese Empire.[18]

This principle of China's territorial integrity was not new in the language of American policy. It had been expressed by Humphrey Marshall in 1853, and by Anson Burlingame in 1862.[19] It had been absent from, if not repudiated by, the Hay policy of 1899, which tacitly acknowledged the reality of leaseholds and spheres. Now in July, 1900, it was revived in a new and stronger form. Hay invited not only "respect" for China's integrity but also suggested "a collective guarantee" by the powers—a guarantee which was not forthcoming since, with the exception of Great Britain, none of the powers even replied to the July circular.

Yet the important point is that in late 1900 the threatened partition of China was again arrested temporarily. Why was this? The note-writing of Hay probably had some psychological effect, but it does not appear to have been the determining factor. This factor again was the rivalry, the mutual jealousy of the powers, and their retreat from the cooperative policy to bilateral negotiations. England and Japan were slowly drawing together to stop Russia in Manchuria and in the Middle East. Germany's equivocal position in Shantung between Russia and England had, to be sure, resulted on October 16, 1900,[20] in an Anglo-German agreement favoring the open door and the integrity of China, but this was an innocuous affair. John Hay referred to it as "a horrible practical [German] joke on England." He failed, it would seem, to

---

[18] United States, *Foreign Relations, 1900,* 299.
[19] See Clyde, *United States Policy toward China,* 24, 60.
[20] Text of the Anglo-German agreement in MacMurray, *Treaties,* I, 263.

realize that if this were so, it was an equally horrible joke upon himself and everything he had been attempting to do in China. In a word, there was no conversion of the powers to the idea of China's integrity. The business of melon-cutting was stopped temporarily because each of the potential aggressors, fearful of the debacle that would follow, hesitated to make the first move. Then, ironically, in the midst of this lull, Hay himself joined the concession hunters. In December, 1900, under pressure from the American Navy, he sought a naval coaling station at Samsah Inlet, north of Foochow on the coast of Fukien province. Japan when consulted blocked the move, reminding Hay, presumably with some delight, of his own recent efforts to preserve the territorial integrity of China.[21] The incident did not strengthen in subsequent years the moral influence of the United States in the Far East.

THE BOXER PROTOCOL, SEPTEMBER, 1901

The final settlement of the Boxer troubles as set forth in the Peace Protocol of September, 1901, was achieved only after prolonged and involved negotiations. The jealousies of the powers being as they were, it was with the utmost difficulty that agreement was at length reached on the kind and degree of punishment China should suffer.

During the advance of the international relief expedition on Peking there was relative harmony, for the plight of the besieged foreigners in the capital was desperate. The international relief army was one of the most remarkable ever assembled: 8,000 Japanese, 4,500 Russians, 3,000 British, 2,500 Americans, and 800 French. Available German troops were held back to protect Kiaochow and the coast. The honor of commanding the allied forces had been given, to please the Kaiser, to Field-Marshal Count von Waldersee, who, perhaps fortunately, did not arrive until after Peking was in allied hands.[22] This was a severe blow to German imperialistic pride. The Kaiser, who was somewhat rabid on the subject of the yellow peril, had instructed his troops "to give no quarter and take no prisoners," and was now forced to see the glory of leadership go to General Linevich, the Russian commander.[23] The

---

[21] Hay consulted Japan because the latter regarded the province of Fukien, opposite Formosa, as a Japanese sphere of influence. The Chinese Foreign Office in response to a Japanese note had pledged itself, April 26, 1898, never to "cede or lease" any part of the province (MacMurray, *Treaties*, I, 126). Hay's effort to secure Samsah was not made public until 24 years after the event (United States, *Foreign Relations, 1925*, 113-115). The Navy again urged the project on Hay in December, 1901, and in May, 1902 (Griswold, *Far Eastern Policy of the United States*, 83-84; Alfred Vagts, *Deutschland und die Vereinigten Staaten in der Weltpolitik* [2 vols., New York, 1935], II, 1096-97, 1134-35).

[22] Clements, *The Boxer Rebellion*, 135-136.

[23] Langer, *Diplomacy of Imperialism*, II, 699-700.

tension was increased during the autumn and winter of 1900-1901, when the powers became convinced that Russia was preparing to control not only Manchuria but also the metropolitan province of Chihli. This led to all manner of attempts by the powers for additional concessions. In these unhappy circumstances, suggesting another partition of the empire, the Boxer Protocol was concluded, September 7, 1901.[24]

The terms were severe and humiliating. The wisdom of the settlement has often been called in question. From the standpoint of the powers it could be argued that Peking's responsibility was great. The Manchu government had regarded itself as at war and therefore must now pay the price of its defeat and its treachery. The terms therefore were dictated against a background of punitive expeditions against many localities where foreigners had been attacked, and allied troops occupied the Imperial City within Peking itself.[25]

In the long view the Boxer uprising was to exert a profound influence upon China's political future. It hastened the end of the Manchu dynasty and the creation of the Republic. In this respect it was a dynamic step in the progress of China's revolution. To be sure, the Boxers were inspired by little more than a "blind and ignorant patriotism," while their patron and defender, Yü Hsien, the Manchu governor of Shantung, was distinguished by nothing save a "policy of blind reaction." The Boxers had no constructive program of reform to offer. They merely attributed China's ills to the "foreign devils" who must be destroyed along with their machines and inventions, "their strange and intolerant religion, their insufferable airs of superiority." [26] Yet with all its weakness, its lack of constructive program, its blind fanaticism and reaction, the Boxer movement was an unmistakable symptom

---

[24] Text of the Protocol in MacMurray, *Treaties,* I, 278-320.

[25] The terms of the Protocol may be summarized as follows: 1) apology to Germany and Japan for the murder of the German minister and the Japanese chancellor of legation, and erection of a memorial to von Ketteler on the spot where he was assassinated; 2) punishment of responsible Chinese officials; 3) erection of monuments in desecrated foreign cemeteries; 4) official examinations to be suspended in all cities where attacks had occurred; 5) China to pay an indemnity of $333,000,000, to create an effective five percent tariff, and to prohibit for at least two years importation of arms, ammunition, and materials for their manufacture; 6) the Taku forts to be destroyed, and a legation quarter to be created in Peking under exclusive control of the powers, which they might make defensible; 7) right of the powers to occupy 13 places as a guarantee of free communication with Peking; 8) China to agree to the amendment of commercial treaties, and to create a ministry of foreign affairs; 9) China to publish preventive edicts against further outbreaks; 10) the right of the allies to maintain legation guards at Peking. The American share of the indemnity, $25,000,000, was, as in the case of all the powers, far in excess of justifiable claims. Substantial portions of it were returned to China in 1907 and 1924.

[26] R. F. Johnston, *Twilight in the Forbidden City* (London, 1934), 44.

of China's growing unrest, of her resentment against foreign intrusion and exploitation, and of her will to resist. It is not to be wondered that the Boxers had little if any understanding of this. It is to be wondered that the Manchu Court understood it so imperfectly, and the foreign powers hardly at all. During the decade which was to elapse between the Boxer troubles and the Revolution of 1911, the Court failed utterly to rid itself of the incubus of decay from within, while the powers intent on the scramble for concessions permitted China's integrity to fade still further into the mists of diplomatic fantasy.

THE ANGLO-JAPANESE ALLIANCE, 1902

The formal diplomatic settlement of the Boxer affair did not stabilize in any permanent sense China's relations with the powers, nor did it end the threat to the American policy of the open door and China's integrity. The renewed attack upon these policies came from Manchuria, which, as already noted, had been occupied by Russia in 1900 consequent on the spread of Boxer outbreaks to areas where the Russians were completing construction of the Chinese Eastern Railway. Before the end of 1900 it was clear that Russia was secretly pressing China for a separate Manchurian agreement that would add greatly to her exclusive rights within her Manchurian sphere. This news was disturbing to Britain, to Japan, and particularly to the United States, for the three powers had regarded the Boxer negotiations at Peking as providing a common and all-inclusive settlement between China and the powers. A separate settlement by Russia covering Manchuria would not only destroy this principle, it would also render nugatory the Hay policy contained in the July, 1900, circular. The case was so urgent that Hay again circularized both China and the powers (February 19, 1901), warning the former

. . . of the impropriety, inexpediency, and even extreme danger to the interests of China of considering any private territorial or financial arrangements, at least without the full knowledge and approval of all the Powers now engaged in [the Boxer] negotiations.[27]

In April, Hay asked Russia for specific assurances that American enterprise in Manchuria would not suffer discrimination. For a brief period this diplomatic pressure was successful. Briefly, the Russian pressure was withdrawn, but in November, 1901, the Russian Minister at Peking was standing over the deathbed of Li Hung-chang attempting to extort

---

[27] Dennis, *Adventures in American Diplomacy*, 243. For texts of Russian agreements and proposed agreements concerning Manchuria, 1900-01, see MacMurray, *Treaties*, I, 88 ff., 274-278, 321-324, 329-331, 661-662.

the dying viceroy's signature on a new Manchurian convention.[28] So matters stood on January 30, 1902, when Great Britain and Japan signed the first Anglo-Japanese Alliance, an agreement which by effecting a complete readjustment in the balance of power was to have tremendous influence on the future of Europe and the Far East.

Like so many agreements before and since, the Anglo-Japanese Alliance pledged the signatories in support of "the *status quo* and general peace in the Extreme East," of the "independence and territorial integrity" of China and Korea, and of the open door there. This was the diplomatic window dressing. The real importance of the alliance was stated in Clause I, which recognized the *special interests* of both powers in China,[29] and the *special interests* of Japan "politically as well as commercially and industrially" in Korea. This was an obvious victory for the principle of spheres of influence; it was an equally obvious defeat for the American policies of the open door and co-operative action for its maintenance. The alliance went on to pledge each signatory to neutrality if the other was at war, and to come to the other's assistance if attacked by more than one power.[30] Since it was clear that the alliance was aimed at St. Petersburg, Russia and France replied with a declaration and agreement (March 16, 1902) taking cognizance of the alliance and reaffirming their adherence to the *status quo* and the integrity of China.[31]

FOUNDATIONS OF THE ANGLO-JAPANESE ALLIANCE

How may the appearance of this vital alliance be explained? Certainly it was not born of far eastern considerations alone. In the broader sense "the treaty was England's first material success in the effort to end her isolation." [32] From the British point of view, the Russian threat to Manchuria and Korea was secondary to the Russian threat "in China generally, in Tibet, in Persia, in Turkey." British efforts toward a

---

[28] Dennis, *Adventures in American Diplomacy,* 350-351.

[29] Here the distinction between the British and the American position, and, consequently, policy, in China is made clear. Both the United States and Britain were concerned principally with protecting their own economic interests in China. Any altruistic concern for China's integrity was a minor consideration. However, whereas the United States was resting its case solely on the principle of China's integrity, the British, by reason of their sphere of influence, in their Yangtze policy had provided a sort of second line of defense to which Britain would retire if the break-up of China came, as seemed only too likely in 1901-02.

[30] Full text of the alliance in G. P. Gooch and H. W. V. Temperley, *British Documents on the Origins of the War, 1898-1914* (London, 1926-1938), II, 115-120.

[31] See MacMurray, *Treaties,* I, 326; C. W. Young, *The International Relations of Manchuria* (Chicago, 1929), 34-35.

[32] Griswold, *Far Eastern Policy of the United States,* 88.

compromise with Russia had failed, the Russians believing presumably that they could reach a settlement with Japan through the pro-Russian Ito. In a word, the English decided upon the alliance with Japan "in order to prevent an understanding between Russia and Japan," an understanding "which would have rendered the British position in the Far East almost hopeless." [33]

In contrast with the British attitude, Japan accepted the alliance for considerations that were predominantly, if not exclusively, far eastern— primarily to advance her interests in Korea, to protect those interests from the Russian threat arising in Manchuria, and, as with the British case, to end her own diplomatic isolation dating back to the Triple Intervention of 1895. Even with these interests at stake there was much opposition to the English alliance led by Ito, the most powerful member of the Genro, who believed that a settlement should and could be reached with Russia.[34] Ito's defeat and the resulting shift in Japan's foreign policy to the British alignment cannot be explained exclusively on the ground of Russia's "glacial pressure" in Manchuria, or of the so-called "community of interests" which had developed between Japan and Britain since the Sino-Japanese War. The two powers were still separated by "a wide geographic and cultural gulf." Japan was still a newcomer among the great powers. These differences in the case of both powers were recognized. They were overcome because, soon after the Sino-Japanese War, a small group of able and vigorous leaders in both London and Tokyo preached the end of isolation and the need for an Anglo-Japanese arrangement.[35]

It is easy to lose perspective and to overestimate the importance of the Anglo-Japanese Alliance. That it was of great significance is obvious. Yet the alliance alone did not change the course of history. Both signatories still hoped for "some sort of arrangement with Russia." In 1902, war between Japan and Russia was not inevitable because of this alliance. In the two years which elapsed between the signing of the alliance and the outbreak of the Russo-Japanese War, Russia could have reached a far eastern settlement with Japan "on attractive terms," and would probably have done so but for the demands of the armed services and the influence of irresponsible adventurers about the Tsar.

---

[33] Langer, The Diplomacy of Imperialism, II, 783.

[34] For Ito's views and his attempts to reach a settlement with Russia on the eve of the alliance see Tatsuji Takeuchi, War and Diplomacy in the Japanese Empire (Garden City, 1935), 124-128.

[35] The work of the alliance propagandists is ably portrayed by C. N. Spinks, "The Background of the Anglo-Japanese Alliance," Pacific Historical Review, VIII (1939), 317-339.

THE ALLIANCE AND UNITED STATES INTERESTS

The key to official American reactions to the alliance and to American policy in the Far East, 1902-04, is suggested by the fact that Secretary Hay, inadequately informed by the diplomatic service, was taken by surprise.[36] When Russia, responding to the pressure of the alliance, agreed (April 8, 1902) to evacuate her troops from Manchuria within eighteen months (that is, by September 8, 1903), Hay appeared to be satisfied.[37] In a letter to President Roosevelt (May 1, 1902), the Secretary of State discussed the purposes of American policy in terms of ungarnished realism.

We are not in any attitude of hostility towards Russia in Manchuria. On the contrary, we recognize her *exceptional position in northern China*. What we have been working for two years to accomplish, and what we have at last accomplished, if assurances are to count for anything, is that, no matter what happens eventually in northern China and Manchuria, the United States shall not be placed in any worse position than while the country was under the unquestioned domination of China.[38]

There were grounds for some of, but not for all, Hay's optimism, for had Russia carried out her convention with China by withdrawing her troops from Manchuria, "there would have been no war. Not a single major power concerned would have disputed the Russian [sphere of] influence" in Manchuria.[39] Furthermore, withdrawal of the Russian troops would have removed the greatest danger to Japanese interests in Korea, thus depriving Japan's warhawks of one of their most effective arguments.

However, Russia did not withdraw. After a partial and temporary retirement, she reoccupied Manchuria, while at Peking she pressed new secret demands upon China.[40] These demands, which if granted would

---

[36] Griswold, *Far Eastern Policy of the United States*, 91.

[37] Text of the Russo-Chinese convention of evacuation of Manchuria is in MacMurray, *Treaties*, I, 326-329.

[38] Roosevelt Papers, printed in Tyler Dennett, *Roosevelt and the Russo-Japanese War* (New York, 1925), 135-136; Dennis, *Adventures in American Diplomacy*, 353. Italics are mine. It would appear that Hay anticipated further encroachment upon China's integrity, and was concerned only in so far as this might infringe upon American rights. China's sovereignty as such was of secondary concern.

[39] W. L. Langer, "Der Russisch-Japanische Krieg," *Europäische Gespräche*, No. VI (1926), 300-304.

[40] By these demands China would have agreed among other things: 1) not to create new treaty ports or admit additional consuls in Manchuria; 2) to employ no foreigners save Russians in Manchuria; and 3) that the Newchwang customs receipts be deposited in the Russo-Chinese Bank. United States, *Foreign Relations, 1903*, 53-54.

have ended any pretense of an open door and China's integrity in Manchuria, were the result of a conflict over policy between two factions at St. Petersburg. One group, headed by Witte, favored a gradual economic penetration of Manchuria which could be achieved without unduly alarming the powers. The second group, which now controlled the Tsar, favored immediate, aggressive economic and political pressure, backed by military force if necessary, to make Russia's position thoroughly secure in Manchuria, and to challenge eventually Japan's position in Korea.[41]

The failure of Russia to carry out the evacuation, and her presentation of new demands implementing the aggressive policy of Bezobrazov, *et al.*, threatened to make the Manchurian question an exclusive Russo-Chinese concern, and to nullify the negotiations for a new Sino-American treaty of commerce which had already been begun. However, the treaty was signed, October 8, 1903, opening Antung and Mukden in Manchuria as treaty ports, after Russia had given Hay another vague assurance that she "had never opposed the development of foreign commerce in Manchuria." [42] Yet neither the treaty nor Russia's assurance was substantial ground for the belief that American policies in China were secure. Hay still faced great obstacles. He knew that Count Cassini, the Russian ambassador in Washington, was a "lying diplomat," that little useful intelligence could be expected from American diplomatic representatives in St. Petersburg, whom the President termed "cloth dolls," and that the Russian government had made "mendacity" a "science." These were poor implements with which to build a policy of the open door and the integrity of China. Throughout the Manchurian dispute Hay played a cautious game, for when China appealed for American good offices, the Secretary declined to be drawn in. He had already told the President that American "public opinion" would not support any such action "openly hostile to Russia."

JAPAN AND RUSSIA

So it was that the way was left open for Japan, backed by the prestige and power of her new alliance with Britain, to challenge Russia, and to do so, ostensibly at least, in defense of the open door. In July, 1903, she opened direct negotiations with Russia for an understanding on both

---

[41] The moving spirit of the group was State Councillor Bezobrazov, supported by many of the grand dukes, the militarists, and Admiral Alexieff, who was later appointed Viceroy of the Far East, in which capacity at Port Arthur he was able to act independently of Count Lamsdorff and the Foreign Office.

[42] Dennis, *Adventures in American Diplomacy*, 358; text of the commercial treaty in Clyde, *United States Policy toward China*, 222-230.

Manchuria and Korea. She proposed an arrangement whereby: 1) Chinese sovereignty and integrity in Manchuria would be respected; 2) the administration of Manchuria would be restored to Chinese hands, Russia retaining only railroad guards; 3) Japan would recognize Russian rights in Manchuria based on recognized treaties; and 4) Russia would recognize Japan's political as well as commercial and industrial interests in Korea as already set forth in the Anglo-Japanese Alliance.[43]

The Russian response was dilatory. At first, having refused to give any assurance on Manchuria, Russia transferred the negotiations to Tokyo, Lamsdorff stating that Baron Rosen, Russian Minister in Japan, would take his instructions from Admiral Alexieff at Port Arthur. This sounded very much like saying that Russia's policy would be dictated by Bezobrazov and his clique. When Japan asked a second time for some assurance on Manchuria, the Russians named the poor health of the Tzarina as the reason for their delay in replying.[44]

Early in January, 1904, the Russian official attitude softened, conceding most, if not all, of what Japan had asked, but at the same time Bezobrazov and those who were in control at Port Arthur were insisting that Russia would not get out of Manchuria and that there would be no open door there.[45] This meant war.

JAPAN'S DECISION

Japan's policy toward Russia had been fixed with some certainty as early as the spring of 1903. At that time it had been determined "to grant Russia a priority right in Manchuria" while insisting on Japan's unique status in Korea. When negotiations were undertaken with Russia in July, 1903, the Japanese cabinet had already decided "to resort to arms, should such negotiations fail." Although this decision was opposed by Ito, it had the vigorous support of General Iwao Oyama, chief of the general staff, who held that Japan's strategic position would deteriorate with time. Meanwhile Japanese public opinion loudly demanded that Russia's advance in Manchuria be stopped. Leading newspapers, such as the *Tokyo Asahi,* the *Osaka Mainichi,* and others, clamored for war. Distinguished scholars and professors of the Imperial University of Tokyo wrote vigorously in the press, spoke from the lecture platform, and presented the government with secret memorials favoring war. By November, 1903, there was little opposition to this

---

[43] United States, *Foreign Relations, 1903,* 616; Dennis, *Adventures in American Diplomacy,* 359.

[44] Hay Papers, Griscom to Hay, Tokyo, Dec. 8, 1903.

[45] Dennis, *Adventures in American Diplomacy,* 362.

popular, public demand. On December 28 the government issued an emergency Imperial ordinance providing for "emergency military expenditures," [46] and on February 4 reached its decision to sever diplomatic relations on February 6. On February 8 a Japanese squadron delivered a surprise attack on Port Arthur. War was declared on February 10. To neither power did it come as a surprise. Many leaders in Japan had long regarded the conflict as inevitable. In Russia the Tsar himself had prophesied as early as 1901 that there would be war in 1904.[47] Nor does history present a better example of a war fought by both powers for imperialistic ends. In this respect history affords little ground for choosing between the belligerents. However, in assessing the relative responsibility, if this be possible,

. . . it can at least be said for Japan that her policy was based upon a real need. The argument for self-preservation is in her favor. However great or small her need for Korea was at that time, it is easy to see that she could not afford to allow the peninsula to fall into the hands of some power which would seal it hermetically against Japanese colonization or trade. With the Russians the case was entirely different. If they are honest with themselves they admit, like Kuropatkin, that Russia had no need of expansion in the Far East. . . . The fact was that the predatory tendency of the Russian autocracy had led to expansion, in many cases senseless expansion, in the Far East as in the Middle East.[48]

THE WAR AND AMERICAN POLICY

The outbreak of war reintensified the so-called Chinese question. There was to be sure little danger that other European powers would enter the conflict. For either France or Germany to have done so would have endangered their European frontiers;[49] but since the war was to be fought on Chinese territory, there was very real danger both to the open door and to China's integrity. Accordingly, President Roosevelt reasserted the Hay policy of 1900, asking the powers to respect "the neutrality of China and in all practical ways her administra-

---

[46] At the same time the chief of the naval general staff was elevated to equal rank with the chief of the army general staff under the direct control of the emperor; a supreme war council was established, and two warships were purchased from Argentina. Takeuchi, *War and Diplomacy in the Japanese Empire*, 137-142.

[47] Dennis, *Adventures in American Diplomacy*, 354.

[48] W. L. Langer, "The Origins of the Russo-Japanese War" [from the original English manuscript], *Europäische Gespräche* (Hamburg, 1926).

[49] No evidence has been forthcoming to support President Roosevelt's statement that: "I notified Germany and France . . . that in the event of a combination against Japan . . . I should promptly side with Japan. . . ." Dennett, *Roosevelt and the Russo-Japanese War*, 2; Vagts, *Deutschland*, II, 1178-79.

tive entity." Since circular notes had little effect prior to hostilities, even less could be hoped of them after war had begun.[50] Nevertheless, "the conception of *de jure* Chinese sovereignty over Manchuria was restored to American diplomacy . . ." by these notes. In this sense American policy in China was reinforced at least formally, but at the same time it was weakened by evident American willingness "to follow Great Britain's example and abandon . . . [Korea] to its Japanese fate." [51]   There was perhaps no other course which America could follow.   Yet the abandonment of Korea weakened the moral foundations of American policy.   Russia was quick to ask why we opposed her in Manchuria while giving Japan a green light in Korea.[52]

At the same time, in far western China the American policy of China's integrity was rebuffed by the British.   The State Department had been disturbed by implications of the British Younghusband mission to Tibet.   In the course of Anglo-American discussions on the subject, the British referred to Chinese sovereignty in Tibet as a "constitutional fiction" and a "political affectation," and when the United States asked that China's territorial integrity be respected there, no assurance was forthcoming from Lord Lansdowne.[53]

While the Russo-Japanese War was yet in progress, the United States made two more efforts to keep alive the principle of China's integrity. The first of these was a diplomatic circular, January 13, 1905, similar to that of the previous year.   The Russian response gave no satisfaction. The second case was President Roosevelt's demand upon Japan for assurance that she "adhere to the position of maintaining Open Door in Manchuria and restoring that province to China."   Without this assurance the President was not prepared to act as mediator.[54]

IN SUMMARY

The Russo-Japanese War closed what may be called the first chapter in the history of the twin American principles of the open door and the

---

[50] On this occasion, as on a later one, the Kaiser hoped to exclude Manchuria from the American proposal in order that he might later share in Russia's Manchurian spoils.

[51] Griswold, *Far Eastern Policy of the United States*, 96.   All our leading diplomats in eastern Asia—Griscom at Tokyo, Allen at Seoul, as well as Hay and Rockhill—looked to Japan as the only, if not the most desirable, solution of the Korean problem.

[52] Griswold, *Far Eastern Policy of the United States*, 97.

[53] Griswold, *Far Eastern Policy of the United States*, 97-102.   The principal motive of the British Tibetan policy was to stop the flirtation between Russia and the Dalai Lama. China lacked the power to do so, and the Indian government took the matter into its own hands though opposed by the British Foreign Office.

[54] See: Dennett, *Roosevelt and the Russo-Japanese War*, 178-180; Griswold, *Far Eastern Policy of the United States*, 103.

integrity of China. Ethically sound, these principles were also in keeping with traditional aspects of American policy, such, for example, as the most-favored-nation principle. It would, however, be foolish to ignore the fact that the open door and the integrity of China meant little in general to other powers or that they were given more than diplomatic lip-service in these years. These American principles struggled for survival against impressive obstacles, some, though not all, of which were of our own making.

Until such time as the United States was prepared and willing to attack the spheres directly, its policies of the open door and China's integrity were destined to savor of the doctrinaire. Certainly in the years 1899 to 1905 there was nothing to indicate that this difficulty could be easily overcome. The American government was not in a position to implement its policy with anything save diplomatic notes and circulars. There is no evidence to indicate that American public opinion would have sanctioned stronger measures even had the Department of State wished to apply them. Finally, American policy did not always remain true to its own doctrinaire principles. Hay himself was urged into being a concession hunter. What is more, he conceded that Chinese integrity in Manchuria was not essential so long as American treaty rights in the area were not infringed.

Recognizing these basic weaknesses and periodic lapses, the historian must also note that the twin principles of American policy were not without their successes. Certainly they were not completely successful in preserving China's integrity. Certainly they did not provide equality of opportunity for capital investment. Yet they did restrain the powers in some measure. They helped to keep alive the ideal of China's nationhood and of free enterprise at a time when both were in serious danger.

CHAPTER 17

CHINA: FROM EMPIRE TO REPUBLIC

THE Manchu dynasty during the nineteenth century suffered a series of terrific shocks and experienced almost overwhelming disasters. It was called upon to withstand not only violent internal rebellions, such as the T'ai-p'ing, but also the Western commercial and military impact with the "unprecedented humiliations" of 1895 to 1900. Yet the dynasty withstood these misfortunes, and, at times, there was evidence that it might even survive them. These evidences of strength, however, were apparent rather than real, for, when in 1912 the collapse finally occurred, it was occasioned by incidents which in themselves were insignificant—an accidental bomb explosion in Hankow and "a mere mutiny" of a garrison at the sister city of Wuchang across the Yangtze River. From these small incidents came the abdication of the proud Manchu house, the troubled beginnings of the republican era and the years subsequent to 1912, so revolutionary in terms of the old China as to defy certain analysis. Obviously these great events did not spring from the accidental explosion of a bomb. They are a product of intellectual, revolutionary trends reaching far back into the nineteenth century. The disasters of the nineteenth century shaped and sharpened those Chinese minds which in the twentieth century were to lead China along the road of political, economic, and social revolution. It is this background of revolution and reform which will be outlined in the pages of this chapter.

THE LATER MANCHU EMPERORS

From 1796 to 1912 China was ruled in succession by six Manchu emperors.[1] The reign of Emperor Jui (1796-1820), a well-intentioned but weak ruler, marked the beginning of widespread rebellion. Repression of these outbreaks was swift, drastic, cruel, and indiscriminate.[2]

---

[1] For complete list of the Manchu emperors, see Reginald F. Johnston, *Twilight in the Forbidden City* (London, 1934), 453; Homer H. Dubbs, "Chinese Imperial Designations," *Journal of the American Oriental Society*, LXV (1945), 32.

[2] E. T. Williams, *A Short History of China* (New York, 1928), ch. x.

The Tao-kuang emperor (1821-1850) was an abler and more vigorous ruler but his government was already deeply encrusted with corruption. Secret political societies were again active. Rebellions occurred in widely separated areas: Kwangsi, Hainan, Formosa, Szechwan, Hupeh, Shansi, and Turkestan. Although the emperor improved conditions at Peking, he could not reach the corruption in the provinces, though he did attempt to stamp out the opium menace.

The reign period name, Hsien-feng, designating the sovereign who ruled 1851 to 1861, means "general prosperity," hardly an appropriate title for one of the most troubled decades in China's long history. Rarely, if ever, have the Chinese considered themselves visited by greater woes. As a prelude to these misfortunes the testing of the first treaties with the Western powers could not be counted a happy experience. But the greatest catastrophe of all was the T'ai-p'ing Rebellion, together with the Nien-fei uprising in North China. The next blow to the dynasty in importance was the war with Britain and France beginning in 1856 and culminating in the destruction of the Summer Palaces near Peking and the humiliating flight of the Court to Jehol. Third in importance in this succession of disasters came the Russian annexations of the left bank of the Amur and of the Maritime Province. Serving as an appropriate background to this wretched picture was the weakness and incompetence of the emperor himself. Indeed it seemed that the death of this dissolute and fugitive sovereign in Jehol was about the one blessing in which the Chinese of 1861 could take comfort.

The Dragon Throne then passed to a child five years of age, the only son of the late emperor. Since the new monarch, the T'ung-chih emperor (1862-74), was a child, a regency was established composed of Prince Kung, brother of the late emperor; the Empress Tz'u-an, the first consort of the deceased emperor; and the Empress Dowager Tz'u-hsi, mother of the child sovereign. Of these, the Empress Dowager was gradually to emerge as the dominating personality at Peking until her death in 1908. This brief reign of Emperor Yi, like those of his predecessors, was marked by violent rebellion.[3] The emperor died childless in his nineteenth year.

In such cases, there were well established rules by which the succession was established, but in this case the rules were not followed. Instead, the strong-willed junior Empress Dowager, Tz'u-hsi, determined to retain and expand the power she had acquired during the reign of her son, chose a four-year-old child, a grandson of the Tao-kuang emperor, and thus of the same generation as the deceased monarch. This

[3] Williams, *A Short History of China*, ch. xii.

was a flagrant violation of the system by which each succeeding emperor was able to perform the appropriate ancestral sacrificial rites. It made possible, among other things, continuation of the regency of the two dowager empresses, Tz'u-an and Tz'u-hsi, from 1875 to 1880, and the sole regency of Tz'u-hsi from 1880 to 1889. For the brief period of nine years, 1889-1898, the Kuang-hsü emperor ruled in his own right. It was this well-intentioned youth who launched the ill-fated Hundred Days of reform which led to his imprisonment and to resumption of the regency by the Empress Dowager, 1898-1908.[4]

Finally in 1909, a two-year-old child became the Hsüan-tung emperor, the last of the Manchu line. He was a nephew of his predecessor, and because he was a minor, his father, Prince Ch'un, a man wholly unprepared for the task, was named regent. His appointment brought from the gossips of the capital the remark: "The Ch'ing [Manchu] House began with a regency and will perish with a regency."[5]

To one who examines critically the last 116 years of Manchu rule, it will be apparent that the dynasty had ceased to produce sovereigns of ability and character. Emperors Ch'eng and Ching were well intentioned, but neither possessed the capacities of greatness. This weakness of the dynastic line might not have proved fatal had the court or government been staffed with able advisers and administrators. The striking thing is, however, that nineteenth-century China revealed very real poverty in statesmanship. Some great names there were: Lin Tse-hsü, who seized the foreign opium at Canton; Tsêng Kuo-fan, who fought the T'ai-p'ings; Prince Kung, who saved the dynasty from grave mistakes after 1860; Li Hung-chang, who enjoyed the respect if not the love of the foreign powers; Chang Chih-tung; and Yüan Shih-k'ai. These were great names, but each and all of them failed to provide the leadership which nineteenth-century China so urgently demanded. They failed even to eradicate the corrupt, enervating influence of the 3,000 eunuchs who infested the Forbidden City, and, too frequently, as in the case of Li Lien-ying, influenced the political decisions of the Empress Dowager.[6] Moreover, it is not easy to estimate correctly the character and the capacity of this woman. For all her faults and frailties, Tz'u-hsi was in many respects a strong ruler. She is sometimes credited with having held the dynasty together during her lifetime, and

---

[4] Princess Der Ling, *Old Buddha* (London, 1928), gives an intimate, sympathetic account from memory of court life and intrigue in these last years of Manchu rule; see also her *Two Years in the Forbidden City* (New York, 1914); see further, J. O. P. Bland and E. Backhouse, *China Under the Empress Dowager* (Philadelphia, 1912).

[5] Johnston, *Twilight in the Forbidden City*, 60.

[6] Johnston, *Twilight in the Forbidden City*, 54, 174.

in spite of her upsetting of Kuang-hsü's reforms, her vacillation during
the Boxer period, and the wasteful building of the Summer Palace with
navy funds, she frequently listened to her abler advisers and more often
than not supported their proposals. But neither she nor her advisers
were equal to the tasks which faced China. The failures of the last
Manchu rulers, however, become more understandable as one examines
the short-comings of the republicans and militarists who were to succeed them.

INFLUENCE OF THE *LITERATI* AND MANDARINS

Quite apart from the personal character of her sovereigns, the collapse
of the old China was hastened by the tradition-bound ruling aristocracy.
Old China was a free society in the sense that its modes of behavior
were so generally accepted by all as to render governmental interference
largely unnecessary and so rather negligible. Centuries of time had
given to China a complete life pattern created by her scholastic bureaucracy, and accepted by the people as natural and proper. The scholars,
the *literati,* and the mandarins not only controlled this traditional system, they were also a vital part of it and subject to it. The system was
one of long established mores. It was not designed to conform quickly
to demands for radical change, nor did it produce a crusading type of
political leadership based on any concept of strong, active government.
However, the impact of the West on nineteenth-century China had
created the need for a positive administration based upon law. This
was precisely what China did not possess, and what her scholar-officials
by the very nature of their training were incapable of providing.[7]

CRITICISM OF GOVERNMENT IN OLD CHINA

From what has already been said it must not be assumed that Old
China had no means of correcting the ills of society. One Chinese critic
has said that though ancient "China, like many other ancient countries,
was blessed with the absence of newspapers," there was always among
the educated class "a current of public opinion, which in times of national crisis, burst forth into regular movements, became organized and
articulate, and wielded an effective power over public affairs." Criticism of government took various forms. There were local "town
strikes" and the "waylaying of [an] official's sedan chair." There were
the official Imperial censors who had the right to speak their minds

[7] P. M. A. Linebarger, *Government in Republican China* (New York, 1938), 1-12; A. F. Legendre, *Modern Chinese Civilization* (London, 1929), ch. x; see also the comments of Lin Yutang, *My Country and My People* (New York, 1935), 206-213.

freely but enjoyed no constitutional protection from the wrath of those whom they criticized. Nevertheless, while the censors enjoyed no constitutional immunity, they were protected by a customary immunity no less powerful than law. While it is true that this immunity was violated by various irresponsible rulers, it still existed. There were also unofficial critics among the scholars who resorted to pamphleteering and posting placards in the streets.[8] These methods were sometimes effective in Old China, but in nineteenth-century China they were inadequate, because China's entire politico-economic structure was being challenged by the West.

THE BEGINNINGS OF THE MODERN CHINESE PRESS

Supplementing these old methods of criticism which reappeared in nineteenth-century China was the birth of China's modern press. It is of interest to note that this modern press, designed for the public, and having its origins in the early years of the nineteenth century, was first developed largely "through the efforts of the early [Protestant] missionaries in China." [9]

After the *Arrow* War (1856-60), Chinese newspapers, as contrasted with the missionary press, made their appearance. The influence exerted by these early papers and the men who edited them was important but should not be overestimated. The papers themselves were not well-balanced journals, and the editors enjoyed little political or social prestige. The great Viceroy Chang Chih-tung referred to them as "literary loafers of Kiangsu and Chekiang." [10]

THE PRE-REVOLUTIONARY REFORM PRESS, 1895-1911

The Sino-Japanese War, 1894-95, has long been recognized as of vital influence in the story of Japan's march to empire. It was equally significant in marking the beginnings of a new China. It helped create a new Chinese periodical literature, "inspired by the highest ideals of patriotism and culminating in the Revolution of 1911." The periodical and daily press, despite repeated suppressions by the Manchu government, became the chief medium for the agitation for national political

---

[8] Lin Yutang, *A History of the Press and Public Opinion in China* (Shanghai, 1937), 1-8.

[9] Lin Yutang, *Press and Public Opinion in China* (Shanghai, 1937), 77-79; H. E. Legge, *James Legge, Missionary and Scholar* (London, 1905); E. A. Morrison, *Memoirs of . . . Robert Morrison. . . .* (2 vols., London, 1839); and Timothy Richard, *Forty-five Years in China* (London, 1916).

[10] Lin Yutang, *Press and Public Opinion in China,* 77-93; see also Roswell S. Britton, *The Chinese Periodical Press 1800-1912* (Shanghai, 1933).

reform. In this persecuted press were mirrored those significant lines of political thought which were taking shape at the turn of the century: 1) the demand for national political reform, the exposure of corrupt officialdom, and the introduction of the Western concepts of liberty, constitutionalism, and democracy, advocated by K'ang Yu-wei and Liang Ch'i-ch'ao; 2) the demand that the alien Manchus be expelled, advocated by Chang T'ai-yen and Sun Yat-sen; 3) the rise of more liberal cosmopolitan philosophies, represented by Yen Fu; and 4) the desire, in the turmoil of revolutionary thought, to preserve China's own national culture, a view advocated by Chang T'ai-yen and Liu Shih-p'ei.[11]

BEGINNINGS OF INDUSTRIALIZATION

Political reform in the structure and philosophy of Chinese government was also promoted in the late nineteenth century by the first Chinese efforts at industrialization. The first efforts to introduce railways, telegraphs, arsenals, and factories were sponsored by men such as Li Hung-chang, Tso Tsung-T'ang, Chang Chih-tung, and others, not of course as preliminary steps to far-reaching political reform, but with the idea of strengthening the defense services and making China less dependent on foreign arms and munitions. Nevertheless, although this industrialization was sponsored by high officialdom, yet it was not without influence on the thinking of the younger generation of political reformers. Although there was violent popular opposition at first both to the railroad and the telegraph, the usefulness of these novelties became in time fairly obvious, at least to the educated and official classes.[12]

OTHER EVIDENCES OF WESTERNIZATION AND REFORM

There was other evidence, too, of China's first faltering steps toward reform. The missions of Pin Ch'un and Burlingame in 1866 and 1868 marked the inception of diplomatic representation abroad (see Chapter

---

[11] Lin Yutang, *Press and Public Opinion in China,* 94.

[12] The depth of opposition to the first railways is illustrated in the case of the Shanghai-Woosung line built by a British firm in 1876. When a Chinese, in public protest, committed suicide by flinging himself beneath the wheels of the engine, the Imperial government purchased the road, tore up the rails and shipped them off to Formosa, and built a temple on the site of the station. See P. H. Kent, *Railway Enterprise in China* (London, 1907), 1-22. On early industrialization see Gideon Chen, *Tso Tsung T'ang; Pioneer Promoter of the Modern Dockyard and the Woollen Mills in China* (Peiping, 1938); and by the same author, *Lin Tse-hsu: Pioneer Promoter of the Adoption of Western Means of Maritime Defense in China* (Peiping, 1935); also W. L. Bales, *Tso Tsung-T'ang: Soldier and Statesman of Old China* (Shanghai, 1937).

11), and the educational mission to the United States, 1872 (Chapter 12), though a failure in itself, was not without importance. Meanwhile mission schools in China were introducing the minds of their students to a new education and a new Western civilization. At Canton, Shanghai, and Peking there were mission language schools. In Peking in 1897 the Chinese government T'ung-wen College, already more than thirty years old, was headed by an American missionary, W. A. P. Martin, who offered instruction in international law, physics, astronomy, anatomy and physiology, chemistry, mineralogy, mathematics, French, Russian, German, English, and Chinese. Many of its graduates subsequently staffed the Chinese diplomatic and consular service.[13]

These and many other evidences of progressive thought were sometimes too liberally interpreted by contemporaries both in China and abroad. The righteous enthusiasm of Burlingame and many others created the impression that the victory of reform and westernization in China was already won. Actually this was far from being so. It is no stigma on the nineteenth-century personalities and agencies of reform to note that they had scarcely scratched the surface of China's problem.[14]

THE SINO-JAPANESE WAR STIMULATES REFORM

More than any event which preceded it, the Sino-Japanese War, 1894-95, forced a considerable body of educated Chinese to recognize the imperative need of reform. The humiliating Treaty of Shimonoseki brought forth a flood of memorials to the throne. No previous humiliation had so inspired thoughtful men.

Three years later the young Kuang-hsü emperor, mortified by the threatened subjection of his country through the scramble of the powers for leaseholds and spheres (1897-98), fell under the influence of K'ang Yu-wei and instituted the abortive Hundred Days of Reform.[15]

Indeed, the years 1895 to 1911 saw an unprecedented growth in the development of a Chinese periodical press devoted to revolutionary thought. The most important of the new periodicals were published in widely separated cities such as Peking, Shanghai, Changsha, Hangchow, Chungking, Tientsin, Chengtu, Amoy, Canton; and in foreign cities such as Macao, Hongkong, Yokohama, and Tokyo. Frequently banned by government decree, many of them continued to survive and to appeal to an increasing clientele on a wide variety of cultural as well

[13] M. E. Cameron, *The Reform Movement in China* (Stanford University, 1931), 17-22.
[14] Cameron, *The Reform Movement in China*, 22.
[15] Lin Yutang, *Press and Public Opinion in China*, 94-98.

as political, agricultural, commercial, and industrial subjects. Some even discussed a feminist movement, and in 1898 a magazine in the vernacular tongue, the *Wusih Paihuapao* made its appearance, edited by China's first woman journalist, Miss Ch'in Yüfang.[16]

THE REVOLUTIONARY PRESS AND THE MANCHUS

While virtually all of China's young press was concerned with the general problem of national reform, specific organs were direct in their political attacks upon the Manchu government. Chief among these was the *Su-pao* ("Soochow Paper"), founded in the International Settlement of Shanghai in 1897, and registered with the Japanese consulate-general in the name of the publisher's Japanese wife. Edited by a Chinese scholar who had been dismissed from office, it attacked fearlessly the whole coterie of corrupt officialdom, and though originally monarchist in its views, it came to advocate the expulsion of the Manchu rulers.

After 1905 new revolutionary journals appeared in Tokyo, where Monarchist Party exiles like K'ang Yu-wei and Liang Ch'i-ch'ao were engaged in journalistic warfare with the republican adherents of Sun Yat-sen, Wang Ching-wei, and Hu Han-min. Much of this debate was soon echoed in the "Chinatowns" of great cities throughout the world —in New York, San Francisco, Paris, London, and Singapore.[17]

THE CONVERSION OF THE EMPRESS DOWAGER

Until the imminent collapse of the dynasty during that "midsummer madness" known as the Boxer Rebellion, the Empress Dowager had set her face steadfastly against any significant attempts at reform. The failure of the One Hundred Days in 1898 was due directly to her. Her return to power in the capacity of regent signalized an intensification of reaction. This tendency was given its fullest expression in the policies and actions of the Court as the Boxer movement got under way. The Empress Dowager was in full sympathy with the anti-foreign, anti-Christian philosophy of the blind and ignorant Boxer patriots. It was

[16] For a list of important periodicals of the period see Lin Yutang, *Press and Public Opinion in China,* 107-113.

[17] For a discussion of K'ang Yu-wei's place in the revolutionary philosophy of the period see W. F. Hummel, "K'ang Yü-wei, Historical Critic and Social Philosopher, 1858-1927," *Pacific Historical Review,* IV (1935), 343-355. Very suggestive material on the background of the reform movement is in E. R. Hughes, *The Invasion of China by the Western World* (London, 1937). On outstanding Chinese leaders of the period, see A. W. Hummel, ed., *Eminent Chinese of the Ch'ing Period* (2 vols., Washington, 1943, 1944).

not by accident therefore that "government troops under Tung Fu-hsiang and other sympathizers with reaction were allowed by the Court to join forces with the Boxers." [18]   In a word, the Empress Dowager had set her course not only against reform at home but also against the treaty powers that personified the impact of all things Western.

Conversion, however, may come late in life. When, in the midst of the Boxer troubles foreign armies again entered Peking, and the Empress Dowager fled for a second time, as in 1860, from the capital, it appeared to her that nothing short of changed policies could save her proud Manchu house. Even before her return to Peking in January, 1902, Tz'u-hsi was a converted woman. She had not become a liberal, far less a democrat, for she had no understanding of such things, but she was converted to "reform," at least as she defined that term, and for her this was a profound change. From 1901 until her death in 1908, the Regent turned in principle to a program which bore striking resemblance to the reforms she had so ruthlessly suppressed in 1898. During 1902, as indicative of things to come, reform edicts removed the ban on intermarriage between Chinese and Manchus, advised the Chinese to abandon the practice of binding the feet of their women, ordered the sending of intelligent Manchus abroad for study, and abolished a number of sinecures. All this seemed to indicate that the Empress Dowager was intent on a thorough house-cleaning. There was still, however, the question of the depth, sincerity, and understanding of her conversion, and whether this masterful but unscrupulous woman had the capacity to rebuild the fortunes of the dynasty.[19]

THE MANCHU REFORM PROGRAM, 1902-1911

The comprehensive program of reform which the Empress Dowager attempted to implement may be considered under the following headings:

a) Educational Reform
b) The New Army and Navy
c) Constitutional Reform
d) The Campaign against Opium
e) Miscellaneous Aspects.[20]

---

[18] R. F. Johnston, *Twilight in the Forbidden City* (London, 1934), 46.

[19] Cameron, *The Reform Movement in China*, ch. iii, gives an excellent account of Tz'u-hsi's conversion.

[20] I have here drawn heavily on the work of M. E. Cameron, *The Reform Movement in China* (Stanford University, 1931).

EDUCATIONAL REFORM

There could be little prospect for any constructive reform in China along Western lines so long as there was no appropriate educational basis on which to build. China's traditional Confucian education (see Chapter 2), had, it seemed, little relation to problems of the twentieth century. Fortunately for the reformers, the Boxer Protocol (1901), by suspending for five years the civil service examinations in cities where foreigners had been attacked, made easier the introduction of a westernized curriculum, which many Chinese were now demanding. In 1901 an Imperial edict called for the building of a national school system. Instruction was still to be primarily in the Confucian classics but it was also to include Chinese and Western history, government, and science. In 1904 this educational plan was revised and extended on the model of the educational system then prevailing in Japan. It was designed to provide for kindergartens, primary schools, middle schools, high schools or provincial colleges, and an Imperial university at Peking. There was a notable lack of provision for the education of women. Then in 1905 one of the most effective obstacles to the new system was removed when the old civil service examinations were abolished, a move for which Yüan Shih-k'ai was in part responsible. This was followed by creation of a Board of Education to seek some uniformity of standards and administration.

There was substantial evidence that many Chinese accepted the new educational reforms with enthusiasm if not always with understanding, but there was also persistent opposition. Fitful waves of reaction followed the first waves of reform. While temples were being turned into schools, and the Empress Dowager was curtailing her theatricals to equip an academy for girls, some of the erstwhile reformers turned conservative, re-emphasized Confucian studies, and belittled the Western learning. Still greater opposition came from the local mandarins. Peking might decree centralization in education, but it would remain a dead letter until the local officials were prepared to implement it. Even where the local official attitude was favorable, it frequently dissipated itself in the construction of colleges rather than primary schools.

Of equal difficulty were the problems of financing the new schools and staffing them with trained teachers. Finance was left to the ingenuity of the local community with results that were "precarious and unsatisfactory." In the teacher problem, the missionaries and the native graduates of the mission schools offered the greatest hope. The missionaries, however, were deterred from accepting appointment by a rule forbidding the teaching of religion in government schools. As a result, a large proportion of the new teachers came from Japan. These worked for lower salaries than Westerners, and culturally they fitted more easily into the Chinese environment. •

Meanwhile, in 1905, the Empress Dowager, intent on building through education a new body of public servants capable of strengthening the dynasty and resisting the pressure of the foreign powers, urged more students to study abroad. At one time there were probably 15,000 Chinese students in Japan.[21] Some undoubtedly profited by the experience, while others were mere adventurers seeking the prestige that a few months of foreign residence would give. A lesser number of students went to Europe or to the United States. Those who came to America were assisted through Boxer Indemnity funds which the American government returned to China after 1907.[22] On the eve of the Revolution of 1911 there were some 800 Chinese students in the United States and about 400 in Europe.

On their return to China, the foreign-trained students did not always prove to be an unqualified blessing. Few persons of any nationality who have studied abroad are apt to be willing to teach children to read and write. Certainly those students who returned to China were not expected to do this. To stimulate applicants for teaching posts and to eliminate incompetents, the government found it necessary to provide examinations, and to reward the successful teacher with appointment to official rank. In these examinations, held after 1906, it was discovered that many of the foreign-trained students could not write their native Chinese tongue with facility.

These were discouraging signs. Yet in the years 1909-10 China could point to 57,267 schools, 89,362 teachers, and 1,626,529 enrolled students. In the light of only ten years of educational reform the figures seem reasonably impressive until one recalls that China's population was in excess of 400,000,000, of whom some 65,000,000 were children of school age. "The Empress Dowager and her advisers judged well the slowness with which educational change would come in China when they set a 5 per cent literacy as all that could be hoped for in 1917, the year in which the constitution was to be proclaimed."[23] In quality as well

---

[21] J. M. Clinton, "Chinese Students in Japan," *Chinese Recorder and Missionary Journal*, Oct., 1909; A. J. Brown, *The Chinese Revolution* (New York, 1912), 79-80.

[22] In 1908 the American Congress by joint resolution authorized President Roosevelt to reduce the United States share of the Boxer Indemnity from $24,440,000 to $13,655,-492. The original figure had far exceeded American claims. (United States, *Foreign Relations, 1907*, Pt. I, 174-175; *ibid., 1908*, 64-65, 71-72.)

[23] Cameron, *The Reform Movement in China*, 87.

as in quantity the new education left much to be desired, but a beginning had been made and this beginning was the herald of even greater changes to come.

THE NEW ARMY

The Imperial government had acquired the nucleus of an excellent army in the 1860's in the troops with which Li Hung-chang and Tsêng Kuo-fan had put down the T'ai-p'ing Rebellion; but, when the immediate emergency was passed, the old ways again prevailed. China returned to what was largely, and with some exceptions, a paper army recruited from the highways and byways for inspection day, and then promptly disbanded. This militia was useless for purposes of war or defense. The Manchu bannermen, descendants of the conquerors of 1644, a force distinct from the Chinese militia, were efficient enough as horsemen and archers, but these skills had little bearing on modern warfare.[24] Between 1860 and 1894 Li Hung-chang did attempt to build a reputable fighting force. China's need for such a force was obvious to the outside world long before 1900; but it was not so obvious to the Old China that honored the scholar while suspecting the soldier. Not until after the Japanese victory of 1895, and the disasters of the Boxer rising was the Manchu court stirred to action. Here the credit for progress was due to the Empress Dowager and the indefatigable Yüan Shih-k'ai. An attempt was made in 1902 to put the autonomous provincial forces under a central command in Peking. This and many other plans met with vigorous opposition, both domestic and foreign.

After 1907 army reform became uneven at best. For some time enthusiasm of the reformers was high and a series of ambitious plans was proposed and in some cases tried. Military schools were established. Instruction was provided even for the common soldier in elementary subjects and patriotism. Other factors proved less favorable. In 1907 Yüan, able and popular with the troops, was deprived of control over much of the army he had built. In general, it was clear that relatively little had been done to create an Imperial army which would defend the dynasty and the throne, a conclusion which was soon to be borne out by the events of 1911 and 1912. Nevertheless, the military reforms were not without significance. They marked the appearance

[24] E. T. Williams, *China Yesterday and Today* (5th ed., rev., New York, 1935), 526-527. For detailed treatment of the subject see A. M. Kotenev, *The Chinese Soldier* (Shanghai, 1937), chs. iv-vi.

of a new spirit of militarism which was to serve China both ill and well in years to come.[25]

THE CHINESE NAVY

China's first experiences with a modern navy were disquieting. During the T'ai-p'ing Rebellion, H. N. Lay, Inspector-General of the Chinese Imperial Maritime Customs, was commissioned to purchase a fleet in England to be used against the rebels. Lay secured the services of a Captain Sherard Osborn to command the fleet, and attempted to install himself as a sort of first and sole lord of the Chinese admiralty responsible to the emperor alone. China could properly raise objection to this scheme on a number of grounds. In the first place it struck squarely against the principle of provincial autonomy. More important to the Chinese government, however, was the fact that Lay tried to control the fleet independently of any Chinese governmental authority below the emperor. Thus Prince Kung, who was head of the central government, bitterly opposed the Lay proposal and met it by appointing a Chinese commander-in-chief nominated by Tsêng Kuo-fan and Li Hung-chang, with Osborn as assistant commander. This meant that the fleet was to be controlled by the great provincial viceroys, not by a foreigner responsible to the emperor. In the confusion that followed, the Chinese finally decided to disband the whole enterprise. The venture had cost China £550,000. She had acquired some experience but not a navy.[26]

A second naval disaster overtook China in 1884. Hostilities had broken out as a result of the clash of Franco-Chinese interests in Indo-China. In August, 1884, a French force destroyed what passed for the Chinese fleet at Foochow.[27] The entire action lasted about 10 minutes.

When the Sino-Japanese War broke in 1894, China had nevertheless gotten together a navy consisting of four squadrons which on paper was "decidedly, if not decisively," superior to Japan's. European naval experts conceded this superiority. What they failed to anticipate was the superior strategic and tactical skill of the Japanese, plus the fact that because of her lack of centralized national control China was to fight the

[25] For a full discussion of the military reforms see Cameron, *The Reform Movement in China*, 88-97. For a discussion of the character of the Chinese fighting man, 1900-12, see Kotenev, *The Chinese Soldier*, chs. vi-vii.

[26] H. B. Morse and H. F. MacNair, *Far Eastern International Relations* (Boston, 1931), 247-250.

[27] Morse and MacNair, *Far Eastern International Relations*, 352; L. C. Arlington, *Through the Dragon's Eyes* (London, 1934), 99-101.

naval war with only one of her four squadrons—Li's northern fleet.[28]
Following the defeat of 1894-95 nothing was done to create a new navy
until after the Russo-Japanese War. In 1907 a Department of the Navy
was created as a branch of the Ministry of War, and a few students
were sent to train with the British Navy. By 1909 futile efforts were
again being made to put government vessels under the control of Peking
instead of under the provinces.[29]

POLITICAL AND CONSTITUTIONAL REFORM

The constitutional reforms by which the Manchu dynasty attempted
to save itself after the Boxer debacle were foreshadowed by the Empress
Dowager's edict issued from Sianfu, January 28, 1901. In this edict
"Old Buddha" appeared in the usual role of political philosopher and reformer:

The Empress Dowager has now decided that we should correct our short-
comings by adopting the best methods and systems which obtain in foreign
countries.[30]

Accordingly, in 1905 a commission proceeded abroad to study foreign
constitutional systems.

The feeling had gradually been growing that there must be some germ of
strength in Occidental governments that was unknown to the Chinese. To
locate and introduce that source, it was thought, was all that was needed to
enable China to regain her position of superiority in the world.[31]

The commission was particularly impressed by what it saw in Japan.
To the investigators it seemed clear: 1) that Japan's strength was due
to her adoption of Western institutions, and 2) that Japan had provided
herself with a constitution without sacrificing the power of the Imperial
House. Why then could not the Empress Dowager by similar reforms
satisfy her subjects, strengthen the Empire, and preserve her own
power? She therefore proceeded on the assumption that real power
was to be reserved to the Throne, with the people tendering advice when
requested to do so through their representatives. Furthermore, she proposed to act slowly in order to placate the conservative opposition. By
the close of 1907 three cautious steps had been taken on the road to con-

[28] Edwin A. Falk, *Togo and the Rise of Japanese Sea Power* (New York, 1936), 157-160.
[29] Cameron, *The Reform Movement in China*, 99.
[30] Bland and Backhouse, *China Under the Empress Dowager*, 419-424.
[31] Harold M. Vinacke, *Modern Constitutional Development in China* (Princeton, 1920), 54.

stitutional government: 1) the principle itself had been accepted; 2) a commission had been created to advise on procedure; and 3) an edict had been issued authorizing a national assembly and also provincial assemblies.[32] Constitutional reform was still in the blue print stage.

During 1908 these rather vague preliminaries assumed more tangible shape. The Throne approved specific regulations for the provincial assemblies that were to meet within a year. Underlying principles of the future constitution were decided upon and promulgated. A national parliament was to meet after nine years, and a preliminary constitutional program to this end was adopted. The new provincial assemblies were to be an integral part of the national machinery, their powers in no case infringing the Imperial prerogatives, an indication that the official reformers were under the influence of the Japanese and German models. The assemblies were conceived as sounding boards of provincial opinion. Furthermore, in large part, their discussions were to be limited to matters submitted to them by the viceroy or governor. The right to vote for electors who in turn would choose members of the assembly was strictly limited by property or scholastic qualifications. As time was to show, these assemblies proved effective in two ways: 1) they reflected a considerable degree of public opinion, and 2) they checked the efforts of the central government to increase its own power.

On the subject of constitutional principles the reformers were perfectly clear in their position. "The government of China," so said a memorial, "is to be constitutional by Imperial decree. . . . The principles of the constitution are the great laws which may not be lightly altered. . . . The constitution is designed to conserve the power of the sovereign and protect the officials and the people."[33] All legislative, executive, and judicial authority was reserved to the Manchu sovereign.

Parliament was given power to propose legislation . . . ; it might adopt measures of government; and it might impeach ministers for illegal acts, but no action it took had any weight or validity save that derived from the Imperial sanction.[34]

As W. W. Rockhill, American Minister at Peking, commented, the purpose of the Imperial reformers was "a perpetuation of the existing system under a thin veil of constitutional guarantees."[35]

---

[32] Vinacke, *Modern Constitutional Development in China*, ch. iii.

[33] See United States, *Foreign Relations, 1908*, 192.

[34] Vinacke, *Modern Constitutional Development in China*, 77.

[35] Quoted by Vinacke, *Modern Constitutional Development in China*, 79.

Application of this program of political reform was to take place gradually over a period of nine years. In 1909 the provincial assemblies met for the first time, conducted themselves with considerable dignity, and led in the public agitation for the early calling of a parliament. The following year the National Assembly held its first meeting (October 3, 1910). Of the 200 members, 100 were chosen by the Throne, the remainder by the provincial assemblies from their own members. Contrary to expectation, this Assembly, far from proving a mere rubber stamp, forced the government's decision to convoke a parliament in 1913 instead of 1917. It also forced the Throne to consider concessions toward establishment of a responsible ministry. In general it showed a remarkably progressive attitude.[36]

OPIUM SUPPRESSION

One of the most notable Manchu efforts in reform was directed against the opium traffic which for a century and a half had played havoc with the physical and intellectual well-being of the Chinese people. Under the legalized trade after 1858, importation had continued to increase, reaching 77,966 piculs (a picul equals 133⅓ pounds) in 1888. After this date importations declined substantially but were replaced in part by production within China. The difficulties of the Chinese government in controlling the business were many. Even if it could have suppressed domestic cultivation in the provinces, which is doubtful, the deficit would have been promptly made up by foreign importation which under the treaties China was powerless to control. Furthermore, Peking needed the revenue derived from the import duties and from the taxes on domestic production. In India, from which most of the foreign opium came, the British government saw no reason to discourage production merely to enrich Chinese growers and venal officials. In China there was no disposition to suppress domestic cultivation merely to enrich foreign producers and traders. The heart of the trouble was the Chinese willingness to use opium, and little improvement could be expected until moral sentiment could be linked with effective administrative reforms.

The Chinese program of reform which took shape in the first decade of the twentieth century drew its inspiration from a number of sources. Chinese public sentiment against the drug was stimulated by the report of an American committee seeking to control the traffic in the Philippines. The Indian government, responding to moral sentiment

---

[36] See also the summary of constitutional reform given by Cameron, *The Reform Movement in China*, ch. vi.

in Britain, showed a disposition to co-operate with China. The first practical step was taken by the Imperial government in 1906 when it adopted a policy of taxing domestic opium out of existence. This was followed almost immediately by a policy designed to stop both cultivation and use of opium by gradual prohibition. By 1907 encouraging progress had been achieved. Then, as a result of Anglo-Chinese negotiations, an agreement was reached in January, 1908, whereby Britain would decrease annually the opium exports to China. The arrangement was to run for three years, and to be continued for an additional seven if it was found that China had meanwhile continued effective measures of suppression at home. In 1911 the British government consented to renew the agreement. As a result too of findings of an official opium commission which met at Shanghai in 1909, the International Opium Conference, which met at The Hague, December 1, 1911, reached an agreement among the powers having treaties with China whereby they agreed to take more effective measures to stop the smuggling of drugs into China, to close shops and dens in the foreign controlled areas, and to prevent opium passing through the foreign post offices in China.

It was just at this moment, when a victory over opium appeared in prospect, that the Revolution of 1911 occurred, turning, for the time being at least, the thoughts of the nation from social reform to political revolution.

MISCELLANEOUS REFORMS

Many other reforms were attempted during the last decade of Manchu rule. If for the time being most of these reforms failed or in some cases enjoyed but a meager success, they nevertheless served the useful purpose of agitating the public mind, and preparing it in some degree for great changes to come. Among these miscellaneous efforts at reform the most important dealt with the financial system. The nation's fiscal or taxation system had long been run

. . . on a sort of gentlemen's agreement that Peking would not expect more than a certain customary amount from a particular region; what became of the rest collected from the peoples may easily be guessed from the inevitable connection between the terms "mandarin" and "squeeze." [37]

Little was done to remedy this vicious circle.

There was also the need of bringing some order into China's chaotic system of currency. A comprehensive plan, proposed by Professor Jeremiah W. Jenks of Cornell University, whereby a uniform Im-

---

[37] Cameron, *The Reform Movement in China*, 161.

perial coinage was to be created, made little progress, though the government did seek foreign financial assistance to carry through some minor reforms.

Beginnings were also made in reforming the judicial system. Some Chinese realized that this was a necessary preliminary to abolition of extraterritoriality. However, the first new draft codes, based on rather indiscriminate borrowing from Western codes, were not accepted by the government. Nevertheless, a new system of courts was approved in 1907, separating the judicial from other functions of government, and in 1911 a new criminal code based largely on the Japanese was approved by the National Assembly. It remained in force under the young republic after 1912.

In 1910 slavery was officially abolished, while in some sections popular movements discouraged foot-binding in Chinese women and the wearing of the queue by Chinese men.

A DECADE OF REFORM IN SUMMARY

China in the years 1901 to 1911 experienced one of the most critical periods in her modern history. Her government faced social, political, economic, and international problems of great magnitude. In the main these problems had been occasioned by the inability of old Confucian China to adjust her society to the nineteenth-century Western impact. The Manchu dynasty failed to recognize the need of adjustment and also to provide the leadership to execute it. When the need was finally recognized by the Manchus, it was too late. The prestige of the dynasty had already been destroyed. Its conversion was at best halfhearted—an eleventh hour attempt to preserve itself. At the same time its program of reform, though failing to save the dynasty, did prepare the way, however inadequately, for the republican era.

CHAPTER 18

MANCHURIA AND KOREA, 1904-1910

THE Russo-Japanese War was precipitated by a Japanese naval attack on Port Arthur, February 8, 1904. Two days later, February 10, the Emperor Meiji issued a declaration of war.[1] Admiral Heichachiro Togo's naval assault on Port Arthur employed every device of *surprise* attack, preceding, as it did, by two days the formal declaration of war.[2] The war, however, which followed was a *surprise* only to those who had failed to appreciate the growing intensity of imperialistic rivalry in the Far East since 1895.[3] Viewed in the perspective of the years 1894 to 1904 the Russo-Japanese War was a logical climax in the struggle for empire and, more specifically, in the bitter international competition to control a decadent China and a helplessly corrupt Korea.[4]

The background out of which this war had arisen has already been covered in some detail in preceding chapters. It will be necessary here only to recapitulate the major issues involved. These issues were not exclusively far eastern. On the contrary, they involved the interests and policies of all the great European powers and the United States. For the moment, however, the complexities of the scene as a whole were overshadowed by the specific purposes of Russia and Japan in Korea and Manchuria. These purposes involved the question of Korea's in-

---

[1] Tatsuji Takeuchi, *War and Diplomacy in the Japanese Empire* (Garden City, 1935), 144-145. Diplomatic relations had been severed by Japan, February 6.

[2] Edwin A. Falk, *Togo and the Rise of Japanese Sea Power* (New York, 1936), 278-306. "Neither Japanese bad faith, which remains unproved, nor Russian diplomatic gullibility constituted an excuse for the utter unpreparedness of the [Russian] Port Arthur squadron that night of February 8." (P. 296.) The Japanese naval victory at Port Arthur was by no means as complete as it should have been had Togo used his full strength. Cf. the Japanese attack on Pearl Harbor, December 7, 1941.

[3] Even among newspaper correspondents who had "covered" Manchuria and Korea in the years 1901-03 there were some who came to believe that historical events have no meaning and thus that there would be no war between Japan and Russia. See H. G. Whigham, *Manchuria and Korea* (New York, 1904), 49.

[4] See F. H. Harrington, *God, Mammon and the Japanese* (Madison, 1944), for Korean conditions.

dependence and of China's territorial integrity. These questions in turn had already been prejudiced in the case of China by the widespread creation after 1897 of spheres of economic and political interest, and in the case of Korea by Britain's recognition there of Japan's primary interests as expressed in the first Anglo-Japanese Alliance. Control of Manchuria and Korea was the key to control of China. After 1902 Japan held in Korea the advantage given her by the Anglo-Japanese Alliance. After 1900 Russia held in Manchuria the advantage bestowed upon her by the Boxer troubles. She was in a position not only to claim Manchuria as a *de facto* sphere of influence but also to proceed to its political conquest. Neither was she prepared to acknowledge Japan's exclusive primacy in Korea. Japan in turn was unwilling to share her political interest in Korea with any power. As to Manchuria, though Japan's interests and purposes there were still in the formative stage, it is clear that she wanted a Manchurian foothold. The chance of securing this foothold in the future could be safeguarded only by confining Russia's Manchurian interests within the narrowest interpretation of a sphere of influence, thus blocking any Russian scheme for a protectorate or for annexation of Manchuria. Consequently, for the moment, as in 1899 and 1900, Japan became the spokesman of the open door and the integrity of China in the Three Eastern Provinces.[5]

DEFINITION OF RUSSIA'S POSITION IN MANCHURIA, 1895-1905

The specific position which Russia had acquired in Manchuria between 1895 and 1904, and from which Japan sought to drive her in the Russo-Japanese War, was involved in the extreme. It may be summarized in simplified form as follows:

1. A twenty-five-year lease of the southern part of the Liaotung Territory (Dalny and Port Arthur).
2. Railway concessions including the Chinese Eastern Railway "with an administrative zone in which Russian jurisdiction was paramount wherever the Russian officials chose to exercise it."
3. Administrative rights in the Manchurian customs, native and maritime, and preferential land frontier customs rates on the railways.
4. A military alliance with China concluded in 1896.

[5] For full discussions of the background of the war see: K. Asakawa, *The Russo-Japanese Conflict* (Boston, 1904) (scholarly, but stresses the Japanese case); Alexander Hosie, *Manchuria: Its People, Resources and Recent History* (London, 1904); W. L. Langer, "The Origin of the Russo-Japanese War," English original of an article published in *Europäische Gespräche* (Hamburg, 1926).

5. Maintenance of troops and railway guards in Manchuria in increasing numbers after 1900.

Writing in 1929, a student of Manchurian affairs noted that: "At no time since 1905 has Manchuria been so nearly on the verge of practical absorption as during the closing years of the Russian period before 1905." [6]

THE BELLIGERENT POWERS

At the outbreak of hostilities the belligerents appeared unevenly matched. The area of Russia's territory (more than 8,250,000 square miles), with vast though largely undeveloped resources, with a population estimated in 1904 at nearly 140,000,000, and with a national ordinary revenue of £208,000,000, appeared overwhelming when contrasted with Japan's small islands, limited in resources and with a population at that time of some 47,000,000, and an annual revenue of £25,500,000. Russia's available army was in excess of 4,500,000 men. Japan's army, including trained reserves, numbered some 850,000, with a reservoir of untrained manpower available for military service of some 4,000,000. Russia's naval strength, superior on paper to Japan's, was weakened by its division into a Pacific and a Baltic fleet. From the outset this enabled Japan to control the Yellow Sea and the Sea of Japan, to consolidate her base in Korea, thus forcing the battle in Manchuria, and to have time to prepare for the Russian Baltic fleet, which after its famous trip to the Far East was destroyed by Togo in the Battle of the Sea of Japan (May 27 and 28, 1905). This success was partly due to General Nogi's costly victory in forcing the surrender of Port Arthur (January 2, 1905) and of the remnants of the Russian far eastern fleet. [7] In addition, Russia's land communications stretched along 5,000 miles of single-track railway from Moscow to Harbin. Until the Japanese had taken Port Arthur they could avail themselves of little railroad transport. In Korea at the outbreak of hostilities there was a short line from Chemulpo (Jinsen) to Seoul (Keijo), while some forty miles of the longer line from Fusan to Seoul had also been built.

Whatever the relative balance between the belligerents in material resources and position, the moral advantages weighed heavily in favor of Japan. The training and morale of her armed forces were excellent. The army had been prepared in the school of Karl von Clausewitz; [8] successive Japanese ministries after the Triple Intervention of 1895, and

[6] C. W. Young, *The International Relations of Manchuria* (Chicago, 1929), 6-7.

[7] W. D. Puleston, *The Armed Forces of the Pacific* (New Haven, 1941), 58-61.

[8] E. L. V. Cordonnier, *The Japanese in Manchuria, 1904* (London, 1912).

particularly after 1900, never lost sight of the possibility of war, and prepared systematically for it;[9] and the Japanese public was convinced of the national righteousness of its cause.[10] Russia's military machine, in contrast, had not prepared effectively for this war; her government was in the hands of factions; and her illiterate peasant soldiers, brave as fighters, had no understanding of why they should be warring on the distant frontier of far eastern Asia.

LAND SPHERE OF MAJOR HOSTILITIES

A major peculiarity of the Russo-Japanese War was that it was fought in Manchuria, territory under the sovereignty of China, hence neutral territory. However, since Russia after 1900 was in partial military occupation of Manchuria, and since Peking lacked the military power, if not the will, to defend the Three Eastern Provinces, there was nothing for China to do but recognize this part of her territory as an area of hostilities and thereby to imply her consent to military operations by the belligerents in her territory.[11]

MILITARY CAMPAIGNS IN MANCHURIA

Only a few of the military events of the war can be mentioned in passing. Japanese troops landed in Korea at Chemulpo, February 8 and 9. Other forces landed at Gensan on Korea's northeastern coast. General Kuroki's army crossed the Yalu River into Manchuria, May 1. A week later a second Japanese army under General Oku landed in South Manchuria (Liaotung) near the Russian leased territory, while another army under General Nodzu landed further east. On May 26 the Japanese cut the Russian lines at Nanchan, thus forcing them to withdraw on Port Arthur, July 31, and a month later the remaining Japanese armies (125,-000) faced the main Russian forces (158,000) under General Kuropatkin south of Mukden. At the Battle of Liaoyang (August 23-September 3), the Russians were forced back, but were not routed. At Sha-ho (October 9-17) the Russians attacked but failed to break the Japanese lines. The campaign was then halted during the bitter Manchurian winter, save at Port Arthur, which fell to the Japanese at terrific cost, January 2, 1905. Japan was thus able to reinforce her northern armies for the Battle of Mukden (February 23-March 10, 1905), in which for the first time she had superiority in numbers (400,000 to 325,000). Again the

[9] Tatsuji Takeuchi, *War and Diplomacy in the Japanese Empire,* 132-141.

[10] Puleston, *Armed Forces of the Pacific,* 61.

[11] Sakuye Takahashi, *International Law Applied to the Russo-Japanese War* (London, 1908), 250; and Amos S. Hershey, *The International Law and Diplomacy of the Russo-Japanese War* (New York, 1906), in particular, ch. ix, on China's neutrality.

Russians were forced to retire, this time to Tiehling, north of Mukden. At his own request Kuropatkin was now replaced as commander-in-chief by General Linievitch. Two months later, as already noted, came Russia's most severe reverse—the destruction of her Baltic fleet in the Sea of Japan.[12]

THE UNITED STATES AND THE PROBLEM OF PEACE

Efforts to find a basis for peace were undertaken early in the war. While winning technical military victories on land, and having destroyed Russian sea-power, Japan had failed to break the Russian armies. Each victory removed Japanese armies further from their base. At home the nation's economy had been strained to the point of danger. In a military sense, as the war dragged on Russia's position showed some improvement, but her funds were exhausted and French bankers were not disposed to extend further credits. In addition, revolutionary movements within Russia threatened the entire war effort.

Nevertheless, it was Japan that made the first formal proposal for peace on May 31, 1905, when she requested President Theodore Roosevelt on his own "initiative to invite the two belligerents to come together for the purpose of direct negotiation." Roosevelt's subsequent approach to the Tsar was accepted June 6, and two days later the United States sent formal invitations to the belligerents, offering good offices. Now for a second time, as in 1898, the United States was to play a significant role in world affairs. There was to be sure no general understanding on the part of Americans of the issues involved in the Far East. By and large the American people simply believed "that Japan was fighting a war in self-defense" and "for an altruistic cause." [13] Far different was the view of the President, expressed in a letter to President Wheeler of the University of California:

I believe that our future history will be more determined by our position on the Pacific facing China than our position on the Atlantic facing Europe.[14]

---

[12] Among contemporary accounts of the military and naval campaigns see: Frederick Palmer, *With Kuroki in Manchuria* (New York, 1906); Charles A'Court Repington, *The War in the Far East 1904-1905* (London, 1905); Sir Ian Hamilton, *A Staff Officer's Scrap-Book* (2 vols., London, 1905); Louis L. Seaman, *From Tokio Through Manchuria* (New York, 1905). Note also: General Kuropatkin, *The Russian Army and the Japanese War* (2 vols., London, 1909); A. Novikoff-Priboy, *Tsushima* (New York, 1937), the story of the voyage to the Far East of the second Russian squadron.

[13] Eleanor Tupper and George E. McReynolds, *Japan in American Public Opinion* (New York, 1937), 6-7.

[14] Quoted by A. L. P. Dennis, *Adventures in American Diplomacy, 1896-1906* (New York, 1928), 406.

It is unnecessary here to treat in any detail the preliminaries of the peace settlement at Portsmouth, New Hampshire: the appointment of delegates, Witte and Rosen for Russia, Komura and Takahira for Japan; the death of Secretary Hay, July 1, 1905; the renewal of the Anglo-Japanese Alliance, August 12, 1905, recognizing Japan's "paramount political, military, and economic" interests in Korea; the signing of the secret treaty of Björkö between the Kaiser and the Tsar; the success of Witte in capturing American sympathy for Russia's case; the capacity of the Japanese "by their stiffness and taciturnity" to lose in the negotiations the advantage won by their military and naval victories; and the other repeated crises into which the negotiations fell.[15]

THE TREATY OF PORTSMOUTH, SEPTEMBER 5, 1905

The Treaty of Portsmouth, September 5, 1905, was destined to become one of the most consequential agreements in the modern history of the Far East. Indeed for many years it was to be in a very real sense the heart, the kernel, of the so-called far eastern question. By it Japan acquired from Russia, subject to the consent of China, the Liaotung leased territory, the southern section of the Chinese Eastern Railroad from Kuan-ch'eng-tzu (near Changchun) to Port Arthur, along with certain coal mines which belonged to or were worked by the Russians. Both powers agreed "to evacuate completely and simultaneously Manchuria," except the Liaotung leasehold, within eighteen months after the Treaty became effective. Both powers, however, reserved the right "to maintain guards" to protect their respective railway lines in Manchuria, the number not to exceed 15 per kilometer. Administrative rights in Manchuria, usurped by the belligerents during the war, were to be restored to China. Russia declared that she had not in Manchuria "any territorial advantages or preferential or exclusive concessions in impairment of Chinese sovereignty or inconsistent with the principle of equal opportunity." Both Japan and Russia engaged "not to obstruct any general measures common to all countries, which China may take for the development of the commerce and industry of Manchuria." The two powers also agreed to "exploit their respective railways in Manchuria exclusively for commercial and industrial purposes and in no wise for strategic purposes with the exception of the railways in the Liaotung leased territory." With regard to Korea, Russia acknowledged that Japan possessed in Korea paramount political, military, and

---

[15] For detailed discussions of these matters consult: Tyler Dennett, *Roosevelt and the Russo-Japanese War* (New York, 1925); and Dennis, *Adventures in American Diplomacy,* ch. xiv.

economic interests, and engaged not to obstruct such measures as Japan might deem it necessary to take there. The southern half (Karafuto) of the island of Sakhalin was ceded to Japan in lieu of a war indemnity, and Japan was granted fishing rights in certain territorial waters of Siberia on the Pacific.[16]

JAPAN'S NEW POSITION IN KOREA

Prior to 1905 Japan considered her primary interests to be in Korea rather than Manchuria. It was to be expected therefore that a Japanese victory in the Russian war would serve to clarify the nature and intent of Japan's purposes in Korea.

It will be recalled that the decade 1894-1904 was a period of intense but intermittent Russo-Japanese economic rivalry in Korea, scarcely softened by the innocuous Yamagata-Lobanov, and Nishi-Rosen agreements of 1896 and 1898. The political color of this rivalry had already been well illustrated at the southern Korean port of Masampo, where the Russians attempted to pre-empt strategic lands only to discover that they had been purchased previously from Korean owners by some Japanese.[17] During the preliminary conversations looking to the first Anglo-Japanese Alliance, Count Hayashi told Lord Lansdowne that Japan's primary purpose was "protection of its interests in Korea."[18] The subsequent alliance (1902) recognized that Japan was "interested in a peculiar degree politically as well as commercially and industrially in Korea." Then for a few months it seemed that the Korean emperor would bestir himself to a program of reform as a self-protective measure against Russian and Japanese penetration, but nothing came of these efforts, the Korean court settling back again into its accustomed corruption and extravagance.[19] By 1903 Japan's instructions to her ministers abroad were referring to Korea as "an important outpost in Japan's line of defense."[20]

With the outbreak of the Russo-Japanese War, Korea proclaimed her neutrality,[21] but took no steps to defend it, believing, it would seem, that

---

[16] Text with additional articles in MacMurray, *Treaties,* I, 522 ff.

[17] G. P. Gooch and Harold Temperley, *British Documents on the Origin of the War* (11 vols., London, 1929), II, 32-33; A. J. Brown, *The Mastery of the Far East* (New York, 1921), 143-144.

[18] A. M. Pooley, ed., *The Secret Memoirs of Count Tadasu Hayashi* (New York, 1915), 134.

[19] See: Harrington, *God, Mammon and the Japanese,* chs. xvi, xvii; United States, Department of State, *Korean Dispatches,* Vol. 18, No. 470, Horace Allen to John Hay, May 31, 1902.

[20] *Archives Diplomatiques* (Paris, 1904), XCI, 844.

[21] United States, *Senate Documents,* Ser. 6952, 8-9.

benevolent protection would come from the United States and the great powers of western Europe.[22] Japan, however, was no longer concerned with Korean neutrality or Korean independence. In the military sphere, Korea was now looked upon as a necessary base of operations against Russia, and in the political sphere the peninsula was soon to be subjected to intimate Japanese control. The process was to be the removal of a legal fiction. Although Korea had been legally independent since 1895, she had in fact become a pawn in Russo-Japanese policy, each of these contending powers professing support for Korea's independence as a means of checking the designs of the other.

Japanese forces occupied Seoul (February 8, 1904), the day Togo attacked Port Arthur, and a protocol signed February 23 laid the ground work for the subsequent Japanese protectorate.[23] Korea was to place "full confidence" in Japan and to "adopt the advice of the latter with regard to improvements in administration." Japan would "definitely guarantee the independence and territorial integrity" of Korea and to this end might interfere in Korean affairs. Korea was pledged not to conclude with third powers any agreement "contrary to the principles" of the protocol.

In additional agreements (August 19-22, 1904) Japan was empowered to appoint advisers to the Korean departments of finance and of foreign affairs.[24] By the beginning of 1905 Japan had assumed responsibility for policing the Korean capital and had placed a Japanese police inspector in each province.[25]

International sanction was given in July, August, and September, 1905, to Japan's new position in Korea. In July, William Howard Taft, Roosevelt's Secretary of War, in conversations with the Japanese Prime Minister, General Count Katsura, gave his approval, later confirmed by the President, to a Japanese suzerainty in Korea.[26] In August, the re-

---

[22] F. A. McKenzie, Korea's Fight for Freedom (New York, 1928), 77-78.

[23] Text in United States, Foreign Relations, 1904, 437. On the nature of protectorates see: A. H. Feller, "Proctectorate," Encyclopedia of Social Science (New York, 1934), XII, 567; M. F. Lindley, The Acquisition and Government of Backward Territory in International Law (London, 1926).

[24] Text in United States, Foreign Relations, 1904, 439. Under the agreement a Japanese, Mr. Megata, was appointed to the finance department, and D. W. Stevens, an American, to the foreign office. A Japanese also became adviser to the Korean royal household department.

[25] United States, Department of State (Archive section), Korea, Despatches, Vol. 21, No. 799.

[26] Dennett, Roosevelt and the Russo-Japanese War, 113-114; H. F. Pringle, Theodore Roosevelt (London, 1932), 384. Japan in turn satisfied Roosevelt by a disavowal of any aggressive purpose in the Philippines.

newed Anglo-Japanese Alliance referred to Japan's "paramount" interests at Seoul,[27] and in September, Russia in Article II of the Treaty
of Portsmouth likewise acknowledged Japan's "paramount" position.
With this international sanction Japan, through pressure exerted at
Seoul, secured from the Korean government an agreement (made public November 23) giving Japan control of Korea's foreign relations and
the right to appoint a Japanese resident-general at Seoul. On the following day the United States instructed its Minister at Seoul to close
the legation.[28] Willard Straight described this diplomatic retreat as
"like the stampede of rats from a sinking ship." The establishment of
the Japanese protectorate in Korea was thus complete. Having consolidated her position at Seoul, Japan was now prepared to implement in
South Manchuria the new position there which the Treaty of Portsmouth had given her.[29]

STEEL RAILS AND POLITICS IN MANCHURIA

The Treaty of Portsmouth was the herald of far-reaching changes in
Manchuria. After 1905 it became convenient to refer to "North Manchuria," where Russia still claimed a sphere of influence, and to "South
Manchuria," where Japan was about to create her sphere.[30] Since both
before and during the Russo-Japanese War Japan had professed to be
fighting for the open door and the integrity of China in Manchuria, the
conclusion of peace was greeted with general popular enthusiasm by the
American people, but "American investors and merchants in the Far
East disapproved of the treaty because they were afraid that Japan
would now curb their own activity in the Orient," [31] and particularly in
the promising frontier area of South Manchuria. It was in this setting
after 1905 that the Manchurian question became acute, though the principles involved had not changed. In its simplest form the question
was whether under Chinese sovereignty and administrative integrity,
Manchuria was to be open on terms of equality to the commerce, in-

[27] *British and Foreign State Papers*, XCVIII, 136-138.
[28] Text of the Korean-Japanese agreement in United States, *Foreign Relations, 1905*, 612-613.
[29] For a Japanese account of the Korean negotiations see Tatsuji Takeuchi, *War and Diplomacy in the Japanese Empire*, 160-162.
[30] The line of demarcation between these spheres (North and South Manchuria) ran, from Hunchun in the east, approximately parallel to the main line of the Chinese Eastern Railway. This line was defined in the secret Russo-Japanese treaties of 1907, 1910, and 1912. See E. B. Price, *The Russo-Japanese Treaties of 1907-1916. . . .* (Baltimore, 1933), map on 124.
[31] Eleanor Tupper and George E. McReynolds, *Japan in American Public Opinion* (New York, 1937), 15.

dustry, and capital of all nations, or whether it was to become again an exclusive economic preserve, this time of Russian and Japanese capital, buttressed by Russian and Japanese political control in derogation of Chinese sovereignty and administration. The answer to this question and indeed the key to the entire problem of modern far eastern history requires examination of the specific and complex issues which arose in Manchuria between 1905 and 1910.

MILITARY OCCUPATION OF MANCHURIA

Although ratifications of the Treaty of Portsmouth were exchanged at Washington (November 25, 1905), the former belligerents had agreed to an 18-month period in which to complete evacuation of their armies. This meant that for more than a year Manchuria remained partly under military occupation.[32]   Although agreements of this type are common at the termination of hostilities, they may become the subject of abuse or of misunderstanding, and in the case of South Manchuria as early as March, 1906, the United States called to Japan's attention charges from American interests in China that

. . . action of the Japanese authorities in Manchuria during Japanese [military] occupation is so generally directed towards establishing Japanese commercial interests in the principal towns, and toward acquiring property rights for Japanese in all available quarters as to leave little or no opening for other foreign trade by the time the territory is evacuated.[33]

Thus within six months of the conclusion of peace the United States was calling upon Japan, as it had previously called upon Russia, to respect the principal of equal commercial opportunity.

THE SINO-JAPANESE TREATY OF PEKING, DECEMBER 22, 1905

The Treaty of Portsmouth had provided that the transfer to Japan of Russian territorial, railway, and other rights in South Manchuria was to be conditional on the consent of China. This consent was secured by Japan's Foreign Minister, Baron Komura, in negotiations with Yüan Shih-k'ai at Peking in a treaty dated December 22, 1905.

An additional Sino-Japanese agreement of the same date contained important provisions: 1) China agreed to open 16 cities in Manchuria to

---

[32] MacMurray, *Treaties*, I, 527.
[33] United States, *Foreign Relations, 1906*, Pt. I, 171-172.

international residence and trade;[34] 2) Japan agreed to withdraw her troops and railway guards (if Russia would withdraw her railway guards) when "China shall have become herself capable of affording full protection to the lives and property of foreigners"; 3) Japan secured the right to maintain the military railway she had built from Antung on the Korean border to Mukden; and 4) China consented to formation of a Sino-Japanese corporation to exploit the Yalu forests.[35]

SECRET "PROTOCOLS" OF THE PEKING CONFERENCE

The formal Sino-Japanese treaty and additional agreement were later claimed by the Japanese government to be supplemented by certain alleged secret "protocols," the most important of which pledged the Chinese government not to construct any mainline railway "in the neighborhood of and parallel to" the Japanese South Manchuria Railway (running from Changchun to Port Arthur and Dalny, now Dairen), or any branch line "which might be prejudicial" to the Japanese line. These "protocols," the legality of which has never been fully established, appear to have taken the form of memoranda or minutes on the proceedings of the Komura-Yüan conference. Their significance, however, lies not so much in the question of their legality as in the fact that they revealed the intent (legal or otherwise) of Japan to create a railway monopoly in South Manchuria.[36]

THE SOUTH MANCHURIA RAILWAY COMPANY

The intimate relation between Japanese interests in South Manchuria and the Japanese government was revealed (June 7, 1906) by the creation of the South Manchuria Railway Company—a joint stock company to own and manage all Japanese and Japanese operated railroads in Manchuria. The Japanese government owned one half of the capital stock and controlled appointment of the principal officers. Under the Company's articles of incorporation shareholders were limited to the Chinese and Japanese governments and subjects of these two countries. The president and vice-president, appointed as indicated by the Japanese government, were responsible to the Japanese prime minister. The company was empowered to engage in subsidiary enterprises such as

[34] Feng huang cheng, Liaoyang, Hsinmintun, Tiehling, Tang kangtzu, Fakumen, Changchun, Kirin, Harbin, Ninguta, Hunchun, Sanhsing, Tsitsihar, Hailar, Aigun, and Manchouli.
[35] Texts in MacMurray, *Treaties,* I, 549.
[36] For a text of the alleged "protocols," see MacMurray, *Treaties,* I, 554. A discussion of their validity is in Young, *The International Relations of Manchuria,* 258-265.

mining, water transportation, electric power, real estate, and warehousing within the railway zone. In addition the company possessed broad civil administrative powers and authority to collect taxes within the railroad zone.[37]

GOVERNMENT IN THE KWANTUNG LEASEHOLD

By the Treaty of Portmouth Japan had acquired from Russia the Liaotung leased territory, now to be known as Kwantung; and at Peking in December, 1905, Japan had agreed to "conform to the original agreements concluded between China and Russia" concerning this territory and concerning the matter of railway construction "so far as circumstances permit." Japan promptly set up an administrative machinery for her leasehold known as the Government General of Kwantung (*Kwanto Totoku Fu*). A governor-general who was to be of high military rank was to protect railways and exercise civil administrative power in the leased territory. He was responsible, in his appointment to the prime minister in Tokyo, in questions relating to foreign affairs to the minister for foreign affairs, in matters of military administration to the minister of war, and in matters of mobilization and operations to the general staff. He commanded the Kwantung garrison, controlled civil administration in the leased territory, and police jurisdiction in the South Manchuria Railway zone.[38]

RAILWAY AGREEMENTS BETWEEN CHINA AND JAPAN

After the Russo-Japanese War, the contemplated development of the resources, agricultural and mineral, of South Manchuria, and the keener recognition of the strategic and political importance of the area led to an unprecedented interest and rivalry in railroad enterprise. The energy, the efficiency, and the spirit of monopoly which the Japanese poured into the South Manchuria Railway not only excited the jealousy of other foreign nationals, principally British and American, but also inspired the fear that Japanese railroads using the S.M.R. as the trunk would branch out east and west to the exclusion of all non-Japanese

---

[37] Texts relating to creation and powers of the S.M.R. Company, in MacMurray, *Treaties,* I, 555, 557, 559. The Chinese government did not exercise its privilege to purchase shares.

[38] Texts of relevant documents in MacMurray, *Treaties,* I, 558 ff. In 1919 the union of military and civil functions was abolished by creation of the Kwantung Government instead of the Government General, headed by a governor with civil jurisdiction over Kwantung and authority to police the railway, and "to supervise the business" of the S.M.R. Co. This governor retained control of police but not of the Kwantung garrison.

enterprise. It appeared indeed that Japan both in the light of her geographical position and her national policy was in a position to exploit her new-found sphere of influence on a scale undreamed of by other sphere-holding powers in China.

Development of Japan's sphere involved in the first instance certain railway agreements with China, arising out of the recent war and the Treaty of Peking of December, 1905. In 1907, for instance, China acquired from Japan the Hsinmintun-Mukden Railway, which the Japanese army had built during the war. The purchase was effected in part with funds loaned China by the South Manchuria Railway, China being required to employ for the line during the life of the loan a Japanese engineer-in-chief and a Japanese accountant. By 1927, the loan having been met, the Hsinmintun-Mukden line had become an integral part of the Chinese government's Peking-Mukden Railway. In 1909 the Japanese permitted the railroad to reach the walled city of Mukden by passing under the tracks of the S.M.R., a circumstance which set the stage for dramatic events in 1928.[39] China also agreed in 1907 to borrow from the S.M.R. half the funds needed for a railroad connecting Changchun, northern terminus of the S.M.R., with Kirin. After construction of the line, the loan repayment fell in arrears, and in 1917 management of the line was undertaken by the Japanese S.M.R.[40]

More important was the case of the Antung-Mukden Railway built by the Japanese as a narrow gauge military line during the Russo-Japanese War. In December, 1905, China agreed that Japan might maintain and operate the line for 15 years subject to completion of certain improvements. Japan did not complete these improvements within the time limit (that is, by 1908), but did subsequently present Peking with an ultimatum. As a result of this ultimatum China signed a new agreement (August 19, 1909) permitting Japan to reconstruct the line as a standard gauge road. It was completed in November, 1911. In 1915 Japan's control was extended from the original 15 years to 99 years, that is, to 2007.[41]

Japan also attempted to secure control over all new railroad construction in South Manchuria. By the secret "protocols" of 1905 she hoped to protect the S.M.R. from "parallel" and "prejudicial" lines. The

[39] Texts of relevant documents in MacMurray, *Treaties,* I, 627, 632, 767, 782. For the history of British and Russian interests in the Peking-Shanhaikwan and Shanhaikwan-Hsinmintun sections of the Peking-Mukden line, see Percy H. Kent, *Railway Enterprise in China* (London, 1907).

[40] Texts of relevant documents in MacMurray, *Treaties,* I, 627, 767, 785; II, 1054, 1220, 1390.

[41] Texts of relevant documents in MacMurray, *Treaties,* I, 551, 787; II, 1220.

S.M.R. also had the right to supply any capital China needed for branch lines or extensions of the Kiren-Changchun system. Then in 1913 Japan secured a provisional agreement to finance for China three lines connecting with the S.M.R.: the Ssupingkai-Chengchiatun-Taonan Railway, the Kaiyuan-Hailungcheng Railway, and the Changchun-Taonan Railway; and in addition a line from Taonan to Jehol, and one from Kirin to Hailungcheng.[42]

MINING, LUMBERING, CABLES, TELEGRAPHS

Supplementing further the picture of Japan's new position in South Manchuria were a number of Sino-Japanese agreements covering mining and lumbering concessions and the construction and control of cables and telegraphs. Prior to 1905 the Russians had operated coal mines at Fushun and Yentai near Mukden;[43] these mining rights in South Manchuria passed to Japan in the Treaty of Portsmouth. After considerable controversy China and Japan reached agreement (September 4, 1909) for Japanese exploitation of the Fushun and Yentai mines, China to be paid a tax on all coal so mined. A separate agreement covered Japanese interests in the Penhsihu mines on the Antung-Mukden Railway.[44]

China, in the Sino-Japanese agreement of December, 1905, consented to the formation of a joint Sino-Japanese stock company "for the exploitation of the forests in the regions on the right bank of the River Yalu," a concession of great value in view of the vast timber wealth of southeastern Manchuria.[45]

China and Japan agreed (October 12, 1908) that the two governments would lay and maintain a submarine cable from Kwantung province across the Gulf of Pechihli connecting with the Japanese post office at Chefoo in Shantung province. In the same agreement all land telegraphs acquired by the Japanese from the Russians or constructed by Japan during the Russo-Japanese War outside the leased territory and the railroad zone were to be returned to China for the sum of ¥ 50,000. Lines within the railroad zone were retained by Japan.[46]

[42] Relevant documents in MacMurray, Treaties, II, 1054. For the subsequent history of these proposed lines see Young, The International Relations of Manchuria, 74-76.
[43] Sino-Russian agreements in MacMurray, Treaties, I, 74, 154.
[44] Relevant documents in MacMurray, Treaties, I, 790-793.
[45] Relevant documents covering earlier Russian concessions and the later Japanese, in MacMurray, Treaties, I, 154, 549, 731, 733.
[46] Relevant documents covering these and additional Japanese telegraph concessions in MacMurray, Treaties, I, 760-765.

CUSTOMS REGULATIONS: KWANTUNG AND RAILROAD ZONE

After the Russo-Japanese War, Dairen (the former Dalny) and the leased territory under Japanese control continued to be a duty-free zone as they had been under the previous Russian occupation. Japan, however, secured from China (May 29, 1913) a duty reduction of one-third on imports and exports to and from Manchuria via the S.M.R. and Chosen Railway. Precedent for this advantage was the similar preferential land frontier tariff rate on goods entering Manchuria from Russia over the Chinese Eastern Railway.[47]

JAPANESE JURISDICTION IN MANCHURIA AFTER 1905

Among the more significant features of Japan's position in South Manchuria after 1905 were certain jurisdictional powers. Within the Kwantung leased territory she possessed all rights of administration pertaining to sovereignty except the power to alienate the territory.[48]

Far more controversial from the legal point of view were the jurisdictional powers exercised in the railway zones by Russia and by Japan. The railway zones, defined as lands "actually necessary for the construction, operation, and protection" of the original Chinese Eastern Railway, were areas in which first Russia and, after 1905, Japan (in South Manchuria) exercised very broad administrative powers, the legal validity of which has in some measure been questioned.[49] Powers *exercised* by Japan (apart from questions of legality) included: ordinary rights of administration pertaining to sovereignty, taxation, police, and transfer of real property; employment of a limited number of railroad guards to protect the railway; and the exercise of ordinary police power and of customary functions of municipal and local administration.

Over and above the foregoing powers, Japan enjoyed, as did also other "treaty powers," extraterritoriality and consular jurisdiction long established in China's treaties with foreign powers. Japanese consular police, attached to various Japanese consulates in Manchuria, exercised authority beyond the railroad zones. Special arrangements too pertained

---

[47] Relevant documents in MacMurray, *Treaties,* I, 634, 638, 683; II, 1039.

[48] An exception to this general statement of powers was the city of Chinchow in the leased territory, where the Chinese retained the right of administration and police. China also retained administrative authority in the neutral zone on the border of Kwantung and Manchuria, but Chinese troops could not enter this area without the consent of Japan.

[49] For a strictly legalistic discussion of this subject, note C. W. Young, *Japanese Jurisdiction in the South Manchuria Railway Areas* (Baltimore, 1931).

to designated areas in the Chientao regions where large numbers of Koreans had settled. These Koreans were subject to Chinese laws and courts, but in certain cases a Japanese consular officer was entitled to attend court in the interest of Korean defendants. This system continued until 1915, even after the Japanese annexation of Korea in 1910 had made all Koreans Japanese nationals.[50]

---

[50] MacMurray, *Treaties,* I, 796-797.

CHAPTER 19

MANCHURIA AND KOREA, 1904-1910 (CONTINUED)

RUSSIA IN NORTH MANCHURIA AFTER 1905

IN GENERAL, Russia's special position in North Manchuria remained unchanged by the Russo-Japanese War. Russia continued to assume that she possessed in the Chinese Eastern Railway zone "practically complete civil administrative rights (as taxation, police jurisdiction, and the right to possess and dispose of real property), and, likewise, civil and criminal jurisdiction over certain Chinese nationals, and involving all cases either 'directly or indirectly' affecting the interests of the railway." [1]   After 1908 China contested this interpretation, and in 1909 the two powers reached agreement whereby Chinese were to share in the municipal administration of towns of the railway zone. [2]   Russian mining and lumbering concessions were clarified and extended in Heilungkiang and Kiren provinces. [3]   As already noted in South Manchuria, so in North Manchuria China recovered all telegraph lines operated by Russia outside the railway area. [4]

INTENSIFICATION OF INTERNATIONAL RIVALRY

The foregoing pages have presented some of the specific features of the Japanese and the Russian position in Manchuria following the Russo-Japanese War.   Even so brief a survey indicates that while China's sovereign rights were specifically reserved in the Kwantung territory and the various railway zones, *de facto* administration was exercised by Russia (the Chinese Eastern Railway) in North Manchuria, and in South Manchuria by Japan (the Government General of Kwantung and the S.M.R.).   Far from decreasing foreign (Russian) control in Manchuria, the Russo-Japanese War had paved the way for Sino-Russian and Sino-Japanese agreements by which two powers instead of

---

[1] C. W. Young, *The International Relations of Manchuria* (Chicago, 1929), 93-94.

[2] MacMurray, *Treaties,* II, 1181 ff.   This and subsequent agreements led to varying interpretations, and to complications with other foreign powers (Belgium, France, Great Britain, Japan, the Netherlands, and Spain).

[3] MacMurray, *Treaties,* I, 658, 671, 721.

[4] MacMurray, *Treaties,* I, 631.

one were to claim spheres of influence there. In these circumstances
the future of the open door doctrine and the integrity of China appeared
as unpredictable as when Russia was the sole intruder. Foreign business interests in China, British and American in particular, had anticipated great opportunities for their goods and capital in South Manchuria
once peace was restored. It was therefore of the utmost importance to
discover how far Japan and Russia were bent on a policy of preference,
if not monopoly, for their own commerce, industry, and capital. A test
case was soon forthcoming.

GREAT BRITAIN AND MANCHURIA, 1907

The Chinese government in November, 1907, contracted with a British firm, Pauling and Company, to build a short railroad from Hsinmintun to Fakumen. In its origins this contract was a natural outgrowth
of agreements made as early as 1898 between the Chinese government
and the (British) Hongkong and Shanghai Banking Corporation for
the construction of certain railways in Manchuria. These British concessions were given qualified recognition by Russia in 1899 and again
in 1902.[5] When, however, these early concessions were revived by
the specific Hsinmintun-Fakumen project, the Japanese government
promptly protested that the proposed line violated the secret "protocols"
of 1905, the new road being in the Japanese view "parallel" and "prejudicial" to the S.M.R. The success of the Japanese protest was assured
when the British government refused to support the British concession-
aires or to call in question the validity of the "protocol" on which Japan's
protest was based. The incident encouraged Japan in the effort to
create a railroad-construction monopoly in South Manchuria.[6] Japan
also refused China's later proposal that the question be referred to the
Hague Court of Arbitration, and in 1909 secured from China a pledge
to be consulted prior to any undertaking by China to construct the
line.[7]

FRANCO-JAPANESE TREATY, JUNE 10, 1907

Japan's post-war problem in Manchuria was already being solved by
diplomatic measures far more fundamental than the blocking of a small

[5] See MacMurray, *Treaties*, I, 173, 179, 204, 326.
[6] See C. W. Young, *Japan's Special Position in Manchuria* (Baltimore, 1931), 107-123;
P. H. Clyde, *International Rivalries in Manchuria* (Columbus, 1928), 179-187; Hsü Shuhsi, *China and Her Political Entity* (New York, 1926), 292-296; Herbert Croly, *Willard
Straight* (New York, 1924), 243; Great Britain, *Parliamentary Debates* (March 3, 1908),
185, p. 527; and United States, *Foreign Relations, 1910,* 269.
[7] MacMurray, *Treaties*, I, 790.

proposed railway. It was the problem of consolidating her position both in Korea and South Manchuria, and in coming to workable terms with her late enemy, Russia. This latter object was rendered easier since statesmen friendly to an entente were in power at Tokyo (Saionji, Hayashi, and Motono) and at St. Petersburg (Iswolsky). The road to a general Russo-Japanese *rapprochement* was to be paved by France. France was not without experience in the processes by which territory (Annam) could be detached from China and spheres of influence acquired. France had opposed Japan in 1895 (the Triple Intervention); she was allied with Russia during 1904-05; and therefore it was now good policy, in view of Japan's victory, for France to clarify her relations with Tokyo, and to aid in creating a Russo-Japanese entente. The Franco-Japanese treaty which materialized on June 10, 1907, and which was to provide the formula for subsequent Russo-Japanese agreements is notable ". . . for its complete *sang-froid,* its subtle implications, and its bold assumptions." [8] The two powers, after agreeing "to respect the independence and integrity of China, as well as the principle of equal treatment in that country for the commerce and subjects or citizens of all nations," went on to assert that they possessed "a special interest" in preserving peace and order "especially in the regions of the Chinese Empire adjoining the territories where they possess rights of sovereignty, protection or occupation." [9] These signatory powers then proceeded to constitute themselves as the guardians of peace in vast areas of China which they later defined as including, in the case of France, Kwangtung, Kwangsi, and Yünnan; and, in the case of Japan, Fukien, and "the regions of Manchuria and Mongolia." [10]

THE RUSSO-JAPANESE TREATIES, 1907

Following promptly this remarkable Franco-Japanese treaty came four Russo-Japanese agreements: June 13, a convention providing for through traffic at the junction of the Russian and Japanese railways at Changchun;[11] July 28, a treaty of commerce and navigation, and a fisheries convention;[12] and July 30, two political conventions, one public, the other secret. The public convention subscribed (it had now become

---

[8] E. B. Price, *The Russo-Japanese Treaties concerning Manchuria and Mongolia* (Baltimore, 1933), 26-31.

[9] In the case of Japan: Korea, Kwantung, and the S.M.R. zone; in the case of France: Annam and French Indo-China in general.

[10] Price, *The Russo-Japanese Treaties,* 28-33.

[11] MacMurray, *Treaties,* I, 643-648.

[12] Japan, Ministry for Foreign Affairs, *Recueil de traités et conventions conclus entre l'Empire du Japon et les puissances étrangères* (2 vols., Tokyo, 1918), I, 549 ff., 563.

a sort of international habit) to the "independence and territorial integrity of the Empire of China," and pledged the signatories "to sustain and defend the maintenance of the *Status quo* and respect for this principle by all pacific means within their reach."[13]   The secret convention (not revealed until published by the Bolshevik government, 1918) established precedents of the greatest importance:

1. It drew a line of demarcation between North and South Manchuria (the Russian and the Japanese spheres).
2. North of this line Japan undertook not to seek for herself or her subjects, nor to obstruct Russian efforts there to secure, concessions for railroads or telegraphs.
3. Russia undertook neither "to interfere with nor to place any obstacle in the way of the *further development*" of the "relations of Political solidarity between Japan and Korea."
4. Japan "recognizing the special interests of Russia [in Outer Mongolia undertook] . . . to refrain from any interference which might prejudice those interests."[14]

THE UNITED STATES AND MANCHURIA

It was becoming evident at the time, though the public evidence was by no means so conclusive then as it is today, that the Franco-Japanese and the Russo-Japanese agreements of 1907 presented a clearly defined threat to the American doctrine of China's territorial integrity and its corollary, the principle of equal opportunity, popularly known as the open door. The reader of these pages is already aware that the efforts of the American government in the years 1899 to 1905 to insist on the integrity of China were sporadic, periods of positive assertion being followed by silence and even admissions denying the principle.[15] The Franco-Japanese treaty (1907) asserted with clarity that it was the business of Japan and France to maintain peace and order, should this become necessary, in large areas of China. Such responsibility obviously contemplated possible occupation of Chinese territory, a circumstance not to be reconciled easily with China's integrity. And as for the open door in Manchuria after 1905, its status has never been described more

[13] United States, *Foreign Relations, 1907*, II, 765; MacMurray, *Treaties*, I, 657-658.
[14] Text in Price, *The Russo-Japanese Treaties*, 107-111.
[15] As in Secretary Hay's letter to President Roosevelt, May 1, 1902: ". . . We recognize her [Russia's] exceptional position in Northern China. What we have been working for . . . is that, no matter what happens eventually in northern China and Manchuria, the United States shall not be placed in any worse position than while the country was under the unquestioned domination of China." Quoted in A. L. P. Dennis, *Adventures in American Diplomacy, 1896-1906* (New York, 1928), 353.

realistically than by ex-President Roosevelt to his successor, President Taft:[16]

. . . As regards Manchuria, if the Japanese choose to follow a course of conduct to which we are adverse, we cannot stop it unless we are prepared to go to war. . . . The Open Door policy in China was an excellent thing, and I hope it will be a good thing in the future, so far as it can be maintained by general diplomatic agreement; but as has been proved by the whole history of Manchuria, alike under Russia and under Japan, the "Open Door" policy, as a matter of fact, completely disappears as soon as a powerful nation determines to disregard it, and is willing to run the risk of war rather than forego its intention.

The foregoing statement explains why the American government under the presidency of Theodore Roosevelt did not seriously challenge Japan's claim of special interests in South Manchuria. There were Americans, however, both in and outside government who did attempt to challenge the Japanese position sometimes from motives of private and corporate profits, and sometimes from the higher ground of national policy and principle. In 1905 E. H. Harriman, hoping to build a round-the-world transportation system, reached an understanding with Ito and Katsura to finance the reconstruction of the railway (S.M.R.) which Japan hoped to acquire from Russia at the end of the war. After peace came, Japan dropped the scheme. In Tokyo it seemed better policy to secure funds in London, where the Anglo-Japanese Alliance had recently been renewed, than in the United States, against which Japanese public opinion had been embittered by the Portsmouth Treaty, which had denied to the "victors" a war indemnity.[17]

Far more active than Harriman in furthering American commerce and capital in Manchuria was Willard Straight, Consul-General of the United States at Mukden, 1906-08. Straight was convinced that the weakness of the United States in the Far East was due to the relatively small American capital investment in China.[18] He observed with much concern the contrasting growth of Japanese interests in Korea and Manchuria. A Sino-American publicity bureau which he inspired was so active that the Japanese protested and the bureau was liqui-

[16] Roosevelt to Taft, December 22, 1910, quoted by A. W. Griswold, *The Far Eastern Policy of the United States* (New York, 1938), 132.

[17] George Kennan, *E. H. Harriman* (2 vols., Boston, 1922), ch. xviii; Herbert Croly, *Willard Straight* (New York, 1924), 238-250.

[18] For estimated figures see C. F. Remer, *Foreign Investments in China* (New York, 1933), 249-260.

dated.[19] Straight made little progress with his official superiors so long as Roosevelt remained in the White House. Indeed the President was less concerned with Japan and American capital in Manchuria than he was with the possibility of hostile Japanese action against the Philippines.

This was because a crisis had been precipitated in 1906 in American-Japanese relations when the San Francisco School Board segregated Oriental students in the city schools. The "Gentleman's Agreement," 1907-08, restored in part a sense of diplomatic calm, but war talk was such in the summer of 1907, that the President sent General Leonard Wood, commanding the troops in the Philippines, special instructions for meeting a Japanese attack, while Taft was again sent to Tokyo (October, 1907), from where he reported that Japan was anxious to avoid war. To meet the crisis in more fundamental ways, Roosevelt decided on two lines of action: 1) he sent the American fleet on a world cruise including Japanese ports (March 16, 1907, to February 22, 1909); and 2) he made concessions to Japan at the expense of China's integrity in Manchuria. The cruise of the American fleet signalized the arrival of American sea-power, pointedly told the Japanese that the United States was not afraid to put its gun-boats in any part of the Pacific, and pleased both the Canadians and the Australians.[20]

While the American fleet pursued its course in foreign waters the President employed the less provocative arts of diplomacy with the Japanese in Washington. A five-year arbitration treaty was concluded with Japan (May 5, 1908). It was an innocuous affair excluding all questions of "vital interests," but nonetheless a peaceful gesture.[21] This was followed by an exchange of notes between Secretary of State Root and the Japanese Ambassador, Takahira (November 30, 1908), an agreement which "was as important for what it left unsaid as for what it definitely stipulated." [22] Both countries were "firmly resolved reciprocally to respect the territorial possessions belonging to each other" not only in eastern Asia but also in "the region of the Pacific Ocean," abjuring therein "any aggressive tendencies." Each declared its support for the "existing *status quo*," for the open door, and for the independence and

[19] Griswold, *Far Eastern Policy of the United States,* 138.

[20] T. A. Bailey, *Theodore Roosevelt and the Japanese-American Crisis* (Stanford University, 1934), chs. xi, xii; H. F. Pringle, *Theodore Roosevelt* (New York, 1931), ch. x; J. P. Gooch and H. W. V. Temperley, eds., *British Documents on the Origins of the War, 1898-1914* (11 vols., London, 1926-38), VIII, 455 ff.

[21] Bailey, *Japanese-American Crisis,* 292; United States, *Foreign Relations, 1908,* 503-505.

[22] Griswold, *Far Eastern Policy of the United States,* 129; text in United States, *Foreign Relations, 1908,* 511-12.

integrity of China. In case of threat to these principles, the two powers agreed to "communicate" with each other in search of an "understanding." Since the meaning of phraseology so general is ambiguous, there has been no agreed interpretation on the Root-Takahira exchange. A legalistic view would hold that Japan had again pledged herself to the open door and the integrity of China; but the narrative of events leading to the exchange would support the view that Japan had given a renewed pledge on the Philippines, and in return "the United States had given Japan a free hand in Manchuria." [23]

In the broader sphere of world politics, as contrasted with American-Japanese issues, the Root-Takahira agreement made a fiasco of the Kaiser's attempt in 1907 and 1908 to create "a German-American-Chinese entente, supported by Russia, to counteract the Anglo-French-Japanese agreements" of 1904-07. As a part of this project, T'ang Shao-yi was sent by China to Washington in 1908 "ostensibly to render thanks for the reduction of the [American-Boxer] indemnity, but really to pave the way for the entente with Germany and America." This was what T'ang sought; what he got was the privilege of reading the Root-Takahira notes on the eve of their signature.[24]

THE SHIFT TO DOLLAR DIPLOMACY

Whatever the strength or the weakness of the Roosevelt-Root policy toward Japan and Manchuria, it was soon to give place to a new American strategy. William Howard Taft and Philander C. Knox became President and Secretary of State respectively at a time when American capital was to look increasingly to foreign fields for investment. Government was sympathetic, and as Taft said later, policy substituted "dollars for bullets" and combined "idealistic humanitarian sentiments" with "legitimate commercial aims." The commercial machinery of the Department of State was enlarged, and from November, 1908, until June, 1909, its Far Eastern Division was headed by Willard Straight, who worked incessantly to maintain Harriman's interest in Manchurian railway finance, and to enlist the interest of New York bankers. Early in 1909 these efforts bore fruit. At the instance of the State Department a banking group was designated "as the official agent of American railway financing in China" with Straight as its Peking representative.[25]

[23] Griswold, *Far Eastern Policy of the United States*, 129-131; T. A. Bailey, "The Root-Takahira Agreement of 1908," *Pacific Historical Review*, IX (March, 1940), 19-36.

[24] See Luella J. Hall, "The Abortive German-American-Chinese Entente of 1907-08," *Journal of Modern History*, I (1929), 219-235.

[25] The banks included were: J. P. Morgan and Co., the First National Bank and the National City Bank, Kuhn, Loeb and Co., and the Harriman interests. See F. V. Field, *American Participation in the China Consortiums* (Chicago, 1931), 34-36.

The next step taken by the Department was to demand of China that the American bankers be admitted to the Hukuang railway loan then under negotiation between China and three banking groups representing British, French, and German interests. The new American policy was thus striking at European financial monopoly in China Proper as well as at the Japanese in Manchuria. This was in line with the objects of Taft and Knox "to force American capital by diplomatic pressure" into a region of the world where it would not go of its own accord.[26] As applied to Manchuria it meant that Secretary Knox was to attempt what was diplomatically impossible, to "smoke Japan out" of her position in Manchuria despite the fact that Japan by 1907 "had given general notice of her determination to dominate as much of Manchuria as she could." [27]

THE CHINCHOW-AIGUN RAILWAY PROJECT

Implementation of the experiment was begun by Straight and Harriman, who in 1909 were attempting to buy the Chinese Eastern Railway from Russia. What Harriman really wanted was the Japanese S.M.R., but the Japanese had refused to sell. Therefore Harriman would force the sale by buying the Russian road and connecting it with the Gulf of Pechihli by a new line parallel to the S.M.R. from Chinchow (near Shanhaikwan where the Great Wall meets the sea) to Aigun on the Amur. If the threat of construction did not bring the Japanese to terms, then actual construction of the Chinchow-Aigun line would be undertaken. "He [Harriman] would smash competitors in Manchuria exactly as he had smashed them at home." [28]

But Harriman died on September 10, 1909; and although Straight secured from the Manchurian government on October 2, 1909, a preliminary agreement to finance (by the American group) and construct (Pauling and Co.) the Chinchow-Aigun line, the bankers in New York without Harriman's leadership became timid. Harriman's railroad politics had failed.

THE KNOX NEUTRALIZATION PROPOSAL

It seemed therefore that if dollar diplomacy had any resources, this was the time to use them. Accordingly, on November 6, 1909, Secre-

---

[26] Griswold, *Far Eastern Policy of the United States,* 146.

[27] J. G. Reid, *The Manchu Abdication and the Powers* (Berkeley, 1935), 75; Griswold, *Far Eastern Policy of the United States,* 150.

[28] Griswold, *Far Eastern Policy of the United States,* 152-153; Reid, *Manchu Abdication,* 42.

tary Knox made two striking (some would say fantastic) proposals to
Great Britain: 1) that the foreign-owned Manchurian railways (C.E.R.
and S.M.R. systems) be "neutralized" by providing China with funds
to purchase them through a great multi-power loan, during the life of
which the railroads would be under foreign, international control; 2)
in case "neutralization" proved impracticable, that Great Britain join
with the United States in supporting the Chinchow-Aigun project and
in inviting powers "friendly to complete commercial neutralization of
Manchuria to participate." [29] These propositions were nothing if not
Gargantuan.

Sir Edward Grey approved "the general principle" of the neutralization proposal but thought it "wiser to postpone" any consideration
of its application. As to the Chinchow-Aigun proposal, Sir Edward
thought nothing should be done until China had agreed to Japanese
participation. With this British approval in principle, but refusal in
fact, Knox approached the Chinese, French, German, Japanese, and
Russian governments.

Russia and Japan after consulting with each other rejected the neutralization scheme in notes which showed a marked similarity (January
21, 1910). Russia found that "nothing appears at the present time to
threaten either his [China's] sovereignty or the open door policy in
Manchuria," and added that "establishment of an international administration and control of the Manchurian railroads . . . would seriously
injure Russian interests." As for the Chinchow-Aigun proposal, the
Russians labelled it as "strategic and political." Indeed, the Russians
made it clear that they proposed to examine with great care any and all
future proposals that might be made for financing railroads in Manchuria.[30]

Japan replied that "the most serious objection to the proposal in question lies in the fact that it contemplates a very important departure from
the terms of the Treaty of Portsmouth." In the Japanese view, the
open door was not threatened, and the interests of economy and efficiency would not be served by substituting international for national
control of the Manchurian railroads.

Japan and Russia then addressed China, protesting against the Chinchow-Aigun project and demanding that they be consulted before foreign capital was employed in Manchurian railway enterprise.[31] As a
result France and Great Britain gave notice that they would not support

[29] United States, *Foreign Relations, 1910*, 234 ff.
[30] United States, *Foreign Relations, 1910*, 234 ff.
[31] United States, *Foreign Relations, 1910*, 257.

the United States in this line.[32] The Gargantuan plans of Harriman, Straight, and Knox had miscarried. But this was not all.[33]

RUSSO-JAPANESE TREATIES OF 1910

Secretary Knox, in the view of the British government, had hastened, if he did not actually cause, a tightening of the Russian and the Japanese spheres in Manchuria.[34] On July 4, 1910 (of all days!), Russia and Japan signed two conventions, again as in 1907, one public, the other secret. They announced to the world "the perfecting" of their connecting railway service in Manchuria; refrained from any mention of China's integrity and the open door; but engaged publicly in case the *status quo* should be menaced to decide "the measures that they may judge it necessary to take for the maintenance of the said *status quo*."

Secretly the two powers reaffirmed the line of demarcation drawn between their spheres in 1907, and strengthened their "special position" by recognizing "the right of each, within its own sphere, freely to take all measures necessary for the safeguarding and the defense of those interests." Neither would hinder "the consolidation and further development of the special interests of the other," while each would "refrain from all political activity" within the other's sphere. Finally, the secret convention provided for "common action" in defense of their special interests.[35]

The significance of dollar diplomacy as practiced by Knox in this instance is that it had not opened, on the contrary, it had closed, the door to American capital in Manchuria. Russia and Japan had, with the approval of England and France, been drawn together to protect their "special interests." Germany gave the United States some "moral" support, not because she cared for American principles but because of her own isolation among the big powers—Britain, France, Russia, and Japan —in China.[36] Even Straight and the bankers turned on Knox, accused him of using them as instruments of an aggressive policy, and threatened to withdraw from the far eastern field.[37]

---

[32] United States, *Foreign Relations, 1910*, 256, 268.

[33] The best treatment of the international politics combatting the Knox proposals are: Price, *The Russo-Japanese Treaties*, 46 ff.; and Reid, *Manchu Abdication*, chs. iv-vi.

[34] Reid, *Manchu Abdication*, 142; *British Documents*, VIII, 485.

[35] Price, *The Russo-Japanese Treaties*, 42-46; text of secret convention, 113-116. The evidence of these authorities and many others would seem to discredit the conclusion of C. W. Young that reference to "Russian and Japanese 'spheres of influence' there [in Manchuria], where none has ever existed" is unwarranted. Cf. his *Japan's Special Position in Manchuria*, 6.

[36] Griswold, *Far Eastern Policy of the United States*, 157.

[37] Croly, *Willard Straight*, 339-344. Straight and the Department of State also blamed the British for not co-operating with the United States. Griswold, however, holds that "it

CHINESE ADMINISTRATION IN MANCHURIA, 1905-1910

Meanwhile, as Russia and Japan delimited their spheres of "special interest" in Manchuria, what had become of Chinese administration there? After 1905, when the zeal of Chinese reformers was at its height in Peking, the old Manchurian military regime was abolished (1907) in favor of a viceroyalty, each of the Three Provinces being placed under a civil-governor.[38]

The function of these officials was to save Manchuria for the dynasty. The degree of success they enjoyed (1907-10) against the Russians and the Japanese has been indicated in the preceding pages.

THE ANNEXATION OF KOREA

In the struggle for empire which has been traced in this and the preceding chapter, it will be recalled that by 1905 Korea had become a Japanese protectorate, so recognized internationally. Roosevelt had written to Hay (January 29, 1905): "We cannot possibly interfere for the Koreans against Japan. They could not strike a blow in their own defense." [39] Nevertheless the emperor of Korea persisted in the belief during 1905 that the United States would come to his country's rescue because of the "good offices" clause in the Korean-American treaty of 1882.[40] The Department of State, however, had taken the view that the earlier Japanese-Korean agreements of 1904 had already created a Japanese protectorate, which Korea had not protested; she had thus deprived herself of any further grounds for appeal under the good offices clause of 1882. Such was the legal status of the case. But these legalities, it should be noted, do not present an adequate picture of the political aspects of American policy in 1905. In the political sense, American policy was not opposed to Japanese control of Korea. Roosevelt held that realistic politics demanded the sacrifice of Korean independence, and that a Korea controlled by Japan was preferable to a Korea controlled by Russia.[41]

---

is difficult to resist the conclusion that Knox deliberately misinterpreted Grey's replies, a well-known diplomatic practice to which Hay had also had recourse." *Far Eastern Policy of the United States,* 158. See also Reid, *Manchu Abdication,* 126-127.

[38] H. S. Brunnert and V. V. Hagelstrom, *Present-Day Political Organization of China* (Shanghai, 1912), 382-395.

[39] Tyler Dennett, *Roosevelt and the Russo-Japanese War* (Garden City, 1925), 110.

[40] Text in United States, *Statutes at Large,* XXIII, 720.

[41] Tyler Dennett, "American Good Offices in Asia," *American Journal of International Law,* XVI (1922), 22-24.

KOREA: A RESIDENCY-GENERAL

For the administration of her protectorate Japan created a residency-general (December 20, 1905) with one of her ablest statesmen, Hirobumi Ito, as resident-general. The resident-general was to control and direct matters relating to diplomatic affairs in addition to supervising other phases of the Korean government, such as the department of finance, previously subject to Japanese advice.[42] Within certain limits he had authority to issue ordinances and to suspend the operation of certain laws. He could control the appointment of Korean office-holders, but not the palace advisers with whom the emperor surrounded himself. It was through these that the emperor secretly maintained anti-Japanese contacts with Koreans in Russia and China.

EPISODE OF THE HAGUE PEACE CONFERENCE, 1907

Despite the fact that by 1907 the Korean royal palace was guarded by Japanese police, an official Korean delegation, bearing credentials from the emperor, and advised by H. B. Hulbert, an American teacher long resident in Korea, arrived at the Hague Peace Conference. The mission was to make known "the violation of our [Korean] rights by the Japanese" and to re-establish "direct diplomatic relations" with the powers.[43] Neither the Conference nor the Dutch government would receive the mission.

Japan acted promptly. Foreign Minister Tadasu Hayashi went to Seoul to confer with Ito. With the Elder Statesmen they agreed that "the hour had not yet come to push to extreme limits [annexation] the chastisement for the felony committed." Instead "the [Korean emperor] king was forced to abdicate the throne in favor of his son," and a new agreement was concluded "whereby the Japanese resident-general became a virtual regent." [44] Under this agreement all matters of internal administration as well as foreign relations were to be controlled by the resident-general.

With Japanese control tightening its grip on the entire Korean administration, the Korean problem as seen by the Japanese government again became an integral part of the larger Manchurian scene where, as we have noted, Japan and Russia had come to an understanding (in the 1907 and 1910 secret treaties) in order to block the financial and political

---

[42] United States, *Foreign Relations, 1906,* II, 1025 ff.

[43] *The Independent* (New York), LXIII (1907), 425.

[44] Price, *The Russo-Japanese Treaties,* 33; Tatsuji Takeuchi, *War and Diplomacy in the Japanese Empire* (Garden City, 1935), 162-163.

policies of Straight, Harriman, and Knox, with their dollar diplomacy. As early as the spring of 1909 Foreign Minister Komura had secured the approval of Premier Katsura and Prince Ito to a memorandum "strongly recommending" Korean annexation,[45] and by July the proposal had the approval of the cabinet and the emperor. Meanwhile Ito, having resigned as resident-general (June 14, 1909) to become president of the Privy Council, went to Harbin (October, 1909) to confer with Russian Minister of Finance Kokovtseff to prepare the way for a closer understanding with Russia.[46] On July 12, 1909, Viscount Sone, who had replaced Ito in Korea, had already secured an agreement placing the administration of Korean courts and prisons under direct Japanese control. Indeed, every preparation had been made for executing the predetermined policy of annexation. The assassination of Ito by a Korean (fanatic or patriot?) in Harbin (October 26, 1909) served only to increase the popular and public demand in Japan for immediate annexation.[47] On May 30, 1910, General Terauchi, retaining his post as Japanese minister of war, succeeded Sone as resident-general in Korea. On June 18, Prime Minister Katsura announced the intended annexation of Korea to the press. On June 22, the Tokyo government created "the Imperial Colonial Board, with Prime Minister Katsura as President, having under it the administration of Formosa, Sakhalin, the [Kwantung] Leased Territory, and Korea." [48] Then on June 24, the day on which the draft Russo-Japanese treaties of July 4, 1910, were shown to the British and French governments, the Korean police were placed under the command of the Japanese resident-general and minister of war. General Terauchi, "under heavy guard," reached Seoul on July 23. "All organs of public opinion" had been "suspended or ruthlessly suppressed." [49] In the audience that followed, Terauchi presented the young Korean sovereign with a face-saving means of escape: a request for annexation from the emperor of Korea to the emperor of Japan.[50] The treaty of annexation was signed August 22, 1910, and proclaimed seven days later.[51] In Japan annexation was "acclaimed as a great achievement." [52]

---

[45] Tatsuji Takeuchi, *War and Diplomacy in the Japanese Empire*, 164.

[46] Straight, it will be recalled, had negotiated the preliminary agreement for Anglo-American financing of the Chinchow-Aigun railway on October 2, 1909, after nearly three years of sporadic effort.

[47] Tatsuji Takeuchi, *War and Diplomacy in the Japanese Empire*, 164.

[48] Price, *The Russo-Japanese Treaties*, 59.

[49] Tatsuji Takeuchi, *War and Diplomacy in the Japanese Empire*, 165.

[50] Price, *The Russo-Japanese Treaties*, 60.

[51] Text in *British and Foreign State Papers, 1909-1910*, 992-993.

[52] Tatsuji Takeuchi, *War and Diplomacy in the Japanese Empire*, 167.

CHAPTER 20

FIRST YEARS OF REPUBLICANISM IN CHINA

IN 1911 the Manchu dynasty had ruled China for 267 years. Like other successful conquerors of the Middle Kingdom, it had recognized the superior cultural attainments of the conquered people, and it had associated Chinese with Manchus in government. Thus the dynasty not only held the Mandate of Heaven but also ruled at times with distinction. By mid-nineteenth century, however, the Manchus faced economic dislocation at home and the impact of the Western world of ideas on their seaboard. These conditions called for radical adjustments in China's political, economic, and social structure—adjustments which the Sino-Manchu political hierarchy could neither conceive nor execute. To be sure, in the face of impending disaster, the aging and incompetent Empress Dowager sought refuge in reform, but as was noted in the discussion of these measures (Chapter 17) her conversion was more apparent than real. To the last it was her purpose to give the shadow and not the substance of reform.

IMMEDIATE CAUSES OF THE REVOLUTION

A series of events which may be described as the immediate causes of the Revolution of 1911 began with the year 1908. There was the death of the unfortunate young emperor, Kuang-hsü, followed shortly by the passing of the old Empress Dowager herself. She had already provided for the succession by unwisely placing an infant on the throne, with the Manchu, Prince Ch'un, as nominal regent. Thus when death removed the strong, if unscrupulous hand of Old Buddha, the helm of state was legally in the keeping of a child directed by a regent who although well-meaning enough was almost completely devoid of political wisdom and the capacities of leadership. The seriousness of these events should be considered in relation to the complete Chinese picture during the first decade of the century: the abortive reforms of 1898, the disasters of the Boxer Revolt, the inroads of the Western powers and Japan, the use of Chinese soil as battlegrounds in the Russo-Japanese War, and the reduction of Manchuria to the status of Russian and Japanese spheres of influence. All of these events called for the appearance of dynamic and far-sighted leadership at Peking. Adding to the political void at Peking was the retirement of Yüan Shih-k'ai. Yüan had been the main support of the Empress Dowager. Among the high officers of the court and the metropolitan administration, he alone had some appreciation of the need of reform and some capacity to carry it into effect. With Yüan, there also went into retirement many of the abler lesser officials whom he had trained and who were responsive to his leadership. In October, 1909, Chang Chih-tung, the great Yangtze viceroy, died. The result was that while officially the reform program was continued, it became little more than a succession of edicts and blueprints.

THE NATIONAL ASSEMBLY

As already noted (Chapter 17), the reform program called for the creation of a national assembly. This body met for the first time in October, 1910. Since half of its members were Imperial appointees, and the remainder were chosen by a very narrow electorate, it was assumed that the assembly would be largely a rubber stamp for the government. Actually it proved to be anything but docile. It forced the government to promise a parliament in 1913 instead of after the longer nine-year period of preparation provided in the reform program. It threatened to impeach members of the government, and attacked its fiscal and administrative policies with vigor. Early in 1911 it demanded a responsible cabinet, winning the demand in principle at least before adjournment. At this point the weather vane of Chinese politics was pointing, albeit somewhat uncertainly, toward evolutionary constitutional reform rather than to political revolution. Yet within a few months the Manchu dynasty had abdicated, and a new government, republican in name, had taken its place.

THE RETURN OF FLOOD AND FAMINE

Conditions favorable to revolution were present in the China of 1910 and 1911. Pressure of population on the means of subsistence together with recurring crises of famine occasioned by flood and drought was in no sense a new feature of the Chinese scene. Such disasters had occurred many times in Chinese history, and, in the modern period, they had returned with startling frequency. In the twenty-five years preceding the Revolution of 1911, population had increased by perhaps as many as 50,000,000 persons, and while some of these found new homes in Manchuria and other sparsely populated areas of the empire or migrated abroad to Indo-China and the Malay States, these movements provided no relief for the basic problem of livelihood in China's populous regions. The years 1910 and 1911 marked the culmination of a series of bad seasons. Floods and drought in varying degree of intensity destroyed crops over a wide area. Estimates of the ravages and the toll of human life vary, but it is clear that hundreds of thousands died, and several millions were on the verge of starvation. Those who survived were psychologically prepared for any movement, rebellious or otherwise, which promised relief.

Throughout China discontent had also been fanned by rising taxes. Every measure in the reform program of 1901 and after had called for expenditure: the new army, new railroads, the new educational system. In addition, there were the charges on the Japanese war indemnity of 1895, and the more onerous charges of the Boxer Indemnity of 1901.

CENTRALIZATION VERSUS PROVINCIAL AUTONOMY

Closely linked with popular criticism of tax policies was the tendency of certain features of the reform program to encroach on the traditional autonomy of the provinces. In so far as the reform program possessed a real purpose, other than that of saving the dynasty, it was to give China a national progressive government capable of holding the sovereignty of the state, and of protecting it from foreign encroachment. This could only be done by sacrificing in large measure the autonomy of the provinces where, however, vested local interests were loathe to part with the prerogatives which time and custom had given them. It was the time-honored question of centralization versus decentralization, and the mores of China leaned heavily toward the latter.

The issue came to focus on the question of financing and thus controlling proposed trunk line railroads designed to be the first step in solving China's problem of communications. In the midst of the general agitation for reform after 1905, usually known as the "rights recovery" movement, there was a strong demand for railroad construction on a provincial rather than a national basis, and for financing these lines with Chinese rather than foreign funds. It was a natural reaction to foreign concession grabbing and foreign financial control, while at the same time it was an equally natural expression of traditional Chinese political habits. But it was an impractical policy. The huge sums necessary could not be raised in the provinces, and even such sums as were collected were dissipated in faulty speculation or unadulterated graft. Likewise, it was beginning to dawn on the Peking government that a program of national reform, if it were to be dominated by Peking, must presuppose national communications such as railroads. Accordingly, early in 1911, Peking began to prosecute with vigor its policy of railroad centralization. Foreign loans were contracted for the Hankow-Canton and Hankow-Szechwan trunk lines. At the same time the government sought to reach a settlement with the provincial interests involved. This proved to be difficult. Although the bonds with which Peking proposed to recompense the provinces concerned represented a reasonably liberal settlement, it did not satisfy the local interests. Official protests were lodged at Peking, and in Szechwan there were public demonstrations on a wide scale. Discontent took the form of an open, if, indeed, a minor, rebellion. It was a situation in which Peking, fearful lest the movement spread to other provinces, hesitated to act promptly or with force.[1]

THE REVOLUTION OF 1911

While the Imperial government was debating measures to settle the railroad troubles in Szechwan, an event of momentous import occurred in the central Yangtze Valley. At Hankow, on October 9, an explosion occurred within the Russian concession in a bomb factory operated by followers of Sun Yat-sen. Investigations led to the arrest and execution of a number of republican revolutionaries. These events precipitated a military revolt among troops at Wuchang across the river from Hankow, where leaders of the revolt dragged their commander, Colonel Li Yuan-hung, from under his bed, presenting him with the choice of immediate death or leadership of the rebellion. Being a practical man, though at the time far from a revolutionist, Colonel Li chose the latter. Within a brief period the three major cities of the middle Yangtze— Hankow, Hanyang, and Wuchang—were in rebel hands.

From this center, the revolt spread rapidly, particularly in the provinces south of the Yangtze. While revolts occurred in some regions of the north, such as Shensi, Shantung, and Chihli, generally speaking the north remained loyal to the Imperial government. The pattern was that of a series of local and largely bloodless rebellions seemingly uncoordinated and without unified leadership. The disclosure of revolutionary plans at Hankow had been premature. Revolutionists in widely scattered areas were not acting on a predetermined national plan.[2] While the Wuchang group was attempting to co-ordinate the movement by requesting provinces which had declared their independence to send delegates to a Wuchang revolutionary council, the revolution spread to Shanghai, where a new rebel government, led for the

---

[1] For a full discussion see P. H. Kent, *The Passing of the Manchus* (London, 1912).

[2] P. M. A. Linebarger, *Government in Republican China* (New York, 1938), 145.

moment by Wu T'ing-fang, a Cantonese and former Minister to the United States, attempted to speak for the revolution as a whole. Inter-revolutionary politics was thus making its appearance. The Shanghai group was dominated by Cantonese who were determined that leadership in the rebellion should not remain with the Yangtze provinces centered at Wuchang. Fortunately all the revolutionary groups were at one in their determination that the Manchus must go. This and Li Yuan-hung's willingness to give way to Shanghai's so-called "military government prevented an open break and permitted the Canton elements to lead." [3]

EFFECTS OF THE REVOLUTION IN PEKING

Peking, fearful of dealing vigorously with the revolt against its railway policies in Szechwan, was even less capable of meeting wisely the anti-dynastic revolts begun at Hankow. The government was embarrassed not only by rebellion, which was spreading to practically every region of South China, but also by the reconvening on October 22, less than two weeks after the Wuchang rising, of the National Assembly. Heartened by the general spirit of rebellion, the Assembly forced the dismissal of those who had pushed the national railroad policy; again demanded responsible cabinet government; insisted that a constitution be adopted only with the consent of the Assembly, and that political offenders be pardoned. Since many of the northern troops refused to move south to suppress the rebellions until these questions had been settled, the government had no recourse other than to grant the demands. On November 3, the dynasty gave its approval in edicts establishing a constitutional monarchy. Meanwhile the regent, Prince Ch'un, had induced Yüan Shih-k'ai to return to Peking by promising him unlimited powers. Yüan promptly resumed his command of the military forces, and on November 8 the National Assembly elected him premier.

THE POLICY OF YÜAN SHIH-K'AI

Yüan Shih-k'ai's critics have dealt harshly with his record. He has been characterized as "a soldier and diplomat from the North, narrow in outlook, altogether a tradition-bound official despite his up-to-date ideas—an opportunist and a realist in politics." [4] Actually Yüan was far more than these. While he had his limitations, and they were exceedingly large, he had shown genuinely progressive tendencies. He

---

[3] H. M. Vinacke, *Modern Constitutional Development in China* (Princeton, 1920), 102.
[4] Linebarger, *Government in Republican China*, 147.

was an opportunist and a realist but he was not altogether tradition-bound. Some of his non-military ideas were as up-to-date as his military ones. He was a progressive, capable of carrying out needed reforms, as the previous decade had shown, and a tried administrator in civil and particularly in military affairs. He was not a republican and did not believe in 1911 that republicanism was the answer to China's ills, in which view he was by no means alone among China's abler men. Like many other Chinese of sober thought, Yüan seems to have held to the view that it would be fatal for China to attempt a complete break with the spirit or the political machinery of the past, and that the stability of reform would depend in some major degree on Confucian mores and not exclusively on the adoption of Western ideologies.[5] Invested by the dynasty with supreme powers, and endowed by the National Assembly with the post of prime minister, Yüan's task was to put a stop to rebellion, and then to carry on the constitutional reforms of the Assembly. Yüan, however, appears to have entertained purposes more subtle than these. While not seeking the destruction of the dynasty, Yüan was for the time willing to permit the spread of the southern rebellions in order to force the Manchus to accept and play the role of the passive, constitutional monarchy. There appears to be no doubt that Yüan's Imperial forces were superior in every respect to the revolutionary armies of Li, yet the northern armies were never permitted to push their advantages to ultimate and decisive victory. So long as these conditions prevailed, Yüan was able to impose his will in Peking and also in the subsequent negotiations with the republican rebels.

THE REPUBLICAN LEADERSHIP

Opposed to Yüan, to the dynasty, and to the National Assembly stood the republican rebel armies of Li Yuan-hung, the so-called "military government" (Cantonese) at Shanghai, and the southern provinces which had declared their independence. Half of China was in the grip of a "spontaneous" revolt which lacked personal leadership. On October 10, when the Hankow incident occurred, Sun Yat-sen, a Cantonese revolutionist and exile, and the ideological leader of the revolution, was in the United States. Not until two months later (December 24, 1911) did this man, who had been the leader of the revolutionary movement since its inception, and who, more than any other, was to shape the political thinking of twentieth-century China, reach Shanghai.

Born in 1866 or 1867, Sun Yat-sen was reared in the rebellious Cantonese atmosphere which had nurtured the T'ai-p'ing and other revolts.

---

[5] A. M. Kotenev, *The Chinese Soldier* (Shanghai, 1937), 82-83.

Sun was introduced to Western life and learning through his attendance at school in Honolulu and medical college in Hongkong. Through these experiences his early rebel-patriotism was developed and matured into a philosophy of nationalism for China. His object was the creation of a modern nation-state. By the time of the Sino-Japanese War, 1894-95, Sun's ideas were finding expression through secret revolutionary organizations. The movement was first known as the *Hsing Chung Hui,* or Society for the Regeneration of China (1894-1905); for the next seven years (1905-1912), as the *T'ung Mêng Hui,* or League of Common Alliance; the *Kuomintang,* or National People's Party (1912-1914); the *Chung Hua Kê Ming Tang,* or Chinese Revolutionary Party (1914-1920); and, after 1920, the *Kuomintang.* The ideology of the movement was nationalistic, anti-dynastic, increasingly anti-monarchial, and, finally, republican.

THE PEACE NEGOTIATIONS

The return of Sun Yat-sen, while inspiring to the revolutionists, did not alter the fact that for the moment at least they were incapable of carrying the revolution to a successful conclusion or of holding its leadership. In the previous two decades the republican leaders had made the intellectual transition from Confucian to Western political ideology. This did not mean that Confucian ideology was absent from Sun's thought, nor did it signify that the Chinese masses had any understanding of the new philosophy. The balance between the hoary traditions of dynastic rule and the mysteries of republicanism was held not by Sun Yat-sen but by Yüan Shih-k'ai. With subtle appreciation of his political and military advantage, Yüan attempted to negotiate a settlement with Li Yuan-hung, finally agreeing with Li's consent to deal with the republican group at Shanghai. This was in December, 1911. Meanwhile, at Li's suggestion, delegates from the "independent" southern provinces assembled at a national convention in Nanking and elected Sun Yat-sen provisional president. It was this more unified republican regime which finally concluded the peace settlement with Yüan's representative, T'ang Shao-yi, an American-educated Cantonese.

In the ensuing negotiations the monarchy was brought to an end and a republic, in name at least, was created. Sun Yat-sen stepped down from the presidency, and at his suggestion the Nanking Convention elected Yüan Shih-k'ai first provisional president of the Republic of China. Sun's relinquishment of the presidency may have been due in some degree to his desire to remain solely the ideological leader of the new China, but the more decisive factor in his decision was the political and military power of Yüan.

The new regime was to be inaugurated with the arrival of Yüan at Nanking. However, Nanking represented the south and was controlled by the southern Republicans, while Yüan's armies were in the vicinity of Peking. This explains why a military mutiny engineered by Yüan near Peking made it inconvenient for the new president to leave the old capital. By this means Yüan was able to force the Republic under his own leadership to come to Peking, the home of tradition and conservatism. Furthermore, the abdication edicts, dictated by Yüan himself and promulgated on February 12, 1912, implied clearly that the new president derived his power by transfer from the throne rather than by mandate of the Republic, thus strengthening his position in the view of the tradition-minded masses.[6]

THE FOREIGN POWERS AND THE END OF THE DYNASTY

The end of the Manchu dynasty and the emergence of Yüan Shih-k'ai in a new position of power as president of the Republic of China were not due solely to the political and military advantages enjoyed by Yüan within China. Both the Republic and Yüan's leadership therein were in part the creation of the great foreign powers. From 1908 and even earlier, the fate of the Manchu dynasty rested on its capacity to prevent further disintegration in the political and social fabric of China, to arrest foreign concession hunters, and to forestall the ultimate partition of the empire by the foreign powers. In those crucial years between 1908 and 1912 the powers failed both singly and collectively to support the Imperial government to these ends. Indeed, the rivalries of the powers in their efforts to control China politically and economically weakened what little prestige was left to the dynasty and thereby invited provincial opposition to Peking's national railway policies. Again, the reforms which Peking planned for the border territories of Tibet, Mongolia, and Manchuria—reforms designed eventually to bring these areas into a national China—were frowned upon by England, Russia, and Japan. From the Wuchang rebellion in October, 1911, until the abdication edicts of February 12, 1912, the powers did nothing to prevent the collapse of the Imperial regime. On the contrary, they assisted Yüan Shih-k'ai in his ambitions to head the new Republic. As a result of

[6] Texts of the abdication edicts are in *The China Year Book, 1913* (Shanghai, 1913), 481-484.

conflicting power-interests and of commitments from some of the powers, Yüan was able to count on diplomatic and financial support before the conclusion of his negotiations with the southern republicans and before he had been elevated to the presidency. In a word:

> The powers were willing to permit a republic under Yüan; for they could bargain with him to recognize the *status quo* in exchange for political recognition and foreign loans; and such an arrangement would not interfere with autonomous Tibet, Turkistan, and outer Mongolia, nor with the special position of Russia and Japan in Manchuria, nor with the consortium's financial control plans for China.[7]

EARLY PHASES OF YÜAN'S GOVERNMENT

With the establishment of the Republic, China did not enter an era of republicanism but rather one of militarism. This is accounted for by a number of considerations.[8] The national army organized by Li Hung-chang and Yüan Shih-k'ai was a northern army; it was not truly national in character, and its officers thought of themselves as the servants of Yüan, not of the State. In the southern provinces during the revolution, authority tended to shift to those provincial leaders who could command the personal allegiance of troops in their respective areas. Thus both during and succeeding the Revolution, military authority was also political authority. Since as a result of revolutionary conditions the number of men under arms increased rapidly, there were few checks upon the power of these personal, and, in most cases, irresponsible, armies.

Not being in a position to destroy or disband these independent provincial armies, Yüan's only recourse was to make allies of them. This he did in a measure by appointing their commanders as provincial governors. Eventually he hoped to replace them by civil administrations responsive to his Peking government. This would be done by coaxing the provincial militarists into various government posts in the capital, thus separating them from their armies, the source of their strength. In these circumstances China was faced with militarism, national or local or a combination of both. There was no strong middle class to oppose the spread of militarism, and as for the masses, their

---

[7] John Gilbert Reid, *The Manchu Abdication and the Powers, 1908-1912* (Berkeley, 1935), 313. Note in particular the summary of the policies of the respective powers, 300 ff.

[8] For a contemporary discussion of the situation see Frank J. Goodnow, "Reform in China," *American Political Science Review*, IX (1915), 209-224. Goodnow, President of Johns Hopkins University, was constitutional adviser to President Yüan.

understanding of the Revolution was little more than a naïve belief that it meant the end of taxation.

Meanwhile, the new government was attempting to get under way at Peking under the terms of a Provisional Constitution adopted at Nanking in March, 1912. Being the product of southern republicanism, this Constitution was shaped with the idea of making the president subject to parliamentary will. Under it, the Nanking Convention or Council was to act as a parliament until elections had been held. Yüan's first cabinet represented a compromise between his own wishes and those of the parliament, but as early as the summer of 1912 the clash between executive and parliament was becoming apparent. In August, Sun Yat-sen's republican followers announced organization of their political party, the *Kuomintang,* to which Yüan replied by organizing his own Progressive Party, the *Chinputang.* When the new and first National Assembly under the Provisional Constitution met early in 1913, the *Kuomintang* held the strongest position but did not have absolute control. In July, a second republican revolt was suppressed by Yüan. Yet on October 10, 1913, the Assembly removed Yüan's provisional status by electing him president of the Republic. Less than a month later, November 4, Yüan suppressed the *Kuomintang.* Then by presidential decree, January 10, 1914, he "suspended" the Assembly and replaced it with his own Constitutional Council. This body brought forth on May 1, 1914, its own constitution, known as the Constitutional Compact. It created a "presidential government, and legitimatized" Yüan's dictatorship.

In this manner Yüan was attempting to pave the way for a restoration of monarchy with himself on the throne. In theory at least, constitutional monarchy as proposed in 1898 by K'ang Yu-wei seemed more likely to succeed than republicanism. This view was presented to Yüan in a memorandum, August 9, 1915, by his constitutional adviser, Professor Frank Goodnow. Goodnow pointed out the desirability, viewing China's problems of government in the abstract, "of establishing a constitutional monarchy *if* there was general demand for it rather than of maintaining the trappings of Republicanism without operative democracy." [9] As a result therefore of "a circus of plebiscites and constitutional councils," constitutional monarchy was proclaimed in December, 1915. It was short-lived. No considerable body of the Chinese people had any understanding of the relative merits of constitutional monarchy versus republicanism but there were provincial and republican leaders

---

[9] Linebarger, *Government in Republican China,* 153-154.

with following enough to oppose Yüan as a monarch of any kind. Revolt promptly flared in Yünnan and spread rapidly through the south. Yüan renounced the throne in March, and died three months later, on June 6, 1916.[10]

DOLLAR DIPLOMACY AND THE REVOLUTION

The collapse of the Manchu dynasty, as noted, was due in part to the acquiescence of the powers. In like manner, the hope of a stable republic would depend in great measure on the diplomatic and financial policies of the same great powers. China's new republican government of 1912 was "without funds and with increasing unpaid obligations." [11] It was inevitable that China should seek foreign financial aid which, however, could not be divorced from implications of foreign political control. It should be recalled that the Revolution of 1911 was, among other things, a reaction and protest against the foreign scramble for concessions which followed the Sino-Japanese War of 1894-95, and which continued with increasing intensity until the outbreak of the Revolution. Indeed the politico-financial rivalry of the powers was so great that they themselves began to favor pooling certain types of loans to China through an international banking agency called the consortium. This agency was to be composed of groups of bankers designated by their respective governments. Thus loans made through the consortium would be subject to a double test: their acceptability to the bankers on economic grounds, and to the powers on political grounds. In its embryonic stage in 1909 the consortium included only British, French, and German banking groups who were proposing to finance and construct for the Chinese government the so-called Hukuang railways in Central and South China.[12]

The Hukuang railways were to reach southward from Hankow to Canton, and also westward from Hankow into Szechwan. When, however, in the spring of 1909, the British, French, and German banking groups signed the contract for the construction of these lines, they encountered diplomatic opposition first from the United States and then from Russia and Japan. As early as 1898, United States interests represented by the American-China Development Company had secured a contract from the Chinese government to build a railroad from Hankow to Canton. Later, in 1904 and 1905, the Chinese, the British,

---

[10] For a more detailed discussion of the monarchy movement, see Vinacke, *Modern Constitutional Development in China,* 179-211.

[11] C. F. Remer, *Foreign Investments in China* (New York, 1933), 126.

[12] See F. V. Field, *American Participation in the China Consortiums* (New York, 1931).

and the French governments admitted the right of American capital to a share in a loan for another railroad from Hankow to Chengtu, but as late as 1909 "no American financial interests had expressed a desire to participate." [13]   But, while American financiers had shown no desire to follow up these early American concessions or to compete with European capital in China, the Taft administration for purposes of high policy was determined that they should enter the field actively. At the instance of the State Department an American banking group was formed, headed by J. P. Morgan and Company, and, when opposition to the entry of this group into the consortium and the Hukuang loan was encountered, President Taft appealed directly to Prince Ch'un, the regent.[14]   The Taft policy in Central China, as previously noted in the case of Manchuria, was to inject American capital into China as a means of creating an open door policy and preserving the territorial integrity of the empire.   Finally, in May, 1911, on the eve of the Revolution, the American group was admitted to the consortium, but at the price of bitter European resentment.[15]

With the progress of the Revolution and the establishment of the Republic, the interest of the consortium, on the surface at least, was directed toward providing the impecunious government at Peking with funds to maintain itself and to create stable conditions throughout the empire.   In principle, the Republic was to be assisted through international financial co-operation.   However, the road to this objective was beset with many obstacles.   Russia and Japan, though borrowing countries, demanded admission to the consortium.   Their banking groups were admitted in June, 1912.   Here it should be emphasized that this expanded six-power consortium represented not merely an interest in investment banking but also the political interests of their respective governments relative to China.   New difficulties appeared as this larger consortium renewed its negotiations with Peking.   The Chinese administration objected to several features of the consortium.   The loan terms demanded by the bankers and the control measures which they proposed to exercise over expenditures were regarded by the Chinese as excessive.   Furthermore, in the view of the Chinese government and of foreign bankers who were not included in the various groups, the consortium was really an attempt to create a monopoly controlling

[13] William Phillips, Chief of the Far Eastern Division of the State Department, to Secretary Knox, June 10, 1909.   Knox papers, quoted by A. Whitney Griswold, *Far Eastern Policy of the United States* (New York, 1938), 143.
[14] United States, *Foreign Relations, 1909*, 178.
[15] Herbert Croly, *Willard Straight* (New York, 1924), 390-394.

the Chinese loan market.[16]   Therefore, while the consortium was ready
to advance to China a large reorganization loan, the Peking government
attempted to negotiate on more favorable terms with independent
bankers in London.

In the midst of this complicated political-financial wire-pulling at Peking, the Wilson administration had come into power at Washington.
The timid American banking group asked whether it would continue
to enjoy in its China investments the active support of the Department
of State. President Wilson replied on March 18, 1913, withdrawing
official support from the American group because he found the control
measures of the proposed reorganization loan "to touch very nearly the
administrative independence of China itself." [17] Taft had pushed
American bankers into China to preserve the open door. Wilson refused to support them there because their activities, along with the activities of the other groups, threatened China's independence.

The Reorganization Loan Agreement was concluded without American participation on April 26, 1913.[18] Thereby China did acquire funds
in an hour of great need, but the negotiations preceding the loan agreement were a revelation of power politics. The consortium was designed to stabilize the new Chinese Republic, but Sun Yat-sen regarded
the reorganization loan as a means whereby President Yüan would
destroy his political opponents in the *Kuomintang*.[19] Yüan himself
regarded the terms of the loan as incompatible with China's administrative integrity.[20] Finally, the consortium, concerned with China as a
political problem rather than a financial one,[21] resulted in "impairing
rather than strengthening the territorial integrity of China." [22] The
young and nominal Republic of China was facing a hazardous childhood.

SEPARATIST MOVEMENTS IN BORDER TERRITORIES

The transition from Manchu empire to Chinese republic was the occasion too for various rebellions and "independence" movements in the
former empire dependencies of Mongolia and Tibet. During the decade preceding the Revolution of 1911, the Mongol nobility had grown
restive as Chinese settlers encroached on Inner Mongolia, and as Peking

[16] Remer, *Foreign Investments in China,* 126.
[17] See MacMurray, *Treaties,* II, 1025.
[18] MacMurray, *Treaties,* II, 1007-1038.
[19] See Sun's public appeal, *The Times* (London), May 3, 1913.
[20] Griswold, *Far Eastern Policy of the United States,* 171.
[21] Remer, *Foreign Investments in China,* 127.
[22] Griswold, *Far Eastern Policy of the United States,* 174.

attempted to extend the government of China Proper to this area. Mongol disaffection was encouraged by Russia, whose agents stimulated a nationalist movement. In December, 1911, an independent Mongol government came into being at Urga. China combatted the movement by attempting to re-establish her authority in Inner Mongolia, only to be countered by Russian recognition of the Urga government in November, 1912. A year later (November, 1913) Russia and the Republic of China agreed that Outer Mongolia was "autonomous" but not "independent." Nearly two years later (June, 1915) Mongolia accepted this status in an agreement between herself, Russia, and China.

The Revolution of 1911 was also the signal for trouble in Tibet. The Tibetans drove the Chinese garrison from the country, and, as an independent people, proceeded to conclude an agreement (January, 1913) with the new and independent Mongolian government. When Yüan Shih-k'ai sought to re-establish by force China's authority at Lhasa, he encountered British diplomatic opposition. It was not until 1914 that an agreement was worked out among Tibet, China, and Britain whereby western Tibet (Tibet Proper) was to be autonomous, the Chinese maintaining a resident and small guard at Lhasa, while in eastern Tibet the authority of China was to be retained. Although this convention was not ratified by China, it set the pattern for future political controls in Tibet.[23]

These disturbances in the border territories of Mongolia and Tibet were symptomatic of many of the major political ills from which China was suffering. The fall of the Manchu dynasty brought with it the collapse of the ideology which had held its heterogeneous peoples together. China's retention of nominal suzerainty in these areas was due in no sense to her own strength but to the fact that Britain and Russia, content with the substance of power, were indifferent to relics of Confucian political theory.

IN CONCLUSION

The first years of revolution and nominal republicanism in China (1911-16) were essentially years of confusion. The old, alien, Confucian monarchy had lost the Mandate of Heaven, but there had not been adequate preparation for a successor. There was "no victorious leader to assert that the heavenly commission had fallen to him." [24] On the contrary, the only *immediate* leadership produced by the Revolution was that of the military politician and adventurer. The followers of

---

[23] M. J. Bau, *The Foreign Relations of China* (New York, 1922), 104, 140.
[24] E. R. Hughes, *The Invasion of China by the Western World* (London, 1937), 131.

Sun Yat-sen and other intellectual groups, carried away by their enthusiasm for foreign institutions and having no practical knowledge as
to how to make them work, failed to control the new Republic because
in the first place they did not command the military power, and in the
second their concepts of republicanism were not yet intelligible to the
masses.

Cohesive political qualities basic to national patriotism were as strange
to the China of 1911 as were the theory and practice of republicanism.
Consequently, power remained where the Revolution had left it: in the
hands of military leaders. The "twilight" of dynasty had given place
to the "grey dawn" of a republic.[25]

---

[25] Discussions of the passing of the Manchu dynasty by many modern writers, including
spokesmen of the *Kuomintang,* frequently employ such terms in reference to the Manchus
as "foreign Manchu rulers," "foreign dynasty," and "alien dynasty," which at worst are
inaccurate, and at best lead to confusion in thought. The point is that those who characterize the Manchu dynasty as "foreign" or "alien" also frequently claim the Manchu
people and country as Chinese and subject to Chinese rule. Logically, if the Manchus
are a part of China (and in modern times this would certainly seem to be so), then the
Manchu dynasty is also Chinese as of 1644, when its rule in China began. If the Manchu
dynasty was foreign, then there was no Chinese state between 1644 and 1912; it was a
Manchu empire employing Chinese subjects in office, etc. There could be no China other
than a Manchu China during that period. The official designation was the Ta Ch'ing
Kuo (Great Pure Empire or Realm).

CHAPTER 21

THE FAR EAST AND THE FIRST WORLD WAR

CONSIDERED in terms of its immediate causes and in terms of its military and naval campaigns, World War I was primarily a European conflict. Germany, to be sure, did hold some scattered insular colonies in the Pacific and the leased territory of Kiaochow in Shantung, China, but as these were soon taken over by Allied forces, the military aspects of the war were confined to the European theater. No major battles were fought on Asiatic soil or in Asiatic waters. Nevertheless, at one time or another during the conflict, all the major lands and peoples of Asia were aligned with the Allied and Associated Powers. By their participation in the war, the peoples of eastern Asia were united, formally at least, with the Western democracies in the crusade against German militarism, and, after 1917, in the Wilsonian crusade to "make the world safe for democracy." Thus eastern Asia became a participant in the war despite the fact that it was not intimately concerned with the war's immediate causes.

In contrast with the immediate causes, the more remote or underlying causes of the war involved the Far East intimately just as they came eventually to involve the interests of the United States and other powers of the Western Hemisphere. These remote, underlying causes, reaching far back into the traditions and practices of European history, were extraordinarily complex. They involved "the psychology of fear, and all other factors which go to make up the somewhat vague conceptions of 'militarism' and 'navalism' as causes of war."[1] They involved the powerful and disruptive forces of nationalism as they developed in the century following the French Revolution, encompassing, as they did, the political and prejudicial questions of race, religion, democracy, and education. With these were mingled grave problems created by the new industrialization of the more "advanced" powers: "excess population, food supply, foreign markets and raw materials,

---

[1] For a detailed discussion of underlying causes, see Sidney B. Fay, *The Origins of the World War* (2 vols. in one, New York, 1931), I, 32-49.

colonial possessions, and the accumulation of capital seeking investment abroad," as, for example, in the spheres of influence in China.

All of these underlying causes of conflict had taken root in the political, the economic, and the cultural soil of the Far East. By 1914 all the great peoples of Asia, the Japanese excepted, were in colonial or semi-colonial status to one or more of the great Western powers or Japan. The Republic of China, though referred to as an independent, sovereign state, was far from being one. Its authority had already been challenged in the border areas of Tibet, Mongolia, and Manchuria, by Britain, Russia, and Japan. Within China Proper, all the great powers, including Japan, enjoyed the fruits of the so-called unequal treaties: extraterritoriality, the conventional tariff, concessions or settlements, and the right to maintain gunboats and troops in Chinese waters and on limited areas of Chinese soil.

From these underlying conditions, briefly suggested, were to arise the involvements of the Far East in World War I.

JAPAN ENTERS THE WAR

Japan's entrance into World War I derived its sanction from a double basis: the nation's commitments under the Anglo-Japanese Alliance, and the larger political and military purposes of Japan's emerging Asiatic policy.

Prior to Great Britain's entry into the war, Japanese public opinion, regarding the conflict as purely a European affair, favored, as did public sentiment in the United States, a policy of neutrality. But as Britain entered the conflict, the Japanese press assumed a new and militant tone. It recalled Germany's role in the Triple Intervention of 1895; it reminded the public of Japan's obligations to Great Britain under the Alliance, and to France and Russia under the treaties of 1907 and later; it charged that German naval power in the Pacific was a threat to all neutral shipping, and that German military preparations at Kiaochow were a menace to the peace of the Far East; and finally, it advocated attack on Germany's far eastern possessions.[2] By rapid steps, the Japanese press, never wholly free from official inspiration, was finding cause for entering the war in the purposes of the Anglo-Japanese Alliance, the preamble of which was dedicated to the maintenance of peace and the territorial rights of the signatories and their special interests in eastern Asia and India.

Great Britain, however, approached the matter of Japanese assistance

---

[2] The campaign of the Japanese press is summarized in "Why Japan Attacks Germany," *The Literary Digest*, XLIX (September 19, 1914).

under the Alliance with the utmost caution. The British plan of grand strategy in the Pacific, calling for seizure by the Australian navy of German wireless stations in New Guinea, Yap, and Nauru, was blocked unexpectedly by the Australian demand for destruction of the German Pacific squadron as of first concern. Whether British naval forces in the Pacific could have dealt decisively with the powerful fleet of the German admiral, von Spee, is a question on which naval authorities have differed. It is at least doubtful whether it could have done so without assistance from Japan.[3]

On the diplomatic front prior to Britain's declaration of war, the Japanese government had assured Sir Edward Grey that a German attack on Hongkong or Wei-hai-wei would be grounds for invoking the Alliance. Grey had replied to this "generous offer of assistance" saying it was hoped Japan's involvement would not be necessary. This was before Britain's declaration of war and before she was aware of Australian views on naval plans. On August 4, Britain declared war, and three days later, August 7, she requested Japan to destroy the German fleet in Pacific waters. The decision of the Japanese government, made August 8, was to demand of Germany not only surrender of its armed ships in Asiatic waters (thus complying with the British request), but also to demand surrender of the Kiaochow leasehold in Shantung. This momentous decision to join Great Britain in the war (as explained by Count Komei Kato, the Foreign Minister) was not based on legal obligations of the Anglo-Japanese Alliance, for "the general conditions were not such as to impose upon Japan the duty to join the war under treaty obligations," but "as a voluntary expression of friendship toward Great Britain under the alliance."[4] In addition, Japan also welcomed the occasion "as an opportunity to destroy the German influence from eastern Asia and to enhance the international position of Japan."[5]

The inclusion of Kiaochow in the Japanese reply brought prompt reactions in London. The British felt that a Japanese attack on Kiaochow would imply a full extension of the war to Chinese territory, ad-

---

[3] For the naval situation in the Pacific see Julian Corbett, *History of the Great War. . . . Naval Operations* (3 vols., London, 1920-23), I; and Thomas G. Frothingham, *The Naval History of the World War: Offensive Operations, 1914-15* (Cambridge, 1924). Winston Churchill, then First Lord of the British Admiralty, believed that Britain could cope with Germany's naval power in the Pacific. Other naval authorities, including Admiral von Tirpitz, have differed with him. For various aspects of the debate see: Arthur W. Jose, *The Royal Australian Navy* (Sydney, 1928); Winston Churchill, *The World Crisis, 1911-1914* (New York, 1924); M. D. Kennedy, *Some Aspects of Japan and Her Defense Forces* (London, 1928); and Grand Admiral A. von Tirpitz, *My Memoirs* (London, 1919).

[4] Tatsuji Takeuchi, *War and Diplomacy in the Japanese Empire* (Chicago, 1935). 169.

[5] Takeuchi, 169-170.

versely affecting British commercial interests there. Therefore Britain hoped Japan would confine her activities "to protection of the sea trade and postpone her declaration of war." Japan countered with the statement that her Kiaochow proposal was conceived as the best means of safeguarding this sea trade. Britain now reversed her position completely; on August 11, she withdrew her request for assistance under the Alliance.

It was then Japan's turn to feel embarrassment. Public opinion favored war; the cabinet had already made its decision, sanctioned by the Throne; and tension had been heightened by reports that the German ambassador in Tokyo had used threatening language at the foreign office. To have reversed its decision would have rendered untenable the position of the Okuma cabinet.[6] From this dilemma Kato was partly relieved on August 13, when Grey, again reversing himself, agreed to a Japanese ultimatum to Germany for surrender of armed vessels and also of Kiaochow. Grey requested, however, that Japan confine her zone of activity "to the German base and the neighboring China seas," and that this limitation be stated in the ultimatum to Germany. However, on August 15, with Britain's consent the Japanese ultimatum was dispatched without the reservation. It reviewed the peaceful aims of the Anglo-Japanese Alliance; it advised Germany to withdraw all armed vessels from Chinese and Japanese waters, to disarm any that could not be withdrawn, and to deliver to Japan by September 15 "without condition or compensation," the Kiaochow leasehold "with a view to eventual restoration of the same to China." An answer was required not within the customary 48-hour period but within eight days, namely, by August 23.[7]

Barring an improbable German acceptance of the ultimatum, Japan was committed to war, yet the British government made a further effort to limit the sphere of Japanese action. In a press release, August 18, it described the ultimatum as designed "to protect the general interests in the Far East contemplated by the Anglo-Japanese Alliance," and referred in particular to the independence and the integrity of China. The statement continued:

It is understood that the action of Japan will not extend to the Pacific Ocean beyond the China Seas, except in so far as it may be necessary to protect Japanese shipping lines in the Pacific, nor beyond Asiatic waters west-

[6] See the detailed discussion by Charles Nelson Spinks, "Japan's Entrance into the World War," *Pacific Historical Review,* V (1936), 297-311; also Thomas E. LaFargue, *China and the World War* (Stanford University, 1937), 3-27.
[7] Spinks, "Japan's Entrance into the World War," 308-309.

ward of the China Seas, nor to any foreign territory except territory in German occupation on the Continent of Eastern Asia.[8]

The implications of this statement brought forth from Count Shigenobu Okuma, the Japanese premier, a denial of territorial ambitions and the assurance that Japan's war activities would be limited to "self-defense." At the same time Kato protested the British statement, and, as a result, the British government gave public assurance that Japan's purpose was to eliminate German influence from China, thereby removing a menace to the peace of the Far East. "She [Japan] harbours no designs for territorial aggrandizement and entertains no desire to promote any other selfish end." [9]

On August 23, Germany having ignored the ultimatum, Japan entered the war. From August 7, when Great Britain first requested assistance, the eventual entry of Japan was never in doubt. It is equally clear that Britain's hope of limiting Japan's field of action was foredoomed to fail. As noted, Kato's policy was not confined by considerations of the Anglo-Japanese Alliance alone. Of at least equal weight was the opportunity to destroy German influence in the Far East "and to enhance the international position of Japan." Neither of these objectives in the Japanese view would have been served by limitations upon her freedom of military and naval action.

THE NEUTRALITY OF CHINA AND THE PACIFIC

The outbreak of war in Europe had aroused great alarm in Peking. If hostilities spread to the Far East, China's foreign trade would be adversely affected; customs revenues would shrink; and Yüan Shih-k'ai's government would thereby lose its most important source of revenue. Peking would be forced to seek loans abroad. Little could be expected from the United States in view of Wilson's policy toward the consortium bankers. If the war were prolonged, less and less capital could be expected from Europe. Thus a weakened China would rest more and more on the dictates of Japanese policy. China's interests, reasoned Peking, would best be served by exclusion of her territories and waters from the zone of hostilities.

With the outbreak of hostilities, therefore, China attempted to enlist American diplomatic action as an instrument "of her own national policy." She proposed, August 3, 1914, that the United States "endeavor to obtain the consent of the belligerent European nations to an

[8] *The Times* (London), August 18, 1914, quoted by Spinks, "Japan's Entrance into the World War," 309.

[9] *The Times* (London), August 21, 1914.

understanding not to engage in hostilities either in Chinese territory
and marginal waters or in adjacent leased territories." [10]   On the assumption presumably that the neutrality of China was closely linked
with the principle of territorial integrity dear to American official policy,
Secretary of State Bryan approved the neutralization of foreign settlements and concessions in China but not of leased territories, and he
approached the European powers on an even more ambitious scheme
designed to neutralize the entire Pacific Ocean as well as China and its
adjacent waters.   However, none of the belligerents favored the idea
save Germany.[11]   Furthermore, while the Bryan proposal for neutralization of the Pacific rested on a plane of high moral policy, the United
States was not prepared to enforce its suggestion with sanctions.

KIAOCHOW

Following promptly on her declaration of war on August 23, 1914,
Japan proceeded to the investment of the Kiaochow leased territory and
its port of Tsingtao.   With this port under naval blockade, Japanese
military forces, landing on Chinese soil far to the north, moved to attack
Tsingtao from the rear and to occupy the railway zone reaching from
Tsingtao to Tsinan far in the interior of the province.[12]   As in previous
cases, China was unprepared physically and in morale to defend her
neutrality.   She had already formally declared this neutrality and she
now protested Japan's action, but she followed this protest with a proclamation delimiting a war zone in areas adjacent to Kiaochow.   In so doing she was following the precedent established in Manchuria in 1904 at
the suggestion of the United States.   Since Japan promptly ignored the
war zone, it was again patent that China could neither keep the war
from her shores nor control its course within her borders.[13]

Kiaochow surrendered on November 10, and Japan proceeded to take
over not only the leased territory but also all German interests in Shantung, including the Tsingtao-Tsinan Railway and branch lines, mining
properties, and other miscellaneous German holdings, including public

---

[10] United States, *Foreign Relations, 1914* (Supplement), 162 ff.
[11] For a more detailed discussion of China's efforts to enlist American aid in the neutralization proposal, see A. W. Griswold, *The Far Eastern Policy of the United States* (New
York, 1938), 176-180.
[12] A small British force was also engaged for "token" purposes.
[13] Both the Allies and Germany ignored the fundamental issue of China's neutrality.
The Germans used the Tsingtao-Tsinan Railway to carry troops from Tientsin and reservists from other areas into the leased territory.   The European powers also used Chinese
railroads to reach their fighting fronts.   Moreover, for the Germans at this time it should
be said that they were going to defend Tsingtao from attack and not to launch an offensive, as were Japan and England, across Chinese neutral territory.

works.   Japan also took over from the Chinese, on the plea of military necessity, the policing of the railroads outside the leased territory.   Japanese replaced Germans in the Chinese customs office at Tsingtao.   The ousting of Germany was thorough and complete, and when in December members of the Japanese Diet called on the government for a declaration of policy, Count Kato, though declining to give a definite statement of policy, declared emphatically "that Japan was not committed to any power" on the future of Kiaochow.[14]   While the Okuma government was thus reserving to itself full liberty of action, on January 7, 1915, China cancelled the war zone on the ground that it was no longer necessary, all German resistance in Shantung having ceased. This cancellation, it will be seen, was to provide the pretext for further Japanese action.

NATURE OF THE GERMAN RIGHTS IN SHANTUNG

Since the ultimate disposition of the German rights in Shantung was to claim worldwide attention, and since these German rights were typical in many respects of the system of special privilege, particularly economic privilege, in South Manchuria after 1898, the nature and scope of these rights which Japan was to claim as a result of her military victory are matters of importance.   They included among others the following: 1) China had conferred upon Germany a 99-year lease of both sides of Kiaochow Bay, on which Germany erected fortifications and in which Germany had exercised "rights of administration"; 2) within a zone of 50 kilometers of the bay, German troops held the right of freedom of passage, and Chinese administration was subject to German approval; 3) Germany acquired the right to construct certain railroads in Shantung, a provision which resulted in the building of the Tsingtao-Tsinan Railway by a Sino-German concern, the Shantung Railway Company; 4) Germany also acquired the right to mine coal within 30 *li* of the railroads; 5) if Germany desired to return Kiaochow to China before the expiration of the lease, China engaged to lease "to Germany a more suitable place"; 6) Germany engaged not to sublet the territory to another power, but there was no provision regarding the transfer of the territory by Germany to another power as a result of conquest such as the Japanese action of 1914; 7) if assistance in the form of capital or services or materials were needed for any undertaking in Shantung province, China had agreed to approach German nationals.   Under these suggestive privileges, Germany had built a modern port at Tsingtao, had extended a railroad far into the interior of the province, and

[14] Tatsuji Takeuchi, *War and Diplomacy in the Japanese Empire*, 180-181.

had developed broad commercial undertakings, while at Kiaochow she possessed a naval base from which her Pacific squadron operated. It should be recalled, however, that her position in this respect was comparable in its *political* implications with that of Great Britain at Kowloon, with France at Kwangchow, and with Japan at Port Arthur.[15] So far as these powers were concerned in 1914, the question raised was not primarily one of returning these German rights in Shantung to China. Rather it was the question: How would Japan's acquisition of these rights affect the balance of power at Peking?[16]

JAPAN'S NAVAL OPERATIONS

While Japanese naval and military forces were engaged in the reduction of Tsingtao and in taking over other German interests in Shantung, units of the Japanese navy were operating in the Pacific and Indian Oceans in co-operation with the British against German commerce raiders. Early in these operations, while the Australians were occupying German colonies and islands south of the equator, the Japanese occupied the German islands north of the equator. These included the Marianas (excepting Guam), the Carolines, and the Marshalls. Consisting of more than two thousand small islands and coral reefs, the three groups were widely scattered over a vast area of the western Pacific Ocean—an area almost as large as continental United States. By occupying these stepping stones Japan extended her territorial conquests

---

[15] The British at Kowloon did not have the extensive economic rights in the Chinese hinterland that Germany had in Shantung.

[16] For texts of the German-Chinese agreements affecting Shantung see MacMurray, *Treaties,* I, 112, 189; and Ge-Zay Wood, *The Shantung Question* (New York, 1922), Appendix A. The English text of the leasehold agreement translated from the German in contrast with that translated from the Chinese employs the term "cede" instead of "lease" and the phrase "rights of sovereignty" as against "rights of administration."

The problem of 1915 from the standpoint of the Western powers may be compared with later events of 1937 (see Chapter 36). On each occasion the European powers were impotent in the Far East because of war or imminent war. The only great power free to act was the United States and on each occasion it refrained. Japan as a result had a free field.

However, no analogy here should be pushed too far for in many respects the two situations were quite different. In 1915 the European powers were at war and were in no position to act thousands of miles away in an area that was highly peripheral. In 1937 the European powers were not at war (though war was certainly threatening), and therefore had more freedom of action. Moreover, in 1915 the actions carried out by Japan were launched at a time when Japan was allied with Britain, France, and Russia. In 1937 Japan was not allied with any of these, but on the contrary was moving closer to Germany. Thus, whereas in 1915 action against Japan might have had the effect of impeding the European war effort, in 1937 measures to curb Japanese expansion would have been thoroughly consistent with opposition to German expansion. The problems of Germany and Japan were of one piece in 1937, something which was not true in 1915.

and influence to a zone of the Pacific which previously had been controlled exclusively by Europe and the United States. Japan's flag had penetrated eastward and southward into the Pacific 2,800 miles from Tokyo to Jaluit in the Marshalls, more than half the distance to the American naval outpost at Pearl Harbor in the Hawaiian Islands. In like manner Japan became a close neighbor of British and French colonies in the South Pacific. More important, however, in the view of the time, was the control which Japan acquired over the network of German-Dutch submarine telegraph cables linking the East Indies and China by way of the tiny island of Yap in the Carolines. The implications of this Japanese penetration of the Pacific were overshadowed at the time by reason of Japan's military alignment with the European democracies (at the time it was convenient to forget that Russia was not a democracy), but these same implications along with Japan's penetration of Shantung suggest the grounds for Great Britain's desire to limit the zone of Japan's military action.[17]

With the occupation of the Pacific islands and the elimination of German commerce raiders from the Pacific and Indian Oceans, Japan's major military contributions to the war were completed. She continued, however, to convoy Australian and New Zealand troops to the European theater, and during the German submarine campaigns of 1917, Japan sent three destroyer divisions to the Mediterranean. Nevertheless, from the beginning of 1915, Japan's relationship to the war was essentially non-military. In the first instance, Japanese factories became the great supply depots for the Russian armies on the eastern European front; in the second, Japan's policies in China appeared as a threat not only to Western commercial interests there but also to certain political principles emerging in the pattern of Allied war aims.

THE BACKGROUND OF THE TWENTY-ONE DEMANDS

On January 18, 1915, Japanese Minister Hioki at Peking presented to President Yüan Shih-k'ai a group of twenty-one demands designed to "insure" Japan's position in China at a time when Europe was preoccupied with war. The fundamental policy behind the demands was not new. In its origins, it dated back to the beginnings of Japanese expansion in the 1870's. What was now to happen in 1915 was a more intensi-

---

[17] On the Pacific islands taken over by Japan in 1914 see: Paul H. Clyde, *Japan's Pacific Mandate* (New York, 1935), 14-26; Paul H. Clyde, "Stepping-Stones to Empire," *Amerasia,* VI (1943), 522-529; Willard Price, *Pacific Adventure* (New York, 1936); *The Japan Year Book, 1938-39* (Tokyo, 1939), 1001-1016; and Willard Price, *Japan's Islands of Mystery* (New York, 1944).

fied, a brazenly far-reaching application of the principles of power politics which, although employed by European powers against China on numerous occasions, had never been used with the spirit of reckless abandon which was to characterize the Twenty-One Demands.

The reader will recall that though the Russo-Japanese War of 1904-05 may have settled some far eastern problems, it likewise created new ones. These new and vexing problems were concerned principally with the clash of Sino-Japanese interests in South Manchuria, the sphere of influence which Japan had taken over from Russia in 1905. After the annexation of Korea in 1910, both the Japanese government and the Japanese public became more vitally concerned with the status and future of Japanese interests in Manchuria. As early as January, 1913, Count Taka-akira Kato, before leaving London to become foreign minister in the Okuma cabinet, informed Grey that "Japan entertained vital political and psychological concern in the Kwantung Peninsula . . . and South Manchuria"; that Japan was "determined to maintain a permanent occupation of the Kwantung Province"; and that if a "psychological moment" arrived, Japan would seek to extend her leasehold and concessions there.[18] Thus, long before 1915 it was Japan's policy to insure the nation's paramount interests in South Manchuria by means of more specific and inclusive treaty concessions from China.

Closely linked with these Manchurian interests, a second phase of Japanese policy in January, 1915, concerned itself with the nation's position and influence south of the Great Wall in China Proper. In the scramble there for railway and mining concessions, Japan as a debtor nation had found herself at a disadvantage against European and American competitors. Her vexation was the greater because Yüan Shih-k'ai appeared to favor Western rather than Japanese concession hunters. It was humiliating to note that even Belgian capitalists fared better in China Proper than did Japanese. The entry of Japan into the first consortium had not altered matters materially because the consortium as finally constituted dealt only with loans covering political and currency reform, leaving industrial loans (railways, mines, etc.) open to general competition by the powers. Success would be with the powers having the largest purse and offering the most generous credit. It all added up to the fact that successive Japanese governments, recognizing the handicap under which Japanese capital operated, were unwilling to acquiesce in a European financial and railway monopoly in China Proper.[19]

---

[18] Tatsuji Takeuchi, *War and Diplomacy in the Japanese Empire*, 183-185.
[19] LaFargue, *China and the World War*, 28-32.

The European war offered Japan an opportunity to challenge this European advantage in China Proper. At the same time, however, Japan's military action in Shantung placed a further strain on diplomatic relations between Peking and Tokyo—relations already endangered by the clash of interests in South Manchuria.

This increasing tension between Tokyo and Peking had been aggravated late in 1914 by China's various appeals to the United States. The first of these, as already noted, was the effort to secure through American action an inter-power declaration neutralizing Chinese territory. When this failed, and when it became evident that Japan proposed to attack in Shantung, China again sought to protect herself through American intervention. In this case the Chinese government strongly intimated that the Root-Takahira notes of 1908 [20] established in favor of the United States a *right* to be consulted by Japan before the latter embarked on any military action affecting Chinese territory. Although the American government entertained no such view of its "rights," many "serious and responsible" Chinese were convinced by a campaign of rumors (many of which originated in Japan) that the United States was preparing to act in opposition to Japanese interests in China. Upon this delusion, China

. . . founded extravagant hopes that the United States would undertake to guarantee China against any territorial aggression or disregard of its sovereignty.[21]

The point is that China's evident eagerness to enlist American diplomatic aid proved to be particularly irritating to Japan.[22]

. It was against this background that China on January 7, 1915, abolished "abruptly and without previous notification" the war zone in Shantung province. It was against the same background that Japan responded, declaring that China's action revealed a lack of "international good faith" and disregard of "friendly relations." The "psychological moment" of which Kato had spoken two years previously had arrived. Japan now proposed to use it not only to adjust what she regarded as

---

[20] See page 350.

[21] United States, *Foreign Relations, 1914* (Supplement), 186-7. How fantastic these Chinese hopes were was revealed by Acting Secretary of State Lansing when he informed the American legation in Peking that while the United States was prepared to promote China's welfare by peaceful methods, "it would be quixotic in the extreme to allow the question of China's territorial integrity to entangle the United States in international difficulties." *Ibid.,* 190.

[22] For Japanese reactions toward the growth of American influence at Peking, see A. M. Pooley, *Japan's Foreign Policies* (London, 1920), 117-123.

specific grievances but also to establish if possible a general and paramount influence over all China.

SPECIFIC OBJECTIVES OF THE DEMANDS

The Twenty-One Demands, as presented to President Yüan Shih-k'ai on January 18, 1915, were divided in five groups: Group 1 concerned the disposition of the former German rights in Shantung; Group 2 related to Japan's position in South Manchuria and eastern Inner Mongolia; Group 3 dealt with a program for Japanese industrial capital in regions of the Yangtze Valley; Group 4 concerned the non-alienation of Chinese coastal territory; and Group 5 included a variety of subjects, designated as "requests" rather than "demands." [23] Since these demands and the resulting treaties are the measure of Japanese policy during World War I, their specific content justifies examination in some detail.

GROUP 1: SHANTUNG

Under these demands, China was required to assent to any subsequent German-Japanese agreement disposing of German rights in Shantung; to agree not to cede or lease any part of Shantung "to any other power"; to agree to Japanese construction of a railroad connecting Chefoo with the Tsingtao-Tsinan line; and finally to consent to the opening of certain cities to "the residence and commerce of foreigners." By these provisions Japan would preclude the return of Germany to Shantung at the close of the war. Also, the acceptance by China of Group 4, by which China was to engage not "to cede or lease to any other Power" any coast territory, would prevent Germany from acquiring an alternative to Shantung and other powers from securing new holdings elsewhere. But Japan was interested in more than this. She was determined to succeed to certain of the German rights in Shantung, and equally determined not to be deprived of them by the peace conference at the end of the war.[24] Finally, the demands relative to Shantung were in part a response to Japanese public opinion. The capture of Kiaochow had cost 2,000 Japanese lives and 50 million yen. The press demanded a *quid pro quo*.[25] However, this inspired demand of the Japanese press was both illogical and deceptive. The demands were made on neutral China, not on enemy Germany. Whatever demands Japan proposed

---

[23] Text of the Twenty-One Demands, *Foreign Relations, 1915*, 99-103.

[24] The Triple Intervention of 1895, and the Portsmouth Conference of 1905, were usually considered by Japanese statesmen as instances of diplomacy depriving Japan of the rewards of military victory.

[25] United States, *Foreign Relations, 1914* (Supplement), 202-211.

to make on the German enemy could be presented at the peace conference. Instead, to meet the realities of politics, the demands were
made on China, a friendly nation.

GROUP 2: SOUTH MANCHURIA AND
EASTERN INNER MONGOLIA

In Group 2 Japan demanded: that the lease of Port Arthur and Dairen be extended from 25 to 99 years, as also her agreements covering the
South Manchurian Railway and the Antung-Mukden Railway; that
Japanese subjects be permitted "to lease or own land" for "commercial
and industrial uses or for farming"; that Japanese subjects be accorded
"liberty to enter, reside and travel" in South Manchuria and eastern
Inner Mongolia; that Japanese subjects be accorded the right to engage
in mining; that China engage to secure Japan's consent before granting
to any third power a concession to construct railroads or to extend industrial credits in these areas; that Japan be consulted first if China required
foreign advisers in these areas; and finally that control and management
of the Kirin-Changchun Railway be placed in Japan's hands for 99 years.

These were perhaps the most important of all the Japanese demands.
Their purpose was to fulfill a policy that had been pursued since 1904:
namely, to establish beyond question Japan's *paramount* interests in
these regions. In part, Japan had already won recognition of special
position, for by the secret treaties of 1907, 1910, and 1912, Russia had
acknowledged Japan's special position.[26] Moreover, the Anglo-Japanese Alliance implied that there would be no interference from Great
Britain. Nevertheless, after 1906, British and American capital had
contested the Manchurian field against Japan's exclusive pretensions,
and Chinese governments, both monarchist and republican, had attempted to obstruct Japan's encroachments.[27] The Manchurian demands in Group 2 were thus designed to make permanent Japan's control
of Kwantung, Dairen, Port Arthur, the zones of the South Manchurian
Railway, the Antung-Mukden Railway, and the Kirin-Changchun Railway, which latter was eventually to be connected with the Japanese
ports of Seishen, Rashin, and Yuki in northern Korea. It was all a
part of the developing Japanese theory that South Manchuria was Japan's first line of defense, and, though this was not so publicized, an area
for Japanese expansion.

---

[26] Cf. Ernest B. Price, *The Russo-Japanese Treaties of 1907-1916 Concerning Manchuria
and Mongolia* (Baltimore, 1933).

[27] The attempt of Secretary Knox in 1909-10 to "smoke out" Japan was still fresh in the
official Japanese memory in 1915.

The application of certain demands in this group to eastern Inner Mongolia was evidence too of a growing international contest in this "backward" area. Here again, Russia and Japan had already delimited their spheres in the secret treaties of 1907, 1910, and 1912, Russian interests being confined to Outer Mongolia. However, after 1911, China attempted to formalize her control in Inner Mongolia, and sought to stem the tide of advancing Russian and Japanese interests by opening towns to the residence and trade of foreigners, by encouraging British capital to construct railways, and by extending the boundaries of Chihli province far to the north in Mongolian lands. By 1915 Russia had created an effective sphere in Outer Mongolia. Japan now proposed to do the same in Inner Mongolia.[28]

GROUP 3: THE HAN-YEH-PING COMPANY

The third group in the Twenty-One Demands was designed to insure to Japan a more adequate source of iron ore by making the Han-Yeh-Ping Company a Sino-Japanese concern, and by giving the Company a mining monopoly in certain regions of the Yangtze Valley. This Chinese company owned some of the richest iron and coal properties in Central China. Japanese concerns had made extensive purchases of these ores since 1899. In 1903 Japanese interests extended to the Company a loan of 15 million yen to be repaid over a period of 40 years in iron ore and crude iron. The enormous amounts of ore involved led to adverse criticism in China and to a demand for the nationalization of mines, which was effected by presidential mandate in November, 1914. This development appeared to threaten the contemplated ore deliveries under the Japanese loan. Accordingly, in her Twenty-One Demands Japan sought to acquire control of the Company, and thus of major mineral resources of the central Yangtze.[29]

GROUP 4: NON-ALIENATION OF TERRITORY

This group consisted of a single article by which China was to engage "not to cede or lease to any other Power any harbour or bay on or any island along the coast of China." This would not only prevent the return of Germany at the close of the war, it would also preclude China from making territorial grants to other powers, including the United States.[30]

---

[28] Cf. LaFargue, *China and the World War*, 29-41.

[29] F. R. Tegengren, "The Iron Ores and Iron Industry of China," *The Geological Survey of China*, Ser. A, No. 2, 366-380.

[30] In this case Japan had in mind Hay's overtures of 1900 relative to Sam-Sah Inlet.

GROUP 5: "WISHES" OR "DESIRES"

These "desires" included: 1) that China engage influential Japanese as political, financial, and military advisers; 2) that China grant the right to own land to Japanese hospitals, temples, and schools situated in the interior; 3) that China place her police under joint Sino-Japanese administration in designated regions where Sino-Japanese disputes had occurred; 4) that China obtain from Japan a supply of arms, or that an arsenal be established under Sino-Japanese administration; 5) that Japan be granted a concession to construct certain railways in South China; 6) that Japanese be granted "the right of preaching in China."

Only one article of this group, that dealing with Fukien, became a part of the eventual Sino-Japanese treaty settlement in May, 1915, yet as a result of the sweeping objectives revealed by them, it was with these "wishes" or "desires" that world opinion identified Japanese policy, rather than with the more specific demands relating to Shantung and Manchuria.

Japan's pretexts for asking that Fukien be declared a Japanese sphere rested upon: 1) the geographical relation of the province to Formosa; 2) John Hay's efforts to secure an American coaling station at Sam-Sah in 1900; and 3) rumors current in 1914 that the Bethlehem Steel Corporation was to construct a naval dock-yard near Foochow.[31]

The clause in Group 5 relating to railroad concessions was a direct result of previous Japanese ambitions to build a rail network in Kiangsi, Chekiang, and Fukien, thereby diverting traffic from the central Yangtze to the South China coast at Swatow. In these plans Japanese interests had suffered a setback in 1914 when certain railroad concessions in this general area were granted by China to British capital.[32]

Various interpretations have been advanced to account for the inclusion of the remaining proposals in Group 5, and there is conflicting evidence on the point whether the Japanese government at first intended to make any distinction between "demands" and "desires."[33] In part, the chauvinism of Group 5 has been attributed to efforts of the Okuma government to win an election through appeals to a "strong" policy. However this may be, the fact remains that these "wishes" justified extravagant speculation as to Japan's real purposes, not excluding the pos-

---

[31] MacMurray, *Treaties,* II, 1230.

[32] MacMurray, *Treaties,* II, 1113.

[33] Cf. despatches Guthrie to Bryan, February 21, 1915, and Reinsch to Bryan, April 2, 1915, in United States, *Foreign Relations, 1915,* 96 and 118.

sibility that her motive was creation of a Japanese protectorate over China.[34]

THE SINO-JAPANESE NEGOTIATIONS, 1915

In two particulars Japanese diplomacy misjudged the problem it faced in China. In the first place, the Okuma cabinet does not appear to have anticipated the violent reaction which was to come from the Chinese people—a reaction "so widespread and so generally felt that it truly can be said to mark the birth of nationalism in modern China."[35] In the second place, Japan's method of conducting the negotiations with China from January to May, when the resulting treaties were signed, was calculated to increase the apprehension both of China and of the Western powers. The demands were presented directly to the President, Yüan Shih-k'ai, with insistence upon secrecy. This encouraged China to protect herself by permitting the demands to become known through unofficial channels. Within a few days of their presentation various garbled accounts appeared in the Chinese and the foreign press.

The negotiations extended from February 2 to May 7. By April 26 Japan had accepted a number of China's counter proposals and had agreed to return Kiaochow to China following the war. China, however, did not regard the terms under which Kiaochow was to be returned as satisfactory, and accordingly countered with new proposals on May 1. Finally, Japan, finding some of China's counter proposals unsatisfactory, resorted to an ultimatum on May 7. Two weeks later, on May 25, China and Japan signed a number of treaties and notes embodying many, though by no means all, of the objectives set forth in the original Twenty-One Demands. Most of these new concessions embodied in the treaties had been agreed to by China before presentation of Japan's ultimatum.

The more important treaty concessions gained by Japan included: 1) the German leasehold in Shantung, which was to be returned to China after the close of the war in return for recognition of Shantung as a Japanese sphere; 2) extension of the Kwantung leasehold to 99 years, together with increased railroad and other privileges in South Manchuria; and 3) the right of Japan to be consulted first in case China required foreign capital for railway or harbor construction in Fukien.[36]

[34] United States, *Foreign Relations, 1915*, 86.

[35] It is a mistake, however, to describe it as "the birth" of nationalism. Cf. LaFargue, *China and the World War*, 33. There had been an important nationalistic element in the 1911 revolution, and evidences of nationalism previously. The events of 1915 stimulated and spread what was already begun earlier.

[36] Text of the treaties and notes of May 25, 1915, in MacMurray, *Treaties*, II, 1215-1230.

"At one fell swoop" these agreements had brought Japan "to a commanding position in China."

THE UNITED STATES AND THE
TWENTY-ONE DEMANDS

Since Japan had sought to implement her policy in China at a time when Europe was completely involved in war, the United States alone of all the great powers was in a position to act in the Far East if she desired to do so. President Wilson had already shown his concern for China. He had been the first to extend formal recognition to the Republic;[37] he had repudiated the Taft-Knox policy in the consortium which in his view infringed China's administrative independence. His policy in the case of the Twenty-One Demands was "to protect China out of sympathy, and American rights out of interest, but to move cautiously lest Japan be antagonized against the United States and be more severe with China." [38]

The demands created a most unfavorable impression at Washington both by reason of their content and also because Japan attempted at first to conceal Group 5. Nevertheless, the policy of the American government was formulated with restraint in a detailed memorandum from Secretary Bryan to the Japanese Ambassador on March 13.[39] The memorandum raised specific objection to several of Japan's demands. Those concerning Fukien and the purchase of arms were regarded as in violation of the open door; those concerning non-alienation of territory, the employment of Japanese subjects as advisers, and the employment by China of Japanese police officers were described by Secretary Bryan as "clearly derogatory to the political independence and administrative entity" of China. Accordingly, Japan met the American objections by modification or withdrawal of these articles.

Of much greater importance, however, was the position taken by Secretary Bryan on the demands concerning Shantung, South Manchuria, and eastern Inner Mongolia. With respect to these he observed that:

While on principle and under the treaties of 1844, 1858, 1868 and 1903 with China the United States has ground upon which to base objections to the Japanese "demands" relative to Shantung, South Manchuria, and East

[37] Meribeth E. Cameron, "American Recognition Policy Toward the Republic of China, 1912-1913," *Pacific Historical Review*, II (1933), 214-230.

[38] Harley Notter, *The Origins of the Foreign Policy of Woodrow Wilson* (Baltimore, 1937), 233-234, 241-243, 385-386, 410-411.

[39] Text in United States, *Foreign Relations, 1915*, 105-111.

Mongolia, nevertheless, *the United States frankly recognizes that territorial contiguity creates special relations between Japan and these districts.*[40]

Although this voluntary recognition of "special relations" based on geographical contiguity was far from representing Japan's desires, nevertheless, "to get any recognition at all of her special relations to these two areas from the power which had hitherto offered the greatest resistance to such recognition represented a distinct diplomatic gain."[41] The danger lay in the likelihood that Japan would interpret this recognition of her "special relations" in ways not intended or implied by the American government.

The second step in American policy toward the demands was taken on May 11, two days after China had accepted the Japanese ultimatum. In identical notes to China and Japan, Secretary Bryan informed these powers that the United States would not recognize

. . . any agreement or undertaking which has been entered into or which may be entered into between the governments of Japan and China, impairing the treaty rights of the United States and its citizens in China, the political or territorial integrity of the Republic of China, or the international policy relative to China commonly known as the open door policy.[42]

This note, it will be observed, was sent following China's acceptance of the ultimatum, but two weeks before the signing of the Sino-Japanese treaties and notes of May 25. The procedure was unusual, and the doctrine set forth—that of non-recognition—though it was later to play a most conspicuous part in American policy, had no immediate effect upon Japan. This is explained by the nature of Wilson's policy "to move cautiously." The United States in 1915, while sympathetic to China, and concerned for American interests therein, was not prepared to challenge Japan openly. The result was an enunciation of policy which on the one hand threatened non-recognition if American treaty rights or policies were infringed, but which on the other hand softened the blow by conceding to Japan "special relations" in large areas of North China.

The "psychological moment" had indeed been timed nicely. Europe was powerless to oppose Japan because of the war. To questions raised in the Commons, the British government indicated that Japan's demands would not be opposed so long as they did not infringe on British

---

[40] The italics are mine.
[41] LaFargue, *China and the World War*, 64-65.
[42] United States, *Foreign Relations, 1915*, 146.

rights in the Yangtze.[43] France and Russia were too deeply involved in the European struggle to offer opposition. Moreover, they were not opposed to the principles of Japanese policy, though they were jealous of her growing influence in China. All these considerations suggest that effective opposition to Japan could come only from China herself. Would China rise to meet this challenge, or would she, as in times past, continue the doubtful strategy of seeking to protect her own weakness by playing the powers against each other?

[43] Great Britain, *Parliamentary Debates,* 5th Ser., 1915, Vol. 70, 1722.

CHAPTER 22

CHINA AND THE STAKES OF THE FIRST WORLD WAR

THE birth of the Chinese Republic in 1912 was greeted in the United States with undisguised and ill-informed optimism. The traditional and popular though somewhat vaporous friendship of Americans for a China with which they were almost wholly unacquainted found satisfaction in the thought that the new China, being republican, would seek above all to shape its national life on American precepts, habits, and institutions. The attitude was undoubtedly well-intentioned, but it was also unrealistic. It took no account of the fact that the Chinese outbreaks of 1911-1912 occurred spontaneously and for differing reasons, and that the principles of constitutional republicanism were neither understood nor desired by the overwhelming majority. By 1916, following Yüan's attempt to restore the monarchy, the forms of constitutional government were still being maintained, but they functioned under the threat of irresponsible military power. Popular government had not replaced "the paternal despotism of the past." [1]

CHINESE POLITICS, 1915-1917

Although the political and diplomatic turmoil stirred up by Japan's Twenty-One Demands aroused unprecedented resentment among the Chinese people, this popular display of an infant nationalism did not produce an effective national government at Peking. The popular anti-Japanese enthusiasm served for the moment to bring a semblance of greater unity among the politicians, but this was short-lived. The President, Yüan Shih-k'ai, was already planning in the spring of 1915 to set up a monarchy with himself as emperor. Factions representative of the old-style politicians promptly contended with one another for power under the new dispensation. However, Yüan's colorful scheme was wrecked by a combination of powerful forces. The first of these involved international pressure upon China; the second, rebellion within

---

[1] Cf. H. M. Vinacke, "Military Power and Constitutional Development in China," *American Political Science Review*, XV (1921), 233.

China. Early in 1915 Russia and France were already hoping to bring China into the European war. They considered striking a bargain by which, if China aligned herself with the Entente, the Allies would give their blessing to Yüan and his proposed monarchy. When this scheme failed because of Japanese opposition, the Allies advised Yüan to defer the monarchy plan.[2] Yüan was indeed forced to hesitate, for the Allies could always threaten to withhold the funds so essential to Peking's virtually bankrupt treasury.[3]

Opposition to Yüan's proposed monarchy came also from within China and was perhaps as important a factor as foreign pressure. During the early months of 1916, rebellions occurred in many of the southern provinces. These outbreaks were so serious that Peking officially dropped the monarchy plan toward the end of March.

China's political ills, however, were not to be cured by a mere discarding of the monarchy plan. Political disaffection continued to spread through most of the south. At Canton, rebellious provinces organized their own provisional government. Then, in June, death put an end to Yüan Shih-k'ai, and Li Yuan-hung succeeded to the presidency. Again there was a move toward unity, for Li was accepted by most of the rebellious southern provinces. The Provisional Constitution of 1912 was restored, and on August 1, 1916, the parliament which Yüan had disbanded in 1914 met again in Peking. This session, like the former one, was doomed to fail, for the parliament possessed neither mandate from the people nor military power. Five years of nominal republicanism had not served to transfer the politico-military power either to parliament or to the people. Once held by Yüan, it had now passed to the military governors whom he had appointed and controlled.

THE ERA OF THE *TUCHUNS*, 1917-1927

As will be seen in succeeding pages, these military governors, or *tuchuns,* as they came to be known, were to monopolize the political stage in China for a decade, 1917-1927. Usually pictured as the villains of the modern Chinese scene, the *tuchuns* were in many cases as much sinned against as sinning. During the decade in which one combination or another of the war-lords controlled the Peking government, Chinese politics became a sink of corruption, and although the nation's young spirit of nationalism grew stronger, the forms of national govern-

---

[2] It would appear that Japan, hostile to Yüan, insisted that her allies refuse him loans, and that they were forced to agree since they needed Japan's help against Germany.

[3] For a detailed discussion see Thomas E. LaFargue, *China and the World War* (Stanford University, 1937), 78-83; also United States, *Foreign Relations, 1915,* 63-76.

ment established in 1912 were all but wiped out, and the cultural heritage all but submerged under foreign pressures. Nevertheless, the *tuchuns,* viewed historically, were the natural, the inevitable, inheritors of Yüan's politico-military power. In a China which had destroyed an ancient political edifice without creating a new one, they held sway, usually independent of one another, because they commanded personal armies. The area a war-lord might control depended on the size of his personal army, whereas the army he could pay was dependent on the richness and area of land from which tribute and plunder could be drawn. This meant that the centralized dictatorship of Yüan had given place to local military dictatorships.

Many of the war-lords exercised virtually no influence on China's national politics or upon her relations with the foreign powers; they need not be mentioned here. Others succeeded at various times in heading or controlling the Peking administration and thus they did play a part in shaping both domestic politics and foreign relations. Among these were: Tuan Chi-jui, Premier in 1917 and head of the so-called Anhui group; Fêng Kuo-chang, President in 1918 and head of the Chihli faction; Chang Tso-lin, war-lord of Manchuria; General Tsao Kun of Chihli; General Wu Pei-fu; and the picturesque so-called "Christian General," Feng Yu-hsiang. All these colorful figures and many others were to cross Peking with their armies in the troubled decade upon which China was entering in 1917.[4]

BREAKING DIPLOMATIC RELATIONS WITH GERMANY

In the midst of her domestic political chaos, China was called upon in February, 1917, to resolve the question of breaking diplomatic relations with Germany. President Wilson, having announced the severance of American relations with Germany, called upon neutral powers to follow the American example. The American Minister at Peking, Paul S. Reinsch, not only conveyed the appeal to Premier Tuan's government, but also proceeded with great zeal to urge its adoption. When Tuan's government showed a disposition to bargain, asking for a $10,-000,000 American loan for military purposes and a funding of the American share of the Boxer indemnity, Reinsch, without authority from his government, gave assurances. The result was that while China sent a mild note of protest against Germany's unrestricted submarine warfare, it was made to appear that the American government was attempting

---

[4] For colorful contemporary comments on the early years of war-lordism see B. L. Putnam Weale [B. L. Simpson], *The Fight for the Republic in China* (New York, 1917).

to purchase China's support. This was certainly not the case, and the State Department promptly warned its Minister against giving further unauthorized "promises or assurances." The episode was the more disturbing since it led to the assumption that the United States, or at least its Minister, was attempting to take the lead in advising China relative to the European war, which again was contrary to the fact. Actually the real fear in Peking and Washington was that China's military establishment would fall under Japanese control in the event that China severed relations with Germany.[5]

It was now China's turn to take the lead. Tuan's government informed the European Allies and Japan that no further steps toward war could be taken until China was assured that the powers would grant "certain financial benefits, particularly the postponement of the Boxer indemnity installments . . . , and an increase of the customs duties." [6]

Meanwhile, Japan had accepted the idea of a diplomatic break between China and Germany. Japan's greatest concern was to secure from her European Allies a pledge of support for her claims in Shantung and the German islands in the North Pacific (the Marianas, Carolines, and Marshalls). In February and March, assurances were received by Japan from Britain, Russia, and France; the French reply stipulated that "Japan give its support to obtain from China the breaking of its diplomatic relations with Germany." [7] Thus the way for a diplomatic break between China and Germany had already been paved when on February 24 the torpedoing by a German submarine of the French ship *Athos* in the Mediterranean resulted in the death of 543 Chinese coolies.

On March 14 China formally severed relations with Germany. The action precipitated another political crisis in Peking, for the new policy was pushed through by Premier Tuan while being opposed vigorously by President Li. Although Tuan's policy had the support of Parliament, it was received with little enthusiasm by the Chinese people in general. Indeed the break with Germany had been engineered by Tuan and the northern militarists with the primary purpose of reinforcing their own power and with the ultimate view "to getting the upper hand over Parliament and the President." [8]

---

[5] United States, *Foreign Relations, 1917,* Supplement 1, for extensive correspondence covering the period.
[6] United States, *Foreign Relations, 1917,* Supplement 1, 442.
[7] MacMurray, *Treaties,* II, 1169.
[8] United States, *Foreign Relations, 1917,* Supplement 1, 424-425.

CHINA ENTERS THE WAR

Diplomatic relations having been broken, the question of China's entering the war could not be delayed for long, particularly after the American declaration of war on Germany, April 6, 1917. This question, however, raised problems of the gravest import for China. To begin with, the Chinese people, in so far as they understood the war at all, were "distinctly pro-German in their sympathies and remained relatively so up to the signing of the armistice." [9]

Moreover, the delicate equilibrium in China's domestic politics was not fashioned to withstand the shocks of war. Certainly there was no popular demand for war, and at best Peking could claim only a very nominal allegiance on the part of many of the southern provinces. In these circumstances, a declaration of war might well prove hazardous. Be this as it may, Tuan's cabinet was prepared to take even this step if a favorable bargain could be struck with the Allied powers and the United States. The difficulty was that the powers were not in agreement on the concessions to be made to China, and they were vexed by China's mild policy toward German residents.

In April, 1917, the question of a Chinese declaration of war became still more deeply involved in the political struggle between Tuan and the Parliament for control of the government. Briefly, Tuan's strategy was to place China in the war in return for Allied loans to maintain himself and his colleagues in power. The *Kuomintang* majority in Parliament was opposed to any such bargain since it would probably result in enabling Tuan to rule with no parliament at all. From this simple impasse there was now staged in Peking a fantastic political drama, absurdly human and tragic.

Late in April, many of the provincial military governors assembled in Peking at the invitation of Tuan. These gentlemen, after being socially cultivated by the Allied and the American Ministers, announced that they favored war with Germany. They also made it clear that they were opposed to the new draft constitution, then in preparation, since they preferred a government free from parliamentary interference. Then, on May 10, while the legislators were debating a war resolution, a mob of government hirelings surrounded Parliament and by intimidation attempted to frighten the representatives into affirmative action. But Parliament stood its ground, and in response to its demand, the

---

[9] LaFargue, *China and the World War*, 101. LaFargue bases his statement on the official French source, *Bulletin périodique de la presse chinoise* (Paris, 1917-1923), No. 1, 2-3.

entire cabinet save Tuan and one minister resigned. Parliament, not regarding Tuan and one minister as a government, refused to treat with him, whereupon Tuan and his military backers demanded that Parliament disband. At this point President Li stepped into the foreground in aid of Parliament by dismissing Premier Tuan. This inspired the military governors to spring to the support of Tuan by threatening to invade Peking with their armies unless Li disbanded the Parliament. The hapless President, now pretty well beside himself, appealed for mediation to Chang Hsün, an old-line *tuchun,* but Chang Hsün refused to act until Li dissolved Parliament, which he finally did on June 11. Less than three weeks later (June 30), the busy Chang Hsün stole a march on all concerned by restoring the young Manchu emperor, Hsüan Tung, to the throne. This was too much even for the war-lords. Under Tuan's leadership, they invaded Peking; Chang Hsün fled; the boy emperor went back into retirement; *Kuomintang* members of the dissolved Parliament scurried to southern ports, while tired and disheartened President Li, harried by forces which he could not control, resigned. Tuan was now free to re-establish his cabinet. The new government, in which there was no representation of the southern provinces, was dominated by militarists and by pro-Japanese factions. On August 14, the new acting president, Fêng Kuo-chang, declared war on Germany.

China, like Japan in 1914, had entered the war for reasons which were peculiarly her own, and which bore at best only the remotest relationship to the politico-moral issues professed by the Allied and Associated Powers. Tuan's government had two objectives: 1) financial aid from the Allies; 2) international prestige as protection against the new independent government which the southern provinces had by this time set up at Canton.[10]

CHINA'S DECLARATION AND THE ATTITUDE OF THE POWERS

China's decision to enter the war was primarily the work of the illegal, unconstitutional, militaristic regime which controlled Peking in August, 1917. Moreover, the war decision was furthered rather than retarded by the policies of the Western powers and the behavior of their Ministers in the Chinese capital. Furthermore, the upsetting of Li's government, the first promising one China had had since 1913, was due directly to the question whether China should enter the war. Both Li

---

[10] The American diplomatic correspondence covering these events is given in considerable detail in United States, *Foreign Relations, 1917,* and *ibid.,* Supplement 1.

and Sun Yat-sen, neither of whom was a *tuchun,* were opposed to China's joining the conflict. Tuan, *tuchun* and premier, favored war and, in this, was supported in the main by Japan and the Entente Powers. On the top of all this, Reinsch, the American Minister, was competing with the Japanese at Peking for the greater influence over China if she did declare war, while the British and the French awaited the opportunity which a Chinese declaration of war would give to liquidate German far eastern assets. American advice to China, given June 4, that her entry "into war with Germany" was "of secondary consideration" to the question of achieving political unity at home carried no weight with the Peking militarists.[11]

In approaching China, the United States had proposed that similar advice be given by Britain, France, and Japan. All declined.[12] And finally, it should be noted that when China issued her declaration of war, she did so without definite assurance of concessions, financial or otherwise, from the Allied Powers.

THE LANSING-ISHII NOTES

While China's rulers and would-be rulers played a political game of "now-you-see-me, now-you-don't" in Peking, foreign governments were playing for whatever advantages might accrue to them from China's status as a belligerent. Here it should be recalled that China, in her semi-colonial status, was still a major commercial and industrial frontier for capital investment, where rival powers claimed spheres of economic and political influence. Now, however, Germany was isolated in Europe, while the resources of the British and French groups were fully employed in the war. Consequently, by 1917, Japan and the United States were the only powers with funds that might be used in China; and, as the war in Europe began to draw more deeply on American financial resources, it appeared that Japan, now for the first time a creditor nation, would be free to control Peking through the well-known channels of financial imperialism.

The first round in this diplomatic battle had already ended in a qualified American victory, since the Sino-Japanese Treaties and Notes of May 25, 1915, had not given Japan the exclusive control of Peking which she desired. Nevertheless, Japan's gains were substantial enough

---

[11] United States, *Foreign Relations, 1917,* 48-49.

[12] France, in reply to the American overture, observed that: "It did not, in fact, appear happy . . . to say to the Chinese Government that we consider the entry of China into the war . . . as of entirely secondary importance. . . ." United States, *Foreign Relations, 1917,* 75-76.

to bring about a reorientation in official American policy. Whereas in 1913 Wilson had advised the American consortium bankers that they could no longer count on official support, in 1916 the President was urging the American group as well as other American banks to enter the field of Chinese government loans. Two factors explain this change: the first was the steady growth of American business holdings in China; the second was the desire to head off a Japanese financial monopoly at Peking.

Tangible results soon began to appear in the wake of this new policy. Several American banks did extend loans to the Chinese government, while China extended concessions to American firms to construct a far-flung system of railroads in Inner Mongolia, Kwangsi, and Chekiang, where Russia, France, and Great Britain, respectively, claimed spheres of influence. All these governments promptly protested the right of Americans to accept railway concessions in these pre-empted areas.[13]

In spite of this clash of views on the subject of spheres of influence, Great Britain and France were urging the United States to re-enter the old consortium to counter the loan monopoly which their ally Japan seemed destined to acquire in China. Accordingly the United States did participate in the wearisome negotiations which resulted, but not until 1920, in creating a new Four-Power Consortium of American, British, French, and Japanese banking groups. The American government also undertook to carry the British and French shares in certain Chinese loans during the war, and in return wrung from the British a qualified declaration condemning the principle of spheres of influence.[14]

Japan, intent on using the European war to strengthen her own position in China, followed closely all evidences of growing American activity there; but it was the activities of the American Minister, Paul S. Reinsch, that precipitated Japanese action.

Minister Reinsch, like Willard Straight, was a zealous if not always prudent champion of American "rights" in China. Like Straight, too, he held that American "rights" could only be safeguarded and China's integrity preserved by a vigorous opposition to Japan's pretensions. On a number of occasions Reinsch attempted to transplant these views into specific action. For example, in the summer of 1916 when American rights to build railways in certain sections of China were being challenged by Britain, Russia, and France, Reinsch, without authorization

[13] United States, *Foreign Relations, 1917*, 191-195.
[14] Paul H. Clyde, "Railway Politics and the Open Door in China, 1916-1917," *American Journal of International Law*, XXV (1931), 642-657.

from the State Department, boldly attacked Japan's exclusive railway claims in Manchuria by suggesting to the Japanese Minister in Peking that Americans and Japanese co-operate in railway construction in South Manchuria, which Japan claimed as a sphere of influence. The American rights on which Reinsch based this approach were those which had been reserved under the old Chinchow-Aigun Railway Agreement between the United States and China, October 6, 1909. Reinsch's unauthorized action led to inquiries by the Japanese Ambassador in Washington. Secretary Lansing informed the Ambassador that "he did not recollect any such instruction" to Reinsch on railway co-operation, and added that:

. . . The Ambassador must be aware that the American Government recognized that Japan had special interests in Manchuria. Although no declaration to that effect had been made by the United States, yet this Government had repeatedly shown a practical recognition of the fact and did not desire to do anything to interfere with Japan's interests.[15]

In these words, Secretary Lansing gave the Japanese just the kind of opening they desired. They were not long in taking advantage of it.

Moreover, in June, 1917, when the United States advised China that her entry into the war was of "secondary consideration," the Japanese government, taking the view that America was following a consciously unfriendly policy, set about to secure from the United States an official recognition not only of Japan's "special interests" in Manchuria (the phrase which had been used by Lansing) but rather of her "paramount" interests in China. As a first step to this end, Lansing was asked by the Japanese Ambassador to confirm the Bryan statement of March 13, 1915, on "territorial contiguity" (p. 389), and to reassert "its friendly attitude toward Japan in respect of Chinese problems." [16]

This preliminary move by Japan was followed in the summer of 1917 by the arrival in the United States of a special Japanese mission headed by one of Japan's ablest diplomats, Viscount Kikujiro Ishii. The professed purpose of the mission was to bring unity and co-operation into the combined war efforts of the United States and Japan. Ishii's real purpose was to grapple with the complex problem of American-Japanese rivalry concerning China. More specifically, this meant that he was seeking two objectives: 1) to allay popular American suspicions concerning Japan's motives; 2) to secure from the American government

---

[15] United States, *Foreign Relations, 1917,* 117-118.
[16] United States, *Foreign Relations, 1917,* 259.

a public admission of Japan's "paramount interests" in China. Relying on his knowledge of popular American psychology and encouraged by a hospitable public reception, Ishii went far in disarming American public opinion.[17]

In Washington the ensuing Lansing-Ishii conversations took place against a background of feverish American war activity. Ishii sounded off by asserting that Oriental immigration and the China problem were effective weapons in the hands of German propaganda. Lansing countered by saying that Japan's allies and associates feared she was using the war to close the open door and to destroy the integrity of China. Therefore Lansing favored a joint declaration reasserting the open door. In this, Lansing was prepared to give public recognition to Japan's "special interests." Accordingly, on November 2, 1917, the conversations were given formal effects in an exchange of notes which acknowledged Japan's "special interests" in China and endorsed once again the already much endorsed open door policy.[18]

EFFECTS OF THE LANSING-ISHII EXCHANGE

Publication of the notes did not prove to be an unqualified blessing either as a war measure or as a clarification of American policy toward China. Lansing's purpose was merely to repeat the sense of the Bryan statement of March 13, 1915, namely, that geographical propinquity creates special relations between countries. But Bryan's statement had never been made public and the American people was unaware of its existence. Therefore Lansing's concession of "special interests" came as something of a shock to a public imbued with a traditional, if somewhat vague, friendship for China. Even to that small section of the American public which had long realized that Japan claimed and indeed possessed a "special position" in China, it seemed that Lansing's action was ill-advised since it would encourage Japan to close the door.

In Japan the exchange was received with enthusiasm. Government circles referred to Viscount Ishii's "great diplomatic victory," and in general the Japanese press gave the phrase "special interests" a very broad definition, which, contrary to Lansing's intent, could mean "political special interests." Far from reconciling American and Japanese policies in China, the notes served rather to intensify popular suspicion

---

[17] Kikujiro Ishii, *Diplomatic Commentaries,* edited and translated by W. R. Langdon (Baltimore, 1936), 118; Eleanor Tupper and George E. McReynolds, *Japan in American Public Opinion* (New York, 1937), 121.

[18] United States, *Foreign Relations, 1917,* 264.

in the United States that there was a deep, underlying conflict of interests.[19]

Moreover, at the time of the exchange, the American government was more realistic in explanations given to the Chinese government than in those it gave to the American people. Discussing the notes with the Chinese Minister, Lansing said he assumed China preferred us to join with Japan rather than to leave China to that country alone.[20]

Chinese public opinion interpreted the notes quite generally "as indicating a withdrawal of the American Government, in favor of Japan, from any desire to exercise any influence in Chinese affairs." [21]

CHINA'S WAR EFFORT

China was neither able nor anxious to contribute much to the war as a belligerent. Her behavior in this respect was subject to much criticism, particularly by England and France. She was accused of being lax in her control of enemy aliens and of failing in general to co-operate effectively with the Allies,[22] despite concessions made by them after her declaration of war.[23]

Contributions by China to the war effort were, however, not wholly lacking. Both before and during her entry into the war, 190,000 laborers and artisans were recruited in China for labor of various kinds behind the lines in France.[24] But it appears that not until the latter part of 1918, when the collapse of Germany seemed assured, did Tuan's

---

[19] Tatsuji Takeuchi, *War and Diplomacy in the Japanese Empire* (Chicago, 1935), 201-203.

[20] United States, *Foreign Relations, 1917*, 273.

[21] United States, *Foreign Relations, 1918*, 93.

Two other features of the Lansing-Ishii negotiations deserve mention. First: In the beginning Ishii was prepared to accept a general renunciation of spheres of influence, in return for recognition by the United States of Japan's special interests in the form of a Japanese Monroe Doctrine for China. Second: Behind the published Lansing-Ishii notes was a secret protocol in which Japan and the United States agreed that "they will not take advantage of the present conditions to seek special rights or privileges in China which would abridge the rights of the subjects or citizens of other friendly states." It was the Japanese who insisted on secrecy. Existence of the protocol was not revealed until the publication of the *War Memoirs of Robert Lansing* (Indianapolis, 1935); the text of the protocol was published three years later in United States, *Foreign Relations, 1922*, II, 595.

[22] United States, *Foreign Relations, 1917*, Supplement 2, II, 687.

[23] The Allies and the United States agreed among other things to postpone for five years payments on the Boxer indemnity of 1901. Russia, however, only agreed to postponement of one third of the installments due her. China was also conceded an upward revision of the customs tariff to an effective 5 percent, though the revised rates did not go into effect until August, 1919. United States, *Foreign Relations, 1917*, Supplement 2, I, 685-687.

[24] LaFargue, *China and the World War*, 151-152.

government bestir itself to adopt a vigorous war policy through more effective control of enemy aliens and through liquidation of enemy property.[25] These tardy steps were interpreted as a last minute bid by China's government for consideration at the forthcoming peace conference. They were also a recognition by the Chinese war-lords that Chinese public opinion was becoming more sympathetic to the cause of the Allied and Associated Powers.

China, however, was not solely responsible for what appeared as the short-comings of her war record. Against the responsibility of her irresponsible *tuchun* government one must weigh the tortuous diplomacy of the European Allies. Britain and France had assisted in pushing China into the war neither for high moral purposes nor in the hope that she would become an effective belligerent, but rather with the specific intent of eliminating German commercial and industrial competition from a post-war China.[26]

THE FAR EAST AND THE VERSAILLES PEACE CONFERENCE

As Japan and China, like other powers, had entered the war for reasons which were peculiarly their own, so they approached the peace conference for purposes of their own. If the war had swept away the old balance of power in Europe, it had also gone far to destroy the balance of power in the Far East. Prior to 1914 Japan had been accorded a nominal status as a so-called great power, a result of her victories over China in 1895 and over Russia in 1905. Actually, however, the great powers of Europe did not consider Japan as a full ranking member of their company.[27] It was the World War which gave Japan the opportunities she sought. A Europe devastated by war was ill prepared to implement its policies in Asia. On the other hand, the war had given Japan a virtual commercial monopoly in the foreign trade of China, India, the Netherlands Indies, and Australia. Japanese factories experienced an unprecedented growth, and, together with war industries, made Japan a creditor nation with surplus capital seeking invest-

---

[25] Proposals by Tuan's government in December, 1917, to send a Chinese expeditionary force to Europe failed for a combination of reasons: 1) the idea, though favored by the United States, was not supported by England; 2) there was a rather general suspicion that Tuan's main purpose was to secure additional foreign loans; and 3) the Russian revolutions as they affected North Manchuria and the Chinese Eastern Railway suggested that any effective troops which China possessed were needed at home.

[26] LaFargue, *China and the World War*, 149. Specific measures which the Allies urged China to adopt are given in United States, *Foreign Relations, 1917*, Supplement 2, I, 687. The United States did not support all these efforts.

[27] Cf. LaFargue, *China and the World War*, 186.

ment abroad. It was a flood-tide of war prosperity where "it hardly seemed possible to do any business without making money." [28] Japan, therefore, approached the peace conference conscious of her newly found economic and political power. She sought general recognition of her status as a great power, and specific recognition of her hegemony in the Far East.

The opposition to Japan's peace conference objectives was to come principally, though not exclusively, from the United States, for the end of World War I witnessed the beginnings of a more intense American-Japanese rivalry concerning China. It was a conflict of Japanese imperialistic expansion versus the traditional American policy of the open door and the integrity of China, and it was to involve not only the specific issues raised by Japan at the Versailles Conferences but also others which were to culminate later in the Washington Conference of 1921-22. The issues in this long range American-Japanese diplomatic battle were to include: 1) the effort to prevent a Japanese capital investment monopoly in China; 2) the effort to prevent annexation of the Russian Maritime Province by Japan, and to prevent establishment of a Japanese sphere in North Manchuria; 3) the effort to restore Shantung to China; and 4) the effort to implement the principles of American far eastern policy by a treaty structure covering the Pacific and the Far East. [29]

JAPAN'S DEMANDS AT VERSAILLES

At the Versailles Conference, Japan presented three demands: 1) she asked for cession of the former German islands in the North Pacific Ocean (the Marianas, the Carolines, and the Marshalls); 2) she asked confirmation of her claims to the former German rights in Shantung province; and 3) she asked for a declaration of racial equality among states as a basic principle of the proposed League of Nations. Unassailable as Japan may have believed these objectives to be, they led nonetheless to widespread and bitter opposition from some of her former allies and associates in arms. The sources of this opposition were many and varied. Japan's claim to the German islands violated the Wilsonian principle of no annexations; her claims to Kiaochow and Shantung ran counter to a young and virile Chinese nationalism; and her demand for a declaration of racial equality raised a storm of protest from some of the British dominions, particularly Australia.

---

[28] A. Morgan Young, *Japan Under Taisho Tenno, 1912-1926* (London, 1928), 110-111.
[29] A. W. Griswold, *Far Eastern Policy of the United States* (New York, 1938), 223.

THE FOUNDATIONS OF JAPAN'S CASE

Japan's representatives, Baron Makino and Viscount Chinda, approached their task with confidence, for Japan's demands in the case of the German islands and Shantung were supported by powerful legal claims, and, in the case of racial equality, by high moral principles.[30]

The German islands and Kiaochow had been captured by Japanese arms and were in Japanese possession. Moreover, in three secret agreements (February and March, 1917) England, France, Italy, and Russia had pledged themselves to support the Japanese claims at the peace conference.[31] Likewise, in 1915 Japan had forced China to agree to the transfer of Kiaochow. This, as will be recalled, had raised tremendous resentment in China, where the validity of the 1915 treaties was attacked. But whatever moral or legal strength China's resentment against the 1915 treaties may have, it was seriously weakened in 1918, when, on the eve of the armistice, China again gave her explicit consent to the transfer of Kiaochow to Japan on the understanding that Japan would in turn restore the leasehold to China, but would retain in expanded form Germany's economic rights in the province. Peking had further sealed this bargain by accepting "advance payment on large Japanese railway's loans."[32] So matters stood when the war came to an end. Japan's legal case was strong; and, despite the desire of the Allies and the United States to block her further expansion, they were not prepared to challenge the legal basis of her claims, lest this challenge rebound upon the whole system of unequal treaties pertaining to China. Thus armed, legally and politically, Japan faced the peace conference and the idealism of President Wilson. It was to be a contest of legalities and politics versus ideals.

CHINA ENTERS THE CONFERENCE

If the demands on which Japan was to insist were brutally clear, they were also a logical result of the policy on which Japan had embarked in 1914-15 and to which her preparations had been pointed for many years.

In contrast, the role which China might play at the peace table was not so clearly predictable. To realize why this should be, it is only necessary to recall China's recent efforts in political revolution after 1911,

---

[30] Japan's ranking delegate was Prince Kimmochi Saionji, ex-Premier and Genro. Included also was Ambassador Matsui at Paris.

[31] Texts of the British and French notes to Japan in MacMurray, *Treaties*, II, 1167-1169. Note also the discussions in F. S. Cocks, *The Secret Treaties* (2nd ed., London, 1918), 84-88; Chung-fu Chang, *The Anglo-Japanese Alliance* (Baltimore, 1931), 179-186.

[32] United States, *Foreign Relations, 1919*, I, 571-576.

the resulting internal political confusion, and the war-lord governments which seized Peking. Indeed, as the European war came to a close, there was little, if any, substantial evidence indicating that China was approaching political stability. The insurgent Canton government, organized by Sun Yat-sen and the *Kuomintang,* professed its faith in constitutional government, but in reality it was as subservient to the *tuchuns* of the south as Peking was to those of the north.[33] Neither north nor south at this time was concerned primarily with constitutionalism, but rather with the job of getting or keeping control of whatever administration was recognized by the foreign powers.

THE CHINESE DELEGATION AT PARIS

To a very considerable degree the program which China did present at Paris was a product of opportunism and of particular personalities in her peace delegation. Although the Peking and Canton governments had not achieved unity at home, they presented a façade of unity at Paris, for the Chinese peace delegation was composed of representatives of both governments, Canton as well as Peking.[34] In terms of political strategy and showmanship, this Chinese delegation was unsurpassed at Paris, for to the able political strategy of C. T. Wang was added the eloquent English of Wellington Koo. These men fashioned the Chinese program as presented at Paris. It was the program of a young, progressive, revolutionary, and idealistic China—a program which must have sounded strange in the ears of Peking's parochial *tuchuns.* Yet these *tuchuns* were the government *de facto* of China; they controlled the administration which was recognized by all the powers; and they were the authority to which the Chinese delegation was responsible. It may be added, too, that no spokesman supported with greater eloquence the Wilsonian program. Nevertheless, China's delegation was regarded with suspicion by the European Allies and Japan: first, because in the light of China's internal politics it was questionable whether any delegation could speak for the country; and second, because it was soon evident that Wang and Koo were less concerned with the problem of making peace with Germany than with using the conference to free China from her semi-colonial status. To statesmen of the traditional and conservative school, this purpose was alarming, for it implied an attack not only on Japan's "special interests"

---

[33] China's internal politics of the period is discussed in detail in United States, *Foreign Relations, 1919,* I, 270-358; cf. LaFargue, *China and the World War,* 173-174.

[34] It included such able representatives of the new China as Alfred Sze, Wellington Koo, and C. T. Wang.

but also upon the larger system of spheres of influence and the "unequal treaties" in general, to which all the victorious great powers were parties.[35] In addition, the mistrust of Japan, England, and France was further aroused because both before and during the Paris Conference, Wang and Koo "set out systematically to cultivate the sympathies and enlist the support" of the American delegation, which in turn was not loathe to give the Chinese the encouragement they desired.[36]

THE DEBATE BEGINS AT PARIS

Japan's demand for the "unconditional cession" of the German rights in Shantung was made on January 27, 1919. The following day, China's counter demand that Kiaochow and the German rights be restored directly to China was presented.[37] To President Wilson, the obvious answer to this deadlock between China and Japan was to be found in his own program which promised a new world of international justice under a league of nations. But Wilson could make no progress against the Japanese on this score while Australia, New Zealand, South Africa, France, Italy, and Belgium remained as insistent on annexing the German colonies in their respective regions as were the Japanese in theirs. The best that Wilson could get eventually was the system of mandates which, with the exception of those in Class A, gave to the mandatory power a control which for practical purposes was hardly to be distinguished from annexation.[38] Under this form, a Class C mandate, Japan acquired the former German islands in the North Pacific, and the British dominions got those in the South Pacific. This was not to Wilson's liking, for the Japanese mandate lay directly across the ocean highway from the Hawaiian Islands to the Philippines, and, in his opinion, was of value only in a strategic sense.[39]

---

[35] Cf. LaFargue, *China and the World War*, 175, who suggests that Peking *tuchuns* permitted Wang and Koo to raise idealistic issues, which had little chance of being met, in order to satisfy the Young China elements and "to provide a smoke-screen for the realistic maneuvering which was taking place at the Shanghai conference."

[36] Griswold, *Far Eastern Policy of the United States*, 243; David Hunter Miller, *My Diary at the Peace Conference of Paris* (21 vols., New York, 1924), I, 60, 88; III, 527.

[37] In the weeks that followed Koo's brilliant appeal, both the United States and Japan brought diplomatic pressure to bear at Peking, the former seeking to have the *tuchun* government stand firmly on the program of its young delegates, the latter seeking repudiation of that program. (Lansing papers, cited by Griswold, *Far Eastern Policy of the United States*, 245.)

[38] For the mandate principle see Quincy Wright, *Mandates under the League of Nations* (Chicago, 1930); D. H. Miller, "The Origin of the Mandates System," *Foreign Affairs*, VI (1928), 277-289; G. H Blakeslee, "The Mandates of the Pacific," *Foreign Affairs*, I (1922), 98-115; Paul H. Clyde, *Japan's Pacific Mandate* (New York, 1935), 27-44.

[39] Miller, *Diary*, I, 100.

RACIAL EQUALITY: A "HOT POTATO"

Having "compromised" by accepting a mandate instead of annexation in the Pacific islands, Japan turned to her second objective. With the approval and aid of President Wilson and Colonel House, her delegation presented as an amendment to the draft covenant of the League of Nations a resolution on racial equality. It provided that:

The equality of nations being a basic principle of the League of Nations, the High Contracting Parties agree to accord as soon as possible, to all alien nationals of States members of the League equal and just treatment in every respect, making no distinction, either in law or in fact, on account of their race or nationality.[40]

This resolution, which, it should be emphasized, had the approval of the President, was a logical, if not an essential, complement to the whole spirit of the Wilsonian program as well as to the League itself; but, in news room parlance, it was also a "hot potato." It aroused the unrelenting opposition of Premier Hughes of Australia, who was supported by the chief British delegates, Arthur Balfour and Robert Cecil. The argument advanced against any provision on racial equality was that it implied the right of the League to interfere in questions concerning immigration and the rights of aliens, which were regarded as matters of purely domestic concern. England feared embarrassment in some of the middle eastern colonies if such a resolution were adopted. Hughes saw in the resolution a threat to the "white" Australia policy, and he threatened to arouse through public addresses an outraged public opinion in the British dominions and the United States unless the amendment were dropped. At the same time he stooped to convince the Japanese press that it was the United States and not Australia that was blocking the amendment. Regardless of Hughes' principles and methods, he held a powerful club over Wilson, and he was apparently prepared to use it without restraint.

Wilson's dilemma was real. If the racial equality debate were brought into the open, as Hughes threatened to do, what would be the reaction on the American Pacific Coast and especially in California, which had already enacted the discriminatory alien land law of 1913 aimed at the Japanese,[41] and where influential politicians who did not

---

[40] Miller in his *Diary*, I, 244-245, notes that: "The presentation of the Japanese amendment by Baron Makino and by Viscount Chinda was admirably done, and it seemed to me that they had the support of the entire room."

[41] T. A. Bailey, "California, Japan, and the Alien Land Legislation of 1913," *Pacific Historical Review*, I (1932), 36-59.

share Wilson's ideals or his scruples were planning further legislation along these lines? But this was not all, it was only half of Wilson's problem. American policy at Paris was attempting to hold Japan in check on many fronts. There was Shantung, which Wilson wanted to restore directly to China. There was the prospective Four-Power Consortium into which he hoped to entice Japan in order to preserve a financial open door in China. There was eastern Siberia, which it was hoped could be rescued from Japan's military expansionists despite its occupation at the time by more than 70,000 Japanese troops. And there was the Island of Yap in the Japanese mandate, where it was hoped the United States might be given submarine cable privileges. The State Department was of the opinion that American policy would have a better chance of achieving these objectives, particularly the restoration of Shantung, if Japanese racial pride were satisfied by even an emasculated concession to the principle of racial equality. Thus, on grounds of high principle and of practical politics as applied to American policy, Wilson desired adoption of the amendment.

The vote on Japan's amendment[42] was favorable, eleven to six, but Wilson ruled against adoption of the amendment because the vote was not unanimous.[43] For reasons which to him seemed good, Wilson announced defeat of the measure. The news men had been right: racial equality was a "hot potato." Wilson could not risk the issue in open debate, and he feared that Hughes would force it into the open if it could be defeated in no other way.

SHANTUNG: "OR ELSE"

Two of Japan's objectives at Paris had now been disposed of: in the Pacific islands there had been a "compromise" which the Japanese had accepted but did not like; on racial equality Japan had accepted a defeat particularly galling to Japanese pride since the race issue was "the symbol of discrimination, the label of an inferior people."[44] Japan's government was therefore in no mood to accept further reverses as it approached the debate on its third objective: transfer to Japan, in terms of the peace treaty, of the former German rights in Shantung. Here Japan was determined to accept neither compromise nor defeat. The problem was the more difficult because Wang and Koo had by this time

[42] It had become merely an "endorsement of the principle of equality of nations and just treatment of their nationals."
[43] This was one of those rare occasions at Paris when the Chinese and Japanese were in agreement.
[44] Paul Birdsall, *Versailles Twenty Years After* (New York, 1941), 90.

gone far beyond their original and earlier demand for the direct restoration of Kiaochow and the German rights. Their work at Paris had aroused not only the sympathies of Western peoples, but also a public consciousness within China itself. A new patriotic pride appeared to be taking possession of the Chinese people, expressing itself "in a spontaneous mass movement" in support of the Paris delegation.[45] Encouraged by the support of this spontaneous public opinion, Wang and Koo were now calling for abrogation of all the 1915 treaties and notes. This was a direct thrust not only at Japan's pretensions in Shantung but also at her "special position" in South Manchuria and eastern Inner Mongolia and to her general ambitions in China as a whole. It was a challenge which the Japanese promptly accepted. They stood firm and demanded Shantung, their "pound of flesh," threatening to withdraw from the Conference if it were denied them.

The Japanese position at this time was virtually impregnable except on the high moral ground of Wilson's principles. Much as he disliked it, there seemed to be but one decision that Wilson could make without wrecking the Conference, namely: acceptance of the Japanese demands. In Wilson's own mind, this "settlement was the best that could be had out of a dirty past." [46] In this he differed from some of his close advisers who felt that the Japanese were bluffing.[47]

CHINA LEARNS TO SAY "NO!"

China was now faced with what to her was an unhappy choice. She could accept in the peace treaty a direct cession to Japan of the German rights, or she could accept the obligation to carry out the even larger concessions Japan claimed under the treaties of 1915 and 1918. The Chinese delegation, however, refused to accept either, on the theory: 1) that China's declaration of war had cancelled Germany's rights in Shantung, and 2) that the 1915 and 1918 treaties were invalid on grounds of equity. Right here lay the main significance of the whole bitter contest over Shantung. The real issue was the question of the validity of the 1915 and 1918 treaties. A denial of Japan's claims to Shantung would have opened the way for questioning the validity of the entire treaty structure of 1915 and 1918. Not to question that structure implied international approval of Japan's attempts to dominate China. On this issue, the Western powers were as widely separated

---

[45] LaFargue, *China and the World War*, 233.

[46] Ray Stannard Baker, *Woodrow Wilson and World Settlement* (3 vols., Garden City, 1922), II, 266.

[47] Griswold, *Far Eastern Policy of the United States*, 253.

as were China and Japan. While Wilson was careful to refrain from any admission that the 1915 treaties were valid, he was equally careful not to deny positively their validity. As in the Lansing-Ishii exchange of 1917, there was vagueness and ambiguity in the American position on the legal question. England and France, on the other hand, did not question either Japan's right to Shantung or the validity of the Sino-Japanese treaties in general. Indeed, since in terms of the Treaty of Versailles the policy of Japan was "to hand back the Shantung Peninsula in full sovereignty to China, retaining only the economic privileges granted to Germany," the British took the position that "China, without the expenditure of a single shilling, or the loss of a single life, had restored to her rights which she could never have recovered for herself." [48]

CHINA'S BALANCE SHEET OF WAR

Although China refused to sign the Treaty of Versailles between the Allied and Associated Powers and Germany, and although her defeat in the Shantung issue was a reverse of great magnitude, her balance sheet of war was not written wholly in red ink. Indeed, she had achieved results which, if not clearly apparent at the time, were none the less real. Her appeals to public opinion had elicited deep sympathy for China's cause—sympathies which, though sometimes founded on misconceptions, were to be of inestimable value in the revolutionary years ahead. Within China itself, the stand of Wang and Koo at Paris had produced stirrings of a new national pride. And, more than this, the war had terminated China's old "unequal" treaties with Germany, Austria, and Hungary, thus opening the way for new treaties with these powers negotiated on a basis of equality. [49]

---

[48] Blanche E. C. Dugdale, *Arthur James Balfour* (2 vols., New York, 1936), II, 245.

[49] Robert T. Pollard, *China's Foreign Relations, 1917-1931* (New York, 1933), 86-87. China did sign the Treaty of St. Germain with Austria, September 10, 1919; the Treaty of Neuilly with Bulgaria; and the Treaty of Trianon with Hungary. China's war with Germany was ended officially September 15, 1919, by proclamation of the Chinese president.

CHAPTER 23

LEGACIES OF WORLD WAR I

THE end of World War I did not bring peace, military or diplomatic, in the Far East. The war, as already suggested, had effected a major shift in the far eastern balance of power. Germany was no longer a force in eastern Asia, but in her place there had appeared a newly rich and powerful Japan whose energies had not been depleted by the war. In China there were rumblings of discontent and the first uneasy stirrings of an infant nationalism made more vocal by the oratory of Wellington Koo at Paris. For the first time, a China humiliated by nearly a century of foreign pressure appeared to be on the point of asserting its right to sovereign independence. Would this mean an immediate frontal diplomatic assault by China on the entire system of "unequal treaties," as well as upon the "special position" of Japan?

SIBERIA AND THE RUSSIAN REVOLUTION

Late in 1917, and in the years which succeeded, the Russian Revolutions had created what may best be described as a political vacuum in Siberia and to a lesser degree in the zone of the Chinese Eastern Railway in north-central Manchuria. During the years 1918 to 1920 and after, Siberia, North Manchuria, and Outer Mongolia became a confused and cruel battle ground for armies, political creeds, and irresponsible brigands, in which all the major powers, England, France, Japan, and the United States, became actively involved with their politics and their armies.

In tracing these various developments in some detail, it will be necessary first to recall some aspects of Russo-Japanese relations in the Far East.

RUSSIA AND THE FAR EAST, 1916

After the Russo-Japanese War, Russia retained her important sphere of influence in North Manchuria and her control of the Chinese Eastern Railway with the branch line running south from Harbin to Kwanchengtzu (Changchun), where it connected with Japan's South Manchuria Railway.[1] There was evidence too of the vitality of Russian policy in the secret Russo-Japanese treaties of 1907, 1910, and 1912, in which the two powers defined more specifically their spheres of influence and agreed upon methods of close co-operation in defense of their "special rights." (Chapter 19, pp. 347-354). By 1915, Russia had also consolidated her position in the Far East through a "protectorate" over Outer Mongolia. Although the tripartite treaty of 1915 again acknowledged Chinese suzerainty in Outer Mongolia, it was Russian influence *de facto* which prevailed there.

By 1916 Russia and Japan, now allies in the World War, came to a further agreement in defense of their contiguous spheres of influence. A new secret convention provided for co-operation in defense of their "vital interests" in the Far East to the end that "China should not fall under the political domination of any third Power hostile to Russia or Japan."[2]

THE RUSSIAN REVOLUTIONS, 1917 AND AFTER

The functioning of these nicely laid Russo-Japanese plans was soon to be disturbed by events within Russia itself. The Russian Revolutions of 1917 were as striking in their impact upon the Far East as was the World War. The ousting of the Tsarist Imperial regime, the subsequent collapse of Kerensky's provisional government, and the resulting chaotic warfare between revolutionary and anti-revolutionary forces either weakened or destroyed the political bonds which had held these vast Siberian territorial and political interests together. The resulting political vacuum posed questions of the greatest magnitude, and in the first instance most of these questions concerned Russia's altered relationship to the European war. Could Russia be maintained as an effective ally in the war against Germany? Would not a defeated and a politically helpless Russia become the granary of a revived and possibly victorious Germany? How could Russia be restored as a fighting ally? With what Russians, White, Pink, or Red, should the Allies deal? As the power of the old Russian Imperial regime collapsed, what authority would fall heir to those vast Russian interests on Chinese soil, such as the strategic Chinese Eastern Railway? These and many other similar questions were to worry leaders of the Allied and Associated Powers from 1917 on to the autumn of 1918, while their armies were still locked

---

[1] C. W. Young, *The International Relations of Manchuria* (Chicago, 1929), 93.

[2] E. B. Price, *The Russo-Japanese Treaties* (Baltimore, 1933), 77-90. Note that in this convention, "special interests" had become "vital interests."

in a desperate battle on the western front and while the decisive power of the American war effort was yet to be felt.

CHINA AND THE RUSSIAN REVOLUTIONS

The most immediate effect in the Far East arising from the Russian revolutions was a temporary reassertion of Chinese authority in areas previously dominated by the Tsarist government: North Manchuria, Outer Mongolia, and the Barga territory.[3]

POLITICAL CONDITIONS IN SIBERIA, 1917-1920

Political affairs throughout Siberia from late 1917 to 1920 presented a picture of unmeasurable confusion. The collapse of the Imperial government in the spring of 1917 brought first a revival of the late nineteenth-century movement for Siberian autonomy—a movement supported by "socialists of various complexions, liberals, and even moderate conservatives."[4] Opposed to these "regionalists," there was from November, 1917, to the summer of 1918 the rising influence of the local soviets. The defeat of these groups in the summer of 1918 paved the way for the Kolchak White government at Omsk, which "claimed" all power in Siberia from November, 1918, to January, 1920. Although Kolchak's government was accorded a "kind of defacto recognition" from the Supreme Council of the Allied and Associated Powers, it was opposed by a nondescript array of Siberian factions great and small. In the end Kolchak's government fell before the rising tide of the Red armies, but meanwhile it was also opposed more or less openly by a variety of self-appointed "saviors" of Siberia. There was, for example, Cossack Captain Grigorii Semenov, who had been commissioned by Kerensky's provisional government to recruit troops in Trans-Baikalia. With the fall of Kerensky, Semenov, seizing the Trans-Siberian Railway in the Chita region, preyed upon the inhabitants with a nice lack of discrimination, butchering anyone suspected of being a Red. His unspeakable brutalities contributed to "the popular hatred of all 'White' organizations." He was supported openly by the Japanese army.[5] There was Baron Ungern von Sternberg, who used Mongolia as a base from which to attack the Reds and helpless peasants in general, and who had visions of setting up a Pan-Mongolian empire. Many of the

[3] Robert T. Pollard, *China's Foreign Relations* (New York, 1933).

[4] Elena Varneck and H. H. Fisher, eds., *The Testimony of Kolchak* (Stanford University, 1935), 247.

[5] Varneck and Fisher, *The Testimony of Kolchak*, 231, 261; William S. Graves, *America's Siberian Adventure* (New York, 1931), 86 ff.; Dimitri Alioshin, *Asian Odyssey* (New York, 1940), 48.

Baron's victims were disposed of by feeding them to a pack of wolves maintained for this purpose.[6] There were Social-Revolutionists of divergent shades, some of whom co-operated reluctantly with Kolchak, others with the Bolsheviks. In the Russian railway zone at Harbin there were two principal factions. In July, 1918, Lieut. General Dimitrii Leonidovich Horvath, who had been general manager of the Chinese Eastern Railway and administrator of the railroad zone since 1903, proclaimed an all-Russian, anti-Red government. Horvath's conservative regime was opposed at Harbin and later at Vladivostok by a group of political opportunists representing the center-left Social-Revolutionists who formed another "government" headed by Petr Yakovlivich Derber. In addition to these there were many other groups led by Cossack adventurers more concerned with opportunities for pillage and plunder than with the political future of Russia. Finally, there were almost innumerable bands of peasant "partisans" who had no understanding of the mad political currents by which they were enmeshed and impoverished.[7]

In the midst of this political confusion of contending factions, cruelties that tax the imagination were perpetrated by Whites and Reds alike; but if distinctions can be drawn in such matters, it would appear that the most frightful inhumanities were those practiced by Semenov and his "Whites." [8]

THE CZECHOSLOVAKS IN SIBERIA

Another factor complicated conditions in Siberia. Early in World War I a Czechoslovak detachment was formed in Russia and fought as a part of the Russian army against the Central Powers. During the period of Kerensky's provisional government, this Czech force was increased to nearly 50,000 men. As the Russian armies disintegrated in the first months of Bolshevik rule, the Czech legions remained intact; they were placed under the Supreme French Command by the Czech National Council in Paris, where the decision was made to transport the force around the world by way of Vladivostok and the Pacific to serve with the French armies on the western front. Permission was granted the Czechs by the Bolsheviks to cross Siberia to Vladivostok en route to France. In the chaotic conditions prevailing, clashes soon occurred between Czech and Bolshevik forces. During May and June,

[6] Alioshin, *Asian Odyssey,* 48; Pollard, *China's Foreign Relations,* 162-163; Louis Fischer, *The Soviets in World Affairs* (2 vols., New York, 1930), II, 534-537.
[7] See "Memoirs of the Red Partisan Movement," in Varneck and Fisher, *The Testimony of Kolchak,* 265-328.
[8] Varneck and Fisher, *The Testimony of Kolchak,* 325.

1918, anti-Bolshevik governments appeared at Samara and Omsk sheltered by Czech arms.[9]

THE QUESTION OF ALLIED INTERVENTION IN RUSSIA

While this checkered pattern of events outlined in preceding pages was developing, the Allied Powers considered the question of military intervention in Russia to re-establish a new eastern front against Germany. Basically, the object was to keep Russia in the war against the Central Powers; but Allied representatives in Russia were divided as to the means that should be used to this end. While some favored assistance to anti-revolutionary White elements, others conferred with the Reds. At the close of 1917 opinion among the powers themselves was widely divided. Japan and France favored intervention against the Bolsheviks; Britain favored intervention with Russian consent against the Germans; and the United States was opposed to any intervention at all. During the early months of 1918, the Allies considered the possibility of Japan acting alone as their mandatory in the occupation of Siberia, and when on April 4, 1918, two Japanese were killed at Vladivostok, Japan landed troops to police the city, and the British sent a small legation guard. In Moscow this was viewed as the beginning of an anti-Bolshevik intervention. Shortly following this came open warfare between the Czechs and the Bolsheviks in the region of the Volga.[10]

AUSTRO-GERMAN PRISONERS IN SIBERIA

Another stimulus in Allied countries toward the cause of intervention was the reports that German and Austro-Hungarian prisoners of war in Siberia were being recruited into the Red armies "for defense of the Soviet regime and the expected world revolution." The measure of truth in these reports has never been determined with accuracy. Although in general these reports appear to have been greatly exaggerated, the tendency in Allied countries was to accept them at face value. Thus they had immense effect on both official and public opinion and certainly influenced President Wilson's final decision in favor of intervention.[11]

---

[9] James Bunyan, *Intervention, Civil War, and Communism in Russia* (Baltimore, 1936), 75-87.

[10] Bunyan, 60-75, 87-92.

[11] United States, *Foreign Relations, 1918, Russia,* II, 52, 57, 63-64, 83-84, *passim;* F. L. Schuman, *American Policy toward Russia* (New York, 1928), 87-88; Fischer, *The Soviets in World Affairs,* I, 103-106.

THE DECISION ON INTERVENTION

The break between the Czechs and the Bolsheviks was one of the most decisive factors in the final decision of the Allies to intervene, for the hold of the Czechs on the Siberian Railway and their strategic positions in the Volga region appeared as the first substantial footholds from which a new eastern front might be built. On June 1, 1918, the Supreme War Council at Versailles decided to reinforce Murmansk in northwestern Russia, already held by British troops since March, and to occupy Archangel also. The United States offered no objection to this move, though it was as yet unwilling to agree to intervention in Siberia.[12] A month later, on July 2, the Allied decision to intervene in Siberia was made final, the basic argument advanced being that the Allies could not win on the western front even in 1919 unless the Germans were forced to divert troops to the East.[13]

WILSON'S RELUCTANCE TO INTERVENE

It remained to secure President Wilson's approval of intervention in Siberia and his consent to have the United States participate in it. For Wilson, this was a difficult and complex problem. The President was already on record in a declaration of friendship for Russia. But for what Russia? White, Pink, or Red? Moreover, American policy was opposed to any intervention that would place Japan in Siberia.

It was British, French, and Japanese pressure and the determination of these governments to act anyway which finally forced Wilson's hand. On July 17, 1918, the United States informed the Allied ambassadors of its decision to intervene, and of its objectives, to which it asked their adherence.

Military action is admissible in Russia . . . only to help the Czecho-Slovaks consolidate their forces and to get into successful cooperation with their Slavic kinsmen and to steady any efforts at self-government or self-defense in which the Russians themselves may be willing to accept assistance. . . . The only legitimate object for which Americans or Allied troops can be employed . . . is to guard military stores which may subsequently be needed by Russian forces and to render such aid as may be acceptable to the Russians in the organization of their own self-defense.[14]

[12] American troops were dispatched to Murmansk in June. United States, *Foreign Relations, 1918, Russia*, II, 484-485.
[13] United States, *Foreign Relations, 1918, Russia*, II, 243-244.
[14] United States, *Foreign Relations, 1918, Russia*, II, 288.

From August until November, 1918, troops of the Allied Powers, British, Japanese, French, and Americans, were landed at Vladivostok. It was Wilson's intention to curb the Japanese by an agreement limiting the American and Japanese contingents to some 7,000 troops each. In the end the United States sent 9,000 troops; the Japanese something in excess of 72,000.[15]

THEORY AND PRACTICE IN SIBERIA

Now that the Allied contingents were in Siberia, what were they to do? There was as much disagreement on this question as there had been on the original point of intervention. The policy of the American military forces, commanded by Major General William S. Graves, had been determined by President Wilson. It required that they refrain from "any interference of any kind with the political sovereignty of Russia" and from "any intervention in her internal affairs."[16] Since these American troops were already on Russian soil, these were admittedly difficult instructions to follow. Nevertheless, General Graves did his best to carry them out. Where American troops patrolled the railroads, they did so for all Russians, whether White or Red. Graves' actions in this respect appear to have been proper, but they led to a tense situation, since of all the key personalities in the intervening armies, he alone held unswervingly to his instructions and to the announced purposes of the intervention. On the other hand most of the Allied representatives, including many Americans, disregarded completely the principles of non-interference and neutrality in Russian affairs. The European governments, the Japanese, and some American officials had reached the view that the purpose of the intervention was to fight the Reds. The announced purposes of the intervention were no longer to be the real purposes. Thus England, France, and Japan, with the willing support of certain American consular officials and members of the Department of State, became the de facto allies of the Cossack brigands and murderers: Semenov, Kalmikov, and Rozanov, who masqueraded as the leaders of the Russian people. Moreover, the Allies, mainly the British and French, were responsible for bringing Admiral Aleksandr Vasilevich Kolchak to Siberia where they installed him as head of the White government at Omsk. There this well-meaning but mild and ineffectual reactionary was surrounded by discredited Russian

---

[15] Contrary to the general belief that Japan agreed to this limitation, it appears that she was careful to reserve the liberty to send additional troops if in her view circumstances demanded it. United States, *Foreign Relations, 1918, Russia*, II, 324-326.

[16] United States, *Foreign Relations, 1918, Russia*, II, 289.

Whites whose sole thought was to get back into power, and by the British and French military missions which appear to have been unaware that Russia could not be pressed back into the political and economic mold of the tsars. From November, 1918, until January, 1920, Kolchak, the Czechs, and their British and French allies fought the Bolsheviks, long after Germany had fallen and the need of an eastern front had disappeared.[17] On the part of the European Allies and Japan, the original stated purposes of the intervention had been sidetracked without Wilson's consent for very different purposes, that is, for interference in the internal politics of Russia.[18]

THE DEVELOPMENT OF RAILWAY POLITICS

It was inevitable that the Siberian adventure, regardless of its real or stated purposes, should become involved with the control of the Siberian Railway system and with that integral segment of it, the Chinese Eastern Railway. Whoever controlled these railways, controlled Siberia.

In March, 1917, after the United States had severed diplomatic relations with Germany but before the declaration of war (April 6), the strategic importance of the Trans-Siberian system had been impressed upon the American government. On April 2, after the fall of the tsarist regime, the United States approached Kerensky's government asking whether it would welcome an inspection of Russia's railroad systems, then in a state of virtual collapse, with a view to their rehabilitation for war purposes through American technical assistance. The British government had gone so far as to suggest American management of the Siberian system as a war measure, a proposal which Ambassador Page in London sent to Washington with the comment:

This seems so important a suggestion looking towards future American-Russian trade that I send it for your investigation if you think wise.[19]

---

[17] United States, *Foreign Relations, 1918, Russia*, II, 324-329. Graves' refusal to cooperate with Semenov's White brigands or with Kolchak led to unsuccessful British pressure at Washington for his recall. (Graves, *America's Siberian Adventure*, 195.) For alleged efforts of certain members of the State Department to force Graves into line with the White factions, see *ibid.*, 296-7. The most influential foreign representative in Siberia was General Alfred William Fortescue Knox, chief of the British military mission, and a pillar of support to Kolchak until the latter's cause became hopeless. Knox's qualifications are suggested by his remark to General Graves: "I [Graves] was getting the reputation of being a friend of the poor and didn't I know they were only swine." Graves, 87.

[18] Graves, 192-193.

[19] United States, *Foreign Relations, 1918, Russia*, III, 184.

Shortly after this a special American diplomatic mission went to Russia. It was headed by the distinguished Republican ex-Secretary of State, Elihu Root. Its purpose was to gain a better understanding of how the United States might co-operate in the solution of Russian war problems. This mission returned from Moscow with enthusiastic reports of what Russia would yet do in the war. In reality the mission, and this was not entirely its fault, had achieved no real success at all. From the first, it was viewed as skeptically by most of the Russians as it had been previously by its critics in the United States.[20]

THE RAILROAD COMMISSION

Meanwhile, in May, 1917, a second American mission, known as the Railroad Commission, had entered Russia at Vladivostok. It was headed by John F. Stevens, formerly chief engineer of the Panama Canal. Its task was to find means of rehabilitating the Russian railways, and it began its work by attempting to relieve the congestion in the Vladivostok region. The broad proposals of this commission were accepted by the Russian government in August. These included a program for railway assembly plants to be set up by American technicians with American equipment and under the supervision of American railway engineers. For this purpose a Railway Service Corps of technical experts, headed by Colonel George Emerson, proceeded to the Far East to carry out the recommendations of the Stevens Commission. The work was to be financed by a Russian loan floated in the United States. The entire business was supposed to be a Russian affair. Secretary Lansing had cautioned Stevens that he must in no way create the impression that the Railway Commission either represented or spoke for the American government.

By December, 1917, however, Kerensky's government, with which these plans had been made, had been thrown out by the Bolsheviks, and political conditions were such at Vladivostok that for a time the Railway Service Corps was unable to land. Stevens thought the United States ought to send a warship and 5,000 troops to Siberia. The "time is coming," he said, "to put [the fear?] of God into these people [the Russians]." So matters stood until April, 1918, when, as already noted (p. 416), the Japanese first landed troops to police Vladivostok—an act which gave substance to the prediction of the American Ambassador at Tokyo, Roland S. Morris:

---

[20] United States, *Foreign Relations, 1918, Russia,* I, 107-152. F. L. Schuman, *American Policy toward Russia* (New York, 1928), 40-44.

. . . The [Japanese] army is powerful and the General Staff, I believe, would welcome and probably exaggerate any occurrence which might afford an excuse [for action in Siberia].

By this time, Stevens, now in Harbin, was trying to discover what, if anything, could be done to restore traffic on the Chinese Eastern Railway, which was laboring along in a half-hearted way under General Horvath's White government. Emerson meanwhile had been authorized to confer on railway matters with the Reds where this seemed desirable. This situation led Stevens to comment that:

The new [Horvath] administration of the Chinese Eastern are bitterly anti-Soviet. . . . We are thus placed in impossible situations of trying to help two bitterly opposing [Russian factions] with the usual result facing us [of] antagonizing both.

Nevertheless, Stevens' presence at Harbin seemed necessary if control of the entire transportation system of Manchuria was not to fall into Japanese hands.

Moreover, Japan was legally, as well as strategically, in a position to take advantage of the political uncertainties in Manchuria and Siberia. In May, 1918, she signed two treaties with the *tuchun* government of Peking providing for Sino-Japanese military co-operation if "the general peace and tranquility" of the Far East were menaced.[21]   Thus, late in July, when Semenov's brigands were hard pressed by the Reds, Japan invoked these military agreements with China and dispatched troops to the zone of the Chinese Eastern Railway. This made it appear that Japan was already well on the way to make North Manchuria a Japanese sphere. If this was Japan's purpose, it was blocked by the insistence of the United States that inter-Allied, not exclusive Japanese, control be maintained on the Chinese Eastern Railway. Not, however, until January 9, 1919, was an inter-Allied railroad agreement reached. By it, the operation of railroads under Allied military control was to be in the hands of an inter-Allied commission which in turn was to be advised by Stevens and a technical board.[22]

---

[21] Text of these treaties in United States, *Foreign Relations, 1918,* 222-226. Supplementary Sino-Japanese agreements were signed in September, 1918, and February, 1919.
[22] United States, *Foreign Relations, 1918, Russia,* II, 433-461; III, 239-249; *1919,* I, 590-615; Graves, *America's Siberian Adventure,* 175-207; Thomas E. LaFargue, *China and the World War* (Stanford University, 1937), 170-172; Schuman, *American Policy toward Russia,* 139-143.

THE END OF THE INTER-ALLIED INTERVENTION

As the wearied months of 1919 dragged on, evil days settled upon the entire Siberian adventure. The high purposes of military strategy for which it was conceived no longer had any meaning, for Germany had long since collapsed and the war in Europe was over. The ill-concealed desire of the Western powers and Japan to crush Bolshevism in Russia had resulted in dismal failure. By the end of 1919 the remnants of Kolchak's armies were in complete rout before the rising Red tide and the infuriated peasant partisans. The White elements both within and outside Russia had failed to provide any program or any leadership which the Russians would accept. Ambassador Morris in Tokyo went far to explain this when he said:

The advent of Allied forces [in Siberia] has led to the hope among former [Russian] officials, civil and military, that they will regain the power and influence they had before the revolution. The attitude of these officials indicates that they will be relentless in their endeavor to suppress all liberal or moderate movements. Possibly nothing but their inevitable failure will bring them to reason.

Morris believed that only a correction of "industrial inequalities will modify the existing bitter class feeling of the Bolsheviks." [23]

As for the Western Allies, by 1920 they were tired of the whole business. The war in Europe had been ended more than a year. They therefore withdrew their armies and left Siberia to the Russians—and to the Japanese.[24]

For two years the Japanese remained. The Japanese government and the army regarded the whole eastern Siberian question as being still very decidedly Japan's business. There were many reasons which account for this attitude. The growth of the revolutionary ferment in Russia and the discrediting of the Whites appeared as the prelude to a possible communist society touching the shores of the Pacific which would be a threat to Japan's position in South Manchuria and even to the social fabric and political structure of her society at home. The massacre of Japanese at Nikolaevsk in 1920 seemed to confirm the wisdom of army expansionists who desired to annex the Maritime Province with Vladivostok.[25] So Japan stayed on, temporarily in control of a

[23] United States, *Foreign Relations, 1918, Russia*, II, 414.

[24] Even before the withdrawal, the Canadian contingent in Siberia was "in a state bordering on mutiny." The American troops were "in much the same frame of mind." A. Morgan Young, *Japan under Taisho Tenno* (London, 1928), 179.

[25] On the Nikolaevsk massacre see: Young, *Japan under Taisho Tenno*, 177-187; Varneck and Fisher, *The Testimony of Kolchak*, 331-372.

great circular area reaching from Vladivostok to Chita, an area traversed by the Chinese Eastern and the Amur Railways. She entertained the hope that a buffer state, friendly to Japan, and free of Bolshevik contagion would yet arise in the Far East. But whatever justification there may ever have been for this hope had already been destroyed by the inter-Allied intervention itself, for in general the Russians appear to have been as happy to see the Allies go as the Allied soldiers themselves were to get out of Siberia. Writing in 1931, General Graves noted that the participating governments seemed to take "very little pride in this venture. Who can blame them?" [26]

THE FOUR-POWER CONSORTIUM

Throughout the two years (1918-1920) of international wrangling in Siberia there had been an almost continuous succession of clashes between American and Japanese policy. Virtually the one common ground between the *Gaimusho* and the Department of State was the mutual desire to crush Bolshevism with its program of world revolution. In every other respect American policy in Siberia and North Manchuria was firmly set against Japan's efforts to implement her policy of "special" or "vital interests." This conflict between policies was not new. It was simply growing more intense as American and Japanese aims and interests clashed in many theaters: in Shantung, in North Manchuria, in Siberia, and, as will now appear, in the broader scene of international finance in China as a whole.

It will be recalled that in 1913, President Wilson, disapproving of the control measures employed by the First or Six-Power Consortium as infringements upon the "administrative integrity" of China, informed the American banking group that it would not enjoy the official support of the American government. In the five years which followed, the basic principles of Wilson's policy toward China—territorial and administrative integrity and the open door—did not change, but his views on the means of achieving and maintaining these principles did change materially. By November, 1917, the President, though not fully convinced that independent loans to China were impractical as political weapons, had decided to encourage the organization of a new four-power consortium. The following year, on the initiative of the American government, a new American banking group was formed. The bankers, however, were not of a mind to enter the field of Chinese investments save in concert with British, French, and Japanese banking groups, and with the public support of the American government.

---

[26] Graves, *America's Siberian Adventure*, 356.

These conditions the American government accepted, and on its part insisted that in turn the prospective consortium must respect the well-established principles of American policy in China—principles which were well known to be at variance with Japan's theory of "special interests" and with the theory of the British and the French toward spheres of influence.

The reasons for this complete reversal of method by the Wilson administration are significant. The World War had given Japan a free hand in financing China, and it had also destroyed temporarily any possibility of China's receiving British or French credits. But more was involved than the mere matter of investment. Wilson was forced to recognize that, China's political position being what it was, the political aspects of American policy could no longer be detached with safety from economic considerations. This was made particularly clear during 1918, when as a result of the mysterious maneuverings of K. Nishihara, personal representative in China of Premier Count Terauchi, the Peking *tuchun* government contracted Japanese loans in the amount of some Yen 120 million. These were not investments in the usual meaning of that word. Rather they were payments to officials then in power in exchange for certain agreements that would promote Japanese policy, particularly in Manchuria.[27] Japan was thus buying an economic and political stake from a Chinese *tuchun* government that was willing to sell.[28]

Against Sino-Japanese financial politics of this type, doctrinaire slogans of American policy on the open door and the integrity of China were of little value unless implemented by more realistic factors. Therefore Wilson sought to revive and apply international co-operative action through a new consortium, his hope being that with British and French support, Japan could be held in line and her efforts to gain a financial monopoly at Peking frustrated. Japan's adherence, however, was easier asked than secured, for the new consortium, as conceived by the United States, was a revival and an extension of the international principle basic to the Knox neutralization scheme of 1909-10.[29] Japan was no more prepared to accept the unqualified application of this principle in 1919 than she had been ten years earlier. Indeed it required two years of dreary negotiation, 1918-1920, before a compromise agree-

---

[27] C. F. Remer, *Foreign Investments in China* (New York, 1933), 539-545.

[28] See the reports of J. V. A. MacMurray at Peking, United States, *Foreign Relations, 1918*, 123.

[29] A. W. Griswold, *Far Eastern Policy of the United States* (New York, 1938), 224-225. For detailed discussion of the whole consortium problem see F. V. Field, *American Participation in the China Consortiums* (Chicago, 1931).

ment for the new four-power consortium could be reached. In this compromise the United States, England, and France pledged their "good faith" to "refuse their countenance to any operation [of the consortium] inimical to the vital interests of Japan." These powers also agreed to exclusion from the joint activities of the consortium of the zone of the South Manchuria Railway and a number of other railway, mining, and industrial projects in the Japanese sphere.[30] This was a vital reservation. It meant that while the powers would now pool all loans, administrative and industrial, in China Proper south of the Wall, Japan still retained her "special position" in South Manchuria.

CHINA AND THE CONSORTIUM

The revival of the consortium in 1920 has been interpreted in a number of ways. In part it was due to the new position, political and financial, of the United States in world commerce, industry, and finance. In part it was a specific effort by three powers to block Japan's politico-financial conquest of China, and thus in the American view, to implement the traditional doctrines of the open door and the integrity of China. The idea was that the consortium could be regarded not only as an important piece of financial machinery for the industrial development of China but also as an international pledge of China's integrity and thus of American policy. In this sense the consortium appealed to American public opinion and to traditional concepts of American friendship for China. There were other advantages too, because the idea of a revived consortium had enabled the United States to bring pressure on Britain and France to relinquish in some measure their exclusive options in their respective spheres of influence. In all these ways the consortium was publicized as an instrumentality to preserve China's political and administrative integrity.

Contrary, however, to official and popular expectations, China showed no enthusiasm for the consortium and refused to do business with it. The Chinese government and Chinese political leaders in general took the view that the consortium was a "threat of international control of Chinese finance" and "a monopoly or an attempted monopoly" designed to deprive China of a free world market where she could borrow on the best terms available.[31] Again it was evident that the problem of "pre-

---

[30] Selected correspondence on these negotiations in Paul H. Clyde, *United States Policy toward China*, 271-280. See also United States, *Foreign Relations, 1918*, 169-199; *1919*, I, 420-555; *1920*, I, 497-605; and Field, *American Participation in the China Consortiums*, 142-166.

[31] Remer, *Foreign Investments in China*, 331. For American reactions to the consortium see Eleanor Tupper and G. E. McReynolds, *Japan in American Public Opinion* (New York, 1937), 118-120.

serving" China and of serving American interests at the same time was not a simple task.

THE UNITED STATES SENATE AND SHANTUNG

If the intricacies and complexities of America's position in the Far East were apparent in the years under review, 1918-1920, the motives which fashioned policy were not so apparent as they are today. The debates in the United States Senate on the Shantung clauses of the Treaty of Versailles provide a case in point.[32]

The Treaty, with a long list of amendments, was reported to the Senate on September 10, 1919. Among the amendments was the proposal to reverse the Treaty by restoring Shantung directly to China. The importance of this proposal is clear when it is recalled that it was the Shantung articles on which Japan had been most insistent at Paris.

The Senate now plunged into a long and verbose debate in which the Shantung amendment played a conspicuous part. But the debate was not confined to the Senate chamber. . It was carried on simultaneously in the daily and periodical press, on the lecture platform, and in the pulpit. Although public sentiment was divided, the overwhelming opinion appears to have been that the transfer of German rights to Japan was an outrageous affront to international morality.[33]

On Capitol Hill, those Senators who opposed the Shantung clauses of the Treaty advanced two basic arguments: 1) the absence of equity or morality in permitting Japan to succeed to German rights; 2) the increased power Japan would enjoy at the expense of American far eastern interests. Those Senators who favored accepting the Shantung clauses as drafted at Paris admitted the moral weakness of the solution, but insisted: 1) that it was the only agreement which could be reached at Paris—that it was already made and could not be reversed unless the United States was prepared to go to war to do so; and 2) that the creation of the League more than balanced any temporary injustice to China ("temporary" because Japan had promised to return Shantung).[34]

The Treaty of Versailles was defeated by the Senate in March, 1920, but it remains to raise the question whether the senatorial arguments

---

[32] On the Senate's handling of the Treaty of Versailles see: D. F. Fleming, *The United States and the League of Nations, 1918-1920* (New York, 1932); Dexter Perkins, *Hands Off: A History of the Monroe Doctrine* (Boston, 1941), ch. viii; H. C. Lodge, *The Senate and the League of Nations* (New York, 1925).

[33] Tupper and McReynolds, *Japan in American Public Opinion*, 145-150.

[34] Robert E. Hosack, "The Shantung Question and the Senate," *South Atlantic Quarterly*, XLIII (1944), 181-193. These supporters of the Shantung clauses "poured their most derisive scorn, however, on those who opposed the Shantung clauses as a betrayal of ethical principles at the same time that they attacked the politics of President Wilson as too visionary and idealistic."

on behalf of the birthplace of Confucius represented a genuine and sincere senatorial interest in the hopes and aspirations of China. The answer would appear to be that "it is doubtful whether the Senate was genuinely interested in the fate of Shantung" at all. The moral arguments advanced in the Senate and the oratorical appeals to traditional popular sympathy for China were "basically an effort to protect the moral reputation of the United States rather than an effort to apply ethical standards in world affairs." The question of practical and "actual relief for China was of less importance than the abstract moral integrity of the United States." Furthermore, both proponents and opponents of the Shantung clauses viewed the "question in the light of its effect upon the passage or rejection of the Treaty as a whole." [35] In other words, the fate of Shantung so far as the Senate was concerned was a subordinate issue, despite the fact that it was Shantung which prompted some of the more glowing flights of oratory. With some few exceptions, the opinions of Senators upon the Shantung question were not determined by the merits of the Shantung question itself or upon the relation of the Shantung question to American far eastern policy but rather upon their views on whether the United States should accept or reject Wilson's League of Nations. This was certainly true of many of the small group of "irreconcilables," the men who were irreconcilably against the Treaty in any form and who were prepared to defeat it by fair means or foul. The motives of some of them at least may have been sincere—the belief that the United States must "be rescued from imminent peril." [36] Shantung was merely one convenient weapon among others to achieve this end.

But while Shantung was injected into the senatorial debates primarily for reasons not germane to the interests of American far eastern policy, the effects of the debates bore very directly on later efforts to implement Asiatic policy. Indeed, the loud debating of China's senatorial "friends" contributed fuel to far eastern fires. The loud debating riled the Japanese, encouraged the Chinese to hope for what was then impossible, made more difficult the ultimate return of Shantung to China, and weakened rather than strengthened the influence of the United States in eastern Asia.[37]

[35] Hosack, "The Shantung Question and the Senate," 189-193.

[36] T. A. Bailey, *Woodrow Wilson and the Great Betrayal* (New York, 1945), 59-61.

[37] Bailey, *Woodrow Wilson and the Great Betrayal,* 161-164. Note in particular Bailey's discussion of the degree to which misrepresentation may enter discussions of foreign policy; of the ironical aspects of senatorial indignation after twenty years in which the Senate had accepted leaseholds and spheres without becoming "unduly concerned"; and of how Senator W. E. Borah could fight to keep the United States out of the entanglements of a League in Europe while at the same moment he strove to push the United States into the broils of Asia.

CHAPTER 24

POLITICAL PHILOSOPHY AND
GOVERNMENT IN JAPAN, 1889-1918

IT WILL be recalled that in 1889 the Meiji emperor presented his
people with a constitution. This document was the symbol and the
measure of Japan's modernization and her westernization. But it was
more than this. The Constitution was promulgated on February 11.
This was the official though legendary anniversary of the day on which
in the year 660 B.C. the divinely descended Emperor Jimmu proclaimed
his kingdom in Yamato. This coincidence was not a matter of chance.
It symbolized the purposes of the makers of modern Japan, for it was
their intent to erect a nation-state, modern and Western in the forms
of its material life, but controlled by an intellectual and spiritual philosophy that was neither modern nor Western.

In the larger sense, this Japanese experiment with Western constitutional forms appeared to reflect the general progressiveness of the modern Japanese state. By the close of World War I, Japan had achieved a
place among the select company of the so-called great powers. She had
created a modern army and navy. She had participated in three major
wars. Though a relatively new member in the family of nations, she
had shown considerable aptitude as a student of power politics. In the
material shape of her domestic life she had gone far along the road of
modernization, westernization, and even industrialization. This vitality in her new national life created both friends and foes among the
nations who watched her progress, but even among foes there was a
general admiration for a people frequently described as able, intelligent,
progressive, and patriotic. Nevertheless, the seeming ease with which
Japan made these material and political adjustments tended to create
unwarrantable assumptions among Western peoples. There was, for
example, the tendency to assume that Japan, having acquired a constitution and a parliament, desired to set up Western liberal and democratic
institutions, and that she would seek Western democracy with the same
covetous regard that marked her adoption of railways, steamships, telegraphs, paved roads, and Scotch whisky. This is merely to say that

there was a general tendency to assume that the spirit as well as certain forms of Western democracy would soon prevail in Japan and that this spirit along with the principles of democracy would mean to the Orient what it had meant to the West.[1]

Actually, the political Japan that was being shaped in the years 1889 to 1918 was a curious complex of the new and the old, of the Occidental and the Oriental, of forces liberal and conservative, representative and autocratic, mundane and theocratic. In general, it is a period in which Japan's political history was controlled by a powerful oligarchy against which proponents of liberal and representative government waged a persistent political warfare and achieved measurable results. But it should be noted that the struggle toward liberalism was fought not against a long background of Anglo-Saxon political ideology but against a Japanese background of military dictatorship and feudal clan government. It is against this background that the history of Japanese political thought in the late nineteenth and early twentieth centuries should be seen.

MODERN JAPANESE POLITICAL THOUGHT

Japanese civilization in the broadest historical sense has been built to a very notable degree on alien cultures. During most of her history, certainly from the fifth to the eighteenth century, Japan drew heavily upon the wealth of Confucian China.[2] Since the middle of the nineteenth century, Western civilization has all but transformed completely the material face of Japan, and has also influenced, though in lesser degree, her intellectual outlook. Nevertheless, the realities of her dominating political thought in modern times have been peculiarly Japanese.

DISTORTIONS OF CONFUCIAN DOCTRINE

In two vital ways Japanese political philosophy has since early times changed and distorted some of the fundamentals of Confucian political thought. It is true that in a general sense Japan has accepted the basic concepts which hold that society is more important than the individual, that all men are by nature unequal, that politics is synonymous with ethics, that government by man is superior to government by law, and that the patriarchal family is the model of the ideal political state.[3] In China, however, there were certain safeguards. Although the Chinese

---

[1] The attitude in the United States was somewhat analogous to that which later greeted establishment of the Chinese Republic in 1912.

[2] Sir George Sansom, *Japan: A Short Cultural History* (London, 1932), in particular chs. iv-ix. (A revised edition was published in New York, 1943).

[3] R. K. Reischauer, *Japan: Government-Politics* (New York, 1939), 21-33.

emperor was a theocratic sovereign who ruled because he possessed the "Mandate of Heaven," it is notable that heaven might deprive an unworthy sovereign of the mandate. It thereupon became the duty of his subjects to be disloyal, to rebel, to overthrow the unworthy ruler, and to replace him by a virtuous sovereign. Furthermore, in China, the highest and most coveted honors in society and government were reserved for the civilian-scholars, the *literati*. These men, comprising the ruling class, owed their position not solely to any accident of birth, but to a system of competitive examinations, for which in theory at least every educated person was eligible. Japan, in contrast, distorted these principles to create a "line of emperors unbroken through ages eternal." She thereby produced a theory of absolute loyalty, Confucian in basis, but wholly lacking in Confucian safeguards. In addition, the guardians of this theory of patriotism, the historic Japanese ruling class, were not scholars selected by competitive examination, but feudal warriors who ruled by force of arms and by hereditary title.[4]

THE NINETEENTH-CENTURY REVOLUTION

The opening of Japan to Western intercourse in mid-nineteenth century, coinciding with the rise of a powerful mercantile class, precipitated the downfall of the shoguns, and of feudalism itself, thus paving the way for the creation of a new Japan based not on feudal clan loyalties but rather on a unique nationalism inspired by the restoration of the emperor to *de facto* power.[5] The Restoration leaders sought in creating a unified and nationalistic Japan to preserve their power by directing the absolute loyalty of a people toward a sovereign who was to be regarded as the descendant of the gods, and whose will was to be interpreted as that of "the state." [6]

This new political structure and the theories on which it rested were devised and evolved by men who were political theorists and office holders at one and the same time. In 1867, before the abolition of feudalism, most of them were *samurai,* military-feudal retainers of the

---

[4] Sansom, *Japan: A Short Cultural History,* chs. xiv, xv, xvii, xix, xxi.

[5] See H. S. Quigley, *Japanese Government and Politics* (New York, 1932), ch. ii, for a full discussion of the Restoration.

[6] For conflicting interpretations of the theory of Imperial powers, see: Quigley, *Japanese Government and Politics,* 67-68; Reischauer, *Japan: Government-Politics,* 167-169; G. E. Uyehara, *The Political Development of Japan 1867-1909* (London, 1910), 19; Tomio Nakano, *The Ordinance Power of the Japanese Emperor* (Baltimore, 1923), 5; H. Sato, *Democracy and the Japanese Government* (New York, 1920), 1; E. W. Clement, "Constitutional Imperialism in Japan," *Proceedings of the Academy of Pol. Science,* VI (1916), 325; U. Iwasaki, *Working Forces in Japanese Politics* (New York, 1921), ch. ii. The Japanese doctrine postulating the identity of the emperor and the state is known as *kokutai.*

Western Clans (Satsuma, Chochu, etc.).[7] These men engineered the Restoration (1867) and the formal abolition of feudalism (1871), enveloped the new Japan with the theory of unqualified loyalty to a "divinely descended" emperor in such a way that "the modern Japanese state was deliberately established on a foundation which unified government and religion."[8] The ancient mythology of prehistoric Japan was resurrected where convenient to provide the ultimate sanction for a theory of absolutism through divine right. State Shinto (the way of the gods) was revived and developed to serve a particular political end: namely, to justify belief in the omnipotence of an emperor whose throne was bequeathed by "the Heavenly Deities and the Great Ancestress."[9]

Twenty-two years after the Restoration, the Meiji emperor presented his people with a constitution (1889). It was the work primarily of a younger generation of the former *samurai* class who had been trained by the Restoration leaders and who remained true to the theory of theocratic absolutism which the latter had promoted. These men not only created the Constitution, they directed and controlled its functioning for some thirty years (1889-1918). The document which they devised was clearly a product of "Japanese political principles under the cloak of representative institutions."[10]

THE STRUGGLES OF LIBERALISM

Although the framers of the Constitution had no intent to create a liberal parliamentary regime, they recognized both the practical expediency of Western political forms, and the necessity of placating the growth within Japan of Western political thought, particularly liberalism. Indeed, three major currents of Western thought acquired significant influence in Japan following the Restoration: English utilitarian free thought, French social liberalism, and German political absolutism. At his Mita School (Keio University), Fukuzawa Yukichi taught that "Heaven does not create man above man, nor man under man."[11] Masanao Nakamura introduced concepts of subjective morality based on Christian standards. After 1880 French liberalism found a congenial

---

[7] Typical examples include: Takamori Saigo, Toshiminchi Okubo, Koin Kido. Reischauer, *Japan: Government-Politics*, 64.

[8] D. C. Holtom, *Modern Japan and Shinto Nationalism* (Chicago, 1943), 5.

[9] Holtom, 6.

[10] Uyehara, *The Political Development of Japan*, 110; Reischauer, *Japan: Government-Politics*, 75. The more influential of the men who shaped and controlled the working of the Constitution came later to be known as the Genro (Elder Statesmen): Hirobumi Ito, Aritomo Yamagata, Kaoru Inouye, Iwao Oyama, and Masayoshi Matsukata.

[11] Fukuzawa was the most distinguished intellectual of those who sought westernization at the time. *The Autobiography of Fukuzawa Yukichi* (Tokyo, 1934).

setting in the intellectual turmoil of the post-Restoration era. It inspired the platform of the first political party, the *Jiyuto* (Liberal Party)
in 1881, and in part prompted the Imperial rescript promising a constitution and a parliament in 1889. Rousseau's *Social Contract* had
already been translated by Tokusuke (Chōmin) Nakae. Montesquieu
and Voltaire were read widely, and for a brief period Kimmochi Saionji,
one of the greatest of Japan's liberals, reflected the democratic spirit in
his *Eastern Free Press*. English as opposed to French political influence was seen' in the appearance in 1882 of the second political party, the
Rikken Kaishinto (Progressive or Reform Party), with a parliamentary
program somewhat more conservative than that of the *Jiyuto*.[12]

Reaction, inspired by the government, was, however, already at work.
The indigenous nationalistic and absolutist trends were strengthened by
German influence. Many Japanese were already turning to the writings
of Stein, Gneist, Bluntschli, Jhering, and others. Ito drafted the Constitution under the spell of Bismarck and Prussia.[13] On the eve of
promulgation of the Constitution, Ito and Yamagata banished from the
capital more than 500 liberals. This move was designed to extinguish
all social and democratic thought.[14] The Constitution was thus introduced in an atmosphere of Bismarckian constitutional imperialism.
For nearly three decades this influence fused with State Shinto was sustained as the orthodox political philosophy. As a result, most liberal
political thought was driven into the literary channel of the political
novel. Ryukei Yano in his *Keikoku Bidan* glorified the democratic
zeal of heroes of ancient Greece. Tokaisanshi in his *Kajin-no-Kigu*
presented his hero standing in deep reverence before the Liberty Bell
in Philadelphia.[15] Yet, it would be easy to overestimate the influence
of such works, particularly in view of the fact that a new, and in part,
spontaneous resistance to European thought had already set in before
the turn of the twentieth century. This movement paraded under the
banner of "Preservation of national [Shinto] virtues." As early as 1892
Christianity was attacked by Tetsujiro Inouye on the ground that it did
"not conform to traditional Japanese ideas concerning the State." [16]

Nevertheless, Japan in the early twentieth century appeared to be
moving toward a responsible parliamentary government. From 1918
until 1932 the party politicians, as spokesmen of the new and powerful

---

[12] Kyoson Tsuchida, *Contemporary Thought of Japan and China* (London, 1927), 21-29.
[13] Quigley, *Japanese Government and Politics*, 40.
[14] Tsuchida, *Contemporary Thought of Japan and China*, 29.
[15] Tadao Kunitomo, *Japanese Literature since 1868* (Tokyo, 1938), 13, 23-28.
[16] Tsuchida, *Contemporary Thought of Japan and China*, 32.

industrialists, were in power.[17]   Liberals hailed it as the dawn of *kensei no jodo* (period of normal government).   In 1918 precedent was broken when Takashi Hara, a commoner, became prime minister.   Manhood suffrage was achieved in 1925.   Significant as were these changes, they by no means represented the extreme left wing of Japanese political thought.   While academic philosophers followed neo-Kantian individ-ualism and remained aloof from the so-called practical political prob-lems of society, many of the younger professional, political, and social scientists were turning to socialism as the answer to new problems aris-ing from Japan's industrialization and the consequent disintegration of the traditional family system.

LEFT WING THEORIES

The foundations of a new political and social philosophy had already been laid in the late Meiji and early Taisho eras (*ca.* 1910-1920).   Ōdo Tanaka demanded a sweeping reinterpretation of Japanese philosophy.   Kōjirō Sugimori saw the need for a new evaluation of political theory in the light of Japan's industrialization and social needs.   His basic politico-ethical concept described man as "a free agent."   Jirō Abe found in "freedom" his ideal society.   Reikichi Kita advocated a democracy and "the right of revolution." [18]   By 1920 political thinkers outside of government had swung far to the left.   Some of these men were critics who shunned the ideological approach, such as, for example, Manjiro Hasegawa, who attacked the concept of the State based on Shinto mythology.   In Takanobu Murobuse's *The Downfall of Civilization* (1923), there was the clear reflection of Spengler's influence.   Sakuzo Yoshino and Tokuzo Fukuda were direct in their attacks on the con-trolling oligarchy and bureaucracy.[19]

From these critics it was but a short road to the advocates of socialism. Although socialistic pamphlets appeared in Japan as early as 1881, it was not until 1901 that the Social Democratic [Marxian] Party was formed by Denjiro Kōtoku, Iso Abe, and Sen Katayama.   Suppression of the party by government was not surprising, for its anti-imperialistic phi-losophy made little popular appeal during the era of two wars, the Russo-Japanese (1904-05) and World War I (1914-19).   Radical so-cieties and their publications were banned almost as rapidly as they ap-peared and socialist and anarchist leaders were put to death with little discrimination.   After 1919, however, Marxian doctrine gained rapidly

[17] Reischauer, *Japan: Government-Politics,* ch. vi.
[18] Tsuchida, *Contemporary Thought of Japan and China,* ch. vii.
[19] Tsuchida, *Contemporary Thought of Japan and China,* ch. viii.

in popularity. *Das Kapital* was translated in full by Motoyuki Take-batake. The Russian Revolutions found their chief Japanese spokesmen in Toshihiko Sakai and Kin Yamakawa. Hajime Kawakami, while yet a member of the faculty of the Imperial University, began in 1919 a socialist periodical, *Studies in the Social Problem*. In 1923 students of Waseda University, under the leadership of Professor Ikuo Oyama, campaigned against the introduction of military training. Gradually this post-war peace movement became identified with general progressive and socialistic movements. Professor Sakuzo Yoshino of the Imperial University of Tokyo led in organizing the *Shakai Kagaku Rengokai* (Intercollegiate Association for the Study of Social Science).[20] Thus the fusion of pacifism and socialism appeared as a challenge to the orthodox political philosophy of the oligarchy and to the tradition of militarism which had survived the collapse of feudalism.

THE JAPANESE GOVERNMENT IN ACTION

The foregoing brief sketch of Japanese political thought suggests the dual aspect of Japanese politics in the period of constitutional government from 1889 to 1918. An oligarchy of the Genro, the Elder Statesmen, had fashioned the new political Japan, and it was these men who continued to control political destinies during the first three decades of government under the Constitution. Their power, however, was subjected to persistent attack from the "liberals," better termed the parliamentarians, who sought to reduce the oligarchic and clan statesmen to parliamentary and party control. It is a period in which aristocrats, oligarchs, and their servants, the bureaucrats, attempted, and for a time succeeded in, preserving the essentially autocratic and theocratic ideology in which the Constitution had been framed. The chief characteristics of this document and of the groups through which it functioned have already been outlined. The questions which now present themselves are: What was the experience of this constitutional government in action? What new forces challenged its control?

THE LEADERS IN GOVERNMENT

As already suggested in Chapter 10, it was the Genro who made the decisions and who executed them in the first thirty years of constitutional government. Between 1889 and 1918 the post of Prime Minister in a rapidly shifting series of seventeen governments was held by only

---

[20] K. W. Colegrove, *Militarism in Japan* (Boston, 1936), 15. Influential organs of the press (*Ashi* (Tokyo) and *Nichi Nichi* (Tokyo)) supported this anti-militaristic movement.

eight men, all of whom were Genro, quasi-Genro (in the case of Okuma),
or loyal protégés of Genro, as in the cases of Katsura, Yamamoto, and
Terauchi. With two exceptions, every president of the Privy Council,
the highest constitutional advisory body to the emperor, was also a
Genro.[21] Moreover, certain members of the Genro (Yamagata, Oyama,
and Katsura) carried over into the constitutional regime the military and
clan traditions of feudal days. Yamagata, as master of the Japanese army
until his death in 1922, measured every political decision of government in
terms of its effects upon army power and prestige.[22] This principle was
only slightly less pronounced in Matsukata's control of the navy. As a
result, the influence of the Genro was supreme in government because
the Genro controlled not only the cabinet but also the Privy Council, the
army, and the navy, and such key positions as Lord Keeper of the Privy
Seal, Minister of the Imperial Household, and the presidency of the
House of Peers.[23]

THE BEGINNINGS OF CONSTITUTIONAL GOVERNMENT

Constitutional government had its beginnings at a time when Japanese "patriots," dissatisfied with government policy toward the unequal
treaties, were resorting to attempted assassination of government leaders.
It was in this atmosphere that Yamagata, arch-militarist, faced the first
House of Representatives, in which Itagaki of the *Jiyuto* and Okuma of
the *Kaishinto* were smarting with resentment because they and their
party followings had been excluded from all key positions in the new
government. It was a stormy first session; a dissolution was avoided
largely by the inability of the political parties to combine effectively.
It marked the beginning also of efforts by Okuma and Itagaki to make
the government responsible to the Diet. When they failed to make any
progress on this point they turned to tactics of obstruction. When government was forced to dissolve the House, the opposition felt its first
major victory had been won.[24]

THE ELECTIONS OF 1892

After Yamagata's resignation, Premier Matsukata and his hench-
men, through their grip on the Ministry of Home Affairs, employed

[21] Count Takato of Hizen, 1890-92, and Count Kiyotaka Kuroda of Satsuma, 1895-99,
though not Genro, represented the interests of that group.
[22] For the perpetuation of the military tradition see: Colegrove, *Militarism in Japan,*
1-16; and E. E. Causton, *Militarism and Foreign Policy in Japan* (London, 1936), 13-46,
75-99.
[23] Tatsuji Takeuchi, *War and Diplomacy in the Japanese Empire* (Chicago, 1935), 11-19,
31-42.
[24] Reischauer, *Japan: Government-Politics,* 110, 113.

every devious device by which elections are controlled, yet, when in spite of this the party opposition was victorious, the Prime Minister refused to resign. However, his cabinet survived only one session. Ito, who now (1892) succeeded to the premiership, proved to be abler than his predecessors as a political manipulator. He used the power of the Imperial rescript to establish the principle that the Diet cannot change fixed expenditures. Furthermore, he used the power of the Throne to make the appointment or removal of ministers of state a matter subject only to the will of the sovereign.[25]

THE OLIGARCHY SAVED BY WAR

The resulting deadlock between Ito's government and the opposition in 1894 was relieved only by the outbreak of the Sino-Japanese War. The elections of this year were free from the strife and bloodshed that had stained previous ballots. Extraordinary war budgets were passed without parliamentary opposition. This temporary parliamentary peace was accompanied by a renewed shifting of political influence within the ranks of the Genro. While war enhanced the reputations of Yamagata and Oyama, the stigma of accepting the Triple Intervention of Russia, France, and Germany rested heavily upon Ito. Increased taxation added to Ito's unpopularity. He continued in power, however, until 1896, on the basis of concessions to Itagaki and the *Jiyuto.* When later in the year Matsukata succeeded to the premiership, he too found it expedient to offer political favors to Okuma and his *Shimpoto,* succession party to the *Kaishinto.* Thus was precedent established for opportunistic deals between the oligarchy and the major political parties. But Matsukata's efforts failed as ripidly as Ito's. A new Ito government succeeded Matsukata, but again collapsed within six months.

In the summer of 1898 Okuma and Itagaki, the party leaders, were called upon to form a government. Ito, who led the Genro to this decision, was influenced not only by the failure of the previous non-party governments but also by his jealousy of the growing influence of the militarists under Yamagata. The new government supported by the *Kenseito* (a union of the *Jiyuto* and *Shimpoto*) was short-lived. Party strife over the spoils of office destroyed the union; the cabinet resigned; and by November, 1898, after four months of party government, Yamagata was again premier. In their first government, the party politicians had proved themselves as irresponsible as the oligarchs. Yet even Yamagata had learned that he could not rule without some party support.

[25] For the constitutional relationship of the government and the Throne, see Takeuchi, *War and Diplomacy in the Japanese Empire,* 3-13.

He continued therefore the precedent of opportunistic alliances with chosen party leaders. Holding party politicians in contempt, he was nonetheless ready to purchase their votes in order to secure army appropriations.[26]

THE WAR AND NAVY MINISTRIES

It was at this time that Yamagata performed his most significant political work. It was he who devised the system whereby the Ministries of War and the Navy were to be headed only by high-ranking generals and admirals on the active list. From the strengthening of this tradition in later years arose the power of the army and navy to make and to break cabinets by the simple device of causing a service minister to resign, and refusing to appoint a successor until the demands of the General Staff had been met. This peculiar army and navy control was built on the theory of "the supreme command" embodied in an Imperial rescript of 1889, and in Articles 11 and 12 of the Constitution. Under these authorities, the Ministers of War and the Navy and the Chiefs of Staff had direct access to the Throne on matters within the compass of the supreme command. The service ministers thus enjoyed unique political power. They functioned: 1) as members of the cabinet reporting to the Throne through the Prime Minister; 2) as representatives of the supreme command reporting directly to the Throne.[27]

ITO AND THE SEIYUKAI, 1900

By 1899 there was a wide gulf of personal political dissension between Ito and the military wing of the Genro. Accordingly, in 1900 it is less surprising to find Ito accepting the presidency of a new political party, the *Seiyukai,* successor to the *Kenseito* which, ridiculously enough, had previously supported Yamagata. Deprived once again of party support, Yamagata resigned in 1900 and was promptly succeeded as premier by Ito, who selected an all-party cabinet save for the foreign and service ministries. But this government too suffered an early death, when Ito was accused of using the Throne to force his policies upon the House of Peers. This was the fourth and last of Ito's ministries. His failure spelled new advantages for the militarists within the Genro.[28]

---

[26] Quigley, *Japanese Government and Politics,* 210.

[27] On the theory of the supreme command see: Hirobumi Ito, *Commentaries on the Constitution of the Empire of Japan* (2nd edition, Tokyo, 1906), 28; Quigley, *Japanese Government and Politics,* 87-89; Takeuchi, *War and Diplomacy in the Japanese Empire,* 14-16; Colegrove, *Militarism in Japan,* 16-26; Tomio Nakano, *The Ordinance Power of the Japanese Emperor* (Baltimore, 1923), 154-156.

[28] Reischauer, *Japan: Government-Politics,* 119-120.

Yamagata, who was the natural successor to Ito in the now well established process of shuffling premiers, refused to head the new government. A number of factors influenced this decision: 1) the power of the military-clan Genro was for the time being secure; 2) Yamagata was of no mind to face the political attacks of Ito and the hostile *Seiyukai* in the Diet; and 3) the time was at hand when younger men were to hold the premiership while the older Genro continued their control behind the scenes. Accordingly, it was a military protégé of Yamagata, General Taro Katsura of Choshu, who became premier in June, 1901. Katsura, faced by parliamentary opposition, was forced like others before him to fall back on the budget of the preceding year. During 1903 the militarists continued to strengthen their position. Ito was made president of the Privy Council and thus removed from party affiliation. His place as president of the *Seiyukai* went to his civilian (Kuge) protégé, Kimmochi Saionji, who was eventually to become a full-ranking Genro and the last member of the august body. Here too, as in 1894, war came to the aid of the militarists. As the tension with Russia increased, the Diet sprang to the financial support of the army. This fervent patriotism continued unchecked until the signing of the Treaty of Portsmouth. Then political peace promptly gave place to violent attacks on government resulting in declarations of martial law. Unwilling to face the hostile Diet, Katsura resigned, and was succeeded by Saionji.

For two and one-half years (January, 1906–July, 1908) Saionji's government, supported by the *Seiyukai,* maintained itself in office. Its fall was due primarily to financial policies which failed to satisfy the military oligarchs. Katsura again succeeded to the premiership, and when in 1909 Ito was assassinated in Harbin, Yamagata, militarist and archenemy of all liberal and representative trends, was left as supreme directing head of the Genro. Against this newly entrenched position of the oligarchy, the parliamentarians could exert but little pressure, since political discord within the ranks of the *Seiyukai* precluded any vigorous attack upon the government. As a consequence, Katsura was left free to carry through the annexation of Korea. Far from attacking the policy, the House of Representatives urged Katsura to use the "big stick" in Korea.[29]

The annexation of Korea was another major victory for the militarists. Katsura therefore retired, and Saionji again headed the government in August, 1911. It was in this administration that the growing inner conflict of principle within Japan's political machinery was clearly exposed. Yamagata and the Army wanted the creation of two divisions for Korea.

[29] Takeuchi, *War and Diplomacy in the Japanese Empire,* 166-167.

Saionji, with the civilians of his cabinet, refused to support this policy. Thereupon, the Minister of War resigned, and when Yamagata and the General Staff refused to name a successor, there was nothing for Saionji and his cabinet to do but resign. The army oligarchs had given a practical demonstration of their power to dominate over the civilian wing of government.[30]

With doleful regularity, Katsura again became Prime Minister (1912), though by this time he was no longer the disciple but rather the rival of the aging Yamagata. This estrangement and his unpopularity with the parliamentarians led Katsura to form his own political party, the *Rikken Doshikai* (Constitutional Fellow-thinker's Society). However, even with lavish use of funds he was unable to secure a majority. He had failed in his challenge to the power of Yamagata and in his efforts to buy parliamentary support.

YAMAMOTO AND NAVAL SCANDALS

The Genro now turned to Admiral Count Gombei Yamamoto (Satsuma), but when it was discovered that the Navy was implicated in financial scandals touching battleship construction, the Diet refused to pass the budget, and Yamamoto resigned.

The new premier was Marquis Shigenobu Okuma (1914), whose command of the Diet during two and a half years was in part due to a new coalition party, the *Kenseikai*. By this time the opposition *Seiyukai* had passed under the able leadership of a commoner, Kei Hara. Though Okuma had been one of the early champions of popular government, his administration from 1914 to 1916 was also marked by unprecedented chauvinistic nationalism: Japan's entry into World War I, and presentation of the Twenty-One Demands upon China. It is significant, however, that the government under Okuma recognized in a measure its responsibility to the Diet.[31]

TERAUCHI AND THE MOB

When Okuma resigned in 1916, the premiership passed with unfailing monotony to one of Yamagata's men, General Seiki Terauchi, a soldier of some reputation but wholly unprepared to meet the political, economic, and social dislocations of a Japan undergoing wartime industrialization. War profiteers had already been the occasion of popular in-

---

[30] Quigley, *Japanese Government and Politics,* 214; A. Morgan Young, *Japan under Taisho Tenno* (London, 1928), 21; Reischauer, *Japan: Government-Politics,* 126-127.
[31] For a Japanese interpretation of Okuma see Smimasi Idditti, *The Life of Marquis Shigenobu Okuma* (Tokyo, 1940), ch. xv.

dignation, and, when the government failed to control the price of rice, the authorities were defied, and rioting spread from city to city.[32] These rice riots, as they were called, were symbolic of new forces stirring within Japan—forces with which the military oligarchy lacked the capacity to deal. Accordingly, in May, 1918, Kei (Takashi) Hara, the first untitled man to hold the office, became premier. Often referred to as Japan's "Great Commoner," Hara was a gifted politician who had achieved leadership of the *Seiyukai* through his ability to command the personal loyalty of his followers. Like many of the military oligarchs who preceded him, Hara was unscrupulous, recognizing only loyalty to party rather than to any abstract program of political ideology. Yet his elevation to the premiership was a significant event. It marked the end of rule by the Genro and the clansmen of Satsuma and Choshu. It marked the beginnings of rule by party politicians—men of a new Japan in which the commerce, industry, and finance of a bourgeois society seemed destined to replace the feudal and military traditions perpetuated by the Genro.[33]

---

[32] Young, *Japan under Taisho Tenno,* 116-118.

[33] The economic and industrial background of the politics discussed in this chapter will be presented in Chapter 28.

CHAPTER 25

THE FAR EAST AND THE WASHINGTON CONFERENCE

A S WORLD WAR I receded into the category of things past, and as
mankind welcomed the new years of peace, thoughtful men could
evaluate with greater perspective the popular slogans of the war years.
It was already becoming clear that decisive victories on the battlefield
had not been followed by equally decisive victories at the conference
table. There was the suspicion that the world had not been made "safe
for democracy." The public mind was troubled with foreboding questions. Had man witnessed the "war to end war"? Had militarism
been crushed? Where were "the open covenants openly arrived at"?
What of "freedom of the seas," and the removal of economic barriers
among the nations? Did the revelations of nationalism at the Paris
Peace Conference forecast a better world? Was there to be implementation of the principle of arms reduction? Was the United States,
which had deserted its traditional neutrality in 1917, and whose president had given vitality to the concept of a League of Nations, now to
return to isolation under cover of "the rhetorical mirage of normalcy"?
Indeed, the entire program of Wilsonian principles in which humble
men and women had placed their faith seemed, like the war itself, to
recede into a past compounded of pleasant but impractical idealism.
The new post-war statesmanship would recruit its ranks from the
apostles of "normalcy." There were Hardings in every major capital.[1]

By 1920, to this fundamental questioning of the overall post-war picture had been added new and specific problems, international in character, some created by the war, others magnified by it. These new focal
points of friction were by no means limited to particular geographical
areas, for they were found in the Old World and the New World alike,

---

[1] For the background of the immediate post-war period see: D. F. Fleming, *The United
States and the League of Nations, 1918-1920* (New York, 1932); C. O. Johnson, *Borah
of Idaho* (New York, 1936); H. B. Learned, "The Attitude of the United States Senate
towards the Versailles Treaty: 1918-1920," H. W. V. Temperley, editor, *A History of
the Peace Conference of Paris* (5 vols., London, 1924), VI, ch. v; W. Stull Holt, *Treaties
Defeated by the Senate* (Baltimore, 1933).

but they were particularly acute in the sphere of American-Japanese relations. The co-belligerency of the United States and Japan had not served to harmonize their respective far eastern policies. As the reader is aware, the roots of American-Japanese friction had grown lustily since the days of the Russo-Japanese War in 1904-05. Dollar diplomacy in Manchuria, Oriental immigration in California, special interests versus the open door in China had already made it quite clear that there was a growing coolness in the traditional nineteenth-century friendship between Japan and the United States. By 1920 there was a widespread popular conviction in the United States and Canada, and to a lesser degree in Great Britain and France, that Japan had shown little interest in the defeat of German militarism, and that she had used the war primarily to advance Japanese hegemony in China. This is simply to say that between 1918 and 1920 cordiality in American-Japanese relations had reached an all-time low. This record was traceable directly and in an immediate sense to the differences which had arisen out of the Twenty-One Demands of 1915, the Lansing-Ishii exchange of 1917, the Japanese program as presented at Paris with respect to Shantung and the German islands in the Pacific, and finally, to Japanese military and railway policies in Siberia and Manchuria during the Inter-Allied Intervention of 1918.[2]

"GIVE US YAP! GIVE US YAP!"

Although there is ample evidence to support the marked deterioration in American-Japanese relations, it should be noted that neither the Senate nor the American public at large can be said to have felt any deep concern over far eastern politics in the early post-war years. It will be recalled that the most impassioned senatorial pleas for the restoration of China's rights in Shantung do not appear to have been prompted by any real concern for the birthplace of Confucius. Even in the case of questions which had a direct and immediate bearing upon real and tangible American interests in the Pacific, the American public showed at best a rather half-hearted interest. As a case in point, reference may be made to a controversy that arose with Japan over the hitherto obscure little island of Yap. Located in the western Carolines, Yap was one of the former German islands of the North Pacific taken over by the Japanese. Its peculiar virtue lay in the fact that it was a submarine cable center in the German-Dutch system which connected the Netherlands Indies with Shanghai, and also in the fact that it was linked by cable with the trans-Pacific American cable running through Guam to Ma-

[2] See Chapter 23.

nila. At Paris, Wilson had expressed the hope that Yap be internationalized. This would have prevented the Japanese from gaining a monopoly control over the former German cable system. However, the Peace Conference mandated Yap along with the other German islands in the North Pacific to Japan. American claims were presented subsequently in a long diplomatic correspondence with Tokyo which was not concluded until 1922. Here it is sufficient to note that while the American public was not inclined to regard the Yap affair as a crisis, it was concerned over the island's importance as a cable center for American communications with the Philippines. However, some part of Yap's fame in 1919 was not due to the politics of empire but rather to an American parody on a popular war song entitled, "Yap for Yappers":

> Give us Yap! Give us Yap!
> The Yanks have put it,
> The Yanks have put it,
> The Yanks have put it,
> On the map! [3]

THE TRIANGULAR NAVAL RACE

More tangible in American eyes, and more significant in the American mind, was the appalling naval race in which the United States, Great Britain, and Japan found themselves involved as the war came to a close. Building programs launched during the war were reaching the peak of implementation. To what end was this construction now that the war was over? Amicable relations between Great Britain and the United States gave credence to the open secret that America and Japan were preparing to fight each other in the Pacific.[4] The prospect suggested the complete negation of every ideal for which the war had been fought. Actually, if there was to be a naval race, the United States was better prepared than its potential enemies to face the financial burdens involved. The war had seriously affected British resources, and though Japan had grown wealthy in the war years, her industrial structure was no match for America's. These maritime powers were there-

---

[3] Quoted by Yamato Ichihashi, *The Washington Conference and After* (Stanford University, 1928), 334-335. See also Paul H. Clyde, *Japan's Pacific Mandate* (New York, 1935), ch. iv; Quincy Wright, *Mandates under the League of Nations* (Chicago, 1930), 43-44.

[4] In the United States current inflammatory literature was plentiful. For surveys of this material, see: Iichiro Tokutomi, *Japanese-American Relations* (New York, 1922), 140-143; Eleanor Tupper and G. E. McReynolds, *Japan in American Public Opinion* (New York, 1937), 156-157.

fore faced with the prospect of an American navy which by 1924 would equal, if it did not surpass, the British fleet.[5] The only doubt lay in the question whether the American voter would support the naval appropriations called for by the Naval Appropriation Act of 1916. Both Republicans and Democrats hesitated to add to the nation's gigantic war debt. Furthermore, the fact that the United States had repudiated the League of Nations did not mean that the American people had forsaken the ideals of peace for which they believed they had fought. The scrapping of the Versailles Treaty and the election of Harding in 1920 did not mean that the Wilsonian program had been blotted from the American consciousness. Among Harding's advisers and in the Republican Party at large were many leaders such as Charles Evans Hughes, the new Secretary of State, who were committed to the principle of arms reduction among the great powers, and to American leadership to this end.[6]

THE TROUBLESOME ANGLO-JAPANESE ALLIANCE

On the international political front no problem of the immediate post-war years was more perplexing than that presented by the Anglo-Japanese Alliance. During nearly two decades this Alliance had remained as the keystone of Anglo-Japanese policy. By 1920, however, when Russia and Germany, the powers against which the Alliance was originally directed, were no longer threatening British or Japanese interests, big navy advocates in the United States, supported by the yellow press and by brochures of more substantial scholarship,[7] had taken the position that the Alliance was aimed at the United States and would eventually involve this country in war against Japan and Great Britain in eastern Asia. The idea was one which the British had sought to allay over a period of years. In 1911, as the Alliance was being renewed for a second time, the British made it clear that the obligation of belligerency would not apply against a power with which either signatory had concluded a treaty of general arbitration. However, the Anglo-American arbitration treaty of August 3, 1911, was not approved by the

---

[5] R. L. Buell, *The Washington Conference* (New York, 1922), 139-144; H. C. Bywater, *Sea Power in the Pacific* (New York, 1921), 10; Ichihashi, *The Washington Conference and After*, ch. i.

[6] Fleming, *The United States and the League of Nations*, ch. xii. The Republican platform of 1920, while repudiating the League, had called for "an international association" designed to preserve the peace.

[7] See for example the study by A. L. P. Dennis, *The Anglo-Japanese Alliance* (Berkeley, 1923). Though not published until after the Washington Conference, this study exercised considerable influence on the American delegation.

United States Senate.[8] The subsequent Anglo-American Treaty of
1914 (Bryan Peace Commission Treaty) was not one of general arbitration as interpreted in the Anglo-Japanese Alliance.[9] Finally, Japan's
position at Paris relative to Shantung, and her relations with the British
in Siberia (1918-1920), led once again to the growing conviction that
the Anglo-Japanese Alliance was a bulwark of Japanese policy in Asia.
Even British assurances given in 1920 that the Alliance would not be
binding in the event of war between the United States and Japan did
not dispel these fears.[10] Moreover, official American apprehension was
heightened during 1920 by the belief that Anglo-Japanese negotiations
looking to further renewal of the Alliance were in progress. Finally,
it is to be observed that in Canada the Alliance was regarded with equal
apprehension. Like the states of the Pacific Coast, Canada was showing
increased concern with Oriental, particularly Japanese, immigration.
Canadians readily believed that in an Anglo-American war, Canada
would be a principal theater of operations. How strong this Canadian
sentiment was may best be judged by the success of Premier Arthur
Meighen, who literally forced the London Imperial Conference of June,
1921, to agree that the Alliance must be ended and replaced by a new
and broader agreement covering the Pacific.[11]

THE EARLY BIRD CATCHES THE WORM

Sufficient has been said to indicate how little had been contributed
by World War I to the hopes for peace and tranquility in the Pacific.
It is hardly an exaggeration to say that the Pacific rather than the Atlantic had become, temporarily at least, the center of world politics involving a threatened naval race and increased tension between the
United States and Japan. Here, in part, lay the explanation of why a
Republican administration which had repudiated Wilson's League now
turned to the idea of an international conference on arms reduction.
Even before Harding was inaugurated, Senator W. E. Borah of Idaho
introduced (February 24, 1921) a resolution for a three-power conference. Despite Harding's opposition, the resolution, widely supported
by the press and by public demonstrations throughout the country, was
approved by the Senate and House by overwhelming votes (May 25 and
June 29). By this time both Britain and the United States were moving

[8] See A. W. Griswold, *Far Eastern Policy of the United States* (New York, 1938), 168.
[9] Text of the Bryan Treaty in United States, *Foreign Relations, 1914,* 304-307.
[10] C. N. Spinks, "The Termination of the Anglo-Japanese Alliance," *Pacific Historical Review,* VI (1937), 326.
[11] J. B. Brebner, "Canada, the Anglo-Japanese Alliance and the Washington Conference," *Political Science Quarterly,* L (1935), 45.

rapidly toward the idea of a conference. So far as these two powers were concerned, it was becoming a question as to which should gain the prestige of calling the nations together. But behind this superficial rivalry lay a fundamental political question transcending the more obvious problem of arms reduction. It was the question whether Great Britain under a new Anglo-Japanese Alliance "was to support the special interests of Japan" in the Far East or to align herself more solidly with the traditional American principles of the open door and the integrity of China.[12]

The sequence of events leading to the calling of the Washington Conference may now be briefly told. On March 16, 1921, Lord Lee, First Lord of the British Admiralty, proposed publicly a naval agreement with the United States recognizing the principle of parity.[13] Shortly thereafter, Adolph Ochs, publisher of *The New York Times,* became the medium of a British proposal to the United States whereby the two states would accept naval "equality," the British navy guarding the Atlantic while the American navy would be concentrated in the Pacific. Thus, Britain, while moving cautiously toward renewal of the Anglo-Japanese Alliance, was also suggesting concentration of American seapower against Japan. Nevertheless, the proposal was welcomed in Washington, where it was becoming clear that Britain was prepared to modify the Japanese alliance to meet the wishes of Canada and the United States. As a consequence, on July 5, Lord Curzon suggested to Ambassador George Harvey

. . . that the President [Harding] invite [the] powers directly concerned to take part in a conference to be held to consider all essential matters bearing on [the] Far East and [the] Pacific Ocean with a view to arriving at a common understanding designed to assure settlement by peaceful means, the elimination of naval warfare, [and] consequent elimination of arms, etc.[14]

The British also conveyed this proposal to Japan. Harvey's cable to Washington carrying the British suggestion was crossed by one from Secretary Hughes asking whether the British would receive favorably an invitation to a conference called by the United States.[15] Meanwhile, Hughes' concept of the proposed meeting was growing both in point of agenda and membership, and on July 11, 1921, the press of the world

---

[12] United States, *Foreign Relations, 1921,* II, 314-316. Also, the Republicans called the Washington Conference in part because they had troubled consciences growing out of their failure to find a way into the League.

[13] E. J. Young, *Powerful America* (New York, 1936), 47-54.

[14] United States, *Foreign Relations, 1921,* I, 19-21.

[15] United States, *Foreign Relations, 1921,* I, 18.

announced that President Harding was inviting the powers to an international conference.

THE RELUCTANT GUEST

The response of the powers to America's informal overtures was for the most part cordial, but there were some discordant notes. The Belgians protested that they had been ignored.[16] Russia, unrecognized at this time by the "respectable" society of nations, asserted her undeniable interest in the Far East and proclaimed her own non-recognition doctrine applicable to "any decision taken" by the proposed conference.[17] Japan, too, as was to be expected, showed her reluctance to rush into a conference which was to discuss questions of the Far East. Japanese opinion, both official and public, was critical. It was impossible to disguise the fact that the conference was designed in considerable measure to apply the brakes to policies which Japan had followed since the Twenty-One Demands of 1915. Moreover, the most influential forces in Japanese politics still favored retention of the Anglo-Japanese Alliance. For various reasons Japan was favorable to the idea of arms reduction, but on the subject of political questions concerning the Far East she suspected that a trap had been set, and she wanted a bill of particulars on the agenda. This, Hughes refused, and it was not until July 26 that Japan finally gave her reluctant consent to attend a conference on questions of the Pacific and the Far East as well as on the limitation of armament.[18] In accepting the invitation, the Japanese government gave notice that "problems such as are the sole concern to certain particular powers or such matters that may be regarded [as] accomplished facts should be scrupulously avoided." [19]

STATESMEN OR POLITICIANS?

The formal invitations went out to the powers on August 11, 1921. Nine powers were on the guest list. The great powers included Great Britain, France, Italy, Japan, and the United States. The lesser powers were Belgium, China, the Netherlands, and Portugal. These were included because of their real or supposed interests in the Pacific. It was not anticipated that they would participate in the arms conference. Since German and Austrian interests in the Far East had been liqui-

---

[16] United States, *Foreign Relations, 1921*, I, 30.

[17] United States, *Foreign Relations, 1921*, I, 40-43.

[18] On these preliminary negotiations with Japan see: United States, *Foreign Relations, 1920*, II, 682-685; *1921*, I, 31-53 *passim;* Dennis, *The Anglo-Japanese Alliance*, 64-93; Tatsuji Takeuchi, *War and Diplomacy in the Japanese Empire* (New York, 1935), ch. xx; Kikujiro Ishii, *Diplomatic Commentaries* (Baltimore, 1936).

[19] United States, *Foreign Relations, 1921*, I, 45.

dated by the war, these powers were excluded. The absence of Russia from the list of invited guests could be explained, however, only on the basis of a blind and irrational quarantine with which the victorious powers hoped to isolate the Soviet government.[20]

In terms of personalities, the conference was an assemblage of political and diplomatic stars. The American delegation, headed by Secretary of State Charles Evans Hughes, included Elihu Root, long associated with the conduct of American foreign policy; Henry Cabot Lodge, chairman of the Senate Foreign Relations Committee, a politician who more than any other American was responsible for the repudiation of Versailles and the League; and Senator Oscar W. Underwood, Democratic minority leader on the Foreign Relations Committee. Britain's delegation was headed by the Tory aristocrat and scholar-statesman, Arthur Balfour, a former Prime Minister and Foreign Secretary. Japan sent Admiral Baron Tomosaburo Kato, who in 1922 was to become premier. Leadership of the French delegation was held first by Aristide Briand, Minister for Foreign Affairs, a diplomat "shrewd and skillful in emergencies," and later, after Briand's departure, by René Viviani, a member of the Chamber, and eloquent in his appeals to foreign sympathy. Out of this group came the "Big Three"—Hughes, Balfour, and Kato—who in secret negotiations guided the conference and in general determined its decisions.[21]

THE WAY TO DISARM IS TO DISARM

It was an illustrious assembly of notables that gathered in Memorial Continental Hall on November 12, 1921, to hear President Harding's exuberant remarks of welcome. He was followed immediately by Secretary Hughes, chairman of the conference, who, avoiding the triteness of diplomacy's language, declared that the nations had come together "not for general resolutions . . . but for action." [22] Thereupon he presented to the startled delegates and the galleries a plan for immediate slashing of naval strength. In brief, the American proposal called for:

a) a naval holiday for 10 years in capital ship construction;
b) the scrapping of many ships, including some already in commission and others in process of building;

---

[20] Russia, of course, as noted, protested against her exclusion, and promised in advance not to be bound by any of the decisions. United States, *Foreign Relations, 1921*, I, 40-43.

[21] Ichihashi, *The Washington Conference and After*, chs. i, ii; Buell, *The Washington Conference*, chs. i, ii, iii.

[22] *Conference on the Limitation of Armament, Washington, November 12, 1921–February 6, 1922* (Washington, D. C., 1922), 58.

c) application of the program of scrapping so as to leave the navies of the United States, Great Britain, and Japan in a ratio of 5-5-3; France and Italy, without scrapping, would fit into this ratio as 1.75-1.75;
d) capital ship replacements would be limited by treaty to 500,000 tons each for the United States and Great Britain, and to 300,000 tons for Japan;
e) similar ratios would be applied to aircraft carriers, cruisers, destroyers, and submarines.[23]

The measured words of Secretary Hughes electrified not only the audience which sat before him but the far larger audience of press and public opinion. While delegates threw off their complacency and reporters flashed the news to their papers, the galleries burst into wild applause. No diplomatic conference in the world's history had opened in this way. Yet in reality, the surprise of the delegates lay not so much in the cards that Hughes held as in the boldness of his opening play. No matter how distasteful the idea of naval parity may have been to the British, the fact was that the British government had conceded the principle of parity several months in advance of the conference. Moreover, since the naval ratio proposal could not be detached from political problems of the Far East, Japan's efforts to establish the autonomy of the two conferences was all but defeated from the beginning. In any event, Hughes seems to have been justified in playing most of his cards in the first move instead of holding them in reserve for bargaining purposes. This conclusion seems justified in the light of the final outcome of the conference. But for the moment the future of the Washington Conference would be determined by the measured responses of Britain and Japan to the Hughes proposal. Since Japan was asked to accept an inferior ratio, since her army was "opposed to any reduction," since her government did not believe there could be "any lasting friendship with the United States,"[24] the fate of the Hughes' proposal was doubtful at best.

METAMORPHOSIS OF THE ANGLO-JAPANESE ALLIANCE

Moreover, British acceptance, though likely, could not be taken for granted. Since the question of naval power could not be divorced from political policy as represented by the Anglo-Japanese Alliance,

[23] United States, Sen. doc. 126, 67th Cong., 2nd sess., *Conference on the Limitation of Armament,* 41-63. In addition to the proceedings cited in the Conference document (cf. footnote 22) the Senate document contains certain minutes of committees, the report of the American delegation, and texts of treaties and resolutions.
[24] B. E. C. Dugdale, *Arthur James Balfour* (2 vols., New York, 1936), II, 237-242.

Balfour had come to Washington hoping to substitute "a tri-partite agreement with America" for the old two-power alliance.[25] He was convinced that the Japanese would accept this if they could not have the old alliance intact. However, Secretary Hughes would have none of this proposal, for it would have amounted to American recognition of the "special interests" of Japan and Britain in the Far East.[26] Rather, he hoped the alliance could be replaced by an agreement embodying the principles of the Root-Takahira notes of 1908. Opposed at first by both Balfour and Kato, Hughes not only won his case but secured the inclusion of France in the Four-Power Pacific Treaty, signed December 13, 1921. By this 10-year treaty, superseding the Anglo-Japanese Alliance, the signatory powers agreed:

a) to respect one another's rights in the regions of the Pacific in respect to their "insular possessions and insular dominions";
b) to meet in joint conference "for consideration and adjustment" of any "controversy arising out of any Pacific question and involving their said rights which is not satisfactorily settled by diplomacy"; and
c) if the rights of the contracting parties "are threatened by the aggressive action of any other Power" to "communicate with one another fully. . . ."[27]

The early signature of the Four-Power Treaty materially advanced the fortunes of the conference. The inclusion of France was one of the moves designed to win that country to acceptance of the inferior naval ratio (1.75 as against 5-5-3 for the great powers) assigned to it by the Hughes plan. By ending the Anglo-Japanese Alliance and substituting the broader pledge of "consultation," the Treaty went far to remove American and Canadian fears of Anglo-Japanese co-operation in some future war. Furthermore, by combining principles of the Root-Takahira notes of 1908 with those of the Bryan treaties of 1914, the United States had been given a renewed pledge against aggression in the Philippines, a fact of consequence since Japan, now in possession of the Marshall, Mariana, and Caroline Islands, lay athwart direct American approaches to Manila.[28]

---

[25] Dugdale, *Balfour*, II, 242.
[26] Griswold, *Far Eastern Policy of the United States,* 309.
[27] United States, *Foreign Relations, 1922,* I, 7-36.
[28] There was a long wrangle between the Big Three, involving a question of national pride, as to whether the Four-Power Treaty applied to the Japanese homeland. Hughes and Balfour claimed that it did; Kato that it did not. The Japanese argument was that their homeland did not wish to profit by a pledge usually granted to weaker nations. In the end the Japanese had their way. United States, *Foreign Relations, 1922,* I, 13-39.

THE *STATUS QUO* IN PACIFIC FORTIFICATIONS

Japan's assent to the Four-Power Treaty did not mean that Tokyo was prepared to accept the Hughes program of naval reduction. Japan regarded the western Pacific as her home waters. Here she proposed to achieve and maintain her own naval supremacy. She found little virtue in the consultative principles of the Four-Power Treaty if these were to function side by side with expanding British and American naval bases at Hongkong, Manila, Guam, and other Pacific islands. Accordingly, Kato, who personified Japanese naval philosophy, suggested that Japan would be more likely to look with favor on the Hughes plan if agreement could be reached on maintenance of the *status quo* in Pacific fortifications and if Japan should be permitted to keep the battleship *Mutsu,* which was virtually ready to be launched, and instead scrap the older *Settsu.* On December 15, 1921, the Big Three reached agreement on the non-fortification principle which later became Article XIX of the Five-Power Naval Treaty (February 5, 1922). The three powers agreed that: "The *status quo* at the time of the signing of the present Treaty, with regard to fortifications and naval bases, shall be maintained" in specific possessions. Specifically, the territories in which new fortifications were prohibited included:

a) for the United States: the Aleutians, Guam, Pago-Pago, and the Philippines;
b) for Great Britain: Hongkong and British insular possessions in the Pacific, east of 110 east longitude, excepting islands adjacent to Canada, Australia, and New Zealand;
c) for Japan: the Kurile Islands, Bonin Islands, Amami-Oshima, the Loochoo (Ryukyu) Islands, Formosa, and the Pescadores.

THE FIVE-POWER NAVAL TREATY

This was the price for Japan's acceptance in principle of the Hughes naval plan. Even then the plan was not wholly acceptable to Britain or Japan. On the contrary, it was whittled down to apply only to capital ships before it could be embodied along with the non-fortification agreement in the Five-Power Naval Treaty noted above. As finally concluded, the Naval Treaty provided for:

a) a 10-year holiday in capital ship construction;
b) the scrapping of specified vessels in commission and building (United States, 845,000 tons; Great Britain, 583,000 tons; Japan, 435,000 tons);

c) limiting the tonnage of capital ships and aircraft carriers to 35,000 and 27,000 respectively, and the caliber of their guns to 16 and 8 inches respectively.

The Treaty was to apply until December 31, 1936, and might be terminated thereafter through two years' notice by any signatory.[29]

The terms of this epochal treaty are easily stated, but its immediate effect upon the interplay of national policies in the Pacific and the Far East is not susceptible of simple evaluation. With the exception of Italy, all of the five powers professed their dissatisfaction. Italy's case was unique. Throughout the conference she had been vexingly agreeable, insisting only that she be accorded naval parity with France. France, on the other hand, was piqued not only by this Italian attitude but also by the determined policy of the Big Three to keep France as a third-class naval power. To France, the naval ratio was primarily a matter of national pride, for her policy of security was based on land armaments. Nevertheless, France did not accept the ratio until Hughes had appealed over the heads of the French delegation to Briand in Paris.[30] Likewise, the British, Japanese, and American delegations were far from satisfied. The naval men in particular grumbled that they had given more than they had received.

Granting that the results of the naval conference cannot be measured with mathematical precision, it may nonetheless be conceded that Japan had won tangible and specific advantages. If her sensitive national pride was wounded by the inferior capital ship ratio, her security was greatly increased by the same ratio, by the non-fortification agreement, by her possession of the former German islands in the North Pacific, and by the resulting liberty she enjoyed to pursue her own specific aims in China.

Britain also profited. Although she did forego the right to add to the fortifications of Hongkong and islands in the Central Pacific, she retained full liberty to fortify Singapore, Australia, and New Zealand,

[29] For the negotiations, drafts, and final text of the treaty: United States, *Foreign Relations, 1922*, I, 53-267.

[30] Prior to World War I, France had been a first-class naval power. During the war, however, she had concentrated on land power while the British, vastly expanding their navy, took responsibility for the war at sea. Thus at the end of the war French naval power was at low ebb. French pride was hurt by the Hughes proposal to freeze French naval power by ratio at this inferior level. Hughes was convinced, however, that "existing strength" was the only basis on which any general limitation could be made. The sensitivity of the French was also piqued when, at the first session of the conference, all chairs at the head table were occupied by members of the American, British, and Japanese delegations. This arrangement was corrected at later meetings.

which were not likely to be threatened so long as Japan observed the non-fortification clause. In a word, Britain gave up little and received much in return. Her advantage was the more striking because the Far East, while of great importance, was of much less significance in British policy than were the Middle East or Europe.[31]

Did the United States win advantages comparable to those gained by Britain and Japan? Conceding that the conference had made Japan the naval master of the western Pacific, the arbiter of China's future, and that the United States in terms of naval fortifications had agreed to remain east of Pearl Harbor, it would seem that Secretary Hughes had given much in return for a 10-year naval holiday in capital ship construction. But the foregoing discussion by no means gives a complete picture of either the American position in 1922 or of the realities of American public opinion with which Hughes had to deal. As will be seen in subsequent pages, the Five-Power Naval Treaty was not to be regarded as an isolated agreement but as an integral part of a larger settlement embodying the decisions of the concurrent conference on problems of the Pacific and the Far East from which emerged the Nine-Power Open Door Treaty concerning China—a treaty which bound the signatories to respect the traditional principles of American policy in China. Again one must raise the question as to what alternatives Hughes could have proposed to Kato's suggestion for the non-fortification clause? The evidence on this question is reasonably clear. In the first place, it was not Hughes who surrendered the idea of a strong American military and naval base in the Philippines. That surrender had been made in 1905 when Theodore Roosevelt gave his approval to the Taft-Katsura understanding.[32] In the second place, the alternative to the non-fortification clause was an American naval building program which would have blocked any program of naval limitation and thus have made the conference itself unnecessary and futile. Moreover, at the time of the conference, senatorial leaders were convinced that Congress would not vote the appropriations that a large building program would have entailed.[33] This was the view not only of Republicans and Democrats who had favored the League's machinery for peace, but also of the "irreconcilables" and the former advocates of the "large policy," including Henry Cabot Lodge. These are the factors that must be

---

[31] Note in particular the discussion by Griswold, *The Far Eastern Policy of the United States,* ch. viii, especially 317-322.

[32] See pp. 465.

[33] Cf. Griswold, *The Far Eastern Policy of the United States,* 320, citing Philip C. Jessup, *Elihu Root* (2 vols., New York, 1938), ch. xlvii.

weighed in any effort to determine whether Hughes surrendered too much and gained too little.[34]

THE FAR EASTERN CONFERENCE

The answer, of course, to the critics who maintained that the United States had not struck a good bargain on naval power in the Pacific was the Nine-Power Open Door Treaty concerning China which emerged from the concurrent conference on far eastern questions. This treaty in both its weakness and its strength will be understood best by those who view it as the culmination of nearly a century of American policy in the Far East. That policy had rested essentially on three principles. The first of these was most-favored-nation treatment, to which in 1899 and 1900 had been added the commercial open door and the integrity of China. The resulting composite policy was one of self-interest, not sentiment. Practically, it was vulnerable in the highest degree, because American commercial interests in China were relatively small and because the American people had never shown a willingness to defend by force the open door or the integrity of China. The result was that American policy was never fully implemented. Between 1900 and the end of World War I, the powers had violated the open door and China's integrity whenever they regarded it as advantageous to do so and whenever they were not restrained by their mutual jealousies and fears. American policy had served to retard these encroachments; it did not prevent them.

THE REASSERTION OF TRADITIONAL AMERICAN POLICY

In the light of the foregoing historical background, the American delegation had little choice in the course it should pursue. The Conference itself was based on the idea of naval limitation. The Congress and public opinion were opposed to large naval appropriations. Therefore Hughes was limited from the beginning to diplomatic and legal implementation of American principles respecting China. Here, as in the case of the open door notes of 1899, it was the British who made the first positive overtures.[35] Balfour had come to Washington not only with the proposal of a three-power agreement to take the place of the Anglo-Japanese Alliance, but also with a suggested five-power agree-

---

[34] Another factor, beyond the scope of this discussion, is that the extra-League Washington Arms Conference interrupted the disarmament plans of the League, and had something to do with their final failure, though they probably would have failed anyhow.
[35] Cf. the Hippisley-Rockhill conversations, p. 295.

ment among the United States, Britain, France, Japan, and China. It was designed to insure four principles: 1) the peace of eastern Asia, 2) the independence and territorial integrity of China, 3) equality of commercial opportunity in China, and 4) international co-operation toward China.[36] Using this British suggestion as a starting point, Hughes set about "to give new vigor and reality to the co-ordinated principles of territorial and administrative integrity of China and of the 'open door' or equality of opportunity for all nations in China."[37] He proposed to do this by writing these principles into a multilateral treaty, thus making them for the first time a part of the body of international law. Even here, the obstacles in Hughes' path might well have seemed insurmountable. First, there was Japan's well publicized claim to a "special position." Second, there was the general confusion in China's domestic politics in which an "independent" government at Canton under Sun Yat-sen was contesting the claims of the recognized war-lord government in Peking. And thirdly, there was the general habit of the powers to give lip service to such ideas as China's integrity, while they clung tenaciously to all those special privileges derogatory to China's integrity which they possessed under the so-called unequal treaties. To put it another way, the revolutionary tendencies within China were as unpopular with the Western powers as they were in official circles in Japan.[38] Adding to Hughes' difficulties was the fact that a chaotic and revolutionary China was represented at Washington by a delegation which, as at Paris in 1919, was demanding a "bill of rights" quashing all the unequal treaties. This would have meant abolition not only of Japan's "special position," but also of the conventional tariff, extraterritoriality, and so forth, enjoyed by all the treaty powers.[39]

THE NINE-POWER OPEN DOOR TREATY

When these obstacles are assessed in their full measure, the extent of America's diplomatic triumph resulting in the Nine-Power Open Door Treaty is more apparent. Here too is revealed the basis for Hughes' concessions on Pacific fortifications.

The Nine-Power Treaty was to be so vital to the future of American policy in the Far East that some of its articles must be given in full. The signatory powers (the United States, Great Britain, France, Japan,

[36] United States, *Foreign Relations, 1922,* I, 1-2, 271-272.
[37] United States, Sen. doc. 126, 67th Cong., 2nd sess., 820.
[38] Owen Lattimore, *Solution in Asia* (Boston, 1945), 73.
[39] United States, Sen. doc. 126, 67th Cong., 2nd sess., 444-445; United States, *Foreign Relations, 1922,* I, 272-274.

Italy, Belgium, the Netherlands, Portugal, and China) consented to the following articles:

Article I:

The Contracting Powers, other than China, agree:

(1) To respect the sovereignty, the independence, and the territorial and administrative integrity of China;

(2) To provide the fullest and most unembarrassed opportunity to China to develop and maintain for herself an effective and stable government;

(3) To use their influence for the purpose of effectually establishing and maintaining the principle of equal opportunity for the commerce and industry of all nations throughout the territory of China;

(4) To refrain from taking advantage of conditions in China in order to seek special rights or privileges which would abridge the rights of subjects or citizens of friendly States, and from countenancing action inimical to the security of such States.

Article II:

Not to enter into any treaty, agreement, arrangement, or understanding, either with one another, or, individually or collectively, with any Power or Powers, which would infringe or impair the principles stated in Article I.

Article III:

With a view to applying more effectually the principles of the Open Door or equality of opportunity in China for the trade and industry of all nations, the Contracting Powers, other than China, agree that they will not seek, nor support their respective nationals in seeking:

(a) any arrangement which might purport to establish in favour of their interests any general superiority of rights with respect to commercial or economic development in any designated region of China;

(b) any such monopoly or preference as would deprive the nationals of any other Power of the right of undertaking any legitimate trade or industry in China, or of participating with the Chinese Government, or with any local authority, in any category of public enterprise, or which by reason of its scope, duration or geographical extent is calculated to frustrate the practical application of the principle of equal opportunity.

It is understood that the foregoing stipulations of this Article are not to be so construed as to prohibit the acquisition of such properties or rights as may be necessary to the conduct of a particular commercial, industrial, or financial undertaking or to the encouragement of invention and research.

China undertakes to be guided by the principles stated in the foregoing stipulations of this Article in dealing with applications for economic rights and privileges from Governments and nationals of all foreign countries whether parties to the present Treaty or not.

Other articles bound the signatories: 1) to refrain from supporting their nationals in seeking spheres of influence or "mutually exclusive opportunities in designated parts of Chinese territory"; 2) to respect China's neutrality; 3) to consult fully in circumstances requiring the application of the Treaty. China agreed not to permit discrimination in railroad rates. Powers not signatory to the Treaty were invited to adhere to it.[40]

The Nine-Power Treaty was, beyond any question, a tangible advance over any previous enunciation of American policy in the Far East. By it, historic American principles had been made a part of international law binding upon each of the signatories. However, the Treaty was marked by striking limitations. Far from being a renunciation of "rights" acquired in the past, it was merely a contract limiting future action. Furthermore, the Treaty was wholly lacking in sanctions other than the good faith of the signatory powers. Finally, it was a treaty concerned primarily with principles upon whose definition the powers had more often than not been in disagreement. If, on the basis of these limitations, American policy in 1922 as represented by the Nine-Power Treaty is to stand condemned, the question must still be raised: Was there an alternative policy which the American people would have accepted at that time? To this question, the answer supplied by available evidence is an emphatic, No.

TARIFFS, EXTRATERRITORIALITY, SHANTUNG

Several other major Chinese problems were tackled before the Far Eastern Conference adjourned. The first of these was China's demand for tariff autonomy. To meet this the conference agreed to the Nine-Power Treaty on the Chinese Tariff (February 6, 1922), which, while not granting tariff autonomy, did permit substantial increases in the rates and thus in China's revenue. The basic, though unpublicized, reasons why the conference was not prepared to concede more included a number of considerations: 1) the opposition of foreign commercial interests to increased tariffs, and 2) the conviction that increased revenues would be squandered by numerous war-lord factions in fruitless civil wars. However, the Treaty, in setting up a commission for study and reform of the Chinese tariff administration, kept the door open for further concessions if and when China's government showed itself capable of assuming fuller responsibility.[41]

---

[40] Text of the Nine-Power Treaty is in: United States, *Foreign Relations, 1922,* I, 276-282; Sen. doc. 126, 67th Cong., 2nd sess., 893-897. Clause 4 of Article I amounted in substance to the secret protocol attached to the Lansing-Ishii notes of 1917. Cf. p. 402.

[41] Text of the Tariff Treaty, United States, *Foreign Relations, 1922,* I, 948-957.

On the vexed question of extraterritoriality, which the Chinese hoped to abolish, the conference resorted to a resolution setting up a commission which was to study the entire complex problem and to prepare the way for abolition in the future. This was far from being what Chinese spokesmen wanted, but it was all that any of the foreign powers at this time were willing to concede. Indeed, for many years after the Washington Conference even the United States remained unwilling to submit its nationals to the mercies of China's system of courts and police.[42] Other resolutions adopted by the conference abolished foreign post offices in China, except those in the leased territories, with, however, the proviso that China must set up a satisfactory postal service. The powers also restricted by resolution foreign-owned and operated radio stations on Chinese soil.[43]

Although the Washington Conference itself did not attempt to deal with the Shantung question, Hughes and Balfour were responsible for bringing the Chinese and Japanese together and for breaking the deadlock which threatened to result. At Washington the Chinese were still demanding, as they had at Paris three years earlier, full and direct restoration of the former German rights. The Japanese were equally emphatic. They were prepared to restore the leasehold, but only under the terms of the 1915 and 1918 treaties and through direct negotiations with China.[44] The good offices of Hughes and Balfour finally resulted in Sino-Japanese discussions extending through thirty-six meetings with British and American "observers." Even then the negotiations were only sustained through persistent and powerful British and American pressure at Peking and Tokyo.[45] By the Sino-Japanese treaty which resulted (February 4, 1922), Shantung was returned to China. However, Japan would retain control of the Tsinan-Tsingtao Railway for

---

[42] Paul H. Clyde, *United States Policy toward China* (Durham, 1940), statement by Secretary of State, Frank B. Kellogg, 286-291. The United States and Great Britain relinquished their extraterritorial rights in China in 1943.

[43] On these various resolutions see the discussions in Yamato Ichihashi, *The Washington Conference and After,* chs. xiii-xvi; and R. L. Buell, *The Washington Conference,* chs. viii-ix.

[44] The principle was one on which the Japanese had insisted ever since the Shimonoseki negotiations of 1895.

[45] President Harding told the Chinese Minister that "it would be a colossal blunder in statecraft if China were not to take advantage of the opportunity now afforded her for the settlement of the Shantung question as the alternative might involve a risk of losing the Province." United States, *Foreign Relations, 1922,* I, 945.
Balfour had meanwhile attempted to draw concessions from the Japanese by agreeing to return Wei-hai-wei to China, a gesture which appeared more generous than it was in reality, since this leasehold had already lost much of its strategic value.

fifteen years during the life of a loan through which China purchased the road. The settlement was obviously a compromise. Japan retained temporarily a considerable measure of economic and political control while China had won something more than the mere principle of her claim.

China made less headway in her efforts to abrogate the Manchurian clauses of the treaties and notes of May, 1915. None of the great powers at Washington was prepared to concede officially the Chinese claim that these treaties were invalid because they had been forced upon China. Such a concession might well have opened the way for attack on many other treaties. Moreover, invalidation of the Japanese sphere in South Manchuria would have undermined the foundations of the British and French spheres, to say nothing of the Russians in North Manchuria who were not represented at Washington. Thus China's case against Japan in Manchuria was doomed from the start. Japan, it is true, made a gesture of concessions which was largely meaningless since she had already conceded two of the points mentioned. She opened her railway options to the joint activities of the consortium (this she had already done in 1920 under careful limitations); she withdrew Group V of the Twenty-One Demands which she had previously "postponed" because of the unanimous opposition of the powers; and she denied any intention to impose political, military, or financial advisers upon the Chinese government in South Manchuria.

The position of the United States relative to this diplomatic battle between China and the sphere-holding powers was, however, given explicit statement by Secretary Hughes. He stated: first, that under most-favored-nation treatment, the United States would claim from China all benefits enjoyed by Japan under the 1915 treaties; and second, he carefully reserved any American expression as to the validity of those treaties.[46]

Before the conference adjourned, the United States also appeared in what may seem as the curious role of defender of Russia's territorial integrity in eastern Siberia. At this time, it will be recalled, Russia was not recognized by the United States, nor had she been invited to the conference. Nevertheless, repercussions of the Siberian Intervention of 1918 still possessed weight as Hughes won from the Japanese (January 23, 1922) another assurance that their military forces would soon be withdrawn from Siberia and North Sakhalin. It appears, however, that pressure from within Japan rather than the diplomacy of Hughes

[46] United States, Sen. doc. 126, 67th Cong., 2nd sess., 779-780.

was responsible for Japan's subsequent withdrawal from Soviet territory.[47]

YAP AGAIN!

During, but not as a part of the conference, the United States raised again with Japan its claims concerning the island of Yap. These negotiations brought forth an American-Japanese treaty, February 11, 1922, whereby the United States recognized the Japanese mandate over the former German islands in the North Pacific, while Japan in return granted to American citizens residential, cable, and radio rights on Yap.[48]

IN CONCLUSION

When Harding convoked the Washington Conference, much was expected of its labors. When the conference adjourned, much had been accomplished. Outstanding were major steps in the limitation of naval armament and in writing American principles vis-à-vis China into the treaty structure of international law. These were positive contributions, but they should be assessed in the light of conditions as they existed at the time of the conference. These conditions, political, economic, and diplomatic, did not suggest that the conference possessed a clear mandate either for disarmament or for the scrapping of historic policies of nationalism and imperialism in Asia or elsewhere. It is true that the conference met at a time when a war-weary world, disillusioned by Versailles, was demanding some tangible evidence that the war had not been fought in vain. On the other hand, there was ill-disguised and world-wide skepticism of the League of Nations as an instrument for peace, particularly after its repudiation by the United States Senate. Harding was not wide of the mark when in 1920 he estimated American opinion by saying:

America's present need is not for heroics but healing; not nostrums but normalcy; not revolution but restoration; . . . not surgery but serenity.[49]

There was an irresistible, if unseen, pressure to return to ways which men thought of as tried and tested. Men wanted a better world but also illogically a world that had returned to "normalcy." Naturally this

---

[47] Tatsuji Takeuchi, War and Diplomacy in the Japanese Empire, ch. xviii, in particular 214-215.

[48] Text of the Yap treaty, United States, Foreign Relations, 1922, I, 599-604.

[49] F. L. Allen, Only Yesterday (New York, 1931), 41-42.

jumbled post-war philosophy was reflected in the Washington Conference. While the powers were prepared to make limited concessions toward a naval holiday in capital ships, and toward the principle of consultation in future disputes arising in the Pacific and the Far East, they were not prepared to extend naval limitation to other categories of ships or to land armies, nor were they prepared to surrender in China their special rights resting on nearly a century of unequal treaties. A world which wanted peace still placed its trust in nationalism and special alliances rather than in disarmament and collective security. In China, the conference did little more than freeze the *status quo*.

Finally, it must be concluded that America's policy from Versailles to Washington is a curious commentary on the logic of facts. In 1919-1920 the United States had turned its back on the League of Nations and the principle of collective security. It was thereupon thrown back on its *own* national military and naval power for the implementation of its policies whether in Europe or in Asia. Then at Washington in 1922, the United States effectively curbed the offensive arm of its navy by capital ship limitation. By making Japan supreme in the western Pacific, the fate of American policy in China was placed in Japanese hands. True, there was the Nine-Power Open Door Treaty, but this was a sad substitute, completely lacking in sanctions, for the system of collective security which might well have emerged had the United States assumed leadership in the League of Nations. The fact that America had not assumed this leadership cannot be attributed solely to Lodge and the "irreconcilables." Rather it must be explained by the weight of historic traditions. It was natural that policies which in the nineteenth century had served this country well, should be surrendered reluctantly as a new world called for new policies.[50]

---

[50] As an aftermath to the conference, the Lansing-Ishii Agreement was cancelled on December 27, 1922.

CHAPTER 26

FROM FREE IMMIGRATION TO DISCRIMINATION AND EXCLUSION

JUST as World War I bequeathed a legacy of international rivalry and suspicion touching every major area of the globe, so also it bequeathed national domestic problems of the most serious import. As will be seen, these domestic questions, by their very nature, did not recognize national boundaries. Though domestic in their origins, they were international in their immediate and ultimate consequences.

THE REVIVAL OF NATIONALISM

The war, which was to have made the world "safe for democracy," and was to have created an international philosophy suggested by the League of Nations, had created instead an intense, and often unreasoning, nationalism.[1] This new nationalism became a sort of popular hysteria. Responsible American officials warned the public that "ten million people were ready to leave Europe" for America. Bills were proposed to stop immigration entirely since the influx would lower American standards of living and demoralize American character.[2] Moreover, the impression grew that the new immigrant tide would bring to America the contagion of European revolution, in particular the radicalism of the Bolshevist Russian revolutions.[3]

Indeed, the immigrant scare assumed a vast variety of forms. Sectarian groups saw in immigration a possible "menace to prohibition and even Protestantism."[4]

In reality these flamboyant manifestations were more than the extreme symptoms of racial, religious, economic, or political prejudice.

---

[1] Arthur M. Schlesinger, *Political and Social Growth of the American People, 1865-1940* (New York, 1941), 494.

[2] O. Fritiof Ander, "The Effects of the Immigration Law of 1924 upon a Minority Immigrant Group," *Annual Report of the American Historical Association,* III (1942), 343-352; H. B. Parkes, *Recent America* (New York, 1941), 440; John D. Hicks, *The American Nation* (Cambridge, 1941), 561.

[3] Ander, "The Effects of the Immigration Law of 1924," 345.

[4] *Congressional Record,* 68th Cong., 1st sess., 6271.

They were signs of America's post-war and "post-frontier search for a stable and an indigenous civilization." The war had served to emphasize that the era of free land was now past and that the nation's new task was to produce "a civilization peculiar to the American race and suited to a static society." [5]   This, of course, would involve modification, if not repudiation, of official American attitudes toward foreign peoples. It would challenge the historic concept that America was the "asylum for the oppressed." [6]   The high peak of the earlier philosophy of free immigration had been reached in the Seward-Burlingame negotiations of 1868. These had imbedded in the solemn words of a treaty the dictum that "man has an inalienable right to change his home and his allegiance." But the "march of events" had overtaken and passed Seward and Burlingame and their treaty. A nineteenth-century shibboleth had lost its appeal to the generation of post-war Americans.

BEGINNINGS OF EXCLUSION

The story of the exclusion of Chinese laborers from the United States and its possessions and of the barring of Chinese nationals from American citizenship has already been told.[7]   This principle of Chinese exclusion had seemingly been made final by 1904 when Congress re-enacted the statutes covering Chinese immigration. The occasion was the expiration of the Sino-American treaty of 1894. The result was an outraged Chinese opinion which expressed itself in 1905 in a systematic boycott of American business in China.[8]   While the Chinese phase was thus disposed of, the specter of Oriental immigration had raised its head in another quarter.

THE JAPANESE IN HAWAII

By 1900 there were 61,111 resident Japanese in the Hawaiian Islands, or about 40 percent of the total population. Most of these had come under the terms of a Hawaiian-Japanese cheap labor convention signed in 1896 at the instigation of Hawaiian sugar growers. The political implications of this fast-growing Japanese population were not lost on

---

[5] Rodman W. Paul, *The Abrogation of the Gentlemen's Agreement* (Cambridge, 1936), 3; see also Ander, "The Effects of the Immigration Law of 1924," 345; H. P. Fairchild, *Immigration* (New York, 1925), 460.

[6] Evidences of intolerance—racial, religious, and political—in the post-war years pointed not only to the foreign immigrant but also toward domestic groups in the United States that were considered radical. The period was personified by the work of A. Mitchell Palmer, Attorney-General of the United States. F. L. Allen, *Only Yesterday* (New York, 1931), 46.

[7] See Chapter 12.

[8] C. F. Remer, *A Study of Chinese Boycotts* (Baltimore, 1933), 29-39.

those Americans who had now become interested in annexation of the islands.[9] It was not surprising, then, that in March, 1897, the revolutionary Hawaiian government, dominated by Americans, created something of a crisis when it refused entry to 1,174 Japanese immigrants. Japan protested and sent a warship to Honolulu where its actions were watched by three American warships. Under American mediation, Japan's claims against the Hawaiian government were soon settled, but the importance of the incident was its effect in hastening American annexation of the islands, August 12, 1898.[10]

THE JAPANESE IN THE UNITED STATES

The disposal of Chinese immigration by the Congressional enactments of 1904, and the crisis in Japanese-Hawaiian relations in 1897-98, coincided with the rise of a new problem—the Japanese immigrant in the United States. Until 1900 there were virtually no Japanese in the United States. The census reports for 1870 listed 55 Japanese; for 1880, 148; for 1890, 2,039; but for 1900, 24,326.[11] The tendency of Japanese immigration to the United States to show marked increases had been noted as early as 1892 when United States immigration officers protested the wholesale importation of Japanese laborers to the Pacific Coast. As a result of this protest the Japanese government took steps to discourage the movement.[12] Then, in the American-Japanese commercial treaty of 1894, the United States was careful to stipulate that while in matters "of residence and travel" Japanese were to enjoy all the privileges of the most favored nation, nevertheless, such rights were in no way to

affect the laws, ordinances and regulations with regard to trade, the immigration of laborers, police and public security which are in force or which may hereafter be enacted in either of the two countries.[13]

Anti-Japanese agitation first took shape in San Francisco in 1900 when public meetings demanded application to the Japanese of the Chinese

---

[9] The first abortive American attempt at annexation was the Marcy Treaty of 1854. In 1875 the United States secured from the Hawaiian government a favored commercial status and a pledge that no Hawaiian territory would be alienated to any other power. In 1884 the United States secured the right to use Pearl Harbor as a naval base. In 1893 a revolution against the Hawaiian government resulted in a second attempt at annexation.

[10] R. L. Buell, *Japanese Immigration* (Boston, 1924), 286; A. W. Griswold, *Far Eastern Policy of the United States* (New York, 1938), 339-344; T. A. Bailey, "Japan's Protest Against the Annexation of Hawaii," *Journal of Modern History,* III (1931), 46-61.

[11] Buell, *Japanese Immigration,* 284.

[12] P. J. Treat, *Diplomatic Relations between the United States and Japan, 1853-1895* (2 vols., Stanford University, 1932), II, 383-385.

[13] W. M. Malloy, *Treaties* (2 vols., Washington, 1910), I, 1030.

exclusion laws. Responsive to this agitation, Japan announced her intention to suspend entirely "for the present" emigration of her laborers to both the United States and Canada. However, Japanese continued to enter the United States from Hawaii. Renewed agitations led by the Japanese and Korean Exclusion League occurred in San Francisco early in 1905. Discriminatory legislation was introduced in Congress and, when these bills failed, owing to the opposition of the executive, the San Francisco School Board, in October, 1906, ordered by resolution all Japanese children to attend the Oriental school located in Chinatown. Meanwhile, the California legislature had been joined by the legislatures of Nevada, Idaho, and Montana, in petitioning Congress to stop Japanese immigration. Japan countered by restricting and then temporarily suspending emigration to Hawaii, but by this time the San Francisco School Board was on record

. . . for the higher end that our children should not be placed in any position where their youthful impression may be affected by association with pupils of the Mongolian race.[14]

ROOSEVELT'S ANALYSIS OF AMERICAN INTERESTS

As the immigration crisis in California continued to mount, President Roosevelt sought to adjust it to the general picture of American interests in the Pacific and the Far East where he was fast becoming the key personality in the hoped-for peace conference between Japan and Russia.

After considerable experimentation he rated peace, amicable trade relations, the security of American territory in the Pacific and the effective restriction of oriental immigration all ahead of the territorial integrity of China in the category of American national interests.[15]

In essence, Roosevelt concluded: 1) that Philippine security depended on an understanding with Japan (Taft-Katsura conversations, p. 336); 2) that discrimination against a vigorous Oriental state would destroy commercial most-favored-nation treatment for American commerce in the Far East and render illusory the open door in China and the security of the Philippines. These broader aspects of statecraft were, however, receiving little attention in San Francisco and on the Pacific Coast where the Japanese immigrant had fallen heir to the charges which thirty years

---

[14] T. A. Bailey, *Theodore Roosevelt and the Japanese-American Crises* (Stanford University, 1934), 14.
[15] Griswold, *Far Eastern Policy of the United States,* 349.

earlier had been heaped upon the Chinese immigrant. The Japanese
were said to be immoral and vicious, and as children in the schools they
were too old to associate with American youth. The charges were
either unfounded or deliberately exaggerated.[16]

JAPAN PROTESTS

On October 25, 1906, basing her action on the treaty of 1894, Japan
formally protested "the condition of affairs in San Francisco," pointing
out that the segregation of Japanese children because of nationality was
"an act of discrimination carrying with it a stigma and odium which it
is impossible to overlook."[17]   The President, recognizing the seriousness of the crisis, took prompt action. Victor H. Metcalf, Secretary of
Commerce and Labor, was sent to the Pacific Coast to investigate. The
Secretary of the Navy was instructed to submit comparative data on
American and Japanese naval strength. The President assured the Japanese Ambassador privately that the question would be placed before
Congress; this was done in the message of December 4, 1906. The message bristled with Rooseveltian vigor. It touched upon the progress
and growing power of Japan, upon the historic friendship between the
two nations, and upon the School Board resolution as a "wicked absurd-
ity." It ended with a plea that Japanese be admitted to citizenship by
naturalization, and threatened use of the army to protect Japanese in
their treaty rights.[18] While the message was received with enthusiasm
in Japan, and with favor in eastern United States, it brought forth fresh
bursts of wrath from California, where, after all, a settlement would
eventually have to be reached. Accordingly, the President turned to the
softer methods of compromise. He tried but failed in securing Japan's
assent to a treaty mutually excluding the laborers of both countries.
With the San Francisco Board of Education, which he had invited to
Washington, he was more successful. In return for Roosevelt's promise
to end the immigration of Japanese laborers, the Board agreed to rescind
the obnoxious resolution.

The problem before the President was now two-fold. The first was
to stop the migration of Japanese laborers from Hawaii to the mainland
of the United States. This was accomplished by amendment to the

---

[16] Bailey, *Roosevelt*, ch. ii; United States Sen. doc. 147, 59th Cong., 2nd sess. At
the time the School Board resolution was adopted there were 93 Japanese pupils in San
Francisco's public schools. Of these, 25 were American citizens; 28 were girls; 33 were
between 15 and 20 years of age. The charges of immorality were never substantiated.
There were some instances of twenty-one-year-old Japanese seeking to enter the first grade
with six-year olds.
[17] Bailey, *Roosevelt*, 64.
[18] United States, *Foreign Relations, 1906*, vii ff.

immigration law of 1907 providing at the President's discretion for exclusion of immigrants carrying passports "to any country other than the United States or to any insular possession of the United States or to the Canal Zone." [19] The more difficult problem remained—the stoppage of direct labor migration from Japan to continental United States.

THE GENTLEMEN'S AGREEMENT, 1907-1908

The first proposal made by President Roosevelt and Secretary Root was for a treaty prohibiting immigration of Japanese laborers to the United States and American laborers to Japan. Japan was agreeable if the United States would recognize the naturalization of Japanese immigrants other than laborers. This was unacceptable to Root, who in turn proposed that Japan herself impose the restrictions desired by the United States.[20] Accordingly, on February 24, 1907, the Japanese government indicated its intention to continue the policy then in force of not issuing passports for continental United States for laborers except to those

who, in coming to the Continent, seek to resume a formerly acquired domicile, to join a parent, wife, or children residing there, or to assume active control of an already possessed interest in a farming enterprise in this country.[21]

Details of this Gentlemen's Agreement were not complete until February, 1908, and it was not until the following October that departures of Japanese immigrants exceeded arrivals. Meanwhile, anti-Japanese agitation in California had continued. All in all, it was patent that no matter how successful the Gentlemen's Agreement might be in curbing the influx of Japanese, it was not regarded as a wholly acceptable answer to the problem. Writing in 1908, Professor A. C. Coolidge said "it would be idle to pretend that the outcome is wholly satisfactory." While the Gentlemen's Agreement would give the United States the protection demanded, it rested "not on the efficiency of its own [American] laws, but on the fulfilment of obligations voluntarily assumed by a foreign state." [22]

[19] *Congressional Record*, 59th Cong., 2nd sess., 2809.

[20] Griswold, *Far Eastern Policy of the United States*, 354.

[21] *Annual Report of the Commissioner-General of Immigration, 1908* (Washington, 1908), 125-126. The Gentlemen's Agreement is not contained in a single document. Its text, on the contrary, consists of correspondence exchanged between the United States and Japan during 1907 and 1908. A résumé is printed in United States, *Foreign Relations, 1924,* II, 339-369. It was published in 1939.

[22] A. C. Coolidge, *The United States as a World Power* (New York, 1917; first published in 1908), 355-356.

The Gentlemen's Agreement, however, was far more than an important executive agreement whereby Japanese immigration was to be controlled. In the mind of the President it was a necessary part of the complex of delicate forces supporting American far eastern policy. If there were to be renewed outbursts of anti-Japanese violence on the Pacific Coast, new campaigns for discriminatory legislation and eventual abrogation of the Agreement, then the whole framework of American far eastern policy would again be in jeopardy. There would be no security for the American flag in the Philippines or for the open door in China.

THE PACIFIC COAST WANTS SECURITY TOO

As events were soon to prove, the vocal elements in Pacific Coast politics did not find the Gentlemen's Agreement to their liking. They continued to find in the presence of Japanese communities a threat to American institutions and ways of life. Although the Agreement did provide effective control of the flow of Japanese immigrants, it was found wanting in other respects. From the inception of the Agreement until 1924, total entries of Japanese into the United States were 120,317; departures, 111,636. For the United States and Hawaii the figures were: arrivals, 171,584; departures, 155,488. This was a net increase of only 16,096, or 7,415 for Hawaii and 8,681 for continental United States.[23] Nevertheless, although immigration was controlled, the Japanese population in the United States multiplied with what was considered alarming rapidity. From 24,326 in 1900, it rose to 72,157 in 1910, and to 111,010 in 1920. Those who viewed with alarm could assert that whereas between 1910 and 1920 the total population of the United States increased 4.9 percent, that of the Japanese had increased 53.8 percent. Related figures appeared equally arresting. The excess of Japanese births over deaths in California in 1911 was 523; in 1921 it was 4,379. Actually, these figures taken by themselves were misleading. They represented temporary trends due in part to the fact that virtually all Japanese women in the United States were of child-bearing age.[24]

Renewed troubles were not long in appearing. When the California Commissioner of Labor issued in 1910 a favorable report on the contribution of the Japanese to California agriculture, the document was suppressed as not representing "the wishes of the people of this common-

---

[23] Buell, *Japanese Immigration*, 291.
[24] *14th Annual Census of the United States*, II, 779; Buell, *Japanese Immigration*, 285; "The Fecundity of Immigrant Women," *Immigration Commission Reports*, XXVIII (1910-11), 146, 805.

wealth." [25]   However, when in 1911 the American-Japanese treaty (1894) of navigation and commerce was renewed, the United States conceded to Japan's wishes by amending the clause which had given the United States the right to legislate the exclusion of Japanese labor. Secretary Knox regarded this as merely an appropriate gesture to Japanese pride since Congress had the inherent right to control immigration whether or not the right was expressed in treaty provisions.[26]

THE ALIEN LAND LAWS

California's legislature returned to the anti-Japanese campaign in 1913 when it passed a law prohibiting land ownership by aliens ineligible to citizenship, and limiting leaseholds to three years.   While the Japanese were not mentioned by name, and while the law carefully reserved all rights held by treaty, it was no secret that the legislators had the Japanese in mind.   The attack was legally sound, for the American-Japanese treaty of 1911 did not confer on Japanese the right to ownership in land.   The Department of State therefore maintained the position that California's act had not violated the treaty.   On the other hand, the Department was unable to meet with the same firmness the Japanese charge that the state law was discriminatory.   Then, in 1920, California went further by denying to aliens ineligible to citizenship the right to lease land.   The passage of both laws was opposed by the government of the United States on grounds of policy, but without success.[27]   In general the federal government held to the view that the passage of such laws by the states was "unwise, impolitic and dangerous." [28]   Likewise, from Ambassador Roland S. Morris in Japan came a warning to the State Department in January, 1921, that there "can be no reasonable doubt of the deep feeling of resentment which has been aroused among the people of Japan by the California legislation."   He added, "Racial discrimination will seriously threaten our country's best interests on the Pacific and in the Far East."   To meet the situation, Morris and Baron Shidehara.for Japan drafted in 1921 a treaty revising the Gentlemen's Agreement.   This would have prevented the immigration of wives, children, or parents of resident Japanese laborers and would have conferred on the United States the power of enforcement through deporta-

---

[25] Eleanor Tupper and G. E. McReynolds, *Japan in American Public Opinion* (New York, 1937), 52-53.

[26] Griswold, *Far Eastern Policy of the United States*, 361.

[27] United States, *Foreign Relations, 1913*, 625-628; *ibid., 1920*, III, 1-2; *ibid., 1921*, II, 323-349; T. A. Bailey, "California, Japan, and the Alien Land Legislation of 1913," *Pacific Historical Review*, I (1932), 36-59.

[28] United States, *Foreign Relations, 1921*, II, 340-343.

tion. In return for this effective exclusion the United States was to guarantee resident Japanese from discriminatory treatment. They would enjoy all rights possessed by other foreigners save naturalization. These proposals, however, were swamped by the rising tide of anti-immigration sentiment which followed the World War. The crusade for alien land laws was no longer confined to the Pacific Coast. Fourteen states reaching from Montana to Delaware to Louisiana and Washington enacted legislation on the California model between 1921 and 1925. If there still remained any doubts as to the legality, the constitutionality, of these proceedings, that doubt was removed in 1922 when the United States Supreme Court ruled in the famous Ozawa Case that Japanese were ineligible to citizenship by naturalization. In 1923 the principles of this case were held to apply to all Orientals. Lastly, the constitutionality of the California alien land laws was upheld.[29]

Another factor in creating sentiment against the Japanese was the institution known as the "picture brides." The great bulk of Japanese immigrants who entered the United States before 1907 were men. After 1907, however, passports were issued to Japanese women married in Japan by proxy through an exchange of photographs to Japanese men who were already in the United States. The institution was perfectly proper according to Japanese custom, and if the Japanese male population was to remain in the United States, it was desirable that this population should acquire wives. The fact that the Chinese in the nineteenth century had not been accompanied by their women had opened the way for charges of immorality against the Chinese. But whatever the merits of the "picture brides" as a social institution may have been, the arrival of these women on the Pacific Coast (legally under the Gentlemen's Agreement) was directly responsible for the rapid increase in the Japanese population between 1900 and 1921.[30]

THE EMERGENCE OF A NATIONAL POLICY

It will be recalled then that by 1904 the principle of Chinese exclusion had become an established fact of American policy. To this by 1907 had been added the diluted principle of Japanese exclusion—diluted, because it was disguised in the form of an executive agreement enforceable not by the United States but by Japan. This arrangement, regardless of its merits in terms of high policy, had not been acceptable to public opinion on the Pacific Coast, and as World War I came to an end, discrimi-

---

[29] 260 U. S. 178; 261 U. S. 204; 263 U. S. 197; 263 U. S. 225.

[30] For a discussion of the "picture brides," see Yamato Ichihashi, *Japanese in the United States* (Stanford University, 1932), 291-296.

nation against Orientals was fused with the general demand for more rigid controls on all immigration on a basis of discriminatory selection. The first step in this direction was the law of 1921, by which Congress limited the admission of aliens of each nationality to 3 percent "of the number of foreign-born persons of such nationality resident in the United States" in 1910. This was the Emergency Quota Act of May 19, 1921, renewed in 1922 for two years. In its revised form the Act reduced admissions to 2 percent based on the foreign-born resident population of each nationality in 1890.[31] The particular years selected for determining the percentage of admissions favored the immigrant quotas from northern and western Europe as against southern and eastern Europe.

In other words, by 1921 the principle of discriminating against immigrants of certain nationalities on the presumption of their inferiority to others—the very principle to which Japan had so consistently and so strenuously objected—was being applied by Congress to Europeans as well as to Asiatics, and written into the national immigration laws of the United States.[32]

By December, 1923, the Congress undertook the business of drafting a permanent immigration law to replace these hurried statutes which had been rushed through to stem the immigrant tide from war-torn Europe. It was proposed that the new law be based on the quota system of the recent legislation, but in addition, the new bills in both House and Senate denied entry to aliens ineligible to citizenship. The Japanese, although not named, were the obvious target. Secretary Hughes, now thoroughly alarmed, argued with the House Committee on Immigration that while Japanese immigration should be effectively controlled, the method proposed was inadvisable. In his opinion, it was bad policy to offend Japan unnecessarily when, by assigning Japan a quota, not more than 250 would be admitted annually. Furthermore, the proposed legislation would, the Secretary felt, "largely undo the work of the Washington Conference."[33] Nevertheless, in March, 1924, the House Committee recommended legislation excluding all aliens ineligible to citizenship. The bill passed the House on April 12, by the overwhelming majority of 326 to 71.[34]

[31] United States, Department of Labor, *Immigration Rules and Regulations* (Washington, 1937), 37 ff.
[32] Griswold, *Far Eastern Policy of the United States*, 370.
[33] Buell, *Japanese Immigration*, 353-356; also House of Representatives, 68th Cong., 1st sess., *Report No. 350*.
[34] For full discussion of the House debate see Paul, *The Abrogation of the Gentlemen's Agreement*, ch. ii, 13-33.

Meanwhile, apprehension was mounting both at the State Department and at the Japanese Embassy. To straighten the case which he proposed to present to the Congress, Hughes had prevailed on Japanese Ambassador Hanihara to give the Secretary a memorandum clarifying Japan's understanding of the Gentlemen's Agreement. This was done in a Japanese note, prepared with the collaboration of the State Department, and given to Hughes on April 10. The note reviewed the history of the Agreement, defined Japan's objections to legislation embodying exclusion, and in conclusion "truthfully but most ill-advisedly" referred to "the grave consequences which the enactment of the measure [exclusion clause] retaining that particular provision would inevitably bring upon the otherwise happy and mutually advantageous relations between our two countries." Hughes disliked the phrase "grave consequences" for there were few stronger phrases in diplomatic language, but he regarded the Japanese analysis of the Gentlemen's Agreement as excellent, and so sent the note to Congress.[35]

It was several days after the Hughes letter accompanied by the Hanihara note had reached Congress before the phrase "grave consequences" appears to have been noted. Indeed, the Senate was considering rather favorably Hughes' suggestion that the Gentlemen's Agreement be recognized and thus that Japan be omitted from any exclusion clause. Then on April 14, behind locked doors, the Senate turned its attack on the Hanihara letter. It was described as "impertinent," as not to be "tolerated" by even a fourth-class power, and as a "veiled threat." The Hughes compromise was voted down, and on April 16 the Senate followed the House by voting 71 to 4 to exclude aliens ineligible to citizenship.[36] Last-minute efforts of President Coolidge to delay application to Japan of the exclusion clause in the hope that a new treaty might be negotiated also failed, and on May 15, the immigration bill emerging from conference was passed by House and Senate, the votes being 308 to 62 and 69 to 9. It was to become effective July 1, 1924. The President in signing the bill on May 26 announced that had the exclusion clause not been an integral part of the larger bill, he would have vetoed it on the ground that the method adopted by Congress in securing Japanese exclusion was "unnecessary and deplorable at this time." [37]

With passage of the new immigration bill into law, including the ex-

---

[35] For sources on some of these particulars see T. A. Bailey, *A Diplomatic History of the American People* (2nd ed., New York, 1942), 705 and note.

[36] Paul, *The Abrogation of the Gentlemen's Agreement,* chs. iii-v.

[37] Buell, *Japanese Immigration,* 371.

clusion clause, the United States had entered upon a new phase in its far eastern policy. The principle of exclusion, first applied to the Chinese, a weak power, had now been extended to Japan, a proud, sensitive, and powerful state. Only two years previously at the Washington Conference, American policy had been based on the assumption that this country's interests in the Far East could best be preserved by the limitation of naval armaments and by multilateral treaty commitments (without armed sanctions) to preserve the American open door in China and American sovereignty in the Philippines. It would now remain for the "march of events" to determine whether the new immigration policy adopted by Congress would serve to strengthen or to weaken the foundations of that larger policy.

Immediate reactions to the abrogation of the Gentlemen's Agreement were more pronounced in Japan than in the United States. Japan's official protest was a mild reflection of bitter outbursts in the Japanese press and of deep resentment in the Japanese popular mind. In the United States, reactions were varied because the issues involved were more complex. Public opinion throughout the country, though favoring rigid control of Japanese immigration, does not appear to have favored the method used by Congress. Naturally this view was more pronounced in the East than on the Pacific Coast.[38] The Senate, however, was not guided by the *general* flavor of public opinion, but rather by known public reactions to specific domestic issues. The immigration debate was largely controlled by concurrent domestic reactions that might be expected from "the Southern vote in its relation to the Dyer anti-lynching bill, the issue of Congressional prerogative, the questions of the senatorial investigations and of party loyalty, the need of thinking of the Pacific Coast's presidential vote, to say nothing of the Pacific Coast's racial future." [39] It was hardly surprising that in a post-war period, in which the United States was shunning the idea of collective security, local group pressures in domestic politics should outweigh the broader considerations of foreign policy. Undoubtedly many Americans believed, as did *The Cincinnati Enquirer*, that "the crux of this matter is that the United States, like Canada and Australia, must be kept a white man's country." [40] An heroic step, so it was thought, had been

---

[38] Bailey, *A Diplomatic History*, 706, note 12. Both Roumania and Italy protested the act of 1924 as discriminatory against their nationals.

[39] Paul, *Abrogation of the Gentlemen's Agreement*, 99.

[40] In this opinion, *The Los Angeles Times, The Kansas City Star*, and *The Chicago Tribune* concurred. *Literary Digest*, April 26, 1924, 13-14.

taken, not in the implementation of race prejudice but in "producing a civilization peculiar to the American race and suited to a static society." [41]

POLICIES OF OTHER COUNTRIES

The United States was by no means alone in excluding Asiatics from its shores. By 1924, many, though by no means all, of the countries of Latin America had erected barriers against the Oriental immigrant.[42]

Prior to 1900, the Australian colonies had enacted various anti-Chinese laws. The following year the Commonwealth government passed the Immigration Restriction Act prohibiting the entrance of any person unable to pass a dictation test in a European language prescribed by the examining officer. The law was administered to exclude Asiatics but not Europeans. After 1905 Japanese tourists, merchants, and students entering for temporary visits were exempted from the test. At the same time the phraseology of the law was amended to read "any prescribed language" instead of "any European language." [43] The law and the administration of it were designed to implement the so-called "White Australia Policy" without what might be called legal discrimination in the letter of the statute. That the policy itself was discriminatory has never been open to question.

From 1908 to 1920 New Zealand applied a similar dictation test, but in the latter year the admission or exclusion of immigrants was made a matter of executive discretion administered by the governor-general.

The dictation test, which was apparently acceptable to the Japanese government, was also welcomed by the British government, which frequently reminded the Dominions of its policy of avoiding discriminatory legislation on a basis of race or color. At the turn of the century it recommended the adoption of the dictation test by Canada where, in 1897, anti-Japanese demonstrations in British Columbia had resulted in a flood of anti-Japanese legislation, all of which was disallowed. By 1921, when the control of the Dominions over immigration had been recognized, there was a wide gulf on the one hand between British immigration policy in principle and, on the other, public sentiment in Canada toward Chinese and Japanese immigration or, more embarrass-

---

[41] After 1924 influential American groups, business and professional, advocated revision which would give Japan and China a quota. The move was halted by the Manchurian crisis, 1931. Chinese exclusion was ended in 1943.

[42] Sen. doc. 761, 61st Cong., 3rd sess., Report of the Immigration Commission, *Immigration Situation in Other Countries* (1910); League of Nations, International Labour Office, *Emigration and Immigration: Legislation and Treaties* (Geneva, 1922), 177-188.

[43] Buell, *Japanese Immigration*, 339-340.

ingly, toward British Indians.   The year 1907 brought a marked increase
in the number of Japanese immigrants, the major portion coming from
Hawaii.   As a result Canada and Japan entered into a Gentlemen's
Agreement whereby Japan agreed to issue passports only to 1) previous
residents, their wives and children, 2) not more than 400 domestic and
agricultural laborers annually, and 3) contract emigrants.[44]   In 1910
Canada passed an immigration act giving the governor-general discre-
tionary power to exclude immigrants, and in 1913 adhered to the Anglo-
Japanese treaty of 1911 on the understanding that this act was not to
rescind Canada's rights under the immigration act.   While the Canadian
Gentlemen's Agreement was defended vigorously by the Dominion
government, it was attacked in the press and particularly in the provincial
legislature of British Columbia.   In the spring of 1924 it was amended,
reducing from 400 to 150 the number of agricultural laborers and domestic servants to be admitted annually.   At the time of these developments,
there was no racial bar to naturalization in Canada or New Zealand.

---

[44] Buell, *Japanese Immigration*, 334-336.

CHAPTER 27

THE NEW JAPAN TO 1918: ECONOMIC AND INDUSTRIAL FOUNDATIONS AND POLITICAL AFFAIRS

JAPAN, it will be remembered, had not played a major role as a belligerent in World War I, yet no nation was more profoundly affected by the war than was Japan. It was the war which made Japan an industrial state; which placed her among the world's three greatest naval powers; which prompted her greatest strides toward economic and political liberalism; but which likewise created unprecedented social problems and eventually opened the way for the suppression of liberal thought and the resurgence of reaction and fascism. In a word, the decade which followed World War I was a period of deep significance in Japan's modern history. In the historical background of these years may be seen both the lights and shades which will undoubtedly affect Japan's future. However, the social and economic road which Japan followed after 1918, though determined in part by the war, was also a result of policies adopted and followed during the Meiji era from 1867 to 1912. The political philosophy and constitutional machinery of Japan's government have been discussed in Chapters 10 and 24. Here it will be helpful, before entering on Japan's post-war industrial and social development, to explore the Meiji social and economic foundations of which this development was a natural outgrowth. This is simply to say that the Japan which at Washington in 1922 could demand recognition as one of the Big Three owed her position as a great power not only to the opportunities of World War I but also to the economic and social policies bequeathed by Meiji statesmen.[1]

THE IMPERIAL RESTORATION AND THE END OF FORMAL FEUDALISM

By 1871, with the framework of feudalism already destroyed, Japan was creating a new and unified political regime which would make in-

---

[1] E. F. Penrose, *Population Theories and Their Application with Special Reference to Japan* (Stanford University, 1934), 160.

vasion from abroad too dangerous and too uncertain an undertaking. This new Restoration government, replacing feudalism and resting on a centralized machinery of state, derived its power from the financial backing of the merchant-capitalists, and its leadership from the lesser but capable *samurai* of the Western Clans. In the face of violent domestic opposition, these leaders pursued steadfastly until 1894 the goal of internal reconstruction. Only after the foundations of the new economic, social, and political Japan had been laid did they venture into the field of foreign expansion.[2] What then were the economic and social foundations of the new state?

FOUNDATIONS FOR INDUSTRIALIZATION

At the close of the Tokugawa period, although rice was still the standard of exchange, money had become the principal means of exchange. In the great castle towns (eighteenth-century Yedo had a population of some 1,300,000) there was a thriving trade in the products of the skilled handicraft industries of Kyoto and other centers. A division of labor was also becoming apparent between those who produced raw materials as against the finished products. This division, however, was restricted by the dominance of household industry which has prevailed, though in lesser relative degree, into contemporary, twentieth-century Japan. Commercial capital was concentrated in the hands of traders and usurers, dominated by the *fudasahi* (rice brokers) of Osaka, among which were numbered such families as Mitsui. In general, the economic system which had developed was a kind of primitive monopoly mercantilism between the great cities and the adjacent rural areas.

In other words, one might say that the mercantile system with

. . . its monopoly of trade and reliance on the absolutist state (as in 16th-17th century France and England) was the crutch with which capitalism learned to walk. Grown to full strength, European capitalism discarded the crutch, absolute state power, and finding it a hindrance, turned against it and destroyed it.[3]

But in Japan the young capitalist class, far from dispensing with the crutch of state absolute power, leaned more completely upon it in the

---

[2] For detailed treatment of the decay of feudalism, of the rise of the merchant-capitalists, and of the lower *samurai* as political leaders of early Restoration Japan see: E. Herbert Norman, *Japan's Emergence as a Modern State* (New York, 1940), 1-104; Sansom, *Japan: A Short Cultural History,* ch. xxiii; Eijiro Honjo, *Social and Economic History of Japan* (Kyoto, 1935).

[3] Norman, *Japan's Emergence as a Modern State,* 110.

Meiji era than in the days of the Tokugawas. The reasons for this are readily discernible. In the first place, early Meiji Japan, intent upon overtaking the Western states in point of industrial progress, did not possess any great reservoir of skilled labor. In the second place, the merchant-capitalists who had financed the Restoration and who were in a financial position to set up factory industry on the Western model, hesitated to assume the vast risks involved. As a result, factory industry was undertaken in early Meiji *by the government itself* drawing its capital from merchant loans and from the labor of the peasants in the form of land tax revenue.[4] Private capital, in contrast, tended to remain in the field of trade or in banking, where it found a safe and profitable outlet in government loans. This policy of government-in-industry was followed closely until 1880, when the principle of "direct control" began to give place to "indirect protection." It was at this time that the government, which had carried on the initial development of industry, began to turn over some specific enterprises to the financial oligarchy, the *Zaibatsu,* "at amazingly low rates."[5] By this means, industrial as well as financial capital came to be concentrated in the same hands. Finally, it may be added that the economic structure of nineteenth-century Meiji Japan was fashioned without a major resort to foreign loans.

THE MEIJI GOVERNMENT AND THE STRATEGIC INDUSTRIES

In applying the economic policy outlined above, the interest of the Meiji government was centered first upon those industries directly concerned with the armed defense of the nation; this course would save Japan from the unhappy plight of China. These were in general the heavy industries: mining, steel, shipbuilding, etc. They were also the *strategic* industries, and "from the very first in modern Japan they were government owned and inextricably interwoven with the military problem."[6] The same principle was followed in transportation. The principle of nationalization of railroads was recognized in 1892, and by 1906

---

[4] In general, a system was emerging in which agriculture bore a disproportionate share of taxes as compared with industries.

[5] Norman, *Japan's Emergence as a Modern State,* 114. The principal families which during Meiji Japan came to be known as the *Zaibatsu* are: Mitsui, Mitsubishi, Sumitomo, and Yasuda.

[6] Norman, *Japan's Emergence as a Modern State,* 118. Note in particular three chapters in Shigenobu Okuma, ed., *Fifty Years of New Japan* (2 vols., London, 1910): 1) Aritomo Yamagata, "The Japanese Army"; 2) Gombei Yamamoto, "The Japanese Navy"; and 3) Kanetake Oura, "The Police of Japan."

most of the lines were nationalized.[7] As early as 1872, the nationalization of telegraphs was likewise recognized on strategic grounds.[8]
These developments do not necessarily suggest that Meiji Japan from
the beginning was bent on an ultimate policy of foreign conquest.
They do suggest, however, that the leaders of Meiji were conscious of
the "political necessity" of defending the Restoration government from
attack, foreign or domestic, and that, as a result, industrialization and
strategic security became not a dual but a unified single concept.[9] Another consequence was that, contrary to what had occurred in the West,
in Japan it was the heavy rather than the light industries that first assumed importance. Then, as already indicated, after 1880 the government, while maintaining its rigid grip upon basic military industries,
disposed of others to its financial friends, principally the *Zaibatsu*, continuing to support them with generous subsidies. This dual form of government control, direct or indirect, was still a predominant feature of
Japanese industry at the outbreak of World War II.

LAND AND LABOR IN THE JAPANESE ECONOMY

This pattern of industrialization for early Meiji Japan was applied,
however, in a society which was overwhelmingly agricultural. It is not
surprising therefore that the leaders of Meiji applied themselves to the
agricultural settlement with the same revolutionary vigor they were
showing in politics and industry. The importance of their agricultural
settlement can scarcely be overestimated, for it fashioned the unique
features of much of Japan's twentieth-century social, as well as economic, structure.

PRIVATE LAND OWNERSHIP

In the later years of the Tokugawa *Bakufu*, the illegal alienation of
land to a new landlord class had gone on at a considerable rate. Then,
after 1867, the Restoration legalized the sale of land. Although this
made the peasant a nominal free-holder, it also created the means
through which he could be dispossessed through foreclosures on mort-
gaged land. This was a matter of significance, since in 1870 many of
the peasants were small, independent cultivators. Meanwhile, the

---

[7] Toshiharu Watarai, *The Nationalization of Railways in Japan* (New York, 1914),
57-62.
[8] See Kenjiro Den, "Japanese Communications: The Post, Telegraph and Telephone,"
in Okuma, *Fifty Years of New Japan*, I, 408-423.
[9] Norman, *Japan's Emergence as a Modern State*, 123-124.

Restoration government was seeking a unified and workable system of taxation to provide the revenue with which it hoped to carry the burden of military expenditure, and the capital necessary for the new strategic industries. The answer was found in the land tax policy of 1873, which effected a radical revision in previous methods of taxation. It involved three principal changes: 1) the tax was to be fixed by the *value* of the land, not as formerly by the yield of the harvest; 2) the tax would be at a fixed rate (3 percent), not adjustable as it had been in feudal times to good or bad seasons; and 3) the tax would be paid in money and not as formerly in kind (rice). From the standpoint of government, these changes were logical, particularly in a country not enjoying tariff autonomy, where a fixed and predictable revenue was the more essential. Moreover, the new tax could be administered more efficiently since it was now paid by the landowner without regard to who worked the land.[10]

THE LAND TAX AND THE PEASANTRY

How did the new policy of taxation affect the peasant? It meant in general a steady dispossession of the landowning peasantry and the accumulation of land in a new, wealthy, landowning class.[11] Yet, unlike the eighteenth-century enclosures in England, this did not mean that the Japanese peasantry deserted the countryside and moved to the cities. Since from the beginning Japanese landlords were able to collect excessively high rents, they preferred to retain the tenant on the land rather than to oust him and exploit the land themselves as capitalists. Thus the tradition and habit-bound peasant remained upon the land, paying exorbitant rents and sinking into deeper and deeper poverty. During Meiji Japan his economic decline, caused principally by fantastic rents, was aided and abetted by other factors: 1) the decline of the older household industries; and 2) a marked increase in the rural population. The resulting conditions of extreme agricultural poverty were closely related to developments marking the expansion of the Japanese textile industries in the twentieth century. The younger generation in the tenant households, the girls in particular, moved to the cities seeking to increase the *family* income. The textile industry was thereby provided with extremely low-cost labor. In periods of unemployment, this new

[10] Norman, *Japan's Emergence as a Modern State,* 136-142; Yeijiro Ono, *The Industrial Transition in Japan* (Baltimore, 1890), Publications of the American Economic Society, II, No. 1.

[11] For details on the dispossession of the peasantry see Norman, *Japan's Emergence as a Modern State,* 144-148.

factory labor tended to return to the family homes in the rural villages. In consequence, the burden of unemployment relief was removed in large part from the employers and from the state, while the pressure of population in the villages maintained the high rents on land.[12]

Again, the depressed position of the peasant was conditioned by the size of the average unit of land cultivated by a single household. The growth of tenancy in Japan was not accompanied by any marked increase in the size of the lots cultivated. In 1874 the average holding cultivated by a peasant household was 2.35 acres. In 1909 it was 2.38 acres, and in 1914 (including the larger individual holdings in Hokkaido and Ryukyu) it was 2.61 acres. These figures, covering both paddy and dry fields, are considerably larger than the averages for paddy field holdings alone. The perpetuation of small holdings was partly traceable to Japanese topography, but it is also a direct result of the agrarian settlement made in the early Meiji period. Furthermore, while the Japanese tenant-farmer assumed all the risks involved in crop raising, the landlord, through high rent, took most of the profit. The composite results of this subsistence economy were far-reaching. Those members of what Norman calls the "stagnant surplus population" not protected by the family system were forced into part-time labor on roads, railroads, etc., and into the cities as unskilled labor, where their presence lowered the general wage level. This was occurring at a time when Japanese industry though expanding rapidly was not keeping pace with the growth of surplus population, and when for various reasons emigration was not providing a safety valve. It was a situation of which industry could and did take advantage. The peasant could no longer resort to the common lands for fodder, wood, implements, etc. His household cotton industry was destroyed first by imported cotton and then by the rise of the urban industry in Japan; thus he was forced to turn chiefly to sericulture as the principal supplementary household industry. The partial destruction of the old domestic industry created a home market for the products of Japan's new factory industries, but this expanding home market was subject to limitations:

. . . The extremely high rent and land tax, which left very little surplus in the hands of the peasantry, whether tenant or proprietor, the limited extent to which the separation of industry from agriculture was carried out and the existence of the huge, impoverished surplus population all combined to keep this home market relatively narrow.[13]

---

[12] D. H. Buchanan, "Rural Economy in Japan," *Quarterly Journal of Economics,* XXVII (1923); Norman, *Japan's Emergence as a Modern State,* 149-153.

[13] Norman, *Japan's Emergence as a Modern State,* 165.

This limited purchasing power of the Japanese home market became in the late nineteenth as in the twentieth century one of the chief factors impelling Japanese industry to seek foreign markets for its goods and impelling the nation to use war to this end.[14] Japan's case was not of course unique. Nevertheless, the direction of her national policy could not be unaffected by the fact that the masses of rural labor and unskilled industrial labor were unable to buy the products of their nation's industry.

INDUSTRY IN AN ERA OF THREE WARS, 1894-1919

Between 1894 and 1919, Japan was involved in three major wars: the Sino-Japanese War, 1894-95; the Russo-Japanese War, 1904-05; and World War I, 1914-19. From each of these wars Japan emerged with greatly expanded industrial power. Her first major industrial boom reached its height in 1897 when the system of gold coinage was introduced. During the decade 1894-1903, while imports increased six-fold in value and four-fold in volume, the export trade increased five-fold in value and three-fold in volume compared with the years 1884-88. Paid-up capital rose from ¥232,000,000 in 1893 to ¥887,000,000 in 1903. Following the Russian war, Japan's industrial and trading position revealed marked changes. Whereas in 1900 Japanese investment in China was negligible, probably not more than $1,000,000, by 1914 this figure was swollen to some $220,000,000, largely because of the growth of Japanese interests in South Manchuria, the newly acquired sphere of influence.[15] By 1930 the figure for Japanese investment in China, including direct business investments, investments in Chinese corporations, and obligations of the Chinese government, was $1,136,921,000.[16]

During World War I Japan's industrial expansion showed unprecedented growth. Modern industrial techniques were applied more generally than before; modern machinery was installed in new factories; and the volume of foreign trade continued to increase. Removed as she was from the areas of major combat, Japan entered world markets where previously her goods were unknown, markets which for the time being were deprived of goods supplied formerly by European factories.

---

[14] Norman, *Japan's Emergence as a Modern State*, 166, cites "Hompo Bosekigyo no Hattatsu" [The Development of the Cotton Industry in Our Country], in *Nihon Sangyo Shiryo*, edited by Mukai and Takimoto, which relates how the Sino-Japanese War, 1894-95, gave the Japanese cotton industry a greatly expanded market in Korea and the Yangtze Valley.

[15] S. Uyehara, *The Industry and Trade of Japan* (2nd rev. ed., London, 1936), 5-15; C. F. Remer, *Foreign Investments in China* (New York, 1933), 408-446.

[16] Remer, *Foreign Investments in China*, 548.

It was the great period of Japanese industrialization, but the unprecedented expansion was followed in the immediate post-war years by depression, by contraction of investment, and by the return temporarily of unfavorable balances in foreign trade, leading to what has been described as the most critical period—the decade of the 1920's—in Japan's economic, social, and political history.[17]

EVOLUTION OF THE POLITICAL PARTIES

Before entering on a discussion of the economic and social problems of Japanese society in the post-war decade, it will be well to note briefly the historical role of Japanese political parties in their relationship to the economic life of the nation. The reader will recall that political parties appeared in Japan soon after the Restoration, the three most important in the nineteenth century being the *Jiyuto* (Liberal Party), the *Kaishinto* (Reform Party), and the *Teiseito* (Constitutional Imperial Party).[18] All these parties boasted of their adherence to stated political principles and platforms. These principles and platforms, however, were usually exceedingly vague and broad, and, in any case, were of secondary importance, since in Japanese political thought the emphasis was on the political leader rather than upon any body of principles. It followed then that political parties tended to be aggregations of individuals bound by personal loyalty to a particular man, as was the case in feudal times, rather than a group held together by loyalty to any set of political principles.[19] Although this was the generally prevailing tendency, it should not be assumed that Western political theory in terms of constitutionalism, liberalism, etc., played no part in the thinking of Japanese politicians and intellectuals, for indeed quite the contrary was the case.[20] Yet, at the same time, it would be a mistake to assume that Japanese political parties have been inspired primarily by Western concepts of constitutionalism, or that the early "liberal" in Japanese politics was a replica of the nineteenth-century English liberal. From 1881, when the first party appeared, until about 1900, there appears to have been some genuine enthusiasm among the party politicians for the principles of responsible government. But after 1900 and on until 1918 the power of the Genro and the special groups that supported them—aristocrats, bureaucrats, and militarists—was so entrenched that in general the party

[17] Statistics indicative of the expansion of Japanese industry and trade during the era of three wars, 1894-1919, are given in S. Uyehara, *The Trade and Industry of Japan*.
[18] Cf. Chapter 10.
[19] R. K. Reischauer, *Japan: Government-Politics* (New York, 1939), 29-30, 95-97.
[20] Cf. Chapter 24.

politicians gave up the struggle for liberal principles (for which there was no long background of tradition as in England), and sought the spoils of office by selling their parliamentary support to the oligarchy. In turn, oligarchs such as Hirobumi Ito, and militarists such as Taro Katsura, accepted the presidency of major political parties. With such leaders, it becomes obvious why the parties could no longer stand effectively for liberal or responsible government. It should not be surprising then to discover that in the first two decades of this century, the parties came to merit little distinction in their respective political and social philosophies. Between 1881 and 1928, the lack of stability in political thought and of loyalty to political principle is revealed in the appearance of more than twenty-five parties, not counting many minor groups. However, it would be unwise to assume that the barren character of the parties was due to an inherent or moral incapacity of political leaders to appreciate principles of responsible government. Many factors played their part: lack of tradition, lack of experience, the feudal-clan spirit of the Restoration leaders, the autocratic philosophy in which the Constitution was conceived, and finally the fact that the *economic* foundations on which the first political parties were built were not designed to foster the orderly and healthy development of liberal, responsible, or democratic government.

THE ECONOMIC BASE OF THE FIRST POLITICAL PARTIES

The *Jiyuto* or Liberal Party of 1881 presented the seemingly incongruous spectacle of liberalism promoted by a class of rural landowners. This was due to the peculiar character of Japan's rural economy in the Restoration era. Landed proprietors occupied a dual position. They collected the profits of agriculture in the form of land rent paid by tenants in rice. These profits, which the proprietors converted into money at the best possible rate, were usually invested either in land or in rural industries such as the manufacture of *sake* (rice wine) or *miso* (bean paste). Thus the landowner became a local rural industrialist, or rice-broker, or merchant. He thereby combined the functions of "semi-feudal landlord" with those of the commercial capitalist. It was in this latter capacity of commercial capitalist that the manufacturing-landlord entered politics in 1881, combining his efforts with other groups in the formation of the *Jiyuto*. He did so because he was opposed to the government's policy of financing its military and naval program by increasing taxation on the products he manufactured, and because he objected to paying the bulk of the nation's income in the form of the land tax,[21] while government bestowed its favors and protection on the financial oligarchy of the cities. Other rural groups also had their special complaints. The tenant cultivator wanted reduction in his rent. Those who owned their land were already threatened with dispossession at the hands of larger landowners. Thus from these various groups, particularly from the landed, rural manufacturers came the crusade for "Liberty and the People's Rights" with its subsequent development into the constitutional movement culminating in the Constitution of 1889. In this sense Japanese liberalism sprang from the countryside and not from the cities. In contrast the ideological leadership of the movement came from quite a different group. This was a nucleus of *samurai* from Hizen and Tosa who had been pushed out of the new government bureaucracy by the *samurai* politicians of Satsuma and Choshu. These men of Tosa and Hizen, no longer enjoying office, became the ideological leaders in the demand for a people's assembly.

The second and rival political party, the *Kaishinto*, led by Okuma, included in its membership other disgruntled bureaucrats who were out of office, a scattering of liberal intellectuals who favored the British parliamentary system, and significantly from the economic point of view, some of the wealthier urban merchants and industrialists, including representatives of the Mitsubishi interests. The *Kaishinto* in ideology was a mild reflection of the current English liberalism and utilitarianism.

From 1880 until 1918 the oligarchy, led by the Genro, was able to channel within narrow limits all movements of political liberalism, and thus to uphold its authoritarian concepts on the economic and social structure of society. It accomplished this in a number of ways. It neutralized the parties by playing one against another. It won over to its own fold some of the party leaders by various means, not excluding that of bribing them with offices. Freedom of speech and of the press were seriously hampered long before the Constitution was promulgated. The Press Law of 1875 and the Peace Preservation Law of 1887 were the nineteenth-century manifestations of what came to be known in the twentieth century as the control of "dangerous thoughts." The first liberal political parties were for a time suppressed entirely, thus depriving the economically and socially depressed masses of any political leadership. What is more, when the resurrected Liberal Party (*Jiyuto*) took its place in the first Diet of 1890, it had been shorn of its liberalism and its democratic ideology. By 1900, when it became the *Seiyukai*, it

---

[21] The land tax made up 80.5 percent of the national revenue, 1875-79; 65.6 percent during 1880-84; and 69.4 percent during 1885-89. Norman, *Japan's Emergence as a Modern State*, 171.

was the party of the great landlords and rural capitalists. As such, it became a bulwark of the rural economic settlement which impoverished the small farmer.[22]

A number of tendencies therefore stand out clearly in Japan's political and economic history from 1890 to 1918. First, there was a pronounced willingness on the part of liberal leaders to forsake their liberal principles and "to join in the scramble for office with little regard for basic political principles." [23] Second, party politicians, having compromised the principles for which their parties were supposed to stand, usually found it expedient to support the government's plans and economic measures for military and naval expansion. Third, the former liberal and progressive parties became increasingly subservient to the most powerful *Zaibatsu* families—the financial oligarchy. Mitsui contributed heavily to *Seiyukai* campaign funds; Mitsubishi, to the campaign chest of the *Kenseikai* and later of the *Minseito*. For the first two decades after the turn of the twentieth century the basic principles involved in this situation did not change materially. As Japan's industrialization progressed, the newly created wealth gravitated more and more to the landed aristocracy and to the *Zaibatsu*. As this process went on, it made little difference from the standpoint of economic and social philosophy whether the government was headed by Katsura, a protégé of Yamagata and an avowed champion of the militarists and the bureaucrats, or by Saionji, a Genro and simultaneously president of the *Seiyukai*, which drew its support from an aristocracy of landed capitalists.

These relations among an autocratic and oligarchic government, weak political parties, and the great mass of economically submerged tenant farmers and industrial laborers were the result of a conscious national policy on which government had embarked. The Meiji leaders sought consistently to enrich the national treasury through government-owned or -controlled industry. The object was to provide for a strong military and naval defense.[24] All groups in Japanese society supported the

---

[22] Norman, *Japan's Emergence as a Modern State*, 174-185; G. E. Uyehara, *The Political Development of Japan, 1867-1909* (London, 1910), 89-106, 215-253; Yusuke Tsurumi, *The Liberal Movement in Japan* (New Haven, 1925), 68 ff.; W. W. McLaren, *A Political History of Japan during the Meiji Era, 1867-1912* (New York, 1916), 153-177.

[23] Norman, *Japan's Emergence as a Modern State*, 185.

[24] See Aritomo Yamagata, "The Japanese Army," in Okuma, *Fifty Years of New Japan*, I, 194-217; E. H. Norman, *Soldier and Peasant in Japan* (New York, 1943), a study of the origins of conscription; and Gombei Yamamoto, "The Japanese Navy," in Okuma, *Fifty Years of New Japan*, I, 218-30.

policy, for it was looked upon as essential to the nation's political and economic independence. The military victories which followed Japanese arms in 1895 and 1905 increased further the prestige of the oligarchy and the politico-economic system it had fashioned.

The oligarchs could also claim other achievements of great importance. By the revision of the treaties in 1894 the nation had won tariff autonomy and the abolition of extraterritoriality. It was also well on the way to being recognized as a great power. These were among the primary objectives of the Meiji leaders. Tariff autonomy was essential to national independence. Tariff autonomy plus recognition as a great power opened the way for new commercial advantages in the nation's search for foreign markets. In turn the search for foreign markets was conditioned by both political and economic conditions at home and abroad. Europe's economic imperialism in China was an invitation to Japan to join in the same game. But Japan was also pushed into a policy of economic expansion by conditions within her homeland. Since the social and economic order created in Japan by the Meiji leaders precluded the development of a large home market and thus limited the profits of industry, expansion to create foreign markets and to find raw materials was the obvious, if not the wise, policy. Thus, considered in the economic sense, the policy of expansion was something far more fundamental than the militaristic whim of *samurai* who had become political generals.[25]

A related factor of importance was the speed with which Japan attempted to push forward her economic revolution. As Norman has said, she passed rapidly from a

restricted type of town-against-country mercantilism to a social organization compounded of monopoly control in private industry and state control in vital industries, thus permitting no economic freedom of the *laissez-faire* variety and consequently very little political freedom.[26]

From this it must be concluded that Japan's late entry into the family of nations affected deeply the course of her subsequent history.

[25] The economic basis of Japanese expansion is given in Norman, *Japan's Emergence as a Modern State*, 194-198.
[26] Norman, *Japan's Emergence as a Modern State*, 199. Account should also be taken of the tendency of dependent peoples in Asia to sacrifice much in the way of liberty for the sake of independence and security. On the other hand, all party leaders of Meiji did not intend that liberalism should fail. They were hampered by their past and they tended to be opportunistic.

INDUSTRIAL DEVELOPMENT AND POLITICS, 1914-1918

After 1895, Japan used the same policies to develop her new colonial empire (Formosa, 1895; the South Manchurian sphere, 1905; and Korea, 1905-10) as she had used previously to build industry at home. Railway construction, banking, and industry were conducted by the government or by semi-governmental corporations such as the Bank of Chosen and the South Manchuria Railway Company. In Japan itself, although some government industries were sold to private firms, the change was hardly fundamental since the firms selected were intimately associated with government. In some lines government control increased. The nationalization of railroads in 1906 [27] was a prelude to government monopolies in tobacco, salt, and camphor. It was government again which built the first steel works. Even where industries were turned over to private enterprise, government continued to bolster them through high protective tariffs and generous subsidies.

Some new factors also appeared in Japan's economic structure between 1895 and 1914. After 1897 foreign capital entered Japan in increasing amounts. These loans were floated on the London and later on the New York market.[28] In addition, the nation now possessed a larger and growing class of commercial and industrial entrepeneurs skilled in Western techniques of large-scale production. This was the period when the Japanese cotton industry developed with amazing speed. The new foreign capital opened the way for the development of new industries: hydro-electric power, mechanical engineering, etc. With this background of industrial training, Japan was able to achieve industrial maturity during World War I. Industries which previously had lagged because of foreign competition now were able to enter world markets which a warring Europe could no longer supply. Pre-eminent in this respect were the Japanese woolen industry,[29] the chemical industry, and the artificial silk industry. The pottery and "china" industries, hitherto conducted by small-scale organization, moved into large factory production.[30] The munitions and shipping industries were also expanded to meet the demands of the Allied powers. In the silk industry machine reeling began to replace traditional methods.[31]

---

[27] Masaru Inouye, "Japanese Communications: Railroads," in Okuma, *Fifty Years of New Japan*, I, 424-446.

[28] Masayoshi Matsukata, "Japan's Finance," in Okuma, *Fifty Years of New Japan*, I, 374-376.

[29] Teijiro Uyeda, *The Small Industries of Japan* (New York, 1938), ch. iv.

[30] Uyeda, ch. iii.

[31] G. C. Allen, *Modern Japan and Its Problems* (New York, 1927), 111-115.

THE RICE RIOTS AND THE END OF AN ERA

By 1917 manifestations of war prosperity in Japan were widespread. Ostentation and extravagance flaunted themselves openly without the refinement and asceticism which persisted even in the worst days of *Genroku*, those lavish years of the late seventeenth century. Side by side with this extravagance there was also full employment, but wages did not keep pace with the cost of living, and the pinch of rising prices was soon felt by labor. Prior to 1917 there was virtually no labor movement in Japan. The first modern union of railway workers had been organized as late as 1898 by Sen Katayama. The first major strike had not occurred until 1912, when Tokyo's streetcar employees walked out. Yet in 1917 there were nearly 400 strikes involving 57,000 workers. This was symptomatic of radical changes in social and economic conditions, and of the growing discontent among the poorer classes "whose lot had become intolerable" owing to the high price of the staple food.[32] During 1917-1918 the price of rice had more than doubled; the trouble broke on August 4, 1918, when women raided the rice shops in the province of Toyama. As if by magic (for there was rigid censorship of the news), the rice riots spread to almost every part of Japan, including the great seaport of Kobe, where violence was greatest. Soldiers were called to quell the riots in twenty cities and towns; more than 100 demonstrators were killed in the process. Order, however, was soon restored, for the movement was spontaneous, without organized leadership, a protest by an outraged populace. Nevertheless, the rice riots were a turning point in Japan's modern history. They showed, as no previous incident had shown, the presence of new economic and social forces. When on September 17, the ministry of General Terauchi resigned, Japan had ended the first period of constitutional government—the end of government by the Genro. The new administration was headed by Takashi Hara, a commoner, the first man without title to hold the office of Prime Minister. Japan had turned from the oligarchic control so carefully fashioned by the Meiji leaders to the rule of party politicians.

---

[32] Allen, *Modern Japan and Its Problems,* 144.

CHAPTER 28

JAPAN, 1918-1930: AN ERA OF INDECISION

THE YEAR 1918 seemed to hold the promise of a new Japan in which liberalism and democracy would have some chance to triumph over the oligarchy and the aristocracy of birth and class so carefully preserved by the Meiji leaders. The end of the World War found Japan more intimately associated with the great Western powers than ever before. Her membership among the Allied and Associated Powers brought her within the orbit of the Wilsonian program for a democratic and free world. Within Japan the new and unprecedented industrialization, together with the new social groups and classes thus created, increased the nation's wealth and foreshadowed the appearance of new political leadership in government. The new literature of the war years discarded the former sordid naturalism for new concepts of idealism.[1] The Genro as a group was passing from the scene, and no successors of equal stature had appeared to take its place. Both Yamagata (who died in 1922) and Matsukata (who died in 1924) were aged. Saionji, the only other surviving Genro, was a political liberal, as were other key figures in the aristocracy, such as Makino. Consequently, the failure of the militarist, Terauchi, and the subsequent selection of Hara, a commoner and president of the political party *Seiyukai,* to head the new ministry was hailed by liberals as the dawn of *kensei no jodo* (period of normal government). This implied that rule by the oligarchy had ended and that henceforth Japan, under the Constitution, would develop representative government patterned on a democratic ideal.

THE CONSERVATIVE AND REACTIONARY HERITAGE

But between this hopeful prospect and its ultimate fulfillment lay obstacles of great magnitude. The nation had long accustomed itself to rely for political leadership on the genius and the prestige of the Genro. The political parties had developed no aggressive independent leadership. The army and the militarists enjoyed a privileged position in the Japanese political scheme, but Yamagata's leadership in the army had

---

[1] Tadao Kunitomo, *Japanese Literature since 1868* (Tokyo, 1938), 139.

acted as a brake on the abuse of this power. It was now clear that Yamagata's days were numbered, and equally clear that there was no successor with comparable prestige to restrain the militarists. This all seemed to suggest that liberalism would not be given a free hand, but rather that it would be opposed vehemently by the oligarchy and by those special groups, such as the army, associated with it.

THE HARA ADMINISTRATION AND THE *SEIYUKAI*

The first genuinely party cabinet in Japan's constitutional history began its career against a background of economic and social unrest, of rapidly increasing wealth in the hands of the few, and of inadequate income if not abject poverty for the many. Since it was the economic maladjustment which had brought Terauchi's cabinet to an end, it was to this problem that the new government first turned its attention. Nothing in the nature of radical reform was adopted, but the national finances did reflect the genius of Korekiyo Takahashi, the new Minister of Finance, and the labor situation was relieved by wage increases in many industries. These gestures, however, fell far short of the need. From 1919 to 1922 bitter labor disputes occurred in a number of key industries.[2] By 1921, the infant labor union movement comprised 300 unions with a total membership of more than 100,000. Side by side with this struggle of labor to free itself from what Uyehara has described as "the most miserable conditions," [3] there appeared a type of reactionary organization whose concern was the suppression of "dangerous thoughts." Their major function was to intimidate the liberal and labor movement.[4]

Yet during 1920 some members of Japan's Diet revealed a grasp of world politics and a sense of responsibility rarely revealed in that body. Members of the House of Representatives charged that the Siberian expedition had been a failure from the first; that the purpose was to fight the "Reds" and to assist the "Whites"; and that Japan's participation was a result of machinations of the Genro and the militarists. Probably never before had Japanese liberals spoken with such vehemence. Their views, too, were shared by the informed public. The trouble was that most of the public was not informed, because Hara's embarrassed government, caught between the Diet and the oligarchy, turned to the time-honored expedient of suppressing the press. It was not until 1922 that Hara's successor, Premier Admiral Kato, a member of the oligarchy,

---

[2] Mitsu Kohno, *Labour Movement in Japan* (Tokyo, 1938), 15.

[3] S. Uyehara, *The Industry and Trade of Japan* (2nd rev. ed., London, 1936), 37.

[4] R. K. Reischauer, *Japan: Government-Politics* (New York, 1939), 138.

was able to get the army out of Siberia.[5]   Meanwhile Hara was harassed by squabbles within the *Seiyukai* and by the persistent demands of the army for a free hand in Siberia.   In the midst of this political turmoil, the cause of representative government was threatened when on November 24, 1921, Hara was assassinated by a fanatic.   Political assassination was a hoary institution in the politics of feudal Japan, but its revival in the first days of party government was not a hopeful sign.   In the person of Hara, it had removed an able and a practical politician.   Referred to as Japan's "Great Commoner," Hara possessed great force of character by which he attached men to him.   What his political views were it is hardly possible to say.   Though patriotic in a conventional sense, he was not a great reformer, and in many respects he was not even a liberal.   Nevertheless, as a staunch party man and a commoner, Hara was the agent of representative forces far greater than himself, and his death was thus a loss to the liberalizing of the new Japan.[6]

TAKAHASHI AND THE *SEIYUKAI*

With Hara's death, the premiership was passed to his brilliant Minister of Finance, Korekiyo Takahashi, also a commoner but certainly no politician.   Thereupon, the dissensions which had already weakened the *Seiyukai* broke out afresh; Takahashi resigned; the party split into factions; and the surviving Genro called a navy bureaucrat, Admiral Tomosaburo Kato, to form a government.   Kato had been navy minister in the two preceding cabinets and was Japan's chief delegate at the Washington Conference.   When he died late in the summer of 1923, the Genro again turned to the navy, selecting as Premier, Admiral Count Yamamoto, who in turn chose a second non-party cabinet.   This cabinet survived less than three months, September 2 to December 27, 1923, when it was succeeded by the so-called "Peers Cabinet" headed by Viscount Kiyoura, president of the Privy Council, and composed of conservatives from the House of Peers.

This temporary revival of conservative, non-party cabinets was of course not unrelated to intense currents of social unrest.   Beginning with Hara's murder in 1921, the Japanese public was treated to a succession of assassinations.   Liberal associations were attacked by organized bullies (*soshi*).   The House of Representatives was the scene of fist fights as Diet members charged each other with all manner of

---

[5] For the debates in the House of Representatives, see Tatsuji Takeuchi, *War and Diplomacy in the Japanese Empire* (Chicago, 1935), 214-215.   Unfortunately the "liberalism" of the Hara period was marred, since it was also a period notorious for spoils and corruption.

[6] A. Morgan Young, *Japan under Taisho Tenno 1912-1926* (London, 1928), 120.

scandalous conduct. Current literature, to the chagrin of government, was filled with "dangerous thoughts," some of which ventured the notion that "Soviets are better than Diets."[7] In the midst of this incipient battle between Right and Left, when no liberal editor was safe from attacks by hired bullies, the heart of metropolitan Tokyo was destroyed by earthquake and fire, on September 1, 1923.

The appointment of Kiyoura and the "Peers Cabinet" did not restore national confidence in the oligarchy. Instead, it served to unite the party factions in their determination to restore party cabinets.[8] The Premier therefore resigned and was succeeded by Takaakira Kato, president of the *Kenseikai*. Kato's party cabinet presented a curious balance of forces in terms of broad policy. The liberal policy which it pursued at home was generally acceptable to the nation, but in part this was due to the fact that Kato as Foreign Minister nine years earlier had formulated the Twenty-One Demands. He could therefore be counted on to pursue a strong foreign policy toward China. This idea was popular, but his appointment of Baron Kijuro Shidehara as Foreign Minister was equally unpopular, since Shidehara was known to favor conciliation and, in general, decent treatment of the Chinese.[9]

KATO, THE *KENSEIKAI*, AND THE MITSUBISHI

Indeed, Kato's premiership represented a distinct advance in the theory and practice of Japanese government. Kato had been Minister in England; he was thoroughly versed in the English party system and believed that its major principles could be applied in Japan. He was now head of the strongest political party, and had had long experience as an administrator. Furthermore, he had the backing of the powerful Mitsubishi interests, having served this house as a young man and having married the sister of Baron Iwasaki, Mitsubishi president. Indeed the Kato cabinet was known popularly as the "Mitsubishi government," because of this connection, because Shidehara had also married into the family, and because Hamaguchi, the Minister of Finance, came from the province of Tosa, the native place of the Iwasaki clan.[10] These connections were of importance, since the Mitsubishi interests were at least more inclined toward a liberal foreign policy and responsible government at home than any other group, including their greatest rivals, the

---

[7] Reischauer, *Japan: Government-Politics,* 140.

[8] During Takahashi's premiership the former *Seiyukai* had split into the *Seiyuhonto* and the *Seiyukai*.

[9] Reischauer, *Japan: Government-Politics,* 142.

[10] H. S. Quigley, *Japanese Government and Politics* (New York, 1932), 216, 223.

Mitsui interests, which normally supported the *Seiyukai*. The outstanding act of the administration was the passage of the manhood suffrage bill on March 29, 1925. This was the most substantial victory yet claimed by the forces of liberalism. But it was soon evident that the party unity which had made possible the passage of the bill was a marriage of convenience. A rift was already apparent in Kato's coalition. The *Seiyukai,* backed by the army, was already attacking the financial reforms and retrenchment of Yuko Hamaguchi, the Minister of Finance, and the liberalism of the manhood suffrage law was balanced by the passage of a "Peace Preservation Law" (April, 1925), which threatened imprisonment to those who proposed to alter the form of government or attacked the system of private property. Most of the liberals, who had voted for manhood suffrage also voted for the Peace Preservation Law. Liberalism was not without its limitations.

This was again apparent when the government tackled the delicate matter of army reorganization and reduction. In March the government did do away with four divisions. Against this there was practically no popular clamor, for after the Siberian fiasco the army had sunk somewhat in the national esteem. However, the reduction was not so substantial as it appeared to be. Actually, the military indoctrination and training of the nation were increased. Many officers of the disbanded divisions were sent as instructors to the schools where an enlarged system of military training was set up. In addition, the funds saved by disbanding the new divisions were devoted to new equipment and to modernizing the army. The result was that while the army was reduced, it was placed on a more efficient basis.

Then, on Kato's death in December, 1925, Reijiro Wakatsuki succeeded to both the premiership and the presidency of the party. The Wakatsuki cabinet remained in office until April 18, 1927. Its record, reflecting the irresolute personality of the Premier, was colored by nothing more important than incessant wranglings within the Diet. Seemingly the government lacked both the plan and the leadership for constructive or progressive policies both at home and abroad. Instead of assuming leadership itself, the *Kenseikai* majority and the cabinet attempted to forestall criticism by attacking alleged scandals within the *Seiyukai* opposition. "Trivia" and "nonsense," to quote Reischauer, formed the basis of politics.[11] Wakatsuki and the *Kenseikai* satisfied neither sincere liberals nor the conservatives and the militarists. When the cabinet resigned (April, 1927), it was under violent attack for its failure to formulate a "positive" policy toward China and for its timidity

---

[11] Reischauer, *Japan: Government-Politics,* 147.

in failing to meet certain financial problems in Japan's colony of Formosa.

TANAKA AND THE *SEIYUKAI*

It was now the turn of the Seiyukai. Its problem was to satisfy the conservatives and the militarists, to formulate a "strong" policy toward China, and to re-establish the prestige of party government. Responsibility in seeking to achieve this political miracle rested primarily with General Baron Giichi Tanaka, president of the *Seiyukai,* who now became the new premier. The prospects for liberalism were not bright, for Tanaka, as leader of the *Seiyukai* with its backing of landed barons, was also a prominent member of the Choshu militarists, who were still the most influential group controlling the army. Early in 1928 the first general election under the manhood suffrage law was held with indecisive results. The broader franchise exercised for the first time in the 1928 election appeared not to affect the quality of the legislators. The election of 8 out of 88 proletarian candidates infused some new blood into the legislature, but in general the House of Representatives remained as boisterous as it had been before. Sterility in domestic policy was, however, to be matched by considerable notoriety in foreign affairs.

THE "POSITIVE POLICY" IN CHINA

Ever since the Washington Conference, and particularly while Baron Shidehara had been Foreign Minister, there had been much criticism of Japan's "mild" policy toward China. Critics held that Japan's vested rights in China would be lost unless vigorously protected against a rising Chinese nationalism that was becoming more and more difficult to deal with. Accordingly, Tanaka, as Premier and Foreign Minister, called an important conference of key officials (June 27–July 7, 1927) which framed the principles of "the positive policy towards China." This policy distinguished between Japan's attitude toward China Proper and toward Manchuria and eastern Inner Mongolia. In the latter areas it was held that Japan had "special interests" and that it was therefore her duty to maintain peace there.[12] It seemed too that the policy was to have immediate implementation, for, in the spring of 1928 Japanese troops were dispatched to Tsinan in Shantung. The announced purpose was to protect Japanese residents during the northern march of the

---

[12] Takeuchi, *War and Diplomacy in the Japanese Empire,* 247-248. A document later published in China as the "Tanaka Memorial," and said to have been presented to the emperor, July 25, 1927, purports to be the findings of Tanaka's conference.

Chinese Nationalist armies. Then on June 4 the Manchurian war-lord, Chang Tso-lin, was assassinated near Mukden in the center of Japan's sphere of influence. Circumstances surrounding the assassination were such as to suggest Japanese connivance. The Japanese public, the more liberal organs of the press, and the parliamentary opposition soon formed a substantial block against Tanaka's China policy. Even members of the House of Peers and the Privy Council joined the opposition. In an effort to placate his political adversaries, Tanaka finally withdrew the troops, and, as a gesture to China, accepted the revised tariff schedules of the Nanking government.[13]

THE PACT OF PARIS

The prestige of Tanaka and his *Seiyukai* cabinet was thus already at a low ebb when it exposed itself to further attack both from the Diet opposition and from the conservatives on the delicate question of the emperor's constitutional position. On July 20, 1928, the Tanaka government had agreed to sign the Treaty for the Renunciation of War (The Kellogg-Briand Peace Pact) on the understanding that the phrase "in the names of their respective peoples" did not signify that the emperor signed "as the agent of his people" but rather meant "on behalf of the people," or "on behalf of the state." Once the treaty had been signed, the *Minseito* opposition promptly made political capital of the phrase "in the names of their respective peoples." The words were declared to violate the spirit of Japan's Constitution and to encroach on the Imperial prerogative of the emperor. The ensuing debate raged through the press and finally reached the Privy Council. On the advice of this conservative body, the emperor ratified the treaty with the declaration that the objectionable phrase "is understood to be inapplicable in so far as Japan is concerned." [14] The incident threw much light on the character of Japanese government. It indicated that the liberal *Minseito* was master of the most realistic techniques known to party politics. It also revealed the chauvinism of the "patriots" and indeed of large sections of the press and the populace to anything touching the sovereign authority of the emperor.[15] On July 2, 1929, the Tanaka ministry came to an end. It had satisfied the nation neither in the domestic nor in the foreign field. The overall result was highly injurious to the cause of representative government. Wakatsuji's ministry had been thoroughly irresolute and without a program. Tanaka's government in contrast

---

[13] Takeuchi, *War and Diplomacy in the Japanese Empire*, 248-258.
[14] Takeuchi, *War and Diplomacy in the Japanese Empire*, 262-274.
[15] See the Constitution of the Empire of Japan, Ch. I, Articles I-XVII.

had an over-abundance of both resolution and program which it had applied with astonishing ineptitude. The weakening of popular government by the failure of these two ministries was not apparent immediately, but the groundwork was already being laid for the revival of authoritarian controls.

HAMAGUCHI AND THE *MINSEITO*, 1929

The fall of Tanaka brought the *Minseito* back to power with Yuko Hamaguchi as Premier and Baron Shidehara as Foreign Minister. Both appointments were welcomed generally by the press and the nation for it was recognized that Tanaka's strong-arm methods had reaped nothing but hatred in China as well as costing a great deal of money. So the public was inclined to look with greater favor on the formerly unpopular "weak" policy of Shidehara. The Hamaguchi cabinet, composed of "reasonable and statesmanlike men," was undoubtedly the most liberal which Japan had known. Even the service ministers, General K. Ugaki and Admiral K. Takarabe, were moderates and by no means popular with the aggressive elements in the army and navy. However, the generally high caliber of the cabinet was compromised by the presence of Kenzo Adachi in the important post of Home Minister. Adachi was a "strutting patriot" and a protégé of Viscount Miura, whose empire-plotting had resulted in the murder of the Korean queen in 1895. Despite this background, Miura had remained a sort of political oracle. His disciple, Adachi, had been in Kato's cabinet, and now Hamaguchi, for whatever reasons, found it expedient to elevate him to the powerful Home Ministry. It was this ministry which controlled elections through the appointment of the prefectural governors, and which likewise administered the censorship. Adachi was a master hand at both.[16] Moreover, through the governors, the Home Ministry controlled the workings of the conservative and centralized educational system.

The conciliatory policy of the new government toward China was soon evident and there was decided improvement in Sino-Japanese relations. This did not mean, however, that Japan's objectives in China had changed. It meant rather a change in method toward the same ends represented by the familiar phrase "special position" or "special interests."[17]

On the home front, Hamaguchi campaigned for economy; sought to reduce the budget to prepare for the depression which was just then be-

[16] A. Morgan Young, *Imperial Japan* (New York, 1938), 48-50.
[17] Reischauer, *Japan: Government-Politics*, 152-153.

ginning to be felt; strove to impart some political ideals to a Diet well nigh destitute of them; and, together with Shidehara, attempted to implement the principle of civil control in government. This was a big order if viewed in the light of Japan's past politics. Nevertheless, Hamaguchi was as fearless and resolute as Wakatsuki, his predecessor in the *Minseito,* was timid. In the midst of the growing depression the government signed the London Naval Treaty, banned the export of gold, and effected economies through reorganization of the administration, not excepting the army. All this was laudable and pleasing to many elements in business as well as to political liberals, but it stirred the resentment of the army, of the conservatives in the bureaucracy, and of the ubiquitous and chauvinistic "patriots" with which Japan was overly supplied. Again, as in 1921 when Hara was murdered, fanaticism was permitted to have its day. On November 14, 1930, Yuko Hamaguchi was shot at Tokyo's central railroad station. Though he survived until April of the following year, he was unable to carry on as Premier. His post was filled for the time being by Shidehara, and then after April by Wakatsuki, who also succeeded to the presidency of the *Minseito.* Hamaguchi's passing signified that the cause of representative government was deprived of its most promising leadership. It was a blow from which Japanese political liberalism never recovered. In Western countries, liberalism had been able to survive the assassin's dagger or gun. This was because liberalism in the West was based on political principles which appealed to high ideals of human dignity and character and because of the presence of a monied and conscious middle class. But in Japan, the parties had developed no such ideals, though they had often given them lip service. Party behavior in Japan depended to an extraordinary degree therefore on the quality of its leadership. Up to 1918 when Hara became Premier, development of leadership from among the commoners had been all but precluded by the influence of the Genro and by the survival of aristocratic, feudal, and clan traditions. In these circumstances the emergence of Hamaguchi revealed the potentialities of the liberal and constitutional movement. Hamaguchi, a believer in civil authority in government, was able and honest, simple in his tastes, and steadfast in his beliefs. He was among Japan's greatest men, and when he died the hope for great political principles died with him.[18]

INDUSTRY, COMMERCE, AND FINANCE

During the decade following 1918, Japan felt the effects of those general economic maladjustments which trailed in the wake of World War

---

[18] Young, *Imperial Japan,* 61-62.

I. In part these maladjustments were inherent in the Japanese economic structure; in part they arose from world conditions. The rapid expansion of industry during the war was followed by the liquidation or reduction of capital, by a decline in exports, and by the reappearance of an adverse balance in trade. Along with this came continued inflation of the currency, soaring food prices, and, as a consequence, a great increase in labor disputes. In 1923 the Tokyo earthquake resulted in perhaps as many as 156,000 deaths and a property damage of more than ¥5,000,000,000. In 1927 a financial panic resulted in the closing of many private banks and in the liquidation of a number of industrial plants. These were the general conditions which Hamaguchi sought to correct by a policy of administrative reorganization and economy and by the lifting of the gold embargo in January, 1930.[19] It is not possible here to enter into any detailed discussion of the causes of Japan's economic distress, but it should be noted that conditions in the decade of the 1920's had their immediate origin in the rapid expansion of Japanese industry occasioned by the war. Only after 1928 with the adoption by government of a deflationary policy and the return to gold did Japanese industry "make serious efforts to improve its organization and technical efficiency."[20]

THE GROWTH OF THE LABOR MOVEMENT

In the light of Japan's political and economic conditions described in preceding pages, it is not surprising that the decade of the 1920's witnessed a remarkable expansion of the labor movement, an increase in the number of industrial disputes involving labor, an awakening interest in the theories of socialism and communism, and finally, in the appearance of proletarian political parties.

The earliest labor unions in Japan were socialistic. The movement began about 1897 when Sen Katayama, a Japanese who had acquired his Marxian indoctrination in the United States, organized the *Rodo Kumiai Kiseikai* (Association to Form Labor Unions). The first unions were formed in Tokyo among iron workers and railway engineers and firemen. A society for the study of socialism (*Shakai Shugi Kenkyukai*) was also formed, counting in its membership such names as Katayama, Iso Abe, Denjiro Kōtoku, and Kiyoshi Kawakami. The joint activities of this group and the Iron Workers' Union resulted, in 1901, in a political party, the *Shakai Minshuto* (Social Democratic

---

[19] Uyehara, *The Industry and Trade of Japan*, 18-20.

[20] G. C. Allen, "The Rise in Productive Efficiency," *The Industrialization of Japan and Manchukuo, 1930-1940*, edited by E. B. Schumpeter (New York, 1940), 648-649.

Party), whose platform called for disarmament, universal suffrage, and nationalization of land and industry.[21]

This early appearance of socialism went far to reveal by contrast the basic philosophy and purposes of the Meiji oligarchy and the elements in society allied with them. In 1900 the government passed the *Chian Keisatsuho* (Police Peace Law). This virtually ended the labor and socialist movement since it was now illegal to organize in any movement "to raise wages, shorten hours, or lower land rents." The Home Minister was endowed with authority "to suppress the meetings of any association which he considered dangerous to the peace and order of the community."

The industrial expansion and prosperity of World War I brought rebirth to the labor movement. The awakened movement centered about Bunji Suzuki's *Yuaikai* (Friendly Society of Workers), an organization dominated by intellectuals. Working on the idea of federation, the society was undoubtedly influenced by the theories of Samuel Gompers. In 1921 the name was changed to *Nippon Rodo Sodomei* (Japanese Federation of Labor).

The gains made by Japanese labor toward the end of World War I were achieved despite growing discord within the ranks of labor and its intellectual leadership. There were the conflict over federation, the disputes over labor's entry into politics, and the ideological conflict springing from the Russian revolutions of 1917 and after. Following 1919 the intellectual base of a radical movement was strengthened by the campaign of Sakuzo Yoshino, professor in the Tokyo Imperial University, against militarism, by the organization of societies to study liberal government and socialism, and by the popularity among student groups of Marxian socialism and pacifism. This more radical trend of thought was reflected among the labor unions, some of which were accused of "Bolshevism." In 1922 the Federation of Labor was among the strongest advocates of withdrawing the army from Siberia.

The national emergency created by the earthquake of 1923 was seized upon by the reactionaries as a glorious opportunity for suppression of anything that could be described as radical. The new trend was aided rather than retarded by the Federation of Labor, which in general floated along with the tide of reaction. Homes of socialists were in-

---

[21] The best brief account is Kenneth Colegrove, "Labor Parties in Japan," *American Political Science Review,* XXIII (1929), 329-363, on which I have drawn heavily. See also Sen Katayama, *The Labor Movement in Japan* (Chicago, 1918); Iso Abe, "Socialism in Japan," in *Fifty Years of New Japan,* Shigenobu Okuma, ed. (2 vols., New York, 1909), II, 494-512. The *Shakaito* (Socialist Party) organized at Nagasaki in 1882 by Tokichi Tarui was immediately suppressed by the government.

vaded by hired ruffians who confiscated socialistic literature. A Captain Amakasu of the emperor's gendarmerie strangled with his own hands labor leader Sakae Osugi along with his wife and a seven-year-old nephew.[22] To curb these scandalous proceedings or at least to bring them within the bounds of legal respectability, the same government which passed the manhood suffrage bill of 1925, also enacted the *Chian Ijiho* (Peace Preservation Law), which provided, in Article I:

To organize an association with the object of changing the fundamental character of the state or to deny the system of private property, or to join such an association with knowledge of the nature of its purpose, shall be punished by imprisonment of not more than ten years.

The law was understandable in view of the fear created among both conservatives and liberals by Bolshevist propaganda; but its phraseology (fundamental character of the state), together with the arbitrary powers possessed by the Home Ministry, made it possible for this legislation to be used indiscriminately against moderate as well as radical freedom of thought. The whole business was disastrous in its effects upon the development of a sound, moderate, and law-abiding labor movement. Trimming its sails to the conservatism of government, the Federation of Labor expelled some unions regarded as too radical. The expelled unions formed the *Nippon Rodo Kumiai Hyogikai* (Japan Council of Trade Unions), which now became the left wing of labor. Then other unions seceded from the Federation in protest against its harsh treatment of the communists. Other splits followed, until by 1926 organized labor was hopelessly divided into "four camps—one representing the right, two the center, and one the left. . . ." [23]

JAPANESE LABOR AND POLITICS

Japanese labor, particularly the *Nippon Rodo Sodomei* (the Federation) had avoided politics for a number of reasons. The Federation was conservative and cautious; the working classes did not have the vote; and the government had not consulted the unions in the appointment of delegates to the labor conference at Geneva. Moreover, the government's announcement in 1923 that it proposed to introduce manhood suffrage, far from creating unity, revealed that there was no unity in the ranks of Japanese labor. Conflicts which divided and subdivided

---

[22] Reischauer, *Japan: Government-Politics,* 140-141; Colegrove, "Labor Parties in Japan," 340-341.

[23] Colegrove, "Labor Parties in Japan," 341-342.

the proletarian parties revealed that in Japan as elsewhere the struggle among the socialists was between those who aimed "at a state socialized by constitutional processes and the radicals who are not so particular as to how the revolution comes." [25]

LABOR AND THE ELECTION OF 1928

The general election of 1928, the first held under the manhood suffrage law, which had increased the electorate from 3,341,000 voters to 12,534,000, gave the proletarian parties only eight seats out of the total of 466 in the House of Representatives. This indicated serious weaknesses in the politics of the labor movement, since the new voters included most of the male factory workers and a large part of agricultural labor. Colegrove attributes this near political impotence to five basic factors: 1) the absence of class consciousness due to labor's lack of political experience and its primitive techniques in trade-unionism; 2) the limited number of recognized and experienced leaders among labor; 3) the absence of campaign funds to compete with the financial resources of the *Seiyukai* and the *Minseito,* who were supported by the Mitsui and the Mitsubishi interests respectively; 4) the long history of oppression of the labor movement by arbitrary government decree and by intimidation by hired *soshi;* 5) the electorate's fear of radicalism; and 6) the disputes within the ranks of labor itself. It may also be said that the importance of the labor movement in the decade of the 1920's lay not so much in its own limited development as in the fear which it engendered in other groups. It frightened the old-style aristocrats and conservatives; it diluted the liberalism of the major political parties always fearful of socialistic doctrine; it stimulated a revival of the crusade against "dangerous thoughts"; and it played directly into the hands of the militarists, the super-patriots, and of all who fed on fascist doctrine.[26]

THE NIGHTMARE OF DANGEROUS THOUGHTS

Although the government had some success in suppressing the organized labor movement as such, it found it more difficult to control the spread of proletarian thought.[27] The Russian revolutions had stimulated proletarian thought, and, on the eve of the earthquake in 1923, the Japanese Communist Party was secretly organized. The Party was strengthened in 1926 with the return of Japanese students from the

---

[25] Colegrove, "Labor Parties in Japan," 346-347.
[26] For a discussion of radical ideology see Hugh Byas, "The Communist Movement in Japan," *The Contemporary Review,* CXLI (1932), 190-197.
[27] Tadao Kunitomo, *Japanese Literature since 1868,* 221-242.

Lenin University in Moscow. The developments were soon felt in the left wing of the labor movement. During March, 1928, more than one thousand persons suspected of communist sympathies were detained for examination in police stations. Larger numbers were detained in 1929 and 1930. By 1932 virtually every alleged communist had been arrested. The police campaign led to the discovery of "an alarming growth of communism among students." Included in the group of students arrested was "the heir of a viscount," "the son of a general," and "two sons of a university president." It was this aspect of "dangerous thoughts" that gave the authorities greater concern than any other.[28] Could it be that a society thought to be rigidly indoctrinated with emperor-worship, Shintoism, and government by the privileged, was nevertheless honeycombed with an intelligentsia of communists? Actually the situation was not so serious as it was pictured in official quarters. "As prohibition of alcohol had made drinking fashionable in some American universities," so the frowns of the government had "made Marx fashionable in Japan, and the term 'Marx-boy'" became the label, not of the serious socialist, but rather of those who wished to be in style. When brutal third-degree methods used by the police did not prove wholly successful, milder methods were tried. Government officials met with university faculties to discuss "means of directing students' thoughts into safer channels." Out of these conferences arose the belief that the failure of students to find suitable employment after graduation was a principal cause of student communism.[29]

THE OPEN DOOR TO FASCISM

Among the Japanese themselves, there were some able men who foresaw the dangers ahead. A judge of the Supreme Court who had presided at the trials of many communists described the nation's feelings and its plight when he said:

There is no doubt that the public in general has no sympathy with extreme ideas which aim to establish a proletarian dictatorship. Most people know that change can only come gradually if it is to be lasting, but everyone knows that change must come, and reactionaries who try to retard progress and hamper freedom may lead this growing nation into paths which are more dangerous than their own short-sighted vision can perceive. What the result of this struggle between the longing for freedom and justice and the desire to preserve the old order will be only the future can tell.[30]

[28] Byas, "The Communist Movement in Japan," 192.
[29] Byas, "The Communist Movement in Japan," 196.
[30] Byas, "The Communist Movement in Japan," 197.

These were timely words, because long before the adoption of the "positive policy" by Tanaka's administration there were signs that the reactionaries were making their bid for control. In Japan this was a peculiarly dangerous sign, for the national character, a product of the family system, was steeped in shibboleths of loyalty, discipline, and responsibility. The public was thus indoctrinated toward the right rather than the left, toward respect for established authority rather than toward change, toward the "respectability" of fascism rather than the "subversion" of communism.

THE MILITARY TRADITION

Militarism was the element which made Japan's soil so suitable to the growth of authoritarian ideals. All great modern states of course have a military tradition. In Japan the tradition is unique only in the degree to which it has shaped and controlled the national character and the national destiny.[31]

It must not be supposed, however, that modern Japanese militarism has existed solely as a result of tradition, habit, or philosophy. The Constitution of 1889 and the political structure and machinery emanating from it gave militarism a legal foundation and a functional role of the greatest importance. Of first concern in this connection was the concept of the supreme command (*iaku no gunmu*). This was the absolute control of the armed forces by the emperor, reserved to him by Articles XI and XII of the Constitution. If this were a constitutional formality, little significance would be attached to it, but in this case formality had no place in the purposes which Ito, the framer of the Constitution, had in mind.[32] The removal of the supreme command from all agencies of popular control has perpetuated in modern Japan an institution which flourished during the centuries of feudalism, namely, dual government. In the case where the civil wing of the government differed from the military there were in reality two governments advising the emperor; the Prime Minister representing the civil government, and the service ministers representing the military government. Finally, resignation of one or both of the service ministers rendered the government powerless since the militarists could refuse the service of a

---

[31] Kenneth W. Colegrove, *Militarism in Japan* (Boston, 1936), 10. This brochure is the best brief treatment of the subject in English. See also E. H. Norman, *Soldier and Peasant in Japan* (New York, 1943).

[32] Hirobumi Ito, *Commentaries on the Constitution of the Empire of Japan,* trans. by Miyoji Ito (3rd ed., Tokyo, 1931), 24-25.

successor until their wishes in terms of policy were accepted by the government.[33]

THE MILITARY-FASCIST ALLIANCE

Closely allied with Japan's tradition of militarism were a motley array of reactionary groups with many and divers aims. Some were imperialistic, others extolled patriotism, some were of a pseudo-religious nature, and nearly all professed concern in preserving "the Japanese spirit" and "the fundamental character of the Japanese state." It is easier to tell what these factions opposed than it is to describe what they supported. In general their opposition could be counted upon in any movement which had as its objective liberalism in government or business, the development of representative political institutions, the strengthening of responsible parliamentary government, and, finally, any strengthening of the labor movement, socialism, communism, and social reforms which rested on democratic control. The support of these groups could usually be counted upon in all movements extolling Shintoism and emperor-worship, in policies advocated by the army, in imperialistic movements, and in all forms of chauvinism. However, the background of some of these groups was more complex than this since they claimed a social philosophy which demanded reforms for farmers and workers. These attitudes, however, were not fixed or static. They changed frequently and oftentimes the programs of various groups were contradictory. By the decade of the 1920's when the liberal movement was struggling to establish itself, what, for want of a better name, we may call Japan's fascist societies already had a long and colorful history. The "patriot" was usually in opposition to international co-operation in any useful form.[34]

THE GROWTH OF REACTIONARY SOCIETIES

Parliamentarians also played their part in the creation of fascist societies. The Society of the Imperial Way (*Odo Gikai*) was founded in 1918 by a group of *Seiyukai* politicians and officials of the South Manchuria Railway. The Society of the Spirit of Great Japan (*Dai Nippon Kokusuikai*) promoted "harmony between capital and labor" by breaking up union meetings. The Society of the Foundations of the State (*Kokuhonsha*) was organized in 1919 at the time of the great outbreak

---

[33] For an analysis of the supreme command and dual government see Colegrove, *Militarism in Japan*, 16-27.

[34] Colegrove, *Militarism in Japan*, 27-29.

of labor troubles. One of its organizers was Kiichiro (later Baron) Hiranuma, who was seeking to destroy the democratic movement at the Imperial University of Tokyo. Later in its career the society supported Hiranuma for the premiership. Although the society claimed to be seeking harmony between capital and labor, its record was decidedly anti-democratic.[35]

Other aspects of the fascist trend were evident in the pronounced militarism of Japan's youth movement.

IN SUMMARY

The years from the end of World War I to the assassination of Hamaguchi were among the most vital in Japan's recent history. In many respects they revealed the best and the worst in Japanese life. They were years of democratic progress and of awakening social consciousness stirred by the maladjustments of a young industrial society. But they were also years which revealed the barrenness of party politics and the paucity of great political leadership among the commoners. These were fatal weaknesses in a land where reactionary patriotic societies had long flourished and where the political assassin was too often regarded as a savior of the state.

[35] E. E. N. Causton, *Militarism and Foreign Policy in Japan* (London, 1936), 53, 163; Colegrove, *Militarism in Japan*, 30-32.

CHAPTER 29

CHINA: THE *KUOMINTANG* AND THE RUSSIAN ORIENTATION, 1917-1927

THE decade following World War I, which witnessed in Japan the political and social turmoil traced in the two preceding chapters, is also one of the most significant periods in the history of modern and contemporary China. It was during these years that the Chinese revolution entered upon a new, a vibrant, and a critical stage in its development. The position in which the Chinese found themselves at the Versailles Conference of 1918-1919 emphasized the tragic failure of China's republican revolution of 1911 and of the regime of militarism which followed it. Out of this humiliation there was to come, however, a reborn revolutionary party, the *Kuomintang,* whose mission was to make of nationalism a living political force in Chinese life.[1] Moreover, the new revolutionary fervor which appeared after 1918 was not solely political and national. After 1920 there were signs of a social upheaval which for a time seemed destined to transform the ancient and moribund Confucian society into a proletarian dictatorship. In reality, this was the reflection of a fear prevalent among foreigners rather than a potentiality inherent in Chinese political forces at that time. For a time, as will be seen shortly, the nationalist and the proletarian movements joined forces in a brief and unstable marriage of convenience; but for the moment it is sufficient to suggest that these stirring events, here to be related, were manifestations of profound and complex revolutionary unrest in the entire structure of Chinese life. By 1920, China was entering not merely a political revolution but rather a complex of revolutions taking place simultaneously.[2]

---

[1] *Kuomintang* is a combination of three Chinese words meaning country, people, and party. It is translated variously, National People's Party being perhaps the most acceptable rendering.

The failure of China's revolution, 1911, was not solely the fault of the Chinese themselves. In part the failure, and its consequences, must be attributed to the tenacious belief of the foreign powers that only a "strong man" could handle China. This led the powers to support Yüan Shih-k'ai to an extent which upset the natural balances in Chinese politics.

[2] It is hardly possible in a few words to indicate with accuracy the degree to which the Chinese people in recent decades have become more articulate in the political sense.

507

A SINO-JAPANESE CONTRAST

In approaching the subject of China's revitalized revolution, one should note that the problem of readjustment in China was far more difficult than in Japan. In China, no political leadership comparable to the Genro had yet been developed. The confused and divided leadership of the republican revolution of 1911 did not appreciate that the gap between the crumbling Confucian society and a modern parliamentary republic could not be bridged in one step. The old Imperial regime of the Manchus had been swept away or had crumbled from the weight of its incapacity for adjustment, but there was nothing capable of taking its place save the dictatorship of Yüan Shih-k'ai and the later chaos of tuchunism. In these circumstances it was inevitable that revolutionary forces should again arise as an answer to China's plight. As in 1911, these revolutionary forces were personalized in the character and name of Sun Wen, or, as he is better known to history, Sun Yat-sen, who as provisional president of the Republic in 1912 had stepped aside in favor of a so-called national settlement under Yüan Shih-k'ai.

Sun Yat-sen was born in 1866 or 1867 at Hsiang Shan, Canton delta, in the southern China which had nurtured the T'ai-p'ing Rebellion in the neighboring province of Kwangsi. While still a youth he was educated in Honolulu, acquired a knowledge of English, was converted to Christianity, and became impressed by the power of the great Western states, a power which he attributed to their philosophy of nationalism. In contrast, he saw a vast and populous but weak China resting on what Sun regarded as the worn-out Confucian theory of the world community. Sun was determined that this China should be transformed into a modern nation-state. His work was begun while he studied medicine at British Hongkong, and later when he practiced briefly at Canton and Macao. His early political methods followed an accustomed Chinese pattern: the formation of a small group of fol-

During their long history, the Chinese developed their own political methods for political protest. Their methods, however, were not those of Western nations, and, as a consequence, the Westerner has often described the Chinese as being inarticulate in the political sense. Thus, during the early years of the Nationalist movement it seemed that the Chinese masses, if they did anything at all, merely followed their leaders. As a people they tended to be onlookers rather than an active force rising against their government. Many of them still remain in this category of onlookers. Nevertheless, in the years since 1911, there has also been an amazing political awakening among the people. One cannot measure with accuracy the degree to which, or the rapidity with which, the Chinese people is discarding the role of onlooker for that of active political participant, yet the evidence is certainly clear that the movement is in this direction.

For much of the interpretation which follows in this chapter, I am indebted to Arthur H. Holcombe's study *The Chinese Revolution* (2nd ed., Cambridge, Mass., 1931).

lowers, which took him back to the roots of the T'ai-p'ing Rebellion; affiliation with other groups; petitions to the authorities; and terroristic attacks. By the time of the Sino-Japanese War, 1894-1895, the revolutionary organization of Sun Yat-sen had become "modernist, nationalist, and antimonarchical, instead of merely patriotic and antidynastic." [3] His original revolutionary body, the Society for the Regeneration of China (*Hsing Chung Hui*), 1894-1905, soon began to draw strength from overseas Chinese who had acquired wealth abroad and who were determined to end the old order in China. By 1905, when the movement was reorganized as the League of Common Alliance (*T'ung Mêng Hui*), 1905-1912, republicanism was receiving greater stress through formulation of an ideology which was later formalized in the *San Min Chu I*, or the Three People's Principles: nationalism, democracy, and livelihood (sometimes interpreted as socialism in some form). The hope of the *T'ung Mêng Hui* was the overthrow of the Manchus, the establishment of a republic, and control of the parliamentary regime which would follow. At this stage there was a naïve though perhaps natural tendency on the part of the revolutionists to assume that once the old system was destroyed, democracy would naturally follow.

From 1912 to 1914, Sun Yat-sen's revolutionists adopted the name *Kuomintang,* or National People's Party. From 1914 to 1920 they became the *Chung Hua Kê Ming Tang,* or Chinese Revolutionary Party. But this was a period in which the revolutionary cause was almost as chaotic as the Chinese society in which it struggled to exist. In an effort to meet and capitalize on the disintegration that followed the collapse of Li's government at Peking, Sun Yat-sen and a few of his followers in 1917 set up their own administration at Canton which claimed to be the true or lawful republic, since it was composed of remnants of the Peking parliament dissolved by Li Yuan-hung. Actually the real power in the south rested not with Sun, who, although elected generalissimo, had no army, but with T'ang Chi-yao, the governor of Yünnan and Kweichow, and with Lu Yung-t'ing, who controlled the troops in Kwangtung and Kwangsi. This trio was united only in the sense that it was opposed to the government of Tuan Ch'i-jui at Peking and that government's policy of carrying China into the World War. The result was intermittent warfare between Peking and Canton and the failure of all efforts to unite.[4]

---

[3] P. M. A. Linebarger, *Government in Republican China* (New York, 1938), 34.
[4] T'ang Leang-li, *The Inner History of the Chinese Revolution* (London, 1930), 121-137. Both at this time and later, T'ang was closely associated with Wang Ching-wei as a traitor in the service of the Japanese.

PRESIDENT OF THE SOUTHERN REPUBLIC

For a time the southern Canton government maintained a precarious existence; and in April, 1921, Sun Yat-sen was able to summon a special parliament which elected him president of the "Chinese Republic." There were now two republics and two presidents. Canton itself seemed on the road to becoming a modern municipality under the leadership of Sun Fo, son of Sun Yat-sen, as mayor. But politically conditions were not stable. The revolutionists had all but ceased to exist as a party since 1912. They were held together almost solely by the personality of Sun Yat-sen. Efforts to right this situation in 1920 by readopting *Kuomintang* as the party name were not successful. From the standpoint of revolutionary action the weakness was that little connection existed between the party on the one hand and the military and political power on the other. Some members of Sun's Canton government were not members of the party at all. An additional weakness lay in the fact that the new Kwangtung army, created by two party leaders, Wang Ching-wei and Hu Han-min, and commanded by Ch'en Ch'iung-ming, governor of Kwangtung, received no political indoctrination and, in temper, was hardly distinguishable from the armies of the war-lords. Sun was thus largely dependent on the whims of a southern militarist.[5]

Against the free bootery of militarists, Sun Yat-sen was helpless. While he remained high in the esteem of all who hoped for a better China, he had no effective contact with the masses of the Chinese people, and his party was weak and lacking a program of action. Furthermore, in the view of some of Sun's immediate following, the cause of reform in China could look for no help from the capitalistic Western powers. The Washington Conference, which had just concluded its deliberations, had refused to recognize Sun's Canton government and had continued to deal with the Peking militarists. As a result, its work was seen at Canton as freeing "China from the Japanese policy of independent violent encroachment" while subjecting it "to the co-operative slow encroachment" of all the powers.[6] It was against this background of military jobbery within China and the policies of the Western democracies at Washington that Sun Yat-sen turned to Russia for aid.

---

[5] T'ang Leang-li, *The Inner History of the Chinese Revolution,* 144, recounts the loss at this time of Sun's manuscripts, on which a monumental work, *The Reconstruction of the State,* was to be based. "The loss of 'The Principle of Livelihood' especially was unfortunate, as in the absence of any authoritative guidance, his followers had only their own interpretation of this principle."

[6] Wang Ching-wei, *China and the Powers,* quoted by Harold R. Isaacs, *The Tragedy of the Chinese Revolution* (London, 1938), 63.

REORGANIZATION AND REORIENTATION OF THE KUOMINTANG

Early in 1923 the way had been opened for collaboration between Russia and the Kuomintang through a meeting at Shanghai of Sun Yat-sen and Adolph Joffe, Soviet emissary to the Far East. A joint statement which resulted from this meeting set forth their understanding: 1) that communism and the soviet system were unsuited to China's present needs; 2) that China's immediate goal was the realization of political unity and independence, to which ends Russia would lend her assistance; and 3) that Russia reaffirmed her declaration of 1919 in which she had renounced the imperialism of the tsars though carefully reserving certain rights in the Chinese Eastern Railway.[7] Late in 1923 Michael Borodin arrived at Canton, where he set about creating a new Kuomintang characterized by rigid party organization and discipline and pledged to a program of action. Implementation of this new program would end the days when the Kuomintang was held together largely by bonds of personal loyalty to Sun Yat-sen. The change, however, meant more than this; it meant that the new Russia had become the model for the new revolutionary plan of action in China. The model of the new party at Canton was the Russian Communist Party. That some members of the old Kuomintang would not accept the new membership was more than made up by admitting to the Kuomintang members of the newly formed Chinese Communist Party.

The constitution of the revitalized party reflected the purpose of broadening the base of the revolutionary authority. At the base of the organizational chart were the local groups empowered to promote the revolutionary cause, to conduct necessary local business of the party, and to discipline the members of the group. Above the local groups were district and then provincial organizations culminating in a National Party Congress designed to meet annually and to be the ultimate authority on policy. With the Congress was a Central Executive Committee and a Supervisory Committee to direct when the Congress was not in session. Although the purpose of this new machinery was in part at least to get away from the old personalized relation of mem-

---

[7] The Sun-Joffe joint statement is printed in *The China Year Book, 1924* (Shanghai), 863.

In further explanation of the beginnings of collaboration between China and Russia, there was the fact that Russia was not admitted to the Washington Conference and that most Western countries were hostile to Russia and were still acting on the assumption that the Bolshevist regime was doomed to fall. Ostracized Russia and disappointed, frustrated China had reasons for making common cause over and above any merely willful intervention of Russia in China's affairs.

bers to Sun Yat-sen, the prestige of Sun was such that he was made president of the party for life.[8] His constitutional powers remained large, including the right to veto resolutions of the Party Congress. In general, then, the party organization as it had evolved by the beginning of 1924 was a compromise between the former exclusive personalized control by Sun and the ideal of thorough democratic control originating in the local party cells. Actually, however, conditions within China after 1924 were such that in the conduct of party affairs more and more responsibility gravitated to the Central Executive Committee.[9]

SUN YAT-SEN'S PHILOSOPHY OF THE REVOLUTION

The reorganization of the Kuomintang was but one phase of the new revolutionary activity at Canton. An understandable program of principles that could be popularized among the people was also imperative if the new party machinery was to have meaning. Thus it became necessary for Sun Yat-sen to give more attention to the philosophy and the principles of his program for the new China. Most of his thought was therefore committed to writing during the years 1917 to 1925—the years in which the newly organized Kuomintang was taking shape.

As the social thought of early China is linked with the name of Confucius, so the revolutionary political thought of early twentieth-century China is inseparable from the name of Sun Yat-sen. Although in many passages Sun's writings are neither clear, nor precise, nor complete, they provide when taken as a whole "a systematic and remarkably complete program for the regeneration of China." [10] Sun's revolutionary philosophy and his program of action are set forth in: 1) *Plans for National Reconstruction;* 2) the *San Min Chu I,* or *Three Principles of the People;* 3) the *Fundamentals of National Reconstruction;* and 4) the *Manifesto* of the Kuomintang issued at the First Party Congress in 1924.

In the first of his three-volume *Plans for Reconstruction*[11] Sun reveals

---

[8] The party reorganization may also have been intended to give more effectiveness to a characteristic of Sun's methods of politics which was already well marked. Sun had long shown an aptitude for a type of coalition politics in which he used in his following men of widely different interests and ultimate aims. The party reorganization would at this time provide to some extent both for keeping this diverse following together and for keeping its component parts in balance.

[9] T'ang Leang-li, *The Inner History of the Chinese Revolution,* 175-178.

[10] Arthur N. Holcombe, *The Chinese Revolution* (Cambridge, 1931), 123. Note all of Holcombe's chapter v for a discussion of Sun's writings and his political thought.

[11] Part of this work has been published in English under the titles *Memoirs of a Chinese Revolutionary* (London, 1919), and *The International Development of China* (London, 1922).

the influence of the Confucian background. It was good Confucian theory to say, as Sun did, that those who would govern must first learn to govern themselves through the pursuit of knowledge. Operating on this theory of education, the old Chinese scholars had assumed that the people were to be ruled. Sun, however, held that education was the essence of democracy, and that the best way for the people to learn democracy was to practice it, even if imperfectly at first. Although in these first writings Sun was not unmindful of the importance of China's material reconstruction, he appears to have rejected the economic interpretation as the most important base of politics. He was Confucian in his belief that Heaven is more apt to be impressed by virtue rather than by the material power of brute force.

By far the most famous enunciation of Sun's political principles for the reconstruction of China is the *San Min Chu I* (Three Principles of the People). These materials were first delivered as lectures in 1924 after the reorganization of the Kuomintang. They were a part of the campaign of propaganda designed to reach the popular mind. But they were more than this. The fact that they contained a wide range of statements and interpretations which in part represent conflict between a number of theories and in part compromises between different theories suggests the interpretation that they were designed to hold together a coalition which was growing diverse and which, because of that fact, included components which oscillated between collaboration with each other and rivalry. The lectures, hastily composed, present many imperfections of thought and style, but remain nevertheless a basic portrayal of Sun's philosophy and of the ideological goal of his revolution. Although the lectures were not delivered until after the Russian orientation had taken place, most of the ideas contained in them had long been in Sun's mind and thus do not appear to have been inspired primarily by Moscow. However, as revolutionary propaganda the Three Principles had immense effect upon the thinking of the Chinese people. It gave them for the first time a positive approach to the revolutionary cause in place of the former negative approach which prevailed during the anti-dynastic, anti-Manchu phase of the revolution.[12]

THE FIRST PRINCIPLE: NATIONALISM

The first of Sun's principles was peculiarly alien to the traditional habits of Chinese thought. It will be recalled that the old China was held together by bonds of a common social and cultural heritage rather than by any machinery of centralized political authority. The idea that

---

[12] Linebarger, *Government in Republican China*, 41-44.

the Chinese were to learn to think of themselves not as a society but as a nation-state was in itself daring, and, perhaps, the most revolutionary of all Sun Yat-sen's proposals. Its achievement would be the more difficult since all Greater China was to be incorporated into the new nation-state. Even in the simplest classification, Greater China consisted not of one people but of five: Chinese, Manchus, Mongols, Tibetans, and the Mohammedans, each represented by the five-bar flag of the Republic of 1912. Thus, when Sun talked of a nationalism incorporating all these peoples, he was not thinking of what the West originally termed nationalism but rather of a new patriotism to the state transcending these racial complexities. Patriotism to the state was to take precedence over the customary Chinese loyalties to family, clan, and village.[13]

It may be granted that Sun's nationalism rested upon lofty ideals and upon appreciation of China's great past, yet he also appealed to those arguments which have been the stock in trade of young nationalism throughout modern times. He was alarmed by "the white peril," was attracted by protectionist theories of trade, and looked to the time when China, assuming "the white man's burden," would bring civilization and light to weak and less fortunate neighbors. When this background of Sun's nationalism is borne in mind, the anti-imperialistic and the anti-foreign-control aspects of China's revolution become understandable.

THE SECOND PRINCIPLE: DEMOCRACY

In contrast with the absence of political nationalism or patriotism, certain democratic concepts had played their part in Chinese thought from ancient times. A society devoid of democratic impulses could not have developed or practiced the theory of the Mandate of Heaven. In theory at least, the highest as well as the lowest offices in Old China had

---

[13] When Sun talked of nationalism within a nation which included Mongols, Tibetans, and Mohammedans (the Manchus were of lesser importance), he faced a problem of extreme delicacy. The question involved not only patriotism to the state but also the problem of what kind of state. Was it to be a state in which the Chinese, as the overwhelming majority, were to have a corresponding ascendancy over such people as the Mongols? Or was it to be a federated state in which the Mongols and the Tibetans were to have the standing of majorities within their own territories? A number of the Mongol-Kuomintang followers of Sun at this time believed that the eventual outcome would be a federated state. The subsequent failure to create such a state, and the more recent emphasis on policies which, if successful, would result in the compulsory conversion of such peoples as the Mongols from a status of "sub-standard Chinese" to a status of "standard Chinese" has deeply alienated Mongols and Tibetans, and has given their nationalism a trend which is increasingly anti-Chinese. For Sun, in 1924, it was extraordinarily difficult to come to grips with this problem. If he had advocated too openly a federated status for the frontier peoples, he would, in view of China's weakness at the time, have exposed them to the danger of annexation or near-annexation by foreign powers.

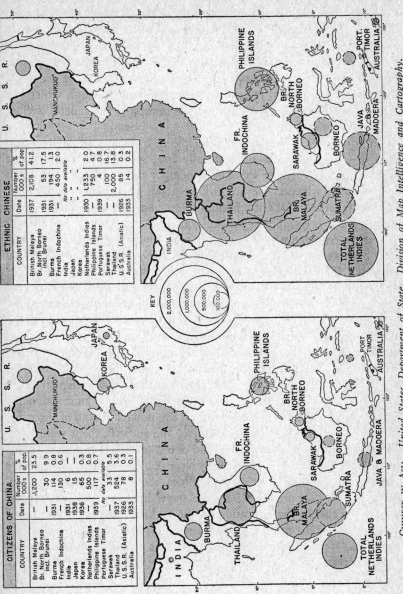

CHINESE IN ASIA. *United States, Department of State. Division of Map Intelligence and Cartography.*

been open to any Chinese who could pass the civil service examinations.
Local government, too, had been a thing of the people in the local community. Yet even here it should be remembered that loyalties and responsibilities were to the family, clan, or guild and not to the people of
the community as a whole, much less to the people of the whole state.
Sun argued that the Chinese in achieving democracy must acquire a
new concept of liberty, recognizing it as the ideal through which the
individual curbs his own freedom in the interest of the general welfare
of all the people of the state.

On equality, the companion principle in a democratic society, Sun
held that since men are not naturally free, neither did nature create
them equal. "When we speak of democracy and equality but yet want
the world to advance, we are talking about political equality. For
equality is an artificial not a natural thing, and the only equality which
we can create is equality in political status." [13]

The government which Sun therefore proposed to erect was to rest
on the sovereignty of the people but was to be run by men of political
capacity. The government of a nation must be built upon the rights
of the people, but the administration of public affairs must be entrusted
to experts. It was to be temporarily an authoritarian administration,
but one which even in the beginning was to be held responsible to the
people through certain mechanisms of control such as the election and
recall of officials who determined policy, and through the initiative and
referendum. Ultimately, the exercise of these mechanisms was intended to make possible the replacement of the authoritarian structure
by a democratic structure of elected representatives. Constitutionally,
the proposed government would rest on five powers instead of three, for
in addition to the legislative, executive, and judicial, there were to be
added the powers of examination and of censorship.[14] Since the events
of 1911-1912 had made it abundantly clear that the Chinese masses were
unprepared for these new responsibilities, the new revolutionary program of 1923-1924 provided for three stages in the development of the
revolution and in the education of the Chinese people. The first of
these would be the military period, lasting for as long as extensive field
operations were still under way. During this period the military power
would necessarily be supreme. The second would be the period of po-

---

[13] Sun Yat-sen, *San Min Chu I*, trans. by F. W. Price (Shanghai, 1927), 243-245.
[14] The principle involved here was not new. The Censorate under the Manchus exercised the function of criticizing officials from the highest, including the emperor, to
the lowest. This right was not always exercised without bias, nor always with impunity,
but in general the very existence of the Censorate had a salutary effect upon officialdom.

litical tutelage, during which the people would receive instruction in the use of their new political powers while the actual power of government remained in the hands of the Kuomintang. With the completion of the educational process would come the third and last period—the inauguration of democratic, constitutional government.[15]

THE THIRD PRINCIPLE: LIVELIHOOD OR "SOCIALISM"

The full exposition of Sun's third principle was never completed, and therefore the full implications of his thought on this important matter continue to be a subject of intense disagreement among his followers both inside and outside China. The principle of livelihood, broadly stated, was that the state should so direct or control the affairs of men that "the needs of all should be supplied as far as possible by the efforts of all." A principle stated in such general terms might be said to point toward any one of our numerous schools of socialistic thought from arbitrary Marxism to the lukewarm theories of Utopians. Sun, while not accepting Marx, treated him both warily and with patience, and even at times with deference. Therefore, instead of following Marx, Sun appears to have been attracted by vigorous but moderate movements of social reform as he had observed these in Western countries. He favored the nationalization of systems of transportation and communication, the improvement of working conditions, a fuller education for workers, and the development of consumers' co-operatives. Livelihood, as Sun expounded it, is definitely socialistic, but it is not Marxian communism. In a word, as Holcombe has said, Sun Yat-sen "should be described as a social reformer with a disposition to favor socialistic measures or, better, as a social revolutionist with a disposition to temporize with capitalism." [16]

Such, in brief, were the main principles and the program of Sun Yatsen. Sun was a visionary, an exhorter, and a teacher. As a leader of rebels in action, and as a political manipulator, he was a failure; but as a herald of new life and inspiration for a bewildered people, he may claim pre-eminent success. Even while he still lived and was unrecognized by perhaps the great bulk of his own people, it was his philosophy which gave point and meaning to the revolutionary cause. Of all modern Chinese, it was Sun Yat-sen who first saw that the Mandate of Heaven might rest upon a sovereign people.

---

[15] Note Holcombe's discussion of the three stages in Sun's plan of revolution. *The Chinese Revolution*, 312-319.

[16] Holcombe, *The Chinese Revolution*, 149.

NEGOTIATIONS WITH PEKING, 1924-25

While Sun's control at Canton continued to be precarious,[17] he had never abandoned hope of reaching a peaceful settlement with the militarists who controlled Peking. For some two years he had engaged in intermittent negotiation with the north, and by 1924 he hoped to strike a bargain with Tuan Chi-jui, provisional chief executive in November, and the Manchurian war-lord, Chang Tso-lin, and to have combined with them in attacking the armies of the rival militarist, Wu P'ei-fu. Because he could not even control the militarists at Canton, Sun was obviously unable to send any forces from the south against Wu, but, in December, 1924, he went to Peking to work out with Tuan, Chang, and the so-called Christian General, Feng Yu-hsiang, a plan for a united China. Arrived in the capital, already a sick man, Sun was now to discover that the militarists had fixed upon terms of a settlement which he could not approve. His final effort to create a government for a united China had failed. On March 12, 1925, Sun Yat-sen died at Peking in the private residence of Wellington Koo which had been taken over and to which Sun was removed from the Union College Medical Hospital where he had undergone an operation for malignant cancer.

The passing of Sun Yat-sen had pronounced and conflicting effects upon the nationalist movement and upon the fortunes of the Kuomintang. So long as Sun lived, his shortcomings, his mistakes, and his lack of practical political acumen had been obvious not only to many of his immediate followers but also to his enemies. Now that he was gone, all this was changed. The failures of the man whom many had regarded as a visionary were forgotten. Sun became the embodiment of all the idealism within the nationalist movement, and the personification of all the revolutionary fervor of the reconstituted Kuomintang. As Confucius had become the sage of ancient China, so would Sun Yat-sen inherit the role in twentieth-century China. Confucianism would give place to Sun Yat-senism.

On the other hand, no single leader had emerged to take Sun's place. Rivalry among his immediate associates was therefore a natural consequence—a rivalry which tended to rest its case on divergent interpretations of Sun's political and economic philosophy. Here there was ample ground for ideological warfare and party strife because of the vague, general, uncertain terms in which Sun had so frequently expressed his ideas. The immediate victory in this intra-party contest for power rested with the left wing and its Russian communist advisers. The

---

[17] T'ang Leang-li, *Wang Ching-wei* (Peiping, 1931), 97-100.

party machinery was in the hands of the left wingers. This enabled them to guide the decisions of the Second National Party Congress in January, 1926. As a consequence, the Congress decided to continue the Russian collaboration and to continue admitting communists to membership in the Kuomintang. Against this radical orientation, the right wing, which met in the so-called Western Hills Conference outside Peking, was for the time being powerless. Here, too, it should be noted that events involving the Western powers played directly into the hands of the radical wing. Beginning with the incident on May 30, 1925, at Shanghai, when the police of the International Settlement fired upon demonstrating Chinese students, coastal China was swept by a wave of resentment against the British (an Englishman commanded and had ordered the police to fire at Shanghai). A boycott of British trade became general and was particularly effective in Hongkong. The spontaneity with which this boycott was applied suggested to Kuomintang leaders that one road to Sun's nationalism lay in direct attack upon the position of the so-called imperialistic powers in China. Since Russia was supposed to be anti-imperialistic, this was another reason strengthening the Kuomintang-Soviet Entente.[18]

THE BASES OF THE KUOMINTANG-SOVIET ENTENTE, 1923-27

The influence which Soviet Russia had won at Canton following the meeting of Sun Yat-sen and Adolph Joffe at Shanghai is traceable to a number of circumstances prevailing in China and also to developments within the Russian Revolution itself. From as early as 1919, the Russians had courted China.[19] Lenin recognized the principle of self-determination in dealing with the diverse peoples of Asia, the right of these peoples to equality in the Communist Party, and to a large measure of autonomy in the Soviet system of states.

The wisdom of this policy soon produced dividends. Outer Mongolia, after a successful revolt in 1921, became the Mongolian Peoples' Republic; but in view of Russia's desire to preserve amicable relations with China, the new republic was not admitted to the Soviet Union.[20] In 1922, after the Japanese withdrawal from Siberia, the Far Eastern Republic entered the Soviet system, and Russia was thus in a new and strategic territorial position to pursue a more vigorous propaganda campaign within China. It was in January of the following year, 1923, that

---

[18] For a discussion of the international aspects of the revolution see Chapter 30.
[19] See the discussion in K. Fuse, *Soviet Policy in the Orient* (Peking, 1927), ch. i.
[20] See page 540.

Adolph Joffe met with Sun Yat-sen in Shanghai.[21]   Only a few months later, Michael Borodin, one of the most successful and tried of Russia's agents of revolution, arrived at Canton.   Born in Russia, he had come to the United States as a boy bearing the name of Grusenberg; he had later, under the name of Berg, conducted a business school in Chicago. But, abandoning the quiet profession of teaching for the more active life of a revolutionist, he appeared as an agitator in Mexico and Turkey under the name of Borodin.   He was possessed of energy, charm, and intelligence.   Moscow could hardly have found a better man to promote its purposes at Canton.

There was a twofold objective in Borodin's Canton mission: 1) to give Chinese revolutionaries the benefit of Russia's experience in the techniques of revolutionary action; and 2) to find ways of putting Chinese communists in control of the Kuomintang.   Under Borodin's guidance, the reorganization of the Kuomintang, already referred to (p. 511), was soon under way.

In the second phase of his work, Borodin was equally successful. The first Kuomintang National Congress admitted Chinese communists to membership provided they took the oath of allegiance to the Party.   This was a deeply significant victory for Borodin and his Russian backers.   The Chinese communists were weak numerically, but in their ideology, organization, and discipline they were comparatively strong.   Once within the Kuomintang, they were able to exert an influence disproportionate to their numbers.   For the moment they were pledged to support the Kuomintang program, but their ultimate goal was a communist-controlled China.[22]

THE AUDIENCE OF THE NEW KUOMINTANG

The audience to which this new Kuomintang was to address itself may be roughly described as made up of two major and many lesser groups.   By far the largest was the vast agricultural population of the countryside.   Next in size was the city population of masters, journey-

---

[21] See page 511.

[22] The statement is, of course, an over-simplification since it does not deal with the complex and speculative question of intermediate forms which the communists may have had in mind to apply before the ultimate goal was reached.   Nor does it take into account the span of time which the communists contemplated should elapse before achieving their full purposes.   It should not be assumed, however, that the communists believed (unless they were extraordinarily naïve) that they would at some propitious moment be able to execute a quick switch from a communist-influenced program to an all-communist program.   It should also be noted that at this time conflict had appeared both among Chinese and foreign communists.   In particular, the rivalry between followers of Trotzky and followers of Stalin was already bitter.

men, and apprentices of the guilds, where industry was still conducted
in small shops and on a pattern essentially medieval. In a few of
China's larger cities such as Shanghai where there were modern, large-
scale textile factories, there were also the beginnings of an urban, industrial proletariat, and here the conventional communist line—the dictatorship of the proletariat—could be used with great effect. But this appeal
could have little meaning among the masters and workers of small-scale
guild industry throughout China as a whole. To these artisans, whose
position was already threatened by the beginnings of factory industry,
the Kuomintang slogan of nationalism was far more understandable.
Where modern industry already had gained a footing there were also the
beginnings of an organized labor movement. It had first manifested
itself among the transport workers of the treaty ports toward the close
of World War I. Later the movement made some progress among
workers in the cotton textile factories at Shanghai and Hankow and in
the flour mills at Tientsin and Harbin. The first Chinese national labor
conference met at Canton in 1922 and, shortly thereafter, the Seamen's
Union at Hongkong gained recognition. Thus by 1924, the labor union
movement in China though still in its infancy was making notable
progress.

The problem of reaching China's numberless peasant-farmers, still
clinging to customs hallowed by forty centuries, was a task which the
Kuomintang had not faced prior to the new Russian orientation. By
1924, however, vast numbers of China's peasantry were ready to lend
a willing ear to almost any gospel that promised relief.[23] In spite of all
his innate conservatism and his slavish acceptance of custom, the peasant
was beginning to react against the inequalities within his village, and
against the manifold forms of extortion that had enabled *tuchuns,* lesser
militarists, and small-fry brigands in general to collect taxes for as much
as twenty years in advance. The peasant was therefore receptive to the
propaganda of the new Kuomintang, and in South China after 1924
there was a remarkable growth of peasant unions.[24]

THE YOUTH AND STUDENT MOVEMENT

As the new Kuomintang with its new Soviet adherents reached out to
capture the latent revolutionary potential of farmers and laborers, much

[23] This is not to say that the hard-pressed peasantry was wholly lacking in discrimination. To an increasing extent in recent times Chinese peasants have responded most
directly to those programs that were specific in proposing measures comprehensible to the
peasants in terms of their own needs and desires rather than in terms of nebulous ideological generalities.
[24] The subject is developed in C. L'Estrange Malone, *New China: A Report of an
Investigation* (London, 1926), Pt. II.

of its most effective propaganda was carried into the treaty ports and to the interior by what has been called the student movement. The marked influence that students have exerted at times upon China's nationalist revolution is traceable in part to the historic position of scholarship and the scholar in Old China. It was natural for the Chinese to look to the student for answers to the manifold political questions that plagued China in the chaotic revolutionary years after 1911. It was also natural for the students to voice their political opinions with an air of authority. This was particularly true of those who had received a modern education in Japan, in Europe, or in America. After 1911, too, China's modern schools increased with great rapidity, as did also the number of students. In the turmoil of prevailing conditions, many in this increasing body of graduates could not find positions they considered commensurate with their training. These readily became active critics of government. So it was that a growing body of students, inspired by Western learning, became the most likely revolutionary material within China. Many students were fanatical supporters of Sun Yat-sen, and the most enthusiastic, if at times irresponsible, members of the Kuomintang. Many, too, were ardent supporters of the Russo-communist orientation at Canton which promised action and results. Yet while many students supported Borodin's program for the new Kuomintang, they were less interested in its Soviet implications than in its immediate promise of a vigorous Chinese nationalism. Far, too, from confining their doings to politics, the students were in the forefront of the intellectual and literary renaissance of the time, and in the movement for emancipation of Chinese women. Since, in the view of the students, the new Chinese woman was to enjoy political equality (a strange and terrifying idea to Chinese of the old school), she was likewise to have a new social freedom to bob her hair, to choose her own husband, and to express her own mind in public.[25]

There were many other sources as well which the Kuomintang-Soviet Entente sought to cultivate, and from which it drew support for the revolutionary cause. The wealthy overseas Chinese communities, long backers of Sun Yat-sen, were still courted by the left wing in power at Canton. Disaffected soldiers of the *tuchun* armies were also a convenient target for Canton's propaganda. At first the agents for this work were hastily trained in speed-up courses at Canton, but after 1925 the abler personnel received special schooling at the new Sun Yat-sen University for Chinese revolutionaries in Moscow. And, all the while,

[25] The subject is developed by T. C. Wang, *The Youth Movement in China* (New York, 1927).

the fiction was maintained of the complete separation between the Soviet Government and the Communist International, so much so, that during 1924, while Borodin and his associates were planning the destruction of the Peking government, Moscow negotiated a treaty with Peking in which the latter recognized the Soviet regime.[26] There could be no question of the realism in Moscow's strategy.

CHINA'S SEMI-COLONIAL STATUS AIDS THE LEFT

The way in which events involving Britain and other Western powers, such as the Shanghai incident of May 30, 1925, played into the hands of the communists at Canton has already been noted. In addition, the Chinese militarists themselves gave aid and comfort to the Soviet orientation at Canton. After the death of Sun Yat-sen, Peking's political bankruptcy became even more apparent than previously, and by 1926 its political incapacity was an international scandal. Many thoughtful Chinese, indeed, were convinced that certain of the major powers (England, France, Japan, and Russia) were secretly supporting their favorite *tuchuns,* and that they expected to be rewarded for so doing with further concessions at the expense of China's sovereignty. There were good and sufficient reasons for these Chinese fears. The general and deep-seated confusion so characteristic of almost every phase of Chinese life during the decade of tuchunism, 1917-27, had led to a prevalent conclusion among foreigners that the Chinese were politically inept and incapable of putting their house in order. If there was ever to be a Chinese house-cleaning, so the opinion ran, it would be done by the Western powers working through one or another of the various war-lords. Japan, too, might have a part in this business. Chang Tso-lin in Manchuria was considered to be her tool; Feng Yu-hsiang, the so-called Christian General, had spent 1926 in Moscow and was regarded as a convert to the Soviet view though not at first an ally of the Kuomintang at Canton; Wu P'ei-fu, the scholar-war-lord, was considered to be the favorite potential instrument of the British. Moreover, the failure of the Peking conferences of 1926 on the Chinese tariff and extraterritoriality confirmed the conviction of many Chinese that China had no government, that the Western powers were unsympathetic toward her, and that the only real hope lay in Canton and its Soviet allies. By the summer of 1926, the Kuomintang had not only completed its own reorganization in Canton but also had created a new model army and a "National Government."

---

[20] See Chapter 31.

THE CANTON REVOLUTIONARY "NATIONAL GOVERNMENT"

This new government created by the reorganized Kuomintang was headed by a deliberative body, the Political Council, composed of all the outstanding Party leaders, and an Administrative Council, composed of the heads of the executive departments. Both councils were appointed by and responsible to the Central Executive Committee of the Kuomintang. Government was therefore wholly in the hands of the Party. The danger and the great weakness in the status of affairs at Canton lay in the ill-defined union and relations between the Kuomintang and the Chinese Communist Party, and also within each of these parties. But those who entertained such fears were pushed aside by the revolutionists of the left wing. The principal of these was Wang Ching-wei, a devoted follower of Sun, who by 1926 had become the official head of the Party. This was the man whose egotism and ambition eventually led him to become a traitor in the service of the Japanese. Canton itself was not only in the grip of a revolutionary fervor, it was also enjoying a wave of unprecedented civic progress and prosperity. While young political agents were being recruited and trained to use the latest invective against imperialism and capitalism, other revolutionaries were making a new and "model" city of Canton. New and striking personalities that caught the public eye were appearing in public office. T. V. Soong, a brother-in-law of Sun Yat-sen, and a Harvard graduate, had already brought a new efficiency into the handling of public finances. C. C. Wu, a son of Wu Ting-fang, one-time Minister to Washington, was handling with skill Canton's unofficial relations with the powers in the face of the great strike and boycott which had brought British trade at Hongkong to virtual stagnation.[27]

CRISES IN KUOMINTANG LEADERSHIP

Yet in the midst of this new revolutionary prosperity, new crises arose on the question of left versus right wing dominance. A new factor was injected when Chiang K'ai-shek in March, 1926, arrested some members of the extreme left wing. Wang Ching-wei and Hu Han-min (the

---

[27] Hu Han-min, another of Sun's devoted disciples who had not favored the extreme Soviet orientation, was forced into exile in 1926 after the Second Party Congress had voted to continue the collaboration with Moscow. The program of the defeated right wing, the so-called Western Hills Groups, had called for: 1) expulsion of the communists from the Kuomintang; 2) dismissal of Borodin and other Russian advisers; and 3) meetings of the Central Executive Committee in Shanghai instead of Canton. See T'ang Leang-li, *Wang Ching-wei*, 120-123.

latter now returned from exile) both fled from Canton, and a *modus vivendi* was patched up whereby Borodin was to remain as adviser while Chiang K'ai-shek was to take the chairmanship of the Standing Committee of the Central Executive Committee and thus become acting leader of the Party. It was a compromise settlement representing a delicate balance. It meant in substance that the recognized Kuomintang political leaders had surrendered, and that the revolution now appeared to be in the hands of two groups: 1) the Soviet left wing elements that controlled the unions (workers' and peasants'); 2) the new military leadership of the Nationalist armies. How long would Borodin and Chiang K'ai-shek continue to work together? [28]

THE ADVANCE TO THE YANGTZE

This new accord at Canton, though far from guaranteeing stability in the ranks of the revolutionists, had given a new prominence and power to Chiang K'ai-shek and his new Kuomintang army led by young officers trained at the Whampoa Military Academy. It was this military leadership which made the decision by the summer of 1926 that the time was ripe to launch a military campaign to oust the war-lords of the north.[29] Assuming supreme command of the expedition, Chiang K'ai-shek handed over nominal leadership of the Party to an intimate friend of Sun Yat-sen, Chang Ching-kiang, while to the Foreign Office at Canton came Eugene Chen, vituperative journalist and native of the British West Indies. The stage was set for a great adventure in revolutionary politics and war.

Paced by political agitators who appealed to peasants and workers, the Kuomintang armies moved north over the route which the T'ai-p'ings had followed less than a century before. In August a Soviet regime

[28] In reality, the controlling forces of the revolution were not wholly within this simple classification. For instance, the unions, workers, and peasants were not controlled entirely by the Soviet left wing elements. There was in particular an agrarian radical group, especially strong in the Fourth Army which marched from Canton through Changsha to Hankow, which for a time worked in alliance with the communists but was never dominated or controlled by them. This army was in large part recruited from the original strongholds of the T'ai-p'ing Rebellion, and it produced men who, even after the later split between the communists and the Kuomintang, were reluctant to cooperate unquestioningly with the right wing of the Kuomintang.

[29] At the time, Peking politics was in total chaos, as revealed by the fall of Tuan Ch'i-jui and the substitution of a military dictatorship headed by Chang Tso-lin, the Manchurian war-lord. The real power of this government extended only as far as Chang's armies. Shantung was controlled by Chang Tsung-chang, a thoroughly rapacious *tuchun;* Shansi by Yen Hsi-shan, the so-called model governor; the Nanking area by Sun Chuanfang; and the central Yangtze by Wu Pei-fu. Another war-lord, Tang Sheng-chi in Hunan, professed himself an ally of the Kuomintang.

was set up in Hunan. Hankow on the Yangtze was in Nationalist hands in September, and the sister city of Wuchang in October. Shortly thereafter, the province of Kiangsi fell to the Nationalists. In the spring of 1927 Anhui and Kiangsu were invaded and the old southern capital of Nanking was taken. Other Nationalist armies moving up the coast overran Fukien and Chekiang. Aid, too, came from the north where Feng Yu-hsiang, now back from Moscow, had joined the battle as an ally of the Nationalists, had occupied Shensi, and had aided in the taking of Honan. Less than a year after Chiang's armies had left Canton, they could regard themselves as masters of half of China. Their victory to this point was a product of: 1) superior military training, leadership, and morale; 2) the propaganda of the left wing and the communists; and 3) the incompetence of the political and military opponents.[30]

THE CANTON NATIONALIST SOVIET MOVES TO HANKOW

While these military campaigns were yet in progress, the Canton Nationalist Soviet government also moved north to Hankow. It was a step of great consequence, since it meant a victory for Borodin and the left over Chiang K'ai-shek. This was so because the Wuhan cities (Hankow, Hanyang, and Wuchang) were the center of the most highly developed capitalistic industry in all China outside of Shanghai. Here there was a large body of industrial wage earners who could be easily reached by Borodin's agitators. Here, too, were large foreign concessions held by the British, the French, and the Japanese.[31] The move to Hankow was therefore a definite advantage for the left wing and for Russian influence, but it threatened the right wing and the moderates and also the chances of the Chinese controlling their own revolution. The complete control of the left wing and the communists at Hankow was soon apparent. Peasant unions, the product of an astonishing mushroom growth, were soon in a position to threaten landlords with confiscation of their property. In Hankow and Kiukiang workers from the new industrial unions took over the British concessions by force, a clash being avoided only because the British marines withdrew to their

---

[30] H. F. MacNair, *China in Revolution* (Chicago, 1931).

The growing friction within the Kuomintang-Communist Entente which was eventually to lead to the dramatic split between Hankow and Nanking in 1927 has been allowed to obscure the fact that the cleavage between the communists and Chiang K'ai-shek was not the only important cleavage of the time. A factor of much neglected significance was the rivalry between the Fourth Army which marched to Hankow, and the First Army which took Shanghai and Nanking.

[31] The German and the Russian concessions had been surrendered to China at the end of World War I.

river gunboats. For the moment Hankow was directing its anti-imperialist attack exclusively against the British, as had been the case during 1925-26 at Canton.

The unprecedented success attending the rise of the Hankow regime was made doubly evident when the British government, in December, 1926, sent a new Minister, Sir Miles Lampson, to China, instructing him to visit Hankow en route to Peking. Britain also issued a striking "Memorandum on Policy in China," calling for a new and sympathetic approach to its problems, to the Nationalist cause, and to policies that would implement the spirit of the Washington Conference treaties and resolutions. This memorandum was presently implemented in an agreement between Britain and the Hankow government for formal rendition of the British concessions at Hankow and Kiukiang to the Hankow regime. This was tantamount to *de facto* recognition.[32] Coupled with the military laurels already won by the Nationalist armies, this diplomatic triumph over Britain's imperialistic interests brought enormous prestige to the revolutionary cause. It was pictured as the unwilling but inescapable retreat of British imperialism.

The left wing and the communists exploited this new prestige to swell the number of workers' and peasants' unions and to win new members for the Chinese Communist Party. Although the number of Communist Party members in 1927 was still small, perhaps 50,000, the vigor of the Party leadership at Hankow under Chen Tu-hsiu, gave it disproportionate influence. At the same time the labor, and more particularly, the peasant, unions enjoyed a remarkable growth in number and membership. The former claimed to have doubled their membership to a total of 2,500,000 in the single year 1926-27, and peasant unions in Nationalist-controlled areas claimed a membership of some 12,000,000. This swelling proletarian movement gladdened the hearts of the left wing of the Kuomintang and of the communists, but created intense apprehension among all conservatives, including the right wing of the Kuomintang. On the surface, relations between the Kuomintang and the communists suggested a continued and still more intimate union. Actually, a rupture was already in the making. When in March, 1927, Chiang K'ai-shek and others refused to attend the Central Executive Committee at Hankow, he was deprived of the chairmanship of the new Standing Committee and was replaced by Wang Ching-wei. This placed the radical group of the Kuomintang and the communists in complete control of the Hankow government. The Nationalist revolution had not become the Red revolution, but it seemed to be headed toward that goal.

[32] Cf. *China Year Book*, 1928, ch. xii.

CHAPTER 30

CHINA'S NEW NATIONALISM
AND THE POWERS, 1922-1927

SINCE the fate of China's revolution after the triumph of the "National" Soviet at Hankow in 1927 was not dependent solely upon the course of domestic politics, it is now appropriate to resume the story of China's relations with the Western powers and Japan in the years which followed the Washington Conference of 1921-22.

It has been noted (Chapter 25) that the Washington Conference produced, among other things, a reassertion of traditional American principles respecting China, among which were such ideas as equality of opportunity (the open door), and the territorial integrity of the Chinese state. The hope was that the framework of China's so-called republicanism could be saved from collapse, and that China herself would be able to offer effective resistance to the new imperial power of Japan, and to the Soviet "contagion" which lurked beyond the long Sino-Russian frontier.

To this end, as early as March, 1922, the conference powers undertook to execute at least some of the pledges given to China at Washington.

REVISION OF THE CHINESE TARIFF

The first concrete accomplishment took the form of a revision of the Chinese tariff rates to yield an effective five percent as contemplated by the treaties. The new rates provided a measure of financial relief to China by raising the specific duties to the approximate 5 percent *ad valorem* provided by the old commercial treaties, but they did not meet the Chinese desire voiced at Versailles and Washington that the treaty tariff be abolished since it limited the income of the Chinese government preventing higher duties for luxuries or for protection.[1]

---

[1] The negotiations of the Shanghai commission are dealt with by C. S. K. Chow, "The Revision of the Chinese Treaty Tariff in 1922," *Chinese Soc. and Pol. Science Review,* *VII* (1923).

THE FOREIGN POST OFFICES

At Washington the powers had also agreed to relinquish the post offices which they had maintained on Chinese soil for many years before there was any adequate postal service. Before the end of 1922 the British had closed their twelve post offices, the Japanese, sixty-six, the French, thirteen, and the United States, one. This latter had been maintained at Shanghai. By the Washington Conference resolution, the powers were still permitted to maintain post offices in leased territories "or as otherwise specifically provided by treaty." Under this provision, the Japanese continued to maintain post offices in the zone of the South Manchuria Railway, pending further negotiations with China.[2]

THE CHINESE EASTERN RAILWAY

In 1922, also, the Japanese fulfilled the pledge given at Washington by withdrawing their troops from Siberia, and the former Allied and Associated Powers terminated their control of the Chinese Eastern Railway, thus bringing to a close the futile intervention undertaken in 1918, and clearing the way for such future settlements China might reach with whatever Russian government eventually emerged in eastern Siberia.[3]

JAPAN AND SHANTUNG

During 1922, the Sino-Japanese agreement concluded at Washington relative to Japan's position in Shantung was carried into effect. Thus the political aspects of Sino-Japanese relations in Shantung had progressed toward a substantial settlement, though Japan's economic influence in the province remained paramount.[4]

THE 1915 TREATIES AND NOTES

These favorable developments in Sino-Japanese relations were balanced, however, by China's unsuccessful efforts in 1923 to reopen the question of termination of the Sino-Japanese treaties and notes of May, 1915. Japan was presented anew (March 10, 1923) with the well-worn

---

[2] *The China Year Book, 1925*, 402. Sino-Japanese agreements on post offices are in League of Nations, *Treaty Series*, XX, 224, 246, 278, 318.

[3] The report of John F. Stevens, president of the Inter-allied Technical Board for the supervision of the Chinese Eastern and Siberian Railways, is printed in United States, *Foreign Relations, 1923*, I, 758-775.

[4] Texts of the agreements are in *Treaties and Agreements with and concerning China* (Washington: Carnegie Endowment for International Peace, 1929), 100-101, 114-126, 127-129. A Japanese garrison stationed at Hankow since the Revolution of 1911 was withdrawn in 1922.

arguments Chinese delegates had used at Versailles and Washington. Japan replied expressing her oft-repeated views that the treaties had been signed by China's recognized government, that they were valid, and were not "susceptible of further modification." [5]

BRITAIN AND RETROCESSION OF WEI-HAI-WEI

During the Washington Conference, in response to China's demand for retrocession of the leased territories, the British had agreed to surrender Wei-hai-wei as a means of facilitating a Sino-Japanese settlement on Shantung.[6] Intermittent negotiations were conducted by an Anglo-Chinese commission at Wei-hai-wei and Peking during 1923 and 1924, but complete agreement was not reached until April 18, 1930, by which time the Nationalist government at Nanking had replaced the war-lord regime at Peking. The incident was suggestive again of the reluctance of the powers to surrender the special privilege they had acquired in China.[7]

FRANCE AND THE GOLD FRANC ISSUE

Difficulties were also developing between China and France. After China's entry into World War I her payments on the Boxer Indemnity had been suspended by agreement with the Allied powers. Payments were to be resumed in 1922, at which time France desired to use the funds due her in paying creditors of the Banque Industrielle de Chine, the recent failure of which had seriously affected French prestige. The balance of payments, if any, were to go to Sino-French educational and charitable foundations. To this China agreed, but trouble appeared when the French government demanded that China pay in "gold" francs at a pre-war rate of exchange. Previous payments, determined by an agreement of 1905, had always been made by China in the currencies of the creditor nations. The franc, however, had now depreciated as a result of the war, and thus France was demanding payment in gold, a demand in which she enjoyed the support of the Boxer Protocol powers. This impasse between China and France was far-reaching in its results, for while it continued France refused ratification of the Washington agreement on the conventional tariff, refused to join the commis-

---

[5] R. T. Pollard, *China's Foreign Relations, 1917-1931* (New York, 1933), 252-254.

[6] *Conference on the Limitation of Armaments* (Washington, 1922), 226, 1070.

[7] For pertinent documents see: Arthur Balfour's letter to Alfred Sze, Feb. 3, 1922, *British and Foreign State Papers,* CXVI (1922), 435-438; text of the draft agreement of May 31, 1923, *The China Year Book, 1924,* 831-837; British statement on Britain's demands relative to Wei-hai-wei in *Parliamentary Debates,* 5th ser., Vol. 172, 1387; text of the 1930 agreement, *The China Year Book, 1931,* 483-486.

sion to investigate extraterritoriality, or to consider relinquishment of the Kwangchow leasehold. Finally, in April, 1925, a compromise agreement was reached. Payments were to be made by China in gold dollars and were to be resumed as of December 1, 1924, instead of 1922. With this settlement at last achieved, France gave belated ratification in July, 1925, to the Nine-Power Open Door Treaty and to the Washington Treaty on the Chinese tariff. The treaties thus came into full force on August 5, 1925.[8]

EXTRATERRITORIALITY

At the Washington Conference China had asked the powers to end their exercise of extraterritorial rights at the end of a limited period, meanwhile adopting a plan of progressive modification. A resolution adopted by the conference provided for a commission to inquire into the practice of extraterritorial jurisdiction in China, into the judicial system and administration of that country, and to make recommendations for improving the system to the end that the several powers might be warranted "in relinquishing, either progressively or otherwise, their respective rights of extraterritoriality." By May, 1923, after the Chinese government had undertaken at the suggestion of the United States to prepare translations of its codes and of other judicial data, the Peking administration notified the powers that it wished the commission on extraterritoriality to meet at Peking on November 1. A number of the powers, however, considered the time ill-chosen, for political chaos within China by the summer of 1923 had exceeded all precedent. To Chinese protests against rumored postponement of the conference, Secretary Hughes informed the Chinese Minister in Washington, Alfred Sze, that it "was idle for China to declaim, as she had at the Washington

---

[8] Relevant documents will be found in *Treaties and Agreements, 1919-1929*, 103-104, 160-164; for excerpts of the 1905 correspondence on rates of exchange and methods of payment see MacMurray, *Treaties*, I, 319; texts of various notes in the intermittent correspondence, 1923-25, between China and France, and China and the powers are printed in *The China Year Book, 1924*, 841-849, and *1925*, 1297-1300. By 1925 all the powers had agreed to a settlement by which Boxer payments in part at least were to be devoted to educational and philanthropical purposes mutually beneficial. Britain had announced such a policy in 1922, details being worked out by an Anglo-Chinese committee. For its recommendations see *The China Year Book, 1928*, 631-634. The Japanese government in March, 1923, agreed to devote a small part of the payments due it to cultural purposes; see *The China Year Book, 1929-30*, 669-670. The United States by Congressional Act, May 21, 1924, agreed to remit to China for educational purposes, the balance of Boxer payments due to this country; see *Treaties and Agreements, 1919-1929*, 132, 147, 156. The Netherlands proposed to devote its share for a survey of flood prevention measures in the Yellow River Valley; see *The China Year Book, 1928*, 634-635. Portions of the Belgian and the Italian shares were also to be devoted to philanthropic work.

Conference" about her sovereignty and her rights as a nation while she
failed to provide herself with a government with national authority or
competence to discharge its international obligations. China, the Secretary added, could hardly expect foreign consideration while she exhibited "before the world inability to protect even the lives and safety of
foreigners." [9] Accordingly the United States proposed that the commission should not meet until November, 1924. But France had not
as yet settled the gold franc question, nor ratified the Washington treaties, and, as a consequence, the first meeting of the extraterritorial commission was not held until January 12, 1926.[10] The commission's investigations were limited to North China since the Canton government,
holding that extraterritoriality should be promptly ended without investigation, would not receive it. It will be recalled that at this time
Soviet influence was dominant at Canton. The commission's report
was a qualified tribute to China's efforts in legal reform. It acknowledged the new modern courts and their procedure but criticized the
continued use of military courts and magistrates courts, in the latter of
which no line had been drawn between judicial and administrative
functions. The commission asserted that China must entrust justice
"to a judiciary which shall be effectively protected against any unwarranted interference by the executive or other branches of the government, whether civil or military." It was recommended that China proceed to the completion and further revision of her modern codes, that
she modernize her prisons, and make adequate financial provision for
her whole judicial system. Further, the commission agreed to certain
modifications in the consular courts, and indicated that the powers
would consider abolition of extraterritoriality when China had made
substantial progress on the principal reforms suggested.[11]

[9] United States, *Foreign Relations, 1923*, I, 625-626. Mr. Hughes had reference to the
prevalence of banditry in the spring and summer of 1923. In May a group of foreigners
had been kidnapped from the famous Pukow-Tientsin Express. Nobody but the Chinese
appreciated the humor of a situation in which the foreigners were held captive in the
mountains of Shantung while the question was argued whether the bandits should be
accepted into the Chinese army.
[10] The powers represented included: the United States, Belgium, China, Denmark,
France, Great Britain, Italy, Japan, the Netherlands, Norway, Portugal, Spain, and Sweden.
Silas Strawn, representing the United States, was chairman. China's case was presented
by her distinguished jurist, Wang Ch'ung-hui.
[11] Relevant documents include: "Memorandum of the Chinese Commissioner on the
Present Practice of Extra-territorial Jurisdiction in China," Great Britain, *Parliamentary
Papers, China,* No. 1 (1927), Cmd. 2797, 3-11; United States Dept. of State, *Report of the
Commission on Extraterritoriality in China* (Washington, 1926). Detailed American
documents and correspondence will be found in United States, *Foreign Relations, 1926,*
I, 966-983.

THE TARIFF CONFERENCE OF 1925

The eventual ratification by France in 1925 of the Nine-Power Treaty on the Chinese tariff cleared the way for the meeting of a tariff conference which assembled at Peking in October. China had already reiterated her position, which had made clear at the Washington Conference, that she would demand complete tariff autonomy. Within a month the conference had recognized "China's right to enjoy tariff autonomy"; had agreed to remove the tariff restrictions contained in the treaties, and to accept the Chinese National Tariff Law as of January 1, 1929. China on her part agreed to the effective abolition of *likin* as of this date.[12]

NATIONALISM AND ANTI-FOREIGNISM

In the three years from 1922 to 1925 the solution of the Chinese problem for which the Washington Conference was supposed to provide had not been achieved. Indeed, conditions within China seemed to grow worse rather than better. It was abundantly clear, as Secretary Hughes had said to Minister Sze in 1923, that China had shown no disposition to put her house in order, that she had no discernible government, and that consideration could not be expected from the powers until China herself showed some regard for the duties as well as privileges of nationhood. Yet as early as June, 1924, in a note addressed to the Washington treaty powers the Chinese government "seemed to imply that the program adopted at Washington should be scrapped," and that without more ado China should be accorded full equality among the nations.[13] This view was unacceptable to the Washington powers. Nevertheless, while political confusion and the failure of the Chinese to create a national government appeared to justify the powers in clinging to the treaty rights, the emergence of a new Chinese nationalism was making of the treaties an issue which the powers would be forced to meet regardless of China's good faith or their own desires.[14]

The appearance of a new and vigorous nationalism associated with

---

[12] Documents and statements on the 1925-26 tariff conference are printed in *The China Year Book, 1926*. See also the correspondence in United States, *Foreign Relations, 1925*, I, 833-835; *1926*, I, 743-862. The most complete study of the history of the conventional tariff in China is Stanley F. Wright, *China's Struggle for Tariff Autonomy, 1843-1938* (Shanghai, 1938); aspects of the problem that developed in the twentieth century are covered in chapters v-vii.

[13] Pollard, *China's Foreign Relations, 1917-1931*, 269.

[14] Chinese police methods and the conduct of many of the Chinese courts in practice made reasonable, from the standpoint of Western trader and diplomat, the unwillingness of the Western powers to surrender their special privileges.

the revitalized Kuomintang, the labor and peasant unions, the student movement, and the new cultural renaissance have already been discussed (Chapter 29). In so far as these movements were concentrated in the great treaty ports, they were bound sooner or later to clash with foreign business interests. In particular the nationalism of the Chinese student movement was both anti-imperialistic and anti-Christian.[15] More than any pronouncements from the governments either at Peking or Canton, it was the agitation by the students which aroused and directed the fury of the Chinese populace in the treaty ports against the foreigners and the system they represented. This new Chinese popular nationalism "drew no fine distinctions." All the treaty powers were looked upon as "obnoxious imperialists, whether the imperialism stopped at consular jurisdiction or whether, as in the case of Japan, it contemplated the alienation of substantial portions of Chinese territory."[16] Thus it was that while China as late as 1925 had failed to create a respectable national government, her people, particularly on the coast, had achieved an unmistakable national consciousness sensitive to all the indignities real and imaginary which China, a quasi-colonial area, had suffered at the hands of the powers.

THE SHANGHAI AFFAIR, MAY 30, 1925

On May 30, 1925, a Chinese mob in the International Settlement attracted by student agitators declaiming against labor conditions in Japanese cotton mills was fired upon by Sikh and Chinese constables. The order to fire, given by a police inspector of British nationality, resulted in the death of nine Chinese. Chinese anger at this "inexcusable outrage" took the form of a general strike supported by virtually all sections of the populace. Business in Shanghai was at a standstill and remained so during most of the summer.[17] However, repercussions of the May 30 incident were not confined to Shanghai. Anti-foreign outbreaks resulting in loss of life and property damage occurred at widely

---

[15] The anti-Christian aspects of the student movement which were particularly strong from 1922 to 1927 are explained by: 1) the association of Christianity with the imperialistic powers responsible for the unequal treaties; 2) the developing interest of Chinese students in science and philosophies of skepticism; 3) the conservatism and intolerance of some of the missionaries; 4) the persistence of Confucian philosophy and tradition; and 5) the growing influence of communism. The subject is discussed in detail in Chao-kwang Wu, *The International Aspect of the Missionary Movement in China* (Baltimore, 1930).

[16] A. Whitney Griswold, *The Far Eastern Policy of the United States* (New York, 1938), 385-386; and Chang Yun-yo, "American Imperialism," *Pacific Affairs,* III (1930), 284.

[17] *The China Year Book, 1926,* 919 ff.

separated points spreading far into the interior, even to Chungking. The most serious disturbances took place, as was to be expected, in the Canton area, the headquarters of the Soviet-dominated Kuomintang. A few foreigners and more than a hundred Chinese were killed when Chinese demonstrators paraded, June 23, on the Shakee bund opposite the British and French concessions on the island of Shameen. Canton instituted a successful boycott of all British goods, and a general strike of Chinese workmen paralyzed business in British Hongkong. Not a houseboy or cook remained in the palatial homes of Hongkong's millionaires.[18] In the face of these "alarming developments" relations between China and the Washington treaty powers reached a new high point of tension. In general, while the foreign merchants, whether British, Japanese, French, or American, protested that force had been used only in defense of their lives and property, their governments, puzzled as to what course to pursue, fell back on the customary appeal to the sanctity of treaties and China's obligation to protect foreigners and their property. Doubtless many informed Chinese also believed in the sanctity of treaties, but in new treaties among equals, and not in the old unequal treaties, a product of the nineteenth century. Even the moribund Peking government protested the May 30 incident,[19] asking a complete revision of the treaties in the name "of the legitimate national aspirations of the Chinese people."

THE CANTON SOVIET AND THE POWERS

When therefore in 1926 the Nationalists at Canton were preparing for the northern march, they were able to capitalize not only upon the unhappy events just related but also upon a long series of blunders by which the principal powers had shaped their policies toward China. World War I had already done much to destroy the prestige of the white man in the Far East. After the war there was the failure to apply the Wilsonian program of equality and self-determination to Asiatic peoples. Then in 1919 came the failure to restore Kiaochow to China. Lastly, the Washington Conference, while voicing the principle of Chinese sovereignty, perpetuated the unequal treaties under a modest program of prospective revision. The net effect, as we have seen, though

---

[18] *The China Year Book, 1926*, 965 ff.; United States, *Foreign Relations, 1925*, I, 647-721, 749-760. See also the excellent study by Lennox A. Mills, *British Rule in Eastern Asia* (Minneapolis, 1942). It should be noted that popular anti-foreign outbreaks, boycotts, etc., were not entirely spontaneous. There was often much organized intimidation of the populace.

[19] *The China Year Book, 1926*, 930.

not wittingly designed by the powers, was to drive Sun Yat-sen to make anti-imperialism a clarion call of the Nationalist revolution.[20]

From 1915 to 1925 the principal target of the Nationalist invective was Japan; from 1925 to 1927 it was Great Britain. The great anti-British strike and boycott at Hongkong and Canton continued for fifteen months under the lively inspiration of the Canton Nationalists, a government which both Britain and the other Washington treaty powers had consistently refused to recognize. Indeed, when the strike and boycott were ended, it was Canton which made the decision, not because it wished to placate British feeling but in order to gain strength for the contemplated northern expedition. Meanwhile the powers knew not what course to pursue since the end of the unequal treaties was demanded not only by the communists and the left wing of the Kuomintang but also by conservatives and militarists, including Chiang K'aishek.[21]

THE ANTI-BRITISH CAMPAIGN AT HANKOW

The drive of revolutionary forces against British imperialism, so successfully begun at Canton, was continued with like success at Hankow when in December, 1926, the Nationalist capital moved there from Canton. A general strike of industrial labor in the Wuhan cities called in November was followed by mass demonstrations, and Nationalist orators intensified the anti-British crusade. The agitation was so effective that on December 18, 1926, the British government proposed that the Washington treaty powers: 1) legalize what Canton was already doing, by agreeing to immediate collection of the Washington surtaxes; 2) recognize and deal with regional governments; 3) implement a grant of tariff autonomy immediately upon China's promulgation of a national tariff; and 4) seek to develop better relations with China even while no national government existed.[22]

Britain's gesture of concession, far from satisfying the Nationalists, spurred them to new outbursts of fury. The British policy was described as a design to weaken China by creating regional governments, and by encouraging militarists to seize the ports and to profit by collection of the proposed surtaxes.[23]

Meanwhile, before the powers could reply to the British proposal, the

---

[20] Various aspects of the Nationalist movement are ably discussed in H. F. MacNair, *China's New Nationalism and Other Essays* (Shanghai, 1925).

[21] Pollard, *China's Foreign Relations,* 295.

[22] Text in *Treaties and Agreements, 1919-1929,* 186-192.

[23] See detailed American diplomatic correspondence, United States, *Foreign Relations, 1926,* I, 618-663.

anti-British crusade on the upper Yangtze had been carried still further. During the first week of January, 1927, under the threat of mob violence, the British abandoned their concessions in Hankow and Kiukiang. Both concessions were immediately taken over for administrative purposes by the Chinese. Likewise, without waiting for action by the powers, whatever Chinese groups happened to be in control of the treaty ports applied the surtaxes without further ado. In January, this developing situation brought forth hurried assurances from the Japanese government and the American government expressing sympathy with China's "just aspirations" and indicating willingness to aid their attainment in an orderly fashion.[24] In the light of this rising tide of nationalism, Great Britain, already disposed to find a new basis for her relations with China, concluded agreements with the Nationalists during February and March, 1927, handing over the Hankow and Kiukiang concessions to China.[25]

THE NANKING INCIDENT, 1927

Almost immediately following these agreements, Britain's policy of conciliation faced new trials at Nanking late in March. No sooner had the old southern capital been captured by the Nationalists than it became the scene of violent and seemingly premeditated attacks by Kuomintang troops upon foreign persons and property. American, British, French, Italian, and Japanese nationals were killed, wounded, or subjected to less fatal outrageous treatment. Foreign property was looted. Nor was there an end to these doings of the Kuomintang soldiery until British and American gunboats laid a protective barrage about the properties of the Standard Oil Company where surviving foreigners had taken refuge.[26] The United States, England, France, Italy, and Japan demanded (April 11) apology, reparations, and guarantees for the future.[27] China's reply was evasive, but despite this the powers did not press for an immediate settlement. To have done so would have strengthened the radical wing of the Kuomintang-Soviet leaders at Hankow. Actually the powers were hoping for the success of a new, conservative, and non-Soviet national regime at Nanking.

---

[24] Texts in *Japan Chronicle*, weekly, Jan. 27, 1927; *Treaties and Agreements, 1919-1929*, 193-197; United States, *Foreign Relations, 1927*, II, 44 ff.

[25] *Treaties and Agreements, 1919-1929*, 203-215. This left at Hankow only the Japanese and French concessions, the German having been surrendered in 1917 and the Russian in 1920.

[26] Arnold J. Toynbee, ed., *Survey of International Affairs, 1927*, 382-391.

[27] Toynbee, 392; *Treaties and Agreements, 1919-1929*, 216; United States, *Foreign Relations, 1927*, II, 146-235.

It was with this government at Nanking a year later (February 26, 1928) that a settlement of the Nanking incident was concluded.[28]

PEKING AND TREATY NEGOTIATIONS

During the advance of the Nationalists on Hankow and Nanking, the war-lord government at Peking had continued to bid for popular favor at home by an almost equally aggressive assertion of China's right to be rid of the old treaties. Between 1925 and 1928 Peking was as much concerned with the question of the treaties as were the Nationalists of the south. The chief difference lay in the fact that while the Nationalists did not hesitate to use violence against the foreigners, Peking was disposed to seek new treaties through diplomacy. In this, if in nothing else, its work was eminently significant.

Peking's first success was a new treaty of commerce with Austria, October 19, 1925, confirming the wartime ending of Austria's extraterritorial rights.[29] A second treaty between equals was concluded with Finland, October 29, 1926.[30] Encouraged by these minor successes, during 1926 Peking became bolder, asserting its right, when certain clauses of a given treaty were subject to revision, to demand revision of the entire treaty, and failing this, to abrogate the treaty by unilateral action.[31] This policy was first applied to Belgium. In November, 1926, China announced by presidential mandate the abrogation of the Belgian treaty, that country having refused China's demand for complete revision. As a result, in January, 1927, Belgium indicated her willingness to negotiate a new treaty.[32] In August, 1927, the Peking government, still further emboldened, after some correspondence with France gave notice that the Franco-Chinese commercial conventions of 1886-1887 and 1895 were no longer regarded as in effect. France, too, then agreed to join in negotiations for a new convention on the understanding that the old conventions would remain in force in the interim period. The negotiations continued until Peking fell to the Nationalist armies in 1928.[33] Peking was also able to initiate negotiations with Japan for revision of

[28] Treaties and Agreements, 1919-1929, 216-226; David Bryn-Jones, Frank B. Kellogg (New York, 1937), 215-219; Pollard, China's Foreign Relations, 307.

[29] League of Nations, Treaty Series, Vol. 55, 9.

[30] League of Nations, Treaty Series, Vol. 67, 345.

[31] Most of the old treaties with China provided for periodic revision of specified clauses at the request of either contracting party. In 1926 Peking appealed not only to this provision but also to the principle of rebus sic stantibus (Pollard, China's Foreign Relations, 312).

[32] United States, Foreign Relations, 1926, I, 984-1000; and The China Year Book, 1928, 785-86.

[33] The China Year Book, 1929-1930, 830-31.

the treaty of 1896, and with Spain for the treaty of 1864.[34] Furthermore, Peking was able during 1927 to apply the Washington surtaxes in areas under its control. When Sir Francis Aglen, British Inspector-General of the Chinese Maritime Customs, refused to collect them, the Chinese dismissed him from office and appointed another Britisher, A. H. F. Edwardes, to succeed him.[35]

THE YEARS 1922 TO 1927 IN REVIEW

During the early months of 1927 China could still be described in the frank and uncomplimentary terms used by Secretary Hughes to Minister Sze in June of 1923. There was no national government. The war-lords were still contending for Peking. The Nationalists, despite their victorious march to the Yangtze, were torn by internal dissension between the left wing which dominated Hankow and a right wing which was yet to emerge at Nanking. Foreign life and property, far from being safe, had been subjected to repeated outrage. Yet there could no longer be any doubt, and this the Washington powers were slowly beginning to perceive, that China's peoples were in revolt. Whither this revolution would lead was by no means clear. A regeneration in Chinese politics resulting in a stable national government able to enforce its treaty obligations would have satisfied the Washington powers. But already by the beginning of 1927 the revolution had gone far beyond this: its ideology under Soviet inspiration had turned proletarian; its processes, no longer defensive, were now rooted in aggressive attacks upon the imperialism of the West and of Japan. Indeed, the revolution had gone too far and too fast. The social implications of the left-wing revolutionists had frightened the conservatives. Reaction was already at work. If the revolution turned conservative, the Washington powers might yet salvage a part of their traditional position in China.

---

[34] *The China Year Book, 1928*, 1402.
[35] *The China Year Book, 1928*, 1077.

CHAPTER 31

CHINA, 1927-1931: THE NATIONAL GOVERNMENT AND THE COLLAPSE OF THE RUSSIAN ORIENTATION

IN THE year 1927 control of the Nationalist revolution was lost by the coalition of the left wing of the Kuomintang and the communists. The new masters were to be the Kuomintang conservatives led by Chiang K'ai-shek. Under their guidance, the revolution became in certain of its aspects a counterrevolution, and the Russian-Soviet orientation was discarded in favor of new alignments with the Western capitalistic states and Japan. The processes by which this change came about necessitate some further discussion of Russo-Chinese relations.

After 1920, Russia's relations with China were twofold. There was the phase (already related in Chapter 29) in which Soviet Russia and the Chinese communists brought aid and comfort to Sun Yat-sen and the Kuomintang at Canton and later at Hankow. At the same time, Russia, after discouraging beginnings, succeeded also in establishing formal relations with the government of Peking.[1] Mongolia and North Manchuria are the keys to this phase of the story.

THE OUTER MONGOLIAN PUZZLE

The general confusion prevailing in Outer Mongolia from 1919 to 1921 was a particularly serious obstacle to Chinese recognition of the Soviets. Outer Mongolia, it will be recalled, had achieved autonomy in 1912 at the time of the republican revolution in China. Then, in 1919, China, taking advantage of the general chaos in Siberia and the border lands, succeeded in briefly re-establishing her military ascendancy, largely limited to the city of Urga, and more uneasily maintained in some other areas of the territory.[2] This was accomplished by a Chinese general, Hsü Shu-tseng, an able and unscrupulous marauder, who was

---

[1] The Russians suffered from fewer diplomatic inhibitions than did the Western powers and Japan. Britain, it will be recalled, did not approach the Nationalists directly and formally until the affair of the Hankow and Kiukiang concessions in 1927.

[2] R. T. Pollard, *China's Foreign Relations* (New York, 1933), 118-119.

affiliated with the notorious pro-Japanese Anfu clique in Peking. Hsü's exploits drove the local Mongol princes into the arms of a White Russian soldier of fortune, one Baron von Ungern Sternberg, who also had Japanese backing. The maraudings of this brigand and his motley army of mercenaries opened the way for the Living Buddha of Urga, as nominal ruler of the area, to declare Outer and Inner Mongolia an empire, and to declare himself the emperor. It thus appeared that the Mongols wanted independence; von Sternberg wanted to attack the Soviets, and the Chinese wanted to reassert their control.[3] Behind this rather amazing confusion stemming from outside Mongolia were important political phenomena within the country. Here there were two rather distinct though related movements. 1) The traditional conservative leadership in Outer Mongolia was rapidly passing from the ineffective hands of the princes to the hands of ecclesiastical functionaries of the Lama Church. The Urga Living Buddha, already referred to, was grossly incompetent, being far gone with syphilis, but the Church as an institution was from this time forward to prove itself a much more centralized and well-organized bulwark of the whole conservative society in Mongolia than were the princes. 2) Moreover, there was already in Mongolia a revolutionary independence movement as well as the conservative independence movement. The interaction between these two movements became an essential part of later developments. For the time being, however (that is, for the period 1919-1921), it was the Russians who clarified the picture. They invaded Mongolia, executed von Sternberg, and stood by while the Mongols set up a Peoples' Revolutionary Government. This government in turn requested Russia to assist in restoring peace between the new Mongolian state and China.[4]

THE MISSION OF ADOLPH A. JOFFE

Soviet assistance in the creation of this "independent" Mongolia widened still further the breach between China and Russia.[5] It was now clear that Mongolia had been detached from China, partly as a result of Russian intervention, and also as a result of efforts made by the Mongols themselves to achieve their own independence. Nevertheless, it was not Russia's desire that this should prevent efforts toward a resumption of formal Sino-Russian relations.

For this purpose, Adolph A. Joffe, among the ablest of the early Soviet

---

[3] Pollard, *China's Foreign Relations*, 162-163.
[4] George Stewart, *The White Armies of Russia* (New York, 1933), 400-405.
[5] *Treaties and Agreements, 1919-1929*, 102-103.

diplomats, arrived at Peking in August, 1922. Chinese intellectuals received him with enthusiasm; the government, with considerable reserve. Joffe's objectives were: 1) to establish diplomatic relations; 2) to preserve the new Russian influence in Mongolia; and 3) to salvage Russian interests in the Chinese Eastern Railway which the Chinese assumed to have been surrendered by the L. M. Karakhan declarations of Soviet policy toward China in 1919 and 1920.[6] Wellington Koo, Peking's Foreign Minister, wanted a Russian withdrawal from Mongolia as a precedent to any negotiation. Joffe countered with the accusation that China permitted White Russians to use Chinese soil as a base for attacking "the Russian people." This was for Peking an embarrassing thrust, for at the time Manchuria, where most of the White Russians were, was controlled not by any authority in Peking but by Chang Tso-lin, the Manchurian war-lord, who asserted his independence whenever it suited his purposes to do so. This gave point to Joffe's second thrust that the Chinese Eastern Railway was being ruined by the economic and financial policies of its manager Boris Ostroumoff, a White Russian, who had been appointed in 1920 by the Russo-Asiatic Bank, successor to the Russo-Chinese Bank. The Bank was the ostensible guardian of the interests of the original French and other stockholders in the Chinese Eastern Railway Company.[7] When Koo recalled that Russia had already voluntarily renounced the works of imperialism, Joffe made haste to explain that Russia had not surrendered all her interests in China but rather only those which derived from the "predatory and violent policy of the Tsar's." All Russia's legal rights remained until such time as they were surrendered by Russia or until

----

[6] Russian policy as announced by Chicherin in 1918 appeared to concede China's exclusive political rights in the railway zone while reserving Russia's financial and economic rights. The Karakhan note of October 2, 1920, asserted as "null and void all the treaties concluded with China by the former governments of Russia," and suggested, among other things, a special treaty on the Chinese Eastern Railway. See R. T. Pollard, *China's Foreign Relations, 1917-1931* (New York, 1933), 124-7, 129-30, 135-7. It would seem that the difference between the Karakhan declarations of Soviet policy toward China and other more cautious Russian statements can be to some extent explained by the fact that Karakhan was identified with the Trotsky wing, for which he was later purged. The Trotsky world revolution view, holding to the likelihood or at least the desirability of a complete overturn of the existing world order, allowed for more reckless and sweeping denunciations of old treaties; while the Stalin view which was already beginning to shape the future policy of revolution within a given country required more caution in the wording of statements dealing with external rights and treaties.

[7] At the Washington Conference China had defeated the efforts of the powers to establish international control of the railway, but the powers in turn had insisted by resolution that: 1) China give better protection to the line; 2) China was responsible for the obligations toward the foreign stockholders, bondholders, and creditors of the line. *Conference on the Limitation of Armament*, 1376-80, 1502-04.

new and mutually satisfactory agreements were negotiated. The policy enunciated by Joffe could appear at first glance to be a mere reassertion of the political significance of the Chinese Eastern Railway to Russia, and thus identical in principle with the earlier policy of the tsars, but closer examination compels recognition of a distinction between Russian surrender of political rights and Russian efforts to retain economic interests in the Chinese Eastern Railway. In January, 1923, the Joffe negotiations came to an end. Joffe left for Shanghai to meet Sun Yat-sen (see p. 511) having first advised Koo that the time had come for China to choose between Russia's Whites and Reds.[8]

During 1923, the rigid, stand-fast *status quo* policy of the great powers, plus a train of events in the Far East played directly into the hands of Soviet policy. Joffe's meeting with Sun at Shanghai was a preface to the remarkable growth of Soviet influence in the Kuomintang. Moreover, Joffe's subsequent visit to Japan suggested a *rapprochement* in Russo-Japanese relations. In Siberia the Soviet position had been strengthened in November of 1922 when the Far Eastern Republic formally joined the Soviet Union.[9] Finally, in the late spring of 1923 the inability of Peking to protect foreign lives and property in China suggested the possibility of intervention by the Western powers. Accordingly, China was in no position to refuse further Russian overtures when in September, 1923, L. M. Karakhan, the new Russian envoy, arrived at Peking.

THE RUSSO-CHINESE TREATY, 1924

Not until May 31, 1924, were the subsequent Koo-Karakhan negotiations crowned with success in a treaty and supplementary agreements through which the two powers resumed formal relations.[10] Russia gave up her extraterritorial rights and her concessions at Tientsin and Hankow. The Russian legation and consulates were restored; property of the Orthodox Church was turned over to the Russian government; Russia's remaining shares of the Boxer Indemnity were to be devoted to education of the Chinese people; Russia recognized China's sovereignty in Outer Mongolia and a commission was to arrange for the withdrawal of Russian troops. Concerning the Chinese Eastern Railway it was agreed: that the line was a "purely commercial enterprise"; that Chinese sovereignty prevailed in the railroad zone; that

---

[8] Pollard, *China's Foreign Relations,* 172-177.

[9] See H. K. Norton, *The Far Eastern Republic of Siberia* (London, 1923), and Louis Fischer, *The Soviets in World Affairs* (2 vols., New York, 1930), I, 373; II, 541.

[10] *Treaties and Agreements, 1919-1929,* 133-144; Harriet L. Moore, *Soviet Far Eastern Policy* (Princeton, 1945), 156-167.

China might redeem the line "with Chinese capital"; that the fate of the line would be determined by China and Russia to the exclusion of third parties; and that management of the road would be a joint Russo-Chinese concern.[11]

THE RUSSO-MANCHURIAN AGREEMENT, 1924

Since the Chinese Eastern Railway lay in the Manchurian territories of Chang Tso-lin, over which at the time Peking had no control, Karakhan negotiated (September 20, 1924) a separate agreement with the Manchurian dictator.[12] Though containing differences in detail, this agreement followed in general the previous Peking settlement.

The agreements, however, did not solve anything. During 1925 and 1926 Sino-Russian relations, as they revolved about the Chinese Eastern Railway and were aggravated by one dispute after another, grew steadily worse.[13] Moreover, by 1926 the Peking government was no longer controlled by the pro-Russian *tuchun,* Feng Yu-hsiang, but by the anti-Bolshevik, Chang Tso-lin of Manchuria.[14] Once in Peking, Chang asked for the recall of Karakhan, and announced that he would rid North China of Bolshevik influence. Russia, however, could afford to accept this reverse with equanimity, for at Canton her influence was increasing steadily and, as the reader will recall (Chapter 29), it was paramount when the Nationalists removed their capital to Hankow, January 1, 1927.

HANKOW VERSUS NANKING

Having traced China's relations with the powers (Chapter 30) and Peking's particular difficulties with Russia, we may now resume the narrative of the Nationalist revolution. The reader is already aware

---

[11] Protests were lodged at Peking against the railway agreement by the Russo-Asiatic Bank, Japan, France, and the United States, all of whom claimed a financial interest in the line. United States, *Foreign Relations, 1924,* I, 482-513.

[12] Text in Moore, *Soviet Far Eastern Policy,* 168-174; *Treaties and Agreements, 1919-1929,* 148-152.

[13] For the nature of these disputes see Pollard, *China's Foreign Relations,* 198-204.

[14] The "pro-Russian" and "anti-Bolshevik" attitudes of Feng and Chang respectively are understandable. Feng, though a war-lord, represented a Chinese nationalism which was based inland, having no secure access to a treaty port through which to receive arms from abroad. Feng, therefore, was receptive to deals with Russia for the receipt of arms by an overland route. This consideration was much more important than any predisposition on Feng's part to deal with Russia because of sympathy with Russian ideas. Chang, on the other hand, depended primarily on the Japanese in the matter of securing foreign arms, and while in any case there was no reason for him to throw himself into Russian arms, his active anti-Bolshevist attitude was in some part a reflection of Japanese policy as well as of Chang's own ideas.

that dissension had been obvious in the Kuomintang-communist united front from the beginning. These divisions were intensified once the Nationalists, victorious on the battlefield, were able to move the government to Hankow.[15] Conservative, propertied members of the Kuomintang, apprehensive because of the growth of labor and peasant unions bent on industrial and rural reform, foresaw that the Nationalist movement under Russian inspiration was leading to independence and social revolution instead of to "an independent China in which the people would be docile."[16] Therefore, once the Nationalists had reached the Yangtze, the gulf between the right and left wings became wider. Instead of the two groups seeking accommodation in a mutually acceptable and truly national program, they moved farther apart. Hankow, it will be remembered, dropped Chiang K'ai-shek from membership of the Central Executive Committee of the Kuomintang, and threatened to deprive him of his military powers. Chiang in turn defied Hankow. His troops were soon in control of the wealthy Shanghai area, and by April he was able to set up at Nanking a government rivalling the Hankow regime.[17]

EXIT COMRADE BORODIN

At this point, events in Peking rather than on the Yangtze determined the immediate future of the Nationalist cause which seemed so hopelessly divided. As a result of raids on the Russian embassy in Peking, carried out on April 6 by order of Chang Tso-lin, it was revealed that Borodin, the chief Russian adviser to Hankow, was under direct orders from Moscow, and that the Communist International had approved plans for the sovietization of China.[18] Peking promptly broke relations

---

[15] Hankow, 600 miles inland on the Yangtze from Shanghai, was with its sister cities of Wuchang and Hanyang the greatest urban center of interior China. They were known collectively as the Wuhan cities. Because of their early industrial development and their large laboring population, they constituted a strategic center in the revolutionary plans of the left wing.

[16] Lawrence K. Rosinger, *China's Crisis* (New York, 1945), 13.

[17] These seemingly clear and definite moves were the external manifestations of far more involved political struggles in which many of the details are still obscure. It is clear, however, that the dropping of Chiang from the Central Executive Committee must be seen in the light of earlier events. Toward the end of January, 1927, Chiang had refused to go to Hankow, insisting that the Central Executive Committee meet at Nanchang where he had his own military headquarters. The Central Executive Committee therefore had at least a technical reason for dropping him for insubordination to a party decision. Thereupon Chiang made a deal with Chen Tiao-yuan, war-lord of Anhui, moved his troops down the Yangtze, and got into negotiation with the Shanghai merchants, who agreed to back him for leadership of the Kuomintang on terms which were understandable to the merchants and bankers.

[18] Texts in *Chinese Soc. and Pol. Science Review*, XI (1927), 193-272.

with Moscow. These and other revelations brought to an end the Russian orientation. It was now generally accepted that Borodin had plotted to overthrow the Kuomintang and to establish a communist state. Borodin, his corps of advisers, Eugene Chen, and others fled to Russia where they were soon followed by Madam Sun, the widow of Sun Yat-sen.

Cleansed of the Russian influence, the Kuomintang was still a house divided against itself. Right and left wings were still irreconcilable. Neither the victories of the Nationalist armies over Chang Tso-lin nor the resentment occasioned when in May and June Japan sent more than 4,000 troops to guard her interests in Shantung served to weld the Party together. In August the intra-party estrangement was eased when Chiang K'ai-shek went into temporary exile in Japan. He returned in November to head again the Nationalist armies. The resulting regime which emerged at Nanking was one in which the Kuomintang conservatives had the upper hand. Moreover, the use of force by Chiang at Shanghai to suppress the communists, left-wing elements, and labor unions, gave warning that the social phases of the revolution were to be curbed. Chiang's repressive policy on this occasion was soon to become a major left-wing point of historical reference, and was thus to develop a significant bearing on future relations between the right wing of the Kuomintang and the varying parties and groups of the left.

THE NATIONAL GOVERNMENT AT NANKING, 1927

The National government of China which was progressively taking shape at Nanking toward the close of 1927 was to prove by far the most substantial China had known since the time of Yüan Shih-k'ai. Many factors contributed to this stability. The new government played very successfully on the name of Sun Yat-sen, the patron saint of the revolution, and his philosophy of the state, *San Min Chu I*. Its armies had already proved their superiority. Its treasury was financed by the Chinese bourgeoisie, in particular the bankers of Shanghai. Moreover, the foreign capitalistic powers, since the retreat of the Russians, looked upon the new government with some favor. Its bureaucracy of civil servants had already acquired some experience at Canton and Hankow. Lastly, when in 1928 its armies drove Chang Tso-lin from Peking, Nanking was accorded diplomatic recognition by the Western powers and Japan.[19]

[19] The best general reference for this period is H. F. MacNair, *China in Revolution* (Chicago, 1931). See also P. M. A. Linebarger, *Government in Republican China* (New York, 1938).

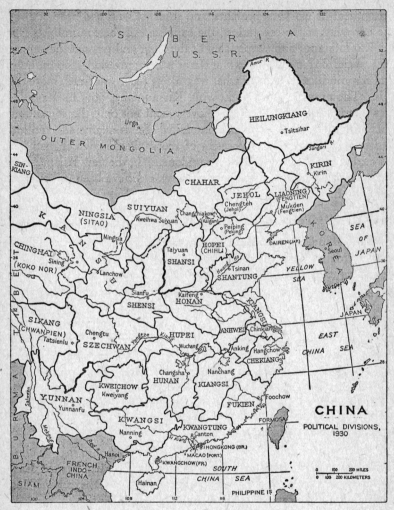

Courtesy of George B. Cressey and of the "Geographical Review," published by the American Geographical Society of New York.

THE PRICE OF SUCCESS

Therefore, by the close of 1927 it seemed probable that China might soon enjoy a new unity and political stability at home and a more workable relationship with the foreign powers. For a time indeed these desiderata were achieved, but the success of the Nationalists at Nanking was purchased at a heavy price. The cost included: the suppression of all radical, and most liberal, groups; the slaughter or imprisonment of workers, peasants, and students who had been active in the left wing of the revolution; the expulsion of the communists from the Kuomintang; and suppression of the labor and peasant movements. The official slogan of this reign of terror was suppression of communism and communists. Actually what was taking place was much more than this. The purpose of the right-wing Kuomintang, now in the saddle, was to eradicate from party and government not only the communists but also all liberal elements interested in fundamental, political and social reform. The processes of reorganization which had been effected at Canton in 1923-24 were undone. "In the new Kuomintang" as it now appeared at Nanking "there would have been no place for Sun Yat-sen." [20]

NANKING: THE POLITICAL STRUCTURE

The National Government as it was established at Nanking (1927-28) was created by and was responsible to the now purged Kuomintang. Its constitution (1928-31) was the so-called First Organic Law of the National Government. Under this instrument power was concentrated at the top, and was exercised through five yüan (departments or divisions), rather than the three—legislative, executive, and judicial—common to Western government. Finally there was no parliamentary body. Until 1931 the president of the National Government exercised extensive powers controlled by a council of state. The system was altered somewhat in 1931 when the Kuomintang promulgated a provisional constitution. Under this the president lost practically all power to the Executive Yüan. [21]

THE FIVE-FOLD DIVISION OF POWERS

The five-fold division of powers known as the yüan system was a distinctive feature of Sun Yat-sen's political plan. The Executive Yüan was in a sense the cabinet of the National Government.

The Legislative Yüan, a body of eighty-eight members, was neither a parliament nor a legislature as the term is commonly understood in the West. Basically its function was research and the drafting of legislation.

---

[20] Lawrence K. Rosinger, *China's Crisis* (New York, 1945), 14.

[21] The principle of party rule and not the people's rule is expressed in Art. I of the First Organic Law: "The National Government shall administer affairs of the nation under the direction and supervision of the Kuomintang." For descriptions of the organization of the National Government see Shih Chao-ying and Chang Chi-hsien, editors, *The Chinese Year Book, 1936-37*, 223-362, 946-955; Linebarger, *Government in Republican China*, 173-182.

The Judicial Yüan comprised the Supreme Court, Administrative Court, the Ministry of Justice, and a Commission for the Disciplinary Punishment of Public Functionaries. It dealt with cases of government personnel in the civil service.

The Examination Yüan was concerned with applying a merit system to all government officials, excepting the top political positions. There were two divisions in this yüan: the Examination Commission and the Ministry of Personnel. Merit systems are of course difficult to apply even in the most advanced democracies and in circumstances where there is a real will to make them work. It is not surprising then that in contemporary China the work of the Examination Yüan has not been outstanding. Merit alone apart from considerations of hewing to the party line, be it Kuomintang or Communist, is not an effective key to the doors of public office.

The last of the five divisions, the Control Yüan, suggests the Censorate in Old China. Its functions, as that of its ancient predecessor, was to denounce (in the modern sense bring suit) against irresponsible officials. It also included a Ministry of Audit.

Because of the political, social, and economic conditions of stress which have prevailed in China in recent decades, it is impossible as yet to pass considered judgment on the effectiveness of the division of powers under the yüan system. Certainly the "elaborate scheme of bureaucratic departmentalization" was too cumbersome to permit ready adjustment to circumstances of foreign war and domestic revolution. Furthermore, the relative effectiveness of Chinese government at this time is to be attributed not so much to constitutional forms as to the greatest concentration of military power since 1911.[22]

THE PERIOD OF POLITICAL TUTELAGE

In the summer of 1928, when Peking had fallen to the Nationalists, the Kuomintang instituted formally a Program of Political Tutelage. Sun Yat-sen, it will be remembered, had foreseen the revolution as passing through three stages: military rule, political tutelage, and lastly, constitutional democracy. Once Kuomintang armies had taken Peking, and the government had been established at Nanking, the first or military period was considered to be ended; the period of political tutelage had begun. Thus only parts of Sun Yat-sen's program were implemented, with the result that his program as a whole cannot be said to

---

[22] The growth of China's armies is suggested by the following figures. Men under arms: 1912, 400,000; 1929, 1,600,000; 1930, 2,600,000, exclusive of Red armies and communist bands. United States, *Foreign Relations, 1930*, II, 43-44.

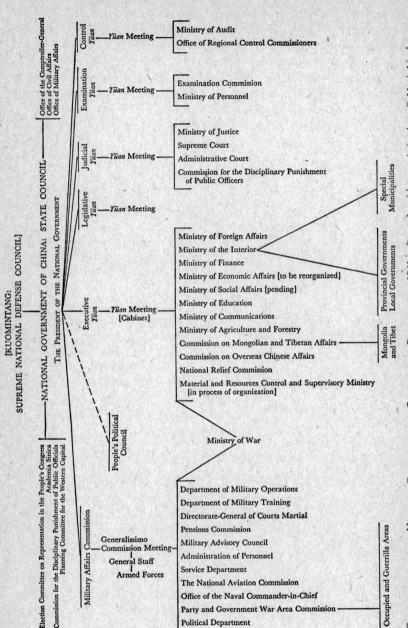

ORGANIZATION OF THE NATIONAL GOVERNMENT OF CHINA AT THE BEGINNING OF 1941. *Reproduced by permission from P. M. A. Linebarger, "The China of Chiang K'ai-shek" (Boston, 1941).*

have been given a fair trial. Whereas Sun had co-operated with all elements who supported the National revolution, the men who controlled Nanking after 1927 held that China's education for democracy during the period of tutelage must be left solely to the Kuomintang. This attitude was a reflection of the chief elements in the Party after the expulsion or the subordination of liberals and left-wingers in 1927.

NANKING AS A "NATIONAL" GOVERNMENT

The fact that the Nanking regime was known as the National Government suggested that it was national as Western peoples usually understand that term. Only in a limited sense was this true. As the administration which was soon recognized by the powers, it was the National Government, but in a geographical sense it was not master of all of China Proper within the Wall. Its power was based primarily on the lower Yangtze and diminished as it radiated into more remote areas. The Peking area was controlled by Generals Yen Hsi-shan and Feng Yu-hsiang, two erstwhile northern militarists who had joined the Nationalist cause. Nanking's control in Manchuria was nominal and dependent on the good will of Chang Hsueh-liang, the Young Marshal.[23] In the same way, a number of southern and western provinces within the Wall gave no more than nominal recognition to Nanking. Yet even with these qualifications Nanking ruled a larger area than any government since the collapse of the Yüan Shih-k'ai military regime. The immediate force making possible this wider but not inclusive territorial control was the power of the Nationalist army under Chiang K'ai-shek. Nationalist soldiers, as a result of indoctrination and training, possessed fighting qualities and a revolutionary spirit completely lacking among the troops of the old-type war-lords. It is significant too that their leader, Chiang K'ai-shek, had risen to prominence, "not as a civilian politician, but as a soldier." At this time there was no conclusive evidence that as generalissimo in the National Government he was more than the most successful of all China's numerous war-lords— one who paid lip-service to the slogans of the revolution, but also crushed his opponents with the same ruthlessness as a provincial *tuchun*. It was not yet clear that Chiang, because of his greater power and the extent of territory he controlled, would rise above the mere expression of military power and become the symbol of a united nation.[24]

---

[23] His father, Chang Tso-lin, had died in June from injuries received when his train was bombed entering Mukden.

[24] Rosinger, *China's Crisis*, 47.

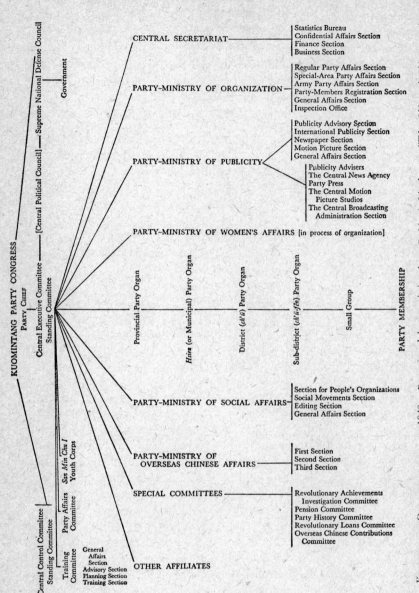

CENTRAL SECRETARIAT
- Statistics Bureau
- Confidential Affairs Section
- Finance Section
- Business Section

PARTY-MINISTRY OF ORGANIZATION
- Regular Party Affairs Section
- Special-Area Party Affairs Section
- Army Party Affairs Section
- Party-Members Registration Section
- General Affairs Section
- Inspection Office

PARTY-MINISTRY OF PUBLICITY
- Publicity Advisory Section
- International Publicity Section
- Newspaper Section
- Motion Picture Section
- General Affairs Section
- Publicity Advisers
- The Central News Agency
- Party Press
- The Central Motion Picture Studios
- The Central Broadcasting Administration Section

PARTY-MINISTRY OF WOMEN'S AFFAIRS [in process of organization]

Provincial Party Organ — Hsien (or Municipal) Party Organ — District (chü) Party Organ — Sub-district (chü-fen) Party Organ — Small Group — PARTY MEMBERSHIP

PARTY-MINISTRY OF SOCIAL AFFAIRS
- Section for People's Organizations
- Social Movements Section
- Editing Section
- General Affairs Section

PARTY-MINISTRY OF OVERSEAS CHINESE AFFAIRS
- First Section
- Second Section
- Third Section

SPECIAL COMMITTEES
- Revolutionary Achievements Investigation Committee
- Pension Committee
- Party History Committee
- Revolutionary Loans Committee
- Overseas Chinese Contributions Committee

OTHER AFFILIATES

KUOMINTANG PARTY CONGRESS
PARTY CHIEF
Central Executive Committee
Standing Committee
[Central Political Council] — Supreme National Defense Council
Government

Central Control Committee
Standing Committee

Training Committee

Party Affairs Committee

San Min Chu I Youth Corps

General Affairs Section
Advisory Section
Planning Section
Training Section

KUOMINTANG ORGANIZATION AS OF 1940. *Reproduced by permission from P. M. A. Linebarger, "The China of Chiang K'ai-shek," (Boston, 1941).*

NANKING'S NEW TREATY RELATIONS

With the ousting of the old Peking regime, June, 1928, the National Government at Nanking promptly took over the conduct of China's foreign relations. It issued a declaration (June 16) calling for new treaties negotiated with full regard to the sovereignty and equality of states.[25] Then the government gave notice that those unequal treaties, which had expired, were regarded as abrogated. Interim regulations denying extraterritoriality would control the nationals of these countries until new treaties were negotiated.[26]

Although these declarations were by no means welcome in the view of the capitalistic powers, nevertheless they were disposed to negotiate. Indeed, there was no alternative unless they proposed to use force to impose the old treaties. Moreover, China's break with Russia, and the new conservative orientation of the Kuomintang were pleasing to the foreign business groups and in the main to their governments. It was felt therefore that in negotiation the National Government would be more "reasonable" than its declarations implied.

The United States was the first power to act. By a treaty concluded at Peking on July 25, 1928, this country conceded tariff autonomy to China, subject of course to most-favored-nation treatment.[27] The agreement was one of the most significant in China's recent foreign relations for "it shattered the old international bloc" long opposed to any concessions.[28] On February 1, 1929, the National Government revealed its new-found strength by enforcing a new import tariff, the first to be drawn by the Chinese themselves free from foreign interference since 1843.

The tariff agreement with the United States was followed before the end of 1928 by similar agreements with other powers. Indeed, by January, 1929, Japan was the only power which had not concluded a new tariff agreement. This situation was due to a number of questions outstanding between the two countries. Not until Japanese troops had retired from Shantung and China had agreed to revenue allotments for the security of certain Japanese loans was an agreement reached (May 6, 1930).[29]

---

[25] *The Chinese Soc. and Pol. Science Review,* XII (1928), Supplement, 47-48.

[26] *The China Year Book, 1929-30,* 824.

[27] Text of the MacMurray-Soong treaty and correspondence in United States, *Foreign Relations, 1928,* II, 449-491.

[28] S. F. Wright, *China's Struggle for Tariff Autonomy, 1843-1938* (Shanghai, 1938), 633-634.

[29] Wright, *China's Struggle for Tariff Autonomy,* 635-641.

EXTRATERRITORIALITY CONTINUES

The new China tariff treaties with Belgium, Denmark, Italy, Portugal, and Spain contained provisions for abolition of extraterritoriality subject to a similar concession by all the powers. Accordingly, on April 27, 1929, China addressed identical notes to the United States, Great Britain, and France requesting abolition at the earliest possible date. Japan, whose new tariff treaty had not yet been signed, was not included, but similar notes were sent to Brazil, the Netherlands, and Norway. The replies of Britain, France, and the United States (August 10) were an emphatic denial that China was as yet entitled to full jurisdictional sovereignty. While complimenting China on the progress she had made, they noted that the recommendations of the Commission on Extraterritoriality had not been carried out.[30] In September, 1929, China protested this attitude both directly to the powers and in the Assembly of the League of Nations. In December, Nanking went a step further, announcing the unilateral ending of extraterritoriality as of January 1, 1930, but softening the blow with the assurance that China would negotiate with powers willing to do so. Britain then entered the game of verbal strategy, announcing her willingness "to agree that January 1, 1930, should be treated as the date from which the process of the gradual abolition of extraterritoriality should be regarded as having commenced in principle." With this idea the United States and Japan fell in line.[31]

THE RUSSO-CHINESE CRISIS IN MANCHURIA, 1929

While the National Government at Nanking was regaining tariff autonomy and was seeking to abolish the extraterritorial rights of the great capitalistic powers, it faced a new crisis in Manchuria with communistic Russia on the recurrent problem of the Chinese Eastern Railway. Since the expulsion of the communists from the Kuomintang in 1927, Sino-Russian relations had grown progressively worse. In Manchuria these relations had never been happy even after Chang Tso-lin's agreement with the Soviets in 1924. Chang was bitterly anti-communist. The Soviet was determined to maintain its right in the railway and was not averse to using the railroad zone as a base for propa-

---

[30] United States, *Foreign Relations, 1929*, II, 597. The American note said that: "To exchange an assured and tried system of administration of justice, under which it is acknowledged that life and property have been protected and commerce has grown and prospered, for uncertainties in the absence of an adequate body of law and an experienced and independent judiciary would be fraught with danger. . . ."

[31] The American correspondence is in *Foreign Relations, 1929*, II, 543-674.

ganda. When the Old Marshal was succeeded by his son, Chang
Hsueh-liang, in 1928, the potential danger in this delicate situation
became real and immediate. Young Chang was as opposed to Soviet
influence in Manchuria as was his father, and he strengthened his position, morally at least, by announcing his allegiance to Nanking. It was
against this background that the joint Russo-Chinese management of
the Chinese Eastern Railway operated under terms of the Peking and
Mukden agreements of 1924 with the Soviets.

The latent conflict inherent in this delicate situation was first brought
into the open in 1927 when Chang Tso-lin, then master of Peking,
raided buildings adjacent to the Russian Embassy. He justified his
action by citing the alleged Russian violation of the non-propaganda
clauses of the 1924 agreements (see page 543).[32] Two years later, May
27, 1929, on the orders of the Young Marshal, now an acknowledged
servant of the National Government, Chinese police entered Soviet
consulates in a number of cities along the Chinese Eastern Railway,
arrested some officials and communist agents, and seized various documents which were interpreted as evidence of Russian propaganda in
violation of the treaties. Then in July the Manchurian authorities
seized the telegraph and telephone systems of the railway, arrested more
than two hundred of its employees, and replaced them with Chinese or
White Russians. Russia replied very promptly with an ultimatum address both to Nanking and Mukden. It demanded that China reinstate
the Soviet employees, rescind her arbitrary actions, and agree to negotiate immediately on all outstanding questions affecting the railroad.
Four days later, July 17, since China had not met these terms, Russia
broke off relations. China did the same on July 20. Both powers had
only recently signed the so-called Treaty of Paris (Kellogg Pact) re-
nouncing war as an instrument of national policy. Both now showed
considerable energy in moving troops to the border in preparation for
a settlement by force. Before the end of July an informal sort of warfare marked by raids and counter raids back and forth across the Man-
churian-Siberian border was under way.[33]

[32] Art. VI of the Peking agreement, and Art. V of the Mukden agreement. Moore,
Soviet Far Eastern Policy, 157, 172.
[33] The American diplomatic correspondence is in United States, *Foreign Relations, 1929,*
II, 186-434. Secondary accounts include: Russell M. Cooper, *American Consultation in
World Affairs* (New York, 1934), 86-88; Louis Fischer, *The Soviets in World Affairs* (2
vols., London, 1930), II, ch. xxx; A. W. Griswold, *The Far Eastern Policy of the United
States* (New York, 1938), 389-391; H. L. Kingman, *Effects of Chinese Nationalism Upon
Manchurian Railway Developments, 1925-1931* (Berkeley, 1932), 61-78; R. T. Pollard,
China's Foreign Relations, 1917-1931 (New York, 1933), 387-399; Arnold J. Toynbee,
ed., *Survey of International Affairs, 1929* (London, 1930), 344-351.

TESTING OF TREATY FOR THE RENUNCIATION OF WAR

The peace of the Far East was again at stake. Peace machinery applicable to the situation was inadequate. Russia was not a member of the League of Nations and she was not a party to the Washington Conference treaties. However, both Russia and China had signed the Treaty for the Renunciation of War concluded at Paris in August, 1928, and currently known as the Pact of Paris, or the Briand-Kellogg Treaty.[34] In this treaty the signatories had "condemned recourse to war for the solution of international controversies" and had renounced war "as an instrument of national policy," agreeing thereby "that the settlement or solution of all disputes or conflicts of whatever nature or of whatever origin they may be . . . shall never be sought except by pacific means." However, all parties recognized that the treaty did not impair the right of self defense which the British in particular interpreted very broadly.[35] These reservations "reduced the pact to a collection of individual declarations of the intention not to fight except in defense of whatever national interests each signatory might consider vital."[36]

Despite the innocuous nature of the Briand-Kellogg Treaty, Henry L. Stimson, who when the Manchurian trouble arose had succeeded Kellogg as Secretary of State, believed it was in the American interest to implement the agreement by reading into it consultative obligations and by marshalling world public opinion to its support. He refused to accept the pact as a mere declaration of pious purpose, very much as John Hay in 1899 had attempted to make something real out of the slippery replies of the powers to his open door notes.[37] Believing that the treaty could become "a practical instrument for preserving the peace," Stimson reminded both Russia and China of their obligations to use pacific means.[38] This appeal was formally approved by all the major powers signatory to the pact and by China and Russia, who gave assurance that they would not resort to force—save in self defense. Meanwhile, negotiations between the Soviet and local Manchurian officials, and between

---

[34] United States, *Foreign Relations, 1928*, I, 1-234, contains the extensive official correspondence incident to negotiating the treaty.

[35] United States, Department of State, *Treaty for the Renunciation of War* (Washington, 1933), 43-46, 72-73.

[36] Griswold, *Far Eastern Policy of the United States*, 393.

[37] Henry L. Stimson, "The Pact of Paris" (Washington, Council on Foreign Relations, an address, Aug. 8, 1932).

[38] United States, *Foreign Relations, 1929*, II, 186-434; precedent for the action is discussed by Stanley K. Hornbeck, "American Policy and the Chinese-Russian Dispute," *The Chinese Soc. and Pol. Science Review*, XIV (1930), 41-60.

the Russian Ambassador and the Chinese Minister in Berlin had proved abortive. Further efforts by Stimson looking to mediation also failed. By November there was open though undeclared warfare on the Manchurian border. A Soviet army invaded Manchuria from the west. The forces of Chang Hsueh-liang retreated in confusion. On December 3, Chang agreed to Russia's demands, and this act was approved by Nanking on December 22.

The brief undeclared war had demonstrated: 1) that in Manchuria, Soviet Russia was as jealous of what she considered to be her interests and as ready to defend them by force as was tsarist Russia before her, although the interests had become somewhat different in form; 2) that the Briand-Kellogg Treaty faced with its first test case was meaningless as an effective preventive of war; and 3) that the National Government at Nanking, involved in suppressing opposition in central and northwest China, was incapable of exerting its power in the border provinces of the northeast.[39] Moreover, it appears likely that among Japanese leaders there were some who soon entertained the belief that if the Russians, who had no international friends, could get away with so much in North Manchuria without international intervention, Japan, who did have friends, could get away with much more.

---

[39] Pollard, *China's Foreign Relations,* 396. Details on the Sino-Russian negotiations and the unstable settlement which followed the undeclared war are in *ibid.,* 396-399.

CHAPTER 32

JAPAN IN WORLD POLITICS, 1922-1930

IT MAY appear as something of a paradox that the decade of the 1920's, a decade in which Japan appeared to be moving steadily toward such concepts as liberalism, representative government, and democracy, was also the decade which failed to resolve conflicts in policy between Japan and her greatest and most immediate neighbor, China.[1] From the outset therefore it should be noted that in the case of Japan, as well as of other countries, the development of liberalism and representative government at home did not preclude a vigorous policy of expansion and imperialism abroad.[2] Between the years 1922 and 1931, as will shortly be seen, there was no essential difference *of purpose* between Japanese liberals as against conservatives and militarists in matters concerning Japan's policy in China. The fundamental character of the policy had long been fixed. It was a policy of imperialism and expansion resting on well publicized assumptions of a "special position" and "special interests." The crux of the policy was Japan's economic and political stake in South Manchuria dating back to her victory in the Russo-Japanese War. No Japanese government, no matter how tinged with liberalism, had ever proposed to relinquish the essentials of the policy. The principal differences among Japanese statesmen concerned *methods* to be used in implementing policy, and the *time* when these should be applied.[3]

FOCAL POINTS OF JAPANESE POLICY

World War I not only projected Japan into the company of the great powers, it also increased materially the economic and political power she could bring to bear on far eastern politics.

---

[1] In following the story related in this chapter, the reader will find it desirable to refer frequently to the account of Japan's domestic politics, 1918 to 1930, as told in Chapter 28.

[2] The assertion of Japan's "special interests" in Manchuria and in other parts of China, as well as the implementation of these interests, had at times occurred when the government in Tokyo was headed by men who were thought of as "liberals": Saionji after the Russo-Japanese War, and Okuma when the Twenty-One Demands were presented to China.

[3] Owen Lattimore, *Solution in Asia* (Boston, 1945), 48.

Appearing in the wake of World War I were three major issues which successive Japanese governments regarded as of supreme importance. All three of these issues called for fundamental long-range decisions in terms of Japanese foreign policy. The first of these was the question of seapower in the Pacific, a question with which the world's greatest naval powers, Great Britain and the United States, felt an equal concern. The second was the new situation created by the failure of the inter-Allied Siberian Intervention to pave the way for the destruction of Bolshevism in Russia. This meant that Japan as well as China must look to a frontier in northeastern Asia separating a capitalistic from a communistic society. The third was the rapid development of a Chinese nationalism which, if it prospered, must collide sooner or later with Japan's special position in South Manchuria. To all of these major problems, Japanese statesmen found answers in the decade that followed the Washington Conference, but whether they were good answers must be judged in the light of Japan's developing diplomacy.

In retrospect, the overall picture of Japanese foreign policy from 1922 to 1931 compares favorably with the record of other great powers. Even her severest critics have attested to this. It has been noted that

. . . whatever may have been the unwillingness of Japan to attend the Washington Conference, and whatever may have been her hesitation in affixing her signature to the Nine Power Treaty, it is to be conceded that, during the nine succeeding years, that is, until the Fall of 1931, Japan appeared to have adopted a foreign policy that was in substantial conformity with the undertakings to which she had pledged herself.[4]

But, as we have already seen, a scrupulous regard for treaty commitments was not by itself an answer to the far eastern question. The British discovered this at Shanghai and Hongkong in 1925, at Hankow and Kiukiang in 1926, and the British and the Americans at Nanking in 1927. The trouble was that the Washington Conference agreements were "primarily a recognition of existing, if brutal, facts, a consolidation of the *status quo*."[5] By themselves alone they could not achieve definitive solution for a part of the world which was already in open revolt against the *status quo*. To be sure, in 1922 Chinese nationalism was

[4] W. W. Willoughby, *Japan's Case Examined* (Baltimore, 1940), 8; see also Henry L. Stimson, *The Far Eastern Crisis* (New York, 1936), 36: "The Japanese Government had thus for ten years given an exceptional record of good citizenship in the life of the international world."

[5] A. W. Griswold, *The Far Eastern Policy of the United States* (New York, 1938), 331.

not as yet organized politically, nor was the course of Japan's "hungry expansionism" clearly predictable. Yet the potentialities of conflict between these movements were obvious. Thus in signing the Washington agreements Japan undertook an extremely difficult task. She was committed by treaty to the broad principle of China's political integrity while at the same time she clung to a policy of maintaining her special position in South Manchuria.

The first favorable developments in Japanese policy after the Washington Conference occurred late in 1922 and early in January, 1923, when the government carried out the restoration to China of Kiaochow in accordance with the Shantung treaty signed at Washington.[6] Then on April 14, 1923, the Lansing-Ishii notes of 1917, regarded by public opinion in the United States and China as thoroughly obnoxious, were cancelled by the mutual consent of the two governments. While in the press of America and China this was trumpeted as a great victory for China and American policy, its real significance was limited because the Japanese government accepted the view of Ishii to the effect that Japan's "special position was not based upon the discredited agreement but upon concrete realities of history and geography." Ishii held that Japan's special position was not a question of "benefits conferred on Japan by the United States."[7]

JAPAN AND RUSSIA, 1922-1929

A second striking development in the immediate post-Washington Conference period was the formal improvement in Japan's relations with Soviet Russia. At the end of 1922 the last Japanese forces left the mainland of Siberia. Their withdrawal was due to many pressures. In addition to diplomatic pressure exerted on Japan at the Washington Conference, the Japanese public no longer supported a policy which had cost the taxpayer some 700,000,000 yen, had alienated the Russians and aroused the suspicions of the Western powers, and which finally had served to hasten rather than retard the union of eastern Siberia with communistic Moscow. The net result was that when the last Japanese soldier left Siberia the diplomatic gulf between Tokyo and Moscow was wide and deep. Yet the economic as well as the political interests of both Japan and Russia demanded an end to the chaos created by revolution and intervention.

As a consequence, then, of protracted negotiations begun in June,

---

[6] Details are in W. L. Godshall, *Tsingtao under Three Flags* (Shanghai, 1929), ch. xi.

[7] Tatsuji Takeuchi, *War and Diplomacy in the Japanese Empire* (New York, 1935), 203; see also Kikujiro Ishii, *Diplomatic Commentaries* (Baltimore, 1936), 134-135.

1923, a treaty was signed, January 20, 1925, restoring relations between the two powers.[8]

THE RUSSO-JAPANESE TREATY, 1925

The treaty covered a wide range of subjects, political and economic. First in importance were the provisions for mutual *de jure* recognition, and Russia's recognition of the Treaty of Portsmouth (1905), on the basic provisions of which depended most of Japan's legal claims to a special position in South Manchuria. Other Russo-Japanese agreements made subsequently with the tsarist government were to be subject to review. Pending the conclusion of a treaty of commerce, the rights of entry, travel, residence, private ownership, and the liberty to engage in peaceful pursuits of commerce and industry were to be mutually enjoyed by the respective nationals in accordance with the laws of each country. In view of "the needs of Japan with regard to natural resources" Russia agreed to grant concessions to Japanese for the exploitation of mineral, forest, and other natural resources of eastern Siberia. Japanese would continue to fish in Siberian coastal waters under terms of a temporary agreement made in 1924 pending revision of the Russo-Japanese fisheries convention of 1907. Both countries pledged themselves to restrain all their officials and all organizations officially subsidized from engaging in propaganda likely "to endanger the order and security" of either. Russia agreed to adjust on terms favorable to Japan debts due Tokyo by the tsarist government, and Japan in turn agreed to withdraw her troops from northern Sakhalin by May 15. In this territory she would be granted various oil, coal, and lumber concessions. Finally, in a note annexed to the treaty, Russia expressed "sincere regret for the Nikolaievsk incident of 1920." [9] At the same time she disclaimed all "political responsibility" for situations arising out of the Portsmouth Treaty concluded by the tsar's government.[10]

The *rapprochement* represented by this treaty was a product of significant and varied forces playing upon Japanese policy. It had become evident even to Japan's chauvinists that military and political intervention had failed utterly to isolate eastern Siberia from the advance of

---

[8] For further details on the background of the Russo-Japanese *rapprochement* see V. A. Yakhontoff, *Russia and the Soviet Union in the Far East* (New York, 1931), 233-253; Roy H. Akagi, *Japan's Foreign Relations* (Tokyo, 1936), 418-425.

[9] See p. 422.

[10] W. H. Chamberlin, *Soviet Russia* (Boston, 1930), ch. x; Yakhontoff, *Russia and the Soviet Union in the Far East*, ch. xvi; also Louis Fischer, *The Soviets in World Affairs* (2 vols., London, 1930).

Bolshevism. Furthermore, since there was in Japan an increasing demand for the products of Siberia's mines, forests, and waters, the reestablishment of normal relations in which commerce and industry might develop with some freedom was the natural alternative despite Japan's fear of the infiltration of "dangerous thoughts." Moreover, the success of Russian influence with the Chinese Nationalists at Canton and the conclusion of the Russian treaties with Peking and Mukden in 1924 emphasized Japan's isolation. Indeed, this isolation was now looming much larger in Japanese eyes than it had at the time of the Washington Conference. There was no longer an Anglo-Japanese alliance as a prop to Japanese policy, and "the insensate method" taken by the American Senate in the Quota Immigration Act of May, 1924, to exclude Japanese from the United States was interpreted by the Japanese press, the government, and public opinion as again indicative of an American attitude basically unfriendly to Japan's interests and purposes. Probably to most Japanese, the American of that day was an incomprehensible being. During 1923 this American had contributed money and supplies in the amount of some $7,000,000 for relief and reconstruction in the Yokohama earthquake disaster of September 1. Less than a year later the government of this same American passed an immigration act which to the Japanese appeared as a willful affront to a friendly nation. It was the combination of all these forces playing together upon the feudal-capitalistic mind of Japan's government that had directed it somewhat timorously into a renewal of normal relations with Bolshevik Russia.[11]

THE RUSSO-JAPANESE FISHERIES

In general, Russo-Japanese relations maintained a relative calm from 1925 to 1931, subject to some aggravating and protracted negotiations on the old problem of Japanese fishing rights in Russian waters.[12]

THE PERIOD OF SINO-JAPANESE AMITY

The period in which normal diplomatic relations were restored between Japan and Soviet Russia also saw the growth of happier prospects in Sino-Japanese affairs. During the greater part of the decade, 1922-1931, Japan's foreign policy was colored by the personality and the lib-

---

[11] The process was encouraged also by British and Italian recognition of the Soviet government and by the liberal conciliatory policy of Baron Kijuro Shidehara who became Foreign Minister in Japan in 1924.

[12] Robert Mossé, ed., *Soviet Far East and Pacific Northwest* (Seattle, 1944), 33-40, gives a convenient brief survey of Soviet foreign policy in the Pacific.

eral philosophy of Baron Kijuro Shidehara, a career diplomat who had married into the Iwasaki family, which controlled the powerful Mitsubishi trust. Shidehara had become the spokesman of those elements which saw the future of Japan's commercial and industrial expansion in terms of membership in the League of Nations, limitation of naval armament, and the development of a policy of conciliation and adjustment to China's new nationalism without renunciation of Japan's "life line" in South Manchuria. From 1924 to 1927 and from 1929 to 1931 while he was Foreign Minister, he pursued in general what came to be known as the "Shidehara policy." Shidehara summarized the principles of the policy before the Japanese Diet in January, 1927:

1) To respect the sovereignty and territorial integrity of China, and scrupulously avoid all interference in her domestic strife.
2) To promote solidarity and economic *rapprochement* between the two countries.
3) To entertain sympathetically and helpfully the just aspirations of the Chinese people, and to co-operate in the efforts for realization of such aspirations.
4) To maintain an attitude of patience and toleration in the present situation in China, and, at the same time, to protect Japan's legitimate and essential rights and interests by all reasonable means at the disposal of the Government.

The crux of the Shidehara policy depended, among other things, upon whether the two nations could find a common interpretation of such phrases as "the just aspirations of the Chinese people" and "Japan's legitimate and essential rights and interests." Shidehara's efforts to reconcile China's aspirations with "Japan's interests" came at a time when an underlying conflict between the two was increasing rather than diminishing in intensity.[13]

First steps in the policy of "conciliation" toward China had been taken, as already noted, in 1923 when Kiaochow was restored and a number of Japanese post offices on Chinese soil were closed.[14] Further precedent for the Shidehara policy was given in the case of the 1923 Chinese boycott of Japanese goods arising out of China's renewed request for retrocession of the Liaotung leasehold. Although this boycott occasioned "an important temporary disturbance of trade," it called

---

[13] For a discussion of constitutional and other forces determining foreign policy in Japan see Takeuchi, *War and Diplomacy in the Japanese Empire,* ch. xxix.
[14] The postal agreement is discussed by Takeuchi, *War and Diplomacy in the Japanese Empire,* ch. xxi.

forth no change in Japanese policy.[15]   Again, in 1925, although conditions in Japanese cotton mills occasioned the Shanghai demonstrations and the killing of Chinese by police of the International Settlement, Japan hastily paid an indemnity to bereaved Chinese families. Japanese interests, too, though affected, escaped the excessive pressures exerted on the British in the great boycott which followed. This was especially notable since in 1925 "the Japanese were originally singled out as the nation to be subjected to the boycott." [16]

On two occasions during Shidehara's first term at the Foreign Office Japan did resort to the use of troops "for the protection of Japanese interests in China." In December, 1925, when Kuo Sung-ling, a lesser militarist in Manchuria, revolted against Chang Tso-lin, Japan dispatched some troops to the Mukden area. Again in April, 1927, Japanese marines were used to resist Chinese mobs attacking the Japanese concession at Hankow. But as against these cases, the Japanese naval forces did not join in the Anglo-American bombardment of Nanking in March, 1927, despite the fact that the Japanese consulate had been attacked by the Chinese and several Japanese nationals had been wounded.[17]

TANAKA AND THE POSITIVE POLICY

Shidehara's "weak" policy, which had been pursued in the face of mounting civil war and anti-foreignism in China, aroused bitter opposition among Japanese militarists and conservatives in the services, in the government, and in business circles. The sentiment was particularly strong among the aristocratic reactionaries of the powerful Privy

---

[15] C. F. Remer, *A Study of Chinese Boycotts* (Baltimore, 1933), 80-91.

[16] The political as well as the economic implications of this boycott and their relation to the Nationalist movement and the campaigns on anti-imperialism, anti-foreignism, etc., are discussed by Remer, *A Study of Chinese Boycotts*, 92-127.

[17] These manifestations of policy are not entirely self explanatory. The case of Kuo Sung-ling involved a form of duplicity in Japanese policy recalling the phase of intervention in Outer Mongolia (see p. 541). In the case of Outer Mongolia, the "Little Hsu" adventure was backed by Japan; Baron von Ungern-Sternberg was also backed by Japan, although the forces of Hsu and the Baron fought each other. Similarly, in Manchuria Chang Tso-lin was backed by Japan in general as a long-term policy; but Kuo Sung-ling was also backed in his revolt against Chang Tso-lin by Japan for particular and short-term reasons.

In the Hankow case, the Japanese were engaged in local defense; there was no question of Japanese instigation of Chinese agents. Thus the Hankow case and the dispatch of Japanese troops to the Mukden area were not completely parallel.

The Nanking case, where the Japanese naval forces did not join with the British and the Americans, was a distinct third situation. In this case, the Japanese were following the same policy which they had used at Shanghai in 1925—the policy of stepping aside and hoping that Chinese wrath would be concentrated on others.

Council. In April, 1927, a most critical period in the Nationalist movement in China, the Council, by rejecting measures of the Wakatsuki cabinet designed to bolster the Bank of Japan, forced the resignation of the government, thus opening the way for appointment of an aggressive *Seiyukai* cabinet headed by General Baron Giichi Tanaka, who since 1925 had been head of the *Seiyukai* Party.

Tanaka was one of those who aspired to the mantle until lately worn by Aritomo Yamagata, who for so many years as militarist and politician among the Genro had kept alive the martial traditions of Choshu clansmen. A veteran of the Russo-Japanese War, Tanaka had served as Minister of War during the inter-Allied Siberian adventure. Now, in 1927, as leader of the *Seiyukai,* Prime Minister, and Minister for Foreign Affairs, he voiced the rising opposition to the "weak" Shidehara by enunciating a strong or, as it was called, "positive," policy toward China.[18]

TANAKA'S TWO-FOLD POLICY IN CHINA

The "positive" policy distinguished between the attitude Japan would adopt toward China Proper and her attitude toward Manchuria and eastern Mongolia. Tanaka re-emphasized that Japan had "special interests" in these latter areas, "that it was her duty to maintain peace and order there," and that her rights and interests in these areas would be protected if threatened by disturbances incident to the Nationalist move-

---

[18] The "positive" policy was given definite form at a conference, June 27-July 7, at the Foreign Office, presided over by Tanaka, and attended by representatives of the Finance, Foreign, Navy, and War Departments, the chiefs of the general staffs, the commander of the Kwantung army, the Japanese Minister to China and three consuls-general in China. (Takeuchi, *War and Diplomacy in the Japanese Empire,* 247-248). Associated with the decisions of this conference is the enigmatic history of the so-called "Tanaka Memorial," a document which, purporting to contain the decisions reached at Tanaka's conference, first made its appearance in 1929, and after 1931 was reprinted many times and widely circulated as evidence of Japan's pre-determined policy vis-à-vis China in general and Manchuria in particular.

Japanese policy in Manchuria and China after 1931 bore a striking resemblance to specific points in the "Memorial." The disputed authenticity of the document is discussed by Willoughby, *Japan's Case Examined,* 146-153.

The "weak" versus the "positive" policies of Shidehara and Tanaka respectively involved more than an argument over principles to be applied in foreign policy toward China. In some considerable measure, Shidehara represented the commercialism of Japan's light industries and their quest for expanding export markets. Tanaka was more closely identified with Japan's heavy industries. A strong armament policy enabled the army and navy to place large contracts with Japan's heavy industries, thus in fact subsidizing them, for which reason the heavy industries tended to be willing to go along with the Tanaka policy. But in order to justify armaments and preparedness, Tanaka was forced to adopt a "positive" policy, to maintain that a war-like crisis was perpetually just around the corner on the continent of Asia.

ment or other civil strife. The earliest manifestations of the strong policy had occurred in May and June, 1927, when portions of Japan's Manchurian garrison were sent to Shantung ostensibly to protect Japanese life and property said to be threatened by the northern march of Nationalist troops who by this time, it will be recalled, were in control of the Yangtze Valley. Nearly a year later, April, 1928, the success of the advancing Nationalists was so marked that the downfall of Chang Tso-lin, Manchurian war-lord, Generalissimo of the Peking government, and friend of Tanaka, seemed assured. Chang's survival appeared to rest on the intervention of a third power. It was in these circumstances that further Japanese troops were sent to Tsinan, capital of Shantung and terminus of the Kiaochow railway, where Japanese economic interests were extensive. The decision to send the troops was made by a special council consisting of Tanaka as Prime Minister and Foreign Minister, General Shirakawa, Minister of War, and Admiral Okada, Minister of the Navy, without the presence of "any civilian representative of the Foreign Office." Once the decision had been made, the government disclaimed any intention to interfere with China's domestic affairs. This disclaimer was obviously meaningless, as was pointed out by Japan's opposition press, which labelled the decision as unwarranted and detrimental.[19] Seemingly the government's purpose was to strengthen its position at home by giving tangible implementation to the strong policy while at the same time it protected Chang Tso-lin from the advancing Nationalists.

Complicating events now crowded fast upon the scene. At Tsinan the first clash between Nationalist and Japanese troops occurred on May 3. There were casualties among civilians and soldiers on both sides. Within a week the Japanese commander had issued an ultimatum demanding withdrawal of Chinese Nationalist forces from Tsinan and from the zone of the Shantung railroad. On May 8 the Japanese government approved the dispatch to Shantung of additional troops —a division at war strength. In China the National Government presented its case to the League of Nations, May 11. On June 4 Chang Tso-lin, fleeing from Peking to his provincial capital at Mukden, died as a result of injuries sustained when his special train was bombed as it passed under the tracks of the Japanese-owned South Manchuria Railway. Then, on July 17, under instructions from Tanaka, Japan's consul general at Mukden, "in his individual capacity," advised Marshal Chang Hsueh-liang, who had succeeded his father as ruler of Man-

---

[19] *Tokyo Asahi*, April 19, 1928, cited by Takeuchi, *War and Diplomacy in the Japanese Empire*, 250.

churia, to postpone announcing his proposed allegiance to the Nationalist cause and government at Nanking.

Despite rigid censorship of the Japanese press, a deluge of criticism was heaped upon the Tanaka government for the extravagant and militaristic course into which it was dragging the nation. In the House of Peers, Baron Shidehara compared his own handling of the Nanking incident with the strong-arm policy now being pursued. In the face of this criticism Tanaka was forced to abandon the positive policy. The Tsinan incident was formally settled by an exchange of notes, March 28, 1929. These contained mutual expressions of regret, provided for the withdrawal of Japanese troops from Shantung within two months, and set up a joint commission to determine the losses sustained.

JAPAN AND THE KELLOGG-BRIAND TREATY

Meanwhile, the Tanaka government had adhered to the Treaty for the Renunciation of War on the understanding that the phrase in the treaty, "in the names of their respective peoples," did not signify that the emperor signed "as the agent of this people." The government regarded this reservation as necessary, since under the Japanese constitution the emperor was held to sign a treaty in his own name and not that of the people. The precaution, however, did not shield Tanaka's *Seiyukai* government from violent attacks by the *Minseito* opposition and by the Privy Council. The treaty was finally ratified with the declaration that the phrase "in the names of their respective peoples" was "inapplicable in so far as Japan is concerned." [20]

TANAKA AND THE DEATH OF CHANG TSO-LIN

A culminating blow to Tanaka's prestige was the death of Chang Tso-lin, June 4, 1928, following the bombing of his train as it passed under a Japanese-controlled railway bridge on the outskirts of Mukden. Again there was rigid press censorship, and eight months after the incident had occurred, Tanaka could only reply to inquiries in the Diet that the incident was still under investigation. Finally, when the government's investigation was completed, it was rumored that the Japanese commander of the Kwantung garrison was to be placed on the reserve list as a disciplinary measure. The report itself was not made public, but the incident and its political aftermath in Japan, coming in conjunction with the bungling of the "positive" policy in China and the constitutional issues raised by the Kellogg-Briand Treaty, forced the

---

[20] The subject is treated by Takeuchi, *War and Diplomacy in the Japanese Empire,* 262-274.

resignation of the Tanaka government in July, 1929. Again the way was opened for a resumption of the more conciliatory policy under Yuko Hamaguchi as Premier with Shidehara again at the Foreign Office.[21]

JAPAN AND THE LEAGUE OF NATIONS

As the pendulum of Japanese politics swung uneasily between the "weak" and "strong" policies of Shidehara and Tanaka, Japan had continued to play a respectable and in some cases a distinguished role as a member of the League of Nations. A number of Japan's most distinguished statesmen, jurists, diplomats, and public men served with the League. Until 1926 Inazo Nitobe, one of the best known of Japan's liberals abroad, served as an Under-Secretary-General and as a Director of the International Bureau. He was succeeded by Yotaro Sugimura as Under-Secretary-General and Director of the Political Section.

JAPAN AND THE WORLD COURT

Japan was also active in the field of arbitration and adjudication of international disputes. She was a signatory of the Convention for the Pacific Settlement of International Disputes, a product of the Hague Peace Congress of 1899 and 1907. When, under the League of Nations, the principle of international adjudication acquired new life, Mineichiro Adachi was named a member of the League committee which drafted the statutes for the new Permanent Court of International Justice, commonly known as the World Court. A Japanese, Yorozu Oda, was one of the original eleven judges of the Court. He in turn was succeeded in 1930 by Mineichiro Adachi, who served also as President of the Court. However, on account of the so-called optional clause in the statutes of the Court imposing compulsory acceptance of its jurisdiction in specified cases, Japan did not accept the Court's full jurisdiction.[22]

NAVAL RIVALRY IN THE PACIFIC

The Washington Conference, as will be recalled, had made a beginning in holding within bounds the race in naval armament among the great powers. However, after 1924, when the United States passed the general immigration act excluding aliens ineligible to citizenship, there was noticeable tension in American-Japanese relations and a grow-

---

[21] The effects upon Japanese politics of the death of Chang Tso-lin, referred to in Japan only as "a grave Manchurian incident," are treated by Takeuchi, *War and Diplomacy in the Japanese Empire*, 275-282.

[22] Akagi, *Japan's Foreign Relations*, 458-462.

ing interest in the question of armaments. A naval race was still quite possible, for the Washington Conference ratio, 5-5-3 for the United States, Great Britain, and Japan, was applicable only to capital ships. Indeed, the naval race was already under way, for while the United States failed to maintain its naval strength either in auxiliary categories or in the capital ships to which it was entitled under the Washington agreement, the other powers, Japan and Great Britain, continued to build.[23]

THE GENEVA DISARMAMENT CONFERENCE, 1927

Without adequate preparation, President Coolidge on February 10, 1927, invited the powers to a disarmament conference at Geneva. Although France and Italy declined to attend, Great Britain, the United States, and Japan attempted to extend and supplement the principles adopted at Washington. The United States wanted to apply the 5-5-3 ratio to all categories and to reduce total cruiser tonnage. No agreement, however, was reached and the conference ended in failure.

This was the more lamentable since there appears little doubt that public opinion at this time in all three countries favored further limitation. The conference was defeated both by the naval experts and by lobbyists of special groups.[24]

THE LONDON NAVAL CONFERENCE, 1930

Anglo-American-Japanese relations continued to deteriorate after the Geneva Conference. There appeared to be no solution to the naval problem so long as Great Britain and the United States remained as far apart as they were at Geneva. By late 1929 this doleful picture had been retouched and brightened. Shidehara was back at the Japanese Foreign Office, and President Herbert Hoover and Prime Minister Ramsey Mac-Donald had talked amicably at the President's fishing camp at Rapidan, Virginia. Evidence of the improved international temper came with a British invitation to the powers, October 7, 1929, to a disarmament conference in London. As at Geneva, this conference was soon mired in the technical details of the experts who again seemed to be "on top" instead of merely "on tap." Yet, on April 22, 1930, the London Naval Treaty was signed by Britain, the United States, and Japan. France,

[23] For discussions of the growing armament problem: B. H. Williams, *The United States and Disarmament* (New York, 1931); J. W. Wheeler-Bennett, *Disarmament and Security since Locarno, 1925-1931* (London, 1932), chs. i and ii; Giovanni Engely, *The Politics of Naval Disarmament*, trans. by H. V. Rhodes (London, 1932), chs. i, ii, iii.

[24] Williams, *The United States and Disarmament*, 175-184.

who had demanded a political agreement assuring her of military support, and Italy accepted only parts of the Treaty.[25] Nevertheless, the results of the conference were positive if limited. The three major powers had accepted a maximum upper limit in all categories of vessels. Britain acceded to an overall principle of parity with the United States. Japan accepted a 10-10-6 ratio in heavy cruisers, was granted a 10-10-7 ratio in light cruisers and other auxiliary ships, and parity with the larger powers in submarines. An escalator clause could release any signatory from its obligations if its position was jeopardized by the naval construction of a non-signatory.[26]

JAPAN AND THE LONDON TREATY

At the London Naval Conference Japan had sought "three fundamental claims": 1) a 70 percent ratio relative to the United States in 10,000-ton 8-inch-gun heavy cruisers; 2) a 70 percent ratio in gross tonnage relative to the United States in all auxiliary craft; and 3) parity with Britain and the United States in submarine tonnage at the then high existing strength of some 78,000 tons. This program of the Japanese naval staff, supported by the press, was designed to give the nation greater relative strength in far eastern waters than was provided by the 5-5-3 capital ship ratio of the Washington Treaty. In Japan it was generally regarded as "adequate for defense in any contingency." As against this the United States proposed for Japan a 60 percent ratio in total tonnage for auxiliary craft. The ultimate settlement embodied in the treaty was a compromise. Since any compromise which would save the conference from failure would be essentially political in character, Wakatsuki and Matsudaira recognized the necessity of modifying "the three fundamental claims." To do this they were forced to ignore the advice of the Japanese naval experts.[27] In Tokyo, the Hamaguchi government, which favored acceptance of the compromise, met violent opposition from the naval staff and all ultra-nationalistic groups. Admiral Kanji Kato, chief of the naval general staff, personified the resolute position of the military services and their supporters. The decision to accept the compromise was therefore a major victory for civilian as opposed to military dominance in the government. Furthermore, it strengthened the liberal constitutional theories of Tatsukichi Minobe, a distinguished jurist, who held that the power to determine the military

---

[25] Wheeler-Bennett, *Disarmament and Security*, 127-214.

[26] Portions of the voluminous American correspondence on the conference are in U. S., *Foreign Relations, 1930*, I 1-131. For the text of the Treaty, see 107-125.

[27] See Takeuchi, *War and Diplomacy in the Japanese Empire*, 293.

and naval strength of the state did not belong to the supreme command. In this view, it was the prerogative of the cabinet and not of the military services to advise the emperor.[28]

Japan's adherence to the London Treaty marked the high point in the nation's struggle toward liberal, civilian, and responsible government, but it also marked a decision by the militarists to oppose, by force if necessary, any further challenge to their "special position" in the constitutional and political life of the nation.

In summary, it may be noted that the recognition of Japan as a great power, and, after 1919, as the dominant power in the Far East, stemmed directly from her wartime-created industrialization, and from Europe's wartime preoccupation and exhaustion. After World War I, Japan, moving toward liberalism and responsible government at home, was regarded by Western capitalistic states as a bulwark against communism in Asia, and as a protector of the common treaty rights of foreigners against the extreme demands of Chinese nationalism. On the other hand, in so far as Japan sought to maintain for herself an exclusive position in South Manchuria, and to increase her relative naval power in auxiliary ships beyond the 5-5-3 capital ship ratio granted her by the Washington Naval Treaty, her policies were distinctly at variance with those of the United States and Great Britain. Moreover, any tendencies such as Tanaka's "positive" policy suggestive of Japanese hegemony in China would negate the American principles of the open door and territorial integrity, and jeopardize Britain's commercial and investment primacy in China.

Assuredly also, it was significant that Japan, the power most deeply and intimately involved, had shown under the Shidehara policy a disposition to recognize "the just aspirations" of the Chinese people. Nevertheless, the decade of opportunity ended in the gloom of ominous shadows. Tanaka's positive policy of 1927-28, Russia's resort to force in Manchuria, 1929, and finally the resurgence of war-lordism and militarism in China in 1930, with their irresponsible attacks upon foreign persons, property, and treaty privileges—all these were a forecast of danger, if not imminent crisis, as the world of 1930 sank into the most devastating economic depression of modern times.

---

[28] Takeuchi, *War and Diplomacy in the Japanese Empire,* 310-311.

Chapter 33

THE MANCHURIAN CRISIS AND THE LEAGUE OF NATIONS

MANCHURIA, in the year 1931, was an exceedingly fertile region of some 380,000 square miles, as large as the combined area of France and Germany, with an estimated population of 30,000,000 persons of whom some 28,000,000 were Chinese (including a small percentage of native Manchus), 800,000 were Koreans, 150,000 Russians, and some 230,000 Japanese.[1] Until the beginning of the twentieth century Manchuria had remained almost completely undeveloped. About 1895, Russia, and later Japan, thought of Manchuria as an area occupation of which would imply domination of far eastern politics. After the Chinese Eastern Railway was built, Manchuria assumed importance because of its own natural wealth. In 1928 the total value of Manchuria's agricultural products, including such principal crops as soya beans, kaoliang, wheat, millet, and barley, most of which were exported, was some $650,000,000. There had also been extensive exploitation of the rich timber lands and of such minerals as coal, iron, and gold. This extraordinarily rapid development of a frontier region was made possible by the capital and managerial investments of Russia and Japan and by the toil and industry of millions of Chinese immigrant farmers from Shantung who, after the turn of the century, settled in increasing numbers on the newly opened lands. Indeed, it was this Chinese peasant rather than any government under which he lived, be it the Manchu dynasty or the Republic after 1911, who determined the ultimate course of Manchurian history. Neither the feeble Manchu dynasty nor the later struggling Republic under Yüan Shih-k'ai could do more than

---

[1] One important fact relating to estimated population statistics of Manchuria is often overlooked. As of 1931, the Manchurian population included a Mongol minority estimated from 500,000 to 2,000,000 scattered throughout something like one fourth of the territory. Though weak in numbers and organization, the Mongols were strengthened by a rapidly growing nationalism among all the Mongols of Inner Mongolia backed by the existence of an unrecognized but *de facto* independent Mongolian state in Outer Mongolia. The continuing importance of this Mongol question in western Manchuria is shown by a recrudescent Mongolian nationalism since VJ-Day stimulated by the existence of an Outer Mongolia whose prestige has been high among the Mongols generally.

merely assert Chinese sovereignty in Manchuria, whereas Russia and Japan continued to define and delimit it into their respective spheres of influence. Yet while all this was going on, millions of Chinese peasants had taken possession of Manchuria's soil and in this sense had made it irrevocably Chinese. During the years 1905 to 1928, Manchurian poli-

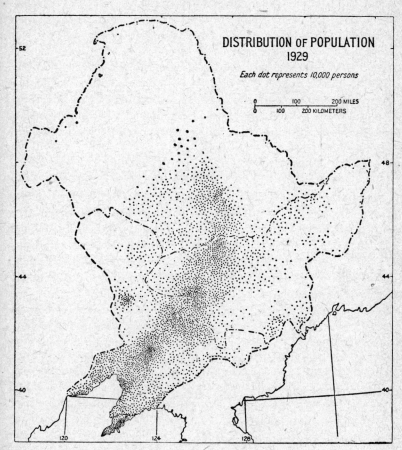

MANCHURIA. *Courtesy of the "Geographical Review," published by the American Geographical Society of New York.*

tics, in so far as it was not controlled by Russia or Japan, was run by Chang Tso-lin, an erstwhile bandit who had turned statesman. Chang, like the war-lords of any other province, "alternately supported, attacked, or declared his territory independent of the Central Government," but this did not mean that the people of Manchuria "wished to be separated from China" or that the goal of Chang himself was to set up a separate nation-state. On the contrary, it was a part of the strategy by which one *tuchun* or another hoped to exterminate his rivals and to emerge as head of a unified national China. Although Chang's armies acted at times as though they were allied with the forces of the Kuomintang, the Old Marshal was not in general a supporter of the Party's doctrines; yet he favored the unification of China, and, if he had possessed the power to do so, he would have ousted both the Russians and the Japanese from their Manchurian spheres of influence. It was he who prepared the way for the attack on the Chinese Eastern Railway in 1929, and who initiated a policy of Chinese railway construction "which was to cut off the [Japanese] South Manchuria Railway from some of its feeder districts." Although he was long reputed a friend of Japan, he appeared less willing in his last years to permit Japan's "special position" to go unchallenged.[2]

MANCHURIA UNDER CHANG HSUEH-LIANG, 1928

The Young Marshal, Chang Hsueh-liang, who succeeded as ruler of Manchuria after his father came to a violent end in 1928, was in many respects an ardent Nationalist. He, too, resented the presence of Russia and Japan, and in particular the tendency of the latter to give gratuitous advice.[3] Accordingly, in December, 1928, he announced his allegiance to the Nanking Government, accepted the Nationalist flag, and in turn was made commander-in-chief of the North-Eastern Frontier Army and was confirmed as chief of administration of Manchuria, of Jehol, and part of Inner Mongolia. So far as the internal administration of Manchuria was involved, the new allegiance to Nanking was nominal rather than real. To be sure, a Manchurian headquarters of the Kuomintang was established but, in reality, "the old system and its personnel continued to function as before"; the Nanking Government merely confirmed what the Manchurian authorities were pleased to do. There was nothing particularly unusual about this system for it was in conformity with well-established Chinese habits and practice.

However, if there was little change in domestic policy, the allegiance of Manchuria to the National Government produced results of great consequence in foreign policy. To the "forward policy" adopted by the Old Marshal before his death was now added a "well-organized and

---

[2] League of Nations, *Report of the Commission of Inquiry* [The Lytton Commission] (Geneva, 1932), 24-30.

[3] See p. 566.

systematic Kuomintang propaganda" which dwelt ceaselessly "on the primary importance of the recovery of lost sovereign rights, the abolition of unequal treaties and the wickedness of imperialism." This propaganda was extremely effective in Manchuria, where the presence of the foreigner with his special rights was more obtrusive than in any other part of China, with the possible exception of Shanghai. As a result, Russians, both Reds and Whites, and Japanese, including Koreans as Japanese subjects, soon felt the effects of a "systematic persecution" manifesting itself through popular agitation or in specific acts such as the raising of rents or refusals to renew contracts.[4]

In Manchuria, as in other parts of China, there was the tendency for the official Kuomintang "line" to focus upon the foreigner and imperialism as the cause of all China's trouble, to the exclusion of other contributing factors. Among these contributory factors were the military dictatorship and the administrative bureaucracy through which the Young Marshal ruled the Three Eastern Provinces. Under the system, military expenses consumed about 80 percent of total expenditure. The Manchurian armies numbered about one fourth of a million men equipped from an arsenal reputed to have cost $200,000,000 (silver). "The treasury was not capable of paying adequate salaries to the officials. As all power rested in the hands of a few military men, office could be owned only through them. Nepotism, corruption, and maladministration continued to be unavoidable consequences of this state of affairs." Taxes were progressively raised, and when even these revenues proved inadequate, there was the handy practice by which the authorities steadily depreciated irredeemable provincial currencies. To a very great extent by 1930, the Manchurian militarists controlled the banks, which in turn bought the harvests with irredeemable and depreciating paper with the idea of forcing the foreign buyers, notably the Japanese, to pay higher prices. The result was to impoverish the Chinese farmer and to infuriate the Japanese.[5] Yet in all this maladjustment there were some signs of improvement. The Chinese peasant and Chinese capital were playing under the Changs a greater part than ever before in Manchurian development. There were signs of stronger social and economic relations with China Proper. Chinese capital had undertaken river conservancy, a harbor project at Hulutao, and extensive railroad construction. The Chinese, too, had created an extensive flour milling industry at Harbin. Trade with China Proper was increasing and was

[4] *Report of the Commission of Inquiry,* 30.
[5] *Report of the Commission of Inquiry,* 31.

financed in part by Chinese banks. This increasing interdependence was in itself an encouragement to a nationalistic policy directed against the special privileges of Japan.[6]

SINO-JAPANESE ISSUES IN MANCHURIA PRIOR TO SEPTEMBER 18, 1931

During the quarter of a century before September 1931, the ties which bound Manchuria to the rest of China were growing stronger and, at the same time, the interests of Japan in Manchuria were increasing. Manchuria was admittedly a part of China, but it was a part in which Japan had acquired or claimed such exceptional rights, so restricting the exercise of China's sovereign rights, that a conflict between the two countries was a natural result.[7]

With many of these Japanese rights and concessions the reader is already familiar. They dated back to the Russo-Japanese Treaty of Portsmouth of September, 1905, and the Sino-Japanese Treaty of Peking of December, 1905.[8] They included the Kwantung leased territory, the former Russian railroad from Dairen (Dalny) to Changchun, and the Antung-Mukden Railway. These lines were operated by the South Manchuria Railway Company, which the Japanese government controlled. In addition to working valuable coal mines at Fushun and Yentai, the company administered the railroad zone, where it collected taxes and engaged in many forms of business. By the Sino-Japanese Treaties and Notes of May 25, 1915,[9] the leasehold and the railroad concessions were extended to 99 years, and Japanese subjects in South Manchuria were accorded the right to travel and reside and engage in business, and to lease land for trade, industry, and agriculture. Japan was given rights of priority for railway and certain other loans in South Manchuria and eastern Inner Mongolia. She also acquired preferential rights in the appointment of advisers to the Manchurian government.[10] As a result of these treaties and special concessions, Japan held "an im-

---

[6] The most convenient brief studies on these aspects of Manchurian development are to be found in League of Nations, *Supplementary Documents to the Report of the Commission of Inquiry* (Geneva, 1932). Note especially: Study No. 3, "Chinese Migrations to Manchuria"; No. 4, "Public Finance in Manchuria"; No. 5, "The Currencies of the North-Eastern Provinces"; and No. 6, "Manchuria's Trade with China Proper and with Foreign Countries."

[7] *Report of the Commission of Inquiry,* 37.

[8] See pp. 334 and 339.

[9] See p. 388.

[10] These preferences in loans and advisers were surrendered by Japan at the Washington Conference.

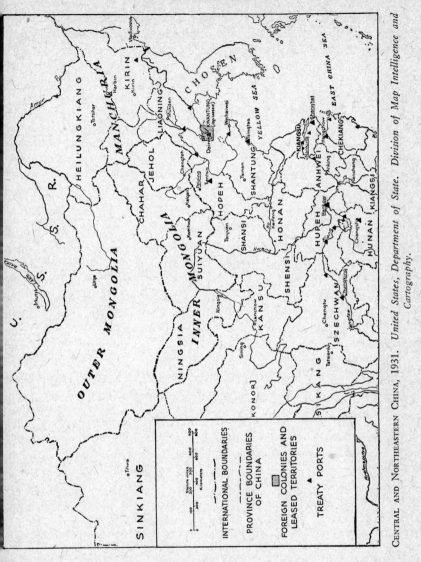

CENTRAL AND NORTHEASTERN CHINA, 1931. *United States, Department of State. Division of Map Intelligence and Cartography.*

portant and unusual position in Manchuria." In the leased territory and the railroad zone she exercised many of the prerogatives of sovereignty. In those portions of larger cities which grew up within the railroad zone, Mukden and Changchun for example, "she controlled the police, taxation, education and public utilities." Her position was protected by the Kwantung army in the leased territory, by railway

guards in the railway zone, and by consular police in various districts.[11]
This enjoyment of economic and administrative privileges by Japan in
the territory of China was a product of stormy historical development
and war. Had it been freely desired or accepted by both sides or had
it been the result of a policy of close collaboration, it is conceivable that
it might have worked smoothly. "But, in the absence of those conditions, it could only lead to friction and conflict." [12]

Manchuria had come to represent, therefore, a fundamental clash of
Sino-Japanese interests. Chinese governments regarded it as their "first
line of defence"; Japanese governments, as their "life-line." Chinese
called it the "granary of China," while the migration of Chinese peasants to it was a sort of safety valve easing the pressure in over-crowded
areas such as Shantung.[13] Japanese stressed that they had won Liaotung in 1895; that they had saved Manchuria from Russia in 1905; that
Japanese capital was principally responsible for the development of the
country; and thus that by reason of patriotic sentiment, needs of defense,
and exceptional treaty rights they had acquired there a "special position." Japan's fixed policy therefore was to secure her Manchurian
vested interests, expand them when and where possible, and to protect
them by fostering the idea that Manchuria and eastern Inner Mongolia
were special areas, distinct from China Proper, and that in these it was
Japan's obligation to maintain peace and order. Efforts of Japan to
implement this policy led to diplomatic conflict on specific issues.

THE SINO-JAPANESE TREATIES OF 1915

Principal among these issues were the conflicts arising out of the Sino-
Japanese Manchurian treaty and notes of May, 1915, with the general
background and history of which the reader is already familiar.[14] After
1915, whereas Japan insisted upon the fulfillment of the treaty, the
Chinese persistently denied its validity. The issues tended to become
more acute after 1928 when the Kuomintang was established in Man-

---

[11] The police power which Japan exercised under extraterritoriality made possible a large
Japanese traffic in opium and in arms. There was a flourishing business in the smuggling
of arms to Chinese bandits, while bandit activities in turn provided the pretext for bringing pressure on the Chinese government. Throughout the South Manchuria Railroad
zone there were Japanese "drug stores" under the protection of extraterritoriality which
were the centers for dispensing opium and smuggled arms. League of Nations, Advisory
Committee on Traffic in Opium and Other Dangerous Drugs, *Report to the Council on the
Work of the Twenty-Third Session*, Geneva, June 7 to 24, 1938. (Official No. C237.M.-
136, 1938. XI).

[12] *Report of the Commission of Inquiry*, 37-38.

[13] *Supplementary Documents to the Report of the Commission of Inquiry*, Study No. 3.

[14] See p. 381.

churia. After 1927, too, there was a movement among the Chinese to divest the South Manchuria Railway of its political and administrative functions, making of it a purely commercial enterprise. This was a very natural nationalistic aspiration but it struck at the very basis of Japan's position, which in Manchuria was definitely political. Furthermore, although the original Russo-Chinese Railway Agreement of 1896 conferred upon the original Chinese Eastern Railway Company the "absolute and exclusive administration of its [railway] lands," the Chinese government denied on legal grounds that this conferred political control in the railway zone. They pointed to other clauses of the agreement which suggested it was never intended that Russia or Japan should exercise broad administrative rights such as police, taxation, education, and public utilities.[15] In addition, the activities of Japanese railway guards, both in and outside the railway zone, and of the Japanese consular police became increasingly irritating as Nationalist sentiment in Manchuria grew. These police were located not only in the railroad areas but also at Japanese consulates in various towns, Harbin, Manchouli, and the Chientao District on the Korean border. Japan claimed that consular police were a proper feature of the extraterritorial system and that they were an extension of the consular courts. The practice was not followed generally by other powers in China but the Japanese justified it by reason of the greater number of their nationals, especially Koreans, living in Manchuria. China claimed that the practice was unnecessary and unwarranted by treaty. Whatever the legalities, the fact was that conflicts occurred between the Chinese police and the Japanese consular police.

The 1915 treaty also conferred on Japanese subjects the right to reside and travel in South Manchuria and to engage in business and industry. In the rest of China under the extraterritorial system foreigners as a class were not permitted to reside or to engage in business outside the treaty ports. China took the view that this right should be withheld until extraterritoriality was abolished and foreigners were subject to China's laws and courts. Because of this view and because they regarded the treaty of 1915 as invalid anyway, the Manchurian authorities adopted various measures to defeat the "residence" clause, such as refusal to issue passports to Japanese and by subjecting them to special taxes.[16]

[15] C. Walter Young, *Japanese Jurisdiction in the South Manchuria Railway Areas* (Baltimore, 1931), 25 ff.
[16] Conflicts over the terms by which Japanese might lease land in Manchuria are treated in the *Report of the Commission of Inquiry*, 54.

KOREANS IN MANCHURIA

A further source of conflict was the presence in Manchuria of 800,000 Koreans who after 1910 were Japanese subjects. As in the case of Japanese, the Chinese opposed acquisition of land in Manchuria by Koreans. Japan, on the other hand, refused to recognize the naturalization of

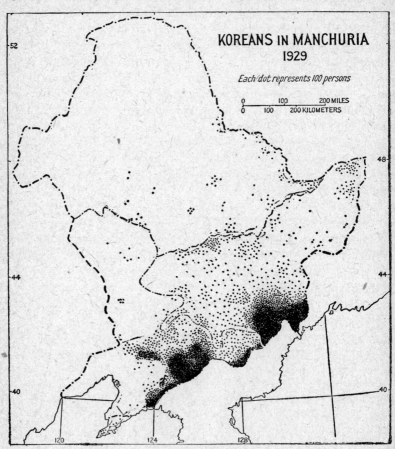

Courtesy of the "Geographical Review," published by the American Geographical Society of New York.

Koreans as Chinese. China resented the use of Japanese consular police to protect the Koreans. In the Chientao District on the Manchurian side of the Korean border, where Koreans greatly outnumbered the Chinese, China attempted various methods of "restriction" which Japan regarded as "unjustifiable." Finally, by 1927 the Manchurian authorities had taken the view that Japan was using the Koreans as "a vanguard of Japanese penetration and absorption." [17]

RAILWAY POLITICS IN MANCHURIA

Railways were one of the sorest spots in Sino-Japanese relations in Manchuria in the years just preceding 1931. Railways in Manchuria were constructed quite as much for political as for economic reasons. This was true of the Russians when they built the Chinese Eastern after 1896; of the Japanese when they took over the South Manchurian line in 1905; and of the Chinese, who began to build in the decade of the 1920's. Following the Russo-Japanese War, the semi-official, efficient, profitable, and wealthy S.M.R. (South Manchuria Railway) made it a policy to finance the construction of only such Chinese lines as would be "feeders" to its own road terminating in the great port of Dairen. The increasing power of this transportation system under Japanese ownership and control, and in fact its very existence, were repugnant to China. The success of the Japanese system, and the resentment which it provoked, stimulated the Chinese after 1924 to embark on their own program of railway construction quite independent of Japanese capital.

The Chinese effort to overcome the Japanese railway monopoly in South Manchuria intensified Sino-Japanese friction and precipitated a conflict on the question of so-called "parallel lines." At the Sino-Japanese conference in Peking, December, 1905, there was entered in the minutes a declaration:

The Chinese Government engages, for the purpose of protecting the interests of the South Manchuria Railway, not to construct, prior to the recovery by it of the said railway, any main line in the neighborhood of and parallel to that railway, or any branch line which might be prejudicial to the interests of the above-mentioned railway.

This engagement was not contained in any formal treaty, but it was at least "a declaration or statement of intention on the part of the Chinese plenipotentiaries." This so-called "protocol" became a bone of Sino-Japanese contention because Japan and China disagreed as to what the statement meant. Japan claimed under it the right to preclude the construction of any Chinese line which the S.M.R. regarded as prejudicial to its system. China's contention was that she was only precluded from building "lines with the deliberate object of unduly impairing the commercial usefulness and value of the South Manchuria Railway."

---

[17] For additional aspects of the Korean problem in Manchuria, see *Report of the Commission of Inquiry*, 55-61, and *Supplementary Documents*, Study No. 9.

The matter was complicated, since there was no mutually acceptable definition as to what constituted a "parallel" line.[18] At all events, China did build railways paralleling the S.M.R. and connecting with Yingkow and Hulutao, and these lines, moreover, were quite successful in diverting traffic away from the S.M.R.

RAILWAY LOAN ISSUES

Further Sino-Japanese trouble in Manchuria was a result of Japanese financing of certain Chinese Government railways. By 1931, Japanese capital and interest to the value of ¥150,000,000 had been expended in the construction of four major and a number of lesser lines.[19] Japan complained that China would not pay the loans or appoint Japanese railway advisers as required by the agreements. China countered Japan's arguments with the contention that the loans were primarily strategic and political; that they had been made by the S.M.R. with the idea of monopolizing railroad construction; that the lines were heavily over-capitalized and for the present could not be put on a paying basis. But here again it was clear that the issues at stake were political. The S.M.R. had made the loans in order to build up feeders to its own system and to preclude an independent Chinese system, even when it was known that the new lines would be unprofitable for many years. On the other hand Chinese Nationalists remembered that some of the Manchurian loans were a part of the Nishihara loans of 1918 made to the Anfu clique government which at that time controlled Peking and which was regarded as having sold out to Japan. Many Nationalists therefore felt justified in repudiating the loan contracts.

A related issue was the controversy over the construction of the important projected railway from Tunhua to Kwainei designed to link Central Manchuria with the northern Korean border and its seaports at Seishin, Rashin, and Yuki. Japan insisted that this line should be built and that China had agreed that Japan should participate in financing it. The Chinese were opposed to the building because they feared Japan would use the new line as an additional means of controlling Manchuria.[20]

[18] Railroad experts attached to the Lytton Commission were of the opinion that "the terminology used is so indefinite that it can be stretched to mean almost anything." It was thus of advantage to Japan not to have a judicial interpretation of the precise meaning of the "protocol." See *Supplementary Documents,* 49.

[19] The four standard-[gauge] lines included: the Kirin-Changchun, the Kirin-Tunhua, the Ssupingkai-Taonan, and the Taonan-Anganchi Railways. The original Sino-Japanese agreements, 1913, for the financing of such lines are in MacMurray, *Treaties,* II, 1054.

[20] Japan rested her basic claim on the Chientao Agreement, Sept. 4, 1909, MacMurray, *Treaties,* I, 796; for the subsequent alleged Sino-Japanese negotiations see *Report of the*

Complicating the situation further was a "war of railway rates" between Japanese and Chinese lines beginning in 1929. The Japanese asserted that the Chinese rates constituted "unfair competition," to which the Chinese replied that their lines, unlike the S.M.R., were not concerned primarily with making profits but rather with assisting the Chinese rural population to reach markets as cheaply as possible. Each side, with ample grounds, accused the other of rate discrimination, secret rebates, etc. Such questions of course were highly technical and there was little possibility of a satisfactory settlement so long as neither side desired settlement by some regularly constituted body such as a railroad commission.

Additional friction centered in the rivalry between the great Japanese port of Dairen in the Kwantung leased territory and the Chinese ports of Yingkow and Hulutao toward which Chinese railway construction was focussed.

Finally, it should be noted that Sino-Japanese negotiations during the first six months of 1931 on the whole complicated problem of railroads resulted in complete failure. In January there was some reason to believe that both sides desired a settlement. By mid-summer it was doubtful whether either side wanted the kind of solution which was attainable through negotiation and compromise.

WANPAOSHAN AND THE KOREAN RIOTS, 1931

Among the immediate incidents forming a prelude to armed conflict in Manchuria was the so-called Wanpaoshan affair and the case of Captain Nakamura. Neither was intrinsically important in itself, yet both demonstrate the way in which incidents may be used to inflame national sentiment when relations are already strained by more fundamental issues.

At Wanpaoshan, a small Manchurian village not far from Changchun, a dispute had arisen in the spring of 1931 between Chinese and Korean farmers over the disputed rights of the latter to construct an irrigation ditch across the lands of the former. Chinese police appeared to protect the Chinese; Japanese consular police, to protect the Koreans. A joint Sino-Japanese investigation having failed to produce an agreement, the Koreans were continuing to dig their ditch assisted by the consular police, when the Chinese farmers drove off the Koreans, filled in part of the ditch, and were in turn dispersed without casualties by fire of the consular police. Then, under police protection, the Koreans

---

Commission of Inquiry, 47; C. Walter Young, The International Relations of Manchuria (Chicago, 1929), 212-215.

again went to work on their ditch and finished it. It was all a perfect example of the kind of petty dispute inevitable under the extraterritorial and consular police system as applied by Japan.[21]

Of much significance, however, was the use that was made of this incident. As a result of sensational accounts in the Japanese and the Korean press, Korea was soon aflame with anti-Chinese riots in which, according to Chinese official accounts, 127 Chinese were killed, 393 were injured, and Chinese property valued at ¥2,500,000 was destroyed. Japan held that the riots were a spontaneous outburst resulting from China's mistreatment of Koreans in Manchuria. The Chinese government on the other hand claimed that Japan had encouraged the outbreak by permitting inaccurate and inflammatory press reports of the Wanpaoshan affair, and that no adequate steps had been taken to suppress the riots until much life and property were destroyed. Japan expressed regret and offered compensation for the bereaved families, but in September, 1931, a settlement of the Wanpaoshan incident had not been reached by the two governments.[22] But this was not all; the events in Korea precipitated a boycott of Japanese goods in China which, with the possible exception of the 1919-21 boycott, was soon to become "the most intense, the most effective, and the most prolonged" of China's efforts to employ this weapon.[23]

THE CASE OF CAPTAIN NAKAMURA

Captain Nakamura, a Japanese military officer on active duty who, while on a mission in Manchuria for the Japanese army, represented himself as an agricultural expert, was killed by Chinese soldiers in northwestern Manchuria, June 27, 1931. The case was broadcast in Japan as a willful insult to the Japanese army. Although the Chinese were dilatory at first in pursuing an investigation, Marshal Chang later sent a mission to Tokyo endeavoring to find a basis for settlement of this and other outstanding questions in Manchuria. By September 18, the Nakamura case had not been settled, but the Manchurian authorities had admitted that Chinese soldiers had killed Nakamura. Negotiations thus seemed to be "progressing favourably" to a settlement.[24]

---

[21] For the legal technicalities involved in the dispute see *Report of the Commission of Inquiry,* 61-62.

[22] Later Chinese reports placed the number killed in the Korean riots at 142 and property damage at more than ¥4,000,000. China, *Memoranda Presented to the Lytton Commission,* I, 262.

[23] C. F. Remer, *A Study of Chinese Boycotts* (Baltimore, 1933), 155-159. Prior to September 18, 1931, this boycott was effective only in Shanghai, Tientsin, and parts of the middle Yangtze region.

[24] Additional details on the Nakamura case will be found in *Report of the Commission of Inquiry,* 63-66. Nakamura was an intelligence officer one of whose primary assign-

SUMMARY: MANCHURIAN ISSUES, SEPTEMBER 18, 1931

The Sino-Japanese Manchurian question as it existed on September 18, 1931, was basically a collision of "irreconcilable policies." The fundamental conflict had been inherent in the general situation since 1905, when Japan first acquired a sphere of influence in South Manchuria. After 1924, and particularly after 1927, the collision of interests became more intense and more apparent. As the tension increased, both sides made some efforts to find solutions by peaceful means through diplomatic negotiations. On the other hand, by 1931 the more extreme Japanese military elements and the more rabid of the young Chinese Nationalists had so aroused public opinion as to render negotiation and compromise virtually impossible. Even had the best of intentions prevailed, peaceful settlement would have required restraint and wisdom. In its simplest form the issue was a contest for political control. As in China Proper, so in Manchuria, the goal of the Nationalists was complete sovereignty, *de facto* as well as *de jure*. This was a goal which Japan, jealously guarding her "special position," was not prepared to concede. It went beyond the concessions which even a Shidehara could make.

Indeed, though Japan was still clinging to the policy of conciliation, internal problems, as well as the Chinese attack upon Japan's vested interests, were preparing the Japanese people for a resumption of the "positive policy" in Manchuria.[25]

Moreover, if in either China or Japan there were those who favored and planned a policy of force to settle Manchurian issues, September, 1931, was a time well chosen. The full force of a great world-wide depression was being felt by every major power. Everywhere the prospects for Europe's proposed disarmament conference were "as dark as they well could be." In Europe there was economic chaos which had called forth the Hoover Moratorium. England deserted the gold standard in September, and in both England and the United States there was economic distress with which neither government seemed able to deal. If force were applied in Manchuria, it was unlikely that Europe or America would interfere effectively to stop it.

SEPTEMBER 18, 1931, AND AFTER

The tension over Sino-Japanese relations in Manchuria was shared by the Chinese and Japanese military forces in the Three Eastern Prov-

---

ments was to estimate the strength of Mongol nationalism and Mongol opposition to Chinese colonization of Mongol lands in western Manchuria.

[25] *Report of the Commission of Inquiry*, 66-67.

inces. On the night of September 18, 1931, Japanese forces seized the city of Mukden. The hostilities were precipitated, according to the Japanese version, by a Chinese attempt to blow up the tracks of the S.M.R. However, the Lytton Commission, appointed later by the League of Nations to investigate conditions in Manchuria, found that

the Japanese . . . had a carefully prepared plan to meet the case of possible hostilities between themselves and the Chinese. On the night of September 18th-19th, this plan was put into operation with swiftness and precision. The Chinese . . . had no plan of attacking the Japanese troops, or of endangering the lives and property of Japanese nationals at this particular time or place. They made no concerted or authorized attack on the Japanese forces and were surprised by the Japanese attack and subsequent operations. . . . The military operations of the Japanese troops during this night . . . cannot be regarded as measures of legitimate self-defense.[26]

In these initial military operations, the Japanese also seized Changchun on September 19, and Kirin on September 21. Also on September 21 China appealed to the League of Nations under Article XI, and requested the United States, a champion of the Briand-Kellogg Pact, to aid in preserving far eastern peace and the principle of peaceful settlement of international disputes.[27] This led to immediate consultation between the Secretary General of the League and the American State Department; the Secretary of State, Henry L. Stimson, gave assurance of American "co-operation and frankness," and expressed the opinion that the Japanese military had ignored the Japanese Foreign Office. It was thus the opinion of the American government that preparation should be made to uphold treaty obligations but that it would be wise for the Western powers "to avoid action which might excite nationalistic feeling in Japan in support of the military and against Shidehara." [28] From this point on, the United States and the major League powers were in virtually constant but hardly effective consultation on the Manchurian dispute. On its part, the League, which had just assembled when the outbreak occurred, requested both China and Japan, September 22, to seek a peaceful settlement by withdrawing their troops. At the same time the League considered sending a commission to investi-

---

[26] *Report of the Commission of Inquiry,* 71. The Commission found that an explosion undoubtedly occurred on or near the railroad, but that the damage, if any, was so slight as not to interfere with the passage of the night express.

[27] Detailed treatment is in W. W. Willoughby, *The Sino-Japanese Controversy and the League of Nations* (Baltimore, 1935), ch. iii; note also U. S., Sen. Doc. No. 55, 72-1, "Conditions in Manchuria," 3.

[28] Henry L. Stimson, *The Far Eastern Crisis* (New York, 1936), 41-42.

gate, and it suggested that the United States make similar proposals to the disputants. For the moment, Stimson did not take to this proposal or to the appointment of an American on the commission as proposed by the League, but, independently, he informed the Japanese, September 22, "that the responsibility for determining the course of events with regard to the liquidating of this [Manchurian] situation rests largely upon Japan," and he hinted that both the Kellogg Pact and the Nine Power Open Door Treaty were at stake.[29] Stimson held that the road to this liquidation lay in "giving Shidehara and the Foreign Office an opportunity, free from anything approaching a threat or even public criticism, to get control of the situation." It was the difficult problem of letting "the Japanese know that we are watching them and at the same time to do it in a way which will help Shidehara."[30]

THE SPREAD OF HOSTILITIES IN MANCHURIA

Meanwhile, affairs were not progressing smoothly in Manchuria. Japanese troops did not withdraw as a result of the League's discreet request. Indeed the Kwantung army announced that it no longer recognized the government of Chang Hsueh-liang, and on October 8, the city of Chinchow, near the border of China Proper, was bombed by Japanese planes. The purpose was to disperse the remnants of Chang's government and army, but its effect was much broader than this, for it was clear indication that the Kwantung army was not to be stopped by fine words and that the League hesitated to take any vigorous action. Simultaneously the United States took a more vigorous stand in supporting "independently" the efforts of the League and in suggesting the course to be pursued. The American Consul at Geneva, Prentiss Gilbert, was authorized to participate in meetings of the League Council involving applicants of the Briand-Kellogg Pact.[31]

Back in Manchuria Japanese forces, ignoring a League resolution of October 24 directing Japan to withdraw her army within the railroad zone by November 16, proceeded to extend their conquests into North Manchuria to the town of Tsitsihar beyond the main line of the Russian-controlled Chinese Eastern Railway, and also to move southward toward Chinchow. With these conquests safely achieved, Japan proposed that the League send the often discussed commission of investigation. On December 10, supported by the Japanese delegate, the

---

[29] Sen. Doc. No. 55, "Conditions in Manchuria," 4-5; Stimson, *Far Eastern Crisis,* 42-47; Russell M. Cooper, *American Consultation in World Affairs* (New York, 1934), 198-201.

[30] Stimson, *Far Eastern Crisis,* 34-37.

[31] *Report of the Commission of Inquiry,* 72; Cooper, *American Consultation in World Affairs,* 207; Willoughby, *The Sino-Japanese Controversy,* 104-110.

League decided to do so. On the following day in Tokyo the Wakat-suki-Shidehara cabinet fell amid a rising tide of popular nationalism. Only a few weeks later the triumph of militarism seemed assured when the Kwantung army, dispersing the last southern remnants of Chang's armies, captured the city of Chinchow, January 2, 1932.[32] The effort to solve the Manchurian conflict by peaceful means had failed. As 1932 advanced Japan completed her military conquest.[33]

REVIVAL OF THE AMERICAN NON-RECOGNITION DOCTRINE

Many and complex circumstances had produced this tragic outcome. Two great powers had clashed on "longstanding problems in Man-churia." Problems of this character, in the words of Secretary Stimson, could "only be settled by the parties concerned." [34] On this basis it be-came the function of the League and other interested powers to find a means of bringing China and Japan together in peaceful negotiation. This seemingly simple goal was not reached. The approaches to it were blocked by the pre-determined purposes of the Japanese army, by the at times unwise diplomacy of China, by the inability of the Western pow-ers to agree readily and with confidence on what should and could be done, by the natural timidity and caution with which governments con-sidered action, the results of which could not be wholly foreseen, and by the confusion of the public mind both in the United States and abroad as to the real issues and how they should be faced.

From the beginning of Manchurian conflict in September, the League powers as well as the United States were well aware of the dangers in-volved. Open conflict between Japan and China was a threat to the Nine-Power Treaty, to the Treaty for the Renunciation of War, to the prestige of the League of Nations itself, and indeed to all governments

[32] For the extension of the Japanese conquest, see the *Report of the Commission of Inquiry*, 72-83: on the resolution of December 10 and subsequent appointment of the Commission, *ibid.*, 6-12.

[33] There were also efforts toward "appeasement" made by the Nanking Government which form a part of the general international effort to solve the Manchurian conflict by peaceful means. Wellington Koo as Foreign Minister suggested a neutral zone around Chinchow. Such efforts at appeasement had important bearing on later events. Among other things these efforts constituted the beginnings of what became a growing suspicion among many Chinese against their government. It might be compared with the later growth of anti-appeasement sentiment in Britain against Chamberlain. The popular opinion in China which eventually welcomed a united front between the government and the communists after the Sian incident of 1936 (see p. 616) owed much of its strength to the fact that this opinion had been in process of growth since 1931-32.

[34] United States, *Foreign Relations, 1931*, III, "The Far East" (Washington, 1946), 411. "We do not care what solution is reached between China and Japan so long as it is done by pacific means." Stimson to Dawes, November 10, 1931.

who regarded their interests as synonymous with the upholding of world peace and the implementation of the principle of collective security. Yet as the closing months of 1931 passed by, and as Japan's military action progressed, neither the League nor the United States applied economic or military sanctions. It was the hope of the American government that peaceful elements in the Japanese government would be encouraged to reassert their influence over the army and its supporters. During 1931, Secretary Stimson did not propose to the powers any anti-Japanese action which Britain or France rejected. Indeed, it was the League powers that sounded out cautiously the American Secretary of State as to whether the United States would support a policy of sanctions. Secretary Stimson gave no encouragement to these inquiries; in fact, his expositions of policy and his instructions to American representatives at Geneva, London, and Paris were hostile to sanctions of any kind involving the United States, other than the sanctions of adverse public opinion and official non-recognition of conquests or settlements achieved by other than peaceful means.

The course which the American government attempted to follow is now quite clear. It was a policy which required the utmost delicacy in its diplomatic application. The attempt was to act "independently" of the League, "reserving full independence of judgment as to each step to be taken," while at the same time "endeavoring to support the general objective of the League, namely, the preservation of peace in Manchuria." As early as November 19 the American government had determined these limits to its policy and actions. Instructing Charles G. Dawes in Paris, Secretary Stimson said:

We do not see how we can do anything more ourselves as a government than to announce our disapproval and to announce that we will not recognize any treaties which may be forced by Japan under the pressure of military occupation. We do not ourselves believe in the enforcement of any embargo by our own government, although we would not probably in any way allow our government to interfere through the fleet with any embargo by anyone else. We believe an embargo is a step to war and if an embargo is decided upon by the League, it would be very likely for that embargo to lead to war.[35]

---

[35] United States, *Foreign Relations, 1931*, III, "The Far East," 494-496. In his search for a policy, Secretary Stimson was limited from the beginning by this country's military unpreparedness for war, and by the anti-war temper of both Congress and the people as well as other factors. Nevertheless, the Secretary's hope of strengthening the Japanese moderates by adopting a mild policy was soon shown by the sequence of events to be fundamentally unsound as a solution of the crisis. Its principal effect was to encourage the Japanese militarists.

Japan's course in Manchuria was, in the Secretary's view, a flagrant violation of treaties and a threat to the whole structure of peace, but he did not at this time regard war against Japan as the proper solution.[36]

Such was in brief the background of the action taken by Secretary Stimson on January 7, 1932, when, after informing the British and the French of his intentions but without waiting for their concurrence, he informed China and Japan that the United States

. . . cannot admit the legality of any situation de facto nor does it intend to recognize any treaty or agreement entered into between those governments, or agents thereof, which may impair the treaty rights of the United States or its citizens in China, including those which relate to the sovereignty, the independence, or the territorial and administrative integrity of the Republic of China, or to the international policy relative to China, commonly known as the open-door policy; and that it does not intend to recognize any situation, treaty, or agreement which may be brought about by means contrary to the covenants and obligations of the Pact of Paris, of August 27, 1928, to which treaty both China and Japan, as well as the United States, are parties.[37]

The United States was moving slowly from a policy of conciliation toward one of diplomatic coercion. The non-recognition doctrine was a reassertion of Secretary Bryan's position of May, 1915, whereas the note as a whole was a reassertion of traditional American policy since the time of Secretary Hay. As in former cases, the note assumed erroneously that Britain and France would see their far eastern interests as identical with those of the United States.[38] Neither Britain nor France associated themselves with this American move. Neither power was any more prepared to stop Japan in Manchuria in 1932 than it was when Japan first entered Manchuria between 1905 and 1910.

HOSTILITIES SPREAD TO SHANGHAI

Toward the end of January, 1932, Sino-Japanese hostilities spread from Manchuria to Shanghai, where a most effective boycott of Japa-

---

[36] A general war against Japan does appear to have been favored by some of China's representatives, including Dr. Alfred Sze, at Paris, as indicated by a telephonic exchange between Stimson in Washington and Dawes in Paris, November 19, 1931:

Dawes: That [an embargo leading to war] is what Sze wants to do.
Secretary [Stimson]: Yes, Sze would like very much to get all the nations of the world in war with Japan.
Dawes: Exactly.
Secretary [Stimson]: We have no sympathy with that and we do not intend to get into war with Japan. (Foreign Relations, 1931, III, 496-497.)

[37] Sen. Doc. No. 55, "Conditions in Manchuria," 53-54.

[38] A. W. Griswold, The Far Eastern Policy of the United States (New York, 1938), 422-425; also Foster Rhea Dulles, China and America (Princeton, 1946), 189-201, for American public reactions.

nese goods was in progress. Here too incidents led to demands by the Japanese navy and eventually to a naval offensive against Chinese sections of the city. But unlike the policy of retreat in Manchuria, at Shanghai, a Chinese army (the 19th Route Army) held its position until the arrival early in March of heavy Japanese army reinforcements. These hostilities at Shanghai, however, were of greater effect upon British opinion than anything which had happened in Manchuria, for, as Stimson hoped, they startled "the merchants of Great Britain into a realization of what Japanese aggression towards China ultimately meant to them." [39] As a result there was a greater disposition to co-operate with the United States. The British protested Japanese bombings at Shanghai, and concurrently with the United States sent naval and marine reinforcements to the International Settlement. Meanwhile, China invoked Articles X and XV of the Covenant, under which the League would be required to assess responsibility and eventually perhaps to apply sanctions. This led to appointment of a League committee at Shanghai consisting of the local consular representatives of the League states to report directly on conditions there. [40] When the Japanese requested the good offices of the neutral powers to re-establish peace at Shanghai, it seemed that Anglo-American efforts were succeeding, but since the terms proposed by the powers were not acceptable to Japan, the effort failed. [41] Meanwhile, in Manchuria the Japanese had moved rapidly to consolidate their political as well as their military position. They had encouraged and promoted the organization of local self-governing administrations throughout Manchuria which were gradually combined in a new "State" that declared its independence of China and the Kuomintang on February 18, 1932. [42] Six days later, February 24, the developing policy of the United States was revealed in a letter from Secretary Stimson to Senator William E. Borah, Chairman of the Senate Foreign Relations Committee. It set forth that a situation had been created in the Far East in clear violation of the Nine-Power Treaty and the Briand-Kellogg Pact; that the Nine-Power Treaty was merely one of a group of "interrelated and interdependent" treaties; that the willingness of the United States in 1922 to restrict the fortifications of the Philippines and to surrender its freedom in capital ship construction was predicated on the assumption that other powers would accept the self-

[39] Stimson, *Far Eastern Crisis*, 134.

[40] League of Nations, *Report of the Committee of Inquiry*. The Committee was set up at Shanghai under Art. XV, Paragraph 1, of the Covenant. (A [Extr.] 3. Geneva, 1932).

[41] Willoughby, *The Sino-Japanese Controversy*, 320-323.

[42] For the development of this movement, see *Report of the Commission of Inquiry*, 88-93.

denying ordinances imposed by the Nine-Power Treaty. While this letter was a general appeal to the powers to join the United States in the non-recognition doctrine, it had other specific objectives. Stimson hoped to encourage China; to clarify policy to the American public; to influence the coming Assembly of the League of Nations; to remind the Conservative British government of its responsibilities under the Nine-Power Open Door Treaty which Balfour had helped to write; and finally he hoped it would be a suggestion to Japan that if the Nine-Power Treaty was of no importance to her, other powers might decide that other treaties of great consequence to Japan were of little importance to them.[43]

For a time there appeared to be some slight improvement in the far eastern problem. On March 12, 1932, the League Assembly aligned itself with the non-recognition doctrine through a resolution proposed by the British. This resolution declared

. . . that it is incumbent upon the members of the League of Nations not to recognize any situation, treaty or agreement which may be brought about by any means contrary to the Covenant of the League of Nations or to the Pact of Paris.[44]

Then, in May, China and Japan made peace at Shanghai on terms worked out by the consular committee of the League. The subsequent withdrawal of the Japanese forces did not, however, indicate any major change in Japanese policy. The withdrawal was due rather to the stubborn resistance of the 19th Route Army and the danger of too great involvement with the other powers at Shanghai while the Manchurian situation was as yet unstabilized.[45]

These improvements, if such they could be called, were at best temporary. The League's disarmament conference in the spring of 1932 revealed the inability of Europe and America to unite on that fundamental problem, let alone present an effective united front against Japan. As a result Japan was accorded a virtual free hand in Manchuria. On March 9, the former and last Manchu emperor of China, now known as Mr. Henry Pu-yi, became regent of the new state of Manchukuo, and on September 15, Japan in a treaty extended formal recognition to that "offspring of aggression." Less than a month later, October 2, the report of the League's investigating body, the Lytton Commission, was

---

[43] Stimson, *Far Eastern Crisis*, 175.

[44] Willoughby, *The Sino-Japanese Controversy*, 299-301.

[45] Negotiations of the peace at Shanghai are treated by A. J. Toynbee, ed., *Survey of International Affairs, 1932*, 502-515; Willoughby, *Sino-Japanese Controversy*, ch. xiv.

published. Its appearance could not but be anti-climactic in the light of all that had happened since September 18, 1931.

THE REPORT OF THE COMMISSION OF INQUIRY

On the course of immediate events, the influence of the report was nil, but as an historic document, as a clarification of the real issues at stake, and as a plan for peaceful settlement (for anyone who wanted a peaceful settlement), its importance can hardly be overestimated.[46]

The report presented Manchuria as a complex product of historical development involving conditions unparalleled elsewhere, and found that neither a restoration of the *status quo ante* nor the continued maintenance of Manchukuo provided a satisfactory solution. On the contrary the report proposed ten conditions regarded as indispensable to any satisfactory solution.

1. A solution which did not find a compatible basis for the interests of both China and Japan would not be a gain for the cause of peace.

2. There must be consideration of the interests of the U. S. S. R.

3. There should be conformity with existing multilateral treaties: the Covenant of the League, the Pact of Paris, and the Nine-Power Open Door Treaty.

4. Recognition of the rights and interests of Japan which "are facts and which cannot be ignored."

5. The establishment of new and clarifying treaty relations between Japan and China.

6. Effective provision for the settlement of future disputes through machinery "facilitating the prompt settlement of minor disputes as they arise."

7. "The government in Manchuria should be modified in such a way as to secure, consistently with the sovereignty and administrative integrity of China, a large measure of autonomy designed to meet the local conditions and special characteristics of the Three Provinces."

8. Establishment of internal order and security from aggression through an effective local gendarmerie and the withdrawal of all armed forces other than gendarmerie.

9. Encouragement of an economic *rapprochement* between China and Japan on the basis of a new commercial treaty.

[46] Members of the Commission included: H. E. Count Aldrovandi (Italian), Général de Division Henri Claudel (French); the Rt. Hon. the Earl of Lytton (British), who served as chairman; H. E. Dr. Heinrich Schnee (German); and Major-General Frank Ross McCoy (American), who served with the approval of the United States Department of State but as an official representative of the League and not of the United States. This was a nice distinction, since the United States was not a member of the League, though so far as the Manchurian dispute was concerned the United States in the opinion of many had gone a long way toward entering the League by the back door.

10. Finally, "since the present political instability of China is an obstacle to friendship with Japan and an anxiety to the rest of the world (as the maintenance of peace in the Far East is a matter of international concern), and since the conditions enumerated above cannot be fulfilled without a strong Central Government in China, the final requisite for a satisfactory solution is temporary international co-operation in the internal reconstruction of China, as suggested by the late Dr. Sun Yat-sen."

JAPAN'S REPLY TO THE REPORT

Japan's reply to the findings of the Commission was presented to the Council of the League, November 21, 1932. It insisted that Japan alone was the judge as to whether her military action was justifiable self defense; that the creation of Manchukuo resulted from the "spontaneous character of the independence movement among the people of Manchuria"; that there had been no violation of the Nine-Power Treaty or the Covenant of the League of Nations; and finally that the solutions proposed by the Commission were "too refined and intricate" to meet conditions as they existed in the Far East. The Japanese government therefore asserted that since in the view of the Commission its proposals could not be applied "without a strong Central Government in China," and since there was no assurance of such a government even under international control, Japan could not "idly wait for such an uncertain eventuality in order to solve the Manchurian question." [47]

THE LEAGUE AND THE LYTTON REPORT

In the League, the report of the Commission of Inquiry was considered by a special Committee of Nineteen which in February, 1933, recommended: 1) non-recognition of Manchukuo, 2) a Manchurian government compatible with Chinese sovereignty, and 3) an invitation to Japan and China to undertake direct negotiations under the good offices of a League commission. Japan's response was the invasion of Jehol province in January, 1933; a dramatic scene at Geneva where the Japanese delegation walked out of the Assembly, February 24; and finally, March 27, Japan's announcement of her resignation from the League which under terms of the Covenant would become effective in two years time. Meanwhile, Japanese armies were completing the conquest of Jehol province, capturing Chengteh, the capital, March 4. Other forces invaded the Pei-p'ing (Bei-ping) area south of the Great Wall, where at Tangku a truce was signed, May 31, 1933, creating a broad "demilitarized neutral" zone from which all Chinese military forces were excluded. This invasion of North China pointed directly

---

[47] League of Nations, *Observations of the Japanese Government on the Report of the Commission of Inquiry* (Geneva, 1932).

to new phases in the problem created by Japan's conquest of Manchuria. This was the question of who was to control North China. Was it to become an integral part of an expanding national China centered at Nanking; was it to be swallowed up by an expanding Manchukuo; or was it to be molded into some kind of autonomous buffer state between the two? [48] The Japanese had long made it clear "that they considered North China to be an essential partner in the Japan-Manchukuo economic bloc" then emerging. By 1935, therefore, the Kwantung army was attempting to create a five-province autonomous North China comprising Chahar, Suiyuan, Shansi, Hopei, and Shantung, an area which if fully exploited would add much to Japan's economic requirements in coal, iron ore, and raw cotton.[49]

IN SUMMARY

The events described in preceding pages of this chapter constituted war in every sense save the legal one recognized by international law. By the application of force, by large-scale hostilities, Japan had gained control of nearly half a million square miles of Chinese territory, yet here was something which the international legal opinion of governments did not regard as war, and which the Japanese euphemistically termed an "incident." [50] It was in reality one of those extraordinary phenomena of the twentieth century—peaceful war, or war that is not war at all.[51] Nevertheless, whatever one might call these events, their effect was to reshape the Far East more radically than any previous "incident" since the British in 1842 had fashioned the Treaty of Nanking as the gauge of China's relations with the powers. This becomes more evident when it is recognized that Japan's creation of Manchukuo was an effort to establish a continental power in Asia as a counterbalance to the maritime power which Western nations had exercised over China through nearly a century.[52] The task was more difficult than anything the West had essayed in China during the nineteenth century because Japanese plans ran counter to the new twentieth-century force of Chinese nationalism. Yet in one respect the problem itself had not changed, for it was still a question of who should control China and of

---

[48] George E. Taylor, *The Struggle for North China* (New York, 1940), 17. On Japan's withdrawal from the League, see League of Nations, *Official Journal*, XIV (1933), 657-658.

[49] Taylor, *The Struggle for North China*, 119.

[50] On the legal nature of war, see C. C. Hyde, *International Law* (3 vols., 2nd rev. ed., Boston, 1945), III, 1679 ff.

[51] See L. H. Woolsey, "Peaceful War in China," *American Journal of International Law*, XXXII (1938), 314-319; and C. G. Fenwick, "War without a Declaration," *ibid.*, XXXI (1937), 694-696.

[52] Owen Lattimore, *The Mongols of Manchuria* (New York, 1934), 15.

how that control should be exercised, just as it had been back in 1897 and 1898 when the Western powers delimited their spheres of influence and guarded them with their own naval bases on Chinese soil.

In a broader sense, the Manchurian "incident" was a second and more disheartening test of collective security as a principle, and of the means of enforcing it. As Russia used direct action in North Manchuria in 1929, so Japan used force in South Manchuria and North China from 1931 to 1933. Although the League of Nations performed a most useful task through the investigations of the Lytton Commission, neither France nor Great Britain, the powers which dominated the League, was prepared to apply sanctions against Japan without the active support of the United States.

The premises on which American policy rested have already been stated, and, it would seem, the question of applying sanctions was settled for all the powers when they received no encouragement from Washington in 1931. Moreover, any attempt to evaluate the events of 1931 as a test of collective security is complicated by the fact that though the United States co-operated to a limited degree with the League, this country remained outside the world's only permanent machinery dedicated to the principle of collective security, and the American administration was constantly fearful of the public reaction should it appear that this country was using Manchuria as a back-door entry into the League. In reality, American policy, as the Manchurian affair developed in 1931, remained true to traditional principles of the open door and the integrity of China as embodied in the Washington Treaties, and it called upon Japan to observe these covenants and the Treaty for the Renunciation of War. It prodded the League toward similar action. Whether more could have been expected from a government representative of the same political party which a decade earlier had repudiated the Wilsonian program of collective security is a matter on which there is no general agreement. At all events, neither the League nor the United States nor the two together stopped Japan, and, as on a previous occasion in 1915, the integrity of China was not preserved by reassertion of the non-recognition doctrine. This meant that the forces motivating Japan's drive on the continent were stronger than the forces which the powers were prepared to use in an effort to stop her. Japan had chosen her time well. She was convinced that though the world might use fair and even vigorous words, it would oppose her with neither economic nor military sanctions. In this her judgment proved to be only too sound. Collective security as an effective weapon, judged in the light of the Manchurian affair of 1931, was still a distant ideal.

CHAPTER 34

THE TRUCE BETWEEN TWO UNDECLARED WARS: 1933-1937

FROM the Tangku agreement of 1933 until July, 1937, the Far East re-lapsed into an uneasy, an uncertain, and an unstable period of peace. For Japan there was the problem of digesting the political and economic harvest garnered under the name Manchukuo. For China there was the problem of salvaging and re-creating material and spiritual strength in anticipation of further Japanese expansion. For the League of Nations and the United States there was the perplexing question of how to implement the non-recognition doctrine which thus far had failed utterly to curb Japan's armies. Could some compromise yet be found between the aspirations of Chinese nationalism and the expansive fever of Japanese imperialism? The emphatic answer given to this question in 1937 will be more understandable in the light of some relevant discussion of: 1) the policies of the United States and the League after 1931; 2) Japan's political and economic development during the same period; and 3) the effects of the Manchurian Incident on China's domestic politics.

THE NEW ORIENTATION IN AMERICAN POLICY

The Roosevelt-Hull administration of 1933 recognized the failure of the Stimson efforts. While surrendering no principles, the new administration turned to new tactics. While desisting from provocative note-writing, which had seemed only to encourage the militarists, it sought to relieve the tension left by Stimson in American-Japanese relations. On the other hand, it continued to co-operate and to bolster the timid efforts of the League for collective security; and on November 16, 1933, it officially recognized Soviet Russia. While this recognition was aimed basically toward a revival of foreign trade and toward ending the anomaly in which for more than a decade there had been no formal relations between the United States and the *de facto* government of 160,000,000 peoples, its significance was not lost upon Japan. Beyond these mild efforts the United States was not prepared to go. Like the

597

League, the United States had found no effective means of opposing Japan short of war. At home, the administration was involved in efforts to defeat the disastrous depression. The American people were in no mood for war and, as the Japanese judged their temper, were too busy with domestic affairs to pay serious attention to the Far East.[1] From 1932 until after 1937, the United States did not contemplate the use of force to implement its far eastern policy. It was not until 1938 that this country really began to acquire a treaty-strength navy.[2] These were years in which the perspective of Americans was circumscribed within domestic efforts to end the depression and in which American political philosophy leaned heavily toward the doctrines of pacifism and isolationism.[3] Prior to 1937, no act imposing isolationism on the administration was vetoed by Roosevelt.[4] Even after the renewal of war in the Far East in July, 1937, the policy of the United States, as expressed by Secretary Hull, was perforce one of moralizing on the virtues of peace and on the exercise of self-restraint among nations.[5] The American public was in the dangerous position of believing that Japan should be punished, of approving the public condemnation of her aggression, yet of warning its own government not to become involved in war.[6] The Nye Munitions Investigation of 1934 intensified the already strong predisposition to isolationism, and the Neutrality Act of 1935 was meant to make it impossible for the country "to be dragged into war."[7] Though American sympathy for China remained firm, there were many who, when hostilities again broke in China in 1937, were prepared to invoke the neutrality law, even though this would preclude China from receiving from us the sinews of war. Moreover, the decision of the United States, made in the Tydings-McDuffie Act, March 24, 1934, to grant independence to the Philippines appeared to confirm the prevalent conviction that the isolationists were in control of Amer-

---

[1] The attitude was typical of many of Japan's leaders after the Manchurian affair of 1931-32.

[2] Basil Rauch, *The History of the New Deal: 1933-1938* (New York, 1944), 152.

[3] These forces were felt keenly by American diplomatic representatives in the Far East. Cf. Joseph C. Grew, *Ten Years in Japan* (New York, 1944), 23, 71.

[4] Rauch, *The History of the New Deal*, 155.

[5] "This country constantly and consistently advocates maintenance of peace. We advocate national international self-restraint. We advocate abstinence of all nations from use of force in pursuit of policy and from interference in the internal affairs of other nations." United States, Department of State, *Press Releases* (Washington, D. C., 1937), July 16, 1937, 41-42.

[6] Eleanor Tupper and G. E. McReynolds, *Japan in American Public Opinion* (New York, 1937), 357, 398-401.

[7] United States, Department of State, *Peace and War: United States Foreign Policy, 1931-1941* (Washington, D. C., 1942), 24.

ican foreign policy, and that the United States was about to pull out of the Far East.[8]

Indeed, in the six years which followed the invasion of Manchuria there was no serious threat from the outside world to Japan's conquests. Whatever the public opinion of the world may have been, this opinion was never translated into practical sanctions against Japan. No Western government either within or without the League was ready to apply economic sanctions against Japan, much less to make war upon her for the sake of China's integrity. To this degree, China and Japan were left to their own devices. What these devices were must now be our purpose to relate.

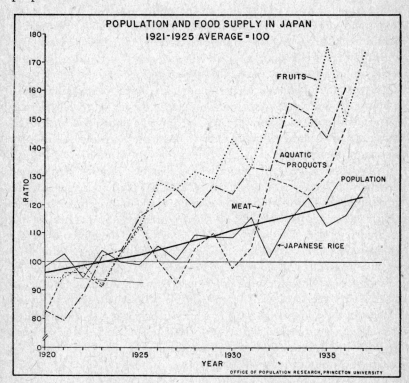

United States, Department of State. Division of Map Intelligence and Cartography.

JAPANESE POLITICS AND GOVERNMENT, 1931-1937

In June, 1932, shortly after his arrival in Tokyo as the new Ambassador of the United States, Joseph Clark Grew noted that "one thing is

[8] A. W. Griswold, *The Far Eastern Policy of the United States* (New York, 1938), 454.

certain and that is that the military are distinctly running the Government and that no step can be taken without their approval." [9]

It will be recalled that the decade from 1920 onward had been notable as a period in which representative and responsible government appeared to be making steady headway. With the fall of Tanaka's "positive policy" cabinet in 1929, the less provocative *Minseito* returned to power with a cabinet headed by Yuko (the Lion) Hamaguchi as Premier and Shidehara again at the Foreign Office. It was this government which accepted the London Naval Treaty despite powerful domestic opposition from the navy and patriotic societies; it advocated retrenchment and reform at home—a platform which was by no means pleasing to the party politicians or the militarists who wanted more troops and more weapons; and it finally resumed the policy of conciliation toward China. Although the Hamaguchi government found favor with the liberal elements of Japanese society, it was thoroughly hated by the militarists and by the bulk of the aristocracy and the bureaucrats. To these latter, Hamaguchi personified a political philosophy which if pursued to its logical conclusion would lead the nation toward democracy, would curb the more radical and unscrupulous advocates of expansion, and would eventually deprive the aristocracy and the military services of their special privileges under the Constitution.

In November, 1930, Hamaguchi was shot by a young fanatic, and although he lived until the following April, he could no longer lead the government. The loss of his leadership was a blow from which his policies never recovered. The *ad interim* premiership was held at first by Shidehara and later by Wakatsuki. Neither of these men possessed Hamaguchi's skill in holding the party politicians in line. Shidehara was a bureaucrat with no party popularity. Wakatsuki, irresolute and relying heavily on compromise, was in no sense a dynamic leader. In other words, the passing of Hamaguchi left Shidehara without strong support in the cabinet on his China policy. This was one of the circumstances which prompted the army to act in Manchuria in September, 1931, leaving it to the Foreign Office to explain to the powers as best it could. Beginning then in 1931, there was a sharp revival of dual government as the army continued to pursue its policies in China largely independent of the Foreign Office. As Secretary Stimson had noted, after September 18, 1931, the Japanese Foreign Office no longer controlled Japanese foreign policy.

In December, 1931, the helpless *Minseito* government resigned, and was followed by a *Seiyukai* ministry under Ki Inukai, who in 1929 had succeeded Tanaka as president of the party. The general election of

[9] Grew, *Ten Years in Japan*, 6-14.

January, 1932, returned a large *Seiyukai* majority, and this encouraged
the cabinet to play with the army by reasserting the positive policy
which the army was already practicing in the field. But the tide of
officially inspired opinion in Japan was now running fast toward an
ultra-nationalism which even the chauvinism of the *Seiyukai* could not
satisfy. Beginning in February, 1932, Japan witnessed a series of political assassinations, culminating in the murder of Premier Inukai on
May 15. Korekiyo Takahashi, Finance Minister, temporarily succeeded
to the premiership. The nation was already in the midst of a political
crisis, hastened by the Manchurian Incident. The day of the party politicians was all but ended. The day of the reactionary, of the militarist,
and of Japan's unique type of fascism had begun.[10]

THE MILITARY CLASS IN POWER

In 1932, then, the movement toward civilian representative government dominated by political parties and financed by the *Zaibatsu,* the

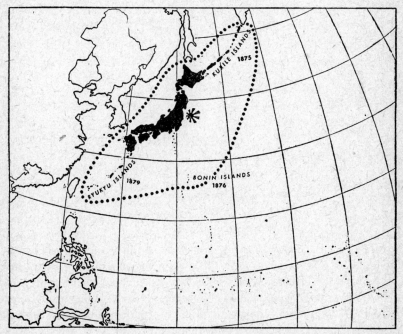

JAPAN, 1875-1890. *Maps appearing on pages 601-608 are reproduced from "A War
Atlas for Americans," Simon and Schuster, Inc., New York, 1944. They are reproduced
by permission from Simon and Schuster, Inc., and from United States, Department of
State, Division of Map Intelligence and Cartography.*

[10] R. K. Reischauer, *Japan: Government-Politics* (New York, 1939), 154-157.

wealthy industrial and landed families, came to an end. More and more in the succeeding decade political power was to gravitate into the hands of the military caste which in foreign affairs was ambitious to further Japan's conquests in China and which at home was to emerge as the advocate of political, economic, and social reforms expounded as the principle of *Kodo*, the Imperial Way. This was the concept of a totalitarian and divine state of which a divine emperor following the Imperial Way was the living embodiment. The instrument of this re-

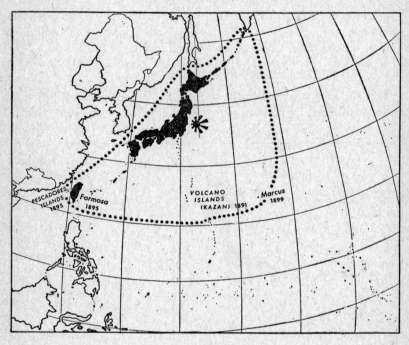

JAPAN, 1891-1904.

vival of divine dictatorship was, as noted, the military caste, not an individual. Thus there was never in Japan a personal dictatorship in the sense in which Hitler and Mussolini might be so described, or even in the milder sense in which Chiang K'ai-shek resolved factionalism within China's Kuomintang. Apart therefore from the emperor's "divine" leadership, always impersonal and supposedly far removed from politics and the people, dictatorship in Japan, in so far as it has existed, has been the rule of a group, or caste, or a coalition of groups. Even in the case of this military caste, after 1931 there was never complete unity or complete and exclusive control. The political picture remained confused, since civil bureaucrats representing many shades of political thought continued to hold high ministerial posts.

NATIONAL CABINETS

Moreover, there was no immediate victory for the extreme militarists. Instead, in 1932, upon the advice of the aged Prince Saionji, the last of the Genro, Japan turned to so-called "national cabinets" designed to

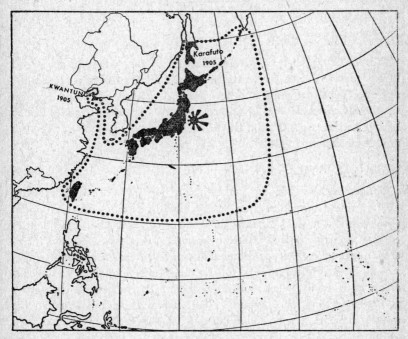

JAPAN, 1905-1909.

represent a compromise between the party "liberals" on the one hand and the extreme militarists, chauvinists, and ultra-nationalistic patriots on the other. As an example, the new cabinet formed in 1932 after Inukai's assassination was headed by Admiral Viscount Makoto Saito. Saito was the answer to those who wanted "safe" statesmanship to bring the nation through the current foreign and domestic crisis. He was acceptable to the militarists because he was an admiral; to privileged society because he was a member of the aristocracy; to the seemingly bankrupt political parties because, although not a party man, he had shown no violent opposition to the parties; and to the nation as a whole because he might be expected to follow the middle of the road.[11]   The Saito cabinet included five party members (three from the *Seiyukai,* two from the *Minseito*), two bureaucrats, three militarists, and three members of the House of Peers.   In general, this was the type of political coalition which appeared in the succeeding cabinet of Admiral Keisuke Okada, July 8, 1934, and the later cabinet of Koki Hirota, March 9, 1936.   By 1937, however, the trend against the political parties was intensified. The cabinet formed by General Senjuro Hayashi in February contained no party members.[12]

RESHUFFLING THE POLITICAL PARTIES

Meanwhile the party politicians, alarmed by the growing influence of the militarists, sought to revive their prestige through new leadership, new aggressive platforms, and new parties.   Typical of the new parties was the *Kokumin Domei* (National Union Party) organized by Kenzo Adachi and insurgents from the *Minseito,* which advocated a vigorous totalitarian, fascist regime.[13]

ARAKI AS SPOKESMAN OF THE NEW POLITICAL TIMES

The decline and the later final eclipse of Japan's political parties after 1930 are understandable when it is recalled that parties in the modern sense were still in their infancy; that their allegiance was to personalities and not to firmly rooted political principles; that they had sold themselves to the great *Zaibatsu* houses, Mitsui and Mitsubishi in particular, and thus had forfeited any claim to broad popular support from the electorate; and, finally, when it is remembered that in general the parties lacked leadership.   To be sure, Hara, Hamaguchi, and Inukai were commoners with a wide following, but, of the three, only Hamaguchi combined political idealism with the craft of the politician.   Too frequently the parties had found it expedient to accept the leadership of an avowed militarist such as Tanaka.   Compromise of this kind was not only to be expected, it was inevitable under the unique constitutional system which Ito had devised to preserve ultimate political power within the hands of the military-feudal aristocracy.   When therefore at the time of the Manchurian Incident, Japan faced an accumulation of political, economic, and social maladjustments at home and a crisis in her

---

[11] Ippei Fukuda, *Sketches of Men and Life* (Tokyo, 1933), 27-35.

[12] *The Japan Year Book, 1938-39* (Tokyo, 1938), 144.

[13] On the parties in this period note Hugh Borton, *Japan Since 1931* (New York, 1940), 16-20.

relations with China and the powers abroad, no voice which the political parties could raise commanded either the respect or the faith of the nation.[14]

There were voices, however, to which an increasing number of Japanese were ready to listen, because these expressed a politico-religious philosophy deeply rooted in Japanese history and tradition. Most eloquent of these voices was that of General Sadao Araki, who had risen from

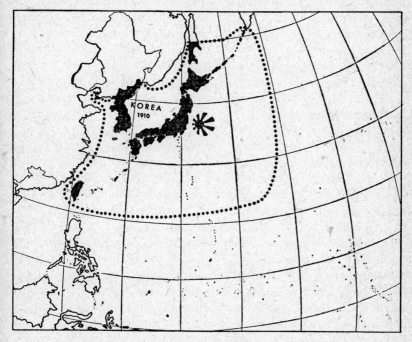

JAPAN, 1910-1919.

humble birth and from labor in a soya bean sauce factory to become Minister of War, 1931-1934. In appearance and temperament a mild and ascetic priest rather than a saber-rattling *samurai*, Araki was nevertheless at heart a soldier, simple in his personal habits and single-minded in his devotion to *Kodo*, the Imperial Way. It was Araki who now became the spiritual leader and the politico-ethical spokesman of a new Japan. As this Japan faced a world hostile because of her continental expansion, Araki rationalized ultra-nationalism and foreign conquest in terms of the high ethical principles which clothed the traditional Japa-

---

[14] Note the discussion by Borton, *Japan Since 1931*, 16-20.

nese doctrines of *Kodo* and *Kokutai* (National Polity).[15] The implications of *Kodo* and of *Hako ichiu* (The world under one roof) were reinterpreted as Japan's universal and benign mission designed to bring peace to the world. In the Far East, this mission would spread the beneficent rule of the emperor to those benighted peoples whose rulers had failed them or who had fallen a prey to Western exploitation and the doctrines of capitalism and liberalism. At home *Kodo* would direct Japanese footsteps into the forsaken paths of her own indigenous culture. From these paths she had been enticed, so it was said, by pernicious Western cults: liberalism, capitalism, democracy, individualism, and even communism. The result was a Japan where political life was usurped by corrupt political parties, where capitalists grew wealthy while peasants could not eat the rice they grew—a Japan weakened at home and thus denied the right to rescue Asia from European and American exploitation.[16]

THE GROWTH OF THE "PATRIOTIC" SOCIETIES

In the vogue of nationalism, which grew as the influence of the older political parties and of labor declined, there was a corresponding increase in the number and influence of so-called patriotic societies. The increase of such societies, whether ultra-patriotic or terroristic, dated from World War I, but the most phenomenal growth occurred in the years 1930 to 1932. By 1936 there were some 235 such organizations, of which 19 were formed in 1930, 42 in 1931, and 58 in 1932. While the real purposes of these societies were not always clear, they one and all loudly proclaimed the sanctity of the Imperial House, advocated *Kodo* and *Kokutai,* took a special interest in training the youth of the nation, and supported militarism with vehemence. The more important of the patriotic societies were associated with the military services such, for example, as the Ex-Service Men's Association (*Zaigo Gunjinkai*); the Imperial League of Young Officers (*Kokoku Seinen Shoko Domei*); and the Black Ocean Society (*Genyosha*), which included both civilians and military under the leadership of Mitsuru Toyama. Many of the patriotic societies drew much of their membership from rural Japan, from which areas came most of the conscripts for the army. Such societies were apt to denounce capitalism and to favor vaguely some form of state socialism under the emperor. Another type of society, more

---

[15] *Kokutai* as used by the Japanese is meant to suggest that unity of the state which results from the unqualified loyalty of the people to the Imperial line "unbroken through ages eternal."

[16] D. C. Holton, *Modern Japan and Shinto Nationalism* (Chicago, 1943), 21-23.

national in scope, was the Young Men's Association (*Nippon Seinen-dan*). This was open to any young man 13 to 25 years of age who was possessed of "purity and genuineness," who was devoted to loyalty and filial piety, and who was willing to sacrifice himself in the interest of the state. This organization claimed a membership of nearly two and one-half million in 1934. Its complement was a young women's organization with one and one-half million members.[17]

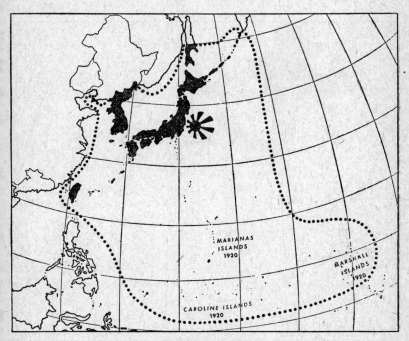

JAPAN, 1920-1930.

THE MILITARY PATRIOTS SEEK CONTROL

When elements within the Japanese army took matters into their own hands by seizing control of Manchuria in 1931-1932, their object was not only to spread Japanese conquest on the mainland but also to seize political power within Japan itself. Prior to World War I, the Imperial Rescript (1882) of the Meiji emperor forbidding persons in active military service to engage in politics had in general been honored;

---

[17] Borton, *Japan Since 1931*, 30-35; Kenneth Colegrove, *Militarism in Japan* (Boston, 1936).

but after the war, army temper was typified by a younger group of militant officers drawn largely from the rural districts. These officers were politically minded, and they "were intent on reforming the country." Although in many cases sincere and well-intentioned, their mental background was parochial, and their vehement denunciations of liberalism and capitalism were without restraint. Nevertheless, their reverence for the emperor, their championship of the depressed classes (particularly the peasants who were their fathers and brothers), and their indis-

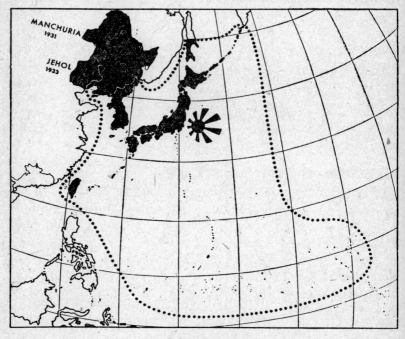

JAPAN, 1931-1933.

criminate clamor against corrupt party politicians won them a large following. Furthermore, although their cures for Japan's ills were often voiced in such vague phrases as "stabilization of the national livelihood," they never failed to appeal to the virtues of *Bushido*. The contrast between the wealthy industrialist and corrupt politician on the one hand and the "simple, pure, impecunious" officer on the other was meant to be striking—and it was.[18]

---

[18] Sakuzo Yoshino, "Fascism in Japan," *Contemporary Japan,* I (1932), 190 ff.

Out of this welter of patriotic societies, civilian and military, came the succession of terroristic plots, *coup d'états,* and assassinations which punctuated Japan's political life from 1931 to 1936. The earliest of these schemes came to light in October and November, 1931, when a plan to establish a military dictatorship was discovered by the police.[19] In February, 1932, Junnosuke Inouye, a former Finance Minister closely associated with the *Minseito,* and Baron Takuma Dan, head of the Mitsui, were assassinated. Inouye and Dan were singled out as representative of the capitalists, industrialists, and politicians who were said to be ruining the nation.[20] On May 15, 1932, came the assassination of Premier Inukai, abortive attacks on other officials, and an attempt to blow up the Bank of Japan, the offices of the political parties, the Tokyo Metropolitan police building, and electrical power stations. When these outrages failed to produce a military-fascist dictatorship, army extremists turned to pamphleteering. Their booklets stressed the coming "crisis of 1936" when the Washington and London naval treaties would expire, the menace to Japan from Soviet Russia and capitalistic America, and Japan's mission to defend the Orient.[21]

RUNNING DOWN THE LIBERALS

Despite public denials by the Minister of War, it was now evident that powerful elements within the army had determined to take a hand in politics by direct pamphleteering appeals to the nation. As a result, during 1935 relations between the military and the government were strained. This in turn led to further verbal attacks by the ultra-nationalists on whatever remnants of liberalism still survived. The new target of the crusaders for *Kokutai* (the National Polity) was a distinguished professor of constitutional law, Tatsukichi Minobe. The professor had spent a lifetime teaching in the Imperial University of Tokyo, but only now was it discovered that his theory which held the emperor to be an organ of the state and not the state itself was a pernicious doctrine. In the public clamor which forced Minobe's resignation from the House

---

[19] T. A. Bisson, *Japan in China* (New York, 1938), 207; Borton, *Japan Since 1931,* 38-39.

[20] A. Morgan Young, *Imperial Japan* (New York, 1938), 115-118.

[21] Capitalists and politicians were not alone victims of army and patriotic extremists. There were many divisions and cliques within the army. After 1934, Generals Araki and Mazaki, strong advocates of *Kodo,* were retired by General Hayashi, then Minister of War, and General Nagata, of the Military Affairs Bureau. Colonel Aizawa, a junior officer, protested to General Nagata against these reforms, and then murdered Nagata to remove a "degenerate" influence from the army. Borton, *Japan Since 1931,* 45.

of Peers, the *Seiyukai* outdid even the militarists in condemnation of Minobe and in demands for "clarification of the national polity." [22]

Meanwhile the more conservative elements in the army and the bureaucracy hoped to quiet the growing unrest by creating a Cabinet Inquiry Council (*Naikaku Shigikai*), May 11, 1935, designed to give "stabilizing" advice to the government. This body was dominated by conservative and cautious bureaucrats. In July significant shifts were made in the high command of the army; these were intended to produce greater unity by removing some of the more fiery advocates of *Kodo*. Amid sweeping changes of command General Jinzaburo Mazaki was shifted from the office of Inspector General of Military Education. Extremists interpreted this as an attempt to replace the Araki-Mazaki group, known to be friendly to the younger and more rabid officers, with General Kazushige Ugaki and those in the army who had shown a greater disposition to work with the industrialists and to respect at least the forms of representative government and the political parties. A franker explanation would have recognized the need of controlling the political activities of the young officers if army discipline were to be maintained at all.

In February, 1936, the Japanese electorate expressed approval of these modest reforms when the *Kodo*-conscious *Seiyukai* was defeated by the *Minseito,* which had appealed for parliamentary government to save the country from fascism. Ultra-nationalist candidates were defeated, whereas labor doubled the votes cast for it in 1932. The election was in no sense a repudiation of Japan's policy in Manchuria or China, but in domestic politics it was a direct rebuff to the army extremists and the super-patriots. These latter accepted the challenge promptly. On February 26, four days after the announcement of the election returns, some twenty junior officers and a regiment of troops en route to Manchuria attempted by force to overthrow the Okada cabinet. The mutineers murdered Korekiyo Takahashi, the Minister of Finance, Admiral Viscount Makoto Saito, Lord Keeper of the Privy Seal, and General Jotaro Watanabe, Inspector General of Military Education. They attempted to kill Premier Okada but murdered his brother-in-law by mistake. For three days the heart of Tokyo was held by the mutinous troops. Although for the moment the army's prestige was shattered by

---

[22] The position of the emperor in the constitutional system is treated by Kenneth Colegrove, "The Japanese Emperor," *American Political Science Review*, XXVI (1932), 642-659, 828-845; the Minobe affair is treated by Borton, *Japan Since 1931*, 10-11, and Reischauer, *Japan: Government-Politics*, 167-168.

these outrages, it soon recovered when apologists painted the assassins as young men pure in heart whose sole motive was to restore the "national spirit." Fundamentally the political picture had not been changed; for although the new government formed by Koki Hirota, March 9, 1936, was composed of moderate militarists and civilian bureaucrats, the influence of the army remained high, each minister having been approved by General Count Juichi Terauchi, the Minister of War. Perhaps more important was the way in which the maneuverings of the moderates versus the extreme militarists added to the confusion of thought and alignment among civilian groups. Factionalism was already present in the bureaucracy, some of whose members were avowedly fascist, and within the major political parties the *Seiyukai* had long since shown its willingness to support extremes of nationalism. Now there were signs that the great Mitsui house was beginning to look with qualified favor toward extremists at home who could be counted as expansionists abroad. Younger and lesser known capitalists such as R. Aikawa, heading army-sponsored industry in Manchukuo, had already accepted army backing as a convenient means of breaking into the industrial monopoly of the established *Zaibatsu* houses. The net result was, as the cross currents of domestic conflict increased, that the Hirota cabinet moved steadily toward "bureaucratic totalitarianism." The influence of the Diet declined while military and naval budgets reached an all-time high. Before the end of the year Japan had signed an anti-communist pact with Germany, November 25, 1936.[23] Further evidence of the army's involvement in politics came in January, 1937. When the Hirota cabinet resigned, the emperor called upon a moderate, General Kazushige Ugaki, to form a government; but Ugaki was blocked when the army refused to appoint a Minister of War. In February, however, the army did accept the elevation to the premiership of General Senjuro Hayashi, who had been Minister of War. In June, after Hayashi had failed to win the nation's unified support, he was succeeded by Prince Fumimaro Konoye, a member of one of Japan's oldest and most aristocratic families. It was the expectation that Konoye's close family relationship with the Imperial Household would lead the nation to unite politically behind his policies.[24]

The unhealthy pass which Japan's domestic politics had reached by

[23] The Anti-Comintern Pact expressed the desire of the signatories to co-operate against the influence of communism. Text in H. S. Quigley and G. H. Blakeslee, *The Far East* (Boston, 1938), 304-305. It was renewed for a second 5-year period, November 25, 1941.
[24] Reischauer, *Japan: Government-Politics*, 178-182.

June, 1937, needs no further emphasis. Political assassins and terrorists were not a new feature of Japanese life, but their reappearance beginning with the attack on Hamaguchi in 1929 bore a special significance. Always garbed in the role of guardians of the emperor, of the Imperial Way, and of the National Spirit, they served as the shock troops for all those who favored reaction, ultra-nationalism, fascism, or military dictatorship. Each time the terrorists struck, the army and its sympathizers won at least a psychological victory, for the very existence of political terrorism was taken as proof of the depths to which the nation had sunk under the rule of "corrupt" industrial capitalists and political parties. Until 1937 the Japanese electorate showed a surprisingly healthy skepticism toward all moves in the direction of fascism or military dictatorship, but their reluctance to give way to the army at home was forever being weakened by the appeal of military conquest abroad, of the expanding empire in China, and of Japan's benevolent mission to insure the peace and tranquility of the Far East. In the case of Japan, as in that of other countries before her, this appeal was too strong for the advocates of liberalism and parliamentary government.

THE EMPIRE AND BUSINESS

Japan's invasion of Manchuria in 1931 and her subsequent defiance of the League of Nations were repugnant to public sentiment in the major Western countries, but they aroused less concern than did another phase of Japan's expanding empire. This was the progress of Japan's industrialization and the deeper penetration of foreign markets by the finished products of her machines. By 1936, Japan led the world as an *exporter* of textiles in addition to many miscellaneous items. The new imports were raw materials—cotton, wool, rubber—much of which was re-exported as finished products. This was an industrial revolution in the truest sense of the word. Between 1931 and 1936, Japan's exports more than doubled in volume and value, though the yen lost about two thirds of its gold value during the same years. Nevertheless, by 1936 Japan's share of world trade was still only about 3.5 percent. Yet the expansion of Japan's foreign trade in these years created great apprehension among competitors principally because of the ability of the Japanese to undercut all comers. This ability was frequently attributed to what Western countries and business men liked to call unfair and unscrupulous business practice. A more intelligible explanation appears to be the capacity which Japan showed after 1930: 1) to rationalize and thus increase the efficiency of her industry; 2) to profit by the national capacity to work long hours for little pay; and 3) to combine a simple

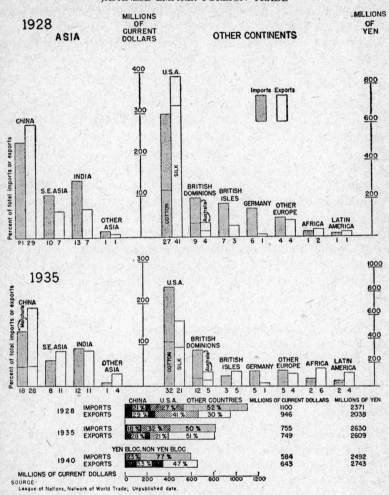

JAPANESE EMPIRE: FOREIGN TRADE

United States Department of State, Division of Map Intelligence and Cartography.

Oriental standard of living with a high Occidental standard of industrial productivity.[25]

To summarize then, it may be said that between 1931 and 1937 tensions within Japan had not been eased. Manchukuo under Japanese tutelage was an established fact, and here Japan was pushing an un-

---

[25] W. H. Chamberlain, *Japan Over Asia* (London, 1938), 171-175.   G. C. Allen, "Japanese Industry: Its Organization and Development to 1937," in *The Industrialization of Japan and Manchoukuo,* edited by E. B. Schumpeter (New York, 1940), 489-490.

precedented industrial development. Relations with China, however, had not improved. Japan's invasion of foreign markets was creating greater apprehension abroad, while at home her political life revealed restlessness, lack of stability, and a pronounced trend toward totalitarianism.

JAPAN'S MONROE DOCTRINE BECOMES EXPLICIT

All these factors were related to policies which Japan had long pursued. Japan had long aspired to be "the guardian of the peace and security of the Far East," and in pursuit of this goal had developed her doctrines of "special interests" and "paramount interests." As far back as the close of World War I, many Japanese had written and had spoken of Japan's "Monroe Doctrine" in eastern Asia. Although there was little similarity between the principles which Japan was applying in Asia and those which were inherent in the American doctrine, the use of the term had a considerable propaganda value for Japan. Now in the wake of the Manchurian invasion, Japan gave more formal expression to her concept of her position in Asia. In April, 1934, the spokesman of the Japanese Foreign Office, Eji Amau, enunciated the principles of Japan's policy toward China:

1) The unification of China must be achieved by China's own efforts.
2) Japan would oppose any joint efforts by the powers (League of Nations) to assist China since such joint efforts would acquire *political* significance.
3) Individual countries might assist China if their assistance was "not detrimental to the maintenance of peace in the Far East."

This was a clear enunciation of Japan's claim to "paramount interest" in all that concerned the future of China. In 1932, Japan had successfully defied the League of Nations in Manchuria. In 1934, she asserted her right to pursue a similar policy with respect to China as a whole.[26]

CHINA, 1931-1937

The China which felt the weight of Japanese expansion in these years was a society too complex to be described in a few generalizations, yet some suggestions of its main characteristics must be given.

Chinese society represented many classes or groups whose interests appeared to be frequently at variance. Yet between 1933 and 1937 these differences were in part subordinated to a rising popular demand for

---

[26] The Amau statement is printed in *The China Year Book, 1934*, 725-726.

resistance to Japanese aggression. In varying degree this popular movement was felt by almost all classes: by the small middle class and workers of the cities, and also by the peasants and landlords of the countryside. This was distinctly a people's movement. It derived its power
from conditions within China as well as from Japanese pressures. At
the time of the Manchurian invasion, the National Government at Nanking had determined to limit its resistance to Japan to appeals to the
League. From then on it followed a policy of appeasement dictated by
its own military weakness against the superior force of Japan and by the
fact that its authority was seriously challenged by the establishment in
November, 1931, of a central Soviet (Communist) government in Kiangsi under the leadership of Mao Tse-tung and Chu Teh. There were
also bitter divisions within the Kuomintang, as exemplified by a revolt
of the 19th Route Army inspired by its leader General Tsai Ting-kai
and a group of Kuomintang liberals. The 19th Route Army had fought
gloriously against the Japanese at Shanghai in 1932. Tsai and Kuomintang liberals wanted a united front, including Communists, to be
formed in the name of resistance to Japan. But among the conservatives, the reactionaries, and the fascists of the Kuomintang, it was more
important to crush the Communists than to resist Japan. As a result, all
Nanking's military strength, organized by German military advisers
and employing nearly a million troops, was centered upon a succession
of five anti-Communist campaigns. Under this pressure, the Communists undertook the long march to the northwest, where by 1936 they had
established themselves in what was later to be known as the Shensi-
Kansu-Ningsia Border Region with its Communist capital at Yenan.
For a time the Communists were weakened, but they had not been destroyed. On the other hand, Nanking, while failing in its objective to
destroy a rival, did increase its power in a number of provinces such as
Hunan, Yünnan, Kweichow, and Szechuan, where previously its rule
had been only nominal.[27] Accordingly, between 1935 and 1937 the
National Government was able further to strengthen its power by
developing communications (highways and railroads) by laudable reforms in currency and taxation,[28] and by profiting through the technical
counsel of experts sent out by the League of Nations.

Nevertheless, the policy of appeasement toward Japan grew increasingly unpopular. In November, 1935, there was an attempt to assassinate Wang Ching-wei, the Foreign Minister, who to the public mind

---

[27] L. K. Rosinger, *China's Wartime Politics* (Princeton, 1944), ch. i.
[28] W. Y. Lin, *The New Monetary System of China* (Shanghai, 1936), especially chapters
i–iii.

personified the official policy. At the same time, Japan's efforts to establish an autonomous North China fomented demonstrations and protests from university students in practically all parts of the country. The students demanded civil liberties, an end to political oppression at home, and national leadership by Nanking against any further Japanese encroachment. The movement spread rapidly among professional classes and the urban workers, the latter of whom organized in Shanghai the Anti-Japanese National Salvation Association, which Nanking promptly attempted to suppress. In May, 1936, the Student's National Salvation Union was formed; it sought: 1) an immediate end to civil war, 2) freedom for all political prisoners, and 3) formation of a national united front.[29]

THE GILBERTIAN COUP D'ÉTAT

No national front was possible without agreement between the Kuomintang and the Communists. The first steps toward such an agreement were taken by the Communists in the spring of 1936 when they abandoned the policy of confiscating land and when they reduced taxes on merchants and industrialists and proposed cessation of the Kuomintang-Communist civil war. Nothing came of this at the moment for Nanking was involved in attempting to implement its control of the Canton area; when this was accomplished, a new threat to the National Government appeared in the north.

The headquarters of the Kuomintang-Nationalist armies in the north was the city of Sian; here in December, 1936, Chiang K'ai-shek was seized by the troops of his northern commander and erstwhile dictator of Manchuria, Chang Hsueh-liang. After he was driven from Manchuria by the Japanese in 1932, Chang and his Tungpei or northeastern army had been ordered by Chiang to fight the Communists in the northwest. This proved to be an unprofitable and unpopular undertaking. Chang suffered a number of defeats, and his soldiers, who were interested in regaining their Manchurian home, had little stomach for fighting their fellow countrymen. Actually a sort of truce had come to prevail between the Tungpei-Communist armies. In November, 1936, Japan invaded Suiyuan province with puppet Manchurian and Mongolian troops. Throughout China there was a popular cry for resistance, but Nanking's response was to send more Nationalist troops against the Communists in Kansu. Moreover, when anti-Japanese strikes broke out in Shanghai and other cities, Nanking arrested a number of leaders of the patriotic National Salvation movement.

---

[20] Rosinger, *China's Wartime Politics*, 14-17, 19-21.

Meanwhile Chiang K'ai-shek went to Sian to end the Tungpei-Communist truce. Failing, he threatened to move the Tungpei army to the south. Two days later, December 12, 1936, Chiang was arrested by the Young Marshal. In a public statement the Sian leaders announced that their purpose was to effect a national front against Japan.[30] During the thirteen days that Chiang remained a prisoner, China's future lay in an unsteady balance. Many of the Tungpei leaders (not including the Young Marshal) appear to have been willing to murder Chiang. In Nanking some of the Kuomintang were willing to make assassination certain by launching a military expedition to rescue the Generalissimo. Ironically, it would appear to be the Communists, whose comrades Chiang had slaughtered at Shanghai in 1927 and whose armies he had fought consistently ever since, who were responsible for his release. They better than the Tungpei group realized that Chiang, despite his policy of appeasement, was the indispensable symbol of national unity.

What the results of the Sian coup d'état would be was not immediately apparent. There was no immediate sign that Chiang had agreed to change his policies. Nevertheless, while to the outside world the Sian kidnapping seemed like an act in a Gilbert and Sullivan opera, its significance in Chinese politics was great. It emphasized the growing popular demand to end civil war and resist Japan. It suggested that under continued appeasement, Nanking would soon lose the moral leadership of the nation. It revealed the depth of disloyalties within the Nanking regime itself as well as the superb political strategy of the Communists.[31] Sian did not effect an immediate agreement, but it prepared the way for negotiations which were conducted during 1937 and which were making some progress when Japan renewed hostilities at Peking in July.[32]

[30] This could only be effected, they said, by adoption of a program including: 1) reorganization of the Nanking Government, admitting all parties to joint responsibility in saving the nation; 2) immediate stoppage of all civil war; 3) release of patriotic leaders held by Nanking as political prisoners; 4) support of the people's patriotic movement; 5) guarantees of civil liberties; and 6) convocation of a National Salvation Conference. Full text in Rosinger, *China's Wartime Politics*, 94-95, and in James Bertram, *First Act in China* (New York, 1938), 126-127.

[31] See Rosinger's discussion, *China's Wartime Politics*, 18-24.

[32] The Young Marshal, Chang Hsueh-liang, whose patriotism had outrun his political discretion, became a prisoner of the National Government after Chiang's release.

CHAPTER 35

BUILDING A NATION IN THE PHILIPPINES

AT THIS point in our story, we must digress from the narrative of gathering conflict between China and Japan in order to relate the progress of American administration and policy in the Philippines, where, since the beginning of the century, the United States had undertaken to school an Oriental people in Western principles of self-government looking to possible independence at some future date. After 1899, as we have seen in Chapter 15, the Philippine Islands were the most tangible stake possessed by the American people in the Far East; they constituted the first and the largest responsibility of the American people in that area. The attitudes which Americans adopted from time to time toward their Filipino wards are a measuring stick suggestive at least of the real and the professed interests of the American public in adjacent areas of the Far East. In the years from 1930 to 1934 when Japan was invading Manchuria and beginning her encroachments upon North China, a new chapter was also begun in the history of the Filipino people and of American guardianship in the Islands.

THE LAND AND PEOPLES OF THE PHILIPPINES

During the approximately half a century since Dewey's victory at Manila Bay, the islands and peoples of the Philippines had experienced notable development, but in some respects this growth was not an unqualified blessing, since it created new problems with which the American people was not always prepared to deal. First among the notable changes of the twentieth century has been the increase of population. In 1903 the Islands (115,600 square miles, slightly larger than the state of Arizona) sheltered a population of something more than 7,000,000; by 1918 the figure was 10,314,310; and by 1939 it had reached 16,000,303.[1]

---

[1] Classified according to citizenship there were:

Filipinos	15,833,649
Chinese	117,487
Japanese	29,057
Americans	8,709
Spanish	4,627
German	1,149
British	1,053

Small groups of other nationals completed the total.

618

Along with increased population came a rising standard of living resulting from expanded agriculture, exploitation of forest resources, and the sale of these products in the duty-free American market. The principal Philippine exports were sugar, manila hemp (abaca), copra, and tobacco. After 1930 there was developed a considerable mining industry which produced gold, chrome, copper, iron, and manganese. The possibilities of developing some light industry in the Islands also appeared; but with the absence of coking coal there seemed to be little prospect for heavier industry. Most significant for our story was the phenomenal growth in Philippine-American commerce on the basis of virtually free trade. In 1908, Americans sold some $5,000,000 worth of goods to the Philippines; in 1929, $92,592,000. Philippine exports increased proportionally, and most of these went to the American market. In 1908 total Philippine exports were valued at $32,000,000; in 1929, at $164,446,000. In 1933 American importers were taking 87 percent of all Philippine exports. The bulk of these exports (about 90 percent) was made up of sugar, copra, palm oil, tobacco, and abaca. In some years sugar alone made up 60 percent of the total exports. Thus after some thirty years of American occupation and some twenty years of Philippine-American free trade, the commerce of the Philippine Islands, both export and import, had been channelled almost exclusively with the United States. Trade had indeed followed the flag, and prosperity had been the result. Each year the economic life of the Filipino people became more dependent upon the American market. This condition logically suggested that the Islands were to continue indefinitely as an "unincorporated" territory of the United States.[2]

CHARACTERISTICS OF EARLY AMERICAN POLICY

During the years of what may be termed Republican rule (1900-1913), the official American policy concerned itself primarily with the large and basic tasks of cleaning up the pest- and plague-ridden islands, of promoting their economic development, and of providing their peoples with the beginnings of a public educational system. The Americans

---

Classified on the basis of religion, there were:

Roman Catholics	12,603,365
Aglipayans (the Philippine Independent Church)	1,573,608
Protestants	378,361
Mohammedans	677,903
Pagans or persons not members of any religious group	626,008

[2] As an "unincorporated" territory, the legal and political position of the Islands and the civil and political rights of the Filipinos under the American flag were determined by Congress, limited only by those provisions of the Constitution which are prohibitive. See J. R. Hayden, *The Philippines* (New York, 1942), 763-764.

who pioneered in this work have left a record of accomplishment of which their country may well be proud. Successive presidents, McKinley, Roosevelt, and Taft, assumed that these were the primary tasks; that for some years no purpose was to be served by discussions of independence even as a remote possibility. For the present, it was enough, as Taft had said, that the United States was pursuing a policy of "the Philippines for the Filipinos" and was training them in self-government to open an "era of good feeling."

REVIVAL OF THE INDEPENDENCE MOVEMENT

With the triumph of expansionism, imperialism, and empire, signified by the Republican victory of 1900, the interest of the American electorate in the Philippines all but disappeared. On the other hand, the Anti-Imperialist League attempted to keep up interest, and the Democratic Party platforms of 1904, 1908, and 1912 denounced the idea of permanent American sovereignty in the Islands.[3] The corresponding Republican platforms made no commitments for the future.

Some of the early agitation for independence came from Filipino conservatives who had formed the Federal Party in the Islands. Originally this party favored Philippine autonomy looking toward eventual statehood in the American Union; but as the party leaders sensed that the American people was not likely to approve statehood, independence "in due time" became the goal. By 1907 a number of Filipino political groups, including the nationalist revolutionary leaders of Spanish-American War days, had united in a second and stronger party, the Nationalists, demanding "immediate independence." From 1907 on it was the Nationalists who controlled the Philippine Assembly. The Party's agitation for independence was continuous, and in this it may have represented most of the 3 percent of the population eligible to vote. The great mass of the illiterate, non-voting population probably had little if any understanding of what independence would mean.[4] At all events, it was the Nationalists who carried the campaign for independence to Washington when Manuel Quezon in 1909 became one of the Islands' resident commissioners at the capital. Quezon campaigned actively for

---

[3] W. C. Forbes, *The Philippine Islands* (2 vols., New York, 1928), summarizes some of the party pledges: II, Appendix XXXVII.

[4] To many Nationalist politicians the plank of independence was merely a means of getting votes. "As one Filipino expressed it, 'The peasants remember that they paid heavy taxes under the Spanish regime. They do not pay as much under American rule, and the [Nationalist] politicians have led them to believe that, when and if independence is achieved, there will be no taxes at all.'" Grayson L. Kirk, *Philippine Independence* (New York, 1936), 42.

independence both in Congress and in the columns of *The Filipino People,* a magazine which he founded. The thesis of the Quezon appeal was that the United States had met its responsibilities so well that the Islands were now ready for independence.[5] In so far as the American public took any interest in this campaign, it appears to have entertained a healthy skepticism. The demand for independence was regarded as an encouraging sign of young nationhood, but it was also recognized that perhaps Filipino Nationalists had their eye on the native ballot box and did not wish to be taken too seriously.

THE DEMOCRATS AND THE REVIVAL OF INDEPENDENCE

In 1910 the Republicans lost control of the House of Representatives in Washington, and two years later (March, 1912) the Democrats introduced the first Philippine independence bill. This bill, sponsored by Congressman W. A. Jones of Virginia, was reported favorably by the Committee on Insular Affairs but was not acted on by the House.[6]

The election of Woodrow Wilson to the presidency was followed shortly by the appointment of Francis B. Harrison as the new governor-general of the Philippines. In his inaugural address at Manila, Harrison expressed the new American policy when he said that every official act would be "taken with a view to the ultimate independence of the Islands and as a preparation for that independence." Independence would be approached as rapidly "as the safety and the permanent interests of the Islands will permit." This policy was soon implemented. A native now replaced for the first time the American majority on the Philippine Commission, the upper house of the native legislature; throughout the government Filipinos were appointed to many posts previously held by Americans. On August 29, 1916, President Wilson approved the so-called Jones Bill, which provided for widening autonomy in the Philippines and pledged the United States "to recognize their independence as soon as a stable government can be established therein." [7] Here for the first time the United States went on record in a

---

[5] Quezon's appeals in Congress were usually supported by appeals and resolutions of the Nationalist Party and the Philippine Assembly. *Congressional Record,* 61-2, 6310-6313, and 61-3, 3949-3957.

[6] Representative Jones was chairman of the Committee. House Report 22143, 62-2.

[7] United States, *Statutes At Large,* XXXIX, Pt. I, Public No. 240, p. 545. "An Act to declare the purpose of the people of the United States as to the future political status of the people of the Philippine Islands, and to provide a more autonomous government for those islands."

In creating a "more autonomous government," the Jones Act did away with the Philippine Commission, replacing it with a legislature composed of a senate and a house

qualified promise of eventual independence. After the passage of the
Jones Bill, it became the practice of Philippine Nationalists to assert that
the "stable government" called for by the act had already been achieved,
and that independence should therefore be granted. For the time being,
however, nothing could be done while the United States was absorbed
in World War I.

Immediately following the war, the Philippine government, encouraged by the Wilsonian principle of self-determination, sent a special mission to Washington. From Europe, Wilson informed the mission that
independence was "almost in sight," and, in his annual message to a
hostile Congress (December, 1920), he reminded the legislators of "our
duty to keep our promise to the people of those Islands." No action,
however, was taken; and as the Republicans returned to power, it was
again taken for granted that independence had once more become a
matter of the distant future. Informed American opinion appears to
have been content that this should be so—a sentiment which was undoubtedly shared, though secretly, by some of the Philippine independence leaders themselves.

THE WOOD-FORBES COMMISSION

In 1920 President Harding dispatched a commission headed by
General Leonard Wood and former governor W. Cameron Forbes to
report on conditions in the Islands. The report, submitted the following year, found that the Harrison administration had proceeded too
rapidly in turning the government over to the Filipinos; that this policy
had led to confusion and maladministration; that the Filipino people
lacked adequate education in political matters; that there was great
difference of opinion among Filipinos as to the time and conditions
under which independence would be desirable; that the Islands were not
ready economically or militarily for independence; and finally that the
Filipinos needed more time in which to profit by the autonomy which
they already enjoyed before seeking further autonomy, let alone independence.[8] While General Wood remained in the Islands as governor-general with the unpopular task of imposing stricter American
executive authority, the Filipino politicoes redoubled their independence
propaganda in Washington and throughout the United States. It appears, however, to have made little headway. Unfortunately, the
American people in the early post-war period showed a regrettable lack

---

of representatives. This legislature functioned from 1916 to 1935. For details on the
legislative powers and process in the Philippines, see Hayden, *The Philippines*, ch. viii.
   [8] United States, House Doc. No. 325, 68-2.

of interest in the Philippines; and when in 1924 President Coolidge told a Filipino mission bluntly that the Islands were not ready for independence, there was possibly not one American in a thousand who had any grounds for knowing whether the President was correct or not.[9] The President's opinion was reaffirmed two years later in the report of his special investigator, Colonel Carmi A. Thompson. The Thompson report advised against early independence because of the financial weakness of the Islands, their lack of national solidarity, and the decline which would be inevitable in Filipino-American trade.[10] When in response to these criticisms the Filipino politicians proposed a referendum to determine whether the people wanted independence, the bill was vetoed by Governor Wood and the veto upheld by President Coolidge on the ground that: "A plebiscite on the question of immediate independence would tend to divert the attention of the people toward the pursuit of mere political power rather than to the consideration of the essential steps necessary for the maintenance of a stable, prosperous, well-governed community."[11]

As the Coolidge administration came to a close, the American people appeared content to permit Philippine independence to wait on the indefinite future. This was not in itself an unwise resolve. While the Wood-Forbes and the Thompson reports were political documents, they were likewise able analyses of unhappy conditions prevailing in the Islands. The real trouble was that the American public in general had long since lost interest in the Philippines. Whether we should continue to carry the White Man's Burden there was, as the average American saw it, something which could safely be left to the government to decide. This was a far cry from the popular enthusiasm which some thirty years previously had greeted Dewey's victory at Manila Bay. And if in the meanwhile the United States had, to use Watterson's editorial phrase, become "an imperial republic incomparably greater than Rome," it was not because of any conscious effort or sustained interest on the part of any considerable number of the American people. "Benevolent assimilation" had long since lost the glamour it possessed in the autumn of 1898.

THE ECONOMICS OF BENEVOLENT ASSIMILATION

Yet during the very years when Americans in general were showing scant interest in the political, cultural, and educational burdens of em-

---

[9] *Congressional Record*, 68-1, 3617-3619.

[10] United States, Senate Doc. No. 180, 69-2.

[11] Letter of the President to Governor Wood, April 6, 1927. Forbes, *The Philippine Islands*, II, Appendix XXXVI.

pire, this country was linking the Philippines so closely to the American economic system and market that independence had become a virtual impossibility save at appalling expense to the Islands' political economy.

During the first decade of American rule in the Philippines, there was little change in the Islands' tariff policy; the treaty of peace with Spain had provided that for ten years Spanish ships and merchandise would be admitted to Philippine ports "on the same terms as ships and merchandise of the United States." Other states were protected in this arrangement by the most-favored-nation clause. During the same period duties paid on imports to the United States from the Philippines were reduced 25 percent of the regular rates. Then in 1909, Congress established virtually free trade with the Islands.[12] Full free trade was achieved in 1913 when the quota limitations of the earlier legislation were removed. Under free trade, Philippine-American trade enjoyed unprecedented growth, and the United States acquired almost a monopoly of both the Philippine import and export trade. As a result, too, of free trade, and through stimulation by other factors, such as wartime demands, a number of Filipino agricultural industries experienced a remarkable expansion, thus acquiring a new importance in the export trade and in the financial structure of the Islands. Between 1922 and 1934 sugar, cocoanut, and tobacco exports increased rapidly. It was these developments which enabled the Islands to buy increasing quantities of American manufacturers. Thus at one and the same time the political policy of the United States was to confer a larger measure of autonomy and the hope of ultimate independence on the Filipino, whereas the economic policy was to fashion a Philippine economy dependent upon a free American market—a market which would be seriously curtailed if not closed completely once the Islands had gained their independence.[13]

THE AMERICAN FARMER AND THE PHILIPPINE "MENACE"

As early as 1921 some farm groups[14] in the United States had showed an interest in curtailing the importation of Philippine cocoanut prod-

---

[12] The fact that quotas were fixed on certain imports such as sugar, tobacco, etc., and that full duties would be paid on all imports above these quotas was of no significance at the time since the quotas fixed were in excess of what the Islands could then produce for export.

[13] For tariff policy, note United States Tariff Commission, *United States-Philippine Tariff and Trade Relations,* 2nd ser. (1931), Report No. 18.

[14] The dairy industry and the cottonseed oil interests. United States, Senate Finance Committee, *Hearings on the Proposed Tariff Act of 1921.*

ucts, but it was not until 1928-29 that the business of putting a stop to the free importation of Philippine agricultural products was undertaken seriously by pressure groups. In part, this time element is explained by the fact that the prosperity of the 1920's had been enjoyed by American industry and not by agriculture. Both major parties were pledged to farm relief, the Republicans by the promise of a high protective tariff. Moreover, farm organizations in seeking relief by legislation laid increasing emphasis on the menace of Philippine imports.[15] From 1929 onward, American attitudes toward Philippine independence were shaped by a peculiar mixture of our sense of moral responsibility to our wards and our desire to be free from the alleged competition of Philippine agricultural products.

Groups other than the farm organizations now became interested as it was discovered by patriotic societies and labor that independence was perhaps the speediest and certainly the surest way of putting an end to Philippine immigration. During the decade of the '20's, Filipinos had migrated to the United States at an average annual rate of slightly less than 5,000. There was wide difference of opinion as to how serious this immigration was either as a labor problem or as a general social problem, but its effect was to revive many of the arguments which had been used effectively in the late nineteenth century against the Chinese, and in the early twentieth century against the Japanese. The immediate threat, if such it was, from Philippine immigration was not, however, the sole reason for labor's joining the new crusade for independence. For many years the American Federation of Labor had denounced our continued occupation of the Philippines as a policy of imperialism.

INDEPENDENCE AND POLITICAL EXPEDIENCY

As the fate of the Philippines was debated in Congress from 1930 on, the question of their independence became less and less a matter of political principle and more and more one of political expediency. The pressure groups whose interest has been noted wanted to be rid of the Philippines. Only to a minor degree were they interested in whether the American task of preparing the Islands for self-government had been carried to a point where independence might now safely be granted.

In December, 1932, Congress enacted the Hare-Hawes-Cutting Bill. It provided for independence after a transition period of ten years; quota limits were to be applied to Philippine imports; there was to be a

---

[15] For an excellent brief discussion, see Kirk, *Philippine Independence*, 78-95.

gradual application of the American tariff; and finally, the Philippines were to be granted an annual immigrant quota of 50.[16]

The Hoover presidential veto which promptly followed was no surprise, for the firm opposition of the administration to early independence was well known. In one of the ablest state papers of the Hoover regime, the President challenged the statesmanship of virtually every clause of the bill. His over-all denunciation condemned it as a repudiation of the government's moral responsibility to the American people, to the Filipinos, and to the world. He noted that it was particularly unfortunate that nationhood should be thrust upon the Islands on the spurious ground that it would achieve American farm relief at a time when the outlook in international relations gave little promise that the Filipinos could maintain their independence. As positive alternate proposals the President suggested: 1) a plebiscite to be held in fifteen or twenty years to test Philippine sentiment, 2) immediate restriction of immigration, 3) gradual reduction of free imports, and 4) gradual enlargement of political autonomy. Eventually commercial relationships would be stabilized on the basis of a fixed mutual preference similar to but broader than that between the United States and Cuba.[17] The Hoover veto was immediately overridden by heavy majorities, and the bill became law, though in reality it satisfied no one. By those who had opposed independence it was regarded as a betrayal of trust. The pressure groups that had favored independence in order to exclude Philippine products regarded the immediate restrictive measures as inadequate. In the Philippines, the dominant political opinion was that the act would be ruinous to the economy of the Islands and that the political collapse which would likely follow would be attributed to the inability of the Filipinos to govern themselves rather than to the economic clauses of an "unjust" independence bill. Accordingly, under the leadership of Manuel Quezon, the offer of independence was rejected by the Philippine legislature on October 17, 1933.[18] There were also American pressure groups in the Islands that opposed independence for reasons of self-interest: shippers, trading and investment firms, as

---

[16] Hayden, *The Philippines*, 354.

[17] The veto message is printed in Kirk, *Philippine Independence*, 227-234.

[18] The principal objections of the Philippine government were: a) that the commercial settlement would "seriously imperil the economic, social, and political institutions" of the Philippines; b) that the immigration question had been handled in a manner "objectionable and offensive" to the Filipinos; c) that the military and naval privileges retained by the United States were "inconsistent with true independence, violate national dignity, and are subject to misunderstanding"; and finally, d) that the powers to be held by the American High Commissioner during the transition period were not definitely circumscribed.

well as army and navy groups. These added to the general confusion
in American attitudes toward the Philippine problem.

THE TYDINGS-McDUFFIE BILL, 1934

Since there was no likelihood that Congress would change the economic provisions of the Law, President Roosevelt suggested the only concession to Philippine sentiment which was likely to win congressional
approval. He proposed amendment of the Hare-Hawes-Cutting Act by
striking out the provision for a permanent American military base in
the Islands. The question of the future of the American naval establishment was to be left to future negotiations. With this change and
some minor revisions of the sugar and cocoanut oil quotas, the old act,
now repassed as the Tydings-McDuffie Law, received presidential approval, March 24, 1934.[19] The law was accepted by the Philippine legislature on May 1; the native leaders were now convinced that no better
terms would be granted. Then, after having thus provided for Philippine independence following a period of economic transition, Congress
surrendered completely to the lobbyists through legislation providing
for immediate drastic limitations on Philippine sugar and by authorizing a processing tax on all cocoanut oil imports.[20] The conclusion expressed by *The New York Times* was inescapable: "Congress is indifferent to what may truthfully be called the 'plighted word of the United
States Government.'"[21]

THE PHILIPPINES ACCEPT

The Philippines accepted the Tydings-McDuffie Law, May 1, 1934.
On July 10 elections for the Constitutional Convention provided for by
the Law were held. The Constitution framed by this body was approved
by President Roosevelt, and was ratified by the Philippine electorate on
May 14, following. As the Commonwealth of the Philippines was thus
inaugurated, Quezon was elected the first President and Osmeña Vice-
President. An amendment to the Tydings-McDuffie Law, the Philippine Economic Adjustment (the so-called Tydings-Kocialkowski) Act,
was approved by President Roosevelt, August 7, 1939, and accepted by
the Islands. This was the result of continued efforts to modify the
economic clauses of the Independence Law and also of the findings of
a Joint Preparatory Committee on Philippine Affairs. A report of this

[19] Text in United States, *Statutes At Large*, XLVIII, Pt. I, Public No. 127.
[20] United States, *Statutes At Large*, XLVIII, Pt. I, Public No. 213, p. 670, and Public
No. 216, p. 763.
[21] Quoted by Kirk, *Philippine Independence*, 134.

committee showed that even in a period of generally amicable international relations, the abrupt ending of Philippine-American trade preference in 1946 "would endanger the economic and political stability of the independent Philippine state." [22]   The 1939 amendment was designed to extend to Philippine export industry "a stay of execution."

AMENDMENT OF THE PHILIPPINE CONSTITUTION

Three amendments were also incorporated in the Commonwealth Constitution and approved by the President of the United States, December 2, 1940. The first provided for a return to the bicameral legislature to be known as the Congress of the Philippines. The second reduced the term of the president from six to four years, providing for re-election with the limitation that no president may hold office for more than eight consecutive years. The third set up an independent commission to supervise elections.[23]

THE PHILIPPINE GOVERNMENT IN EXILE

After the Japanese invasion of the Philippines, December 8, 1941, the President, the Vice-President, and the United States High Commissioner in the Philippines withdrew to the United States, where in Washington a government in exile was set up. On August 2, 1944, Sergio Osmeña succeeded to the presidency, following the death of Quezon. The new President was installed at Tacloban, the capital of Leyte, October 10, 1944, during the reconquest of the Islands.

THE NATIONAL DEVELOPMENT OF THE PHILIPPINES

The forty-three years from the American occupation of the Philippines in 1898 until the Japanese invasion of 1941 have been called very properly the period of national development. They are the years in which the ideal of nationhood, born in the late years of the Spanish regime, was permitted and encouraged to grow to maturity under the inspiration of American political principles and philosophy. There are of course no absolute standards of measurement by which the American political record in the Philippines may be tested. However, if it may be said that the American people has had an overall policy toward the Filipino, that policy has been prefaced by the assumption that the Islands were ultimately to be free, and that it was the task of America to prepare them politically for that independence. Although this was

[22] Hayden, The Philippines, 795.
[23] Text of amendments in Hayden, The Philippines, 848-859.

the popular purpose, American official policy in the Islands was never quite so simple as this would suggest; for, as we have seen, the Philippines were our first great outpost of empire. With our right hand we often pointed the way to political independence; with our left we held the Islands to economic dependence. This was not a case of sinister design, but rather of what McKinley would have called "the march of events." Recognizing then that American economic policy had not prepared the Islands for independence, we may still examine some features of the political policy that were attended with more success. Did the period of American tutelage, 1898 to 1934, give the Islands adequate preparation for the Commonwealth, established in 1935, and, in turn, is the record of the Commonwealth such as to justify optimism as an infant nation proceeds to charter its own course?

CULTURAL AND RACIAL DIVERSITY

A basic problem to be tested under any regime of Philippine independence is that presented by the cultural and racial diversity of the Philippine people.[24] The presence of more than forty ethnographic groups, more than eighty languages and dialects, together with the contrasts separating Christian, Mohammedan, and pagan, have created serious problems for the young Philippine Commonwealth. Yet the differences have been minimized by the fact that the vast majority of the Filipinos are members of one great racial group, the Malays. At the time of the Japanese invasion in 1941, it was as yet too early to evaluate Filipino efforts to win the political allegiance of the culturally heterogeneous "South" and to make it integrally a part of the Philippine nation. It should be remembered, too, that the absence of a common native language remains an obstacle to the development of strong national and democratic institutions. The small educated and wealthy classes have a common language in English or Spanish, but the masses of the people know for the most part only their own local idiom. But the real strength of Philippine national unity remains yet to be tested. Whether it is strong enough to overcome the disruptive issues of economic, social, and religious policy within the Islands is a question which only the future will answer. It is to be remembered, too, that although under the Constitution of the Commonwealth all Filipinos are equal before the law, only the merest beginnings had been made toward social, economic, or political equality. In the Philippines, as in all Oriental

---

[24] Marcelo Tangco, "Racial and Cultural History of the Philippines," *Philippine Social Science Review*, X (1938), 110-127.

countries, the gulf between the small educated and wealthy class at the top and the masses at the bottom is both the danger and the challenge to future Philippine statesmanship.[25]

THE CONSTITUTION OF THE COMMONWEALTH

The evolution of Philippine political institutions since the end of the Spanish regime takes account of six basic constitutional documents. The first was the so-called "Malolos Constitution" of the First Philippine Republic of 1899. It was a liberal and democratic document written by Filipino intellectuals voicing their protest against Spanish and American rule.[26] Although somewhat doctrinaire, this constitution revealed broad knowledge of Western political institutions and capacity to modify them to meet Philippine conditions. A second document of constitutional importance was the Instructions to the Second Philippine Commission drawn up by Elihu Root as Secretary of War. These Instructions set forth the principles on which major American policies in and toward the Philippines were to be based. The third and fourth documents are the Organic Act of 1902 and the Organic Act of 1916; both were laws of the United States Congress creating the legal structure within which Philippine government was to be developed. The fifth was the Revised Administrative Code of 1917, an enactment of the Filipino legislature, whereby it created a government taking full advantage of the increased autonomy permitted under the Jones Law. Sixth, and finally, is the Constitution of the Commonwealth of the Philippines of 1935, which, unlike the Constitution of 1899, was drafted by a constitutional convention composed largely of practical and experienced Filipino politicians.[27]

In the Tydings-McDuffie Law, under authority of which the Constitution of the Commonwealth was drafted, the Filipinos were required to provide a constitution, republican in form, containing a bill of rights, and providing for complete religious toleration. Since these requirements would have been met regardless of the American mandate, the Islands may be said to have been free to form a government expressive of their own political ideals. The result was a constitution resting on the basic political philosophy of Western democracy and providing for a republican state in which sovereignty is declared to reside with the

[25] For an able discussion see Hayden, *The Philippines*, 3-31.

[26] The Malolos Constitution is in the *Report of the Philippine Commission*, 1900, I, 189.

[27] José M. Aruego, *The Framing of the Philippine Constitution* (2 vols., Manila, 1936), I, 22-23; and Miguel Cauderno, *The Framing of the Constitution of the Philippines* (Manila, 1937), describe the Constitution and the character of the membership of the constitutional convention.

people, from whom all governmental authority emanates. The Filipino bill of rights is more "extended and explicit" than those contained in American constitutions. Reflecting the period in which it was written, the Constitution of the Commonwealth includes concepts designed to create "social justice" for all the people. It stresses the duties as well as the rights of citizenship and confers upon the state large powers over persons and property. Indeed it represents "Rooseveltian rather than Jeffersonian Democracy." [28] Although the Philippine Constitution embodies the American doctrine of the separation of powers, this is not likely to mean what it has in the United States, for the reason that the powers of the Philippine president are predominant.[29] As indicated, the unicameral national assembly provided for in the Constitution as first adopted was discarded in favor of a bicameral legislature by an amendment of 1939. In general the Constitution reveals not only American but also Filipino and Spanish influence, and in particular reflects the political philosophy of recent as well as traditional American political thought.

THE PHILIPPINE PRESIDENCY

Under the Constitution, the Philippine president, elected by the direct vote of the people, has virtually all the powers possessed by his predecessor, the American governor-general. He does not share his power with other elective executive officials. In the great powers which the Philippine president exercises over appropriations for the operation of government, his position is comparable to that of the British cabinet, and, indeed, in a sense is stronger, since he cannot be turned out of office.[30]

THE CIVIL SERVICE

The American civil service which functioned in the Islands from the American conquest until 1913 was notable for its morale and efficiency. Later, the Wood-Forbes Report noted "a marked deterioration due to politics," and accused the Philippine legislature of passing laws

---

[28] Hayden, *The Philippines*, 42. In the constitutional declaration of principles it is said that: "The promotion of social justice to insure the well-being and economic security of all the people should be the concern of the State." The Philippine Constitution, Art. II, Sec. 5.

The government is also empowered to limit the rights of property in the interests of the general welfare and to expropriate land at just compensation to be subdivided and sold in small lots at cost. This reflected Filipino determination to prevent a recurrence of large estates once held by religious orders.

[29] V. G. Sinco, "The Separation of Powers in the Philippine Constitution," *Philippine Law Journal*, XV (1935), 281-290.

[30] On the position of the president see Hayden, *The Philippines*, 60-86.

"tending to demoralize" the civil service and to inject into it "the infection of politics." During the 1920's Governor-General Wood did much to restore and strengthen the merit system, but he could not secure improvement in the civil service law. Nevertheless, without pressure from the United States, the Filipinos wrote into their Constitution the principle of the independence and permanence of the merit system as applied to civil service. More important perhaps were the steps subsequently taken by the Commonwealth government to give immediate effect to the civil service provisions of the Constitution. These included amendment of the Civil Service Law and reorganization of the Bureau of Civil Service. This resulted in substantial improvement; but, as in the United States so in the Philippines, the legislature at times refused to classify positions which it was politically expedient to preserve as a part of the spoils system. Unfortunately, too, for the merit system, Philippine society, being quasi-feudal in its family and class relationships, has encouraged the rapid advancement of young men who have the protection of powerful patrons. But in general this evil has not been as marked as might have been anticipated.[31] It was the considered judgment of the late Professor J. R. Hayden that "the Philippine Civil Service is one of the most successful products of American-Filipino collaboration in the building of the Philippine state." [32]

LEGISLATURES IN THE PHILIPPINES

It is likewise as yet too early to pass judgment on the history of the legislative process in the Philippines. Until the establishment of the Commonwealth in 1935, the various legislatures of the Islands, from the first elective Assembly of 1907, were marked by two significant characteristics. In the first instance, they were colonial legislatures, in the second, they developed as instruments for the securing of independence rather than as the law-making body in a state whose constitutional structure was already determined. From 1907 until 1935, with the exception of the Harrison period, the position of the American executive in the Philippine government enabled the governor-general to tender advice on legislative policy and indeed to impose decisions with far greater freedom than could have been exercised by a native executive.

---

[31] The nationalization of the Philippine civil service is suggested by figures covering the years 1913 to 1917. Americans in the insular service in 1913 numbered about 2,600; in 1915 the figure was 1,978; in 1917 it was further reduced to 1,475.

The Philippine civil service is treated in detail in Hayden, *The Philippines*, 87-143.

[32] Hayden, *The Philippines*, 143.

While in terms of rules and organization the Philippine legislatures have followed the American model, they have nevertheless been Filipino in spirit. Their history is in no sense a slavish imitation of American practice, for Filipino legislators have been free from accumulated precedent. Moreover, one party, the *Nacionalistas,* has enjoyed almost unchallenged control and has written the legislative record of the young nation. Under the colonial period before 1935 and in the period of the Commonwealth after that date, the processes of Philippine law-making have too often served the causes of political expediency and corruption. Despite the spirit of the Constitution and the political oratory that flourishes at election time, Philippine legislatures have been handpicked, elected by controlled processes, and in every sense a tool of the president.

LAW AND THE ADMINISTRATION OF JUSTICE

The law of the Philippines and the legal institutions which have been created since 1899 have derived their form and substance from a number of sources: from Roman law of Spanish days; from English common law as revealed in American practice; from native Filipino customary law; and from the legal code of the Koran as it prevails among the Mohammedans of Mindanao and Sulu. From the beginning of the American occupation, the substance of the Bill of Rights of the American Constitution was extended to the Islands. With certain specific exceptions, such as trial by jury, it was included in the Organic Acts of 1902 and 1916; and, with additions, it constituted the new bill of rights in the Commonwealth Constitution of 1935. While the body of Philippine law consists of many codes, there has been an increasing tendency to interpret Philippine statutes according to the dictum of Anglo-American authorities and decisions.[33]

Under the Commonwealth, the Supreme Court is established by the Constitution; inferior courts are provided for by law. All judges are appointed by the president with the consent of a Commission on Appointments of the Congress. In a number of ways the Constitution seeks to guarantee the independence of the courts.[34] The gradual strengthening of the legal system and of the administration of justice

---

[33] Philippine law under the Commonwealth has comprised many hundred statutes and six codes: those of Spanish origin being the Civil Code, the Revised Penal Code, and the Code of Commerce; those of American origin being the Code of Criminal Procedure, and the Code of Civil Procedure, and finally the Revised Administrative Code of 1916 with later amendments.

[34] On the Philippine system of law note in particular Eugene A. Gilmore, "The Development of Law in the Philippines," *Iowa Law Review,* XVI (1931), 465-479; George A. Malcolm, *The Commonwealth of the Philippines* (New York, 1936).

has been as notable under the Commonwealth as it was in the days of American rule.[35]

POLITICAL PARTIES IN THE PHILIPPINES

During the period of American rule, Filipinos looked upon their political parties as instruments for political independence. The exception to this generalization was the *Partido Federalista* (Federal Party), which in the days of the insurrection was the party favoring immediate peace with the United States. Since peace could only be had by accepting American sovereignty, this party favored statehood in the American Union as the highest status to which the Philippines could aspire because they could not resist American arms successfully. The Federalists were conservatives of the upper-classes. The Party gave unstinted aid to American authorities in their efforts to end the insurrection. By 1905, however, the Federalists were favoring "ultimate independence." [36]

From 1900 to 1905, sometimes called the "period of suppressed nationalism," a great many political groups appeared which favored immediate or early independence; but it was not until 1907 that these abortive efforts resulted in the union of various groups to form the *Partido Nacionalista*. At the same time the Federalists adopted the name *Partido Nacional Progresista*, and thus became the conservative nationalist and independence party. Beginning with the election of the first Philippine Assembly by a semi-popular electorate in 1907, the *Partido Nacionalista* won a majority which it not only held but increased in successive elections. It was this party which succeeded in identifying itself most closely with the cause of independence. It was also this party which took the position that it was responsible to the Filipino voters as well as to the American sovereign power which had created the Assembly in which this majority party now functioned. A third party, the *Partido Democrata Nacional*, making its appearance in 1917, was composed of some members of the discredited *Progresistas* and dissatisfied *Nacionalistas*. It functioned as the opposition party until 1931.

Until 1934-35, when the Tydings-McDuffie Law was accepted by the Filipino people, the history of political parties in the Islands was affected and controlled primarily by: 1) the issue of independence and 2) political rivalries within a small group of able leaders. During the Commonwealth the factor of personalities did not disappear, but in

---

[35] The important subject of local self-government in the Philippines and of the tendencies toward greater centralization are treated by Hayden, *The Philippines*, 261-312.

[36] Dapen Liang, *The Development of Philippine Parties* (Hongkong, 1939).

some degree it was subordinated to the major task of constructing a government capable of meeting new problems inseparable from independence. The need for statesmanship was emphasized by the *Sakdalista* rebellion of May 2, 1935. This was an abortive attempt by underprivileged elements to overthrow the government in Manila. The result was to hasten formation of a limited coalition between the dominant leaders, Quezon and Osmeña, and their respective political followings or parties.[37] With Quezon as President and Osmeña as Vice-President, the Commonwealth moved toward the Republic of the Philippines under the same nationalist party and the same leaders who had guided the campaigns for independence since 1907. In the 1941 elections there was no opposition party; to be on the *Nacionalista* list was to be elected.

EDUCATION IN THE PHILIPPINES

Since the beginning of the American occupation of the Philippines Filipino leaders have favored free public education and the separation of church and state. The broad objectives of the American educational program were: to abolish illiteracy, to provide every child with a modern elementary education, to provide a limited secondary and higher education, and to give instruction in the English language for all. In 1925 the accomplishments and failures of the program were revealed by a commission of recognized American educators.[38] In 1939 there were 1,861,861 students in the Philippine public school system, or only 45 percent of the estimated school population between the ages of 7 and 17. This percentage, as Hayden points out, should be judged in the light of other factors: 1) the inability of the Islands to pay for high-school education for all and 2) consideration for the social, economic, and political problems which would arise if secondary and higher education were extended to greatly increased numbers under present conditions.[39] Whatever the limitations in educational progress may have been, it is worth noting that the Constitution of the Commonwealth and the Republic requires that:

All educational institutions shall be under the supervision of and subject to regulation by the State. The Government shall establish and maintain a

---

[37] By this time constant shifts and reunions among political groups had complicated party terminology. Quezon's party was now known as the *Nacionalista-Democrata;* Osmeña's as the *Nacionalista-Democrata Pro-Independencia.*

[38] Board of Educational Survey, *A Survey of the Educational System of the Philippine Islands* (Manila, 1925).

[39] Hayden, *The Philippines,* 469-470.

complete and adequate system of public education, and shall provide at least free public primary instruction, and citizenship training to adult citizens. All schools shall aim to develop moral character, personal discipline, civic conscience, and vocational efficiency, and to teach the duties of citizenship. Optional religious instruction shall be maintained in the public schools as now authorized by law. Universities established by the State shall enjoy academic freedom. The State shall create scholarships in arts, science, and letters for specially gifted citizens.[40]

One of the principal tasks of the Commonwealth has been to re-organize its vocational schools and courses, to elevate the prestige of vocational training, and to adjust these courses to the practical needs of the country. Despite these efforts, Filipino students still showed a marked preference for the academic course and the prestige which it has carried. In addition, the Commonwealth has been confronted with the tremendous task of adult education, on which it had been able to make little more than a beginning at the outbreak of World War II. In 1940 there were more than 5,000,000 Filipinos who had been unable to attend school during childhood.

PRINCIPLES VERSUS REALITIES

To recapitulate, it may be freely acknowledged that the period of American rule in the Philippines, 1898-1935, brought great and good changes in the life of the Islands, and laid a substantial foundation for a democratic society. On this foundation the Filipino may continue to build if his leadership is so minded. That this will be the case is, how-ever, by no means certain, for Filipino "democracy" in practice is dis-tinctly different from its formal structure in terms of the Constitution. In appearance, this government, whether of the Republic or of the Com-monwealth which preceded it, possesses the outward forms of an Ameri-can-styled democracy. Yet competent students aver that in "operation it is evolving into a quasi-dictatorship with democratic embellish-ments."[41] Part of the explanation lies in the fact that the Filipino is still a Malay far more than he is an American. Many still prefer a society in which a leader does the political thinking. Politics is still a matter of personalities rather than principles, and the voter is apt to choose the most eloquent speaker. Of course, American politics is not immune to these tendencies, but here they are at least frowned upon. Other ways in which Philippine democracy has far to travel are ex-

[40] Art. XIII, Sec. 5.
[41] Lennox A. Mills, "The Governments of Southeast Asia," *Government and Nationalism in Southeast Asia* (New York, 1942), 65.

emplified by experiences of the new Republic and by certain social movements which made their appearance about 1930.

THE PHILIPPINE REPUBLIC

On July 4, 1946, the Commonwealth of the Philippines, inaugurated in 1935, became the Philippine Republic when Manuel A. Roxas took office as its first president in the presence of General Douglas MacArthur and Paul V. McNutt, the American Ambassador and formerly a high commissioner to the Commonwealth. In the presidential election of April, 1946, Roxas had received a majority of some 200,000 out of a total vote of 2,500,000 over Commonwealth President Sergio Osmeña. The Republic was inaugurated against a political background of charges, denials, and counter-charges. The new president, an active leader in Philippine politics prior to World War II, had been captured by the Japanese after the fall of Corregidor. His record during the Japanese occupation was a question on which there was violent and bitter dispute. The view of his supporters, and, presumably, the official view of the United States, was that he resisted Japanese efforts to place him in the puppet government, finally accepting with reluctance a post connected with the collection of food. By his critics he was regarded as a collaborationist who should have been brought to trial for holding important offices in Japan's puppet regime.[42]

After his "liberation" by American forces, Roxas "was put on active duty with the rank of brigadier general in General MacArthur's headquarters,"[43] until in June, 1945, he returned to political life. Given a clean bill of political health by General MacArthur, Roxas and his political supporters carried the presidential election, and the collaborationist issue was presumably closed.[44] Other troubles, however, confronted the new president. The national treasury was empty. There was a large budgetary deficit, and the country as a whole faced shortages of staple foodstuffs to an extent even threatening famine. The sugar in-

---

[42] Monroe Hall, "Collaborator's Candidate," *Far Eastern Survey*, XV (1946), 72-73. See also Claude A. Buss, "The Philippines: Problems of Independence," *Pacific Islands* (Boulder, Colorado, 1946), 17-18.

[43] Monroe Hall, "Collaborator's Candidate," 73.

[44] The clear majority which Roxas received in the election suggests implications that are broader than politics alone. The Filipino people chose to applaud Roxas "for his motives rather than to criticise him for his acts. A vote for Mr. Roxas was salve to the conscience of the individual Filipino. Most Filipinos were not able to live as guerrillas. They had to stay at home, face the enemy, and match wits against him for their lives and welfare. It was impossible to defy him and expect to exist. . . . In voting for Mr. Roxas they rationalized their own decisions, and in placing the stamp of approval upon him, they placed it upon themselves." Buss, "The Philippines: Problems of Independence," 17.

dustry had been so wrecked by the war that production for 1945-46 was below one tenth of domestic requirements. Rice production was crippled because of the loss of draft animals killed during the Japanese occupation. These conditions were an immediate and direct consequence of the war, but linked with them was a deep-seated social unrest manifesting itself in armed rebellion against the government of the new Republic. This social unrest, though aggravated by the war, long antedated the Japanese invasion. It was a direct result not of the war but of the socio-economic structure dating back to Spanish days, and which the period of American rule failed to eradicate.

THE ECONOMIC CLASS STRUCTURE OF THE PHILIPPINES

Unlike the United States and other Western democracies, in the Philippine Islands there is no large Filipino middle class. Much of the commerce and trade of the Islands has been in the hands of the Chinese, who have also to some extent been the money lenders. While many of the Chinese returned to China and were replaced by newcomers, others remained in the Islands and married Filipino women. Many Spaniards also married Filipinos, and it is the descendants of these mixed marriages, the mestizos, who compose the core of the native ruling class. Former President Quezon was a Spanish mestizo, his successor, President Osmeña, a Chinese mestizo. In general the mestizos, numbering some 900,000, a very small proportion of the total population, appear to be abler and more active than the native pure-blooded Filipino. It is the mestizo class which has profited most by the introduction of self-government. It holds most of the important posts in politics, the professions, business, and agriculture, and controls most of the wealth. The native Filipino in contrast is generally a peasant or manual laborer, and "a high percentage of them are heavily in debt to the propertied class." [45] Since 1930, as the peasant has acquired some little political consciousness, his tendency to resist those whom he regards as his oppressors arises both from the fact that he is frequently incapable of freeing himself from debt and also because this debt is frequently held by the same class which controls politics and government, namely, the large landowner. It is the landed proprietor who controls local candidates and tells the peasant for whom to vote. This influence is not of course surprising in a land where nearly half the population is still illiterate and where only about 15 percent has some education beyond the primary school.

---

[45] Mills, "The Governments of Southeast Asia," 66.

Until 1934, politics in the Philippines was almost exclusively a question of achieving independence. When this was disposed of by 1934 the political picture shifted to considerations of the future of the Islands' economy when independence had deprived them of a free American market. It happened, however, that this shift coincided with the full impact of the depression of the early thirties which aggravated the already unhappy condition of the underprivileged peasant. This was the setting which nurtured the *Sakdal,* Labor, and Communist parties which rose in the thirties to challenge the established political groups.[46]

The *Sakdal* Party led by Benigno Ramos which appeared in the depression years of the early 1930's aimed its program directly at the tenant-landlord problem with its concomitants of farm debt and low standards of life among rural dwellers. The *Sakdal* movement was also a protest against the control of the national life by the traditional parties composed primarily of the aristocracy and the intelligentsia. The willingness of the *Sakdalistas* to resort to force when their demands for reform were ignored led to the charge by the aristocracy and business interests that the party was communist. Regardless of the validity of the charge, the *Sakdals* revealed surprising strength with the electorate, and for this reason were feared all the more by the traditional politicians.

The same years brought forth an infant communist party led by Crisanto Evangelista. It opposed acceptance, as did also the *Sakdals,* of the Constitution of the Commonwealth and the Republic, advocating instead a Soviet form of government. At the outbreak of World War II, the *Sakdal,* the Communist, and a small labor union movement were still nourished by economic and social maladjustments which the government had done little to cure, and which to far too great a degree it had sought to ignore.[47]

Neither the liberation of the Philippines nor the establishment of the Republic could of themselves remove the fundamental causes of this social unrest. Indeed the experiences of the war tended to aggravate the problem. The young Republic was faced at its inception with armed revolt throughout the great rice bowl of Central Luzon. The Hukbalahaps (army of the people for fighting Japan), an armed peasant group of ex-guerrillas between 100,000 and 200,000 strong had waged merciless war against the Japanese. When peace came and the Japanese were removed, the Huks, who in part at least inherit the program of the pre-war *Sakdals,* were not prepared to lay down their arms until the

[46] See Karl Pelzer, *Pioneer Settlement in the Asiatic Tropics* (New York, 1945), 88-114.
[47] Note the discussion by Virginia Thompson "Nationalism and Nationalist Movements in Southeast Asia," in *Government and Nationalism in Southeast Asia,* 154-156.

grievances of the peasants had been met by the absentee proprietors of Manila who own the land and whose political record has not been of a kind to inspire peasant confidence.[48]   While appealing to the Huks to surrender their arms and seek a peaceful adjustment of grievances, the Roxas government prepared to crush the rebellion by force if necessary. Only the future could reveal whether the Philippine Republic could meet the real problem: removal of the economic and social causes that were sustaining the Huk movement.

THE UNITED STATES AND THE PHILIPPINES

Although the Philippines are now an independent nation, the ties between the United States and the Islands remain exceedingly strong. In 1946 this country gave the Philippine Army $50,000,000 worth of equipment.   The United States Congress authorized grants of $620,-000,000 for Philippine reconstruction necessitated by the war.   In addition, the Bell Act provided for free trade for eight years and for a gradually increasing tariff during the succeeding 20 years with special inducements for American capital in the Islands.   These measures suggest a policy of continued close connections, and some elements in the policy have led to Filipino charges that the young Republic is to become "another Cuba."   The Islands remain an important factor in the thinking of American naval and military authorities, and America retains rights in army, navy, and air bases in the Republic.   An old pre-war dilemma still confronts the Filipino politician in these post-war years. He appreciates and covets American protection, yet he wishes to be unhampered and unconfined in the control of his own political affairs.

----

[48] The Hukbalahaps were "organized in March, 1942, in an area in Luzon where the gap between landlord and tenant was widest.   The Huks did fight against the Japanese, and they absorbed into their organization Communists, liberal educators, labor leaders, peasants, and 'commercial bandits.'   They killed landlords as well as Japs, but they killed landlords because they were collaborators and not because they were landlords. The landlords looked to the invading [Japanese] army for protection of their privileges, and the Japs looked to the landlords for the continued production of sugar, tobacco, or cotton and for the continued collection of taxes.   Some landlords managed to survive. During the battle of liberation they absented themselves and the peasants took over." The Huks sought the friendship of the liberating Americans but were suspected of wishing to overthrow the government by force, and so their organization was outlawed by American military officials.   Buss, "The Philippines: Problems of Independence," 18.

CHAPTER 36

THE SINO-JAPANESE UNDECLARED WAR, 1937-1941, AND THE NEW ORDER IN EASTERN ASIA

THE new phase of continental expansion which the Japanese army had undertaken in September, 1931, and to which it had since committed the Japanese government was not designed to be limited, and indeed could not be limited, within the old borders of China's Three Eastern Provinces—Fengtien, Kirin, and Heilungkiang. Manchuria, while valuable in itself, was of still greater significance to Japan as a base from which to dominate the politics and the economics of China. These ends, however, could not be achieved satisfactorily in the Japanese view until the Kuomintang-Nationalist government was brought to terms, and the "menace" of Communism in China was removed. The creation of Manchukuo was therefore a step toward greater expansion into North China and westward toward Outer and especially Inner Mongolia. From these movements, which, as will be seen, were to prove abortive, came the renewal of general Sino-Japanese hostilities in the bloody though undeclared war of 1937-1941, and the final merging of this conflict with the world conflagration that began with Pearl Harbor.

CONSOLIDATION IN MANCHUKUO AFTER 1932

Although unrecognized at first by any great power save Japan, the new state of Manchukuo was the scene of striking developments in the years following 1932. In 1933 its borders were extended by the Japanese conquest of Jehol province in eastern Inner Mongolia. On March 1, 1934, Henry Pu-yi, the last Manchu emperor of China, was enthroned as the Emperor Kangtê. Under a constitution of the same date, Manchukuo became a monarchy with both executive and legislative authority exercised by the emperor, though the latter powers were subject to the approval of a Legislative Council. Real power, however, remained in the hands of the Japanese Ambassador to Manchukuo who was at the same time commander of Japanese and Manchukuo troops

641

and governor of the Kwantung Territory. Simultaneously with these events Japan encouraged the settlement of Japanese and Korean farmers in northeastern Manchukuo against the Soviet frontier, and encouraged the investment of Japanese capital for the development of Manchurian resources in general and mineral resources in particular.

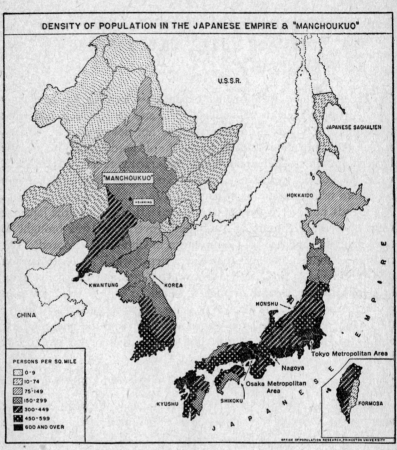

DENSITY OF POPULATION IN THE JAPANESE EMPIRE & "MANCHOUKUO"

United States, Department of State. Division of Map Intelligence and Cartography.

The objectives of this policy appear to have been both economic and strategic. During 1932 to 1937 the foundations were also laid for a huge industrial expansion. New pioneer construction included: the building of a new capital city, Hsinking (the former Changchun), construction of new railways, highways, and ports (such as Rashin), the construction of hydro-electric plants, the opening of new mines. All these activities were actively encouraged by the Japanese-dominated Manchukuo government; but the response of private Japanese capital from the great *Zaibatsu* families and the wealthy South Manchuria Railroad were insufficient to meet the demands of the Kwantung Army militarists who hoped to build in Manchuria not only a great arsenal against Communist Russia but also to establish a species of model state built on principles akin to national socialism and thus free from the "corrupt" influences of Japan's capitalists and party politicians.[1] Accordingly, late in 1937, the coal, iron, steel, light metals, automobile, and airplane industries were placed under the management of a new corporation, the Manchuria Industrial Development Company, in which half the stock was held by the Manchukuo government. Transportation, including railways, highways, harbors, etc., remained under the management of the South Manchuria Railway controlled by the Japanese government. These developments were in line with the fundamental policy announced in March, 1933, through which the Kwantung Army hoped "to avoid the baneful effects of unbridled capitalism through the application of a certain measure of national control so that a sound development in all branches of the people's economy may be realized."[2] The private as opposed to the government stock of the new Manchuria Industrial Development Company was taken largely by a younger group of Japanese capitalists headed by Yoshisuke Aikawa and known as the Nissan interests. This great holding company was advertised as representing the "capitalism of the people" and was regarded as a junior rival of the older and more conservative corporations such as Mitsui and Mitsubishi.[3] The move served the additional purpose of bringing pressure on the older concerns to support the economic policies of the militarists.

JAPANESE INVESTMENTS IN MANCHURIA AND MANCHUKUO

This industrial exploitation of Manchukuo represented a fantastic influx of Japanese capital. Prior to the Manchurian Incident of 1931, Japanese investments in the South Manchurian sphere of influence amounted to ¥1,617,000,000, nearly 50 percent of which represented outlays of the South Manchuria Railway. In 1938 total Japanese invest-

---

[1] Paul H. Clyde, "Japan's Investment in Manchuria," *Geographical Magazine,* Nov., 1939.

[2] South Manchuria Railway, *Fifth Report on Progress in Manchuria to 1936* (Dairen, 1937), 98.

[3] Hugh Borton, *Japan Since 1931* (New York, 1940), 51.

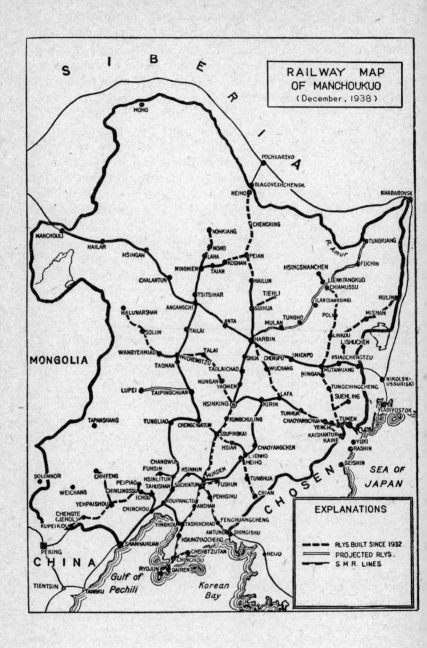

ments in Manchukuo were about ¥3,441,000,000 and by the end of 1939 the figure had probably reached ¥4,500,000,000. Much of this investment took the form of imports of mining, factory, and textile machinery, and of consumption goods.[4]

MANCHUKUO'S FOREIGN RELATIONS

In line with the American Non-Recognition Doctrine, none of the great powers, save Japan, at first recognized Manchukuo, and of the small powers, only El Salvador, the Papacy, and the Dominion Republic had extended recognition by 1934. Germany, however, gave qualified recognition in a trade agreement of the same year, renewed for a second three years in 1937, and in November, 1937, Italy formally recognized the puppet state.[5] Full German recognition came on May 12, 1938, and was soon followed by recognition from Poland and Hungary. On February 24, 1939, Manchukuo became a signatory of the Anti-Comintern Pact concluded by Germany and Japan on November 25, 1936. For the time being, however, these political niceties of recognition were of less significance than the fundamental economic conflict over the open door in Manchuria brought to light by the Manchukuo Oil Monopoly Law of November, 1934. Under this law the Manchuria Petroleum Company formed in February, 1934, by the Manchukuo government was "to monopolize the exploitation and refining of crude petroleum." The Law made refined petroleum products a government monopoly, permitting their manufacture, exportation, and importation only by authorized dealers. The object, again, was both economic and strategic, "to develop Manchurian resources and refining capacity at the expense of the importers of refined products." The large foreign oil companies, American, British, and Dutch, charged that they were being forced out of the Manchurian market. The American, British, and Dutch governments protested to Japan that the open door was being violated. Japan denied responsibility and suggested that the powers negotiate with Manchukuo. This of course they could not do under the non-recognition policy.[6]

[4] E. B. Schumpeter, ed., *The Industrialization of Japan and Manchukuo, 1930-1940* (New York, 1940), 398.

[5] Russia in selling its Chinese Eastern Railway interests to Manchukuo in 1935 thereby presumably extended *de facto* recognition to the new state. Moreover, Manchukuo maintained consular agents in Siberia with, of course, Moscow's consent.

[6] Schumpeter, *Industrialization of Japan and Manchukuo*, 394; Irving S. Friedman, *British Relations with China: 1931-1939* (New York, 1940), 47-49.

A WELL-ORDERED PUPPET

During the decade of the 1930's the internal politics and government of Manchukuo were ordered better than the outside world of non-recognizing powers was prepared to admit. Under an authoritarian,

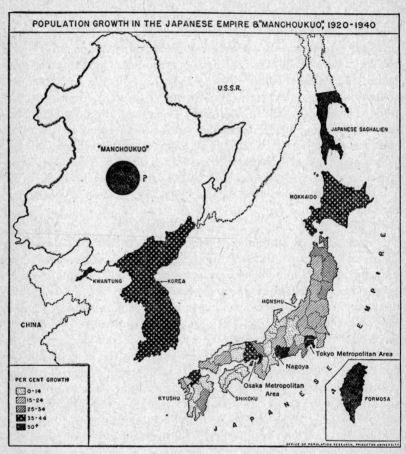

United States, Department of State. Division of Map Intelligence and Cartography.

highly regimented regime, Manchuria possessed greater stability than at any time in its modern history. Chinese who resisted were hunted down and disposed of. For those who accepted the regime, there was increased security for life and property;[7] the government now operated

---

[7] While in general this was true, there is also evidence that those who suffered from Japanese rule were not solely those who resisted. See in particular the picture presented

on a budget in contrast to the whimsical finance followed in previous years by the Old Marshal, Chang Tso-lin, and his son, Chang Hsueh-liang; taxes were reduced and more honestly collected, and a new uniform currency, the Manchurian yuan, was created and given stability by tying it to the Japanese yen. The opium business, long a plague in Manchuria, was not wiped out, but it was brought under rigid government control and limitation. The political philosophy on which the Japanese sought to rest the new state was a revival of the Confucian principle of *Wang Tao,* the kingly way. This made a strong appeal to all traditionally minded elements in the overwhelming Chinese population. The weakness lay in the inability of the Japanese to conceal the complete control which they always exercised. Although the "front" positions in government were held by Chinese, Manchus, and Mongols, all vice-ministerial and key executive posts were held by Japanese vice-ministers or advisers. With this unbroken control in their hands it was possible, as the Japanese did in 1935, to surrender their extraterritorial rights to Manchukuo, and to use this as further evidence of Japan's "friendly" purposes not only as regards Manchukuo but also toward China.

By 1937 Japan had made considerable progress toward integrating the economic and strategic values of Manchukuo with those of the homeland. In general, the idea had been that Manchuria would provide the raw materials in minerals and foodstuffs lacked by Japan's growing industrial society. On the credit side, so far as Japan was concerned, Manchurian population was rapidly increasing, new farm lands were opened, industry, particularly coal, iron, and steel, were expanding. On the debit side was the instability of the international picture pervaded by the insatiable fever of the Kwantung Army to insure the borders of the new state by pushing its boundaries into Mongolia and by forcing the establishment of friendly governments in North China.[8]

THE JAPANESE ADVANCE IN INNER MONGOLIA

Having established herself in Manchuria, it was inevitable that Japan should also move into Inner Mongolia. It will be recalled that Japan's interests in that region had been clearly expressed in the Twenty-One

by W. I. Ladejinsky, "Manchurian Agriculture under Japanese Control," *Foreign Agriculture,* V (1941), 309-340. Moreover, there was great economic pressure on the people of Manchuria as Japan's war program developed. These factors all served to keep alive a Manchurian resistance movement.

[8] The conclusion is developed by Schumpeter in *Industrialization of Japan and Manchukuo,* 3-37.

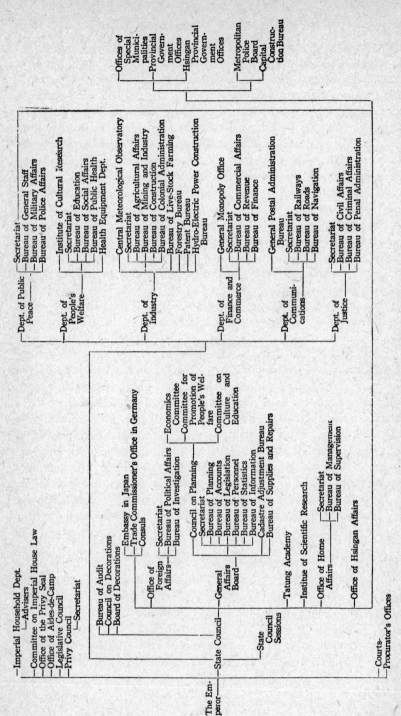

CHART OF THE GOVERNMENT OF MANCHUKUO.

Demands of 1915. With Inner Mongolia under her control Japan would be in a stronger position to control North China, and to prevent the extension of Russian influence from Outer Mongolia. Moreover, the Kwantung Army believed that it could play upon the existing friction between the Mongol herdsmen and Chinese farmer colonists. After 1912 Chinese farmers encroached upon Inner Mongolia's lands that are marginal between farming and grazing. In the period of republican China after 1912 Inner Mongolia had been incorporated as provinces of China—Jehol, Chahar, Suiyuan, and Ningsia. To these areas Chinese farmers from heavily populated areas south of the Wall had been encouraged to migrate. This influx and the consequent loss by the Mongols of much of their grazing land increased the inherent enmity between the two groups.

Hoping to further its plans by taking advantage of this situation, the Kwantung Army moved to the support of the most aristocratic and conservative Mongol groups: the Mongol princes and the priesthood of the Lama Buddhist Church, both of which were prepared to see in Japan a possible protector against the Chinese farmer and against Russian Communists from Outer Mongolia. The first step was the creation of a virtually autonomous Mongol province in western Manchuria incorporating part of Jehol, which had been added to Manchukuo in 1933.[9] Here, by guaranteeing the Mongols possession of their grazing lands, by insuring and respecting their autonomous government, and by fostering the privileges of the Lama priests, the Japanese hoped to appeal to the Mongols in general, including those in Outer Mongolia. The scheme was not entirely successful since the Mongol princes bargained also with the Chinese Nationalists at Nanking. For a time, beginning in 1934, the princes maintained an autonomous government in Inner Mongolia which accepted Chinese advisers. It had, however, little military power and so was unable to resist the Kwantung Army which by 1937 had occupied most of Chahar.

THE JAPANESE IN THE PEI-P'ING AND TIENTSIN AREA

Just as the Kwantung Army felt it necessary to move westward into Inner Mongolia, so it became even more essential to establish friendly governments in the northeastern sections of China Proper, especially in the provinces of Hopei, Shantung, and Shansi. These provinces could be linked, so it was thought, with the Inner Mongolian provinces of Chahar and Suiyuan (yet to be conquered), to give Japan control of all bordering territory to the south and west of Manchukuo. Also, as

[9] T. A. Bisson, *Japan in China* (New York, 1938), 60-63.

in the case of Inner Mongolia, Japanese action was declared to be in self defense. In North China this argument was more plausible since here the country was controlled after 1932 by Chang Hsueh-liang and his armies, which had retreated from Manchuria. His hopes of regaining his home land, and his resistance to the Japanese in Jehol provided the occasion though not the cause for bringing the Kwantung Army south of the Wall into the Pei-p'ing and Tientsin area where, as already noted, in May, 1933, the Tangku truce was signed. This provided for demilitarization of portions of Hopei province but not for

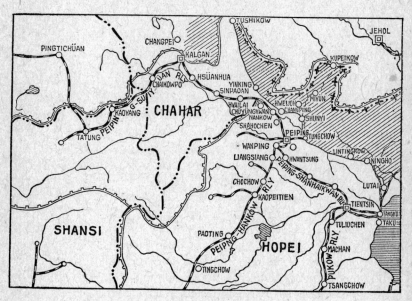

THE DEMILITARIZED ZONE OF THE TANGKU TRUCE.

removal of Japanese troops maintained between Pei-p'ing and Tientsin under the Boxer Protocol. Chinese police "friendly" to Japan were to maintain order in the demilitarized areas. Confusion was compounded by the fact that the Tangku truce and other agreements subsequently reached were negotiated with local officials whose relationship to the Nanking Government was not always clear. Nevertheless, there was temporary improvement, since in the two years following the truce postal service and rail traffic, passenger and freight, was resumed between Manchukuo and China, though without the latter extending formal recognition. Underlying friction, however, was unabated, and by 1935 the Kwantung Army had exerted enough pressure to force the

retirement of more Chinese troops from Hopei and to liquidate the
Kuomintang in the region.

It was at this juncture, when General Kenji Doihara, the so-called
Lawrence of Manchuria, was a chief spokesman of the Kwantung

The New York Times.

IN 1935, IMPERIALISTIC GROUPS IN JAPAN FAVORED CREATION OF AN AUTONOMOUS
NORTH CHINA, FREE FROM THE POLITICAL CONTROL OF NANKING AND UNDER THE
TUTELAGE OF MANCHUKUO.

Army, that there was much talk of an "autonomous North China state"
to be composed of the five provinces of Chahar, Suiyuan, Shansi, Hopei,
and Shantung. The area was presumably to be annexed from the uncertain control of Nanking and governed by Chinese willing to co-

operate with Japan. Seeking to prevent his *démarche,* the Nanking Government encouraged the organization of new local governments which would be acceptable to the Japanese. As a consequence, by 1936 Chang Hsueh-liang's armies had moved further to the west; the more pronouncedly anti-Japanese organs of government, such as the Pei-p'ing Political Council, had been dissolved, their functions being taken over by two new local governments, the East Hopei Autonomous Council, clearly dominated by the Japanese, and the Hopei-Chahar Political Council, which was supposedly friendly to Japan.[10] But unlike the previous course of events in Manchuria, the new autonomous state did not materialize. Had the Kwantung Army been better schooled in the fundamental relations of China Proper and Manchuria, it might have realized that what could be done north of the Wall could not, as a matter of course, be done south of the Wall. At all events, Japanese interests sought temporary profits through the new indirect control of East Hopei where Japanese goods in huge quantities were smuggled into the territory or were permitted to enter at one fourth the regular tariff rates. Most notorious of all was the growth of the opium traffic in the hands of Japanese and Koreans. Here a primary objective was not immediate profits to private traders but demoralization of the entire customs administration in North China, thus detaching the area from reliance on Nanking and creating a new dependence upon Japan.[11]

Simultaneously with the Japanese infiltration into North China came renewed efforts of Japanese diplomacy to reach an understanding with China as a whole. There was always the hope among Japanese statesmen that a workable arrangement could be reached for close political and economic planning among Japan, Manchukuo, and China. The fact that the rise of a new Chinese nationalism had already precluded such a scheme of Japanese domination does not appear to have been fully appreciated in Tokyo. However, Japan's success in Manchukuo and the continued factional strife within China lent a rational plausibility to the Japanese hope. Indeed, on the surface, Japan appeared to make some progress. There were elements within the Kuomintang-National Government prepared to adopt a policy of appeasement either from personal conviction on the principle of a Pan-Asiatic policy or because they regarded resistance by China as hopeless. Consequently, during 1935 Nanking made some efforts to stop anti-Japanese boycotts,

[10] Bisson, *Japan in China,* 97-98, 100-110.
[11] *The China Year Book, 1936,* 140.

to prevent publication of inflammatory anti-Japanese articles, and to suppress the student movement.[12]

Nanking, however, was not entirely subservient. When in 1934 Japan warned the League powers and the United States to follow a policy of "hands off" China, the Nanking Government denied the right of Japan to assert a monopoly of political interest in the Far East. Manifestly, there was nothing in the general situation as it was developing to indicate that the Chinese people were prepared to submit humbly to Japan or that Japan had found any effective way to limit the advance into China begun in 1931. Furthermore, by 1937 the international situation in the Far East, particularly as it affected Great Britain's financial empire there, had been revolutionized. Since of all Western

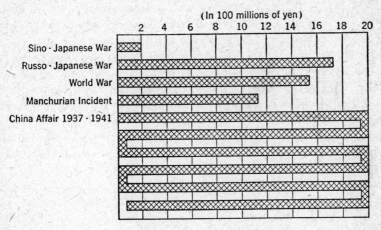

EXPENSES OF JAPAN'S WARS.

nations Great Britain still held the largest financial stake in China, it is essential to trace briefly the course of British policy as it developed after the Manchurian Incident of 1931.

BRITISH POLICY IN THE FAR EAST, 1931-1937

The historic cleavage which had frequently existed between British and American policy in the Far East was not ended with Japan's invasion of Manchuria in 1931. In January, 1932, Great Britain declined to give its formal support when the United States enunciated the so-called Stimson Non-Recognition Doctrine covering Japan's con-

[12] See the Ho-Umetsu agreement, and Nanking's "Good-Will Mandate," 1935, Bisson, *Japan in China*, 55-58.

quests. British policy as interpreted by *The Times* was that it was not the business of the British government to defend "the 'administrative integrity' of China until that integrity" was "something more than an ideal." Although as the Manchurian affair progressed through the counsels of the League, Great Britain showed greater disposition to support co-operative action, her course from 1931 to 1933 was "on the whole favorable to Japan rather than to China," and she "acted more vigorously and promptly when Shanghai, the center of British interests, was attacked than when Manchuria, in which she had substantial but relatively less important interests, was invaded." Defenders of British policy in this period maintain that her position was logical since she "could not rely on the United States for more than moral support."[13]

During 1934, Britain, confronted with an increasingly turbulent situation in Europe and a constitutional crisis in India, continued the policy of appeasing Japan at the expense of British prestige in China. The futility of this was the more evident since during 1933-1935 Japan continued, as noted in previous pages, to pursue a positive and aggressive policy. But by the close of 1934, when Japan denounced the Washington and the London Naval Treaties, previous to which a Japanese naval training squadron had been hospitably received by Hitler, the British government began to show greater concern for its position in China. This concern was further increased by an economic depression which struck Shanghai and Hongkong in 1934, where British financial interests predominated.[14] This precipitated anew in Britain an unofficial debate on the merits of Anglo-American versus Anglo-Japanese co-operation.[15] For the time being, during 1934 and the early part of 1935, Britain's official policy continued to see avenues of Anglo-Japanese co-operation while simultaneously attempting to re-establish Britain's diplomatic prestige at Nanking and to increase British financial and technical aid in China's economic reconstruction. Supporting the policy of Anglo-Japanese co-operation was the Mission of the Federation of British Industries to Japan and Manchukuo, October and November, 1934, which produced no positive results.[16]

---

[13] Friedman, *British Relations with China: 1931-1939*, 18-42.

[14] This financial crisis was in part a result of the World Economic Conference silver agreement, July, 1933, and the United States Silver Purchase Act of June, 1934, of the increasing tendency of China's silver to leave the country, and of a decrease in China's foreign trade. In 1935 the National Government embargoed the export of silver. For details on the silver question in China see Friedman, *British Relations with China: 1931-1939*, 51-54.

[15] The arguments in this debate are developed by Friedman, 54-58.

[16] See Federation of British Industries, *Report of the Mission to the Far East, August-November, 1934.*

It was in late 1935 and in 1936 that British diplomacy in China finally initiated a new policy which, perhaps more than any other single factor, clarified the basic issue of the coming struggle. In June, 1935, the British government announced it was sending its chief economic adviser, Sir Frederick Leith-Ross, to the Far East, and it invited the American, French, and Japanese governments to send similar missions. This request was declined, and in Tokyo the Japanese government rebuffed Sir Frederick's proposals for *joint* financial aid to the Nanking Government. The inspired Japanese press expressed the official view that the time had passed when Japan could co-operate with other powers in China on "an equal footing." [17] This Japanese principle, by no means new in 1935, had long precluded and was to continue to preclude an amicable far eastern settlement.

The arrival of the British mission in China coincided with decrees by the National Government nationalizing silver and stabilizing its currency, a program which would probably not have been practical but for "the support given to it by the British government." [18] There was thus emerging a new British policy which recognized "that Britain's position depended on an independent Nanking." British finance would seek to rehabilitate Nationalist China and thus strengthen her against Japan.

The Japanese reaction was one of bitter hostility, particularly from the militarists. The Japanese War Office accused Nanking of selling the country to foreigners.[19] By the spring of 1937 there had been some improvement in Anglo-Japanese relations but Britain's new fundamental policy had not been changed. London was now committed with some degree of certainty to the support of Nanking and to the success of its new financial program.

TIGHTENING LINES OF CLEAVAGE

The new British backing bolstered resistance forces within the Kuomintang-Nationalist government at Nanking and indirectly stimulated the movement for a popular front against Japan as manifested in the Sian kidnapping episode of December, 1936, already discussed (p. 616). It also stimulated the Japanese to renewed but fruitless efforts to bring

---

[17] Discussions of the British mission and of Anglo-American as well as Anglo-Japanese rivalry are in G. E. Taylor, "The Powers and the Unity of China," *Pacific Affairs*, IX (1936), 532-543; "Japan in China: the Far Eastern Problem," *Round Table* (London), XXV (1935), 684-696; L. T. K. Wu, "China's Monetary Dilemma," *Far Eastern Survey*, IV (1935), 190-194.

[18] Friedman, *British Relations with China: 1931-1939*, 66-67.

[19] *Survey of International Affairs, 1935* (2 vols., London, 1936), I, 323.

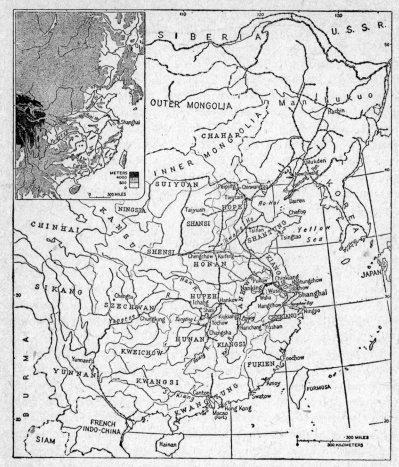

CHINA AND NORTHEASTERN ASIA, 1936.   Illustrating the complicated politico-geographical relations of China, Soviet Russia, and Japan (Manchoukuo).   The inset emphasizes the high mountain and plateau barriers that focus the Yangtze Valley on
Shanghai.   *Courtesy of John E. Orchard and of the "Geographical Review," published
by the American Geographical Society of New York.*

China to terms.   In October, 1935, the Hirota government suggested a
Sino-Japanese settlement based on three principles.   China was to abandon the policy of playing one country against another; she must recognize Manchukuo; and she must devise joint measures with Japan for
the suppression of communism.[20]   To implement diplomatically this
program, Japan, in 1936, sent a succession of special ambassadors to

[20] Bisson, *Japan in China*, 126.

Nanking, but without success. By the close of 1936, Japan was also demanding of Nanking recognition of Japan's "special position" in North China, where, as already noted, she had failed to establish an autonomous government. Meanwhile at Berlin, Japan and Germany on November 25, 1936, signed the Anti-Comintern Pact designed to provide for co-operation in "defense against the disintegrating influence of communism." [21] Furthermore, at Shanghai the Japanese were declaiming against Britain's predominant position on the Municipal Council of the International Settlement; at home the Japanese press was denouncing Canada and Australia because of the commercial restrictions and the exclusion policies applied respectively against Japanese goods and immigrants, both being labelled as evidence of the hostility of British imperialism to Japanese interests. Finally, it was also in 1936 that Japan withdrew from the London Naval Conference as the Washington and London Naval Treaties expired.

THE COLLAPSE OF NAVAL LIMITATION

It will be recalled that the London Naval Conference of 1930 had produced a rather meager victory for the principle of arms limitation. Two years later at the World Disarmament Conference at Geneva, the United States had proposed abolition of all offensive weapons with the alternate proposal that existing armaments be reduced by 33 percent. Contributing to the failure of these proposals was the situation already prevailing in the Far East, where Japan had invaded Manchuria and was engaged in hostilities at Shanghai. In 1933 the failure of the International Economic Conference at London delivered another blow to the principle of international co-operation and stimulated movements toward economic and political nationalism and their concomitant of big navies. The effects were only partially relieved by the American Trade Agreements Act, June, 1934, designed to give relief from the Smoot-Hawley Tariff Act of the Hoover administration, by authorizing the President to raise or lower substantially existing rates in the case of nations prepared to make reciprocal concessions.

Meanwhile, the United States had fallen behind in naval construction, and in March, 1934, Congress passed the Vinson Bill authorizing construction of a treaty-strength navy. In December, 1934, Japan exercised her privilege of giving two years' notice of her intent to denounce the Washington Naval Treaty of 1922. At the same time Japan made it

---

[21] H. S. Quigley, *Far Eastern War, 1937-1941* (Boston, 1942), 168. Italy became a co-signatory, Nov. 6, 1937, the agreement being renewed with additional signatories at Berlin, Nov. 25, 1941.

clear that at the next naval conference, scheduled for 1935, she would insist on naval parity. Accordingly, when their demand was denied, the Japanese withdrew from the London Conference which met in 1935-36. The treaty agreed upon by Britain, the United States, and France, March 25, 1936, without the adherence of Japan and Italy, thus became a sort of death gasp of naval limitation. The whole structure of international naval co-operation so painstakingly erected since 1922 was shattered.

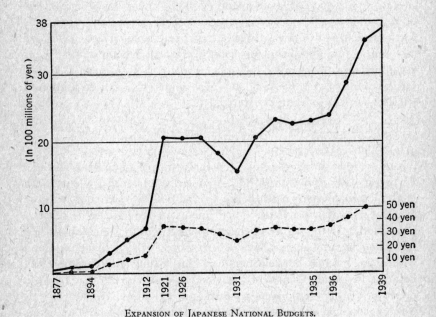

EXPANSION OF JAPANESE NATIONAL BUDGETS.

THE RENEWAL OF HOSTILITIES, JULY 7, 1937

The year 1937 was one of acute crises throughout the world. It was a year in which fascism and naziism became bolder in their verbal and diplomatic attacks upon democracy, communism, the territorial *status quo,* and the system of collective security as represented by the League of Nations. In contrast, the democracies were divided at home and unable to unite in opposition to the growing totalitarian group. Russia, rocked by the anti-Stalin conspiracies and purge, remained isolated from both groups. In this atmosphere of crisis occurred the incident which precipitated hostilities anew in China.

LUKOUCHIAO: HOSTILITIES BUT NOT WAR

Fighting broke out on the night of July 7, 1937, at the town of Wanp'ing near the Lukouchiao or Marco Polo Bridge not far from Peip'ing. The contestants were a Chinese garrison and a Japanese force. The latter were conducting maneuvers here beyond the localities where foreign troops might be stationed under the Boxer Protocol. The area was strategically important, being crossed by a connecting railway between the Pei-p'ing-Tientsin and the Pei-p'ing-Hankow mainlines. Moreover, without treaty right, the neighboring town of Fengt'ai, through which the short line passed, had been garrisoned for more than a year by Japanese troops. Although in 1913 the Chinese government had authorized foreign commanders to drill their troops in the Lukouchiao district, the magnitude of the Japanese maneuvers following the long period of tension since the Tangku truce was an invitation to trouble. As on many previous occasions, the matter might have been settled as a local incident,[22] but the issue was now manifestly the political control of North China, and both sides believed that "war was inevitable." By the end of July, the Pei-p'ing and Tientsin areas were in Japanese hands. By the beginning of August, Japanese troops had driven into Inner Mongolia, occupying Kalgan and thus severing China's principal line of overland communication with Soviet Russia; Suiyuan province and its capital Kweihua were overrun and occupied; this placed the Pei-p'ing-Suiyuan railway in Japanese hands. Other Japanese forces moved south into Shansi to strike at strongholds of the Chinese Communists both there and in bordering Shensi. Here, however, the Japanese met their first significant reverses at the hands of the 8th Route (Communist) Army, so-called since its theoretical incorporation with the Nationalist armies in August, 1937. It was here that guerrilla tactics first revealed their power against overwhelmingly superior Japanese forces both in number and weapons. The result was complete frustration of Japan's attempt to drive into Northwest China. "At the end of 1941 the Japanese were no further into Shansi than they had been in 1938." [23]

---

[22] The Chinese government was willing to settle the Marco Polo Bridge incident as a local matter and made strong efforts to induce the Japanese to regard it as such.

[23] For additional details see the excellent account by Quigley, *Far Eastern War, 1937-1941*, 65-70; and Reports of the League of Nations on the outbreak of hostilities and the subsequent fighting in China to October, 1937, in United States, *Foreign Relations: Japan, 1931-1941*, I, 384-396.

HOSTILITIES SPREAD TO SHANGHAI

The Japanese hope that the new conflict could be localized and confined to bringing North China under Japanese control was not realized. Hostilities in the north aroused bitter resentment throughout many parts of China, particularly in the Yangtze Valley. Then, while the two powers augmented their forces at Shanghai, came the incident necessary to precipitate hostilities there.[24]   It seems probable that the Japanese wished to avoid immediate spread of the conflict to the Shanghai region.   The Chinese, on the contrary, hoped to relieve the pressure in the north by spreading the conflict to the Yangtze.   Here, too, there was greater likelihood of other powers being involved if Japan disregarded the neutrality of the International Settlement.   Again, as in 1932, the Chinese at Shanghai were defeated after heroic resistance, and the Japanese moved up the Yangtze to capture Nanking, December 12-13, 1937.   The National Government had already moved to Hankow and was eventually to retire further westward to Chungking.   Chinese resistance had already infuriated the Japanese, and this fury was given free reign at Nanking where local Japanese commanders permitted wholesale acts of brutality against the local Chinese populace.[25]

Japan's next move was to join her North China armies with those in the Yangtze by gaining control of the two north-south railroads: the Pei-p'ing-Hankow and the Tientsin-Pukow lines.   This was not accomplished until May, 1938, after the Japanese had recovered from a humiliating defeat at Taierchwang.   It required another five months for the Japanese to reach Hankow on the upper Yangtze, which they took on October 25, 1938.   Less than a week earlier, October 21, Canton, the great port of South China, had fallen to the Japanese.   The surrender of Canton without effective resistance was not only a blow from which China never recovered, since the city was a major gateway for war materials, it was also indicative of the failure of the National Government to provide overall planning in defense, and it lent some credence to reports that the city had been "sold."   Meanwhile in Central China the war had reached a seeming stalemate.   In November, 1939, the Japanese landed at Pakhoi in Kwantung, invading the neighboring province of Kwangsi to capture the capital at Nanning.   However,

---

[24] When a Japanese sub-lieutenant and seaman attempted to enter the Hungjao aerodrome near Shanghai, and were refused admittance, shooting occurred in which the Japanese and a Chinese sentry were killed.

[25] L. S. C. Smythe, *War Damage in the Nanking Area* (Nanking, 1938); H. J. Timperley, *What War Means: The Japanese Terror in China* (London, 1938); and Quigley, *Far Eastern War, 1937-1941*, 74.

China's overall strategy showed some improvement. In Hunan province the Japanese were forced to stop in their drive on Changsha, though in June of 1940 they were able to move up the Yangtze to capture Ichang. They had now invaded China on three major fronts, yet China's resistance seemed only to stiffen. To meet this stalemate, the Japanese resorted to widespread bombing, much of which was centered on the new temporary capital at Chungking, and on key points on the Burma Road. In February, 1939, the Japanese navy seized the island of Hainan off the South China coast, occupied the Spratley Islands a month later, and continued to maintain a blockade of Chinese shipping at principal Chinese ports.[26]

PEACE FEELERS

After the fall of Nanking early in 1938, the Japanese began a series of efforts to sound the Chinese on proposals for peace. All these proposals involved Japanese control of strategic Chinese areas, recognition of Manchukuo, and the formation of an economic bloc of China, Japan, and Manchukuo. Although these peace feelers played upon existing dissension within the Kuomintang, they were definitely refused by Chiang K'ai-shek in December, 1938.

THE PROPAGATION OF PUPPET REGIMES

Having failed to conquer China or to bring her government to acceptance of peace, Japan decided henceforth to ignore the Kuomintang-Nationalists as a government and to seek the establishment of "a new Chinese regime" which would "do away with the folly of anti-Japanism."[27] To this end Japan proposed to set up a puppet government similar to the regime which had functioned in Manchukuo since 1932. The first of these was the Provisional Government of the Republic of China proclaimed at Peking in December, 1937. Its authority and ability to govern the people of North China were successfully challenged from the beginning by a new and patriotic Chinese administration called the Border Government of Hopei, Shansi, and Chahar, organized by Chinese Communists with the original approval of the National Gov-

---

[26] Military and naval aspects of the Sino-Japanese conflict are given in greater detail in Quigley, *Far Eastern War, 1937-1941,* 66-81. From July 7, 1937, until December 9, 1941, when China declared war on Japan, the far eastern conflict was not war in the technical sense. For a discussion of the question why nations fight without a declaration of war see C. G. Fenwick, "War Without a Declaration," *American Journal of International Law,* XXXI (1937), and L. H. Woolsey, "Peaceful War in China," *American Journal of International Law,* XXXII (1938).

[27] Nevertheless, Japan thereafter continued to maintain some contacts with the National Government and to launch occasional peace feelers behind the scenes.

ernment. This border government became one of the great forces of guerrilla resistance to Japanese penetration in the north.[28]

The Provisional Government at Peking never possessed more than a wavering local appeal. It was therefore incumbent on Japan to find a Chinese of national personality who could head a new puppet regime at Nanking with some prospect of claiming the allegiance of the Chinese people. The Japanese finally settled upon Wang Ching-wei as their man. Wang had a long and distinguished, if erratic, revolutionary record. An intimate of Sun Yat-sen, he had held many of the highest posts in the Kuomintang and the National Government. Although originally a leader of the left wing in the Kuomintang, he had come to oppose the Communists, had developed a bitter spirit of rivalry toward Chiang K'ai-shek, and was recognized as the leader of appeasement. Yet in all this he was not "far apart from many other leaders who remained in Chungking and continued to participate in the war of resistance." His desertion to the Japanese appears to be explained by "his inordinate ambition, and his lack of any means of satisfying his lust for power." [29] Moreover, prior to 1941 Wang, by political rationalization and personal vanity, had probably convinced himself that China's future lay in co-operation with Japan and that his own political wisdom could be relied on to preserve China's freedom. At all events, at Nanking, March 30, 1940, the new National (Puppet) Government, under the leadership of Wang, was proclaimed. Declared to be the true guardian of the principles of Sun Yat-sen, this "returned" and "Reorganized Government" retained the Kuomintang ideology and the structure of the National Government as it had previously existed at Nanking. Its personnel was composed in considerable part, though not exclusively, of Kuomintang members who had deserted with Wang. Wang's government, soon recognized by Japan, concluded a treaty with Tokyo, November 30, 1940, providing for joint defense against communism and for co-operation in economic development. Recognition was also accorded to the Wang regime, July 1, 1941, by Germany, Italy, Spain, Rumania, and other totalitarian governments of Europe.[30]

FASHIONING A CO-PROSPERITY SPHERE

Occupied China, measured in terms of the penetration of Japanese arms, constituted principally a rich block of territory comprising the Yangtze Valley from Shanghai to Hankow in the south, to Pei-p'ing

---

[28] The techniques of resistance as they developed in North China are ably portrayed by George E. Taylor, *The Struggle for North China* (New York, 1940).

[29] L. K. Rosinger, *China's Wartime Politics* (Princeton, 1944), 33-34.

[30] Quigley, *Far Eastern War*, 114-122.

and Chahar province in the north.   Here Wang's nominal jurisdiction extended over more than a half million square miles of territory with a population of close to 200 million.   It included much of the wealthiest and most densely populated areas of China.   With a puppet state erected for its political control, Japan now turned to economic exploitation which would integrate the area into the co-prosperity framework with Manchukuo and Japan.   The groundwork was prepared by intensive campaigns of propaganda to eliminate anti-Japanese sentiment and to provide proper education in the schools.   Against this background the whole economic and commercial structure of central and northeastern China was reorganized.   All forms of communication, and all features of industry, including mining, were to be capitalized and directed by new companies in which Japan held half the stock.   Ultimate authority rested with the newly organized China Affairs Board created in Tokyo on December 16, 1938.[31]   The general plan contemplated concentrations of high precision industry in Japan, heavy, chemical, and electrical industry in Manchukuo, salt production and light industry in North China.[32]

TOTALITARIAN TRENDS IN JAPAN, 1937-1941

The spread of warfare in China coupled with increasing tension between Japan and the Western democracies created lively pressures within Japan's domestic political structure.   Nevertheless, it was not until the summer of 1940 that a precipitate trend toward totalitarian state socialism was under way.   The entire period, however, was one of political instability.   Between February, 1937, and October, 1941, eight cabinets presided over Japan's destinies.   For some time, however, the inspired clamor for a "new national structure," a polite phrase for totalitarianism, was resisted.   In the parliamentary elections of April, 1937, the militarists and fascists suffered severe defeat, and until his death in November, 1940, Prince Kimmochi Saionji, the last of the Genro, sought to check the wilder extremists.   Yet the political influence of the military organs of the Supreme Command tended in general to increase. This was natural in view of the war Japan was waging in China. Moreover, it should be noted that the measures of greater control which Japan's government adopted up to the summer of 1940 "were similar to those observable in democratic states under conditions of depression and war." [33]   By the late summer of 1940 the ultimate defeat of the

---

[31] C. B. Fahs, *Government in Japan* (New York, 1940), 65-66.
[32] Quigley, *Far Eastern War*, 123-131.
[33] Quigley. *Far Eastern War*, 158.

liberal parliamentarians seemed assured. In July and August the major
political parties, the *Seiyukai* and the *Minseito*, dissolved themselves,
and in the following October, Prince Konoye announced the birth of
the Imperial Rule Assistance Association, described as a nationally representative body which was to assist the government in creating the
"new national structure." Its essential nature was that of a "patriotic"
society; its function, political propaganda.[34] The Association was to
be a means of liquidating the remnants of democratic constitutionalism
and of substituting complete control by an oligarchy of military and
fascist bureaucrats applying the principles of *Kodo*.

JAPAN AND THE AXIS ALLIANCE

A tendency for Japan and Germany to unite diplomatically was accelerated as both withdrew from the League of Nations in 1935. Promoting a closer relation was a kinship in political ideology and their
mutual hostility to the democracies and the Soviet Union. Opposing it
were German commercial ambitions in the Far East, not to mention the
respective German and Japanese claims to exclusive racial superiority.
The German-Japanese Anti-Comintern Pact, November 25, 1936, which
did little more than express the intent to co-operate against communism,
was an answer to the "popular front" movement endorsed by the Com-
intern in 1935. There was presumably an accompanying but secret
German-Japanese political agreement concerning China and the Soviet
Union. Italy, as noted, joined the Anti-Comintern Pact, November 6,
1937. As the war in China developed, it was the German Ambassador
to China, Oscar Trautmann, who conveyed Japan's peace terms of January, 1938. Shortly thereafter in May, 1938, the German military
mission was withdrawn from China. The German Ambassador left
Chungking a month later. Many Japanese remained critical of the
Pact, especially after Germany concluded a non-aggression treaty with
the Soviet Union in 1939. However, on September 27, 1940, when, as
noted, the extremists were gaining control in Tokyo, Japan, represented
by Yosuke Matsuoka, her Foreign Minister, concluded a treaty of alliance with Germany and Italy that recognized Japan's leadership in a
new order in Greater East Asia, the same primacy being accorded to
Germany and Italy in Europe.[35]

---

[34] T. A. Bisson, "Japan's 'New Structure,'" *Foreign Policy Association Reports*, April
15, 1941.
[35] Text of the Anti-Comintern Pact, United States, *Foreign Relations: Japan, 1931-1941*,
II, 153-155; summary of text of the Japan-German-Italian alliance, in *ibid.*, 165-166.

SINO-SOVIET-JAPANESE RELATIONS, 1931-1941

The four years of undeclared war (1937-1941) between Japan and China brought major changes in their relations with Soviet Russia. Japan's invasion and conquest of Manchuria, 1931-1932, had all but eliminated Russia as a factor in North Manchuria and led to the Soviet sale of the Chinese Eastern Railway to Manchukuo in 1935.[36] There was much force to the Soviet view that the report of the Lytton Commission was "genuinely anti-Japanese" but not "genuinely pro-Chinese," and that the Western powers, while willing to condemn Japan, were unwilling to take any effective steps against her. Countering Russian reverses in Manchuria were the resumption of Russo-American diplomatic relations, November 16, 1933, and Russia's entry into the League of Nations, September, 1934. These moves brought Russia into closer relations with the Western democracies, whereas her relations with Japan deteriorated. During 1935-36 there was constant and increasingly dangerous friction between the two powers. These disputes involved the payments for the Chinese Eastern Railway, the slippery question of Japanese fisheries in Soviet waters, successive boundary disputes on the Amur River and on the elusive boundary between Manchukuo and Outer Mongolia, and lesser differences over the oil concessions held by Japanese in Russian Sakhalin.[37] The Manchukuo-Outer Mongolia border disputes led directly to more intimate relations between the Mongol People's Republic and the Soviet Union. There had already been close military, political, and economic collaboration between the two since 1921. Now, on March 12, 1936, they concluded a Protocol of Mutual Assistance, promising military aid in the event either was threatened with military aggression.[38] To China's immediate protest, Russia replied that the pact was not a violation of Chinese sovereignty and that the agreement was analogous to the one Russia had made with the Manchurian authorities in 1924 (see p. 544).

The renewal of Sino-Japanese hostilities in July, 1937, soon affected the interests of the U.S.S.R. In the first instance, China appealed to Russia as well as to the signatories of the Nine-Power Treaty, and in August White Russians raided the Soviet Consulate at Tientsin, presumably at the instigation of the Japanese. On August 21, Russia and China concluded a general non-aggression treaty.[39] From this time

---

[36] Harriet L. Moore, *Soviet Far Eastern Policy, 1931-1945* (Princeton, 1945), 5-46.
[37] The subjects are treated in detail in Moore, *Soviet Far Eastern Policy*, 47-76.
[38] Text in Moore, *Soviet Far Eastern Policy*, 185-186.
[39] Text in Moore, 187-188.

until 1940, Soviet-Japanese relations continued to deteriorate. During July and August, 1938, a full-scale battle occurred between Soviet and Japanese troops at Changkufeng where the Korean, Manchukuo, and Soviet borders meet. The truce which finally ended the hostilities did not settle the frontier questions in dispute since both sides were more interested in a test of strength than in the territorial issue.[40] Meanwhile the two powers resumed negotiations on the fisheries. Previous Japanese efforts to secure a long-term agreement had been interrupted in 1936 because of Russian resentment at the Anti-Comintern Pact. Now only temporary agreements were possible. Russia was content that Japanese fishing rights should continue, but only on terms which guaranteed Russia's sovereignty and the development of her own fisheries.[41] Again in 1939 a series of battles occurred between Soviet-Mongol forces and Japanese-Manchukuo troops in the Nomonhan district east of Lake Buir on the Manchukuo-Outer Mongolian border. Here as at Changkufeng, Soviet resistance was temporarily chastening to the ambitions of the Kwantung Army.[42]

Simultaneously, Russia's relations with Japan were affected by the unexpected Russo-German non-aggression pact, August 23, 1939, and the outbreak of a general European war in September. Although these events brought no immediate change in Sino-Soviet relations, they had appreciable effects on Japanese policy. With the democracies preoccupied in Europe, the way was open for Japanese expansion in southeastern Asia; Tokyo looked to improved relations with the Soviet Union. Such a move was also welcome to Russia, for she believed that the democracies still hoped for a Soviet-Japanese embroilment over Manchuria and Mongolia. The result was the Russo-Japanese neutrality agreement of April 13, 1941.[43] A major victory for Soviet diplomacy, the pact was a pledge of neutrality by Japan toward Siberia and Outer Mongolia, and of Russia toward Japan and Manchukuo. The pact was followed in June by a Soviet-Japanese commercial convention.

This improvement in Soviet-Japanese relations effected no fundamental change in Russia's complex relationship with China. This relationship involved: 1) formally friendly relations with Chungking and material aid in credits and goods; 2) acceptance of Chiang K'ai-shek's leadership of the Kuomintang-Communist united front in the war of national salvation; 3) refusal to recognize Wang Ching-wei's puppet

[40] Details in Moore, 98-101.
[41] Quigley, Far Eastern War, 256.
[42] Moore, Soviet Far Eastern Policy, 113.
[43] Text in Moore, Soviet Far Eastern Policy, 200-201.

regime at Nanking. Yet at the same time Russia had reached basic settlements with Japan, had seemingly recognized Manchukuo in the neutrality pact of 1941, and had completed the process of making Outer Mongolia a Soviet satellite by concluding with this state, over which China claimed sovereignty, an alliance of mutual assistance. Like the democracies, Soviet Russia wished "to save" China; but as will appear, the China which each hoped to preserve was not one and the same.

RESISTANCE IN INDEPENDENT CHINA

Both for China herself and for the world at large the most significant and compelling fact of the four years of undeclared warfare, 1937-1941, was the resistance of independent China, its refusal to submit. Considerably more than half of the territory and the population of China Proper remained beyond the control of Japanese arms. In terms of economic wealth, it was much the poorer half of China. All of the great coastal cities, much of the seaboard provinces, and the lower Yang-tze Valley—the more heavily industrialized and commercialized areas—were controlled if not occupied by Japan. Chinese nationalism thus had no alternative but to base its resistance, both political and economic, on the great interior hinterland of the west where political and economic modernization were all but unknown. To this ancient west country, into the provinces of Szechwan, Kweichow, and Yünnan, trekked an astonishing migration of the wealthy, the educated, the politically influential, students, professors, skilled laborers, and some with no other designation than that of patriot. They travelled by boat, by cart, and on foot, carrying what possessions they could. In the old interior where ancient and feudal traditions were still predominant, they set up the wartime capital at Chungking, reassembled transplanted schools, universities, and factories.[44] Although the movement was basically one of survival, it was also inspired by the will to create a new and a better China.

THE UNITY OF COMPULSION

But China's magnificent unity of resistance was clouded by internal dissensions of the gravest import. The most important of these was the rivalry between the Kuomintang-National Government and the Chinese Communists. The latter, by 1937, were the second political power within the nation and their relations with the Kuomintang-Nationalists were embittered by ten years of relentless and cruel civil

---

[44] On transplanted industry see the study by Kuo-heng Shih, *China Enters the Machine Age* (Cambridge, 1944).

war. The unity which the two groups achieved in 1937 was a product not of any basic political settlement of China's internal politics, but rather of "the unrelenting pressure of a foreign foe." [45] There were rifts also between the Kuomintang and lesser political groups. Although in the spring of 1938 the decision of the Kuomintang to create the People's Political Council indicated a wartime trend to more representative government, the Kuomintang one-party control was not seriously affected. Moreover, after the fall of Hankow in October, 1938, China's desperate military situation, while promoting temporarily closer Kuomintang-Communist unity, led eventually to deeper conflicts between the two parties. To understand an important factor bringing this about, it should be noted that in 1937, few Kuomintang leaders believed a long war of resistance possible. The strategy of prolonged resistance through guerrilla warfare, first suggested by the Communists, proved eventually to be one of China's strongest military weapons, but in employing it, the political and economic betterment which it was necessary to offer the peasantry to enlist the latter's support had "far-reaching social implications" by no means welcome to the conservatives of the Kuomintang.[46] After 1938 the success of the Communists in organizing guerrilla resistance in North China behind the Japanese lines, and the historically understandable refusal of the Communists to submit wholly to the Kuomintang dictatorship, widened the breach between the two parties. From then on there were periodic clashes between Kuomintang and Communist armies.

THE "NEW ORDER" IN "GREATER EAST ASIA"

Amid the stalemate in Japan's undeclared war in China, and with the outbreak of war in Europe in 1939, came further steps in Japan's policy of expansion, the new moves centering in southeastern Asia, which is to say, in French Indo-China, in Thailand, and in the Netherlands Indies. Japanese expansionists had for many years argued the relative merits of continental expansion in northeastern Asia versus maritime expansion in the southeast. After 1939 the problem was resolved by expansion in both. The new developments involved a new phraseology descriptive of broadened horizons. Labels such as the "economic bloc of Japan, Manchukuo, and China," "co-prosperity," and the "new order in East Asia," soon gave place to "the new order" and "co-prosperity in Greater East Asia." [47] Accordingly, while France was collapsing before Ger-

---

[45] Bases of the Kuomintang-Communist Entente of 1937 are given in Rosinger, *China's Wartime Politics*, 25-28.

[46] Rosinger, *China's Wartime Politics*, 30-33.

[47] E. O. Reischauer, *Japan Past and Present* (New York, 1946), 182.

man arms in Europe, pressure was brought to bear by Japan on the French Indo-Chinese colony. A limited occupation of the northern areas, designed to prevent importation of supplies to the Chinese, was effected in the summer and autumn of 1940. This was followed by Japanese military occupation of the entire colony in 1941. The way for all this was paved through Berlin's influence with the Vichy government. By the spring of 1941, this "peaceful" occupation had borne fruit in two agreements for economic collaboration which gave Japan a preferred position in the importation of capital and goods and in the export of grains and minerals.[48]

Japan's control in Indo-China gave her the opportunity to play the role of mediator in international disputes in that area and thus to implement her role as "stabilizing force in East Asia." She had concluded a new treaty of friendship and neutrality with Thailand, June 12, 1940. This emboldened Thailand, in November, 1940, to revive claims to the territory of Laos, west of the Mekong River, and to northeastern Cambodia, which France had occupied in the late nineteenth and early twentieth centuries. Thai troops invaded the areas, and in March, 1941, Japan presided over negotiations in Tokyo by which the areas in question were ceded to Thailand.[49] From then until the end of 1941, Thailand attempted to pursue a course of neutrality between Japan and the democracies.

Simultaneously the Japanese government was attempting to dominate the Netherlands Indies through political pressure and economic infiltration. In March, 1941, Japanese women and children began to withdraw from the Netherlands Indies.

THE UNITED STATES OPPOSES THE NEW ORDER

During the first three months of the Manchurian crisis (1931), the Hoover administration followed an extremely cautious policy.

The Roosevelt administration in 1933, while standing firm on the treaties, as Stimson had done, and while surrendering no principles, did adopt new tactics. It stopped talking about Manchuria; it recognized Soviet Russia; it began to build up the American fleet; and, through the Reconstruction Finance Corporation, it made available $50,000,000 in credits to the Chinese government. But the diplomacy of silence was short-lived. The Amau statement, April 17, 1934, by which Japan extended her theory of "special interests" to China as a whole, and the oil monopoly law in Manchukuo which followed later in the year were re-

---

[48] Quigley, *Far Eastern War*, 181-186.
[49] Quigley, *Far Eastern War*, 183, 186-7, 190-1.

garded by the United States as the most serious challenge yet to the open door, and were vigorously though vainly protested.[50]

From 1934 onward, American-Japanese relations subsisted on stony ground. American credits to China, coupled with the new British policy toward China which developed in 1935, and the increase in Japanese-American naval rivalry which went with the collapse of naval limitation in 1935-36, all appeared to Japan as inimical to her "special position." To the American government it was becoming clearer that if American diplomacy was to have any effect in implementing basic American policies, it would have to rest on a program of national preparedness.[51] By "so lightly casting off the Nine-Power Treaty," [52] and by refusal to continue the system of naval ratios in any form, Japan was giving the impression that nothing short of force would dissuade her from an exclusive *Pax Japonica* in the Far East.[53]

A NERVOUS SPECTATOR OF THE UNDECLARED WAR

For nearly six months after the outbreak of the undeclared war at Peip'ing in July, 1937, the press reports of this new and hideous bloodshed fell on the ears of an American public whose reactions were clearly apathetic. Though there was sympathy for China, 55 percent of those polled by the American Institute of Public Opinion declined to play favorites. It was not until 1939 that opinion became overwhelming pro-Chinese. While American life and property within China entered a period of unprecedented danger, administrative moves were governed with a cautious eye on public opinion, which had produced the neutrality acts of 1935 and 1937.[54]   The act of 1937 was not invoked in the Far

---

[50] Correspondence on the Amau statement is in United States, *Foreign Relations: Japan, 1931-1941*, I, 223-225; for the protest on the oil monopoly see *ibid.*, I, 130-131.

[51] Grew, *Ten Years in Japan*, 147.

[52] Tyler Dennett, "America and Japanese Aims," *Current History*, XXXIX (1934), 766.

[53] J. P. Capua, *American Policies Toward Japan: 1932-37* (Duke University, an unpublished manuscript study, 1945). The peace which Japan was seeking involved prevention: 1) of the "inevitable" unification of China, 2) of the potential "economic" conquest of China by the United States, and 3) of the socialistic industrialization of Siberia by Russia. Karl Radek, "The War in the Far East," *Foreign Affairs*, X (1932), 545.

[54] Inspired by the Italo-Ethiopian crisis, May, 1935, the first act provided that in cases where the President proclaimed the existence of a state of war, it would be unlawful for Americans to sell or transport munitions to the belligerents. There was no provision enabling the President to discriminate against "aggressor" nations. The act was later broadened to prohibit loans to belligerents and to prohibit export of munitions to opposing forces in a civil war (Spain). A new neutrality law, May 1, 1937, went further by prohibiting American travel on belligerent vessels. The "cash and carry" provision insured continued profits to the American seller. As a compromise to the proposal of embargoing sale of raw materials to belligerents, it empowered the President to specify

East, for it would have operated to the advantage of Japan, not China.[55]
And when, on October 5, 1937, Roosevelt appealed in Chicago for a
quarantine against the "international anarchy" of the aggressors and
asked for "positive endeavors to preserve peace," American public opinion, while applauding the principle, was still unprepared to approve
armed sanctions either in Europe or the Far East.[56]

THE BRUSSELS CONFERENCE

The diplomacy of words continued. The League of Nations, October
6, 1937, expressed "its moral support for China." [57] In November the
United States and eighteen other powers met at Brussels, to which the
Belgian government at British suggestion had invited, among others,
the signatories of the Nine-Power Treaty. Since Germany and Japan
refused to attend, and those who were present were unprepared to use
force, the conference broke up on November 24 without result on the
far eastern conflict.[58]

THE *U. S. S. PANAY* "INCIDENT"

In the early afternoon of December 12, 1937, in weather that "was
clear, sunny and still," the *U. S. S. Panay,* a river gunboat plainly displaying her American colors, which had evacuated the last of American
embassy personnel at Nanking, was bombed and sunk by Japanese
planes[59] on the Yangtze some twenty-seven miles above Nanking. The
casualties numbered two killed, eleven seriously injured, thirty-two
slightly injured.[60] On the same day a number of British ships were fired
upon,[61] and three tankers of an American oil company were destroyed.

articles which were to be paid for on delivery and carried from the United States by the
buyer.
[55] Secretary Hull said on March 17, 1938, that the act "was designed primarily to keep
our Nation out of war. . . . Application of the law [in the Far East] would be most
likely to endanger the very objectives which the law was designed to promote." United
States, *Foreign Relations: Japan, 1931-1941,* I, 457-458.
[56] Text of the Quarantine Address in United States, *Foreign Relations: Japan, 1931-1941,*
I, 379-383.
[57] *Documents on American Foreign Relations, 1938-1939,* 162.
[58] Japan's view placed before the conference in a memorandum, Nov. 12, was that
"since it has been obliged to resort to its present action as a measure of defense against
Chinese acts of provocation, this action does not come within the scope of the Nine-Power
Treaty. . . ." *Documents on American Foreign Relations, 1938-1939,* 173.
[59] Report of George Atcheson, Jr., United States, *Foreign Relations: Japan, 1931-1941,*
I, 532-541.
[60] Report of the Commander-in-Chief, U. S. Asiatic Fleet, United States, *Foreign
Relations: Japan, 1931-1941,* I, 546.
[61] Friedman, *British Relations with China,* 112-116, discusses how "this inexcusable
attack was glossed over by the British Government."

The United States promptly demanded apology, reparations, and guarantees for the future.   The Japanese hastened to provide them; Foreign Minister Hirota called on the American Ambassador on the following day.[62]   While American opinion was outraged by the *Panay* affair, its public expressions were marked by a stoical reserve and a fixed resolve not to be drawn into the far eastern war.[63]

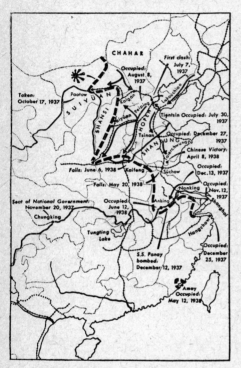

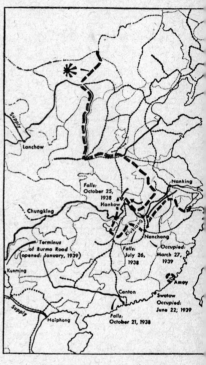

THE FIRST YEAR, 1937-1938.   THE SECOND YEAR, 1938-1939.

Maps appearing on pages 672-674, inclusive, are from "A War Atlas for Americans," Simon and Schuster, Inc., 1944.   They are reproduced by permission from Simon and Schuster, Inc., and from United States, Department of State, Division of Map Intelligence and Cartography.

During most of 1938, after the *Panay* affair had subsided, American-Japanese relations relapsed into a state of uneasy calm, although the

---

[62] The American demands and the Japanese efforts to meet them are reproduced in extensive correspondence in United States, *Foreign Relations: Japan, 1931-1941*, I, 517-563.   Before the responsibility was finally fixed on the Japanese officers involved, Hirota confided to Ambassador Grew: "I am having a very difficult time." *Ibid.*, 550. Damages paid by Japan were $2,214,007.36.

[63] The proposed Ludlow amendment to the Constitution, making a declaration of war dependent on a national referendum save in cases of invasion, was defeated shortly thereafter by the narrow margin of 21 votes, and in a public opinion poll 53.9 percent favored complete American withdrawal from the Far East.

basic facts of conflict in policy continued unabated, and, indeed, were aggravated by Japan's course of action in China. The United States attempted to keep the record clear by repeated formal protests against: 1) bombing of civilians and other acts by the Japanese endangering the life and welfare of Americans in China; 2) Japan's efforts to destroy the administrative integrity of the Chinese Maritime Customs; and 3) the in-

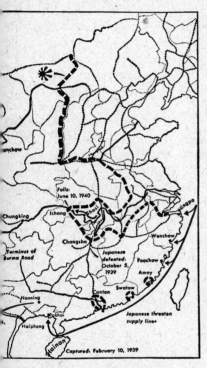

THE THIRD YEAR, 1939-1940.

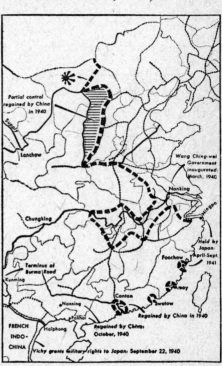

THE FOURTH YEAR, 1940-1941.

creasing acts by Japan in occupied China interfering with American treaty rights and equality of commercial opportunity.[64] The year closed with a vigorous protest, December 30, from the United States, in which this country rejected Japan's fiat that non-discriminatory treatment in China and the treaty rights of the powers in general must henceforth be contingent upon recognition of a "new situation" and a "new order" in East Asia.[65]

Japan had meanwhile been implementing her attack upon China by diplomatic and other forms of pressure upon foreign settlement and concession areas. The move was a two-edged weapon by which Japan

---

[64] Extensive selections from the American-Japanese correspondence on these subjects are in United States, *Foreign Relations: Japan, 1931-1941*, I, 564-641, 729-826.

[65] United States, *Foreign Relations: Japan, 1931-1941*, I, 820-826.

might pose as the champion of restoration of these areas to China, while at the same time humiliating the foreigners within them, revealing their lack of protection by their home governments, and thus causing them to lose "face" in the eyes of the Chinese.[66]

ABROGATING "PROVISIONS WHICH NEED NEW CONSIDERATION"

This form of Japanese pressure helped to prompt the most vigorous action yet taken by the United States, which, on July 26, 1939, notified Japan that it was giving the requisite six-month notice of abrogation of the American-Japanese Treaty of Commerce and Navigation signed February 21, 1911. In the niceties of diplomatic language, Japan was advised that the treaty "contains provisions which need new consideration." [67] It meant that the United States was preparing the way to combat Japan's "new order" by economic means. A month later Japan was also confronted by the Russo-German non-aggression pact which gave Moscow a relatively free hand in the Far East.

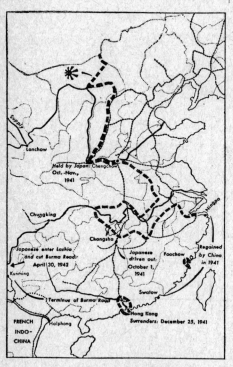

THE FIFTH YEAR, 1941-1942.

Nevertheless, the fall of Poland and France, the desperate plight of Britain, and the menace of Hitler's Germany appeared to give Japan a free hand to work her will in creating the "co-prosperity sphere in Greater East Asia." Thus, although free

---

[66] Friedman, *British Relations with China*, 195-211; L. H. Woolsey, "Japanese in Kulangsu," *American Journal of International Law*, XXXIII (1939), 526-530; for a very able study of the complex status of Shanghai in the nineteenth and twentieth centuries, see W. C. Johnstone, Jr., *The Shanghai Problem* (Stanford University, 1937).

[67] United States, *Foreign Relations: Japan, 1931-1941*, I, 189.

by January, 1940, to embargo shipments to Japan, the American government was forced to proceed with caution. There was the fear that American economic sanctions would drive the Japanese into the oil fields of the all but defenseless Netherlands Indies. Consequently, the United States fell back on arguments of desperation: Japan was reminded of her obligations under the Root-Takahira Notes of 1908 and the Four-Power Pacific Treaty of 1921, and additional credits were made available to China.

CHAPTER 37

THE FAR EAST IN WORLD WAR II

THE year 1941 climaxed the most sobering crisis the people of the United States had known since the threat to dissolve the Union in 1861. The climax came with Japan's astounding attack on Pearl Harbor, December 7; but on that date, the crisis was already more than two years old. It had begun in the summer of 1939 when war engulfed Europe. As that struggle got under way with Hitler's invasion of Poland (September 1, 1939) and the British and French declarations of war on Germany (September 3), the United States attempted to assume, for the moment at least, its traditional position of neutrality bolstered by the special neutrality legislation passed by Congress in 1937.

In many respects, however, this was not merely a reassertion of traditional concepts of American foreign policy. In 1939 the American people was more politically conscious of the crisis, of the dangers to American neutrality, and indeed to American independence than had been the case in 1914. Moreover, the majority of Americans, unlike those of 1914, were not of a mind to be neutral in thought. They were not friendly to totalitarianism; they were opposed to Hitler; they hoped the democracies would win. Although traditional isolationists as well as those with fascist leanings recalled "the mistake" of 1917, appealed to all the traditions of isolationism, and labelled the European struggle as just another war of imperialism, most Americans were deeply disturbed by the Axis theory of international relations: its disregard of international law, its cynical justifications for the use of force, and the mechanized might of its armies. Although the full implications of these things were not realized by the public as a whole, there was a growing presentiment by the spring of 1940 that the Axis no longer recognized international law, that Hitler had abolished neutral rights and unofficially declared war on all the democracies—including the United States. The problem as the American people's government saw it was how to aid the democracies effectively without being drawn into the war.

As Germany's early victories brought one disaster after another to democracy in western Europe thus opening the way for an assault on democracy in America, the United States found little sense of security in traditional neutrality. In November, 1939, Congress lifted the arms embargo but still compromised with isolationism by creating "danger zones" in European waters into which American ships might not enter. Meanwhile, by the Declaration of Panama (October 3, 1939), the American republics warned belligerents not to carry hostilities into a "safety belt" surrounding the American continents from Canada southward.[1] In Europe, as Hitler's armies advanced, customary neutral rights were fast disappearing in a war of edicts and of counter-edicts. By June, 1940, Americans were forced to recognize the unbelievable: France had fallen. Denmark, Norway, Belgium, Holland, and Luxembourg were already in Hitler's hands. Battered Britain alone remained between Hitler's Germany and an American people who did not want war, and were unprepared for it. In July, 1940, the American republics again reacted to the danger when at Havana they set up a "collective trusteeship" to administer colonial areas in the western hemisphere that were in danger of falling into Axis hands.[2] A month later, in August, Canada and the United States established a Permanent Joint Board of Defense.[3] In September a frightened American Congress at last passed a conscription law, and by October had voted appropriations of more than $17,000,000,-000 for defense. Meanwhile the American government was freezing the credits of those countries Germany had occupied. In September, too, came the unprecedented destroyer deal by which this country through executive agreement gave Great Britain 50 overage but serviceable destroyers in return for the right to establish military bases in British territory from Newfoundland to Guiana.[4] The crisis in Europe was impelling the American people and its government toward a status of quasi-belligerency. In November, the no-third-term tradition was shattered, in part because Americans believed that Hitler hoped for Roosevelt's defeat; and in January, 1941, Congress passed the Lend-Lease Act by which the United States undertook to give direct aid to those powers resisting aggression. This meant that the danger from the Axis was considered so great as not only to justify the complete abandonment of neutrality but also to warrant "an unofficial declaration of war."[5]

In the early months of 1941, Balkan Europe fell to Hitler. In April,

---

[1] Text in *Documents on American Foreign Relations*, II, 115-117.

[2] Text in *Documents on American Foreign Relations*, III, 85-90. This was to preclude German occupation of Danish, Dutch, or French territory in the New World.

[3] *Documents on American Foreign Relations*, III, 160-161. Canada was already a belligerent when this agreement was made.

[4] *Documents on American Foreign Relations*, III, 203 ff.

[5] *Documents on American Foreign Relations*, III, 711-723.

Nazi penetration of Greenland led to American occupation of that Danish colony. In May, President Roosevelt proclaimed an unlimited national emergency. The shooting had already started. The *Robin Moor,* an American ship, had been sunk (May 21) in the South Atlantic. From then on the United States and Germany moved steadily toward a condition of undeclared war. In June, German and Italian assets were frozen and their consulates closed as Hitler invaded Russia. Soon after (July), the United States took over from Britain the defense of Iceland, and a month later, in August, President Roosevelt and Prime Minister Churchill made public the joint declaration known as the Atlantic Charter.[6] The Charter meant in reality that the United States was committed to the defeat of Hitler and the principles for which totalitarian Germany stood. At the same time this country took the logical step of beginning to convoy Lend-Lease to assure its arrival in Britain. On October 27, 1941, the President in a Navy Day address warned the American people that "the shooting has started." In all but name, the United States and Germany were at war.

THE FAR EAST EARLY IN 1941

It was against this background of America's inevitable involvement to save what remained of democratic power in Europe that the United States also faced, after September, 1940, an intensified threat to its interests and to those of other democratic states in the Far East.

Toward the beginning of that fateful year, 1941, diplomatic tensions were not confined to war-torn Europe and to relations between Germany and the United States. The military victories of naziism in Europe were complemented by a political and diplomatic victory spanning the Eurasian continent. The Tripartite Pact of September, 1940, between Germany, Italy, and Japan, achieved a united front for totalitarianism in Europe and Asia. Against this alliance, the anti-Axis grouping of powers remained unorganized, although it was no longer possible to assume that there were two wars, one in Europe and another in Asia. The Tripartite Pact was a clear enunciation of the political, economic, and military union of the three powers to achieve the "New Order" in Europe and in the Far East.[7]

Early in 1941, the prospect in the Far East facing the anti-Axis powers was not encouraging. Japan's ruling castes believed that the "golden opportunity" to consummate the program of Greater East Asia was at

---

[6] *Documents on American Foreign Relations,* IV, 10-11.
[7] For the provisions of the Pact, see United States, *Foreign Relations: Japan, 1931-1941,* II, 165-166.

hand. The democracies were ill-prepared for defense; they were confused by and preoccupied with the war in Europe and with domestic issues. As a result, Japan had already begun "to follow in the Far East Germany's pattern in the Balkans and to 'Bulgarize' Indo-China, Thailand, and the Netherlands East Indies." [8]

The center of anti-Axis resistance in the Far East at this time continued to be a China exhausted by war, plagued by lack of supplies, by internal factionalism, corruption, and growing inflation, yet withal a China that continued to resist. The Burma Road, one of the last remaining supply routes, was exposed by late 1940 to Japanese air attack. In anti-Axis capitals it was believed that if Germany reached the Near East, Japan would move to join with her Axis ally in the Indian Ocean. This potential threat created ever-growing defensive needs in the Philippines, the Indies, Malaya, Burma, New Zealand, and Australia—needs which, when added to the existing requirements of Britain in the Near East, far exceeded the immediate capacity of the democracies to fill. Indeed, the American people and their government had probably never faced a greater national crisis.[9]

AMERICAN-JAPANESE NEGOTIATIONS, 1941

From March until December, 1941, the United States and Japan conducted "informal conversations" in Washington covering their conflicting interests and policies in the Pacific and the Far East.[10] These conversations progressed through six stages:

1. The preliminary phase (January to May) in which both powers indicated a willingness to seek a peaceful solution of differences through direct discussions.

2. Second phase (May to July) involved consideration of Japan's proposal of May 12, and the interruption of the conversations following the movement of Japanese troops into southern Indo-China.

3. Third phase (August to October) in which, following Japan's insistence on its peaceful purposes, conversations were resumed.

4. Fourth phase (October to November) began with the advent of the Tojo cabinet and its greater insistence upon acceptance of Japan's terms of settlement.

5. Fifth phase (November 20 to December 1) in which were dissipated whatever vague hopes of a settlement may have previously been entertained.

6. Sixth and final phase (December 2-7) in which the language of diplomacy gave way to the language of war.

---

[8] United States, *Foreign Relations: Japan, 1931-1941*, II, 326-7.
[9] *Foreign Relations: Japan, 1931-1941*, II, 328. Hereafter cited as *Conversations*.
[10] *Conversations*, 325-386.

SUBSTANCE OF THE CONVERSATIONS

The substance of these prolonged conversations contained nothing which was essentially new to American or to Japanese policy in the Far East. These respective policies had been in process of clarification for forty years. The goals of American policy were the complementary principles of equal opportunity (the open door) and the integrity (territorial and administrative) of China. The goal of Japanese policy was implementation of the principle of Japan's "special interests" in China (special position and paramount influence). This policy, remaining unaltered in principle, had grown, however, from the early concept of a sphere of influence to a policy of the "New Order" at first in "East Asia" and then in "Greater East Asia." Thus the key to an examination of the conversations must lie in the question: What in 1941 were the prospects of finding a mutually acceptable accommodation between these diametrically opposed policies?

In seeking a basis for opening the conversations, the United States government took the view that there was "one paramount preliminary question." This was "a definite assurance in advance that the Japanese Government had the willingness and power to go forward . . . to abandon its present doctrine of conquest by force," and to adopt four principles:

1. Respect for the territorial integrity and the sovereignty of each and all nations.
2. Support of the principle of non-interference in the internal affairs of other countries.
3. Support of the principle of equality including equality of commercial opportunity.
4. Non-disturbance of the *status quo* in the Pacific except as the *status quo* may be altered by peaceful means.[11]

Admiral Kichisaburo Nomura, Japan's recently arrived ambassador, replied that "he believed that his Government desired peace."

Japan's proposal for a general settlement was presented to the American government on May 12. It "appeared to carry out a concept of a joint overlordship by Japan and the United States of the Pacific area." Although the American government found little in Japan's proposals to justify prolonging the conversations, it decided to continue them for certain broader considerations of policy. These considerations included:

---

[11] *Conversations*, 332.

1. Information that conservative Japanese leaders hoped sincerely for a settlement with the United States.

2. "Consideration of the world situation," and recognition of the results that would follow from a "Japanese armed attack on British and Dutch territories in the Far East."

3. "The hope of defeating Hitlerism in Europe would be greatly enhanced if the more conservative elements in Japan should succeed."

JAPAN MOVES INTO SOUTHERN INDO-CHINA

This general impasse in the American-Japanese conversations was further heightened in July when Japanese armed forces moved into southern Indo-China.[12] This advance had been preceded by "the calling up of from one to two million reservists and conscripts"; the recall of Japanese merchant vessels from the Atlantic Ocean; and charges in the Japanese press that the United States was using the Philippine Islands as a "pistol aimed at Japan's heart."[13]

The Japanese Ambassador was promptly informed by the United States that the occupation of southern Indo-China could only be regarded as "the last step before proceeding on a policy of expansion and conquest," and thus there remained no "basis for pursuing further the conversations." This diplomatic frankness did not stop the Japanese advance which soon became "a vigorous under-cover movement of Japanese infiltration into Thailand." President Roosevelt's suggestion that Indo-China be "neutralized" was also unacceptable to Japan[14] and accordingly, on July 26 the President by executive order froze Japanese assets in the United States. This led to renewed protestations of Japan's desire for a peaceful settlement, but simultaneously Japan continued mobilization; she augmented her forces in Manchuria, Indo-China, and South China; and indulged in further bombings of American property in China.

Japan's reply to the Indo-China neutralization proposal came on August 6. The United States was asked "expressly or by implication": 1) to remove its restrictions on trade with Japan; 2) to suspend defensive preparations in the Philippines; 3) to stop furnishing equipment to

---

[12] Japan gave varying explanations of this move: 1) that it was designed to end hostilities in China; 2) that it was a precautionary measure against "certain foreign powers [that] were determined to encircle Japan."

[13] "Later on August 8 and again on August 15, an official Japanese spokesman declared that encirclement of Japan by the ABCD powers—the United States, Great Britain, China, and the Netherlands—was an actual fact." The Japanese press insisted that though friendship with the United States was desirable, it must not be achieved at the expense of "any change in Japan's policies." *Conversations*, 338-340.

[14] *Conversations*, 341-342.

Britain and the Netherlands for arming their far eastern possessions; 4) to discontinue aid to China; and 5) to agree to Japan's assertion and exercise of a special military position and a permanent preferential political and economic status in Indo-China. Although this was not regarded as meeting in any sense the President's neutralization proposal, events between August 8 and September 6 were interpreted by Washington as grounds for again continuing the conversations. For one thing, Russia in the European war had demonstrated an unhoped for capacity for resistance; the United States and Britain had agreed to take parallel action in warning Japan against new moves of aggression; and finally on August 28 the Japanese Prime Minister had proposed a meeting with the President.

The President was prepared to welcome a meeting with Japan's Prime Minister if there could be "a meeting of minds on fundamental principles." That this was impossible again seemed to be made clear on September 6 when the Japanese presented a new proposal. In every way it was unsatisfactory. It "clearly implied . . . that the conditions under which American trade and commerce in China were henceforth to be conducted was a matter of decision by Japan." Although at the same time Japan did accept "in principle" America's four basic principles of policy, a month later it was announced that "certain adjustments would be necessary in applying these principles to actual conditions."

Again on October 2, the United States asked for a preliminary agreement on principles. Japan countered that she had made all the "concessions" possible, and she urged a speedy agreement. On October 17 General Hideki Tojo became Japan's new Prime Minister, and although his cabinet professed its desire to continue the conversations, the developing tension led Secretary Hull (November 7) to inform the American cabinet that "a crisis was imminent in the Far East." Nevertheless, the Secretary advanced further proposals (November 15) for a possible joint American-Japanese declaration on economic policy based on unconditional most-favored-nation treatment. On the same day new impetus appeared to be given to the conversations with the arrival in Washington of Saburo Kurusu to assist Ambassador Nomura. It was soon evident, however, that Kurusu brought no new "concessions." America's position was also unchanged. Briefly, this position was that no peaceful gestures on Japan's part "would be taken seriously by anyone" so long as Japan was "clinging to the Tripartite Pact," continuing to make war on China and insisting on a preferred economic and political position in China.

Seeking once more to circumvent this wall of American principles, the Japanese brought forward a new proposition November 20. In return for unlimited quantities of oil, suspension of American freezing orders, and discontinuance of American aid to China, Japan would shift her armed forces from southern Indo-China to northern Indo-China. The United States countered with a comprehensive proposal (November 26) which in essence was a summary of the familiar basic principles and objectives of American policy.[15] The Japanese negotiators expressed the view that this reply seemed tantamount to ending the conversations. However, further exchanges occurred during the first week of December, and on December 6 President Roosevelt telegraphed a personal message to the Japanese Emperor appealing for a course of action to avert "tragic possibilities." On the following afternoon, Sunday, December 7 at 2:20, Ambassador Nomura delivered Japan's detailed denunciation of American policy in the Far East—a denunciation which Secretary Hull characterized as a document filled with "infamous falsehoods and distortions on a scale so huge that I never imagined until today that any government on this planet was capable of uttering them." More than an hour earlier, Japan's airforces had delivered a crushing blow to the American Pacific fleet as it lay in Pearl Harbor. America was now facing war across two oceans. On December 8, the Congress declared that a state of war existed between the United States and Japan. Four days later Germany and Italy declared war on the United States.

The American-Japanese conversations of 1941 were the final chapter in a diplomatic conflict which began in 1905 when Japan acquired a sphere of influence in South Manchuria. Despite her professions supporting the open door, Japan, for reasons which to her seemed good, had followed a policy promoting her own "special position" and her "special interests" in China. American diplomacy over the years failed to stop Japan, and there was an ironic touch in the fact that the United States had contributed to making the Treaty of Portsmouth, the basic settlement on which Japan rested her claims to a "special position." Although the open door and the integrity of China had remained consistently the policy of the United States, this country had never been in a position to insist on its application. The weakness lay not in the principles of the policy itself but in the fact that the American people had never been prepared to implement it since implementation would have meant war. Neither the Manchurian Incident of 1931 nor the undeclared war of 1937 had convinced America that the open door and China's integrity were worth fighting for.

[15] Text in *Conversations*, 371-374.

THE PEARL HARBOR DISASTER

On the morning of December 7, 1941, Japanese bombing planes launched from carriers crippled the United States Pacific Fleet in Pearl Harbor and destroyed most American aircraft in the Hawaiian Islands. The casualties were as staggering as the damage to the fleet: 2,343 dead, 1,272 wounded, 960 missing, among American service forces. That much of the crippled fleet was back in service within a year was belated compensation for the greatest naval disaster in all American history. Providentially, the Japanese did not follow up their victory with an effort to invade the Hawaiian Islands. Having for the time being paralyzed American naval power in the Pacific, Japan was free to pursue her immediate objective, the conquest of southeastern Asia—Hongkong, Malaya, the Philippines, and the Indies.

Responsibility for the Pearl Harbor disaster presents a complex problem with which historians will wrestle for many years, if not generations, to come. By July, 1946, there had already been eight official investigations; yet it seemed to many that the full story had not been revealed. Although the earliest investigation, made by the then Secretary of the Navy, Frank Knox, and Associate Supreme Court Justice Owen Roberts, laid the major responsibility on the Pearl Harbor commanders, Admiral Husband S. Kimmel and General Walter C. Short, later investigations, including that of a joint Congressional committee, tended to lay less blame on the commanders and more upon various departments and personalities in the government at Washington.[16] Whatever the ultimate verdict of history may be, the Pearl Harbor attack was

---

[16] For the several Pearl Harbor investigations see: United States, Sen. doc. 244, 79th Cong., 2nd sess., "Investigation of the Pearl Harbor Attack. Report of the Joint Committee on the Investigation of the Pearl Harbor Attack." (Washington, 1946.) Previous investigations included: 1) The Roberts Commission, organized under presidential order, December 18, 1941. 2) The Hart inquiry conducted by Admiral Thomas C. Hart by order of Secretary of the Navy Frank Knox. Initiated February 12, 1944, this investigation was concluded, June 15, 1944. 3) The Army Pearl Harbor Board investigation, extending from July 20, 1944, to October 20, 1944, was held pursuant to Public Law 339, 78th Cong., approved June 13, 1944. 4) The Navy Court of Inquiry investigation begun June 13, 1944, was also pursuant to Public Law 339, 78th Congress. 5) The Clark inquiry. This was an investigation conducted by Colonel Carter W. Clark by order of General George C. Marshall regarding the manner in which certain "top secret" communications were handled. The investigation was conducted September 14-16, 1944, and July 13 to August 4, 1945. 6) The Clausen investigation, conducted by Major Henry C. Clausen, JADG, under instructions of the Secretary of War, Henry L. Stimson. Conducted November 23, 1944 to September 12, 1945, this investigation was supplementary to the findings of the Army Pearl Harbor Board. 7) The Hewitt inquiry conducted by Admiral H. Kent Hewitt supplemented the findings of the Navy Court of Inquiry investigation. This was conducted May 14 to July 11, 1945.

of tremendous importance not merely as a military catastrophe but also in its political implications.[17]   If in the American mind there remained on the morning of December 7 any lingering doubts as to the role of the United States in the struggle against totalitarianism, Pearl Harbor removed them.

THE TRADITIONAL DEMOCRACIES ON THE DEFENSIVE

Just as the democracies had been on the defensive ideologically and diplomatically since 1937 and earlier, so now for many tense and uncertain months after Pearl Harbor they were to remain militarily on the defensive.   The Axis fought with many advantages: it had planned and prepared for war; its armies were not only mobilized, but many of its troops had already been tested in battle; finally, it possessed interior lines of supply contrasting with the far-flung ocean routes on which the anti-Axis group depended.   The weakness of the Axis lay in its two territorial spheres, the German-Italian in Europe and the Japanese in the Far East; but this disadvantage was for the time being more than overcome by the momentum of the Axis attack.   Since the democracies were on the defensive, the Anglo-American chiefs of staff determined early in 1942 to concentrate first on the defeat of Hitler, and simply to hold Japan. Time was to prove the wisdom of this decision though at the moment it was an anathema to the Chinese and others threatened by imminent Japanese invasion.[18]

BEGINNINGS OF THE UNITED NATIONS

Within a month of Pearl Harbor the anti-Axis nations sought to give political as well as military purpose and cohesion to their belated preparations for war.   On January 1, 1942, in response to an American proposal, twenty-six governments that were now at war with the Axis pledged their united action in prosecuting the conflict, agreeing to conclude no separate peace.[19]   By this means the principles of the Atlantic Charter became a basic manifesto of these United Nations and the pre-

---

[17] United States, *Foreign Relations: Japan, 1931-1941*, II, 133.

[18] For a factual narrative of naval, ground, and air campaigns of the war in the Pacific and Far East, see Roger W. Shugg and H. A. De Weerd, *World War II* (Washington, 1946).

[19] These powers included: the United States, Great Britain, Russia, Australia, Belgium, Canada, China, Costa Rica, Cuba, Czechoslovakia, Dominician Republic, El Salvador, Greece, Guatemala, Haiti, Honduras, India, Luxembourg, the Netherlands, New Zealand, Nicaragua, Norway, Panama, Poland, South Africa, and Yugoslavia. Later adherents included: Mexico, the Philippines, and Ethiopia during 1942; Brazil, Bolivia, the Free French, and Iraq in 1943.

liminary blueprint for war and eventual peace in Asia as well as in Europe.[20]   The immediate problem, however, was to hold the Axis offensive within limits until the productive power of America as the "arsenal of democracy" should enable the United States to assume the offensive first in Europe and then in the Pacific and Asia.   To this end Anglo-American unity of military action was assured from the beginning through a joint strategic command exercised by the Combined Chiefs of Staff dating from February 6, 1942.   Liaison with Russia and China was maintained through military missions in Moscow and Chungking.

JAPAN'S OFFENSIVE: THE PACIFIC AND
SOUTHEAST ASIA, 1941-42

Japan's attack immediately following Pearl Harbor spread like a great fan southward and westward to encompass southeastern Asia and the island empires which lay off its shores—the East Indies and the Philippines.   Co-ordinated attacks were launched not only from the Caroline Islands and Formosa but also from naval bases and airfields which the Vichy French had permitted Japan to acquire in French Indo-China, and from bases in Thailand acquired after December 8.   While Britain fought with her back to the wall in Europe and while American naval power in the Pacific lay crumpled at Pearl Harbor, Japan moved swiftly to the conquest of the peoples and the great natural wealth of Southeast Asia, her immediate objectives being Midway, Wake, and Guam, Hongkong, the Philippines, Thailand, and Malaya.

Japan's attack on Hongkong came at almost the identical hour of the attack on Pearl Harbor.   The island fortress and one of the great commercial ports of the world surrendered to the Japanese on December 25, 1941.   It had been a British colony for just a century.   Its garrison of some 12,000 men, ill-equipped and with no adequate support of sea or air power, was powerless against the attack protected by control of the seas and launched by land and air.[21]

Far more sensational than the fall of Hongkong, which had been anticipated, was Japan's conquest of the Malay peninsula and Singapore. After seizing a number of airfields, Japanese troops trained specially for tropical and jungle warfare entered Malaya in the north from Thailand and Indo-China and moved south in three lines to converge just north of Singapore.   Already on December 10, British naval power had been

---

[20] *Documents on American Foreign Relations,* IV (1941-42), 203-8.

[21] For the techniques of the Japanese occupation, military, political, and economic, see Robert S. Ward, *Asia for the Asiatics* (Chicago, 1945).

crippled when Japanese planes sank the *Prince of Wales* and the *Repulse*. This made Singapore a naval base without a navy. On the peninsula, retreating British ground forces fought bravely but hopelessly. On February 15, 1942, the city which Stamford Raffles had founded in 1819 surrendered. Japan's road to Burma and India was open.

The attack on Burma had already begun. Simultaneously with the campaign in Malaya Japan had invaded Burma, occupied lower Burma, taken Rangoon, cut the Burma Road, and by June, 1942, was in possession of the entire country. Save for the air route, "the Hump," over the Himalayas, there was now no communications line between the Anglo-American front and China. Even this route was threatened as Japanese planes based on carriers struck as far west as Colombo in Ceylon.

THE CONQUEST OF THE PHILIPPINES

Japan's first attack on the Philippines also came within a few hours of the assault on Pearl Harbor. Here as in Malaya, despite the bravery of Americans and Filipinos, it was for the defenders a story of "too little and too late." There were less than 20,000 American troops in the Islands under General Douglas MacArthur. Manila was occupied January 2 as American and Filipino forces (covered by the guns of Corregidor) retired to the Bataan peninsula. Here a heroic defense was maintained by Lieut. General Jonathan M. Wainwright until the inevitable surrender, April 9. Meanwhile General MacArthur had been ordered to Australia, which was to become the base for the later counteroffensive. Corregidor, reinforced by remnants that crossed the channel from Bataan, held out for some weeks, but was finally taken on May 6. Japan's conquest of the remaining islands was soon completed. At no time in their history had Americans shown greater courage than in the defense of the Philippines; but at best their effort was a delaying action. Bataan was a costly sacrifice to unpreparedness.

With speed unabated, Japan moved on to the conquest of the rich Netherlands Indies. Here her campaigns were virtually complete by March, 1942. Allied naval forces and aircraft again fought delaying actions. Simultaneously the Japanese had moved south and east of the Philippines with the ultimate objective of invading Australia, where General MacArthur had set up defense headquarters in March. Only after the invaders had occupied the Bismarck and Solomon Islands and parts of New Guinea was their progress checked. Meanwhile the American Navy had executed tactical thrusts at Japanese outposts in the Marshall and Gilbert Islands, culminating in the famous air raid on Tokyo, April 18, 1942, by army bombers commanded by Colonel James

H. Doolittle. Later on May 7 and 8, in a naval air battle over the Coral Sea, American naval planes broke up a Japanese attempt to cut the Australian supply lines across the southwestern Pacific to Honolulu and the American Pacific Coast.

THE BATTLE OF MIDWAY

The first major Japanese reverse of the war was the naval air battle of Midway, June 3-6, 1942, which inflicted enormous losses on the enemy fleet and prevented the occupation of Midway and possibly of the Hawaiian Islands. After Midway, save for their invasion of the Aleutians, the Japanese were no longer a menace in the central or eastern Pacific. This impotence in turn added greater security to the 8,000-mile supply line from the United States to the new military bases in Australia. However, these bases remained under constant threat from the Japanese in the Solomons and New Guinea. To meet this danger American forces struck first at the Solomons. The largest of the Solomons, Guadalcanal, was won after fierce air, naval, and ground campaigns lasting from August 7, 1942, to February, 1943. At the same time, Australian and American troops turned back the Japanese in Papua (southeastern New Guinea) thus finally halting the Japanese advance in the Southwest Pacific. Far to the west, British, American, and Chinese forces were striving to hold and strengthen bases in India and China, the area which came to be known as the CBI (China-Burma-India) Theater. After Japan's conquest of Burma, all supplies reaching China went by air over the Hump. Here, too, after great effort extending over many months, the battle of supply was won. By January, 1944, air-borne supplies to China exceeded peak capacities carried over the Burma Road, and American airforces were operating from fields in India and in China. At the far eastern extremity, too, of the Asiatic and Pacific battlefront in the Aleutian Islands, where the Japanese had first landed in June, 1942, American forces took the offensive in May, 1943, and by August had retaken the entire archipelago. Later, these islands provided bases for bombing raids on northern Japan.

THE TURN OF THE TIDE OF BATTLE

The year 1943 marked the end of Japan's march to conquest and the beginnings of her ultimate defeat. In the Pacific and in Asia as in Europe, this defeat could not come until the United Nations had achieved a realistic unity in overall policy and strategy, had won the battle of production, and had brought this newly created power to bear on far-flung battlefronts on the land, the sea, and in the air. In the battle against Japan, the contributions of China, Australia, and New Zealand are not to be minimized; yet for reasons which are clear the major responsibility fell to the United States. Until May, 1942, these Pacific allies waged a desperate defensive struggle. The victory at Midway in the summer of 1942 restored something of a balance in naval power. The campaigns of the succeeding year until August, 1943, halted Japan in the Southwest Pacific. The line of battle was thus being stabilized against the day of counteroffensive.

THE DIPLOMATIC BACKGROUND OF THE COMING VICTORY

From the beginning of the war in Europe and the Far East, it had been the ill-concealed boast of the totalitarian powers that their opponents were incapable of uniting in resistance, and that historic nationalistic rivalries and ideological conflicts could not be submerged. Nevertheless, in a series of momentous conferences the principal powers of the United Nations did achieve a common policy aimed at winning a speedy military victory and the bases of a durable peace.

THE QUEBEC CONFERENCE

At Quebec, Canada, August 11-24, 1943, Roosevelt, Churchill, and T. V. Soong approved policies designed: 1) to strike at Japan through greater aid to China, 2) to achieve closer collaboration with Russia, and 3) to speed the invasion of Italy.[22]

THE MOSCOW CONFERENCE

The Moscow Conference of Foreign Ministers was a logical sequel. There, October 19-30, 1943, Britain, the Soviet Union, and the United States proclaimed among other things the principles of the coming peace, noting that "it was essential . . . to continue the present close collaboration and cooperation in the conduct of the war into the period following the end of hostilities. . . ."[23] Fascism was to be destroyed and war criminals brought to justice. China also joined in declarations demanding "unconditional surrender" by the Axis and promising a post-war international organization based on the sovereign equality of states to maintain peace and security. Fear that the United States, reverting as it had in 1919 to a policy of isolation, would not honor the Moscow declaration,

---

[22] *Documents on American Foreign Relations,* VI (1943-44), 224-226.
[23] *Documents on American Foreign Relations,* VI (1943-44), 226-232.

was removed when both Houses of Congress passed resolutions favoring American membership in the proposed international organization.[24]

THE CAIRO MEETING

Since Russia was not at war with Japan, the Moscow Conference of Foreign Ministers had not dealt specifically with war plans and purposes in the Far East. Such plans and purposes were the subject of the meeting of Roosevelt, Churchill, and Chiang K'ai-shek at Cairo, November 22-26, 1943. The war was to be prosecuted until Japan accepted "unconditional surrender." Japan was to be deprived of all the lands which she had seized since 1894. Korea was "in due course" to be free and independent.[25]

Following immediately on Cairo came the first meeting of Stalin with Roosevelt and Churchill at Teheran, November 26-December 2, which gave final shape to plans for destruction of Hitler's Germany.[26]

THE DUMBARTON OAKS PROPOSALS

Meanwhile at Dumbarton Oaks in Washington, D. C., representatives of the United States, Great Britain, Russia, and China drafted preliminary proposals for an international organization to replace the League of Nations. It was later to materialize as the United Nations Organization. The stated purpose was to maintain international peace and security.[27] Subsequently, at Yalta in the Crimea, February, 1945, Roosevelt, Churchill, and Stalin again met and, among other things, announced a coming international conference at San Francisco to create a charter for the permanent organization of the United Nations.[28]

MILITARY OFFENSIVE OF THE UNITED NATIONS, 1943-44

Even before the achievement of a complete diplomatic and military coalition, the United Nations were winning their first campaigns as the prelude to eventual victory. In the Pacific, these included, as already noted, the Battle of Midway and the campaigns at Guadalcanal and in the Aleutians. Simultaneously, British and American forces broke the

---

[24] The Fullbright Resolution, H. of Rep., Sept. 21, 1943, and the Connally Resolution, U. S. Senate, Nov. 5, 1943.

[25] *Documents on American Foreign Relations,* VI (1943-44), 232-234.

[26] *Documents on American Foreign Relations,* VI (1943-44), 234-237. See also Foster Rhea Dulles, *The Road to Teheran* (Princeton, 1944).

[27] Leland M. Goodrich and Edvard Hambro, *Charter of the United Nations* (Boston, 1946), 5-9.

[28] Goodrich and Hambro, 9-10. Russia agreed at Yalta to enter the war against Japan following the defeat of Germany. Text in United States, Department of State, *Occupation of Japan* (Washington, D. C., 1946), 52-53.

German and Italian armies in North Africa (May, 1943). Meanwhile Soviet armies had stopped the German advance at Stalingrad (September-November, 1942), and in 1943 were engaged in the first great Soviet counteroffensive. In September, 1943, came the unconditional surrender of Italy. By the spring of 1944 the Germans had been driven from all of southern Russia.

THE ADVANCE IN THE PACIFIC AND FAR EAST, 1943-44

In the summer of 1943, American forces, military and naval, were prepared to advance from the toe-holds at Guadalcanal and in New Guinea. Through some of the cruelest campaigns of the war, fought in New Georgia, Bougainville, and New Guinea, American and Australian armies moved to neutralize Rabaul, Japan's principal military and naval base in the Southwest Pacific. This, the first great offensive of the Pacific war ("climbing the Solomons-New Guinea ladder"), revealed the astounding new weight of American naval and military striking power developed since Pearl Harbor. It was this power which enabled the Navy to take Makin and Tarawa Islands in the Gilberts (November, 1943), and Kwajalein in the Marshalls (February, 1944), and to bomb far to the west the Japanese bases on Truk in the Carolines, and Saipan in the Marianas, in a drive destined eventually to cut Japan's communications with her empire in Southeast Asia.

THE CBI FRONT, 1943-44

For the first two years of the war, the Japanese were in virtually undisputed control of the China-Burma-India front. The seemingly impenetrable jungle, devastating heat and disease, distance, lack of transportation, paucity of supplies and troops, all conspired to delay the day of counteroffensive. Nevertheless, even here the Japanese were beginning to feel the first Allied blows. In the winter and spring of 1943-44, air-borne invasions of the northern Burma jungle were launched by Wingate's British Raiders and Merrill's American Marauders. Bitter campaigns were fought by the British on the Manipur-Imphal front, but most successful for the United Nations was the work of American and Chinese forces in northern Burma (1944) covering construction of the Ledo Road, the new supply route from India to China.

American occupation of the Gilbert and Marshall Islands was the prelude to a great naval offensive which developed in the summer of 1944. Striking westward toward the China coast, American forces moved to the conquest of the major islands of the Mariana group (Saipan, July 9, and Tinian, July 23) and to the reconquest of Guam, August 3. All were taken after bitter fighting and great loss of life, both American and Japanese.

Meanwhile, in the spring and early summer, American and Australian land and air forces, with naval support, under General MacArthur had broken Japan's New Guinea armies into isolated and powerless groups, thus opening the way for the invasion and reconquest of the Philippines.

Other pressures, too, were operating and reducing Japan's power to resist. By the summer of 1944, American submarines had sunk a total of nearly 700 Japanese vessels. These losses diminished Japan's power to hold her newly won empire in Southeast Asia, and contributed to the eventual collapse of Japanese war production at home. To this latter task the United States brought the world's mightiest airplane, the B-29 bomber, based on secret airfields deep in independent China. The first raid by these flying superfortresses against southern Japan was made on June 15, 1944. Later raids struck at the eastern part of North China and Manchuria. Subsequently, Saipan became the principal base for super-fortress raids on the length and breadth of Japan's industrial homeland.

THE RECONQUEST OF THE PHILIPPINES

In the closing months of 1944 and during the first six months of 1945, the carnage of war returned to the Philippines. Preliminary to the re-conquest of the Islands, American forces battled their way into the Palau group of the western Carolines and the Halmahera group off north-ern New Guinea in September, 1944. Then, after air operations had neutralized Japan's airforce in the Philippines, American forces in-vaded Leyte, October 21. A series of fierce naval battles which followed ended Japan's naval efforts to prevent a full-scale invasion. Long and costly military campaigns followed in Leyte and Mindoro, leading finally to the invasion of Luzon and the siege of Manila, February 8-24, 1945. Not until July had American and Filipino forces destroyed the last effective Japanese resistance in northern Luzon. In the liberation of the Philippines, some twenty-three Japanese divisions were virtually annihilated. By July, also, Australian and Dutch forces had completed the reconquest of the rich oil lands of Borneo.

IWO JIMA AND OKINAWA

As the reconquest of the Philippines became merely a matter of time, American land, sea, and air forces pressed the attack closer to Japan it-self. On March 16, 1945, the capture of tiny, desolate Iwo Jima, the most costly operation in the history of the United States Marine Corps, removed at least one danger from the path of the increasing raids of

B-29 bombers now based on Saipan.   Almost simultaneously the Americans landed on Okinawa in the Loochoos (Ryukyus) and, again in some of the costliest fighting of the war, from April through June, crushed Japanese resistance in spite of damaging attacks by Japanese suicide planes.   Possession of Okinawa enabled the American air forces to bring the weight of their full striking power to bear on Japan's home islands.

THE SEA AND AIR ASSAULT ON JAPAN

As the weight of American military and naval power moved closer to Japan Proper in 1945, the devastating effect of the B-29 superfortress raids over Tokyo was brought home to the Japanese populace.   The tempo of the air attack on Japanese targets increased 500 percent in the twelve months following June, 1944.   The new bases on Iwo Jima and Okinawa made possible, by the summer of 1945, co-ordination of attack of "land-based medium and heavy bombers with B-29s, and with carrier and land-based fighters."   As the great air assault developed, Japan's defenders were struck not only in Japan itself but also on the farther edges of her conquered and now crumbling empire—in Bangkok, Formosa, Saigon, Singapore, Rangoon, Penang, and Kuala Lumpur.   In the early months of 1945, the attacks on Japan itself were concentrated on industrial centers: Tokyo, Nagoya, Osaka, Kobe, Akashi, Hachijo, Omuta, Shizuoka, Koizumi, and Tachikawa; and on the destruction of Japanese airfields, principally in Kyushu.   Although American losses in all these attacks were heavy, they could not be compared with the frightful destruction wrought in Japan.   By June 1, 1945, more than fifty square miles of Tokyo had been reduced to rubble and ashes, so effective had been the incendiary bomb against the match-box construction of large parts of the Japanese cities.   As the larger cities were systematically reduced, the attack turned to small secondary industrial targets.   In July, 1945, British carrier planes joined the attack.   By the same month, more than 2,000 American planes were sometimes over Japan in a single day.   The land-based attacks were ably supported by naval carrier-plane attacks and by naval bombardment of Japan's coastal cities.   The combined Anglo-American Third Fleet in the final two and one-half months of the war destroyed or damaged nearly 3,000 Japanese planes and sank or damaged some 1,600 enemy naval and merchant vessels, thus completing the virtual destruction by August 1, 1945, of Japan's power on the sea and in the air.   The final blows to the Japanese fleet were delivered as it lay in its Inland Sea bases.

Thus by the summer of 1945, Japan's military position was hopeless.

In Europe, Germany had already collapsed (May 7-8, 1945). It was now possible to warn the Japanese people that particular cities would be destroyed. The resulting raids carrying out these threats made it increasingly clear to the Japanese populace that their own defenders were powerless. Yet as late as June 9, Premier Kentaro Suzuki, who had succeeded General Kuniaki Koiso in April, 1945, replying to President Truman's warning that Japan would be destroyed unless she surrendered, declared that Japan would fight on. Then on July 26 during the Potsdam Conference, the United States, Britain, and China delivered a final ultimatum to Japan demanding immediate unconditional surrender.[29] Japan replied (July 30) that she would ignore the demands of the Potsdam Declaration.

THE ATOMIC BOMB

Japan's words of rejection were brave, but they were far removed from the realities of her actual situation: military, economic, or psychological. The overwhelming, irresistible weight of American-British arms had already broken Japan's power for successful resistance. She now faced the futile slaughter which would attend the coming day of invasion. How costly in lives and human suffering this day would have been will never be known, for other events conspired to end hostilities without an invasion. On August 6 the Japanese city of Hiroshima and its army base were destroyed in the space of minutes by a bomb dropped from an American superfortress—the first atomic bomb used in warfare. Nearly a month earlier (July 13), the Japanese government had asked Russia to intervene with Britain and the United States to bring about peace. Russia's reply, not delivered until August 8, announced immediate severance of her diplomatic relations with Japan and that "from August 9 the Soviet Government will consider itself to be at war with Japan." Within hours of Russia's severance of relations, a second atomic bomb destroyed the city of Nagasaki and its naval base (August

---

[29] Terms of the Potsdam ultimatum included: 1) elimination of those elements in Japan that had led the nation into world conquest; 2) destruction of Japan's war-making power; 3) implementation of the Cairo Declaration; 4) disarming of all Japanese military forces; 5) the declaration disclaimed any intent that "the Japanese shall be enslaved as a race or destroyed as a nation, but stern justice shall be meted out to all war criminals"; 6) all obstacles would be removed "to the revival and strengthening of democratic tendencies among the Japanese people"; 7) Japan would be permitted to retain such industries "as will sustain her economy and permit the exaction of just reparations in kind," but not those which would enable her to rearm for war; 8) military occupation of Japan until these objectives should be achieved; and finally 9) Japan should immediately surrender unconditionally or be utterly destroyed. Text in *Occupation of Japan* (Washington, D. C., 1946), 53-55.

9). On the same day Russian armies invaded Manchuria, seized the Korean ports of Rashin and Yuki (August 12), and advanced in the southern or Japanese half of Sakhalin Island.

JAPAN SURRENDERS

On August 10, the Japanese government announced its willingness to accept the Potsdam terms (to which Russia had now subscribed) provided they comprised no "demand which prejudices the prerogatives of His Majesty [the Emperor] as a sovereign ruler." The reply of the United States (August 11) stated that "the authority of the Emperor and the Japanese Government to rule the State shall be subject to the Supreme Commander of the Allied Powers." Japan accepted these terms August 14, and the surrender was effected on board the U. S. battleship *Missouri* in Tokyo Bay, September 2, 1945.[30]

---

[30] Terms for the surrender of all Japanese armed forces are in Shugg and De Weerd, *World War II,* 429-434. Texts of relevant documents are in *Occupation of Japan* (Washington, D. C., 1946), 4-6, 56-67.

CHAPTER 38

CHINA IN WAR AND IN VICTORY

IT IS far from satisfying to attempt a conclusion to this story of modern China. The Chinese Revolution which began on the Yangtze in 1911 has not completed its course. The conditions which created it have not yet been removed, and Sun Yat-sen's philosophy—the Three Principles of the People—which gave the revolution life and purpose has not been built into the tangible framework of an acceptable government. The failure as yet to reach Sun's goal is understandable, for the road on which China's Revolution has travelled has been a particularly rough one. Two road-blocks have frequently obstructed its progress. The first of these is the weight of Chinese tradition itself. Habit and custom of thought and action sanctified by the centuries do not give way easily to what is new. Moreover, as Sun Yat-sen indicated, much of what is old should be preserved; but it has not been easy for the Chinese to decide to which of the old things they should cling, nor what of the new should be adopted. The second obstacle which has often seemed to halt China's Revolution is the same force which has had much to do with creating it—the impact on China of the modern Western world. The world of Western thought and action inspired the revolutionary philosophy of Sun Yat-sen, yet the great Western powers and Japan have often feared China's Revolution, have interfered with it, and have sought to direct it into this or that particular channel. Nevertheless, China in the most recent years of revolution has stood the test. During the four and one-half years of the undeclared war with Japan, 1937-1941, "resistance was created by the will of the Chinese people." The unity of a people, regardless of party, whether Kuomintang, Communist, or other, has been preserved. Advocates of appeasement there have been, but they have failed to carry the people with them.[1]

But the trials of the undeclared Sino-Japanese War, 1937-1941, were but a prelude and a testing ground for even greater trials to come. With December, 1941, China, for the second time in the era of the re-

---

[1] Lawrence K. Rosinger, *China's Crisis* (New York, 1945), 3-24. It is worthwhile noting that the idea of unity is not only a principle of modern nationalism but also of Confucian political theory.

696

publican revolution, became engulfed in a world conflict. She promptly followed the American and British declarations by herself declaring war on Japan. Her own long conflict with Japan thus became merged with the world-wide struggle against the Axis powers. As in 1917, China was ill-equipped in the material weapons with which modern nations fight, yet she proved to be exceedingly strong while the enemy remained within her gates. Her moral strength was symbolized by her ready adherence to the Declaration of the United Nations on January 1, 1942. The darker side of the picture was that China's new allies, the United States and Britain, were in no position to give her immediate aid. Independent China still remained locked in the great western interior, and was governed from the fugitive capital at Chungking. Nearly a third of the richest parts of China, including the lower Yangtze Valley and most of the seacoast were controlled by Japan, and, if the Japanese were unable to advance further, so were the Chinese unable to regain the lost territory. Indeed for nearly two years, China's plight grew progressively worse. Isolation from her allies became almost complete as all of Southeast Asia fell to Japan. Even for many months after the tide of battle in the Pacific had turned, there was no substantial relief in munitions, guns, or planes for China. Furthermore, the strategy of the great powers, the United States, Britain, and Russia, called first for defeat of the Axis in Europe.

FIRST AMERICAN AID TO CHINA

Yet within the limitations set by early defeat in Southeast Asia and the Pacific, and the requirements of global strategy, the United States did go to China's aid. At first this aid was little more than verbal assurance to China that the war would be fought until Japan was defeated. There followed financial aid, a $500,000,000 loan in 1942, practically without strings attached. There was also implementation of long-range planning to reopen communications with Chungking. The chief of the American military mission to China, General Joseph Stilwell, became chief-of-staff to Generalissimo Chiang K'ai-shek and commander of ground forces in the CBI (China-Burma-India) theater. After the retreat from Burma, it was Stilwell's task to train Chinese troops for the reconquest, to open air transport from India over the Hump of the Himalayas to Chungking, and to construct the Ledo Road (later known as the Stilwell Road) from Assam through northern Burma to link with the upper Burma Road. One of the heroic stories of the war was written by the Americans who, beginning with virtually no equipment, flew lend-lease supplies across the roof of the world to Chungking. There

CHINA IN WAR AND VICTORY

was also aid to China from the American Volunteer Group. Under Colonel, later General, Claire L. Chennault, these American "Flying Tigers" had operated prior to Pearl Harbor under contracts with the Chinese government to protect the Burma Road. Later they continued to operate in China as the Fourteenth Air Force of the United States Army Air Forces. However, although this aid was significant, China's resistance still rested on her own resources—the spirit which remained in a war-weary and sorely tried people.

THE REBIRTH OF CHINA'S SOVEREIGNTY

On the political and diplomatic front, the United States also moved to bolster Chinese confidence. It was felt that the time had come to discard the last remnants of the so-called unequal treaties, some of them now a century old. What remained of these treaties was a particularly sore spot in the thinking of all Chinese nationalists. Tariff autonomy had already been conceded to China more than a decade earlier. Now, on January 11, 1943, both the United States and Great Britain concluded treaties with China providing for immediate relinquishment of their extraterritorial rights and for the settlement of related questions. This act and the virtual relinquishment of special rights by all the remaining "treaty powers" completed the long process of restoring and recognizing the full sovereignty of China.[2] This meant, among other things, that the time had arrived when the powers would no longer maintain troops on Chinese soil or garrison the legation quarter at Pei-p'ing and the international settlements at Shanghai and Amoy. American public opinion certainly approved these gestures to China's partnership in the United Nations. Moreover, there were Americans who felt it was unfortunate this country had waited until, so far as the Western powers were concerned, their special privileges had already been lost as a result of Japan's aggression.

REPEAL OF THE CHINESE EXCLUSION LAWS

More striking, however, than the demise of extraterritoriality, was America's repeal of the Chinese exclusion laws. It was a far cry from west coast slogans of the late nineteenth century that "John Chinaman" who could live on "the smell of a greasy rag" "must go," to the urgent message of President Roosevelt to Congress, October 11, 1943, that

---

[2] L. M. Goodrich and M. J. Carroll, *Documents on American Foreign Relations,* V (Boston, 1944), 485-501. A year earlier the U. S. Congress authorized $500,000,000 in credits to China to stabilize her currency, combat inflation, and finance production of war supplies.

America "correct a historic mistake," and "silence Japanese propaganda," by repealing the laws which had barred Chinese, now our allies, from American shores. Impelled by the pressures of war, Congress ended Chinese exclusion by a bill which became law on December 17, 1943. Under the new law, a presidential proclamation fixed an annual quota of Chinese immigrants at 105. There can be little doubt that the vast majority of Americans approved this belated atonement for "a historic mistake." Yet there was still opposition. Even the pressures of war and the emphasis on the principles for which Americans were fighting had not completely removed the old prejudices. Opposition to ending exclusion voiced itself in the Senate and especially in the House of Representatives. It was based on apprehension that the bill was the opening wedge for large Asiatic immigration. In China the new law was greeted with enthusiasm. Sun Fo, son of Sun Yat-sen, and President of the Legislative Yüan, described it as "reaffirming our faith in American fair play and American friendship."[3]

The fuller significance of abolition of extraterritoriality and the exclusion laws was given at the Cairo Conference, November 22-26, 1943, where President Roosevelt and Prime Minister Churchill met with Generalissimo Chiang K'ai-shek to consider problems of war and peace in the Far East. The implication was that China was now accepted as one of the great powers; that the National Government had the full support of Britain and America; and that the post-war Far East would be built around a fully sovereign, independent, and strong China. If these goals could be attained, it would be the fulfillment of principles to which American policy had adhered for nearly a century. Indeed, the year 1943 revealed new heights in America's traditional admiration of and friendship for China. In part, this newly aroused enthusiasm was due to the visit of Madame Chiang K'ai-shek, who had come to the United States early in 1943 to win American support for the National Government and to criticize the strategy of merely holding the front against Japan until the defeat of Hitler had been achieved. Her eloquence and charm appeared to personify the heroism of a China that had refused to be beaten. This was enough. "Chinese unity and Chinese democracy were accepted uncritically under the spell of her magnetic personality."[4] Madame Chiang had spoken of the high lights in the Chinese picture. She had avoided the shadows. Neither she nor other eloquent Chinese spokesmen of the National Government were in

---

[3] Relevant documents are in Goodrich and Carroll, *Documents on American Foreign Relations,* VI (Boston, 1945), 607-617.

[4] Foster Rhea Dulles, *China and America* (Princeton, 1946), 240.

a position to say what all knew—that China's prosecution of the war had reached its lowest point since Japan struck at Lukouchiao in July, 1937.

FACTORS IN CHINA'S DETERIORATING WAR EFFORT

Basic in China's collapsing war effort by 1943 was the fact that the Chinese, as a people, had been worn down and disillusioned by six years of war. Millions had lost their homes and all their worldly possessions. The early hopes that aid would soon be at hand from America and Britain were shattered. The news of early Axis victories in the first year of war dispelled much of what hope was left. Discouragement was natural, and at times it vented itself in resentment against democracies.

A more immediate factor in China's declining morale was the nation's economic crisis, immeasurably aggravated, though not wholly created, by the war. Even in times of general world peace, China's economy provided no surplus. Now, in years of war, as productivity declined prices rose in an inflation which was soon beyond control; profiteering became rampant not only in business circles but among many high officials in the National Government. "National goals were dissipated in making money and protecting special privilege." [5] For a time Chinese censors were able to prevent news of the skyrocketing cost of living from reaching the outside world. Within independent or "Free" China wholesale prices increased over 500 percent between June, 1937, and June, 1944.[6] The disaster of inflation struck first at all groups with fixed incomes, perhaps the worst sufferers being China's all too few school teachers. The peasant, the great bulk of China's masses, also felt the heavy hand of inflation because the average Chinese peasant never does have a surplus of rice to sell, and thus cannot profit by a rising market.[7] Given the nature of Chinese economy with the added difficulties of wartime, inflation was to be expected. That it developed into an uncontrolled spiral was due to the fact that hoarders and profiteers had sufficient influence with the National Government to block effective preventive measures. A situation grew in which government revenue came principally from the land tax on the mass of the people while wealthier classes failed to share in China's war expenses.[8] In addition, the administration of the land tax in kind was estimated to

---

[5] Dulles, *China and America*, 241.
[6] Rosinger, *China's Crisis*, 160.
[7] Note the more optimistic view developed by J. E. Baker, "China Will Carry On," *Far Eastern Survey*, XI (1942), 127-128.
[8] Rosinger, *China's Crisis*, 176.

cost two-fifths of the value of the grain collected. No phase of China's war economy escaped the effects of these disastrous conditions. As a result, even the Chinese Industrial Co-operatives, organized in 1938-39 to encourage and speed war production among local groups and recognized as one of the finest examples of the war effort of the Chinese people, were hampered at every turn by the declining value of their limited capital.[9] Where famine was added to the shortages of war, inflation, which was here a synonym for lack of food, led the peasantry to revolt and to disarm their own soldiers. Chinese intellectuals who dared to protest against the official policies that tolerated these conditions felt the heavy hand of the anti-democratic Ministry of Education in Chungking or of one or another of the various bodies of secret police. Not even the Chinese peasantry whose ancestors for centuries had taken privation for granted could be induced to resist the invader indefinitely in the face of these economic odds.

Faced with economic crisis, increasing numbers of Chinese placed responsibility for the nation's plight on the National Government and the Kuomintang. Whatever the shortcomings of this Kuomintang government were, and they were certainly considerable, it had continued for more than a decade to justify its claim as the government of the Republic.

THE NATURE OF THE NATIONAL GOVERNMENT

In form, China's government, while differing rather widely from governments in Britain and America, contained structural features readily comprehended by Westerners: a president, a state council, a national military council, five divisions or yüan for the exercise of certain powers (executive, legislative, judicial, examination, and censor), and numerous ministries such as finance, foreign affairs, and so on. But the realities of politics operating through this structure represent political practices which are quite different from the American or British model. Since the establishment of the National Government, the highest officials of that government have been at the same time the highest officials of the party, and, in addition, many of the most important decisions of government were made by the Central Executive Committee of the Party. Thus the first factor of political power has been the political machine of the Kuomintang. In turn, the power of the Kuomintang machine has rested in part at least on its control of China's armies, a control that is often furthered by appointing generals as provincial gov-

---

[9] On the Chinese Industrial Co-operatives see, Nym Wales, *The Chinese Labor Movement* (New York, 1945), 96-100.

ernors. Finally, political power in China, as in other parts of the Orient, is a highly personal thing. This personal element may play a large part in any country, but it is particularly strong in China both for traditional reasons and also because constitutionalism in practice does not yet exist there. This explains one of the reasons why there was little change in the structure of China's government or in the personnel of her leadership during eight years of devastating war from 1937 to 1945.[10]

THE KUOMINTANG

The position and the character of the Kuomintang as the party developed after 1927 was also a major determinant in China's varying ability to maintain her morale and the struggle against Japan. After Sun Yat-sen's death the character of the party underwent radical change. After 1927, the liberals, those inclined democratically, the left wing members, and Communists were either expelled or gradually removed from posts where they could exert effective influence on policy. To an increasing degree the party came to be representative of the personal oligarchy at the top rather than of the broader membership at the bottom. Even this membership is less than one percent of China's population. The Kuomintang had thus never been a political party in the American or British sense. It has never been responsible to an electorate of the public in even a limited sense, and as time went on it became less responsive to the wishes of liberals within its own ranks. The result was that the nation's revolutionary party tended to trail behind trends of thought in the nation, while the government in turn trailed behind the party.[11]

---

[10] Lawrence K. Rosinger, *China's Wartime Politics* (Princeton, 1944), 45-47, for changes effected in government structure. On the structure of the National Government as affected by the Japanese invasion see Liu Nai-chen, "The Framework of Government in Unoccupied China," in *Voices from Unoccupied China,* edited by H. F. MacNair (Chicago, 1944), 1-15.

[11] Rosinger, *China's Crisis,* 38-39; Rosinger, *China's Wartime Politics,* 49; and in particular the penetrating analysis of government and social organization in China in D. N. Rowe, *China Among the Powers* (New York, 1945), 125-146. Note especially the thesis that Dr. Sun's doctrines have been robbed of any real significance "for the decision of concrete [political] questions." The Kuomintang Nationalists claim to be orthodox and at the same time they confirm landlords in property rights and liquidate Communists. Other parties, such as the Communists, profess equal orthodoxy while liquidating landlords and their estates. Rowe, 133.

Among China's principal minor political parties whose members include many middle-of-the-road elements, liberals, progressives, intellectuals, writers, socialists, etc., were the following:

1. The Democratic League founded in 1941 by liberals of the People's Political Council. Its claims to the name democratic are perhaps more valid than those of any other party. In the Kuomintang-Communist conflict, the attitude of the League has been divided

FACTIONALISM IN POLITICS

A further important feature of the political scene is the factionalism characteristic of Chinese politics, and exemplified notably within the personal oligarchy that has controlled the Kuomintang and the National Government. The most powerful of these factions control the party machine. Their leaders are the political bosses. Outstanding among these in Kuomintang history has been the so-called "C. C. Clique," which takes its name from Ch'en Li-fu, who became Minister of Education in 1938, and his brother, Ch'en Kuo-fu, Minister of Organization of the Kuomintang. This clique has obstructed freedom of teaching and has promoted "what may properly be characterized as an undemocratic ideology." [12] Another Kuomintang faction was the Whampoa or military clique controlled by generals. The military group, however, has not always been a unit. It has been associated with super reactionaries, such as Ho Ying-chin, who was Minister of War, and progressives, such as Ch'en Ch'eng, who have advocated thorough modernization of China's armies. A third faction, whose position is difficult to define, included representatives of capital and business, and was led by H. H. Kung, who has held such posts as Minister of Finance and Chairman of the Board of Directors of the Bank of China. While he

between those inclined to close co-operation with the Communists and those who favor the position of a neutral mediator.

2. The Young China Party was organized in Paris in 1923 and for some years drew its membership from Chinese students in France. Labelling itself "democratic," its emphasis on state capitalism and social co-operation has led some critics to regard it as fascist, others as left-wing. In practice it has acted closely in sympathy with the Kuomintang.

3. The National Socialist Party. Led by Carson Chang (Chang Chia-sheng), and not to be confused with national socialism of the German variety, this party has been largely an attempt to restore traditional values somewhat modified by Western thought.

4. The National Salvationists' Association, begun in 1935, was formally organized by Shanghai intellectuals in 1937 to urge the government to offer armed resistance against Japan. By that time a number of its leaders had already been imprisoned by the government. These able and patriotic leaders were later released, but the movement continued to be suppressed. The National Salvationists have represented a movement rather than a political party. Their political thinking has been somewhat leftist, but their principal objective has been unity of the country above all party considerations.

5. The National Association of Vocational Education, organized in 1917, seeks national revitalization through popularizing vocational education.

6. The Local Self-Government Institute is a group which advocates rural reform and reconstruction.

7. Two parties closely related in aims and ideology were the Social Democratic Party, 1925, the Chinese affiliate of the Second International, and The Third Party organized in 1927-28 by dissident Communists and left Kuomintang members after the Kuomintang purge of the Communists. The party has been the advocate of a leftist interpretation of the *San Min Chu I*, of socialism, and land reform.

[12] Rosinger, *China's Crisis*, 40.

advocated strong co-operation with the Allies, Kung's domestic policies have generally revealed the semi-feudal view of the more conservative banking groups. These are but examples of many groups and personalities within the Kuomintang. In general the continuous conflicts that occurred between cliques and personalities did not get into the political news. The objective was not to eliminate an opponent but to play for relative position.[13]

THE ROLE OF CHIANG K'AI-SHEK

Given the personal character of the Chinese government, one is able to comprehend more readily the role which has been played by Generalissimo Chiang K'ai-shek, the most important personality in recent Chinese history. Chiang cannot be dismissed simply as a reactionary among reactionaries any more than he can be described as a liberal or a democrat. Moreover, account must be taken of the way in which Chiang rose throughout the revolutionary period to the unrivalled position of prestige he enjoyed during the war and into the post-war period. To begin with, he was a trusted disciple of Sun Yat-sen, but unlike other of Sun's lieutenants who were civilian politicians, Chiang was a soldier whose principal military education was received in Japan. Since the National Government, established in 1927, resulted directly from military victories won by the Kuomintang armies which Chiang led, it was natural that he should emerge as leader of the new government. Nevertheless, both in China and abroad at that time, Chiang was regarded not as the successor of Sun Yat-sen but as the newest and most successful of the many war-lords who had fought for control of China during the previous decade. History, however, was soon to cast Chiang in a new role. As Japan's aggressions increased, military and political factionalism gave way to a growing popular demand for national resistance. To achieve political unity under military resistance, the nation naturally turned to Chiang K'ai-shek. For Chiang the decision was a difficult one, for he had been prosecuting a bloody and unsuccessful civil war against the Communists. Yet he did alter his policies, accepted the nation's mandate, and became truly the national leader, thus demonstrating his capacity to achieve heights of real statesmanship. Nevertheless, it was not Chiang who led the way in 1935-1937, but the Chinese who led Chiang.[14]

[13] Rowe, *China Among the Powers,* 138; for further discussion of factions in Chinese politics, Sun Keewong, "Chiang Picks a Governor for Szechwan," *Asia,* XLI (1941), 193-194.
[14] Rosinger, *China's Crisis,* 17.

What have been the political characteristics and the philosophy of this national leader of wartime China? Having made the decision to resist aggression, he remained inflexible in this purpose. A virtue in wartime, this inflexibility has not been so useful in the problems of peace. He is not deeply versed in political or economic thought, but is adept in listening to the thoughts of others and in shifting the weight of his own influence to maintain a balance among the factions that surround him. While undoubtedly a professing Methodist, he has appeared to be more influenced by the moral ideas of his own native background. Concepts such as uniformity in opinion, obedience to authority, loyalty, propriety, and willing acceptance of one's proper place in life strongly appeal to him. This is not simply because these concepts might further his personal ambitions, but rather because he devoutly believes in them. As yet, the most revealing document on Chiang's political philosophy is his book *China's Destiny,* published in 1943. It treats of life and government in the Old China, of the history of the unequal treaties, of the Kuomintang, but it stresses the exploitation suffered at the hands of foreign powers, and develops a detailed blueprint for China's reconstruction. Features of the book which have a direct bearing on the current problems of post-war China are: 1) its repeated attacks on Chinese democrats and liberals as well as Communists; 2) its anti-foreignism: the great powers are held to be primarily responsible for China's troubles, a view never accepted by Sun Yat-sen and never established by any kind of historical proof; 3) a glorification of China's past in terms of respect for the official class which ruled Old China. There is thus a definite lack of evidence to indicate that Chiang has desired the people of China to become the positive political force which democracy would demand.[15]

Finally, what of the dictatorship Chiang is said to have wielded?

---

[15] The Chinese edition of this very revealing work on Chiang's political thinking and his political objectives is Chiang K'ai-shek, *China's Destiny* [Chung Kuo Chih Ming Yün] (Chungking, 1943). For further analysis see Rosinger, *China's Crisis,* 50-57. Although the first Chinese edition was 200,000 and was followed by more than 200 printings, Chungking censors would not permit foreign correspondents to quote from the book in their dispatches, and even as late as 1946 a translation held by the State Department was denied by Secretary Byrnes to Congressmen who requested to see it on the ground that the time was not "propitious" for making public the document (see H. F. MacNair in *The Chicago Sun Book Week,* Feb. 23, 1947). In January, 1947, this ill-advised official secrecy and censorship, both Chinese and American, were brought to an abrupt end with the simultaneous publication in translation of two rival American editions. The first of these is an officially authorized translation by Wang Chung-hui with an introduction by Lin Yutang. The second, unofficial edition, contains notes and commentary by Philip Jaffe, and includes in addition a fifty-page translation of an essential companion work by Chiang, *Chinese Economic Theory.*

Chiang K'ai-shek has not been a dictator in the sense in which Germany, Italy, Spain, Russia, and Portugal have provided us with examples. China does not yet possess the machinery of political communication and control out of which that kind of dictatorship may be built. In so far as China has had anything resembling a dictatorship, it has been held by the Kuomintang oligarchy rather than by any individual. Moreover, this hierarchy is, as noted, essentially a collection of cliques. That Generalissimo Chiang is the moderator who balances one group against another does not detract from his prestige as the only living individual who has been able to personify the ideal of China's unity. Rather, to state this fact is merely to describe a normal, traditional Chinese system of political operation. Indeed it is a system that is natural in the "almost total absence of fixed political formalism in the Chinese scene." [16]

REVIVAL OF THE CONSTITUTIONAL MOVEMENT

The increasing privations and hardships of war and the declining prestige of the National Government served both directly and indirectly to revive the question of constitutionalism in the most gloomy hours of war. In the vanguard of this movement were China's liberals and democrats drawn from intellectual and middle-class groups. They were not numerous, and their survival as liberals had been difficult. Freedom of speech and assembly, as understood by Western democracies, have never been nationally recognized in China as an inalienable right of citizenship. There was nothing new therefore in the National Government's suppression of liberty; rather it was a case of suppression becoming more rigid as the war dragged on and the government revealed itself as incapable of providing effective leadership. Consequently, occasion arose in 1943-1944 for the revival of liberal demands that constitutional machinery be created through which more of the people might speak.

In 1931 a Provisional Constitution had been adopted [17] which with amendments continued to operate throughout the subsequent years of war.[18] Proposals looking to a permanent constitution resulted in 1936 in the formal promulgation of the Draft Constitution.[19] Hostilities in 1937 blocked the convening of a National Congress to consider the draft. The spread of war suggested indefinite delay, but as the Sino-Japanese

---

[16] Rowe, *China Among the Powers,* 139.

[17] The Chinese Ministry of Information, *China Handbook, 1937-1943* (New York, 1943), 40.

[18] Text of the Provisional Constitution in *The China Year Book, 1932,* 688-690.

[19] Text in *China Handbook, 1937-1943,* 120-127.

conflict reached a seeming stalemate in 1939, questions of constitutionalism were again raised. Already the National Government through its
Program of Resistance and Reconstruction had announced it would establish a People's Political Council, comprising "the best minds of the
nation" to advise the government.[20] When in the first meeting of the
Peoples Political Council, September, 1939, there were requests from
councilors of all parties, Kuomintang, Communist, Nationalist Socialist,
Young China, and National Salvationists, for immediate steps toward
constitutional democracy, Chiang K'ai-shek appointed a Constitutionalism Promotion Committee representing divergent views within the
Council to stimulate discussion of constitutional issues. Meanwhile the
Kuomintang leadership decided to call the National Congress late in
1940. For reasons of both war and politics this meeting was not held;
but in 1943, when Chiang K'ai-shek again emphasized the importance
of constitutionalism, the Kuomintang Central Executive Committee decided to call the Congress within a year of the end of war to adopt a
constitution. These were indeed signs of progress toward constitutionalism, but they did not mean that solution had yet been reached on
any of the fundamental issues such, for example, as the legal recognition
of political groups other than the Kuomintang and their right to participate in politics. Moreover, it should be noted that the constitutional
issue, as such, had no interest for the masses of the Chinese people.
Nevertheless, the years since 1923 have made it clear that the Chinese
masses have a very real interest in taxes, prices, and income, and a growing sense that in some way these matters are connected with good and
bad government. The point is that too few of China's people understood the relation of constitutionalism to government. As China's
eight long years of war with Japan came to an end, the conservative
Kuomintang oligarchy was faced with the fact that the work of popular
political organization of the people had "been left, in the main, to the
Communists." [21]

---

[20] On the organization, reorganizations, and meetings of the Peoples Political Council:
China Handbook, 1937-1943, 109-110; Guenther Stein, "Peoples Political Council Re-
organizing," *Far Eastern Survey,* XI (1942), 158-160.

[21] Rosinger, *China's Crisis,* 78. Neither the existence of the Kuomintang New Life
Movement, nor of the *San Min Chu I* Youth Corps, both of which are principal social
instruments of the Kuomintang, would appear to weaken the conclusion noted above.
The New Life Movement in its inception at least owed much of its inspiration to German
and Italian fascist models. Its later exhortations to public "morality" have had little influence because this campaign was not co-ordinated with basic material reforms in economics and politics. The Youth Corps, as Sun Fo has said, is an example of excessive
military regimentation, and does not train its members for the practical responsibilities of
self-government. Rowe, *China and the Powers,* 137-138; and Sun Fo, *China Looks
Forward* (New York, 1944), ch. ix.

REVIVAL OF KUOMINTANG-COMMUNIST STRIFE

The final and, in some respects, the major factor in China's declining capacity to resist Japan was the gradual disintegration of the united front which had been forced into being in 1937 under the duress of Japanese aggression. The effectiveness of this united resistance depended from the beginning on maintaining an understanding between the Kuomintang and the Chinese Communist Party.[22] This made the problem exceedingly difficult not only because the united front had been imposed from without by Japan's aggression, but also because of the bitter memories of the Kuomintang-Communist warfare from 1927 to 1937. Beginning in 1931 with its Soviet government in Kiangsi, the "Chinese Soviet Republic" had pursued relentlessly its policy of land expropriation and rural reform under the political leadership of Mao Tse-tung and the military skill of Chu Teh, commander of the Chinese Red Army. This development coincided with Japan's invasion of Manchuria. The Kuomintang Nationalists thus faced two enemies: the Communists in the interior and the Japanese on the eastern frontier. Faced with this dilemma, the National Government, frequently indecisive in policy, attempted to exterminate the Communists and to appease, though reluctantly, the Japanese. Within and without the Kuomintang, however, there was violent disagreement on this policy, but the significant fact was that Chiang K'ai-shek failed to exterminate the Communists, who by 1935 had completed the long march and established themselves in the northwest in what was to become known as the Shensi-Kansu-Ninghsia Border Region, with its Capital at Yenan.[23]

Within the two succeeding years, the growing popular will for resistance, the Sian incident, and the renewal of Japan's military action resulted in the Kuomintang-Communist truce. Advocating a united struggle for independence, enforcement of democracy, and improvement in the people's livelihood, the Chinese Communist Party described its program of co-operation with the Kuomintang as: 1) seeking en-

[22] In countries where democratic constitutionalism and national patriotism are taken for granted, the union of all major political factions in a wartime united front is expected, and its achievement is comparatively simple. Such was not the case in China, where the patterns of human behavior had not been shaped by democratic constitutionalism and its related ideal of political patriotism.

[23] The ablest treatment of Communists in this period is Edgar Snow, *Red Star Over China* (New York, 1938). On the organization of the Chinese Communist Party, P. Miff, *Heroic China* (New York, 1937), a Marxian interpretation. Harold Isaacs, *The Tragedy of The Chinese Revolution* (London, 1938), a Trotskyist critique of the rise of the Communist movement in China.

forcement of the Three Principles of the People; 2) abandonment of its
policies of overthrowing the Kuomintang by force, of sovietization, and
of forcible land confiscation; 3) abolition of the Soviet Government and
of the Red Army, which would be reorganized as the National Revolutionary Army of the National Government. This program was wel-

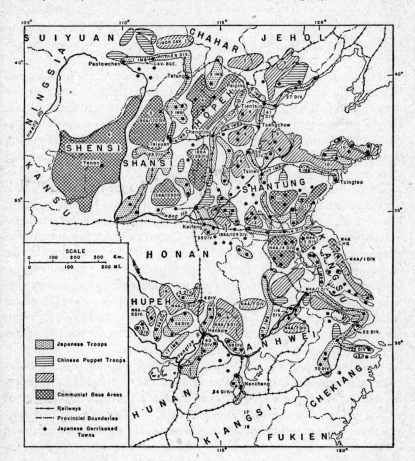

CHINESE COMMUNIST AND JAPANESE POSITIONS IN CHINA, FEBRUARY, 1944. *United
States, Department of State, Division of Map Intelligence and Cartography.*

comed in a guarded declaration by Generalissimo Chiang. As a result,
resistance to Japan was strengthened as the Red Army, now the Eighth
Route Army, operated under guerrilla tactics in the north while Communist guerrillas still in the Yangtze became the New Fourth Army.
Even greater unity seemed forecast by the first meeting of the People's

Political Council with representatives from all parties, July, 1938. From that time onward, however, the unification movement was gripped by a creeping paralysis. Both the National Government and the Communists continued to fight Japan, but the united front became merely a name, and eventually, by 1944, not even that. The total effect was to cripple China's limited powers to resist Japan and to pave the way for a renewal of civil war if and when the invader was expelled.

BASES OF THE KUOMINTANG-COMMUNIST SPLIT

In the ensuing battle of words between Chungking and Yenan, each side accused the other of bad faith, of sabotaging the war, and of seeking to build its own political strength instead of fighting the common enemy. Symptomatic of conditions was the use of as many as half a million Nationalist troops, not to fight the Japanese, but to blockade the Communist controlled areas of the north. Neither side trusted the other.

The chief reasons for the widening rift between the Kuomintang and the Communists lay first, in the bitterness of the historical background just recited, and second, in the ideological conflict between the two. To many it appeared that the National Government, as the instrument of the extreme right wing in the Kuomintang oligarchy, no longer adhered to Sun Yat-sen's Three Principles, but was, on the contrary, a conservative, reactionary regime bent on preserving an oligarchic rule with special privilege for the landed and financial classes. On the other hand, it was equally clear in the light of events of 1931-1937, that the men who directed Yenan and the Communist Party regarded themselves as Marxians. The fact that they modified their policies after 1937 by ceasing to expropriate and redistribute land was regarded by their enemies as a clever compromise and as a first step toward the "new democracy," a phrase which suggests a radical left wing interpretation of Sun Yat-sen's principles. These extreme views suggest the gulf that separated Chungking from Yenan. The tension was heightened, too, by the seeming success which the Communists enjoyed. After 1937, their radical agrarian reforms, which for the time being at least replaced their former Marxianism, made a wide, popular appeal in the northern areas which they ruled.[24]

---

[24] The most detailed report on conditions in the Yenan area is Guenther Stein, *The Challenge of Red China* (New York, 1945). The popularity which the Communists enjoyed as a result of their agrarian reforms should not be taken to mean that they, any more than the Nationalists, have a remedy for one of China's most difficult problems— increasing population. See Rowe, *China Among the Powers*, 53.

The charges which the Communists levelled against the National Government and the Kuomintang were serious, and in many important cases, the truth of these charges was established by impartial evidence. The Kuomintang was accused of breaking the agreement (the truce) which was to create the united front; of attacking and attempting to exterminate the Communist Fourth Route Army in the lower Yangtze, an attempt which was made but which failed; of failing to replace the party dictatorship with democratic government. Against this background, the Communists declined to turn over to Chungking control of their own armies.

On its part, too, Chungking made its own accusations. It charged the Communists with bad faith in the 1937 truce, of refusing to obey orders of the National Government, and of revolutionary and treasonable intent in attempting to maintain a state within a state. The view of those who controlled the Kuomintang was that there could be no political settlement until the Communist armies were handed over to Generalissimo Chiang's command. The nature of the conflict between the two groups being what it was, there was never the slightest prospect that the Communists would surrender control of their armies until the Kuomintang had led the way by setting up a truly representative government.

THE ALLIES SENSE THE DANGER

Although there had been warnings in 1943, it was not until early in 1944 that this picture of Chinese conditions broke through the Chungking censorship and reached the American public.[25] The almost immediate reversal in American public opinion was perhaps a natural, but an unreasoning, shift from emotional and sentimental attachment and admiration for China's war effort to one of almost unqualified denunciation.[26] The concern of the American government, if less vocal than that of the public, was directed through more useful channels. Although the Yenan regime was not recognized as a government by the United States or any other power, its importance in the war could no longer be ignored. An American military mission visited the Communist area in July, 1944. At the same time, the United States sought to bring its influence to bear on Chungking, to which, in the summer

---

[25] See among others the following articles: Pearl Buck, "A Warning about China," *Life,* May 10 (1943), 53-58; Hanson W. Baldwin, "Too Much Wishful Thinking About China," *Reader's Digest,* XLIV (1943), 63-67; T. A. Bisson, "China's Part in a Coalition War," *Far Eastern Survey,* XII (1943), 135-141.

[26] Note the analysis of Congressman Walter H. Judd, "Our Ally China," *Time,* June 18, 1945.

of 1944, went Vice-President Henry A. Wallace and Donald Nelson, Chairman of the War Production Board. There was a fear that the Kuomintang-Communist rift would lead to estrangement between Chungking and Moscow and ultimately between Moscow and the United States. American policy wanted a China united under a Nationalist regime which would be strong because it was moving in the direction of democracy and not away from it. The Wallace visit was designed to impress upon Generalissimo Chiang the imperative need of Chinese unity and of continued amicable relations between China and Russia and between China and the United States. Donald Nelson's visit resulted in the formation of a Chinese War Production Board, December, 1944, which did increase China's war production; the ultimate results were disappointing, however, because the National Government showed no disposition to tackle the problems of hoarding or profiteering and thus to move toward fundamental improvement.[27]

TENSION IN SINO-AMERICAN RELATIONS

The hope that these moves would lead to a healing of China's maladies was destroyed in the autumn of 1944. At this time a Japanese military advance had intensified the political crisis in Chungking and nearly resulted in a reorganization of the government as desired by the United States. The checking of this Japanese advance lessened the imminent danger and thereby contributed to the breakdown in the half-hearted negotiations between Nationalists and Communists which had dragged on for some months without any useful results. In October came the disturbing news that at the request of Generalissimo Chiang, General Joseph W. Stilwell, commander of the China-Burma-India theater and Chiang's chief of staff, was being recalled to the United States. Shortly thereafter came the resignation of the American Ambassador, C. E. Gauss. The high praise given Stilwell by President Roosevelt and clearance by the War Department's censorship of newspaper articles, deeply critical of the Chungking regime, gave credence to the belief that Stilwell's recall was related directly to severe tensions in Sino-American relations. It was interpreted as Chiang's refusal to push through the political, economic, and military reforms which the United States had been urging upon the National Government. Specifically, these reforms appear to have included: 1) that General Stilwell be made commander-in-chief of all Allied forces in China in order to insure the most effective possible distribution of arms and supplies for

---

[27] On problems of China's industrial development, Rowe, *China Among the Powers,* 75-124. Industrial labor in Chinese war industry is treated by Kuo-Heng Shih, *China Enters the Machine Age* (Cambridge, 1944).

the entire theater; 2) that the Chinese army be reorganized and the dead wood in the Chinese high command eliminated; 3) that the war effort of the Kuomintang and Communist armies be unified under Stilwell's command.[28]

This crisis was to bring far-reaching results in the application of American policy in China. America continued its support of Chungking and its efforts to bring about changes in Chungking's domestic policies, but it did so through personalities who, it was felt, would employ diplomatic methods even in wartime. Major General Albert C. Wedemeyer now became Chiang's chief of staff, and Major General Patrick J. Hurley assumed the post of American Ambassador in Chungking. Donald Nelson also returned to China to carry through the reorganization of her war industry. A visit by General Hurley to Yenan brought a resumption in negotiations between the two capitals, but the basic questions remained unsolved. The fact was that there were still two governments in China. The function of American policy was to find a means through which they might unite to create a strong and a more democratic China. This was the situation at the beginning of 1945. In succeeding months, however, under the influence of Ambassador Hurley there appeared to be a shift toward more outright support for the Nationalists. Far from winning general American approval, this apparent shift in American policy was attacked even by conservative segments of the American press which pointed out again that the so-called Communist areas were the most democratic in China and the most stubborn in their resistance to Japan. Thus matters stood as, with Japan's sudden surrender, hostilities in the Pacific came to an end. China, along with other of the United Nations, shared in the glory of this military triumph. In point of time and in depth of suffering from hunger, disease, and the general ravages of war, no people had borne greater years of trial than China's peasantry and those of her patriots who hoped for a better and a more democratic China. The catastrophe of the Japanese invasion was now a thing of the past, but the problems of China's rehabilitation remained. An impoverished country and people faced the prospect of civil war—a struggle of opposing ideologies and of major factions contending for power.[29]

---

[28] On the background of General Stilwell's position and responsibility in China, and the crisis which occasioned the demand for his recall, Theodore H. White and Annalee Jacoby, *Thunder Out of China* (New York, 1946), 145-165, 214-225. See also M. S. Stewart, "Divided China," *Behind the Headlines* pamphlets, V (1946), No. 5 (Toronto, 1946).

[29] The story of the Nanking puppet regime under Wang Ching-wei and of other forces of appeasement will be found in P. M. A. Linebarger, *The China of Chiang K'ai-shek* (Boston, 1941), 183-210; in Rosinger, *China's Wartime Politics,* 33-35, and in the same

THE POST-WAR ERA

With the end of the war, peace became for China a desperate requirement if the nation was to recover from the Japanese invasion and from
the effects of intermittent domestic strife. All through the first year
following Japan's surrender, foreign correspondents in China were virtually unanimous in the view that the overwhelming majority of the
Chinese people wanted an end of civil conflict and were as one in their
opposition to belligerent leaders in both Kuomintang and Communist
factions. There were also other and equally pressing reasons why peace
within China was a desperate requirement. During World War II,
China, as has been noted, regained her full sovereignty and became a
member of that select company, the so-called great powers. However,
there was a striking discrepancy between China's real strength and her
nominal position among the big nations. So long as she remained
divided and weak at home, so long would she be an arena for the rival
maneuvers of the United States and Russia, and thus a threat to renewed
world conflict. This potential danger became an ominous reality in the
post-war period as the ideological conflict between the United States and
Russia was implemented in the actions of practical politics both in Europe and in the Far East. The American public was more awake to
the difficulties of this post-war period than had been the case in 1919,
but it was not so clear whether the same public understood that victory
in the Pacific had been won in the midst of Asia's contemporary revolution, and thus, even less than in 1920, there could be no safe return to
what a former American president liked to call "normalcy."

The end of the war in the Pacific produced in China a state of affairs
which, for the moment, could hardly be described as either peace or war.
During the months that preceded the Japanese surrender, the Chung-
king-Yenan negotiations sponsored by Ambassador Hurley had reached
a stalemate. The Communists were convinced that expediency was
driving the United States into ever closer relations with Chungking.
The rulers of the Kuomintang, for their part, appeared to have felt
that Ambassador Hurley and General Wedemeyer could be made to
serve Chungking's purposes. Both Chungking and the Communists
were bidding for American support. In Chungking there had been
some shifts in personalities designed to create the impression of reform.
Yenan's bid for American favor had taken the form of a show of military strength against Japan's positions. Neither side was now concerned with the dream of a united China. Then came the unexpected
Japanese surrender, the news of which gave no pleasure to official

author's *China's Crisis,* 58-64. For a pro-Nanking interpretation, see Don Bate, *Wang
Ching-wei: Puppet or Patriot* (Chicago, 1941).

Chungking. Its armies were in the west and south; the northeastern provinces from Shanghai to Peking, held by Japan, would thus surrender to the Communists, who were already in that area where their armies and the guerrillas had been stubbornly fighting Japan throughout the war. The Communists would thereby control China's vital northeastern seaboard unless Chiang's armies were moved in by the United States army, air forces, and navy. Such assistance to Chiang was given with all the resources the American services could muster. Technically, the aid was quite proper. It meant simply that the United States was assisting the recognized government of its ally, China, to accept the surrender of the Japanese armies of occupation. By Yenan and Moscow, however, the move was regarded as political, namely, that United States policy as implemented by Ambassador Hurley and General Wedemeyer was now solidly behind Chungking, and was bent on placing Kuomintang armies in a position to crush the Communists, thus achieving a united China by force and not by the democratic union of all major parties.

THE POSITION OF RUSSIA, 1945

If American policy appeared to shift, so also did Russia's. In August, 1945, Russia's post-war position in Asia had been defined in a Sino-Soviet treaty. Some major terms had already been agreed to by the United States and Russia at the Yalta Conference. This agreement was the price America paid for Russia's promise to enter the war against Japan. Far from being understandable simply in terms of Soviet-Marxian ideology, the terms of this treaty harked back to Manchurian history of the 1890's and the early years of the twentieth century when Russia was ruled by the Tsars. By the new treaty, China recognized what had long been a reality, the independence of Outer Mongolia; Russia acquired joint control of the principal Manchurian railways (the Chinese Eastern and the South Manchuria); Dairen was to be made an international free port with special rights for Russia; historic Port Arthur was to be available as a Russian naval base; and finally, as in the days of the "good," old-fashioned imperialism, Russia pledged full support and recognition of the National Government, and respect for its sovereignty in Manchuria. This treaty coincided with Russia's entry into the war against Japan and with the Russian invasion and military occupation of Manchuria, which Japan had made the richest industrial area of all China. The treaty was the price Chungking paid for continued Russian recognition. To this point the situation added up to one in which the United States was moving Kuomintang armies into the Communist-controlled areas of the northeast, while Russia did not prevent Chinese Communist forces from entering Manchuria and gaining possession of most of that country. Moreover, the industrial wealth of Manchuria proved too great a temptation to machine-hungry Russia. The charge was that Manchuria was sacked to bolster Siberian industry.[30]

Meanwhile, as was to be expected, hostilities had broken out between the Nationalist and Communist forces in widely separated areas of the northeast. The civil war which so many had predicted had begun. Furthermore, it could not be described as simply another of China's civil wars, for both the United States and Russia were betting heavily, and their money was not on the same horse. Unless the crisis could be halted, the principles which had underscored American policy throughout the Pacific war would be bankrupt. In November, 1945, Ambassador Hurley, now back in Washington, resigned, publicly charging his failure to the State Department. The harassed American public thereby had grounds for the belief that the United States and Russia were no longer mediators among China's factions but partisans on opposite sides of a civil war.

THE MARSHALL MISSION

To meet this crisis, President Truman appointed General George C. Marshall as a presidential special envoy to China and in a public state-

---

[30] On the political and social philosophy and record of Chungking and Yenan during the Pacific war see John K. Fairbank, "Our Chances in China," *Atlantic*, CLXXVIII (1946), 37-42.

Note the report by Frank E. Taylor on "Censorship of Writers and Publishers in China," *Publisher's Weekly*, CL (1946), 2596-2599. Mr. Taylor, who returned from China in October, 1946, reported on the "contrast between growing suppression of freedom in the Nationalist parts of China, and the lack of restraints in the North." "Mr. Taylor's information was given to him directly by leading [Chinese] writers and critics to whom he talked in Shanghai, Kunming and Peiping; and in the Communist capital, Yenan. Most Chinese writers belong to the unofficial China Writers' Association and virtually all of them said they oppose the Chiang K'ai-shek government, which the writers told Mr. Taylor is as much opposed to the Democratic League and other middle-of-the-road groups of intellectuals as it is to the Communists." A statement from a representative group of China's writers, brought to this country by Mr. Taylor, reads: "The Generalissimo's four promises of liberty to the people, pledged in the Political Consultation Conference not long ago—one of these dedicated to the liberty of speech and publication—have never been and are never meant to be carried out. Instead, severe measures are taken to control all liberal voices, not legislatively nor judicially, nor by the police authorities, but through the hands of secret service men. This form of persecution leaves no trace behind."

A critical estimate of Ambassador Hurley and an analysis of the reasons for his failure are in White and Jacoby, *Thunder Out of China*, 243-256. The Chinese Communists dubbed the Ambassador, "Little Whiskers"; his Kuomintang associates referred to him as the "Second Big Wind."

Text of the Sino-Soviet Treaty and documents on the railway and port agreements are in *American Review on the Soviet Union*, VII (Nov., 1945), 66-73. Text of the Yalta Agreement is in U. S. Dept. of State, *Occupation of Japan* (Washington, 1946), 52-53.

ment reaffirmed the major bases of American policy. The President stressed the need for: 1) a strong, united, and democratic China; 2) continued American recognition of the National Government and abstention from interference in China's internal affairs; 3) cessation of hostilities between Kuomintang and Communist forces; and 4) calling of a Chinese national congress representative of all parties to achieve national unification on a democratic basis and to end what the President called Chungking's "one-party government." There was also the suggestion that in the event China did not carry out the reforms, American aid would be withheld. Within a few weeks this policy had been confirmed by the Moscow Conference of Foreign Ministers of Great Britain, Russia, and the United States.

The choice of General Marshall was a measure of the imminent disaster facing American policy in Asia. His acceptance of a task which now appeared hopeless was the measure of his own self-sacrifice. During the year of Hurley diplomacy, the United States had lost its nonpartisan position. Marshall was asked to re-establish American nonpartisanship and a new faith in the integrity of American diplomacy. The miracle was that by January, 1946, the prestige of Marshall's integrity had produced a truce.[31]

This truce between the Central Government and the Communists resulted in the calling of a Political Consultative Conference, January, 1946, representing all parties, Kuomintang, Communists, the Democratic League, as well as nonpartisans, which was able to reach what appeared to be a basic understanding acceptable to all for a transitional government, for a democratic revision of the Kuomintang-proposed draft constitution, and for unification of the armies. By April, however, this apparent progress under General Marshall's good offices was well on the way to liquidation. Whatever the mixed and complex causes of this tragedy, its more obvious results were not in question. It was clear that the right-wing Kuomintang was determined to nullify the Political Consultative Conference accords; that hostilities had broken out again on various Government-Communist fronts; and that the whole situation was involved with increasing tension in Russo-American relations in the Far East and elsewhere. As against Russia's unwillingness to prevent the Chinese Communists from tightening their grip on Manchuria was the fact that the United States, advocating the role of mediation, was nevertheless selling some $800,000,000 of surplus war property to the Central Government. Before the close of 1946 inter-

[31] On the obstacles, American, Chinese, and Russian, confronting Marshall, see White and Jacoby, *Thunder Out of China*, 269-308.

mittent civil war was again in progress. By the end of the year General Marshall's efforts to bring the warring factions together in a working agreement had failed. Meanwhile the National Government convoked the National Assembly to adopt the draft constitution. The Communists refused to attend but some of the lesser parties did join the Kuomintang-dominated Assembly. In December, 1946, the draft constitution was adopted to go into effect on December 25, 1947.

Early in January, 1947, at the close of his 13-month mission, General Marshall, already designated as America's new Secretary of State, issued a public report summarizing his views with respect to China. This report has become a state document of the utmost importance. It is a clear portrayal of the contending forces within China with assessment of responsibility upon those guilty of perpetuating turmoil. It also laid down specific suggestions to guide American policy in seeking further to achieve a united and a more democratic China. Among General Marshall's findings the following were particularly notable:

1) The greatest obstacle to peace in China has been the complete, almost overwhelming, suspicion with which the Chinese Communist Party and the Kuomintang regard each other. As a result it has been common practice for distortion of the facts to be utilized by both sides in order to heap condemnation on the other.

2) On the side of the National Government, which is in effect the Kuomintang Party, there is a dominant group of reactionaries which in General Marshall's belief has opposed almost every effort he made to influence the formation of a genuine coalition government.

3) On the side of the Chinese Communists, General Marshall found two groups: a) liberals who are prepared to place the interests of China before those of a Communist state; b) radicals who are prepared to use any measures to gain their ends, to wreck the economy of the country, to overthrow the government without any regard to the immediate suffering of the people.

4) The Political Consultative Conference, January, 1946, and the agreements reached by it offered China a liberal and forward-looking charter for peace and reconstruction, but irreconcilable groups within the Kuomintang Party, interested in the preservation of their own feudal control of China, evidently had no real intention of implementing them, and the course which the Chinese Communist Party pursued in later months indicated an unwillingness on its part to make a fair compromise.

5) China's salvation as General Marshall saw it could be found in the assumption of leadership by the liberals in the government and in the

minority parties, who unfortunately lacked the political power necessary to exercise a controlling influence.

6) General Marshall found the newly adopted Constitution to be in accord in all major respects with the principles laid down by the Political Consultative Conference. China's future, he believed, would depend on the degree to which the government gives substance to this constitutional form by a genuine welcome to all groups to share in the responsibility of government.

By midsummer of 1947, China's political, economic, and social plight had shown no improvement. On the contrary, it called forth from President Truman a fact-finding mission headed by Lieutenant General Albert C. Wedemeyer. On the conclusion of his investigations in China, General Wedemeyer was quoted by the press as saying: 1) that China must effect far-reaching political and economic reforms, 2) that the Chinese Communists could not be eliminated by military force alone, and 3) that the National Government could yet win and hold the confidence of the Chinese people by removing from posts of responsibility incompetent and corrupt officials.

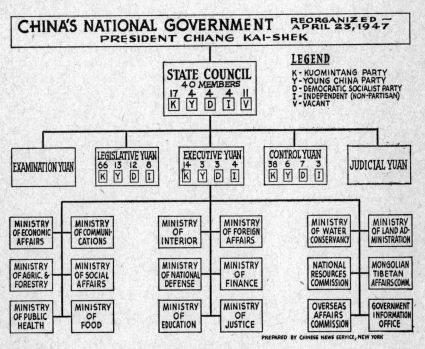

CHINA'S MULTI-PARTY GOVERNMENT.

CHAPTER 39

JAPAN SINCE 1941: IN WAR AND IN DEFEAT

THE people of Japan have been faced in the years since 1941 with two of the great crises of their history. In the first, these people were called upon by their political and military masters to wage total war for the achievement of Japan's divine mission: establishment of the "New National Structure" at home and the "New Order in Greater East Asia" abroad. The latter of these objectives has already been discussed in previous pages. It will remain here to note some of the final steps taken in the years after 1937 to complete the "New National Structure." In the second crisis, a proud and sensitive people, having met complete military defeat in 1945, was called upon to face a future compounded of social confusion in its homeland and of uncertainty in its relations with the outside world of conquerors. These events are as yet too close, too clouded by the censorship imposed by war and by the victors, to permit definite analysis or evaluation. Yet it is possible to see a considerable portion of wartime and post-wartime Japan and to indicate some of the directions in which she is moving and is being permitted to move. What manner of nation is emerging from the war? What status is being assigned to her by those who have won the military victory? Since Japan's defeat was achieved chiefly by American arms, and since the occupation of Japan is essentially an occupation by Americans, what are the policies this country is applying, and to what end are they being applied? To these questions and to others related to them in Japan's most recent and contemporary history the following pages must be addressed.

CREATING THE "NEW NATIONAL STRUCTURE"

The political philosophy and the structure of government which had developed in Japan by 1941 and which were to persist throughout the war were in many respects logical developments of earlier steps taken after 1931 toward totalitarian control. Yet neither before 1941 nor after that date did Japan become a fullfledged corporate state in the manner of Germany or Italy. She produced no all-powerful Nazi or Fascist party, and she produced no single political leader capable of emerging as an individual or personal dictator. Likewise in matters of economics and production, she failed to create the full corporate state in the manner of her European allies. What happened in Japan both before and during the war was, of course, influenced by these European pace-setters; but Japanese conditions, problems, and the methods of dealing with them remained essentially Japanese. In general, the similarities to the totalitarian powers of Europe were apparent rather than real.

THE DICTATORSHIP OF THE BUREAUCRACY

When by her attack on Pearl Harbor Japan engulfed the Pacific area in World War II, she was operating under a governmental structure which had been altered vastly since the invasion of Manchuria a decade earlier in September, 1931. Liberalism and parliamentary government, from which so much had been expected in the decade 1920 to 1930, had been extinguished. The Imperial Diet had declined in political importance, though its entire influence had not been destroyed. The traditional political parties, the *Seiyukai* and the *Minseito,* had abolished themselves under the pressure of extremists in 1940, and the country had returned to nonparty ministries long before the abolition of the parties themselves. The armed services had secured increasing control over the civil administration but had been unable to gain a monopoly on political power. There was, however, an increasing concentration of political power in the cabinet and especially in the office of the prime minister. After 1931 and more particularly after 1937, the functions of government had been increased greatly, in part by cabinet-inspired legislation in the Diet and by a much greater use of Imperial ordinances, ministerial orders, and departmental regulations. Increasingly as individualistic and democratic ideals were ostracized and suppressed, Japan appeared to be looking to the central European dictatorships for her political inspiration. When she attacked Pearl Harbor, she seemed to be not far from the goal of the corporate state. While this was in part true, the corporate state that was appearing was peculiarly Japanese in character. It was not simply an imitation of a European counterpart. Certainly the most important results of the governmental changes from 1931 to 1941, which have here been summarized, were to increase the number and the power of bureaucratic agencies, to enhance the prestige and the political influence of the bureaucracy as a whole, and thus to create in wartime Japan what may best be called "a dictatorship of the bureaucracy." [1]

---

[1] Charles Nelson Spinks, "Bureaucratic Japan," *Far Eastern Survey,* X (1941), 219-225. The term "bureaucracy" as applied to government in Japan is used in a much

PECULIARITIES OF THE JAPANESE BUREAUCRACY

The growth of bureaucratic agencies and of bureaucratic power in Japan after 1931 suggests comparison with similar tendencies in the Western world and particularly in the United States under the New Deal. In Japan, in Europe, and in the United States, these parallel tendencies may be attributed to the economic plight of the depression years. Nevertheless, bureaucracy in Japan has possessed indigenous qualities which give it a degree of uniqueness and distinguish it in significant measure from bureaucracy, for example, in the United States. That throughout the history of modern Japan bureaucracy has been a greater political force, a broader and more complex mechanism, than in other countries is explained by a number of considerations. During the entire constitutional period, with the exception of the decade of the 1920's, the ministers of state (the cabinet) were always linked more intimately with bureaucratic elements than with the Diet which was supposed to represent the people. In the second place, some factions of the bureaucracy, the army and the navy, enjoyed a position of political independence and power guaranteed by constitutional organization. As a third element, Japan's bureaucrats enjoyed a unique political strength because of the influence they have wielded in the formulation as well as in the execution of policies. Ministers of state in Japan's bureaucratic cabinets long recognized that government's fortunes depended less on the adoption of important national policies than on giving appropriate political recognition to each major bureaucratic group and maintaining a balance among these groups. Fourth, membership in the bureaucracy was equivalent to membership in a privileged class. Dating from the early years of the Meiji period, the bureaucracy absorbed and retained many characteristics of feudal Japan, such as clan loyalties and a supreme contempt for popular control in government. Perhaps the outstanding example of this contempt for the popular will was the army's long opposition to the principle of popular government represented by the lower house of the Diet. This opposition was often less a characteristic of militarism than an expression of bureaucratic resentment against anything savoring of democracy. The sacrosanct position of the bureaucracy was also typified by the respect with which the private citizen approached the common policeman or the petty clerk in some obscure government bureau. Moreover, the independent, if

---

broader sense than is common in Western usage. It includes not only the civil servants but also the agents of the military services, and at times of the political parties and the *Zaibatsu*.

not the irresponsible, position of the bureaucracy was fortified by laws which assured the permanency of officeholders.

THE BUREAUCRACY NOT A UNIT

The sources of political power in Japan, still numerous in 1941, included the emperor, the cabinet, the army and navy, and even the Diet; yet all these had come to be overshadowed by the bureaucracy of which the army and navy were merely parts, albeit important and powerful parts. This statement suggests that the bureaucracy as a whole was not a unit but a collection of rival factions. Moreover, as the bureaucratic agencies of government increased in size and number after 1931 and as the political parties lost influence and finally disappeared, it became more and more the function of the prime minister to act as a sort of mediating officer between these factions of permanent officeholders. Indeed from the standpoint of the highest executive officers of government, the problem created by an enlarged and increasingly powerful bureaucracy was more difficult to deal with than the former political parties had ever been. The parties could always be met in the open arena of the Diet, where the government knew their strength and how to deal with it; but the multi-factional character of the bureaucracy defied accurate analysis, for it was shifting and unstable in its alignments. As a result of this and of other factors, no individual was able to dominate the entire bureaucracy sufficiently to create a unified political machine or to create a one-man dictatorship comparable to those that appeared in Europe. Even had a supremely capable leader appeared—and this was never probable in a Japan where individualism had been systematically frowned upon—his path to one-man dictatorship would have been obstructed, perhaps effectively, by the unique position of the emperor and of the Imperial Constitution of 1889.

THE ABSENCE OF COMMANDING POLITICAL LEADERSHIP

The absence of commanding political leadership in recent Japan is indeed as notable as the rising power of the bureaucracy. In this respect the reign-eras of Taisho and Showa since 1912 fail to stand comparison with the Meiji period, 1867-1912. It was the Meiji period which gave to Japan that remarkable group of extraconstitutional but all-powerful advisers of the Throne who guided the nation, not always wisely but usually with ability, through the most notable years of modernization. The influence of the Genro was all but unchallenged until after General Yamagata's death in 1924. From then on Prince Kimmochi Saionji, as the sole surviving Genro, continued to exert an influence on the side of moderation and restraint. After 1931 even Saionji's prestige declined rapidly in the clamor raised by the extremists, so that his influence could do little more than temper and delay the most aggressive tendencies of the times. When, on November 24, 1940, Saionji died, the Genro as an institution passed into history; Saionji's passing meant that the last symbol of liberalism in high places was removed from Japanese politics; the nation itself was without commanding political leadership.

There were significant efforts to perpetuate the Genro system. In a limited way it did live on in a loose organization made up of the Lord Keeper of the Privy Seal, all former prime ministers, and high representatives of the army and navy. Its influence, however, never equalled or even rivalled that of the Meiji Genro. The new group possessed neither the same qualities of statesmanship nor the record of achievement of its predecessor. The personnel of the new Genro as this body took shape after 1934 is a measure of the political mediocrity which governed Japan, which involved her in the undeclared war with China, and which eventually carried her into World War II. Outstanding among the so-called new Genro was Prince Fumimaro Konoye, who upon three occasions was called to head Japanese cabinets on the eve of World War II. Konoye was chosen not because of his ability to lead but because of the aristocratic prestige of his family and his capacity, despite his nebulous political thinking, to keep on reasonably good terms with all factions.[2]

---

[2] While Saionji still lived he consulted with the earlier members of the new Genro as far back as 1934, when the Saito cabinet fell. Some of the members of the new group at that time and in succeeding years included: 1) Kurahei Yuasa, Lord Keeper of the Privy Seal, a man of moderate though conservative views whom the fanatics forced out of office in June, 1940; 2) Marquis Koichi Kido, Yuasa's successor, a man in sympathy with totalitarian trends though not an extremist; 3) Baron Kiichiro Hiranuma, a confidant and mentor of Konoye, a legalist, organizer and president of the *Kokuhonsha*, a powerful nationalistic society which was deeply involved in the political assassinations of 1936, a reactionary but again not an extremist as indicated by the fact that the extremists attempted to assassinate him on August 14, 1941; 4) Admiral Mitsumasa Yonai, a liberal who opposed Japan's alliance with Germany, but not a statesman of great caliber; 5) Koki Hirota, an extreme, polished nationalist and a protégé of Mitsuru Toyama; 6) Baron Reijiro Wakatsuki, a former premier and head of the *Minseito* but of little political influence after 1932; 7) Admiral Keisuke Okada, whom the extremists attempted to assassinate in 1936; 8) General Nobuyuki Abe, whose political influence was nebulous; 9) General Senjuro Hayashi, who carried some weight with army extremists. See Charles Nelson Spinks, "The Elder Statesmen of Japan," *Asia*, XLI (1941), 565-566. The term "extremists" is used here to designate those favoring an unqualified corporate state.

EFFORTS TO STRENGTHEN POLITICAL LEADERSHIP

As the power of the bureaucracy increased, successive governments after 1932 sought to provide the prime minister with various agencies and devices through which he might exercise more effective leadership. The first of these was the five-minister conference or inner cabinet which had become fully established by 1940. It included the prime minister and the ministers of war, navy, foreign affairs, and finance. Later there were added the incumbent of the unique office of vice-premier and certain ministers without portfolio. This inner cabinet failed to solve the twofold problem of the prime minister: 1) that of managing the cumbersome machinery of government and 2) that of maintaining some degree of equilibrium among bureaucratic factions and extragovernmental groups, such as patriotic societies and the business interests. Accordingly, in the spring of 1941, Premier Konoye turned to a second expedient, the creation of an unofficial but informally recognized "Big Three of the Cabinet." This included the premier, the vice-premier, and the minister of finance. Although more flexible than the five-minister conference, this device also failed to produce satisfying results.[3]

THE IMPERIAL RULE ASSISTANCE ASSOCIATION

A third device designed to increase the efficiency of Japan's top bureaucratic leadership was the *Taisei Yokusan Kai* or Imperial Rule Assistance Association, which made its appearance on the demise of the traditional political parties in 1940. The idea of a single national party had been inspired by the European fascist model. Prince Konoye was eventually prevailed upon to lead the movement, but by the time the party took shape, the extremists had been forced out of key positions. The new association emerged as little more than an agency of "spiritual mobilization."[4]

THE IMPERIAL RULE ASSISTANCE POLITICAL SOCIETY

Early in the war, the political impotence of the IRAA led to the creation of a new and closely related organization, the Imperial Rule Assistance Political Society. This body, at first associated with the efforts of the government to pack the Diet with "approved candidates"

[3] With himself as premier, Konoye's first triumvirate included Baron Hiranuma, vice-premier, and Masatsune Ogura, minister of finance. Ogura was a member of the Sumitomo banking group.

[4] Andrew J. Grajdanzev, "The 'Ethical Elevation' of Japanese Politics," *Far Eastern Survey*, XII (1943), 67-71.

and to regiment their activities after election, enjoyed only a very limited success. As the war progressed, the IRAPS tended to become a species of Diet members' club dominated by conservative, but not extremist, party leaders.[5]

THE NEW, EXPANDED BUREAUCRACY

The new, expanded bureaucracy, which slowly created its own dictatorship after 1931 and which created a problem of political leadership that was never wholly solved, may be described under two main divisions: 1) at first there was an expansion of ministerial agencies and the creation of certain extraministerial boards under the jurisdiction of the Cabinet, and 2) there was the formation of the so-called national policy companies.

The decade following 1930 witnessed a marked bureaucratic expansion within the ministerial departments to handle the increase functions which the government had taken over. One principal result was a confused multiplying of offices and an equally confused redistribution of functions. There was also the addition of one new ministry, the Ministry of Welfare, 1938, under which were five major bureaus.

Some of the more important extraministerial agencies created in the immediate pre-war years included: the Manchurian Affairs Board, 1934; the Cabinet Planning Board, 1937; the Cabinet Advisory Council, 1937; the China Affairs Board, 1938; the National Mobilization Council, 1938; the Price Policy Council, 1940; and the National Spiritual Mobilization Movement, 1940. The Manchurian Affairs Board was entrusted with the co-ordination of policy between Japan and Manchukuo. The Cabinet Planning Board, headed by a president of rank equal to that of a minister of state, functioned "as a sort of politico-economic general staff." Designed as a co-ordinating and directing agency, it might instruct ministers and even override their decisions. The China Affairs Board (the *Koa-in* or Uplift Asia Board) was responsible for furthering the New Order in occupied China. In this respect, it assumed some of the functions of the Foreign Office and was the link between the home government and Japan's continental military commands. Finally, the Cabinet Advisory Council was an effort to recognize the modern would-be Genro and through them to find a means of reconciling rival bureaucratic factions.[6]

---

[5] T. A. Bisson, *Japan's War Economy* (New York, 1945), 103.

[6] Membership in this body sometimes included such irreconcilable political personalities as Yosuke Matsuoka, General Kazushige Ugaki, Admiral Nobumasa Suetsugu, and General Sadao Araki. See Charles Nelson Spinks, "Bureaucratic Japan," *Far Eastern Survey*, X (1941), 223.

THE NATIONAL POLICY COMPANIES

The national policy companies, the number of which was multiplied on the eve of World War II, were the instruments of Japan's expansion at first in Manchuria and then in occupied China. The idea involved in this form of financial organization was not new. It had been employed early in the Meiji era in such cases as the Hokkaido Development Company and the Yawata Iron Works. As an instrument of national expansion abroad, the system was first fully matured in the South Manchuria Railway Company, founded in 1906, in whose hands Japan's exploitation of the South Manchurian sphere remained a virtual monopoly until 1932. The pattern of organization for which the S. M. R. provided the model was that of an official corporation in which the government held a controlling number of shares. In the later national policy companies, particularly those which operated in occupied China, the companies were merely holding concerns controlling subsidiary companies which conducted the business enterprises involved. An example of this kind was the North China Development Company, which took over the economic exploitation of North China after the Japanese conquest. Other national policy companies were promotion concerns designed to finance private companies, for example, the Japan Gold Production Promotion Company. Most of the more than forty national policy companies, the majority of which appeared after 1935, were monopolies in their respective spheres. All of them were subject to direct executive control of the Japanese government. In addition to these companies, there were also many commercial and industrial associations of a private character engaged in co-ordinating and regulating production and distribution in Japan's domestic and foreign trade. All these private associations were also under government regulation and control. Moreover, behind all this growth of bureaucracy were the much older government controlled or "national policy banks" such as the Bank of Japan, the Bank of Taiwan, and the Bank of Chosen, dating back to 1882, 1897, and 1911, respectively.

THE LACK OF A PLANNED ECONOMY

Although political power in pre-war Japan had gravitated toward this cumbersome and leaderless bureaucracy and although there was increasing state intervention in economic life, the nation was still far from possessing a planned economy. As late as 1941, most of the nation's business was financed and operated by private enterprise with only limited government interference.[7] From the autumn of 1940, however,

[7] *The Oriental Economist,* Sept., 1941, 458.

as Japan moved closer to war with the democracies, the need for national control of industry became more pressing. Virtually all factions recognized the need for greater control, but there was no agreement as to the degree of control desirable or as to who should exercise this control. Extremists in the army, the navy, and some factions of the bureaucracy clamored for total control in which the state would simply take over all industry. The business interests, particularly the *Zaibatsu,* were opposed to this program and remained so throughout the war. They were not hostile to greater wartime integration of industry, enforced by the state; in fact, they perceived some advantages to themselves in such a system, but they were determined that their ownership and their prerogatives of management should be safeguarded and preserved. The key questions argued in 1941 were: 1) What is to be the kind and the extent of economic controls? and 2) Who is to administer them? [8] Easy answers to these were not available. Nevertheless, on the eve of the Pearl Harbor attack, virtually all influential groups were paying lip service to the idea of a "new economic structure" as a necessary basis for total war in the Pacific.

THE TOJO CABINET

The Tojo cabinet, which replaced the third Konoye ministry on October 18, 1941, was supposed to be the answer to this riddle. The former Konoye cabinet, which had held office from the summer of 1940, had moved steadily toward implementation of the "new national structure" in Japan's politics at home and in relation to her expanding empire; but its contributions to the "new economic structure" were less notable.

General Hideki Tojo was a product of the Kwantung Army School, a former commander of the gendarmerie in Manchukuo, Chief of Staff of the Kwantung Army, Vice-Minister of War in the first Konoye cabinet (later he had become Inspector-General of Military Aviation), and finally Minister of War in the third Konoye cabinet. He enjoyed a record as an able administrator, and in his political and economic thinking it was assumed that he shared the attitude of the "state planners" who had dominated the philosophy of the Kwantung Army in Manchukuo. He was thus acceptable to the militarists and the fascist extremists, but in addition he appears to have been regarded by the *Zaibatsu* as a reliable leader for the greater war ahead. As Japan's wartime premier, Tojo held more offices and acquired greater power than any prime minister in Japan's history. He held concurrently the posts

[8] Bisson, *Japan's War Economy,* 3-9.

of Premier, War Minister, and Home Minister. After he had relinquished the last of these, he took over the new Ministry of Munitions
and became also Chief of Staff. Under his regime Japan not only won
her sweeping victories of 1942 but also suffered her first major defeats.
Tojo's accession to power seemed to guarantee the creation in wartime
Japan of a full-fledged, military, corporate state, if not a personal dictatorship. This expectation was not fulfilled, and the Tojo government
did not long survive Japan's first major reverses.

BASIC WARTIME CHANGES IN ECONOMY

The Pacific war forced great changes on Japan's economy. The war
created a vast expansion of heavy industry and a corresponding shrink-
age in light industry.[9] The war also brought equally far-reaching
changes in the administrative control of Japan's industry. Until the
war, the general industrial monopolies of the *Zaibatsu* operated in general as semi-autonomous units "linked neither with each other nor with
the government through any effectively coercive administrative authority." Before the close of the war, that is by 1944-45, the major enterprises of Japan's industrial economy were under the control of a newly
created wartime ministry, the Ministry of Munitions, operating under the
provisions of the Munitions Company Act. This centralized control
and relatively efficient management of war production was secured,
however, only after two war years, 1942-43, of the chaotic administration
which Tojo had been unable to overcome. This early failure on Japan's
home-production front contributed to her first military and naval reverses. The new centralization of administrative power over production which the government finally acquired in January, 1944, does not
appear to have been a political victory for the militarists and the extreme
"state planners," but rather an acceptance by the government of control
measures proposed by and acceptable to the monopoly industrialists, the
Zaibatsu. In a word, the key questions on the extent of controls and
who should administer them had been answered favorably to the industrialists. After the fall of the Tojo cabinet, Ginjiro Fujihara, a
member of the *Zaibatsu*, became Munitions Minister in the next cabinet.
The evidence suggests that although at the beginning of the war the army
was the most powerful single faction in Japan's bureaucracy, its place
had been taken before the close of the struggle by the captains of industry.

---

[9] Bisson, *Japan's War Economy*, 201; also the more recent analysis by J. B. Cohen, "The
Japanese War Economy: 1940-1945," *Far Eastern Survey*, XV (1946), 361-370.

THE RETURN TO TRADITIONALISM IN POLITICS

Although the war thus forced a greater concentration of administrative power than Japan had ever previously known, the failure of these belated measures to achieve victory, together with the rising specter of defeat, encouraged a return to traditional politics under more conservative guidance of the new Genro. In July, 1944, one month after American forces invaded Saipan, the Tojo cabinet fell. The new ministry which succeeded was still essentially a military cabinet headed by a Kwantung Army extremist, General Kuniaki Koiso, but tempered by the presence of Admiral Mitsumasa Yonai as Deputy Prime Minister and Navy Minister. Koiso's cabinet survived less than a year in the face of mounting military reverses. On April 7, 1945, it was succeeded by a ministry headed by Admiral Baron Kantaro Suzuki as Premier. Suzuki was a former Lord Chamberlain who had been attacked by the extremist assassins in 1936. This cabinet to an even greater extent than that of its predecessor represented a careful balancing of conservative bureaucrats, the military services, and the business interests, and a conscious effort by the Elder Statesmen to defeat all extreme forms of political control. It was the Suzuki cabinet which tendered Japan's surrender in August and then, in the midst of the greatest crisis of Japan's history, gave place, September 16, 1945, to a new ministry under a prince of the Imperial Household, Naruhiko Higashi-kuni, a cousin of Emperor Hirohito. The selection of an Imperial prince as Premier was an effort to stabilize and quiet public opinion as the Japanese people witnessed the occupation of their homeland by a foreign army. Once the first phase of the occupation and demobilization was complete, Higashi-kuni resigned, October 5. He was succeeded the following day by one of Japan's few surviving "liberals," a man whom the nation had repudiated in 1931, Baron Kijuro Shidehara, who remained in office until April 22, 1946. It was Shidehara who faced the first problems of a defeated and broken Japan, the problems of food, of housing, of inflation, and of a nation without leadership and without purpose. These were beyond the grasp of the aged Shidehara, and in May the premiership passed to Shigeru Yoshida.[10] Yoshida had been Foreign Minister in the Shidehara cabinet. He had also succeeded to the presidency of the Liberal Party after the disqualification of Ichiro Hatoyama. The Yoshida government, formed May 22, 1946, was succeeded, June, 1947, by the ministry of Tetsu Katayama, socialist and Christian.

[10] On these successive cabinet changes see *Far Eastern Survey,* XIV (1945), 105-108; XV (1946), 177-180.

THE STATE STRUCTURE AND JAPAN'S DEFEAT

Although Japan's collapse, her acceptance of unconditional surrender, was brought about by the overwhelming power of American armament, the time and the manner of the surrender were conditioned by the political, economic, and bureaucratic character of the Japanese state which has been described briefly in these pages. Indeed, Japan's surrender would probably have come earlier had the political structure of the nation permitted a more rapid and decisive determination of national policies.[11] At least some of the reasons which determined the time and the manner of the Japanese surrender have already been revealed by the *Summary Report* (Pacific War) of the United States Strategic Bombing Survey. It is clear that as early as mid-1944 those Japanese leaders who possessed the basic information foresaw the economic collapse which was already underway and which assured the coming military disaster. By August, 1945, even without direct air attack, the level of Japan's production would have declined below the peak of 1944 by forty to fifty percent solely as a result of the interdiction of overseas imports. As it was, the damage from air attacks approximated that which was suffered by Germany. Something like thirty percent of the urban population of Japan lost its homes and much of its possessions. With this appalling physical disaster came declining morale. Japan's civilian casualties numbered about 806,000, of which 333,000 resulted in death. As late as June, 1944, only two percent of the population believed in the possibility of defeat; by June, 1945, however, forty-six percent believed Japan could not win; and by August, just before the surrender, the figure had risen to sixty-eight percent. This declining belief in the power to win was accompanied by loss of confidence in both the military and the civilian leaders. Although a few of Japan's statesmen foresaw the ultimate defeat as early as February, 1944, it was not until May, 1945, that the Supreme War Direction Council, a creation of the Koiso cabinet, considered seriously means to end the war. Negotiations seeking Soviet mediation were initiated with Russia. Emperor Hirohito on June 20 instructed the Council to devise a plan for ending the war immediately. A move to send Prince Konoye to Moscow was abandoned when news of the Potsdam Declaration reached Japan. Even after the destruction of Hiroshima, August 6, by the first atomic bomb attack and the Russian entry into the war on August 9, the Minister of War and the Chiefs

---

[11] A. W. Burks, "Survey of Japan's Defeat," *Far Eastern Survey*, XV (1946), 248-250.

of Staff were opposing unconditional surrender. It was the Emperor who finally resolved the conflict in favor of unconditional surrender.[12]

THE AMERICAN OCCUPATION OF JAPAN

The original American plan for the occupation and the military government of Japan was fashioned out of experience gained in Germany, Italy, and in Pacific islands. The assumption was that the invasion of Japan would be accompanied by great loss of life, physical destruction, and the complete disorganization of the Japanese government. Japan's sudden surrender and the resulting peaceful occupation by American forces completely altered the problem. The decision was made not to administer Japan directly through a numerous corps of American military government officers, but to exercise authority through the Emperor's government. This decision meant that there would be as little tampering as possible with the existing machinery of Japanese administration. "The Japanese Cabinet would operate subject to directions from General MacArthur's headquarters." [13]

Under this conception of the problem there was to be no large military government establishment, but rather a much smaller organization of staff sections created as a part of General MacArthur's headquarters to plan the execution of occupation policy in respect to political, economic, and social problems involved in the remaking of Japan.[14] Un-

[12] From the findings of the *Strategic Bombing Survey* it may be concluded that the Hiroshima atomic bomb attack merely hastened a Japanese political decision which was already inevitable.

[13] The original plan of military government and the changes brought about by Japan's sudden surrender is discussed in detail by Merle Fainsod, "Military Government and the Occupation of Japan," *Japan's Prospect* (Cambridge, Mass., 1946), 287-304.

[14] The following suggest the scope of these staff sections which were to study their appropriate fields and prepare recommendations for General MacArthur.

1. A General Procurement Office governing the acquisition of supplies by the occupation forces.

2. A Natural Resources Section concerned with formulating policies for the rehabilitation of Japan's economy.

3. An Economic and Scientific Section concerned with the distribution of essential goods, with transportation, utilities, banking, price stabilization, and conversion of war plants.

4. A Civil Communications Section to recommend policies in this field.

5. A Public Health and Welfare Section.

6. A Legal Section concerned with general legal matters and with war crimes and war criminals.

7. A Civil Information and Education Section designed to plan the remaking of "Japan's thinking, impress war guilt on the nation, and expedite the Four Freedoms."

8. A Government Section to "advise the Supreme Commander on the status and policies of the military government in Korea and the internal structure of Japan's civil military government"; and to "recommend steps in demilitarization of the Japanese government and the elimination of feudal and totalitarian practices." (See Fainsod, 293-294.)

der this plan of occupation, the military government acts not directly upon the Japanese populace but through the constituted Japanese government. The private Japanese citizen acts on the instructions of his own government.

UNITED STATES POLICY TOWARD DEFEATED AND OCCUPIED JAPAN

While many of the day-to-day steps in the occupation of Japan have been determined by events in Japan and by personalities which dominate in the occupation forces, the American government regards the occupation forces as "the instruments of policy and not the determinants of policy." [15] The official statement of this policy, September 22, 1945, came in the form of instructions to General MacArthur, the Supreme Commander.[16] The ultimate objectives were stated to be:

1. To insure that Japan will not again become a menace to the United States or to the peace and security of the world.
2. To bring about the eventual establishment of a peaceful and responsible government. . . . The United States desires that this government should conform as closely as may be to principles of democratic self-government, but it is not the responsibility of the Allied Powers to impose upon Japan any form of government not supported by the freely expressed will of the people.

Implementation of these objectives was to be secured by limiting Japan's sovereignty to her main islands and a few outlying minor ones by complete demilitarization, by elimination of the militarists and encouragement of democratic associations, and by affording opportunity for the building of an economy adequate for peacetime requirements.

The relationship that was to prevail between the Supreme Commander of the Allied Nations and the Japanese government was to be one of employing the already constituted agencies, including the Emperor, to the extent that this method satisfactorily furthered the objectives of the United States. The policy, however, was not to

. . . commit the Supreme Commander to support the Emperor or any other Japanese governmental authority in opposition to evolutionary changes looking toward the attainment of United States objectives. The policy is to use the existing form of government in Japan, not to support it. Changes in the form of government initiated by the Japanese people or government in

[15] *Department of State Bulletin,* Sept. 23, 1945, 427.
[16] *Department of State Bulletin,* Sept. 23, 1945, 423-427.

the direction of modifying its feudal and authoritarian tendencies are to be permitted and favored.

The more notable political objectives of the occupation were declared to be: 1) prompt disarmament; 2) suppression of militaristic and ultra-nationalistic organizations and the exclusion of their leaders from public office; 3) elimination of doctrines of ultra-nationalism and militarism from the educational system; 4) the arrest and trial of war criminals; 5) establishment of religious freedom and the abolition of Shinto as a state-directed and -supported religion; 6) abrogation of laws that discriminate on a basis of race, nationality, religion, or political opinion; and 7) the release of political prisoners and reform of the police, legal, and judicial systems to guarantee individual liberties and civil rights.

The economic objectives of the occupation were set forth as including: 1) destruction of the economic base of Japan's military strength; 2) reduction of heavy industry to the minimum requirements of an economy for peace; 3) encouragement to "the development of organizations in labor, industry, and agriculture, organized on a democratic basis"; 4) encouragement to policies "which permit a wide distribution of income and of the ownership of the means of production and trade"; 5) dissolution of the great family combines that have controlled Japanese industry and trade; 6) provision by Japan of goods and services needed by the occupying forces "to the extent that this can be effected without causing starvation, widespread disease and acute physical stress"; 7) the development by Japanese authorities of programs that will avoid acute economic distress, assure impartial distribution of available supplies, provide reparations, and restore a reasonable peace-time economy; 8) restoration of looted property; and 9) eventual resumption of normal international trade.

THE EXECUTION OF POLICY

During the first year of the occupation of Japan some notable progress was made in applying these policies. There was indeed a veritable stream of directives from General MacArthur's headquarters to the Japanese government. Among the tangible accomplishments were: the demobilization and disarmament of Japan, the arrest of many war criminals and the beginnings of their trials, the release of political prisoners and the abrogation of discriminatory political laws, and initial steps in revision of the educational system and toward the dissolution of the *Zaibatsu*. But by the end of 1947 it was still too early to appraise with any certainty the theory on which the occupation was proceeding or the thoroughness with which the Japanese were doing their own house cleaning.

INTERNATIONAL "CONTROL" OF JAPAN

From the moment of Japan's defeat it had been made clear that the United States would assume a predominant position in the occupation. Although this country gave assurance that it would consider the wishes of the principal Allied powers, it was made emphatic that "in the event of any differences of opinion among them, the policies of the United States will govern." [17] Nevertheless, the idea of a completely free hand for the United States in fashioning the new Japan did not meet with international favor. Since the control of Japan would have a direct bearing on larger questions concerning the Far East, it was to be expected that China, Russia, Australia, Great Britain, and France would seek a voice in policies applied in Tokyo. Anticipating such demands, the United States government seized the initiative by inviting participation, but the original American proposal for a purely advisory committee representing the chief Allied powers was not received favorably. The problem was eventually resolved in December, 1945, when the foreign ministers of Great Britain, Russia, and the United States, after consultation with China, agreed upon the creation of a Far Eastern Commission and an Allied Council for Japan. The functions of the Commission, which meets in Washington, are to formulate policies, to review on the request of any member any directive issued to the Supreme Commander, and to consider other matters which may be referred to it by agreement among the participating powers. Military operations and territorial adjustments are beyond the Commission's powers. After establishment of the Commission, it still remained the task of the United States to issue the directives to the Supreme Commander, now, however, in accordance with the policy decisions of the Commission. In theory at least, the Commission was a severe limitation on the freedom of the United States to formulate policies, but this did not mean that the United States had lost its predominant position, since American directives to General MacArthur continued to be issued in accord with American interpretation of policy decisions, and the Supreme Commander continued to apply the directives according to his own interpretation of them. The Allied Council in Toyko was designed to be a consultative and advisory body without power to act. Thus, beginning

---

[17] *Department of State Bulletin,* Sept. 23, 1945, 424.

with 1946, the exclusive control of the United States was tempered by a degree of international co-operation.[18]

POST-WAR POLITICS IN JAPAN

Among the fragments of evidence throwing some light on the national character of post-war Japan are those provided by the general election of April 12, 1946, and the rebirth of political parties which accompanied it. This election was notable in many respects: in absolute numbers more Japanese voted than in any previous election; women enjoyed the franchise for the first time; of 80 women candidates for the Diet nearly half were elected; the more than 2,700 candidates represented all shades of political opinion from ultra-nationalists of the right to avowed Communists of the left; and finally, under the weight of the occupation control, the election was reasonably free from pressure and corruption. The Japanese voters leaned heavily toward conservative candidates of the traditional Japanese type. This conservatism, however, was probably less an expression of views on tangible political and economic issues —for today most Japanese appear to favor reform—than an effort to cling to a national institution, the Throne. To most Japanese voters, the conservative parties were the ones most likely to preserve the Throne, which most Japanese still reverence highly despite the Emperor's post-war denial of his divinity.

THE REBIRTH OF THE POLITICAL PARTIES

The most compelling fact in Japan's post-war politics is that more than a year after surrender no new and fresh political leadership had appeared. This was testimony to Japan's political immaturity in terms of the development of democratic thought. "Political direction in Japan still comes from above, not from below." [19] None of Japan's post-war political parties, including the Communist Party, represent a basically new force in Japanese politics, or an expression of the popular will. On the contrary these parties suggest a continuity in Japan's political life. Certainly, since any democratic development in Japan will not be unrelated to political parties, the origins of these new groupings are likely to have a close bearing on Japan's political future.

In general, the new parties have revealed a close resemblance to pre-war parties and, in the main, are continuations and regroupings of them.

---

[18] Werner Levi, "International Control of Japan," *Far Eastern Survey*, XV (1946), 299-302. Texts of relevant documents in *Occupation of Japan* (Washington, D. C., 1946), 7-11, 67-73.

[19] Charles Nelson Spinks, "Postwar Political Parties in Japan," *Pacific Affairs*, XIX (1946), 252; also *Occupation of Japan* (Washington, D. C., 1946), 22.

The new parties like the old ones tend to be followings of individual leaders or groups of leaders. In reality, the pre-war parties, dissolved in 1940, disappeared only in name. In most cases they continued to live in or near the IRAA and its successor the Japan Political Association. When the war ended, many of the old party politicians stepped again into the political foreground; and their pre-war followings, somewhat reshuffled by the war, gravitated again toward them. The principal post-war parties as they appeared in the election months of the spring of 1946 included the following:

1. The Progressive Party. This was principally a coalition of the pre-war Machida faction of the old *Minseito* and the Nakajima faction of the old *Seiyukai*. This group was responsible in 1945 for the conservative reorganization of the IRAA which produced the Japan Political Association controlled by former members of the *Minseito* and the *Seiyukai*. It supported the peace movement leading to Japan's surrender.

2. The Liberal Party. Drawn from the Kuhara faction of the old *Seiyukai* and from the center and right of the former Social Mass Party, this party existed during the war as the *Dokokai* under the leadership of Ichiro Hatoyama, maintaining a mild rightist opposition to the IRAA. Neither the Liberal Party nor the Progressive Party is liberal or progressive. Both are coalitions of extremely conservative politicians and their followings. Their political thinking is nebulous apart from its insistence upon all ultra-conservative elements in Japanese life. Both parties support the emperor system, oppose Communism, and while in a vague sort of way they have advocated democracy they have tended to shun the reforms that would lead in the direction of democracy. Early in 1946 most of the original Progressive Party leaders and members were disqualified politically by General MacArthur because of their open support of the IRAA. In similar manner, Hatoyama, the Liberal Party chief, was disqualified because of his previous nationalistic record. He was replaced by Shigeru Yoshida, who after much difficulty succeeded in forming a Liberal-Progressive coalition ministry in May, 1946. The April, 1946, elections gave the Liberals 141 seats in the lower house and the Progressives, 92, the combination representing just half the total seats in the house.

3. The Social Democratic Party. This was the most unstable of all the parties because of the diverse political elements that compose it. It is a conglomerate re-creation of the pre-war proletarian movement. It represents a marriage of convenience of pre-war parties whose political purposes have often been openly hostile. Five principal pre-war parties

contribute to the membership of this group: 1) conservative and center elements from the former Social Mass Party; 2) leftist elements derived from the former Labor-Farmer Party (*Rodo Nomin To*), the Japan Proletarian Party (*Nippon Musan To*), and the pre-war left wing of the labor movement; 3) right wing elements from the former *Nippon Kokka Shakai To* (Japan National-Socialist Party), the *Kodokai* (Imperial Way Society), and other old right wing groups. During 1946 this heterogeneous socialist party, dominated by the right and center, decided to uphold the emperor system, and rejected the popular front movement with the Communists.

4. The Japan Communist Party (*Nippon Kyosan To*). Organized in October, 1945, and certainly the newest and most radical force in Japanese politics, the party is basically a revival of the pre-war Communist movement and party. It has the most definite political program of all Japan's parties, but, like the other parties, is still colored more by the characteristics of its leaders than by political principles. The leaders themselves, such men as Kyuichi Tokuda, Yoshio Shida, and Sanzo Nozaka (known during the war as Susuma Okano), are self-appointed politicians with personal followings. The party's activities have been characterized by rivalries among the party bosses, by public appeals to all discontented elements (the strategy of chaos), and by condemnation of the emperor system. The party is as yet no more an expression of the popular will than are the other parties, and at the close of 1946 it still remained a minority group.

5. Finally there is a multitude of lesser minority parties, mostly rightist in complexion.

THE NEW CONSTITUTION

Formally at least, Japanese politics is now an expression of a reformed political philosophy expressed in a new constitution made public by Premier Shidehara before the resignation of his cabinet. This Constitution, which had the approval of General MacArthur's headquarters and which was subsequently ratified by the House of Representatives on August 24, 1946, contrasts sharply with the authoritarian tone of its predecessor. With the exception of the Constitution of the Philippine Republic, it is the first wholly democratic charter to be acquired by an Asiatic people.

The new Constitution provides among other things: 1) "that government is a sacred trust, the authority for which is derived from the people"; 2) "that no people is responsible to itself alone but that laws of political morality are universal and that obedience to such laws is in-

cumbent upon all people who would sustain their own sovereignty";
3) that "the Emperor shall be the symbol of the state, . . . deriving his
position from the sovereign will of the people"; 4) that "the advice and
approval of the Cabinet shall be required for all acts of the Emperor in
matters of State," and "the Emperor shall perform only such state functions as are provided for in the Constitution"; 5) that "war, as a sovereign right of the nation, and the threat or use of force is forever renounced as a means of settling disputes with other nations"; 6) that "all
of the people shall be respected as individuals and that the right to life,
liberty and the pursuit of happiness shall within the limits of the public
welfare be the supreme consideration"; 7) that a bicameral legislature
consisting of elected members representative of all the people "shall be
the highest organ of state power"; 8) that the Cabinet shall be responsible to the Diet; 9) that the power to administer national finance shall
be exercised as the Diet shall determine; and 10) that amendments to
the Constitution shall be initiated by the Diet and require a concurring
vote of two-thirds of all the members of each house before submission
to ratification to the electorate.

As an expression of democratic political philosophy and of a new nationalism dedicated to peace and not war, Japan's new Constitution
stands without rival among the world's great charters. Whether this
Constitution will promote democracy within Japan and whether it will
prove to be a true reflection of the political genius and the political aspirations of the Japanese people, rather than an artificial importation of
alien values, are questions which only the future can answer. It is perhaps well to remember in this connection that forty years of American
occupation of the Philippines and a constitution based primarily on
American political concepts have not as yet produced democracy in the
Philippines.[20]

THE REFORM OF JAPANESE EDUCATION

Inseparable from the reform of Japanese politics and government was
the status of Japanese education. Because Japan's centralized, bureaucratic educational system was one of the principal foundation stones supporting the edifice of militarism and Shinto nationalism, and because
the hope of a future democratic Japan lies in her scholars, teachers, and
the generation of youth now in her schools, the reconstruction of Japa-

---

[20] On Japan's first post-war Diet and the political parties, K. K. Kurihara, "Japan's New
Diet," *Far Eastern Survey*, XV (1946), 145-148; and C. N. Spinks, "Postwar Political
Parties in Japan," *Pacific Affairs*, XIX (1946), 250-259. Text of the revised Draft Con-
stitution in *Occupation of Japan* (Washington, D. C., 1946), 117-132.

nese education is a primary responsibility of the occupation. Policy respecting reform in education has been of two kinds: 1) policies of negation expressed in the directives of the Supreme Command ordering the eradication of militarism and nationalistic Shintoism from the schools;[21] 2) positive proposals to aid the Japanese themselves in setting up the conditions of a sound educational system within their culture.

THE UNITED STATES EDUCATION MISSION TO JAPAN

The groundwork for the second and positive phase of policy was laid by the investigations and recommendations of a United States Education Mission which visited Japan during March, 1946. Its recommendations included proposals for: 1) decentralization, in order that teachers may develop professionally without regimentation; 2) development of a curriculum through co-operative action involving teachers, calling on their experience and releasing their creative talents; 3) the teaching of morals as an interpenetrating part of the varied activities of the democratic school; 4) the rewriting of textbooks in geography and history to recognize mythology for what it is; 5) the encouragement of health programs and vocational education; 6) fundamental reform of the Japanese language looking to the common use of some form of Romaji in writing and "a more democratic form of the spoken language"; 7) an upward revision of compulsory education with provision for teacher training, for adult education, and for expanding the facilities for higher education.   These changes, if and when they are applied, will constitute a fundamental revolution in the Japanese approach to national and international life.[22]

THE ECONOMIC SETTLEMENT IN JAPAN

One of the most significant phases of the economic reconstruction of Japan is the "program for the dissolution of the large industrial and banking combines [the *Zaibatsu*] which have exercised control over a great part of Japan's trade and industry." [23]   The purpose behind this policy is to create a wider distribution of income and ownership and more varied forms of economic activity and ownership which "are deemed likely to strengthen the peaceful disposition of the Japanese

[21] On some of the problems involved in the eradication of political Shinto, Daniel C. Holtom, "Shinto in the Postwar World," *Far Eastern Survey*, XIV (1945), 29-33.

[22] Department of State, *Report of the United States Education Mission to Japan* (Washington, D. C., 1946, Department of State, Publication 2579, Far Eastern Series 11).

[23] "U. S. Initial Post-Surrender Policy for Japan," *Department of State Bulletin*, September 23, 1945, 423-427.

people and to make it difficult to command or direct economic activity in support of military ends." The expressed object was "psychological and institutional demilitarization." A secondary effect will be to weaken materially the competitive power of Japanese industry when it is readmitted to world markets. The business reorganization thus does not rest primarily on a basis of the personal war guilt of Japan's big business leaders. Indeed, the responsibility of the *Zaibatsu* for Japanese aggression "is primarily institutional rather than personal." [24] Instead, the implications of the reorganization are to be seen as political as well as economic. The *Zaibatsu* system encouraged the perpetuation of "semi-feudal relations between the employer and employee, held down wages, and blocked the development of labor unions." It also discouraged independent business ventures and "retarded the rise of a Japanese middle class." This situation was one of the reasons explaining the lack of a free base for independence in Japanese politics.[25]

The following measures taken immediately after the surrender constituted the first step in reducing indirectly *Zaibatsu* power: the seizure of Japan's overseas assets, the seizure of properties within Japan for reparations, and the levy of special taxes in the fall of 1946. Under these pressures and in anticipation of others to come, some of the large combines submitted a voluntary dissolution plan, known as the Yasuda Plan, which with revisions was given provisional approval by the Supreme Commander. However, if the *Zaibatsu* are to be destroyed as the wielders of great economic power, the Yasuda Plan must be regarded merely as a first step; for it "is obviously insufficient to destroy the power of the great Japanese combines." [26]

THE TRIAL OF JAPAN'S MAJOR WAR CRIMINALS

In the Philippines early in 1946 a number of Japan's military leaders were tried for war crimes committed in the Islands, were sentenced to death, and executed. Among these were Lieut. General Tomoyuki Yamashita, and Lieut. General Masaharu Homma, the conqueror of

---

[24] Corwin D. Edwards, "The Dissolution of the Japanese Combines," *Pacific Affairs*, XIX (1946), 227-228.

[25] At the close of the war the *Zaibatsu* consisted of three major groups: 1) the traditional big families, the Mitsui, Mitsubishi, Sumitomo, and Yasuda; 2) lesser combines which had become important before the war, Nomura, Riken, Okura, Nippon Nitrogenous Fertilizer, and Oji Paper; 3) combines created primarily by the war and the colonial adventures which immediately preceded it, Nakajima Aircraft, Nissan, etc.

[26] Edwards, "The Dissolution of the Japanese Combines," 227-240; and *Report of the Mission on Japanese Combines*, Part I (Washington, D. C., Department of State, Publication 2628, Far Eastern Series 14).

Corregidor who ordered the Bataan "death march." Other trials were held in Shanghai; nevertheless, the most important of all were those involving Japan's major planners of war which opened in Tokyo.

The Tokyo trials of principal war criminals were instituted pursuant to the Potsdam Declaration of July 20, 1945, and the Instrument of Surrender of September 2, 1945, and were conducted under the terms of the Charter of the International Military Tribunal for the Far East, approved by the Supreme Commander of the Allied Powers on January 19, 1946, with amendments of April 26. In the indictment, Japan's "major war criminals" were charged with: 1) crimes against peace, 2) murder, and 3) conventional war crimes and crimes against humanity. The specific purpose of the trials as expressed by Joseph B. Keenan, Chief of Counsel, in the opening statement of the prosecution was to confirm the already recognized rule that such individuals of a nation who, either in official positions or otherwise, plan aggressive warfare, especially in contravention of sound treaties, assurances, and agreements of their nations to the contrary, are common felons and deserve and will receive the punishment of ages meted out in every land to murderers, brigands, pirates, and plunderers.[27]

---

[27] Documents, including the opening statement of the prosecution, the Charter of the International Military Tribunal, and the indictment, are in *Trial of Japanese War Criminals* (Washington, D. C., 1946, Department of State, Publication 2613, Far Eastern Series 12).

The participating nations include: the United States, China, Great Britain, Soviet Russia, Australia, Canada, France, the Netherlands, New Zealand, India, and the Philippines.

The "criminal, militaristic clique" charged with dominating and directing the internal and foreign policies of Japan includes: Sadao Araki, Kenji Doihara, Kingoro Hashimoto, Shunroku Hata, Kiichiro Hiranuma, Koki Hirota, Naoki Hoshino, Seishiro Itagaki, Okinori Kaya, Koichi Kido, Heitaro Kimura, Kuniaki Koiso, Iwane Matsui, Yosuke Matsuoka, Jiro Minami, Akira Muto, Osami Nagano, Takasumi Oka, Shumei Okawa, Hiroshi Oshima, Kenryo Sato, Mamoru Shigemitsu, Shigetaro Shimada, Toshio Shiratori, Teiichi Suzuki, Shigenori Togo, Hideki Tojo, Yoshijiro Umezu.

The juridical basis of the Nürnberg War Crimes Trial and of the corresponding trial in Tokyo has been warmly defended and vigorously attacked by outstanding American legal authorities. The ablest defense of the trials has been given by Henry L. Stimson, "The Nuremberg Trial: Landmark in Law," *Foreign Affairs,* XXV (1947), 179-189. The essence of the Stimson argument follows:

"International law is not a body of authoritative codes or statutes; it is the gradual expression, case by case, of the moral judgments of the civilized world. As such it corresponds precisely to the common law of Anglo-Saxon tradition. . . ."

"It is clear that until quite recently any legal judgment against a war-maker would have been absurd. Throughout the centuries the choice between war and peace remained entirely in the hands of each sovereign state and neither the law nor the ordinary conscience of humanity ventured to deny that right. For the loser in a war, punishment was certain. But this was not a matter of law; it was simply a matter of course."

Following World War I, efforts to outlaw war reached "their climax in the Kellogg-Briand Pact of 1928, in which 63 nations, including Germany [and Japan], renounced aggressive warfare. During that period the whole world was one, [but] we lacked the

KOREA: INDEPENDENCE "IN DUE COURSE"

When Japan surrendered, her principal colony, Korea, was promptly divided, pursuant to a military decision reached at Potsdam, into two zones separated from each other by the 38th parallel. The division was for purposes of the military occupation'. American forces under Lieut. General John R. Hodge took possession of the southern zone and Soviet

---

courage to enforce the authoritative decision. . . . We did not reach the second half of the question: What will you do to an aggressor when you catch him? That answer escaped us for it implied a duty to catch the criminal, and such a chase meant war. . . ."

"What has been done at Nuremberg . . . is a new judicial process but it is not *ex post facto* law. It is the enforcement of a moral judgment which dates back a generation. It is a growth in the application of law that any student of our common law should recognize as natural and proper, for it is just in this manner that the common law grew up. All case law grows by new decisions, and where those decisions match the conscience of the community, they are law as truly as the law of murder. . . ."

A test of the validity of the Stimson theory would only come as the nations by their actions give convincing proof that they are behaving in conformity with that "conscience of the community" assumed to be the basis of the war trials.

For an able attack on the theory of the trials see Nathan April, "An Inquiry into the Juridical Basis for the Nuernberg War Crimes Trial," *Minnesota Law Review,* XXX (1946), 313-331.

"We are thus forced to the conclusion that the IMT [The International Military Tribunal] has no legitimacy. . . . It was not constituted under the law of the several nations whom it purports to represent."

"By whose commission do the members of the IMT sit? . . . The appointment of Mr. Biddle and his alternate was the private act of an individual who happened at the time to be President of the United States."

"Does the indictment charge a juridically cognizable offense? . . . Unless the meaning of the word 'law' is to be expanded so as to embrace every postulated consensus of moral and sociological judgment, so that 'law' comes to mean whatever people in general are supposed to believe is right, there can be no pretense that there is or ever was any 'law' prohibiting the waging of wars of conquest."

Alluding to the concept that the Pact of Paris is supposed to have "outlawed" wars of aggression, April points out that: "By a process of unique ratiocination this Pact or Contract has been transformed into a 'law'; a process which for some reason had never been applied to the scores of treaties of international friendship and alliance that had preceded it in world history. . . . No verbiage, however mellifluous, can serve to transmute an agreement into a 'law';—there may be a law which provides a remedy for the breach of an agreement, but the law is not the agreement nor is it generated by it. Prior to the Pact of Paris, the observance of international treaties rested upon the honor of those who were parties there-to and upon a decent respect for their military potential—and upon nothing else. The Pact of Paris did not change the situation one iota. . . . There isn't the remotest suggestion in the Kellogg-Briand Pact that a breach of it would constitute a 'crime.' "

"Because we have no World-State there can be no world law; and because there is no world law, there can be no world crime. An act which is not a crime is not justiciable before a judicial tribunal."

"But, because an act is not justiciable, it does not follow that it must be tolerated regardless of its moral infamy." The recourse here lies in direct political action to which the perpetrators of infamy are amenable.

forces occupied the north. The situation in Korea was already chaotic, if not desperate, when the occupation took place in August and September, 1945. Japan's monopolistic control of the economy was on the point of collapse. A debased currency had led to an uncontrolled inflation; and the arbitrary division of the country by the victors into two zones, on grounds of political expediency and lack of an acceptable alternative, provided from the beginning a thoroughly artificial approach to achieving the declared purposes of the victors, namely, laying the foundations for an independent nation.[28]

Moreover, the government of the United States appears to have been inadequately prepared for the task of occupying and governing Korea, a task which had been long foreseen, and the peculiar difficulties of which were no secret. "No arrangements were made to train American military government officers for the specific purpose of occupying Korea," [29] and General Hodge "landed in Korea with only a draft directive, which did not include specific recommendations as to immediate steps to be taken in political and economic matters." [30] This unfortunate situation was aggravated by one of the first orders of the American Command to the effect that Japanese administrators would be retained temporarily in office though without the power of independent action. This order aroused bitter Korean resentment and diminished materially Korean faith in the immediate and the ultimate purposes of the United States. This loss of prestige was not fully regained as the American

---

[28] For an analysis of the social and economic differences in the two zones and their bearing on political problems, see Andrew J. Grajdanzev, "Korea Divided," *Far Eastern Survey*, XIV (1945), 281-283. At the time of the occupation, the division of Korea into two zones was more involved with social than with economic dangers. In 1945 a survey of the available statistics indicated "that in the Russian zone the social relations in the villages are less strained than in the south, prosperous middle-sized farms are more numerous, and there are still available some uncultivated but cultivable lands. Industrial plants were almost all in Japanese hands and by now [October, 1945] there is no doubt that the question of Japanese ownership there does not even arise. . . . As to the American zone, it has more than its proper share of 1) rich and conservative landlords who will leave excellent impressions on the forces of occupation—the American officials will understand their desire for social peace and stability; 2) a multitude of lawyers (since the capital is in the American zone of occupation), well-to-do persons, and old aristocracy; 3) a substantial number of the Japanese who were businessmen and were not in the government, and who would ask for and may receive protection of their legitimate rights, especially of their private property; 4) a substantial number of unemployed or partially employed artisans catering to the refined tastes of the upper groups; 5) poverty-stricken farming population, previously voiceless and poorly organized; and 6) under-paid and dissatisfied workers in private enterprises." Grajdanzev, *ibid*.

[29] Merle Fainsod, "Military Government and the Occupation of Japan," *Japan's Prospect*, 302.

[30] George M. McCune, "Occupation Politics in Korea," *Far Eastern Survey*, XV (1946), 34.

Command, on orders from the Supreme Commander, hastened to undo the damage by removing as rapidly as possible the Japanese administrators.[31]

KOREAN POLITICS AT THE MOMENT OF SURRENDER

Although Japanese rule in Korea had contributed much of a purely material character, such as the development of transportation, industry, and reforestation, it had left a legacy of economic exploitation, political and social oppression, and decay of the native culture. Korean national aspirations, however, had continued to live through an underground movement which the Japanese were never able to suppress completely.[32] Between August 14, when Japan surrendered, and September 8, when the American occupation forces landed, the Japanese governor-general, fearful of Korean violence, appealed to a Korean independence leader, Yo Unhyong (Lyuh Woon Hyung), long a political prisoner, to restrain his countrymen in the hour of their new freedom. Yo Unhyong and his associates did appeal for moderation, organized committees to promote order, and convened a congress which on September 6, two days before the American landing, established the so-called People's Republic, which expected to work with the occupation forces and to receive some degree of recognition from them. In this the "Republic" was disappointed, for the American Command, limited by the terms of its directive, was concerned primarily with the military task of accepting the Japanese surrender, whereas the real tasks in Korea were political and economic. In contrast with the American expedient of dealing at first through Japanese administrators, the Russians, who had invaded northeastern Korea before the end of hostilities, were reported to have imprisoned whatever Japanese administrators they caught and then to have worked with Korean "People's Committees." Against these contrasting beginnings, the 38th parallel soon became equivalent to a closed international boundary across which Americans and Russians viewed each other with increasing suspicion while Koreans grew more impatient for their independence and the "new freedom."

THE MOSCOW AGREEMENT ON TRUSTEESHIP

In December, 1945, the three great powers (Great Britain, Russia, and the United States) decided to place Korea under a four-power trusteeship for a period of up to five years. The agreement provided that the

---

[31] Head of the Japanese administration at the time of the surrender was Governor-General Nobuyuki Abe, who had previously been president of the IRAA in Japan.

[32] Andrew J. Grajdanzev, *Modern Korea* (New York, 1944).

American and the Soviet Commands in Korea form a Joint Soviet-American Commission to assist in the establishment of a provisional democratic Korean government. This decision proved most unpopular in Korea, but what was of even greater consequence was that deep and genuine differences soon developed between the Americans and the Russians on the Joint Commission and brought a complete breakdown of negotiations on May 8, 1946. Korea in the view of many Koreans had become "a victim of Soviet-American dissension," and as a result was gaining "neither freedom nor independence." [33]

Specifically, the breakdown in the negotiations of the Joint Commission developed from the question of which Koreans should be consulted in setting up the interim provisional government for Korea. The United States, in line with its basic and over-all policy, took the ground that all Koreans should be consulted. The Russians held that consultation should be denied those Koreans who had criticized the Moscow agreement on trusteeship. In the abstract, the American position was unimpeachable.

It is not the purpose of the American delegation [said the official American announcement] to defend any school of political thought or to permit obstruction to the fulfilment of the Moscow decision. Nor is the American delegation defending the views of those who believe trusteeship might unduly delay the Koreans' independence. However, it will not and cannot agree to any action by the Joint Commission that would deny to over a hundred Korean democratic parties and social organizations the right guaranteed by the Moscow decision to participate in the formation of their own government, simply because they have expressed honestly and openly their preference for immediate independence rather than for a trusteeship.

Although the Russians did not make a similarly clear statement, their position did not appear to rest equivocally on the principle that any Korean opposing the Allies and the Moscow agreement should on that account forfeit all right of political activity during the trusteeship. The Russian objections were apparently aimed at specific Korean leaders whom the Russians regarded as avowed political enemies; to these the Russians showed no disposition to open the political field. The position of these Korean political leaders and the Russian attitude toward them will be made clearer by an account of the development of Korea's postwar political parties.

---

[33] A letter of Yongjeung Kim, appealing to the United Nations, appears in *The Voice of Korea,* III (1946), October 24.

POLITICAL PARTIES IN POST-WAR KOREA

From the beginning of the Korean occupation, one of the most difficult tasks faced by the American Command was the building of a workable relationship with the multitude of Korean political parties, associations, and societies which promptly sprang into being. Some of these parties dated back to the independence movement of 1919. Some were mushroom growths, the opportunistic creations of Japan's defeat and Korea's "liberation." In other cases the leaders of political independence and their "governments" were in exile, and had not yet reached Korea. The task of the American Command was the more difficult because American policy required that the Command be impartial among all native groups and encourage political freedom of expression and because a vicious rivalry had persisted among Korean factions, particularly within the Korean independence movement abroad. In the American zone, after the occupation was underway, the politics of independence was soon dominated by two of these rival factions: 1) "the People's Republic," dominated by left-wing elements, including Socialists and Communists; and 2) the "Korean Provisional Government," composed principally of conservatives.[34]

THE KOREAN PROVISIONAL GOVERNMENT

It has already been noted that the People's Republic, organized by Yo Unhyong prior to the American occupation, had aspired to recognition by the American Command. However, a rival group, the Korean Provisional Government, which had maintained a shadowy existence in China since the independence movement of 1919, also aspired to national leadership and recognition. On October 20, 1945, Dr. Syngman Rhee, for many years an exile and the representative in Washington of the Provisional Government, reached Seoul. To many Korean patriots Rhee had become almost a legendary figure; but, far from proving to be an instrument for welding together Korea's political groups, Rhee "turned out to be a sentimental old man with uninhibited animosity

---

[34] The principal political parties behind these so-called governments may be listed as follows: the New People's Party (*Sinmin-dang*) and the Communist Party (*Kongsan-dang*) supported the Republic; the conservative Nationalist Party (*Kungmin-dang*), composed largely of professional men; and the ultra-conservative Democratic Party (*Minju-dang*), which included persons of wealth, many of whom collaborated notoriously with the Japanese, and supported the Provisional Government. All these parties favored nationalization of industry. The real issue with them was "not that of public versus private industry but rather a question as to what group is to get into power and to administer public industries." McCune, "Occupation Politics in Korea," 35.

toward the Soviet Union and the [Korean] leftists." A month later, in November, 1945, Rhee was joined by Kim Ku, the president of the Provisional Government, now returned from exile in China. Like Rhee, Kim Ku failed to win over the leaders of the People's Republic, which continued to gain in strength until it enjoyed "far more popular support than any other single political group." [35]

In this arena of native political factionalism, American policy continued to be based on the abstract democratic principle of giving the Korean people an absolutely free choice in the selection of their interim government under the trusteeship. In practice, however, if the overwhelming weight of reports from Korea could be believed, the policy of attempting to maintain neutrality had failed, with the result that the American occupation authorities more and more appeared to be in support of the conservative minority. Moreover, the words and behavior of Syngman Rhee and Kim Ku influenced the attitude of Russia and helped to bring the negotiations of the Joint Commission to an untimely end. Realists in politics, the Russians refused to be tolerant of men who were not only openly anti-Russian but who hoped in addition to have American support in Korea against the Russians.[36]

By midsummer of 1947, freedom and independence for Korea were yet to be achieved. Historic Sino-Japanese and later Russo-Japanese rivalry in Korea had given place to Russo-American rivalry.

[35] Gordon Walker in The Christian Science Monitor, January 3, 1946, quoted by McCune, "Occupation Politics in Korea," 36.

[36] Note the analysis by Raymond Swing in The Voice of Korea, III (1946), May, 22.

CHAPTER 40

SOUTHEAST ASIA

FOUR centuries ago adventurous navigators and empire-builders seeking a new and more profitable way to put spices on the dinner tables of Europe founded their first trading posts on the shores of Southeast Asia. From these beginnings there grew in time European colonial empires of great size and wealth comprising the lands known today as Netherlands India, the Philippines, Malaya, Indo-China, and Burma. With the single exception of Siam (Thailand), these, the principal lands of what is commonly called Southeast Asia, became the colonial possessions of great European powers.[1] For some three centuries or more, that is until late in the nineteenth century, the importance of the general area of Southeast Asia rested primarily on the spice trade, on coffee, and tobacco. In those days, the meat and fish which Europeans ate in winter had been preserved without benefit of refrigeration by salting them away in the fall. When later they were brought to the dinner table, the richly aged taste which had been acquired meanwhile was softened by heavy doses of spices: pepper, mustard, nutmeg, cinnamon, and cloves. Spices therefore commanded a price for which men would risk their fortunes and their lives in the building of empires. Control of the spice trade was a major avenue to wealth and power for men and for nations. Since most spices came from the East Indies, as they do even today, Southeast Asia acquired immense political as well as economic importance. In more recent years, that is, since the latter part of the nineteenth century, the spice trade has declined in relative importance, but this has not decreased the significance of Southeast Asia,

---

[1] The character of the early colonial settlements in Southeast Asia was pre-eminently commercial rather than political. For example, after two centuries of occupation, the Dutch residents in Java still looked upon themselves as merchants staying abroad for the purposes of trade. While on occasion they used their constabulary to subdue unruly native peoples in the neighborhood of the commercial settlements, the Dutch trader remained a merchant rather than a colonizer. In general, too, the Portuguese and British settlements in Southeast Asia were for long merely outposts of their Indian settlements. Thus it should be noted that nowhere in Southeast Asia did Europeans go with the conscious or deliberate purpose of building empires, though in the long run that was what they eventually did.

which in contemporary times has become a source of the world's rubber, tin, oil, sugar, and many other products. This fact in part explains why colonial control of Southeast Asia in one form or another was an issue in World War II. One of Japan's chief objectives was to break the colonial bonds between Europe and America and Southeast Asia, and under the guise of bringing freedom to this area to incorporate it into the Japanese sphere known as Greater East Asia. Even before this colonial struggle came to a crisis in World War II, other conflicting forces of great moment were stirring among the native peoples of Southeast Asia. Principal among these was the appearance of nationalistic

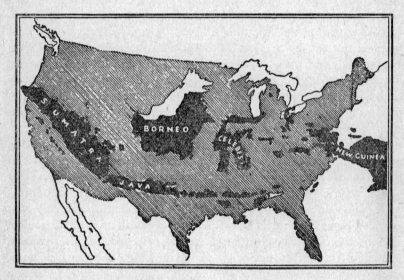

THE AREA OF NETHERLANDS EAST INDIES COMPARED WITH THAT OF THE UNITED STATES. *Netherlands Information Bureau, New York.*

movements rebelling against colonial control. These movements were further complicated by economic and social class struggles revealing themselves politically in communistic risings. Revolts against colonialism and oppressive social conditions were scattered and rarely involved large numbers, but they were vitalized and unified by the opportunities for organization and propaganda afforded by World War II. As one Western colonial regime after another fell before the onslaught of Japanese arms, so the prestige of Western, the white man's, civilization suffered in the eyes of Asiatic peoples and stirred their latent, often vague resentment against alien control. Thus, as Southeast Asia emerged from the world conflict, its social, economic, and political patterns were in flux and revealed a far more widespread discontent than had been known to exist. The problems represented by this demand for self-rule on the part of large numbers with little previous experience were not likely to yield to simple or easy solutions. Some of the historical aspects which lie behind this confused picture will be suggested briefly in the pages that follow.

COLONIAL STATUS: NINETEENTH AND TWENTIETH CENTURIES

The colonial empires of Spain, Portugal, and the Netherlands in the East Indies were founded in the sixteenth and seventeenth centuries, but it was not until the nineteenth century that the colonial pattern of Southeast Asia as it has come to be known in the twentieth century was fully achieved and matured as a result of the French acquisition of Indo-China, the spread of Dutch rule over more distant parts of the archipelago, and by the advent of British rule in the Malay States and in Burma.

THE PORTUGUESE AND THE DUTCH

The Portuguese in the spice trade first established themselves at Malacca in 1511, but in 1522 set up a trading post at Ternate in the Moluccas, or Spice Islands. At the beginning of the seventeenth century, the Dutch drove the Portuguese from Amboyna, also in the Moluccas, and to secure further this newly won position in the Spice Islands, set up a protective base in Java far to the west, annexed adjacent territory, supported native buffer states, and thus from beginnings as merchant adventurers, "dependent on the favour of native rulers for their trade," emerged in time as merchant princes wielding supreme political power in the archipelago.[2] All this was the work of the Dutch East India Company, which continued as the sole arm of Dutch authority in the Islands until the Company was abolished in 1800. Following years of uncertainty and confusion in Dutch policy incident to the Napoleonic Wars and their aftermath (1800-1830), the Dutch government experimented for a time with the so-called Culture System (1830-1850), the theory of which was that taxes would be paid in produce rather than in money and that the economy should rest on the intensive development of export crops. This system built up the agricultural production of Java, and in Europe restored the commercial prosperity of the Netherlands, but the administrative policy by which

---

[2] In the eastern half of Timor, Portugal still retains a remnant of her once lucrative commercial empire in the Indies.

it was enforced, though establishing order, was arbitrary and did violence to native cultural patterns. From 1850 to 1870, Netherlands India passed through a further period of transition to a regime of economic liberalism which latter remained the prevailing policy until the end of the century. Essentially this was a shift from a mercantile system to one of private exploitation. As in the case of the Culture System, the initial years of free enterprise brought seemingly great prosperity. Plantation agriculture expanded rapidly, but this was a result of corporate, not individual, enterprise, and was potentially at the expense of the natives and of manufacturers in the Netherlands whose goods could not be sold to natives who had nothing with which to buy. In a word, the period of liberalism was one in which Europeans and Chinese in the Islands increased in numbers and wealth, whereas the natives faced a deteriorating economic status and a disorganized social life.[3] After 1900 Dutch policy, while continuing to stress the liberal tradition, recognized the need for state intervention. The purpose, however, was often to stimulate material wealth rather than to foster human welfare among the natives. Even when paternalistic measures were planned the attitude was one of discovering what could be done for the Javanese rather than one of finding what the Javanese could do for themselves.[4]

GOVERNMENT IN NETHERLANDS INDIA

Government in the Indies is a product of long historical development in which a European power gradually assumed control over Asiatic peoples in widely scattered islands of the far eastern tropics. The traditional European attitude was that these were alien, heathen, and backward peoples. The business of ruling over them was the white man's burden. This general philosophy, applied in all the lands of Southeast Asia, does not imply that the colonial governments maintained there by the United States, France, Britain, and Holland have all been the same. On the contrary, there have been marked differences in the application of colonial policies.

Netherlands India has always been divided into two areas for purposes of government and administration. The first and more important area was composed of the islands of Java and Madura with their dense population and highly developed economy of native agriculture. The second was the Outer Territories or Outer Provinces, including all the remaining islands with their sparse population and their uneven cul-

---

[3] Politically the natives gained in protection against extortions by their native rulers.

[4] Among the best accounts is J. S. Furnivall, *Netherlands India* (New York, 1944); for the historical survey see chs. i-viii.

tural development.[5] In this connection it should be noted that "while the Dutch have been in the East Indies for over three centuries, their control over much of the area was only nominal until recent years. Outside of Java, only Amboyna, the Minahasa [northern Celebes], and a few other small areas were subject to Dutch administrative penetration." Most of the Outer Territories were brought under effective administrative control only at the turn of the twentieth century. Moreover the receptivity of the native peoples to alien and Western cultural influences has varied greatly. In general, resistance has been greatest in Java with its dense population, Moslem religion, and generally higher civilization than that possessed by the Outer Territories.[6]

Whereas during the first years of the twentieth century under the theory of state intervention the Indies were closely regulated by the government in Holland, later years witnessed the growth of greater autonomy for the colonial administration, though, of course, subject to Holland's ultimate control. This administration was more cautious than either of the neighboring colonial regimes (the British in Burma, the Americans in the Philippines) toward questions of self-government and education. Dutch administration continued to be strongly paternalistic, insisting that it "and not the Indonesians shall judge how fast the political advance shall be." [7]

The educational policy of the Dutch colonial administration has also

---

[5] Not all the culture in the Outer Territories can be described as backward. This is to be noted in the case of some of the peoples of Sumatra and the Celebes. Minangkabau architecture, Bugi seamanship, etc., are cases in point. The student should not mistake lack of modern technical equipment for cultural inferiority.

[6] For an excellent discussion of Dutch colonial policy see Amry Vandenbosch, *The Dutch East Indies* (Berkeley, 1942), 51-73. The best brief account of government is Lennox A. Mills, "The Governments of Southeast Asia," in *Government and Nationalism in Southeast Asia* (New York, 1942), 97-106. Note also Raymond Kennedy, *The Ageless Indies* (New York, 1942), 114-125. The contrast in problems of government between Java-Madura and the Outer Territories is suggested by population figures. Total population of Netherlands India, 1930, was 60,700,000; of Java-Madura, 41,719,000. Total estimated population of Netherlands India, 1940, was 70,000,000. The overwhelming population is native (Indonesian, speaking the Malay language), 59,143,000; Chinese number about 1,233,000; other foreign Asiatics, mostly Arabs, 111,000; Europeans and Eurasians or Indo-Europeans, 242,000. The greater Javanese resistance to Western cultural influence must be measured against the fact that they have been exposed to more of it.

[7] Mills, "The Governments of Southeast Asia," 4. It should be remembered that the situation in respect to the Volksraad was not unique in Southeast Asia. In the last analysis the Philippine legislature, to note a comparison, could not control the Governor-General. As a matter of fact the United States government had three successive checks on the Philippine legislature: 1) the veto power of the Governor-General, 2) the veto power of the President, and 3) the veto power of the United States Congress. In either colonial area the essential question was apt to be the extent to which these powers were used.

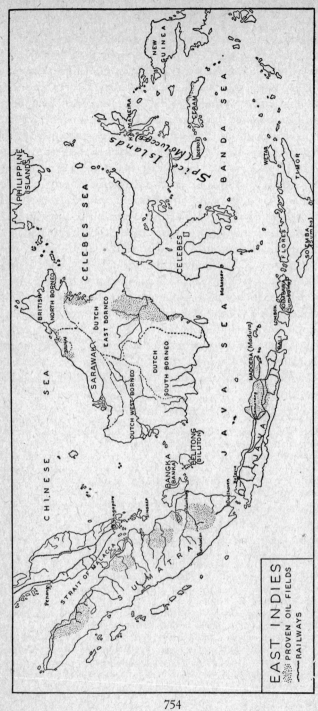

EAST INDIES
∴∴∴ PROVEN OIL FIELDS
⌒⌒⌒ RAILWAYS

MAP OF THE EAST INDIES SHOWING RELATIVE POSITION OF ISLANDS, CHIEF RAILWAYS, AND PROVEN OIL FIELDS. *After U. S. Department of Commerce.*

been an integral part of the colonial philosophy applied in the Indies. In the Philippines it was the American theory that an ever-expanding system of schools would provide democratic training for the masses. Dutch educational policy, in contrast, has been aimed at giving the native greater skill in his traditional calling of agriculture, a Dutch education being reserved for a few potential native leaders and for minor official posts in government. The policy, though thoroughly justified in the Dutch view, has not been popular, for many an Indonesian, like the Burmese and the Filipinos, would prefer a literary education leading to the sedentary pursuits of government official or lawyer. The Dutch have defended their system by saying that freedom of educational choice would mean dislocation and loss to the economic and social structure, and the creation of an idle intellectual proletariat. On the other hand, although Dutch policy has not encouraged the Western concept of democratic education, it has been much concerned with improving the native standard of living. Emphasis has been placed on the importance of economic literacy for the farmer, whereby he might protect himself from the moneylender, and on the importance of rural credit, health, irrigation, communications, and protection of native land rights.[8]

World War II brought major changes in the enunciation of Dutch policy. Impelled by discontent in the Indies, by Japan's invasion, and the collapse of Dutch authority, the helpless Netherlands government already in exile in Europe issued a new declaration of policy for the empire which was to be reorganized in four great divisions (the Netherlands, Surinam, Curaçao, and Indonesia), each part completely autonomous in internal affairs, but in empire affairs bound by ties of mutual responsibility. This declaration was not taken at face value by Indonesian nationalists, who, as the war came to an end in 1945, established the independent Indonesian Republic just as British troops were opening the way for the restoration of Dutch authority. The strength of the nationalist movement, however, was apparently sufficient to prevent a return to the pre-war *status quo,* for in February, 1946, the policy of dominion partnership was reaffirmed by the Netherlands government and expanded somewhat vaguely to include the possibility of eventual self-rule for Indonesia.[9]

---

[8] Mills, "The Governments of Southeast Asia," 44-45. Even this limited agricultural education was far from being universal among the natives.

[9] The plan for a quadripartite kingdom is discussed by Raymond Kennedy, "Dutch Plan for the Indies," *Far Eastern Survey,* XV (1946), 97-102. No definitive judgments can as yet be given on 1) the real strength of the Indonesian nationalist movement, or 2) on the conviction held by many Dutchmen that the British instead of using their power to restore Dutch authority have employed it to favor the Indonesians.

NATIONALISM IN NETHERLANDS INDIA

The nationalistic movement in Netherlands India is a development of the twentieth century, and, until the close of World War II, when Indonesian nationalists forcibly resisted the return of Dutch authority, the movement had attracted relatively little attention among Western peoples. Nevertheless, as in the Philippines, nationalism in varying forms and degrees has become a force to be reckoned with not only in Indonesia but also in all colonial areas of Southeast Asia—in French Indo-China, and in British Burma and Malaya. However, in the discussion of nationalism which follows, it should be remembered that the movement has never embraced the Indies as a whole but flourished rather in urban centers, such as Java, where Western influence was intense.[10] Moreover, nationalism in the Indies cannot be evaluated simply in terms of the history of nationalism in Europe or the Americas. This is because nationalism in Asia, a product, to be sure, of westernization, is developing nevertheless in an Oriental setting of very uneven cultural levels where philosophical values as to what is good are derived from the traditional Eastern philosophies of politics and religion, be they Confucian, Buddhist, Hindu, or Moslem. It would thus be a mistake to assume that nationalism in Asia will or should take on precisely the forms that have been associated with it in the West.[11]

HISTORY OF THE NATIONALIST MOVEMENT

In a formal sense the nationalist movement originated in 1908 when the first native political society was formed in Java. The advent of Western industry had hastened the process by which many a native communal village farmer had become an agricultural or factory "coolie." Thereby the economic and political gulf between the alien populace

---

[10] Note in particular the essay by Rupert Emerson, "Introduction," in *Government and Nationalism in Southeast Asia* (New York, 1942), 3-33.

[11] In point of origins, the fabric of the so-called "nationalistic" movement includes a number of strands: 1) the discontent of exploited workers in the sweated industries operated by both natives and Chinese; 2) the discontent of professional men, students, and workers who have come somehow in contact with Western thought; 3) the native cultural revival, usually linked with the self-interest of cultural institutions of a traditional kind that have difficulty in maintaining their prestige and income as popular native contacts become more cosmopolitan. In Java, this cultural revival again has three sources. It is partly Mohammedan; partly a looking back to the great era of the Majapahit (Hindu) empire; partly a deliberate attempt of the colonial authorities to divert the minds of the people from ideas dangerous to the ruling class. Events in the Indies both prior to and during World War II would seem to indicate that the attempt has miscarried; that no revival of puppet plays and legends is effective in rendering the mind of the native populace immune to social and economic questions.

(Europeans and Chinese) was enlarged and emphasized, and at the same time native society was becoming more conscious of the political and economic controls exercised by the alien planter, industrial manager, and business man. Thus, the rather moderate objective of this first political society, *Boedi Oetomo* (Beautiful Striving), was educational and economic advancement for the masses under the leadership of native intellectuals.

Within two decades, however, nationalism had become a complex mixture of demands for political, economic, and social change. By 1929 the colonial government was imprisoning nationalists as well as Communists. This again only served to unite elements of discontent. On the eve of World War II the principal native political parties had formed a union known as *Gapi*. For the time being this union, in the face of Dutch determination against secession, took the practical course of dropping independence and advocating self-government within the empire.[12]

FACTORS CONDITIONING INDONESIAN NATIONALISM

Whatever the future course of Indonesian nationalism may be, it will be conditioned in terms of political theory and social reform by its own complex historical heritage. Pre-eminent in this heritage is the fact that most Indonesians are small farmers, conservative, provincial, with interests confined to crops, taxes, and village affairs. Traditionally they expect government to come from above, not from below. There is a wide cultural gulf between this farmer and the Western-educated native of the towns, be he lawyer, teacher, journalist, or government official. There is an even wider chasm between this farmer and the Chinese middleman, and between the farmer and the European. It becomes clear, therefore, that in the Indies there is no strong native middle class which can emerge as the champion of nationalism and democracy. The Western-educated native intellectual demands democracy and nationalism in the name of the whole people, but the native has no understanding of what democracy is. The middleclass petty capitalists of the islands are the Chinese, whose loyalties are to China

---

[12] Vandenbosch, *The Dutch East Indies,* 310-340; Raymond Kennedy, "Indonesian Politics and Parties," *Far Eastern Survey,* XIV (1945), 129-132. The cases of arrest and imprisonment of Indonesian nationalists as well as Communists do not attest a unique situation in the Indies. A colonial government like any other, so long as it is in power, seeks to maintain what it regards as law and order. The student should note the measures of arrest and imprisonment which American colonial authorities have used in the cases of Porto Rican nationalists. In the case of colonial dependencies, the line between a nationalist and a revolutionist may become an exceedingly thin one.

rather than to the Indies.[13] The great natural resources, the wealth of the Indies, rubber, oil, etc., are owned and operated by the capital and the technical skill of the West. This is simply to say that Indonesia is a plural society comprising three social orders: the native Indonesians, the Chinese, and the Europeans. These social orders live side by side but at the same time they live separately, "rarely meeting save in the material and economic sphere." Culturally their backgrounds are diverse in the extreme. These facts go far to explain why the developing history of Indonesian nationalism has been marked by lack of purpose on the part of government and lack of confidence on the part of the people. The resulting estrangement slowed the pace of government toward reform and stimulated extreme demands and violent measures on the part of the nationalists. On the other hand, it should not be forgotten that there are some strong bases for Indonesian nationalism. The islands have not been plagued with a caste system such as prevails in India, and at least in the Java-Madura area of concentration the culture is homogeneous.[14]

THE POST-WAR STRUGGLE FOR INDEPENDENCE

When the war in the Pacific ended, British troops in the absence of Dutch forces entered Indonesia to liberate it from the Japanese and presumably to restore the islands to Netherlands sovereignty. This plan was frustrated by troops of the newly formed independent but unrecognized Indonesian Republic, formed, as already noted, in 1945. Indonesia then entered a new period of slaughter in which the British, eventually joined by Dutch troops, did battle against the native nationalists. Late in 1946, having failed in their efforts to mediate between the Dutch and the Indonesians, the British announced that their troops would be withdrawn. This move spurred negotiations between the Indonesians and the Dutch with the result that by the end of 1946 the Netherlands Indies were in the process of becoming a sovereign nation. The plan which looks to implementation by 1949 foreshadows an East Indian archipelago composed of three autonomous states: 1) the Republic of Indonesia, consisting of Java, Sumatra, Madura; 2) Dutch Borneo; and 3) the "Great East," comprising the Celebes, the Moluccas, Dutch New Guinea, and the Sunda Islands. The three states are to

---

[13] The statement is qualified by the fact that there is a considerable Chinese-speaking population which intermarried with Malays, and belongs to the Malay middle class in the Indies, in Malaya, and in the Philippines. These groups have looked to China when oppressive measures were passed against them by colonial or native governments. They have manifested little loyalty to China when they were permitted to live in peace.

[14] Note the discussion by Furnivall, *Netherlands India,* 238-239.

form a federation, the United States of Indonesia, which will remain a part of the Dutch empire through an alliance with the Kingdom of the Netherlands, the whole to be known as the Netherlands-Indonesian Union.[15] During the interim period while the Union is in process of formation, the Dutch will retain sovereignty over the Indies, the Republic of Indonesia will exercise a qualified sovereignty in its own territory, and the two will co-operate as partners in forming the Union. Finally, the plan of settlement calls for the Netherlands to sponsor the United States of Indonesia for admission to the United Nations.

BRITISH MALAYA

On the eve of World War II, Great Britain held a large and wealthy empire cutting across the tropics of Southeast Asia, composed of Burma, British Malaya, and portions of the great island of Borneo (Sarawak, Brunei, and British North Borneo). Of this empire, the most important area in economic terms was that combination of small colonial settlements and protectorates known as British Malaya. Like many another region, remote from the Western world, British Malaya was thrust upon public attention by the early military disasters of the war. Previously this tropical empire was largely taken for granted by Britishers and, even among them, all the average man knew of it was that it produced tin and rubber and had a strong naval base.[16]

Like many events of modern times in eastern Asia, Great Britain's first inroads into Malaya were precipitated by political happenings in Europe. During the eighteenth century, after its earlier and vain efforts to break the Dutch monopoly in the East Indies, the English East India Company had turned to the consolidation of its position in India. Subsequently, by the time of the French Revolution, the Company was more conscious of the need to protect the eastern Indian coast, and later, when Napoleon seized Holland, the British once again turned to Malaya, seeking to share in the rich trade between that region and Europe and the Far East. From this broad historical background was to come one of the most colorful chapters in the history of Great Britain's com-

---

[15] At the end of 1946 the plan awaited the final approval of the Dutch government. As 1947 advanced, the problem of setting up the interim government proved exceedingly difficult. In July hostilities broke out between Dutch and Indonesian troops. While the Council of the United Nations called upon the Dutch and the "Republic of Indonesia" to settle their dispute by arbitration or other peaceful means, each side continued to charge the other with bad faith. These developments were renewed signs of the birth pains of nationalism in Southeast Asia.

[16] The standard study is Lennox A. Mills, *British Rule in Eastern Asia* (Minneapolis, 1942).

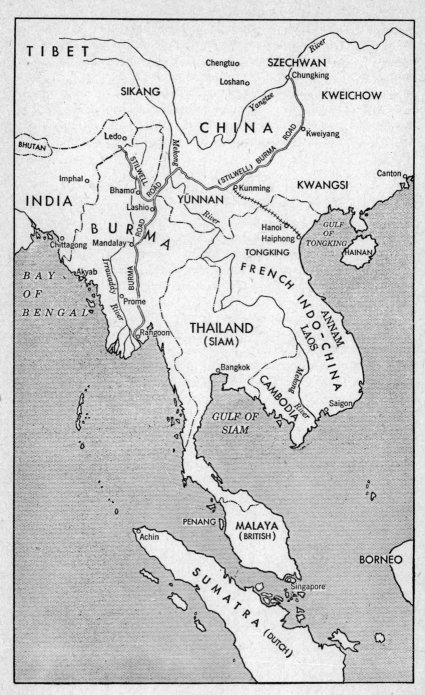

SOUTHEAST ASIA.

mercial, colonial, and industrial expansion—a chapter inextricably bound up with the name Singapore, a small island which lies off the southern tip of the Malay Peninsula. In 1819, this island, circled with mangrove swamps and virtually uninhabited, was chosen by Thomas Stamford Raffles, a young Company agent "insatiable in ambition," as the site for a factory of the English East India Company. A century later, Singapore had become a city of almost half a million inhabitants and one of the greatest commercial crossroads of the world, its harbor sheltering the ships of every maritime power. Here, too, Britain had built the world's most publicized naval base, a base which surrendered to Japan in February, 1942, because it had no navy to service.

THE PHYSICAL CHARACTERISTICS

The Malay Peninsula, with an area of 53,000 square miles, approximately the size of the state of Florida, and with an estimated population in 1937 of 5,112,000, is a region characterized by a central mountain chain with altitudes ranging from 4,000 to 8,000 feet, below which are the rolling foothill country and the coastal plains that in some places are extremely narrow while in others they broaden out to as much as thirty miles in width. It is here on the western shore, in the coastal plains, and in the undulating terrain of the lower foothills, that the rubber-growing lands of Malaya are found. Here, too, in the valleys of the lowlands are the deposits of tin washed down from the high granite ranges.

Malaya is a tropical land, with only slight year-round variations of temperature; Singapore is only ninety miles from the equator. The even temperature is partly accounted for by the fact that the peninsula is all but surrounded by tropical seas which exert a moderating influence and provide an abundant source of moisture. The rainfall, influenced by the monsoons, is well distributed throughout the year, there being no essentially dry season such as prevails in most tropical lands of the monsoon area. It is this climatic factor that has contributed much to making Malaya the world's foremost area in rubber culture. Although much of the land is covered with dense tropical forests containing a great variety of species, there are relatively few of commercial value, and, as a result, much of the timber used in recent years in Malaya has been imported from Sumatra.[17] An excellent system of roads has been constructed since World War I.

---

[17] See Daniel R. Bergsmark, *Economic Geography of Asia* (New York, 1935), 276-280; United States, *Commerce Reports,* "Forest Resources and Lumber Industry of British Malaya," Washington, D. C., Jan. 6, 1930, 34-35.

In modern times, agriculture in Malaya has consisted of two principal kinds: 1) the small plots of the natives (Malays), where, in many cases, rubber is produced, and where rice and tropical vegetables are grown, and 2) the large-scale plantations of Europeans and Chinese, where, prior to World War II, about 45 percent of the world supply of rubber was produced. Here too it may be noted that in the decade of the 1930's Malaya held first place in the world's production of tin with 28 percent of the total output.[18]

RACIAL STOCKS IN MALAYA

The principal native people of the peninsula is the Malay. He is a descendant of the Proto-Malay[19] with a considerable mixture of Arab, Indian, and Chinese blood. At the end of 1937, the Asiatic population of Malaya was estimated to be 5,112,000, of which Malays numbered 2,169,000, or 42.4 percent; Chinese, 2,114,000, or 41.3 percent; East Indians, 755,000, or 14.8 percent; Eurasians, 18,000, or .4 percent; and others, 56,000, or 1.1 percent. Most of the Malays are British subjects or British-protected persons, whereas in the case of the Chinese, the majority has been composed of foreign residents: 1,000,000 out of a total Chinese population of 1,709,000 in 1931.[20] But although the Chinese have formed the overwhelming foreign group in Malaya in the twentieth century, it has been Indian rather than Chinese culture which has influenced the historic patterns of Malayan life. Indian commerce, Indian Buddhism, and Hinduism had reached Malaya by sea in the early centuries of the Christian Era. Out of these early contacts arose a number of rival empires which for many centuries struggled for control of the Straits and the wealth which passed through them.

THE EUROPEANS REACH MALAYA

The Portuguese, the first Europeans to reach China by the all-sea route, had seized Malacca, as the reader is aware, in 1511, some four

---

[18] Bergsmark, 280-283; H. S. Hotchkiss, "The Evolution of the World Rubber Situation," *Harvard Business Review*, II (1924), 129-138; C. E. Akers, *The Rubber Industry in Brazil and the Orient* (London, 1914); J. B. Scrivenor, "The Physical Geography of the Southern Part of the Malay Peninsula," *Geographical Review*, XI (1921), 351-371; R. O. Winstedt, *Malaya* (London, 1928); and for a popular description, Frederick Simpich, "Singapore, Crossroads of the East," *The National Geographic Magazine*, XLIX (1926), 235-269.

[19] The Proto-Malay stock was formed by the addition of a Mongol strain to the early Indonesian or Nesiot peoples who at a remote time entered the peninsula from Yünnan. This Indonesian strain persists today in the Sakai people found in limited numbers in the Malayan mountains.

[20] Sir Richard Winstedt, *Britain and Malaya, 1786-1941* (London, 1944), 6.

years before they reached Canton. Under Portuguese control, Malacca soon became the great entrepôt of Lisbon's commerce in the East. Here were handled the nutmegs, mace, pepper, camphor, gold, and silk which for a century made Portugal master of the Eastern trade. A little more than a century later, in 1641, Malacca was captured by the Dutch, who were already strongly entrenched at Batavia. Malacca now remained in Dutch hands until the period of the French Revolution when, the Dutch and French Republics having formed an alliance, Malacca was seized and held by the British until 1818, when it was returned to Holland, only to be finally ceded to Britain in 1824. By the beginning of the twentieth century therefore, Malacca had been continuously a European colony for four centuries.

Meanwhile, the British had acquired another outpost in Malaya. During the eighteenth century, the Malay empire had entered a period of decline marked by rivalries among contending state dynasties. The Sultan of Kedah's fear of a rival in Selangor had enabled an agent of the English East India Company to raise the British flag over the island of Penang in 1786, and to acquire a strip of land on the opposite mainland, known as Province Wellesley, in 1800. In 1819 Thomas Stamford Raffles, who had become agent of the English East India Company at Malacca in 1810, and governor of Java when it was captured the following year from the Dutch, made the first agreements with the Sultan of Johore whereby land was granted for factories on the island of Singapore in return for a small annual allowance. In 1824 Singapore was ceded to Britain in perpetuity. Thus by that year the English East India Company held in Malaya in the name of Britain, the island of Penang and Province Wellesley, Malacca, and the island of Singapore, all of which were to be known as the Straits Settlements.

STATUS OF MALAYA, 1786-1867

The history of Great Britain in Malaya from 1786, when Penang was occupied, until 1858 is a chapter in the history of the English East India Company. The Company's business was commerce, not social service, or for that matter the extension of colonial control. The Company's posts in Malaya were simply the markets to which were drawn the rich resources of the peninsula. The English Company, like the Dutch before it, operated at first on the principle of monopoly, but Raffles, far in advance of the economic thought of his day, made Singapore a free port. Economically this was a policy which bore rich returns. However, in its general policies of government and especially in the administration of land in the Straits Settlements, the record of the Company left much to be desired. The servants of the Company were often inexperienced in the governing of new territory, and the land system which they administered was a hodge-podge of the systems left by their Portuguese and Dutch predecessors.[21]

When the East India Company was abolished in 1858, the Straits Settlements passed for nine years under the control of the India Office without any significant change being effected in the structure of their administration. This was an interlude of virtual stagnation which came to an end in 1867, when the decision was made to divorce the Straits Settlements from India and to give them a separate existence as a crown colony under the Colonial Office.

THE CONSTITUTION OF THE STRAITS SETTLEMENTS

The Straits Settlements constituting a crown colony were administered by a governor who in time was assisted by an executive council composed of the commandant of the British garrison, leading officials of the administration, and three appointed members supposedly representative of the public. Whereas final legislative authority in the crown colony remained with the British Parliament, this authority was exercised only in emergency. Customarily, local legislation was passed by a local legislative council in the crown colony. In recent years this council has consisted of the governor, thirteen officials of his administration, and thirteen non-officials (British subjects), representatives of the public and appointed by the governor. These latter representatives usually have included Chinese, British Indian, and Eurasian elements of the population. The governor plus the official members of the council constituted a majority and thus had the controlling voice in all legislation. The nomination rather than the election of the non-official members of the council was a logical answer to conditions distinguished by "a floating population of many races." The policy of maintaining an official majority on the council was in the British view necessary, since members of the council were concerned with ruling a plural society in which the desire for democratic self-government was found only among "a few Europeans and Straits-born Chinese."[22]

CREATION OF THE MALAY PROTECTORATES

Prior to the last quarter of the nineteenth century, Britain's control in Malay was limited, as noted, to the Straits Settlements. However, much earlier in the century officials of the East India Company, acting

---

[21] Winstedt, *Britain and Malaya,* 25.
[22] Winstedt, *Britain and Malaya,* 39.

in the interest of peace among the native states, had arbitrated in boundary disputes, had used force to repel invasions by Siamese forces, had offered protection to certain states in case of attack, and had sometimes determined the succession to native thrones. After 1857, and despite almost constant war among the native states of the peninsula, the British government did not encourage a policy of interference in native affairs. As late as 1872 the Colonial Office held to the view that traders who placed their persons and property in jeopardy did so at their own risk. However, in the following year local pressure brought abandonment of this policy for one of intervention in native affairs. The new policy, euphoniously phrased, noted that:

Her Majesty's Government find it incumbent to employ such influence as they possess with the native princes to rescue, if possible, these fertile and productive countries from the ruin which must befall them if the present disorders continue unchecked.

Within a matter of months after the adoption of this new policy, British advisers had been placed by the governor of the Straits Settlements in the native states of Perak, Selangor, and Negri Sembilan, and a few years later, in 1887, Pahang also received a British adviser. Thus was initiated the process by which the native states were to become British protectorates, a process which ended finally the insecurity and lawlessness that preceded British rule.

THE CONSTITUTION OF THE FEDERATED MALAY STATES

The Federated Malay States (Perak, Selangor, Negri Sembilan, and Pahang) each became a British protectorate as a result of treaties signed with their respective rulers between 1874 and 1880. These treaties provided: 1) that each native ruler accept a British resident whose advice was mandatory in all matters "other than those touching Malay religion and customs"; and 2) that revenues be collected and all appointments made in the name of the respective state sultans. Each of these states had a state council combining legislative and executive functions, but there was no over-all inter-state control, with the result that there were in fact wide variations in law, in taxation, and in administration of land in the various states despite the presence of a British adviser in each.

To achieve greater uniformity and more effective administration, the four states were federated in 1895 under a common civil service controlled by a resident-general. A federal durbar was also formed with advisory but no legislative powers. In 1909 a federal council was created which, with the purpose of protecting the vested interests of the tin and rubber industries, curtailed further the autonomy of the states. These various moves toward centralization soon led to abuse and eventually to criticism of the entire administration. As a result, in 1935, reforms looking to decentralization were effected. Legislation was again placed in the hands of the state councils, though a number of public services, such as the public debt, remained under federal control. First steps in liberalizing the federal council had been taken in 1927 when the sultans retired from its membership and were replaced by four Malay appointees and one Indian, who sat with five Europeans and two Chinese.

THE UNFEDERATED MALAY STATES

Five states, Johore, Kedah, Perlis, Kelantan, and Trengganu, remained outside the Federation. Although the international status (protectorates) of these states was fixed by treaties similar to those between Britain and the federated states, the administrative tie was not so close. Corresponding to the resident in the federated state was the adviser in the unfederated state. This distinction was a measure of a more advanced civilization in the case of Johore and Kedah, and of remoteness and poverty in the case of Kelantan and Trengganu, where little foreign capital was invested and where a Malay population was all but untouched by European interests.

BRITISH ADMINISTRATION IN THE LATE
NINETEENTH CENTURY

After 1867, when the Straits Settlements passed under the Colonial Office, major reforms were effected in the administration of law in the colony. The executive and judicial functions, previously combined, were separated.

A special civil service was also created for Malay after 1867 designed to provide officials trained in the language and native customs of the Malays and the Chinese. By 1910 a special local civil service open to Malays only was also begun. On the eve of World War II, Malays and other Asiatics occupied all minor posts in departments of government. Malays constituted a majority of the police, and in the vernacular schools there were some 3,000 Malay and 4,000 Chinese teachers.[23]

---

[23] British administration in the period is summarized by Winstedt, *Britain and Malaya*, 47-51. The Chinese teachers were for the most part in private Chinese schools rather than in the official or subsidized Malay schools.

RECENT AND CONTEMPORARY GOVERNMENT IN MALAYA

Thus, British Malaya emerged into the twentieth century as ten separate governments under three different varieties of colonial administration. The practical difference between the Straits Settlements, a crown colony of the traditional type, and the protected states was not very great, for in both areas the actual administration has adhered closely to the crown colony pattern. This complexity of governmental organization has arisen as an evolutionary process, in most respects a result of a growing mixture of races. British control in Malaya was followed by a large immigration of Chinese and Indians until in 1937 the number of Chinese, as noted, almost equalled the Malay population. The process was one in which rubber and tin (developed by Western capitalists, Chinese traders, and laborers) suddenly transformed medieval Malaya into a twentieth-century state. In this process the Malays, one of the least politically minded of peoples, were destined to be submerged unless their political and economic interests received special protection. Thus the fundamental problem of government in Malaya has been "to discharge this obligation, and at the same time give legitimate weight to the interests which have been created by the Chinese and Indian immigrants and the British owners of tin mines and rubber plantations." [24]

DEMOCRACY AND NATIONALISM IN BRITISH MALAYA

British "Malaya is one of the few parts of Asia where the demand for democratic government hardly exists," and where on the eve of World War II there was no strongly assertive movement of nationalism. Historically this circumstance may be traced to the fact that the Malay States were not the unwilling victims of European colonial conquest but rather "sought the protection of European powers against the encroachments of foreign Asiatics." As a result there has been an absence of resentment toward the colonial overlord. Moreover, there was no strong tradition of Malay national control, and with two rather unimportant exceptions there have been no Malay revolts against British rule. On the contrary, the *pax Britannica* was welcomed by the peasantry and ultimately by the native sultans who came to enjoy under it greater prestige, security, and wealth.[25]

---

[24] Mills, "The Governments of Southeast Asia," 78-80.
[25] Virginia Thompson, "Nationalism and Nationalist Movements in Southeast Asia," in *Government and Nationalism in Southeast Asia* (New York, 1942), 169-172; Mills, *British Rule in Eastern Asia*, 3.

Such manifestations of nationalism as have occurred in Malaya are to be traced to "a small but growing middle class of [Malay] professional men and government employees which feels that such privileges as have been left or granted to Malaya have benefited solely the ruling class," by which is meant the native sultan aristocrats, and the foreign population of Westerners, Chinese, and Indians who control the economy. The vast majority of the Malays, the peasants, have remained largely apathetic in political matters. The political philosophy of the Malay has been to hope for benevolent despotism and to obey. What the small middle class was seeking was greater government effort to train Malays for self-government. Here, too, the Malay grievance is economic rather than political. Under British control economic opportunity in Malaya was "theoretically open to all alike, but the passive Malays did not seek them, while Chinese and Indians swarmed over their country," and by their greater aggressiveness reaped the rewards. Even Britain's protective and paternalistic legislation was not wholly successful in protecting the peasant from agrarian indebtedness to Indian moneylenders. To meet the threat of a landless peasantry modern British policy was seeking to educate the peasantry to co-operation and thrift through co-operative societies.[26]

The events of World War II, however, would seem to suggest that for the practical working purposes of politics it will no longer be possible to regard the Malays as the only settled, native inhabitants of the country, dismissing the Chinese and the Indians as outsiders. Much more is likely to be heard on the very real question of whose country Malaya is. The Japanese occupation appears to have intensified greatly both racial and class sentiment and hostility.

BURMA

Burma, long a subject of song and story, and more recently the scene of wartime romance and tragedy clustering around the Burma and Stilwell Roads, has an area of 261,000 square miles, about the size of Texas, and an extremely important geographical location between the two great civilizations of Asia, the Indian and the Chinese. On the west Burma is bordered by the Indian province and the Bay of Bengal; on the north, by Tibet; on the east, by southwestern China and French Indo-China; on the south, by Siam and the Malay Peninsula. It is this unique geographical location which goes far to explain why Burma, es-

---

[26] The whole problem of peasant debt and the Malay standard of living is treated by Mills, *British Rule in Eastern Asia,* 275-290.

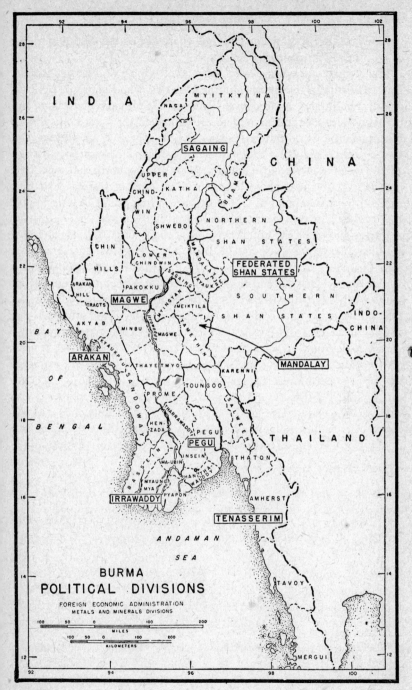

BURMA
POLITICAL DIVISIONS

FOREIGN ECONOMIC ADMINISTRATION
METALS AND MINERALS DIVISIONS

100 50 0 100 200
MILES

100 50 0 100 200
KILOMETERS

United States, Department of State. Department of Map Intelligence and Cartography.

769

sentially neither Indian nor Chinese, "partakes of the culture and life of both her more populous neighbors." [27]

The country has two well-defined regions, Upper and Lower Burma. Lower Burma in the south comprises the deltas and plains of the Irrawaddy, the Sittang, and the lower Salween, the province of Arakan, and the Tenasserim Peninsula. Here are produced the great crops of rice (Burma is the world's greatest exporter of this grain), tin, and lumber. Upper Burma is a vastly different country, formed of successive narrow valleys and the towering mountain systems of the north and northwest regions. With the exception of tin and oil, most of Burma's extensive mineral wealth is found in Upper Burma. Only coal is lacking to give Burma the common requisites of industrial civilization.

Burma's population, numbering more than 16,000,000, consists of a considerable number of language groups, of which the outstanding are the Burmese, numbering about 10,000,000; the Karen, 1,350,000; the Tai or Shan, 1,000,000; and more than 1,000,000 that use various Indian languages. Many non-Burmese use the Burmese language, and the fact that Burmese has not become the universal tongue of the country is due in part to the general hesitancy of the Burmese people to enter business. As a people, the Burmese, concentrated in Central and Lower Burma, are buoyant and spontaneous in temperament and have been described as "perhaps the most attractive people in the whole of the British Empire." Their critics regard them as "light-hearted, irresponsible, and even lacking in perseverance and ambition." Certainly they are possessed of racial pride and a growing sense of nationalism. The religion of the Burmese and Shans is Buddhism.

HISTORICAL BURMA

The long and earlier, as distinct from the short, modern, history of Burma is a story of migrations of peoples who came primarily from eastern Tibet and western China. To this racial tie with China was added in the eleventh century an even stronger cultural bond with India through the conquest of Burma by Hinayana Buddhism. After the thirteenth century, when the Mongols invaded the country, Burmese history is marked by successive periods of political disintegration interspersed with the appearance of aggressive and strong military rulers whose conquests spread at times far beyond the borders of present day

---

[27] The most convenient and comprehensive scholarly treatment is John L. Christian, *Modern Burma* (Berkeley, 1942), on which I have relied heavily in the following brief sketch.

Burma. At the close of the eighteenth and during the early years of the nineteenth century, Burma was a military power of consequence. It was during this period that her armies twice invaded Siam, conquered parts of Assam, and defeated invading Chinese forces. Significantly, this era of military power and expansion coincided with the consolidation of British power in India. Thus the stage was set for Anglo-Burmese conflict on the ill-defined Burma-Bengal frontier.

THE ANGLO-BURMESE WARS

Long before the nineteenth century, European traders in the East had a secondary interest in Burmese commerce. As far back as the beginning of the seventeenth century, the English, French, and Dutch had exported teakwood from Burma, but the country lay beyond the interests of the spice trade and therefore did not become a major center of European commerce. However, as a prelude to European involvement in Burma's internal affairs, the British and the French, contending for supremacy in India, gave aid respectively to opposing Burmese factions in the decade of 1750. During the next 75 years exaggerated reports reached the outer world of Burma's power and wealth, and eventually frontier incidents provided the occasion for the First Anglo-Burmese War. As a result of three conflicts, the First, the Second, and the Third Anglo-Burmese Wars, 1824, 1852, and 1885, respectively, Burma became a British colony; the final steps in annexation (1886) were hastened as a result of French intrigue in Upper Burma.[28]

The new colony was made a province of the British Indian Empire, a status which it retained until 1937, when it was separated from India and became virtually a self-governing dominion, though a colony in form. During the colonial years, Burma revealed marked growth toward modernization in her economic, and to a somewhat lesser degree, in her political, life. As a measure of this growth, by 1940 no colonial area of Southeast Asia, excepting only the Philippines, enjoyed so wide a measure of political autonomy. The development, however, was rudely interrupted by World War II, by the Japanese invasion and conquest, and by the long campaigns in the China-Burma-India theater of war. For good or ill, the war served to enhance the political maturity of many Burmese leaders and thus contributed to the rebirth of Burmese nationalism which had been evident in pre-war years. The national movement must be seen as a product of Burmese historical tradi-

---

[28] The story of Anglo-French rivalry over Burma is given in Christian, *Modern Burma*, ch. iv, 43-56.

tion, of economic development under British rule, and of political forces of nationalism dominating world thought in the twentieth century.

BURMA'S ECONOMIC DEVELOPMENT

The attitude of the Western world toward Burma in the nineteenth century was primarily that the country was a geographical area whose resources invited economic development. It was natural that this should be the attitude of the English East India Company not only because commerce was the business of the company but also because Burma with rich resources possessed neither capital, technological training, nor modern commercial experience, and her peoples had not developed an aptitude for business. Whatever may have been the merits or shortcomings of the economic approach, its achievements in Burma under British rule were indeed great.[29]

After World War I, the emphasis on the colonial-economic approach met its first serious challenge, and, in keeping with public sentiment of the post-war years, British policy became more responsive to the idea of self-determination of colonial peoples and, more specifically, to the idea of self-government. Nevertheless, "the need for economic and political reform in Burma outran the speed of adjustment. Inertia had to be overcome, and it was not easy to decide exactly what to do." Thus many basic economic problems (agricultural credit, farm tenancy, immigration) were not grappled with until after 1937. As a result, prolonged economic maladjustment had created much popular unrest by the time of the Japanese invasion of 1942. Behind this picture were fundamental evolutionary changes in Burma's economy covering more than a century of British rule.

Burma's economy in pre-British days was semi-feudal, based not so much on the country's frequently predatory central government as on the social groupings involved in a subsistence agriculture. The creation of surplus wealth was not a primary object, and such earnings as the peasant might spare went for the support of the Buddhist church. By the beginning of the twentieth century, this simple, agricultural society had been invaded by the aggressive, *laissez-faire* commercialism of British, Indian, and Chinese traders and businessmen. The development of the teak industry, and the transformation of the Irrawaddy delta jungles into rice fields created a new economic picture involving

---

[29] John F. Cady, "Economic Development in Burma," *Far Eastern Survey*, XV (1946), 1-4. The pioneer comprehensive economic study of Burma is J. S. Furnivall, *The Political Economy of Burma* (Rangoon, 1931).

Burmese and Indian labor, Indian merchants and moneylenders, British capital, and a British-Burmese civil service. Huge profits made possible increasing colonial revenues from which came better roads, improved public health, etc. Little was done, however, to create an import market. Standards of living failed to keep pace with productivity. Since business was not concerned with the social consequences of its activity, and since the bulk of the native peoples did not understand the commercial and industrial revolution taking place about them, the result was a major degree of social dislocation. Instability became typical of the old native village life; the educational influence of the Buddhist clergy declined; a migrant laboring class appeared and contributed to increasing lawlessness. In a word, the new prosperity was not in general shared by the Burmese peasant. After the Indian moneylender, the landlord, the tax collector, and the Chinese merchant had each taken his toll or his profit, the peasant had less than enough on which to live until the next crop. Wholesale foreclosures on land mortgages in the decade of the 1930's created intense anti-Indian feeling. This was aggravated by the inability of the Burmese to compete with Indian labor, and by the inability of government prior to 1940 to deal with Indian immigration. The bitter anti-Indian race riots of 1930 and 1938 were the result. The British were also a target for this resentment, because British courts gave Indians the protection of the law to which they were legally entitled.

SELF-GOVERNMENT, POLITICS, AND NATIONALISM

Burmese manifestations of nationalism are, in the main, a recent, twentieth-century development. During the nineteenth century most Burmese appear in general to have welcomed the stability and peace of British control which replaced the factional strife which had existed under native rule. By the later years of the century there was a measure of local self-government exercised through the agency of the village headmen and later through representative district councils. Neither system enjoyed much success. The council system might have contributed something to Burma's training in representative government but for the fact that in Burma there was no public-spirited group willing to perform public service without pay. The record of municipal councils in the cities was equally bad. In general, Burmese councilmen preferred to dispense with civic improvement rather than vote the taxes to pay for it.[30]

[30] John F. Cady, "Conflicting Attitudes toward Burma," *Far Eastern Survey*, XV (1946), 27-29.

The central government of the colony acquired a new constitution in 1922 which provided for a legislative council instead of the previous advisory one. More than 17 percent of the Burmese population enjoyed the suffrage, and more than a majority of the council was elected from Burmese constituencies. The constitution, however, was extremely unpopular, allegedly because it set up a dyarchy dividing executive authority into powers reserved to the governor (defense, foreign affairs, finance, higher education, justice, communications), and those transferred to responsible ministers (agriculture, forests, health, primary education, and local government). Burmese opposition to the constitution was continuous and reached to the point where most candidates elected to the council were pledged not to accept posts in the transferred ministries.

By 1930, when economic distress had added its weight to the general political discontent, political groups outside the council had become more noisy than the council itself. A serious rebellion against British authority led by Saya San in 1930 revealed the degree to which popular sentiment was prepared to challenge the established order. Out of the rebellion came the organization of the *Dobama* (We Burmans) Society of young nationalists demanding independence and calling themselves *Thakin* (Lord) in derision of the earlier custom of addressing Britishers by this term. By 1940, the *Dobama* party had won substantial popular influence, its purposefulness being in marked contrast with motives of personal rivalry which appeared to control so many Burmese politicians in the legislative council.

The Imperial Commission of 1929, investigating constitutional reform for the Indian Empire, recommended that Burma be separated from India and that a program of extending representative government be carried out in spite of the fact that in the Commission's view Burma's record with self-government was not encouraging to the future of representative government. The new Burmese constitution of 1935 which resulted gave to Burma a qualified dominion status. Ministerial responsibility to an elected legislature was limited by extensive powers reserved by the governor.[31] The new constitution went into effect in 1937 with the active support of the Burmese electorate, though the qualifications on full dominion status, as the Burmese saw them, were not popular. Nevertheless, the operation of the new government was marred from the outset by intense partisan rivalry between political

[31] These included power to veto legislation, to put in force essential regulations not passed by the legislature, and to assume all necessary powers in situations of emergency.

leaders who spent so much time corralling personal followings that they contributed little to policy or administration. Corruption and bribery increased to an alarming extent in all branches of the government where political patronage entered in.[36]

There can be little doubt that Burmese nationalism was further matured by the experiences of the war, and by war and post-war developments in India. Nevertheless, this growth has not simplified the issues now being faced. These issues, like post-war problems in other areas, are exceedingly complex and are not to be resolved by the single issue of immediate and complete independence. Whatever the future political structure may be, those who are responsible for Burma's public life will be called upon to deal with a vast array of tasks: rehabilitation, Indian immigration, farm debts and credit, and foreign sources for capital, to say nothing of the political difficulties in any adjustment to full dominion status.[37]

POST-WAR BURMESE POLITICS

The formal surrender of Burma was signed by the Japanese at Rangoon in September, 1945, and the country was immediately placed under a British emergency administration headed by Governor Dorman Smith and an executive council. This administration was opposed violently by General Aung San's Anti-Fascist People's Freedom League, which appeared to be the most powerful force in Burmese public opinion.[38] By April, 1946, Burma's vigorous nationalism brought the assurance of the British government that Burma would be given "full self-government." Unrest, however, continued, revealing in debates in the British House of Commons that Burma was torn by robbery, violence, and murder, partly inspired by the effects of "Japanese-stirred nationalism," and that British land and naval forces were in action against guerrilla bands. There had been further mass demonstrations in Rangoon by the Anti-Fascist League. As 1946 ended, British policy revealed marked

[36] John F. Cady, "Conflicting Attitudes toward Burma," *Far Eastern Survey,* XV (1946), 30-31.
[37] Mutual oppression among different ethnic groups in Burma is too recent to permit of optimism as to what would happen if European control were removed entirely. The evidence is clear that the protection of minorities in Southeast Asia, and especially in Burma, is a vital contemporary issue.
[38] Prior to World War II, Aung San was on the British blacklist for Burma. During the war he led Burmese troops first against the British and then against the Japanese. He was Minister of Defense in the puppet cabinet of Ba Maw, and as a civilian later held office as Vice-President of the Executive Council under the British.

concessions to this violent nationalism. Major General Sir Hubert Rance, the new governor, had formed a coalition executive council including representatives of all Burmese political parties. Burma was entering a new political future, but she had not yet begun to deal with the grave social and economic questions which are the heritage of her past. As widespread nationalist protests continued, Prime Minister Attlee, after announcing that "it is for the Burmese people to decide their own future," received Aung San and a Burmese delegation in London (January, 1947) to speed the processes of independence. The resulting agreement "by which the people of Burma may achieve their independence within or without the Commonwealth," provided for a constituent assembly to take immediate control of Burma's armed forces. Implementation of this agreement resulted in further unrest in Burma. On July 19, 1947, "terrorists" using machine guns killed six and wounded two members of Burma's new fourteen-man Executive Council in the Council Chamber in Rangoon. The dead included Nationalist leader U Aung Sang. These events were the more disturbing since British-Burmese agreement on arrangements for Burmese independence had been reached shortly before the assassinations.

FRENCH INDO-CHINA

The fourth major colony of Europe in Southeast Asia is French Indo-China, which during the twentieth century has included five political and administrative divisions. These are: the colony of Cochin China, and the protectorates of Tonkin, Annam, Laos, and Cambodia. The total area, 286,000 square miles, is approximately the combined area of Texas and West Virginia. The population is some 24,000,000, including nearly 500,000 Chinese, and 42,000 Europeans, nearly all of whom are French. The concentrations of population are in the Mekong Delta and valleys of the south and the Red River Valley in the north. The central mountainous area harbors settlements along the seacoast and in the Mekong Valley of the interior. Each of the five states has its own peculiar geographical setting. Life in Tonkin, the northern state, centers in the valley of the Red River and in the cities of Hanoi and Haipong. Annam is a long, coastal, mountainous area with limited and isolated coastal plains. Laos to the west in the interior includes the hill country of the upper central Mekong. Cambodia covers the plain of the lower Mekong, and Cochin China covers the delta of this great river with its important city of Saigon. Rice culture is the predominant form of agriculture, followed by the plantation culture of rubber, tea, and coffee. Mineral wealth is extensive in the north where coal, tin, zinc, tungsten, chromium, iron, and other ores are mined. In Indo-China as in Burma there is an extensive export trade in rice.[39]

The political divisions of the area are not coterminous with the complex of racial groups and cultures which are found in Indo-China. Of these groups the Annamese predominate, making up about 70 percent of the population. Culturally, Annamese civilization reveals a strong Chinese influence; Annam was for many centuries a tributary state of China. Confucian concepts dominate most phases of Annamite life. Buddhism in modified forms also has a foothold, though it commands little popular prestige. Taoism is present in some of its lower forms, particularly sorcery. Mixed with these formal religious importations are substantial remnants of many indigenous cults. The resulting religious picture, though somewhat obscure, is distinguished by a comforting absence of fanaticism.[40]

The peoples of Cambodia and Laos, in contrast to the Annamese, are predominantly Indian in culture. The Cambodians, the second major racial group, representing some 6 percent of Indo-China's population, include descendants of ancient Khmer stock. At Angkor in Cambodia still remain the magnificent ruins of temples and palaces, built by forced labor, evidence of the Khmer civilization of eight centuries ago. Feudal relationships, with emphasis on powerful ties of clan, have tended to persist strongly among the Cambodians. Brahmanism and Buddhism have been the dominating religious philosophies.

The people of Laos, the long belt of territory of the central and upper Mekong Valley, are probably the descendants of early immigrants from China and Tibet. Tribal and family organization still predominates among them. Brahman and Buddhistic influence is found here also.

THE COMING OF THE FRENCH

The Portuguese, who arrived in the sixteenth century, were the first modern Europeans to reach Indo-China.[41] Their objectives here, as in

---

[39] Note the discussion of geography and resources in George B. Cressey, *Asia's Lands and Peoples* (New York, 1944), 515-520. The intensive agriculture of Tonkin and northern Annam, carried to excess by pressure of population, has created underemployment and poverty and the pushing out of population into less hospitable sections of Cambodia.

[40] Virginia Thompson, *French Indo-China* (New York, 1937), 43.

[41] Chinese colonization here as in Malaya, the Philippines, and Netherlands India, long antedated European colonization, but in some respects was similar to it. The early Chinese colonizers were controlled by the seasons which prevented merchant vessels from crossing the seas in the months of the typhoons. Hence "factories," or trading posts, were established and grew into Chinese colonies. In general they were not militant, and they were unsupported by the home government. Thus in time they disappeared. The Europeans in contrast were armed, able to fight off pirates, able to pit local princes against each other, and thereby to establish permanent posts.

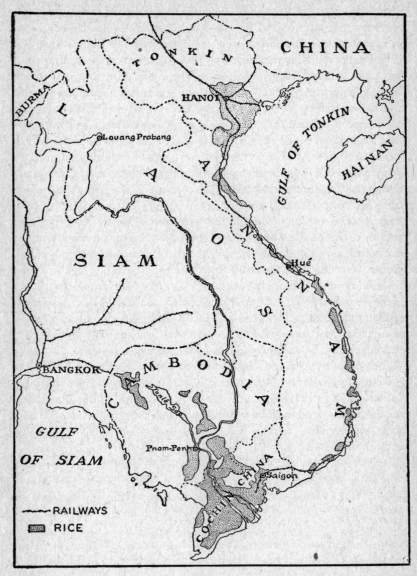

MAP OF FRENCH INDO-CHINA, SHOWING POLITICAL DIVISIONS, RAILWAYS, AND CHIEF RICE-PRODUCING REGIONS. *From Daniel R. Bergsmark, "Economic Geography of Asia."*

China, were trade and the establishment of Jesuit missions. French missionaries and traders appeared in the seventeenth century, but the real foundations of French political power in Indo-China were laid in the years from 1747 to 1858. In the earlier years of this period, 1747-1774, France made diplomatic contact with Annam in the hope of opening trade and of using the region as a base for attacks on Dutch and British commerce. In 1787 the first treaty between France and Cochin China was signed. This was the work of Pigneau de Behaine, Bishop of Adran, ecclesiastic, diplomat, and soldier of fortune, who aided the king of Cochin China against rebels in the hope of furthering French territorial expansion and in turn the spread of Catholic missions in the peninsula. The early nineteenth century, however, was marked by violent anti-Christian movements and the refusal of native rulers to receive French diplomatic and naval missions. Later, Napoleon III, failing in 1855 to secure a treaty with Annam that would put an end to the executions of French and Spanish ecclesiastics, in co-operation with Spain dispatched a naval expedition, 1858, at the time of the *Arrow* War in China. Successful campaigns were conducted against Tourane and Saigon. In 1862, France wrested a treaty from Annam which guaranteed religious toleration, opened three ports to French and Spanish trade, and provided that Annam pay an indemnity of $4,000,000, and cede portions of Cochin China to France. The following year Cambodia was made a French protectorate, and in 1867 remaining provinces of Cochin China were annexed.

From this time until the beginning of the present century, France moved steadily forward to complete the conquest of Indo-China, each move seemingly timed nicely by intervals of a decade as though there were some peculiar magic in this regularity. After the French had applied military pressure in 1874, France formally recognized the independence of Annam, and in return Annam opened the Red River in Tonkin to French trade, named a number of ports open to French commerce, and granted extraterritoriality to Europeans. By the close of another decade, 1884, Annam was forced to recognize herself a protectorate of France. Since Annam, at least formally, had been a tributary state of China, this development precipitated Franco-Chinese hostilities ending in inevitable Chinese defeat. In still another decade, 1893, France demanded of Siam, in the name of Annam, certain inland territories to the east of the Mekong which were organized as the new protectorate of Laos. Again in a decade, 1904, further territory held by Siam was ceded to both Cambodia and Laos, and an additional grant to Cambodia at Siam's expense was made in 1907. Thus by the beginning of the twentieth century, France by military force had become the military master of an empire in Indo-China.[42]

GOVERNMENT IN FRENCH INDO-CHINA

Government in French Indo-China has been designed to attain objectives quite different from those sought in neighboring British colonies of Southeast Asia. Whereas in the latter, autonomy within the Empire has been the goal during the past twenty-five years with self-government being introduced by progressive stages, in the former "the intention has been that the dependency should be drawn progressively closer to France as an integral part of a closely knit empire dominated by the mother country."[43] In practice this has meant: that the governor-general has little local independence; that most natives do not acquire French citizenship but remain subjects; that colonial legislative councils have little authority; and that the very limited representation of the colony (Cochin China) in the French Chamber of Deputies is chosen by and speaks for the French and not for the native community.

While Cochin China, a colony, was administered directly by French officials, the other four provinces of Indo-China, which were technically protectorates, maintained their native administrations operating under close French supervision and control. Although the native mandarins in the protectorates were not simple figureheads, the power of the French officials there was hardly less than in the colony of Cochin China, where direct rule prevailed.

NATIONALISM IN FRENCH INDO-CHINA

It is at least as difficult to generalize on nationalism in French Indo-China as it is to do so in the case of other colonial areas of Southeast Asia. Divergences of race and culture, a product of the many migrations that peopled Indo-China, means that nationalism struggles in "an inextricable tangle of minorities of race, language, and religion."[44]

[42] French penetration, like that of the British in Malaya, was spasmodic and opportunistic, but in addition it was influenced by a desire to gain a foothold in China. French administrators in Indo-China tended to be more militant than the British in Malaya. They were less thorough in working out administrative methods, and they exerted less control over matters of no direct interest to themselves.

The political and diplomatic history of the French conquest is covered adequately by Thomas E. Ennis, *French Policy and Developments in Indochina* (Chicago, 1936), 1-51; and by Herbert I. Priestley, *France Overseas: A Study of Modern Imperialism* (New York, 1938), 102-118, 216-243.

[43] Mills, "The Governments of Southeast Asia," in *Government and Nationalism in Southeast Asia* (New York, 1942), 108.

[44] Rupert Emerson, "Introduction," *Government and Nationalism in Southeast Asia,* 19. The seeming strength of Indo-China's "nationalism" in recent years is explained

The roots of Annamese nationalism in varying forms may be traced to the distant past when Annam was under the political as well as the cultural sway of China. In modern times, Annamese nationalism derives from influences of the French conquest. Although French colonial administrators never consciously promoted nationalism, "French institutions were so impregnated with the liberal ideas of 1789 that they unconsciously fostered patriotism and a love of political liberty in subject peoples." [45]

Moreover, French rule was the result of a long and bitter conquest in which native resistance was compounded of diverse elements: patriotism, brigandage, and piracy.

Unrest, political and economic in its base, was typical of Indo-China in the decade prior to World War I. Stimulation came from Japan's victory in the Russo-Japanese War, but more particularly from a new interest among Annamese intellectuals in the eighteenth-century French political philosophy of Rousseau and Montesquieu. Many native intellectuals, however, were disillusioned in 1908 when, as the result of a conservative reaction among the French in Indo-China, Hanoi University was closed. This reactionary trend in French policy was further emphasized a few years later when France used forced Indo-Chinese labor in Europe during World War I. During and after the war, too, the more rapid economic development of Indo-China created additional causes of native resentment.

As in other parts of Southeast Asia, the Chinese in French Indo-China were a focal point of native attack. An outstanding case was the Chinese boycott of 1919. The Chinese in Indo-China showed little interest in politics, but they controlled the native rice and fish trade and the sources of native credit. In general the Annamite attitude toward the Chinese has been one of admiration of Chinese culture and business acumen but also of deep resentment against Chinese control of native commercial economy. Annamite nationalists were as much opposed to Chinese economic as to French political control. An additional factor closely linked with the nationalist agitations of the 1920's was the rapid development of the Communist movement.

partly by the nearness to China: each country affords refuge to the revolutionaries of the other, and hence there is mutual stimulation of nationalistic discontent. A further stimulus to discontent and nationalism has been the inferior labor legislation of Indo-China, compared with that of other colonies, and the difficulty of enforcing laws because of the diffusion of mines and lumber concessions over a large mountainous hinterland. The result has been shown in many strikes and minor outbreaks of revolt.

[45] Virginia Thompson, "Nationalism and Nationalistic Movements in Southeast Asia," in *Government and Nationalism in Southeast Asia,* 198; and the same author's larger study, *French Indo-China,* 475-494.

Prior to World War II, however, the nationalist movement had enjoyed only a very limited success. This was not wholly due to French opposition. The Indo-Chinese nationalist movement itself was not basically constructive. In the first place, it possessed distinct racial limitations, since it was confined to the Annamese, who continued to regard Cambodians and Laotians as fit only to be subject peoples. Moreover, Annamese nationalists were divided among themselves by mutual jealousies and by the lack of a constructive national program, and they were unsupported by any vital public spirit. On the other hand, French policy in the pre-war years was none too wholesome in its rigid and often cruel suppression of nationalist and, in particular, Communist groups. By the eve of World War II, France had succeeded in indoctrinating native intellectuals with French culture, but by her failure to embody the concepts of this culture in native political institutions, she failed to win native loyalty against the Japanese invasion. The war was thus an occasion for a reassertion of nationalism.[46]

THE INDO-CHINESE FEDERATION

Extending qualified recognition to this reassertive native nationalism, the French government in March, 1945, announced that French Indo-China would be given partial self-government at the close of the war. The plan called for an Indo-Chinese Federation in which native citizens would also be citizens of the "French Union," a new term to include France and all parts of "the imperial community." Indo-China was to have a federal government, under a governor-general, composed of Indo-Chinese and resident French ministers. As the war in the Pacific ended, Indo-China was occupied by Allied, including French and Chinese, troops. Initial clashes between the French and Annamese nationalists were halted by a truce, September 28, 1945. Five months later, March 6, 1946, France concluded an agreement recognizing the Viet Nam Republic (the former Annam and Tonkin) as "a free state within the Indo-Chinese Federation and the French Union." Later, in March, Ho Chi-minh, president of the new republic, unsuccessfully re-

---

[46] Of all Western colonizers in Southeast Asia, the French have been outstanding for their lack of racial feeling, and for their willingness to treat Asiatics as equals when in fact they are equals in education, refinement, or attainment. Hence, there has been no antagonism to Indo-Chinese nationalists of French education as long as they abstained from trying to propagandize the simple peasants. What led to persecution was that the Indo-Chinese nationalists, French in almost everything but appearance, learned, principally from China, that their own political futility would end the moment they could bring large masses of the working people behind their banners.

quested American recognition. On June 1, 1946, French authorities announced formation of an "independent Cochin-Chinese Republic" within the Federation and the Union. These were significant if also qualified steps toward self-government. Indo-China appeared to be entering a new and what is likely to prove a difficult period in her history.

SIAM

For the better part of the past century, Siam has been something of a political curiosity in Southeast Asia—a small independent state wedged between and hedged about by the colonial possessions of Europe and the United States. On the west and northwest, Siam borders on Burma; on the east and northeast, on French Indo-China; on the south, it is open to the Gulf of Siam, beyond which lie Britain's Malay Peninsula, the South China Seas, the Dutch Indies, and the Philippines. This legal, and to a degree actual, independence, however, has not been a result of the military prowess of Siam or the wisdom of its rulers, but rather of agreement between European colonial rivals—England in Burma and Malaya, and France in Indo-China—to preserve this small kingdom as a buffer state. In terms of cold-blooded politics, Siamese independence has been therefore a measure of European suffrance rather than an expression of the cultural entity of an Asiatic people.

THE GEOGRAPHIC SCENE

Siam, with an area of some 200,000 square miles, approximately the combined area of Colorado and Wyoming, has a natural border of mountains on the west, north, and northwest. To the central east, the Mekong forms the boundary; on the southeast, Cambodia. One major river, the Menam Chao Bhraya, usually known as the Menam, lies wholly in Siamese territory. In general, the country falls into three geographical areas. The southwestern delta and plain in the vicinity of Bangkok, the capital, is the region of rice culture; the north is mountainous with steep valleys running north and south; the remainder of the country, chiefly the northeast, is an area of rolling hills. Siam, of course, is a land of the monsoon, featured by two rather distinct seasons: the rainy season of the southwest monsoon, May through October; and the dry season of winter, November through February, followed by the hot weather of early spring.[47]

---

[47] Cressey, *Asia's Lands and Peoples,* 507-509.

SIAMESE ECONOMY

Life in Siam depends almost exclusively on rice culture. Some 95 percent of the crop land produces rice and, prior to 1940, about one third of the crop was exported. In the earlier years of the century this export trade went primarily to Europe. After World War I it was diverted to China and India. Siam also produces some rubber and copra. Hardwood forests and some tin deposits are among the principal natural resources. Coal is scarce and no petroleum has been discovered.[48]

PEOPLES OF SIAM

In the course of history successive waves of immigrant Mongol peoples entered Siam from the north; remnants of many of these groups survive. The linguistics of the early settlers were as varied as their ethnology. Of the main languages and dialects spoken in Siam, the Thai, used by the people of the same name, who are among the more recent comers to the peninsula, is the most important. The Thai probably entered Siam from Yünnan. In time their language was adopted by many of the earlier migrants.[49]

SIAM'S FOREIGN RELATIONS

Any discussion of the interminable disputes which long marked the relations of Siam with her immediate neighbors, such as Burma and Cambodia, is beyond the scope of this discussion. Her relations with China are extremely old, antedating the twelfth century; as a result of these contacts Siam came to occupy the status of a tributary state. The Portuguese established commercial relations with Siam in the sixteenth century after their capture of Malacca. The first Dutch and English merchants arrived at the beginning of the seventeenth century. When the French appeared, somewhat later, a number of Siamese embassies visited the Court of Versailles. Toward the close of the eighteenth cen-

---

[48] The present agricultural (rice) economy in Siam and also in Burma provides almost no clue to the potential richness and diversity possible in the uses of these lands once enough capital has been invested in the hilly and highland areas. The pre-eminence of rice cultivation rests in part on the fact that it was the quickest means of bringing revenue to governments. Only in very recent times have the governments of Southeast Asia directed their attention to improved dairy farming, horticulture, and improved food production for domestic consumption.

The most definitive study of rice in the economy of Southeast Asia is V. D. Wickizer and M. K. Bennett, *The Rice Economy of Monsoon Asia* (Stanford University, 1941).

[49] For accounts of the ethnological and linguistic groups in Siam note Virginia Thompson, *Thailand: The New Siam* (New York, 1941), 7-15; H. G. Deignan, *Siam: Land of Free Men* (Washington, 1943).

tury, Siam was all but completely despoiled by her Asiatic neighbors, Burma and Cambodia, yet finally, under a series of able though erratic leaders, she repelled the invaders. During this period of conflict (the late eighteenth century), Siam's contacts with Europe virtually ceased. She continued, however, to send embassies to China at irregular intervals. China regarded these envoys as bearers of tribute from a dependent state. Siam's continued interest in them arose from the fact that they were successful and profitable commercial ventures.

Just as in the seventeenth century it was Siam's almost incessant military involvement with her neighbors that prompted her to seek aid from Europeans, so it was again in the early nineteenth century when she again began to exchange native products for firearms secured at first from the Portuguese. Her first major commercial treaties were made with Great Britain in 1822 and 1826, and with the United States in 1833. This was the first treaty concluded by the United States with a nation of the Far East. In 1855-56, Britain, France, and the United States concluded further treaties with Siam containing rights of extraterritoriality and a conventional tariff. On this occasion Townsend Harris was the American envoy.[50]

During most of the nineteenth century, despite these commercial accords, the fate of Siam as a nation hung in the uneasy scales of Anglo-French rivalry in Southeast Asia. Britain's successive annexations of Burma made her a territorial neighbor of Siam on the west and north; the advent of France in Cochin-China, Cambodia, and Annam brought her to Siam's border on the north, east, and southeast. Indeed, the French protectorate in Cambodia was achieved by breaking the control of Siam over that state. Much later in the century, 1893, Siam, in a treaty with France, renounced her claims to territory east of the Mekong (Laos); this territory was ceded technically to Annam, already a French protectorate, and then organized by France as the separate protectorate of Laos. In 1896 growing friction between the European rivals on the borders of Siam was abated by an Anglo-French treaty which created British and French spheres in western and eastern Siam respectively. A little later, 1904, France secured at Siam's expense further cessions of territory to Cambodia and Laos. After these transfers the Anglo-French rivals agreed to annex no further territory in their respective zones of influence. Nevertheless, in 1907, some 7,000 square miles were added to Cambodia, though France restored some territory previously

---

[50] For the American-Siamese treaties see Hunter Miller, ed., *Treaties and Other International Acts of the United States of America* (Washington, D. C., 1931-42), III, 741-788; VII, 329-400.

acquired, and agreed that Siamese courts should exercise jurisdiction over French Asiatic subjects and protected persons on Siamese soil. Two years later, 1909, Britain added territory to her protected Malay states of Trengganu, Kelantan, and Kedah. In return Siam regained jurisdiction over British subjects in her territory. Later treaties following World War I provided for the complete relinquishment of extraterritoriality when Siam's new and modernized codes should go into effect. As against these gains, Siam gave up her claims to some 90,000 square miles of territory on the east, and some 15,000 on the southwest.

POLITICS IN MODERN SIAM

Politics in twentieth-century Siam has been concerned with three major problems: 1) with a movement from autocracy to some form of representative government; 2) with efforts to create a national unification; and 3) with the task of maintaining the country's independence, so frequently threatened in the nineteenth and the twentieth centuries— at first by the missionary, mercantile, and the political interests of the Western powers, and more recently by the expansion of Japan. All these problems were closely related.

It was in the middle nineteenth century that a rather remarkable ruler, King Mongkut, while attempting to preserve his territory by playing against each other the English and French rivals, recognized the need for modernizing the country. The longer reign of his son, Chulalongkorn, 1868-1910, was a period of domestic reform. Progress was hastened because the people were accustomed to accept without question the commands of an absolute sovereign, and because the administration itself was largely a family affair, since various departments of the government were being headed by princes of the royal house.

FROM ABSOLUTISM TO CONSTITUTIONALISM

The program of reform and modernization effected many changes in Siam. Slavery was abolished. Many Siamese studied abroad and returned with a knowledge of new technical skills and new viewpoints toward politics, thus preparing the way for the downfall of absolutism. The gradual creation of a new and more widely selected body of civil servants provided the beginnings of a new political group and ultimately a revolutionary party. When in the depression years of the late 1920's, the dynasty applied a policy of retrenchment, the "Promoters," as the revolutionary group called itself, including a number of army officers, took over the government, June, 1932, and imposed a constitution upon the king, who himself favored constitutionalism but who had been restrained up to this time by members of the royal house. The revolution was entirely peaceful, for both the royal and the revolutionary parties hoped to avoid giving any pretext for foreign intervention.

THE CONSTITUTIONAL REGIME

The new constitution virtually excluded the royal family from political power which, by reason of the large number of appointed members in the new Assembly, was now in the hands of the Promoters. The power of the latter, so long as they remained united, was now as absolute as had been the king's.

The new government promoted education as an ultimate test for the franchise; sought to implement a program of a national economic policy to provide remunerative work for all; and attempted to stimulate a political consciousness which would eventually express itself through political parties.

Meanwhile, however, factionalism had appeared between the civilian and the military wings of the Promoters' party. For five years, 1932-37, Phya Bahol, as Prime Minister, held the two groups in unsteady balance. When he was succeeded by Luang Pibul Songkran, Siam entered upon a program of extreme nationalism implemented by the methods of the dictator.

Within limitations prescribed by the mild temperament of Siam's Buddhist tradition, and aided by his own personal attractiveness and diplomatic skill, Luang Pibul Songkran aped the procedures of the Central European dictators. Foreigners were pushed out of the nation's economic life and, as World War II developed, Pibul was able to take over the investments of United Nations nationals. Educational and cultural nationalization was now stressed more than ever. It met little opposition among the many ethnic groups already closely assimilated with the Thai people, but this was not the case when the program was applied to the Moslem Malays and to the Chinese. An already acute Malay irritation was aggravated in 1943 when Japan prompted Siam to annex four of the Malay states from which Japanese arms had driven the British in 1942. This added nearly a million Malays to Siam's population. The Chinese also presented a problem to the new disciplined nationalism. Composed both of immigrants and of many born in Siam, they numbered in the neighborhood of two million. Lack of normal diplomatic relations between Siam and China in recent years complicated this problem. In general, the Siamese policy was to tolerate the adult Chinese population but to apply a rigid policy of assimilation to the children. Finally, the new nationalism of Pibul sought the return of all lost territory where Thai people resided in numbers. Suggestive of this revived policy of expansion was Pibul's edict of 1939, which changed the name of the country from Siam to Thailand. With Japan's consent, demands on France for territorial retrocessions were carried out in 1940. From this event dated Japan's domination of the country's policy. Although Pibul had concluded a treaty of neutrality with Britain in 1940, he made Thailand an active ally of Japan, ultimately declaring war on Great Britain and the United States. Great Britain retaliated with a declaration of war, but the United States ignored the Siamese declaration on the professed ground that it was unconstitutional. The Japanese army that occupied Thailand interfered little with the administration, but their presence increased Pibul's power. Nevertheless, his regime came to an end, July, 1944, as a result of economic dislocation caused by the war. Siam's foreign trade other than with Japan had disappeared at the beginning of the war. Now the trade with Japan was lost as Tokyo began to face defeat. This trade had become Thailand's only source for manufactured goods.

The succeeding government of Luang Khovid Abhaiwongse restored civilian influence, repealed discriminatory measures against Malays and Chinese, restored freedom of speech, secretly hampered the Japanese, though they could not be resisted openly, and even sheltered an American Office of Strategic Services mission in Bangkok. The information which this mission sent out to its government was dispatched from a radio station located, of all places, in the Bangkok police headquarters.

As World War II drew to a close, the Regent, Luang Pradit, proclaimed peace in the name of the king, annulled Thailand's declarations of war, and offered to restore Malay and Shan territories and to refer the Cambodian annexations to the United Nations. The name Siam was restored as Indian troops entered the country to accept the surrender of the Japanese. Siam could turn once again to her problems of government and the national economy. In neither field had the difficulties to be met been lessened by war,[51] or by the efforts of the United States to idealize the Siamese.

SIAM'S ECONOMIC STRUCTURE

Siam's political development and prospects are closely linked with the country's traditional economy. Siam has neither an urban nor an industrial society. Bangkok, the only major city, is supported by a rural

---

[51] H. M. Spitzer, "Siam's Political Problems," *Far Eastern Survey*, XV (1946), 105-109, is an able survey of political developments since 1937. The Cambodian annexations were later annulled by direct agreement with France.

population of rice growers. Moreover, the development of trade with foreign powers in the nineteenth century did not produce a large middle or mercantile-industrial class. The export trade was created and managed largely by foreigners: tin, rubber, and teak wood largely by Europeans; rice by the Chinese. Siam's modernization involved in the development of this export trade created a demand for imports, including machinery and miscellaneous manufactured goods, but these changes did not interfere materially with native rural economy save for an adverse influence on domestic textile production. During World War II there was at first a dislocation and finally a complete stoppage of foreign trade. The country's communication system was partially paralyzed, creating an acute shortage of all manufactured goods. The net result was some increase in agricultural diversification, cotton for example, and some accumulation of surplus export products: rice, rubber, and tin.[52]

[52] H. M. Spitzer, "Siam's Economic Problems," *Far Eastern Survey*, XV (1946), 139-141.

CHAPTER 41

THE FAR EAST TODAY AND TOMORROW: PEACE OR WAR?

V-J DAY, August 14, 1945, which ended the hostilities of World War II in the Pacific and the Far East, did not bring peace to eastern Asia in any fundamental sense. To be sure, victory in war had freed the Orient of the incubus of Japanese militarism, fascism, and imperialistic expansion; but the war had not and could not of itself rid Asia of all the ills from which it suffered. In many areas of the Far East men were still prepared to fight, and they continued to fight to achieve the things they desired. Many of their goals were old and revived aspirations not traceable exclusively to the recent policies and behavior of Japan. Rather, they were the recurring manifestations of an Asia stirred by political and social revolution, and it was this revolution, in process before World War II, that remained as the most characteristic feature of the post-war Far East. Throughout the entire area there was not a single country or a single people unaffected by dynamic forces of change. The processes of westernization and modernization, present before the war, were in many respects accelerated by the conflict, and they continued to operate with even greater force after hostilities had ceased. Thus Japan's surrender was but the first step (to be sure an important one) toward meeting a vast array of perplexing questions which war had not solved, and which in some cases were the creation of the war.

THE ECONOMIC COLLAPSE

Basic in Asia's contemporary unrest are its traditional "low" standards of living made even lower by the ravages of war: the destruction of life savings and property, the interruption of trade with the West, the cessation of imports of consumer goods, the displacement of large segments of population, and indeed the general dislocation resulting from extreme shortages and uncontrolled inflation. Some areas of eastern Asia were more adversely and radically affected by the war than others. Yet in general the words of President Manuel Roxas that war and the

790

Japanese had brought "physical ruin" to the Philippines could as well be applied to large areas of the Far East. This is not to say of course that the economic problems of the Far East are insuperable. It is to say that they will prove to be exceedingly difficult. The relative poverty of eastern Asia in resources for an industrial society, her historic problems of population, the sub-subsistence income of the peasant masses, the lack of industrial capital, all these and many other factors suggest that Asia's economic recovery is a long-range task. Moreover, the rate of economic recovery in the Far East is and will continue to be conditioned by traditional historic social habits which have as yet by no means adjusted themselves fully to a Western and modern world. Much of Asia's economic thinking and acting, as is natural, still rests on Confucian concepts of family loyalty, on economic relations that are feudal, on political theories that government is a matter of men rather than law, and that government comes from above, not from below. These concepts are changing, but they change slowly, and what now appears as permanent mass dissatisfaction is evidence that the new base for economic as well as other values has not as yet been found. Asia's poverty, while not necessarily an incitement to war, creates fertile ground for continued social and political unrest.

THE POLITICAL TURMOIL

Politics no less than economics presents an eastern Asia shaken by war. Traditional views of Asia's political status are no longer tenable. Japan, the one "great power" of the Far East, is being reduced to the status of a third- or fourth-class power. China, for one hundred years a quasi-colonial area, has regained her full sovereignty and has been dignified with nominal inclusion among the great states. The Philippines have become an independent republic. Other native republics, semi-independent in fact, have been born in French Indo-China and Netherlands India, and independence "in due course" has been promised to Korea. The Mongolian People's Republic has acquired nationhood under Soviet patronage. Burma and India stand on the threshold of a new and independent political future. These signs of vital political consciousness are partly a result of what may loosely be called nationalism, of a refusal to be governed longer by traditional forms of colonialism, but they are also and perhaps more fundamentally the symptoms of a much broader social unrest. Westernization and modernization have brought eastern Asia out of her seclusion, have affected her intellectual as well as her material life, have created the stirrings of a new social consciousness, and have supplied her with a new intellectual and social leadership, whether it be in the person of a Sun Yat-sen, a Chiang K'ai-shek, or a Mao Tse-tung in China, a Roxas or a Taruc in the Philippines, a Soekarno in Indonesia, a Ho Chi-minh of the Viet Nam Republic in Indo-China, a Syngman Rhee or a Yo Unhyong in Korea. The principle common to all these leaders is the concept of Asia's inherent right to political independence. Their disagreements, at times violent, concern the political, economic, and social structure in which independence shall function.

REALIGNMENT OF WESTERN POWERS

Quite as striking as Asia's new and changing political status is the new and evolving alignment of the great Western powers in and with respect to the Far East. During the late nineteenth and the early twentieth centuries, the place of the Far East among the nations was fixed in a major degree by the policies of Great Britain, France, Russia, and Germany. When the Washington Conference met in 1921-22, control of the Far East had shifted to Great Britain, Japan, and the United States. When World War II ended, the alignment had again changed and rivalries had been intensified by the appearance of ideological conflict. This meant that the post-war Far East, deeply involved in evolutionary and revolutionary change, would not be allowed to seek its own solutions in its own ways. Westernization and modernization were not arrested by the war. On the contrary, the influence of these forces was increased, and, in addition, it is now exercised primarily through the power, prestige, and policies of the United States and the Soviet Union. Put in other words, this is to say that the two great historic frontiers of the Far East are now controlled by the world's most powerful states. The northern and western frontier against Siberia and Central Asia, where the ancient silk caravans passed from China, the back door to the East, is the sphere of influence of Soviet Russia. The newer frontier, the maritime gateway to China on the Pacific, is the sphere of the United States. These frontiers meet along the 38th parallel in Korea. This remote geographical line, unheralded and unsung in the records of history, has become the most strategic symbol in eastern Asia. It is this line, figuratively at least, which will divide or unite America and Russia in the creation of the future Far East.

THE NATURE OF THE ISSUES

As these concluding pages are written, nearly two years following V-J Day, it is again abundantly clear that the making of peace is more difficult than the making of war. In 1946-47, as in 1918-20, statesmen were attempting to reconcile the political nature of nations with the moral aspirations of men. During World War II, as in most wars, the moral purposes were readily expressed. Even the Japanese professed to be fighting for peace, stability, and justice in Greater East Asia. The high goals of the United Nations were expressed in President Roosevelt's interpretation of the Atlantic Charter pledging to all the world

. . . disarmament of aggressors, self-determination of nations and peoples, and the four freedoms—freedom of speech, freedom of religion, freedom from want, and freedom from fear.[1]

During the conflict men were supported by these moral aspirations toward a better world. When peace came they faced the practical problem of implementing their moral aspirations through political action. Again, as in World War I, this was proving to be a discouraging task. Although World War II like its predecessor arose, in the belief of most Americans, out of complex forces called nationalism, imperialism, power politics, etc., the war did not destroy these things. In some ways it was discovered that men had even fought to preserve them. The evidence did not suggest that nationalism had grown weaker than it had been in 1939, that nations were less fearful of surrendering their sovereign independence, that they no longer sought what they supposed to be their national interest, or that they were less concerned with promoting a balance of power which they regarded as advantageous.[2] As a consequence, the end of World War II signified to many men merely a new opportunity to resume the old techniques in pursuit of the old and "inevitable" struggle of power politics.

THE NEW EFFORT TOWARD COLLECTIVE SECURITY

Could this "inevitable" struggle that must end once again in another world catastrophe be avoided? Most men hoped and some believed that it could. At least it was clear that the goal of a stable world peace had become more imperative and perhaps more difficult to achieve than at any previous time in modern history. It was equally clear that revolutionary changes in the modern world of industry, technology, and science had so altered the nature of contacts between nations as to render "a world community possible and a world organization necessary." [3] The new world of industry, science, and technology was creating new

---

[1] *Documents on American Foreign Relations,* IV (1941-42), 61.

[2] See Carl L. Becker, *How New Will the Better World Be?* (New York, 1944), 3-21.

[3] Harold H. Fisher, *America and Russia in the World Community* (Claremont, Calif., 1946), 7-28.

theories of politics and of international relations. Symptomatic of these
changes were: 1) the declining prestige in Europe and Asia, including
the Far East, of pre-war, capitalist, democratic institutions; 2) a growing recognition of a one-world concept; and 3) a fuller understanding
of the dreadful implications of total war in an atomic age. In this new
world of atomic politics, the weaker powers were tending to become the
economic and political satellites of the most powerful states—more specifically, of the only great military powers surviving the war—the United
States and the Soviet Union. This development in turn emphasized the
factor of regionalism with its resulting international rivalries, and suggested that the possibilities of world peace rested to an alarming degree
on the ability of the United States and the Soviet Union to live as good
neighbors.[4] Against this satellite regionalism of the world's great powers, which is the contemporary form taken by the old pre-war ailments
of nationalism, imperialism, and power politics, the moral aspirations of
men and nations for a better world of peace were seeking to express
themselves through the Charter of the United Nations Organization.

THE UNITED NATIONS ORGANIZATION

The United Nations, created in 1942 as a wartime coalition, has since
become the instrumentality designed to implement the moral aspirations
of nations by marshalling vital world forces in support of peace, security,
and human welfare. Its origins in terms of immediate background are
to be found in:

1. The Moscow Conference of October 19-30, 1943, at which the
United States, Great Britain, the Soviet Union, and China recognized
"the necessity of establishing at the earliest possible date a general international organization, based on the principle of the sovereign equality of
all peace-loving states, and open to membership by all such states, large
and small, for the maintenance of peace and security."

2. The Dumbarton Oaks Conference, 1943, at which the four powers
engaged in exploratory conversations looking specifically to the creation
of an international organization, and drawing up proposals to that end.

3. The Yalta Conference, February 3-11, 1945, which, in addition to

---

[4] American versus Soviet regionalism in the Far East was exemplified in the first two
years following World War II by the developing American military, economic, and
political relations with the Philippine Republic, with the National Government of China,
and in the virtually exclusive American control of occupied Japan and exclusive control in
southern Korea, as against Soviet sponsorship of the Mongolian People's Republic, Russia's
special treaty rights in Manchuria, her exclusive occupation of northern Korea, and her
potential power to enter the politics of Sinkiang and to support the Yenan government of
the Chinese Communists.

other matters, announced a conference to be held at San Francisco, April 25, 1945, to prepare a charter for the United Nations along the lines suggested by the Dumbarton Oaks proposals and the Yalta agreements.

THE CHARTER OF THE UNITED NATIONS

Since the United Nations is designed as an instrumentality of *world* peace and security, its responsibilities and its functions pertain to the Far East as to other regions. Like the Covenant of the League of Nations, the Charter created at the San Francisco Conference, 1945, is an agreement partaking of the character of a treaty among those governments that voluntarily adhered to it.[5] The organization which the Charter creates is based on the principle of voluntary co-operation among states seeking common objectives. While recognizing "the principle of the sovereign equality" of all member states, the Charter, also taking into account inequalities among states, recognizes that the larger powers have special rights and must therefore assume special responsibilities. The purposes of the United Nations Organization (UNO) as expressed in the Charter are exceedingly broad and include the purpose of developing friendly relations as well as the maintenance of international peace and security, always excluding the principle of intervention "in matters which are essentially within the domestic jurisdiction of any state."

The principal organs and related agencies of the UNO are represented graphically in the accompanying chart. Of these organs, the most important are the General Assembly and the Security Council.

The General Assembly is sometimes described as the parliament of the United Nations, but this is misleading, because, since the UNO is not a state, the Assembly is not a legislative body in the generally understood sense. It is a deliberative, supervisory, financial, elective, and constituent body which may initiate studies and make recommendations but which cannot adopt legislation which is binding on the member states or their citizens.[6]

Likewise, the second principal organ of the UNO, the Security Council, is sometimes described as the executive. This, too, is apt to be misleading not only for the same reason but in addition because the field of

[5] In addition to a number of Central and South American republics, the principal far eastern and Pacific area countries participating in the San Francisco Conference and thereby in the framing of the Charter included: Australia, Canada, China, France, Mexico, the Netherlands, New Zealand, the Philippine Commonwealth, Union of Soviet Socialist Republics, United Kingdom, and the United States of America.

[6] On the detailed functions and powers of the Assembly, L. M. Goodrich and Edvard Hambro, *Charter of the United Nations* (Boston, 1946), 24-38, 53-116.

Trusteeship Council

Provided for by the Charter and established by General Assembly in Dec., 1946.
Includes members of Security Council, Members that administer trustee territories, and some others elected by General Assembly. Carries out functions prescribed in trusteeship agreements.

General Assembly

Composed of delegates from all the Members of the U. N.
Studies and discusses questions relating to peace, security, etc.
Has power to make recommendations to Members of the U. N. or to the Security Council. Recommendations in a given dispute may not be made to the Security Council (save with its consent) when in such dispute the Council is exercising functions assigned to it under the Charter.
There were 54 Member Nations at the beginning of 1947.
Meets annually or on special call.

World Health Organ

Research organ on medical development.

International Refugee Organization

In part a successor to UNRRA. Resettlement of displaced persons.

Economic and Social Council

Membership, 18, elected by General Assembly.
Studies and reports with respect to international economic, social, cultural, educational, health, and other matters, and makes recommendations to the General Assembly and to special agencies (see below).
Assists Security Council on latter's request.
May make recommendations for purpose of promoting respect for and observance of human rights and fundamental freedoms for all.

Educational, Scientific, and Cultural Organization

Promotes world understanding thru these fields.

". . . specialized agencies, established by intergovernmental agreement . . . , shall be brought into relationship with the United Nations. . . ." [See Articles 57 and 63.]

International Labor Organization

Organized at end of World War I as part of League of Nations system. Designed to improve labor standards. Delegates from labor, management, and governments.

International Monetary Fund

A result of Bretton Woods proposals. To assist in the stabilization of currencies and deal with other monetary problems.

International Bank

A result of Bretton Woods agreement. To assist reconstruction, foreign investment, and balanced growth of international trade.

International Civil Aviation Organization

Deals with legal and economic problems of commercial air transportation.

Security Council

Eleven members. Permanent members include: United States, Great Britain, Soviet Russia, France, China. Non-permanent members elected for 2-year terms by the Assembly.
Meets in permanent session.
May investigate any dispute threatening international peace, recommend appropriate procedures for adjustment, determine the existence of any threat to peace, and determine action by military forces of U. N. Members to restore peace.
Members of U. N. undertake under terms to make forces available to S. C.

U. N. Secretariat

Headed by the Secretary-General appointed by the General Assembly on recommendation of the Security Council. He is chief administrative officer of the U. N.
Work of the Secretariat is continuous, serving both General Assembly and Security Council.

International Court of Justice

The principal judicial organ of the U. N. Functions in accordance with a statute which is based upon the Statute of the Permanent Court of International Justice.
Judges are elected by the Security Council and the General Assembly voting concurrently.
Members of the U. N. parties to a case undertake to comply with the decision of the Court.
Member nations may by declaration accept the compulsory jurisdiction of the Court, conditionally or unconditionally.

International Armed Forces

Forces provided by all Members for the suppression of threats to peace and security.

Atomic Energy Commission

Eleven Members of the Security Council and Canada. Plans the handling of problems relating to atomic energy.

U. N. Food and Agriculture Organization

Engages in research with the view of raising levels of nutrition and standards of living.

UNRRA

United Nations Relief and Rehabilitation Administration. Organized by agreement, Nov. 9, 1943. Non-permanent, termination of work began in 1947.

Military Staff Committee

Chiefs of Staff of the five great powers. On orders of the Security Council it directs military action against aggressors.

CHARTER AND SPECIALIZED AGENCIES RELATED TO THE UNITED NATIONS.

executive action, so far as it is provided for in the Charter, is divided between the Security Council, the Economic and Social Council, and the Trusteeship Council. This is a wide departure from the practice under the Covenant of the League of Nations where functions of an executive character were centered in the Council of the League. Nevertheless, the primary responsibility for peace and security rests with the Security Council. Its permanent members, the so-called Big Five, include China, France, the Soviet Union, the United Kingdom, and the United States. Unlike the Assembly, the Security Council functions continuously. It has the power to intervene in any situation whose continuance is regarded as endangering peace and security, and to decide what measures are to be taken to maintain or restore peace. The members of the UNO are obligated to accept and carry out the decisions of the Security Council taken in conformity with the Charter. The Security Council is also charged with formulating plans for establishing a system for the regulation of armaments. In the voting procedure of the Security Council the larger responsibility of the great powers is recognized in that action by the Council on all non-procedural questions requires concurrence of all the permanent or big power members. This has the effect of making the UNO "a league of peace-loving nations with an alliance of great powers for keeping the peace as its hard core of military strength and political reality." This voting procedure, involving the power to veto, expressed the belief of the big powers that enforcement measures for peace and security could not be regarded as practical unless concurred in by the major powers.[7]

The third organ created by the Charter is the International Court of Justice, a new court replacing the Permanent Court of International Justice created under the Covenant of the League of Nations. Since some states were not ready to accept a general system of compulsory jurisdiction, the Charter provides that each member state may by declaration accept the compulsory jurisdiction of the new Court conditionally or unconditionally.[8]

The principle which underlies the system provided by the Charter for the pacific settlement of disputes places primary responsibility on the parties to a dispute themselves; the Council has authority to intervene when a dispute is held to endanger the maintenance of international peace and security. The Council does not impose an obligatory settlement but acts as an agency of conciliation. When, however, the presence of a threat to peace has been recognized by the Security Council,

[7] Goodrich and Hambro, *Charter of the United Nations,* 28-30, 117-188.
[8] Goodrich and Hambro, *Charter of the United Nations,* 30-32, 257-267.

enforcement action is primarily the responsibility of the Council. It determines the form of sanction to be employed, such as economic or military measures.

THE PRINCIPLE OF TRUSTEESHIP

Of particular importance in the Pacific area are the Charter provisions on the administration of non-self-governing territories. These provisions include: 1) a declaration regarding such areas, setting forth the principle that "the interests of the inhabitants of these territories are paramount" and accepting the obligation "to promote to the utmost . . . the well-being of the inhabitants"; 2) provision for an international trusteeship system; and 3) provision for a Trusteeship Council. The general system of trusteeship applies to such of the following categories of territories as may be placed thereunder by means of trusteeship agreements: 1) territories previously held under mandate; 2) territories detached from enemy states as a result of World War II; and 3) territories voluntarily placed under the system by states responsible for their administration. Under this system there is no expressed obligation for UNO members to place territories they control under trusteeship. The placing of a territory in the system and the terms applicable depend on individual agreements subject to approval by the Assembly. Moreover, in any trusteeship agreement, an area or areas of special strategic importance may be designated "a strategic area or areas." The inclusion of this provision is a measure of the degree to which the thinking of the great powers was still influenced by the politics of war rather than by the politics of peace. The measure is of paramount importance since designation as a "strategic area" brings the territory under the jurisdiction of the Security Council (where the veto applies). Nevertheless, in point of principles and purposes, the trusteeship system is a progressive step over the mandate system of the League of Nations. In point of practice, however, there is less assurance that trusteeship will mean anything where the strategic interests of the great powers are involved.

THE ECONOMIC AND SOCIAL COUNCIL

From the beginning, the United Nations recognized formally that world peace and security would depend fundamentally on creating conditions of stability and well-being in the economic and social spheres. Thus the UNO is pledged to foster "higher standards of living," "full employment," etc. Planning for these objectives is the responsibility of the Economic and Social Council. In the Far East the potential field for the action of this council is all but unlimited. It is particularly significant that the UNO has given general recognition to the interrelation between socio-economic problems and the political conditions that are likely to contribute to peace.[9]

THE UNO: THE PROSPECT

The United Nations Organization and the Charter under which it functions are a first step only toward the implementing of international peace and security. As late as the early months of 1947, although the powers had not yet begun to speak officially of a peace treaty with Japan, their tendencies toward regionalism and to renewed rivalries of power politics were, as noted, all too evident. These tendencies toward power alignments, particularly when backed by ideological conflict and prejudice, present the most formidable obstacle which the UNO must surmount if it is to survive as an effective agency for peace. The success or failure of the United Nations in the Far East as elsewhere will be determined by the use that is made of it, by the policies which individual governments pursue, and finally by whether the major peoples of the world desire to be good neighbors and approach the Charter as a workable instrument to that end. If peoples and governments want a better world, and look upon the business of getting it as a continuing process, the Charter of the United Nations may well become a useful instrument. It does not appear, however, that the late war, with the colossal destruction and human misery it entailed, has made the task any easier.

Moreover, it has already become certain that the United Nations will be tested as severely in the Far East as in Europe. In the Far East as elsewhere, it must face the problems of armament and security, of trusteeship,[10] of general rehabilitation and relief of economic distress, and, lastly, problems of social maladjustment in which millions of people have nothing to lose by social change save their ignorance, disease, and poverty.

The future for these Asiatic peoples is closely linked with the present and future behavior of Soviet Russia on the one hand and the traditional

---

[9] For further features of the UNO not treated here see Goodrich and Hambro, *Charter of the United Nations.*

[10] At the beginning of 1947 the UNO was faced with an argument on whether the transfer of mandated and ex-enemy territories to U. N. trusteeship is obligatory or optional for the administering power. Russia, which held no mandate, was insisting that it is obligatory. Britain (holding the Palestine mandate) and the United States (holding the former Japanese mandated islands in the Pacific) held it to be optional. Eight transfers of former mandated territories to trusteeship had, however, been approved. In the Pacific these included: the Australian mandate in New Guinea, and the New Zealand mandate in western Samoa.

democracies, now led by the United States, on the other. Furthermore, conflicts of ideology, such as democracy versus communism, which have divided the Western world are also in the business of dividing Asia and the Far East. There the resulting conflicts are, if anything, more confused than in the West, because they are involved with Asia's indigenous, ancient, and traditional cultures and philosophies. Thus the Far East, and indeed Asia as a whole, now faces a climactic point in the supreme crisis which the history of the past century, recounted in these pages, has created. In the past one hundred years, Western thought and action, and Western philosophical values have striven to conquer the East. The aggressiveness, often the ruthlessness, of the Western impact created a problem for the Orient. Since the middle of the nineteenth century this problem has been how to achieve a strong, independent nationalism in the Western sense, not for its own sake, but in order to enable the Orient to preserve its own intuitive, aesthetic, and unique philosophical values. As the Far East seeks to find its way among the tangled influences of Western democracy and Western communism, the basic purpose is to be strong in defense of its own philosophical values.[11]

During the past century, the three major countries of Asia (China, Japan, and India) have attempted, each in its own way, to achieve Western nationalistic independence. Each has done this in "terms of its own philosophical background and attendant cultural materials." [12] Unhappily, in the nineteenth and twentieth centuries, in which Asia has learned so much from the West, the West in turn, impressed with its own material power and carried away by the crusading zeals of its own philosophies, has had little time or disposition *to learn from Asia*. And so it would appear that in the long struggle which began with the Treaty of Nanking it is the East rather than the West which has travelled further along the road of human experience and appreciation. If it be true that the key to world peace and security is an "informed realism of philosophical and cultural understanding," [13] then it must follow that Asia is closer to the goal of the United Nations than are the great powers and the peoples of the West.

---

[11] "Whatever political system evolves in China, you cannot tear out of Chinese life the Confucian tradition and manners, the family and clan spirit, the dignity of farmer and laborer, the respect for intellectual aristocracy, and the well-balanced combination of individual enterprise and community pride." Frank W. Price [translator of Sun Yat-sen's Three Principles of the People], "China in Perspective," *The China Magazine*, XVI (1946), 10.

[12] F. S. C. Northrop, *The Meeting of the East and West* (New York, 1946), 428.

[13] Northrop, *The Meeting of the East and West*, 428-429.

FOR FURTHER READING

CHAPTER 1

The geography and people of Asia. Daniel R. Bergsmark, *Economic Geography of Asia* (New York, 1935); Lionel W. Lyde, *The Continent of Asia* (London, 1933); L. Dudley Stamp, *Asia* (3rd ed., New York, 1935); L. H. D. Buxton, *The Peoples of Asia* (New York, 1925); George B. Cressey, *Asia's Lands and Peoples* (New York, 1944), the best work for those seeking a general introduction to the subject.

China. General. L. H. D. Buxton, *China: The Land and the People* (Oxford, 1929); George B. Cressey, *China's Geographic Foundations* (New York, 1934); Walter H. Mallory, *China: Land of Famine* (New York, 1926); G. W. Prothero, Historical Section, British Foreign Office, Handbook No. 67, *China;* No. 68, *Mongolia;* No. 69, *Manchuria;* No. 70, *Tibet* (London, 1920); L. Richard, *Comprehensive Geography of the Chinese Empire* (Shanghai, 1908).

Configuration and climate. Carl W. Bishop, "The Geographic Factor in the Development of Chinese Civilization," *Geographical Rev.,* XII (1922), 19-41; Carl W. Bishop, "The Rise of Civilization in China with Reference to its Geographical Aspects," *Geographical Rev.,* XXII (1932), 617-631.

Soils and minerals. H. Foster Bain, *Ores and Industry in the Far East* (rev. ed., New York, 1933); O. E. Baker, "Land Utilization in China," *Problems of the Pacific* (Chicago, 1928), 324-338; J. L. Buck, "Agriculture and the Future of China," *Annals of the American Academy of Pol. and Soc. Science,* CLII (1930), 109-115; J. L. Buck, *Chinese Farm Economy* (Chicago, 1930); F. H. King, *Farmers for Forty Centuries* (New York, 1926), an excellent introductory study.

Resources and foreign trade. C. F. Remer, *The Foreign Trade of China* (Shanghai, 1926).

North China. F. G. Clapp, "The Hwang Ho, Yellow River," *Geographical Rev.,* XII (1922), 1-18; C. K. Edmunds, "Shantung, China's Holy Land," *Nat. Geographic Magazine,* XXXVI (1919), 231-252.

Manchuria. Hsiao Chu, "Manchuria, A Statistical Survey," *Problems of the Pacific, 1929* (Chicago, 1930), 380-422; Economic Bureau of the Chinese Eastern Railway, *North Manchuria and the Chinese Eastern Railway* (Harbin, 1924); Owen Lattimore, *Manchuria: Cradle of Conflict* (New York, 1932); Owen Lattimore, "The Unknown Frontier of Manchuria," *Foreign Affairs,* XI (1933), 315-330; South Manchuria Railway, *Report[s] on Progress in Manchuria* (Dairen).

Mongolia and Sinkiang. R. C. Andrews, "Explorations in Mongolia," *Geographical Journal,* LXIX (1927), 1-23; R. C. Andrews, "Explorations in the Gobi Desert," *Nat. Geographic Magazine,* LXIII (1933), 653-716; R. C. Andrews, *On the Trail of Ancient Man* (New York, 1927); R. C. Andrews and others, *The New Conquest of Central Asia* (New York, 1933); L. H. D. Buxton, "Present Conditions in Inner Mongolia," *Geographical Journal,* LXI (1923), 393-413; Owen Lattimore, "Caravan Routes of Inner Asia," *Geographical Journal,* LXXII (1928), 497-531; Owen Lattimore, "Chinese Colonization in Inner Mongolia: Its History and Present Development," *Pioneer Settlement* (New York, 1932), 288-313; Owen Lattimore, *The Desert Road to Turkestan* (London, 1928); Sir M. Aurel Stein, "Innermost Asia, Its Geography as a Factor in History," *Geographical Journal,* LXV (1925), 377-403, 473-501; Sir M. Aurel Stein, *On Central-Asian Tracks* (London, 1933); E. S. Sykes and Percy Sykes, *Through Deserts and Oases of Central Asia* (London, 1920); Langdon Warner, *The Long Old Road in China* (New York, 1926); Sven Hedin, *The Silk Road* (London, 1938); G. B. Cressey, "The Ordos Desert of Inner Mongolia," *Denison University Bulletin,* 1933.

Tibet. Charles Bell, *Tibet, Past and Present* (Oxford, 1924), the author was a British resident in Lhasa; Charles Bell, *The People of Tibet* (Oxford, 1928).

Siberia: the Soviet Union in general. Nicholas Mikhailov, *Soviet Geography* (London, 1935), and *Land of the Soviets* (New York, 1939); Samuel N. Harper, *The Soviet Union and World Problems* (Chicago, 1935).

Middle and Far Eastern Siberia. R. A. Davies and Andrew J. Steiger, *Soviet Asia* (New York, 1942); Emil Lengyel, *Siberia* (New York, 1943); William Mandel, *The Soviets in the Far East* (New York, 1943).

Japan: configuration and climate. Glenn T. Trewartha, *Japan: A Physical, Cultural and Regional Geography* (Madison, 1945), chs. i-ii; *The Climatic Atlas of Japan and Her Neighboring Countries* (Tokyo, 1929); T. Okada, *The Climate of Japan* (Tokyo, 1931); C. W. Thornthwaite, "The Climates of Japan," *Geographical Rev.,* XXIV (1934), 494-496.

Soils and minerals. Shiroshi Nausu, *Aspects of Japanese Agriculture* (New York, 1941); E. B. Schumpeter, ed., *The Industrialization of Japan and Manchukuo, 1930-1940* (New York, 1940); H. Foster Bain, *Ores and Industry of the Far East* (2nd ed., New York, 1933); Guy Harold Smith and Dorothy Good, *Japan: A Geographical View* (New York, 1943).

Population. W. R. Crocker, *The Japanese Population Problem* (London, 1932); Ryoichi Ishii, *Population Pressure and Economic Life in Japan* (London, 1937); E. F. Penrose, *Population Theories and Their Application with Special Reference to Japan* (Stanford University, 1934), the best work on the subject.

Agriculture and the rural community. John F. Embree, *Suye Mura: A Japanese Village* (Chicago, 1939), an excellent study; Andrew Grajdanzev, *Statistics of Japanese Agriculture* (New York, 1941); Shiroshi Nasu, *Land Utilization of Japan* (Tokyo, 1929), the standard work.

Industrial geography. G. C. Allen, *Japanese Industry: Its Recent Develop-*

ment and Present Condition (New York, 1940), the best work covering the entire subject; Teijiro Uyeda, *The Small Industries of Japan* (New York, 1938); S. Uyehara, *The Industry and Trade of Japan* (2nd rev. ed., London, 1936).

Burma. The most definitive, critical work is G. E. Harvey, *British Rule in Burma 1824-1942* (London, 1946); the best general introductory study covering the modern period is John L. Christian, *Modern Burma* (Berkeley, 1942), see ch. ii on "The Land and the People"; see also Sir Herbert Thirkell, *Burma* (Cambridge, 1923).

Siam (Thailand). K. P. Landon, *Siam in Transition* (Chicago, 1939); Sir Josiah Crosby, *Siam: The Cross Roads* (London, 1944); U. S. Dept. of Commerce, *Economic Development of Siam* (Washington, 1929); Daniel R. Bergsmark, *Economic Geography of Asia* (New York, 1935), ch. xv; Ernest Young, *Siam* (New York, 1908); Lionel W. Lyde, *The Continent of Asia* (London, 1933), ch. xxix; V. D. Wickizer and M. K. Bennett, *The Rice Economy of Monsoon Asia* (Stanford University, 1941); H. G. Deignan, *Siam—Land of Free Men* (Washington, 1943).

Indo-China. V. D. Wickizer and M. K. Bennett, *The Rice Economy of Monsoon Asia* (Stanford University, 1941); Virginia Thompson, *French Indo-China* (New York, 1937); Shannon McCune, "Saïgon, French Indo-China," *Journal of Geography,* XXXVI (1937), 24-33; Kate Mitchell, *Industrialization of the Western Pacific* (New York, 1942).

Malaya. Rupert Emerson, *Malaysia: A Study in Direct and Indirect Rule* (New York, 1937); L. A. Mills, *British Rule in Eastern Asia* (London, 1942).

Netherlands India. Jan O. M. Broek, *Economic Development of the Netherlands Indies* (New York, 1942); J. H. Boeke, *The Structure of Netherlands Indian Economy* (New York, 1942); Rupert Emerson, *Malaysia: A Study in Direct and Indirect Rule* (New York, 1937); J. S. Furnivall, *Progress and Welfare in Southeast Asia* (New York, 1941), and *Netherlands India: A Study of Plural Economy* (New York, 1944); A. D. de Kat Angelino, *Colonial Policy* (2 vols., The Hague, 1931); R. Kennedy, *The Ageless Indies* (New York, 1942); Amry Vandenbosch, *The Dutch East Indies: Its Government, Problems, and Politics* (Berkeley, 1941).

New Guinea. Stephen W. Reed, *The Making of Modern New Guinea* (Philadelphia, 1943), the outstanding work on the subject.

The Philippines. Commonwealth of the Philippines, Dept. of Agriculture and Commerce, *Atlas of Philippine Statistics* (Manila, 1939); A. L. Kroeber, *Peoples of the Philippines* (New York, 1919); Dean C. Worcester and Ralston Hayden, *The Philippines Past and Present* (New York, 1930), treatment of the non-Christian peoples in chs. xx-xxiii, treatment of the people of the Mountain Province in appendix v, 806-817; for the character of the Filipino people, see Charles Derbyshire, *The Social Cancer* (Manila, 1912), a translation of José Rizal's *Noli me Tangere,* in which Rizal, crusading for self-government, stresses unfavorable traits of the national character; Camilo Osias, *The Filipino Way of Life* (Boston, 1940), an excellent character study; W. Cameron Forbes, *The Philippine Islands* (Boston, 1928);

James A. Le Roy, *Philippine Life in Town and Country* (New York, 1905), a picture of the Filipino people at the end of the Spanish regime.

Chapter 2

General works on Chinese history and culture. K. S. Latourette, *The Chinese: Their History and Culture* (3rd ed., New York, 1946), a very competent portrayal with excellent bibliographical suggestions; L. Carrington Goodrich, *A Short History of the Chinese People* (New York, 1943), a brief and popular interpretation; C. P. Fitzgerald, *China: A Short Cultural History* (London, 1935), one of the best treatments of Chinese culture in a single volume; Richard Wilhelm, *A Short History of Chinese Civilization* (New York, 1929); Paul Monroe, *China: A Nation in Evolution* (New York, 1928), by an American educator who visited China frequently; S. Wells Williams, *The Middle Kingdom* (2 vols., New York, 1901; 1st ed., 1848; final revision, 1883), by a distinguished nineteenth-century American missionary and diplomat—the work on China most widely read by Americans in the nineteenth and early twentieth centuries; E. T. Williams, *China: Yesterday and Today* (New York, 1923), a survey of many aspects of Chinese life by an American Foreign Service officer who lived many years in China; Marcel Granet, *Chinese Civilization* (New York, 1930), a very stimulating work on political and social organization though regarded as uncritical by some sinologists; Sophia H. Chen Zen, ed., *Symposium on Chinese Culture* (Shanghai, 1931), excellent essays on many aspects of China's cultural development; A. H. Smith, *Chinese Characteristics* (New York, 1894), a revealing portrayal of Chinese habits and character by an able American observer long resident in China; E. T. C. Werner, *China of the Chinese* (London, 1919), emphasizes the importance of the family.

Origins and racial composition of the Chinese. H. G. Creel, *The Birth of China* (London, 1936), a scholarly work.

History and philosophy of ancient China. Derk Bodde, *China's First Unifier: A Study of the Ch'in Dynasty as Seen in the Life of Li Ssŭ* (Leiden, 1938); T. F. Carter, *The Invention of Printing in China and Its Spread Westward* (New York, 1931); H. H. Dubs, *Hsüntze, the Moulder of Ancient Confucianism* (London, 1927); H. H. Dubs, *The Works of Hsüntze* (London, 1928); James Legge, *The Chinese Classics* (5 vols., rev. ed., Oxford, 1893, 1895), translations of many of the great works of the Chou period; James Legge, "The Texts of Taoism," *The Sacred Books of the East* (Oxford, 1891), Vols. XXXIX, XL; Liang Ch'i-ch'ao, *History of Chinese Political Thought during the Early Tsin Period,* trans. by L. T. Chen (New York, 1930); Y. P. Mei, *The Ethical and Political Works of Motse* (London, 1929); Pan Ku, *The History of the Former Han Dynasty,* critical translation with annotations by H. H. Dubs (2 vols., Baltimore, 1938, 1944); W. E. Soothill, *The Analects of Confucius* (Oxford, 1937); J. J. Shryock, *The Origin and Development of the State Cult of Confucius* (New York, 1932).

Chinese history from the third to the nineteenth century: religion.
Charles Eliot, *Hinduism and Buddhism* (London, 1921); J. Foster, *The Church of the T'ang Dynasty* (London, 1939); K. S. Latourette, *A History of Christian Missions in China* (New York, 1929); J. B. Pratt, *The Pilgrimage of Buddhism* (New York, 1928); W. E. Soothill, *The Three Religions of China* (London, 1913).

Barbarian pressures and invasions on the frontiers. Sir Henry Yule, *Cathay and the Way Thither* (new ed., London, 1913-1916); Sir Henry Yule, *The Book of Ser Marco Polo* (3rd ed. rev., 2 vols., London, 1921); Franz Michael, *The Origin of Manchu Rule in China* (Baltimore, 1942); Adolf Reichwein, *China and Europe: Intellectual and Artistic Contacts in the Eighteenth Century* (New York, 1925).

Government and politics. H. S. Brunnert and V. V. Hagelstrom, *Present Day Political Organization of China* (Shanghai, 1912); Pao Chao Hsieh, *The Government of China, 1644-1911* (Baltimore, 1925); Han Liang Huang, *The Land Tax in China* (New York, 1918); Leonard S. Hsu, *The Political Philosophy of Confucianism* (New York, 1932), marred by a tendency to read Sung philosophy into ancient Confucianism; Liang Ch'i-ch'ao, *History of Chinese Political Thought* (New York, 1930); W. F. Mayers, *The Chinese Government* (Shanghai, 1897); H. B. Morse, *The Gilds of China* (London, 1909); H. B. Morse, *The Trade and Administration of the Chinese Empire* (London, 1908); A. W. Hummel, ed., *Eminent Chinese of the Ch'ing Period* (Washington, 1943, 1944).

Economic and social organization. J. L. Buck, *Chinese Farm Economy* (Chicago, 1930); J. L. Buck, *Land Utilization in China* (Chicago, 1937); Pearl S. Buck, *The Good Earth* (New York, 1931), a novel; Fei Hsiao-tung, *Peasant Life in China* ((London, 1939), a social and economic analysis of life in the Chinese village; S. D. Gamble, *Peking: A Social Survey* (New York, 1921); F. H. King, *Farmers for Forty Centuries* (New York, 1926), agriculture in China, Japan, and Korea at the beginning of the twentieth century; V. K. Leong and L. K. Tao, *Village and Town Life in China* (London, 1915); Mabel Ping-hua Lee, *The Economic History of China* (New York, 1921), with emphasis on agriculture; Arthur H. Smith, *Village Life in China* (New York, 1899).

Chinese literature. H. A. Giles, *A History of Chinese Literature* (New York, 1927); Marcel Granet, *Festivals and Songs of Ancient China* (New York, 1932).

Chinese art and architecture. L. Ashton, *Introduction to the Study of Chinese Sculpture* (London, 1924); L. Binyon, *Painting in the Far East* (London, 1908); S. W. Bushell, *Chinese Art* (London, 1910); E. F. Fenollosa, *Epochs of Chinese and Japanese Art* (2 vols., London, 1912).

Chapter 3

General works. Two brief but competent surveys: E. O. Reischauer, *Japan, Past and Present* (New York, 1946), and K. S. Latourette, *The History of Japan* (New York, 1947). See also: B. H. Chamberlain, *Things Japanese* (6th ed., rev., Kobe, 1939), notes on a multitude of Japanese topics; E. W. Clement, *A Short History of Japan* (Tokyo, 1936), an elementary account, useful for lists of sovereigns, shoguns, etc.; W. E. Griffis, *The Mikado's Empire* (2 vols., 12th ed., New York, 1913), one of the most popular works introducing Japan to the American public in the late nineteenth century; Engelbert Kaempfer, *The History of Japan, Together with a Description of the Kingdom of Siam, 1690-92* (3 vols., Glasgow, 1906), the author was physician to the Dutch mission at Nagasaki during the days of exclusion; Yoshi S. Kuno, *Japanese Expansion on the Asiatic Continent* (Berkeley, 1937, 1940), Vol. I covers to 1600, Vol. II covers 1600-1850; James Murdoch, *A History of Japan* (3 vols., Kobe and London, 1903-1926), Vol. I covers from the beginnings to the arrival of the Portuguese, Vol. II (with the collaboration of Isoh Yamagata) covers from the arrival of the Portuguese, 1542, to 1651, and Vol. III, 1652-1868; G. B. Sansom, *Japan: A Short Cultural History* (rev. ed., London, 1932), the best single volume in English covering the subject from earliest times to the middle of the nineteenth century.

Early Japanese history. K. Asakawa, *The Early Institutional Life of Japan* (Tokyo, 1903), a study in the Reform of 645 A.D.; K. Asakawa, "The Life of a Monastic Shō in Medieval Japan," *Annual Report of the American Historical Association,* 1916, I (1919), 311-346, the study of a class of private manor; W. G. Aston, *Nihongi: Chronicles of Japan from the Earliest Times to A.D. 697,* in *Trans. and Proceedings of the Japan Soc. of London,* Supplement I (2 vols., London, 1896); B. H. Chamberlain, trans., *Kojiki or Records of Ancient Matters* (2nd ed., Kobe, 1932); R. K. Reischauer, *Early Japanese History c. 40 B.C.—A.D. 1167* (2 vols., Princeton, 1937).

The first centuries of feudalism, 1192-1600. K. Asakawa, trans. and ed., *The Documents of Iriki, Illustrative of the Development of the Feudal Institution of Japan* (New Haven, 1929), essential source materials translated and edited by a distinguished Japanese scholar.

Tokugawa Japan, 1600-1867. Hugh Borton, "Peasant Uprisings in Japan of the Tokugawa Period," *Trans. of the Asiatic Soc. of Japan,* 2nd series, XVI (1938), xv, 1-258.

Japanese economic history to 1854. Eijiro Honjo, *The Social and Economic History of Japan* (Kyoto, 1935), the most satisfactory single volume on the subject in English; Yosaburo Takekoshi, *The Economic Aspects of the History of the Civilization of Japan* (3 vols., New York, 1930), a digest of a much larger standard work in Japanese; Matsuyo Takizawa, *The Penetration of Money Economy in Japan and Its Effects upon Social and Political Institutions* (New York, 1927), the collapse of feudalism explained in terms of an economic revolution from a rice to a money economy.

Biographies. Walter Dening, *The Life of Toyotomi Hideyoshi,* edited by M. E. Dening (3rd ed., Kobe, 1930); A. L. Sadler, *The Maker of Modern Japan: The Life of Tokugawa Ieyasu (1542-1616)* (London, 1937).

Japanese mythology, religion, and philosophy. Masaharu Anesaki, *History of Japanese Religion with Special Reference to the Social and Moral Life of the Nation* (London, 1930), a scholarly summary by a distinguished Japanese scholar; Inazo Nitobe, *Bushido, the Soul of Japan: An Exposition of Japanese Thought* (rev. and enlarged ed., New York, 1905), a Japanese publicist presents the subject in the ideal rather than the real; D. C. Holton, *National Faith of Japan: A Study in Modern Shinto* (London, 1938), a standard work; Genchi Kato, *A Study of Shinto, the Religion of the Japanese Nation* (Tokyo, 1926); Masaharu Anesaki, *Nichiren the Buddhist Prophet* (Cambridge, 1916), a biography of the founder (1222-1282) of a leading Buddhist sect; H. H. Coates and Ryugaku Ishizuka, *Honen the Buddhist Saint: His Life and Teachings* (2nd ed., Kyoto, 1925), a translation of the official biography of the founder (1133-1212) of a sect of Japanese Buddhism; Sir C. N. E. Eliot, *Japanese Buddhism* (London, 1935), an excellent work.

Japanese literature. W. G. Aston, *A History of Japanese Literature* (London, 1933; 1st ed., 1899), a brief pioneer work; A. S. Omori and Kochi Doi, trans., *Diaries of Court Ladies of Old Japan* (Tokyo, 1935); W. N. Porter, trans., *The Tosa Diary* (London, 1912), a translation from the work of one of the first masters of Japanese prose; Arthur Waley, trans., *The Tale of Genji: A Novel in Six Parts Translated from the Japanese* (London, 1935), the greatest of Japanese novels, by Lady Murasaki; A. B. Mitford (Lord Redesdale), *Tales of Old Japan* (London, 1910); Thomas Satchell, trans., *Hizakurige* (Kobe, 1929), an excellent translation of the boisterous adventures of Yagi and Kita on the Tokaido, by Jippensha Ikku (1775-1831).

The Arts. Masaharu Anesaki, *Buddhist Art in its Relation to Buddhist Ideals, with special reference to Buddhism in Japan* (Boston, 1915).

Additional references. Hugh Borton, Serge Elisséef, and Edwin O. Reischauer, *A Selected List of Books and Articles on Japan* (Washington, 1940).

Chapter 4

Western contacts with China. Owen Lattimore, *Inner Asian Frontiers* (New York, 1940); F. J. Teggart, *Rome and China* (Berkeley, 1939); G. F. Hudson, *Europe and China: A Survey of Their Relations from the Earliest Times to 1800* (London, 1931); T. F. Carter, *Invention of Printing in China and its Spread Westward* (rev. ed., New York, 1931); Sir Mark A. Stein, *On Ancient Central-Asian Tracks* (London, 1933); A. C. Moule, *Christians in China before the Year 1550* (New York, 1930); A. C. Moule and Paul Pelliot, *Marco Polo* (London, 1938); Henry H. Hart, *Venetian Adventurer*

(Stanford University, 1942); Sir Henry Yule, *Cathay and the Way Thither* (2 vols., London, 1866).

Western contacts with Japan. Richard Hildreth, *Japan As It Was and Is* (2 vols., Chicago, 1906), covers Western intercourse to 1858; M. Paske-Smith, *Western Barbarians in Japan and Formosa in Tokugawa Days 1603-1868* (Kobe, 1930), deals in particular with the English; Peter Pratt, *History of Japan, Compiled from the Records of the English East India Company . . .*, edited by M. Paske-Smith (2 vols., Kobe, 1931); John Saris, *The Voyage of Captain John Saris to Japan 1613*, ed. by Sir Ernest Satow (London, 1900); Sir Ernest Satow, *The Jesuit Mission Press in Japan 1591-1610* (Tokyo, 1888); Engelbert Kaempfer, *The History of Japan* (3 vols., New York, 1906).

CHAPTER 5

For many years following its publication in 1910, H. B. Morse's *The International Relations of the Chinese Empire*, Vol. I, covering the period 1834-1860, provided the best general background account of the Canton Trade. This was followed in 1926 by the same author's monumental work, *The Chronicles of the East India Company Trading to China, 1635-1834* (4 vols., Oxford, 1926, and a fifth supplementary volume, *1742-74*, 1929), a virtually inexhaustible source on all aspects of the trade assembled from the records of the Company. Additional contributions to the subject drawn from British sources are found in the recent work of W. C. Costin, *Great Britain and China, 1833-1860* (Oxford, 1937). To these accounts must be added two authoritative works by Earl H. Pritchard, *Anglo-Chinese Relations during the Seventeenth and Eighteenth Centuries* (Urbana, 1929), and *The Crucial Years of Early Anglo-Chinese Relations, 1750-1800* (Pullman, Wash., 1936), which use some Chinese as well as the British sources. The first work in English resting primarily on Chinese official sources is P. C. Kuo, *A Critical Study of the First Anglo-Chinese War (With Documents)* (Shanghai, 1935). This work is a material supplement and revision of all previous studies because of its use of *Ch'ou Pan Yi Wu Shih Mo* (Reign of Tao-kuang) [The Beginning and End of the Management of Barbarian Affairs], a comprehensive collection of documents on Chinese diplomatic history beginning with the year 1836, which was published in 1930. It also draws upon two other major Chinese works: *The Political Works of Lin Tsê-hsü*, in Chinese (16 vols., Shanghai, 1876), and *Tung Hua Lu* [Annals of the Reigning Dynasty] (155 vols., Peking, 1887). Invaluable source material in English will be found in the British Parliamentary Papers, *Correspondence Relating to China, 1834-1839*, and *Additional Correspondence Relating to China, October-November, 1839* (London, 1840), and in *The Chinese Repository*, a periodical published at Canton, 1832-1851.

For Chinese institutions having a bearing on the foreign trade, the student should consult H. B. Morse, *The Trade and Administration of the Chinese Empire* (London, 1921), and T. R. Jernigan, *China in Law and Commerce*

(New York, 1905). Note should also be taken of W. F. Mayers, *The Chinese Government* (Shanghai, 1897); and G. W. Keeton, *The Development of Extraterritoriality in China* (2 vols., London, 1928).

Canton social conditions in the days before the first Anglo-Chinese war are described in W. C. Hunter, *The 'Fan-Kwae' in Canton before Treaty Days, 1825-1844* (Shanghai, 1911), and C. T. Downing, *The Fan-Qui in China in 1836-1837* (3 vols., London, 1838).

CHAPTER 6

Many of the basic works on the period covered by this chapter have been listed in the reading suggestions for Chapter 5. Note in particular: Morse, *International Relations;* Costin, *Great Britain and China,* and especially Kuo, *Critical Study of the First Anglo-Chinese War.*

Military aspects of the conflict between England and China are treated in a considerable number of contemporary works of uneven value. William D. Bernard, *Narrative of the Voyages and Services of the Nemesis from 1840 to 1843; and of the Combined Naval and Military Operations in China* (2 vols., London, 1844). Edward Belcher, *Narrative of a Voyage Around the World . . . 1836-1842: Including Naval Operations in China* (2 vols., London, 1843). John E. Bingham, *Narrative of the Expedition to China* . . . (2 vols., London, 1842), is rich in material but sometimes inaccurate in detail. *The Chinese Repository* (20 vols., Canton, 1833-1851), a journal edited by E. C. Bridgman and S. Wells Williams, contains in Volumes IX-XII some of the best contemporary material on the war. Arthur Cunynghame, *An Aide-de-Camp's Recollections of Services in China* (2 vols., London, 1844). John Francis Davis, *China during the War and since the Peace* (2 vols., London, 1852), an able account by a distinguished British official. John Ouchterlony, *The Chinese War* (London, 1844).

For sources and secondary materials on the peace settlement see footnote citations to this chapter.

CHAPTER 7

W. J. Hail, *Tseng Kuo-fan and the Taiping Rebellion* (New Haven, 1927); Alexander Michie, *The Englishman in China* (2 vols., Edinburgh, 1900), the life in the Far East of Sir Rutherford Alcock; Marquis de Moges, *Recollections of Baron Gros's Embassy to China and Japan in 1857-58* (London, 1860); L. Oliphant, *Narrative of the Earl of Elgin's Mission to China and Japan in the Years 1857, '58, '59* (Edinburgh, 1859).

Chapter 8

There are very few satisfactory general accounts of the period in English. The basic work is Frank A. Golder, *Russian Expansion on the Pacific, 1641-1850* (Cleveland, 1914), by a distinguished American scholar. In addition to citations in footnotes to this chapter see: T. W. Atkinson, *Travels in the Regions of the Upper and Lower Amoor* . . . (London, 1860); A. Krausse, *Russia in Asia* . . . *1558-1899* (New York, 1899); H. B. Morse, *The International Relations of the Chinese Empire* (3 vols., London, 1910-18), I, in particular ch. xix; Albert Parry, "Russian Missionaries in China, 1689-1917 . . . ," *Pacific Historical Review,* IX (1940), 401-424; L. Pasvolsky, *Russia in the Far East* (New York, 1922), deals primarily with the later period; E. G. Ravenstein, *The Russians on the Amur* (London, 1861), one of the best contemporary views; A. Lobanov-Rotovsky, *Russia and Asia* (New York, 1933), the author, a member of the former Imperial nobility, gives a popular general survey; F. H. Skrine, *The Expansion of Russia, 1815-1900* (Cambridge, 1904); J. W. Stanton, "Russian Embassies to Peking during the 18th Century," *University of Michigan Historical Essays,* XI (1937), a scholarly study.

Chapter 9

Japanese history, 1800-1865. K. Asakawa, "Some of the Contributions of Feudal Japan to the New Japan," *Journal of Race Development,* III (1912-13), 1-32, by a distinguished Japanese medievalist; Garret Droppers, "The Population of Japan in the Tokugawa Period," *Trans. of the Asiatic Soc. of Japan,* XXII, No. 2 (1894), 253-284, a standard work; Herbert Zachert, "Social Changes during the Tokugawa Period," *Trans. of the Asitic Soc. of Japan,* 2nd series, XVII (1938), 238-254; Sir Rutherford Alcock, *The Capital of the Tycoon* (2 vols., New York, 1863), penetrating descriptions and observations by a British diplomat three years in Japan; J. H. Gubbins, *The Progress of Japan 1853-1871* (Oxford, 1911), an excellent treatment with documents; E. Herbert Norman, *Japan's Emergence as a Modern State* (New York, 1940), perhaps the best book on economic and political problems, 1853-1900.

Economic history. Yosaburo Takekoshi, *The Economic Aspects of the History of the Civilization of Japan* (3 vols., New York, 1930), an abbreviated English translation of a much larger and an authoritative Japanese work; Matsuyo Takizawa, *The Penetration of Money Economy in Japan* (New York, 1927), traces the decline of feudalism to effects of money on political and social institutions.

Foreign relations. M. Paske-Smith, *Western Barbarians in Japan and Formosa in Tokugawa Days 1603-1868* (Kobe, 1930), by no means readable, but contains valuable British source materials; Townsend Harris, *The Complete Journal of Townsend Harris,* introduction and notes by M. E. Cosenza (New York, 1930), the fascinating journal of the first American consul general and minister to Japan; Francis L. Hawks, *Narrative of the Expedition of an American Squadron to the China Seas and Japan* . . . (3 vols., Washington, 1856), the rich though official account of Perry's mission; Arthur Walworth, *Black Ships off Japan* (New York, 1946), the story of the opening of Japan by Perry, 1853; P. J. Treat, *Diplomatic Relations between the United States and Japan, 1853-1895* (2 vols., Stanford University, 1932), I, chs. i-xi, based on extensive use of American diplomatic archives.

Literature. Lord Redesdale, *Tales of Old Japan* (London, 1910); Jippensha Ikku, *Hizakurige,* trans. by Thos. Satchell (Kobe, 1929), an excellent translation of the famous roisterous adventures on the Tokaido of two irresponsible, comic characters.

See also footnotes to this chapter.

CHAPTER 10

In addition to the following, see titles listed for Chapter 9.

History. G. C. Allen, *Modern Japan and its Problems* (New York, 1927), excellent essays on many aspects of Japanese life by a well-informed student; J. H. Gubbins, *The Making of Modern Japan* (London, 1922), a general survey, 1850-1919; W. W. McLaren, *A Political History of Japan* . . . *1867-1912* (London, 1916), a good study by an American authority; W. W. McLaren, "Japanese Government Documents," *Trans. of the Asiatic Soc. of Japan,* XLII, Pt. 1 (1914), an extensive and well selected compilation covering 1867-1889; A. H. Mounsey, *The Satsuma Rebellion* (London, 1879), an account of the rising of 1877; Count Shigenobu Okuma, compiler, *Fifty Years of New Japan* (2 vols., London, 1910), essays by Japanese leaders in a wide variety of fields; Sir Ernest Satow, *A Diplomat in Japan* . . . (London, 1921), observations of a diplomat on the Restoration.

Government and politics. H. S. Quigley, *Japanese Government and Politics* (New York, 1932), the most satisfactory text in English on the subject; R. K. Reischauer, *Japan: Government-Politics* (New York, 1939), a brief but clear treatment; G. E. Uyehara, *The Political Development of Japan 1867-1909* (New York, 1910), a Japanese interpretation of the Constitution of 1889 and its theories; four brief studies by K. W. Colegrove: "The Japanese Privy Council," *American Political Science Review,* XXVII (1933), 885-898, XXVIII (1934), 29-39; "The Japanese Cabinet," *American Political Science Review,* XXX (1936), 903-923; "The Japanese Foreign Office," *American Journal of International Law,* XXX (1936), 585-613; Hirobumi Ito, *Commentaries on the Constitution of the Empire of Japan,* trans. by Miyoji Ito (3rd ed., Tokyo, 1931), remarks of the man most responsible for shaping the Constitution.

Literature. Tadao Kunitomo, *Japanese Literature Since 1868* (Tokyo, 1938), an excellent survey and analysis; *Introduction to Contemporary Japanese Literature,* edited by Kokusai Bunka Shinkokai (Society for International Cultural Relations, Tokyo, 1939); W. G. Aston, *A History of Japanese Literature* (London, 1899), sketchy and out of date but still useful.

CHAPTER 11

General references, China: 1860-1894. E. R. Hughes, *The Invasion of China by the Western World* (London, 1937), the author, instructor in Chinese religion and philosophy, University of Oxford, attempts a pioneer appraisal of the influence of Christian missionaries, Western political thought, science, and medicine. E. T. Williams, *China: Yesterday and To-Day* (5th ed. rev., New York, 1935), by a former member of the American Foreign Service, still of great value as a general survey, note ch. xxi. H. B. Morse, *The International Relations of the Chinese Empire* (3 vols., London, 1910-18), by a distinguished Anglo-American long a member of the Chinese Customs Service, has been superseded in part by more recent research but remains an indispensable source book, containing material, especially from Chinese Customs sources, which cannot be found elsewhere, and providing in readily accessible form much useful material from British sources; see Vols. I and II for this period. S. Wells Williams, *The Middle Kingdom* (rev. ed., 2 vols., New York, 1907), the work on China most widely read by Americans in the nineteenth century, its author distinguished as a missionary and a member of the American foreign service. Henri Cordier, *Histoire des relations de la Chine avec les puissances occidentales, 1860-1900* (3 vols., Paris, 1901-02), though weak in many respects, is based on French archival materials and so presents the French official point of view in many significant connections. C. Wilfred Allan, *Makers of Cathay* (3rd ed., Shanghai, 1936), brief, popular sketches of Chinese leaders; note essays on Tsêng Kuo-fan, Li Hung-chang, and Chang Chih-tung. Gideon Chen, *TsoTsung T'ang* (Peiping, 1938), a brief biography of one of China's first industrialists. Lin Yutang, *A History of the Press and Public Opinion in China* (Shanghai, 1937), ch. viii, "The Beginnings of the Modern Press 1815-95." A. W. Hummel, ed., *Eminent Chinese of the Ch'ing Period* (Washington, 1943-44), contains excellent biographies of distinguished Chinese of the nineteenth century.

The T'ai-p'ing Rebellion. W. J. Hail, *Tsêng Kuo-fan and Taiping Rebellion* (New Haven, 1927), the standard work on the rebellion based on Chinese and foreign sources. T. T. Meadows, *The Chinese and Their Rebellions* (London, 1856), the author, a member of the British consular service, was a witness to many events of the rebellion, and a profound student of Chinese affairs. W. H. Medhurst, *Critical Review of the Books of the Insurgents* (Shanghai, 1853). H. B. Morse, *In the Days of the Taipings* (Salem, Mass., 1927), a novel.

The Burlingame Mission and the co-operative policy. See references cited in footnotes of this chapter.

Commerce, diplomacy, treaty revision and enforcement. S. Lane-Poole, *The Life of Sir Harry Parkes* (2 vols., London, 1894), a good biography of an aggressive exponent of British "rights" in China and Japan. A. Michie, *The Englishman in China During the Victorian Era* (2 vols., Edinburgh, 1900), an illuminating work centered about the life of Sir Rutherford Alcock.

Chapter 12

Note references for Chapter 11.

Chinese immigration and exclusion. The basic works on this subject are M. R. Coolidge, *Chinese Immigration* (New York, 1909), and E. C. Sandmeyer, *The Anti-Chinese Movement in California* (Urbana, 1939), the latter, being notable for its stress on the conflict between local and federal jurisdiction; see also C. C. Tansill, *The Foreign Policy of Thomas F. Bayard, 1885-1887* (New York, 1940), ch. v, for an excellent discussion of diplomatic aspects of Chinese immigration after the treaty of 1880; the most extensive work covering the entire field of Oriental immigration is R. D. McKenzie, *Oriental Exclusion* (Chicago, 1928); see also *Reminiscences of James B. Angell* (New York, 1912), ch. vi; and Charles Denby, *China and Her People* (2 vols., Boston, 1906).

Chapter 13

Korea. For English translations of many documents and diplomatic exchanges concerning Korea, see *British and Foreign State Papers* (London), and *Korea: Treaties and Agreements* (Washington: Carnegie Endowment for International Peace, 1921), and United States, Department of State, *Foreign Relations* (Washington) volumes for the years 1870-1894. See further, H. N. Allen, *Things Korean* (New York, 1908), an interesting work of general reference; Tyler Dennett, *Americans in Eastern Asia* (New York, 1922), contains chapters on Korea's foreign relations, now superseded in part by more recent research; F. H. Harrington, *God, Mammon, and the Japanese* (Madison, 1944), a brilliant and scholarly analysis of missionary activity, economic enterprise, and political intrigue in late nineteenth-century Korea; C. O. Paullin, *Diplomatic Negotiations of American Naval Officers, 1778-1883* (Baltimore, 1912), a good account of the negotiation of the first American treaty with Korea; W. W. Rockhill, *China's Intercourse with Korea from the XVth Century to 1895* (London, 1905), the author was one of the best informed American students and diplomats in the Far East; W. F. Sands, *Undiplomatic Memories* (New York, 1930), chatty memoirs of an

American diplomat in Korea; P. J. Treat, "China and Korea, 1885-1894," *Political Science Quarterly,* XLIX (1934), 506-543, makes extensive use of American diplomatic correspondence.

Sino-Japanese War. In addition to many of the references listed above, see: Tatsuji Takeuchi, *War and Diplomacy in the Japanese Empire* (Garden City, 1935), ch. x, an able and penetrating study of Japan's policy; G. A. Ballard, *Influence of the Sea on the Political History of Japan* (New York, 1921), chs. v-vi, valuable as the analysis of a British naval authority rather than a historian; A. J. Brown, *The Mastery of the Far East* (New York, 1919), chs. i-vi; J. H. Gubbins, *The Making of Modern Japan* (London, 1922), chs. xxii-xxiii, the author was an able member of the British foreign service in Japan; W. W. McLaren, *A Political History of Japan during the Meiji Era* (London, 1916), ch. x, by an American, is a good account of Japanese political forces leading to war; E. A. Falk, *Togo and the Rise of Japanese Sea Power* (New York, 1936), by an American naval officer, gives an authoritative study of the naval strategy of the war.

CHAPTER 14

A. Yarmolinsky, ed., *The Memoirs of Count Witte* (New York, 1921), has been widely used but is unreliable in many respects; Baron Rosen, *Forty Years of Diplomacy* (2 vols., New York, 1922), the considered views of a keen Russian diplomat; A. M. Pooley, ed., *The Secret Memoirs of Count Tadasu Hayashi* (New York, 1915), the most important Japanese source yet available in English; Philip Joseph, *Foreign Diplomacy in China, 1894-1900* (London, 1928), excellent use of all save Russian sources; R. Stanley McCordock, *British Far Eastern Policy 1894-1900* (New York, 1931); K. Asakawa, *The Russo-Japanese Conflict* (Boston, 1904), one of the best statements of the Japanese view; Payson J. Treat, *Diplomatic Relations between the United States and Japan* (3 vols., Stanford University, 1932 and 1938), the most exhaustive treatment of American archival material: Vol. I covers the years 1853-1875, II, 1876-1895, III, 1895-1905; "Vladimir" [Z. Volpicelli], *The China-Japan War* (New York, 1896), a good contemporary account; T. F. Tsiang, "Sino-Japanese Diplomatic Relations, 1870-1894," *Chinese Soc. and Pol. Science Rev.,* XVII (1933), based on Chinese sources.

Auguste Gérard, *Ma Mission en Chine, 1894-1897* (Paris, 1918), very important for both French and Russian policy; Paul H. Clyde, *International Rivalries in Manchuria* (rev. ed., Columbus, 1928), a general survey of international relations affecting Manchuria.

Masanori Ito, *Kato Takaaki* (2 vols., Tokyo, 1929), papers of an important Japanese statesman.

Chapter 15

Alaska. B. P. Thomas, *Russo-American Relations, 1815-1867* (Baltimore, 1938); V. J. Farrar, *The Annexation of Russian America to the United States* (Washington, 1937); F. A. Golder, "The Purchase of Alaska," *American Historical Review,* XXV (1920), 411-425; T. A. Bailey, "Why the United States Purchased Alaska," *Pacific Historical Review,* III (1934), 39-49.

Samoa. G. H. Ryden, *The Foreign Policy of the United States in Relation to Samoa* (New Haven, 1933), a detailed account.

Hawaii. J. W. Pratt, *Expansionists of 1898* (Baltimore, 1936), the most satisfactory account of the development of American policy; C. C. Tansill, *The Foreign Policy of Thomas F. Bayard,* ch. xii; T. A. Bailey, "Japan's Protest against the Annexation of Hawaii," *Journal of Modern History,* III (1931), 46-61; P. J. Treat, *Diplomatic Relations between the United States and Japan 1895-1905* (Stanford University, 1938), 25-50.

The background of the Spanish-American War. A. L. P. Dennis, *Adventures in American Diplomacy 1896-1906* (New York, 1928), ch. iii, with significant documents in appendix.

Political, social, and economic developments in the Philippines, 1895-1913. C. B. Elliott, *The Philippines: to the end of the military régime* (Indianapolis, 1916), treats the Spanish colonial system as well as the American military occupation; C. B. Elliott, *The Philippines: to the end of the Commission government* (Indianapolis, 1917), by the same author who held administrative and judicial posts in the islands and who was a member of the Commission, is an exhaustive analysis of American government in the islands, both Federal and local; Dean C. Worcester, *The Philippines Past and Present* (2 vols., New York, 1914; new edition in one vol., with biographical sketch and four additional chapters by Ralston Hayden, New York, 1930), presents the views of one of the most active American participants in Philippine government; W. Cameron Forbes, *The Philippine Islands* (2 vols., Boston, 1928), is the ably presented case of Taft's governor-general; Maximo M. Kalaw, *The Development of Philippine Politics, 1872-1920* (Manila, 1926), an account of the part played by the Filipino leaders and parties in the political development of the Philippines by the Dean of Liberal Arts, University of the Philippines; David P. Barrows, *History of the Philippines* (rev. ed., Yonkers-on-Hudson, 1925), the author was commissioner of education in the islands; Emma Blair and James A. Robertson, *The Philippine Islands, 1493-1898* (55 vols., Cleveland, 1903-1909), a most exhaustive compilation covering the history of the Philippines to the end of the Spanish regime.

Chapter 16

R. H. Akagi, *Japan's Foreign Relations* (Tokyo, 1936), ch. vii, a conventional Japanese interpretation of the open door; K. Asakawa, *The Russo-Japanese Conflict* (New York, 1904), in spite of its contemporary character this work is still of value; S. F. Bemis, *A Diplomatic History of the United States* (rev. ed., New York, 1942), 479-502; P. H. Clyde, "The Open Door Policy of John Hay," *The Historical Outlook*, XXII (May, 1931), 210-214; Tyler Dennett, *John Hay* (New York, 1933); Feng Djen Djang, *The Diplomatic Relations Between China and Germany Since 1898* (Shanghai, 1936); W. L. Godshall, *The International Aspects of the Shantung Question* (Philadelphia, 1923); A. W. Griswold, *The Far Eastern Policy of the United States* (New York, 1938), 38-86; Philip Joseph, *Foreign Diplomacy in China* (London, 1928); R. S. McCordock, *British Far Eastern Policy, 1894-1900* (New York, 1931); Henry F. Pringle, *Theodore Roosevelt* (New York, 1931); C. F. Remer, *Foreign Investments in China* (New York, 1933), particularly Part II; P. J. Treat, *Diplomatic Relations Between the United States and Japan, 1895-1905* (Stanford University, 1938), especially chs. vi, ix-xii; W. W. Willoughby, *Foreign Rights and Interests in China* (2 vols., rev. ed., Baltimore, 1927), I, ch. iv, on the open door; En Tsung Yen, *The Open Door Policy* (Boston, 1923).   On the developing Russo-American rivalry see E. H. Zabriskie, *American-Russian Rivalry in the Far East* (Philadelphia, 1946), chs. ii-v.

Chapter 17

In addition to the works cited in the text the following contain materials touching wide and varied aspects of the complex reform movements.   G. H. Blakeslee, ed., *China and the Far East* (New York, 1910); H. S. Brunnert and V. V. Hagelstrom, *Present-Day Political Organization of China* (Shanghai, 1912); Margaret E. Burton, *The Education of Women in China* (New York, 1911); Katherine A. Carl, *With the Empress Dowager in China* (New York, 1907); Chen Shao-Kwan, *The System of Taxation in China in the Tsing Dynasty, 1644-1911* (New York, 1914); Dugald Christie, *Thirty Years in the Manchu Capital* (New York, 1914); Sir Alexander Hosie, *On the Trail of the Opium Poppy* (2 vols., London, 1914); Hsieh Pao Chao, *The Government of China, 1644-1911* (Baltimore, 1925); two works by H. B. Morse, *The Trade and Administration of the Chinese Empire* (London, 1908), and *The Trade and Administration of China* (rev. ed., London, 1913); Paul S. Reinsch, *Intellectual and Political Currents in the Far East* (Boston, 1911); E. A. Ross, *The Changing Chinese* (New York, 1911); Wei Wen Pin, *The Currency Problem in China* (New York, 1914).

CHAPTER 18

G. A. Ballard, *The Influence of the Sea on the Political History of Japan* (New York, 1921), chs. vii-ix; Maurice Baring, *With the Russians in Manchuria* (London, 1905), graphic journalistic pictures of the Manchurian battlefields; Paul H. Clyde, *International Rivalries in Manchuria* (Columbus, 1928), chs. iv-vii; Tyler Dennett, *Roosevelt and the Russo-Japanese War* (New York, 1925), the best detailed treatment of the subject including the European aspects; A. L. P. Dennis, *Adventures in American Diplomacy 1896-1906* (New York, 1928), supplementary to Dennett and valuable for the documents printed; A. Whitney Griswold, *The Far Eastern Policy of the United States* (New York, 1938), the best thoroughly documented survey of the period since 1900; J. H. Gubbins, *The Making of Modern Japan* (Philadelphia, 1922), chs. xxiv-xxvi, good brief treatment by a British student; A. S. Hershey, *International Law and Diplomacy of the Russo-Japanese War* (New York, 1906); P. J. Treat, *Diplomatic Relations Between the United States and Japan 1895-1905* (Stanford University, 1938), chs. x and xii, by an outstanding American authority on the subject; C. W. Young, *The International Relations of Manchuria* (Chicago, 1929), essentially a convenient digest with certain supplementary materials of the MacMurray *Treaties* concerning Manchuria; C. W. Young, *Japan's Special Position in Manchuria* (Baltimore, 1931), *The International Legal Status of the Kwantung Leased Territory* (Baltimore, 1931), and *Japanese Jurisdiction in the South Manchuria Railway Areas* (Baltimore, 1931), valuable legalistic studies to be used, however, with great care since, as their author himself states (I, vii), "These studies are not history."

CHAPTER 19

In addition to many of the titles listed for Chapter 18 note the following.

T. A. Bailey, *Theodore Roosevelt and the Japanese-American Crises* (Stanford University, 1934), a complete and scholarly treatment; Owen Lattimore, *Manchuria: Cradle of Conflict* (New York, 1932), a profound study of Manchuria's regional relationship to China; E. B. Price, *The Russo-Japanese Treaties of 1907-1916 concerning Manchuria and Mongolia* (Baltimore, 1933), a definitive study with texts of the treaties; J. G. Reid, *The Manchu Abdication and the Powers* (Berkeley, 1935), a brilliant and an exhaustive study of the role of foreign diplomacy at Peking, 1908-1912.

George H. Blakeslee, *Japan and Japanese-American Relations* (New York, 1912); Henry Chung, *Korean Treaties* (New York, 1919); Tatsuji Takeuchi, *War and Diplomacy in the Japanese Empire* (Garden City, 1935), ch. xii on the Russo-Japanese War and ch. xiii on the annexation of Korea. On

Russo-American relations see E. H. Zabriskie, *American-Russian Rivalry in the Far East* (Philadelphia, 1946), chs. vi-vii.

CHAPTER 20

H. F. MacNair, *Modern Chinese History: Selected Readings* (Shanghai, 1923); Reginald Johnston, *Twilight in the Forbidden City* (London, 1934), throws much light on the political life of Peking both before and after the Revolution; John Gilbert Reid, *The Manchu Abdication and the Powers* (Berkeley, 1935), the most exhaustive and scholarly treatment of the policies of the powers during the last years of the Manchu dynasty; A. M. Kotenev, *The Chinese Soldier* (Shanghai, 1937), treats the subject briefly in broad perspective, covering the nineteenth as well as the twentieth centuries; M. E. Cameron, *The Reform Movement in China, 1898-1912* (Stanford University, 1931), the best treatment of the Manchu reform program. E. R. Hughes, *The Invasion of China by the Western World* (London, 1937), particularly ch. iii, on the influence of Western political thought; George H. Blakeslee, ed., *Recent Developments in China* (New York, 1913), contains, among other notable essays, E. W. Capen's "The Western Influence in China," and Y. S. Tsao's "The Relations of the Returned Students to the Chinese Revolution"; W. W. Willoughby, *Foreign Rights and Interests in China* (2 vols., Baltimore, 1927), valuable as a reference in checking the foreign position in China during the Revolution and in other years; Kalfred Dip Lum, *Chinese Government* (Shanghai, 1934), a brief study by an author whose contacts with Chinese politics were intimate; American Academy of Political and Social Science, *Annals* (Philadelphia, 1930), Vol. 152, brief treatment of practically all phases of the early republican period; H. M. Vinacke, *Modern Constitutional Development in China* (Princeton, 1920), in particular chs. iv-viii; A. H. Holcombe, *The Spirit of the Chinese Revolution* (New York, 1930), a discussion of political theory in China's revolution in which the author attempts to find theory through a study of personalities.

Sun Yat-sen. Henry B. Restarick, *Sun Yat-sen: Liberator of China* (New Haven, 1931), and Lyon Sharman, *Sun Yat-sen: His Life and Its Meaning* (New York, 1934), the most satisfactory biographies of the great revolutionary leader; Stephen Chen and Robert Payne, *Sun Yat-sen: A Portrait* (New York, 1946), not a full biography but a useful brief introduction to Sun's career and his thought; Bernard Martin, *Strange Vigour* (London, 1944), uses the Cantlie papers and press notices.

CHAPTER 21

Japan and World War I. The most adequate brief treatment explaining Japan's participation is Charles N. Spinks, "Japan's Entrance into the World

War," *Pacific Historical Review,* V (1936), 297-311; Tatsuji Takeuchi, *War and Diplomacy in the Japanese Empire* (Chicago, 1935), ch. xiv, not only a survey of successive steps taken by the ministry but also of the discussions in the Diet; Paul S. Reinsch, *An American Diplomat in China* (Garden City, 1922), ch. xi, the interpretations of the American Minister at Peking always zealous to use American influence for the protection of China against Japan —see also ch. xii on the Twenty-One Demands; Kikujiro Ishii, *Diplomatic Commentaries,* translated and edited by William R. Langdon (Baltimore, 1936), scattered but revealing discussions by one of Japan's ablest diplomats; W. L. Godshall, *The International Aspects of the Shantung Question* (Philadelphia, 1923), chs. ii-iii, an able treatment; Jefferson Jones, *The Fall of Tsingtau* (Boston, 1915), interesting as a contemporary account; two valuable background essays are chs. iii and iv in George M. Dutcher, *The Political Awakening of the East* (New York, 1925).

The Twenty-One Demands and the treaties and notes of May 25, 1915. The ablest detailed account is in Thomas E. La Fargue, *China and the World War* (Stanford University, 1937), chs. ii and iii; less detailed but basic is A. W. Griswold, *The Far Eastern Policy of the United States* (New York, 1938), ch. v; *The Sino-Japanese Negotiations of 1915,* Japanese and Chinese documents and the Chinese official statement, edited by the Carnegie Endowment for International Peace, Division of International Law, Pamphlet 45; for a Japanese interpretation of Japan's entry into the war and of the Twenty-One Demands, Smimasa Idditti, *The Life of Marquis Shigenobu Okuma* (Tokyo, 1940), ch. xv; see also chapters in Reinsch and Takeuchi cited above; Paul H. Clyde, "The Open Door in Relation to the Twenty-One Demands," *Pacific Affairs,* III (1930), 834-841.

CHAPTER 22

Chinese politics, 1917-1919. H. F. MacNair, *China in Revolution* (Chicago, 1931), especially good for detail in a confused period; Paul S. Reinsch, *An American Diplomat in China* (New York, 1922), valuable because its author was American Minister at Peking, but should be used with discrimination since it is special pleading rather than history; Robert T. Pollard, *China's Foreign Relations 1917-1931* (New York, 1933), in particular, pp. 1-49.

The Lansing-Ishii Exchange. Robert Lansing, *War Memoirs* (Indianapolis, 1935); Kikujiro Ishii, *Diplomatic Commentaries,* translated and edited by W. R. Langdon (Baltimore, 1936).

The Paris Conference. W. L. Godshall, *The International Aspects of the Shantung Question* (Philadelphia, 1933), a competent study; Paul Birdsall, *Versailles Twenty Years After* (New York, 1941), an excellent study of the Peace Conference in general with a penetrating chapter on Japanese strategy, pp. 83-115; two basic works by David Hunter Miller, *The Drafting of the Covenant* (2 vols., New York, 1928), and *My Diary at the Conference of*

Paris (21 vols., New York, 1924). The most definitive brief study is T. A. Bailey, *Woodrow Wilson and the Lost Peace* (New York, 1944), note in particular ch. xviii.

CHAPTER 23

The Siberian intervention. The most satisfactory documentary treatment of the period from April to December, 1918, is James Bunyan, *Intervention, Civil War, and Communism in Russia* (Baltimore, 1936). F. L. Schuman, *American Policy toward Russia since 1917* (New York, 1928), is an able and critical study. Elena Varneck and H. H. Fisher, *The Testimony of Kolchak and Other Siberian Materials* (Stanford University, 1935), is particularly valuable for its editorial annotations on the sources printed. William S. Graves, *America's Siberian Adventure 1918-1920* (New York, 1931), by the commanding general of the American forces in Siberia, is poorly organized but nevertheless an invaluable critical document on policy and action in Siberia. Louis Fischer, *The Soviets in World Affairs* (2 vols., London, 1930), is, as the title suggests, a comprehensive work, with valuable chapters on the intervention as related to over-all policy. Note also Charles Seymour, *Intimate Papers of Colonel House* (4 vols., Boston, 1926-1928).

The Consortium. Extensive official correspondence is printed in United States, *Foreign Relations,* volumes for 1917-1920. Selected correspondence is in *The Consortium* (Washington: Carnegie Endowment for International Peace, 1921), and Paul H. Clyde, *United States Policy toward China* (Durham, 1940). A good specialized study is F. V. Field, *American Participation in the China Consortiums* (Chicago, 1931). There is a brief but sound exposition in C. F. Remer, *Foreign Investments in China* (New York, 1933).

CHAPTER 24

For a penetrating picture of the pattern of Japanese culture see Ruth Benedict, *The Chrysanthemum and the Sword* (Boston, 1946).

History of political thought. Hirobumi Ito, *Commentaries on the Constitution of the Empire of Japan,* translated by Miyoji Ito (Tokyo, 1889); Rikitaro Fujisawa, *Recent Aims and Political Development of Japan* (New Haven, 1923); *The Autobiography of Fukuzawa Yukichi* (Tokyo, 1934); Tatsuo Kawai, *The Goal of Japanese Expansion* (Tokyo, 1938), for the so-called philosophy of *musubi;* H. L. Keenleyside and A. F. Thomas, *History of Japanese Education* (Tokyo, 1937), for the political philosophy behind the educational system; *Introduction to Contemporary Japanese Literature* (Tokyo, 1939); Iichiro Tokutomi, "The Life of Yoshida Shoin," *Transactions of the Asiatic Society of Japan,* XLV (1917), Part I.

Political history and government. C. B. Fahs, *Government in Japan* (New York, 1940); Shinichi Fujii, *The Essentials of Japanese Constitutional Law* (Tokyo, 1940); Uichi Iwasaki, *The Working Forces in Japanese Politics . . . 1867-1920* (New York, 1921); W. W. McLaren, *A Political History of Japan During the Meiji Era, 1867-1912* (London, 1916); E. H. Norman, *Japan's Emergence as a Modern State* (New York, 1940); E. H. Norman, *Soldier and Peasant in Japan: The Origins of Conscription* (New York, 1943).

Political parties. Shoji Iizawa, *Politics and Political Parties in Japan* (Tokyo, 1938); Kenneth Colegrove, "Labor Parties in Japan," *American Political Science Review,* XXIII (1929), 329-363; Sen Katayama, *The Labor Movement in Japan* (Chicago [c. 1918]); Mitsu Kohno, *Labour Movement in Japan* (Tokyo, 1938).

Liberalism and democracy. Sir George Sansom, "Liberalism in Japan," *Foreign Affairs,* XIX (1941), 551-560; Yagoro Hirao, *Social Policy in Japan* (Tokyo, 1937); Tetsu Katayama, *Women's Movement in Japan* (Tokyo, 1938); Tsunejiro Miyaoka, *Growth of Liberalism in Japan* (Washington, 1918); C. N. Spinks, "The Liberal Myth in Japan," *Pacific Affairs,* XV (1942), 450-456; K. Colegrove, "Parliamentary Government in Japan," *American Political Science Review,* XXI (1927), 835-852.

Militarism, fascism, communism. T. A. Bisson, "Japan's New Structure," Foreign Policy Association, *Reports,* XVII (1941), 26-36; Hugh Byas, *Government by Assassination* (New York, 1942); Carl Crow, editor, *Japan's Dream of World Empire: The Tanaka Memorial* (New York, 1942).

Chapter 25

A. W. Griswold, *The Far Eastern Policy of the United States* (New York, 1938), presents a very able treatment of the Conference and its background. Yamato Ichihashi, *The Washington Conference and After* (Stanford University, 1928), by a Japanese scholar, long professor of Japanese history and government at Stanford University, and secretary to Admiral Kato, Japan's chief delegate at the Conference. R. L. Buell, *The Washington Conference* (New York, 1922), though contemporary is valuable in presenting the historical background out of which the Conference grew. Two important articles are: J. B. Brebner, "Canada, the Anglo-Japanese Alliance and the Washington Conference," *Political Science Quarterly,* L (1935), 45-58, and C. N. Spinks, "The Termination of the Anglo-Japanese Alliance," *Pacific Historical Review,* VI (1937), 321-340.

Chapter 26

Note in particular the diplomatic correspondence and memoranda in United States, *Foreign Relations, 1924,* II, 333-411, on the Gentlemen's Agreement and the exclusion provisions of the Immigration Act of 1924. The Gentlemen's Agreement is treated ably in T. A. Bailey, *Theodore Roosevelt and the Japanese-American Crises* (Stanford University, 1934). Articles which are basic studies are those by R. L. Buell, "The Development of the Anti-Japanese Agitation in the United States," *Political Science Quarterly,* XXXVII (1922), 605-638, and XXXVIII (1923), 57-81. For a brief summary, factual in nature, Buell's *Japanese Immigration* (Boston, 1924) is still good.

For the issue in Congress in 1924, the best treatment is Rodman W. Paul, *The Abrogation of the Gentlemen's Agreement* (Cambridge, 1936). The relation of the immigration question to the larger aspects of American foreign policy in the Far East is best treated by A. W. Griswold, *The Far Eastern Policy of the United States* (New York, 1938), ch. ix. A Japanese interpretation is presented in Yamato Ichihashi, *Japanese in the United States* (Stanford University, 1932). R. D. McKenzie, *Oriental Exclusion* (Chicago, 1928), presents an able analysis of the working of the 1924 law. E. G. Mears, *Resident Orientals on the American-Pacific Coast* (Chicago, 1928), surveys legal and other relationships of the white population and the Orientals. The broad outlines of immigration in the entire Pacific area are given in J. B. Condliffe, ed., *Problems of the Pacific* (Chicago, 1928), 146-161. A brief but thorough analysis of the Japanese in Hawaii in 1924 is Romanzo Adams, *The Japanese in Hawaii* (New York, 1924). Basic statistical material on Japanese migration is given in Walter F. Wilcox, ed., *International Migrations* (New York, 1929), I, 160-166. An excellent sociological study of the Japanese in Hawaii is Andrew W. Lind, *Hawaii's Japanese* (Princeton, 1946).

Chapter 27

Economic history of Meiji. Although no single volume in English is devoted to this subject, chapters or larger sections of many works dealing with modern Japan are devoted to the subject. The outstanding interpretation of the politico-economic foundations of modern Japan is E. Herbert Norman, *Japan's Emergence as a Modern State* (New York, 1940). Other works of value stress political rather than economic history. G. C. Allen, *Modern Japan and Its Problems* (New York, 1938), is a series of excellent introductory essays on political, social, economic topics. E. E. N. Causton, *Militarism and Foreign Policy in Japan* (London, 1936), while dealing with the more recent period gives valuable background. W. R. Crocker, *The Japanese Population Problem* (London, 1931), traces the history of the problem during the Meiji period. Yukichi Fukuzawa, *Autobiography,* trans. by E. Kiyooka (Tokyo, 1934), contains the reflections of one of the greatest intellectuals of the Meiji period. J. H. Gubbins, *Progress of Japan, 1853-1871* (Oxford, 1911), and *The Making of Modern Japan* (London, 1922), are valuable political interpretations. W. W. McLaren, *A Political History of Japan during the Meiji Era, 1867-1912* (New York, 1916), is a most useful study, as is the same author's "Japanese Government Documents," *Transactions of the Asiatic Society of Japan,* XLII (1914), Pt. I. See also S. Nasu, *Land Utilization in Japan* (Tokyo, 1929). John E. Orchard, *Japan's Economic Position* (New York, 1930). J. W. Robertson Scott, *The Foundations of Japan* (London, 1922).

Chapter 28

R. K. Reischauer, *Japan: Government-Politics* (New York, 1939), 133-157, an excellent brief chapter on "The Party Politicians in Power, 1918-1932." Tatsuji Takeuchi, *War and Diplomacy in the Japanese Empire* (Chicago, 1935), has two excellent chapters: xxii, on the Tsinan Incident in its relation to the Japanese government, and xxiii, on the government and the Pact of Paris. A. Morgan Young, *Japan under Taisho Tenno 1912-1926* (London, 1928), and *Imperial Japan 1926-1938* (New York, 1938), though journalistic are packed with valuable material and observations on Japanese politics and the social order. H. S. Quigley, *Japanese Government and Politics* (New York, 1932), is still the most satisfactory reference work on the subject. E. B. Schumpeter, ed., *The Industrialization of Japan and Manchukuo, 1930-1940* (New York, 1940), though dealing with the later decade contains much material on the decade of the 1920's, particularly in the chapters by G. C. Allen and E. F. Penrose. The social and cultural pattern of Japan is surveyed admirably by John F. Embree, *The Japanese Nation* (New York, 1945). Militarism and fascism are covered by: Kenneth W. Colegrove, *Militarism in Japan* (Boston, 1936); E. E. N. Causton, *Militarism and Foreign Policy in Japan* (London, 1936); O. Tanin and E. Yohan, *Militarism and Fascism in Japan* (New York, 1934), and *When Japan Goes to War* (New York, 1936). Note also Edwin O. Reischauer, *Japan Past and Present* (New York, 1946), chs. x and xi.

Chapter 29

For influences stemming from the pre-revolutionary period: E. R. Hughes, *The Invasion of China by the Western World* (London, 1937), ch. iii, on the effects of Western political thought.

P. M. A. Linebarger, *The Political Doctrines of Sun Yat-sen: An Exposition of the San Min Chu I* (Baltimore, 1937); Lyon Sharman, *Sun Yat-sen: His Life and its Meaning* (New York, 1934), a full-length critical biography; Stephen Chen and Robert Payne, *Sun Yat-sen: A Portrait* (New York, 1946), a briefer but suggestive study.

On the period 1919-1927: T'ang Leang-li, *The Inner History of the Chinese Revolution* (London, 1930), a favorable interpretation of the rise of the Kuomintang and a justification of both the Soviet orientation and its later repudiation; T. C. Woo, *The Kuomintang and the Future of the Chinese Revolution* (London, 1928), deals in particular with the period 1924-1927 and strongly supports the Russian Orientation; Ren Yen Lo, *China's Revolution from the Inside* (New York, 1930), an inadequate general survey, but does contain chapters on special phases such as the anti-opium movement, woman's movement, etc.

Marxian interpretations include: Harry Gannes, *When China Unites: An Interpretative History of the Chinese Revolution* (New York, 1937), a completely undocumented work filled with questionable generalizations; Anna Louise Strong, *China's Millions: The Revolutionary Struggles from 1927 to 1935* (New York, 1935), a Stalinist interpretation by an observer present when the Hankow Soviet fell in 1927, and who left Hankow with Borodin; Harold R. Isaacs, *The Tragedy of the Chinese Revolution* (London, 1938), presents an anti-Stalin, pro-Trotsky interpretation, brilliantly written but inadequately documented on points of interpretation.

CHAPTER 30

The most satisfactory study of China's relations with the powers is Robert T. Pollard, *China's Foreign Relations, 1917-1931* (New York, 1933). For the special role of the United States, see A. Whitney Griswold, *The Far Eastern Policy of the United States* (New York, 1938), ch. x; Henry K. Norton, *China and the Powers* (New York, 1927), interprets China's relations in terms of the industrial revolution as it affected the nation in the post-war years. H. G. W. Woodhead, *The Truth about the Chinese Republic* (London, *ca.* 1925), presents the contemporary views of a Britisher, long resident in China, editor of *The China Year Book*, who opposed abrogation of the unequal treaties. J. B. Taylor, *Farm and Factory in China* (London, 1928), is a good though brief discussion of the agricultural and industrial background against which the Nationalist movement developed. The emergence of a new social order is portrayed by T'ang Leang-li, *The Foundations of Modern China* (London, 1928). T. C. Chao, *China Today Through Chinese Eyes* (London, 1927), is a symposium on varied phases of Chinese life with suggestive chapters on politics, industry and labor, the intellectual renaissance, religion and education. Raymond T. Rich gives a convenient introductory survey in *Extraterritoriality and Tariff Autonomy in China* (Shanghai, 1925). Other conveniently brief accounts are: Harold S. Quigley, *Chinese*

Politics and Foreign Powers (Worcester: International Conciliation Pamphlet, No. 227, Feb. 1927); and S. K. Hornbeck, *China To-Day: Political* (Boston: World Peace Foundation Pamphlets, No. 5, 1927), dealing with the rise of nationalism and China's revolt against the treaties.

CHAPTER 31

The National Government at Nanking. P. M. A. Linebarger, *Government in Republican China* (New York, 1938), gives an able and sympathetic account of the new government's philosophy and structure, chapter viii. K. D. Lum, *Chinese Government* (Shanghai, 1934), is an account by a member of the National People's Convention of 1931. Early biographies of Chiang K'ai-shek include: Chen Tsung-hsi, Wang An-tsiang, and Wang I-ting, *General Chiang Kai-shek, the Builder of New China* (Shanghai, 1929); H. K. Tong, *Chiang Kai-shek* (2 vols., Shanghai, 1937); Robert Berkov, *Strong Man of China* (Boston, 1938). See also H. F. MacNair, *China in Revolution* (Chicago, 1931), an able narrative. See too the interpretative studies by A. N. Holcombe, *The Chinese Revolution* (Cambridge, 1930), and *The Spirit of the Chinese Revolution* (New York, 1931).

The National Government and treaty relations, 1927-1931. The best account is R. T. Pollard, *China's Foreign Relations, 1917-1931* (New York, 1933), ch. x. For the special subject of tariff autonomy see S. F. Wright, *China's Struggle for Tariff Autonomy 1843-1938* (Shanghai, 1938), ch. vii.

The Sino-Russian dispute concerning the Chinese Eastern Railway. A. W. Griswold, *Far Eastern Policy of the United States* (New York, 1938), gives a particularly good analysis of American policy, 389-400. Substantial portions of the American diplomatic correspondence are printed in United States, *Foreign Relations, 1929*, II, 186-434; *1930*, II, 298-302. For additional accounts see footnotes to this chapter.

CHAPTER 32

United States, *Foreign Relations,* volumes covering the years 1922 to 1930, a particularly rich source on political conditions in China, on the policies of the various powers toward China, and on inter-power relations as focused in the Geneva Conference, the London Conference, the negotiations for the Treaty for the Renunciation of War, etc.

Russo-Japanese relations. A. A. P. Dennis, *The Foreign Policies of Soviet Russia* (New York, 1924), a pioneer work in English now superseded by later studies; Louis Fischer, *The Soviets in World Affairs* (2 vols., New York, 1930); Henry K. Norton, *The Far Eastern Republic of Siberia* (New York, 1927).

Sino-Japanese relations. Arnold J. Toynbee, ed., *Survey of International Affairs* (annual volumes, London, 1925-31); H. K. Norton, *China and the Powers* (New York, 1927); R. T. Pollard, *China's Foreign Relations, 1917-1931* (New York, 1933); H. S. Quigley, *Chinese Politics and Foreign Powers* (New York, 1927); Sir Frederick Whyte, *China and the Foreign Powers* (London, 1928).

Naval limitation. On the Geneva Conference, see B. H. Williams, *The United States and Disarmament* (New York, 1931). The London Conference is treated by J. W. Wheeler-Bennett, *Disarmament and Security* (London, 1932); Giovanni Engely, *The Politics of Disarmament* (London, 1932); Tatsuji Takeuchi, *War and Diplomacy in the Japanese Empire* (Chicago, 1935)—this latter work is based largely on Japanese sources.

Chapter 33

The basic treatment of the Manchurian "Incident" is League of Nations, *Report of the Commission of Inquiry* (Geneva, 1932), and the *Supplementary Documents* (Geneva, 1932). The outstanding studies on Manchurian culture and civilization in relation to China are Owen Lattimore, *Manchuria: Cradle of Conflict* (New York, 1932) and *The Mongols of Manchuria* (New York, 1934). The historical development of the Manchurian question is treated by Paul H. Clyde, *International Rivalries in Manchuria* (Columbus, 1928). H. L. Kingman, *Effects of Chinese Nationalism upon Manchurian Railway Developments, 1925-1931* (Berkeley, 1932), is a brief but convenient study. See also H. Feis, *The International Trade of Manchuria* (Worcester, 1931). For a digest and analysis of treaties, agreements, and negotiations concerning Manchuria, see C. W. Young, *The International Relations of Manchuria* (Chicago, 1929). Japan's legal position in Manchuria as it had developed to 1931 is treated in three volumes by C. W. Young, *Japan's Special Position in Manchuria, Japanese Jurisdiction in the South Manchuria Railway Areas,* and *The International Legal Status of the Kwantung Leased Territory* (Baltimore, 1931). These are detailed studies, excellent within their limited legalistic approach, but lacking in appreciation or evaluation of the broader historical forces which determined the course of events. An able Japanese apology is given by K. K. Kawakami, *Manchoukuo: Child of Conflict* (New York, 1933). The official Chinese case as presented to the Lytton Commission is *Memoranda Presented to the Lytton Commission* (2 vols., New York, 1932); the official Japanese case is *The Present Condition of China* and *Relations of Japan with Manchuria and Mongolia* (2 vols., Tokyo, 1932). The controversy as presented and argued before the League is treated legalistically by W. W. Willoughby, *The Sino-Japanese Controversy and the League of Nations* (Baltimore, 1935).

CHAPTER 34

Japan and Japanese policy, 1931 to 1937, and the relations of other powers to Japan. G. C. Allen, *Japan the Hungry Guest* (London, 1938), and *Japanese Industry: Its Recent Development and Present Condition* (New York, 1939), are indispensable for the study of Japan's economic structure. See also Isoshi Asahi, *The Economic Strength of Japan* (Tokyo, 1939). T. A. Bisson, *American Far Eastern Policy, 1931-1940* (New York, 1940), is convenient as a factual summary. The same author's *Japan in China* (New York, 1938), is a good contemporary study. E. E. N. Causton, *Militarism and Foreign Policy in Japan* (London, 1936), is an introductory general study. It should be read with Kenneth Colegrove's *Militarism in Japan* (Boston, 1936). W. H. Chamberlain, *Japan over Asia* (Boston, 1937, and London, 1938), is a competent survey by an able American journalist. Charles B. Fahs, *Government in Japan* (New York, 1940), Hugh Borton, *Japan Since 1931* (New York, 1940), and R. K. Reischauer, *Japan: Government-Politics* (New York, 1939), especially ch. vii, are three studies which supplement each other. A. E. Hindmarsh, *The Basis of Japanese Foreign Policy* (Cambridge, 1936), and A. M. Young, *Imperial Japan 1926-1938* (New York, 1938), present two approaches to Japan's foreign policy. On the Japanese population question the outstanding studies are E. F. Penrose, *Population Theories and Their Application with Special Reference to Japan* (Stanford University, 1934), and W. R. Crocker, *The Japanese Population Problem* (London, 1931), which present differing conclusions.

Additional material on the important and complex character of Japan's economic development include the following: E. B. Schumpeter, ed., *The Industrialization of Japan and Manchukuo* (New York, 1940), with contributions by the editor, G. C. Allen, E. F. Penrose, and M. S. Gordon. See too E. F. Penrose, *Food Supply and Raw Materials in Japan* (Chicago, 1930).

China, 1931-1937. On the theory of government, P. M. A. Linebarger, *Government in Republican China* (New York, 1938). On the position of military forces, E. F. Carlson, *The Chinese Army: Its Organization and Military Efficiency* (New York, 1940). See also G. E. Taylor, "The Reconstruction Movement in China," *Problems of the Pacific* (New York, 1936); G. E. Hubbard, *Eastern Industrialization and Its Effect on the West* (London, 1935); Edgar Snow, *Red Star Over China* (New York, 1938).

CHAPTER 35

The standard work on the development of the independence movement and nationalism in the Philippines both before and during the period of the Commonwealth is J. R. Hayden, *The Philippines: A Study in National De-*

velopment (New York, 1942). On the independence movement as an aspect of American politics and pressure groups a brief convenient study is Grayson L. Kirk, *Philippine Independence* (New York, 1936).

The population, peoples, and resources of the Philippines. Herbert W. Krieger, *Peoples of the Philippines* (Washington, 1942).

The Philippine Constitution. José M. Aruego, *The Framing of the Philippine Constitution* (2 vols., Manila, 1936); the author was Dean of the College of Liberal Arts, University of Manila, and a member of the Constitutional Convention, 1935. See also Miguel Cauderno, *The Framing of the Constitution of the Philippines* (2 vols., Manila, 1937); José P. Laurel, *The Three Powers of Government under the Philippine Constitution* (Manila, 1936).

The Philippine presidency. Isabelo P. Caballero and M. de Gracia, *Quezon: The Story of a Nation and Its Foremost Statesman* (Manila, 1935), and Carlos Quirino, *Quezon: Man of Destiny* (Manila, 1935), are uncritical biographies of the first President.

Administration and the civil service in the Philippines. See the *Report[s] of the Philippine Commission,* 1901-1908; J. R. Hayden, "Higher Officials in the Philippine Civil Service," *American Political Science Review,* XXVII (April, 1933).

The Philippine legislature. Sergio Osmeña, *The Problem of Democratic Government in the Philippines: Its Salient Aspects* (Washington, 1925).

Law and the administration of justice. Eugene A. Gilmore, "The Development of Law in the Philippines," *Iowa Law Review,* XVI (1931), 465-479; George A. Malcolm, *The Commonwealth of the Philippines* (New York, 1936).

Philippine political parties. Dapen Liang, *The Development of Philippine Parties* (Hong Kong, 1939); M. M. Kalaw, *The Development of Philippine Politics, 1872-1920* (Manila, 1926).

Education. Antonio Isidro and others, *Education in the Philippines* (Manila, 1939).

Chapter 36

Manchuria (Manchukuo), Mongolia. John R. Stewart, *Manchuria Since 1931* (New York, 1936), a competent survey. E. B. Schumpeter and others, *The Industrialization of Japan and Manchukuo, 1930-1940* (New York, 1940), is of great value.

British policy in China, 1930-1940. The most convenient survey is Irving S. Friedman, *British Relations with China: 1931-1939* (New York, 1940).

The Far East and the end of naval limitation. Walter Lippmann, W. H. Shepardson, W. O. Scroggs, eds., *The United States in World Affairs,* vols. for 1933, 1934-35, 1936, 1937, and 1938 (New York).

China and the Undeclared War, 1937-1941. H. S. Quigley, *Far Eastern War, 1937-1941* (Boston, 1942), is an excellent general introduction. The best brief survey of Chinese politics during the war is Lawrence K. Rosinger, *China's Wartime Politics 1937-1944* (Princeton, 1944).

Japan and the New Order. Excellent in content and among the most readable books on the subject is Hugh Byas, *Government by Assassination* (New York, 1942). Joseph C. Grew, *Ten Years in Japan* (New York, 1944), is compiled from the diary of an American ambassador. On the developments in Japanese government note in particular: Hugh Borton, *Japan Since 1931* (New York, 1940), and C. B. Fahs, *Government in Japan* (New York, 1940). Japan's politico-religious policy is portrayed by D. C. Holtom, *Modern Japan and Shinto Nationalism* (Chicago, 1943), and G. C. Allen, *Japan the Hungry Guest* (New York, 1938). On Japan's activities in China, T. A. Bisson, *Japan in China* (New York, 1938); George E. Taylor, *The Struggle for North China* (New York, 1940).

The United States and Japan's New Order. W. C. Johnstone, *The United States and Japan's New Order* (New York, 1941), is an able account of the effects of Japanese policy on American interests. For American policy in China see F. R. Dulles, *China and America* (Princeton, 1946), chs. xiii-xviii.

CHAPTER 37

General. *General Marshall's Report: The Winning of the War in Europe and the Pacific* (New York, 1945), a report by the Chief of Staff covering July 1, 1941 to August, 1945.

The Pacific Theater. W. H. Hobbs, *The Fortress Islands of the Pacific* (Ann Arbor, 1945), a description of their geography and strategic importance; Felix M. Keesing, *The South Seas in the Modern World* (New York, 1941), the economy and culture of Pacific islands.

Southeast Asia and the Philippines. Robert Considine, ed., *General Wainwright's Story* (Garden City, 1946), contains the General's account of four years of humiliating defeat, surrender, and captivity, told with brevity, clarity, and humanity; Colonel Carlos P. Romulo, *I Saw the Fall of the Philippines* (Garden City, 1943); Tan Pei-ying, *The Building of the Burma Road* (New York, 1945), an absorbing narrative; G. S. Seagrave, *Burma Surgeon* (New York, 1943), the story of a doctor in the retreat from Burma.

Naval campaigns. Fletcher Pratt, *The Navy's War* (3rd ed., New York, 1944); Fletcher Pratt, *Night Work* (New York, 1946), the story of how the naval war in the Southwest Pacific was changed from a long war of island-hopping to a faster one of by-passing and cutting off the enemy; Rear Admiral Yates Sterling, Jr., *Why Sea Power Will Win the War* (New York, 1944), a presentation of the argument of naval versus air power; Walter Karig and Welbourn Kelley, *Battle Report: Pearl Harbor to Coral Sea*, Vol. I (New York, 1944), prepared from official sources; A. Kroese, *The Dutch*

Navy at War (London, 1945), a Dutch naval officer describes the failure to defend the Netherlands Indies from the Japanese in 1942.

Air power. A. H. Narracott, *Air Power in War* (London, 1945), portrays the strategic conceptions of the principal powers; Donald Hough and Elliott Arnold, *Big Distance* (New York, 1945), an account of the contribution of the AAF to victory in the Pacific between the Battle of the Coral Sea and the Battle of the Bismarck Sea; T. W. Lawson, *Thirty Seconds Over Tokyo* (New York, 1943), an account of the Doolittle raid by a participant.

The atomic war. Henry De Wolf Smyth, *Atomic Energy for Military Purposes* (Princeton, 1945), a commercial edition of the official report on development of the atomic bomb; John J. O'Neill, *Almighty Atom* (New York, 1945), a chronicle of man's developing control of the atom by the science editor of the *New York Herald Tribune;* Harrison Brown, *Must Destruction Be Our Destiny?* (New York, 1946), a discussion by an atomic scientist of the Manhattan Project; William L. Laurence, *Dawn Over Zero* (New York, 1946), contains a graphic story of the development of the atomic bomb and its use over Hiroshima.

Miscellaneous topics. H. L. Childs and John B. Whitton, *Propaganda by Short Wave* (Princeton, 1943), an analysis of short wave propaganda; Robert E. Summers, *Wartime Censorship of Press and Radio* (New York, 1942), a history of American censorship; Stewart Alsop and Thomas Barden, *Sub Rosa: The O. S. S. and American Espionage* (New York, 1946), an account of American agents in enemy territory; Ellis M. Zacharias, *Secret Missions* (New York, 1946), a critical account of U. S. naval intelligence, preceding and during the war.

CHAPTER 38

General. Knight Biggerstaff, *China: Revolutionary Changes in an Ancient Civilization* (Ithaca, 1945); Owen and Eleanor Lattimore, *The Making of Modern China* (New York, 1944), a short history; Maxwell S. Stewart, *War-time China* (New York, 1944), a brief picture.

The United States and China. T. A. Bisson, *America's Far Eastern Policy* (rev. and enlarged ed., New York, 1945), a presentation of American policy, 1931-1944; Arthur E. Christy, *The Asian Legacy and American Life* (New York, 1945), a panel of authorities describes what America owes to the Orient; Nathaniel Peffer, *Basis for Peace in the Far East* (New York, 1942); George E. Taylor, *America in the New Pacific* (New York, 1942), an analysis of American interests at the outbreak of World War II; Wendell L. Willkie, *One World* (New York, 1943), observations and ideas from the wartime mission that began in August, 1942; Quincy Wright, H. Lauterpacht, E. M. Borchard, Phoebe Morrison, *Legal Problems in the Far Eastern Conflict* (New York, 1941). The documentary history of American aid to China may be followed conveniently in L. M. Goodrich and others, eds., *Documents on American Foreign Relations* (Boston, 1939-1947) Vols. I-VII.

United States, Treaty Series 984, *Relinquishment of Extraterritorial Rights in China . . .* (Washington, 1943).

The Chinese economic crisis, inflation, profiteering, agricultural and industrial conditions. Hubert Freyn, *Free China's New Deal* (New York, 1943), an optimistic account of economic development in independent China since 1937; Fei Hsiao-tung, *Peasant Life in China* (New York, 1939); Fei Hsiao-tung and Chang Chih-i, *Earthbound China* (Chicago, 1945), a socio-anthropological study of a rural community in southwest China; Bruno Lasker, *Asia on the Move* (New York, 1945), an account of population pressure, migration, and resettlement as a result of want and war; Eleanor Hinder, *Life and Labour in Shanghai* (New York, 1944), a study of a decade of social administration in the International Settlement; Augusta Wagner, *Labor Legislation in China* (Peking, 1938); Shih Kuo-heng, *China Enters the Machine Age,* trans. and ed. by Fei Hsiao-tung and F. L. K. Hsu (Cambridge, 1944), a study of labor in Chinese war industry; Lao-t'ai-t'ai Ning and Ida Pruitt, *A Daughter of Han* (New Haven, 1945), the autobiography of a Chinese working woman as told by her to Ida Pruitt; Tsang Chih, *China's Postwar Markets* (New York, 1945), a study of China's economic needs and the financial and technical means by which they may be filled.

Chinese politics and government. Wei-tung Pan, *The Chinese Constitution* (Washington, 1945), a study of forty years of effort in constitution making; H. F. MacNair, ed., *Voices from Unoccupied China* (Chicago, 1944), Harris Foundation lectures at the University of Chicago by a group of Chinese scholars, semi-official representatives of the National Government; Stephen Chen and Robert Payne, *Sun Yat-sen: A Portrait* (New York, 1946), a political biography which throws much light on the position of Sun's Kuomintang after his death in 1925; Guenther Stein, *The Challenge of Red China* (New York, 1945), a competent journalistic report on the Communist areas in wartime China; Theodore H. White and Annalee Jacoby, *Thunder Out of China* (New York, 1946), a graphic narrative and interpretation of wartime China; P. M. A. Linebarger, *Government in Republican China* (New York, 1938), particularly good on the theory of political power; Sun Fo, *China Looks Forward* (New York, 1944), the son of the "Father of the Chinese Revolution" gives his estimate of Kuomintang accomplishments and failures; Madame Wellington Koo, *Hui-lan Koo* (New York, 1943), the social and diplomatic career of the wife of a Chinese diplomat—the first issue of the book was withdrawn from circulation.

Materials on Chiang K'ai-shek and the Soong family. Robert Berkov, *Strong Man of China* (Boston, 1938), a journalistic account of Chiang's rise to power by a manager of the Shanghai bureau of the United Press; H. H. Chang, *Chiang K'ai-shek: Asia's Man of Destiny* (New York, 1944), warmly sympathetic to Chiang but deficient in the use of available sources, and inaccurate in detail; Sven Hedin, *Chiang K'ai-shek* (New York, 1940), a eulogy by the Swedish explorer; H. K. Tong, *Chiang K'ai-shek: Soldier and Statesman* (2 vols., London, 1938), an authorized biography by an enthusiastic admirer; Mayling Soong Chiang and Chiang K'ai-shek, *Sian: A Coup d'Etat* (Shanghai, 1937), Madame Chiang's account of her husband's captivity with extracts from his Sian diary; P. M. A. Linebarger, *The China of Chiang K'ai-shek* (Boston, 1941), an able political study sympathetic to the Kuomintang; Emily Hahn, *The Soong Sisters* (New York, 1941).

The United States and Russia in China. Foster Rhea Dulles, *The Road to Teheran* (Princeton, 1944), a readable survey of American-Russian relations, 1781-1943; Harold H. Fisher, *America and Russia in the World Community* (Claremont, Calif., 1946), by the director of the Hoover Library at Stanford University.

Chapter 39

General accounts on Japanese reconstruction. Carl L. Becker, *How New Will The Better World Be?* (New York, 1944), a sound historical background for realistic peace planning; Wilfred Fleisher, *What to Do with Japan* (New York, 1945), proposals by a former publisher of a Tokyo English-language newspaper; Douglas G. Haring, ed., *Japan's Prospect* (Cambridge, 1946), a composite work by scholars who trained personnel for military government, which aims to inform the American public on the nature of the task in Japan; D. G. Haring, *Blood on the Rising Sun* (Philadelphia, 1943), important principally for its discussion of social problems; W. C. Johnstone, *The Future of Japan* (New York, 1945), a forecast of the problem of remaking Japan; Matsuo Kato, *The Lost War* (New York, 1946), an able account by a Japanese journalist of Japan's lost cause, and of the horrors of total war; F. S. C. Northrop, *The Meeting of East and West* (New York, 1946), a brilliant inquiry into the problem of world understanding.

Politics and government. Herman Beukema and others, *Contemporary Foreign Governments* (New York, 1946), includes material on the military occupation government in Japan; Paul H. Clyde, "The Far East," in *Twentieth Century Political Thought,* edited by Joseph S. Roucek (New York, 1946).

The social structure. John F. Embree, *Suye Mura* (Chicago, 1939), an able sociological study of a Japanese rural village; John F. Embree, *The Japanese Nation* (New York, 1945), a penetrating social survey of contemporary Japanese life; Toru Matsumoto and Marion O. Lerrigo, *A Brother Is a Stranger* (New York, 1946), a life story of a contemporary Japanese Christian and a study of the Japanese national psychology.

Shinto nationalism. D. C. Holtom, *Modern Japan and Shinto Nationalism* (Chicago, 1943), the ablest presentation of the subject.

Militarism. Hillis Lory, *Japan's Military Master* (New York, 1943), an account of the integrating of the Japanese army into the life of the people; John McGilvrey Maki, *Japanese Militarism* (New York, 1945), a *Nisei* who served with the Office of War Information portrays the causes and prescribes a cure for Japan's military spirit.

Japan's economy. T. A. Bisson, *Japan's War Economy* (New York, 1945), a study which emphasizes the importance of the *Zaibatsu* in Japan's plans for war; C. D. Carus and C. L. McNichols, *Japan: Its Resources and Industries* (New York, 1944); H. G. Moulton and L. Marlio, *The Control of Germany and Japan* (Washington, 1944); E. F. Penrose, *Population Theories and Their Application to Japan* (Stanford University, 1934); O. D. Russell, *The House of Mitsui* (Boston, 1939), a history of one of the most powerful *Zaibatsu;* Guy-Harold Smith and Dorothy Good, *Japan, a Geographical View* (New York, 1943), an excellent, concise survey of the land, people, and resources.

The Japanese in America. Forrest E. La Violette, *Americans of Japanese Ancestry* (Toronto, 1945); Carey McWilliams, *Prejudice: The Japanese-Americans* (Boston, 1944), a study of the treatment of the *Nisei* during World War II.

Korea. Andrew J. Grajdanzev, *Korea Looks Ahead* (New York, 1944), a survey of the country, people, and their prospects; Andrew J. Grajdanzev, *Modern Korea* (New York, 1944), emphasizes social and economic life under Japanese rule; Younghill Kang, *The Grass Roof* (New York, 1931), an autobiographical novel of great power; San Kim and Nym Wales, *Song of Ariran* (New York, 1941), the story of San Kim, a Korean revolutionist, as told by him to Nym Wales.

Formosa. A. J. Grajdanzev, *Formosa Today* (New York, 1942).

CHAPTER 40

General works on Southeast Asia. Rupert Emerson, Lennox A. Mills, and Virginia Thompson, *Government and Nationalism in Southeast Asia* (New York, 1942), is an excellent introduction. J. S. Furnivall, *Progress and Welfare in Southeast Asia* (New York, 1941), by a recognized British authority. Bruno Lasker, *Peoples of Southeast Asia* (New York, 1944), a readable introduction by an exceptionally well qualified American student of the area. V. D. Wickizer and M. K. Bennett, *The Rice Economy of Monsoon Asia* (Stanford University, 1941), is a definitive economic study.

Netherlands India. Rupert Emerson, *Malaysia: A Study in Direct and Indirect Rule* (New York, 1937), a comprehensive and scholarly study of Dutch colonial administration; A. D. de Kat Angelino, *Colonial Policy* (2 vols., Chicago, 1931), abridged from the standard Dutch edition; Hubertus J. Van Mook, *The Netherlands Indies and Japan* (New York, 1944), an official view by a Dutch minister of colonies.

British Malaya. Lennox A. Mills, *British Malaya* (Singapore, 1925); Sir Frank Swettenham, *British Malaya* (London, 1929); L. R. Wheeler, *The Modern Malay* (London, 1928); Rupert Emerson, *Malaysia: A Study in Direct and Indirect Rule* (New York, 1937), an excellent treatment.

Burma. J. S. Furnivall, *The Political Economy of Burma* (Rangoon, 1931), by one of the outstanding authorities on the country; W. J. Grant,

The New Burma (New York, 1940), a journalistic account by a former editor of *The Rangoon Times;* G. E. Harvey, *History of Burma from the Earliest Times to the Beginning of the English Conquest* (London, 1925), a standard work; Alleyne Ireland, *The Province of Burma* (2 vols., New York, 1907), very detailed on economic and administrative problems; Sir George Scott, *Burma from the Earliest Times to the Present Day* (London, 1924), a history by an outstanding authority.

French Indo-China. The growth of the French Empire in the Far East has only a limited literature in English. Thomas E. Ennis, *French Policy and Developments in Indochina* (Chicago, 1936), surveys the historical development of the French conquest, and treats at some length economic and social problems. Herbert I. Priestley, *France Overseas* (New York, 1938), is a study in modern imperialism which devotes two chapters to Indo-China. Virginia Thompson, *French Indo-China* (New York, 1937), is an extensive work treating of Annamite civilization and French administration and economy, as well as the peninsula's peoples of Indian culture in Cambodia and Laos.

Siam. K. P. Landon, *Siam in Transition: A Brief Survey of Cultural Trends in the Five Years Since the Revolution of 1932* (Shanghai, 1939), and *The Chinese in Thailand* (London, 1941), both excellent studies; Reginald Le May, *An Asian Arcady* (Cambridge, 1926), and *Siamese Tales Old and New* (London, 1930); Anna H. Leonowens, *The English Governess at the Siamese Court* (Boston, 1870), and *The Romance of the Harem* (Boston, 1873); these two books by Anna H. Leonowens, picturing Siam in the 1860's and now out of print, form the basis of the delightful story by Margaret Landon, *Anna and the King of Siam* (New York, 1943); Virginia Thompson, *Thailand: The New Siam* (New York, 1941), the most convenient general survey. The colorful story of the underground in Siam during the Japanese occupation of World War II is given by Nicol Smith and Blake Clark, *Into Siam: Underground Kingdom* (Indianapolis, 1946).

CHAPTER 41

Hernando J. Abaya, *Betrayal in the Philippines* (New York, 1946); Carl L. Becker, *How New Will the Better World Be?* (New York, 1944), the most penetrating historical analysis of the things for which Americans fought in World War II, and of the post-war world with which they are faced; Ruth Benedict, *The Chrysanthemum and the Sword* (Boston, 1946), a profound work on the motivations of Japanese behavior; *The Pattern of Pacific Security* (London, 1946), a discussion by Chatham House experts suggesting for the Pacific area a regional organization within the United Nations; David Dallin, *The Big Three, The United States, Britain, and Russia* (New York, 1945); Vera Micheles Dean, *The Four Cornerstones of Peace* (New York, 1946), a clear portrayal of the organization of world peace from Dumbarton Oaks to the San Francisco Conference by the Research Director of the Foreign Policy Association; Harold H. Fisher, *America and Russia in the World Community* (Claremont, Calif., 1946), an able analysis of Russo-American problems; J. S. Furnivall, *Educational Progress in Southeast Asia* (New York, 1943); Leland M. Goodrich and Edvard Hambro, *Charter of the United Nations* (Boston, 1946); Huntington Gilchrist, "The Japanese Islands: Annexation or Trusteeship," *Foreign Affairs,* XXII (1944) 635-642; John Hersey, *Hiroshima* (New York, 1946), a graphic account of the effects of the atomic bomb; Felix M. Keesing, *Native Peoples in the Pacific World* (New York, 1945); Kenneth K. Kurihara, *Labor in the Philippine Economy* (Stanford University, 1945), a study of rural and industrial labor conditions, and of government labor policies in the pre-war years; Owen Lattimore, *Solution in Asia* (Boston, 1945), an able analysis of some Asiatic reactions to the Anglo-Saxon and to the Russian theory and practice of "democracy"; Hans J. Morgenthau, *Scientific Man vs. Power Politics* (Chicago, 1946), suggests that power politics is inseparable from human society, that it is not a result of ignorance or misunderstanding, that its problems are not technical and to be solved by the blueprinters of world peace, that it results from irrational forces eternally dominating the aspirations of men; F. S. C. Northrop, *The Meeting of East and West* (New York, 1946), a penetrating philosophical inquiry concerning the obstacles to world understanding; K. M. Pannikar, *The Future of Southeast Asia* (New York, 1943), an Indian view; Carlos P. Romulo, *I See the Philippines Rise* (Garden City, 1946), presents reflections of a Filipino editor on the liberation of his homeland; Frederick L. Schuman, *Soviet Politics at Home and Abroad* (New York, 1946), an appraisal of Russian affairs since 1917; Warren S. Thompson, *Population and Peace in the Pacific* (Chicago, 1946), a penetrating study of the relation of population and resources to the maintenance of peace by the Director of the Scripps Foundation of Population Research; Laura Thompson, *Guam and Its People* (rev. ed., Princeton, 1946); Henry A. Wallace, *Soviet Asia Mission* (New York, 1946); Sumner Welles, *Where Are We Heading?* (New York, 1946); K. Zilliacus, *Mirror of the Past* (New York, 1946), a former official with the League of Nations highlights some parallels between the role of the victors in 1919 with that of 1945-46; H. F. MacNair, ed., *China* (Berkeley, 1946), Part 5, on economics and reconstruction, 455-520.

INDEX

INDEX

A

Abe, General Nobuyuki, 724 *n.*
Abeel, David, 128
Abhaiwongse, Luang Khovid, 788
Aconcagua, Mount, 4
Adachi, Kenzo, 497
Adachi, Mineichiro, as president of the World Court, 568
Adams, John Quincy, 126
Aglen, Sir Francis, 539
Aguinaldo, Emilio, 281-282
Alaska:
air route over, 27
Seward's purchase of, 274
Albazin, 162
Alcock, Sir Rutherford:
expedition on Choshu, 186
opposes coercion, 220
Aleutian Islands, 276
Japanese occupation and American re-conquest of, 688
Alien Land Laws, 469, 470
Allied Council for Japan, 735
All-sea route to China, discovery of, 87 *ff.*
Amaterasu-omi Kami (Sun Goddess), 66
American Baptist Missionary Union, 221
American Bible Society, 221
American Board of Commissioners for Foreign Missions, 221
American Volunteer Group, 698
Amherst mission, 1816, 106-107
Amoy, 25, 132
Amur River, 11
and Jewish province of Birobidjan, 25
and Russian boundary, 160
in Russo-Chinese diplomacy, nineteenth century, 165
Andes Mountains, 4
Angell, James B., 234
Anglo-Burmese Wars, 771
Anglo-Japanese Alliance:
in relation to Russian and Japanese policy, 330
in the years 1919-21, 444-445

Anglo-Japanese Alliance (*Cont.*):
origin of, 303-304
relation of U. S. to, 305-306
replaced by Four-Power Pact, 449-450
Anhui, 8 *n.*
Annam, 35, 37, 776
Annamese nationalism (*see* Indo-China)
Anti-Comintern Pact:
Japan and Germany sign, 655, 664
Manchukuo becomes signatory of, 645
Anti-foreignism (China):
during Boxer uprising, 297
following Washington Conference, 510
in the nineteenth century, 108
Anti-foreignism (Japan):
and the Perry mission, 180
aroused by Perry and Harris treaties, 183 *ff.*
Antung, 25
Anyang, 43
Arabian Sea, 4
Arab trade with China, 85
Araki, General Sadao, 604-606
Arctic Circle, 26
Aristeas of Proconnesus, 83
Arrow affair, 150-151
Arrow War, 152-153
burning of the Summer Palace, 157-158
renewal of hostilities, 156-157
Ashikaga civilization, 75-77
Ashikaga shogunate, 75
Asia:
climate in, 5-6
comparison in size with North America, 4
extent of, 4
isolation of, 6
population, 4, 5
Asian plateau, 4
Assam, Burma and, 771
Atlantic seaboard, American, as boundary of American political interest, 1
Atomic bomb, 694
Audience question, 225-227
Australia, policy of, on Oriental immigration, 474

China (*Cont.*):

and Manchuria, administration in, 1905-10, 355

and Nanking incident, 1927, 537-538

and Russia:

in Manchuria, 1929, 554 *ff.*

relations with, 1917-20, 511 *ff.*

Russo-Japanese War, 332

and Shanghai affair, 1925, 534-535

and United States:

aid to China, after 1941, 697

exclusion law, repeal of, 698-700

U. S. aid to, after 1941, 697

and Versailles treaty, refusal of, to accept, 410-411

and World War II, 696-713

postwar period, 714-715

war effort, deteriorating, 700-701

anti-Christian movement in, 534

anti-British campaign, Hankow, 1926, 536-537

as society, 8

border territories, separatist movements in, 1912-13, 370-371

Boxer uprising in, 296-302

Canton Soviet, and foreign powers, 535-536

centralization vs. provincial autonomy in, 1911, 360-361

Chiang K'ai-shek, 704-706

Christian missions in, late nineteenth century, 221

climatic regions of, 12

commercial interest in, growth of, 104

conservative nationalists, triumph of, 1927, 546 *ff.*

Constitution of, 706 *n.*

constitutional movement, revival of, 706-708

dependencies of, 17-23

relation of, to China, 242-243

early European knowledge of, 83

early history of, traditional accounts, 42

education in, traditional, 62-64

European interest in, renewal of, 85-86

extraterritoriality, conference on, 1926, 531-532

foreign loans to, Sino-Japanese War, 260-261

geographical limits of, 8-9

Gilbertian *coup d'état,* 616-617

government of:

basis of, 58

historic patterns of, 1

China (*Cont.*):

government of (*Cont.*):

influence of *literati* and mandarins in, 314

machinery of, in Old China, 57-58

native criticism of, 314-315

handicraft shops in, 13

Hundred Days of Reform, 270-272

Imperial audience question, 225-227

indemnity loans to, 260-261

industrialization of, 13, 14, 316

influence of, on Europe, eighteenth century, 103

interior of, cultural importance of, 667

Korea, policy in, 1880, 247-248

Kuomintang, 702

history of, 1917-27, 507-527

strife with Communists, revival of, 708-709

loses control of Ili, Annam, Burma, Sikkim, 245-246

Lukuchiao incident, 659

Manchu reform program in, 1902-1903, 319-328

Marshall mission, 716-719

mineral resources of, 12-14

National Assembly, first meeting of, 1910, 359

nationalism, anti-foreignism, development of, 533-534

National Government of, 13

political structure of, after 1927, 546 *ff.*

Nationalist movement, 1927-31, 507 *ff.*

Old China:

central government in, 58-61

local government in, 61-62

machinery of government in, 57-58

political theory in, 55-57

open door policy in, 292-296

People's Political Council, 707

political astrology in, 236-237

political theory concerning, 239-242

political tutelage, period of, 516

politics:

before patriotism, 700 *ff.*

developments, 1931-37, 614-616

factions in, 703-704

1915-17, 392-393

population of, 14

pre-revolutionary reforms in, 1895-1911, 315-316

press in:

modern, beginnings of, 315

revolutionary, and the Manchus, 318

Root, Elihu:
  and Root-Takahira Notes, 350-351
  mission to Russia, 1917, 420
  Taft commission to Philippines, 286
  Washington Conference, 448
Root-Takahira Notes, 350-351
Rousseau, influence of, in Japan, *Jiyuto* party, 198
Roxas, Manuel A., first president of Philippine republic, 637
Rubruck, William de, 86
Russia (Tsarist):
  annexation of Maritime Province, 168-169
  conditions in Siberia, 1918, 414-415
  conflict with China over C.E.R., 1929, 555
  first contacts with China, 95, 162-163
  influence of, in Canton and Hankow governments, 1923-27, 519 *ff*.
  in Manchuria, after 1900, 298, 305-306
  in revolution, 1917 *ff*., 413-414
  interests of, in North Manchuria:
    after 1905, 345
    in 1916, 412-413
  lease of Liaotung, 266-267
  leases Port Arthur, 266-267
  position of, in Manchuria, 1895-1905, 330-331
  relations with China:
    at close of World War II, 715-716
    1917-19, 414-415
  Siberia, exploration and colonization of, 160-162
Russian-American Company, 165
Russian far eastern policy, 27, 162-163, 261-262, 305-306
Russian Soviet Federated Socialist Republic, 25
Russo-Chinese Bank, 261
Russo-Chinese frontier, 26, 160
Russo-Chinese northeastern frontier, first settlement of, 95
Russo-Japanese War:
  and U. S. policy, 333-335
  destruction of Baltic fleet, 331, 333
  issues involved in, 329
  relation of China to, 332
Ryukyu Islands (Loochoo or Liuchiu), 29, 30
  case of, 242

S

Saigo, Tsugumichi, 199
Saigon, 37, 776

Saionji, Prince Kimmochi, 438, 439, 490, 663, 724
Saito, Admiral Viscount Makoto, 602
  assassination of, 610
Sake (rice wine), 484
Sakhalin Island, 28
Sakishima Island, 30
Salween River, 11, 770
Samar, 40, 93
Samarkand, 83
Samoan Islands, U. S. interest in, 275
Samurai:
  affected by abolition of feudalism, 192
  revolt of, against shogunate, 188-189
San Francisco School Board, resolution of racial segregation, 464-466
Sankin kotai, law of, 79
San Min Chu I:
  and Nanking government, 546
  Democracy, second principle of, 514-517
  Nationalism, first principle of, 513-514
  Socialism, third principle of, 517
Sarawak, 759
Satsuma clan, 79
Schurman, J. G., commission of investigation, 285
Seimchan, 27
Sei Shonagon, Lady, 72
Sei tai shogun (*see* Yoritomo)
Seishin, 582
Seiyuhonto, 493
Seiyukai, 495
Selangor, 765
Semenov, Captain Grigorii, 414, 418, 421
Sendai, 66
Seoul (Keijo), 34
Seres, 8
Sesshu, 77
Seward, William H.:
  and Burlingame Treaty, 218
  and purchase of Alaska, 274
  and treaty questions, 229-230
Sha-ho, battle of, 332
Shakai Shugi Kenkyukai, 499
Shan, 17 *n.*
Shang (Yin) dynasty, 43
Shanghai, 9, 13
  as a treaty port, 132
  industrialization of, 14
  map of, 134
  origins of International Settlement, 133-136
  position of, in mid-nineteenth century trade, 133 *ff*.
  seaport, 25